La  5

TAXMANN'S
LAW RELATING TO
SEARCH
&
SEIZURE

TAXMANN®'S

Law Relating To
Search
&
Seizure

As amended by
Finance Act 2023

Dr. Raj K. Agarwal
M.Com., FCA, FCS, AICWA, LLB, LLM, MBA, Ph.D

Dr. Rakesh Gupta
FCA, FCS, AICWA, LLB, LLM, MBA, Ph.D
Ex-Member, Income Tax Appellate Tribunal

9th Edition
2023

© All rights reserved

Price : ₹ 2995

Law stated in this book is as amended by the Finance Act, 2023

Published by :
Taxmann Publications (P.) Ltd.

Sales & Marketing :
59/32, New Rohtak Road, New Delhi-110 005 India
Phone : +91-11-45562222
Website : www.taxmann.com
E-mail : sales@taxmann.com

Regd. Office :
21/35, West Punjabi Bagh, New Delhi-110 026 India

Printed at :
Tan Prints (India) Pvt. Ltd.
44 Km. Mile Stone, National Highway, Rohtak Road
Village Rohad, Distt. Jhajjar (Haryana) India
E-mail : sales@tanprints.com

Disclaimer

Every effort has been made to avoid errors or omissions in this publication. In spite of this, errors may creep in. Any mistake, error or discrepancy noted may be brought to our notice which shall be taken care of in the next edition. It is notified that neither the publisher nor the author or seller will be responsible for any damage or loss of action to any one, of any kind, in any manner, therefrom. It is suggested that to avoid any doubt the reader should cross-check all the facts, law and contents of the publication with original Government publication or notifications.

No part of this book may be reproduced or copied in any form or by any means [graphic, electronic or mechanical, including photocopying, recording, taping, or information retrieval systems] or reproduced on any disc, tape, perforated media or other information storage device, etc., without the written permission of the publishers. Breach of this condition is liable for legal action.

For binding mistake, misprints or for missing pages, etc., the publisher's liability is limited to replacement within seven days of purchase by similar edition. All expenses in this connection are to be borne by the purchaser.

All disputes are subject to Delhi jurisdiction only.

Dr. RAJ K. AGARWAL

Dr. RAKESH GUPTA

ABOUT THE AUTHORS

Dr. Raj K. Agarwal has been meritorious throughout his academic career. He has done M.Com., LL.B., LL.M., MBA and Ph. D. and is Fellow member of Institute of Chartered Accountants of India and Institute of Company Secretaries of India and Associate Member of Institute of Cost Accountants of India. He has been practicing as Chartered Accountant since 1984 as senior partner in M/s. Rakesh Raj & Associates. He has wide experience of handling Income Tax search cases and has poured his practical experience in the form of this well researched book. He has been associated with the academic activities of the Institute of Chartered Accountants of India representing various committees of the Institute and with the Institute of Company Secretaries of India representing its Northern India Regional Council as Chairman in the year 2003. He has been contributing articles and addressing various seminars on topics relating to income-tax, accounting, auditing and business restructuring.

Dr. Rakesh Gupta is a law graduate and Fellow Member of Institute of Chartered Accountants of India and Institute of Company Secretaries of India and Associate Member of Institute of Cost Accountants of India. He has done Ph. D. He was awarded gold medal in LL.B. examination by the University. He along with Dr. Raj started practicing as chartered accountant in the year 1984 in the firm M/s. Rakesh Raj & Associates. He was selected as Member of Income Tax Appellate Tribunal in the year 2000 and thereafter he resigned from the service and started practicing as an advocate as senior partner of M/s. RRA Tax India at Delhi representing income tax cases before various High Courts and Supreme Court of India. He is a prolific speaker and has been contributing to the profession by addressing various seminars on regular basis on legal and practical topics relating to Income Tax. He has been contributing articles in various professional magazines, writing column in newspapers and making appearances at T.V. channels.

PREFACE

The enactment of the provisions of search and seizure in our country under the income-tax law dates back to the year 1956. This is an extreme action undertaken by the Income-tax Department to investigate a person regarding the undisclosed income. With the gradual deterioration in the value system in the society, there is increased tendency to resort to illegal, unethical and corrupt practices for maximization of wealth. This results into the generation and accumulation of unaccounted income. Needless to say, Income-tax Department is becoming more and more vigilant on this issue and the actions of search and seizure are being undertaken frequently. Further, with the introduction of technology in the working of the Income-tax Department, better qualitative information are available which, in turn, lead the tax department to undertake investigation by resorting to income-tax search and seizure actions.

The law relating to income-tax search and seizure is cumbersome and at the same time, the process of search and seizure is painful from the point of view of the taxpayers. The law relating to income-tax search and seizure and particularly assessment procedure with respect to taxpayer who is searched, has undergone several changes in the past. Apart from the legal issues, there are practical complications which are faced by the searched persons. There are several practical aspects which keep on haunting a person regarding handling of income-tax search and seizure. An attempt has been made in this book to comprehend and address various practical aspects relating to search and seizure, apart from discussing and analyzing various complicated and controversial legal issues.

Over a period of time, several landmark judgments have been delivered by Supreme Court, different High Courts and benches of Tribunal. Significant judgments delivered in this regard have been discussed and analyzed at appropriate places. With respect to new assessment procedure in search cases applicable w.e.f. 1st June, 2003, as given under sections

153A to 153D, the law is in the process of being evolved, developed, interpreted and explained by Supreme Court and various High Courts. These provisions have been discussed in this book, keeping in view the various issues which may be analyzed and interpreted by the courts in future.

There are certain issues with respect to which there are divergent views prevailing in the professional circles as well as expressed by different courts while delivering various judgments. An attempt has been made in this book to give both the views so as to bring on surface the different dimensions of the controversy and wherever deemed appropriate, own opinion has been expressed by us also.

Further, on various controversial issues, an attempt has been made to give a balanced view from the point of view of taxpayers as well as department. However, the possibility of having a slight tilt in favour of the taxpayers cannot be ruled out for the reason that the authors do have the background of being practicing tax consultants in their professional career and have throughout represented the cases of the taxpayers at various levels right from Assessing Officer till Supreme Court.

Income-tax Act, 1961 is in the process of being replaced by new Direct Tax Code very shortly. There was a dilemma as to whether a comprehensive commentary on income-tax search and seizure provisions should be published at this juncture. In the mean time, Direct Taxes Code Bill, 2010 has been placed before Parliament and it was observed that conceptually the provisions relating to search and seizure contained in the Bill are on the same lines of the Income-tax Act, 1961 with certain minor amendments. Therefore it was thought appropriate to release the present book which, in our humble opinion, would remain relevant and useful under the existing Act as well as after the enactment of new Code.

In the beginning of the book, few chapters have been devoted to discuss Frequently Asked Questions (FAQs), gist of significant landmark judgments of various courts and checklists to be practiced by the assessee while handling income-tax search and seizure action. Such material may be quite handy and may provide readily available solution to certain practical issues. For detailed analysis and discussion, one may refer to appropriate section in the book.

Development of law is a continuous process and in practice also, it has been observed that new kind of issues and situations keep on emerging. We welcome and invite suggestions and request that any new issue(s) coming to the knowledge of the esteemed readers may be referred to us for discussion and incorporation in future edition of the book. We would further invite feedback with respect to any discrepancy in the book which may be noticed by the esteemed readers despite our sincere efforts to avoid any mistake or error.

The issues have been discussed and analyzed in this book keeping in view the need of different sections of the society. This book may be useful to the practicing tax consultants, taxpayers being individuals or Corporates, senior executives working with the corporate world, academicians and students and at the same time to the tax administrators as well.

SECOND EDITION

It was maiden attempt writing book on the subject 'Income Tax Search and Seizure' incorporating our practical experience of professional practice. The first edition of the book was published in June 2011 and we are extremely happy and satisfied that the book has been well received and appreciated in the professional as well as tax department circle. Direct Taxes Code Bill, 2010 presented in Parliament could not be enacted so far and therefore the provisions introduced in the bill amending certain provisions relating to search and seizure could not be effected. The Finance Act, 2012 has thoroughly amended penalty provision relating to search with certain other minor amendments relating to provisions of sections 153A and 153C of the Income-tax Act, 1961. It is a matter of extreme pleasure and satisfaction to bring out second edition of the book analyzing the amendments introduced by Finance Act, 2012 and further discussing the judgments delivered by different courts during last one year on different aspects relating to provisions of search and seizure.

THIRD EDITION

It is a matter of extreme pleasure and satisfaction that the second edition of the book received overwhelming response from the readers. It has encouraged us to bring the third edition incorporating changes made by the Finance Act, 2013 and latest judicial decisions rendered by different courts and we hope that it will receive the same response.

FOURTH EDITION

It is a matter of extreme pleasure and satisfaction that the third edition of the book received overwhelming response from the readers. It has encouraged us to bring the fourth edition incorporating changes made by the Finance (No. 2) Act, 2014. We hope that it will receive the same response.

FIFTH EDITION

We are pleased to bring fifth edition of the book incorporating amendments made by Finance Act, 2015 & Finance Act, 2016 and judicial decisions rendered by the courts during last two years. Chapter on Direct

Tax Code has been dropped from the book as it is now clear from the government that new Direct Tax Code shall not be introduced. Certain significant amendments proposed in the Direct Tax Code earlier have already been incorporated in the Income Tax Act. We would welcome to your valuable suggestions and feedback on various aspects of the book.

SIXTH EDITION

We are pleased to bring sixth edition of the book incorporating amendments made by Finance Act, 2017 and judicial pronouncements rendered by different courts during the calendar year. The Taxation Laws (Second Amendment) Act, 2016 has amended the penalty provisions relating to search and has amended section 115BBE alongwith introduction of new penalty provision under section 271AAB which have been analysed and discussed in detail in this edition. A new chapter on Income Declaration Scheme, 2016 and The Taxation and Investment Regime for Pradhan Mantri Garib Kalyan Yojana, 2016 alongwith the critical analysis of the schemes has also been incorporated in this edition.

SEVENTH, EIGHTH AND NINTH EDITION

The seventh edition of book was published after a gap of almost 4 years. There was lot of demand of the revised edition of the book in professional circle. The delay was extended due to covid pandemic during the year 2020-21. Finance Act, 2021 has done away with special provision of assessment of search cases as provided u/ss 153A and 153C and now the assessment of search cases has to be undertaken as per normal provisions of the Act by regular assessment or reopening the cases u/s 148. We added a new chapter in the book analyzing the amended reassessment provisions along with discussion on various controversial issues which may arise in future.

In the eighth edition of the book, judicial decisions rendered by different courts on various issues upto March 2022 have also been updated.

The ninth edition of the book is published incorporating the amendments made in the Income-tax Act by Finance Act, 2023 and judicial decisions rendered by different courts on various issues up to March 2023 have also been updated.

We once again request our esteemed readers to keep on sending their valuable suggestions so as to make the book more useful for all of us.

raj@taxindia.net
rakesh@taxindia.net
Mob. : 9810002906, 9810420515

DR. RAJ K. AGARWAL
DR. RAKESH GUPTA

CHAPTER-HEADS

CONTENTS

1

SEARCH AND SEIZURE - NATURE OF PROVISIONS

2

CIRCUMSTANCES WHEN SEARCH CAN BE INITIATED

3

AUTHORIZATION OF SEARCH

4

VALIDITY OF SEARCH - WRIT JURISDICTION

5

ACTUAL CONDUCT OF SEARCH OPERATIONS

CONTENTS

6

SEIZURE OF BOOKS OF ACCOUNT, DOCUMENTS AND ASSETS

7

RESTRAINT ORDER - SECTION 132(3) AND SECTION 132(8A)

8

RECORDING OF STATEMENT - SECTION 132(4)

9

PRESUMPTION UNDER SECTIONS 132(4A) & 292C

10

SECTIONS 132(8)/132(10)/132(9)/132(9A) TO (9D) & 132B

PART 1

MISCELLANEOUS PROVISIONS RELATING TO SEARCH

11

REQUISITION UNDER SECTION 132A

12

NEW ASSESSMENT OR REASSESSMENT SCHEME OF SEARCH CASES AS INTRODUCED BY THE FINANCE ACT, 2021

15

ATTRACTION OF WEALTH TAX IN SEARCH CASES

16

PENALTIES AND PROSECUTION IN SEARCH CASES

17

APPLICATION TO SETTLEMENT COMMISSION IN SEARCH CASES

18

PRECAUTIONS BEFORE FACING SEARCH ACTION

SIGNIFICANT CHECK LISTS ON VARIOUS ISSUES RELATING TO HANDLING OF SEARCH & ASSESSMENT OF SEARCH CASES

1

POWERS AND OBLIGATIONS OF AUTHORISED OFFICER DURING SEARCH

Powers of Authorised Officer

➢ To enter forcibly into the premises if required.

➢ To search each and every part of the premises.

➢ To break open lock of locker, almirah, safe, box etc. in case keys are not available.

➢ To take extreme action *e.g.* tear sofa, dig floor/wall etc. in case of suspicion that incriminating material is kept therein.

➢ To conduct personal search of any person present or entering the premises.

➢ To seize books of account/documents.

➢ To seize undisclosed assets including cash or jewellery.

➢ To make list of stock or other assets not being seized.

➢ To place identification marks on the books of account not being seized.

➤ To put restraint order u/s 132(3), if deemed necessary.

➤ To record statement on oath u/s 132(4).

➤ To take services of police officers or other officers of the Central Government as required.

➤ To intimate to other Government authorities in case any violation of any other statute is found.

Obligations of Authorised Officer

➤ To show search warrant before commencing search and obtain signature of the person searched on search warrant.

➤ To prepare panchnama mentioning the proceedings of search and handover a copy to the assessee.

➤ To call for two witnesses in the presence of whom whole search operation is to be carried out.

➤ Seized articles to be kept in sealed packages bearing identification mark.

➤ To get signature of the person searched and that of the witnesses on seized packages, panchnama, statement recorded and put his signature also.

➤ To permit necessary telephone calls.

➤ To call the valuer for the valuation of jewellery.

➤ To inform and report expeditiously to controlling room and higher authorities on various significant development during search.

➤ Not to confine or put undue pressure on any person.

2

RIGHTS AND DUTIES OF ASSESSEE DURING SEARCH

Rights of assessee during search

- ➤ To see copy of search warrant.
- ➤ To see evidence of identity of officers of search team.
- ➤ To make personal search of the members of search party.
- ➤ To get medical aid, if required.
- ➤ To have regular meals.
- ➤ Right to worship as per custom.
- ➤ Right of the children to go to school.
- ➤ Nobody can be confined.
- ➤ Permission to leave the premises in view of the urgency of matter.
- ➤ Withdrawal by pardanasin women.
- ➤ To remain present during search proceedings or in his absence, to authorize somebody else on his behalf.
- ➤ Right to ensure that the facts stated by person searched during recording of statement u/s 132(4) are correctly incorporated.

Duties of Assessee during Search

- ➤ To allow free and unhindered ingress into the premises to the search team.
- ➤ To make available keys of locker, almirah, safe, boxes, etc.
- ➤ To facilitate operation of computer/laptop or other devices in which data is stored in electronics form.
- ➤ To co-operate with the search team in discharging their functions.
- ➤ Not to remove any article from its place without notice or knowledge of the authorized officer.
- ➤ Not to secret or destroy any document or evidence.
- ➤ To affix his signature on the recorded statement, inventories and panchnama.

3

___

NATURE OF QUESTIONS USUALLY ASKED BY THE AUTHORISED OFFICER DURING RECORDING OF STATEMENT IN SEARCH

➤ The identity, PAN No., sources of income of the assessee and other family members.

➤ Capacity in which the premises under search is occupied *i.e.* whether as owner, employee, tenant or otherwise.

➤ Names and addresses of business concerns, factory, godown, and branches, associate business entities of which assessee or his family members are proprietor, partner, director or shareholder.

➤ Investment in immovable properties with address and year of acquisition and source of acquisition.

➤ Investment in movable assets such as shares, FDRs, Bonds, jewellery, cars, expensive household items and source thereof.

➤ Particulars of Income Tax and Wealth Tax assessment.

➤ Details of cash, jewellery or other valuables lying in the house or in the bank locker, to whom the same belongs and the source thereof.

➤ Particulars of bank lockers maintained by the assessee and other family members, contents therein and the location of the keys of the locker(s).

➤ Details of bank accounts maintained with the banks with account numbers.

➤ Details of household expenses incurred, marriage or functions celebrated, educational expenses of the children and the source of withdrawal for the same.

➤ Details of books of account, including stock registers, maintained and the place where these are kept, password and software used for obtaining data kept in computer or other electronic device.

➤ Details regarding any secret chamber, locker or false sealing in the premises, if any.

➤ Details of any kind of movable assets, books of account or documents of others kept with the assessee or relating to the assessee kept with somebody else.

➤ Details of loans and advances, gifts or other credits given or taken/accepted by the assessee.

➤ Details of foreign travel and source of such expense and copy of passport.

➤ Details relating to undisclosed financial transactions carried by the assessee with respect to which authorized officer has information and the *modus operandi* adopted by the assessee to earn income outside the books.

➤ To seek explanation regarding incriminating material found such as pocket diaries, loose papers containing financial transactions, duplicate set of books of account, unaccounted agreements and properties etc.

➤ Source of acquisition of assets found such as cash, jewellery, electronic gadgets, A.C., refrigerator, music system etc., stock in business in excess of the amount recorded in the books, investment in immovable properties not recorded in the books, investment made in asset in cash, loans or advances, gifts or any other credit given or taken in cash etc.

➤ Authorized officer may cause enquiry to decode the figures or financial transactions recorded by the assessee in some kind of coded form in the seized material.

➤ Enquiry is made regarding any deviation found by the authorized officer in the actual facts and evidences found during search and as stated by the assessee during his preliminary statement.

4

CONTENTS OF SURRENDER LETTER

From the point of view of assessee

In case surrender of undisclosed income is made during the course of search and letter of surrender is submitted separately, it should normally contain the following details and under noted aspects may be taken care of :—

➤ Break up of total amount of undisclosed income surrendered person-wise, entity-wise and year-wise.

➤ A paragraph mentioning that the surrender letter submitted by the assessee is in the nature of statement of the assessee u/s 132(4).

➤ To mention that the declaration is subject to no penal consequences.

➤ To mention broad manner of earning undisclosed income and to substantiate it to the extent possible.

➤ To mention that tax applicable on surrendered income shall be paid in due course of time as and when due.

➤ Surrender letter to be signed by of the person/entity making the surrender. In case a person makes declaration on behalf of other person, he should be authorized to do so.

➤ Surrender of undisclosed income to be made in the hands of the person/entities against whom search warrant has been issued.

➤ To ensure that surrender letter is given prior to the date of conclusion of search with respect to the concerned person/entity.

➤ In case declaration is made amending or improving upon any earlier declaration, this fact should be clearly mentioned.

➤ In case there is seizure of cash, assessee should state and request to treat the amount of cash seized as payment of advance tax in the hands of concerned person/entity.

➤ A line mentioning that surrender of undisclosed income is being made to buy peace and to settle the dispute.

> Before making surrender of undisclosed income of the earlier year, all *pros* and *cons* to be weighed properly.

From the point of view of the department

> To ensure that the corresponding evidences relating to undisclosed income being surrendered are available.

> To obtain authority letter in case, surrender is made by a person on behalf of some other person/entity.

> A line stating that declaration of undisclosed income is over and above normal/regular income of the assessee.

> A line stating that the declaration is being made willingly by the assessee without any pressure or coercion or threat.

> To ensure that contents of surrender are covered in the statement of the assessee recorded u/s 132(4) and such statement is recorded on oath.

5

POST SEARCH LETTERS TO THE AUTHORISED OFFICER/ ASSESSING OFFICERS ON VARIOUS ASPECTS

➢ Request to appropriate cash seized toward advance tax.

➢ Application u/s 132B for release of disclosed assets if any seized along with all the relevant evidences.

➢ Letter requesting to give photocopies of all the documents, papers or books of account seized.

➢ Letter for release by person/entity not covered in the search, in case any books of account or assets belonging to them have been seized.

➢ Letter with complete evidences regarding disclosure of jewellery or assets in case restraint order u/s 132(3) has been passed but assets have not yet been seized.

➢ Letter for release of jewellery against deposit of equivalent amount of cash/furnishing of bank guarantee.

➢ In case of any irregularity or high handedness experienced during search, a letter explaining the actual facts to be brought to the notice of higher authorities.

➢ In case there is undue delay in lifting restraint order passed u/s 132(3), matter to be brought to the notice of higher authorities.

➢ In case any assessment/reassessment proceeding are pending before the Assessing Officer with respect to the person searched, a letter to the Assessing Officer regarding abatement of such proceedings.

6

POST SEARCH PROCEEDINGS BY THE AUTHORISED OFFICER

➤ Preparation of panchnama on completion of search.

➤ Lifting of restraint order passed u/s 132(3).

➤ To operate bank lockers and seizure of assets, if required.

➤ Recording of statement u/s 132(4) for seeking explaining of documents/undisclosed assets.

➤ To obtain break-up of surrendered income, if any.

➤ To collect records from different locations.

➤ To conduct third party inquiries/consequential survey if deemed appropriate.

➤ To send various reports to higher authorities.

➤ To prepare appraisal report.

➤ To prepare a suggestive questionnaire to be issued by Assessing Officer during assessment stage.

➤ To seek information/clarification from assessee on various issues.

➤ To institute prosecution in appropriate cases if deemed necessary.

➤ To recommend for the centralization of cases with appropriate jurisdiction.

7

PREPARATION PRIOR TO ASSESSMENT PROCEEDINGS

After search and before receiving the notices for filing returns of income u/s 153A, assessee usually gets sufficient time which may be utilized for preparing himself for effective representation in assessment proceeding. For this purpose, the following points may be kept in mind:—

➢ Filing the pending returns of income.

➢ Filing the objection for transfer of cases u/s 127.

➢ Organizing the books of account and other records relating to earlier six years properly.

➢ Ledgerization of transactions in case of individuals.

➢ Obtaining photocopies of seized documents.

➢ To prepare the explanation of the seized key documents.

➢ Filing pending returns of related persons.

➢ Going through the appraisal report, if possible.

➢ Proper accounting treatment and planning of surrendered income in the books of account.

➢ Payment of admitted taxes relating to the surrendered income if any.

➢ Filing of writ to High Court, if required.

8

DESIRED AMENDMENT/CLARIFICATION ON VARIOUS CONTROVERSIAL ISSUES

Authorisation and conduct of search

- ➤ Presence of advocate/CA/consultant during search.
- ➤ Pressure not to be exercised by the departmental officers for surrender of undisclosed income.
- ➤ Non-seizure of jewellery even if mismatched but covered within overall quantum of jewellery disclosed.
- ➤ Opportunity to the assessee before issuing requisition u/s 132A.
- ➤ Supply of the copy of search warrant to the person searched.
- ➤ Furnishing of the copy of the statement recorded immediately/expeditiously.
- ➤ Uninterrupted business operations during search.
- ➤ Simplification of the provisions regarding authorization of search.
- ➤ Allowing photocopies of books of account seized by the authorized officer expeditiously.
- ➤ Revoking of restraint orders passed u/s 132(3) within 15-30 days instead of 60 days.
- ➤ Issue of summon u/s 131(1A) by the authorized officers to the person searched during post search enquiry.

Release of assets

- ➤ Immediate release of disclosed assets if seized during search.
- ➤ Release of seized assets against payment of cash or furnishing of bank guarantee.
- ➤ Adjustment of cash seized towards tax liability including advance tax.
- ➤ Payment of interest for delay in release of assets.

Assessment

➢ Recording of satisfaction by Assessing Officer of person searched as well as Assessing Officer of other person before assuming jurisdiction u/s 153C.

➢ No proceedings u/s 153C on the basis of seizure of disclosed assets/regular books of account of other person.

➢ Procedure for release of seized disclosed assets/regular books of account belonging to other person(s).

➢ No proceedings u/s 153C relating to the year(s) for which nothing has been seized.

➢ No proceedings u/s 153A relating to year(s) for which nothing has been seized.

➢ Prescribing the time limit for issuing notices u/s 153C.

➢ Rationalization of time barring assessment limit in case of proceedings u/s 153C/132A, when huge gap exists in intimation of action and conclusion of action/handing over the material.

➢ Nature of additions which can be made during assessment u/s 153A.

➢ Prescribing the time limit for issuing notices u/s 153A.

Penalty

➢ Levy of penalty for concealment of income etc. u/s 271(1)(c) instead of penalty u/s 271AAA relating to the "undisclosed income" of the "specified previous year" once the return of income has been filed for such "specified previous year".

➢ For granting immunity from the levy of penalty for "undisclosed income" relating to "specified previous year" u/s 271AAA, the requirement of substantiating the manner is not practical.

➢ Some mechanism for declaration of "undisclosed income" relating to earlier years along with penalty for concealment of income but having deterrence effect.

➢ Levy of penalty u/s 271(1)(c) if return of income for earlier years could not be filed in time before the date of search for *bona fide* reasons.

LEADING CASE LAWS ON SIGNIFICANT ISSUES

SEARCH AND SEIZURE - NATURE OF PROVISIONS

Power of search to be exercised strictly in terms of law

- ◆ M.P. Sharma *v.* Satish Chandra AIR 1954 SC 300
- ◆ Pooran Mal *v.* Director of Inspection (1974) 93 ITR 505 (SC)
- ◆ Ramkibhai Kalidas *v.* I.G. Desai, ITO (1971) 80 ITR 721 (Guj.)

No power of arrest in the case of income tax search

- ◆ L.R. Gupta *v.* Union of India (1992) 194 ITR 32 (Del.)
- ◆ K. Choyi, ITO *v.* Syed Abdulla Bafakki Thangal (1973) 91 ITR 144 (Ker.)

CIRCUMSTANCES WHEN SEARCH CAN BE INITIATED

Provisions of section 132(1) to be construed strictly

- ◆ ITO *v.* Seth Brothers (1969) 74 ITR 836 (SC)
- ◆ Ganga Prasad Maheshwari *v.* CIT (1983) 139 ITR 1043 (All.)
- ◆ L.R. Gupta *v.* Union of India (1992) 194 ITR 32 (Del.)

Authorisation of search on the basis of assumption of non-compliance of notice/summon as given under section 132(1)(b)

- ◆ Pooran Mal *v.* Director of Inspection (1974) 93 ITR 505 (SC)
- ◆ C. Venkata Reddy *v.* ITO (1967) 66 ITR 212 (Mys.)
- ◆ Lit Light & Co. *v.* CIT (1982) 136 ITR 513 (All.)
- ◆ V.K. Jain *v.* Union of India (1975) 98 ITR 469 (Del.)

- Balwant Singh *v.* R.D. Shah, Director of Inspection (1969) 71 ITR 550 (Del.)

Information in possession of the competent authority on the basis of which search is authorised not to be based upon rumours or suspicion or vague facts

- Dr. Nandlal Tahiliani *v.* CIT (1988) 170 ITR 592 (All.)
- Dr. Sushil Rastogi *v.* Director of Investigation, Income Tax Department (2003) 260 ITR 249 (All.)
- L.R. Gupta *v.* Union of India (1992) 194 ITR 32 (Del.)
- Seniram Doongarmal Agency (P.) Ltd. *v.* K.E. Johnson (1964) 52 ITR 637 (Assam) (FB)
- N.K. Textile Mills *v.* CIT (1966) 62 ITR 58 (Punj.)
- Harmel Singh *v.* Union of India (1993) 204 ITR 334 (P&H)
- Kusum Lata *v.* CIT (1989) 180 ITR 365 (Raj.)
- Jain & Jain *v.* Union of India (1982) 134 ITR 655 (Bom.)
- Pawan Solvent & Chemicals *v.* CIT (1987) 166 ITR 67 (Pat.)
- Tejram Omprakash (HUF) *v.* DIT (2014) 220 Taxman 85 (Mag.) (MP)(HC)
- Rajesh Rajora *v.* UOI (2014) 220 Taxman 146 (Mag.)(MP)(HC)

Information in possession of the competent authority on the basis of which search is authorised not to be general in nature

- Ganga Prasad Maheshwari *v.* CIT (1983) 139 ITR 1043 (All.)
- Dr. Nandlal Tahiliani *v.* CIT (1988) 170 ITR 592 (All.)
- Mahesh Kumar Agarwal *v.* Dy. DIT (2003) 260 ITR 67 (Cal.)
- L.R. Gupta *v.* Union of India (1992) 194 ITR 32 (Del.)

Information in possession of the competent authority on the basis of which search is authorised not for fishing or roving enquiry

- ITO *v.* Seth Bros. (1969) 74 ITR 836 (SC)
- Balwant Singh *v.* R.D. Shah, Director of Inspection (1969) 71 ITR 550 (Del.)
- Bharati (P.) Ltd. *v.* R.S. Chadda (1973) 89 ITR 108 (Cal.)
- I. Devarajan *v.* Tamil Nadu Farmers Services Co-op. Federation (1981) 131 ITR 506 (Mad.)

Information in possession of the competent authority on the basis of which search is authorised can be based upon reports from other authorities

- Sudarshan & Co. *v.* CIT (1983) 139 ITR 1032 (All.)

- Narayan Das v. CIT (1984) 148 ITR 567 (MP)
- Ganga Prasad Maheshwari v. CIT (1983) 139 ITR 1043 (All.)
- Subir Roy v. S.K. Chattopadhyay (1986) 158 ITR 472 (Cal.)
- Orient (Goa) Ltd. v. Union of India (1994) 210 ITR 896 (Bom.)
- Harmel Singh v. Union of India (1993) 204 ITR 334 (P&H)

Before authorizing search information should be verified

- Lajpat Rai v. CIT (1995) 215 ITR 608 (All.)
- Lit Light & Co. v. CIT (1982) 136 ITR 513 (All.)
- Diamondstar Exports Ltd. v. DGIT (Inv.) (2005) 278 ITR 36 (Bom.)
- M.S. Associates v. Union of India (2005) 275 ITR 502 (Gauhati)
- Dr. D.C. Srivastava v. DIT (Inv.) (2007) 212 CTR (All.) 527
- Union of India v. Ajit Jain (2003) 260 ITR 80 (SC)
- Doctor's X Ray & Pathology Institute Pvt. Ltd. v. Director of Investigation (2009) 318 ITR 125 (All.)
- Genom Biotech Pvt. Ltd. v. DIT (Inv.) (2009) 224 CTR (Bom.) 270
- Balwant Singh v. R.D Shah, Director of Inspection (1969) 71 ITR 550 (Del.)
- Ganga Prasad Maheshwari v. CIT (1983) 139 ITR 1043 (All.)
- Gardhara Singh v. CIT (1980) 125 ITR 340 (P&H)
- Dr. Nalini Mahajan v. DIT (Inv.) (2001) 252 ITR 123 (Del.)
- Farshubhai Prabhuram Bhai Kakkad v. DIT (Inv.) (2003) 264 ITR 87 (Guj.)
- Shyam Jewellers v. Chief Commissioner (Admn.) (1992) 196 ITR 243 (All.)
- Anand Swaroop v. CIT (1976) 103 ITR 575 (P&H)

Before authorizing search there has to be reason to believe not reason to suspect

- Balwant Singh v. R.D. Shah, Director of Inspection (1969) 71 ITR 550 (Del.)
- Kusum Lata v. CIT (1989) 180 ITR 365 (Raj.)
- Ganga Prasad Maheshwari v. CIT (1983) 139 ITR 1043 (All.)
- Vindhya Metal Corporation v. CIT (1985) 156 ITR 233 (All.)
- Kalpaka Bazar v. CIT (1990) 186 ITR 617 (Ker.)
- Dr. Partap Singh v. Director of Enforcement (1985) 155 ITR 166 (SC)

- Pooran Mal *v.* Director of Inspection (1974) 93 ITR 505 (SC)
- ITO *v.* Seth Brothers (1969) 74 ITR 836 (SC)
- Hazari Lal Soni *v.* Union of India (1994) 208 ITR 365 (Raj.)
- ITO *v.* Lakhmani Mewal Das (1976) 103 ITR 437 (SC)
- Jain & Jain *v.* Union of India (1982) 134 ITR 655 (Bom.)

Formation of reason to believe separately for each person

- Harihar Shah *v.* CIT (2006) 281 ITR 199 (Gau.)

There has to be nexus between information and reason to believe

- Harvest Gold Foods (India) Pvt. Ltd. *v.* Union of India (2006) 282 ITR 83 (Raj.)
- Dr. Nandlal Tahiliani *v.* CIT (1988) 170 ITR 592 (All.)
- Lit Light & Co. *v.* CIT (1982) 136 ITR 513 (All.)

Reasons recorded for authorizing search need not be communicated

- Mamchand & Co. *v.* CIT (1970) 76 ITR 217 (Cal.)
- Jain & Jain *v.* Union of India (1982) 134 ITR 655 (Bom.)
- Ram Swarup Sahu *v.* CIT (1992) 196 ITR 841 (Pat.)

Circumstances when survey can be converted into search

- Asstt. CIT *v.* Panchuram Deshmukh (2010) 40 DTR 252 (Bilaspur) (Trib.)/(2010) 133 TTJ (Bilaspur) 53
- Vinod Goel *v.* Union of India (2001) 252 ITR 29 (P&H)
- Asstt. CIT *v.* Mangaram Chaudhary HUF (2008) 119 TTJ (Hyd.) 671/ (2010) 123 ITD 359
- Badri Ram Choudhary *v.* Asstt. CIT (2012) 67 DTR 107 (Jd.) (Trib.)/ (2012) 145 TTJ (Jd) 7

AUTHORIZATION OF SEARCH

Search warrant can be issued in joint name

- Dr. Oswald Anthony *v.* CIT (2004) 270 ITR 204 (Pat.)
- Madhupuri Corpn. *v.* Parbhat Jha, Dy. DIT (Investigation) (2002) 256 ITR 498 (Guj.)
- CIT *v.* Smt. Vandana Verma (2010) 186 Taxman 88 (All.)/(2011) 330 ITR 533
- Rajat Tradecom India (P.) Ltd. *v.* Dy. CIT (2009) 23 DTR 311 (Ind.)/ (2009) 120 ITD 48
- Jose Cyriac *v.* CIT (2011) 336 ITR 241 (Ker.)
- Naresh Chand Baid *v.* Asstt. CIT (2012) 66 DTR 221 (Chhattisgarh)

Issue of blank search warrant is illegal and may vitiate the whole process of search

- Jagmohan Mahajan *v.* CIT (1976) 103 ITR 579 (P&H)
- H.L. Sibal *v.* CIT (1975) 101 ITR 112 (P&H)
- Manmohan Krishan Mahajan *v.* CIT (1977) 107 ITR 420 (P&H)

Search warrant is not required to be served to the person under search.

- Jain & Jain *v.* Union of India (1982) 134 ITR 655 (Bom.)
- V.K. Jain *v.* Union of India (1975) 98 ITR 469 (Del.)
- Genom Biotech Pvt. Ltd. *v.* DIT (Investigation) (2009) 224 CTR (Bom.) 270
- Southern Herbals Ltd. *v.* DIT (1994) 207 ITR 55 (Ker.)
- Subir Roy *v.* S.K. Chattopadhyay (1986) 158 ITR 472 (Cal.)

VALIDITY OF SEARCH - WRIT JURISDICTION

Satisfaction note recorded by competent authority not to be shown to the person searched. Validity of satisfaction note cannot be subject matter to be decided by ITAT. Illegality of search can be decided by High Court/ Supreme Court in writ jurisdiction

- Ram Swarup Sahu *v.* CIT (1992) 196 ITR 841 (Pat.)
- Mamchand & Co. *v.* CIT (1970) 76 ITR 217 (Cal.)
- Dr. Partap Singh *v.* Director of Enforcement (1985) 155 ITR 166 (SC)
- Rati Ram Gotte Wala *v.* DCIT (2004) 89 ITD 14 (Del.)
- M.B. Lal *v.* CIT (2005) 279 ITR 298 (Del.)
- Promain Ltd. *v.* Dy. CIT (2006) 281 ITR (AT) 107 (Del.) (SB)
- CIT *v.* Paras Rice Mills (2008) 15 DTR 262 (P&H)/(2009) 313 ITR 0182 (P&H)

Validity of search

- Bhupendra Ratilal Thakkar *v.* CIT (1976) 102 ITR 531 (SC)
- Shyam Jewellers *v.* Chief Commissioner (Admn.) (1992) 196 ITR 243 (All.)
- CIT *v.* Tarsem Kumar (1986) 161 ITR 505 (SC)
- Tomar, I.S. Dr. *v.* DIT (1996) 85 Taxman 468 (All.)
- ITO *v.* Seth Brothers (1969) 74 ITR 836 (SC)
- Pawan Solvent & Chemicals *v.* CIT (1987) 166 ITR 67 (Pat.)
- Shree Krishna Investments *v.* Union of India AIR 1976 Cal. 333

- Dr. Nandlal Tahiliani v. CIT (1988) 170 ITR 592 (All.)
- CIT v. Dr. Nandlal Tahiliani (1988) 172 ITR 627 (SC)
- H.L. Sibal v. CIT (1975) 101 ITR 112 (P&H)
- Harmel Singh v. Union of India (1993) 204 ITR 334 (P&H)
- Chemitex v. Union of India (1982) Tax L.R. 2871 (Goa)
- Kusum Lata v. CIT (1989) 180 ITR 365 (Raj.)

Irregularity during search does not make the search illegal

- E.P. Royappa v. State of Tamil Nadu AIR 1974 SC 555
- Dr. Partap Singh v. Director of Enforcement (1985) 155 ITR 166 (SC)
- Express Newspapers Pvt. Ltd. v. Union of India AIR 1986 SC 872
- Takshila Educational Society v. DIT (Inv.) (2005) 272 ITR 274 (Pat.)
- Naraindas v. CIT (1984) 148 ITR 567 (MP)
- ITO v. Seth Brothers (1969) 74 ITR 836 (SC)
- Balwant Singh v. R.D. Shah, Director of Inspection (1969) 71 ITR 550 (Del.)
- CIT v. Dr. C. Balakrishnan Nair (2005) 282 ITR 158 (Ker.)
- CIT v. S.K. Katyal (2009) 308 ITR 168 (Del.)
- Dr. C. Balakrishnan Nair v. CIT (1999) 237 ITR 70 (Ker.)
- VLS Finance Ltd. v. CIT (2007) 289 ITR 286 (Del.)
- Lan Eseda Steels Ltd. v. Asstt. CIT (1994) 209 ITR 901 (AP)
- Pooran Mal v. Director of Inspection (1974) 93 ITR 505 (SC)

Evidences collected during illegal search can be made use of by the department

- DGIT v. Diamondstar Exports Ltd. (2007) 293 ITR 438 (SC)
- CIT v. Nandlal Tahiliani (1988) 172 ITR 627 (SC)
- Kusum Lata v. CIT (1989) 180 ITR 365 (Raj.)
- Pooran Mal v. Director of Inspection (1974) 93 ITR 505 (SC)
- L.R. Gupta v. Union of India (1992) 194 ITR 32 (Del.)
- Union of India v. Ajit Jain (2003) 260 ITR 80 (SC)
- Rakesh Kumar Agarwal v. DGIT (1996) 221 ITR 818 (Del.)
- Khandani Shafakhana v. Union of India (1989) 175 ITR 408 (Del.)
- ITO v. U.K. Mahapatra & Co. (2009) 225 CTR (SC) 131
- Dr. Partap Singh v. Director of Enforcement (1985) 155 ITR 166 (SC)

◆ Varghese Varghese *v.* Commissioner of Agricultural Income Tax (1976) 105 ITR 732 (Ker.)

◆ Thakursidas Banwarilal *v.* CIT (1998) 232 ITR 846 (Gau.)

◆ New Street Oil Mills *v.* State of Kerala (1978) 111 ITR 463 (Ker.)

◆ Balwant Singh *v.* R.D. Shah, Director of Inspection (1969) 71 ITR 550 (Del.)

◆ Harikisandas Gulabdas & Sons *v.* State of Mysore (1971) 27 STC 434 (Mys.)

◆ Bishnu Krishna Shrestha *v.* Union of India (1987) 168 ITR 815 (Cal.)

High Court cannot examine sufficiency of reasons recorded by competent authority

◆ Balwant Singh *v.* R.D. Shah, Director of Inspection (1969) 71 ITR 550 (Del.)

◆ ITO *v.* Seth Brothers (1969) 74 ITR 836 (SC)

◆ Calcutta Discount Co. Ltd. *v.* ITO (1961) 41 ITR 191 (SC)

◆ Kusum Lata *v.* CIT (1989) 180 ITR 365 (Raj.)

◆ Sudarshan & Co. *v.* CIT (1983) 139 ITR 1032 (All.)

◆ Southern Herbals Ltd. *v.* DIT Investigation (1994) 207 ITR 55 (Kar.)

◆ Shyam Jewellers *v.* Chief Commissioner (Admn.) (1992) 196 ITR 243 (All.)

◆ Suresh Bhai Bhola Bhai Jani *v.* Union of India (2001) 249 ITR 363 (Raj.)

◆ Director General of IT (Investigation) & Ors. *v.* Spacewood Furnishers (P.) Ltd. & Ors. (2015) 119 DTR (SC) 201

Scope of writ petition under article 226

◆ Sriram Jaiswal *v.* Union of India (1989) 176 ITR 261 (AR)

◆ Yogendra Kumar Durlabhji *v.* CIT (1999) 237 ITR 405 (Raj.)

◆ Wakil Kumar *v.* CIT (2003) 259 ITR 698 (Pat.)

◆ Jagdish Prasad Saraogi *v.* Union of India (1997) 225 ITR 642 (Gau.)

◆ Namit Verma *v.* Union of India (2001) 247 ITR 49 (Del.)

ACTUAL CONDUCT OF SEARCH OPERATIONS

Search should be completed expeditiously - No undue delay permitted

◆ Dr. C. Balakrishnan Nair *v.* CIT (1999) 237 ITR 70 (Ker.)

◆ Shri Ganesh Enterprises Pvt. Ltd. *v.* Union of India (1994) 210 ITR 786 (Del.)

- ◆ CIT *v.* Sarb Consulate Marine Products Pvt. Ltd. (2007) 294 ITR 444 (Del.)

Services of police officers permitted during search

- ◆ ITO *v.* Seth Brothers (1969) 74 ITR 836 (SC)
- ◆ Subir Roy *v.* S.K. Chattopadhyay (1986) 158 ITR 472 (Cal.)

SEIZURE OF BOOKS OF ACCOUNT, DOCUMENTS AND ASSETS

Seizure of assets belonging to other persons

- ◆ DIT (Inv.) *v.* S.R. Batliboi & Co. (2009) 224 CTR (Del.) 369/(2009) 315 ITR 137 (Del.)
- ◆ DIT (Inv.) *v.* S.R. Batliboi & Co. (2009) 227 CTR (SC) 238

Opportunity to assessee before seizure is made

- ◆ L.R. Gupta *v.* Union of India (1992) 194 ITR 32 (Del.)

Power to seal whole premises

- ◆ Shyam Jewellers *v.* Chief Commissioner (Admn.) (1992) 196 ITR 243 (All.)

Seizure of title deed of immovable property

- ◆ Bhagwan Das Narain Das *v.* CIT (1975) 98 ITR 194 (Guj.)

Immovable property cannot be seized

- ◆ Sardar Parduman Singh *v.* Union of India (1987) 166 ITR 115 (Del.)
- ◆ M.K. Gabrial Babu *v.* Asstt. DIT (1990) 186 ITR 435 (Ker.)
- ◆ Nand Kishore Mangharani *v.* DIT (1994) 210 ITR 1071 (All.)
- ◆ CIT *v.* M.K. Gabrial Babu (1991) 188 ITR 464 (Ker.)
- ◆ Rajendra Singh Nayak *v.* DCIT (2014) 268 CTR 484/227 Taxman 13 (Mag.) (MP)(HC)

No seizure of assets when source of acquisition is explained

- ◆ CIT *v.* Vindhya Metal Corporation (1997) 224 ITR 614 (SC)
- ◆ Biaora Constructions Pvt. Ltd. *v.* DIT (Inv.) (2006) 281 ITR 247 (MP)

RESTRAINT ORDER- SECTION 132(3) AND SECTION 132(8A)

Restraint order u/s 132(3) can be passed only for books of account, other document or assets which are liable to be seized

- ◆ Windson Electronics Pvt. Ltd. *v.* Union of India (2004) 269 ITR 481 (Cal.)

- Om Prakash Jindal *v.* Union of India (1976) 104 ITR 389 (Cal.)
- Ramesh Chander *v.* CIT (1974) 93 ITR 244 (P&H)
- Smt. Krishna Verma *v.* Asstt. CIT (2008) 113 ITD 655 (Del.) (SB)
- VLS Finance Ltd. *v.* CIT (2007) 289 ITR 286 (Del.)
- Mst. Anisa Bano *v.* CIT (1989) 177 ITR 368 (MP)

Restraint order u/s 132(3) not to be used to keep the search operation pending

- CIT *v.* Sandhya P. Naik (2002) 253 ITR 534 (Bom.)
- CIT *v.* S.K. Katyal (2009) 308 ITR 168 (Del.)
- CIT *v.* Sarb Consulate Marine Products Pvt. Ltd. (2007) 294 ITR 444 (Del.)
- CIT *v.* Deepak Aggarwal (2009) 308 ITR 116 (Del.)
- M.B. Lal *v.* CIT (2005) 279 ITR 298 (Del.)
- VLS Finance Ltd. *v.* CIT (2007) 289 ITR 286 (Del.)
- Dr. C. Balakrishnan Nair *v.* CIT (1999) 237 ITR 70 (Ker.)

Restraint order to be addressed to the assessee

- ITO *v.* M. Shajahan (1976) 104 ITR 347 (Ker.)
- Jain & Jain *v.* Union of India (1981) 134 ITR 655 (Bom.)

Restraint order to expire after 60 days

- Mahesh Kumar Agarwal *v.* Dy. DIT (2003) 260 ITR 67 (Cal.)

Restraint order cannot be renewed from time to time

- Windson Electronics Pvt. Ltd. *v.* Union of India (2004) 269 ITR 481 (Cal.)
- B.K. Nowlakha *v.* Union of India (1991) 192 ITR 436 (Del.)

Restraint order to be lifted expeditiously

- Ganesh Enterprises Pvt. Ltd. *v.* Union of India (1994) 75 Taxman 239 (Del.)/(1994) 210 ITR 786 (Del.)

Whether restraint order can be passed with respect to bank accounts, fixed deposits, etc.

- I. Devarajan *v.* Tamil Nadu Farmers Services Co-op. Federation (1981) 131 ITR 506 (Mad.)
- M.V. Gnanendra Nath *v.* Union of India (2004) 266 ITR 250, 254 (Kar.)
- Bhagwan Das Narayan Dass *v.* CIT (1975) 98 ITR 194 (Guj.)
- Mahesh Kumar Agarwal *v.* Dy. DIT (2003) 260 ITR 67 (Cal.)

Restraint order cannot be put on whole premises

- Shyam Jewellers *v.* Chief Commissioner (Admn.) (1992) 196 ITR 243 (All.)

Restraint order does not amount to seizure

- Mrs. Kanwal Shamsher Singh *v.* Union of India (1974) 95 ITR 80 (Del.)
- Ramesh Chander *v.* CIT (1974) 93 ITR 244 (P&H)
- B.K. Nowlakha *v.* Union of India (1991) 192 ITR 436 (Del.)
- CIT *v.* Sarb Consulate Marine Products Pvt. Ltd. (2007) 294 ITR 444 (Del.)
- CIT *v.* Sandhya P. Nayak (2002) 253 ITR 534 (Bom.)

Prosecution for contravention of restraint order passed under section 132(3)

- State of Maharashtra *v.* Narayan Champalal Bajaj (1993) 201 ITR 315 (Bom.)
- State *v.* Rakesh Aggarwal (1995) 80 Taxman 539 (Del.)

RECORDING OF STATEMENT - SECTION 132(4)

Statement u/s 132(4) recorded on oath can be used as evidence in any proceedings under the Act

- Addl. CIT *v.* Hanuman Agarwal (1984) 17 Taxman 19 (Pat.)/(1985) 151 ITR 150 (Pat.)
- Chowkchand Balabux *v.* CIT (1961) 41 ITR 465 (Assam)

Evidentiary value of statement recorded u/s 132(4)

- Kesri K. Deboo *v.* Asstt. CIT (2009) 313 ITR 186 (Bom.)
- M.S. Aggarwal *v.* Dy. CIT (2004) 90 ITD 80 (Del.)
- Pullangode Rubber Produce Co. Ltd. *v.* State of Kerala (1973) 91 ITR 18 (SC)
- Ravindra D. Trivedi *v.* CIT (2008) 215 CTR (Raj.) 313/(2008) 2 DTR 385 (Raj.)
- Dy. CIT *v.* Pramukh Builders (2008) 115 TTJ (Ahd.) (TM) 330/112 ITD 179 (Ahd.)(TM)
- Dy. CIT *v.* Bhogilal Mulchand Kandoi (2005) 98 TTJ (Ahd.) 108/96 ITD 344 (Ahd.)
- Hokum Chand Jain (2010) 191 Taxman 319/337 ITR 238 (Chhattisgarh)
- Asstt. CIT *v.* Yerra Nagabhushanam (1997) 226 ITR 843 (AP)
- Shree Ganesh Trading Co. *v.* CIT (2013) 214 Taxman 262/257 CTR 159/84 DTR 94 (Jharkhand) (HC)

- Bhagirath Aggarwal *v.* CIT (2013) 351 ITR 143/215 Taxman 229/89 DTR 362 (Delhi) (HC)

Issue of summon under section 131(1A) after the conduct of search

- Dr. Mrs. Anita Sahai *v.* DIT (Inv.) (2004) 136 Taxman 247 (All.)/266 ITR 597 (All.)
- Arti Gases *v.* DIT (2004) 248 ITR 55 (Guj.)
- Dr. V.S. Chauhan *v.* Director of Income-tax (Investigations) (2011) 336 ITR 533 (All.)
- Neesa Leisure Ltd. *v.* Union of India (2011) 338 ITR 460 (Guj.)

Retraction of statement given under section 132(4)

- Nagubai Armul *v.* B. Sharma Rao AIR 1956 SC 100
- Sarwan Singh Rattan Singh *v.* State of Punjab AIR 1957 SC 637
- Avadh Kishore Das *v.* Ram Gopal AIR 1979 SC 861
- Asstt. CIT *v.* Rameshchandra R. Patel (2005) 94 TTJ (Ahd.) (TM) 361/ 89 ITD 203 (Ahd.) (TM)
- Asstt. CIT *v.* Jorawar Singh M. Rathod (2005) 94 TTJ (Ahd.) 867
- Dhunjibhoy Stud & Agricultural Farm *v.* Dy. CIT (2002) 82 ITD 18 (Pune) (TM)
- Hiralal Maganlal & Co. *v.* Dy. CIT (2005) 96 ITD 113 (Mum.)

Consequences of retraction

- CIT *v.* Dr. N. Thippa Setty (2010) 322 ITR 525 (Kar.)
- CIT *v.* Medical Trust Hospital (2008) 220 CTR (Ker.) 166

In case of retraction burden of proof on assessee

- Krishan Lal Shiv Chand Rai *v.* CIT (1973) 88 ITR 293 (P&H)
- Karam Chand *v.* Asstt. CIT (2000) 73 ITD 434 (Chd.)
- Video Master *v.* Jt. CIT (2002) 83 ITD 102 (Mum.)
- Dhanvarsha Builders & Developers Pvt. Ltd. *v.* Dy. CIT (2006) 102 ITD 375 (Pune)
- Kantilal Prabhudas Patel *v.* Dy. CIT (Inv.) (2005) 93 ITD 117 (Indore) (TM)
- Carpenters Classics (Exim) Pvt. Ltd. *v.* Dy. CIT (2007) 108 ITD 142 (Bang.)

Undisclosed income can be assessed having regard to nature of evidences

- ITO *v.* Ashok Kumar Aggarwal (1990) 38 TTJ (Del.) 189
- Pullangode Rubber Produce Co. Ltd. *v.* State of Kerala (1973) 91 ITR 18 (SC)
- Dy. CIT *v.* M.L. Jain (2005) 96 TTJ (Jodh.) 362

- Asstt. CIT *v.* Anoop Kumar (2005) 94 TTJ (Asr.) 288
- S.R.M.T. Ltd. *v.* Dy. CIT (2005) 97 TTJ (Visakha.) 580

PRESUMPTION UNDER SECTION 132(4A)

Legal presumption is against the person having possession or control

- P.K. Narayanan *v.* CIT (1998) 229 ITR 596 (Ker.)
- ITO *v.* Prem Dass (1992) 198 ITR 93 (P&H)
- Kerala Liquor Corporation *v.* CIT (1996) 222 ITR 333 (Ker.)
- CIT *v.* K.I. Pavunny (1998) 232 ITR 837 (Ker.)
- Chuharmal *v.* CIT (1988) 172 ITR 250 (SC)
- CIT *v.* Ashok Kumar (2006) 286 ITR 541 (All.)
- Hemant Kumar Ghosh *v.* Asstt. CIT A. Anr. (2015) 126 DTR (Pat.) 396 (HC)

Possession or control may be different from ownership

- ITO *v.* W.D. Estate Pvt. Ltd. (1993) 45 ITD 473 (Bom.) (TM)/(1993) 46 TTJ (Bom.) 143
- CIT *v.* K.K. Abdul Kareem (1996) 88 Taxman 323 (Ker.)/(1996) 132 CTR 431 (Ker.)
- CIT *v.* Soorajmal Nagarmull (1990) 181 ITR 340 (Cal.)
- Mangilal Agarwal *v.* Asstt. CIT (2008) 300 ITR 372 (Raj.)
- R. Bharathan *v.* ITO (1990) 182 ITR 146 (Ker.)
- Bansal Strips Pvt. Ltd. *v.* Asstt. CIT (2006) 99 ITD 177 (Del.)
- CIT *v.* Shravan Kumar Gurjar (2010) 230 CTR 539 (Del.)

Presumption is a rebuttable presumption

- Asstt. CIT *v.* Thahrayamal Balchand (1980) 124 ITR 111 (Raj.)
- CIT *v.* P.R. Metrani (HUF) (2001) 251 ITR 244 (Kar.)
- Biru Mal Pyare Lal *v.* Asstt. CIT (2001) 79 ITD 169 (Chd.)
- Shashikant M. Zaveri *v.* Sixth ITO (1990) 37 TTJ (Bom.) 120
- Asstt. CIT *v.* Radheyshyam Poddar (1992) 41 ITD 449 (Cal.)
- Bharathan (R.) *v.* ITO (1990) 182 ITR 146 (Ker.)
- CIT *v.* Kishanchand (1993) 45 TTJ (Jp.) 20
- CIT *v.* S.M.S. Investment Corporation Pvt. Ltd. (1994) 207 ITR 364 (Raj.)
- CIT *v.* Raj Pal Singh Ram Avtar (2007) 288 ITR 498 (All.)
- Sukh Ram *v.* Asstt. CIT (2006) 285 ITR 256 (Del.)
- Surendra M. Khandhar *v.* Asstt. CIT (2010) 321 ITR 254 (Bom.)

- ◆ CIT *v.* Ved Prakash Choudhary (2008) 305 ITR 245 (Del.)
- ◆ CIT *v.* D.R. Bansal (2010) 228 CTR (Chhattisgarh) 247/(2010) 327 ITR 44 (Chhattisgarh)
- ◆ CIT *v.* Blue Lines (2015) 231 Taxman 49 (Karn.)(HC)

Presumption is not binding on assessing officer

- ◆ Pradip Chandulal Patel *v.* P.G. Karode (1992) 197 ITR 385 (Guj.)
- ◆ ITO *v.* Abdul Majeed (1987) 64 CTR (Ker.) 266/(1988) 169 ITR 440 (Ker.)
- ◆ S.R.M.T. Ltd. *v.* Dy. CIT (2005) 97 TTJ (Visakha.) 580
- ◆ Anjuga Chit Funds Pvt. Ltd. *v.* Dy. CIT (2008) 113 ITD 67 (Chennai)

Presumption is available under regular assessment proceedings

- ◆ Pushkar Narain Sarraf *v.* CIT (1990) 183 ITR 388 (All.)
- ◆ P.R. Metrani *v.* CIT (2006) 287 ITR 209 (SC)
- ◆ Ashwani Kumar *v.* ITO (1991) 39 ITD 183 (Del.)

Onus to establish income of the assessee remains on assessing officer

- ◆ Doon Valley Roller Flour Mills Pvt. Ltd. *v.* IAC (1989) 31 ITD 238 (Del.)
- ◆ Asstt. CIT *v.* Sri Radheshyam Poddar (1992) 41 ITD 449 (Cal.)
- ◆ Kollipara Subba Rao *v.* ITO (1990) 32 ITD 668 (Hyd.)
- ◆ CIT *v.* D.K. Gupta (2009) 308 ITR 230 (Del.)
- ◆ Amar Natvarlal Shah *v.* Asstt. CIT (1997) 60 ITD 560 (Ahd.)
- ◆ Brijlal Rupchand *v.* ITO (1991) 40 TTJ (Indore) 668
- ◆ Asstt. CIT *v.* Ashok Kumar Poddar (2008) 16 DTR (Kol.) (Trib.) 55

No presumption against third party

- ◆ Straptex (India) Pvt. Ltd. *v.* Dy. CIT (2003) 84 ITD 320 (Mum.)
- ◆ Rama Traders *v.* First ITO (1988) 32 TTJ (Pat.) (TM) 483
- ◆ Kishanchand Sobhrajmal *v.* Asstt. CIT (1992) 41 ITD 97 (Jp.)
- ◆ Asstt. CIT *v.* Kishore Lal Balwant Rai (2007) 17 SOT 380 (Chd.)
- ◆ Sheth Akshay Pushpavadan *v.* Dy. CIT (2010) 130 TTJ (Ahd.) (UO) 42

SECTION 132(8)/132(10)/132(9)/132(9A)

Approval for extension for retention of books of account, documents, etc. to be granted before expiry of the period

- ◆ CIT *v.* Jawahar Lal Rastogi (1970) 78 ITR 486 (SC)
- ◆ Metal Fittings Pvt. Ltd. *v.* Union of India (1983) 141 ITR 758 (Del.)

Application and release of disclosed assets seized

◆ Gordhanbhai Nagardas Patel *v.* Deputy CIT [2017] 82 taxmann.com 455/249 Taxman 604 (Guj.

◆ Fatema Hussain *v.* Union of India [2017] 88 taxmann.com 725 (Patna)

◆ Hyderabad Vanaspathi Ltd. *v.* ITO (1984) 19 Taxman 422 (AP)/(1985) 152 ITR 1 (AP)

◆ Hanuman Pershad Ganeriwala *v.* Director of Inspection (1974) 93 ITR 419 (Del.)

◆ Sampat Lal & Sons *v.* CIT (1984) 150 ITR 191 (MP)

Commissioner's approval for retention to be communicated

◆ Arti Gases *v.* DIT (Inv.) (2001) 248 ITR 55 (Guj.)

◆ State Bank of Patiala *v.* S.K. Sharma AIR 1996 SC 1669

◆ Managing Director, ECIL *v.* B. Karunakar AIR 1994 SC 1074

Extension for retention can be granted repeatedly as may be required

◆ Smt. Vidya Devi *v.* ITO 1972 Tax LR 572

◆ Mohan Magotra *v.* DIT (2002) 177 CTR 352 (J&K)

Release of books of account or documents illegally seized

◆ K.R. Modi & Co. *v.* Dy. DIT (Inv.) (2005) 272 ITR 587 (Cal.)

Release of books of account or documents relating to other persons seized

◆ Wakil Kumar *v.* CIT (2003) 259 ITR 698 (Pat.)

◆ Raj Kumar Sharma *v.* Secretary, Government of India (2002) 175 CTR (P&H) 49

Illegal retention of books of account, other documents

◆ Thanthi Trust *v.* CIT (1987) 167 ITR 397 (Del.)

◆ Krishna Kumari Sharma *v.* CIT (1991) 192 ITR 57 (All.)

◆ Cowasjee Nusserwanji Dinshaw *v.* ITO (1987) 165 ITR 702 (Guj.)

◆ C.K. Wadha *v.* CIT (1970) 78 ITR 782 (Cal.)

◆ Khandani Shafakhana *v.* Union of India (1989) 175 ITR 408 (Del.)

◆ Rakesh Kumar Agarwal *v.* DGIT (1996) 221 ITR 818 (Del.)

◆ Survir Enterprises *v.* CIT (1986) 157 ITR 206 (Del.)

◆ Director of Inspection *v.* K.C. & Co. (1987) 32 Taxman 495 (J&K)/ (1990) 185 ITR 475 (J&K)

◆ Metal Fittings Pvt. Ltd. *v.* Union of India (1983) 141 ITR 758 (Del.)

Right to obtain photocopies of books of account, other documents seized

◆ New Kashmir & Oriental Transport Co. Pvt. Ltd. *v.* CIT (1973) 92 ITR 334 (All.)

◆ Ramesh Chander *v.* CIT (1974) 93 ITR 244 (P&H)

◆ Dhaniram Gupta *v.* Union of India (1973) 89 ITR 281 (Cal.)

Immediate release of deposits seized from disclosed bank accounts

◆ D.R. Benefit Fund Limited *v.* Asstt. DIT (Inv.) (2006) 203 CTR (Mad.) 453/(2008) 297 ITR 346 (Mad.)

Conversion of assets in kind into money

◆ K.C.C. Software Ltd. *v.* DIT (Inv.) (2008) 298 ITR 001 (SC)

◆ Raj Kumar *v.* Union of India (2000) 242 ITR 584 (P&H)

◆ Windson Electronics Pvt. Ltd. *v.* Union of India (2004) 141 Taxman 419 (Cal.)/(2004) 269 ITR 0481 (Cal.)

◆ Jagdishprasad M. Joshi *v.* Dy. CIT (2005) 273 ITR 296 (Bom.)

No retention of seized assets during pendency of appeal by the department

◆ Naresh Kumar Kohli *v.* CIT (2004) 137 Taxman 438 (P&H)

◆ Mukundray K. Shah *v.* DGIT (2004) 141 Taxman 381/269 ITR 529 (Cal.)

◆ Bhagwat Prasad *v.* CIT (1983) 139 ITR 961 (All.)

◆ Asha Devi *v.* CIT (2007) 291 ITR 496 (Del.)

◆ Bhawna Lodha (Smt.) *v.* DGIT (2013) 354 ITR 134/214 Taxman 273/ 257 CTR 176 (Raj.)(HC)

Release of assets against deposit of cash, furnishing of bank guarantee

◆ Hasmukhlal Bagdiya *v.* Asstt. CIT (1992) 195 ITR 50 (MP)

◆ Rajinder Pal Mahajan *v.* Ralson India Ltd. (1995) 211 ITR 828 (P&H)

◆ Subodhchandra & Co. *v.* ITO (1995) 215 ITR 95 (Guj.)

◆ Pooran Sugar Works *v.* Asstt. CIT (1996) 219 ITR 221 (All.)

◆ Smt. Surinder Kaur *v.* Union of India (2000) 245 ITR 135 (Del.)

◆ Ramnath Kapoor *v.* CIT (2011) 57 DTR 311 (MP)

No application of seized assets for liability of subsequent years

◆ Vinod Poddar *v.* CIT (1994) 208 ITR 722 (Pat.)

◆ J.R. Malhotra *v.* Additional Session's Judge AIR 1976 SC 219

No application of seized assets against tax liability of third persons

◆ Naresh Kumar Kohli *v.* CIT (2004) 266 ITR 553 (P&H)

◆ Smt. Shobha Sengar *v.* CIT (2000) 244 ITR 10 (All.)

Mandatory for A.O. to adjust seized amount against demand under section 140A

◆ Ravinder Singh *v.* Asstt. CIT (2004) 89 ITD 477 (Asr.)

Seized amount to be treated as tax paid by the assessee, if requested

◆ Rajesh Kumar Vinit Kumar *v.* CIT (2006) 283 ITR 395 (All.)

◆ Asstt. CIT *v.* Topsel Pvt. Ltd. (1996) 56 TTJ (Cal.) 621/(1996) 56 ITD 186 (Cal.)

◆ Ramjilal Jagannath *v.* Asstt. CIT (2000) 241 ITR 758 (MP)

◆ Satpaul D. Agarwal (HUF) *v.* Asstt. CIT (1998) 62 TTJ (ITAT- Mum.) 98

◆ Gopal Chand Khandelwal *v.* Asstt. CIT (1995) 52 ITD 661 (Del. - Trib.)

◆ Asstt. CIT *v.* Raghunandan Lal (2002) 82 ITD 436 (Chd.)

◆ Iqbal Chand Khurana *v.* Dy. CIT (2001) 70 TTJ (ITAT- Del.) 16

Release of seized assets to whom?

◆ Smt. Kusum Lata Singhal *v.* CIT (1990) 185 ITR 56 (SC)

◆ Assainar *v.* ITO (1975) 101 ITR 854 (Ker.)

◆ Balkrishna Ramgopal Ruia *v.* Union of India (1990) 185 ITR 328 (Bom.)

Payment of interest on release of seized amount

◆ Anilkumar Bhagwandas *v.* P.K. Tiwari (1999) 238 ITR 788 (Guj.)

◆ Anilkumar D. Gajjar *v.* CIT (1996) 220 ITR 470 (Guj.)

◆ Manohar Lal *v.* CIT (2001) 249 ITR 1 (MP)

◆ Mohammed Usman *v.* Union of India (1997) 224 ITR 730 (Del.)

◆ Ashok Kumar Aggarwal *v.* Director (Grievances Cell), CBDT (2005) 279 ITR 161 (Del.)

◆ Bhagwan Prasad Agarwal *v.* CIT (2006) 282 ITR 189 (All.)

◆ Ajay Gupta *v.* CIT (2008) 297 ITR 125 (Del.)

◆ Sandvik Asia Ltd. *v.* CIT (2006) 280 ITR 643 (SC)

◆ Dr. R.M. Saboo *v.* Asstt. CIT (2005) 92 TTJ (Hyd.) 1078/92 ITD 532 (Hyd.)

◆ Kishore Jagjivandas Tanna *v.* K. Rangrajan (2008) 306 ITR 121 (Bom.)

◆ Sitaram Through LRs *v.* CIT 68 DTR 230 (Bom.)/248 CTR 180 (Bom.)/(2012) 341 ITR 549 (Bom.)

◆ Mohit Singh *v.* Asstt. CIT (2011) 53 DTR 153/(2011) 241 CTR 244 (Del.)

- Prem Nath Nagpal *v.* Asstt. CIT (2010) 34 DTR 1/128 TTJ 53 (Del. 'H')
- CIT *v.* Kesr Karyalya (2005) 196 CTR 611 (Del.)/(2005) 278 ITR 596 (Del.)
- CIT *v.* Ashok Kumar (2011) 334 ITR 355 (P&H)
- CIT *v.* Arun Kapoor (2011) 334 ITR 351 (P&H)
- Vishwanath Khanna *v.* Union of India (2011) 335 ITR 548/(2011) 61 DTR 318/(2011) 244 CTR 208 (Del.)
- Chironjilal Sharma (HUF) *v.* UOI (2013) 263 CTR 625/96 DTR 305/ (2014) 360 ITR 237/222 Taxman 352 (SC)
- S.K. Jain *v.* CIT (2013) 354 ITR 84/215 Taxman 237/87 DTR 264 (Delhi)(HC)
- Om Prakash Agrawal *v.* UOI (2013) 81 DTR 341/214 Taxman 5 (Mag.)/255 CTR 445 (MP)(HC)

Damages in case of delay or irregularity in release of assets

- DGIT *v.* Diamond Star Exports Ltd. (2006) 156 Taxman 299 (SC)/ (2007) 293 ITR 438 (SC)
- Kuber Planters Ltd. *v.* Dy. CIT (2006) 150 Taxman 11 (Del.)

REQUISITION UNDER SECTION 132A

Requisition to be made after recording satisfaction in consequence of information in possession of the competent authority

- CIT *v.* Vindhya Metal Corporation (1997) 224 ITR 614 (SC)
- B.R. Metal Ltd. *v.* CIT (1999) 239 ITR 329 (Gau.)
- Ramesh Chander *v.* CIT (1974) 93 ITR 244 (P&H)
- Biaora Constructions Pvt. Ltd. *v.* DIT (Inv.) (2006) 281 ITR 247 (MP)
- Shree Janki Solvent Extractions Ltd. *v.* Dy. DIT (1996) 221 ITR 30 (All.)
- DIT (Inv.) *v.* Payal Selection Co. (2008) 307 ITR 377 (MP)
- Sudarshan & Co. *v.* CIT (1983) 139 ITR 1032 (All.)
- Ibrahim Othayoth *v.* Sub-Inspector of Police (1998) 232 ITR 320 (Ker.)
- Arun Kumar Chajjar *v.* Collector of Customs (Preventive) 1995 (75) ELT 747 (Cal.)
- Ganga Prasad Maheshwari *v.* CIT (1983) 139 ITR 1043 (All.)
- Manju Tandon *v.* T.N. Kapoor, Dy. Superintendent of Police (1978) 115 ITR 473 (All.)

- Krishnagopal v. DI (Inv.) (2009) 308 ITR 273 (MP)
- Amar Agrawal v. DIT (Investigation) (2005) 276 ITR 182 (MP)
- Smt. Suman Singhai v. Director of IT (Investigation) (2011) 335 ITR 188 (MP)
- M. Manoj Kumar & Co. v. Director of IT (Investigation) (2011) 242 CTR 309 (MP)
- Atta Husain v. Director of IT (Inv.) (2011) 60 DTR 25 (MP)/246 CTR 207 (MP)
- Prakash Jaichand Shah v. DIT (Investigations) (2013) 350 ITR 336/ 255 CTR 403/81 DTR 396 (Guj.)(HC)

Requisition can be made to which authority

- Janardan Das v. Bindeshwari Prasad Sah (1999) 238 ITR 65 (Pat)
- Balbir Singh (Decd.) Through L/R Mrs. Dilpati v. CIT (1984) 146 ITR 266 (P&H) affirmed in CIT v. Balbir Singh (1993) 203 ITR 650 (P&H)
- Chander Prakash Agrawal v. State of Rajasthan (1994) 119 CTR 216 (Raj)/205 ITR 562 (Raj.)
- Abdul Khader v. Sub-Inspector of Police (1999) 240 ITR 489 (Ker.)
- CIT v. Balbir Singh (Decd.) (1984) 203 ITR 650 (P&H)
- Samta Constructions Co. v. Pawan Kumar Sharma, Dy. DIT (Inv.) (2000) 244 ITR 845 (MP)
- Srinivasan v. Dy. Superintendent of Police (1973) 91 ITR 308 (Mad.)
- Sadruddin Javeri v. Government of Andhra Pradesh (2000) 243 ITR 579 (AP)
- Suresh Bhai Bhola Bhai Jani v. Union of India (2001) 249 ITR 363 (Raj)
- Amandeep Singh v. DIT (2001) 252 ITR 139 (P&H)
- Parasnath v. Union of India (1997) 225 ITR 365 (MP)
- Babu Rao v. Inspector of Police (1991) 190 ITR 616 (Mad.)
- Union of India v. Judicial Magistrate (1993) 140 ITR 553 (All.)
- Smt. Surinder Kaur v. Union of India (2000) 245 ITR 135 (Del.)
- Babu Lal v. DIT (2006) 281 ITR 70 (All.)

Provision of section 153C may be applicable for requisitioned assets

- Smt. Mithilesh Kumari Jain v. CIT (1994) 209 ITR 337 (All.)

Applicability of provision of section 153A when requisition is made but actual delivery of seized material is not received

- Asstt. CIT v. Sonu Verma (2008) 305 ITR (AT) 406 (Asr.)
- Amandeep Singh v. DIT (Inv.) (2001) 252 ITR 139 (P&H)

- Chandra Prakash Agrawal *v.* State (1994) 205 ITR 562 (Raj.)
- Jageshwar Rosin & Turpentine Factory *v.* Asstt. CIT (2006) 102 TTJ (Del.) 670/100 ITD 399 (Del.)
- Smt. Mahesh Kumari Batra *v.* Jt. CIT (2005) 95 ITD 152 (Asr.)

ASSESSMENT OF SEARCH CASES
UNDER SECTION 153A/153C

Assessment for the preceding seventh year prior to the year of search can be reopened under section 148

- Ramballabh Gupta *v.* Asstt. CIT (2007) 288 ITR 347 (MP)

Pending assessment or reassessment to abate

- Abhay Kumar Shroff *v.* CIT (2007) 290 ITR 114 (Jharkhand)
- CIT v. S. Ajit Kumar [2018] 93 taxmann.com 294/255 Taxman 286

Fresh assessments to be framed for all the preceding six years whether assessment proceedings are abated or not

- Meghmani Organics Ltd. *v.* Dy. CIT (2010) 129 TTJ (Ahd.) 255
- LMJ International Ltd. *v.* Dy. CIT (2008) 119 TTJ (Kol.) 214
- Anil Kumar Bhatia *v.* Asstt. CIT (2010) 1 ITR (Trib.) 484 (Del.)
- Anil P. Khemani *v.* Dy. CIT in ITA 2855 to 2860/Mum/2008 dated 23.2.2010.
- CIT *v.* Raj Kumar Arora (2014) 120 DTR (All) 417 (HC)

Issues regarding filing of return under section 153A

- CIT *v.* B. G. Shirke Construction Technology (P.) Ltd. [2017] 79 taxmann.com 306/246 Taxman 300 (Bom).
- Principal CIT *v.* Vijay Infrastructure Ltd. 402 ITR 363 (All.
- Principal CIT *v.* JSW Steel Ltd. 187 DTR (Bom) 1
- Shrikant Mohta *v.* CIT [2018] 257 Taxman 43/95 taxmann.com 224 (Cal.)
- Mahavir Manakchand Bhansali *v.* CIT [2017] 88 taxmann.com 609 (Bom.)
- CIT *v.* Deepak Kumar Agarwal [2017] 86 taxmann.com 3/251 Taxman 22 (Bom).
- Principal CIT *v.* Ram Avtar Verma [2017] 88 taxmann.com 666
- Principal CIT *v.* Meeta Gutgutia Prop. M/s. Ferns "N" Petals [2017] 82 taxmann.com 287 (Delhi)

- Principal CIT *v.* Dipak Jashvantlal Panchal [2017] 88 taxmann.com 611 (Guj).

- CIT *v.* S. Ajit Kumar [2018] 93 taxmann.com 294/255 Taxman 286 (SC)

- Principal Commissioner of Income Tax *v.* Dipak J Panchal [2017] 98 CCH 0074 (Guj).

- Principal CIT *v.* Best Infrastructure (India) (P.) Ltd. 397 ITR 82/159 DTR 257 (Del)

- CIT *v.* S. Ajit Kumar [2018] 93 taxmann.com 294/255 Taxman 286 (SC)

- Principal *CIT v.* Sunrise Finlease (P.) Ltd. [2018] 89 taxmann.com 1/ 252 Taxman 407 (Guj.)

No other assessment or reassessment proceedings during pendency of proceedings under section 153A

- CIT *v.* Jaideo Jain & Co. (1997) 227 ITR 302 (Raj.)

Revision of returns filed in pursuance to notice under section 153A

- ITO *v.* Banarsi Lal Satya Narain (1995) 55 ITD 372 (Pat.)
- Asstt. CIT *v.* Cavinkare (P) Ltd. [2009] 120 ITD 126 (Chennai)

Seizure of cash during search - Whether adjustable as advance tax

- Satya Prakash Sharma *v.* Asstt. CIT (2009) 20 DTR 561 (Del.) (Trib.)
- Sudhakar M. Shetty *v.* Asstt. CIT (2008) 10 DTR 173 (Mum.)(Trib.)
- CIT *v.* K.K. Marketing (2005) 278 ITR 596 (Del.)
- Gian Chand Gupta *v.* Dy. CIT (2002) 80 ITD 548 (Del.)
- Dy. CIT *v.* Gold Tax Furnishing Industries (2001) 73 TTJ (Del.) 223
- Ramjinath Jagannath *v.* Asstt. CIT (2000) 241 ITR 758 (MP)
- CIT *v.* Pandurang Dayaram Talmale (2004) 135 Taxman 193 (Bom.)/ 187 CTR 625 (Bom.)

Whether assessment in pursuance to notice under section 153A is in the nature of de novo assessment

- Dy. CIT *v.* Sushil Kumar Jain (2010) 48 DTR 185 (Ind.)
- Asstt. CIT *v.* Rajesh Jhaveri Stock Brokers Pvt. Ltd. (2007) 291 ITR 500 (SC)
- CIT *v.* Kelvinator of India Ltd. (2010) 320 ITR 561 (SC)
- Vipan Khanna *v.* CIT (2002) 255 ITR 220 (P&H)
- Suncity Alloys Pvt. Ltd. *v.* Asstt. CIT (2009) 124 TTJ (Jodh.) 674
- CIT *v.* Piara Singh (1980) 124 ITR 40 (SC)
- LMJ International Ltd. *v.* Dy. CIT (2008) 119 TTJ (Kol.) 214

- Meghmani Organics Ltd. *v.* Dy. CIT (2010) 129 TTJ (Ahd.) 255
- Anil Kumar Bhatia *v.* Asstt. CIT (2010) 1 ITR (Trib.) 484 (Del.)
- Shivnath Rai Harnarain (India) Ltd. *v.* Dy. CIT (2008) 117 TTJ (Del.) 480/117 ITD 74 (Del.)
- Shyam Lata Kaushik *v.* Asstt. CIT (2008) 114 TTJ (Del.) 940/114 ITD 305 (Del.)

Notice under section 143(2) within time limit as prescribed is mandatory in case of proceedings under section 153A

- Asstt. CIT *v.* Hotel Blue Moon (2010) 321 ITR 362 (SC)
- Dy. CIT *v.* Sushil Kumar Jain (2010) 48 DTR 185 (Ind.)
- Ashok Chaddha *v.* ITO (2011) 337 ITR 399 (Del.)
- Narendra Singh *v.* ITO (2011) 138 TTJ (Agra) 615/130 ITD 509 (Agra)

Recording of satisfaction before invoking provision of section 153C

- Manish Maheshwari *v.* Asstt. CIT (2007) 289 ITR 341 (SC)
- CIT *v.* Dawn View Farms (P) Ltd. (2009) 178 Taxman 15 (Del.)/224 CTR 504 (Del.)
- Asstt. CIT *v.* R.P. Singh (2007) 111 TTJ (Del.) 880
- CIT *v.* Late Raj Pal Bhatia (2011) 49 DTR 9 (Del.)/333 ITR 315 (Del.)
- Vijay Sehgal (HUF) *v.* Asstt. CIT (2006) 100 ITD 560 (Asr.)
- Y. Subbaraju & Co. *v.* Asstt. CIT (2004) 85 TTJ 670/91 ITD 118 (Bang.) (SB)
- Shoreline Hotel (P) Ltd. *v.* Dy. CIT (2008) 116 TTJ (Mum.) 536
- Manoj Aggarwal *v.* Dy. CIT (2008) 113 ITD 377 (Del.)
- Pepsi Foods (P.) Ltd. *v.* ACIT (2014) 367 ITR 112 (Delhi)(HC)

Analysis of provision of section 153C

- Principal CIT *v.* N.S. Software (Firm) [2018] 93 taxmann.com 21/255 Taxman 230 (Delhi)
- CIT *v.* Smt. Nirmala Keshwani 79 taxmann.com 399
- CIT *v.* Calcutta Knitwears 43 taxmann.com 446/223 Taxman 115 (Mag.) (SC)
- Principal CIT *v.* Jitendra H. Modi [2018] 403 ITR 110 (Guj).
- Ganpati Fincap Services (P.) Ltd. *v.* CIT [2017] 82 taxmann.com 408 (Delhi
- Tapan Kumar Dutta *v.* CIT [2018] 92 taxmann.com 367/255 Taxman 200 (SC)

- Shyamraj Singh *v.* Dy. CIT 411 ITR 709 (Kar)
- Principal CIT *v.* Himanshu Chandulal Patel, C/TAXAP/342/2019 (Guj)
- CIT *v.* Smt. Soudha Gafoor 408 ITR 246 (Ker)
- Super Malls (P) Ltd. *v.* Principal CIT 187 DTR (SC) 257
- Principal CIT *v.* Dreamcity Buildwell (P.) Ltd [2019] 110 taxmann.com 28/266 Taxman 465 (Delhi)
- Asstt. CIT *v.* Dr. Ranjan Pai [2019] 109 taxmann.com 90/178 ITD 647 (Bang.)
- Principal CIT *v.* Vinita Charurasia [2017] 82 taxmann.com 153/248 Taxman 172 (Delhi)
- CIT *v.* Arpit Land P. Ltd. 154 DTR 241 (Bom).
- Canyon Financial Services Ltd. *v.* ITO [2017] 84 taxmann.com 71/249 Taxman 493 (Delhi)
- Principal CIT *v.* Index Securities P Ltd. 304 CTR 67/157 DTR 20 (Delhi)
- CIT *v.* Renu Constructions P. Ltd. [2018] 99 taxmann.com 426 (Delhi)
- CIT *v.* Lavanya Land Pvt. Ltd. [2017] 83 taxmann.com 161/249 Taxman 275 (Bom.)
- Principal CIT *v.* Dreamcity Buildwell Pvt. Ltd. [2019] 110 taxmann.com 28/266 Taxman 465 (Delhi)
- Pr. CIT *v.* Krutika Land (P.) Ltd. [2019] 103 taxmann.com 9/261 Taxman 454 (SC)

Issues regarding assessment under section 153C

- Anil Kumar Gopikishan Agrawal *v.* Asstt. CIT [2019] 106 taxmann.com 137 (Guj.)

Jurisdiction under section 153C can be assumed when seized material belong or belongs to other person

- Vijaybhai N. Chandrani *v.* Asstt. CIT (2010) 38 DTR (Guj.) 225
- P. Srinivas Naik *v.* Asstt. CIT (2008) 114 TTJ (Bang.) 856/117 ITD 201 (Bang.)
- Meghmani Organics Ltd. *v.* Dy. CIT (2010) 129 TTJ (Ahd.) 255
- Bhajan Das & Brothers *v.* Asstt. CIT (2009) 119 ITD 76 (Agra) (TM)
- ITO *v.* Arun Kumar Kapoor (2011) 140 TTJ 249 (Asr.)

Opportunity of hearing not required to be given by additional commissioner before granting approval to assessment orders under section 153A/153C

◆ Kailash Moudgil *v.* Dy. CIT (2000) 72 ITD 97 (Del.) (SB)

◆ Sree Rama Medical & Surgical Agencies *v.* CIT (2000) 243 ITR 245 (AP)

◆ Shaw Wallace & Co. Ltd. *v.* Asstt. CIT (1999) 64 TTJ (Cal.) 719/68 ITD 148 (Cal.)

Time limit for completing assessment in search cases

◆ CIT *v.* Anil Minda (2010) 328 ITR 320 (Del.)

◆ CIT *v.* Sandhya P. Naik (2002) 253 ITR 534 (Bom.)

◆ C. Ramaiah Reddy *v.* Asstt. CIT (2003) 87 ITD 439 (Bang.) (SB)

◆ Mahakoshal Engineers & Contractors Co. (P.) Ltd. *v.* Asstt. CIT (2003) 85 ITD 267 (Nag.)

◆ Babu Lal *v.* DIT (2006) 281 ITR 70 (All.)

◆ DTS Rao *v.* Asstt. CIT (2007) 106 ITD 570 (Bang.)

◆ Dy. CIT *v.* Adolf Patric Pinto (2006) 100 ITD 191 (Mum.)

◆ Shanti Lal Godawat *v.* Asstt. CIT (2009) 30 DTR 413 (Jd.)/126 TTJ (Jd) 135

◆ S. Precision Machines (P.) Ltd. *v.* CIT [2017] 79 taxmann.com 421 (P&H)

◆ Rajan Jewellery *v.* CIT [2019] 109 taxmann.com 104/266 Taxman 357 (Ker.)

◆ K.V. Padmanabhan *v.* Asstt. CIT [2019] 107 taxmann.com 24/265 Taxman 36 (Ker.)

Nature and scope of provisions of section 153A

◆ Bansilal B. Raisoni & Sons *v.* Asstt. CIT 173 DTR 68 (Bom).

Fresh Assessment pursuant to order u/s 263 - Whether fresh approval u/s 153D required - Debatable

◆ Osho Forge Ltd. *v.* CIT [2018] 93 taxmann.com 369/255 Taxman 375 (P&H)

HANDLING OF ASSESSMENT IN SEARCH CASES

Obtaining photocopies of seized material

◆ CIT *v.* Oriental Rubber Works (1984) 145 ITR 477 (SC)

- Jorawar Singh Baid v. Asstt. CIT (1990) 183 ITR 664 (Cal.)
- Dhani Ram Gupta v. Union of India (1973) 89 ITR 281 (Cal.)

Telescoping of additions against general declaration of undisclosed income

- Eagle Seeds & Biotech Ltd. v. Asstt. CIT (2006) 100 ITD 301 (Indore)
- Ram Lubhaya v. Asstt. CIT (1995) 52 TTJ (Del.) 21
- Kantilal & Bros. v. Asstt. CIT (1995) 51 TTJ (Pune) 513/52 ITD 412 (Pune)
- CIT v. K.S.M. Guruswamy Nadar & Sons (1984) 149 ITR 127 (Mad.)

Principal of peak balance

- Addl. CIT v. Chetan Dass (1975) 99 ITR 46 (Del.)
- Addl. CIT v. Dharamdas Agarwal (1983) 144 ITR 143 (MP)
- Addl. CIT v. Mohan Engineering Co. (1985) 151 ITR 571 (Pat.)
- CIT v. Neemar Ram Badlu Ram (1980) 122 ITR 68 (All.)
- Surendra M. Khandar v. Asstt. CIT (2001) 76 ITD 121 (Mum.)
- Essem Intra Port Services (P.) Ltd. v. Asstt. CIT (2000) 72 ITD 228 (Hyd.)

Adjustment against intangible additions

- CIT v. Jawanmal Gemaji Gandhi (1985) 151 ITR 353 (Bom.)
- Anantharam Veerasinghaiah & Co. v. CIT (1980) 123 ITR 457 (SC)
- CIT v. S. Nelliappan (1967) 66 ITR 722 (SC)

Reference to departmental valuation officers in search cases

- Hanemp Properties (P.) Ltd. v. Asstt. CIT (2006) 285 ITR 26 (Del.) (AT)
- ITO v. Hotel Hilltop (1995) 52 TTJ (Jp.) 539

Reference for special audit under section 142(2A)

- Maya Spinners Ltd. v. Dy. CIT (Assessment) (2008) 306 ITR 137 (Indore)
- Rajendra C. Singh v. Jt. CIT (2009) 118 ITD 99 (Mum.)
- Sahara India (Fin.) v. CIT (2008) 300 ITR 403 (SC)

Reliance on statement recorded by authorised officer during search

- Chander Mohan Mehta v. Asstt. CIT (1999) 71 ITD 245 (Pune)
- CIT v. Mrs. Doris S. Luiz (1974) 96 ITR 646 (Kar.)
- Asstt. CIT v. Mrs. Sushila Devi Agarwal (1994) 49 TTJ (Ahd.) 663/ (1994) 50 ITD 524 (Ahd.)

- CIT v. P.V. Kalyanasundaram (2006) 282 ITR 259 (Mad.) affirmed in CIT v. P.V. Kalyanasundaram (2007) 294 ITR 49 (SC)
- Ramesh Pershad v. IAC (1989) 28 ITD 550 (Hyd.)
- Pushpa Vihar v. Asstt. CIT (1994) 48 TTJ (Bom.) 389
- Madras Bangalore Transport v. CIT (1991) 190 ITR 679 (Mad.)
- S. Arjan Singh v. CWT (1989) 175 ITR 91 (Delhi)
- Pullangode Rubber Produce Co. Ltd. v. State of Kerala (1973) 91 ITR 18 (SC)
- CIT v. Ravi Kant Jain (2001) 250 ITR 141 (Del.)
- Hotel Kumar Palace v. CIT (2006) 283 ITR 110 (P&H)
- Kishinchand Chelaram v. CIT (1980) 125 ITR 713 (SC)
- Jindal Stainless Ltd. v. Asstt. CIT (2009) 120 ITD 301 (Del.)
- Kailashben Manharlal Chokshi v. CIT (2008) 14 DTR 257 (Guj.)/328 ITR 411 (Guj.)
- ITO v. Akshay Bhandar (1990) 33 ITD 13 (Gau.)

No addition for investment in jewellery upto specified limit not required to be seized

- Smt. Salochana Devi Jaiswal v. Dy. CIT (2004) 90 TTJ (Jab.) 974
- Smt. Bommana Swarna Rekha v. Asstt. CIT (2005) 95 TTJ (Visakha) 885
- Jai Kumar Jain v. Asstt. CIT (2006) 99 TTJ (Jp.) 744
- Rajendra C. Shah v. Jt. CIT [2007] 158 Taxman 170 (Mum.)
- CIT v. M.S. Agrawal (HUF) (2008) 11 DTR 169 (MP)/236 CTR 538 (MP)
- Dy. CIT v. Gordhandas Lachmandas (2008) 16 DTR 26 (Mum.) (Trib.)
- CIT v. Ratanlal Vyaparilal Jain (2010) 45 DTR 290 (Guj.)/339 ITR 351 (Guj.)
- Lal Chand v. CIT (1992) 194 ITR 399 (All.)
- Dy. CIT v. Arjun Dass Kalwani (2006) 101 ITD 337 (Jodh.)
- Manibhai S. Patel v. WTO (1991) 37 ITD 485 (Ahd.)
- Gautam Laljibhai Gajar v. ITO (1991) 41 TTJ (Ahd.) 542/37 ITD 514 (Ahd.)
- Asstt. CIT v. Smt. Parbati Ganguly (1992) 44 TTJ (Cal.) 108
- V.G.P. Ravidas v. Asstt. CIT (2014) 121 DTR (Mad) 44 (HC)

Assessment in the case of retraction of surrender of undisclosed income

◆ Kailashben Manharlal Chokshi *v.* CIT 14 DTR 257 (Guj.)/328 ITR 711 (Guj.)

◆ ITO *v.* Bua Dass [2006] 155 Taxman 130 (Asr.-Trib.)

◆ CIT *v.* Dhingra Metal Works 48 DTR 230 (Del.)/328 ITR 384 (Del.)

◆ Bachittar Singh *v.* CIT 48 DTR 236 (P&H)/328 ITR 400 (P&H)

◆ CIT *v.* Jagdish Chand Gupta 47 DTR 156 (P&H)/329 ITR 583 (P&H)

◆ Carpenters Classics (Exim) P. Ltd. *v.* Dy. CIT (2008) 299 ITR 124 (Bang.)

◆ Hotel Kiran *v.* Asstt. CIT (2002) 82 ITD 453 (Pune)

◆ Asstt. CIT *v.* Mrs. Sushiladevi S. Agarwal (1994) 50 ITD 524 (Ahd.)

◆ Asstt. CIT *v.* Ravi Agricultural Industries (2009) 117 ITD 338 (Agra) (TM)

◆ Kantilal C. Shah *v.* Asstt. CIT (2011) 142 TTJ 233 (Ahd. 'C')/133 ITD 57 (Ahd.)

◆ Ravindra Kumar Verma *v.* CIT (2013) 214 Taxman 117 (Mag.) (All.) (HC)

◆ Bannalal Jat Constructions (P.) Ltd. *v.* Asstt. CIT [2019] 106 taxmann.com 128/264 Taxman 5 (SC)

◆ Principal CIT *v.* Best Infrastructure (India) (P.) Ltd. [2018] 94 taxmann.com 115/256 Taxman 63 (SC)

◆ Principal CIT *v.* Manoj Hora [2017] 88 taxmann.com 923 (Delhi)

◆ CIT *v.* Dilbagh Rai Arora [2019] 104 taxmann.com 371/263 Taxman 30 (All.)

No addition on the basis of dumb documents

◆ Amar Natvarlal Shah *v.* Asstt. CIT (1997) 60 ITD 560 (Ahd.)

◆ Asstt. CIT *v.* Shailesh S. Shah (1997) 63 ITD 153 (Bom.)

◆ Brijlal Rupchand *v.* ITO (1991) 40 TTJ (Indore) 668

◆ Malabar Oil Marketing Co. *v.* Asstt. CIT (2004) 91 TTJ (Mum.) 348

◆ D.D. Malhan *v.* Dy. CIT (2004) 91 TTJ (Del.) 947

◆ Addl. CIT *v.* Prasant Ahluwalia (2005) 92 TTJ (Ctk.) 464

◆ Smt. Bommana Swarna Rekha *v.* Asstt. CIT (2005) 94 TTJ (Visakha.) 885

◆ Bansal Strips (P) Ltd. *v.* Asstt. CIT (2006) 99 ITD 177 (Del.)

◆ Asstt. CIT *v.* Satyapal Wassan [2007] 295 ITR 352 (AT) (Jab.)

- Nirmal Fashions (P) Ltd. *v.* Dy. CIT (2009) 23 DTR 386 (Kol.)(Trib.)/ 123 TTJ 180 (Kol.)
- CIT *v.* Girish Chaudhary (2008) 296 ITR 619 (Del.)
- Chander Mohan Mehta *v.* Asstt. CIT (1999) 71 ITD 245 (Pune)
- CIT *v.* D.K. Gupta (2009) 308 ITR 230 (Del.)
- T.S. Venkatesan *v.* Asstt. CIT (2000) 174 ITD 298 (Cal.)

On the basis of evidence of specific period, extrapolation of income for the entire search years not sustainable

- Dy. CIT *v.* Royal Marwar Tobacco Product Pvt. Ltd. (2009) 120 TTJ (Ahd.) 387
- ITO *v.* Murlidhar Bhagwan Das (1964) 52 ITR 335 (SC)
- Instalment Supply (P.) Ltd. *v.* Union of India AIR 1962 SC 53
- K. Sadasiva Krishna Rao *v.* CIT (1983) 144 ITR 270 (AP)
- CIT *v.* Mahesh Chand (1993) 199 ITR 247 (All.)
- Asstt. CIT *v.* M.M. Sales Agencies [2006] 97 TTJ 575 (Jp)
- Dr. S. Surendranath Reddy *v.* Asstt. CIT (2000) 72 ITD 205 (Hyd.)
- Samrat Beer Bar *v.* Asstt. CIT (2000) 75 ITD 19 (Pune) (TM)
- D.N. Kamani (HUF) *v.* Dy. CIT (1999) 70 ITD 77 (TM) (Pat.)
- Sunny Jacob Jewellers and Wedding Centre *v.* DCIT (2014) 362 ITR 664/102 DTR 68/267 CTR 361 (Ker.)(HC)

No addition on estimated/ad hoc basis

- Asstt. CIT *v.* Radhey Shyam Poddar (HUF) (2004) 86 TTJ (Asr.) 558
- Asstt. CIT *v.* Nitin Mukesh Mathur (2004) 88 TTJ (Mum.) 220/(2002) 83 ITD 641 (Mum.)
- Bajrang Lal Bansal *v.* Dy. CIT (2005) CIT 94 TTJ (Del.) 1071
- CIT *v.* C.L. Khatri (2005) 197 CTR (MP) 44/(2006) 282 ITR 97 (MP)
- Jagdish Duggal *v.* Asstt. CIT (2009) 24 DTR (Chd.) (Trib.) 174
- Sukh Ram *v.* Asstt. CIT (2006) 99 ITD 227 (Ahd.)
- Anand Autoride Ltd. *v.* Jt. CIT (2006) 99 ITD 227 (Ahd.)
- Kantilal Prabhudas Patel *v.* Dy. CIT (2005) 93 ITD 117 (Indore) (TM)
- Smt. Rajrani Gupta *v.* Dy. CIT (2000) 72 ITD 155 (Mum.)
- Dr. R.M.L. Mehrotra *v.* Asstt. CIT (1999) 64 TTJ (All.) 259/68 ITD 288 (All.)
- Smt. Purnima Beri *v.* Dy. CIT (2003) 264 ITR 54 (Asr.) (TM)
- ITO *v.* Vijay Kumar Khandelwal (1994) 50 TTJ (Jp.) 11/50 ITD 405 (Jp.)

- ◆ ITO *v.* Gurubachasingh J. Juneja (1996) 54 TTJ (Ahd.) (TM) 1/55 ITD 75 (Ahd.)(TM)
- ◆ Mansukhlal Ratanlal Jain (Chopra) *v.* Union of India (2008) 300 ITR 98 (MP)
- ◆ CIT *v.* Manoj Jain (2006) 287 ITR 285 (Del.)
- ◆ Mrs. Deepa Bhatia *v.* Asstt. CIT (2011) 139 TTJ (Del 'B') 329

Whether deduction can be claimed for unrecorded business expenditure

- ◆ Elite Developers *v.* Dy. CIT (2000) 73 ITD 379 (Nag.)
- ◆ Dhanvarsha Builders & Developers P. Ltd. *v.* Dy. CIT (2006) 102 ITD 375 (Pune)

No addition on the basis of newspapers, diaries unless corroborated or suggesting undisclosed income of the assessee

- ◆ Amarjit Singh Bakshi (HUF) *v.* Asstt. CIT (2003) 263 ITR 75 (Del.)
- ◆ Pooja Bhatt *v.* Asstt. CIT (2000) 73 ITD 205 (Mum.)
- ◆ Associated Stone Industries Kotah Ltd. *v.* Dy. CIT (1999) 64 TTJ (Jp.) 708/68 ITD 312 (Jp.)
- ◆ Atul Kumar Jain *v.* Dy. CIT (1999) 64 TTJ (Delhi) 786
- ◆ Daulat Ram *v.* Asstt. CIT (1999) 63 TTJ (Del.) 436
- ◆ S.K. Gupta *v.* Dy. CIT (1999) 63 TTJ (Del.) 532
- ◆ Essem Intra Port Services P. Ltd. *v.* Asstt. CIT (2000) 72 ITD 228 (Hyd.)
- ◆ Asstt. CIT *v.* Prabhat Oil Mills (1995) 52 TTJ (Ahd.) 533
- ◆ CIT *v.* Multi Tech Auto Ltd. (2008) 301 ITR 73 (Jharkhand)
- ◆ CIT *v.* Khazan Singh & Bros (2008) 304 ITR 243 (P&H)
- ◆ CIT *v.* Vivek Aggarwal (2015) 121 DTR 241 (Del.)(HC)
- ◆ CIT *v.* Home Developers (P.) Ltd. (2015) 117 DTR 248 (Del.) (HC)
- ◆ P. Madhurajan (HUF) *v.* ACIT (2015) 373 ITR 630 (Mad.)(HC)
- ◆ CIT *v.* Jalaj Batra (2015) 372 ITR 622 (Bom.)(HC)

Burden of proof

- ◆ Surendra M. Khandar *v.* Asstt. CIT (2001) 76 ITD 121 (Mum.)
- ◆ Asstt. CIT *v.* Sweety Traders (2007) 105 ITD 45 (Chd.)
- ◆ CIT *v.* N. Swamy (2000) 241 ITR 363 (Mad.)
- ◆ G.G. Films *v.* ITO (1993) 45 TTJ (Coch.) 644
- ◆ K. Hari Prasad *v.* IAC (1995) 52 ITD 563 (Hyd.)
- ◆ CIT *v.* Mussadilal Ram Bharose (1987) 165 ITR 14 (SC)
- ◆ Chuharmal *v.* CIT (1988) 172 ITR 250 (SC)

♦ Bafakyh Export House v. ITO (1995) 53 TTJ (Coch.) 293

♦ Dilip N. Shroff v. Jt. CIT (2007) 291 ITR 519 (SC)

♦ Venkataswami Naidu & Co. v. CIT (1959) 35 ITR 594 (SC)

♦ Janki Ram Bahadur Ram v. CIT (1965) 57 ITR 21 (SC)

♦ Saroj Kumar Majumdar v. CIT (1959) 37 ITR 242 (SC)

♦ CIT v. Premji Gopalbhai (1978) 113 ITR 785 (Guj.)

♦ ITO v. Ratnesh Kumari (Rani) (1980) 123 ITR 343 (All.)

♦ Abubucker Sait (Janab) v. CIT (1962) 45 ITR 37 (Mad.)

♦ CIT v. Raunaq Singh Swaran Singh (1972) 85 ITR 220 (Del.)

♦ Dalmia Cement Ltd. v. CIT (1976) 105 ITR 633 (SC)

♦ Virani v. CIT (1973) 90 ITR 255 (Guj.)

♦ Deep Chandra & Co. v. CIT (1977) 107 ITR 716 (All.)

♦ Lalit Ram Mangilal of Cawnpore v. CIT (1930) 1 ITR 286 (All.)

Defect in issue of notice for filing returns

♦ Dr. R.M.L Mehrotra v. Asstt. CIT (1999) 64 TTJ (All.) 259/68 ITD 288 (All.)

♦ VVS Alloys Ltd. v. Asstt. CIT (2000) 68 TTJ (All.) 516

Addition on account of inadequate household expenditure

♦ Microland Ltd. v. Asstt. CIT (1999) 63 TTJ (Bang.) 701/67 ITD 446 (Bang.)

♦ Dhanvarsha Builders & Developers P. Ltd. v. Dy. CIT (2006) 102 ITD 375 (Pune)

♦ Eagle Seeds & Biotech Ltd. v. Asstt. CIT (2006) 100 ITD 301 (Indore)

♦ Manharlal C. Soni v. CIT (1995) 127 CTR (Guj.) 230/(1995) 215 ITR 634 (Guj.)

♦ Basana Rani Saha v. ITO (1990) 37 TTJ (Gau.) 188/33 ITD 574 (Gau.)

♦ CIT v. Guru Bachhan Singh J. Juneja (2008) 302 ITR 63 (Guj.)

♦ CIT v. Rameshwar Lal Ahuja (2009) 312 ITR 217 (P&H)

Addition for difference in stock

♦ ITO v. Jewels Emporium (1994) 48 ITD 164 (Ind.)

♦ CIT v. Hindustan Mills & Electrical Stores (1998) 232 ITR 421 (MP)

♦ Giggles (P) Ltd. v. ITO (1992) 43 ITD 388 (Del.)

♦ Jai Sharda Rice Mills v. ITO (1991) 36 ITD 254 (Asr.)

♦ ITO v. Shyam Sunder Dhoot (1986) 17 ITD 274 (Jp.)

♦ CIT v. Veerdip Rollers P. Ltd. (2008) 307 ITR 3 (SC)

Addition in the year to which incriminating material belongs

◆ Principal CIT *v.* Jayant K. Furnishers [2019] 109 taxmann.com 52/ 266 Taxman 91 (SC)

Addition under section 68 during search cases

◆ Satyapal Wassan *v.* ITO (1991) 39 TTJ (Jab.) 72

◆ Kantilal & Bors. *v.* Asstt. CIT (1995) 52 ITD 412 (Trib.) (Pune)

◆ K. Hari Prasad *v.* IAC (1995) 52 ITD 563 (Hyd.)

◆ Sumati Dayal *v.* CIT (1995) 214 ITR 801 (SC)

Addition under section 69 during search cases

◆ Kewal G. Bajaj *v.* Asstt. CIT (1999) 71 ITD 375 (Mum.)(SMC)

◆ Manoj Aggarwal *v.* Dy. CIT (2008) 113 ITD 377 (Del.) (SB)

◆ Vinod Behari Jain *v.* ITO (2008) 306 ITR (AT) 392 (Del.)/(2009) 117 ITD 220 (Del.)

Delay in supplying copies of seized material - Levy of interest not justified

◆ Bachchubhai S. Antrolia *v.* Asstt. CIT (2007) 288 ITR 57 (Rajkot)(AT)

PENALTIES & PROSECUTION IN SEARCH CASES

Levy of penalty in case of agreed addition during assessment

◆ M.S. Mohammad Marzook *v.* ITO (2006) 283 ITR 254 (Mad.)

◆ CIT *v.* Dharam Chand (1993) 204 ITR 462 (Bom.)

◆ ITO *v.* Akshay Bhandar (1989) 33 ITD 13 (Gau.)

◆ Pullangode Rubber Produce Co. Ltd. *v.* State of Kerala (1973) 91 ITR 18 (SC)

Declaration of undisclosed income during search - Requirement regarding specifying and substantiating the manner

◆ Hissaria Brothers *v.* Dy. CIT (2009) 31 DTR 223 (Jd.)/(2009) 126 TTJ (Jd) 391

◆ Mahendra Chimanlal Shah *v.* Asstt. CIT (1994) 49 TTJ (Ahd.) 677/ (1994) 51 ITD 244 (Ahd.)

◆ CIT *v.* Radha Kishan Goel (2005) 278 ITR 454 (All.)

◆ CIT *v.* Mahendra C. Shah (2008) 215 CTR (Guj.) 493/(2008) 299 ITR 305 (Guj.)

Payment of tax and interest relating to undisclosed income

◆ Ashok Kumar Gupta *v.* CIT (2006) 287 ITR 376/157 Taxman 339 (P&H)

- CIT *v.* Nem Kumar Jain (2006) 151 Taxman 187 (All.)/(2006) 202 CTR 328 (All.)
- Gebilal Kanhaialal (HUF) *v.* Asstt. CIT (2004) 270 ITR 523/(2005) 143 Taxman 42 (Raj.)

Declaration of undisclosed income for earlier years

- CIT *v.* Punjab Tyres (1986) 162 ITR 517 (MP)
- CIT *v.* Suresh Chandra Mittal (2001) 251 ITR 9 (SC)
- CIT *v.* Suresh Chandra Mittal (2000) 241 ITR 124 (MP)
- CIT *v.* Rajiv Garg (2009) 313 ITR 256 (P&H)

Declaration of undisclosed income for earlier years made subject to no penalty

- CIT *v.* D.K.B. & Co. (2000) 243 ITR 618 (Ker.)
- CIT *v.* Rakesh Suri (2010) 233 CTR (All.) 184/(2011) 331 ITR 458 (All.)
- Bhagat & Co. *v.* Asstt. CIT (2006) 101 TTJ (Mum.) 553
- Addl. CIT *v.* Prem Chand Garg (2009) 31 SOT 97 (Del.)(TM)/(2009) 119 ITD 97 (Del.) (TM)
- Asstt. CIT *v.* Indica Exports (2010) 129 TTJ (Del.) 269/(2010) 5 ITR 347 (Del.)(AT)
- Trivium Power Engineers Pvt. Ltd. *v.* ITO (2010) 133 TTJ (Del.) 438
- Sir Shadi Lal Sugar & General Mills Ltd. *v.* CIT (1987) 168 ITR 705 (SC)
- K.P. Madhusudhanan *v.* CIT (2001) 251 ITR 99 (SC)

Penalty in case of revision of return after search having taken place

- CIT *v.* Shyam Lal M. Soni (2005) 144 Taxman 666 (MP)/(2005) 276 ITR 156 (MP)
- Dy. CIT *v.* S. Kumar (2008) 15 DTR 34 (Bang.)/(2009) 120 ITD 201 (Bang.)
- CIT *v.* Suresh Chand Bansal (2009) 22 DTR 1 (Cal.)/(2010) 329 ITR 1 (Cal.)
- Dy. CIT *v.* K. Natarajan (2010) 34 DTR 414 (Bang.)/(2010) 128 TTJ (Bang.) 558
- Asstt. CIT *v.* Rupesh Bholidas Patel (2008) 16 DTR 369 (Ahd.)
- Dy. CIT *v.* Omkareshwar R. Kalantri (2010) 42 DTR 489 (Pune)
- CIT *v.* A. Sreenivasa Pai (2000) 242 ITR 29 (Ker.)

Penalty under section 271AAA not applicable in case of requisition under section 132A

- Vinod Goyal v. Asstt. CIT (2008) 115 TTJ (Nag.) 559/(2008) 6 DTR 23 (Nag.)
- CIT v. Aboo Mohmed (2001) 250 ITR 313/(2000) 111 Taxman 120 (Kar.)
- Principal CIT v. Smt. Ritu Singhal [2018] 92 taxmann.com 224 (Delhi)
- Principal CIT v. Mukeshbhai Ramanlal Prajapati 398 ITR 170 (Guj.)
- Principal CIT v. Phoenix Mills Ltd. 175 DTR 433/307 CTR 700 (Bom).
- Duraipandi & S. Thalavaipandian AOP v. Asstt. CIT [2019] 106 taxmann.com 20 (Mad.)
- Asstt. CIT v. Gebilal Kanhaialal (HUF) [2012] 25 taxmann.com 214/ 210 Taxman 24 (SC)
- Principal CIT v. Surinder Kumar Khindri [2017] 88 taxmann.com 673 (Punj. & Har.)

Attraction of penalty for concealment in cases covered u/s 153C

- Principal CIT v. Rajkumar Gulab Badgujar 111 taxmann.com 257/ 267 Taxman 488 (SC)

APPLICATION TO SETTLEMENT COMMISSION IN SEARCH CASES

No power with the settlement commission to grant waiver from levy of interest

- CIT v. Anjum M.H. Ghaswala (2001) 252 ITR 1 (SC)
- Brij Lal v. CIT (2010) 235 CTR (SC) 417/328 ITR 477 (SC)

Order of settlement commission not appealable

- R.B. Shree Ram Durga Prasad and Fateh Chand Narsing Das v. Settlement Commission (1989) 176 ITR 169/43 Taxman 34 (SC)
- N. Krishnan v. Settlement Commission (1989) 180 ITR 585/47 Taxman 294 (Kar.)

FREQUENTLY ASKED QUESTIONS (FAQs)

Nature of search provisions

Q1. *After recommendations of the Direct Tax Committee found by the Government for simplification and rationalization of direct taxes or enactment of new Direct Tax Code, how far shall the provisions of income tax search and seizure as contained under Income-tax Act, 1961 and the analysis made under this book remain relevant?*

Ans. Provisions relating to income tax search and seizure are likely to remain on the same lines as the provisions contained under Income-tax Act, 1961. Therefore, the analysis and detailed discussion with case laws made in this book relating to the provisions of income tax search and seizure shall remain equally useful and relevant.

Q2. *What is the distinction between income tax search/income tax raid and income tax survey?*

Ans. Income tax search and income tax raid is one and the same thing. Income tax survey is another tool in the hands of the tax authorities for making investigation under the Income-tax Act. Income tax survey is comparatively milder action and can be undertaken only at business premises and no seizure of assets is permitted in the case of survey.

Q3. *Income tax search provisions are quite harsh in nature. Whether similar power for making investigation is available to tax authorities in other countries also?*

Ans. Yes, powers of almost similar nature are available with the tax authorities for making investigation and un-earthing black money in other developed and developing countries. In other developed countries, such powers are more transparent, system driven and technology based than being discretionary in nature.

Q4. *The provisions of income tax search and seizure are quite harsh and it is often said that the powers given to tax authorities are draconian in nature. Are there any checks and balances established by the legislature so as to prevent misuse of such powers?*

Ans. Yes, there are in-built safeguards provided within the provisions of section 132 itself so as to restrict misuse of the powers of search and seizure with the tax authorities. There is no power of arrest given to the income tax authorities in the case of search as is the case with respect to the enforcement of other economic laws such as excise duty, customs, enforcement directorate, etc.

Authorization of Search

Q5. *Whether non-compliance of summons issued by the Assistant Director of Investigation under section 131(1A) can form the basis for initiating search?*

Ans. This is a controversial issue and there is no direct authority available from any court on the above issue. As per literal interpretation of section 132(1), it seems that search action cannot be initiated for non-compliance of summons issued under section 131(1A) but if we go by purposive interpretation, such view is not free from doubt.

Q6. *Whether search can be initiated on the basis of information regarding investment in immovable properties particularly when existence of immovable property is a known fact and cannot be the subject matter of seizure?*

Ans. To take a view that search action cannot be initiated on the basis of information regarding investment in immovable properties, does not seem to be the correct view. The underlying asset may be immovable property which is a visible asset and location of which may be in the knowledge of the department, but the test would lie upon the fact that whether income representing such assets or the assets itself, have been disclosed to the department or not.

Q7. *Whether the identity of the informer, on the basis of whose information, search action was initiated, can be discovered by the person searched?*

Ans. It is very difficult to know the identity of the informer since such information is kept highly confidential in possession of senior officers only. However, in case the informer is a professional informer and claims reward from the Department at a later stage for information supplied by him, assessee may lay hand at such details of reward, though the same is also kept confidential. In case such professional informers approach court for seeking a direction to the tax department to give them the reward, their identity in that case becomes exposed.

Q8. *How much time does it take in preparing a case for taking search action by the income tax department?*

Ans. There is no time limit which can be prescribed for this purpose. It depends upon the nature of information regarding existence of undisclosed income and likelihood of seizure of assets, according to which case may be prepared for taking action of search. However, in all cases, search warrant by competent authority is required to be issued before taking action of search.

In the case of property transaction, when there is information available with the department regarding exchange of huge unaccounted cash consideration, search may be planned even in one day. In yet another case, unless the information received is reliable and verified, search action may not be planned and remain pending for months or sometimes years together.

Q9. *Under what circumstances an action of survey under section 133A may be converted into search under section 132?*

Ans. It is not easy and is not at the whim and fancy of the survey team to convert survey into search, though in practice, it has been observed that sometimes such pressure is exercised by the survey team. It may be possible only on the fulfilment of either of the conditions prescribed under clause (*a*), (*b*) or (*c*) of section 132(1) and after obtaining the search warrant from the competent authority. Survey is generally conducted by assessment wing of the department whereas competent authority to authorize search in such a case would normally be Commissioner of Income Tax. The Additional Commissioner of Income-tax, who may be heading the survey team, may not normally be the competent authority to authorize search and he will have to obtain search warrant from CIT.

Q10. *Whether assessee can get copy of search warrant authorizing search action against him?*

Ans. As per various judicial pronouncements, assessee does not have legal right to get the copy of search warrant authorizing search against him. Copy of search warrant is shown and signature of assessee on search warrant is obtained by the authorized officer before commencing action of search but the copy of search warrant is not supplied to the assessee.

Q11. *Whether assessee can get copy of reasons recorded by the competent authority authorizing search?*

Ans. The reasons recorded by the competent authority authorizing search are kept in confidential folder and the same are not shown to the assessee. The assessee cannot get the copy of the reasons; moreover, he cannot even read the contents of the reasons recorded. In a case when validity of search is challenged in writ petition before the High Court and copy of reasons is summoned by the High Court, the reasons recorded are seen and read by their lordships themselves and the contents are not made public or available to the assessee. In certain judicial cases reported, it has been seen that the reason for conducting search has been reproduced in the judicial orders.

Q12. *Whether authorized officer can enter and search any of the premises relating to the person searched in the course of search action on the basis of suspicion that some kind of incriminating material may be available thereat?*

Ans. Any premises relating to the person searched may be searched on the basis of suspicion but authorized officer is required to obtain search warrant from the competent authority to enter and search such premises. He cannot, at his own, enter and search any of the premises relating to the person searched.

Q13. *Whether consequential search warrant can be issued by the competent authority in the name of some other person, say consultant of the assessee, or employee of the assessee on the basis of suspicion?*

Ans. No search warrant can be issued by the competent authority in the name of some other person merely on the basis of suspicion. For issuing search warrant in the name of some other person, the competent authority has to record "reasons to believe" in consequence of information in his possession.

Q14. *Whether search warrant can be issued in the name of minor/non-resident Indian/foreign national residing in India/Legal heir of the deceased person?*

Ans. Yes, it is possible.

Q15. *Whether blank search warrant signed by the competent authority may be filled and used by the authorized officer for covering some other premises during search?*

Ans. No, use of search warrant in this manner is illegal.

Q16. *Whether search can be conducted with respect to the person who is in joint occupation with the person searched?*

Ans. A person who is in joint occupation with the person searched may also be searched by the authorized officer to find out any incriminating material relating to the person searched available in his possession. However, in case the premises are independent, separate search warrant is required to enter and search such premises. Independence of the premises is a matter of fact and will depend upon particular case.

Q17. *Whether search warrant can be issued in joint name?*

Ans. Yes, search warrant can be issued in joint name and in such a situation, each person covered in the search warrant can be searched and would be liable to be assessed/re-assessed in accordance with the provisions of section 153A. However, in such a case, "reason to believe" is required to be recorded by the competent authority separately for each person before including his or her name in the search warrant.

Q18. *In case of a search with respect to group of companies, if search warrant is issued in the name of the employee of the company and consequently, search is conducted at his residential premises, whether legality of search can be challenged by such employee in the High Court for the reason that search in his case is invalid?*

Ans. For conducting a valid search at the residential premises of the employee, "reason to believe" should be recorded by the competent authority with respect to such person in his individual capacity. "Reason to believe" recorded for the group as a whole may not be sufficient for issuing search warrant in his personal name and conducting search at his residential premises and in such a case search action may be declared as invalid by the High Court if it is found that reason to believe has not been recorded against him in his individual capacity. However, search warrant can be issued in the name of the company to conduct search at his residential premises in case, there is suspicion that incriminating material relating to the company is kept at his residential premises.

Q19. *The person searched is generally tempted to challenge the validity of search in the High Court. Whether it is in his advantage to do so?*

Ans. It is not always advantageous to challenge the validity of the search in the High Court. The decision is required to be taken keeping in view several factors and after weighing all the *pros* and *cons*.

Q20. *Whether incriminating material found and seized during search which is declared as illegal by the High Court, may be used by the department against the assessee?*

Ans. Yes, as per various judicial pronouncements, incriminating material found and seized even in an illegal search action may be used by the income tax department against the assessee in appropriate proceedings.

Q21. *Whether validity of search can be challenged by the assessee during appellate proceedings before CIT(A)/ITAT?*

Ans. No, validity of search cannot be examined by CIT(A)/ITAT during appellate proceedings. The validity of search can be examined by High Court in writ jurisdiction.

Q22. *Whether failure to file the return of income or return of wealth may be a sufficient ground to issue search warrant?*

Ans. No, non-filing of return of income/wealth cannot be a sufficient ground for conducting search.

Conduct of Search

Q23. *Whether action of search can be initiated in the night?*

Ans. There is no restriction provided under the Act with respect to the timings for initiating action for search. Search action can be initiated at any time depending upon the urgency of the matter.

Q24. *Whether search can be conducted at the premises found locked or at the premises where no person is available?*

Ans. Yes, the authorized officer has the power to break open the lock and enter the premises and make the search irrespective of whether the occupant/owner or some other person is available at the premises or not. The authorized officer may call upon two independent witnesses and in the presence of such witnesses; he may conduct the search proceedings.

Q25. *Whether search can be conducted with respect to a person at the premises not belonging to him but occupied by some other person?*

Ans. Yes, search can be conducted at any premises for which search warrant has been issued in consequence of information available with the authorities that incriminating material belonging to the target person is kept at such premises.

Q26. *Whether deleted data from the laptop may be restored and be made use of by the department?*

Ans. Yes, there are softwares available to restore the deleted data and sometimes the department does make use of such technique. The assessee cannot disown such data.

Q27. *Whether a guest staying with the assessee may also be searched?*

Ans. Yes, any person staying in, coming out or going in the premises may be made subject of personal search.

Q28. *Whether assessee is duty bound to disclose password/software for operation of files in the computer?*

Ans. Yes, assessee is duty bound to disclose password/software for operation of files in the computer. In case of non-co-operation in this regard, assessee may be prosecuted.

Q29. *Whether the authorized officer has the power to break open the locker, almirah, box etc. or tear the sofa or dig the wall/floor etc.?*

Ans. Yes, in case of suspicion or non-co-operation from the assessee to make available the keys, the authorized officer has power to take such action.

Q30. *Whether search can be temporarily suspended?*

Ans. Search can be temporarily suspended by passing prohibitory orders as prescribed under section 132(3) of the Act.

Q31. *Whether it is mandatory to appoint two independent witnesses before commencing conduct of search?*

Ans. Yes, it is a mandatory requirement and the entire search proceedings are conducted in the presence of two independent witnesses.

Q32. *Whether witnesses of his choice may be selected by the assessee?*

Ans. No, it is not the right of the assessee to select witnesses of his choice. However, in practice, selection of witnesses is made by the authorized officer with the consent of the assessee so that whole proceedings may be carried out smoothly.

Q33. *Whether authorized officer can forcibly require any person to act as witness?*

Ans. No, it is not possible to forcibly require any person to act as witness. However, a person refusing to act as witness without any justifiable cause, inspite of direction of the authorized officer may be prosecuted for his denial.

Q34. *Whether a person can ask for medical aid during the proceedings of search?*

Ans. Yes, a person under search can ask for medical aid in case he is not feeling well and he requires medical aid. He can call his family doctor to look after him and on the advice of doctor, if required he may be admitted to hospital.

Q35. *Whether assessee may insist for the presence of his counsel at the time of search operation?*

Ans. No, assessee does not have legal right to insist the presence of his counsel at the time of search operations. Search proceedings are the investigation proceedings and are conducted in the presence of two independent witnesses.

Q36. *Whether authorized officer has power to arrest or detain the person during search?*

Ans. No, income tax authorities in the course of income tax search and seizure operation do not have any power to arrest or detain any person.

Q37. *Whether the assessee has right to get copy of panchnama and copy of statement recorded during search?*

Ans. Assessee has the right to get copy of panchnama along with all annexures and generally it is handed over by the authorized officer to the assessee at the time of conclusion of search. But copy of statement recorded is not given to the assessee on the plea that the same shall be given at the time when it is to be used against the assessee.

Q38. *Whether production, purchase and sale of goods can be stopped/restrained by the authorized officer during search operation?*

Ans. No, there is no such power to the authorized officer to stop/restrain the production or movement of the goods during search operation. However, since inventory list of goods is prepared by the search team, assessee is required to make available necessary facilities to the search team so as to enable them to carry out this work smoothly.

Q39. *Whether assessee can ask for identity card of the members of search team?*

Ans. Yes, assessee can ask for production of identity card of the members of search team. In the absence of identity card some other evidence proving identity and genuineness of the person forming part of the search team, may be produced.

Q40. *What is the remedy available with the assessee in case his rights are denied by the authorized officer during search proceedings or excessiveness is exercised upon him?*

Ans. In such a situation assessee should try to resolve the matter after having discussion with the higher authorities. In case the matter is not resolved, he can file writ under Article 226 of the Constitution with the High Court at a later stage.

Q41. *What is the time limit within which search is required to be concluded?*

Ans. As such there is no time limit prescribed for conclusion of search proceedings. However, search proceedings are required to be undertaken at a stretch and be concluded at the earliest. Search proceedings may be temporarily suspended by passing prohibitory order as prescribed under section 132(3) of the Act and such prohibitory order is required to be lifted within a period of 60 days.

Q42. *Whether the authorized officer can prevent the assessee from receiving or making telephone calls during search?*

Ans. There is no specific power with the authorized officer to prevent the assessee from receiving or making telephone calls during search unless he believes that such permission would hinder the very object of search and the assessee may use the telephone calls to spread the message of search or manipulate the evidences. However, in practice it has been observed that such permission is not granted unless the telephone calls are very urgent and personal in nature and are made in the presence of the authorized officer.

Q43. *What is the advantage to the assessee by making declaration of undisclosed income during search in his statement recorded under section 132(4) of the Act?*

Ans. Assessee gets immunity from penalty with respect to undisclosed income relating to specified previous year declared during search while recording statement under section 132(4) in case declaration is made in the manner as prescribed under section 271AAA.

Q44. *Whether declaration of undisclosed income relating to earlier years can also be made during search so as to get immunity from penalty?*

Ans. There is no immunity from penalty by making declaration of undisclosed income relating to earlier years and penalty for concealment under section 271(1) (c) shall be attracted.

Q45. *Whether assessee can make declaration of undisclosed income under section 132(4) after initial action of search is concluded but his locker is under restraint under section 132(3)?*

Ans. Yes, according to CBDT's Instruction No. 1741 dated 24th January, 1986, the words in the "course of search" would include the period during which any locker, godown etc. is put under restraint under section 132(3).

Seizure during search

Q46. *Whether regular books of account and records can be seized?*

Ans. Yes, regular books of account and supporting records relating to the person searched can be seized during search.

Q47. *Whether regular books of account and supporting records relating to some other person/entity found at the premises of the person searched can be seized?*

Ans. Legally speaking, such books of account and records cannot be seized. However, it is seen in practice that these are seized on the ground that the person searched may have nexus with these books of account and supporting records.

Q48. *Whether disclosed assets belonging to the person searched can be seized during search?*

Ans. Seizure of disclosed assets cannot be made during search provided evidences regarding disclosure of assets to the department are produced by the assessee to the satisfaction of the authorized officer. Sometimes, such assets are seized for want of sufficient evidences in this regard available and produced by the assessee.

Q49. *Whether incriminating material consisting of documents and assets belonging to some other person found at the premises of the person searched can be seized during search?*

Ans. Seizure of such incriminating material can be made on the pretext that such material may have connection with the person searched.

Q50. *Whether assets acquired prior to seven years can be seized u/s 132 of the Income-tax Act?*

Ans. Assets acquired prior to seven years representing income relating to those years which cannot be made the subject matter of assessment or reassessment under any of the provisions of the Act cannot be seized legally. However, burden to prove that such asset was acquired during that period would lie upon the assessee.

Q51. *Whether original title deeds of immovable property can be seized?*

Ans. Original title deeds of immovable property which is a disclosed property cannot be seized. However, original title deeds of the undisclosed immovable property can be seized.

Q52. *Whether items of jewellery which do not match with the details of jewellery earlier declared by the assessee under VDIS Scheme or in his wealth tax returns can be seized?*

Ans. It would depend upon the satisfaction of the authorized officer. In case he believes that the jewellery found is different from the jewellery already declared by the assessee, seizure of such jewellery can be made.

Q53. *Whether jewellery worn on person by the assessee or other family members can be valued and seized during search?*

Ans. Such jewellery will form part of total jewellery and will be required to be valued along with total jewellery. But generally, such jewellery is not seized as it forms part of total minimum jewellery not required to be seized as per instructions of CBDT.

Q54. *Whether passport of the assessee can be seized?*

Ans. No, passport of the assessee cannot be seized.

Q55. *Whether operation of regular bank accounts of the assessee can be restrained during pendency of search proceedings?*

Ans. No, operation of regular bank accounts of the assessee cannot be restrained during pendency of search proceedings nor any seizure of money from such bank accounts can be made.

Q56. *Whether operation of bank lockers of the assessee can be restrained during search operation?*

Ans. Yes, operation of bank lockers of the assessee can be restrained during search operations by passing order under section 132(3).

Q57. *Whether stock in trade of the business entity can be seized?*

Ans. No as per amendment made by Finance Act, 2003 w.e.f. 1st June, 2003, no seizure or deemed seizure of stock in trade of the business entity can be made.

Q58. *Whether operation of computers can be restrained during pendency of search?*

Ans. Generally speaking operation of computers and normal working of the business cannot be halted or restrained during search operation. However, necessary steps may be taken so that data in the computer is not manipulated and seizure of such data is made by the search team smoothly.

Q59. *In the case of search with respect to a group of companies, when search is conducted at the residential premises of some employee of group company, whether personal assets of the employee can also be seized?*

Ans. In case, such personal assets of the employee are of undisclosed and/or incriminating nature, such assets are also liable to be seized.

Q60. *In case several companies are having registered office situated at one premises but search has been authorized at such premises with respect to one company only, whether books of account or documents relating to other companies can also be seized?*

Ans. In case any incriminating evidences relating to the other companies are found at such premises, such evidences can also be seized on the pretext that target company may have connection with such evidences.

Q61. *Whether jewellery or some other assets belonging to a friend of the assessee who has deposited it with assessee for safe custody can be seized?*

Ans. No, such assets cannot be seized unless there is reason to believe by the authorized officer that such asset belongs to the assessee and it represents his concealed income.

Q62. *Whether the authorized officer can seize cash or documents which have been thrown at the neighbours' house by the assessee and assessee claims that such assets have not been found at his premises?*

Ans. Yes, the authorized officer can seize such assets after recording the complete facts and circumstances in the presence of the witnesses.

Restraint Order u/s 132(3)

Q63. *Whether search remains pending till all the restraint orders passed are lifted?*

Ans. Yes, technically search is treated as pending till all the restraint orders passed u/s 132(3) are passed. Search is treated as finally concluded when all the restraint orders are lifted.

Q64. *What would happen when restraint order passed u/s 132(3) is not lifted within 60 days?*

Ans. As per sub-section (8A) of section 132, a restraint order passed under sub-section (3) of section 132 shall be in force for a period exceeding 60 days from the date of such order. It implies that in case restraint order is not lifted up to 60 days, it shall become ineffective and no seizure of assets/documents can be made thereafter. Moreover, search shall be treated as concluded on the expiry of the period of 60 days.

Q65. *Whether restraint order u/s 132(3) can be passed for stock in trade or for restricting movement/production of goods?*

Ans. Restraint order cannot be passed for items which are not required to be seized. Since stock in trade cannot be seized, no restraint order with respect to stock in trade can be passed. Further there is no power with the authorized officer to restrict or stop movement/production of goods.

Q66. *Whether security guards can be posted to protect the assets, books of account or documents with respect to which restraint order has been passed?*

Ans. The authorized officer may take such steps as may be necessary for ensuring compliance with the order passed u/s 132(3). In case he apprehends removal, damage or alteration to the items put under restraint, he may take necessary steps, *inter alia*, including posting of security guards.

Q67. *Whether restraint order can be passed with respect to regular books of account or disclosed assets/jewellery?*

Ans. Disclosed assets/jewellery cannot be seized therefore one can say that no restraint order with respect to disclosed assets/jewellery can be passed. However, the authorized officer can pass restraint order till the evidences regarding disclosure of assets/jewellery are produced before him and he is satisfied regarding the fact of disclosure of such assets/jewellery. Regular books of account can be the subject matter of seizure. Therefore, restraint order with respect to the same can be passed.

Q68. *Whether regular bank account of the person searched can be put under restraint u/s 132(3)?*

Ans. No, restraint order u/s 132(3) cannot be passed against regular bank accounts of the person searched.

Recording of Statement

Q69. *Whether a person is bound to answer questions put to him during the course of recording of his statement u/s 132(4)?*

Ans. Yes, statement u/s 132(4) is recorded on oath and a person is duty bound to answer all questions put to him truthfully and honestly. However, answering to questions is not test of his memory and in case assessee does not remember certain facts or he requires to consult his books of account or other records, he can say so and may submit the facts at a later date.

Q70. *Whether statement of other family members or employees of the assessee being the person under search can be recorded u/s 132(4)?*

Ans. Yes, examination of any person may be conducted u/s 132(4) in respect to all the matters which may be relevant and useful for the purpose of any investigation under the Income-tax Act.

Q71. *Whether assessee is duty bound to explain the nature and contents of the documents/notings/slips found at his premises?*

Ans. In case question is asked by the authorized officer while recording statement u/s 132(4) to explain the nature and contents of the documents/notings/slips found at his premises, assessee is required to answer such question to the best of his memory. In case he declines to answer the question, he may be penalized and prosecuted under the Income-tax Act.

Q72. *Whether summons u/s 131 can be issued and statement of the assessee be recorded u/s 131(1A) by the authorized officer?*

Ans. This is a controversial issue and judicial opinion is divided on this aspect. For detailed discussion, kindly refer to chapter on statement u/s 132(4).

Q73. *Whether assessee can amend the statement earlier given, in case he realizes that the statement earlier given is not correct or incomplete?*

Ans. Yes, a person can amend or correct his statement earlier given at any stage before conclusion of statement, whenever he realizes that the statement earlier given is not correct or complete.

Q74. *Whether statement of any visitor can be recorded who may visit the person searched in the course of search proceedings?*

Ans. Yes, authorized officer can examine on oath any visitor visiting the assessee in the course of search proceedings in case he has reason to suspect that any income has been concealed or is likely to be concealed by such person which may have connection with the person searched.

Q75. *Whether retraction of undisclosed income declared by the assessee in the course of search can be made at later stage?*

Ans. There is no legal bar in making retraction of undisclosed income declared by the assessee earlier during his statement in the course of search. The ultimate decision regarding undisclosed income of the assessee shall be taken by the Assessing Officer or higher authorities keeping in view the evidentiary value, relevant evidences and circumstances under which statement declaring undisclosed income and its retraction was made by the assessee.

Presumption regarding evidences found

Q76. *Whether there is presumption under the Act that the figures or details mentioned on the documents/papers/loose sheets/slips, etc. found and seized from the possession of the assessee shall be treated as his undisclosed income?*

Ans. No, there is no such presumption. Presumption u/s 132(4A)/292C is to the extent that evidences found from the possession of the assessee belong to him and the contents mentioned therein are true and correct.

Q77. *Whether such presumption is rebuttable presumption?*

Ans. Yes, such presumption is rebuttable presumption and the assessee can rebut the presumption by leading cogent evidences to this effect. The onus would lie upon the Assessing Officer to establish that undisclosed income can be attached to the assessee emanating from the evidences found from his possession.

Q78. *What is dumb document and what are its implications on the assessee?*

Ans. Dumb document may be said to be a document on which certain figures/details are mentioned but from such details no meaningful interpretation can be drawn. No undisclosed income can be attached to the assessee on the basis of dumb document.

Q79. *Whether a transporter or agent from whose custody the assets are seized can be treated as owner of the assets and undisclosed income can be assessed in his hands?*

Ans. A transporter or agent can shift his burden by leading evidences regarding actual owner of the assets. In such a situation undisclosed income if any, can be assessed in the hands of the actual owner and not in the hands of the agent. In case the transporter or agent fails to prove the identity of actual owner, presumption of undisclosed income can be drawn against him.

Retention and release of books of account, assets etc.

Q80. *Whether computer hardware/laptop seized can be released by the authorized officer?*

Ans. As per departmental internal instructions, computer hardware/laptop is not required to be seized but seizure is required to be made of hard disk or other electronic devices on which data has been stored. As per normal practice adopted now-a-days, computer hardware/laptop is released after seizing hard disk or other electronic device containing data. Copy of such hard disk/other electronic device is also given to the assessee at his request.

Q81. *Whether copy of documents or books of account seized in an illegal action can be retained by the department?*

Ans. Yes, copy of documents or books of account seized in an illegal action can be retained by the department. Such evidences may be made use of by the department wherever required and deemed appropriate in terms of the law.

Q82. *Whether assessee can obtain photocopies of the documents or books of account seized from his premises from the authorized officer?*

Ans. Yes, as per section 132(9) assessee has right to get copies of the documents or books of account seized from his possession from the authorized officer immediately after search. But there is no time limit prescribed for this purpose and, in practice, it has been observed that such copies are seldom supplied by the authorized officer. Assessee gets such photocopies later on from the Assessing Officer when notices for filing returns of income u/s 153A are received by him.

Q83. *What is the procedure for release of disclosed assets if seized during search?*

Ans. In case disclosed assets are seized by the authorized officer for want of satisfactory evidences produced by the assessee in the course of search, such assets cannot be released by the authorized officer but may be released by the Assessing Officer. Assessee can move application to the Assessing Officer within 30 days from the end of the month in which seizure was made with all the evidences for release of such assets. Such assets can be released by the Assessing Officer with the approval of CIT but after adjusting any existing tax liability under all the Direct Tax Acts, if any outstanding for payment by the assessee.

Q84. *Whether cash seized can be treated by the assessee as advance tax paid?*

Ans. After amendment to section 132B, cash seized can not be treated and adjusted towards advance tax payment. However, cash seized can be adjusted towards the self assessment tax liability.

Q85. *Whether remaining seized assets after payment/adjustment of all the tax liabilities including interest and penalty can be retained by the department on the ground that further appeal with higher authorities has been filed by the department?*

Ans. No, seized assets cannot legally be retained on the above ground and department is required to release assets immediately after payment of all the tax liabilities.

Q86. *Whether jewellery can be released immediately after search on deposit of cash of equivalent amount?*

Ans. Yes, it is possible and CBDT has issued Instruction No. 286/97/2003 dated 3-3-2004 prescribing procedure for release of jewellery against deposit of cash or furnishing of bank guarantee of equivalent amount.

Requisition of books of account, documents or assets documents or assets"

Q87. *Whether opportunity is required to be given to the assessee to explain the source of acquisition of assets before making requisition to seize assets?*

Ans. No, there is no such provision u/s 132A to grant opportunity to the assessee before issuing authorization for requisition.

Q88. *Whether a person against whom requisition has been issued is required to be assessed or reassessed for earlier six years in accordance with the provisions of section 153A?*

Ans. Yes, a person against whom requisition has been authorized is required to be assessed or reassessed for earlier six years in accordance with the provisions of section 153A.

Q89. *Whether a person against whom authorization for requisition is issued can make declaration of undisclosed income so as to get immunity from penalty?*

Ans. There is no deeming fiction of "undisclosed income" relating to "specified previous year" as given u/s 271AAA, applicable in the case of requisition. Since no penalty u/s 271AAA is attracted in the case of requisition, there is no need of making declaration by the assessee and therefore provision of section 132(4) is also not applicable in the case of requisition. There is no immunity from penalty u/s 271(1)(c) for undisclosed income relating to earlier years irrespective of declaration made by the assessee during search.

Wealth Tax

Q90. *Whether jewellery for which Wealth Tax return has not been filed but source of acquisition is explained from the Income Tax point of view can be seized?*

Ans. Jewellery, with respect to which there is evasion of wealth tax, can be seized for recovery of wealth tax liability since action of search is generally taken jointly under the Income-tax Act and Wealth-tax Act.

Penalty and Prosecution

Q91. *Whether immunity from penalty can be available to the assessee by making declaration of undisclosed income relating to earlier years?*

Ans. No, there is no immunity from penalty by making declaration of undisclosed income relating to earlier years in the course of search. For any concealment of income relating to earlier years, penalty provisions u/s 271(1)(c) shall be attracted.

Q92. *Whether immunity is not available even when declaration of undisclosed income for earlier years is made by the assessee stating that such declaration is subject to no penalty?*

Ans. This is an established principle that there is no estoppel against law. When there is no specific provision under the Act for such immunity, assessee cannot claim it on the basis of the manner of his declaration.

Q93. *What kind of immunity from penalty is available u/s 271AAA by making declaration of undisclosed income during search?*

Ans. As per section 271AAA there is deeming fiction of undisclosed income and the income relating to current year not recorded in the regular books of account may also be treated as undisclosed income on which penalty at the rate of 10% of such undisclosed income may be attracted as provided u/s 271AAA. By making declaration of undisclosed income during search in the manner as provided under sub-section (2) of section 271AAA, assessee can get immunity from such penalty.

Penalty provision u/s 271AAA has been discontinued in respect of search initiated on or after 1.7.2012 and new provision of section 271AAB has been enacted wherein there is no immunity from penalty but two rates of penalty have been given for different situations.

Settlement Commission

Q94. *Whether assessee can make application to the Settlement Commission for settling the cases relating to search?*

Ans. As per amendment made by Finance Act, 2010 there is one opportunity available to the assessee for making settlement of cases relating to search subject to conditions spelt therein.

Finance Act, 2021 has abolished the institution of Settlement Commission and with effect from 1st February, 2021 no new application may be filed for settlement. Therefore such option is no longer available to the searched person.

Q95. *Whether it is in the interest of the assessee to approach to the Settlement Commission for settling cases relating to search?*

Ans. It will depend on the facts and circumstances of the case. It cannot be said that it would always be advantageous for the assessee to approach the Settlement Commission. Decision will have to be taken by the assessee after weighing all the *pros* and *cons* relating to above issue.

Q96. *Whether Settlement Commission has the power to grant waiver from levy of interest?*

Ans. No, levy of interest is a mandatory requirement provided under the Act and it cannot be waived by Settlement Commission.

Q97. *Whether Settlement Commission has the power to grant immunity from penalty and prosecution?*

Ans. Yes, Settlement Commission has discretion to grant immunity from penalty and prosecution as prescribed under Income-tax Act and Wealth-tax Act, in appropriate cases.

Q98. *Whether order of Settlement Commission is appealable with the High Court/ Supreme Court?*

Ans. No, order of Settlement Commission is final and binding and no appeal with the High Court/Supreme Court can be filed against such order.

Assessment

Q99. *Whether a person who has been searched is mandatorily required to be assessed or reassessed for earlier six years?*

Ans. Yes, as per requirement of the provision of section 153A, a person who has been searched is mandatorily required to be assessed or reassessed for earlier six years.

Q100. *Whether assessment/reassessment u/s 153A is made for undisclosed income found as a result of search as was the case under block assessment regime?*

Ans. No, the concept of assessment/reassessment u/s 153A is entirely different from the concept of block assessment and it is not assessment/reassessment of undisclosed income found as a result of search only.

Q101. *What kind of additions can be made in the case of assessment/reassessment in pursuance to notice u/s 153A?*

Ans. Broadly speaking, nature of assessment/reassessment for earlier six years in pursuance to notice u/s 153A shall be governed by normal provisions of the Act and the additions can be made as applicable in the case of assessment u/s 143(3) or in the case of reassessment u/s 147/148 as the case may be.

Q102. *Is there any separate form prescribed for filing return of income in pursuance to notice u/s 153A?*

Ans. No, there is no separate form prescribed for this purpose. Income Tax return is required to be filed on the same form as applicable in the normal course mentioning that the return is being filed in pursuance to notice u/s 153A.

Q103. *What would happen to the pending assessment/reassessment proceedings relating to any of the earlier six years already under going with the Assessing Officer?*

Ans. Such proceedings shall abate and shall in a way be merged with the new proceedings to be undertaken in pursuance to notice u/s 153A.

Q104. *In case there is any undisclosed income found relating to some other person, whether such person can also be assessed/reassessed for earlier six years as per provisions of section 153C?*

Ans. Such other person can be assessed or reassessed for earlier six years as per provisions of section 153C in case evidences found during search *belong to* such person. In case there is undisclosed income emanating from the evidences belonging to the person searched but such evidences do not *belong to* the other person, such undisclosed income can be assessed or reassessed in the hands of such other person as per provisions and principles of section 147/148 and not as per provisions of section 153C.

Q105. *Whether as per provisions of section 153C, the other person is also required to be assessed or reassessed for earlier six years even when evidences belonging to him seized during search are relating to only one year?*

Ans. Yes, as per provisions of section 153C, in case a person is covered within the ambit of such provision, he is required to be assessed or reassessed in the same manner as the person searched in accordance with the provisions of section 153A. However, Hon'ble Supreme Court has laid down in the case of *CIT* v. *Sinhgad Technical Education Society* 397 ITR 344 (SC) have held that only that year would be subject to assessment u/s 153C relating to which incriminating material has been found.

Q106. *What is the time limit for issuing notice u/s 153C?*

Ans. There is no time limit prescribed under the Act for invoking provision of section 153C. However, as per various judicial pronouncements, notice u/s 153C should be issued before passing order in the case of person searched u/s 153A or within reasonable time.

LIST OF CASES

SEARCH AND SEIZURE - NATURE OF PROVISIONS

1.1 Introduction

Power of search & seizure is an extreme power in the hands of State. Such provisions are generally frowned upon by the taxpayers. The genesis of the power of search and seizure incorporated under the Income-tax Act, 1961 lies in the growing menace of black money in our economy which is popularly known in our country as parallel economy. No body can deny the fact that there are rampant tax evasion practices prevalent in our society and the Government has constitutional duty to prevent such practices for the larger good of the nation. The powers of search and seizure have been given mainly to unearth black money and prevent tax evasion.

The necessity to have the drastic power of search has been felt not only in India but also in other countries where democratic right to privacy is considered supreme. Under U.K. laws, privacy of a citizen is considered sacred and Lord Coke described the then subsisting law as under *"the house of everyone is to him his castle and fortress as well as his defence against injury and violence as for his repose"*. But in the changed circumstances it is no longer a castle or a fortress any more even in developed economy like that of U.K.

(*i*) Meaning of "search" and "seizure"

In the Concise Oxford Dictionary the word *"search"* means *"look for"* or *"seek out"*.

Search means a thorough inspection of the premises or place and of the person. Search indicates an action in which each and every place is looked and checked. Considering the scope and object of section 132(1)(*iii*) of the Act, the word "search" should not be given a far too technical meaning. [*Mohammed Kunhi* v. *Mohammed Koya* [1973] 91 ITR 301 (Mad.)]

1

"Seizure" means forcibly taking possession of property, etc. by law. It means taking possession of the asset or other items contrary to the wishes of the person possessing the same but under the authority of law. Seizure can be actual physical seizure of the assets or it can be constructive seizure under the authority of law.

In common parlance Income-tax search is popularly known as income tax raid also.

(ii) **Search v. Inspection**

All searches are inspections but all inspections are not necessarily searches. A search is a thorough inspection of a man's house, building or premises or of his person, with the object of discovering some material which would furnish evidence of guilt for some offence with which he is charged. It implies looking into hidden places where such material is concealed.

[*CCT* v. *Ramkishan Shrikishan Jhaver* [1967] 66 ITR 664 (SC)]

(iii) **Seizure v. Prohibitory Order**

"Seizure" means the dispossession of the person from whom seizure is made and assumption of possession of the seized article by seizing officer. Where only keys of a locker are seized and an order under section 132(3) is served restraining the owner from opening or operating the locker, the contents of the locker remain in the custody and possession of the owner and not of the seizing officer, and that would be so even after the locker was opened and an inventory of its contents was made by the officer. Order restraining the owner from opening or operating the locker would tantamount to issue of Prohibitory Order.

[*Mrs. Kanwal Shamsher Singh* v. *Union of India* [1974] 95 ITR 80 (Delhi)]

(iv) **Search v. Survey**

Under the Income-tax Act, 1961, various powers of investigation have been provided to the Income Tax authorities as given under Chapter XIII Part C, such as issuing summons under section 131, calling for information under section 133(6), collecting information under section 133B, undertaking search under section 132, undertaking survey under section 133A etc. Income tax search and survey actions are both undertaken by visiting the premises of the assessee and collecting information regarding undisclosed income of the assessee.

Sometimes, nature of action and powers available to the tax authorities during income tax search and income tax survey operation are not properly understood and distinguished by the assessee. Major features of distinction between income tax search and income tax survey may be summarized as under:

1. Income tax survey can be conducted only at business premises and not at residential premises of the assessee while income tax search can be conducted at both the places.

2. No seizure of any kind of assets including unaccounted cash can be made in the case of survey. However, as per amendment made by Finance Act, 2002, with effect from 1st June 2002, impounding of books of account or other documents can be made in survey operation.

3. There is requirement of recording "reason to believe" in consequence of the information in possession of the competent authority and of issuing warrant of authorization as provided under section 132(1) for taking search action. There is no such requirement for undertaking income tax survey action.

4. Income tax survey action can be initiated during business hours when the business premises are open while there is no such restriction for undertaking income tax search action.

5. In the case of income tax search, statements are recorded on oath as provided under section 132(4) and such statements have higher evidentiary value in comparison to statements recorded during income tax survey action which are not required to be recorded on oath.

6. Income tax search action can be concluded within 60 days from the date of initiation of the action and there is power to put temporarily prohibitory orders on the incriminating material likely to be seized. There is no such power of temporary suspension in the case of income tax survey action and it is required to be completed at a stretch.

7. A person against whom income tax search action is undertaken is required to be assessed or re-assessed mandatorily for earlier six years prior to the year of search as provided under section 153A of the Act (in some cases for 9 years). There is no such requirement in the case of survey and the assessee may be required to undergo scrutiny assessment under section 143(3) or 147 depending upon the nature of incriminating evidences found during survey.

1.2 Historical background

In India, the provisions relating to search and seizure were introduced for the first time in the year 1956, in the Indian Income-tax Act, 1922. Prior to this, powers of search and seizure vested in income tax authorities in 1948 as per Taxation of Income Investigation Commission (Amendment) Act, 1948, were struck down as *ultra vires* and violative of Article 14 of the Constitution by the Supreme Court.

By the Taxation of Income (Investigation Commission) Act, 1947, an Investigation Commission was founded conferring powers to track down the cases where substantial tax evasion was involved. For the purpose, the income tax authorities were bestowed with the necessary powers of search and seizure to assist the Investigation Commission to bring the tax evaders into the net. But Hon'ble Supreme Court in the case of *Suraj Mall Mohta & Co.* v. *A.V. Visvanatha Sastri* [1954] 26 ITR 1 held the statutory provisions contained in the above mentioned Act as violative of Article 14 of the Constitution because they were found discriminatory in nature *qua* the persons against whom proceedings under the abovesaid Act were taken. The said view was again reiterated by Hon'ble High Court in the case of *Thangalkunju Musaliar* v. *Authorised Official and ITO* [1954] 25 ITR 120 (Ker.).

Hon'ble Supreme Court in a subsequent decision in the case of *Shree Meenakshi Mills Ltd.* v. *A.V. Visvanatha Sastri* [1954] 26 ITR 713 considered the effect of the subsequent insertion of sub-section (1A) in section 34 of the Indian Income-tax Act, 1922 and held that after introduction of the said sub-section, the defence of valid classification was not available to the State because sub-section (1A) dealt with the same class of persons which were dealt with section 5(1) of the impugned Act and hence provisions of said section being discriminatory in nature, had become void and unenforceable. This view was further reiterated by Hon'ble Supreme Court in the case of *Basheshar Nath* v. *CIT* [1959] 35 ITR 190 in which Hon'ble Supreme Court held that section 8A of the Taxation of Income (Investigation Commission) Act, 1947 was void along with section 5(1) of the said Act as it was discriminatory in character and offended Article 14 of the Constitution and that a settlement arrived at under section 8A of the said Act during the investigation was therefore void and unenforceable.

Section 37 of the 1922 Act, was redrafted based on the recommendation made by Taxation Inquiry Commission 1956 according to which powers of search were invested with income tax officers who were specially authorized by the Commissioner. But these powers of search operated in the limited field to the extent of search and seizure of books of account and other documents which were likely to be useful in making proper assessments under the said Act.

When Income-tax Act, 1961 was enacted, the provisions relating to search and seizure were incorporated u/s 132 of the Act. Originally the powers of search and seizure were confined only in relation to books of account and documents and not for cash or other assets. Since then, there have been numerous amendments in the provisions relating to powers of search and seizure from time to time keeping pace with the value system prevailing in the society and mind set of the authorities regarding the manner how to administer income tax law in the country. Major amendments introduced u/s 132 of the Income-tax Act, 1961 & relating to the assessment of search cases from time to time are, in brief, as under:—

(*i*) **Finance Act, 1964**

Section 132 was substituted and this Act enlarged the scope of powers given u/s 132.

(*ii*) **Income Tax (Amendment) Act, 1965**

Provisions of section 132 were further refined. One of the important provisions incorporated was with regard to the validation of certain searches made. The powers of seizure of unaccounted cash, bullion or jewellery or other valuable articles or things were conferred on the tax authorities.

(*iii*) **Taxation Laws (Amendment) Act, 1975**

As per recommendations made by the Wanchoo Committee, far-reaching changes were made in section 132, enlarging the scope of search to cover vessel, vehicle and aircraft, incorporating section 132(1)(*iia*) so as to search any person present in the premises during search or going out or entering into the premises. The provisions for application of the seized assets were introduced to effectively encounter the generation of black money. Sub-section (4A) was added to section 132 introducing presumptions against the person searched and many more changes were introduced.

(*iv*) **Direct Tax Laws (Amendment) Act, 1987**

Prohibitory order u/s 132(3) was made operative upto 60 days from the date of order subject to extension and it was clarified that order u/s 132(3) shall not be deemed to be seizure of books of account, other documents or assets.

(*v*) **Finance Act, 1988**

The concept of deemed seizure was incorporated by insertion of second proviso to section 132(1).

(*vi*) **Finance Act, 1995**

Concept of block assessment was introduced by inserting Chapter XIVB under the Income-tax Act, 1961. Concept of passing order u/s 132(5) making summary assessment to decide the retention of seized assets was dispensed with.

(vii) Finance Act, 2003

By the time the concept of block assessment could be applied and interpreted by the courts and the provisions were settled, the whole procedure of assessment in the case of search was amended by introducing new assessment procedure u/ss 153A, 153B and 153C. It was also provided that seizure of stock-in-trade in business cannot be made.

(viii) Finance Acts, 2007 & 2012

New penalty regime was introduced in respect of search taking place on or after 1.6.2007 for 'specified previous year' by introducing section 271AAA. Penalty provision in search cases as provided in section 271AAA was overhauled and substituted by new Section 271AAB by Finance Act, 2012 in respect searches taking place on or after 1.7.2012.

1.3 Objective of Search

Over a period of time, income tax department (in short "department") has realized that income tax scrutiny assessment may not yield much result in terms of revenue augmentation and departmental authorities may not be able to detect substantial tax evasion. Even after substantial economic growth, tax base of income tax assessees is very low.

The powers of search and seizure have been given to the tax authorities primarily to achieve the following objectives:

    a. To collect evidences of undisclosed income/wealth not declared by the assessee.

    b. To seize assets representing undisclosed income/wealth.

    c. To have the deterrence effect.

Ground Rule 2 issued by Central Board of Direct Taxes (CBDT) specifying objects of the search, states as under:—

> *"A search is necessary to secure evidence which is not likely to be made available by issue of summons or by visiting, in ordinary course, the premises concerned. Tax authorities have powers to summon persons and documents. Tax authorities have to resort to search and seizure when there is evidence of undisclosed documents or assets which have not been and would not be disclosed in ordinary course".*

The objective of section 132 was thus intended to unearth the hidden or undisclosed income of property and bring it to the assessment as held in *Gulab & Co.* v. *Superintendent of Central Excise (Preventive)* [1975] 98 ITR 581 (Mad.). Thus, the object of the section is not merely to get information of the undisclosed income but also to seize money, bullion representing the undisclosed income and to retain them for purposes of proper realization of taxes or penalty etc. as was held in *Pannalal* v. *ITO* [1974] 93 ITR 480 (MP).

1.4 Features of search provisions

(*i*) Investigation process

The provisions relating to search & seizure are contained u/s 132 of the Income-tax Act, 1961. It is an investigation process undertaken by the department to unearth black money, collect evidences relating to undisclosed income and investments and make seizure of the undisclosed assets.

(*ii*) Harsh in nature

To undertake search & seizure operations is considered a very harsh action on the part of the income tax department with severe consequences and also so recognized by courts from time to time including in the decision titled *Manish Maheshwari* v. *Asstt. CIT* [2007] 159 Taxman 258/289 ITR 341 (SC). Under the Income-tax Act, department has various powers for collecting taxes and verifying correctness of the Income Tax return filed and income declared by the assessee *e.g.*, scrutiny of the cases, summoning the assessee, collecting the evidences from third parties, imposing interest and penalty for defaults committed, conducting survey at the business premises etc. It was felt that these powers are not sufficient enough to prevent tax evasion and therefore, further power of conducting search or raid as it is popularly known, have been vested in the income tax authorities. As per powers conferred for conducting search, the tax officials visit the business and residential premises of the assessee without prior information to collect the evidences, record the statement and seize the undisclosed assets. Such steps by any standard are harsh steps qua the citizens of the country.

(*iii*) Invading privacy

Under search and seizure operation, the privacy of the person is invaded completely. The tax officials have the power to visit and search any place including residential premises of any person at any time even in the mid night, in consequence of information in their possession regarding undisclosed income or wealth but of course by observing certain statutory requirements. They have powers to enter and search each and every corner of the premises of the person being searched.

(*iv*) Deterrence effect

Income tax search is the ultimate action taken by the department to catch hold of the undisclosed asset of the tax evaders but such action is taken in rare circumstances upon fulfilment of necessary ingredients designed to secure the citizens from arbitrary exercise of such power. The other important objective of granting such powers to the tax officials is to create deterrence effect in the society so that those inclined to evade taxes may refrain from doing so, keeping in view harsh consequences of search action.

(*v*) **Severe consequences**

Wide powers have been conferred on the tax officials in the matter of search and seizure and there are severe consequences on the assessee in whose case search is conducted and undisclosed income and wealth is detected. In the case of every person who is searched, detailed procedure of investigation is carried out, enquiries are made, adverse evidences are collected and appraisal report is prepared by the authorities which are ultimately used for fastening the tax liability, imposing the penalties and initiating prosecution in respect of undisclosed income and wealth. Even when no incriminating evidences relating to undisclosed income are found during search operations, income tax cases of the searched person for last six years are scrutinized as per procedure of assessment provided under section 153A of the Income-tax Act.

1.5 In-built safeguards

Since search & seizure provisions are quite harsh in nature, in-built safeguard mechanism has been provided while enacting the provisions relating to authorization and conduct of search by higher authorities and formation of *"reason to believe"* regarding undisclosed income based upon *"information"* in possession of department before authorizing search. Safeguards have been provided at different stages under the provisions of search so as to prevent any possible misuse of the provisions by the authorities.

(*i*) **Authorization by higher authorities**

The powers of authorizing search action have been vested in the higher officials of the department *i.e.*, Principal Director General, Director General, Principal Chief Commissioner, Chief Commissioner, Principal Director, Director, Principal Commissioner, Commissioner or any such Additional/Joint Director or Additional/Joint Commissioner as is empowered by the Board in this regard. Lower rank officers are not empowered to undertake search action at their own. It has been so provided on the ostensible premise that senior officers are prone to take objective decisions by virtue of their experience in the field. By entrusting such power in the hands of officers of sufficient higher rank, objectivity is sought to be lent and it has been attempted to be ensured that possibility of arbitrary exercise of such power is eliminated.

(ii) 'Reason to Believe' in consequence of information in possession

The competent authorities can authorize search only after formation of "*reason to believe*" regarding non-compliance or possible non-compliance of the notice u/s 142(1) or summon u/s 131 or regarding possession of undisclosed income or undisclosed assets by the person against whom search is being authorized. "*Reason to believe*" has to be formed based upon information in possession relating to undisclosed income etc. Existence of material for the purpose of forming "*reason to believe*" is another safeguard built in the system of search.

(iii) Satisfaction at two stages

In case of search and seizure operation, satisfaction by the tax authorities is arrived at two stages, first, by the competent authority before authorizing search, and second, by the authorized officer who actually conducts search, before making seizure of undisclosed assets. The authorized officer has to satisfy himself that assets found during search are undisclosed in nature. Only then he has authority to seize the same. So at each stage, legislature has ensured to maintain the objectivity by making suitable provisions.

(iv) Whole proceeding in the presence of two witnesses

The search operation is required to be conducted in the presence of two independent witnesses selected from the same locality to witness the whole proceedings and to ensure that search operation is conducted in an independent and fair manner.

(v) Strict reporting system and maintaining transparency

During search operation, strict and immediate internal reporting system by authorized officer to the higher authorities is adhered in practice so as to maintain complete transparency and fairness. Various reports are administratively required to be sent by the authorized officer and information of significant nature is passed to the higher authorities immediately so as to maintain transparency and prevent the possibility of any arbitrary use of the power.

(vi) Power of search to be exercised strictly in terms of law

It has been held in number of judicial pronouncements that provisions relating to search have to be construed and implemented strictly in accordance as provided under the statute:

"A search by itself is not a restriction on the right to hold and enjoy property. On the other hand, a seizure and carrying away is a restriction on the possession and enjoyment of the property seized. This, however, is only temporary and for the limited purpose of investigation. A search and seizure is, therefore, only a temporary interference with the right to hold the premises searched and the articles seized. Statutory regulation in this behalf is necessary and reasonable restriction cannot *per se* be considered to be unconstitutional. The search and seizure as effected in that case were neither unreasonable nor constituted a serious restriction on the right of the various petitioners, in as much as their buildings were invaded, their documents taken away and their business and reputation affected by large-scale and allegedly arbitrary searches and that a law (pre-Constitutional to section 96(1) of the Criminal Procedure Code, 1898, corresponding to section 93(1) of the Criminal Procedure Code, 1973), which authorized such searches, did not violate the constitutional guarantee and was valid. The damage, if any, caused by such temporary interference, if found to be in excess of legal authority, is a matter for redress in other proceedings. Indeed, while there is no constitutional guarantee in India against illegal search and seizure as available under the Fourth Amendment of the American Constitution, there are provided sufficient safeguards in almost all the enactments conferring on the authorities' power of search and seizure. Be it noted that the primary power is the power of seizure. The power to enter and search any building or break open the lock of any door, box, locker, safe, almirah or other receptacle is only an incidental power, the exercise of which will be only a means to the primary end, *viz.*, the seizure." [*M.P. Sharma* v. *Satish Chandra* AIR 1954 SC 300, 306]

Since a serious invasion is made upon right of privacy and freedom of the taxpayer, the power must be exercised strictly in accordance with the law and only for the purpose for which the law authorizes it to be exercised.

[*Pooran Mal* v. *Director of Inspection* [1974] 93 ITR 505 (SC)]

Provisions relating to search and seizure in the income tax law, if properly carried out, do not interfere with the right to hold and enjoy property as guaranteed under the Constitution. These powers are not arbitrary and naked powers without any guidance in the matter of their exercise. Limitations are put on its exercise—

   (*i*) It can be authorized by certain defined authorities, high up in the hierarchy;

   (*ii*) Belief is based on information on record and not mere suspicion;

   (*iii*) The belief is concerning the matters stated in clause (*a*), (*b*) or (*c*) of section 132(1) in relation to person, account books, documents, article or things referred to in these clauses;

   (*iv*) The extent of exercise of power is as stated in clause (*i*), (*ii*) or (*iii*) of section 132(1).

[*Ramjibhai Kalidas* v. *I.G. Desai, ITO* [1971] 80 ITR 721 (Guj.)]

1.6 Scope of search provisions

(*i*) Search action only in rare cases

Kelkar Committee has very aptly pointed out in its report on tax reforms, *"Search and seizure has a limited role in the Income Tax proceedings. Search and seizure is not a substitute for investigation. It is only a tool for investigation. It is not an end in itself. Search and seizure cannot be a way of life for any civilized society. Search and seizure should be used in rarest of rare cases, when it is a must and where alternative measures of investigation have failed. And once it is used, it should have its full impact as a deterrent. The tax evader should suffer the penal consequences of interest, penalty and prosecution in respect of the concealed income detected as a result of the search."- (Para 3.25 of the report)*

There are departmental instructions to invoke power of search and seizure only in cases of massive concealment of income say, more than ₹ 1 crore *(Instruction No. 7 dated 30th July 2003).*

(*ii*) A self contained code

Provisions regarding search and seizure under the Income-tax Act and rules constitute a self contained code.

[*H.L. Sibal* v. *CIT* [1975] 101 ITR 112 (P&H)]

The special provisions of sections 132 and 132A along with the relevant rules constitute, by and large, a self-contained comprehensive code in themselves governing the procedure of search and seizure.

[*Mamchand & Co.* v. *CIT* [1968] 69 ITR 631 (Cal.)]

[*Director of Inspections* v. *K.C.A. & Co.* [1987] 32 Taxman 495 (J&K)]

The provisions of section 132 exist in isolation of other provisions of the Act. It is essentially a procedural section empowering the tax authorities to take action where the income and assets are not voluntarily disclosed.

[*Joginder Singh* v. *CIT* [1981] 6 Taxman 245 (P&H)]

[*Jayantilal C. Jhaveri* v. *Asstt. CIT* [1995] 55 ITD 313 (Bom.-Trib.)]

It has been held by Supreme Court that section 132 is self contained code in itself *P. R. Metrani* v. *CIT* [2006] 157 Taxman 325 (SC).

(*iii*) No power of arrest

The income tax authorities during the course of search have no power to arrest or even to detain a person in their custody.

"Person cannot be restrained from attending to his normal duties, after his statement is recorded. The Act does not give any power to the Income Tax department to arrest an individual. Thus, once a statement is recorded during search, the department has no power to restrain such person from attending to his professional work."

[*L.R. Gupta* v. *Union of India* [1991] 59 Taxman 305 (Delhi)]

"Section 132 of the Income-tax Act does not empower the authorized officer to arrest the person who is found or suspected to be in possession of any document or money, etc. The powers under section 132 of the Income-tax Act are much narrower than those conferred under the Foreign Exchange Regulation Act, 1973, and the Customs Act, 1962".

[*K. Choyi, ITO* v. *Syed Abdulla Bafakki Thangal* [1973] 91 ITR 144 (Ker.)]

1.7 Constitutional validity

Keeping in view the harsh character of search and seizure proceedings, a question is always raised as to the constitutional validity of such provisions. Though, this aspect has been dealt at great length in other chapter, yet it would be fruitful to discuss this aspect summarily here as under.

The provisions relating to the law of search and seizure are constitutionally valid as the power is directed to be used for prevention of tax evasion measure.

[*CCT* v. *Ramkishan Shrikishan Jhaver* [1967] 66 ITR 664 (SC)]

"There are adequate safeguards built in section 132 and rules to ensure that the Director of Inspection or the Commissioner cannot lightly or arbitrarily invade the privacy of a subject. Before he acts, he must be reasonably satisfied that it is necessary to do so on the basis of information in his possession."

"There is a valid classification of persons against whom proceedings under Section 132 may be taken and the section does not violate Article 14 of the Constitution of India."

"Search of a premises by itself, no doubt offends the right of a subject to hold property guaranteed under Article 19, but searches necessitated for avoiding tax evasion or facilitating the making of assessments cannot be termed as unreasonable restrictions on the rights of the subjects. Similarly, seizure of documents for a limited period for the purpose of assessment would also constitute a reasonable restriction. Section 132 is not, therefore, hit by Article 19 which guarantees right of a subject to hold property. However, there is no fundamental right under Article 19 to withhold records or information." [*Balwant Singh* v. *R.D. Shah, Director of Inspection* [1969] 71 ITR 550 (Delhi)]

The provision relating to search and seizure u/s 132 of Income-tax Act, 1961 and Rule 112 of the Income-tax Rules, 1962 do not violate the fundamental rights under Article 19(1)(*f*)/(*g*) of the Constitution of India [*Pooran Mal* v. *Director of Inspection* [1974] 93 ITR 505 (SC)].

The restrictions placed by any of the provision of section 132 or 132A or Rule 112 are reasonable restrictions on the freedom under Article 19(1) (*f*)/(*g*). It was further held that provisions of section 132(1) and 132(5) of the Income-tax Act, 1961 are not discriminatory and do not violate Article 14 of the Constitution [*Pooran Mal* v. *Director of Inspection* [1974] 93 ITR 505 (SC)].

The Apex Court in the case of *Pooran Mal* (*supra*) also held as under:

> "Search and seizure are not a new weapon in the armoury of those whose duty it is to maintain social security in its broadest sense. The process is widely recognized in all civilized countries.

> It is now too late in a day to challenge the measure of search and seizure when it is entrusted to Income Tax authorities with a view to prevent large scale tax evasion. Indeed, the measure would be objectionable if its implementation is not accompanied by safeguards against its undue and improper exercise. As a broad proposition it is now possible to state that if the safeguards are generally on the lines adopted by the Criminal Procedure Code they would be regarded as adequate and render the temporary restrictions imposed by the measure reasonable."

The powers of search and seizure are instruments for curbing economic offences which erode the social fabric and cause damage to its social security. While upholding the constitutional validity of the provisions relating to search and seizure in tax laws, Supreme Court thus expressed its concern over parallel economy of black money:

> "As far as direct taxes are concerned, the main objective of conferring the powers of search, seizure and survey on the authorities concerned has been to unearth black money and prevent its proliferation; to fight and curb illegal elimination of tax liability by fraud, wilful default or neglect, *i.e.*, tax evasions; to check avoidance of tax through various legal devices, including the formation of trusts and diversion of income or wealth to members of family; etc. That is to say, mopping up of black money, the magnitude of the effect of which on the national economy has been, and continues to be, horrendous".

> "It is a well known fact of our economic life that huge sums of unaccounted money are in circulation endangering its very fabric. In a country which has adopted high rates of taxation, a major portion of the unaccounted money should normally fill the Government coffers. Instead of doing so, it distorts the economy. Therefore, in the interest of the community, it is only right that fiscal authorities should have sufficient powers to prevent tax evasion. Search and seizure are not a new weapon in the armoury of those whose duty it is to maintain social security in its broadest sense. The process is widely recognized in all civilized countries. Our own criminal law accepted its necessity and usefulness in sections 96 to 103 and section 165

of the Criminal Procedure Code, 1898. Since the object of the search is to get at concealed incomes, any person, who is in custody without enquiring about its true nature, exposes himself to search, and that sub-section (4) of section 132 of the Income-tax Act, 1961, shows the way how such an innocent person can make the impact of the search on him bearable. All that he has to do is to tell the true facts to the searching officer explaining on whose behalf he held custody of the valuables. It will then be for the concerned officer to ascertain the person concerned under sub-section (5) of that section. In the opinion so expressed the safeguards are adequate to render the provisions of search and seizure as less onerous and restrictive as is possible under the circumstance."

[*Pooran Mal* v. *Director of Inspection* [1974] 93 ITR 505 (SC)]

1.8 Applicability of Code of Criminal Procedure, 1973

Sub-section (13) of section 132 provides that the provisions of the Code of Criminal Procedure, 1973 (2 of 1974), relating to searches and seizure shall apply, so far as may be, to searches and seizure under sub-section (1) or sub-section (1A) of section 132.

The objective of inserting specific sub-section to the provisions of income tax search under section 132 is to clarify that the general nature of searches under the Income-tax Act is similar to the nature of searches as provided under Criminal Procedure Code. In case there is any matter relating to which guidance is not available under the provisions of Income-tax Act, reference can be made to the provisions of searches under Criminal Procedure Code, 1973 and to the judicial pronouncements made by the courts in this respect.

The provisions contained in the Income-tax Act and the rules being special provisions, have an overriding effect over the general provisions contained in the Code of Criminal Procedure [*Union of India* v. *Judicial Magistrate (Eastern Railway) Mughal Sarai* [1983] 12 Taxman 76 (All.)]. Also, the criminal court has no authority to order handing over of property *i.e.*, cash or jewellery to persons claiming it, where it is subject-matter of warrant of authorization under section 132 or 132A of the Act.

In actual practice, the provisions of the Code have little bearing on the search proceedings under the Income-tax Act as the income tax provisions are self sufficient to deal with all possible situations. The case laws under the Code can be useful as a general guide only to a limited extent in so far as it deals with the general principles relating to search and seizure.

1.9 Applicability of Civil Procedure Code (CPC), 1908

Section 131(1A) of the Act provides, *inter alia,* that the authorized officer before he starts the actual search and other actions contemplated under clauses (*i*) to (*v*) of section 132(1) has reason to suspect that where any income has been concealed or is likely to be concealed, by any person within his jurisdiction, it shall be permissible for him to exercise powers envisaged u/s 131(1). The Income tax authorities by virtue of section 131(1) have been vested with the powers normally exercised by the Civil Courts under the Code of Civil Procedure in the following matters:

◆ Discovery and inspection,

◆ Enforcing the attendance of a person,

◆ Examining him on oath,

◆ Compelling the production of books and documents, and

◆ Issuing commissions.

Thus, the authorized officer is also empowered to exercise the above stated powers which are vested in a court under the Code of Civil Procedure, 1908.

1.10 Search and Seizure Provisions in Socio-economic Context

The question whether an action under section 132 of the Act is justified and is taken in exercise of the proper authority vested by law or it leads to an outrage of the privacy, liberty, freedom and other fundamental rights of a citizen, has always baffled the Courts. The consensus of judicial opinion which has emerged from time to time seems to apply the test of whether or not the action was *bona fide, i.e.* in the interest of social justice and fulfilment of the objective behind the provisions or it was motivated by collateral purposes and mala fides.

Since a serious invasion is made upon rights, privacy and freedom of the taxpayer, the power must be exercised strictly in accordance with the law and only for the purpose for which the law authorizes it to be exercised. If the action of issue or execution of search warrant is challenged, the authorizing or the authorized officer must satisfy the Court about the regularity of action. If the action is maliciously taken or the power is exercised for collateral purposes, it is liable to be struck down by the Court. If the conditions for the exercise of powers are not satisfied, the proceeding is liable to be quashed. But where the power is exercised *bona fide* and in furtherance of statutory duties, any error of judgment will not vitiate the action. Where the belief is entertained by the authorizing authority for the reasons recorded, Court will not substitute its own opinion. [*ITO* v. *Seth Bros.* [1969] 74 ITR 836 (SC)]

It has been held in the case of *Chief CIT* v. *State of Bihar* [2012] 18 taxmann. com 70/205 Taxman 232 (Patna) that in continuation of interrogation late in the night, there was violation of human rights insofar as interrogation during search and seizure continued till 3.00 a.m. in the second night.

1.11 Powers of Search and Seizure under other Economic Laws

It is not only the Income-tax Act where power of search and seizure has been given to the tax authorities. Similar power or rather more drastic power of search and seizure has been given under various other economic laws.

Such power has been given under Goods & Services Tax Act, Central Excise Act, Customs Act, Prevention of Food Adulteration Act, Essential Commodities Act, Gold Control Act, Foreign Exchange Management Act, Prevention of Money Laundering Act, etc. and so on. Under some of such legislations, even power of arrest has been given to those authorities. However, no such power of arrest is available with the income tax authorities in the case of search u/s 132 of the Income-tax Act, 1961.

The basic provisions relating to search and seizure under various Central Legislations are almost similar. The courts have consistently upheld the powers of search and seizure under various economic laws. However, courts have held that use of such powers is to be in strict compliance of the provisions of the respective laws and rules and cannot be made arbitrarily or *mala fide*.

1.12 Power of Search in other Countries

The power of search and seizure has been given in economic laws of almost all the developed countries.

In U.K., power of search and seizure has been given not only for investigation of criminal offence but also for revenue offences with safeguards provided so as to prevent arbitrary use of the powers. Powers of search and seizure have been made available in U.K for the revenue offences subject to certain safeguards provided therein.

In *Rose Minister* v. *IRC* 3 ALL ER 385, Lord Denning, while supporting the power of search, observed as under:

> "Many will ask:
>
> Why has Parliament done this?
>
> Why have they allowed this search and seizure by the Revenue Officers?
>
> It did it here because the Board of Inland Revenue were very worried by the devices used by some wicked people, such as those and we often see such cases in our courts-
>
> Who keep two sets of books: one for themselves to use; the other to be shown to the revenue,
>
> Those who make out two invoices: one for the customer, the other to be shown to the taxman.
>
> Those who enter into fictitious transactions and write them into their books as genuine.

Those who show losses when they have in fact made gains.

In the tax evasion pool, there are some big fish who do not stop at tax avoidance. They resort to frauds on a large scale. I can well see that if the legislation were confined, or could be confined, to people of that sort, it would be supported by all honest citizens. Those who defraud the revenue in this way are parasites who suck out the life-blood of our society."

"None would wish that any of those who defraud the Revenue should be free. They should be found out and brought to justice. But it is fundamental in our law that the means which are adopted to this end should be lawful means. The means must not be such as to offend against the personal freedom, the privacy and fundamental rights of property. Every man is presumed to be innocent until he is found guilty. If his house is to be searched and his property seized on suspicion of an offence, it must be done by due process of law, and the process involves that there must be a valid warrant specifying the offence of which he is suspected and the seizure is limited to these things authorized by the warrant."

In USA, power of search and seizure had been given under the Inland Revenue but the same are quite restricted with the following objective:

"The right of the people to be secure in their persons, houses, papers and effects, against unreasonable searches and seizures, shall not be violated, and no warrants shall issue but upon probable cause supported by oath or affirmation and particularly describing the place to be searched and the person or things to be seized."

CHAPTER 2

CIRCUMSTANCES WHEN SEARCH CAN BE INITIATED

2.1 Conditions precedent for initiating search

The power of search given to Income Tax authorities under the Income-tax Act, 1961 are well guarded powers and the necessary safeguards are put in place so that this power cannot be used by the authorities arbitrarily. Section 132(1) of the Income-tax Act, 1961 prescribes certain basic requirements to be fulfilled before initiating search action. Search warrant can be issued when any of the conditions prescribed under clause (*a*), (*b*) or (*c*) of section 132(1) is existing.

2.2 Text of section

Section 132(1) of the Act reads as under:

"132. (1) Where the Director General or Director or the Chief Commissioner or Commissioner or Additional Director or Additional Commissioner or Joint Director or Joint Commissioner in consequence of information in his possession, has reason to believe that—

(*a*) any person to whom a summons under sub-section (1) of section 37 of the Indian Income-tax Act, 1922 (11 of 1922), or under sub-section (1) of section 131 of this Act, or a notice under sub-section (4) of section 22 of the Indian Income-tax Act, 1922, or under sub-section (1) of section 142 of this Act was issued to produce, or cause to be produced, any books of account or other documents has omitted or failed to produce, or cause to be produced, such books of account or other documents as required by such summons or notice, or

(*b*) any person to whom a summons or notice as aforesaid has been or might be issued will not, or would not, produce or cause to be produced, any books of account or other documents which will be useful for, or relevant to, any proceeding under the Indian Income-tax Act, 1922 (11 of 1922), or under this Act, or

18

(c) any person is in possession of any money, bullion, jewellery or other valuable article or thing and such money, bullion, jewellery or other valuable article or thing represents either wholly or partly income or property which has not been, or would not be, disclosed for the purposes of the Indian Income-tax Act, 1922 (11 of 1922), or this Act (hereinafter in this section referred to as the undisclosed income or property).

then,—

(A) the Director General or Director or the Chief Commissioner or Commissioner, as the case may be, may authorize any Additional Director or Additional Commissioner or Joint Director, Joint Commissioner, Assistant Director or Deputy Director, Assistant Commissioner or Deputy Commissioner or Income-tax Officer, or

(B) such Additional Director or Additional Commissioner or Joint Director, or Joint Commissioner, as the case may be, may authorize any Assistant Director or Deputy Director, Assistant Commissioner or Deputy Commissioner or Income-tax Officer,

(the officer so authorized in all cases being hereinafter referred to as the authorized officer) to....."

2.3 Legislative History - Significant Amendments

Section 132(1) was introduced under the Income-tax Act, 1961 which was first substituted by the Finance Act, 1964 and again substituted by the Finance Act, 1965. By the Taxation Laws (Amendment) Act, 1975 with effect from 1.10.1975, under clause (c) of section 132(1), the words 'would not be disclosed' were added along with the words 'which has not been disclosed'. The objective of amendment was to cover those assets which the authorizing officer believes, would not be disclosed by the person to the Income Tax department as the same have been acquired out of unaccounted income.

Finance Act, 2017 has incorporated an *Explanation* in sub-section (1) of section 132 clarifying that the reason to believe, as recorded by the competent authority shall not be disclosed to any person or any authority or the appellate tribunal. This *Explanation* has been inserted retrospectively with effect from 1.4.1962.

2.4 Objective

The provision of search is very harsh and is often termed as draconian. Therefore, the legislature has provided safeguards so that the same is not used by the authorities in a mechanical and arbitrary manner. The legislature has provided specific circumstances under which search action can be initiated. It has been provided that search action can be undertaken only when authorizing officer forms *"reason to believe"* in consequence of relevant and cogent information in his possession that the person is having in his possession evidences relating to undisclosed income or undisclosed assets or about the non-compliance of summon or the notice u/s 142(1).

Search action is generally initiated when authorizing officer is satisfied that incriminating evidences relating to undisclosed income or undisclosed assets are likely to be seized. In case no seizure is expected, there is generally no need of search and the affairs of a person can be investigated by way of open enquiry or by other methods.

The other objective of initiating search, sometimes, may be to get hold the books of account or documents which have a bearing on the tax liability of a person which such person seeks to withhold by way of repeated non-compliance of notices or summons issued by the authorities. But even under such circumstances, search action is undertaken with the objective to seize those books of account or other documents which are being repeatedly asked by the authorities to be produced but not being produced by the assessee.

Other objective which is achieved is the automatic spread of deterrence message to all those who seek to withhold the legitimate taxes due on their income so that they may desist and refrain from indulging in tax evasion.

2.5 Broad Framework

For the sake of simplification, the provisions of section 132(1) may be read as under:

> 132. (1) Where the **competent authority** in **consequence of information** in his possession, has **reason to believe** that
>
> (*a*) any person to whom a **summons** was issued to produce, any books of account or other document has failed to produce, such books of account or other document,
>
> (*b*) any person to whom a **summons** has been or might be issued will not produce, any books of account or other document which will be useful for, or relevant to, any proceedings under the Act,
>
> (*c*) any person is in possession of any **asset** and such asset represents undisclosed income or property.
>
> then,
>
> **the competent authority** may authorize any **authorized officer** to................ undertake search action.
>
> **Competent Authority** refers to Principal Director General or Director General or Principal Director or Director or the Principal Chief Commissioner or Chief Commissioner or Principal Commissioner or Commissioner or any such Additional Director or Additional Commissioner or any such Joint Director or Joint Commissioner as may be empowered in this behalf by the Board or

Asset refers to money, bullion, jewellery or any other valuable article or thing.

Authorized Officer refers to Additional Director or Additional Commissioner, Joint Director or Joint Commissioner, Assistant Director or Deputy Director, Assistant Commissioner or Deputy Commissioner or Income Tax Officer as the case may be.

Summons refers to summons under sub-section (1) of section 37 of the Indian Income-tax Act, 1922 or under sub-section (1) of section 131 of this Act, or a notice under sub-section (4) of section 22 of the Indian Income-tax Act, 1922 or under sub-section (1) of section 142 of this Act.

From the above provision, the following points emerge:

♦ Search can be authorized by the competent authority only

♦ Before authorizing search, the competent authority has to form *"reason to believe"*.

♦ *"Reason to believe"* is to be formed in consequence of information in his possession.

♦ The competent authority can authorize to any authorized officer to undertake search action.

♦ *"Reason to believe"* is to be formed when any one or more of the following three conditions exist:

   (*a*) non-compliance of summons u/s 131(1) or notice u/s 142(1) issued to produce books of account or other documents,

   (*b*) belief of likely non-compliance of summons u/s 131(1) or notice u/s 142(1), if issued, for production of books of account or other documents,

   (*c*) possessing assets representing undisclosed income or property.

(*i*) **Compliance of statutory conditions as contemplated under section 132 are mandatory**

Hon'ble Supreme Court in the case of *ITO* v. *Seth Bros.* [1969] 74 ITR 836 laid emphasis on the need for strict compliance of the statutory conditions for exercising powers u/s 132 in the following words:

> "Since by the exercise of the power under section 132 of the Income-tax Act, 1961 a serious invasion is made upon the rights, privacy and freedom of the taxpayer, the power must be exercised strictly in accordance with the law and only for the purposes for which the law authorizes it to be exercised. If the action of the officer issuing the authorization or of the designated officer is challenged, the officer concerned must satisfy the court about the regularity of his action. If the action is maliciously taken or power under the section is exercised for a collateral purpose, it is liable to be struck down by the court. If the conditions for the exercise of the power are not satisfied, the proceeding is liable to quashed."

Hon'ble Allahabad High Court in the case of *Ganga Prasad Mahesh-wari* v. *CIT* [1981] 6 Taxman 363 held that compliance of statutory conditions as contemplated u/s 132 are mandatory in nature and must be unscrupulously adhered to before warrant for search is issued to authorizing officer.

(ii) Provisions of section 132(1) should be strictly construed

A search conducted under section 132 of the Income-tax Act, 1961, is a serious invasion into the privacy of a citizen. Section 132(1) has to be strictly construed and the formation of the *"reason to believe"* by the authorizing officer must be apparent from the note recorded by him. The belief so recorded must clearly show whether the belief falls under clause (*a*), (*b*) or (*c*) of section 132(1). No search can be ordered except for any one of the reasons contained in clause (*a*), (*b*) or (*c*) of section 132(1). The satisfaction note should itself show the application of mind and the formation of belief by the officer ordering the search. If the reasons recorded do not fall under clause (*a*), (*b*) or (*c*), the authorization under section 132(1) is liable to be quashed.

[*L.R. Gupta* v. *Union of India* [1991] 59 Taxman 305 (Delhi)]

It has been held in the case of *Khem Chand Mukim* v. *Principal Director of IT (Inv.)* 186 DTR (Del) 145 that reasons were, firstly, not recorded before undertaking the search and was therefore, completely unauthorized and a high-handed action on the part of the respondents. Also, Respondents do not state that Jewellery was concealed, or was kept by the assessee surreptitiously. Jewellery found in the assessee's possession was his stock-in-trade and consequently, he was entitled to the protection provided in the proviso appearing after sub-cl. (*iii*) to sub-s. (1) of s. 132 & thus search and seizure and *ex post facto* warrant of authorization dt. 11th Sept., 2018 issued by respondent No. 2 under s. 132 was quashed with costs of Rs. 50,000 payable by Revenue.

2.6 Clause (a) of sub-section (1) of section 132

Under clause (*a*), it is necessary that assessee has failed as a matter of fact, to comply with the specified notice issued to him. Issue of a valid notice to the assessee to produce books of account or other documents and assessee's failure to comply with the same, are the pre-requisites under this clause. Thus, historical fact of non-compliance of a valid specified notice may be the ground for issuing warrant of search.

The assessee must have committed the omission or failure to comply with the terms of notices under section 131(1) or 142(1). It is not necessary that the non-compliance of notices should have been committed before the same officer, who is authorizing the search. Non-compliance of the summon u/s 131(1) may be before the Assessing Officer, but search may be authorized on this ground, for example, by Director of Income Tax (Investigation). It is interesting to note that summons referred in this clause are the summons issued u/s 131(1) and not u/s 131(1A) of the Act.

However, we are of the opinion that non-compliance of the summon issued under section 131(1A) would also be covered within the ambit of clause (*a*) of section 132(1) and search operation on this basis can be initiated.

At this stage useful reference may be made to the decision of Delhi Bench of Income Tax Appellate Tribunal in the case of *Young Indian* v. *ADIT* ITA No. 5303/Del/2016, dated 30.8.2018 in which Tribunal held that the provisions of section 131(1A) has to be read along with the provisions of section 131(1) of the Income-tax Act.

In the case of *Jorawar Singh Baid* v. *Asstt. CIT* [1992] 198 ITR 47 (Cal.), it was held that it is the duty of the authorizing officer before issuing the warrant of search, to verify that the said notice or summons were duly served, sufficient time was allowed to comply with them, and the failure was deliberate, repeated and without any circumstance to justify it.

In *L.R. Gupta* v. *Union of India* [1991] 59 Taxman 305, the Delhi High Court observed that clause (*a*) refers to the facts which must exist before a belief is formed for taking action under section 132. In other words, clause (*a*) refers to a situation where the failure to comply with the notice(s) under section 142(1) or summons under section 131(1) has already taken place.

Clauses (*a*) to (*d*) of sub-section (1) of section 131 refer to the following matters:—

  a. Discovery and inspection;

  b. Enforcing attendance of any person, including any officer of a banking company and examining him on oath;

  c. Compelling production of books of account and other documents;

  d. Issuing commissions.

It is interesting to note that it is only the failure to comply with the requirement of above clause (*c*) *viz.* production of books of account & other documents, which is covered under clause (*a*) of Section 132(1). Failure to comply with summon issued merely for personal presence cannot constitute a pre-condition for authorizing a search.

Similarly, clauses (*i*) to (*iii*) of sub-section (1) of section 142 refer to the following matters:

  i. Asking the assessee to file a return in the prescribed form and manner, *ii.* Asking for production of books of account and documents which the Assessing Officer may require,

iii. Asking the assessee to furnish information or total wealth statements.

But it is only the failure to comply with the requirement of above clause (*ii*) *viz.* production of books of account & documents, which is covered under clause (*a*) of section 132(1) and not those covered under clauses (*i*) and (*iii*) above.

(*i*) Non-compliance of invalid summons or notice.

Non-compliance of an invalid summons or notice cannot constitute a pre-condition in terms of clause (*a*) of section 132(1). It is incumbent upon the authorizing officer to satisfy himself *inter alia* about the legal validity, relevance and utility of summons under section 131(1) as well as the notice under section 142(1) before treating the failure as a pre-condition for action under section 132(1).

(*ii*) No search action for non-filing of return of income

Failure to file a return or to furnish information as per notice under section 142(1) cannot be made a basis for issue of warrant of authorization. In the case of *L.R. Gupta* v. *Union of India* [1991] 59 Taxman 305, Delhi High Court held that action under section 132 could not be taken for non-filing of return in respect of income which is not liable to tax. This finding is based on the assessee's contention that the compensation and interest thereon received on compulsory acquisition of land by the Government were not liable to tax, in view of Supreme Court's decision in *CIT* v. *Hindustan Housing & Land Development Trust Ltd.* [1986] 27 Taxman 450A, and that the appeals had been filed against the quantum of enhanced compensation by the Union of India, which were pending before the High Court and that appeals had also been filed by the Gaon Sabha and the owners, challenging the right of the petitioners to get any compensation and that till such time as all these appeals were finally concluded in favour of the petitioners, it could not be held that the petitioners had become the owner of the money or that they had earned any capital gain or income by way of interest or otherwise, and that as receipt of the amount was not taxable, the same was not included in the Income-tax return, nor was shown in the wealth-tax return.

2.7 Clause (b) of section 132(1)

Clause (*b*) of section 132(1) is of wider connotation and covers a situation where it is apprehended by the competent authority that in case summons u/s 131(1) or notice u/s 142(1) is issued to produce any books of account or other documents, assessee will not produce the same.

This may be appreciated with the help of an example - a disgruntled employee who has fallen with his employer, walks to the Dy. Director of Income Tax (Investigation) with the duplicate set of books of account where undisclosed transactions of the employer are recorded and based on his deposition and in view of such books of account, belief can be formed by the competent authority that if summon is issued for the production of such books of account, these would not be produced because such books of account are not meant for production before the tax authorities.

It covers two situations - when notice or summons have been issued but the date of compliance may not have expired and the other is where the notice or summons have not been issued at all. In both the situations, there has to be valid basis to apprehend as to the non-compliance.

Failure to file returns of income or net wealth in response to notice under section 142(1) is not a good ground to conclude that information or document will be withheld. [*L.R. Gupta* v. *Union of India* [1991] 59 Taxman 305 (Delhi)]

In case, there is information in possession of the authorities that assessee is maintaining duplicate set of books of account containing details of transactions of undisclosed income, it can very reasonably be apprehended that in case notice is issued to the assessee to produce such books of account, assessee will not produce the same. However, with respect to regular books of account, bank statements, or registered sale deeds in respect of properties recorded in the books, it cannot be presumed ordinarily that the assessee will not produce the same in case notice is issued. Books of account or other documents referred to in this clause, are those which will be useful, or relevant to any proceeding under the Income-tax Act. Any books of account or documents containing details of financial transactions or supporting documents relating to financial transactions may be useful for or relevant to any proceeding under the Income-tax Act. It is not only the books of account or documents relating to undisclosed business transactions which are intended to be referred in this clause but this clause also refers to various records, files and details of regular business transactions which may be apprehended as not to be produced by the assessee, in case called for by the authorities.

Before making this presumption that assessee will not produce books of account or other documents, there has to be sufficient information or material in possession of the authorities on the basis of which, such *"reason to believe"* can be formed.

It was held that for invoking the provisions of section 132(1)(*b*), it is not a precondition that notice or summons should first be issued to judge, whether it would be complied with or not. [*V.K. Jain* v. *Union of India* [1975] 98 ITR 469 (Delhi) and *Lit Light & Co.* v. *CIT* [1982] 136 ITR 513 (All.)].

(i) **Assumption of non-compliance of notice/summon to be based on material**

Section 132(1)(*b*) refers to cases where there is reason to believe that if any summons or notice has been issued or will be issued, then that person will not produce or cause to be produced the books of account, etc. The competent authority must have some concrete fact, material or circumstances on the basis of which such a belief can reasonably be formed. Such belief must be based on some cogent material or basis.

It has been held that when there is information that a person is hiding or is likely to hide or destroy documents or books of account which are required or are relevant for the purposes of the Act, then, in such a case, it can be said that unless and until a search is conducted, the said books of account or documents will not be recovered. [*Pooran Mal* v. *Director of Inspection* [1974] 93 ITR 505 (SC)]

(ii) **Futility of notices, even if issued**

In a case, where the Commissioner had sufficient information to show both by way of information of the informant and the report of the Additional Director of Inspection that the alleged absence of books or loss of books is not believable and that the books said to have been lost and several statements and documents written in the course of the business are still available which may be of considerable help in determining the correct income, it was held that the Commissioner formed the reasonable belief that the assessee, even if called upon to produce such books and papers, which might still be in his possession would omit or fail to produce the same. [*C. Venkata Reddy* v. *ITO* [1967] 66 ITR 212 (Mys.)]

(iii) **Formal notice is not necessary but basis to be proved.**

Under clause (*a*) of sub-section (1) of section 132, an action can be taken if a person fails to comply with a summons served under section 131(1) or a notice under section 142(1) to produce or cause to be produced specified books of account or other document. Under clause (*b*), however a formal notice is not essential. The authorizing authority must have reason to believe that the person is not likely to produce his books, etc. In the second situation the authority, if challenged, has to prove the basis of his belief. In the case of *Lit Light & Co.* v. *CIT* [1982] 136 ITR 513, Allahabad High Court has held that it is not necessary, before effecting the search and seizure under section 132 of the Act that the officials of the Income Tax Department should have given to the person whose account books and documents are sought to be seized, a notice to produce whatever account books or other documents are needed and that the person should have failed to comply with such a notice. As laid down in clause (*b*) of sub-section (1) of section 132, if the CIT is satisfied that the persons would not produce or cause to be produced any books of account which will be useful for, or relevant to, any proceeding under the Act, he is empowered to direct search and seizure without giving to the persons concerned a notice to produce the account books or other documents needed.

Similar views have been expressed by the Delhi High Court in the case of *V. K. Jain* v. *Union of India* [1975] 98 ITR 469.

(*iv*) Authorization of search on the basis of non-compliance of summons issued under section 131(1A)

The power of issuing summon to the assessee for the purpose of production of evidences or making an enquiry or investigation under the Act has been given under section 131 of the Act. Sub-section (1) of section 131 empowers the Assessing Officer, Joint Commissioner, Chief Commissioner or Commissioner, *inter alia*, to issue summons for enforcing the attendance of any person or for compelling the production of books of account and other documents. This power can be exercised while trying a suit *i.e.* during the pendency of any proceedings under the Act before the authority(ies).

Sub-section (1A) of section 131 empowers the Director General or Director or Joint Director or Deputy Director or Assistant Director of Income Tax to issue summon for the purpose of making any enquiry or investigation under the Income-tax Act and to enforce the attendance of any person or for compelling the production of any books of account or other documents. This power can be exercised by these authorities on the basis of reason to suspect that any income had been concealed or is likely to be concealed by any person and there is no requirement of pendency of proceedings unlike sub-section (1), with respect to such person before him or any other Income Tax Authority for issuing summons under this sub-section.

Clause (*a*) or clause (*b*) of section 132(1) refers, *inter alia*, to summons issued under section 131(1) and not to summons issued under section 131(1A). It gives rise to a very pertinent question whether a search can be authorized on the basis of non-compliance of summons issued under section 131(1A). If we follow the rule of literal interpretation of statute, which should, in fact, be followed in interpreting the drastic power of search, it can be argued that non-compliance of summons issued or to be issued under section 131(1A) cannot result in search action and no search can be authorized merely on the basis of same.

There seems to be rationale too, for this proposition and it cannot be said to be simply an omission on the part of legislature. Summons under section 131(1A) may be issued on the basis of reason to suspect that any income has been concealed or is likely to be concealed. It is not required to be issued during pendency of any proceedings but it can be issued for making any enquiry or investigation on the basis of suspicion. Thus any failure to comply with the summons under section 131(1A) issued merely on the basis of suspicion is not intended by the legislature to be the basis for undertaking drastic action of search and seizure. On the other hand, summon under section 131(1) can be issued only during the pendency of any proceeding and therefore non-compliance of such summons has been envisaged to be the basis for authorization of search.

Conversely, it may be argued that this is only an omission from making reference of summon issued under section 131(1A) in clause (*a*) or clause (*b*) of section 132(1). There cannot be the legislative intent to exclude the non-compliance of summon issued under section 131(1A) for the purpose of authorization of search. It can further be argued that operation of clause (*a*) or clause (*b*) of section 132(1) cannot be restricted to cover the situation of non-compliance of summons or notice only when some proceedings under the Act are pending against a particular person. There may be situation when a person may possess books of account or documents of incriminating nature which are not likely to be produced by him to the Income Tax Department in case called for and even if no proceeding under the Act are pending against such person, search action is intended to be authorized against such person for seizure of such books of account or documents as per object of section 132(1). In case we take the earlier interpretation, it would be a very narrow interpretation and will defeat the very purpose of section 132(1). Therefore there is need to make purposive interpretation under such circumstances. However, since a controversy exists on this issue, it needs to be clarified by the legislature.

In the case of *Balwant Singh* v. *R.D. Shah, Director of Inspection* [1969] 71 ITR 550, Delhi High Court has opined that if there was only a remote possibility of summons or notices being issued, the action would not be justified, not because there was no proceedings imminent, but because a reasonable person could not have in those circumstances reason to believe that the person concerned will not produce the books of account and documents if summons or notices were issued to him.

(v) **Consequential search based upon close relationship - Whether covered under section 132(1)(*b*)**

A report was prepared by ADI (Inv.) stating that he had received information when a search against a company had been started at Jamshedpur. Search was also started against a few of its agents in Calcutta. The report further stated that the petitioner was a person connected with the company and appeared to be in possession of some incriminating documents and assets pertaining to the company. Close relationship between the petitioner No.1 and the persons in control of the said company would certainly lead one to believe that in the ordinary course petitioner No.1 would not comply with the notice under the Income-tax Act and produce material in his possession which would be adverse to the company and the said relatives. Hence, the search was held as properly authorized. [*Lajpat Rai* v. *CIT* [1995] 215 ITR 608 (All.)]

2.8 Clause (c) of section 132(1)

In practice, income tax search is generally authorized, based upon information, relating to condition mentioned under clause (*c*) of section 132(1). Clause (*c*) of section 132(1) contemplates a situation where there is information regarding a person possessing undisclosed assets which have either not been disclosed to the department or there is belief that the same will not be disclosed to the department. The undisclosed assets may be in the nature of money, bullion, jewellery, other valuable article or thing. Mere information of undisclosed income without representing and existence of any undisclosed asset will not be sufficient enough for the purpose of this clause. The existence of undisclosed assets with the assessee is a precondition for invoking clause (*c*).

It contemplates two situations, one where the non-disclosure of asset representing concealed income has already taken place and the other is where no such omission or failure to disclose such asset has taken place, but on the basis of information in possession, the authority has reason to believe that non-disclosure of such asset will take place. The asset must represent secreted and undisclosed funds of the assessee. But, when the department is aware of the existence of income or asset and such income or asset is exempt from tax liability, the provisions of clause (*c*) will not be attracted.

In the case of *H.L. Sibal* v. *CIT* [1975] 101 ITR 112, Punjab and Haryana High Court observed that if a particular assessee had utilized his undisclosed income in constructing a spacious building, his premises could not be subjected to search under section 132 on this basis alone and that a search could be authorized only if information is given to the Commissioner that a person is keeping money, bullion, jewellery, etc., in this building or else-where. However, if information regarding tax evasion and other particulars *e.g.*, map and other evidence for utilization of the undisclosed income in the construction of the building are found, the action under section 132 would be justified.

(*i*) **In Possession - Any money, bullion, jewellery or other valuable article or thing**

Clause (*c*) of section 132(1) contemplates only a situation where any person is in possession of any asset consisting of any money, bullion, jewellery or other valuable article or thing. Books of account or other documents are not covered within this clause. Books of account or other documents which are not expected to be produced by the assessee, are covered within the ambit of condition prescribed under clause (*b*) of section 132(1).

'*In possession*' does not refer to the situation where a person in possession of any asset has to be the owner of the asset also. In case ownership of the asset is not clearly established or in the knowledge of the department, search warrant can still be issued in the name of the person who is in possession of the asset. It may so happen when person carrying unaccounted cash is caught at airport and action under section 132 or under section 132A is initiated against him. At any later stage, when the actual owner of the asset is established, assessment proceedings may be undertaken against the actual owner in accordance with the provisions of section 153C.

But in case a person is having possession of undisclosed asset on behalf of some other person or in fiduciary capacity, *e.g.*, deposits by banker, pledged assets against loan given, etc., search warrant cannot be issued in the name of the person having possession of the asset. For fulfilling conditions under clause (*c*), it is not only pos-session of the asset to be seen but authorizing officer has to satisfy himself that the asset represents undisclosed income. And in such cases undisclosed income cannot be attributed to the person who is keeping possession of the asset on behalf of others. In such a situation, undisclosed income will relate to the person who is the owner of the asset and search warrant can be issued in the name of owner of the asset in whose case *"reason to believe"* that he is having undisclosed asset can be formed. But in such case, the premises or place can be searched relating to the person who is having the possession of the asset.

(*ii*) **In possession - Books of account and other documents**

In the case of books of account or other documents, the ownership is generally established and therefore, cannot be in question. In such a situation, search warrant is to be issued in the name of the person to whom books of account or other documents belong, even if the same are in possession of some other person, *e.g.,* in possession of counsel of the assessee. If department is having information that books of account or other documents of the assessee are kept at the office of his counsel, search warrant has to be issued in the name of the assessee only, for making search and seizure of such books of account or other documents. It cannot be issued in the name of his counsel. Similarly, there may be a situation when assessee is keeping his books of account containing undisclosed transactions at the residence of some of his friend. To make search and seizure at such premises, search warrant has to be issued in the name of assessee and not in the name of his friend who is keeping the books of account or other documents with him.

(iii) No search for disclosed assets

Assets or money known to the department as existing (*i.e.* disclosed assets) cannot be seized. Where the existence of the money or assets is known to the Income Tax Department and where the case of the assessee is that the said money or the valuable asset is not liable to be taxed, provisions of section 132(1)(*c*) relating to undisclosed assets would not be attracted.

L.R. Gupta v. *Union of India* [1991] 59 Taxman 305 (Delhi)

(iv) Whether clause (c) covers undisclosed immovable assets?

In *L.R. Gupta's* case, Delhi High Court has observed that clause (*c*) refers to money, bullion, jewellery or other valuable article which, either wholly or partly, should have been the income of the assessee and which has not been disclosed. For this purpose, the clause pertains only to movable and not immovable assets.

In the case of *Harmel Singh* v. *Union of India* [1993] 69 Taxman 347 (P&H), the High Court found that goods which may be lying concealed alone can be subject matter of search and seizure. The tankers were not lying concealed. The tankers were usually parked at the petrol pump. Action under section 132 can only be taken in order to recover goods which are lying concealed. High Court relied upon decision of Supreme Court in the case of *CIT* v. *Tarsem Kumar* [1986] 27 Taxman 305.

In this connection, with respect, it is submitted that this appears to be a narrow view. The decision of Delhi High Court in the case of *L.R. Gupta* v. *Union of India* [1991] 59 Taxman 305/[1992] 194 ITR 32 cannot be interpreted to mean that no action can be taken in respect of the concealed income which has been invested in immovable property. The underlying asset may be immovable property or visible assets which may be in the knowledge of department, but the test would lie upon the fact that whether income representing such assets or the assets itself, have been disclosed to the department or not. In case the assets are undisclosed or the income representing the assets is undisclosed, the condition is covered by clause (*c*) of section 132(1).

(*v*) **Whether action under section 132(1)(*c*) can be taken on the construction of a building.**

In *Pooran Mal's* case [1974] 93 ITR 505 (SC) a big godown had been newly constructed by the petitioner but his books of account did not reflect the expenditure on account of the construction. It was alleged on behalf of the department that on search, certain documents in the nature of maps, etc., were seized which showed that the petitioner had constructed the building in the month preceding the date of search and the money with which the said building was constructed was unaccounted money. The Court held that there was no substance in the contention that the income tax authorities could not have possibly entertained the required belief. The search and seizure, therefore, could not be regarded as illegal.

In *H.L. Sibal's* case (*supra*), the Punjab & Haryana High Court observed that if particular assessee had utilized his undisclosed income in constructing a spacious building, his premises could not be subjected to search under section 132 on this score alone and that a search could be authorized only if information is given to the Commissioner that a person is keeping money, bullion, jewellery, etc., in this building or elsewhere. When seen in light of the Supreme Court observations in the case of *Pooran Mal*, the ratio laid down by the Punjab & Haryana High Court in *H.L. Sibal's* case, with respect, does not seem to be wholly correct because if the information with regard to tax evasion and that the money has been utilized in the construction of house and that the particulars, e.g., map and other evidence for utilization of the concealed income in the construction of house can be found as a result of action under section 132, the action would be justified and the pre-condition laid down under section 132(1)(*b*) seems to be satisfied. Therefore, the crux of the matter is the information about tax evasion and the existence of concealed income.

2.9 Information in Possession

"Reason to believe" to be formed by the authorizing officer regarding existence of either or more of the conditions as given under clause (*a*), (*b*) or (*c*) of section 132(1), has to be based upon information in his possession.

Information has to be specific with respect to assessee against whom search warrant is issued. Information should not be general in nature without correlating it with the assessee. Information has to be based on actual facts and not merely on rumours, suspicion or gossip. The facts constituting the information must be relevant to the inquiry. Information may have come into the possession of authorizing officer by internal sources or external sources. It may be in writing or oral or gathered form the records available.

(*i*) **Information relating to situation under clause (*a*), (*b*) or (*c*) of section 132(1)**

Information has to be relevant to justify existence of condition either or more under clause (*a*), (*b*) or (*c*) of section 132(1).

Information under clause (*a*) is available easily as non-compliance would have occurred as a matter of fact borne out on departmental record. But, it is not as if that non-compliance of each and every no- tice under section 142(1) or summon under section 131(1) is treated as information to initiate search action. The nature of information required by such notice or summon should be vital in nature and non-compliance is motivated by wilful defiance of law.

Information under clause (*b*) is based upon presumption of non-com- pliance of notice or summons. Information should be in the nature where it can reasonably be anticipated that assessee will not produce books of account or other documents, if called for. Information relating to undisclosed income or property will undoubtedly fall in this category. There can be information even relating to disclosed business which assessee may be expected not to produce or would like to hide from the department.

Information falling under clause (*c*) has to be in the nature of existence of undisclosed assets or assets representing undisclosed income of the assessee. The nature of information in most of the cases falling under this clause forms the basis for initiating search in practice.

In the case of *Tejram Omprakash (HUF)* v. *DIT* [2013] 40 taxmann. com 117/[2014] 220 Taxman 85 (Mag.) (MP), the Court held that merely because originally members of family of other group were engaged in electrical business of larger HUF and that assessee in its business of electrical goods was supplying goods to other group company, assessee could not be implicated. Further, issuance of authorization of search and seizure warrant without there being any information in possession about assessee and without recording satisfaction about not producing relevant books of account and other documents could not be sustained. Thus, in absence of compliance of requirement of section 132, authorization for search and seizure

and consequent search and seizure in respect of assessee's properties
was liable to be quashed.

(ii) **Information not to be based upon rumours or suspicion**

Information has to be based on cogent material or basis. It has not
to be based on hearsay.

"Being known for 'roaring practice' and for *'high rate of fee for operations'* in the absence of any other material could not be construed
as constituting information in consequence of which the Director
could have reason to believe that the petitioner had not disclosed its
income or would not disclose it."

"What could have resulted in an action against the petitioner under
section 132 was a reasonable belief that he was in possession of any
money, bullion or jewellery or other valuable article representing
wholly or partly income or property which has not been disclosed
or would not be disclosed."

".... Information within the meaning of section 132(1) should be
accurate as possible having reference to the precise assets of a
person and not of general nature and that should in all probability,
lead the authorities to have the unmistaken belief that money, bullion, jewellery or other valuable articles or things pointed out by the
informer would be found in the possession of the person named by
the informer."

".... the conditions precedent for action under section 132 is the information in the possession of the authority in consequence of which
he may have reason to believe that any person was in possession of
any money, bullion, jewellery or other valuable articles which represented undisclosed income."

[*Dr. Nand Lal Tahiliani* v. *CIT* [1988] 39 Taxman 127 (All.)]

That the reasons recorded under section 132 were only generalities
based on rumours. It could not be said that the Commissioner had
reason to believe that the petitioner was concealing his income. As
regards the jewellery seized, according to the CBDT guidelines, the
three units residing in the premises could retain 2,500 gms of net gold
jewellery but the total jewellery found was less than 1,000 gms. The
petitioner, admittedly, had a huge practice in his dental profession
and huge income. The cash and articles seized could not be such
which could not be due to his income from his profession and which
would not have been disclosed.

In view of the above, the writ petition was to be allowed. The entire
search and seizure operations conducted were illegal. The respondents
were directed to release cash and other articles and books seized
forthwith to the petitioner.

[*Dr. Sushil Rastogi* v. *Director of Investigation, Income Tax Department* [2003] 128 Taxman 217 (All.)]

The expression *"information"* must be something more than a mere rumour or a gossip or a hunch. The material on record must exist on the file to show that the authorizing officer had taken action for any of the reasons enumerated in clause (*a*), (*b*) or (*c*) of section 132(1).

[*L.R. Gupta* v. *UOI* [1991] 59 Taxman 305 (Delhi)]

The use of the expression *"reasons to believe"* appearing in sub-section (1) of section 132 conveys the idea of a *bona fide* belief based on some reasonable or credible information and not the information which may be imaginary. It must be based on information and not on mere suspicion.

[*Senairam Doongarmal Agency (P.) Ltd.* v. *K.E. Johnson* [1964] 52 ITR 637 (Assam) (FB)] [*N.K. Textile Mills* v. *CIT* [1966] 62 ITR 58 (Punj. & Har.)]

To justify action under section 132, authorities must have relevant material at the time of passing order to take action on the basis of which they could form opinion that they have reason to believe that action under section 132 would be justifiable. In the instant case, search warrant was issued solely on the basis of complaint which is entirely vague and lacks particulars. Authorities considered facts stated in complaint to be sufficient material without collecting material to support complaint. Ordering of raid and issuing warrant under section 132, therefore, was not justified. In addition, the tankers were not lying concealed. The tankers were usually parked at the petrol pump. The action under section 132 can only be taken in order to recover goods which are lying concealed. Thus, warrant and consequential proceedings pursuant thereto were quashed. Authorities directed to return documents/goods seized.

[*Harmel Singh* v. *UOI* [1993] 69 Taxman 347 (P&H)]

Search authorized on the information that certain brand of chewing tobacco and pan masala was selling at high premium in the market as a result of artificial scarcity created by dealers of which the petitioner was one, was held to be invalid by the High Court. There was no reasonable information on the basis of which the Director of Inspection could have formed a *bona fide* belief to issue the authorization under section 132(1). The expression *"has reason to believe"* in sub-section (1) of section 132 means the *bona fide* belief based on some reasonable or credible information and not on the information which may be imaginary.

[*Kusum Lata* v. *CIT* [1990] 48 Taxman 401 (Raj.)]

In the case of *Rajesh Rajora* v. *UOI* [2013] 40 taxmann.com 330/ [2014] 220 Taxman 146 (Mag.) (MP), it has been held that in absence of any cogent reasons in the present matter, warrant of authorization could not have been issued. Issuance of warrant of authorization is a serious action and for this authorization officer should have recorded his satisfaction. Though normally Court does not look for the reasons of satisfaction, but in the present case it appears that the warrant of authorization was issued merely on hypothecated grounds, which is not sustainable under the law.

(*iii*) **Information relevant to enquiry**

The fact that returns were filed and assessments made and completed cannot, by itself, preclude the Department from ordering search and seizure if reliable information reaches the concerned authorities regarding large undisclosed income of the assessee. The Assistant Director studied Income Tax records of the department and also made extensive but discreet enquiries which showed bogus hawala racket. In the face of such detailed report, the Court had no difficulty in upholding the search to be valid.

[*Jain & Jain* v. *Union of India* [1982] 8 Taxman 48 (Bom.)]

(*iv*) **Information not to be based upon vague facts**

It has been held in the case of *Spacewood Furnishers (P.) Ltd.* v. *Director General of IT (Inv.)* [2012] 17 taxmann.com 114/204 Taxman 392 (Bom.) that Director General of IT (Inv.) having approved search and seizure action against the petitioners simply on the basis of satisfaction notes submitted by the Asstt. Director of IT (Inv.) and the Addl. Director of IT (Inv.) which do not disclose the report of the alleged discreet enquiry conducted by them, and there being nothing in the said satisfaction notes to indicate that the said authorities had obtained any information which was suppressed by the petitioners from them, there was no relevant material with the authorities which could enable them to have a "reason to believe" that action under section 132(1) was essential and therefore the impugned authorization issued under section 132(1) is bad and unsustainable, and the search undertaken in pursuance thereof is illegal.

It has been held in the case of *Durgappa Lakkanna* v. *Asstt. CIT* 215 DTR (Kar.) 452 that where satisfaction note refers to the information that the assessee has been receiving unaccounted cash and making cash payment for the land being alienated/sold/purchased & Information refers to specific transaction, It cannot be stated that the exercise of power invoking section 132 in the present case in light of the material produced before the Court is one that would call for interference in exercise of power under Article 226 of the Constitution of India.

(*v*) **Information not based upon generalities**

The CIT issued warrant of authorization without there being any reason to believe that the jewellery which was in possession of the petitioner represented wholly or partly his undisclosed income, therefore his action was without jurisdiction. Mere possession of a thing is not sufficient.

[*Ganga Prasad Maheshwari* v. *CIT* [1981] 6 Taxman 363 (All.)]

Satisfaction of the authorities may be subjective but it must be arrived at objectively on material found on record. Living in posh house or having a high standard of living alone cannot constitute the basis for '*reasonable belief*' without anything on record to demonstrate that the standard of living was not proportionate to the income so as to warrant the conclusion that the person was concealing his income. Information in consequence of which reason to believe is formed has not only to be authentic but capable of giving rise to inference that the person was in possession of undisclosed income, which has not been or would not be disclosed.

[*Dr. Nand Lal Tahiliani* v. *CIT* [1988] 39 Taxman 127 (All.)]

Flourishing of business under a brand name cannot be the reason to believe of evasion of tax law. Section 132 has its independent face value. If one is not to be covered under section 132, then there is no question of any search and seizure or block assessment

[*Mahesh Kumar Agarwal* v. *Dy. DIT* [2003] 133 Taxman 520 (Cal.)].

Merely because an allegedly lavish marriage had taken place can be no basis for forming an opinion under section 132(1). A survey under section 133A of the Income-tax Act was conducted and a statement showing the expenses which had been incurred was submitted to the Department. The source of the expenses was also indicated. Rumour about the lavish expenses cannot be regarded as information under section 132(1).

[*L.R. Gupta* v. *Union of India* [1991] 59 Taxman 305 (Delhi)]

(*vi*) **Information not for fishing or roving enquiry**

If a reasonable person could not have, in certain circumstances, reason to believe that the requisites of the section do exist; search warrants cannot therefore, be issued merely with a view to making a roving or fishing enquiry. [*ITO* v. *Seth Bros.* [1969] 74 ITR 836 (SC)]

[*Balwant Singh* v. *R.D. Shah, Director of Inspection* [1969] 71 ITR 550 (Delhi)]

[*Bharati (P.) Ltd.* v. *R.S. Chadda* [1973] 89 ITR 108 (Cal.)]

[*I. Devarajan* v. *Tamil Nadu Farmers Services Co-op. Federation* [1981] 131 ITR 506 (Mad.)]

(*vii*) **Information based upon reports from other authorities**

In the case of *Sudarshan & Co.* v. *CIT* [1983] 139 ITR 1032, Allahabad High Court held that the information supplied by the ITO could legitimately lead the Commissioner to form the opinion that the person concerned had undisclosed and unaccounted assets liable to tax.

In the case of *Naraindas* v. *CIT* [1983] 14 Taxman 447 Madhya Pradesh High Court held that a detailed report of Assistant Director of Inspection (Intelligence) could be relied upon by the Commissioner as a credible information for taking action under section 132.

In the case of *Ganga Prasad Maheshwari* v. *CIT* [1981] 6 Taxman 363 Allahabad High Court held that the action of the Commissioner to authorize search under section 132 was not valid when the report received from Assistant Director was without any evidence to substantiate the allegations.

In the case of *Subir Roy* v. *S.K Chattopadhyay* [1986] 29 Taxman 13, Calcutta High Court held that the action under section 132 was justified where it was taken in pursuance of information received from the Ministry of Finance regarding tax evasion by the assessee and supplemented by further enquiries by Investigation Wing of the Income Tax Department.

Where on examination of the relevant files it was found that the information received was taken down by the officer concerned and some other information was solicited from some source, and the proposal was discussed with the higher officers, the authorization of search was held to be valid. *Orient (Goa) Ltd.* v. *Union of India* [1995] 81 Taxman 363 (Bom.).

In the case of *Harmel Singh* v. *Union of India* [1993] 69 Taxman 347, Punjab and Haryana High Court held that a mere complaint to the Income Tax Authorities cannot be treated as information for arriving at the conclusion that the action under section 132 is warranted. In this case the High Court observed that Assistant Director and Deputy Director merely acted on the complaint which was entirely vague, indefinite and contained no particulars. It was further observed that no efforts were made to verify the information and the authorities simply assumed that the assessee was having lot of income based upon the complaint received. According to the High Court, there was no material to form a reasonable belief as was essential for satisfaction of the precondition laid down in section 132 of the Act.

(*viii*) **Verification of information**

The report on its very face does not contain any material or reason to justify a search of the locker. The reluctance of assessee to allow the locker to be searched cannot be the basis of the required reason to believe. Therefore, the Income Tax authorities had no justification for proceeding to search the locker and the authorization in question was based on irrelevant considerations. The warrant of authorization is, therefore, against the provisions of section 132 and must be quashed to protect a citizen from unnecessary breach of his privacy.

[*Lajpat Rai* v. *CIT* [1995] 215 ITR 608 (All.)]

CIT having received reliable information from an informant who had intimate knowledge of business dealings of assessee, action under section 132 was justified on that basis. The statement of the main informant, who had intimate knowledge of the business dealings of the petitioners regarding possession of large cash and jewellery, the possible places where they were hidden, registration numbers of benami trucks and cars owned, was recorded on oath. The nature of the information furnished by him could reasonably be accepted as reliable and it was verified to be of substance. On the material furnished by the Department, the contention of the petitioners that the action was *mala fide* or that there was no reliable information in possession of the CIT to justify action under section 132 was rejected as untenable.

[*Lit Light & Co.* v. *CIT* [1982] 136 ITR 513 (All.)]

Merely on the basis of fax message, without anything else, no reasonable person could form a belief that jewellery, etc. carried by the sales manager of assessee represented income which had not been or would not be disclosed, therefore, condition precedent for issuing authorization under section 132 being absent, the authorization under section 132, consequent search and notice under section 158BC are liable to be quashed with direction to return gold and jewellery with 8 per cent interest on its value from the date of seizure till payment.

[*Dimondstar Exports Ltd.* v. *DGIT (Inv.)* [2005] 143 Taxman 16 (Bom.)]

State Legislature having not claimed any privilege in respect of report of Comptroller & Auditor General of India, information derived from the said report, which had not been laid before the legislature, could be acted upon by the Income Tax authorities under section 132(1). It is only when the report of the CAG is published that the same can come into the possession of any one including the authorities mentioned in section 132(1). This subtle, but very fine and firm distinction between the power to issue a warrant of authorization and the power to initiate investigation needs to be kept in mind, while dealing with the question as to whether the CAG's report could have at all been used by the Income Tax Authorities.

[*M.S. Associates* v. *Union of India* [2005] 147 Taxman 172 (Gauhati)]

In the case of *Dr. D.C. Srivastava* v. *DIT (Inv.)* [2007] 162 Taxman 290/212 CTR 527 (All.), it has been held that where information given by the officers of the custom department to the income tax authorities that the petitioner has made a declaration of ₹ 10 lacs at the airport did not constitute sufficient information for forming the belief that the said amount was unaccounted money which was not disclosed or would not be disclosed specially when the petitioner has given his PAN and therefore the authorization u/s 132 was without jurisdiction.

However, it may be noted that this ratio assumes significance since the action of search was taken by the department u/s 132 and not u/s 132A.

In the case of *Union of India* v. *Ajit Jain* [2003] 129 Taxman 74 (SC), it has been held that intimation by the CBI to the income tax authorities alone about recovery of cash from the petitioner could not constitute information within the meaning of section 132(1) particularly when the petitioner had also stated on oath that the money found in his possession was reflected in the books of account of the company of which he was the managing director.

In the case of *Doctors X-Ray & Pathology Institute (P.) Ltd.* v. *Director of Investigation* [2010] 186 Taxman 480 (All.), it has been held that secret information and subsequent verification thereof by the Additional Director of Income tax (Investigation) clearly provide enough foundation and material to the authority to form the basis for reason to believe, proceedings u/s 132 and consequently the notices issued u/s 158BC are valid and have been issued in accordance with law.

In the case of *Genom Biotech (P.) Ltd.* v. *DIT (Investigation)* [2009] 180 Taxman 395 (Bom.), it has been held that in view of specific information in the possession of the department that petitioner No. 1 has been evading tax by fabricating fake/exaggerated invoices and that the investment made by petitioner No. 2 out of the funds brought to India represented the amount said to be paid to foreign companies abroad, designated authority was justified in forming the belief that the conditions set out in clauses (*b*) and (*c*) of section 132(1) are satisfied.

(*ix*) Consequences of false information

Department takes adequate precautions before it acts on the allegations made against a person to ensure that department does not act on any false information given by the informer. Therefore, the ADI or DDI apart from conducting an exhaustive enquiries, records a statement on oath in detail from the informer and a warning is also administered to the informant that if the allegations made by him are found to be false, he will be liable to be prosecuted u/s 182 of the Indian Penal Code which reads as under:

"False information, with intent to cause public servant to use his lawful power to the injury of another person:

Whoever gives to any public servant any information which he knows or believes to be false, intending thereby to cause, or knowing it to be likely that he will thereby cause, such public servant—

a. *to do or omit anything which such public servant ought not to do or omit if the true state of facts respecting which such information is given were known by him, or*

b. *to use the lawful power of such public servant to the injury or annoyance of any person,*

shall be punished with imprisonment of either description for a term which may extend to six months, or with fine which may extend to one thousand rupees, or with both.

a. *A informs a Magistrate that Z, a police officer, subordinate to such Magistrate, has been guilty of neglect of duty or misconduct, knowing such information to be false, and knowing it to be likely that the information will cause the Magistrate of dismiss **Z**. A has committed the offence defined in this section.*

b. *A falsely informs a public servant that Z has contraband salt in a secret place, knowing such information to be false, and knowing that it is likely that the consequence of the information will be a search of Z's premises, attended with annoyance to **Z**. A has committed the offence defined in this section.*

c. *A falsely informs a policeman that he has been assaulted and robbed in the neighbourhood of a particular village. He does not mention the name of any person as one of his assailants, but knows it to be likely that in consequence of this information the police will make enquiries and institute searches in the village to the annoyance of the villagers or some of them. **A** has committed an offence under this section."*

(x) Information to exist prior to issue of authorization

In the case of *Dr. Mrs. Anita Sahai* v. *DIT* [2004] 136 Taxman 247 (All.), it was held that conditions precedent for search and seizure is reason to believe that assets would not be disclosed. Material found during search cannot form basis for such belief and assets found in search cannot justify the action of search.

(xi) Information related with return of income

It was held in the case of *Dy. DIT* v. *Mahesh Kumar Agarwal* [2003] 130 Taxman 674 (Cal.), that in view of enquiry report indicating that the assessee's business involves huge cash transactions and the returns showed small amount of net profit or taxable income as compared to large turnover and the investment being made, there were materials for formation of reason to believe that there was suppression of income and therefore, power of authorization of search was validly exercised.

(xii) Information in case of persons relating to group companies

It was held in the case of *S.K. Industries (P.) Ltd.* v. *DGIT (Investigation)* [2007] 160 Taxman 60 (Delhi) that the petitioners being part of the group companies owned and managed by one family which have been found to be involved in nebulous nature of dealings and not disclosing their true income in the returns filed, there was sufficient material to come to a reasonable belief that the simultaneous search against the individual petitioners along with other family concerns was necessary.

In the case of *Madhu Gupta* v. *DIT (Inv.)* [2013] 30 taxmann.com 92/214 Taxman 246 (Delhi) it has been held that the so-called information was undisclosed and what exactly that information was, was also not known. At one place in the affidavit of the Deputy Director of Income-tax, it had been mentioned that he got information that there was a "likelihood" of the documents belonging to the DS group being found at the residence of the assessee. That by itself would amount only to a surmise and conjecture and not to solid information and since the search on the premises of the assessee was founded on this so-called information, the search would have to be held to be arbitrary. When the search was conducted on January 21, 2011, no documents belonging to the DS group were, in fact, found at the premises of the assessee. The warrant of authorisation was not in the name of the DS group but was in the name of the assessee. In other words, the warrant of authorization under section 132(1) had been issued in the name of the assessee and, therefore, the information and the reason to believe were to be formed in connection with the assessee and not the DS group. None of clause (a), (b) or (c) mentioned in section 132(1) stood satisfied in the assessee's case and, therefore, the warrant of authorisation was without any authority of law. Had the warrant of authorisation been issued in the name of the DS group and in the course of the searches conducted by the authorized officer, the premises of the assessee had also been searched, the position might have been different. But that had not happened in the case of the assessee. The warrant of authorisation was in the name of the assessee and, therefore, it was absolutely necessary that the pre-conditions set out in section 132(1) ought to have been fulfilled. Since those pre-conditions had not been satisfied, the warrant of authorisation would have to be quashed. Once that was the position, the consequence would be that all proceedings pursuant to the search conducted at the premises of the assessee would be illegal and therefore, the prohibitory orders would also be liable to be quashed. The jewellery/other articles/documents were to be unconditionally released to the assessee.

It has been held in the case of *Ameeta Mehra* v. *Addl. DIT (Inv.)* [2017] 82 taxmann.com 279/248 Taxman 308/395 ITR 185 (Delhi) even when key to assessee's locker was found during search of group but no credible information is there leading to reasonable belief that assessee is connected to group or her locker contained undisclosed income, search of locker is invalid & authorization is liable to be quashed & thus notice under section 153A is not valid.

2.10 Collection of Information

(*i*) Source of information

The information may come in possession of the department from internal sources or external sources. Internal sources include income tax returns along with financial statements filed by assessee, replies submitted in response to summons or notice issued under any proceedings under the Act, information available relating to assessee in the files of other persons, associates or sister concerns of the assessee, information relating to the assessee gathered in search or survey action undertaken in the case of other persons, information received through AIR, etc. The external sources will include information received from informers, other government departments such as ROC, SEBI, Excise, Sales-tax and other revenue departments, newspapers, internet, etc. Now a days, lot of information is available relating to any person on internet at different sites and frequent use of the same is made by the department either to get fresh information or for verification of the information collected from any other source.

The income tax department generally gets information from the following sources:

    a. Informers,

    b. Internal sources, and

    c. External sources.

(*a*) Informers

Informers may be professional informers or specific informers. Professional informers are those persons who pass the information relating to the affairs of other persons to the Income Tax department as a matter of carrying the same as their profession/vocation. Since informers are paid reward for valuable and correct information regarding undisclosed income of other persons, certain persons have adopted it as their profession. The information received from the professional informers may not be very reliable, precise or creditworthy. Before relying on such information, income tax officials need to verify the correctness and creditworthiness of the information.

Information passed by the specific informers is much more reliable and accurate. People do pass information relating to undisclosed income of other persons with whom they may have developed enmity, dispute or jealousy. Sometimes, information is passed by business partners, disgruntled employees, brothers, in-laws, family members etc. due to personal disputes. Such information is very specific, useful and creditworthy for the department and search action can very quickly be planned on the basis of such information. Sometimes, such informer provides vital documents to the department such as photocopies or duplicate set of books of account or documents, diaries etc. containing undisclosed transactions, correspondence relating to undisclosed or benami business transactions, evidences relating to sales, outside books of account, information regarding secret bank accounts, secret places where incriminating material is kept, etc.

Validity of information gathered from *'informers'* and its use has been judicially approved by several High Courts as well as by the Supreme Court. The material on which the belief is grounded may be secret, may be obtained through intelligence or occasionally may be conveyed orally by informant. Information given by an informer, being a person intimately connected with the affairs of the assessee, can form information. Only the informer's statement in writing will not form a base for sufficient information; full details about the method of concealment adopted by the assessee must be collected.

The Bombay High Court has upheld the validity of action under section 132 which was taken on the basis of anonymous complaints. The Bombay High Court found that detailed scrutiny of the allegations contained therein was made by the Department before taking action and there was sufficient material to justify the issue of authorization for search - *Narayan R. Bandekar* v. *Second ITO* [1989] 46 Taxman 274 (Bom.).

However, Allahabad High Court administered a word of caution that credibility of the informer and the information supplied by him should be very carefully scrutinized and it would not be correct to act merely on rumour and hearsay - *Dr. Nand Lal Tahiliani* v. *CIT* [1988] 39 Taxman 127 (All.); *Pawan Solvent & Chemicals* v. *CIT* [1987] 32 Taxman 12 (Pat.) and *Kusum Lata* v. *CIT* [1990] 48 Taxman 401 (Raj.).

(*b*) **Internal sources**

Internal sources may comprise of information gathered from the following material-

(1) From the study of Income tax returns and financial statements filed by the assessee, there may be certain unusual features or inherent contradictions indicating existence of undisclosed income which may form basis to develop the case for search. Such information is used very carefully by the investigation wing of the department so as to ensure confidentiality of any action being planned.

(2) Tax evasion petition received by the department which may be anonymous but may provide valuable information regarding undisclosed transactions of a person.

(3) Information obtained through internet. Now a days a lot of information regarding any person, firm or company is available on various sites and may be obtained through internet.

(4) Annual Information Report which is submitted by various agencies such as banks, mutual funds, NBFCs, registration authorities, etc., provide valuable information regarding the financial transactions and business affairs of a person and the same may be used to verify whether the transactions have been duly disclosed by the assessee in the income tax return filed or not.

(5) Information through PAN card - now a days, requirement to quote PAN in big financial transactions is being made mandatory and information may be gathered by the department through PAN card of the assessee so as to further verify the same and then take it to the logical ends.

(*c*) **External sources**

Information is collected by the department from various external sources such as—

(*a*) GST department.

(*b*) Customs, central excise or VAT department.

(c) Civil court cases for financial disputes.

(d) Revenue intelligence and Enforcement Directorate.

(e) Special crime branch of Central Bureau of Investigation.

(f) Serious Fraud Investigation Office.

(g) Police department.

(h) Newspapers, magazines and periodicals.

(i) Advertisement in print and electronic media, hoardings.

(j) Stock exchanges and details relating to Security Transaction Tax.

(k) Banking Cash Transaction Tax (BCTT) used to provide valuable information earlier which was introduced with effect from 1.6.2005 but the same has been discontinued with effect from 1.4.2009.

(l) Social Media

(ii) Reward to Informer

Informers are entitled to reward for parting credible information leading to detection of concealed income and consequent tax evasion. CBDT has issued guidelines from time to time prescribing the basis on which the reward is given. Usually once the search which was conducted on the basis of information provided by the informer is over and is successful, the informer is paid an interim reward depending on how far the information supplied by him has led to the detection of tax evasion. Reward is purely discretionary and the informer cannot claim interim reward as a matter of right. Interim reward is usually given because the assessments pursuant to the search take its own time. When assessment as a result of search becomes final in the sense when all the appeals are over, the final reward is paid to the informer in terms of the guidelines issued by the Board and interim reward if any is deducted. It is interesting to note that the reward is tax free. In fact reward scheme also exists for outstanding work done by the departmental officers and staff in the matter of search and seizure.

(iii) Incentive/Reward to Departmental Officers

This is a matter of fact that some sort of reward/incentive scheme is in operation in income tax department. Reward/Incentive is paid to the departmental officers and staff depending upon the tax evasion detected or declaration of undisclosed income obtained by them in the course of search.

In our opinion, such scheme of reward/incentive to the departmental officials is not in right spirit. Detection of evasion of tax is nothing but part of their official duty. Temptation to get reward/incentive may, in practice, motivate the officials to pressurize the assessee and obtain declaration of undisclosed income in unfair and unjust manner.

2.11 "Reason to Believe"

Formation of belief is an important condition to issue search warrant by the authorizing officer. *"Reason to believe"* is the most significant safeguard on the powers of the authorizing officer to take action under section 132. *'Reason to believe'* implies *"to accept as true or have faith with proper justification"*. *"Reason to believe"* has to be formed with respect to the information in possession. The legislature has used the words *'reason to believe'* and not *'reason to suspect'*. The belief to be formed by the authorizing officer will have subjectivity but it should be based upon cogent objective material.

Before forming belief, the information in possession of the authorizing officer has to be verified. Mere receiving of information is not sufficient to form belief. Cases come to the notice day-in and day-out when false and exaggerated information is passed on to the department due to jealousy, dispute, rivalry, etc. Such information unless verified, cannot form the basis to form belief. The information should be reasonable, reliable and based upon actual facts:

(*i*) **"Reason to believe" for conditions mentioned under clause (*b*) or (*c*)**

Clause (*b*) or clause (*c*) of section 132(1) contemplates a situation that books of account or other documents will not be produced or a person in possession of assets will not disclose the same to the department. To form a belief of future event that compliance would not happen and to read the mindset of an assessee will have to be based on apprehension or anticipation of such situation and will involve some amount of subjectivity on the part of authorizing officer. But such apprehension has to be well reasoned for, based upon actual facts and information in his possession and sufficient enough to form belief of the event happening in normal circumstances.

The phrase *"has reason to believe"* postulates belief and existence of reason for that belief. The belief must be held in good faith and it cannot be merely pretence. The existence of the belief and the reasons for the belief will be justiciable but not the sufficiency of the reasons. Further such belief should not be based on mere suspicion but it must be based upon information. The facts constituting *"information"* must be such as a reasonable and prudent man can arrive at the requisite belief or conclusion therefrom. The belief must not be based on mere suspicion. When challenged, the court has to examine as to whether there was, in fact, information in the possession of the authority authorizing the search and whether there is a rational connection between the information and the belief so formed. The information is required to be of reliable because unless the information is reliable it cannot furnish a reasonable basis for entertaining the belief that any of the circumstances mentioned in section 132 does exist. The information must have a relevant bearing on the formation of the belief and must not be extraneous or irrelevant to the purpose of section 132. If the court is satisfied on these two matters, the adequacy or sufficiency of the material will not be subject to judicial scrutiny.

Hon'ble Delhi High Court in the case of *Balwant Singh* v. *R.D. Shah* [1969] 71 ITR 550 have held that the expression *"reason to believe"* is both subjective and objective but the area of objectivity is limited. It is subject only to a limited scrutiny and the court cannot substitute its own opinion for that of the authority specified in the section.

Hon'ble Rajasthan High Court in the case of *Kusum Lata* v. *CIT* [1990] 48 Taxman 401 have held that the expression *"has reason to believe"* in section 132(1) means the *bona fide* belief based on some reasonable or credible information and not on the information which may be imaginary.

Hon'ble Allahabad High Court in the case of *Ganga Prasad Maheshwari* v. *CIT* [1981] 6 Taxman 363 have held that *"reason to believe"* is a common feature in taxing statutes. It has been considered to be the most salutary safe guard on the exercise of the power by the officer concerned. It is made of two words *"reason" "to believe"*. The word *"reason"* means cause or justification and the word *"believe"* means to accept as true or to have faith in it. Before the officer has faith or accepts a fact to exist, there must be a justification for it. The belief may not be open to scrutiny as it is the final conclusion arrived at by the officer concerned as a result of mental exercise made by him on the information received. But, the reason due to which the decision is reached can always be examined. When it is said that *"reason to believe"* is not open to scrutiny what is meant is that the satisfaction arrived at by the officer concerned is a immune from challenge but where the satisfaction is not based on any material or it cannot withstand the test of reason, which is an integral part of it, then it falls thorough and the court is empowered to strike it down. Belief may be subjective but reason has to be objective.

In a number of cases the phrase *"reason to believe"* has come to be considered and it may be of interest to consider few more of such cases even at the cost of repetition.

In *Vindhya Metal Corporation* v. *CIT* [1985] 156 ITR 233 (All.) it is held that reasons which lead to issue of a warrant are open to judicial review as "it is settled that the existence or otherwise of the conditions precedent to exercise of power under these provisions is open to judicial scrutiny. While the sufficiency or otherwise of the information cannot be examined by the court, the existence of information and its relevance to the formation of the belief can undoubtedly be gone into. Also whether on the material available with the Commissioner, any reasonable person could have arrived at the conclusion that a search, seizure on a requisition should be authorized is a field open to judicial review."

In *Kalpaka Bazar* v. *CIT* [1990] 186 ITR 617 (Ker.), search was held to be valid as it was found that proper reasons had been recorded by the Commissioner of Income Tax about his belief regarding assessee's possession of a huge quantity of unaccounted stock in trade not disclosed to revenue.

In *Dr. Partap Singh* v. *Director of Enforcement* [1985] 22 Taxman 30 (SC), it was observed by the Supreme Court that the material on which the belief is grounded may be secret, may be obtained through intelligence or occasionally may be conveyed orally by informants and it is not obligatory to disclose the material to the petitioner in the writ petition making allegation that there was not material before him on which his reason to believe can be grounded.

In *Pooran Mal* v. *Director of Inspection* [1974] 93 ITR 505 (SC), it is held that undisclosed property found in a search may not be a justification for the authorization of a search, if in fact there were not grounds for entertaining a reasonable belief at the time authorizing the search as required by sub-clauses (*a*), (*b*) and (*c*) of section 132(1).

In *ITO* v. *Seth Bros.* [1969] 74 ITR 836 (SC) it is held that if the conditions for exercise of the power are satisfied and held to be. *bona fide*, any error of judgment will not vitiate the exercise of power. Where the Commissioner entertains the requisite belief and for reasons recorded by him authorizes a designated officer to enter and search premises, the court cannot be asked to substitute its own opinion as to whether an order authorizing search should have been issued.

In *Hazari Lal Soni* v. *Union of India* [1993] 70 Taxman 383 (Raj.), it is held that a search can take place only if the satisfaction of Commissioner is recorded that he has reason to believe that any person is in possession of assets or books which had not been or would not be disclosed for the purpose of Income-tax Act or when called upon to produce the account books or other documents which will be useful for or relevant to any proceedings under the Income-tax Act, such person would not produce the same. The court considered the detailed enquiries conducted and the information collected from informer which was checked up by a personal visit to the place. The court held that *"it was unable to see that it was a case where without recording reasons to believe by the Director of Inspection, a search was conducted."*

In *ITO* v. *Lakhmani Mewal Das* [1976] 103 ITR 437 (SC) it is held that the words *'reasons to believe'* postulate belief and existence of reasons for that belief. The belief must be held in good faith. It cannot be mere pretence. It does not mean a pure subjective satisfaction of the officer. The belief must not be based on mere suspicion.

Hon'ble Bombay High Court in the case of *Jain & Jain* v. *Union of India* [1982] 8 Taxman 48 have held that the belief of course cannot be mere pretence nor can it be a mere doubt or suspicion. It is something much more than that. Section 132 speaks of *"reason to believe"* and not *"reason to suspect"* or *"reason to doubt"*. *"Reason to believe"* is thus a higher test to be fulfilled. If the belief is *bona fide*, if the same is in good faith, if it is not pretence and if it is cogently supported, the court will not interfere there with or sit in appeal over it, rather it has no jurisdiction to interfere.

Hon'ble Supreme Court in the case of *Dr. Partap Singh* v. *Director of Enforcement* [1985] 22 Taxman 30 held that the expression *"reason to believe"* is not synonymous with the subjective satisfaction of the officer. The belief must be held in good faith. It cannot be merely pretence.

It has been held in the case of *Asstt. Director of IT (Inv.)* v. *Apparasu Ravi* [2011] 10 taxmann.com 200/199 Taxman 150 (Mad.) that the assessee himself having made a concrete statement that he was carrying 10 kg. of gold jewellery while travelling from Singapore to Chennai which was handed over to him by an unknown person to hand over the same to another unknown person in Chennai, the IT authorities had reason to believe that the said gold would not have been disclosed for the purposes of the Act and, therefore, the search and seizure operation effected against the assessee was valid. Assessee, an Indian citizen was not governed by clause (*b*) of *Explanation* to section 6(1) but by section 6(1)(*c*) alone and, therefore, the Asstt. Director of IT (Inv.) was well within his jurisdiction in effecting search and seizure on him by invoking section 132(1). Order passed under section 132B refusing to return the seized gold pending the completion of assessment was justified.

It has been held in the case of *Shah-E-Naaz Judge* v. *Addl. Director of IT (Inv.)* [2018] 100 taxmann.com 346/[2019] 260 Taxman 116 (Delhi) that Satisfaction note prior to authorisation under section 132(1) to search locker woefully forms the negative conclusion and finding without referring to material and evidence that had led and prompted the author to reach the denouncement. Hon'ble Court held that the use of the word "may" to presume presence of undisclosed assets in the locker, given the absence of reference to even a single shred of evidence and material to justify the inference, reflects and establishes supine indifference to the statute and Constitutional guarantee that "right to privacy" should not be impinged and violated on mere posturing and pretentiousness & therefore Warrants of authorization for search and seizure operations in respect of the lockers are vitiated and illegal.

Issue of search warrant on the basis of Key of Locker found not valid

It generally happens that in the course of search on a particular person, key of locker belonging to spouse or some other family member may be found. In such cases, it is seen that Revenue issues search authorization for operating the locker in the name of person in whose name the locker stands. This is not in accordance with law and it cannot be said that valid search authorization has been issued. In such cases, search warrant for operating and searching the locker should be issued in the name of the original person searched. The owner of the locker in such cases cannot be covered as the person searched unless 'satisfaction note' or 'reason to believe' recorded in case of searched person includes the name of the owner of the locker also against whom conditions prescribed u/s 132(1) were existing.

It has been held in the case of *Ameeta Mehra* v. *Addl. Director of IT (Inv.)* [2017] 82 taxmann.com 279/248 Taxman 308 (Delhi) that issue of search warrant in the name of assessee on the basis of a key of locker found during search of N Group was not valid when there is nothing in the satisfaction note to indicate that there was any credible information available with the Department that the assessee belonged to the N Group who were being searched or that locker would contain money, jewellery etc. that constituted her undisclosed income.

It has been held in the case of *Adarsh Credit Co-operative Society Ltd.* v. *Jt. Director of IT (Inv.)* 179 DTR (Guj.) 200 that there were sufficient grounds for the authorities to hold the belief that the case of the assessee is covered under sub-cl. (c) of sub-s. (1) of s. 132 and, therefore, there is no reason to interfere with the impugned authorization as well as impounding of documents under s. 133A(3)(*ia*) & necessary care has been taken and the case was properly scrutinized before issuance of the authorization.

It has been held in the case of *Adarsh Credit Co-operative Society Ltd.* v. *Jt. Director of IT (Inv.)* 179 DTR (SC) 199 that the warrant of authorization under s. 132(1) was based on definite information and discreet verification and further holding that the order passed under s. 133A was also in consonance with the provisions of the Act.

(ii) **Reason to believe and not reason to suspect**

"Reason to believe" is a narrower connotation than *"reason to suspect"*. *"Reason to believe"* has to be based upon actual facts while *"reason to suspect"* may be based upon indirect correlation of facts. Search warrant under section 132(1) cannot be issued merely on the basis of suspicion. *"Reason to believe"* is required to be formed before authorizing search with respect to a person.

Search action may be required to be undertaken at various premises with respect to a person. *"Reason to believe"* is not required to be formed *qua* each premises of the assessee against whom search is authorized. Search warrant for any premises with respect to such person can be issued on the basis of suspicion. The words used under clause *(i)* of section 132(1) or under sub-section (1A) of section 132 are *"reason to suspect"*. The requirement is to form *"reason to believe"* *qua* - assessee against whom search is authorized but for covering any of the premises relating to such assessee, it can be on the basis of *"reason to suspect"*.

(iii) **Reason to believe cannot be justified on the basis of assets seized during search**

Reasons are to be based on the evidence found prior to search and not on the basis of articles found during search. *Smt. Kavita Agarwal v. DIT (Investigation)* [2003] 133 Taxman 848 (All.)

Where it is alleged by the assessee that there was no information for issuing of warrant of authorization for search and there is no denial thereof as the search is sought to be justified on the ground that some incriminating documents showing suppression of production were found and seized, search is held illegal. *Ravi Iron Industries* v. *Director of Investigation* [2004] 134 Taxman 138 (All.).

Material found during search cannot form the basis for belief for initiation of action under section 132. *Suresh Chand Agarwal* v. *DGIT* [2004] 139 Taxman 363 (All.).

(iv) **Search warrant for the search of the premises of tenant or business associate or relative or senior employee.**

Whether authorized officer can obtain a search warrant for the search of the premises of a tenant where search is being conducted against the owner of the premises or for the premises of senior employee of the company where search is being conducted against the company or for the premises of brother, parent, counsel or other business associate of a person against whom search is being conducted?

In case authorized officer during search comes to know that certain incriminating material belonging to the assessee is secreted in the premises of some other person and he wants to search that premises, search warrant can be issued in the name of assessee for such premises. No search warrant can be issued in the name of tenant, employee or relative of the assessee for his premises as no *"reason to believe"* can be recorded against them in the facts of the case. On the basis of reason to suspect, any premises relating to or belonging to any other person can be searched but search warrant has to be in the name of assessee in respect of whom *"reason to believe"* has been formed.

It has been held in the case of *Shilpa Chowdhary* v. *Principal Director of IT (Inv.)* [2021] 124 taxmann.com 509/277 Taxman 576/430 ITR 218 (Delhi) that as to the authorisation under section 132(1) or section 132(1A) and validity vis-a-vis search of assessee's premises and bank locker, assessee's premises were searched on the basis of search warrant under s. 132(1) issued against KC Group on the suspicion that the assessee's premises was a location where undisclosed income/assets/documents/other incriminating evidence relating to the KC Group was likely to be found and another warrant was also issued under section 132(1) against the assessees in respect of bank locker which was found during the search of assessee's premises, there was indeed material with the concerned authority to form reasons to believe that the locker contained articles/cash/jewellery/other materials which represented the undisclosed income of the assessee and thus action initiated by the respondents under section 132(1) qua the assessees does not call for any interference by this Court.

(v) Formation of *"reason to believe"* separately for each person.

It has been observed that in certain cases when search is planned against a person, search warrant is issued against him and the names of his wife, father, mother or son who are residing along with him are also included in the search warrant. Sometimes, search warrant is issued in joint names of several persons residing together within the premises. For issuing search warrant in the name of any person, *"reason to believe"* has to be formed against each person separately. There has to be recording of "reason to believe" against each person and how conditions mentioned in either of clauses (*a*), (*b*) and (*c*) of section 132(1) are satisfied personally against that person, needs to be arrived at. Adding name of any person in the search warrant has severe consequences upon such person and he is liable to fresh assessment for last six years (in certain cases 9 years) under section 153A. Therefore, name of any person cannot be included in search warrant casually without recording reasons and forming belief against him specifically.

If in the course of search operation property including jewellery or even books of account are discovered to have a reasonable proximity with the object of the search but such property is located in another premises, a consequential search warrant can be issued authorizing a search of the other premises where such property may be located. The authorized officer recorded his satisfaction to the effect that the fixed deposit certificates of the petitioner represented the property of the account holder, *i.e.*, the petitioner, and not the property of DS, the courier agency, whose premises were authorized to be searched in terms of the initial warrant of authorization issued. There was no satisfaction recorded by the authorized officer to the effect that the amount covered by the fixed deposit certificates was in any way relatable to DS in respect of whom satisfaction as regards suppression of concealment of income had led to the initiation of search on the strength of the original warrant. In the absence of such satisfaction, the consequential warrant authorizing the search of the premises of the Bank could not be held by the court to be authorized under the provisions of section 132. Consequently, the action of the respondents in converting the property of the petitioner in the form of the fixed deposit certificates and the further action of the respondents in obtaining a banker's cheques for the amount covered by the two certificates and the consequential deposit of the amount of the banker's cheques into the account of the Commissioner were unauthorized actions with which the court must interfere. [*Harihar Shah* v. *CIT* [2006] 154 Taxman 18 (Gau.)]

It has been held in the case of *Zinzuwadia and Sons* v. *Deputy CIT* [2019] 108 taxmann.com 42/265 Taxman 261/419 ITR 169 (Guj) that search is person specific and not location specific.

(vi) *"Reason to believe"* **whether open to judicial scrutiny**

The Court has to see if the belief was based on relevant material but it cannot substitute its own opinion as to the reasonableness of the belief in writ jurisdiction. Disclosure of materials or information to the persons against whom action under section 132(1) is taken is not mandatory and at the initial stage of search and seizure, it is sufficient if the Revenue places the material before the Court to examine whether the said material on which search and seizure is ordered, was relevant to the exercise of the power under section 132(1). The scope of the writ jurisdiction while examining the validity of the authorization under section 132(1) is limited to seeing whether the reasonable belief formed by the authority issuing the authorization was a reasonable belief, in the sense whether the said belief was formed only on the basis of relevant material/information.

[*Southern Herbals Ltd.* v. *DIT (Investigation)*[1994] 207 ITR 55 (Kar.)]

There must have to be some material bearing on the question of escapement of income of assessee. Whether the grounds are adequate or not is not a matter for the Court to investigate. Only the existence of belief can be challenged by assessee. Expression *"reason to believe"* does not mean a purely subjective satisfaction on the part of ITO. It must be held in good faith. Powers of ITO to reopen assessment, though wide, are not plenary. Interest was allowed as deduction in original assessment Subsequently ITO found that creditors were name-lenders. There was nothing to show that the confession related to a loan advanced to assessee. The live link or close nexus between material before ITO and belief he was to form regarding escapement of income was missing. The said material could not have led to formation of the belief that income escaped assessment because of assessee's failure or omission to disclose fully and truly all material facts. Pre-conditions for exercise of jurisdiction under section 147 were not fulfilled.

[*ITO* v. *Lakhmani Mewal Das* [1976] 103 ITR 437 (SC)]

[*Manju Tandon* v. *T.N. Kapoor, Dy. Supdt. of Police* [1978] 115 ITR 473 (All.)]

The existence of *"reason to believe"* in section 132 is subject to a limited scrutiny and the Courts cannot substitute their own opinion for that of the Director of Inspection. Of course, the Director of Inspection must not lightly or arbitrarily invade the privacy of a subject. Before he acts, he must be reasonably satisfied that it is necessary to do so but the decision must still remain his and not that of the Courts. If the grounds on which reason to believe is founded are non-existent or are irrelevant or are such on which no reasonable person can come to that belief, the exercise of power would be bad; but short of that, the Courts cannot interfere with the *"reason to believe"* bona fide arrived at by the Director of Inspection. It is also open to the Courts to examine whether the reasons for the belief have a rational connection or a relevant bearing to the formation of the belief. On the facts of the case, the information in possession was held to be relevant and adequate and the writ petition was dismissed.

[*Balwant Singh* v. *R.D. Shah, Director of Inspection* [1969] 71 ITR 550 (Delhi)]

Finance Act, 2017 has incorporated an *Explanation* in sub-section (1) of section 132 as under:

"*Explanation.*—For the removal of doubts, it is hereby declared that the reason to believe, as recorded by the income-tax authority under this sub-section, shall not be disclosed to any person or any authority or the Appellate Tribunal."

The above *Explanation* has been inserted retrospectively with effect from 1st day of April, 1962.

Similarly, in sub-section (1A) of section 132, the following *Explanation* has been inserted with effect from 1st day of October, 1975, the date from which sub-section (1A) was incorporated in the Act:

"*Explanation.*—For the removal of doubts, it is hereby declared that the reason to suspect, as recorded by the income-tax authority under this sub-section, shall not be disclosed to any person or any authority or the Appellate Tribunal."

Though rationale of introducing the clarification is not spelt out in the Memorandum explaining the provisions of Finance Bill, 2017 but the observations of Hon'ble Supreme Court in para 22 of its order in the case of *Director General of IT (Investigation) & Ors.* v. *Spacewood Furnishers (P) Ltd. & Ors.* [2015] 119 DTR (SC) 201 **appear to be the triggering point of such clarificatory Explanation.** Supreme Court in the above case had observed that it is only at stage of commencement of assessment proceedings after completion of search and seizure, if any, that requisite material may have to be disclosed to assessee. Any possible attempt to put the above decision as an authority that Revenue is required to disclose the reason to believe at the stage of assessment on the request of the taxpayer, it appears, is sought to be repelled by the abovementioned clarificatory Explanation.

Above clarifications brought retrospectively thus clarify the intention of the legislature that *"reason to believe"* in sub-section (1) and *'reason to suspect"* in sub-section (1A) of section 132 formed by the competent authority to take the action of search has to be kept confidential. Amendments abovementioned clearly bring out that Reasons recorded for initiating search cannot be disclosed or cannot be reviewed or scrutinized even by the appellate authorities and even by Income Tax Appellate Tribunal.

However, there is nothing in the amendments which put any fetters on the disclosure of such reason before High Courts and Supreme Court if direction is issued by these courts to produce the material. In fact, High Courts and Supreme Court are constitutional courts and shall always have the powers to scrutinize or review the "reason

to believe" etc. recorded by competent authority in Writ/SLP jurisdiction or otherwise.

It has been held in the case of *Prathibha Jewellery House* v. *CIT(A)*
[2017] 88 taxmann.com 94/[2018] 252 Taxman 174 (Kar.) that Power
of CIT(A) to examine validity of search is no longer there in view of
the fact that the decision in the case of *C. Ramaiah Reddy* v. *Asstt.
CIT* [2012] 20 taxmann.com 781 (Kar.) which allowed the appellate
authority to go into the question of validity of search is a subject-matter
of pending appeal before the Supreme Court and an *Explanation* has
been inserted in section 132(1) by Finance Act, 2017 with retrospective
effect from 1st April, 1962 which prohibits the appellate authorities
to go into the reasons recorded by the concerned IT authority for
directing search.

(vii) **The function of formation of** *"reason to believe"* **cannot be delegated**

The authorizing officer may form his opinion or belief on the basis
of the information supplied by the subordinate authorities but the
function of forming the belief cannot be delegated to a subordinate
authority. Issue of authorization by Director of Inspection where
reasons were recorded by Assistant Director of Inspection was not
valid as the formation of belief could not be said to be of the authorizing authority. *Dwarka Prosad Agarwalla* v. *Director of Inspection*
[1981] 7 Taxman 299 (Cal.)

Reason to believe should be of the authorizing officer and not of the
Ministry. *Bishnu Krishna Shrestha* v. *Union of India* [1987] 168 ITR
815 (Cal.)

2.12 Nexus between information and "reason to believe"

The allegations against the petitioner-company were regarding suppression
of sales/production, inflation of expenses or incurring the expenditure in
cash, which were not reflected in the regular books of account maintained
by the assessee. The assessee thus generates quite a substantial unaccounted income. There is ample reason to believe that the petitioner has
not produced material relating to assessment of income unless search is
carried out. It is well established that there is reason to believe to conduct
search and seizure invoking the provisions of sections 131 and 132 and the
power of search and seizure has been exercised after taking due care of
the provisions and on the basis of credible information and after applying
mind, there was reason to believe to conduct search operation.

[*Harvest Gold Foods (India) (P.) Ltd.* v. *UOI* [2006] 152 Taxman 398 (Raj.)]

The information has not only to be authentic but also capable of giving rise
to the inference that the person was in possession of undisclosed income

or assets, which has not been or would not be disclosed. In order that the formation of opinion must be in good faith and not mere pretence, it is necessary that information in consequence of which it is formed must be valid and linked with the ingredients mentioned in section 132, that is, there must be rational connection between the information or material and the belief about existence of undisclosed income.

[*Dr. Nand Lal Tahiliani* v. *CIT* [1988] 39 Taxman 127 (All.)]

In *Lit Light & Co.* v. *CIT* [1982] 136 ITR 513 (All.), the warrant of authorization was issued by the Commissioner, on the basis of the following information:-

  a. That Sri Abdul Hamid was the Mutawalli of Haji Lal Mohd. Biri Works, Waqf, Allahabad.

  b. That Sri Abdul Hamid's brother-in-law, Sri Anwar Ahmad and Sri Maqsood Ahmed, with respective houses (1) Roshan Bagh, Opposite Gulab Badi, Graveyard, Allahabad, and (2) 175, Bhadurganj, Allahabad, had duped Sri Abdul Hamid in collaboration with one Rahmat Ali of Mohalla Shahnoor-Aliganj in Patthar Gali, Allahabad. Details of wealth acquired by these three persons were also given. It was informed that Rahmat Ali could be having large amounts of cash ₹ 3 to 4 lakhs and jewellery of considerable amount. Details of the situation of his house and the place where the cash and the valuable were expected to be kept were also given. I was informed that besides cash and jewellery in boxes and covers (cushions, quilts and pillows) there will also be available from two of the personal rooms of the house, incriminating documents, which would show how the group of three persons had manipulated the accounts of Haji Lal Mohammed Biri Works to divert moneys to themselves.

  c. I was further informed that Anwar Ahmad, the brother-in-law of Abdul Hamid, is looking after the business and was in complete actual control. He has his own Biri business as partner in Swadeshi Biri Works, S.C. Basu Road, Allahabad. It was told that Anwar Ahmad pays tax as partner in Swadeshi Biri Works. I was informed that the entire manufacturing work of Haji Lal Mohd. Biri Works had been taken over by the Hind Tabacco Company and the former only sold the goods and have very nominal manufacturing left to themselves. Manufacture is mostly through other contractors and Anwar Ahmad himself is one of them. I was further informed that Anwar Ahmad has 9 trucks in his own name, his wife's name and his transport manager is Rais Ahmad. The transport business head office in Roshan Bagh, opposite Gulab Badi Graveyard, and that was also the residence of Anwar Ahmad. The building had been put up about 4 years ago at a cost of about ₹ 2 lakhs in the name of his wife. A sketch of his

Roshan Bagh residence was given to me. I was informed that cash and jewellery and diaries will be found at certain specified places of which details were given to me.

d. Maqsood Ahmad, I was informed, is another brother-in-law of Abdul Hamid. He had four trucks and an Ambassador Car UPZ 1683; 2 petrol pumps across Jumuna at Rewa Road, Allahabad, named, New Naini Service Station and Dandi Service Station. I was informed that near Dandi Petrol Pump, he had vast lands converted in Maqsood Ahmad Colony cleared by the town planner. The promoter of the colony is a Sikh from Delhi who has a local office in Dandi. The colony is to have 300 shops and over 600 flats and all plots have been sold out. Maqsood Ahmad lived in 1975-77 in Bahadurganj just close to Haji Lal Mohd. Biri Works, separated only by a gali and the house belongs to the Waqf. He stayed in the upper storey and that at specified places in the house there will be found documents and cash and jewellery and about 3 to 4 lakh of rupees will also be found. I was also informed that at Dandi Petrol Pump his trusted Munim, Maqbool Ahmad, will also have documents at the petrol pump.

e. I was also informed that Maqsood Ahmad's brother, Mahmood Ahmed, had joined him in supply of biris of Hind Tobacco Company Haji Lal Mohd. Biri Works and the two brothers have excise licences in their names. I was informed that he also worked as Lit Light Company, sole kerosene agent for Indian Oil at Allahabad, office at Katju Road and depot at Leader Road and that his oil tanker is also parked there."

In the backdrop of the above reason to believe, Hon'ble Allahabad High Court held that original record of the department contained the information that was made available to the CIT before he issued the warrants of authorization for search. The statement of the main informant who had intimate knowledge of the business dealings of the petitioners, was recorded on oath. The nature of information furnished by him could reasonably be accepted as reliable. On the material furnished by the department the contention of the petitioners that action was *mala fide* or that there was no reliable information in possession of the CIT to justify action u/s 132 must be rejected as untenable.

In *Mamchand & Co.* v. *CIT* [1970] 76 ITR 217 (Cal.), the warrant of authorization was issued by the Commissioner on the basis of the following information:-

"Information was received by me of large scale evasion of income-tax by a section of Members of East India Jute & Hessian Exchange Ltd., Calcutta, including the firm of M/s Mamchand & Co., who are also members of East India Jute and Hessian Exchange. I also had information in my possession that some of members of East India Jute and Hessian Exchange (hereinafter referred to as 'the said Exchange') including the petitioners in collaboration with some other members passed on their actual profit by certain artificial losses through fictitious back-dated transactions and thereby have been evading substantial portion of their Income-tax liabilities. From the information in my possession, it appears that the actual procedure of evasion which is common in every case is to introduce in the books losses due to non-existing speculation transaction with the help of ante-dated bogus contracts in I.S.D.N.T.S.D.P.D.O. or in ready goods. These ante-dated transactions are always intended to neutralize the quantum of profit they intend to wipe out. The purchaser of the profit is often a person who has losses to set off, if not "he passes on the profit by a similar transaction to a third broker in the chain from whom the actual profit is realized by the principal operator, *i.e.,* the beneficiary, in cash. Sometimes even five or more persons are brought in the chain to give the transaction a colour of genuineness. The payments for actual value are often made by cheques operated by the beneficiary in the names of his collaborators....."

Hon'ble High Court held that it cannot be said that the warrant was issued upon conjectures alone and not in good faith. The allegation that CIT had no belief, or had no reason to believe or that he had no information in his possession which could induce him to believe are points of no substance. The test is whether there was reason for the belief for a rational action having a relevant bearing to the formation of the belief. This test has been satisfied.

(i) Application of mind by authorizing officer

The scheme of section 132 shows that the mind has to be applied by two officers at two different stages (1) by the Director of Inspection or the CIT when authorizing officer to search. Such application of mind extends to two matters (a) that the person concerned will not produce the books of account; and (b) he will not produce the books which will be useful or relevant to any proceedings; and (2) by the authorized officer that the books searched or seized will be useful or relevant to any proceedings. Where there was tangible information that the assessee had not disclosed large transactions through bank accounts and business activities in various names and had been filing returns deliberately at places different from the places of business in order to avoid scrutiny and such information was also authenticated by independent enquiries by the departmental officers, the search was held to be valid. [*Balwant Singh* v. *R.D. Shah, Director of Inspection* [1969] 71 ITR 550 (Delhi)]

Any complaint made by person interested or disinterested should not be jumped upon and made an excuse to initiate proceedings unless it is thoroughly examined and the authorities are satisfied about its veracity and authenticity.

[*Ganga Prasad Maheshwari* v. *CIT* [1981] 6 Taxman 363 (All.)]

In the present case, the informer was a co-director of the transport company of which the petitioner, G, was the managing director. He not only furnished some of the duplicate account books of the petitioners showing transactions regarding the undisclosed income, but also stated that more such duplicate books of account were kept in the premises of the said transport company and of its managing director, Gardhara Singh, and in the premises of their sister concerns which are inter-connected belonging to virtually the same family and that huge black income was being generated which had been distributed amongst themselves to the detriment of the Revenue and also some of their partners. It is thus clear that two out of the three requirements stand satisfied in the present case, that is, availability of relevant material and application of mind by the CIT to the same. What is merely lacking is the reasons for his belief that the 'undisclosed income' and the documents would not be produced by the petitioners if required to do and, therefore, an immediate search of their premises in question was warranted to get at the same. The emphasis is on the relevancy of the material and the application of mind before passing the order.

[*Gardhara Singh* v. *CIT* [1979] 2 Taxman 362 (P&H)]

Clause (*b*) or (*c*) of sub-section (1) of section 132 could be taken recourse to only if sufficient materials existed therefor. A search or seizure cannot be sustained unless it is clearly shown that it was done by an authority duly authorized therefor and all conditions precedent in relation thereto exist. Warrant of authorization issued by the Addl. Director converting the survey into a search and seizure operation merely agreeing with the recommendations of the requisitioning officer. Even the requisitioning officer did not disclose any material whereupon his '*reason to belief*' was based. Not only, no material was disclosed, the Addl. Director did not ask for any. No reason has been assigned as to why the survey operation would not serve the purpose and the same was required to be converted into a seizure. There has been no independent application of mind, thus, rendering the action to be invalid.

[*Dr. Nalini Mahajan* v. *DIT (Inv.)* [2002] 122 Taxman 897 (Delhi)]

Simply because a sum of ₹ 4.5 Lacs was found at the residence of one partner of a firm there was no justifiable reason to issue authorization for search at the residence of other partners in the same firm, when there was nothing to show as to why the authorizing officer believed that incriminating documents would be found at the residence of the other partners. The condition precedent for having search under the provisions of section 132 did not exist. In view of the facts stated hereinabove, the authorization issued by the Addl. Director of Income-tax (Investigation) in favour of respondent No. 2 for having search at the residence, where the petitioners reside, does not appear to be legal and proper. The said satisfaction seems to have been arrived at in a mechanical manner and without any application of mind. Therefore, the authorization is quashed and set aside.

[*Farshubhai Prabhurambhai Kakkad* v. *DIT (Inv.)* [2003] 132 Taxman 350 (Guj.)]

There is no provision for sealing of the business premises either under section 133A or 132 or any other section of the Income-tax Act. Sub-section (3) of section 132 also nowhere provides for sealing of a shop. The act of sealing of a particular business premises purported to be in exercise of powers under section 132 is a deliberate act in gross violation of the specific provisions of law which the ITO or a higher officer is supposed to know and the said action was not only an abuse of the power or misuse of the power but was a malicious act with a collateral object. The sealing of the business premises for which there was no provision in law was in violation of the fundamental rights guaranteed to a citizen under Article 19(1)(*g*) of the Constitution of India which guarantees the right to practice any profession, or to carry on any occupation, trade or business and also under Article 300A of the Constitution of India inasmuch as the same amounted to temporary deprivation of property without authority of law.

[*Shyam Jewellers* v. *Chief Commissioner* [1992] 196 ITR 243 (All.)]

CIT issuing authorization under section 132(1) being of the opinion that the assessee, one of the top lawyers, submits return on estimate without correlating fees with briefs and as he is not a wealth-tax assessee and has no jewellery, a search is needed. Such inquisitorial search could not be sanctioned. Further, CIT had also not looked into the orders of assessment which showed non-application of mind as in his assessment for A.Y. 1971-72, the ITO had noted: "The assessee is a practicing lawyer and has maintained register for the fees received. Statement of accounts has been furnished and examined. Bank pass books produced and examined". In the face of this order, one fails to understand how the CIT jumped to the conclusion that the petitioner submits returns on estimate basis. It appears that in his zeal for taking action under section 132(1) he did not even care to have a look at the orders of assessment framed against the assessee by the ITOs. This also shows that the CIT did not at all apply his mind before initiating action against the petitioner. For all these reasons the search of the premises of the petitioner is declared to be illegal. Since there is no valid seizure of assets from the premises of the petitioner in the eyes of law, no order against him could have been passed under section 132(5).

[*Anand Swaroop* v. *CIT* [1976] 103 ITR 575 (P&H)]

Concerned officer had substantial information with regard to certain activities and financial status of the assessee-firm and its partners and he had submitted the relevant facts and figures to the higher authorities. Director of Income Tax (Inv.) had applied his mind thereto and had taken final decision only after arriving at necessary satisfaction. It cannot be said that necessary direction for search was given without sufficient material or without application of mind. Further, authorized officer who had carried out search also having jurisdiction over assessee, provisions of section 132(9A) would not apply. Authorised officer, in his capacity as the officer having jurisdiction over assessee is entitled to retain possession of seized documents.

[*Arti Ship Breaking* v. *DIT* [2000] 110 Taxman 457 (Guj.)]

While exercising extraordinary jurisdiction under Article 226/227, the High Court is required to examine with care and caution whether the reason to believe was based on definable material or materials or whether the act of issuance of authorization under section 132A is arbitrary, *mala fide* and whether the subjective satisfaction which is recorded is such that it indicates lack of application of mind of the appropriate authority. There was definable material available before the CIT to issue warrant of authorization under section 132A. Act of issuing authorization was not based on hunch or incredible information and was not arbitrary or *mala fide*. Police having seized cash of ₹ 12 lacs from the petitioner, and there being definable material available before the CIT to issue warrant of authorization under section 132A; sufficiency of the information before issuing warrant of authorization could not be investigated in writ proceedings.

[*Suresh Bhai Bhola Bhai Jani* v. *UOI* [2001] 249 ITR 363 (Raj.)]

Formation of the belief that the petitioner was in possession of unaccounted money, bullion, etc. should be by the authority issuing authorization. Satisfaction in the present case was recorded by the Addl. Director of Inspection, and not by the Director of Inspection who issued the authorization. Search and seizure accordingly became invalid. Further, the reasons recorded for the initiation of search proceedings barely mentioned that there was specific information as to the petitioner being in possession of unaccounted money, etc. No recording either as to the source or as to the contents of the information was made. Recording of reasons, therefore, could not be relied on for the purposes of section 132(1). Grounds for existence of suspicion cannot be equated with grounds for existence with belief in consequence of any information. Further, the fact that the authorization did not strike out the irrelevant portions, indicates the non-application of mind and stereotype authorization of search which should not be encouraged.

[*Dwarka Prosad Agarwalla* v. *Director of Inspection* [1981] 7 Taxman 299 (Cal.)]

It has been held in the case of *Madhupuri Corpn.* v. *Prabhat Jha, Dy. DIT (Investigation)* [2002] 125 Taxman 309 (Guj.)] that satisfaction note prepared by Dy. Director was approved by Additional Director and Director and it was found that petitioners were dealing with large sums of money running into crores of rupees and still not filing any return, it could not be held that there was non-application of mind by the authority issuing the authorization for search against the petitioners.

2.13 Recording of satisfaction

The recording of reasons is also necessary since the action of search has to be judged by the information and reason to believe recorded prior to search. A search cannot be justified by fresh reasons in the shape of an affidavit filed before the Court.

[*Mahalaxmi Poly Plast (P.) Ltd.* v. *State of U.P.* [1994] 1994 taxmann.com 984 (All.)]

The important words of section 165, CrPC, are *"such officer may after recording in writing the grounds of his belief and specifying in such writing so far as possible the thing for which search is to be made."* It has already been noticed that the CIT has to record in writing the reasons of his belief for any statutory purposes mentioned in clause (*a*), (*b*) or (*c*) of sub-section (1) of section 132 before authorizing the search of the premises of an assessee. Since he failed to do so, his action cannot be justified in the eyes of law. The result would be the same if some part of the record was made earlier and additions were made to it after conducting the search, for, in such a situation the condition precedent of recording reasons based on information before issuing an authorization for search would be violated.

[*H.L. Sibal* v. *CIT* [1975] 101 ITR 112 (Punj. & Har.)]

Section 132 it self does not require the CIT to record any reasons unlike section 131(3) which requires the ITO to record reasons before impounding the documents produced before him. However, Rule 112 requires that reasons should be recorded by the CIT before issuing warrants of authorization to carry out a search and seizure. Rule 112 has been framed by the CBDT in exercise of the powers given to it under sub-section (14) of section 132. These rules, therefore, have statutory force. Any search and seizure made in contravention of rule 112 would thus be illegal. The initial seizure of books of account being illegal, their retention would also be illegal.

[*New Kashmir & Oriental Transport Co. (P.) Ltd.* v. *CIT* [1973] 92 ITR 334 (All.)]

Though Rule 112(2) as substituted, has dispensed with the requirements of recording of the reasons, in view of the language of section 132(1) retaining the words "has reason to believe" and the fact that the affected person can challenge the existence of such "reason" in a Court of law, it continues to be the requirement that the authorizing authority records reasons for the issuance of warrant.

[*Pannalal Binjraj* v. *UOI* [1957] 31 ITR 565 (SC)]

The safeguards incorporated by the legislature in section 165 of Criminal Procedure Code are mandatory and not directory. They must be carried out immediately and fully as nearly as possible in the circumstances of each case. The provisions of clause 5 of section 165 (new) are intended to prevent roving searches. Section 165 (new) of the Code lays down various steps to be followed in making a search. The recording of reasons is an important step in the matter of search and to ignore it, is to ignore the material part of the provisions governing searches.

[*State of Rajasthan* v. *Rehman* AIR 1960 SC 210]

The recording of reason before search is provided for both under the Criminal Procedure Code and under the Excise Act and is intended to protect the liberty of citizens and avoid useless and unjustified searches. If an officer before proceeding to search has to record his reason he will have to apply his mind to the facts and the sufficiency of the information on the basis of which he wants to search.

[*Chander Prasad* v. *Emperor* AIR 1937 Pat. 501]

(i) Whether recording of satisfaction has to be in writing?

Sub-rule (2) of rule 112 prior to its substitution by the Income-tax (Fourth Amendment) Rules, 1975 specifically prescribed that before issuing a search warrant, the authorizing officer has to record reasons for doing so. In the new sub-rule (2) of rule 112 the words *'after recording his reasons for doing so'* have been deleted. This has triggered a controversy whether authorizing officer is required to record reasons before issuing search warrant in writing or not. There are contrary views of Punjab and Haryana High Court and Allahabad High Court on this issue. Punjab and Haryana High Court in the case of *Harmel Singh* v. *Union of India* [1993] 69 Taxman 347 has stated that under new rule 112 the concerned authority need not record the reason. They have held as under-

'The words 'after recording his reasons for doing so' have been omitted but the obligation is still there under section 132 that in consequence of information in his possession the authorizing officer has reason to believe, only then he is empowered to issue a warrant of authorization. The concerned authority, since that amendment, need not record the reason under the new rule 112. Form No. 45 provides that he has information in his possession in consequence whereof he had reason to believe that the search and seizure was necessary.'

On the contrary Allahabad High Court while commenting upon the Amendment of rule 112(2) in the case of *Shyam Jewellers* v. *Chief Commissioner* [1992] 196 ITR 243 observed as under:

'That prior to its amendment in 1975, it specially required authorizing officer to record his satisfaction. But this amendment will not change the position in view of the words 'reason to believe' under rule 112(1) of the Rules. This phrase postulates recording of reasons. In the absence of reasons, the order could not be said to be reasonable and cannot be upheld.

The High Court referred to their earlier decision in the case of *Ganga Prasad Maheshwari* v. *CIT* [1981] 6 Taxman 363 (All.)'

The provisions of section 165(1) of the Code of Criminal Procedure, 1973, which are applicable to search under the Income-tax Act, 1961 as well, require recording of reasons for authorizing search. Ground rule 1 issued by Central Board of Direct Taxes prescribing procedure to be followed in conducting search requires formal order and to be passed by authorizing officer before authorizing search. Ground rule 1 states as under:-

"Authorization for a search can only be......... by competent authority"

Ground rules are the rules prescribed by the highest administrative authority of the income tax and one is supposed to be adhered by the income tax officials in discharge of their functions under the Act. When reasons for authorizing the search are recorded in writing, it becomes easier to ascertain the existence of information and formation of belief, by the Courts in case required at any stage.

In view of the above discussion, our considered opinion, with due respect, is that the view expressed by the Allahabad High Court seems to be correct and practical. In the absence of reasons recorded in writing, it would be very difficult for the Courts to ascertain whether there existed any reason, on what basis reason to believe was formed and what was the nexus between information and reason to believe.

(*ii*) **Existence of relevant information is enough for issuing search warrant**

Even prior to amendment in the rule, action under section 132 was held to be valid where there was information/sufficient material but the reasons were not recorded in the case of *Gardhara Singh* v. *CIT* [1979] 2 Taxman 362 (Punj. & Har.). It was held that where there are cogent reasons and relevant material to justify formation of belief with regard to the conditions laid down in clauses (*a*), (*b*) and (*c*) of sub-section (1) of section 132, the action would not get vitiated merely because the formality of recording the satisfaction by the authority was not done. Two out of three requirements of section 132(1) were satisfied *i.e.* availability of the relevant material and application of mind by the Commissioner to the same. Though this judgment of Punjab & Haryana High Court is at variance with its own judgment earlier in the case of *H.L Sibal* v. *CIT* [1975] 101 ITR 112, in which the Punjab & Haryana High Court while examining the expression, "in consequence of information in his possession has reasons to believe" in section 132, after referring to the decision of Supreme Court in *CCT* v. *Ram Kishan Shri Kishan Jhaver* [1967] 66 ITR 664, held that the obligation to record in writing, the grounds of belief as enjoined by section 151(1) of Code of Criminal Procedure, if not complied with, would vitiate the issuance of search warrant and the seizure of the articles. This view of the Punjab & Haryana High Court did not find favour with the Supreme Court in the case of *Dr. Pratap Singh* v. *Director of Enforcement* [1985] 22 Taxman 30.

(*iii*) **Reasons need not be communicated**

It is well settled that the reasons to believe on the basis of which search is authorized by the authorizing officer need not be communicated to the assessee. However whenever action of the search is challenged, the same may have to be produced before the High Court.

In the case of *Mamchand & Co.* v. *CIT* [1970] 76 ITR 217 (Cal.), it was held that there is no provision in law which requires that reasons to be communicated to the assessee. Similar view has been taken by Bombay High Court in the case of *Jain & Jain* v. *UOI* [1982] 8 Taxman 48, wherein it was held that there is no provision either in the Act or rules providing for supply of a copy of warrant of authorization for search to the assessee. All that the law requires is that the authorization must be produced before the commencement of the search.

The situation regarding supply of reasons to believe recorded for taking action under section 148 is different from the situation in respect to the action under section 132. In the case of search under section 132, information is gathered through informers or other sources confidentially. Secrecy is the main ingredient of successful action under section 132 and the breakdown of the secrecy before or after the search can be disastrous. If secrecy is broken before search, the search action could become a failure and if the secrecy is broken after the search, it may create serious situation with regard to the safety and security of the informer's life. It may erode the confidence of the informers in the Department and in future confidential information may not be received by the Department for taking search action.

Patna High Court dismissing the Writ Petition held that the documents and information on the basis of which the authority had arrived at his satisfaction for conducting the search and seizure could not be disclosed to the assessee as it would hamper the enquiry pending against him.—*Ram Swarup Sahu* v. *CIT* [1992] 196 ITR 841 (Pat.).

In the case of *Director General of IT (Investigation) & Ors.* v. *Spacewood Furnishers (P.) Ltd. & Ors.* [2015] 119 DTR (SC) 201, it has been held that necessity of recording of reasons before issuing warrant of authorisation, has been repeatedly stressed upon by Supreme Court so as to ensure accountability and responsibility in decision making process, this, by itself, would not confer in assessee a right of inspection of documents or to a communication of reasons for belief at stage of issuing of authorization. It is only at stage of commencement of assessment proceedings after completion of search and seizure, if any, that requisite material may have to be disclosed to assessee.

It has been held in the case of *Prathibha Jewellery House* v. *CIT(A) & Ors.* [2017] 88 taxmann.com 94/[2018] 252 Taxman 174 (Kar.) that Power of CIT(A) to examine validity of search is no longer there in view of the fact that the decision in the case of *C. Ramaiah Reddy* v. *Asstt. CIT* [2012] 20 taxmann.com 781 (Kar.) which allowed the appellate authority to go into the question of validity of search is a subject-matter of pending appeal before the Supreme Court and an *Explanation* has been inserted in section 132(1) by Finance Act, 2017 with retrospective effect from 1st April, 1962 which prohibits the appellate authorities to go into the reasons recorded by the concerned IT authority for directing search.

It has been held in the case of *Adarsh Credit Co-operative Society Limited* v. *Joint DIT (Investigation)* [2018] 97 taxmann.com 353/ [2019] 414 ITR 434 (Guj.) that Reason to believe that documents or assets have not been disclosed, need not be communicated to assessee, however Reason must be supplied to writ court. Authorization was based on information & Satisfaction note was examined and approved by higher authority, Search proceedings were held valid.

2.14 Scope of Search and Seizure u/s 132

Gujarat High Court has summarized the scope of the provisions of search and seizure u/s 132 of the Act in the following manner:

(a) The authority must be in possession of information and must form an opinion that there is reason to believe that the article or property has not been or would not be disclosed for the purpose of the Act,

(b) The information must be something more than mere rumour or gossip or hunch,

(c) The information must exist before the opinion is formed,

(d) The authorized person must actively apply his mind to the information in his possession and shall form an opinion whether there is reason to believe or not. The opinion must be formed on the basis of the material available at that time,

(e) The opinion must be based on the material which is available and it should not be formed on the basis of extraneous or irrelevant material,

(f) That the formation of opinion shall have rational connection and bearing to the reasons for such opinion. The formation of opinion should be based on active application of mind and be *bona fide* and not be accentuated by *mala fide*, bias or based on extraneous or irrelevant material. The belief must be *bona fide* and cogently supported. The court have further held that the existence or otherwise of the conditions precedent is open to judicial scrutiny,

(g) The court would examine whether the authorized persons had material before it on which he could form the opinion whether there is rational connection between the information possessed and the opinion formed. However, the court will not sit in appeal over the opinion formed by the authorized person if the authorized person had information in his possession and the opinion formed is on the basis of such material. The court will not examine whether the material possessed was sufficient to form an opinion,

(h) The court cannot go into the question of aptness or sufficiency of the grounds upon which the subjective satisfaction is based,

(i) If the belief is *bona fide* and is cogently supported, the court will not interfere with, or sit in appeal over it.

[*Prabhubhai Vastabhai Patel* v. *R.P. Meena* [2000] 112 Taxman 277 (Guj.)]

(*i*) No pendency of proceedings required in relation to issue of search warrant

No proceedings need be actually pending at the time when warrant is issued under section 132. By virtue of *Explanation 2* to section 132 such warrant may be issued in connection with the proceedings which may be commenced in future. [*Bharati (P.) Ltd.* v. *R.S. Chadda* [1973] 89 ITR 108 (Cal.)]

There was nothing in section 132 to show that the search and seizure under that section could be resorted to only if there were pending proceedings. It was held that the section did not require that the proceedings should be imminent. However, the court observed that if there was only a remote possibility of summons or notices being issued, the action would not be justified, not because there was no proceedings imminent, but because a reasonable person could not have in those circumstances reason to believe that the person concerned will not produce the books of account and documents if summons or notices were issued to him. [*Balwant Singh* v. *R.D. Shah, Director of Inspection* [1969] 71 ITR 550 (Delhi)]

2.15 Conversion of survey into search

There remains a question as to whether survey proceeding u/s 133A can be converted into search proceeding u/s 132. In practice, it is seen that during the course of survey u/s 133A, such pressure is resorted to by the survey team to seek surrender of undisclosed income from the person under survey. The assessee remains under constant pressure & fear of the survey being converted into search.

Legally it is not possible to convert survey into search at mere whim & fancy of the survey team. It may be possible only on the fulfilment of the pre-requisites prescribed under clause (*a*), (*b*) or (*c*) of section 132(1) & after obtaining the search warrant from the competent authority who can issue search warrant only after being satisfied in consequence of the information available and after recording reason to believe as to the existence of either or more of conditions as required under clause (*a*), (*b*) or (*c*) of section 132(1). Since the competent authority to issue search warrant is the higher ranked authority as prescribed u/s 132(1), it is not possible by the officer conducting survey to convert survey into search proceeding just like that.

It has been held in the case of *Badri Ram Choudhary* v. *Asstt. CIT* [2012] 67 DTR 107 (Jodh. - Trib.) that on conversion of survey into search, there being nothing in the satisfaction note to meet the requirements of clauses (*a*), (*b*) and (*c*) of section 132(1) and the concerned authority authorizing the search having neither assigned any reason as to why the survey operation was required to be converted into search and seizure nor recorded any reason to believe that the assessee would not comply with the directions if he is called upon to produce any document relevant to the proceedings, there was thus no material before the Department to justify conversion of survey into search, more so when nothing has been found by the Department during the search other than what was inventorised during the survey and, therefore, the search was not valid.

Generally, survey may be converted in to search by the competent authority as prescribed u/s 132 under the following circumstances but of course after fulfilling the pre-requisites of clause (*a*), (*b*) or (*c*) of section 132(1):—

1. In case when information is obtained in the course of survey that certain incriminating material of serious nature and magnitude is kept at the residence of the assessee and no statement is made during the course of survey so as to cover the residence as extended place of business in terms of *Explanation* to section 133A(1). It is not possible to take action at residential premises under survey proceeding but for conducting action at residential premises, search warrant u/s 132(1) is required.

2. In a case when certain incriminating material is lying at some almirah, box or premises that is lying locked and in spite of request/summon from the survey official, the same is not opened by the person present. In the case of survey proceeding, survey team is not empowered to break the lock/seal of the box, almirah or premises etc. In such a situation, search warrant is obtained.

3. Non-compliance of summon issued under section 131(1) seeking the facility of conducting survey in terms of sub-section (6) of section 133A is also one of the situations which may lead to the conversion of survey into search.

4. In case cash and valuables are found in survey which are required to be seized but since there is no power of impounding or seizure of assets in the survey, search warrant is required to be obtained u/s 132 for effecting seizure of such assets.

Assessee having failed to satisfactorily explain the nature and possession of cash found with him at the time of survey under section 133A conducted at the airport, survey was rightly converted into search.—*Asstt. CIT* v. *Panchuram Deshmukh* [2010] 40 DTR 252 (Bilaspur) (Trib.)

Search was found justified same being in continuation of survey conducted u/s 133A which had resulted in recovery of large number of incriminating documents - *Vinod Goel* v. *Union of India* [2001] 118 Taxman 690 (P&H)

In case survey proceeding is converted into search proceeding u/s 132(1), the material impounded in survey and proceeding initially held u/s 133A shall be merged with search proceeding as held in the case of *Asstt. CIT* v. *Mangaram Chaudhary HUF* [2008] 123 ITD 359 (Hyd.-Trib.)

In the case of *Rich Udyog Network Ltd.* v. *Chief CIT & Ors.* [2016] 140 DTR (All) 200, Director of assessee failing to explain source of huge cash found during survey and documents found indicating that the assessee was engaged in the activity of providing bogus entries to various parties, whereby the assessee was accepting undisclosed cash and issued cheques or *vice versa*, survey proceedings were rightly converted into search after recording satisfaction note in accordance with law.

It has been held in the case of *Pawan Kumar Goel* v. *Union of India* [2019] 107 taxmann.com 21/265 Taxman 25 (P&H) that where copy of summons under section 131 were issued to assessee at its business premises, informing assessee that respondent tax officials wanted to carry a survey operation under section 133A & summons too indicated survey operations but procedure was converted into search and seizure which was impermissible in law. Moreover, summons were absolutely silent as to what information was required from assessee during survey operation. It was found that authorities had not demonstrated from any material as to whether assessee failed to co-operate or there was a suspicion that income had been concealed by assessee warranting resort to process of search and seizure. Therefore, since no satisfaction was ever recorded by authorities that survey had to be converted into search and seizure, action of authorities was bad in eyes of law. Further, summons issued to assessee were totally vague as no documents were mentioned which were required of assessee and neither was any other thing stated & thus, process of search and seizure conducted by respondents on business premises/residence of assessee was to be quashed and set aside.

AUTHORIZATION OF SEARCH

3.1 Authority Empowered to Authorize Search

The provision relating to authorities who are empowered to authorize search and issue search warrant is contained u/s 132(1), 132(1A) and under first and fourth proviso to section 132(1) which reads as under:

3.2 Text of Section

"132. (1) Where the Director General or Director or the Chief Commissioner or Commissioner or Additional Director or Additional Commissioner or Joint Director or Joint Commissioner in consequence of information in his possession, has reason to believe that..............

(a) ....

(b) ....

(c) ....

Then,—

(A) the Director General or Director or the Chief Commissioner or Commissioner, as the case may be, may authorize any Additional Director or Additional Commissioner or Joint Director, Joint Commissioner, Assistant Director or Deputy Director, Assistant Commissioner or Deputy Commissioner or Income-tax Officer........

(B) such Additional Director or Additional Commissioner or Joint Director, or Joint Commissioner, as the case may be, may authorize any Assistant Director or Deputy Director, Assistant Commissioner or Deputy Commissioner or Income-tax Officer,

(the officer so authorized in all cases being hereinafter referred to as the authorized officer) to—

(i) ..... to (v)...........:

Provided that where any building, place, vessel, vehicle or aircraft referred to in clause (i) is within the area of jurisdiction of any Chief Commissioner or Commissioner, but such Chief Commissioner or Commissioner has no jurisdiction over the

73

person referred to in clause (*a*) or clause (*b*) or clause (*c*), then, notwithstanding anything contained in section 120, it shall be competent for him to exercise the powers under this sub-section in all cases where he has reason to believe that any delay in getting the authorization from the Chief Commissioner or Commissioner having jurisdiction over such person may be prejudicial to the interests of the revenue :

Provided...........(second proviso):

Provided............(third proviso):

Provided also that no authorization shall be issued by the Additional Director or Additional Commissioner or Joint Director or Joint Commissioner on or after the 1st day of October, 2009 unless he has been empowered by the Board to do so.

Explanation- For the removal of doubts, it is hereby declared that the reason to believe, as recorded by the income tax authority under this sub-section, shall not be disclosed to any person or any authority or the Appellate Tribunal.

(1A) Where any Chief Commissioner or Commissioner, in consequence of information in his possession, has reason to suspect that any books of account, other documents, money, bullion, jewellery or other valuable article or thing in respect of which an officer has been authorized by the Director General or Director or any other Chief Commissioner or Commissioner or Additional Director or Additional Commissioner or Joint Director or Joint Commissioner to take action under clauses (*i*) to (*v*) of sub-section (1) are or is kept in any building, place, vessel, vehicle or aircraft not mentioned in the authorization under sub-section (1), such Chief Commissioner or Commissioner may, notwithstanding anything contained in section 120, authorize the said officer to take action under any of the clauses aforesaid in respect of such building, place, vessel, vehicle or aircraft...."

3.3 Legislative History - Significant Amendments

(*i*) Taxation Laws (Amendment) Act, 1975

Power to authorize search was granted to any such Joint Director or Joint Commissioner as may be empowered in this behalf by the Board.

First proviso was added to section 132(1) so as to provide power to Chief Commissioner or Commissioner to authorize search on the basis of territorial jurisdiction even when there is no jurisdiction over the person.

Sub-section (1A) was added to section 132 to give power to any Chief Commissioner or Commissioner not having jurisdiction over the person but in respect of any place falling in his jurisdiction when he has reason to suspect that any incriminating material is kept therein.

This sub-section was inserted to overcome a situation like one when search is authorized by Director (Investigation), say, Delhi relating to an assessee having premises, say, at Kolkata. During conduct of search at Kolkata, the authorized officer comes to know some other place within Kolkata where he has reason to suspect that incriminating material might be kept. It may not be possible for the authorized officer to obtain fresh search warrant for such new premises from Director (Investigation), Delhi. Under such situation, there may be requirement of obtaining search warrant immediately. As per section (1A), power was given to Commissioner, Kolkata to issue search warrant for such new premises, to the authorized officer.

(ii) Finance Act, 2009

Fourth proviso to section 132(1) was inserted to give powers to the Board to authorize any Additional or Joint Director or Additional or Joint Commissioner to take action under section 132(1) and all actions taken in the past by such officers even if not authorized by the Board were validated by retrospective amendment to this effect. The effect of this amendment resulted into nullification of the ratio of several judgments such as *Dr. Nalini Mahajan* v. *DIT (Investigation)* [2002] 122 Taxman 897 (Delhi), *CIT* v. *Pawan Kumar Garg* [2009] 178 Taxman 491 (Delhi), *CIT* v. *Capital Power Systems Ltd.* [2009] 222 CTR (Delhi) 47.

3.4 Objective

Search can be authorized by officers of specified higher rank so that search provisions may not be used arbitrarily. The above provisions prescribe the authorities who are empowered to authorize search and the officers who can be authorized to carry out search operation. Since search operations are of investigating nature, powers have been given to authorities having either assessment jurisdiction or territorial jurisdiction over the persons within their area.

Further, since search operations are of utmost urgency, powers have been given to any Chief Commissioner or Commissioner to issue search warrant so as to take quick action lest the evidences should be destroyed/maneuvered.

3.5 Who can issue warrant of authorization?

The above provisions regarding authorization of search are drafted in a complex manner. To understand the same properly, provisions may be summarized in the following manner:—

Section	Authority	Under What Circumstances	Against Whom	For Which Premises	Who can be authorized officer
As per section 132(1) read with fourth proviso	1- DG or D 2- CC or C 3- Addl/J D or Addl/ JC empowered by Board to do so	Has reason to believe	Has jurisdiction over the person as per section 120.	For any premise whether within his jurisdiction or not.	Additional/Joint/ Deputy/Assistant Director of income tax/, Additional/ Joint/Deputy/Assistant Commissioner of income tax, Income Tax Officer.
As per first proviso to Section 132(1)	CC or C	Has reason to believe that any delay may be prejudicial to the interest of revenue.	Not having jurisdiction over the person as per section 120	For the premises within his jurisdictions.	-DO-
As per section 132(1A)	CC or C	Has reason to suspect in respect of any other place not mentioned in the warrant of authorization, may authorize the authorized officer for such other place	Not having jurisdiction over the person as per section 120.	-DO-	-DO-
As per Section 132A	1-DG or D 2-CC or C.	Has reason to believe.	Has jurisdiction over the person as per section 120.	Requisition from the possession of any authority.	-DO-

DG- Director General of Income Tax

CC- Chief Commissioner of Income Tax

D- Director of Income Tax

C- Commissioner of Income Tax

ADDL/JD- Additional or Joint Director of Income Tax

ADDL/JC- Additional or Joint Commissioner of Income Tax

From the above, the following points may be noted:-

1. At the first instance, Director General or Director, Chief Commissioner or Commissioner, such Additional Director/Additional Commissioner, Joint Director/Joint Commissioner as empowered by the Board for this purpose may issue search warrants against

the person over whom they exercise jurisdiction as per section 120. But, once search having been authorized and being in progress, Chief Commissioner or Commissioner of any jurisdiction may issue search warrant against any person in accordance with the provisions contained in first proviso to section 132(1) and section 132(1A).

2. Powers u/s 132(1A) may be exercised by Chief Commissioner or Commissioner while search operations are in progress and the search warrant may be issued on the basis of "reason to suspect".

3. For exercising powers under first proviso to section 132(1) against a person over whom no jurisdiction is exercised as per section 120 by Chief Commissioner or Commissioner, the basic requirement of recording satisfaction on the basis of information in his possession as provided under section 132(1) shall have to be complied with.

4. Powers under section 132(1A) or under first proviso to section 132(1) can be exercised only by Chief Commissioner or Commissioner and not by Director General or Director or any other lower ranked officer.

5. It is not necessary that Commissioner will authorize only to Additional/ Joint Commissioner or Deputy/Assistant Commissioner. Similarly, it is also not necessary that higher authorities of investigation wing will authorize to lower authorities of investigation wing only. There can be authorization by Commissioner to Additional/Joint/Deputy/ Assistant Director. Similarly, Director of Income Tax may authorize to Additional/Joint/Deputy/Assistant Commissioner of Income tax or to Income tax Officer.

Powers under sub-section (1A) or first proviso to section 132 can be invoked by Chief Commissioner/Commissioner authorizing Additional/Joint/ Deputy/Assistant Director irrespective of the fact that original authorizing authority is Director General/Director of Income Tax (Investigation).

It has been held in the case of *Kishore Agrawal* v. *Dy. CIT* [2006] 9 SOT 54 (Agra-Trib.) (URO) that assessee was intercepted by the Trade Tax Author- ities (Mobile Squad) of Mathura (UP) while he was within the State of UP, it was the Director of IT (Inv.), Kanpur who had the jurisdiction and the warrant of requisition under section 132A issued by the Director of IT (Inv.), Delhi for requisition of silver ornaments seized from assessee by Trade Tax Authorities at Mathura to hand over the goods to the Department and consequent block assessment were illegal, bad in law and void *ab initio*.

It has been held in the case of *SRS Mining* v. *Union of India* 217 DTR (Mad.) 321 that as to Authorisation under section 132(1) & competent authority to issue warrant, It is not only that authorization should be of the competent authority, but it is on satisfaction of the authority that search warrant can be issued and it can be only of the competent officer and If the search warrant was not issued by the competent officer, then it would vitiate the search and accordingly, the issue would be analysed by the assessing authority while passing the assessment order afresh on remand of the case.

(i) Controversy regarding search authorized by Additional/Joint Director, Additional/Joint Commissioner

Earlier there was a conflict of opinion between different High Courts on the issue whether Additional Director/Additional Commissioner is also a Joint Director/Joint Commissioner as per section 2(*28C*)/2(*28D*) and whether Additional Director/Additional Commissioner was entitled to issue search warrant. Another controversy was as to whether Board has empowered Joint Director/Joint Commissioner to authorize search or not and in the absence of such empowerment, search authorized by Joint Director/Joint Commissioner can be said to be valid search.

In the case of *Dr. Nalini Mahajan* v. *DIT (Investigation)* [2002] 122 Taxman 897 (Delhi), High Court held that Additional Director could not be treated as Joint Director under section 2(*28D*) and was therefore, not authorized to issue search warrant. This view was reiterated by Hon'ble Delhi High Court in the case of *CIT* v. *Pawan Kumar Garg* [2009] 178 Taxman 491, *CIT* v. *Capital Power Systems Ltd.* [2009] 222 CTR 47 (Delhi) to the effect that in the absence of any empowerment by the Board, search authorized by Joint Director/Joint Commissioner was not a valid search.

It has been held in the case of *Director of IT* v. *Dr. Nalini Mahajan* [2009] 181 Taxman 24 (SC) that in view of the fact that CIT in exercise of powers under section 132B, has released cash, jewellery and books of account seized during search impugned, the question whether the Addl. Director (Inv.) has the requisite jurisdiction to authorize any officer to effect search and seizure in purported exercise of his power conferred upon him under section 132(1) is held to have become in fructuous and is not examined.

However, Allahabad High Court had taken a contrary view in the case of *Arun Kumar Maheshwari* v. *ITO* [2006] 285 ITR 179. Punjab and Haryana High Court also said in the case of *Vinod Goel* v. *Union of India* [2001] 118 Taxman 690 that an Additional Director of Income Tax has power to authorize search.

However this controversy has been sought to be set at rest first by making amendment by the Finance Act, 1998 with effect from 1st October 1998 by way of inserting section 2(*28C*) and 2(*28D*), laying down that Joint Commissioner means and includes Additional Commissioner and Joint Director means and includes Additional Director and later on, by bringing retrospective amendment to section 132(1) by Finance (No. 2) Act, 2009 according to which it was provided to validate all such searches authorized by any Additional Director/

Additional Commissioner, Joint Director or Joint Commissioner. However for prospective searches, it was provided by way of insertion of fourth proviso to section 132(1) by Finance (No. 2) Act, 2009 w.e.f. 1.4.2009 that no authorization shall be issued by the Additional Director/Additional Commissioner or Joint Director/Joint Commissioner or on after the 1st day of April, 2009 unless he has been empowered by the Board to do so.

It may be noted that as per Notification No. 82/2009/F. No./142/23/2009-SO dated 11-11-2009 reported at [2011] 227 CTR (St.) 22 (All.), all Additional Directors of Income Tax and Joint Directors of Income Tax have been authorized to issue search warrant. The notification reads as under:

> "S.O. 2879(E)- In exercise of the powers conferred by the fourth proviso to sub-section (1) of section 132 of the Income-tax Act, 1961 (43 of 1961), the Central Board of Direct Taxes hereby empowers all the Additional Directors of Income Tax and Joint Directors of Income tax working under the Director General of Income-tax (Investigation) and Director General of Income-tax (Intelligence) to issue authorization under sub-section (1) of section 132 of the Income-tax Act, 1961 (43 of 1961)."

It has been held in the case of *Smt. Vijay Dhir* v. *Director of Income-tax* [2012] 20 taxmann.com 827 (All.) that Additional Director of Income-tax had jurisdiction to authorize search in 2003 in view of the retrospective amendment made in 2009 and the fact that Form 45 did not include Director of Income-tax is not relevant. In view of the evidence that there was reason to believe that income had not been disclosed, search was valid.

It has been held in the case of *CIT* v. *Trilochan Pratap Singh* [2013] 30 taxmann.com 405/213 Taxman 424 (All.) that in view of the amendment of section 132(1) w.e.f. 1-6-1994, Additional Director has power to issue authorization.

(*ii*) **Misinterpretation of clause (B) to section 132(1) used for issue of subsequent search warrant**

Clauses (*A*) and (*B*) to section 132(1) have been inserted to provide the competent authority to authorize the other income tax authorities subordinate in rank to them to be appointed as "authorized officer" to conduct search. Clause (*A*) provides that Director General or Director or the Chief Commissioner or Commissioner as the case may be, may authorize any authority subordinate to them in rank *i.e.*, Additional Director or Additional Commissioner or Joint Director or Joint Commissioner or Deputy Director or Deputy Commissioner, Assistant Director or Assistant Commissioner or Income-tax Officer to act as authorized officer to conduct search. Clause (*B*) provides that **such** Additional Director or Joint Director or Additional Commissioner or Joint Commissioner as the case may be, may authorize any authority subordinate to them in rank *i.e.* Deputy Director or Deputy Commissioner, Assistant Director or Assistant Commissioner, or Income Tax Officer to act as authorized officer to conduct search. The use of the word "**such**" before Additional Director or Additional Commissioner or Joint Director or Joint Commissioner in clause (*B*) refers to such Additional Director or Additional Commissioner or Joint Director or Joint Commissioner who are empowered by the Board to authorize search. In certain quarters, the word "**such**" in clause (*B*) is misinterpreted to mean such Additional Director or Additional Commissioner or Joint Director or Joint Commissioner who are authorized by Director General or Director or the Chief Commissioner or Commissioner to conduct search as provided under clause (*A*) and it is interpreted that such Additional Director or Additional Commissioner or Joint Director or Joint Commissioner authorized by Director General or Director or the Chief Commissioner or Commissioner to conduct search may in turn authorize any other officer subordinate in rank to them *i.e.,* Deputy Director or Deputy Commissioner or Assistant Director or Assistant Commissioner or Income Tax Officer to conduct search.

In our considered opinion, the above view is not correct and subsequent search warrant cannot be issued by Additional Director or Additional Commissioner or Joint Director or Joint Commissioner unless they themselves are empowered by the Board to authorize search and "reason to believe" is formed by them with respect to the person before authorizing search.

3.6 Who can be Authorized Officer?

Authorized officer is the officer who is authorized by the competent authority under section 132(1) to conduct search at the premises of the assessee. The name of the authorized officer is mentioned in the search warrant. There can be more than one and as many as required, authorized officers deputed to conduct search at a particular premises. Any of the following officers can be appointed as authorized officer in case search is authorized by Principal Director General or Director General or Principal Director or Director or Principal Chief Commissioner or Chief Commissioner or Principal Commissioner or Commissioner:

1. Joint Director including Additional Director and Joint Commissioner including Additional Commissioner.

2. Deputy Director or Deputy Commissioner.

3. Assistant Director or Assistant Commissioner

4. Income tax Officer

In the case of search warrant being authorized by Additional/Joint Director or Additional/Joint Commissioner under section 132(1), the authorized officer may be

1. Deputy Director or Deputy Commissioner
2. Assistant Director or Assistant Commissioner
3. Income tax Officer

The following points may be noted:

1. Any officer authorized to conduct search is called authorized officer.
2. Under section 132(1A), the same officer who has been authorized originally in the initial authorization or any other officer can be authorized officer.
3. It is not necessary that officer to be authorized should be the subordinate of the authorizing authority posted or working under him in the hierarchy.
4. Income tax inspector cannot be an authorized officer. For this reason, statement recorded under section 132(4) by Income tax Inspector is not a valid statement and does not have any evidentiary value.

The authorized officer is the officer who has to conduct actual search operation. He has to exercise powers and undertake actions as mentioned under clause (*i*) to clause (*v*) of section 132(1).

It has been held in the case of *K.V. Padmanabhan* v. *Asstt. CIT* [2019] 107 taxmann.com 24/265 Taxman 36 (Mag.) that one warrant of authorization can specify more than one officer.

3.7 Search warrant can be issued against whom?

Search warrant can be issued against any person who is falling within the scope of either one or more of the conditions as mentioned under clause (*a*), (*b*) or (*c*) of section 132(1) and against whom "reason to believe" has been formed. Search warrant can be issued against any person who is in possession of incriminating books of account, other documents or assets. The person may be in possession of assets as owner or in some other capacity such as possessing the asset on behalf of some other person such as agent on behalf of principal or employee on behalf of employer. Search warrant in the name of agent or employee, who is in possession of asset, can be issued only when identity of actual owner is not established.

(*i*) **Search warrant against person in possession or owner of the asset**

There may be cases when a person who is owner of the asset is not in possession of the asset and the asset is in possession of some other person on his behalf. For example, cash belonging to the assessee company kept at the residence of employee of the company. In case owner of the asset is known to the department, search warrant has to be issued in the name of the owner and "reason to believe" has to be formed with respect to such person.

But in case actual owner of the asset is not known to the department, search warrant can be issued only in the name of the person who is in possession of the asset *e.g.*, an employee carrying unaccounted cash is caught at airport. Search warrant can be issued in his name since he is in possession of undisclosed asset. When it is found that cash seized from his possession is actually belonging or owned by some company, income relating to the same can be assessed in the hands of the company invoking provisions of section 153C.

In the case of search of bank locker, locker is taken on rent by the assessee from bank. Search warrant is issued in the name of assessee for bank locker giving the address of the premises in which bank locker is situated.

It has been held in the case of *Zinzuwadia and Sons* v. *Deputy CIT* [2019] 108 taxmann.com 42/265 Taxman 261/419 ITR 169 (Guj.) that search is person specific and not location specific.

(ii) Search warrant against NRI

"Any person" includes even a non-resident Indian and he would be amenable to search and seizure.

[*Ram Kumar Dhanuka* v. *Union of India* [2001] 118 Taxman 535 (Raj.)]

(iii) Search warrant in the name of deceased person

Search warrant being issued in the name of a dead person and Panchnama also prepared in the name of dead person, the search and the authorization were invalid and void *ab initio*, so also block assessment under section 158BC read with section 144 in pursuance thereof. [*CIT* v. *Rakesh Kumar Mukesh Kumar* [2008] 13 DTR 209 (P&H)]

It has been held in the case of *Gunjan Girishbhai Mehta* v. *Director of Investigation & Ors.* [2017] 80 taxmann.com 23/247 Taxman 22/150 DTR 65 (SC) that Legal heir of the deceased not having raised the issue of invalidity of the search warrant issued in the name of dead person at any point of time prior to the issuance of notice under section 158BD and even participated in the assessment proceedings under section 158BC, the proceedings under section 158BD are not invalid

(iiia) Search warrant in the name of non-existing company

It has been held in the case of BDR Builders and Developers (P.) Ltd. v. Asstt. CIT [2017] 85 taxmann.com 146 (Delhi) that in search & seizure assessment in search cases, where amalgamation of companies has taken place, warrant of authorisation and panchnama issued in

the name of transferor company after it ceased to exist is bad and proceedings are *void ab initio.*

(iv) Search warrant against minor

A minor is usually not required to file his income tax return. Therefore, he cannot make disclosure of his assets to the Income Tax department. In case there is information available with the department regarding some undisclosed assets owned or possessed by the minor, search warrant should be issued in the name of the parent in whose return of income, income of the minor is required to be clubbed and to be filed with the department. It is only such parent who can be assessed under section 153A with respect to the undisclosed income relating to the minor. However, in case the minor is independently assessed with the income tax department with respect to his income, search warrant can be issued in the name of the minor.

(v) Search warrant against professionals

Board has issued instructions the extracts from which are reproduced below:

Matters relating to search and seizure

    1. With a view to focus on high revenue yielding cases and to make the optimum use of manpower, the Board has decided that officers deployed in the Investigation Wing should restructure their activities. They should henceforth strictly adhere to the following guidelines:

        ***   ***   ***

    (iii) Taxpayers who are professionals of excellence should not be searched without there being compelling evidence and confirmation of substantial tax evasion.

        ***   ***   ***

Instruction : No. 7, dated 30-7-2003.

(vi) Search warrant in joint name

"There is no legal bar in issuance of a common authorization."

[*Dr. Oswald Anthony* v. *CIT* [2004] 141 Taxman 520 (Pat.)]

"There is no merit in contention that whenever any authorization is to be issued, it should be with reference to one single individual or a person and not in respect of a number of persons or individuals."

"It is not necessary that one authorization each should be issued with respect to one single individual or a person. On the other hand, one authorization can be issued in respect of a number of persons or individuals. As per provisions of section 2 of General Clauses Act, 1897, singular includes plural and there is no prohibition against issuance of common authorization when the competent authority has reason to believe that a number of persons are involved in inter-connected transactions as reflected from the *prima facie* material available with the competent authority"

[*Madhupuri Corpn.* v. *Prabhat Jha, Dy. DIT (Investigation)* [2002] 125 Taxman 309 (Guj.)]

In the case of *CIT* v. *Smt. Vandana Verma* [2010] 186 Taxman 88 (All.), it has been held that in case search warrant is issued in the joint names, assessment cannot be made in their individual capacity. In case, Revenue wants to assess the persons in their individual capacity, search warrant should be issued separately with respect to each person. However, in our opinion, this decision requires reconsideration as the issue in question is debatable.

It has been held in the case of *Rajat Tradecom India (P) Ltd.* v. *Dy. CIT* [2009] 120 ITD 48 (Indore-Trib.) as to the joint search warrant including the assessee's name that search warrant having been issued in the joint names of a person and the assessee who were carrying on business from the same premises and the premises having been searched and panchnama so prepared, it could not be said that there was no search in the case of assessee. Hence assessment under section 153A in the case of assessee was valid.

It has been held in the case of *Jose Cyriac* v. *CIT* [2012] 20 taxmann.com 738 (Ker.) that there is nothing wrong in authorizing search of a group of concerns by a warrant issued under section 132. All that are required to be stated in the search warrant is precise details about the assessees and the persons to be searched which are contained in the warrants issued in these cases.

It has been held in the case of *Naresh Chand Baid* v. *Asstt. CIT* [2012] 23 taxmann.com 378/209 Taxman 47 (Mag.) (Chd.) that the authorization under section 132(1) in joint names is valid and the authorities were competent to conduct search in the premises of the partners of the firm when the names of all the partners including the assessee were specifically mentioned in the warrant of authorization issued in the case of firm.

The controversy in this regard has been settled by legislation by retrospective introduction (from 1-4-1976) of section 292CC by Finance Act, 2012. Sub-section (1) of section 292CC provides that "*notwithstanding anything contained in this Act, it shall not be necessary to issue an authorisation under section 132 or make a requisition u/s 132A separately in the name of each person.*" It is further provided that *where an authorisation under section 132 or requisition under section 132A has been issued mentioning therein the name of more than one person, the mention of such names of more than one person*

on such authorisation or requisition shall not be deemed to construe
that it was issued in the name of an Association of Persons or Body of
Individuals consisting of such persons. Such amendment seems to
have been brought to nullify the above decision of Allahabad High
Court in the case of *CIT* v. *Smt. Vandana Verma* [2010] 186 Taxman 88.

It has been held in the case of *CIT* v. *Khyber Foods* [2012] 23 taxmann.
com 27/208 Taxman 140 (Mag.) (Ker.) that as to the validity *vis-à-vis*
warrant in joint names/group name, search warrant issued in the
name of group of concerns, specifically mentioning the premises to
be searched where all the concerns are housed could not be said to
be invalid.

It has been held in the case of *CIT* v. *Devesh Singh* [2012] 24 taxmann.
com 26/209 Taxman 267 (All.) (FB) that in view of insertion of section 292CC with retrospective effect from 1st April, 1976, where the
warrant of authorization is issued jointly, it shall not be construed
that it is issued in the name of AOP or BOI consisting of such person
and assessment can be made individually.

(vii) Premises Jointly Occupied

Instances are very common when residential premises are in joint
occupation of several relatives *i.e.* the warrant may be in the name
of the father but separate portions of that premises may be occupied by his sons/daughter-in-law, daughters/sons-in-law. In such a
situation, immediate steps must be taken by the authorized officer
for securing separate warrants for such persons or such portions of
the residential premises so as to carry out valid search and seizure
against such other persons, if required. However, in practice, search
with respect to other persons residing jointly is also undertaken by
the authorized officer on the pretext that such other persons may
have connection or relation with the affairs of the target person and
they may have secreted with themselves any incriminating material
belonging to the target person.

There may be instances where numbers of companies or firms
belonging to the same group are listed at the common address. In
such a case the search of the whole premises may be valid but for
making a legal seizure of the assets or books of account and documents belonging to the other companies or firms independently in
their name, another warrant of authorization must be secured from
the competent authority and be served upon the chief executive or
partner of the other company or firm. However, in practice, seizure
of books of account and documents or assets belonging to other
entities is made in the Panchnama of the target company itself on
the pretext that such material may have connection or relation with
the affairs of the target company.

Hon'ble Karnataka High Court in the case of *Nenmal Shankarlal Partner* v. *Asstt. CIT* [1992] 62 Taxman 529 have held as under :—

> "There is no reference at all in the warrant of authorization that such documents or money, jewellery or other valuable article or thing is in the possession of the petitioner in his individual capacity. As a necessary consequence, the mere mention of residential premises does not enable the department to effect seizure either of gold jewellery or other articles or documents and hence it must be held that the petitioner's contention that the warrant of authorization does not enable the department to effect search or seizure of the property belonging to him on the basis of warrant issued in the name of the firm, no warrant in the name of the petitioner at all having been issued is valid and tenable. The seizure was held invalid for want of necessary authorization."

In the case of *Harbhajan Singh Chadha & Ors.* v. *Director of IT & Ors.* [2015] 122 DTR (All) 146 (HC), it has been held that where warrant of authorisation indicated premises where search and seizure operation was to be conducted and said premises had not been partitioned by metes and bounds, while searching said premises, search of portions occupied by petitioners in said premises was valid and proper, even though their names were not mentioned in authorisation of search and in such case provisions of section 158BD would be attracted.

3.8 Manner of drawing search warrant

(*i*) **Authorization to be in writing with signature and seal of the authorizing officer.** Sub-rule (2A) of rule 112 states that authorization referred to in sub-rule (2) shall be in writing with the signature of the officer issuing the authorization and shall bear his seal.

(*ii*) **Search warrant to specify name of person**

Warrant of authorization must specify the person in respect of whom it is issued - [*Southern Herbals Ltd.* v. *DIT (Investigation)* [1994] 207 ITR 55 (Kar.)]

In pursuance of a search warrant in the name of the firm, residential premises of a partner cannot be searched under section 132(1). Search of the premises of the partner should have been specifically authorized.

[*Nenmal Shankarlal Partner* v. *Asstt. CIT (Inv.)* [1992] 62 Taxman 529 (Kar.)]

(*iii*) **Correct address of premise/place under search to be mentioned**

It is very important that exact description of the premises to be searched is properly mentioned in the search warrant. Any mistake in mentioning the correct address of the premises may create uncontrollable situation. It may defeat very purpose of conducting search for a particular person.

In search warrant, there is separate column to mention the address of the premises to be searched. Any premises can be covered in search warrant on the basis of reason to suspect, if incriminating material is kept therein.

It has been held in the case of *Principal CIT* v. *Associated Mining Co.* [2019] 108 taxmann.com 564 (Kar.) that authorised officer can search any place mentioned in authorisation where he suspects that books of account belonging to assessee are kept and as such, mere change of address of assessee even being in know how of department by itself would not vitiate or invalidate search conducted under section 132. Search conducted at premises in which assessee may not be carrying on business would not nullify search.

(iv) Mention of name of assessee and premises - Both

In the search warrant, name of the person against whom warrant is being issued is necessary. Mere mention of the premises to be searched is not sufficient. Name of the person with respect to whom premises are to be searched is required to be mentioned for issuing a valid search warrant.

On the other hand, mentioning only the name of assessee without the address of the premises is also not enough. The correct address of the premises which is required to be searched has to be mentioned on the search warrant to get entrance into the premises.

For the purpose of the Act, the firm and its partners are different entities. The firm itself is a person for the purpose of the Act. When the legal title might have been with the person whose income or property is sought to be taxed and physical possession was with another person, it is in respect of such person's premises that warrant of authorization should have been issued. In the present case, legal title is not traced to the firm nor is possession that of the firm but it is purely that of the petitioner partner. Therefore, when a search was effected in the residential premises of the petitioner-partner, the warrant of authorization should have enabled the search of the residential premises of the petitioner. But, on the other hand, the warrant of authorization is only against the petitioner firm for not having produced the books of account or other documents and which are not likely to be produced or are in possession of the firm. There is no reference in the warrant of authorization that such documents or assets are in possession of the petitioner-partner in his individual capacity.

As a necessary consequence, the mere mention of residential premises does not enable the Department to affect seizure either of gold, jewellery or other articles or documents. Hence, it must be held that the petitioner's contention that the warrant of authorization does not enable the Department to effect search or seizure of the property belonging to him on the basis of warrant issued in the name of the firm, no warrant in the name of petitioner-partner at all having been issued, is valid. [*Nenmal Shankarlal Partner* v. *Asstt. CIT (Inv.)* [1992] 62 Taxman 529 (Kar.)]

(v) Subject matter not to be stated

Hon'ble courts have been uniform in holding that it is not necessary to specify the particulars of documents of assets to be seized in the warrant of authorization. Neither the Income-tax Act, nor the Income-tax Rules prescribed any such conditions. In fact, it would be unrealistic to foresee as to what documents would be discovered during search and which of them may be relevant or useful for appropriate proceedings under the Income-tax Act. It is only to find such books of account, documents and assets which would show the undisclosed income, assets or secret activities that the search itself is undertaken. Therefore, to expect that the documents or assets to be seized must find mention in the warrant, is uncalled for.

Warrant of authorization need not to specify documents to be seized. In the following case, Supreme Court reversed High Court's decision of holding issuance of search warrant as invalid. The Apex Court held, on the basis of affidavit filed by the petitioners and revenue officers, that Commissioner was justified in issuing warrant of authorization on the basis of report of the ITO and other information and not on the directions of the officers. Held as under:

> "The Act and the rules do not require that the warrant of authorization should specify the particulars of documents and books of account. A general authorization to search for and seize documents and books of account relevant to or useful for any proceeding complies with the requirements of the Act and the Rules. It is for the officer making the search to exercise his judgment and seize or not to seize any documents or books of account."

[*ITO* v. *Seth Bros.* [1969] 74 ITR 836 (SC)]

> "It was held by Madras High Court that the warrant of search need not specify the particular item or document to be searched. It was also held that the authority need not disclose the reasons or grounds for formation of belief and that actual physical search should precede the seizure."

[*I. Devarajan* v. *Tamil Nadu Farmers Service Co-operative Federation* [1981] 131 ITR 506 (Mad.)]

(vi) Grounds for search action not to be stated

Hon'ble Calcutta High Court in the case of *Mamchand & Company* v. *CIT* [1970] 76 ITR 217 have held that it is not necessary to record in the warrant the reasons which led the competent authority to issue warrant of authorization.

The grounds which induced reasonable belief need not be stated in the warrant of authorization.

[*Dr. Partap Singh* v. *Director of Enforcement* [1985] 22 Taxman 30 (SC)]

> "It is not necessary to state the reasons in the warrant, nor is it necessary to specify the documents or books of account, etc., which would be the subject matter of search and seizure. Provided the Commissioner indicates broadly the nature of the documents and the goods in regard to which the officer authorized by him should make a search, it is not necessary that he should make the search himself when he authorizes such officers to make the search and seizure. It is the officers who are to decide whether the documents and goods are such as to come within the scope of the seizure contemplated under section 132 of the Act. But this must be done on the basis of the reasons communicated to them by the Commissioner and not beyond it. If it is so done, it will be taken to be act of the Commissioner himself."

[*Subir Roy* v. *S.K. Chattopadhyay* [1986] 29 Taxman 13 (Cal.)]

(vii) Separate search warrant for each premises

There has to be separate search warrant for each premises, place, vehicle or bank locker situated independently. Search warrant is a pre-requisite to make entry into the premises. Therefore, there has to be a separate search warrant for each premise. A search warrant against a person may contain addresses of many premises belonging to such person to be searched. In such a situation, there has to be separate copy of search warrant for each premise to get ingress into the premises and for showing and getting signature of the person on the search warrant.

(viii) Issue of blank search warrant

Use of blank search warrant by the authorized officer to be filled later or during the course of search as per new facts coming to his knowledge has been strictly prohibited and held to be illegal. Under such circumstances, it cannot be said that authorizing officer has formed valid reason to believe against the person or for the premises and, therefore, the whole action of search may be vitiated.

The onus to prove would lie on the person who is alleging that blank search warrant has been used by the authorized officer. If there is any such case, proper evidence of the actual facts should be available to prove the allegation:

> "One of the grounds on which the constitutional validity of section 132 of the Income-tax Act, 1961, has been upheld is that no warrant of authorization for search can be issued without the satisfaction of as high an officer in the official hierarchy of the Income Tax department as the Commissioner of Income Tax himself. I cannot conceive of a more serious outrage being committed on the statutory safeguard provided by Parliament than a general warrant of authorization being issued by the Commissioner without filling in the name of the person whose premises are sought to be searched. The issue of such a warrant conclusively proves that the officer who signed it was not satisfied that such a warrant should issue, but merely gave such a general warrant out of some lurking suspicion based either on rumours or on something less serious than that. From the practical point of view, the warrant, on the basis of which the premises of the present petitioner were searched, could at the sweet will of the officer in whose hands it happened to be used for anyone he liked and for conducting a general search for fishing out anything that may fall to his hands so that from the material so found a case could, if necessary, be made out against him. The action of the Commissioner in permitting use of a signed blank warrant is "betraying the confidence reposed in him by the drastic provision of section 132 and throwing all sense of propriety and responsibility to the winds on mere suspicion or pretence." *Jagmohan Mahajan* v. *CIT* [1976] 103 ITR 579 (Punj. & Har.)

Rule 112 implies that the Commissioner should append his signature to the warrant only after it is completely filled up and even the plea that it was filled up after satisfaction required by Commissioner was recorded and communicated, even if true, cannot make it valid. *H.L. Sibal* v. *CIT* [1975] 101 ITR 112 (Punj. & Har.)

Use of such a blank form was held to be illegal and seized materials were ordered to be returned. *Manmohan Krishan Mahajan* v. *CIT* [1977] 107 ITR 420 (Punj. & Har.)

(*ix*) Search warrant for benami business concerns

In the case of *Jai Bhagwan Om Parkash* v. *Director of Inspection* [1993] 67 Taxman 33 (P&H), it was held that search of a premises could be carried out where the assessee carried on its business under distinct trade name on the basis of a warrant of authorization issued in its own name.

(x) Panchnama may be in the name of bank account of the assessee

In the case of *Asstt. CIT* v. *Budhiya Marketing P. Ltd.* [2015] 126 DTR (Kol. 'B') 161 (Trib.), it has been held that Warrant of authorisation having been issued in the name of the assessee *vis-a-vis* Panchnama in the name of bank account of the assessee, the search cannot be held to be invalid simply on the basis that the Panchnama has made in reference to the bank account of the assessee instead of assessee itself.

3.9 Nature of search warrant

(i) Search warrant qua-assessee or qua-premises

There always remains a dilemma in the mind of assessee that search warrant issued in the name of a particular person is only to look into the evidences or material relating to such person or the whole of the premises for which search warrant has been issued is covered within the scope of search. Whether authorized officer has power to look into affairs and belongings relating to any person residing or available in the premises at the time of search?

Primarily search warrant is issued qua-assessee since "reason to believe" is formed with respect to the assessee. The authorized officer is empowered to look into the affairs of the assessee and collect evidences of incriminating material relating to the assessee.

For doing so, he is required to search whole of the premises for which he is authorized and search warrant has been issued. In the process, if any incriminating material is found from the possession of any other person within the premises, the same can be seized by the authorized officer in case he has suspicion that such material may have connection with or relating to the assessee.

In case there is any other material coming to the knowledge of authorized officer which is not relating to the assessee or which cannot have any connection with the assessee, such material does not come within the scope of search and cannot be seized. In case any books of account or document or assets relating to some other person are seized clearly recording the fact that such material belongs to third person and does not have any connection or relation with the assessee, such seizure is liable to be held illegal since the same is not covered within the scope of authorization of search. However, in practice it has been seen that any incriminating material relating to other person is also seized by the authorized officer on the pretext that such material may have some connection or bearing with respect to the person searched.

It has been held in the case of *Principal CIT v. Associated Mining Company* 184 DTR (Kar) 364 that though premises searched were not belonging to assessee but search of the premises took place where the assessee firm earlier carried on its business and where books of account of assessee firm had been found and seized, was valid, more so when premises which has been searched is the same premises as indicated in the authorization.

Various aspects relating to above proposition have been discussed in detail at respective places in various chapters.

(*ii*) No warrant for roving enquiry

Search warrant cannot be issued for roving or fishing enquiries but can be issued only when there exist a good ground for believing that further proceedings may have to be taken. [*Balwant Singh v. R. D. Shah, Director of Inspection* [1969] 71 ITR 550 (Delhi)].

(*iii*) Application of mind

As search and seizure are serious matters, the warrant of authorization should not be issued in a laconic manner.

[*V. S. Kuttan Pillai v. Ramakrishnan* AIR 1980 SC 185]

(*iv*) No search without search warrant

Where there was no search warrant against the firm, no search would be conducted against the firm on the basis of search warrant in the name of the partner. [*K.R. Modi & Co. v. Dy. DIT (Inv.)* [2005] 272 ITR 587 (Cal.)]

(*v*) Source of information not to be disclosed

Source of information need not to be disclosed at the stage of issue of search warrant. It is not a part of the duty of the revenue authorities to disclose to the person who challenges the warrant of authorization as to what materials were available against him, which had led to the issuance of the warrant of authorization. It is only when the authorities concerned resolve to impose tax or penalties, etc., that they would have to disclose to the person concerned as to why tax or penalty was being imposed.

[*M. S. Associates v. Union of India* [2005] 147 Taxman 172 (Gauhati)]

In the case of *Harbhajan Singh Chadha v. DIT* [2015] 58 taxmann.com 21/231 Taxman 735/[2016] 380 ITR 100 (All.), it has been held that disclosure of material or information to persons against whom action under section 132 is taken is not mandatory and it is only where petitioner furnishes adequate and cogent material in support of his denial of a valid information that Court can justifiably call upon department to disclose information.

Where information received on first date of search by itself caused a reasonable belief for issuance of warrant of authorisation against petitioners for search of their lockers, search and seizure of petitioners' lockers was perfectly valid.

3.10 Whether warrant is required to be served

Warrant of authorization is only shown to the person to be searched and his signature in evidence thereof is obtained. There is no requirement to serve copy of search warrant to the assessee. Assessee does not have the right to insist to get the copy of search warrant. Sub-rule (3) of rule 112 only requires production of search warrant and does not require the copy of the same to be supplied.

There is no provision in the Act or Rules for providing copy of authorization of warrant to the assessee. All that the law requires is that the authority or warrant must be produced before the commencement of the proceedings of search.

[*Jain & Jain* v. *Union of India* [1982] 8 Taxman 48 (Bom.), *V.K. Jain* v. *Union of India* [1975] 98 ITR 469 (Delhi)].

In the case of *Genom Biotech (P.) Ltd.* v. *DIT (Investigation)* [2009] 180 Taxman 395/224 CTR 270 (Bom.), it has been held that a copy of the information or the satisfaction note need not be furnished to the petitioners.

Warrant of authorization is not required to be delivered or furnished to the person against whom it is issued. [*Southern Herbals Ltd.* v. *DIT (Investigation)* [1994] 207 ITR 55 (Kar.)]

"This court is of the view that it was not necessary to supply the same to the petitioners beforehand provided they had the occasion to have and see the said warrants at the time of search" [*Subir Roy* v. *S.K. Chattopadhyay* [1986] 29 Taxman 13 (Cal.)]

Vide Para 7 of the Board's Circular Letter F. No. 15/156/65-IT (Inv.), dated 13-8-1965, it was stated that it was not necessary to serve on the person whose premises are searched, a copy of warrant of authorization.

On reconsideration of the matter, in consultation with Ministry of Law, the Board is advised that normally the search warrant is only required to be produced to the person whose premises are searched and it is not necessary that a copy of the search warrant should be supplied to him. If, however, a writ petition is filed in the High Court challenging the validity of the search and the High Court directs that a copy of the search warrant should be furnished to the person whose premises are searched, it should be complied with.

[Circular No. 530 [F. No. 286/30/72-IT *(Inv.)*], dated 22-3-1973 from CBDT].

In our considered opinion, the practice of not serving the copy of authorization of search to the person searched is undesirable. When a drastic action like search is being undertaken against a person, the authorization on the basis of which such action is being undertaken is an important document and there does not seem to be valid rationale for not supplying copy of the authorization to the person searched. There may be rationale in not showing or supplying copy of the satisfaction note prepared by the competent authority to the person searched since the information is collected from the confidential sources and disclosure of the identity of the informers may create lot of other unwanted problems. But, copy of the authorization letter does not contain any such confidential details. It is a document on the basis of which legal authority to conduct search is derived by the authorized officer and in our opinion, assessee should have right to obtain copy of the authorization.

(i) Whether assessee can ask for copy of satisfaction note

Satisfaction note recorded by the authorizing officer forming "reason to believe" regarding undisclosed income etc. u/s 132(1) relating to the assessee, is confidential in nature. Assessee cannot ask for or inspect or obtain copy of the same. Even in the case of writ petition challenging validity of search, when the Courts summon the record from the department, satisfaction note is not shown to the assessee. The judges see the record and satisfaction note by themselves and form their opinion regarding existence of information on the basis of which "reason to believe" has been formed. Confidentiality is one of the significant ingredients of successful action under section 132 and break down of confidentiality before or after the search can be disastrous. If confidentiality is breached before search, the action could become a fiasco and if confidentiality is breached after the search, it may create serious situation with regard to the safety of informer's life and person.

There have been divergent views regarding rationale for not supplying copy of reasons recorded to the assessee in search cases. One can argue that to meet the ends of justice and satisfy the assessee regarding validity of search action taken against him, copy of reasons should be communicated to him. Observations of Delhi High Court in L.R. Gupta's case imply that the reason recorded in the satisfaction note should be made available to the assessee by the court so that the assessee can base his contentions thereon. But this may not be done by a Court in a case where the Court is satisfied about their existence and relevance.

Patna High Court dismissing the writ petition held that the document and information on the basis of which the authority had arrived at a satisfaction for conducting the search and seizure could not be disclosed to the assessee as it would hamper the enquiry pending against them. [*Ram Swarup Sahu* v. *CIT* [1992] 196 ITR 841 (Pat.)]

In the case of *Mamchand & Co.* v. *CIT* [1970] 76 ITR 217 (Cal.), it was held that there is no provision in law which requires reason to be communicated to the assessee.

In the case of *Dr. Partap Singh* v. *Director of Enforcement* [1985] 22 Taxman 30 (SC), it was held that the material on which the belief is founded may be secret, may be obtained through intelligence or occasionally be conveyed orally by informants, and it is not obligatory upon the officer to disclose this material on a mere allegation of the petitioner in his writ petition that there was no material against him on which the reasons to believe could be grounded.

It has been held in the case of *MD Overseas Ltd.* v. *Director General of Income-Tax* [2011] 10 taxmann.com 30/198 Taxman 136 (All.) that assessee is entitled to know reasons for search.

However, the above issue has been set at rest by the amendment made by the Finance Act, 2017 with retrospective effect from 1-4-1962 by inserting an *Explanation* to section 132 by clarifying that the reason to believe, as recorded by the Income tax Authority under section 132(1) shall not be disclosed to any person or any authority or the appellate tribunal.

(*ii*) **Whether copy of search warrant and/or satisfaction note can be obtained under RTI Act**

After enactment of Right to Information Act, 2005, it will be interesting to examine whether copy of search warrant and satisfaction note can be obtained by the person who has been searched.

Right to Information Act, 2005 has been enacted by the Parliament so as to give right to the citizens of the country to obtain the information from any of the government authorities regarding their functioning and the actions taken or not taken. RTI Act has the power to lead to transparency and accountability in governance. However such right of the citizens is protected and made subject to non-disclosure of confidential information as given under section 8 of the said Act. There is no specific mention in the RTI Act regarding the supply or otherwise of the search warrant and the satisfaction note to the person searched under the Income-tax Act.

In our opinion, it may be possible to have certified copy of search warrant since this is the document on the basis of which search was authorized and copy was shown to the assessee and his signature on the warrant was obtained. Such warrant of authorization does not contain any confidential information which can be protected under the exceptions of RTI Act.

Section 8(g) and (h) of RTI Act, 2005 provides that there shall be no obligation to give any citizen any information, the disclosure of which would endanger the life or physical safety of any person or identify the source of information or assistance given in confidence for law enforcement or security purposes or information which would impede the process of investigation or apprehension or prosecution of the offenders.

Thus, "satisfaction note" being confidential in nature may not fall within the purview of RTI Act due to the clauses (g) and (h) of section 8 thereof and the assessee may not be able to get the copy of the same. Even when satisfaction note is called for by the High Court in case of writ to decide validity of search, satisfaction note is not shown to the assessee and its contents are not disclosed to the assessee. Their lordships themselves go through the satisfaction note and decide on the issue whether it has been recorded legally to authorize search.

There seems to be rationale in not supplying the copy of satisfaction note to the assessee but there does not seem to be any justifiable ground for not supplying the copy of search warrant to the assessee.

It has been held in the case of *MD Overseas Ltd.* v. *Director General of Income-Tax* [2011] 10 taxmann.com 30/198 Taxman 136 (All.) that as to the information regarding search, Right to Information Act is not applicable.

3.11 Mistake in drawing search warrant

(i) Non-striking of irrelevant portions of the warrant

Hon'ble Madras High Court in the case of *I. Devarajan* v. *Tamil Nadu Farmers Service Co-operative Federation* [1981] 131 ITR 506 and Hon'ble Calcutta High Court in *Dwarka Prosad Agarwalla* v. *Director of Inspection* [1981] 7 Taxman 299 have held that failure to strike out inapplicable portions in warrants in some cases may be a mere regularity, not vitiating the validity. Hon'ble High Court have further held that where the Commissioner failed to apply his mind and if there is no cogent information of valid reasons for belief, non-scoring out of irrelevant portions of warrant may be considered and illustration of non-application of mind and improper exercise of authority.

Hon'ble Supreme Court in the case of *CCT* v. *Ramkishan Shrikishan Jhaver* [1967] 66 ITR 664 have pointed out that non-striking out of irrelevant portion and non-filling up of blank portions of the warrant would indicate non-application of mind and therefore the search was held to be illegal.

Therefore, while courts have taken the signing of blank warrants by the authorizing officers as illegal and searches conducted in pursuance to such warrants were quashed, whereas on the other hand, where there was only a failure to strike out in applicable portion of the warrant, courts have not taken very strict view. Therefore each such case needs to be examined to find out as to whether the infirmity can be called as irregularity or illegality.

Non-scoring out of the irrelevant portions of the form of warrant of authorization by itself does not affect the validity of the exercise of power under section 132 in case other basic conditions and requirements of law have been fulfilled- [*I. Devarajan* v. *Tamil Nadu Farmers Service Co-operative Federation* [1981] 131 ITR 506 (Mad.)]

However, in those cases where there is no cogent information or valid reasons for belief, non-scoring out of the irrelevant portions of the warrant may be considered as additional factor for lack of proper application of mind by the authorizing authority and improper exercise of power under section 132. [*Dwarka Prosad Agarwalla* v. *Director of Inspection* [1981] 7 Taxman 299/[1982] 137 ITR 456 (Cal.)]

Non-striking of irrelevant portions and non-filling up of blank portions of the warrant would indicate non-application of mind. The search was held to be illegal. [*CCT* v. *Ramkishan Shrikishan Jhaver* [1967] 66 ITR 664 (SC)]

(*ii*) Clerical omission not fatal

"An innocuous mistake in deleting the word 'Deputy' should not be fatal to the legality of the search. No substance was found in the plea that the search conducted was illegal".

[*Sonu Systems (P.) Ltd.* v. *Chairman, CBDT* [2001] 115 Taxman 262 (Delhi)]

(*iii*) Mistake in the name in authorization

In case there is any mistake in mentioning the name of the person to be searched which is of clerical nature or full name is not mentioned but abbreviated name is mentioned, search warrant cannot be held illegal on this ground. However, if there is error in the name to the extent of wrong identification of the person to be searched, search warrant may be held to be illegal on this ground.

It has been held in the case of *Verma Roadways* v. *Asstt. CIT* 165 DTR (All) 377 that where search and seizure actually was conducted at the premises of assessee and whatever was seized included money and document belonged to assessee & Assessee at no point of time, before assessing authority raised any such dispute that authorization as well as Punchnama prepared by search and seizure team relate to another person other than assessee, it is difficult to hold that in the present case, mention of different title in authorization and Punchnama i.e. "Verma Transport Company, Lucknow Banda Transport Company" instead of "Verma Roadways" would be sufficient to hold that proceedings under s. 132(1) were conducted against different person and not assessee & thus proceedings under s. 158BC against assessee cannot be held bad.

3.12 Proforma of search warrant

A search warrant is necessarily required to contain name of the person to be searched, full description of the premises to be searched, seal and signature of the authorizing officer and name of the authorized officers.

Various forms have been prescribed in the rules giving the form of search warrant to be used in different situations.

Various forms to be used are as under:

Section	Form	Authorization
132(1)	45	DG or D
		CC or C
		JDI or JCI as empowered by the Board
132(1) first proviso	45A	CC or C
132(1A)	45B	CC or C
132A	45C	DG or D
		CC or C

In case wrong form is used to issue search warrant, it may not invalidate the whole process of search. However, the powers of authorized officer may be restricted to the extent and in the manner as prescribed in the particular form used. In any case it will depend upon the facts of each case.

3.13 Summarisation

1. Warrant of authorization can be issued only by authorities specifically empowered by section 132(1) of the Income-tax Act.

2. The authorities who can be authorized to conduct the search depend upon who the authorizing authority is.

3. Jurisdiction plays a very important role in deciding the authority who can issue the warrant. However, exceptions have been provided to take care of "emergencies", notwithstanding the jurisdictional restrictions.

4. Warrants for search should be issued in proper form depending upon the facts of the case; issue of warrant in a form that does not suit the facts of the case may result in the search being declared invalid; the

assessees should be careful to verify this aspect before the search begins.

5. Scoring out inapplicable portions of the search warrant is not mandatory but it is advisable to do so to avoid controversies.

6. Reasons need not be recorded in the warrant.

7. Documents or assets to be seized need not be specified in the warrant.

8. Issue of blank warrants is illegal.

9. The assessees or persons whose places or premises, etc. are searched have no right to be supplied with copy of the search warrant, though it is imperative that a warrant should be shown to them before commencing the search; nor are they entitled to be informed of the reasons recorded; and

10. No proceedings need to be pending before issue of the warrant.

VALIDITY OF SEARCH - WRIT JURISDICTION

4.1 Validity of Search

Income tax search is an extreme and very harsh action undertaken by the department against the assessee. Such power needs to be exercised with utmost and due care and caution. Validity of the searches is often challenged by the searched persons. The courts have held that search action should be taken following due process of law strictly in accordance with provisions of section 132. In case there is any lapse, the search action may be held to be illegal.

Search action can be authorized only when *"reason to believe"* has been formed by the authorizing officer in consequence to relevant information in his possession as to the existence of either or more of the conditions prescribed under clause (*a*), (*b*) or (*c*) of section 132(1), and valid search warrant is issued as provided under the law. In the absence of any of such conditions having been fulfilled, search may be held by the courts as illegal. If the exercise of powers is in good faith, a procedural defect may be overlooked. While examining the validity of search, court cannot examine adequacy or sufficiency of information but its existence and relevance become crucial factor.

Constitutional validity of section 132 was considered by the Supreme Court in the case of *Pooran Mal* v. *Director of Inspection* [1974] 93 ITR 505 in which Hon'ble Supreme Court observed that the provisions contained in section 132 and Rule 112 of the Income-tax Rules, 1962 are not violative of Article 19(1)(*f*) and (*g*) because the restrictions placed therein were reasonable restrictions. According to the Supreme Court, the power of search and seizure is directed against persons who are believed on good grounds to have illegally evaded the payment of tax on their income and property and therefore, drastic measures to get such income and property with a view to recover government dues would stand justified in itself.

Hon'ble Supreme Court in the case of *Bhupendra Ratilal Thakkar* v. *CIT* [1976] 102 ITR 531 held that section 132 of the Income-tax Act is neither incompetent nor invalid in infringing any of the fundamental rights guaranteed under Articles 14, 19, 21 and 31 of the Constitution. Hon'ble Court further held that rules 112B and 112C are beneficial rules and their validity cannot be impugned.

Hon'ble Allahabad in the case of *Shyam Jewellers* v. *Chief Commissioner (Administration)* [1992] 196 ITR 243 held that neither the section 133A relating to survey nor section 132(3) provide for sealing of the shop or business and such an act violates the fundamental rights amounting to temporary deprivation of property under Article 19(1)(*g*) which guarantees the citizen the right to carry on any profession or trade or business.

Hon'ble Supreme Court in *CIT* v. *Tarsem Kumar* [1986] 27 Taxman 305 held that if the action of income tax authorities does not fall within the purview of section 132, the consequential action would then be arbitrary and unreasonable and would be violative of Article 14 of the Constitution. Similarly, Hon'ble Allahabad High Court in the case of *Dr. I.S. Tomar* v. *DIT* [1996] 85 Taxman 468 held that where the search was conducted whimsically without any material and without any good information, authorization to conduct search and to make the seizure was wholly illegal.

Hon'ble Supreme Court in the case of *ITO* v. *Seth Brothers* [1969] 74 ITR 836 administered a word of caution regarding the searches. According to Supreme Court, since serious encroachment is made upon the rights, privacy and freedom of taxpayer, the power must be exercised strictly in accordance with law and if the action of the officer is challenged in the court of law, the officer must satisfy about the regularity of action. If the action is maliciously taken or the power is exercised for collateral purpose, it is liable to be struck down by the courts.

Hon'ble Patna High Court in the case of *Pawan Solvent & Chemicals* v. *CIT* [1987] 32 Taxman 12 held that raid, search and seizure operations must be conducted to unearth unaccounted income and wealth from unscrupulous taxpayers, smugglers etc. who are scourge of the society. However, wanton and indiscriminate raid and seizure of honest taxpayers will amount to deprivation of fundamental rights of the persons living in society with dignity and grace and therefore, the same should be avoided.

Hon'ble Calcutta High Court in *Shree Krishna Investments* v. *Union of India* AIR 1976 Cal. 333 observed that it may be that a power vested in an authority may be abused by that authority but no statute or provision can be struck down only on the ground that powers thereunder when abused would result in discrimination. An abuse of powers vested by a statute or provision does not render the source of the power tainted. It only renders such act of abuse liable to be struck down.

In *Dr. Nand Lal Tahiliani* v. *CIT* [1988] 39 Taxman 127 (All.) it was held that there must be rational connection between the information or material and the belief about the undisclosed income. Reputation of roaring practice and high fees is not tangible material for invoking power u/s 132. Satisfaction is to be derived objectively and on the basis of available material.

Hon'ble Supreme Court in *CIT* v. *Dr. Nandlal Tahiliani* [1988] 172 ITR 627 observed while dismissing the departmental SLP that department was entitled to *"take into account any information derived from the inventories prepared in consequence of the search and seizure made u/s 132 of the Income-tax Act and impugned in the present case"*.

In *H.L. Sibal* v. *CIT* [1975] 69 Taxman 112 (P&H), Court was of the view that there should be no indiscriminate issue of search warrant as a matter of search policy and blanket condemnation of persons of diverse activities was wholly outside section 165 of Criminal Procedure Code.

In *Harmel Singh* v. *Union of India* [1993] 69 Taxman 347 (P&H), it was held that *"existence of relevant material for taking action u/s 132 is a condition precedent for the exercise of powers"*. Any wrong action u/s 132 is a serious encroachment on the civil rights of a citizen and once the court is satisfied that there was no material before the concerned authority to form an opinion, then the court can interfere but court cannot go into the sufficiency of the material.

In *Chemitex* v. *Union of India* [1982] Tax L.R. 2871 (Goa) the Court held that the provisions for search and seizure are not hit by Article 19(1)(*g*) of the Constitution simply because search has to be conducted without giving prior hearing to the persons. In fact such an opportunity of being heard to a person before invoking power u/s 132 would render the power of search and seizure meaningless and the very scope of these provisions would be defeated.

In *Kusum Lata* v. *CIT* [1990] 48 Taxman 401 (Raj.), it was held by the Court that where there was no reasonable information on which the Director could have had any *bona fide* belief to issue the authorization u/s 132(1), the proceedings were vitiated. In that case, all that was stated was that a particular brand of chewing tobacco, pan masala etc. were selling at a high premium which was result of artificial scarcity created by the dealers. The authorization being illegal and not being in accordance with law was held illegal and therefore, the search and seizure of the assets were also held to be illegal.

In *Dr. Partap Singh* v. *Director of Enforcement* [1985] 22 Taxman 30 (SC) it was held that the material on which the officer has reason to believe that any documents will be useful or relevant to any investigation or proceedings under Foreign Exchange Regulation Act, need not be disclosed in the search warrant issued by him. The material on which the belief is grounded may be secret, may be obtained through intelligence or occasionally may be conveyed orally by the informers. It is not obligatory upon the officer to disclose his material on the mere allegation of the petitioner that there was no material before him for exercising his power to order search.

It is thus clear from the catena of judicial decisions that the courts have held that power to order search must be exercised strictly in accordance with law and only for the purpose for which these provisions were brought on the statute. The court though is not competent to go into the sufficiency of the material upon which reason to believe for the purpose of search is based but the law does not permit at the same time the indiscriminate search and seizure based on suspicion.

(i) Circumstances when search is held to be valid

1. Where certain CDRs and Banker's cheques valued at ₹ 3 crores were deposited with the District Excise Office as security in the name of a firm to participate in the auction for allotment of privilege of selling country made liquor and the same were seized, the search is held to be valid. [*Babu Lal* v. *DIT (Inv.)* [2005] 147 Taxman 318 (All.)]

2. Search in assessee's premises held to be valid where it was done in connection with clandestine transaction of the group with which the assessee was inter-linked. [*Bandel Traders (P.) Ltd.* v. *Union of India* [2003] 130 Taxman 428 (Delhi)]

3. Allegation that Income Tax authorities had taken a bribe would not invalidate the search. [*Kamal Khosla* v. *DIT (Investigation)* [2002] 123 Taxman 1102 (Delhi)]

4. If a search is otherwise justified, the size of search party is not to be fatal to the validity of search. The enormity of search party could not be a ground for interference. Because of the enormity of the building and the premises it was necessary for the purpose of search and seizure to ensure the presence of a number of persons on behalf of the department. *Mamchand & Co.* v. *CIT* [1968] 69 ITR 631 (Cal.), *Subir Roy* v. *S.K. Chatto-padhyay* [1986] 29 Taxman 13 (Cal.).

It has been held in the case of *Jai Bhagwan Om Parkash* v. *Director of Inspection* [1993] 67 Taxman 33 (P&H), that authenticity of complaint and allegation of tax evasion made by complainant duly checked by department independently by secret enquiry, it could not be said that there were no reason to believe for conducting search.

In the case of *Dr. P.G. Viswanathan* v. *DIT (Inv.)* [2013] 30 tax-mann.com 33/214 Taxman 105 (Mad.)(HC)

V. Muthulakshmi v. *DIT (Inv.)* [2013] 351 ITR 217/88 DTR 33 (Mad.) (HC)

K. Viswanathan alias Kumar v. *DIT (Inv.)* [2013] 351 ITR 217/88 DTR 33 (Mad.)(HC)

Dr. Aruna Viswanathan v. *DIT (Inv.)* [2013] 351 ITR 217/88 DTR 33 (Mad.)(HC)

Dr. Anjana Viswanathan v. *DIT (Inv.)* [2013] 351 ITR 217/88 DTR 33 (Mad.)(HC)

Dr. Vikram Viswanathn v. *DIT (Inv.)* [2013] 351 ITR 217/88 DTR 33 (Mad.)(HC)

The assessee challenged the action under section 132 of the Act by way of writ before the High Court. The Court dismissed the petition by observing that there were materials available before the authority concerned, for the formation of his belief to issue such a warrant. Further, the authority had also reason to believe that such documents and things would not be produced by the persons concerned, in the normal course, to enable the Department to conduct necessary inquiries in the matter. Therefore, it was premature on the part of the assessees to stall further proceedings relating to the allegations of evasion of payment of tax by the assessees, by raising the issues relating to the jurisdiction of the Department to issue the search warrants. Of course, it would be open to the assessees to defend themselves by showing, at the appropriate stage of the proceedings, that they were not liable to pay the tax, as assessed by the authorities of the Department. The belief of the authorities that the assessees had secreted certain documents relevant for the purpose of investigation of the matter relating to the evasion of tax by the assessees, was based on materials available before the authorities. When serious allegations of tax evasion by the assessees, to the tune of several lakhs of rupees, have been made, it would not be appropriate for the court to scuttle the process by placing undue emphasis on the hyper technical pleas put forth on behalf of the assessees, with regard to the procedural formalities in the issuance of the search warrants.

In the case of *Emaar Alloys (P) Ltd.* v. *DGIT (Inv) & Ors.* [2015] 64 taxmann.com 67/235 Taxman 569 (Jharkhand), High Court observed that there was sufficient material before the IT authorities that the assessee had not disclosed huge income. Further, before the issuance of the warrant of authorization by the Director of IT to carry out search and seizure, the procedure prescribed under section 132 had been followed. High Court further observed that it need not approve the subjective satisfaction arrived at by the lower authorities.

It has been held by the High Court that search proceedings initiated cannot be declared illegal if there is sufficient material before the IT authorities on the basis of which satisfaction is arrived at that the assessee has huge undisclosed income.

It has been held in the case of *Rajan Jewellery* v. *CIT* 177 DTR 369 (Ker.) that assessee having not raised the objection on validity of search on the ground of absence of panchas before the AO, it could not raise the same before appellate authority.

It has been held in the case of *Subhash Sharma* v. *CIT* [2020] 121 taxmann.com 83/423 ITR 47 (Chhattisgarh) that before issuance of warrant and the notice under section 153A,when the authority applied its mind to the material and the formation of opinion is honest and *bona fide* and further that it is not based on any extraneous or irrelevant material, there is no illegality or infirmity in the entire process based on which the warrant under section 132 and the notice under section 153A was issued against the assessee.

It has been held in the case of *Principal Director of IT (Inv.)* v. *Laljibhai Kanjibhai Mandalia* 215 DTR (SC) 417 that Revenue authorities having formed the belief that the loan of Rs. 10 crores given by the assessee for a short period to an unconnected company situated in a distant city was a mere accommodation entry, and the cobweb of entries including the trial of money paid by the assessee is required to be unravelled, the prerequisite conditions of section 132 stand satisfied and further that even clause (*c*) of section 132(1) is satisfied as the Revenue wants to find out whether the said amount is an undisclosed income and, therefore, the impugned authorization of search could not be set aside.

(*ii*) Circumstances when search is held to be invalid

1. Mere information from CBI that cash was found in possession of an individual cannot justify a search [*Union of India* v. *Ajit Jain* [2003] 129 Taxman 74 (SC)]

2. Where the authorization to survey was issued initially against the doctor, search operations at the residence of the doctor and in the hospital premises held invalid where the hospital belongs to the trust and where no reasons for conversion of survey operations into search operations were given. [*Dr. Nalini Mahajan* v. *DIT (Investigation)* [2002] 122 Taxman 897 (Delhi)]

3. Where the search was in the name of partner, the search on the firm was held illegal. [*Vishwanath Prasad* v. *Asstt. CIT* [2003] 86 ITD 516 (All.-Trib.)]

4. It was held that where in his zeal for taking action under section 132(1) the Commissioner did not even care to have a look at the orders of Assessing Officers, it was held he did not at all apply his mind before initiating action against the petitioner and therefore, the search of the premises of the petitioner was illegal. [*Anand Swaroop* v. *CIT* [1976] 103 ITR 575 (P&H)]

5. The drastic powers of search and seizure cannot be used in a routine manner and are expected to be pressed into action after due care, caution and consideration. These powers have to be invoked in rarest of rare cases. If the conditions precedent are not satisfied, Courts have not hesitated in quashing the warrant of authorization, the action of seizure and in directing return of seized cash, valuables etc. and also seized books of account and documents. In appropriate cases, the harassed assessees have been awarded damages and costs. The facts constituting the information must be relevant to the enquiry. They must be such from which a reasonable and prudent man can come to the requisite belief or conclusion. If either of the aforementioned elements is missing, the action of the authority shall be regarded as lying outside the ambit and scope of the Act. Such an action would be liable to be struck down on the basis of what is commonly known as "legal malice". [*H.L. Sibal* v. *CIT* [1975] 101 ITR 112 (P&H)]

It has been held in the case of *Madhu Gupta* v. *Director of IT (Inv.)* [2013] 30 taxmann.com 92/214 Taxman 246 (Delhi) that when the so-called information remained undisclosed and what exactly that information was, is also not known, the so-called information that there was a likelihood of the documents belonging to a group being found at the residence of the petitioner amounted only to a surmise and conjecture and not solid information and therefore warrant of authorization was liable to be quashed.

In the case of *Dipen Laljibhai Mandalia* v. *DGIT* [2013] 35 taxmann.com 508/217 Taxman 66 (Mag.) (Guj.), the assessee was carrying gold ornaments worth ₹ 6.42 crores on a flight from Ahmedabad to Chennai to show them to retail owners hoping to procure bulk orders for the same. On basis of information received from the security officials at the airport, revenue authorities conducted inquiries with assessee and also with the Karta of HUF who according to assessee was the owner of gold which was leased to them under certain conditions. Subsequently, on basis of a satisfaction note, search and seizure operations were carried out against the HUF. On Special

Civil Application filed by the HUF, the High Court quashed search and seizure operations. The High Court, allowing the Special Civil Applications filed by the assessee, held that since search proceedings in case of HUF were already quashed, said proceedings on very similar grounds and hence would not be sustainable.

In the case of *LKS Bullion Import & Export (P.) Ltd.* v. *DGIT* [2013] 29 taxmann.com 299/214 Taxman 68 (Guj.), Assessee-company was engaged in business of wholesale trading in bullion. Director of assessee, along with other were found carrying about 23 kilos of gold ornaments by air from Ahmedabad to Chennai. Department seized said gold ornaments under section 132. Director of assessee at spot gave statement that 25 kilos of gold was received by assessee from MG-HUF on lease and gold ornaments in question were made out of said gold. Said statements given by director of assessee at airport matched with that of MG-HUF and goldsmith supported by relevant books of account. On facts, competent authority could not have formed a reasonable belief that such gold jewellery had not been or would not be disclosed for purpose of Income-tax. Therefore, search and seizure operation was to be declared illegal and seizure of gold ornament was also to be quashed.

In the case of *CIT* v. *Smt. Umlesh Goel* [2016] 141 DTR (Raj.) 25, it has been held that all the family members are separate assessable legal entities under the Act and in a case where search warrant has been issued in the name of OP and family. It cannot be stretched to cover all the family members, namely spouse and children. Search warrant has to be in the name of specific person to initiate proceeding. When names of the two assessee do not find mention in the warrant of authorisation, the A.O. has no jurisdiction to issue notice under section 158BC

It has been held in the case of *Laljibhai Kanjibhai Mandalia* v. *Principal DIT* [2019] 105 taxmann.com 260/263 Taxman 604 (Guj.) that Search warrant is invalid if provisions of section 132 not attracted; A search was conducted in case of assessee. Assessee filed petition challenging authorisation issued under section 132. It was noted that no summons or notice as envisaged under clause (*a*) of sub-section (1) of section 132 had been issued. It was also noted that belief of revenue that assessee would not respond to a summons or notice issued as envisaged under clause (*b*) of sub-section (1) of section 132 was not based upon any information or other material but was based upon conjectures and surmises that assessee would take alibi of lack of jurisdiction on part of respondents. Thus, circumstance envisaged under clause (*b*) of sub-section (1) of section 132 also did not exist. Finally, there was nothing on record to indicate that any belief had been formed by competent authority to effect that assessee had in his possession any money, bullion, jewellery or other valuable article or thing which would not have been disclosed by him for purposes of Act. In view of aforesaid, it could be concluded that none of clause (*a*), (*b*), or (*c*) of sub-section (1) of section 132 was attracted and, thus, authorisation being invalid, search proceedings in question deserved to be quashed.

The above decision has been reversed by Hon'ble Supreme Court in the case of *Principal Director of IT (Inv.)* v. *Laljibhai Kanjibhai Mandalia* 215 DTR (SC) 417 and in the above circumstances, search has been held valid.

It has been held in the case of *Mectec* v. *Director of IT (Inv.)* [2021] 125 taxmann.com 96/278 Taxman 214/433 ITR 203 (Telangana) that as to the authorisation under section 132(1) and seizure of cash by Police vis-a-vis validity of search warrant, cash from petitioner's employee was seized by police and handed over to IT Department on 27th Aug., 2019 and therefore search warrant dt. 28th Aug., 2019, that too not mentioning the place to be searched, was a fabricated document and the intimation by the Police to the IT Department on 27th Aug., 2019 would not confer jurisdiction on the IT Department to detain and withhold cash and that too by issuance of an invalid search warrant under section 132 and thus Respondents were directed to refund the cash to the petitioner No. 1 along with interest.

(*iii*) Allegation of *mala fide* or *bias* in search

There is presumption in law that Government authorities while discharging their official duty act *bona fide* and in good faith. Search action is a harsh action on an assessee and at times tough decisions are required to be taken by the authorized officer in discharging this function, but of course, within the parameters of law. Some degree of high handedness or excessiveness may be perceived by the searched person to have been resorted to during search by the search team. In general, courts do not entertain the charge of *mala fide* or personal bias attributed to the authorities during search unless strong evidences are brought on record.

However, this presumption of good faith can be rebutted by the assessee by leading evidences. Heavy burden of proof lies on the person searched who is making such allegation. Such person has to lead cogent, irrefutable and concrete direct or circumstantial evidences to prove the charge. Mere making a statement or filing bald affidavit would not be sufficient.

There may be temptation on the part of assessee to challenge a search on the ground of *mala fide*, high handedness, bias or arbitrariness but such action should be taken only in extreme cases where the facts are very strong in favour of the assessee.

The mere fact that the Assessing Officer was also an authorized officer for conducting the search, does not *ipso facto* justify apprehension of bias. Therefore, search cannot be held to be invalid. [*Union of India* v. *Vipan Kumar Jain* [2003] 129 Taxman 59 (SC)].

A search cannot be treated as *mala fide* merely because certain outsiders were associated at the time of search. Where some inspectors were taken along for doing clerical and ministerial work and some policemen were taken for ensuring the maintenance of peace and order and for preventing obstruction and illicit removal of documents, the search could not be held to be invalid. [*Hindustan Metal Works* v. *CIT* [1968] 68 ITR 798 (All.)]

In the absence of anything to show that the documents were either replaced or tampered, any omission to place identification marks on documents will not by itself supply a ground for holding that the search was *mala fide*. [*ITO* v. *Seth Bros.* [1969] 74 ITR 836 (SC)]

Doubtless, he who seeks to invalidate or nullify any act or order must establish the charge of bad faith, an abuse or misuse by Government of its powers." [*S. Pratap Singh* v. *State of Punjab* AIR 1964 SC 72]

The onus of proving *'malice'* is on the person who levels the allegation. Because of the very serious nature of the allegations, the Courts would demand a highly credible proof. [*E.P. Royappa* v. *State of Tamil Nadu* AIR 1974 SC 555]

In absence of any proof of allegations of *mala fide*, the search was held to be not bad. [*Dr. Partap Singh* v. *Director of Enforcement* [1985] 22 Taxman 30 (SC)]

Vague allegations are not enough to prove *mala fide*. [*Express Newspapers (P.) Ltd.* v. *UOI* AIR 1986 SC 872]

There cannot be any blanket formula in this regard. The question of judicial bias or administrative bias or personal bias would have to be decided on the facts of each case. The party alleging bias must prove the fact and should leave no scope for any other finding.

Where an officer is sought to be condemned on the ground that he was personally biased, then the character of such officer is under assassination. Every person who acts as an officer has to face such situation. Every person who is aggrieved by the action of such an officer would always raise such allegation. If the simple allegations which are devoid of legal proof are allowed to stand, then it would become impossible for an officer, especially administrative officer, to work.

The allegation that an officer is prejudiced or biased would not be sufficient unless the evidence is brought on the record leading to the positive conclusion that the bias is established. If the person who raises an allegation is able to establish that the officer in fact is biased, then the Court would give weight to the allegation. [*Takshila Educational Society* v. *DIT (Inv.)* [2005] 141 Taxman 704 (Pat.)]

4.2 Illegality of Search v. Irregularity during Search

There may be certain procedural irregularities committed by the authorized officer in the conduct of scarch, but this will not vitiate the search action as a whole. Nature of procedural defect will also decide whether it is mere procedural irregularity or it is so fundamental in nature that whole process of search can be said to be illegal.

In the case of *Naraindas* v. *CIT* [1983] 14 Taxman 447 (MP) at page 572, the assessee contended that the action of the authorized officers in making search and seizure was illegal because of the irregularity in not calling respectable persons of the same locality as witnesses. The department in its reply affidavit filed before the High Court stated that the names of the witnesses were suggested by the petitioners. The assessee wanted that the outsiders should not be called as witnesses because that would have affect on their credit and prestige. The High Court observed that the petitioners could not complain that the witnesses suggested by him were not respectable persons of the locality in the situation stated above. The High Court, therefore, rejected the assessee's plea based on this contention and also supplemented their conclusion by referring to the decision of the Supreme Court in the case of *ITO* v. *Seth Bros.* [1969] 74 ITR 836 to the effect that any irregularity in the course of search and seizure committed by the officers will not be sufficient to vitiate the action taken provided the officers had in executing the authorization acted *bona fide*.

In *Dr. Partap Singh* v. *Director of Enforcement* [1985] 22 Taxman 30 (SC) it was held that illegality of the search does not vitiate the evidence collected during illegal search the only requirement is that the court or the authority before which such material or evidence seized during the search shown to be illegal is placed has to be cautious and circumspect dealing with such evidence or material.

In *Balwant Singh* v. *R.D. Shah (Director of Inspection)* [1969] 71 ITR 550 (Delhi) it was held that the information gathered as a result of illegal search and seizure can be used subject to the value to be attached to it or its admissibility in accordance with the law relating to the evidence.

(*i*) Delay in concluding search

Keeping of documents either in room or almirah under seal after issuing an order under section 132(3) cannot be said to be irregular procedure; further where search could not be completed on same day, *i.e.*, 27-10-1995, and it was resumed thereafter on 10-11-1995, in the absence of any time-limit prescribed in the Code of Criminal Procedure, 1973, or in the Act, it could not be said that delay in conducting search had vitiated search and seizure. *CIT* v. *Dr. C. Balakrishnan Nair* [2005] 148 Taxman 172 (Ker.).

Hon'ble Delhi High Court in the case of *CIT* v. *S. K. Katyal* [2009] 177 Taxman 380/308 ITR 168, have held *inter alia* that normally a search must be continuous and if it cannot be continuous for some plausible reason the hiatus in the search must be explained and if no cogent or plausible reason is shown for the hiatus in the search, the second or 'resumed' search should be illegal. Hon'ble High Court in this decision *inter alia* relied upon the case of *Dr. C. Balakrishnan Nair* v. *CIT* [1999] 103 Taxman 242 (Ker).

Hon'ble Delhi High Court in the case of *VLS Finance Ltd.* v. *CIT* [2007] 159 Taxman 102, have held that no fault can be found when search conducted on various dates starting from 23rd June, 1998 till 5th August, 1998 as it was not possible or practicable to seize the books of account u/s 132(1) and in such a case authorised officer may pass a restraint order u/s 132(3). The seizure could have been effected on the first day *i.e.* 22-6-1998 and the last panchnama was drawn on 5-8-1998 well before 60 days period was to expire and therefore no ulterior motives can be attributed to the department in failing to seize the books of account and instead passing the restraint order in this respect.

(*ii*) Bona fide irregularity not fatal

An error of judgment on the part of the officers will not vitiate the exercise of the power. Some irregularity in the course of entry, search and seizure committed by the Officer acting *bona fide* in pursuance of an authorization will not vitiate the action taken. *ITO* v. *Seth Bros.* [1969] 74 ITR 836 (SC), *Lan Eseda Steels Ltd.* v. *Asstt. CIT* [1993] 70 Taxman 46 (AP).

(*iii*) Seizure of irrelevant documents

When in the course of a search voluminous documents and books of account are to be examined with a view to judge whether they would be relevant, a certain amount of latitude must be permitted to the authorities. It is true that when particular documents are asked to be seized, unnecessary examination of other documents may conceivably make the search excessive. But when the documents, pieces of paper, exercise books, account books, small memos, etc., have all to be examined with a view to see how far they are relevant for the proceedings under the Act, an error of judgment is not unlikely. At the most this would be an irregularity- not an illegality. *Pooran Mal v. Director of Inspection* [1974] 93 ITR 505 (SC), *Lan Eseda Steels Ltd. v. Asstt. CIT* [1993] 70 Taxman 46 (AP).

4.3 Illegal Search - Consequences

When a search is held as illegal by High Court, question as to what are its consequences, becomes a very important point in terms of as to what is gained or lost by the assessee or by the department. In case search is held illegal, all the actions taken by the department in the conduct of search may be required to be reversed such as:

a. All assets seized during search consisting of cash, money, bullion, jewellery, article or thing will be required to be given back to the assessee.

b. Original copies of books of account or other documents seized during search will be required to be released to the assessee. However, department may be allowed to keep photocopy of the same.

c. No proceedings under section 153A or under section 153C can be undertaken by the department.

d. No presumption under section 132(4A)/292C shall be available to the department.

e. There will be no evidentiary value as such of the statements recorded during search.

f. Costs may be awarded against the department or against the officer(s) or against the officials to undertake illegal search action.

g. However, department is not precluded from using the documents found during search against the assessee under any other provisions of the Income-tax Act.

Where the very initiation of search and block assessment proceedings are quashed by the High Court directing the Department to return the seized material including gold, diamond, jewellery, etc, and the High Court directed the return of seized material with interest, the Supreme Court while confirming the order of High Court did not decide the question of payment of interest but directed to pay the cost in lieu of interest. [*DGIT v. Diamond Star Exports Ltd.* [2006] 156 Taxman 299 (SC)]

The department was directed to return the seized material to the person from whom it was seized. *CIT v. Dr. Nandlal Tahiliani* [1988] 172 ITR 627 (SC), *Kusum Lata v. CIT* [1990] 48 Taxman 401 (Raj.)

"... that the search and seizure were in contravention of the provisions of section 132 of the Income-tax Act, still the material seized was liable to be used subject to law before the Income Tax authorities against the person from whose custody it was seized and, therefore, held that the High Court was right in dismissing the two writ petitions." [*Pooran Mal* v. *Director of Inspection* [1974] 93 ITR 505 (SC)]

"As we have come to the conclusion that, in the present case, no reasonable person could have come to the conclusion that the ingredients contained in clause (*a*), (*b*) or (*c*) of section 132 were attracted, we issue a writ of man-damus quashing the impugned authorization and also the further action which has been taken by the respondents pursuant to the said authorization including the seizure of all documents, cash and jewellery. The respondents are directed to return the said documents, cash and jewellery seized by them to the petitioners within two weeks from today." [*L.R. Gupta* v. *UOI* [1991] 59 Taxman 305 (Delhi)]

Consequent block assessment also held invalid [*Union of India* v. *Ajit Jain* [2003] 129 Taxman 74 (SC)]

Department was allowed to retain photocopy of the documents even illegally seized. [*Rakesh Kumar Agarwal* v. *DGIT* [1995] 83 Taxman 76 (Delhi), *Khandani Shafakhana* v. *Union of India* [1989] 175 ITR 408 (Delhi)]

In the case of *ITO* v. *U.K. Mahapatra & Co.* [2010] 186 Taxman 181 (SC), where books of account and other documents were illegally impounded in a case of survey under section 133A, Supreme Court directed to return the documents to the assessee within two weeks confirming the order of the Orissa High Court. However, it was further directed that the department would be entitled to take print out of all the pages of document and copies of the CD-ROM, which may be certified by the Deputy Registrar of High Court in whose possession the impounded material was lying:

(*i*) Awarding costs against department

The courts have reacted harsh and rightly so, in case provisions of law have been flouted and authorities have acted arbitrarily and carelessly in the matter of authorization and conduct of search actions. In number of cases, courts have punished the departmental officials by awarding cost for their illegal action.

It is well settled now that the State is responsible for the torturous acts of its employees. [*Saheli, A Women's Resources Centre* v. *Commissioner of Police* AIR 1990 SC 513]

Hon'ble Delhi High Court in the case of *Shri Ganesh Enterprises (P.) Ltd.* v. *UOI* [1994] 75 Taxman 239 observed that utmost care has to be taken by the authorities before exercising the powers u/s 132 and even thereafter the subsequent enquiries and investigation have to be concluded expeditiously and thus awarded the cost to the assessee for harassment and for their business being adversely affected by the restraint order.

(*ii*) No civil suit for claiming damages

Searched person may be tempted to file civil suit claiming damages in case he believes that search action was taken without there being any relevant material to authorize the search and that there was no seizure of any undisclosed income/asset. But, such action on the part of searched person may not be entertained by the Court in view of section 293 of the Act which reads *"No suit shall be brought in any civil court to set aside or modify any proceeding taken or order made under this Act; and no prosecution, suit or other proceeding shall lie against the Government or any officer of the Government for anything in good faith done or intended to be done under this Act".* It means that so long as *mala fide* is not alleged and proved by the searched person, remedy by way of civil suit is clearly barred under the specific provision of the Act.

The assessee could have effectively invoked the provisions of section 132B(4) for claiming interest on the assets and could have asked for payment of interest on the amount of loss, if any, that was caused to it. Such a relief could not be claimed by filing a civil suit against an order made under the Act. The assessee therefore, could have demanded payment of interest in terms of section 132B(4) and in case of non-payment of the same, it could have appropriately moved the Commissioner in revision u/s 264. The assessee could have also made a similar prayer in the writ petition, which apparently was not done.

In the facts and circumstances of the case and in the light of the provisions of section 293, the findings recorded by the Trial Court that a civil suit of the nature, which was filed by the assessee, was not maintainable was to be sustainable. Therefore, there was no merit in the instant appeal and the same was to be dismissed. [*Prem Kumar & Sons (HUF)* v. *UOI* [2005] 148 Taxman 103 (Delhi)]

(*iii*) Damages for undue retention

FDRs made by applicant with a finance company were seized during a raid at finance company's premises. For several years, applicant's claim through Court to get his dues was not successful. The applicant deposited money in the form of FDRs to meet in future the marriage expenses of his daughter. During the search of the petitioner-company's premises, FDRs were seized which included the applicant's money. The applicant was compelled to knock doors of various Courts for several years for getting his dues which were denied for one reason or other. Held, that in view of the suffering and agony which the applicant had undergone for several years for no fault of his, it would be just to award the applicant compensation along with the deposits. [*Kuber Planters Ltd.* v. *Dy. CIT* [2006] 150 Taxman 11 (Delhi)]

There was considerable delay in returning books of account, retained without authority of law. The assessee moved to the High Court for intervention. The department sought adjournments a number of times. Court declined to direct the person searched to sign the photocopies made by the department of the seized books of account. In this background, costs of ₹ 5,000 were awarded. The Court ordered for return of seized books and the jewellery within 10 days. [*Rakesh Kumar Agarwal* v. *DGIT* [1995] 83 Taxman 76 (Delhi)]

(iv) **Damages for illegal restraint**

The series of actions of the department from sealing the shop of the petitioner, passing an order under section 132(3) and finally passing its possession to the Rehabilitation Authorities were held to be without jurisdiction and it was held that the search was liable to be struck down. The Court also granted damages of ₹ 10,000 and a further amount of ₹ 500 per day till they handed back the possession of the shop for the illegal action. [*Sardar Paraduman Singh* v. *UOI* [1987] 31 Taxman 515 (Delhi)]

The restraint order under section 132(3) was belatedly lifted. Besides, there was unexplained delay in conducting enquiries. The petitioner was held entitled to costs. [*Shri Ganesh Enterprises (P.) Ltd.* v. *UOI* [1994] 75 Taxman 239 (Delhi)]

(v) **Search Assessment to be Illegal**

It has been held in the case of *Siksha "O" Anusandhan* v. *CIT* [2012] 20 taxmann.com 798 (Ori.) that the person, in respect of whom search under section 132 is initiated, is the same person against whom notice under section 153A is to be issued for making assessment and if there is any illegality in the search warrant, the same will invalidate the search assessment proceeding initiated under section 153A.

In the case of *Dy. CIT* v. *V. Ram Prasad* [2016] 65 taxmann.com 64/236 Taxman 479 (SC), the assessee challenged the block assessment order on the ground that the search was illegal and contrary to law and therefore the order was *void ab initio*. Tribunal held that it had no jurisdiction to examine the authorization of the search as such authorization does not result in any tax demand on the assessee and as the appeal was with reference to the tax liability imposed on the assessee, the Tribunal could not go into the validity of the authorization of search. High Court remitted the matter to the Tribunal to look into the validity of search for determining jurisdiction for making a block assessment.

Supreme Court granted leave to appeal against the High Court order holding that the Tribunal is bound to consider the validity of search for determining the jurisdiction for making a block assessment.

4.4 Evidentiary value of documents found during illegal search

The courts have consistently taken the view that books of account or documents or any other evidence found and seized even during the course of illegal search can still be used by the department against the assessee under any other applicable provisions of the Act. In some of the cases, contrary view has also been taken but tilt is in favour of the proposition that documents seized even in illegal action can be used by the department. Such documents/evidences cannot be used for framing assessment under section 153A but department is not precluded from using the same to initiate action under section 148, wherever found appropriate.

There is nothing in the Evidence Act so as to exclude relevant evidence on the ground that it was obtained during an illegal search and seizure. The information gathered as a result of search and seizure, even if such operations are held to be illegal in a case, can be used in evidence for the purposes of proceedings under the Income-tax Act, 1961. Even though the search and seizure may be in contravention of section 132, still the material obtained thereby is liable to be used against the person concerned. [*Pooran Mal* v. *Director of Inspection* [1974] 93 ITR 505 (SC)]

The illegality in the method, manner or initiation of a search does not necessarily mean that anything seized during the search has to be returned. After all, in the course of a search, things or documents are required to be seized and such things and documents when seized, may furnish evidence. Illegality of the search does not vitiate the evidence collected during such illegal search. The only requirement is that the Court or the authority before which such material or evidence seized during the search shown to be illegal is placed has to be cautious and circumspect in dealing with such evidence or material. [*Dr. Partap Singh* v. *Director of Enforcement* [1985] 22 Taxman 30 (SC)]

While the Agricultural Income-tax Act, 1950, does not authorize search and seizure, it is not, however, correct to say that materials gathered as a result of illegal search and seizure are inadmissible as evidence. Incriminating materials and documents discovered in the course of inspection of the assessee's business premises can be relied upon by the department for the purpose of making an estimate provided the assessees are given a reasonable opportunity to inspect them and take notes therefrom or copies thereof. [*Varghese* v. *Commissioner of Agricultural Income Tax* [1976] 105 ITR 732 (Ker.)]

Illegality or irregularity in seizure of documents cannot vitiate the materials collected unless the genuineness or correctness of the same is in doubt. The Courts in India persistently refuse to exclude material evidence solely on the ground that it was obtained by illegal search or seizure. Illegal search will not invalidate the seizure of the articles. In such cases only the Court is to scrutinize the evidence carefully. [*Thakursidas Banwarilal* v. *CIT* [1998] 232 ITR 846 (Gau.)]

Even if the search and seizure is held illegal, the materials searched and seized can still be looked into and relied upon for purpose of assessment. [*New Street Oil Mills* v. *State of Kerala* [1978] 111 ITR 463 (Ker.)]

In the context of criminal cases, it has been held that Court had discretion to admit the evidence obtained as a result of the illegal search and the constitutional protection against search of person or property without consent did not take away the discretion of the Court. However, it was open to the Court not to admit the evidence against the accused if the Court was of the view that the evidence had been obtained by conduct of which the prosecution ought not to take advantage. It may be argued in support of the exclusionary rule that Article 19 makes the right to acquire and hold property sacred and any property seized in violation of Article 19 should be completely restored. It is true that in appropriate cases the Court may order restoration of the property illegally seized, but so far as the use of information gathered as a result of such seizure is concerned, the Court are the appropriate authority, has, in any case, acting within the law, the power to call for such information and property and use the same in evidence. If it is done in accordance with law, no violation of Article 19 arises. The information gathered, therefore, can otherwise be reached by the Courts or other concerned authorities. The information gathered serves as a check on the person subjected to search and seizure that will not destroy the records or conceal the information. If he produces it in pursuance of summons or notice, it can undoubtedly be used. If, on the other hand, he withholds it, it cannot be said that Article 19 will exclude such evidence because he had no fundamental right to withhold the records and information. Information gathered as a result of illegal search and seizure can be used subject to the value to be attached to it or its admissibility in accordance with the law relating to evidence. [*Balwant Singh* v. *R. D. Shah, Director of Inspection* [1969] 71 ITR 550 (Delhi)]

It is highly unbecoming of the officers of the department to conduct illegal search and seize documents or accounts and make it appear that they are voluntarily handed over to them. The parties against whom search is to be conducted are entitled to the protection given under the provisions of section 165 (new) of the Code of Criminal Procedure. Any attempt to circumvent those provisions by the authorized officer should not be permitted as it is a serious invasion upon the rights, privacy and freedom of the citizens of India. The power of search must be exercised strictly in accordance with law and no deviation should be tolerated. If the search is illegal, anything recovered therefrom must be returned to its owner. In other words, there should be a complete restoration of the property including the copies and notes, if any, made by any official. To permit the official to retain the copies or notes made from the accounts and documents seized under an illegal search, would be an abuse of the process of law. If that is permitted, the officers concerned could resort to illegal searches, make copies of the documents seized and retain them with impunity and return the original when demanded. That would be defeating the very purpose for which the provisions relating to search and seizure are made and safeguard provided against the illegal searches. Such a practice should not be permitted in our system of law.

The search was declared illegal, the department was directed that the documents, things and goods seized should be returned to the petitioners along with photographs, negatives, translations and notes made by the department from the accounts, etc. [*Harikisandas Gulabdas & Sons* v. *State of Mysore* [1971] 27 STC 434 (Mys.)]

The Calcutta High Court while dealing with a case under section 37 of the Foreign Exchange Regulation Act, 1973, observed that in a case where there was no justification for issuing a search warrant, the fact that incriminating documents were discovered as a result of the search will not lend validity or justification to the search and seizure proceeding which was even at its inception unlawful. If the search and seizure proceeding is initially bad in law, the Government cannot be allowed to enjoy the benefit of the illegal search and seizure proceedings. A man cannot be compelled to be a witness against himself in a criminal trial. If documents are unlawfully seized from a man's residence and used in evidence against him, this will amount to user of coerced evidence. It cannot be said that the duty to supervise zealously the legality of a purported exercise of these powers of search and seizure by the Court can be discharged by merely declaring the search as illegal and allowing the Government to retain the fruits of the illegal search. In such an event, this declaration of illegality by a Court of law would be merely a form of words, valueless and undeserving of mention if the Government could use the evidence obtained by illegal search in a criminal or a quasi-criminal proceeding. [*Bishnu Krishna Shrestha* v. *Union of India* [1987] 168 ITR 815 (Cal.)]

However it may be mentioned that the question whether the illegality of the search and seizure would vitiate the evidence and make the same inadmissible, has been an area of judicial controversy. It is relevant to refer constitution bench decision of Supreme Court in the case of *State of Punjab* v. *Baldev Singh* [1999] 157 CTR (SC) 3/AIR 1999 SC 2378 wherein it was held that illegalities in the action of the authorities concerned in regard to the search and seizure would not only vitiate the proceeding but would also disentitle the prosecution to rely upon such materials, record or evidence as admissible to prove the case against the accused. Failure to adhere to the mandatory requirements of the statute would not only invalidate the proceeding but would also result in the accused being acquitted instead of being convicted. But, this decision was rendered in the backdrop of the criminal proceeding and how far the ratio of this decision would apply to income tax searches is a matter which is not free from debate.

(*i*) Challenging validity of search to weigh pros and cons

Assessee may be tempted to challenge validity of search and seizure operations by way of filing writ petition for any kind of illegality or irregularities committed by tax officials during search. However, before taking any such decision, the advantages and disadvantages of the same should be analyzed carefully. The following factors are worth noting in this connection:—

1. There is cost of litigation in terms of money, time and energy to be devoted.

2. There has to be reasonable basis for challenging legality of search action. Mere bald allegation that department may not be having any information relating to undisclosed income of the assessee is not entertained by the courts. The allegation has to be based upon some cogent reasons.

3. Irregularities committed by the authorized officer in the conduct of search alone cannot form the basis to declare search action as illegal.

4. There is evidentiary value of the material seized during search and department may use it to take action under section 148. Some times based upon facts, action under section 148 may be harsher than the action under section 153A.

5. Department may change, in practice, its approach regarding the nature and extent of enquiry and investigation on certain matters, in case assessee files writ with the High Court challenging validity of search action.

6. By the time writ petition is pending with the High Court, litigation is delayed and if petition of the assessee is dismissed, assessing officer gets extra time to complete the assessment.

7. Department may not take the action of challenging validity of search by assessee in good spirit and assessee may have to face, in practice, other consequences of the "displeasure" of tax officials.

8. In case books of account or documents seized are required to be released, department can use the same against assessee by retaining the photocopies or certified copies of the documents or by invoking provisions of section 131 and impounding such documents.

9. In case there has been illegal seizure of cash, money, bullion, jewellery, or other valuable articles or things during search, there may not be fair chance that the courts may order release of the same, even when search action is held to be valid.

Thus, there cannot be any fixed yardstick to decide as to whether one should go in for challenging the validity of search before the High Court. It depends upon the facts of each case and the consequences to follow. One will have to take appropriate decision in the light of its own facts and circumstances after weighing the pros and cons.

(ii) Who can examine validity of search?

The overwhelming view of the Courts is that validity of search can be examined by High Court in writ petition. Income tax Appellate Tribunal or authorities below do not have power to examine the issue of validity of search.

Initiation and conduct of search are held to be administrative acts which cannot be made subject matter of appeal. [*Rati Ram Gotewala* v. *Dy. CIT* [2004] 89 ITD 14 (Delhi-Trib.)]

Validity of search proceedings cannot be examined by Tribunal. Remedy lies in the writ petition under Article 226 of the Constitution. [*M.B. Lal* v. *CIT* [2005] 149 Taxman 490 (Delhi)]

It has been held in the case of *Brij Mohan Bhatia* v. *ITAT* [2011] 13 taxmann.com 146/[2012] 202 Taxman 32 (Punj. & Har.) that the validity of search and seizure operation could not be gone into by the Tribunal in the appeal proceedings.

The Income Tax Appellate Tribunal has no powers, either express or incidental/implied, to adjudicate upon the issue relating to the validity of the search conducted under section 132 while disposing appeal against block assessment but the only remedy in this matter lies in the form of seeking issue of a writ from the Hon'ble High Court. [*Promain Ltd.* v. *Dy. CIT* [2005] 95 ITD 489/147 Taxman 66 (Mag.)/[2006] 281 ITR (AT) 107 (Delhi-Trib.) (SB)]

Hon'ble Court in the case of *CIT* v. *Paras Rice Mills* [2008] 15 DTR 262 (P&H) have held that while hearing an appeal against an order of assessment, Tribunal cannot go into the question of validity or otherwise of any administrative decision for conducting search and seizure.

The other view available in this regard is that the Tribunal has the power to examine the validity of search and existence of reason to believe as catalogued in clauses (*a*), (*b*), (*c*) of sub-section (1) of section 132.

The Tribunal has jurisdiction to go into the question as to whether the search was conducted consequent upon the authorization having been issued in the background of eventualities as mentioned in section 132(1)(*a*), (*b*), (*c*). According to Rajasthan High Court the question whether there existed any material or not which constituted the reason to believe is the matter which can definitely be looked into by the Tribunal and the absence thereof would vitiate entire action. The only limitation according to Rajasthan High Court is that it is not open to go into the sufficiency of reasons. [*CIT* v. *Smt. Chitra Devi Soni* [2008] 170 Taxman 164 (Raj.)]

It has been held in the case of *Badri Ram Choudhary* v. *Asstt. CIT* [2012] 67 DTR 83 (Raj.) that the Tribunal has the power to decide the legality and propriety of the raid under section 132. The Tribunal is entitled and competent to examine the legality and propriety of the raid in the appeal filed by the appellant.

Revenue, however, in the case of *Ajit Jain* v. *UOI* [2001] 117 Taxman 295 (Delhi) raised one of the contentions that there is an alternative remedy to the assessee by way of an appeal to the Tribunal against the block assessment order, and such plea was raised by the Revenue when assessee raised a ground in the writ that search was without jurisdiction and *void ab initio* and provisions of Chapter XIVB could not be invoked. Hon'ble High Court repelled this contention of the Revenue by holding that the availability of an alternative remedy is not an absolute bar to the entertainment of petition under Article 226 of the Constitution. Thus, it may be taken as an implicit concession made by Revenue to the effect that the issue of validity of search could be raised before the Tribunal in appeal against the block assessment order passed under Chapter XIVB.

It has been held in the case of *Trilok Singh Dhillon* v. *CIT* [2012] 20 taxmann.com 806/54 DTR 129 (Chhattisgarh) that assessee having participated in the assessment proceedings under section 153C and not challenged the validity and legality of the search and seizure proceedings initiated against him by filing any writ petition in the High Court, it was not open to him to question the legality and validity of search and seizure proceedings during the assessment proceedings before the Assessing Officer or in the appeals before the CIT(A) or the Tribunal.

It has been held in the case of *C. Ramaiah Reddy* v. *Asstt. CIT* [2012] 20 taxmann.com 781 (Kar.) that a valid search is a *sine qua non* for initiating block assessment and, though an assessee cannot prefer an appeal against the authorization of search and seizure, once unauthorized or illegal search and seizure culminates in an assessment order, he gets a right to challenge the assessment on several grounds including the validity of authorization and initiation of search.

(*iii*) Whether courts can examine sufficiency of reasons

It has been often held that power of search is an administrative action. Courts can examine existence of reasons but not sufficiency of reasons. It is though subjective satisfaction of the person authorizing search, but is to be based on objective considerations.

Now, it is well settled that the action of the Commissioner, in issuing the authorization is neither judicial nor quasi-judicial. Therefore, while the court cannot sit in judgment as an appellate court and substitute their own opinion for that of the Commissioner, it is always open to them to examine whether there existed any reason for formation of a belief and whether or not the information in possession of the Commissioner was relevant and had any nexus with the formation of belief.

This view has been followed by several courts subsequently. In the case of *Balwant Singh* v. *R.D. Shah, Director of Inspection* [1969] 71 ITR 550 (Delhi), it was held that the reasons to believe, as contemplated under section 132, are subjected only to a limited scrutiny, and the High Court cannot substitute its own opinion for that of the Director of Inspection or the Commissioner. While their existence and relevance are open to question, their adequacy cannot be scrutinized.

The Court cannot go into the question of aptness or sufficiency of the grounds upon which the subjective satisfaction is based. [*ITO* v. *Seth Bros.* [1969] 74 ITR 836 (SC)]

One of the important pre-requisite conditions laid down in section 132(1) is that the department must have in its possession *"information"* which cannot be imaginary or invalid. The words *"information in his possession"* are to mean as some valid, reliable and definite information in possession and not merely any imaginary or invalid information. The information should be credible and if there is some such information, the Court cannot go into the sufficiency of the information. [*Calcutta Discount Co. Ltd.* v. *ITO* [1961] 41 ITR 191 (SC), *Kusum Lata* v. *CIT* [1990] 48 Taxman 401 (Raj.)]

The existence of the belief alone can be challenged before the Court but not sufficiency of reason for the belief. [*Sudarshan & Co.* v. *CIT* [1983] 139 ITR 1032 (All.)]

While examining validity of authorization of search, the scope is limited to see as to whether belief formed by the authority issuing the authorization was a reasonable belief. Court cannot examine sufficiency of material leading to belief of authority that search has to be conducted. [*Southern Herbals Ltd.* v. *DIT (Investigation)* [1994] 207 ITR 55 (Kar.)]

While exercising extraordinary jurisdiction under Article 226/227 of the Constitution, the High Court is required to examine in each case whether the act of issuance of authorization under section 132A of the Act of 1961, is arbitrary, *mala fide* or whether the subjective satisfaction which is recorded is such that it indicates lack of application of mind of the appropriate authority. It is to be examined in each case with care and caution that the reason to believe must be based on definable material or materials and if the information or the reason to believe has no nexus with the belief or there is no definable material or tangible information for formation of such belief then in such a case action taken under section 132A of the said Act would be treated to be arbitrary and illegal. Judicial review conferred upon High Court under Articles 226 and 227 of the Constitution is to be held to be basic feature of the Constitution with an avowed object to ensure that the High Court is to act as bulwark of protection of rights of citizens and it would check on the vagaries negligence and mistakes of the executive or high-handedness of the party before it against another on the anvil of rationality and reasonableness. However, section 132A is subjective in character and Court would not investigate the sufficiency or otherwise of the information produced before issuing warrant of authorization under the aforesaid section. [*Suresh Bhai Bhola Bhai Jani* v. *UOI* [2001] 249 ITR 363 (Raj.)]

The belief may not be open to scrutiny as it is the final conclusion arrived at by the officer concerned as result of mental exercise made by him on the information received. But the reasons due to which the decision is reached can always be examined. When it is said that the reason to believe is not open to scrutiny, what is meant is that the satisfaction arrived at by the officer concerned is immune from challenge, but where the satisfaction is not based on any material or it cannot withstand the test of reason, which is an integral part of it, then it falls through and the Court is empowered to strike it down. *Shyam Jewellers* v. *Chief Commissioner* [1992] 196 ITR 243 (All.)

In the case of *Director General of IT (Investigation)* v. *Spacewood Furnishers (P.) Ltd.* [2015] 119 DTR (SC) 201, it has been held that while exercising writ jurisdiction, High Court cannot go into sufficiency and adequacy of reasons and authenticity and acceptability of information on which satisfaction has been reached by authorities that warrant of authorisation is to be issued under section 132.

4.5 Challenging Validity of Search - Writ Jurisdiction

Validity of search can be challenged before High Courts seeking grant of prayer to issue appropriate writs. In case validity of search action under section 132 is challenged in appeal, it is not a remedy, as Commissioner (Appeals) or to Appellate Tribunal cannot adjudicate the issue as to the validity of search.

(i) Grounds for challenging validity of search

Search and seizure is a very harsh action taken by the department and it breaches privacy of the citizen completely. The wide power has been given to unearth black money and prevent tax evasion but at the same time such wide power has been granted with in-built safeguard mechanism so that there is no misuse of the same.

In case there is a violation of safeguard mechanism provided under section 132 by the authorities, the validity of search action can be challenged by the assessee by filing writ petition before the High Court. It is well settled law that the search and seizure operations should be conducted strictly in accordance with law. Though minor irregularities may not vitiate the search operation, serious irregularities may lead to different conclusion as per the Courts. Following may be some of the grounds whereupon an assessee may challenge validity of search—

1. The information is general in nature and there is no specific information relating to the assessee. The information is just based upon rumors, unreliable or wild allegations.

2. No *"reason to believe"* has been formed by the competent authority satisfying existence of any of the conditions mentioned under clause (*a*), (*b*) or (*c*) of section 132(1).

3. There is absence of nexus between information in possession and reason to believe.

4. Search is carried out with *mala fide* intention.

5. Search is not authorized by the competent authority as prescribed under the law.

6. The objective of search cannot be merely for inquisitional purposes.

7. When search is directed as a matter of general policy by the department to search units following under a particular industry or in a particular area.

8. When search is directed merely on the basis that a person is in the possession of cash or jewellery without any reason to believe that it represents concealed income.

9. When there is no application of mind by the authorizing officer and search is approved in a casual and routine manner.

In practice, it is difficult for a person to challenge the validity of search on the basis of above grounds. The information in possession of the authorizing officer on the basis of which *"reason to believe"* is formed is confidential information which is kept in a confidential folder. The contents of information and reasons recorded for authorizing search are not given to the assessee at any stage. Therefore, it is difficult for the assessee to challenge the validity of search merely based upon the above grounds.

It has been held in the case of *Visa Comtrade Ltd.* v. *Union of India* [2011] 13 taxmann.com 44/201 Taxman 413 (Ori.) that writ petition filed by the petitioner challenging the validity of search and seizure operation raised questions of law involving interpretation of various provisions contained in section 132 and the true effect of the expressions "disclosed income" and "undisclosed income" and, therefore, it is maintainable.

(ii) Observance of safeguards in-built in the provisions of section 132 and rules is essential for exercise of powers

In the case of *Pooran Mal* v. *Director of Inspection* [1974] 93 ITR 505 (SC), it was observed:

We are to see what are the in-built safeguards in section 132 of the Income-tax Act. In the first place, it must be noted that the power to order search and seizure is vested in the highest officers of the Department. Secondly, the exercise of this power can only follow a reasonable belief entertained by such officer that any of the three conditions mentioned in section 132(1)(*a*), (*b*) and (*c*) exists. In this connection, it may be further pointed that under sub-rule (2) of rule 112, Director of Inspection or the Commissioner, as the case may be, has to record his reasons before the authorization is issued to the officers mentioned in sub-section (1) [sub-rule (2) of rule 112 since stands amended deleting the requirement of recording the reasons w.e.f. 1-10-1975].

Thirdly, the authorization of search cannot be in favour of any officer below the rank of an ITO. Fourthly, the authorization is for specific purposes enumerated in clauses (*i*) to (*v*) in sub-section (1), all of which are strictly limited to the object of search.

Fifthly, when money, bullion, etc., is seized, the ITO has to make a summary enquiry with a view to determining how much of what is seized, will be retained by him to cover the estimated tax liability and how much will have to be returned forthwith.

Sixthly, where money, bullion, etc., is seized, it can also be immediately returned to the person concerned after he makes appropriate provision for the payment of the estimated tax dues under sub-section (5) and, lastly this is most important, provisions of the Code of Criminal Procedure relating to search and seizure apply, as far as they may be to all searches and seizures being made with normal decencies and good behaviour. The person in charge of the premises searched is immediately given a copy of the list of articles seized. One copy is forwarded to the authorizing officer. Provision for the safe custody of the articles after seizure is also made under rule 112.

The Court also observed that the argument that section 132(5) is confiscatory, in its effect, has also no force. It must be remembered that the object of this provision is to expedite the return of the seized assets after retaining what is due by way of tax to the individual and has been illegally held by the person concerned. It is needless to add that violation of any one of the safeguards provided by law would give rise to a cause of action under Article 226 of the Constitution.

(iii) Mere allegation of existence of no material - Not a valid ground

It is almost a settled law that mere allegation by the assessee that the authorizing officer did not have any information relating to assessee regarding undisclosed income or undisclosed assets on the basis of which *"reason to believe"* could be formed, cannot be a basis to succeed in writ or to convince the Court to ask for producing the record authorizing search. Mere denial by the assessee that there was no valid information with the authorizing officer issuing search warrant is not enough to quash the proceedings. In *Sriram Jaiswal* v. *Union of India* [1989] 42 Taxman 83, the Allahabad High Court held that the petitioner, who should know whether all his assets were fully disclosed or not, should have supported the denial with cogent material and mere denial by the petitioner that there was no valid information with the Director of Inspection who issued the search warrant, was not enough. When the writ was filed after the order under section 132(5) was passed, it was easier for the petitioner to show that the assets said to be undisclosed under section 132(5) had in fact been disclosed.

Similar view was taken by Hon'ble Supreme Court in the case of *Dr. Partap Singh* v. *Director of Enforcement* [1985] 22 Taxman 30, and it was held that it was not obligatory upon the officer to disclose his material on the mere allegation of the petitioner in such writ petition that there was no material before him on which his reason to believe could be based.

How to Tackle the Situation

This is a tricky situation for assessee how to file writ before the High Court even when he is convinced that no unaccounted transactions have been entered by him or no unrecorded assets are held by him. Assessee may be convinced that he is not having any unaccounted assets and there cannot be any specific information relating to him available with the department. Courts may not direct for producing the satisfaction note or information in possession with the department authorizing search merely on allegation made by the assessee.

Under such circumstances, assessee may be required to draw attention of the Court by pointing out certain irregularities during conduct of search, indiscriminate seizure made flouting the procedure laid down, high handedness exercised by the authorities during search or by way of other circumstantial evidences to demonstrate that search and seizure action has not been conducted in proper and fair manner. It is not that by demonstrating the above facts, assessee would be successful in convincing the Court to hold the search action as invalid, but he would certainly be successful in creating a situation that the court would be compelled to direct the department to produce the record for satisfaction of the Court that there was sufficient material justifying the authorization of search and fairness in the conduct of the search. In that process, the Court will have opportunity to examine the information in possession of the authorizing officer on the basis of which reason to believe was formed and whether the same is fulfilling the test or safeguards as provided under the Act.

The grounds, which are merely illustratively indicative in nature and by no means are exhaustive, for and on which writ can be filed so as to render the effective result may be discussed as under though much would depend upon the facts and circumstances of each case-

(*i*) **Challenging assumption of jurisdiction u/s 153A**

Assessment proceeding under section 153A can be undertaken by the assessing officer in consequence of a valid search. Instead of challenging validity of search directly which may not at times be entertained successfully by the High Court in the absence of sufficient material available with the assessee in this regard, sometimes it may be advisable to challenge assumption of jurisdiction by the assessing officer u/s 153A.

In one of the cases, search warrant was though issued in joint name but Panchnama was prepared only in the name of one person. Other person whose name was not included in the Panchnama, was not having copy of search warrant and was thus not sure of his name being included in search warrant. But AO issued him the notice u/s 153A on the ground that there was search in his case also, as warrant of search contains his name also. On the strength of Panchnama not including his name, assumption of jurisdiction by the assessing officer under section 153A was challenged by such other person by way of writ petition in the High Court. High Court on summoning the records may find that though search warrant included his name but *"reason to believe"* was not formed in his case to initiate search against him and therefore, assessment under section 153A may be liable to be quashed.

(*ii*) **Different circumstantial indicators which may point that search was not in accordance with law thus prompting a challenge to search action in court**

1. Search conducted at the premises of independent director or senior employee of the company, but search warrant issued not in the name of the company but in the personal name of the person.

2. Search warrant issued in joint name of all family members of the assessee while other family members do not have any relation with the affairs of the assessee.

3. Search held in the name of a company having similar name with the larger group on which primarily search has been directed. This can be a case of mistaken identity.

4. Search held at the premises of assessee's brother residing on independent floor having no connection with the assessee. This can be a case of incomplete address and there may not be any valid satisfaction against the brother of the assessee.

5. Consequential search warrant issued without any cogent information or relation with the person originally being searched.

6. Non-compliance of summons issued by ADI under section 131(1A) which alone cannot be the basis for authorizing search.

7. Search conducted as a matter of policy at the premises of all, say, sugar manufacturers of a particular area.

(*iii*) **Search warrant not drawn properly**

1. Blank search warrant already drawn but filled during the conduct of search.

2. Search warrant not shown or got signed from the assessee.

3. Search warrant not duly filled containing signature and seal of authorizing officer, name of assessee or address of his premises.

4. Search warrant not mentioning names of the authorized officers.

(iv) Serious procedural irregularities

1. Search conducted without calling two independent witnesses.

2. Assessee or his representative was not permitted to attend the search proceedings

3. When documents brought from outside are planted and included in the Panchnama of the assessee

4. Where boxes, almirahs, receptacles are broken indiscriminately without any opportunity to the assessee to produce keys and nothing incriminating is found in them.

5. Where assessee or his family members are detained and are not permitted to carry out routine activities, take meals or do prayers, worship, etc.

(v) Indiscriminate seizure

1. Seizure is made of the immovable properties.

2. Seizure of disclosed assets/jewellery is made inspite of complete evidences produced by the assessee.

3. In case there is no seizure of any undisclosed assets, this by itself cannot be a ground. In case no assets are seized, assessee cannot allege that search action was illegal. However coupled with other factors, this can be an indication to draw attention of the Court that there could not be any cogent information against the assessee to authorize search.

4. Seizure of disclosed assets and regular books of account of third party without giving opportunity to such person to explain his position.

5. Panchnama is not drawn properly and the correct facts of the incidents taking place during search are not recorded therein.

6. Where seizure has taken place without application of mind and this is evidenced by the fact that all the books and documents found are seized without looking into whether the same is useful or relevant to any of the proceedings under the Act.

(vi) High Handedness exercised during search

1. Threat is administered or third degree is used during search.

2. The business operations of the assessee are halted during search and thereafter also by putting restraint under section 132(3).

3. Statement of the assessee is recorded under threat and coercion and the actual facts stated by the assessee are not properly recorded.

(*vii*) Statement of Panchas

1. Statement given by the panchas recorded in the Panchnama or even thereafter stating the irregularities or high handedness exercised by the search team.

(*viii*) Illegal restraint under section 132(3)

1. Restraint order passed against business stock in trade or for disclosed assets.
2. Restraint order not lifted beyond reasonable time or in any case upto 60 days from the date of conclusion of search.

(*ix*) Post search irregularities

1. Issuing summons to assessee under section 131(1A) repeatedly who has already been searched and statement recorded under section 132(4).
2. Not allowing inspection of books of account seized and not giving the photocopies of the documents which may be urgently required to carry out normal business activities.
3. Not handing over seized material of the assessee to the assessing officer having jurisdiction over the assessee within the prescribed time limit.

It is again submitted that the above grounds or irregularities may not be sufficient enough to get the search declared as illegal by the courts. A petition by the assessee compositely challenging the validity of search along with demonstration of some or more of the above irregularities may compel the court to call for satisfaction note recorded against the assessee. It will give an opportunity to the Court to examine the information in possession of the department on the basis of which search has been authorized and to decide on the issue whether search is valid or not.

4.6 Writ for other matters

It is not that writ petition can be filed by the assessee with the High Court only for challenging validity of search. Writ petition can be filed by the assessee in all situations where rights of the assessee are being denied and no other remedial mechanism is available to the assessee under the Act. For other matters also, assessee can go in writ proceeding when the administrative measures are of no help to him. Some of such matters may be as under-

1. Seizure of disclosed assets of the assessee and not releasing the same inspite of evidences produced by the assessee.
2. Seizure of the stock in trade

3. Assessment proceedings under section 153A initiated even when search is held illegal.

4. Disclosed assets or books of third parties seized and no opportunity being given to him to plead his case.

5. Proceedings under section 153C initiated against some other person without jurisdiction or without recording reasons.

6. Halting normal business activities of the assessee and to get the same resumed.

7. Sealing or locking business premises of the assessee.

There are various judicial pronouncements on the issues which indicate as to under what circumstances search action can be held to be illegal, as to on what grounds a writ petition can be filed or as to under what circumstances writ petition is not entertained by the Courts. These decisions have been discussed at appropriate places in this chapter and in other chapters of the book and may be referred where discussion on particular issue has been made.

4.7 At what stage writ can be filed

There is no time limit for filing writ petition with the High Court. A writ can be filed at any stage whenever assessee feels aggrieved. However, undue delay in filing writ petition may not only weaken the case of the assessee but may impair the very admission of the writ.

The High Court may issue a writ during the currency of search proceedings and direct the stay of further proceedings under section 132 at any stage prohibiting the department from making any further search or any seizure. However, the Courts are circumspect to show their indulgence and exercise a great restraint in passing such orders.

Search conducted in 1998 but the effective hearing started in 2000- writ petition filed simultaneously- it is held that there was no delay in filing writ petition- Constitution of India, Article 226.[*Vipan Kumar Jain* v. *Union of India* [2001] 117 Taxman 178 (P&H)]

Delay in filing writ petition is fatal where no adequate *explanation* for the delay is furnished. [*Ram Mohan Rastogi* v. *Union of India* [1984] 19 Taxman 178 (All.)]

Search proceedings cannot be quashed where there is delay in writ petition and the block assessment is made and appeal is pending. [*Baldev Raj Mehra* v. *Union of India* [2004] 139 Taxman 324 (P&H)]

Where a search was conducted on October 6, 1982 and cash and jewellery were seized, but no summary assessment was made under section 132(5) and a regular assessment was made almost about 3 years later, *i.e.,* on March 24, 1986, and where a part of the jewellery was returned as a result of the regular assessment, and the appeal filed by the assessee was disposed of by the CIT(A) and the department had gone in appeal before the Tribunal, which was pending for a long time, it was held that since the second appeal was pending for a long time, the assessee was entitled to return/refund of cash and jewellery on furnishing bank guarantees to the satisfaction of the departmental authorities. [*Rameshwar Prasad* v. *Asstt. CIT* [1991] 54 Taxman 94 (All.)]

(i) No injunction

In challenging the issue of warrant, the petitioner grievances might be that the search of his premises would be unfair. But what has to be taken into consideration in such cases is the larger question as to whether the hands of the investigating agency can be fettered by an injunction order of the court on the ground that it would use its power in excess of its right conferred on it under the Act. Keeping in view the interest of the state, it is not desirable to grant an injunction. [*N. Ramakrishnan* v. *CIT* [1985] 20 Taxman 465 (Mad.)]

(ii) Repetitive writ petition

In the earlier petition, exactly similar challenges were made regarding the illegal search by the respondents and the Court declined to interfere. It would neither be legal nor in consonance with the principles of propriety to entertain the petition on identical grounds which were specifically raised in the earlier petition and the court dismissed the petition as withdrawn at that stage. No leave was granted to the petitioner to file another petition. The petitioner could not be permitted to negotiate the issues raised in the earlier petition. [*Anil Kumar Bindal* v. *DGIT* [2002] 122 Taxman 855 (Delhi)]

4.8 Scope of Writ Petition

(i) No factual dispute in writ

In writ jurisdiction, the Court would not go into a factual dispute. Writ is decided on the basis of uncontroverted or admitted facts. When facts are disputed on some plausible basis, Court may refuse to go into those factual aspect of the matter while seized with the writ proceeding.

The petitioner contended that the period of 180 days for retaining the books of account expired on January 18, 1988, whereas the approval to retain the books beyond 180 days was granted by the Commissioner on January 19, 1988, and, therefore, the books of account were liable to be retained forthwith. No such pleading having been raised in the grounds of the petition and the question whether the approval was granted on January 18 or 19, 1988, being a question of fact, the Court could not go into the factual dispute, more so, in view of the fact that the approval accorded by the Commissioner up to December 31, 1988, was on the verge of termination. The Court held that the petitioner was not entitled to the writ of mandamus prayed for. [*Sriram Jaiswal* v. *Union of India* [1989] 42 Taxman 83/176 ITR 261 (All.)]

Enquiry cannot be made into disputed facts by the High Court. [*Yogendra Kumar Durlabhji* v. *CIT* [1998] 100 Taxman 282 (Raj.)]

(ii) **Writ not for deciding ownership of seized money**

The petitioner sought a direction to Assistant Director of Income Tax (Investigation), Muzaffarpur, to release the amount of ₹ 13.90 lakh in his favour which had been seized from the possession of three persons. The petitioner claimed to be the owner of the aforesaid money. Held, that the question as to whether the petitioner was the owner of the money or not could not be gone into in this Court. [*Wakil Kumar* v. *CIT* [2004] 134 Taxman 733 (Pat.)]

(iii) **Jurisdiction of High Court - Cause of action arose wholly or partly**

As a result of insertion of clause (2) by 42nd Amendment, a petition under Article 226 can be presented before any of the High Court if the High Court within whose territorial jurisdiction the person or the authority against whom relief is sought reside or situate and if the High Court within whose territorial jurisdiction the cause of action in respect of which relief is sought under Article 226 has arisen, wholly or in part. Where search and seizure took place in Delhi and no nexus or connection can be established with the assessee in Guwahati and no action arose in Delhi, it was held that no writ will lie at Guwahati. [*Jagdish Prasad Saraogi* v. *Union of India* [1997] 95 Taxman 209 (Gau.)]

(iv) **Public Interest Litigation for not conducting search against influential persons not entertained.**

Namit Verma v. *Union of India* [2001] 115 Taxman 153 (Delhi)

4.9 Powers of Court in Writ Jurisdiction

(i) **Court can mould the remedy to suit the facts of each case.**

Director of Inspection of Income-tax v. *Pooran Mall & Sons* [1974] 96 ITR 390 (SC).

(ii) **Inherent powers of Court under Article 226.**

The Court which exercises its power under Article 226 of the Constitution, has got inherent powers to make all such orders as are necessary for doing complete justice to the parties. [*Grindlays Bank Ltd.* v. *ITO* [1980] 3 Taxman 38 (SC) and *Mangilal Jain* v. *Collector of Customs* [1982] 133 ITR 762 (Mad.) at page 778]

(iii) **Court's Power to Review.**

The Court's power of review while exercising jurisdiction under Article 226 of the Constitution extends to correct all errors to prevent miscarriage of justice. The review can be allowed only on:

    a. discovery of new and important matter of evidence which, after exercise of due diligence, was not within the knowledge of the person seeking review, or could not be produced by him at the time when the order was made, or

        - when some mistake or error on the fact of record is found, or

        - on any analogous ground. But review is not permissible on the ground that the decision was erroneous on the merits as the same would be the province of an appellate court. [*Commissioner of Police* v. *Sadruddin H. Javeri* [1999] 103 Taxman 571/[2000] 243 ITR 602 (AP)]

(iv) **Plea of alternative remedy**

As a matter of general principle, the remedy of writ prescribed under Article 226 of the Constitution is normally barred where an alternative remedy is available to the petitioner either under the Constitution itself or under any statutory law.

For challenging validity of search, there is no alternative remedy available under the Income Tax Act, 1961; therefore, jurisdiction will lie before the High Court directly. In other matters relating to search and seizure, administrative or appellate remedies may be available with Commissioner or Chief Commissioner. Before filing writ in such cases, assessee should exhaust the alternative remedies otherwise writ petition may not be entertained by the High Court. Some of the judicial pronouncements on this issue may be discussed as under—

    1. Plea of alternative remedy is of no avail where an action is wholly without jurisdiction. [*Ajit Jain* v. *Union of India* [2001] 117 Taxman 295 (Delhi)]

    2. An order passed without jurisdiction can be quashed in writ proceedings even if there is an alternative remedy. [*Shaw Wallace & Co. Ltd.* v. *ITAT* [1999] 240 ITR 579 (Cal.)]

    3. Where principles of natural justice have been violated, existence of an alternative remedy is not a bar. [*Sri Balasubramania Traders* v. *Asstt. CIT* [1999] 105 Taxman 429 (Mad.)]

4. Though the Income Tax Act provides a complete machinery for assessment of tax and imposition of penalty and for obtaining relief in respect of any improper orders passed by the Income-tax authorities, the appellant cannot normally be permitted to abandon resort to that machinery and to invoke the jurisdiction of the High Court under Article 226 of the Constitution when he had adequate remedy open to him by an appeal to the Tribunal - *C.A. Abraham* v. *ITO* [1961] 41 ITR 425 (SC), but as has been demonstrated above, the position is substantially different in the matter of challenge of validity of action under section 132 for which no normal channel of appeal is provided under the Income-tax Act.

5. Existence of an alternative remedy is no bar for issue of writ when action is taken without jurisdiction and affects fundamental rights - *Vindhya Metal Corpn.* v. *CIT* [1985] 156 ITR 233 (All.). [Upheld by Supreme Court in *CIT* v. *Vindhya Metal Corpn.* [1997] 91 Taxman 192].

Whether the statute provides an alternative remedy or not where any authority acts without jurisdiction or in excess of jurisdiction which again might result in unnecessary harassment of a person concerned, the High Court can interfere under Article 226 of the Constitution. Alternative remedy even if available is not always bar to High Court acting under Article 226. [*Calcutta Discount Co. Ltd.* v. *ITO* [1961] 41 ITR 191 (SC)]

6. The rule of exhaustion of statutory remedies before writ is granted is self-imposed limitation, a rule of policy and discretion rather than a rule of law and the Court may, therefore, in exceptional cases, issue a writ of certiorari notwithstanding the fact that the statutory remedies have not been exhausted. [*Baburam Prakash Chandra Maheshwari* v. *Antarim Zila Parishad* AIR 1969 SC 556]. The Supreme Court has clarified the rule of exhaustion of remedies with two exceptions, *viz.,* (*i*) where the provision under which the order is purported to be made is *ultra vires,* and (*ii*) where the impugned order is made in violation of the principles of natural justice. There are decisions holding that where there is patent lack of jurisdiction, the court can issue a writ even though there is an alternative remedy available. This is, thus, a third exception. [*Punamchand R. Shah* v. *ITO* [1975] 101 ITR 373 (Mad.)]

4.10 Summing up

Hon'ble Supreme Court in the case of *ITO* v. *Seth Bros.* [1969] 74 ITR 836 examined the scope of section 132 and the relevant rules and following principles were broadly laid down to test the validity of any warrant of search and seizure:-

1. The issue of a search warrant by the Commissioner under section 132 of the Income-tax Act, 1961, is not a judicial or a quasi-judicial act.

2. Since by the exercise of the power under section 132 of the Income-tax Act, 1961, a serious invasion is made upon the rights, privacy and freedom of the taxpayer, the power must be exercised strictly in accordance with the law and only of the purposes for which the law authorizes it to be exercised.

3. If the action of the officer issuing the authorization or of the designated officer is challenged, the officer concerned must satisfy the Court about the regularity of his action.

4. If the action is maliciously taken or power under the section is exercised for a collateral purpose, it is liable to be struck down by the court.

5. If the conditions for the exercise of the power are not satisfied, the proceeding is liable to be quashed. But where power is exercised *bona fide* and in furtherance of the statutory duties of the tax officer, any error of judgment on the part of the officer will not vitiate the exercise of the power.

6. Where the Commissioner entertains the requisite belief and for reasons recorded by him authorizes a designated officer to enter and search premises for books of account and documents relevant to or useful for any proceeding under the Act, the court on a petition by an aggrieved person, cannot be asked to substitute its own opinion whether an order authorizing the search should have been issued.

7. Any irregularity in the course of entry, search and seizure committed by an officer acting in pursuance of the authorization will not be sufficient to vitiate the action taken provided the officer has, in executing the authorization, acted *bona fide*.

8. The Act and the Rules do not require that the warrant of authorization should specify the particulars of documents and books of account, a general authorization to search for and seize documents and books of account relevant to or useful for any proceeding complies with the requirements of the Act and the Rules.

9. It is for the officer making the search to exercise his judgment and seize or not to seize any documents or books of account.

10. An error committed by the officer in seizing documents which may ultimately be found not to be useful for or relevant to the proceeding under the Act will not by itself vitiate the search nor will it entitle the aggrieved person to an omnibus order releasing all documents seized.

11. The aggrieved party may undoubtedly move a competent court to pass an order releasing the documents seized. In such a proceeding, the officer who has made the search will be called upon to prove how the documents seized are likely to be useful for or relevant to a proceeding under the Act.

12. If he is unable to do so, the Court may order that those documents be released.

13. The circumstance that a large number of documents have been seized is not a ground for holding that all the documents seized are irrelevant or the action of the officers is *mala fide.*

14. The provisions of Code of Criminal Procedure, 1898 relating to searches apply, so far as may be, to searches under section 132.

15. Thereby, it is only intended that the officer concerned shall issue the necessary warrant, keep present respectable persons of the locality to witness the search, and generally carry out the search in the manner provided by the Code of Criminal Procedure.

16. But sub-section (13) of section 132 does not imply that the limitations prescribed by section 165 of the Code of Criminal Procedure are also incorporated therein.

17. Where as warrant is issued in relation to a firm, the officer authorized thereunder is not restricted to searching for and taking possession of only those books of account and other documents which directly relate to the business carried on by the partners in the name of the firm.

18. The books of account and other documents in respect of other business carried on by the partners would certainly be relevant because they would tend to show inter-relation between the dealings and supply materials having a bearing on the case of evasion of income-tax by the firm.

19. Merely because the Income-tax Officers made a search for and seized the books of account and documents in relation to business carried on in the names of other firms and companies, the search and seizure would not be illegal.

20. In the absence of anything to show that the documents seized were either replaced or tampered with, the irregularity of failing to place the identification marks on several documents will not by itself supply a ground for holding that the search was mala fide.

21. Keeping of police officers in the house of influential businessmen just to ensure the protection of the officers and the records at the time of search could not amount to employment of force.

ACTUAL CONDUCT OF SEARCH OPERATIONS

5.1 Text of section 132(1)(i) to (v)

Power of search and seizure is contained in clauses (*i*) to (*v*) of section 132(1) which empowers the Authorized Officer to:—

(*i*) enter and search any building, place, vessel, vehicle or aircraft where he has reason to suspect that such books of account, other documents, money, bullion, jewellery or other valuable article or thing are kept;

(*ii*) break open the lock of any door, box, locker, safe, almirah or other receptacle for exercising the powers conferred by clause (*i*) where the keys thereof are not available;

(*iia*) search any person who has got out of, or is about to get into, or is in the building, place, vessel, vehicle or aircraft, if the authorized officer has reason to suspect that such person has secreted about his person any such books of account, other documents, money, bullion, jewellery or other valuable article or thing;

(*iib*) require any person who is found to be in possession or control of any books of account or other documents maintained in the form of electronic record as defined in clause (*t*) of sub-section (1) of section 2 of the Information Technology Act, 2000 (21 of 2000), to afford the authorized officer the necessary facility to inspect such books of account or other documents;

(*iii*) seize any such books of account, other documents, money, bullion, jewellery or other valuable article or thing found as a result of such search:

Provided that bullion, jewellery or other valuable article or thing, being stock-in-trade of the business, found as a result of such search shall not be seized but the authorized officer shall make a note or inventory of such stock-in-trade of the business;

139

(*iv*) place marks of identification on any books of account or other documents or make or cause to be made extracts or copies therefrom;

(*v*) make a note or an inventory of any such money, bullion, jewellery or other valuable article or thing.

5.2 Legislative History - Significant Amendments

◆ In clause (*i*) the words "vessel, vehicle or aircraft" were added along with building or place by the Taxation Laws (Amendment) Act, 1975 w.e.f. 01.10.1975 so as to cover moving vehicles, ship or aircraft for search operations. Prior to the amendment, the authorization could be issued only for the search of a building or a place. The scope of this power was found limited by the Legislature which was then extended to cover the search of a vehicle and aircraft as well.

◆ Clause (*iia*) was inserted by Taxation Laws (Amendment) Act, 1975 w.e.f. 01.10.1975 so as to cover any person coming in, present within or going out of the premises to be searched. The authorized officer has been empowered to search such person, if he has reason to suspect that such person has secreted certain undisclosed assets or documents on his person. CBDT Circular No. 179, dated 30.9.1975 explains this insertion as legislating the power which was already there under rule 112(5). In the absence of such power in the Act it self, the relevant rule 112(5) could have been found *ultra vires* to Act.

◆ Clause (*iib*) had been inserted by Finance Act, 2002 w.e.f. 01.06.2002 so as to empower the authorized officer to inspect books and other documents kept in electronic form. It became necessary in view of more and more use of computers and books being maintained by the assessee in electronic form. This amendment was brought to overcome the difficulty faced by the Authorized Officer during search operation, in not being able to operate and have access to the data stored in computers for want of password and reluctance of the person searched and his staff to part with the password.

◆ Proviso to clause (*iii*) was inserted by Finance Act, 2003 w.e.f. 01.06.2003 providing not to seize stock-in-trade of the business so that normal business operations are not disturbed. Prior to this amendment, deemed seizure was being applied by the department on inventory items of the business which was causing lot of hardships in carrying out the business and on the movement of inventory. On the other side, department was also not able to realize the taxes by such seizure since inventory items used to get obsolete over a period of time.

5.3 Objective

The competent authority may authorize the authorized officer to undertake the actions as provided in above clauses (*i*) to (*v*) of section 132(1). The objective is to equip the authorized officer with powers to undertake the actions as provided in these provisions without which the very efficacy of the search operation would have been affected adversely to the Revenue.

5.4 To enter and search

Clause (*i*) of section 132(1) authorizes the authorized officer to enter and search any building, place, vessel, vehicle or aircraft where **he has reason to suspect** that **such** books of account, other documents, money, bullion, jewellery or other valuable article or things are kept.

(*i*) "He has reason to suspect" and "such" - Significance thereof

◆ In this phrase, 'he' refers to the competent authority who is authorizing to undertake search action and not to the authorized officer. The requirement to form 'reason to believe' in consequence of information in possession is qua-assessee and once the 'reason to believe' is formed against a person and search action is undertaken under section 132(1), specific building or place relating to such person to be covered for search can be done only on the basis of suspicion. In this view of the matter, the authorization to enter and search any building or place may be on the basis of suspicion. For covering any building or place, it is not required to form 'reason to believe' with respect to each building or place separately.

◆ The use of the word 'Such' books of account, other documents, money, bullion, jewellery or other valuable article or thing refers to those books of account, other documents, money, bullion, jewellery or other valuable article or thing which are referred under clause (*a*), (*b*) or (*c*) of section 132(1). Therefore, those books of account, other documents, money, bullion, jewellery or other valuable article or thing which are not covered under clause (*a*), (*b*) or (*c*) of section 132(1), cannot be the basis to "enter and search".

(*ii*) Which premises can be searched

There has to be separate search warrant for each premise or place. If a person has several godowns or residential premises, there has to be separate authorization for each premise. If there are different municipal numbers of different portions of the same building, search of only those portions can be carried out whose number is mentioned in the authorization and not of all the portions. Any search operation undertaken at the premises not authorized by the search warrant would be illegal.

(*iii*) Multi-storied buildings

The authorization of search warrant has to be qua-person as well as qua-premises. For example, a search warrant mentions Mr. A, resident of House No. 123, Sector-45, Delhi and this building is a multi-storied building having three floors and Mr. A resides at ground floor. Ist & IInd floor which have independent entry, are occupied by somebody else. In the search warrant, ground floor is omitted to be mentioned along with his address. In such a case, search operation can be undertaken only at the ground floor premises in occupation of Mr. A and the Ist & IInd floor which are occupied by somebody else, may be in occupation of his father or brother, cannot be covered under the search.

Under such circumstances, in case authorized officer attempts to search Ist & IInd floor, such person(s) occupying the Ist and IInd floors has remedy by way to approach to higher authorities or if he fails with them, he may approach to High Court by way of writ petition under article 226 of the Constitution.

However, in case authorized officer has reason to suspect that incriminating material relating to Mr. A, the person searched, is kept at Ist and IInd floor of the premises and he wants to search those floors also, he is required to obtain separate search warrant for those independent floors.

(*iv*) Premises jointly occupied by several persons

Problems do arise in those cases where the premises are occupied jointly like several brothers along with parents living in a family occupying single residential unit. In case they are occupying distinctively demarcated areas within the floor/premises and the search warrant is only in the name of one of the family members, the portion of the premises occupied by other brothers are not to be covered and those members are within their right to plead that no search operation with respect to them can be carried. However, in practice, it is very difficult to claim and establish distinctively demarcated areas within the floor/premise having common entrance. An authorized officer will be entitled to carry out the personal search or the search operations in relation to co-occupier if he is satisfied that co-occupier has secreted some document or asset belonging to the searched person in whose case search is authorized.

In case several family members live together in joint family with no distinctively demarcated areas, it is difficult to claim immunity in relation to search operation with respect to their belongings or area occupied.

Similarly in the case of premises occupied by different companies or registered office of many companies situated in the same office, the search of the entire premises for which a search warrant is issued shall be valid even if the warrant is in the name of one company. The seizure of books of account or other documents can be made belonging to other companies on the ground that there may be some kind of business relation of those companies with the company in whose case search is authorized.

(*v*) **Timings of search**

Search operation at times may be of utmost urgency and thus, no restriction on commencement or conduct of search operation has been provided in the law. A search may be commenced at any time during day or night and may be continued till next day or thereafter. However in practice, search operation is generally undertaken in the morning hours and planning is made in such a manner so as to strike the operation at different premises of the assessee all over the country at the same time.

(*vi*) **Search of the premises found locked**

As per the powers given under clause (*ii*) of section 132(1) read with sub-rule (4) of rule 112, if any premises is found locked, the authorized officer is empowered to break open the lock to enter the premises and search it, irrespective of whether the owner or occupant of the premises is available or not.

(*vii*) **Free Ingress**

According to sub-rule (3) of rule 112 any person incharge of any building, place, vessel, vehicle or aircraft authorized to be searched shall allow the authorized officer carrying the valid search warrant, free ingress thereto and afford all reasonable facilities for the search. It is immaterial as to what is the relationship of that person with the person in whose case the search has been authorized. Refusal to allow free ingress or, not affording the requisite facility for the search may make a person liable for the prosecution under sections 187 & 188 of the Indian Penal Code. Any obstruction in search procedure may make him further liable for prosecution u/s 186 of the Indian Penal Code.

Sub-rule (8) of rule 112 requires occupant of the premises or some other person on his behalf to be permitted, to attend the proceeding during search operation. It does not however mean that no search can be conducted without their presence. The authorized officer is required to ask for admission in the premises and when he cannot otherwise obtain admission, he is empowered to use his authority to enter after breaking the lock.

It was held in the case of *Hari Narayan Chandra* v. *Emperor* AIR 1928 Cal. 27 that it is not necessary that the occupant must be present at the search. The rule only lays down that he should be permitted to do so if he desires to remain present.

(viii) Search at the premises not belonging to assessee

A search can be conducted at the premises, which is not belonging to the target person. The target person may not even be the owner or occupant of such premises. For issuing search warrant and conducting search at any such premises, the competent authority has to satisfy himself that undisclosed books of account, documents or assets relating to the target person under search have been kept or secreted thereat. In case the authorities are having information or suspicion that the target person is keeping undisclosed books, documents or assets at any place or premises not belonging to him, the same may be covered for the purpose of search. When search warrant is issued in respect of such place in the name of target person, the authorized officer is required to search and seize the material only relating to such person. However, in practice, this restraint is not sometime exercised during search of such premises and assets/documents relating to other person(s) are also seized. This in our opinion can be done only when such documents/assets are having any connection or relation to the target person.

Generally under such circumstances, Department undertakes survey operation u/s 133A instead of action of search u/s 132. However, in case the place is not a business premises but is a residential premises, action has to be taken under section 132 as no survey action can be taken u/s 133A at residential premises.

While searching the target person, premises of other person can be covered but search warrant is required to be made in the name of the target person and such search warrant cannot be issued in such a case in the name of other person.

In case search warrant is issued in the name of other person being occupant of any premises, who is having connection with the affairs of the target person, there has to be separate 'reason to believe' recorded with respect to such other person on the parameters of clause (*a*), (*b*) or (*c*) of section 132(1).

It may so happen, for example, when searched person is having close connection with his counsel, relating to the financial transactions and department is having the information that certain documents relating to such transactions are kept in the office of the counsel & therefore the premises of the counsel are also required to be searched. In another situation, when a search is conducted in the case of a company, senior executives of the company who are closely involved in managing the affairs of the company may also be required to be searched so as to collect evidences relating to the affairs of the company. In such cases, when search warrant is issued in the name of target person/company but search operations being conducted at the premises of other persons, undisclosed assets or documents relating to the personal affairs of other persons cannot be seized. However, if authorized officer wants to seize personal assets or documents of other persons which have no connection with the target person/ company, there has to be separate search warrant in the name of consultant or senior executive whose premises are being searched after forming "reason to believe" on the parameters as prescribed under clause (*a*), (*b*) or (*c*) of section 132(1) with respect to such other person(s).

However, in practice it has been seen that the documents or undisclosed assets relating to personal affairs of such other person are seized by the authorized officer on the pretext that such documents or assets might have some connection with the target person/entity.

(*ix*) Car parked outside the house

When search warrant is issued in the case of a person for his residential premises, the authorized officer is empowered to search any place, almirah, room or vehicle parked inside the house. In case car is parked outside adjoining the house and authorized officer is having suspicion that some undisclosed books of account or documents are secreted therein, in our considered opinion, the same can also be searched and searched person cannot take the plea successfully that there has to be separate search warrant for vehicle parked outside the house. For this purpose, parking area of the car adjoining the house will be treated as part of the house and no separate search warrant for the vehicle is required.

5.5 To break, open locks, etc.

Clause (*ii*) of sub-section (1) of section 132 provides that an authorized officer can break, open the lock of any door, box, locker, safe, almirah or other receptacle for exercising the powers conferred by clause (*i*), where the keys thereof are not available.

It is the duty of authorized officer to provide reasonable opportunity to the assessee to produce keys of the lock. In case assessee fails to produce the same, the authorized officer may use his power to break or open the lock. In case the authorized officer suspects the undisclosed assets hidden inside, he may open or tear sofas, beds, break the wall or dig the floor. The assessee cannot object to such actions, if they are done *bona fide* and in good faith while carrying out the object of the search. A public officer discharging his official duties is presumed to be acting according to fairness and good conscience without any bias unless proved otherwise by the person alleging contrary to it.

However it is seen in practice that use of such power is exercised sparingly by the authorized officer under the circumstances when there is persistent non-cooperation in affording the facility of conducting search of any locked room, door, box, locker, safe, almirah or other receptacle.

Action may however lie against the authorized officer if these acts are done in *mala fide* manner and there was no reason to suspect that items broken or destroyed contained undisclosed assets or incriminating documents etc. hidden therein, either on the basis of information received from the informer or from any other source.

5.6 To conduct personal search

Clause (*iia*) of sub-section (1) of section 132 was inserted with effect from 01.10.1975. It empowers the authorized officer to search any person who has got out of, or is about to get into or is in the building or place etc., if the authorized officer has reason to suspect that such person has secreted about his person, any incriminating documents', papers, money, bullion, etc.

Prior to insertion of the above clause, there were doubts about the power of the authorized officer as to whether such authorized officer had any statutory power under the Act, to search any other person (other than the person in whose name the search warrant is issued) who was inside the building or who comes in or goes out of the building. After insertion of this clause, clarity has been brought and power has been specifically given to the authorized officer to search any person inside the building.

Personal search of any member of family residing in the premises or any guest, customer or other business constituent visiting the assessee during the course of search can be conducted and there is no need for separate search warrant for that purpose. Thus, person entering the premise where search operation is on, is required to be careful and vigilant on this aspect and ought to know that his personal search can be conducted by the authorized officer as it is permitted under the law.

The statutory procedure and requirements of the personal search are listed in sub-rules (5) & (9) of rule 112 and have been discussed in detail while analyzing rule 112.

5.7 To afford facility to inspect electronic record

With the development of information technology, books of account are generally kept in computer or in any other electronic form. The details relating to undisclosed transactions may be kept in electronic form in the computers or in other electronic devices. The data in computers cannot be opened unless software being used or password for opening the file is made available to the authorized officer. Before this power was specifically conferred on the authorized officer, search team at times found itself in difficulty in having access to such books of account or documents due to non-cooperation of the searched person, his family members or his staff. To overcome these hardships, clause (*iib*) was inserted in sub-section (1) of section 132 with effect from 01.06.2002. It requires the searched person or any person in possession of electronic record to afford the authorized officer the necessary facility to inspect books of account, other documents or data kept in electronic form.

The necessary facility will include making available software being used to store data, password being used to open files or access to the server where data is stored.

(*i*) **Restoration of deleted data**

Sometimes data created by a person is deleted from the computers for various reasons such as wrong recording or incorrect recording of some fact etc. There are softwares available which may restore the deleted data and with the help of computer expert, department sometimes resort to such strategy so as to restore the deleted data which may be of incriminating nature. The searched person cannot disown such data as the presumption under section 132(4A)/292C will equally apply to the same. However, the searched person will be at liberty to displace the presumption by explaining the facts and circumstances in which the data was deleted so as to shift the burden of proof.

Therefore, every person should remain aware of the above factual and legal situation before creating any incriminating data in soft form.

(*ii*) **Information in electronic form in possession of searched person received via email**

In the computer or laptop of the searched person, there may be details or files containing financial and/or other information which have been received by him *via* email. In case such data is download-ed and is available in the computer of the searched person, it would tantamount that data is in his possession and control and such data may be inspected by the authorized officer.

There may be another situation where these files or details may not have been downloaded. Such data does not remain on the server of the searched person but may be accessed or opened though internet on the mail account of the searched person.

In such a situation, a pertinent question arises for consideration as to whether such data can be said to be in control or possession of the searched person and can the same be looked into and seized by the authorized officer?

In our considered opinion, such data cannot be said to be in possession or control of the searched person since data can be sent in the email id of any person by anybody. Unless the data is downloaded by the such person on his computer, it cannot be said that such data is in his possession and control. There can be one view that if possession and control of such data is not with the searched person, he may not be required to afford the authorized officer the necessary facility such as disclose the password of email id so as to enable him to inspect such data. However this view is not free from doubt & contrary view may be taken by the department in this regard.

5.8 To make seizure

Clause (*iii*) of sub-section (1) of section 132 empowers the authorized officer to seize any such books of account, other documents, money, bullion, jewellery or other valuable article or thing found as a result of such search. Use of the word 'such' prior to books of account, other documents, money, bullion, jewellery or other valuable article or thing refers to those books of account, documents or assets which are covered under clauses (*a*), (*b*), (*c*) of section 132(1) and for which search warrant has been issued. Therefore, such books of account, other documents, money, bullion, jewellery or other valuable article or thing which are not covered under clauses (*a*), (*b*), (*c*) of section 132(1) cannot be seized. No seizure can be made of those books of account or other documents which are not useful or relevant to any proceedings under the Income-tax Act. Similarly, no seizure can be made of the disclosed assets. Detailed discussion regarding various aspects of seizure has been made in a separate chapter.

5.9 To Place identification marks

Clause (*iv*) of sub-section (1) of section 132 empowers the authorized officer to place marks of identification on any books of account or any other documents or make or cause to be made extracts or copies therefrom.

Here in this clause, prior to the words 'books of account or any other documents' the word 'such' has not been used which implies that marks of identification can be made or photocopies can be obtained relating to any books of account or other documents found in possession of the searched person.

5.10 To make inventory of assets

Clause (v) of sub-section (1) of section 132 empowers the authorized officer to make a note or inventory of any assets including cash found, stock-in-trade in the business or other assets, valuable article or thing found as a result of search. The inventory can be made even of the assets which are not seized so as to make verification during assessment proceedings regarding the source of acquisition of such assets.

5.11 Preparation of panchnama

Panchnama is a document prepared at the conclusion of search operation. It is a document containing details of the events having taken place during search operation, details or lists of all the assets seized, details of all the assets & documents found. Other things found & inventorized but not seized are also part of Panchnama. The place from where the assets seized are respectively found is also mentioned in panchnama. Delhi High Court in the case of *CIT* v. *S.K. Katyal* [2009] 177 Taxman 380 have observed that panchnama is a written record of what has been witnessed by Panchas. A panchnama is nothing but a document recording what has happened in the presence of the witnesses. A panchnama may document search proceedings, with or without seizure. A panchnama may also document the return of the seized articles or removal of the seals.

Sometimes the description of location is extremely relevant and important for the purpose of determining the ownership and source of acquisition of an asset or explaining the incriminating material. Panchnama along with all the annexures is signed by the authorized officer, assessee and the witnesses. Panchnama assumes significance of an independent document having high degree of evidentiary value. It becomes a base document to refer to the events occurred, evidences found and assets seized during search.

A Panchnama is to be prepared in quadruplicate; one copy thereof is to be given to the assessee along with all the annexures, one copy to be sent to the authorizing authority and one copy to be sent to the assessing officer along with the Appraisal Report at a later stage.

(i) In case no Panchnama is made out

Omission to make out a Panchnama did not vitiate the entire search proceedings where the Magistrate was satisfied that the evidence of police officer was true. [*State* v. *Kuppuswami Murgesh Acharya* AIR

1967 Bom. 199, *Sunder Singh* v. *State of UP* AIR 1956 SC 411 and *Radha Kishan* v. *State of UP* AIR 1963 SC 822].

(ii) Irregularity in preparation of Panchnama

Even if there is an irregularity in the Panchnama, that does not vitiate the search. Where there is no allegation that apart from a technical defect, there was in fact no search or that books of account, documents, etc., had not been taken possession of from the custody of certain persons, but on the contrary the persons concerned had jointly applied for return of the documents mentioned in the search list, it was held that this illegality could not vitiate the search and seizure. However, because of the illegality of the search, the court will be inclined to examine carefully the evidence regarding the seizure, *Mamchand & Co.* v. *CIT* [1970] 76 ITR 217 (Cal.), p. 237.

In the case of *MDLR Resorts (P.) Ltd.* v. *CIT* [2013] 40 taxmann.com 365/[2014] 221 Taxman 83 (Mag.) (Delhi)(HC), it has been held that section 153A(1) does not make any reference to panchnama or the date of panchnama. A panchnama is not a pre-condition for invoking section 153A. As regards the argument that the time limit u/s 153B is calculated with reference to the date of the last panchnama, a panchnama was drawn up on the occasion of the search and it referred to documents belonging to the assessee though it did not refer to the assessee by name. The panchnama also does not refer to the conclusion of the search. The non-reference to the name of the assessee and the suspension/conclusion of the search is a lapse and failure to comply with the requirements of the search and seizure manual. However, this does not affect the validity of the search or the assessment order u/s 153A. The department should take remedial steps and ensure that such lapses do not occur in future. Also, the department should give a copy of the search warrant to the person searched so as to curtail allegations of interpolation, addition of names etc.

(iii) One or more Panchnamas

There is no stipulation that there has to be only one Panchnama for each warrant of authorization. It would be necessary to prepare a separate Panchnama on conclusion of every phase of a continuing search which could not be concluded at a stretch and also in a situation of lifting each restraint put u/s 132(3) where seizure is made. In case of personal search as provided under clause (*iia*) of section 132(1), separate Panchnama may be prepared in case seizure is made from the possession of an outsider. But in case such panchnama is prepared in the name of third person, the action of seizure may be held to be illegal.

(*iv*) **Forms of Panchnama**

Panchnama contains various details such as names and addresses of Panchas, owner/occupant or in-charge of premises searched, address of premises searched, name of the authorized officer with designation and other officers assisting him, various declarations and certifications, complete details of assets, books of account or other documents found, inventorised, seized or not seized, valuation report of valuer regarding jewellery or other valuables, particulars of statement recorded, time of commencement and conclusion of search, description of restraint put u/s 132(3) etc. A specimen format of Panchnama which is prepared at the time of search is enclosed in the appendix.

5.12 Analysis of rule 112

Rule 112 prescribes certain procedural aspects relating to search and seizure, which are being summarized as under:—

Sub-rule (2)	-	prescribes forms of search warrant to be issued
Sub-rule (3)	-	power of authorized officer to ingress in the building or place.
Sub-rules (4) & (4A)	-	forceful entry to building or place by authorized officer.
Sub-rule (4B)	-	power of the authorized officer to open lock of door, almirah, box, locker, safe, etc.
Sub-rule (4C)	-	power to put restraint, if seizure not practicable.
Sub-rules (5) & (9)	-	personal search of any person
Sub-rules (6) & (7)	-	power regarding calling witnesses during search and preparation of a list of seized assets.
Sub-rule (8)	-	permission to occupant or his representative to remain present during search
Sub-rules (10) - (12)	-	manner of seizure of assets and custody of seized assets
Sub-rule (13)	-	opening of sealed packages at later stage
Sub-rule (14)	-	powers under sub-rules (11) & (13) may be exercised by assessing officer also.

The important aspects relating to above rules are being discussed as under:—

(*i*) **Power to search and seizure**

Sub-rule (1) of rule 112 lays down that the power of search and seizure under section 132 shall be exercised in accordance with sub-rules (2) - (14) of rule 112.

(*ii*) **Prescribed forms to be used for issue of search warrants**

Sub-rule (2) prescribes different forms of search warrant to be issued under different situations. It requires that the authorization shall be in writing with signature and seal of the officer issuing the same. Detailed discussion and various related issues in this connection have been dealt in the chapter 'Authorization of search warrant'.

(*iii*) Free ingress and obligation of the person present

Sub-rule (3) empowers the authorized officer to make free ingress into the building, place, vehicle, vessel, aircraft for which he has valid search warrant. On production of the search warrant by the authorized officer, any person, incharge of the building or place or who is present therein at that point of time, is duty bound to extend all reasonable facilities to conduct search by the authorized officer.

(*iv*) Power to make forceful entry

Sub-rule (4) empowers the authorized officer to make forceful entry into such building or place with the assistance of police officers or other officers of Central Government in case the entry is not possible in normal course. If building or place is locked, he may break or open any outer or inner door or window so as to make entry. However, this power should be used only when entry is not permitted to him in normal course on demand being made after showing his authority and purpose.

Sometimes, it so happens that the person incharge getting the feel of search team coming for search, may lock the door from inside and try to destroy the evidences of undisclosed income. This may happen in the beginning or even during the course of search. By using the above powers, the authorized officer may take quick action so as to prevent the destruction of evidences.

The door or windows of the building to be searched or of any other adjoining building so as to get entry into the premises required to be searched, may be opened or broken.

(*v*) Withdrawal by pardanasheen women

In case building or place being searched is occupied by a woman who according to custom does not appear in public, the authorized officer before entering into such building or place shall give opportunity to such woman to leave the place and only after that, he shall enter into the building or place. The authorized officer is required to afford her every reasonable facility so as to leave the place before further proceeding to conduct the search is undertaken.

A working woman, who is running business or is a working partner or active director in the company, cannot claim to be a pardanasheen woman.

(*vi*) Authority to stop a moving vehicle, vessel or aircraft

Sub-rule (4A) empowers the authorized officer to stop any moving vehicle or vessel or compel to stop or land moving aircraft so as to get entry into the same and conduct search as authorized. Further, he has the powers to break open the door or window and has duty to allow pardanasheen woman to withdraw in the same manner as in the case of place or building as discussed under sub-rule (4).

(vii) Power to break open locker, almirah, safe, box, etc.

Sub-rule (4B) empowers the authorized officer to break open any box, locker, safe, almirah or any other receptacle, if on demand by the officer, keys of the same are not made available.

(viii) Power to restraint

Sub-rule (4C) empowers the authorized officer, where it is not practicable to seize the books of account or documents or assets, to serve an order putting restraint not to remove, part with or otherwise deal with it, except with the prior permission of the authorized officer.

He may take such steps as may be necessary for ensuring compliance with this sub-rule. In practice, lock and seal are placed on the almirah or room in which such books of account, documents or assets are kept.

This power can be used only with respect to assets which can be seized. Since inventory cannot be seized, restraint on movement of inventory is not valid. Detailed discussion has been held on this issue in chapter relating to 'Restraint under section 132(3)'.

(ix) Personal search

Clause (*iia*) of section 132 empowers the authorized officer to make personal search of any person if he has reason to suspect that such person has secreted about such person any books of account, documents or assets. Sub-rule (5) further prescribes that such search may be done with such assistance as may be required. It may include the assistance of police officer or any other officer present alongwith the search team.

Sub-rule (5) prescribes that if personal search of a woman is to be conducted, search shall be made by woman officer only. It is for this reason that lady officers are always accompanied with the search team. Personal search of woman shall be carried with strict regard to decency.

(x) Two or more witnesses during search operation

Sub-rule (6) of rule 112 provides that search operation shall be conducted in the presence of minimum two witnesses. These witnesses are called panchas and as required under sub-rule (7), the list of the seized books of account, documents or assets prepared shall be signed by such witnesses alongwith the authorized officer and searched person or his representative.

The above procedure of appointing two witnesses has been prescribed in the law to ensure independence, transparency & fairness during search operations. In case of any complaint by the searched person regarding high handedness exercised by department or regarding threats, misbehaviour or third degree used during search or procedure of law laid down for conducting search not properly followed by the authorized officer, the role or statement given by these independent witnesses carry lot of weight and significance. Similarly in case searched person or his representative misbehaves or tries to destroy evidences or does not cooperate in the manner as required for smooth conduct of search operations, statements of these independent witnesses becomes very important.

(a) Witnesses to be appointed before making search

The authorized officer is required to appoint two or more witnesses before starting search proceedings and they should remain present throughout the search proceedings.

In case of search at some building or place, witnesses are required to be called from the locality in which such building or place is situated. In case of search of any vehicle, vessel or aircraft, the witnesses can be any two or more respectable persons.

(b) Order may be passed for witnesses to be present

Under sub-rule (6) of rule 112, authorized officer is empowered to issue an order inviting for the witnesses to attend and remain present in the search proceedings. This power is generally used in rare cases when no witness is available or ready to attend search operations. Refusal on the part of witnesses to comply such order may make them liable for prosecution under section 187 of the Indian Penal Code (*King Emperor* v. *Wunna* AIR 1927 Rang. 241).

(c) Witnesses are not required to attend as a witness of search in any proceedings under the Income-tax Act, 1961

Sub-rule (7) of rule 112 prescribes that the search shall be made in the presence of the witnesses and a list of all assets, books of account, documents seized in the course of search shall be prepared and signed by them but they will not be required to attend any proceedings under the Income-tax Act, 1961, unless specifically summoned.

The above provision has been made so that no undue harassment is caused or time of the witnesses is consumed later for the reason that they were present as witness during search proceedings. They may be summoned by the court in case of dispute between assessee and department or any complaints or FIR filed by either of them under Code of Criminal Procedure. Under such circumstances, statement of witnesses becomes quite significant.

(d) Witnesses to be independent

Sub-rule (6) of rule 112 requires respectable inhabitants of the locality to be taken as witnesses and the word "independent" is not there. However, sub-section (4) of section 100 of the Code of Criminal Procedure which prescribes about the search under the Code, in general, requires the appointment of the witnesses who are independent. Moreover, section 132(13) of the Income-tax Act lays down that the provisions of the Code of Criminal Procedure relating to search and seizure shall, so far as may be possible, apply. Therefore, it is always advisable to take only independent witnesses. Any person who is an employee, partner and director or close relative of the searched person or happens to be his associate should not be taken as a witness. This is important for the legal as well as for practical purpose and is in the interest of both the parties. Such a person being under direct influence of the searched person may turn hostile and may not behave fairly and justly.

It has been held in the case of *Rajan Jewellery* v. *CIT* [2019] 177 DTR 369 (Ker.) that assessee having not raised the objection on validity of search on the ground of absence of panchas before the AO, it could not raise the same before appellate authority.

(xi) Services of Police Officers or Officers of Central Government

Section 132(2) provides that the authorized officer may requisition the services of any police officers or of any officers of the Central Government or of both, to assist him for all or any of the purposes specified in sub-section (1) or (1A) of section 132 and it shall be duty of every such officer to comply with such requisition.

Sub-rules (4) & (4A) of rule 112 further empowers the authorized officer to take the assistance of the police officers or any officer of the Central Government or of both to make entry into the building or place authorized to be searched.

The assistance of police may be taken during the conduct of search for the following purposes:—

a. To enter into the building or place authorized to be searched.

b. To break and/or open any outer door, window or any inner door, window, box, almirah, etc. during the course of search proceedings.

    c. To ensure security and protection of the search party from dogs, muscle men or otherwise.

    d. To prevent destruction of evidences or fleeing away with the evidences.

However police force is not to be used for the following purposes:—

    a. For confinement, detention or arrest of assessee or some other person at the instance of the authorized officer.

    b. For manhandling or physical torture of any kind during search proceedings.

    c. For exercising threat, physical or mental torture with the assistance of police for obtaining confessional statement in the manner desired by the authorized officer.

    d. For normal conduct of search and seizure operations or for collecting the evidence.

The decision regarding extent of the security force to be deployed is entirely within the powers of the authorized officer and so long as this is done in *bona fide* manner, assessee cannot object the same on the ground of excessive use of police force or damage of the personal reputation of the assessee. The police force shall be withdrawn as soon as search operations are complete.

If, the search operations are temporarily suspended to be completed later, the police force may remain deployed at the place where the authorized officer has suspicion that evidences under restraint may be destroyed.

In the case of *ITO* v. *Seth Brothers* [1969] 74 ITR 836 (SC), it has been held by the Apex Court that keeping police officers at the time of search in the house of influential businessmen to ensure protection of the officers and the records will not amount to use of excessive force. This view has been followed in several other decisions including the case of *Subir Roy* v. *S. K. Chattopadhyay* [1986] 29 Taxman 13 (Cal.).

Authorized officer is empowered to take services of any officer of the Central Government. It will include the services of officers of excise department, enforcement directorate or officer of income tax department itself. It is for this reason that the presence of income tax inspectors and clerical staff during search is valid and cannot be objected by the searched person.

(xia) **To call for services of any other person/entity**

Finance Act, 2023 has amended sub-section (2) of section 132 granting power to the authorized officer to requisition the services of any person or entity during the course of search. New sub-clause (*ii*) added to section 132(2) is as under:

"(ii) any person or entity as may be approved by the Principal Chief Commissioner or the Chief Commissioner or the Principal Director General or the Director General, in accordance with the procedure, as may be prescribed, in this regard,"

The objective of adding the above power as explained in the Memorandum annexed to the Finance Bill, 2023 is as under:

"In the recent past, due to the increased use of technology and digitization in every aspect including management and maintenance of accounts, digitization of data, cloud storage etc., the procedure for search & seizure has become complex, requiring the use of data forensics, advanced technologies for decoding data etc., for complete and proper analysis of accounts. Similarly, there is an increasing trend of undisclosed income being held in a vast variety of forms of assets or investments in addition to immovable property. Valuation of such assets and decryption of information often require specific domain experts like digital forensic professionals, valuers, archive experts etc. In addition to this, services of other professionals like locksmiths, carpenters etc. are also required in most of the cases, due to typical nature of the operations."

(xii) **What is "locality"**

Locality means from the neighbourhood or from the immediate vicinity or in case no respectable person is available thereat, from the adjoining locality.

In a densely populated town, locality means persons in the immediate vicinity - *Mahanway* v. *King Emperor* AIR 1925 Rang. 205. In a thinly populated place, locality may include places within three or four miles - *Emperor* v. *Mastram* AIR 1931 Oudh. 115. Therefore, the provision relating to locality should be regarded as directory and not mandatory - *Emperor* v. *Darshan Singh* AIR 1941 Lah. 297.

In the case of *Sunder Singh* v. *State of U.P.* AIR 1956 SC 411, two Rikshawalas were taken as witnesses. The Supreme Court held that although they could not be said to be of locality, the search was not invalidated due to that. At best, it would be an irregularity which would reduce the weight of evidence.

(xiii) **What is respectable witness**

The word "respectable" does not mean that the person should be highly placed or very rich. A common man is a respectable person. He should not be a person of unsound mind or he should not have been convicted for any criminal offence. In other words, the witness should be credible in the eyes of law. He should not be a competitor of the assessee or a person having enmity or conflict of interest with the assessee.

Respectability did not connote any particular status or wealth or anything of that kind.

(xiv) Choice of witness with the assessee or with the authorized officer

It was held in the case of *Queen Empress* v. *Raman* ILR 21 Mad. 83 that the witnesses are to be selected by the authorized officer and by no other person.

In practice, the authorized officer takes into consideration suggestion of the assessee in selecting the witnesses. The authorized officer should take care that any genuine objection raised by the assessee in this connection should be duly considered. The witness should not be a competitor of the assessee or a person having enmity or disputes with the assessee. The witness should be a person who understands the nature and objects of the search proceedings and is not unduly perturbed. As far as possible, he should be literate person who is able to read and write.

It has been held in the case of *Smt. Vijay Dhir* v. *DIT* [2012] 20 taxmann.com 827 (All.) that witnesses requested by assessee being present during search, plea that witnesses were not from the locality could not be raised.

(xv) "Witness" must witness the search proceedings

"Witness" must witness the search proceeding. It will be illegal to call them and then detain them outside the building. They should be given proper opportunity to witness the proceedings being carried on. - *Dinkar Nhanu Mangaonkar* v. *Emperor* AIR 1930 Bom. 169.

(xvi) Witness turning hostile during search proceedings

There may be circumstances when the witness may turn hostile during the course of search proceedings. Under such situation, the authorized officer may take another witness after recording the fact of the previous witness being hostile and narrating the specific circumstances. Such recording should be signed by the authorized officer along with other members of his team or other witness and should be made part of panchnama. If possible, consent of the assessee should also be obtained for doing so.

(xvii) Witness refusing to continue or to sign the panchnama

In a case when witness refuses to continue, attempt should be made to convince him at the first instance and if not possible, another witness should be taken after recording the reason of doing so. Difficulty may arise if it happens towards the end of the search and new witness may not like to witness or sign the proceedings which have already taken place. In case witness refuses to sign due to any disagreement, attempt should be made to sort out the differences or he may be allowed to sign along with his remarks or observations as he may like to mention.

If the disapproval by witness reflects any kind of irregularities by the search party, it may not by itself invalidate the search. However, it would impair the credibility of evidences collected and the seizure made, depending on the fact of each case.

(*xviii*) Presence of assessee during search proceedings

Sub-rule (8) of rule 112 prescribes that the occupant of the building or place being searched including the person in charge of such vessel, vehicle or aircraft shall be permitted to attend the search proceedings. Some other person on his behalf may be permitted to attend search proceeding. Copy of panchnama prepared with the list of all assets seized in the course of search shall be delivered to such person. This is the statutory right of the assessee so as to know the detail of the items seized during search.

It is important to note that the presence of the owner or occupant or someone on his behalf is not a precondition for search and his absence will not vitiate the search proceedings. It was held in the case of *Hari Narayan Chandra* v. *Emperor* AIR 1928 Cal. 27, that it is not necessary that the occupant must be present at the time of search. The rule only lays down that assessee should be permitted to do so, if he desires to remain present. The refusal of the permission to remain present by the authorized officer may constitute an illegality.

It is provided under sub-rule (8) that in lieu of the searched person, some other person on his behalf, as may be authorized by him, may remain present to witness search proceeding. There may be cases when several premises of a person are being searched and he cannot remain present everywhere. In such a situation, some other person may represent him to witness the search proceedings. The capacity of such person to witness search is not in the capacity as his authorized representative or counsel but to witness the search proceedings in place of searched person.

(*xix*) Personal search

Sub-rule (9) of rule 112 prescribes that in case of personal search as provided under clause (*iia*) of section 132(1), a list of all things taken possession of, shall be prepared and a copy thereof shall be delivered to such person.

Such person may be a person other than the assessee or a person staying with the assessee or a guest visiting the assessee during search. No separate search warrant is required to be issued for making personal search of such person. The list so prepared relating to the things seized from his possession will form part of panchnama of the assessee in whose case search is authorized. A specific mention shall be made in the list that such assets or things have been seized in the course of personal search of so and so person.

(xx) Seized articles to be kept in sealed packages bearing identification marks

Sub-rule (10) of rule 112 provides that the bullion, jewellery or other valuable articles or things seized during search shall be placed in a package or packages which shall be listed with details of the seized material. Every such package shall bear an identification mark and seal of the authorised officer or any income tax authority not below the rank of Income-tax Officer.

The occupant or person in-charge or his representative shall also be permitted to place his mark of identification or seal on them. A copy of the list prepared shall be delivered to such occupant or representative and a copy shall be forwarded to the authorizing officer.

In actual practice, the seizure memos form part of panchnama and a specimen of the seal of the authorized officer or the searched person are fixed on the panchnama so that it may be possible to ensure that the packages are not tempered.

This sub-rule does not cover cash or money since the same is not kept in packages but deposited with the bank.

(xxi) To convey the seized books of account or assets to the custodian

Sub-rule (11) of rule 112 provides that the authorized officer may convey the books of account, other documents or assets kept in packages, if any seized, to any income tax authority not below the rank of Income-tax Officer who is referred as custodian for this purpose. It is at the option of the authorized officer whether to appoint custodian or not. The authorized officer himself may remain the custodian. However, the authorized officer who has no jurisdiction over the searched person, shall handover the seized books of account, document and assets to the Assessing Officer having jurisdiction over the searched person as provided under sub-rule (9A) of section 132.

(xxii) Procedure to be followed by the custodian

Sub-rule (12) of rule 112 prescribes the procedure to be followed by the custodian in respect of books of account, other documents, sealed packages and seized cash. The custodian may keep the seized material in his own custody or may deposit with the bank authorized for this purpose. Any money seized has to be deposited with the bank as authorized for this purpose for being credited in the personal deposit account (P.D. Account) of the Chief Commissioner or Commissioner having jurisdiction over the searched person.

(xxiii) Opening of sealed packages

Sub-rule (13)(i) of rule 112 empowers the authorized officer to requisition any sealed packages from the custodian. This may be required at any later stage e.g. to operate computer CD. The authorized officer may break any seal and open such packages in the presence of two witnesses after giving reasonable notice to the person from whose custody the same were seized, to remain present.

Sub-rule (13)(*ii*) of rule 112 further provides that the searched person shall be permitted to remain present till the contents of such packages are placed in a fresh package and sealed in the manner specified earlier or delivered to such person or the custodian as the case may be.

(*xxiv*) Assessing Officer is empowered to exercise the power of sub-rules (11) and (13)

The requirement of handing over the seized material to the custodian as given under sub-rule (11) and opening and again sealing the packages of the seized material as per sub-rule (13) may be needed to be undertaken at any later stage by the Assessing Officer who may assess the searched person. Therefore as per sub-rule (14) of rule 112 such powers have been directed to be given to Assessing Officer as well.

5.13 Rules 112A - 112D

The provisions of rules 112A and 112B were relevant to the proceeding u/s 132(5) which used to be applicable to searches conducted on or before 1st July, 1995. Therefore, the provisions of these rules have become inoperative in relation to searches conducted on or after 1st July, 1995.

Rule 112C provides that any surplus assets or proceeds thereof after discharging the tax liability shall be handed over to the person from whose custody the seizure was made. This rule will continue to operate even in relation to searches which may take place on or after 1st July, 1995. This rule should be read along with section 132B which prescribes the procedure of application of seized assets towards tax-liability and detailed discussion has been held in the chapter on application of seized assets under section 132B.

Rule 112D prescribes a detailed procedure to be followed in proceedings u/s 132A with regard to the requisition of books of account, documents and assets and has been discussed in detail in that chapter.

5.14 Ground rules for search and seizure

Board has also prescribed the ground rules for search and seizure both for the department as well as for the taxpayers. The rules prescribe the objective of search, rights of the taxpayers during search and other procedural aspects relating to search proceedings. The ground rules have been reproduced in **Appendix 2**.

5.15 Taxpayers' Charter - Rights & duties of taxpayers during search

Central Board of Direct Taxes has issued taxpayers' charter prescribing rights and duties of taxpayers during search operations reported at [1994] 208 ITR 5 (St.). This charter does not have the force of law but since the same has been issued by Central Board of Direct Taxes, the highest regulatory authority in the field of income tax, all officers of the department conducting search are supposed to follow the instructions given therein. Text of the taxpayers' charter has been given in the appendix. Some of the significant points arising therefrom are being discussed as below:—

5.16 Rights of the assessee before commencement of search—

(i) Production of search warrant

The first step in the course of initiating and conducting search operations is to show search warrant issued by the competent authority to the occupant of the premises by the authorized officer. The occupant should ensure before permitting search operations to be conducted that the warrant of authorization is duly signed with the seal of the issuing authority and that search has been authorized in the proper name and for the premises in which the search team has made ingress.

In case search warrant is blank and the name and address of the person is filled thereat only by the authorized officer, the person or occupant may object to the same. This fact should be got recorded which may be significant to plead the issue of the validity of search warrant at later stage.

Person or occupant of the premise is not entitled to get the copy of search warrant. Requirement under sub-rule (3) of rule 112 is for production of the search warrant and not for supply of the copy of the same to the person or to the occupant. Detailed discussion in this regard is made under the chapter "Authorization of Search".

(ii) Production of evidence of identity of officers of search team

The searched person or occupant of the premise has right to verify the identity of each member of the search party. For this purpose, he may ask the members of the search team for showing their identity cards. In case identity card is not available with them, there should be some other evidence to satisfy their identity as officers from the income tax department. The identity of the officers whose names are mentioned in the search warrant along with other members of the search party and who are accompanying them to assist in the search operation may be verified. The occupant of the premise will be within his rights not to permit admission to such officers who refuse to prove their identity.

(iii) **To make personal search of search party**

The person or occupant of the premise has right to make personal search of all members of the search party before the start of the search and on conclusion of the search. The right of personal search has been given to the person searched or occupant of the premise also to ensure that no material of incriminating nature is brought in by the search team with them with *mala fide* intention. Similarly, the right to make personal search on conclusion of the search, when the members of the search party leave the premises, has also been given to the searched person to ensure that no asset or valuable articles or thing are carried by them. By virtue of conferring such right, searched person is prevented to plead at any later stage regarding any stolen goods by the search team.

Personal search of lady officer should be carried by the lady members of the household of the searched person with strict sense of decency in the same manner as provided for personal search of lady members of the household of the searched person by the search team under sub-rule (5) of rule 112.

If any member of the search team refuses to give personal search before entering the premises, person to be searched is entitled not to permit entry to such officer of search team. However, in practice, personal search of the members of the search team is generally not conducted by the searched person. But forgoing of his right of personal search voluntarily will not entitle the searched person to put any kind of charge on the search team at later stage and it will be deemed as if personal search was conducted by the searched person.

(iv) **Right of the assessee with respect to personal liberty during search operation**

During the course of search operation, person searched or occupant of the premise is entitled to carry out all his day to day activities unless the same does not obstruct the smooth conduct of search operation.

(v) **Right to Medical Aid**

The searched person is entitled to call for a doctor in case of illness to himself or any of his family members in case of emergency. He is entitled to call the doctor of his choice or his family doctor. In case of advice of the doctor, he or his family member is entitled to be admitted in the hospital.

In practice it has been observed that searched persons do resort to complaint of illness and get admission to the hospital so as to avoid facing the search proceeding or giving the statement during the search. Unless there is genuine need for such medical assistance, it is not a healthy practice in the interest of the searched person. Instead of avoiding the search operation, he should try to face the same and he is the best person to manage the situation at that point of time.

(vi) Children to go to school

Children of the searched person are entitled to go to school or tuition or coaching etc. However, their school bags may be checked by the search team before allowing them to leave the premises.

(vii) To have meals

Searched person and his family members are entitled to take their normal meals i.e. breakfast, lunch and dinner at normal times.

(viii) Right to worship

The searched person is entitled to be respected for his religious sentiments. He and other family members have right to do worship according to family custom and culture.

(ix) Permission to leave the premises

Searched person is duty bound to provide all necessary facilities and cooperate to the search team in carrying out smooth conduct of search operations. His right to leave the premises to attend his job or any other obligation has not been prohibited by law. He is entitled to leave the premises unless he is required by the authorized officer not to do so for the reason of his presence being essential for the conduct of search proceedings. He may be required by the authorized officer for recording statement u/s 132(4) or for making keys of the locks available or for getting the locker operated, valuation of jewellery got done etc. and so on and so forth. In other words, he is entitled to leave the premises but not in defiance of lawful orders of the authorized officer necessary for smooth conduct of search operations.

In the case of *L.R. Gupta* v. *Union of India* [1991] 59 Taxman 305 (Delhi) High Court observed as follows:—

> "Before concluding, we would like to advert to another aspect which has caused us some concern. On March 22, 1991, a large contingent reached the residence of the petitioners to conduct search and seizure. It is an admitted fact that petitioner No. 1 made requests that he may be permitted to attend to his work in the High Court. The permission was not granted. The Income-tax Act does not give any power to the income tax department to arrest an individual. The department has certainly the power of recording the statement of a person in accordance with law. Petitioner No. 1 could, therefore, be

legitimately required to be present for the purpose of recording his statement. Once his statement was recorded, there was no reason or justification for the officers of the department exercising jurisdiction which they did not possess, *viz.*, preventing petitioner No. 1 from attending to his work. An authorization which is issued under section 132(1) only enables the officers of the department to conduct search and seizure. Under section 131, they have, *inter alia*, the authority and the power to enforce the presence of a person for the purpose of examining him on oath. There is no power contained in the Act or the Rules whereby the movement of a person against whom search is ordered can be restricted. By refusing to give permission to the petitioner to attend to his work in effect, it amounted to his confinement which is not permissible in law."

(x) Presence of Legal adviser

The issue relating to the presence of legal adviser of the searched person during search operations has always remained a point of debate and controversy. Provision relating to appearance and representation by an advocate or authorized representative is legislated u/s 288 of the Income-tax Act. Sub-section (1) of section 288 provides—

> "Any assessee who is entitled or required to attend before any income tax authority or the Appellate Tribunal in connection with any proceeding under this Act otherwise than when required u/s 131 to attend personally for examination on oath or affirmation, may, subject to the other provisions of this section, attend by an authorized representative."

The right of the assessee to be represented by an authorized representative has been granted u/s 288 when assessee is entitled or is required to attend before any income tax authority in connection with any proceeding under the Income-tax Act. The right of the assessee to be represented by an authorized representative has been specifically prohibited when required u/s 131 to attend personally for examination on oath or affirmation.

Search proceedings u/s 132 can be divided into two categories:—

a. Personal examination of assessee on oath u/s 132(4).

b. The rest of the proceeding of the search and seizure.

Examination on oath u/s 131 is required to be attended personally by the assessee and not by an authorized representative on behalf of the assessee. The requirement of recording statement on oath u/s 132(4) is analogous to above requirement and therefore, at the time of recording of statement u/s 132(4) it is to be attended personally by the searched person and cannot be through an authorized representative.

With regard to rest of the proceeding of search and seizure, these are in the nature of the proceedings when search team is visiting the assessee's premises to collect evidences of undisclosed income or undisclosed assets, if any. These are not the proceedings in the nature when assessee has been required to attend before any income tax authority to present his case, to show books of account or furnish other information as may be required. In the process of collecting the evidences from the office or residence of the assessee, the presence of authorized representative is not statutorily warranted. Authorized representative, while representing the case on behalf of the assessee, is required to present the case before the income tax authority as per the requirement of law. But in the case of process of collecting the evidences, no such function is involved. Therefore, it can be interpreted that to demand the presence of advocate or legal adviser of the assessee at the time of search, is not the legal right of the assessee.

Moreover, there is no need of legal representative of assessee to remain present alongwith assessee while statement of assessee is being recorded or when other search proceedings are being undertaken. There is already requirement of the presence of two respectable witnesses throughout the search proceedings and to witness the whole search action. In case of any irregularity or excessiveness on part of search team, such witnesses can record their objection. It is not only search team members but at times, assessee or his family members may create nuisance or may misbehave or try to destroy evidences. Therefore in search operation, law has envisaged the need of presence of two independent witnesses and not the presence of legal representative on behalf of assessee.

Sub-rule (8) of rule 112 empowers the assessee to remain personally present during search proceedings. It gives right to personally attend to the following persons:—

    a. The occupant of the building, place, vessel, vehicle or aircraft searched.

    b. Including the person in charge of such vessel, vehicle or air craft.

    c. Or some person on his behalf.

Some person on behalf of the searched person to remain present during search is preceded by the word "or" which implies that in case occupant of the building or place is not present, some other person on his behalf shall be permitted to attend in his absence during search operation. Here the word "or" cannot mean to include "and". Moreover, the objective of sub-rule (8) is to allow the assessee to witness the search proceeding and in case he is absent, option has been given for the same to be witnessed by some other person on his behalf.

Further, it may be noticed that the authority given under sub-rule (8) to some other person on his behalf does not mean legal representative or advocate of the searched person. It can be any other person who may not be a person qualified to be appointed as legal representative as defined u/s 288 of the Act. Therefore, authority given under sub-rule (8) for some other person to be permitted to attend on behalf of the assessee cannot be interpreted to mean that power has been given for legal representative or advocate of the assessee to remain present during search proceeding.

Further, ground sub-rule (5) prescribed by the Board in connection with procedure to be followed during the search states that the searched person is not allowed the services of a lawyer at the stage of examination. Though the ground rules do not carry force of law, yet specific denial regarding the presence of lawyer indicates the legislative intent. In any case, search being investigation proceeding, law has not contemplated the presence of the lawyer or authorized representative during search operation.

On the other hand arguments in favour of presence of legal advisor during search operations may be advanced on the following grounds:-

1. Section 288 of the Act permits authorized representative to represent the assessee before any income tax authority in connection with any proceeding under the Act in the case of

   a. Assessee who is entitled to attend before any income tax authority

   b. Assessee who is required to attend before any income tax authority.

   It may be argued that any proceeding under this Act will cover search proceeding u/s 132 and "assessee entitled to attend before income tax authority" will cover the search proceeding also, since as per sub-rule (8) of rule 112 of the Income Tax Rules, assessee is entitled to attend the search proceedings being conducted by the income tax authority.

2. The law does not specifically bar the presence of legal advisor during search proceedings. There could have been specific mention of this situation in the same manner as is a specific mention u/s 288 that when required u/s 131 to attend personally for examination on oath, assessee is required to attend personally and not through an authorized representative.

In the case of *L. K. Advani* v. *State* [1985] CLJ 1325, Hon'ble Delhi High Court held that by virtue of section 30 of the Advocates Act, an advocate was entitled as a matter of right to appear before authority u/s 40 of Foreign Exchange Regulation Act (FERA). A person summoned under FERA had a right to the presence of an advocate during his interrogation and use of the words "authorized agent" in sub-section (3) also includes an advocate. An advocate can be permitted to be a silent spectator but he can make his objections in writing after the interrogation is over, even against the use of third degree methods.

In case of *Poolpandi* v. *Superintendent, Central Excise* [1992] 62 Taxman 447 (SC), a case u/s 108 of the Customs Act, 1962 read with section 40 of the Foreign Exchange Regulation Act, 1973, Supreme Court opined in negative regarding the presence of lawyer during interrogation and such denial was found not in violation of articles 20(3) and 21 of the Constitution of India.

In view of above discussion, we are of the considered opinion that the presence of legal advisor during search proceeding cannot be claimed by the assessee as a matter of legal right. Looking at the controversial nature of this issue and significance attached to it, it would be desirable that the controversy is set at rest either by a judicial pronouncement or by a legislative incorporation or by administrative instruction.

(xi) Presence of Legal Advisor may facilitate the search proceedings

It may not be legal right of assessee to call legal advisor during search but it has been observed in practice that the presence of legal advisor during search proceedings may facilitate the smooth conduct of search operation.

Generally, it has been experienced in practice that till the evidences are collected/seized and statement of the assessee is recorded, presence of the legal advisor is not usually permitted but once the same has been done, authorized officer himself wants the presence of legal advisor particularly for the following matters:-

1. To advise and convince the assessee for making declaration of undisclosed income, if any, so as to get immunity or concession from penalty u/s 271AAA/271AAB of the Act.

2. To produce the evidences regarding jewellery or other assets disclosed in the income tax returns or wealth tax returns filed by the assessee so that the same are not seized.

3. To stand by the side of the assessee and his family members and boost their confidence so that the search proceedings are concluded in a peaceful manner.

4. To create balance between the assessee and the department.

Presence of legal advisor during search operations is not for the sake of presence but for assisting the assessee as well as the department in all possible manner so long as his presence does not obstruct or interfere in the conduct of smooth operation of search and seizure or with the recording of statements of various persons.

5.17 Case study relating to search operation

In the following paras, case study is being discussed narrating the manner in which actual search proceedings are conducted. Discussion is based upon a standard procedure which is generally adopted in practice in normal search operations even though some of the steps may not strictly be in accordance with the provisions of law.

(i) Authorized officer to enter along with his team

Search is generally started in the morning hours, say at around 8.00 AM or so. First of all, authorized officer reaches the premises, knocks at the door as visitor to meet the person to be searched and as soon as the door is opened, the entire search team which may consist of ten to fifteen officials depending upon the size of the premise and the persons to be covered, waiting at a little distance, enter the premises. It is so done to ensure that after getting know-ledge of search team arriving, door may not be closed/locked by the person to be searched. The members of search team do spread immediately at various places/rooms within the premises to ensure that the same are not locked from inside. They keep watch on the movement of each occupant inside so that there may not be any possibility for anybody to destroy any evidence.

(ii) Police force to accompany

Search team is usually accompanied by policemen who remain out side the premises and in case of any kind of need or emergency, their services are called for by the authorised officer. In one of the searches, as soon as the search team arrived at the residential premises, the assessee having got the news of the same, left open fierce dogs so that nobody could dare to enter the premises. At times, conduct of search may be taken as offensive by a particular group of people which may throw the issue of law and order problem. To control such kind of situations, police assistance may be needed.

(*iii*) Showing of search warrant and obtaining signature

The authorized officer calmly sits along with the person to be searched, tells him the purpose of his visit, shows him the search warrant and obtains his signature on the copy of the search warrant. Copy of search warrant is not given to the person searched.

(*iv*) No telephone calls

The search officials ensure, in practice, that no telephone calls are made by the searched person or any other family member. They request to put off the mobile phones or take control of the same. This is so done to ensure that the information of search is not spread by telephonic calls to other business associates or heads of the business premises which may or may not be under search. Further, it is done so that no panic is created amongst the friends and other well wishers of the searched person who may throng and visit the searched person and create unwarranted situation.

The incoming phone calls are also received by the authorized officer so as to get information relating to any undisclosed business transactions and dealings.

(*v*) Offer for personal search

Authorized officer offers the occupant of the premises to make personal search of himself and other members of his team. Generally, it is not done in practice due to loss of nerve at that time but the same is deemed to have been done as a result of the refusal of the searched person to do so.

(*vi*) Calling for two witnesses

Two respectable persons are called from the neighbourhood to be appointed as panchas to witness the search proceedings. Generally, it is done in consultation with the searched person as per his choice unless the choice is with some collateral motive in the opinion of the authorized officer.

(*vii*) Search of each room, almirah or other place

Search is commenced of each room, almirah or box and other places within the premises, to collect books of account, files, documents, loose paper, cash, money, jewellery, other precious and valuable articles or things. Keys of lockers are specifically looked for by the search team which has special training to identify the keys of locker maintained with bank or other depositories. Bank pass books, cheque books are looked for to identify benami or undisclosed bank accounts. Search is made specifically for the incriminating material relating to information in possession of the department. In case search team has information or knowledge of certain secret place within the premises, specific attention is given to that area. For example, there may be information that searched person keeps papers/documents inside sofa or bed or in the pillar or almirah or such like places. In that case, authorized officer may ask the searched person to open it and if such request is not complied with, authorized officer may tear or break it. Similarly, there may be information that incriminating material is kept in some secret tehkhana underground the floor. Authorized officer may dig the floor. Such extreme act is so done when department has any specific information or suspicion created during search. Searched person cannot claim the expenses of repairs, even if nothing incriminating is found.

(viii) What to search

Normally, following aspects are looked into during search operations at residential premises:-

 a. Unaccounted cash

 b. Unaccounted Jewellery

 c. Diaries

 d. Note books, other documents, electronic storage devices e.g. CDs, pen drives etc. having unaccounted transactions

 e. Unaccounted investments in construction of house

 f. Locker keys

 g. Unaccounted personal expenditure, expenses on domestic servants, guards, gardener

 h. Unaccounted house holds items, refrigerator, LCD, ACs, music system etc.

 i. Evidences relating to specific information in their possession:

◆ In addition to above, in the case of business premises, following items are also looked for.

◆ Unaccounted investment in inventory, plant & machinery or building.

◆ Suppression of production or sale.

◆ Bogus expenditure or inflated consumption of raw material or other consumable items.

◆ Fictitious attendance register for inflating wages bill.

◆ Blank vouchers, bills signed by employees or other persons so as to create fictitious support of expenses.

◆ Signed blank cheque books of benami bank accounts.

◆ Visiting cards of persons supplying bogus bills.

◆ Duplicate set of books of account maintained for unaccounted business transactions.

(ix) Keep an eye on movement of each family member

An eye is kept on the movement of each family member by the search team. Generally, it is done by having person to person marking. The purpose is to prevent destruction or removal of any kind of incriminating material.

(x) Recording preliminary statement

Preliminary statement of the searched person or his family members is recorded by the authorized officer to enquire about the general nature of business and occupation carried on by them, about any cash, stocks or other valuable belonging to others kept with them or such items of searched person kept with somebody else. Inquiries are made relating to nature of transactions for which specific information is available with the authorized officer. Inquiries are made regarding number of lockers maintained and their location. An illustrative list of questions which are or may be generally asked in the preliminary statement are given in the chapter on statement u/s 132(4). Such list is by no means exhaustive and questions are dependant upon the facts and circumstances of each case and the nature of information available with the department.

(xi) Not to allow entry of other persons or exit of persons inside

Generally, movement of the persons in or outside the premises is not allowed so that search operation may be undertaken smoothly. In case any person is visiting the searched person, inquiry is made with regard to the purpose of visit and to know about any kind of undisclosed business transactions of the searched person with such person. In case of any suspicion, personal search of such person is also conducted.

No person is allowed to leave the premises without the permission of the authorized officer when it is reasonable and necessary. Personal search of the person leaving the premises is also conducted by the authorized officer.

(xii) Call the valuer to get the jewellery valued

Approved Valuer is called by the authorized officer and the items of jewellery, other precious stones or other valuables found during search are inventorized, valued and valuation report is prepared by the valuer mentioning the rate, weight, quality and value of such items belonging to person searched and other family members residing with him.

(*xiii*) **Operating bank lockers**

Bank Lockers of the searched person and other family members already in the knowledge of authorized officer or on the basis of new information coming to his possession during search are operated by sending search team along with searched person or his authorised representative to the bank who may operate the locker. All the articles found in the locker which may be in the form of cash, jewellery, documents or any other valuables are brought and separate list regarding the same having been found from the locker is prepared.

(*xiv*) **Intimation to bank for stopping operation of bank locker or other undisclosed bank accounts**

Information is immediately given to the respective banks not to allow operation of any of the locker of the searched person or his family members. As soon as information comes into possession regarding any undisclosed bank accounts, the operation of such bank account is suspended.

(*xv*) **Information coming into possession regarding other premises/lockers**

During the course of search, the authorized officer may come to know about some other business premises, godowns, offices or residential premises of the searched person or bank lockers which have not been covered earlier for conducting search. New team of officials are prepared and immediately sent to such places after obtaining necessary authorization so as to undertake either search or survey operations.

(*xvi*) **Recording statement of the searched person and other persons**

Statement of the searched person is recorded on oath u/s 132(4). Searched person is asked to explain the source of cash, jewellery, or other assets found. Further, he is asked to explain the nature of documents, loose paper found and transactions recorded therein. An attempt is made to decode the information/transactions of financial nature if kept by him in coded form. At this stage, searched person remains tense and does not have the benefit of the consultation from an outsider or his counsel. It is believed that he may come out with the true nature of the transactions and source of the assets found. Apart from the searched person, other persons from whose possession any material is found, may also be questioned by the authorized officer and their statements may be recorded u/s 132(4).

(*xvii*) **Seizure of undisclosed items**

For seizure of incriminating material and assets, based on the statement given by the searched person and evidences produced by him, a decision is taken by the authorized officer as to what is disclosed and what is not disclosed. Disclosed assets including cash, jewellery, bonds, fixed deposit receipts, pass books, and other valuable articles or things are released and handed over to the assessee. Undisclosed assets and documents, loose papers containing undisclosed transactions/details of incriminating nature are seized. In case of jewellery, certain quantity as per Board's instruction is released. Some amount of cash is also left for immediate need and requirement of the assessee. In case of items of large volume, weight etc., power of deemed seizure as provided under the proviso to section 132(1) may also be exercised.

(*xviii*) Preparing inventory of material found

Inventory of cash, bank pass books, cheque books, bonds, FDRs, other certificates, precious stones, jewellery, stock inventory at business premises is prepared. Even when such items are not seized, lists are prepared and made part of panchnama, marking as 'Assets found but not seized'. Some of the books of account are identified and marked so that no alteration can be done and the same may be produced later on by the searched person for verification, whenever required.

(*xix*) Preparation of panchnama

The items required to be seized are properly sealed in packages, numbered and panchnama is prepared which is duly signed by the authorized officer, assessee and both the witnesses. Lists are also prepared as to the items found but not seized and are made part of panchnama. A copy of the panchnama is handed over to the searched person or occupant along with all annexures. Panchnama contains the details of the search proceeding conducted by the authorized officer.

(*xx*) Put restraint u/s 132(3)

In case it is required, restraint u/s 132(3) is put on some Almirah/ room or box with some documents, papers or assets inside, which could not be seized. The fact of putting the restraint u/s 132(3) is mentioned in punchnama. The search is not treated as concluded till all restraints are lifted later on. In practice, restraint is put at some or other place relating to the searched person so as to gain time in concluding the search, recording further statement u/s 132(4), enabling declaration by the searched person regarding undisclosed income, if he is willing to make.

(*xxi*) Continuous reporting to controlling room

A control room is established in the office of the authorized officer who remains in the office to coordinate with all the search teams operating at different business and residential premises under search.

Immediate information relating to any incriminating material, documents, papers, assets coming to the knowledge of the search team is passed to the control room and in turn to the higher authorities. It is so done to keep transparency in the whole operation.

(*xxii*) To keep searched person at ease and carry out whole operation smoothly

Search operation is a harsh operation in which privacy of the searched person is completely invaded. The searched person or his family members may lose temper, may behave harsh or abuse or conduct in unruly manner to search team members. Training is given to the search officials to remain cool and calm and carry out the whole operation politely but firmly and purposefully. Authorized officer tries to satisfy the searched person and to keep him at ease so that no unwarranted situation is created. Officials involved in search are trained not to lose temper and exercise restraint in spite of provocation from the side of searched person.

(*xxiii*) Presence of mind and tackling any contingency

There may be various kinds of unexpected and strange situations which may crop up during search operations. The authorized officer is supposed to tackle the same tactfully, convincing the searched person that he is discharging his official duty and there is nothing personal against the searched person. Authorized officer is required to tackle any kind of emergency or contingency with presence of mind, patience and in a friendly manner but firmly and without losing the objectivity. He is required to keep on communicating with the higher authorities taking their guidance on various matters. At times authorized officer is required to exercise mild pressure if searched person does not cooperate in the conduct of search but it should be done within the parameters of law.

(*xxiv*) Calling counsel of the searched person

Generally at the fag end, when evidences are collected, the presence of counsel of the searched person is not only permitted but is desired by the authorized officer. His presence is desired so as to explain the sources of assets found, advise searched person on various ticklish legal issues and more importantly to prepare and convince him for making declaration of undisclosed income or assets, if any.

(*xxv*) To obtain surrender of undisclosed income

The basic objective of whole exercise of search is to collect evidences of undisclosed income or assets of the searched person. Though department is prohibited under law from pressurizing him to make declaration of undisclosed income, yet in practice it has been observed that he is persuaded for making declaration of undisclosed income or assets based upon the incriminating material found during search. It may be in the interest of the searched person as well, to make declaration of undisclosed income so as to get immunity or concession from penalty u/s 271AAA/271AAB.

(xxvi) Offences under other laws

Sometimes, it is found during search that the person under search has committed offences under other laws and/or incriminating material relating to violation of other laws are found. There may be liquor bottles in excess of what is permitted under State Excise Act. There may be foreign currency found in violation of FEMA or rules of RBI. There may be arms and ammunition available without license. There may be inconvenient photographs found which may disturb peace at home.

Under the law, the authorized officer is required to intimate to the respective authority to take suitable action against such person. However, in practice it is not always done and the authorized officer takes a decision whether to pass the information to the other authorities or not. In case of small kind of violations, information may not be passed for corresponding action by other authorities.

However, it has been experienced that in practice such incriminating material acts as catalyst for the searched person to come out with surrender of undisclosed income.

(xxvii) Conclusion of search

Signature of the assessee, authorized officer and both the witnesses are obtained on panchnama and all of its annexures. A copy of the same is handed over to the person searched. Before leaving the premises, search team members offer themselves for personal search, which is generally not done but it is deemed to have been done under the law.

In this manner, search is concluded or temporarily suspended if any restraints u/s 132(3) are passed by the authorized officer.

5.18 Planning of search by authorized officer

Income tax search is a very harsh action taken against the assessee by the department. It is undertaken in rarest of rare circumstances and after lot of thinking and planning. There are checks and balances in-built within the systems which do not allow the department to take search action in ordinary circumstances. At the end of the department for taking search action, it may take months together for making preparations. In a search action, huge financial expenditure in travelling cost, transportation, requisitioning services of other departments such as police officer, valuer etc., are involved. Gearing up of manpower of required calibre and rank at different locations and cities all over the countries is required and availability is to be ensured and above all the whole operation is to be completed, maintaining strict confidentiality and transparency at each stage. Various stages involved in planning in search may be discussed as under:

(i) Triggering Point

The triggering point for a search action is any information received by the department relating to undisclosed income of the assessee. It may be by way of complaint or Tax Evasion Petition (TEP) filed by some person. Information may be passed by business rivals or some disgruntled employee. It has been observed that generally information is given to the department in case of business dispute amongst partners or in the case of family disputes amongst brothers. Recently many cases of dispute over dowry in divorce petition filed with Civil Court have also been noticed. Sometimes non-compliance of notices issued u/s 131 or 142 may become the initiating point.

On the basis of the information available with the department, at times case is developed for search *suo motu*. It may be on the basis of inconsistency observed in the income tax return filed, information received as per annual information report from different sources. Now a day, lot of information is available regarding any person or business on internet and in public domain. Taking clue from there, case may be selected for further developing.

There are professional informers also who keep on passing information to the investigation wing of the income tax department. But their information is not generally found to be precise, accurate or reliable since they work for getting commission. The information given by the insider is more reliable.

(ii) Verification of facts

The information received from different quarters is verified by the authorized officer and his inspectors. Verification is done by visiting different places of the assessee, obtaining bank accounts statement relating to assessee and copy of returns of the assessee. Copies of returns are generally not obtained from the assessing officer lest the confidentiality should be leaked. In some or the other disguised manner, authorized officer prior to search, visits the main premises of the assessee for verification and planning of the search operation.

(iii) Recording of satisfaction

Detailed satisfaction note is prepared by the tax authority mentioning the nature of undisclosed income or undisclosed asset possessed by the assessee, the methodology being adopted to earn undisclosed income. The persons of the group required to be searched and the premises to be covered are mentioned in the satisfaction note. There has to be 'reason to believe' existing relating to undisclosed income in the case of each person for getting search warrant in his name.

The satisfaction note recorded by the tax authority is forwarded to his superior authority being Addl./Joint Director/Commissioner who after modification, if required alongwith his comments forward the same to Director Investigation or Commissioner of Income-tax for his approval.

Recording Satisfaction note is done in such a manner that the fact of undisclosed income or undisclosed asset accumulated by the assessee is reflected supported with the evidences. If it is based only upon rumors and hearsay, it cannot said to be as 'reason to believe' and in case of challenge of search action in writ petition, the whole action may be struck down.

(*iv*) Approval by Competent Authority

The search warrant is generally issued by Principal Director or Director in most of the cases. In case he is satisfied with the reason recorded, approval may be granted authorizing search. Individual search warrant is issued for each premise mentioning the name of the person. Search warrant is separately signed by the authorizing authority with a seal.

Generally search warrant is signed by the Principal Director. But before signing the search warrant, file is put to the knowledge of the Director General as an administrative control measure.

In the case of sensitive case information is given to the Member (Investigation) in CBDT.

(*v*) Search at the premises of the counsel

There remains an issue as to whether premises of Counsel/Chartered Accountant of assessee can also be searched or surveyed. There is no bar in this regard. But, it has been generally seen that search or survey is not planned at the premises of counsel/Chartered Accountant of the assessee while planning action at some business group. However, in a case where there is credible information available with the department that certain incriminating material relating to the target person is lying at the premises of his counsel/Chartered Accountant, department may undertake search u/s 132 or survey u/s 133A depending upon the nature of information and upon satisfaction recorded by the Competent Authority. Generally, it has been seen that in such cases survey u/s 133A is planned.

Reference is also invited to **Circular No. 7D, dated 3-5-1967** which states that the place where entry can be made under section 133A must not be a place where the assessee does not carry on business. Residential or office premises of third parties including a Chartered Accountant, a pleader or income-tax practitioner of whom the assessee may be a client, are not places which may be entered into for the purposes of section 133A. Above circular is reproduced as under:

"The place which an ITO or an Inspector, authorised by him in this behalf, may enter under the provisions of section 133A, must be either a place within the limits of the area under the jurisdiction of the ITO or any place occupied by any person in respect of whom the ITO exercises jurisdiction, at which a business or profession is carried on. The provisions of section 133A make it clear that, in either case, the place must be one where business or profession of an assessee is carried on, although it is not necessary that it should be the principal place of business or profession. The place where entry can be made under the section, must not be a place where the assessee does not carry on business. Business on residential premises of third parties, including a Chartered Accountant, a Pleader or Income-tax Practitioner, of whom the assessee may be client, are not places which could be entered into for the purpose of section 133A. It would be improper for an ITO or an Inspector, authorised by him in this behalf, to enter the office of a Chartered Account for the purpose of inspecting the books of his client. It is also necessary that the place entered should be the business premises and not residential premises of the assessee and the entry should be during business or office hours. It may, however, be noted that the above restrictions do not apply to cases of search and seizure specifically authorised under section 132 by the CIT/Director of Inspection, which will be governed by the provisions of that section."

But if in course of survey, person attending the business states that the books of account/documents, records, cash or inventory are kept in office of his chartered accountant/lawyer/tax practitioner; then the income-tax authority has power to enter business premises/office of chartered accountant/lawyer/tax practitioner to conduct survey under section 133A in connection with survey of premises of their client.

In the case of *U.K. Mahapatra & Co.* v. *ITO* [2009] 176 Taxman 293 (Orissa) affirmed by the Apex Court in [2010] 186 Taxman 181, it has been held that although *Explanation* to Section 133A allows survey of any other place where the books of account of assessee are kept but the pre-condition for conducting survey u/s 133A, is that the client in the course of survey must state that his books of accountant/documents and records are kept in the office of his chartered accountant/lawyer/tax practitioner.

(*vi*) Search at the premise of the employee

In case of search u/s 132 planned by the department at some business group, it has been observed in practice that some of the senior employees of the company are also roped in and search warrant is issued to search their premises also. Generally, such employees are those employees who occupy important positions and/or are involved in managing unaccounted transactions or cash affairs of the company as per the information of the department.

In case search warrant is issued in the name of the company, 'satisfaction' of undisclosed income against the employee is not required to be recorded by competent authority in order to search the premises of the employee. Premises of the employee may be taken under search on the ground that incriminating material relating to the target person/business house may be found at the premises of the employee. But in case search warrant is issued in the name of employee to search his premises, there has to be recording of satisfaction against the employee by the competent authority in terms of the requirements of section 132(1)(*a*), (*b*), (*c*). Sometimes, department commits mistakes in this respect and in such case search conducted with respect to the employee may be held invalid.

In the case of search at the premises of the assessee under any circumstances as discussed above, the entire premises of the employee is liable to be inspected and searched. Even when search warrant has been issued against the company & premises of the employee are searched, any incriminating material found during search relating to the employee's personal affairs is also liable to be seized. Senior employees or non-working directors of the companies should remain quite vigilant and manage their personal affairs in proper manner otherwise they may have to face serious repercussions, when search is conducted at some business group.

(*vii*) Planning of date of search

After receiving authorization warrants, the date of striking search is planned. The movement of the assessee and his availability on the date of search are also watched. It is ensured that there is not too much time lag in striking the search. Otherwise fresh surveillance may be required. Search teams at various places are gathered and stay together on the eve of day of search. It is so done to ensure that search may commence in the early hours on the next days.

The police officers are also requisitioned to accompany search team so as to ensure the safety and security of team members in case of any un-warranted incidents taking place during search.

(viii) Sending teams

On the day of search the teams are sent at different places. The timing of dispatch of various teams is planned in such a manner that search teams strike at various premises of assessee at the same time. To maintain confidentiality, sometimes different or longer routes are selected. Search teams do not use official vehicle, so that they are not identified and at the time of entry into the premise of the assessee vehicles are usually kept at a distance.

A sealed envelope is generally given to the leader of search team and he is instructed to open the envelope on the way and it is at this time he comes to know at which place search team is required to move. This envelope contains copy of search warrants, map of the premises and a brief description, the nature of investigation to be done or the items required to be searched or the enquiries to be made from the assessee relating to what matters, while recording statement of the assessee.

(ix) Monitoring from control room

Control room is established generally in the office of the ADI/DDI who has planned the search under the supervision of his superior authority *i.e.* Joint DI/Addl. DI. Each and every valuable information coming to the knowledge of different search teams at different locations regarding undisclosed assets, important documents or information regarding undisclosed income found or any significant incident taking place during search are immediately passed to the control room. Each premises wise control charts are maintained in the control room and on real time basis any such information being received is recorded. Vital information or papers are immediately forwarded to the higher authorities. The whole procedure has been administratively prescribing in such a manner that complete confidentiality and transparency is maintained at each stage.

(x) Sending various reports

The authorized officer is required to send various reports to the higher authorities till search operations are finally concluded and further upto the stage of finalization of Appraisal report and handing over all seized material to the concerned assessing officer. The reports are required to be sent promptly within administratively prescribed time limit and periodically.

5.19 How to face search

Income tax search is a life time experience for searched person and his family members. The search operations are undertaken by the Income Tax

Department confidentially without prior intimation. When such harsh action is undertaken against a person all of a sudden, he is not mentally prepared for the same. Such person should try to remain cool, keep patience and face it in an intelligent manner. It should be considered as cost of living in the society, values of which have been set by all of us as citizens of this country.

(i) Immediately informing to related persons

In case a person whose premises are under search, gets the opportunity after ingress of search party, he may try to inform to his business partners, senior employees, in charge of other business premises, other directors of the company etc. so that if there is any time gap by the search team to reach at other premises, they may be mentally prepared to face the search and take legitimate precautions as they may deem fit. Any relative, friend or well wisher of the searched person, who is outside the search premises and comes to know about search operations, may also pass on the information to other related business associates who are also likely to be searched and there is nothing illegal in it.

(ii) Managing documents/papers to the extent possible

There may be documents/loose papers, cash or other assets in the possession of the searched person, who is expected to handle the situation during the search operations with in the parameters of law. Though it is not legally expected and ethically advisable for a person to have incriminating material but parallel economy and "out of the books" transactions are unfortunately part of the life and value system prevailing in the society. Though such practice is deprecated but in practice, searched person at times wishes that income tax department is not able to lay hands on the incriminating material in the hope that anything which does not surface at that point of time may not come to the lime light. Most of the times, such wish remains a wishful thinking of the searched person. One should not resort to any illegal and undesirable practice lest any kind of criminal offence should be charged against such person for any misadventure.

(iii) Assessee outside - Whether to reach or avoid

It may happen that search team reaches to the premises of a person who may not be inside the premises. For example, such person may have gone outside his residence to drop the children to school, for morning walk or to the temple etc. It may well be possible that the person under search or senior executives may not have reached to the office or factory till then.

In such a situation such persons always remain in a dilemma after getting the information that search team has struck at their premises

as to whether they should reach their premises and face the proceedings or avoid the same. Authorized officer always requires and
makes efforts to call such persons or other senior persons to remain
present during search so as to enable him to record their statement,
make enquiries for carrying out search operations smoothly in their
presence.

In our opinion, it is desirable to face the situation instead of avoiding
the same. Such person is always in the best position to handle the
situation with maturity and wisdom. It is also true that there is no
power of arrest to the income tax department during search operation.

In case person under search does not remain available at the premises,
certain adverse actions may be taken by the search team which could
otherwise be avoided. Statement may be recorded of the spouse of
such person or of some junior employee at business premises who
may not answer the queries in proper manner and/or answers given
by them may be damaging or factually incorrect. Certain assets or
documents may be seized which are otherwise disclosed ones but the
evidence of disclosure could not be produced at the relevant time
due to absence of the searched person.

In one of the cases, income tax team reached at the registered office of a company with the authority to undertake survey u/s 133A.
Generally, it so happens that in case of whole search operations, at
certain business premises where undisclosed assets are not likely
to be found and seized; only survey is undertaken. The registered
office of the company was situated there only for name sake and
in fact, it was the office of the associate of the assessee. At the time,
when income tax team reached there, the premises were locked. On
getting the information of income tax team coming there for search,
nobody reached there. The Income-tax Officers kept on calling the
concerned person to come, open the lock and provide the information
throughout the day but nobody responded due to fear and panic.
At the end, competent authority took the decision to convert survey
into search, of course by complying with the mandatory requirement
of law contained in this regard. Search warrant was issued by the
competent authority, lock of the premises was broken and whatever
documents, books, papers relating to the company or other companies
were available thereat, were indiscriminately seized. Later on, action
was taken against other companies also by covering them u/s 153C
of the Act.

The above situation could have been avoided easily, had somebody
reached the premises, opened the same and let the survey been

proceeded. Survey could be in that case, only with the objective to enquire the affairs and look into the records or documents relating to target Company. Whatever the records of the company at all were available there, could have been shown to the survey team and the rigors of conversion of survey into search and seizure of records of other companies could have been avoided.

At the best, such person may have reached the premises after having consultation with his counsel so as to be mentally prepared as to how to handle the situation, answer the probable questions and produce the evidences of the disclosed assets.

(iv) Collection of evidences of disclosed assets

The person who is outside the premise under search or the counsel of the searched person should try to collect the evidences of the asscts availablc with such pcrson, so as to provc that thc samc arc disclosed assets. There may be cash or jewellery or FDs or other valuables available with the searched person, which have been acquired out of the disclosed sources. The evidences of the same may not be available readily with such person. In such a case, the same may be seized by the authorized officer. In case evidences of the assets having been disclosed are properly collected and at the fag end of search operation when decision of seizure is taken by the authorized officer, the evidences are shown to him, there is all likelihood that the same will not be seized.

In the case of cash found, the authorization letter from the company/firm/business entity so as to keep cash of the business entity/company at the residence of the director or partner or employee and cash available in the books of the business entity/company may be convincing evidence. In the case of jewellery items, copy of the wealth tax return, income tax return showing the disclosure of the jewellery, valuation report of the valuer or any other evidence wherein the items of jewellery are shown existing 7 years prior to search may be good evidence so as prevent seizure. At the cost of repetition, it may be said that in case of jewellery or other assets, the evidence of procuring the same prior to seven financial years may be a good evidence so as to prevent the seizure.

(v) Person going inside to ensure that he does not possess any incriminating material

Sometimes it so happens that some friend or well wisher of the searched person reaches to his premises to show sympathy or solidarity with him. The authorized officer may or may not allow his entry into the premises. Sometimes he may entangle with the authorized officer on certain issue. One should always keep in mind that the authorized officer has also got the legal right to search him in person. Therefore, he should ensure that he does not carry any incriminating material with him.

In one of the searches, a friend of the person under search reached at his residence and got entangled in argument with authorized officer on some issue. The authorized officer to show his legal authority and also for this reason that it was considered expedient, searched him and found a slip in his pocket containing details of property transaction of substantial value in cash which was seized. Needless to say, consequential action was taken against such third person on that basis and such person was put to lot of hardship.

In another case, a friend of the person under search reached at the premises during search and it was transpired that he came to deliver cash of ₹ 30 Lacs kept in his car. On enquiry by the authorized officer, cash was brought inside and the same was seized and section 153C action was undertaken against this fellow, thus necessitating the reopening of his cases for seven years as prescribed under that section.

(vi) Misbehaviour or threat by authorized officer

Sometimes authorized officer may use threat techniques to put pressure on the person under search to get the true facts or explain the document properly or decode the information written in the coded form. Sometimes threat is administered on the employees of the searched person threatening them to search their residential premises also or to reopen their cases and so on and so forth. As per law, authorized officer does not have any such power.

Searched person or his employees or family members should never come under such pressure. They should not be fearful or should not make any statement under panic. Rather, they should try to defuse the situation by requesting not to use such tactics. If situation worsens, he may get the same recorded in his statement or take letter/affidavit from the panches witnessing the proceedings so as to challenge the conduct of search under article 226 of the Constitution by way of writ at later stage. The evidentiary value of the statement recorded or material collected in such illegal or irregular manner is considerably reduced. In extreme cases, person under search may choose to lodge complaint with the higher administrative authorities.

(vii) Misbehaviour by person under search

In case misbehaviour is done by the person under search or his family members by abusing or otherwise, authorized officer may choose to remain cool and further try to cool down such person, try to convince him that search team is doing its official duty. In case of physical assault, assistance of police officer is taken to prevent the searched person from doing so. In extreme cases, such person may be charged u/s 187 of Indian Penal Code to be prosecuted for such action.

(viii) Authorized officer occupying chair of person under search

It may so happen in practice that authorized officer reaching the business premises under search, occupy the main chair of searched person, take control of telephone calls, search the drawers and other nearby cupboards. It may be done with several things in mind, *inter alia*, such as to demonstrate his powers and authority and to create an environment and fear in the minds of other junior staff of the company or member of the family. In fact, the authorized officer does not have any such power as to occupy the chair of the searched person etc. Person under search may politely request him to occupy some other chair. However, such person under search is required to provide all facilities to the authorized officer so as to enable him to search drawers, almirahs, cupboards etc.

(ix) Stop from receiving or making telephone calls

As per law, authorized officer does not have any power to prevent the person under search or his family members from receiving or making telephone calls or for that matter, any power to prevent them to carry out their normal business/personal activities. However, if by allowing such normal business or personal activities, the very purpose of search operation is getting defeated or it creates hindrance in carrying out the search operation, the authorized officer would be well within his powers to temporarily suspend the use of telephone calls. No telephone call can be permitted for passing information to others, consulting related search matters or to make manipulation by giving instructions to fabricate false evidence etc. Urgent and necessary calls shall be permitted. The authorized officer may intercept or hear conversation.

(x) Power of arrest

The authorized officer does not have any power to arrest the person under search for any offence under the Income-tax Act. Such power may be available in the case of searches under GST Act and Custom Act to those authorities. However, in case of offences like destruction of documents, physical assault on the search party, falsification or manipulation of documents and other evidences found or giving false statement on oath, an authorized officer can lodge a complaint with the police and the appropriate police authority may take cognizance of the offence and order the arrest as per law.

(xi) **Assessee or his representative fleeing with records or destructing evidences**

Under no circumstances authorized officer may watch such incident happening when searched person or his representative may try to destroy or run away with the evidences. The authorized officer is empowered to prevent the same by all means, taking police assistance or by using tough measures. Evidences thrown at the adjoining house, with the neighbours or running away with, can be brought back. In case the papers are torn, the same are required to be restored back to the extent possible in the presence of witnesses. In such situation, assessee may be charged with criminal offence as well.

(xii) **Whether production, purchase and sale of goods can be stopped**

As per law there is no power to stop the normal business operations, production or purchase and sale of goods. However physical stock inventorization is required to be undertaken of raw material, finished and semi-finished goods and other items of stock. The same may not be possible in case continuous movement of goods keeps on taking place. Therefore, to facilitate the process of physical stock taking, movement of goods can be suspended temporarily till such job is completed.

In practice, it has been observed that the strategy of not permitting the searched person to resume production or purchase and sale of goods is resorted to by the authorized officer to pressurize such person for making surrender of undisclosed income or for eliciting the required cooperation. The operation of factory is not permitted on one or the other pretext. Sometimes, when the job of physical stock taking could not be completed on the day of search and when search is temporarily suspended by putting restraint u/s 132(3), production or dispatch of goods is not permitted on the pretext that physical stock taking is yet pending and therefore movement of goods cannot be allowed.

In our opinion, authorized officer does not have any such powers and stopping the production or dispatch of goods is in violation of law contained in this regard and filing of writ with the High Court may be considered as remedy. Authorized officer cannot put restraint u/s 132(3) of the Act on stock inventory since restraint under section 132(3) can be put only on assets which can be seized and stock inventory is an asset which cannot be seized. Second Proviso to section 132(1) of the Act regarding deemed seizure is also not applicable to stock-in-trade of the business w.e.f. 01.06.2003. The fact that the job of physical stock inventory could not be completed by the search team, cannot be attributed to the searched person and after suspending the search operations and keeping the same pending for 1-2 days due to tiredness or unavailability of staff cannot be a reason for not permitting the production, purchase and dispatch of goods. Now-a-days, customers do operate on zero inventory level and vendors are required to dispatch the goods regularly otherwise production line of the customers may be stopped and heavy penalties may be imposed on the vendor- assessee. Therefore, authorized officer can never be permitted and for that matter does not have any power under law to stop production, purchase or dispatch of goods.

Searched person is entitled to conduct his normal business activities so long as they do not obstruct the search proceedings. The only requirement may be that purchase or sale or movement of goods should be done with the knowledge and after recording the same with the authorized officer.

(*xiii*) Role of counsel or legal representative

At the time of search, the role of the advocate, counsel, chartered accountant or legal advisor of the searched person becomes very important. Searched person seeks advice of his counsel on various matters and then he is guided by such advice. The counsel should play a very balanced role, advising the client on various matters objectively, in accordance with the provisions of law and in his overall interest. Simply to show his loyalty to the client, counsel should not entangle with the authorized officer on petty matters. Rather, he should facilitate in carrying out the search operations smoothly by convincing and putting the person under search at comfort. The following points in this regard may be significant:-

1. As soon as the information of search having taken place with his client is received by the counsel, he may try to reach to the premises under search. It may not be taken in good taste by the authorized officer who may not permit his presence during search operations. Instead of reaching immediately, the counsel should wait till evening and when he reaches at the premises at this point, it is seen in practice that he is welcomed by the authorized officer who would like to take his assistance in concluding the search proceedings, in convincing the assessee on various points including surrender of undisclosed income, if at all, to be made by the person under search.

2. In the mean time, counsel may remain available on phone if permitted, to advise to various persons. In case any irregularity is being done which comes to his knowledge, he may talk to the authorized officer or to other authorities at the control room to get the things right.

3. In case counsel is deeply involved in some financial transactions with the searched person or books of account, records of such person are lying at his office, the possibility of survey or search at his place as well, cannot be ruled out and first of all, he should try to put his house in order.

4. He should collect the evidences of the assets, cash, jewellery etc. available with the searched person so as to show them later to the authorized officer to prevent the seizure.

5. When called or on reaching the premises in late hours, the counsel may assist in explaining the nature of incriminating material found and to advise as to whether any declaration of undisclosed income is required to be made or not. He has to advise to the searched person properly on this matter and sometimes, has to play the role as negotiator between such person and the department as per law. A detailed discussion regarding the manner of surrender of undisclosed income has been discussed at the later part of this chapter.

(xiv) If searched person's rights are denied

We have discussed various rights of the searched person available to him during search. In practice, it has been observed that sometimes high handedness is resorted to or excesses are exercised by the authorized officer. The rights of the searched person are denied or are not permitted to him. The searched person or even at times, counsel of such person is not aware of all the rights which are denied to such person during search operations. Later when consulting to other persons or senior counsels, he may come to know about the rights available.

(xv) Under such circumstances remedies available with the searched person

1. First of all, searched person or his counsel should try to talk and discuss the matter with the authorized officer at the premises or with the concerned authority in the control room or with the higher authorities i.e. Addl. Director of Investigation or Director of Investigation. He should discuss the issue then and there and get the same resolved.

2. In case disclosed assets are being seized or excesses are being exercised, he should resist the same within the parameters of law. Practically, once assets are seized, it takes lot of time and efforts to get the same released.

3. Searched person should try to collect the evidence of such situation and get the same recorded in his statement before

signing the statement. In appropriate cases, he may procure letters from panches, witnessing the proceedings.

4. After the completion of search operation if certain issues come to his knowledge, he should file the objection immediately with the authorized officer with the copies marked to higher authorities.

5. In case all these measures do not work, the last resort available with the searched person may be to file writ under article 226 of the constitution with the jurisdictional High Court. A detailed discussion in this regard is held in a separate chapter.

(*xvi*) Physical cash short found

There may be situation when during the course of search, physical cash found is short than the amount of cash in hand available as per the books of account. In such a case, Authorized Officer may ask the assessee to explain as to where the balance amount has been kept. There may be various reasons for such short fall of cash depending upon the facts and circumstances of the case. Cash found may be short due to certain expenses/payments having been made but not found recorded in the books. Such outgoings should be properly explained and details should be got recorded. There may be certain payments of cash made which may be in the nature of unrecorded transactions. Obviously, assessee may be tempted not to disclose such payments. There may be another situation when cash has been kept for safe custody at residence or some other premises of the director/ senior employees. In case such other premises is also covered under search, assessee should state this fact which would make the things easy at both the ends *i.e.* at the business premises where the cash is short found as well as at the residential premises where cash is found so as to explain the source of such cash at the residence. However, in case cash has been kept at some premises not covered under search, any disclosure of such premises may also lead to the search of such premises. There may be situation where it is explained that cash has been given to some employee/director for the purchase of some capital asset e.g. land etc. and final information about the deal has not yet been received. In such a case, search party would like to have some more evidence in support of this fact. In other words, there can be numerous fact situations where cash is actually found short than the one recorded in the books of account.

However, it is significant to appreciate that during assessment there cannot be any addition for undisclosed income in case cash found is short. If assessee is able to explain the details of cash utilized, it may be to his advantage so as to explain the source of such utilization which may be in the form of certain assets or expenses.

5.20 Post search proceedings

(*i*) Opening of restraints

During the course of search proceeding, certain restraints u/s 132(3) may be imposed which are mentioned in the Panchnama. It may be relating to certain almirah, box or room or locker of the searched person. Sometimes, restraints are put to gain time before concluding the search operations. Technically, till all restraints are lifted, search operation cannot be said to be concluded.

Wherever restraints are put, the authorized officer is expected to lift such restraints the earliest. For lifting the restraint, authorized officer along with 3-4 other officers visits the place where restraints have been put, opens the seal and takes out the material therein. It may be jewellery, other valuable articles or thing or documents, loose papers etc. The same are examined to look into whether any seizure is required to be made. The statement of searched person is normally recorded prior to and/or after opening of the restraint in connection with the contents of the material therein. Two witnesses are also called to witness these proceedings, panchnama prepared and signatures are obtained in the same manner as in the case of original search.

While lifting the restraint, the authorized officer ensures that the seals on the lock of the almirah, box etc. put are intact and no damage has been caused or no attempt has been made by any body to temper the same so as to take out or manipulate the material kept inside. In case of any doubt, suitable action under Indian Penal Code may be taken.

Generally while lifting the restraint, no other place is again searched nor any other aspect is examined but in case of any suspicion, the possibility of the same being undertaken again cannot be ruled out.

(*ii*) Collecting records from different destinations

Search operations are conducted at various premises which may be located in different cities all over the country. The records and the assets, documents or papers seized are called for from different destinations which have been searched by the officer authorized at different places. All records are received by the ADI or DDI initiating the action and having jurisdiction over the searched person who is further required to appraise the evidences collected and prepare the appraisal report.

After sending the records to the officer initiating the search, the role of the other officers authorized to conduct search at various premises of the assessee, generally, comes to an end.

(iii) Operation of lockers

There may be certain lockers of the searched person or his family members in the bank which are also operated. In case keys are not available, the process of getting the same opened through the services of manufacturer of the locker are undertaken and the same process is followed as is there in the case of lifting the restraint put u/s 132(3).

(iv) Recording of statement - Explaining documents

In case the statement of the searched person could not be completed or recorded at the time of search due to his non-availability or for some other reasons, he may be called by the authorized officer in his office and statement is recorded. Till search is concluded by lifting all the restraints, such statement recorded is the statement recorded u/s 132(4).

The statement of the searched person may be recorded to explain the nature and contents of the documents or loose papers or assets found in search. Generally, it is seen in practice that such recording is done intensely and incisively in case no declaration of undisclosed income to the satisfaction of authorized officer is made by such person. Though publicly denied, yet the objective of the authorized officer remains to persuade or to compel the searched person to declare the undisclosed income based upon the material seized.

The assessee should not avoid going to the office of the authorized officer if called, for recording the statement till search is concluded otherwise authorized officer may record the statement of such person by coming to his premises for lifting the restraints.

(v) Breakup of surrendered income

Sometimes during the course of search, undisclosed income is surrendered by the searched person as a lump sum amount. Before concluding the search proceeding, such person is asked to furnish the breakup of the undisclosed income surrendered viz. assessee-wise, year-wise and item-wise. It is in the interest of both the searched person as well as the department to furnish the breakup.

It may be done by submitting a detailed letter by such person signed by all the persons/entities in whose hand surrender is being made. The authorized officer ensures that surrender is made relating to undisclosed income/asset of which proper evidences are in his possession, so that such person may not be tempted to retract the surrender at any later stage. The details of the surrender made are recorded in the statement of such person taken on oath u/s 132(4).

Sometimes, breakup and details of the undisclosed income earlier given at the time of search may be required to be amended in view of the overall planning and after properly appreciating the evidences collected. The earlier statement given can be revised or improved and the later statement may then supersede the same.

(*vi*) Retraction of Statement

During the course of search proceeding, searched person might have made a declaration of undisclosed income but later on after discussing the matter with his associates or counsel or after properly understanding its implications, there may be a situation when such person may wish to retract the earlier declaration of the undisclosed income made.

It may so happen when such person realizes that surrender was made under pressure and there are no evidences of substantive nature suggesting undisclosed income. Such person generally remains under wrong impression that once surrender is made and taxes with respect to surrender of undisclosed income are paid, the proceedings are finally concluded and no further action or assessment proceeding shall be undertaken by the department. Such person might have made surrender for earlier year(s) but later, he is advised that penalty u/s 271(1)(*c*) may not be avoided or it may so happen when such person may realize that by making surrender of undisclosed income in the manner as done by him, there may be severe consequential impact upon other business associates or employees under the Income-tax Act or under some other statutes such as Central Excise, Sales tax etc.

In a situation when decision for retraction of surrendered income is taken by such person, it should be done at the earliest and delay of each day is held against him. The decision of retraction should be taken only in compelling circumstances. Any such decision of such person is usually considered by the department negatively and which may result into deeper investigation into his affairs and may invite intense post search third party inquiries from the business associates of such person.

A detailed discussion regarding retraction of the statement of undisclosed income has been made in the chapter on statement u/s 132(4).

(*vii*) Third party enquiries

Based upon the nature of evidences collected, sometimes third party enquiries are conducted. The objective is to further collect the information from the business associates of searched person and to corroborate the evidences or information relating to the undisclosed income of such person. Third party enquiry can be made by issuing summons u/s 131 to other parties.

Sometimes, consequential action may be planned to be taken by way of survey u/s 133A at the business premises of third parties or other business associates of such person. This may be done when evidences suggest existence of undisclosed income of other parties who may also be roped in.

Sometimes, it is seen in practice that the above actions are undertaken to seek surrender of undisclosed income from the searched person who may come under pressure due to impending adverse impact upon his normal business relations with business associates or other parties, in case enquiries are made from such persons who may feel harassed due to search action on such person.

(*viii*) **Letters to authorized officer on various aspects**

Searched person may be required to make communication to the authorized officer on various aspects which may be quite useful to him in further proceedings. These communications are quite significant from the point of view of such person in case of any dispute and at the time of appreciating the evidences by the higher authorities at later stage.

    a. Request to appropriate cash seized towards advance tax. Such request made would be useful in case cash seized is not treated as advance tax and interest u/s 234B or 234C is imposed.

    b. There may be certain disclosed assets seized. Letter should be written along with complete evidences requesting to release the same. As per law, it is only undisclosed assets which can be seized.

    c. Letter should immediately be written to get photocopies of all the documents, papers or books of account seized. The assessee may be in a better position to plan his affairs after getting the photocopies. The Income-tax return of the assessee and tax audit may be pending on the date of search and unless the photocopies of the document seized are received, it may not be possible to finalize the same. In case of delay in giving the photocopies, case may be made out against imposition of penalty if any levied for such defaults.

    d. Whenever jewellery is seized, ladies of the house are very sentimental and touchy about it. They insist for their jewellery items to be received back at the earliest. Instructions have been issued by the Board to release jewellery against furnishing of bank guarantee or depositing of cash of the equivalent amount. Request for release of jewellery by furnishing bank guarantee or depositing cash may be made immediately, if desired.

e. There may be assets, books of account or documents relating to other persons seized during search. In case the same have been properly disclosed in the return of income to the department or in the books of account by those persons, letter should be written immediately by such person as well as by those persons requesting for release of the same. Such action is immediately required so that no further proceeding against such persons are recommended or undertaken by the department u/s 153C of the Act.

f. In case searched person has experienced any kind of irregularity or high handedness during search, a letter explaining the actual facts should be brought to the notice of the higher authorities immediately. It may so happen, *inter alia*, if statement of such person was not recorded properly, the valuation of jewellery done by the valuer is objected or the physical inventory-taking was not done in proper manner and quantities were written arbitrarily etc. Objection filed by such person mentioning the actual facts and circumstances will be significant in appreciating the evidentiary value of the evidences by the higher authorities at later stage.

g. In case restraint u/s 132(3) is not lifted and undue delay is made by the authorized officer, the matter should be brought to the notice of higher authorities. There are departmental instructions to lift all the restraints as early as possible and conclude the search.

(ix) Sending various reports to higher authorities

There is a very strong internal reporting system established in the income tax department relating to search operation. Various reports are required to be sent by the authorized officer to the higher authorities immediately as soon as certain facts come to his knowledge and various developments taking place at different stages. The objective of such prompt reporting is to maintain transparency and prevent the possibility of any kind of manipulation of the evidences.

(x) Appraisal Report

Appraisal report is an internal report submitted by the authorized officer to the higher authorities and the assessing officer having jurisdiction over the assessee. This is confidential administrative report, copy of which is not given to the assessee.

(a) Finding of investigation

The job of the authorized officer conducting search is to collect evidences and incriminating material relating to undisclosed income and assets of the searched person. He is generally not the assessing authority and is not empowered to frame assessment, levy any tax liability or finalize any tax demand against the searched person.

All that he is required to do is to prepare an Appraisal Report which is forwarded to the assessing officer having jurisdiction over the assessee and who is empowered to frame assessment u/s 153A or 153C as the case may be. Appraisal Report is divided in two parts, that is, Part A and Part B. Part A contains the details of entities, persons and premises covered under search, assets or documents etc. seized and the location/custodian with whom the same are kept. It further elaborates the nature of evidences collected relating to undisclosed income of the assessee, his analysis and interpretation of such evidences. The authorized officer tries to corroborate various evidences so as to make strong case against the assessee. He may record statements of other parties so as to support his analysis & findings in the appraisal report. Copies of statement recorded during search are also made part of the Appraisal Report.

Part B of Appraisal Report gives the broad nature and description of each and every document, loose papers, files or books of account seized during search.

(b) Significance of Appraisal Report

Appraisal Report prepared by the authorized officer is a very important document which may have significant bearing on the ultimate assessment of income of the assessee by the assessing officer. The assessing officer is guided heavily by the findings given in the Appraisal Report. Though assessing officer has powers and is rather required to go through all the documents and papers seized and make his own observations and investigation, yet in practice it has been observed in practice that due to pressure of time barring cases, assessing officer is able to concentrate primarily on the issues highlighted in the Appraisal Report.

As per internal instructions issued by the Board to assessing officers assessing the search cases, it has been directed that the assessing officer should consult to the authorized officer who has prepared the Appraisal Report, in case there is any deviation in the conclusion drawn by the assessing officer relating to the documents found/issues covered by the appraisal report *vis-a-vis* to the conclusion as drawn by the authorized officer in his Appraisal Report. He is required to consult his senior officer *i.e.* Addl. Commissioner or Commissioner who in turn are required to take views of the corresponding senior officers of the investigation wing *i.e.* Addl. Director or Director of investigation.

In view of the above, assessee is expected to ensure that Appraisal Report is prepared by the authorized officer objectively and he should thus try to extend his cooperation to the extent required and possible.

(xi) Decision of Jurisdiction/Centralization

As per internal departmental instruction, search cases are required to be centralized at one place relating to different persons/entities involved in the search. The objective is to make proper assessment after coordinated investigation and analysis of evidences. Generally, search cases are transferred to Central Circle specially meant for this purpose by passing order u/s 127 by respective Commissioner having jurisdiction in the case of different persons or entities spread at different places all over the country.

The authorized officer makes his recommendation for the appropriate jurisdiction to which all the cases should be centralized. Before passing order u/s 127 for transferring the cases to central circle, opportunity is granted to the assessee to make objection if any, as provided u/s 127 and the decision is taken by the Commissioner of Income Tax after due consideration of the objection raised by the assessee. In case of any difference of opinion between two Commissioners or Chief Commissioners, matter is referred to the Board. In case assessee is aggrieved, he can make representation to the Board and in case of his grievance remaining unaddressed, he may file writ petition to the High Court in appropriate case.

The details of the persons or entities covered under search giving their addresses, PAN and jurisdiction whereat presently assessed is asked to be furnished by the authorized officer. The details are also asked relating to other family members, other sister concerns or group companies of the assessee. The assessee should furnish this information carefully only relating to persons or entities covered under search or as required by the authorized officer. Based upon the information furnished regarding other persons or entities, there may be a possibility of centralization of all the cases.

(xii) **Reply to Questionnaire issued by the Authorized Officer**

During the process of preparation of the Appraisal Report, authorized officer may issue questionnaire to the assessee asking for certain information to be furnished, seeking explanation about the nature or contents of the documents/loose papers collected and related to other matters.

There are divergent opinions on the issue whether once search is over, can authorized officer issue notice and ask information/explanations from the assessee and in case assessee does not reply to such notices, whether he may be penalized. This issue has been discussed in great detail in **Chapter 8**.

However, without going in to the merit of the issue, it is expected from the assessee keeping in view overall planning and cooperation by assessee in finalization of the Appraisal Report, not to ignore such questionnaire but to reply it carefully. Assessee can seize this opportunity to explain the nature of documents in his favour so that no adverse inferences are drawn by the authorized officer.

(xiii) **Records belonging to other persons**

There may be books of account, documents or other records belonging to other persons seized during search. Before taking a stand that such records do not belong to the assessee but to somebody else, one should always keep in mind the possibility of Assessing officer invoking section 153C and such other persons are also likely to be roped into the net of search assessments for seven years. In case such other person is wife or close relative of the assessee, strategic decision may be taken to explain the same in the hands of searched person only, so that if at all any adverse inference is to be drawn from such document, let it be in his hand only so as to avoid the possibility of invoking the provisions of section 153C in the hands of other persons.

(xiv) **Questionnaire to be prepared by the Authorized Officer for Assessing Officer**

As per the latest departmental instructions, authorized officer is required to prepare, along with Appraisal Report, a suggestive questionnaire to be issued by assessing officer to the assessee as the authorized officer had already under gone the process of appraising all the seized evidences closely. Generally assessing officer does not get sufficient time to appraise all the evidences so closely again. The objective of this requirement is to make better utilization of the efforts already made by the authorized officer in appreciating the evidences collected.

Such questionnaire can only be suggestive in nature for the assessing officer so that none of his powers and duty for application of independent judicial mind can be undermined by it.

(xv) **Issue of summons to assessee u/s 131 for personal presence**

Once search operation has taken place against an assessee and search has been concluded, a question arises as to whether during the course of preparation of Appraisal Report, an assessee may be called by the authorized officer to appear before him personally by issuing summons u/s 131 for explaining the nature and contents of the documents or loose papers seized. This has been a point of controversy and there are two opinions about it. Income tax search is the most severe and extreme investigation action taken by the department wherein statement of the assessee is already recorded u/s 132(4) during the course of search and now it is for the authorized officer to draw his own inferences and no more enquires from the assessee at this stage are desirable by enforcing his personal presence.

In practice, such situation is required to be handled tactfully keeping in view the overall objective, by the assessee. Detailed discussion on this issue has been held in chapter relating to statement u/s 132(4).

5.21 Preparation prior to assessment proceedings

Once search is concluded and the authorized officer finalises Appraisal Report duly approved by the higher authorities, the authorized officer is required to handover all the seized material to the assessing officer having jurisdiction over assessee within a period of 60 days from the date on which the last of the authorizations for search is executed as per sec. 132(9A). However in practice, it has been observed that the period of 60 days get extended and administrative approval is obtained by the authorized officer from higher authorities. The process of centralization of all search cases at central circle takes considerable time and for this reason also, the handing over of seized material to the assessing officer gets delayed.

Assessee gets lot of time prior to receiving notices from the assessing officer to file returns u/s 153A. Further time remains available with the assessee after filing the returns but before effective assessment proceedings are undertaken and questionnaire is issued by the concerned assessing officer.

The above time available with the assessee may be utilized in planning, gearing up, collecting evidences and preparation for making submission to the assessing officer. Certain other significant decisions may be required to be taken during this period based upon the facts and circumstances of the case and complexities involved therein. Some of such steps may be discussed as under:-

(*i*) **Filing of pending returns or waiting for notices u/s 153A?**

As on the date of search, there may be income tax returns, tax audit report pending to be finalized and filed by the assessee u/s 139. In case search is held, say, in the month of August 20XX and last date of filing income tax return in the case of a company is 30th September 20XX, income tax return for year ending 31st March 20XX may be pending to be filed. In some cases, due date for filing the return u/s 139(1) might have expired but return could not be filed. In such cases, assessee should file the pending income tax return as early as possible. In case balance sheet cannot be finalized and return cannot be filed due to books of account or other records relevant for finalizing the balance sheet or income tax return, having been seized, photocopy of the same should be applied and obtained at the earliest. In case the same are not provided by the authorized officer, proper evidence of the same should be kept so as to plead the case against levy of interest u/s 234A or 234B or against any kind of penalty, if any, imposed due to late filing of income tax returns or tax audit report.

Assessee should not take a decision not to file such returns till notices u/s 153A are received. Assessee is required to make compliance of all the requirement of law in normal course. Such returns should be filed by the assessee with the assessing officer having jurisdiction over the assessee at the time of filing the return.

When notices are received u/s 153A, assessee is required to file the returns again as required u/s 153A with the assessing officer from whom the notices are received, in case jurisdiction of the assessee is transferred to some other officer u/s 127, after centralization of cases.

(*ii*) **Filing objection for transfer of cases u/s 127**

Search cases are generally centralized at one place for all entities/persons involved in a search. In case, cases are required to be transferred from one CIT jurisdiction to the other, order u/s 127 is required to be passed by concerned Commissioner of Income Tax.

As provided, before passing an order u/s 127 for transfer of jurisdiction, opportunity is given to the assessee to file his objection, if any. Assessee may receive such notice for filing his objection and as per the merit of the case and jurisdiction proposed, assessee will have to take a decision whether to file his objection or not. In case order u/s 127 is passed transferring jurisdiction, assessee may choose to challenge such transfer by way of writ to be filed in the jurisdictional High Court.

(iii) Completion of books and other records

Once search takes place, preceding six years' cases are required to be scrutinized as per the mandate of section 153A. Before the notices for filing returns u/s 153A are received, assessee should utilize this period to ensure that the books of account are completely in order with all the vouchers and evidences properly maintained and available. In case any updating or proper arranging is required, the same should be done.

In case of addition of share capital or unsecured loans, evidences as are required to prove the identity and creditworthiness of the creditors/depositors & genuineness of the transaction should be collected. It may be in the form of confirmation/affidavit from the depositors, copy of their Bank Statements and income tax returns filed and other related evidences. Confirmation from other trade creditors may be obtained and accounts may be reconciled with them.

(iv) Ledgerization of individual affairs

In case of individuals, there may be situation when their personal books of account are not maintained and personal statement of affairs is not prepared and filed with the tax department. All personal bank accounts of the assessee for the period covered under search should be collected from respective banks if not available with the assessee and personal books of account should be prepared compiling details of all the transactions made by the assessee, his spouse or other family members. It should be ensured that there is sufficient provision for house-hold expenses, tuition fee, electricity expenses, travelling including foreign trips and for any function or marriage ceremony organized during this period. The assets seized are duly reflected in the books and their source of acquisition is properly explained. Investment made by the assessee in any kind of movable and immovable properties are properly reflected in the books.

In case any unsecured loans or gifts have been taken by the assessee, complete evidences with respect to the same are collected. Cross reconciliations and confirmations are obtained with the third parties relating to financial transactions.

(v) Obtaining photocopy of documents

Assessee should apply to the authorized officer to get photocopy of documents, loose papers or books of account seized. In case complete photocopies are not supplied by the authorized officer, assessee should obtain the same from the assessing officer and in any case before filing the returns u/s 153A.

All the papers or documents seized should carefully be gone through and correlated from the books of account maintained. In case any undisclosed income has been surrendered based upon the papers or documents seized, the same should be properly correlated with and analysed so as to furnish proper explanation at later stage.

(vi) Explanation of key documents

There may be certain key documents found in search. Assessee should consult on such key documents with the senior consultants. These documents should be appraised with the application of independent mind so as to furnish their interpretation and explanation to the assessing officer in convincing manner.

The authorized officer in his appraisal report may have interpreted these documents from revenue's point of view and assessee may interpret them in different manner, correlating from the books of account and showing that no undisclosed income is emanating out of such papers. There may be certain dumb documents or papers containing rough calculation, estimates or certain future projection or planning. Assessee has to prepare convincing explanation with corresponding evidences to prove his point.

(vii) Filing returns of related persons

There may be certain seized documents or assets which may relate to other family members or business associates of the assessee in whose case search has not been authorized u/s 132. Presumption u/s 292C or deeming fiction of undisclosed income unless recorded in the books of account upto the date of search as provided u/s 271AAA/271AAB, is not applicable to other persons in whose case search has not been authorized and search warrant has not been issued. Based upon such papers or details relating to other persons, sometimes decision has to be taken to file returns or revise returns of such other persons showing their undisclosed income.

(viia) Concept of updated returns

There is option of filing updated return as per provisions of section 139(8A) of Income -tax Act, to the persons other than searched person.

(viii) Obtaining appraisal report

Appraisal report prepared by Authorized officer is an internal report and confidential document, copy of which is not supplied to the assessee. However, in case assessee is able to go through the contents of the same, it may be quite useful in facing the assessment proceedings at later stage. Assessee may plan his affairs properly in tune with the thinking and approach according to which the documents or papers seized have been appreciated by the authorized officer. The assessee is able to read the mind of the authorized officer on the basis of which further assessment proceedings may be undertaken or proceeded with.

(*ix*) Passing accounting entry of surrendered income in the books

It becomes a very important and tricky decision how to pass accounting entry of the surrendered income or undisclosed assets in the books of account. There may be several considerations and issues involved in it. Though there cannot be any blanket proposition in this regard and much depends upon the facts and circumstances of the case but sometimes it may be advisable not to pass any accounting entry in the books of account but to show the undisclosed income only in the return of income to be filed and pay the taxes.

As a general rule, it can be said that in case any undisclosed asset is declared, it is advisable to introduce the same in the books of account. In case, declaration has been made for advances given but not found recorded in the books of account, the same may be received back and deposited in the bank/books of account before the end of the year. In case unrecorded expenditure is surrendered, the same may not be needed to be introduced in the books.

In case of companies or other assessees where books of account are required to be audited, it is very important to decide and it will depend from case to case in what manner the undisclosed income declared by the assessee is to be reported in the financial statement and/or how the same is to be disclosed in the notes to accounts or by the auditors in their audit report. The decision has to be taken based upon facts and circumstances and manner of declaration of each case. The corresponding impact under other statutes, for example, Companies Act, Excise and Sales tax laws, Custom and FEMA Act are also to be kept in mind.

(*x*) Payment of taxes

Assessee has to make arrangements and pay the taxes applicable on the income surrendered during search. Sometimes post dated cheques are handed over to the department against the income surrendered as per tax liability due thereon. Assessee is required to honour the cheques or otherwise make payment of taxes e.g., e-payment and submit the evidences thereof to the department in replacement of the cheque earlier given. Sometimes decision may be taken to pay the amount of taxes out of the capital created as a result of declaration of undisclosed income.

(*xi*) Writ to High Court

In certain cases, where any kind of illegality or irregularity is involved in the whole of the search or seizure proceedings, assessee may have to take decision to file writ with the jurisdictional High Court. Such decision should be taken only after analyzing all the *pros* and *cons*.

Even if search is declared illegal and section 153A proceedings cannot be validly undertaken by the department, there remains evidentiary value of documents seized and action u/s 148 may be initiated by the department. The cost involved in filing writ and corresponding benefits have also to be considered. Assessee takes in to account the impact on overall relation with the departmental authorities before taking such decision.

In case decision is taken to file writ with the High Court, it should be done at the earliest stage but after exhausting all the administrative remedies with the higher authorities.

(*xii*) Whether to approach Settlement Commission

As per Finance Act, 2010, doors of Settlement Commission in search cases have been re-opened. Assessee in consultation with his counsel has to take decision whether to undergo normal assessment proceedings u/s 153A or avail one time opportunity available for going to Settlement Commission in accordance with the applicable provisions. The decision has to be taken on case to case basis and as per facts and circumstances involved. As per section 245D, there should be minimum additional tax liability of ₹ 50 lacs, required to be paid by searched person for filing application with Settlement Commission.

It may be advisable, sometimes, to approach Settlement Commission where issue of undisclosed income of earlier years is involved and assessee wants to seek immunity from penalty provisions u/s 271(1) (*c*). Since this is only one time opportunity available to a person, it should be availed carefully after analyzing all the *pros* and *cons*.

Assessee may apply to Settlement Commission at any time before finalization of the assessment order u/s 153A by the assessing officer. Since minimum additional tax of ₹ 50 lacs is required to be paid by the assessee for applying to Settlement Commission, assessee may take decision before making payment of taxes and declaring undisclosed income in the income tax returns to be filed u/s 153A.

Finance Act, 2021 has abolished the institution of Settlement Commission and with effect from 1st February, 2021 no new application may be filed for settlement. Therefore, such option is no longer available to the searched person.

5.22 Declaration of undisclosed income

In the case of search, the issue of declaration of undisclosed income assumes lot of significance and takes centre stage at the fag end of conclusion of search. It is in the interest of both assessee and department that declaration of undisclosed income is made by the assessee. As per the amended penalty provision introduced for search cases under section 271AAB with effect from 1st July, 2012, the assessee may get concessional rate of penalty under section 271AAB on the undisclosed income declared and on the other hand, the quantum of undisclosed income declared by the assessee becomes the yardstick for the department to judge the success of search operation.

Prior to insertion of section 271AAB, there was complete immunity from the levy of penalty on declaration of undisclosed income under section 271AAA subject to fulfilment of certain conditions which is no longer available in view of introduction of section 271AAB. Now, in search cases assessee would have to pay penalty under section 271AAB for the specified previous year in the case of declaration of undisclosed income. As per sub-section (1) of section 271AAB, rate of penalty was staggered from 10% to 30% of undisclosed income which was effective for the searches conducted between the period commencing 1st July, 2012 to 14th December, 2016. However, with effect from 15th December, 2016, sub-section (1A) has been introduced under section 271AAB by the Taxation Laws (Second Amendment) Act, 2016 enhancing the rate of penalty to 30% or 60% of undisclosed income.

The Government has stated repeatedly that no confessional statement for surrender of undisclosed income will be forcibly obtained at the time of search and survey. The Finance Minister had made a statement in the Parliament in 2003 that no forceful surrender should be obtained at the time of search or survey. CBDT has issued instruction dated 10.03.2003 to this effect. Copy of the instruction issued to all Chief Commissioner/Director General of Income Tax is given in **Chapter 8**.

However in practice, it has been observed that directly or indirectly pressure is put on the assessee to make declaration of undisclosed income. At times, assessee also wants to make declaration of undisclosed income to take advantage of concession from penalty provision.

(i) Why to make surrender?

After introduction of sub-section (1A) to section 271AAB, it has been provided that penalty would be leviable minimum at the rate of 30% of undisclosed income even when undisclosed income is declared by the searched person during the statement recorded under section 132(4) along with fulfilment of other conditions as prescribed therein. In view of such provision, there is hardly any motivation for the searched person to make declaration of undisclosed income during search. Only relief may be that in case of declaration of income is not made during search, then penalty may be levied at the rate of 60% of undisclosed income.

It is also pertinent to note that in case of search, undisclosed income to be declared generally is the income referred in sections 68, 69, 69A to 69D attracting effective tax rate including surcharge and cess to the extent of 78% of the undisclosed income. Beside, penalty is also attracted under section 271AAB @ 30% even when declaration of undisclosed income is made. Thus, assessee may have to pay tax and penalty at the rate of 108% of undisclosed income that is an amount higher than the undisclosed income it self. Therefore, there is hardly any motivation for the searched person to make any declaration of undisclosed income.

Penalty for concealment of income is leviable when certain income is not declared by the assessee in the return of income filed. However, in the case of search there is a fiction of undisclosed income as provided u/s 271AAB to the effect that even for the current year or the year for which due date of filing return has not yet expired and return has not been filed, assessee may be penalized by way of penalty u/s 271AAB in case any income is not recorded in the books of account maintained in the normal course before the date of search or has not otherwise been disclosed to the department in some other manner before the date of search. Such undisclosed income if declared in the return of income to be filed after search would not have attracted penalty but for the deeming fiction of undisclosed income there is attraction of penalty as provided under section 271AAB.

It has been provided under sub-section (1A) of section 271AAB which is effective 15.12.2016 that penalty under this section would be leviable:-

   (a) a sum computed at the rate of thirty per cent of the undisclosed income of the specified previous year, if the assessee,

       i. In the course of search, admits the undisclosed income in a statement under sub-sec. (4) of sec. 132, and specifies the manner in which such income has been derived.

       ii. Substantiates the manner in which the undisclosed income was derived and

       iii. on or before the specified date, pays the tax, together with interest, if any, in respect of the undisclosed income & furnishes the return of income for the specified previous year declaring such undisclosed income therein.

   (b) a sum computed at the rate of sixty per cent of the undisclosed income of the specified previous year, if it is not covered under clause (a) above.

Thus, concessional penalty of 30% u/s 271AAB can be availed by the assessee only when declaration of undisclosed income is made by the assessee in his statement recorded u/s 132(4) before the conclusion of search & other conditions as mentioned above are also fulfilled which is quite cumbersome & harsh requirement of the law.

It is pertinent to mention here that section 271AAB is applicable for undisclosed income of specified previous year as per fiction of undisclosed income created. For undisclosed income of earlier years for which return has been filed or due date of filing the return has already expired, imposition of penalty relating to undisclosed income of those years is governed by the provisions of section 271(1)(c) read with its *Explanation (5A)* and there is no immunity granted for the same even when declaration during search is made by the assessee.

To mitigate rigours of search

It has been experienced in practice that in case surrender of undisclosed income is made by the assessee to the satisfaction of the authorized officer, the rigours of investigation by the authorized officer are mitigated and the whole process is smoothened. When authorized officer has the satisfaction of getting declaration of undisclosed income and collection of taxes to the extent as expected, further investigation proceeding and post search inquires may not be taken vigorously as observed in practice. In the appraisal report, the issues relating to undisclosed income declared may only be highlighted and incisive investigation may not be undertaken.

In case surrender of undisclosed income is not made by the assessee, it is seen in practice that the authorized officer may make attempt to investigate the issues deeply and intensely. He may do it by making rigorous post search third party inquiries, summoning other business associates and making inquiries from them, conducting surveys at business premises of other related parties or business associates to collect corroborating evidences. In the appraisal report also, he may try to highlight various issues even when worthwhile evidences of undisclosed income may not be existing/forthcoming.

(ii) **Decision of surrender by assessee**

The decision of surrender of undisclosed income should not be taken by assessee in undue haste under pressure. Assessee should take sufficient time to understand the nature of evidences found after consulting his counsel. He should weigh all the pros and cons, advantages and disadvantages of making surrender and only after giving due consideration to all the factors and appreciating the true nature of evidences found, any decision of surrender of undisclosed income should be taken.

Surrender of undisclosed income can be made u/s 132(4) before lifting all the restraints and before final conclusion of the search. In case search proceeding are temporarily concluded on the day of search but restraint u/s 132(3) is put, it is seen in practice that it generally takes one week to 3-4 weeks in finally concluding the search and during this period, assessee gets sufficient time to think calmly and consult his counsel before taking any decision of making declaration of undisclosed income.

(iia) **Declaration of undisclosed income after introduction of provision of section 115BBE and penalty provision under section 271AAB**

The penalty provision in the case of search has become very harsh. As per sub-section (1A) to section 271AAB introduced with effect from 15.12.2016, there is mandatory penalty of 30% of the undisclosed income of the specified previous year in case any declaration of undisclosed income is made by the assessee in the course of search during statement recorded under section 132(4) of the Act. This Mandatory penalty of 30% is leviable when assessee fulfils other conditions as stipulated in this sub-section *i.e.* assessee specifies & substantiates the manner in which undisclosed income was derived, makes payment of applicable tax and interest and furnishes the return of income within the specified time.

In case searched person does not make declaration of undisclosed income during search and does not fulfil other conditions as specified under section 271AAB, penalty is liable to imposed at the rate of 60% of undisclosed income.

The above penalty provision shall have the effect that in the case of search, total tax liability for undisclosed and unexplained income detected in search may attract tax and surcharge as provided under section 115BBE at the rate of 75% plus applicable cess along with minimum penalty as provided under section 271AAB at the rate of 30% *i.e.* aggregating to 105% plus cess.

As seen in practice, pressure is exercised by the tax authorities for making declaration of undisclosed income by the searched person at the time of search even when evidences relating to undisclosed income of substantive nature are not found. Searched person, it has been seen in practice, due to the pressure makes declaration of undisclosed income so as to buy peace and get the search operation concluded. But, now searched person would think twice before making declaration of undisclosed income after taking into consideration the fact that on any undisclosed income declared during search sources of which cannot be established, he would be liable to pay total tax liability *i.e.* tax, interest, surcharge and penalty of approximately 105% plus cess.

(*iii*) Conditions of surrender

As per sub-section (1A) of section 271AAB effective from 15th December, 2016, surrender of undisclosed income is required to be made in a specific manner fulfilling all the three conditions provided therein for availing concession in the rate of penalty. Assessee is required to state the manner in which undisclosed income has been derived, substantiate the manner and pay the taxes together with interest in respect of undisclosed income & file the return of income of the specified previous year declaring such undisclosed income.

Practically it may be very difficult to disclose the manner and further to substantiate the manner in which undisclosed income has been derived by the assessee. Manner can be specified in broad terms e.g. from business operation outside the books, from property transaction, from lottery or gambling etc. To substantiate the manner may still be more difficult. Assessee may not be in a position to explain the whole methodology of earning the undisclosed income not recorded in the books of account. The term 'to substantiate the manner' should be interpreted in a broad sense.

In practice it has been observed that the courts have taken a liberal and broad view in this regard. The requirement of stating the manner and its substantiation is not emphasized in a very strict sense while taking decision for imposing penalty u/s 271AAB.

The third condition mentioned for a valid declaration of undisclosed income is the payment of tax applicable on undisclosed income. Taxes are required to be paid as and when due and in case of delay along with interest u/s 234B or 234C. But in any case payment of tax with interest should be made before filing the return of income in which undisclosed income so declared is shown.

The requirement of payment of taxes in respect of undisclosed income has to be read in a manner to mean the taxes due, if any. In case there are losses in the business eligible to be set off against undisclosed income to be declared, the calculation of tax due in respect of undisclosed income shall be made only after adjusting the losses or for that matter, any other benefit if available under the Act. It may be important to look the character of undisclosed income declared and whether it would fall under the head "business" income or "income from other source". This characterization may be important when set-off of such income is being considered from unabsorbed business losses or depreciation. In case income declared is of the nature referred in sections 68, 69, 69A to 69D, benefit of set off of losses against such income is not available in view of clear prescription given in section 115BBE.

For making a valid declaration of undisclosed income and claiming concession in the rate of penalty u/s 271AAB, all the three conditions mentioned hereinabove are required to be fulfilled cumulatively.

(iv) Surrender for earlier years

In case surrender of undisclosed income is made for earlier years to the "specified years" as defined u/s 271AAB *i.e.* for the years for which the returns have already been filed or due date of filing the return has expired, penalty provision of section 271(1)(c) are applicable, as provided under *Explanation* (5A) inserted by the Finance Act, 2007 in case of search initiated on or after 1st June 2007.

As per *Explanation* (5A) to section 271(1)(c), any income declared by the assessee in any return of income furnished on or after the date of search for earlier years, shall be deemed to represent such income in respect of which particulars have been concealed or inaccurate particulars have been furnished for the purpose of imposition of penalty. In view of the above, any declaration of undisclosed income made for earlier years is liable to be hit by the provision of section 271(1)(c) and it may become almost a case of admitted concealment. Under such circumstances, it may be difficult to defend against the imposition of penalty u/s 271(1)(c).

It is pertinent to note that with effect from 1st April, 2017 *viz.* A.Y. 2017-18 inserted by the Finance Act, 2016, penalty for concealment of income in the nature of under-reporting and mis-reporting of income would henceforth be leviable under section 270A.

There may be cases where clinching evidences are found during search suggesting undisclosed income for earlier years. In such cases it may be advisable to exercise the option of making application to the Settlement Commission for settling the cases instead of making declaration of undisclosed income during the course of search. The Settlement Commission has power to grant immunity from penalty and prosecution in appropriate cases. The option of settlement commission in search cases which was withdrawn by the Finance Act, 2007 has been reintroduced by the Finance Act, 2010 in a limited manner, with effect from 1st June 2010.

(v) Surrender subject to no penalty

Sometimes, declaration of undisclosed income for earlier years is made by the assessee mentioning that it is subject to no penalty under any of the provisions of the Income Tax Act. The authorized officer may also assure the assessee that no penalty under any provisions of the Act will be levied.

As per latest judicial pronouncements, there is no legal sanctity to such condition of non-imposition of penalty and the assessing officer is not bound by such condition. It is the nature of evidences which will decide whether assessee has concealed the particulars of income or has furnished inaccurate particulars of income and whether penalty u/s 271(1)(c) can be levied or not in accordance with the parameters mentioned under penalty provisions. [*K.P. Madhusudhanan* v. *CIT* [2001] 118 Taxman 324/251 ITR 99 (SC)]

(*vi*) **Surrender of different items - Precautions**

Assessee may make surrender of undisclosed income based upon the details of transactions found in the loose papers and for different kind of assets not recorded in the books of account or otherwise not disclosed to the department. The declaration may have consequential impact upon some other persons or in some other manner to the assessee. While making declaration of undisclosed income relating to different kind of items, assessee may keep in mind some of the points which are being discussed here as under:-

   (*a*) **Cash**

   In case cash is found in the possession of the assessee which is not recorded in the books of account, & the declaration of such cash is made as undisclosed income, it would be in the nature of income as envisaged under section 69 of the Act. As per the provision of section 115BBE, tax rate on such income would be sixty per cent with surcharge and cess, thus making effective tax rate to the tune of 79%. Apart from the tax, applicable interest & minimum penalty of 30% of undisclosed income under section 271AAB is also leviable. Therefore any declaration of cash would attract heavy amount of tax and penalty.

   In case declaration of cash is co-related with the source of income earned from business or profession or any other head of income and assessee is in position to substantiate such co-relation, then such cash would not be separately taxable and only the undisclosed income as discussed above would be liable to be taxed as per the normal provisions of the Act.

   (*b*) **Stock-in-trade**

   At the time of search, physical counting of stock inventory consisting of raw material, finished or semi finished goods, stores or consumable items etc. is done and the same is compared with the inventory reflected in the books of account. The comparison is made from the inventory reflected in the stock records and in the absence of stock record being maintained by the assessee, trading account upto the date of search is casted and value of stocks as per financial books is worked out taking gross profit rate of the earlier year as base.

In case physical stock inventory is found less as compared to the inventory as per the books, it is assumed that goods have been sold outside the books and it is treated as unaccounted sales and in case physical stock inventory is found in excess as compared to book records, it is treated by the department as undisclosed investment in inventory out of unaccounted income.

Before making any declaration of undisclosed income on the basis of difference found in the stock inventory as per physical list prepared and book records, assessee should keep in mind various points:-

a. To verify that the rates of various items of inventory applied for calculating value of physical inventory found are the same which are applied for valuing inventory in the financial statement. In case method of valuation in the books is at cost, the same basis should be adopted for calculating value of physical inventory found. If sale rates as per price list or MRP rates have been applied, it will over value the physical inventory and may create higher difference from the book records.

b. GP Rate applied is correct and the comparability of trading account is also same, otherwise different result may be there. In case there is valid justification for variance in the GP rate, the same should be kept in mind.

c. Obsolete or damaged goods are identified properly and the same are valued as per appropriate basis and as valued in the earlier financial statement, if any.

d. The valuation or calculation part of the inventory can be verified, amended or challenged at any point of time and any declaration made may be modified for this reason at any stage. However, one should ensure that proper quantity and quality of the various items of inventory are mentioned while preparing physical inventory list.

Once stock list is prepared and signed by the assessee or his authorized representative, to challenge the correctness of the same or to take the stand that the physical counting of stock was done on estimated basis or on *ad-hoc* basis, is very difficult to be accepted unless assessee can prove with the credible evidence, the impossibility of physical counting under particular facts and circumstances of the case. Therefore, it is very important to remain vigilant and ensure that physical stock taking is done properly and accurately.

e. Any surrender of undisclosed income due to difference in inventory may call for action by the GST department as well. Recently it has been noticed that information is obtained by the other departments regarding undisclosed income declared by the assessee and based upon its nature and evidences found, possibility of violation and evasion of tax/duty under respective laws is also examined by those authorities.

(c) Investment in Fixed Asset

There may be cases where investments have been made in Plant & Machinery or Building not reflected in the books of account. Such investment may be declared relating to the current year and after introducing such assets in the books, assessee may claim depreciation on such assets as per applicable rates. In case there are any evidences or invoices relating to acquisition of asset or investment made in the earlier years, the same shall be treated as income of earlier years and the consequences thereof will follow. In case of declaration of undisclosed investment in immovable property, issue regarding evasion of stamp duty may arise. Therefore, such declaration should be made or worded very carefully.

One should also keep in mind the implications of section 115BBE & penalty provision while making declaration of such undisclosed income.

(d) Jewellery, bullion or other valuables

There may be unaccounted jewellery, bullion, precious stones, diamonds, antiques, paintings or other valuable articles found during search. In the absence of any evidence regarding the year of acquisition of such items, the same are treated as undisclosed income of the current year and the same may be surrendered as undisclosed income by the assessee. However, one should keep in mind that such valuable items are liable to be seized by the authorized officer unless these are in the nature of stock-in-trade.

One should also keep in mind the implications of section 115BBE & penalty provision while making declaration of such undisclosed income.

(e) Investment in Fixed Deposit/Shares/Bonds

In case assessee is found in possession of fixed deposit, shares, bonds, KVP, NSC etc. which are not disclosed in his books and the source of the funds regarding investment in such asset is not properly explained, any declaration of such asset shall be treated as undisclosed income of the assessee relating to the year during which these assets have been acquired, even if assessee may state in his statement that he is making surrender of such assets as undisclosed income relating to the current year.

One should also keep in mind the implications of section 115BBE & penalty provision while making declaration of such undisclosed income.

(f) Advances given for properties

Surrender can be made for advances given to acquire properties or for other purposes. During assessment proceeding, assessee may be asked to furnish details of the person(s) to whom advances were given. In case assessee is not able to furnish such details, no other adverse inferences are usually drawn, it is seen in practice, against the assessee except taxing the income which is already declared by the assessee. However, amended provision of section 269SS, section 269T & section 269ST should be kept in mind violation of which may lead to the levy of penalty under section 271D, section 271E & section 271DA respectively.

(g) Creditors no longer payable

There may be outstanding balances in the books of the assessee of certain depositors or creditors which are no longer payable or the corresponding balances are not confirmed by other parties. In case surrender of such balances is made stating the same as "no longer payable" due to non-verification or non-substantiation, assessee may plead to have made the surrender for the current year. In case such deposits or creditors are stated to be "bogus", the taxability of income will relate back to the year of inception when deposits were taken or creditors are credited in the books. In case trade creditors are stated to be bogus, the inference can be drawn that the purchases entered are inflated and undisclosed income will relate back to the year in which purchases have been claimed as expense by the assessee.

(*h*) Share capital

In the case of surrender of the amount of share capital received, income shall be treated relating to the year in which amount of share capital was received by the assessee. Moreover, in case of surrender of share capital is made in the hands of company, it may involve the problem with the Department of Company Affairs & other Agencies such as SEBI etc. Therefore, it may be advisable to explore the possibility of making declaration of such investment in share capital as undisclosed income in the hands of the shareholders.

One should also keep in mind the implications of section 115BBE & penalty provision while making declaration of such undisclosed income.

(*i*) Noting in loose papers

In case any income is declared by the assessee on the basis of details of transaction contained in the loose papers or documents found, the dates mentioned along with the transactions are very important and income may relate to the year of which dates are mentioned along with the transaction. It may not be possible for the assessee to plead such undisclosed income to be relating to current year.

One should also keep in mind the implications of section 115BBE & penalty provision while making declaration of such undisclosed income.

(*j*) Household expenses

In case surrender of household expenses is made based upon specific bills of expenses found, it will be treated undisclosed income of the year in which expenses have been incurred. However, in case surrender for household expenses is made in general terms and due to insufficient expenses shown to meet out household expenses in view of standard of living and status of the assessee, such declaration cannot be restricted only for the current year and there is possibility for such expenses being liable to be extrapolated for all the years covered u/s 153A depending upon the facts and circumstances.

One should also keep in mind the implications of section 115BBE & penalty provision while making declaration of such undisclosed income.

(k) Capital gains

There may be transaction of short term or long term capital gains credited in the books of the assessee. Assessee may not be able to substantiate the genuineness of the transaction in certain cases and may decide to make declaration. In such cases undisclosed income shall be treated relating to the year during which amount purporting to be sale proceed of the capital asset resulting in to alleged capital gain is received and credited in the books of the assessee.

(l) Immovable property - Registered Value v. Fair Market Value

In the case of immovable properties, registered value of the property at which sale deed has been executed and sale consideration has been passed by the buyer to the seller as mentioned in the sale deed is the amount of investment made in the property. Fair Market Value of the property of the current date or of the date on which property has been purchased based upon valuation report cannot be presumed to be the amount of investment made in the property. However, in case any evidence regarding higher consideration passed by the buyer to the seller has been found from the possession of the assessee i.e. receipts of cash transaction, agreement along with details of higher consideration paid etc., undisclosed investment in properties can be attributed to the assessee in such a case and any declaration of such income shall relate to the year in which higher consideration has been paid.

One should also keep in mind the implications of section 115BBE & penalty provision while making declaration of such undisclosed income.

(m) Declaration by Corporates/Listed Companies

In case any declaration of undisclosed income is made by the companies or in particular, by the listed companies in which public is substantially interested, assessee should keep in mind that the action by other regulatory authorities and other government departments cannot be ruled out. Ministry of Company Affairs may come into action for defrauding the investors and issuing prosecution notice against the directors. Recently many cases have come to the light where action has been taken by the respective departments for prevention of serious frauds and coordinated investigation.

(n) Dumb document

There may be certain papers or documents found containing some details, notings. Document itself may not be capable of speaking the real nature of transaction. These details may be relating to estimates, future projection, casual discussion or rough calculation. The document may not contain any date or year of any actual transaction happening. Assessee should be very careful before explaining such document and making any declaration of undisclosed income based upon such document. The department may try to relate each and every figure mentioned as undisclosed income of the assessee. Assessee should try to explain the true nature of such document.

Detailed discussion in this respect has been made under the chapter of assessment u/s 153A.

(vii) "Surrender" Letter

At times it has been observed that assessee makes lump-sum surrender of a particular figure on the day of search relating to undisclosed income pertaining to himself, other family members or business entities of the group. Later on, before conclusion of the search, a surrender letter is obtained from the assessee mentioning year wise, entity wise and item wise break-up of the undisclosed income surrendered. In this regard following points are important and may be noted:-

1. Break-up of the total amount surrendered person wise, entity wise and year wise should be mentioned clearly. It is to be decided in whose hands and for which year undisclosed income is to be shown in the return of income to be filed and tax liability is to be calculated.

2. The authorized officer has to ensure that sufficient evidences are available and correlated with the undisclosed income declared. In the absence of the same, assessee may retract the statement at later stage. Mere statement of the assessee without evidences may not be sufficient to assess and justify addition by the assessing officer in the hands of the assessee during assessment proceedings.

3. It should be clearly mentioned in the surrender letter that it is the statement being given by the assessee u/s 132(4) of the Act and it should be made on oath. It should also be ensured that surrender letter is given on a date prior to final conclusion of the search.

It is in the interest of both the assessee and the department to do so. From department's point of view, the evidentiary value of statement recorded on oath u/s 132(4) is enhanced and from assessee's point of view, the benefit of availing concession from penalty u/s 271AAB remains only when statement is made u/s 132(4).

4. While drafting surrender letter it is advisable to mention that the declaration is subject to no penal provision. Though there may not be legal sanctity for not imposing penalty merely due to putting such condition by the assessee as discussed in earlier paras yet in some of the cases, Courts have taken the view that any surrender by the assessee should be accepted in toto. In case any attempt is made by the assessing officer for levying penalty, assessee can plead a case against the same on this ground. Moreover putting such kind of condition gives mental peace and satisfaction to the assessee at the time of surrender.

5. Manner of earning undisclosed income should also be mentioned along with its substantiation to the extent possible. These are the mandatory conditions to avail concessional rate of penalty u/s 271AAB. Further, a line may be added in the declaration that "Applicable tax shall be paid in due course of time as and when due". Payment of tax is also a pre-condition for lower rate of penalty as provided u/s 271AAB.

6. Surrender letter should be signed by all the persons/entities making the surrender. In case a person makes declaration on behalf on other persons, he should be authorized to do so and letter of authorization in favour of such person should be enclosed along with the surrender letter.

7. Surrender of undisclosed income should be made only in the hands of the persons in whose case search warrant has been issued. No surrender should be made in the case of other family members or business concerns where there is no search warrant as they are not covered by the provisions of fiction of income as given u/s 271AAB. In case they wish to declare any undisclosed income, they can do so while filing their income tax returns and no penalty in their case is attracted for 'specified previous year'.

8. From departmental point of view, authorized officer would always wish the assessee to mention that the declaration of undisclosed income is over and above his normal income and the declaration is being made willingly by the assessee without any pressure, coercion or threat.

9. In case any declaration of undisclosed income is made amending or improving upon quantum or manner of the undisclosed income already declared by the assessee in the earlier statement, this fact should be mentioned very clearly in unambiguous terms so that there does not remain any kind of confusion or scope for making double addition.

10. In case any cash has been seized, assessee should state and request to treat the same as self assessment tax in the hands of particular person for particular year. This is required so as to avoid levy of interest u/s 234B till the time amount seized is appropriated by the assessing officer towards adjustment of assessee's tax liability.

11. It is also in the interest of the assessee and sometimes it may be helpful in future proceedings to mention in the surrender letter that the declaration of undisclosed income is being made to buy peace and to make settlement of the dispute with the department.

It has been observed in practice that inspite of surrender letter given by the assessee, the authorized officer gets the declaration of undisclosed income covered in the statement of the assessee being recorded u/s 132(4) separately also so that the evidentiary value of the income surrendered by way of surrendered letter remains intact and the same is not challenged at any later stage by the assessee.

(*viii*) Whether declaration can be made for assets not found during search?

Whether a person can make declaration of assets which are not found in his possession or control during the course of search? This could have been a point of debate and contradictory opinions when declaration was covered under *Explanation* (5) to section 271(1)(*c*) and definition of "undisclosed income" was not incorporated in the present manner u/s 271AAB of the Act.

After introduction of section 271AAB and definition of "undisclosed income" which can be declared, introduced therein, the point is set right. The definition of undisclosed income is very wide and covers all kind of assets or any entry in the books of account or other document or transactions found in the course of search not recorded in the regular books of account. It also includes any kind of false expenses recorded in the normal books of account maintained. In view of such wide definition of undisclosed income, declaration can be made for any asset whether found or not during search, any kind of expenses incurred not recorded in the books or investments made in immovable properties not recorded in the books.

(*ix*) **Whether surrender can be made by a third person visiting the asses-see during search when his personal search is undertaken and asset is seized from him?**

The provision for making declaration of undisclosed income has been provided u/s 132(4) because fiction of undisclosed income is applicable to the assessee in whose name search warrant is issued for assets or transactions not recorded in the normal books of account maintained as on the date of the search. In the case of other persons in whose case no search warrant has been issued, provision of section 271AAB and the concept of fiction of undisclosed income is not applicable. Therefore, such other person need not to make any declaration u/s 132(4) or during statement being recorded by the authorized officer. Even when such undisclosed income is declared by him at the time when filing his return of income, no penalty provision u/s 271AAB is applicable in his case.

5.23 Planning of surrender

Declaration of undisclosed income may be made by the assessee during search for various reasons and at times under compelling circumstances so as to buy peace and get the search proceeding concluded. Sometimes, surrender of lump-sum amount relating to different entities within the group is made on the date of search and break-up of the same is submitted later, after going through the incriminating material found during search. At this stage, the attempt of the assessee remains to plan the amount surrendered properly so that capital may be created in undisputed manner, all the undisclosed assets or papers, documents containing details of undisclosed transactions or other incriminating material found during search is covered by the amount of undisclosed income declared in the manner so that the same may be explained convincingly at the assessment stage. The planning of undisclosed income declared should be done in such a manner that maximum advantage may be derived by the assessee out of the income surrendered and for which he is paying the taxes. Some of the following points may be kept in mind:-

(*i*) **Generation of Income v. Application in Assets**

There may be document or loose paper found during search suggesting undisclosed income not recorded in the books e.g. transactions relating to unrecorded sales, details relating to unaccounted income earned by way of commission, interest or rent etc. At the same time, there may be evidences found relating to undisclosed assets e.g. unrecorded cash found, investment in jewellery or residential property, advances given for buying properties, investment in cash made for buying properties etc.

One should always keep in mind that income generated outside the books may be applied in making investment in assets outside the books. One can always make out a case to plead that income generated outside the books has been applied in acquiring the assets. Instead of making declaration of undisclosed income and undisclosed assets separately, both of these can be linked and declaration can be made only at one place. In case details of unaccounted sales are found and at the same time cash is also found in possession of the assessee, it can always be pleaded that the cash found has been generated out of cash sales not recorded in the books details of which have been found separately and by making the surrender of cash found, the document relating to unrecorded sales is also explained.

The principle of generation of income v. application in asset is very significant principle in explaining the overall incriminating material, in the form of loose papers, documents and assets found during search. The dates mentioned relating to generation of income and its application in assets is also very important to be kept in mind while applying this method.

(ii) Set off of losses

There may be situation when business losses exist in the entity for which declaration of undisclosed income is made. Business losses for the current year are allowed to be set off against the undisclosed income even if it is in the nature of income from other sources. In case unabsorbed business losses are being claimed to be set off, it is possible only when declaration of undisclosed income made in subsequent year is of the business nature. If income declared is of the nature to be taxed as 'Income from other sources', unabsorbed business losses of earlier years cannot be allowed to be set off as per normal provisions of the Income tax Act. However, unabsorbed depreciation of earlier years is allowed to be set off in subsequent years against income under any head of income including "Income from other sources".

Keeping in mind the normal income tax provisions prevailing at particular point of time, planning of set off of losses can be made. In the same manner, planning can be made to take benefit of other kind of incentives/exemptions, if applicable to the assessee.

Finance Act, 2012 w.e.f. 01.04.2013 has introduced a new section 115BBE as modified from time to time, providing that:

"115BBE. *Tax on income referred to in section 68 or section 69 or section 69A or section 69B or section 69C or section 69D.*

(1) Where the total income of an assessee,-

    (*a*) includes any income referred to in section 68, section 69, section 69A, section 69B, section 69C or section 69D, and reflected in the return of income furnished under section 139; or

    (*b*) determined by the Assessing Officer includes any income referred to in section 68, section 69, section 69A, section 69B, section 69C or section 69D, if such income is not covered under clause (*a*),

the income-tax payable shall be the aggregate of—

    (*i*) the amount of income-tax calculated on the income referred to in clause (*a*) and clause (*b*), at the rate of sixty percent; and

    (*ii*) the amount of income-tax with which the assessee would have been chargeable had his total income been reduced by the amount of income referred to in clause (*i*).

(2) Notwithstanding anything contained in this Act, no deduction in respect of any expenditure or allowance *or set off of any loss* shall be allowed to the assessee under any provision of this Act in computing his income referred to in clause (*a*) and clause (*b*) of sub-section (1)."

It would imply that even current year's business loss shall not be permitted to be set off against deemed income referred to in sections 68, 69 to 69D of the Income Tax Act. In the case of search, undisclosed income found is at times taxed as deemed income u/s 68 or 69 and in such cases assessee shall be required to pay tax as provided in section 115BBE.

(*iii*) Assets acquired prior to seven financial years

If there are any assets acquired prior to seven financial years (in certain cases 9 financial years as given in section 153A) or income generated prior to seven financial years which are not covered by the provisions of section 153A or section 148, no declaration of the same is warranted. Assessee is not required to file the income tax return of such years u/s 153A and department can also not assess the same in the hands of the assessee and create any tax liability for such years.

In the case of *CIT* v. *Vivek Aggarwal* [2015] 121 DTR 241 (Delhi), it has been held that CIT(A) having found that the impugned amount pertained to a transaction relatable to A.Y. 1999-2000 which fell beyond the block period, addition thereof could not be made in the assessment under section 153A.

(*iv*) Conditional surrender

There may be circumstances when conditional surrender is made or surrender is made in accordance with the facts prevailing at that point of time. In case there is any change in the circumstances or modification of the facts, surrender of undisclosed income may be amended before filing of the return of income.

For example, an assessee may have surrendered undisclosed income being investment in inventory on the basis of difference in the value of inventory calculated as per physical stock taking and the value of the inventory as per book records. Later on, assessee finds that the value of the physical inventory has not been done properly as per the principle of valuation consistently adopted for the purpose of financial statement and the difference does not exist or it exists at a lesser figure. Such surrender is liable to be corrected. There may be another situation when unsecured loans or long term capital gains credited in the bank account of the assessee was surrendered at the time of search due to non-availability of relevant evidences and proper justification having been explained at the time of search. Later in case assessee is able to collect and produce all the evidences, such surrender is likely to be amended.

(*v*) Current year income not recorded, advance tax not paid

Assessee may have certain incomes in the current year which have not been recorded in the books of account or advance tax relating to the same having become due, has not been paid. Assessee may have intention of showing the same in his return of income and plans to pay the tax later with interest but before filing his return of income. Income of such nature may be planned to be covered for the purpose of making declaration and the same may satisfy the authorized officer for obtaining declaration. Rather in certain cases, if income is not recorded in the books of account & even if assessee intends to show the said income in his regular return of income to be filed, declaration should be made during search, otherwise it may be treated as undisclosed income and may be liable to penalty u/s 271AAA/271AAB.

For example assessee may have earned capital gains on sale of property in the month of April. Search takes place in the month of January following and no advance tax relating to capital gains had been paid so far. Such capital gains may form part of total declaration of undisclosed income. In such a case, facts should be mentioned in the surrender letter in unambiguous terms so that no scope of misinterpretation remains.

(vi) Principle of Peak Balance

There may be numerous transactions of money coming and going on several occasions. The assessee is not able to explain the source of the incomings and not able to substantiate the same properly. However, in such a case principle of peak balance should be kept in mind and the taxability can be pleaded to be fastened on peak balance outstanding as on a particular date during the period of transactions.

(vii) Challenging valuation

In case there is any mistake or inconsistency in the valuation of assets such as jewellery, stock, household goods etc., surrender relating to same may be rectified or amended at any stage before filing the return of income.

(viii) Creation of Capital

Whenever surrender of undisclosed income is made, the details should be given in unambiguous terms correlating with the specific asset intended to be disclosed. The objective remains to account for the assets in the books of account after declaration, regularize the transactions and create capital base. Surrender should be planned in such a manner that these objectives are achieved.

CHAPTER 6

SEIZURE OF BOOKS OF ACCOUNT, DOCUMENTS AND ASSETS

6.1 Seizure of assets

The basic objective of search u/s 132 is to collect evidences relating to undisclosed income and to seize the undisclosed assets found as a result of search. The power of seizure of assets is contained only in the case of search cases. No such power has been given in the case of survey u/s 133A or under any other provisions of the Act.

Clause (*iii*) of section 132(1) empowers the authorized officer to seize any such books of account, other documents, money, bullion, jewellery or other valuable article or thing found as a result of search.

Use of the word "such" before books of account, other document, money, bullion, jewellery or other valuable article or thing is very significant. The word "such" refers to those books of account, other document, money, bullion, jewellery or other valuable article or thing for which search has been authorized to be conducted and search warrant has been issued. Under section 132(1) clauses (*a*), (*b*) and (*c*), search can be authorized in the following situations:-

(*a*) Any person, to whom summons or notice was issued to produce any books of account or other documents, has failed to produce such books of account or other documents as required by such summons or notice.

(*b*) Any person to whom summons or notice is issued, will not produce any books of account or other documents which will be useful for, or relevant to, any proceeding under the Income-tax Act.

(c) Any person is in possession of any money, bullion, jewellery or other valuable article or thing and such money, bullion, jewellery or other valuable article or thing represents undisclosed income or property.

In view of the above, the word "such" under clause (iii) of section 132(1) is to be interpreted to cover those books of account or other documents as mentioned in clause (a) or (b) above and those assets as mentioned in clause (c) above.

For the purpose of further discussion, seizure may be divided in two parts:-

a. Seizure of books of account or other documents.

b. Seizure of assets i.e. money, bullion, jewellery or other valuable article or thing.

6.2 What can be seized?

(i) Whether regular books of account and records can be seized?

Regular books of account herein implies to refer those books of account, cash book, ledger, stock register, purchase & sale register, purchase and sales invoices, bills, vouchers, files relating to such transactions which are maintained in normal course of business and on the basis of which financial statements are prepared and income tax returns are submitted.

It cannot be interpreted that under clause (a) or (b) of section 132(1), regular books of account or other documents cannot be seized under any circumstances. In case search has been authorized on the basis of "reason to believe" mentioned under clause (a), where notice was issued to produce books of account or other documents and the same were not produced by the assessee, it may be referring to the regular books of account. Notice u/s 142(1) or summons u/s 131(1) is generally issued for producing regular books of account and other documents only. Clause (b) refers to the situation when it is expected that in case such notice is issued, assessee will not produce the books of account or other documents which will be useful for or relevant to any proceeding under the Act. Reference to any books of account or other documents in clause (b) primarily seems to refer to the books of account or other documents containing undisclosed transactions. It can reasonably be expected that in case notice is issued to the assessee u/s 131(1) or u/s 142(1), he may produce regular books of account or other documents but will not produce books of account or other documents containing details of undisclosed transaction. But the reference cannot be limited to this extent only. Even in the case of regular books of account or other documents, there may be certain books of account, records, bills, vouchers, files, invoices, supporting evidences, budgetary figures, internal reports which may not be produced by the assessee when notice to produce the same is issued.

Whenever search warrant is issued after satisfaction under any of the three clause (*a*), (*b*) or (*c*) of section 132(1), it is not possible to restrict the search operation & seizure only relating to the items referred in the respective clause on the basis of which satisfaction has been derived. Generally condition of clauses (*a*), (*b*) and (*c*) may co-exist simultaneously. Even when satisfaction is derived based upon either of the clauses, seizure can be made of undisclosed assets along with the books of account and other documents, referred to in clause (*a*) and clause (*b*).

Power of examination and verification of regular books of account during assessment proceeding or during any other proceeding under the Act has been given to the tax department officials. In the course of any proceeding under the Act, power has been granted even to impound and retain regular books of account or other documents u/s 131(3).

The use of the words "which will be useful for, or relevant to, any proceeding under the Act" in clause (*b*) of section 132(1) also intend to include within its ambit regular books of account and other re-cords which may be useful for and relevant to in connection with assessment proceedings at later stage. During assessment proceed-ings, verification of regular books of account, other documents and records is the primary job of the Assessing Officer and it is integral part of the assessment proceeding. When powers have been given to impound regular books of account and other documents in nor-mal circumstances for examination and verification thereof during assessment proceedings or during any other proceedings under the Act, not to allow such powers in search action u/s 132, cannot be the objective and intentions of the legislation.

Further, it may be appreciated that it may be difficult to segregate what are regular and disclosed books of account or other documents and what are undisclosed books of account or other documents. Even within the regular books of account and other documents, there can be material evidences or records of incriminating nature.

Moreover, under sub-section (9) of section 132, it has been provided that the person from whose custody any books of account or other documents are seized may make copies thereof or take extracts therefrom. This specific provision under sub-section (9) is probably with the intention that in case regular books of account or other documents are seized, the copies thereof are made available to the assessee so that normal business operations may not be hampered.

In view of the above discussion, to restrict the powers of seizure of books or other documents in the case of search only to the undisclosed books of account or other documents and to interpret that regular books of account or other documents cannot be seized during search is too narrow an interpretation and the use of word "Such" prior to books of account or other documents in clause (*iii*) of section 132(1) cannot be interpreted to mean that it does not cover regular books of account.

(*ii*) **Whether disclosed assets can be seized?**

Reference of the word "such" in clause (*iii*) of section 132(1) prior to money, bullion, jewellery or other valuable article or thing found as a result of search refers to those assets mentioned in clause (*c*) of section 132(1) for which search is authorized. Clause (*c*) states any person is in possession of any money, bullion, jewellery or other valuable article or thing and such money, bullion, jewellery or other valuable article or thing represents either wholly or partly income or property which has not been or would not be disclosed for the purpose of Income Tax Act (hereinafter in this section refers to as the "undisclosed income or property").

Clause (*c*) of section 132(1) clearly refers only to the undisclosed income or property. Any disclosed income or property are not covered within its ambit and therefore it can be safely interpreted that any disclosed assets consisting of money, bullion, jewellery or other valuable article or thing cannot be seized. Any seizure of the disclosed asset would be illegal and department is required to return the same to the assessee.

(*iii*) **What is disclosed asset?**

If we look at the definition of undisclosed income given u/s 271AAA, it can be said that disclosed assets are those assets -

   a. which have been recorded on or before the date of search in the books of account or other documents maintained in the normal course or

   b. which have otherwise been disclosed to the Chief Commissioner or Commissioner before the date of search.

In the case of a person engaged in some business or professional activity and maintaining regular books of account in normal course, the assets recorded in the books of account or other documents can be said to be disclosed assets and those assets which have not been recorded in the books of account or other documents will be treated as undisclosed assets.

In the case of a person who is not running business or profession and who is not required under the law to maintain the books of account in normal course, question as to what is the disclosed asset, becomes a tricky one. It can be decided on the basis of the other documents maintained in the normal course or information disclosed by the assessee in the return of income filed. In case asset has been acquired making payment from the Bank A/c of the assessee and the said Bank A/c is disclosed in the return of income filed by the assessee - by disclosing the Bank A/c details, by showing the interest received on Bank deposits in the Bank A/c as income in the income tax return or by disclosing the above Bank A/c in the statement of affairs filed by the assessee, if any, along with his return of income. In such situation, it can be said that the assets acquired by making payment from such Bank A/c of the assessee are the disclosed assets. In case of asset acquired by making cash payment, copy of cash memo/invoice along with satisfactory evidence of disclosed source of cash will be required to prove that the asset is disclosed asset.

Individual persons generally do not maintain books of account of their personal affairs and it becomes very difficult, at the time of search, to prove that the personal assets found from their possession are the disclosed assets. In case personal statement of affairs is prepared and filed with the department alongwith details of the assets owned by the assessee, there may not be much difficulty. But in the absence of such details maintained and filed with the department, it takes lot of pains in satisfying to the authorized officer what is disclosed asset. Details of the Bank A/c alongwith the evidence that the Bank A/c is disclosed to the department, may not be readily available and the asset in absence of proper explanation and evidences may be seized by authorized officer.

In case of jewellery, wealth tax return filed, copy of valuation report of the valuer or if wealth tax is not applicable, copy of invoices alongwith evidence of payment from disclosed sources can be the evidences to prove that the jewellery in possession of assessee is disclosed asset.

When cash is found at the residence and assessee takes the plea, *inter alia*, that it is the cash belonging to the business firm, assessee is required in such a situation to produce sufficient evidences to this effect. Even in such case, unless there is authorization letter from the firm in favour of the assessee to keep cash of the firm at his residence and the authorization is found alongwith the cash at his residence, in practice it has been observed that cash is treated as undisclosed and it is seized.

Therefore, to prove that the asset found in possession of the assessee is disclosed asset, very strong evidences are required to be shown at the time of search so as to prevent seizure thereof.

(iv) **Seizure of the assets belonging to other persons**

In case of a search, where the books of account, documents or assets belonging to other persons are found, a question is usually raised - whether the same can be seized or not. In the case of a search authorized against a particular assessee or business entity, books of account, documents or loose papers relating to sister concern or other person(s) may be found. Similarly, jewellery, fixed deposit or shares belonging to spouse, parents or other family members of the assessee may also be found. Assessee usually pleads that the search has since been authorized in his name, the asset, documents etc. belonging to other person(s) cannot be seized. On the other hand, the department takes the view that anything belonging to any person that is found during the course of search at the premises of the assessee may have connection with the assessee and therefore the same can be seized.

Discussion with regard to the seizure in the case of other person can be made under following two situations:-

(*a*) Whether disclosed assets, regular books of account or other documents relating to other persons can be seized?

(*b*) Whether undisclosed assets, books of account or other documents relating to other persons can be seized?

So far as disclosed assets are concerned, the same cannot be seized even in the case of a person against whom search is authorized. Therefore, there is no question of making seizure of the disclosed assets relating to other person in whose case search is not authorized.

The other point *i.e.* the seizure of the regular books of account and documents relating to other person found in the case of search of an assessee is important as in practice such situation is frequently encountered. Seizure of such books or documents have serious ramification for other persons who may be brought under the ambit of section 153C due to such seizure. Regular (disclosed) books of account or other documents belonging to other person cannot be seized in our view.

The rationale which was discussed earlier regarding the seizure of the regular books of account, or other documents relating to the person searched cannot be applied to the seizure of books of account or documents found during search but relating to other person.

The fine point which was made earlier with respect to seizure of regular books of account or other documents relating to the person searched cannot be said to be existing in the case of other person against whom search is not authorized. It is for the reason that in case of other person, any satisfaction of undisclosed income is not recorded and reason to believe as contemplated under clause (*a*) or clause (*b*) of section 132(1) is not formed. It is not the case where any notice or summon having been issued or if issued are not complied with or would not be complied with by such other person as envisaged under clause (*a*) or (*b*) of section 132(1). It cannot be said that such other person will not produce regular books of account or other documents if called for by the tax department. Therefore, any seizure of the regular books of account of the sister concerns, other business entities or other persons cannot be seized.

The issue regarding seizure of undisclosed assets or books of account or other documents which are not maintained in the regular course belonging to other person is a debatable issue. The person searched usually puts forth the argument that search is authorized against him particularly and therefore, assets and books of account etc. belonging to other person(s) even if undisclosed cannot be seized. For example, assets belonging to the parents residing with the person searched or jewellery owned by & found from the locker of his wife or mother cannot be seized. Search is since qua-assessee in whose case search warrant is issued and therefore any asset in the name of other person cannot be roped in within the ambit of search and seizure cannot be made.

Insertion of clause (*iia*) to section 132(1) empowering the authorized officer to make personal search of any person going out, getting in or available at the place of search is with a view to search such other person to find any asset, books of account or other documents secreted by him relating to the assessee only. It is clear from the language in clause (*iia*) to section 132(1) wherein reference to the word "such" before books of account or other documents, money, bullion, jewellery or other valuable article or thing indicates those books of account or assets for which search is authorized and it can only be relating to the assets, books of account etc. of the person in whose case the search is authorized.

However, departmental viewpoint generally remains that the undisclosed assets, books of account etc. might have been held by the assessee as *benami* in the name of other family members or other persons and may have nexus and connection with the undisclosed income and affairs of the assessee. Similarly, the books of account or the documents containing details of undisclosed transaction may be maintained in the name of other family members but may have nexus with the undisclosed income and affairs of the assessee. Further, the undisclosed transactions or assets even if relating to other person, found at the premises of the assessee, may have nexus with the affairs of the assessee and needs to be examined in connection with the person searched.

Further, from the standpoint of the Revenue, the other argument may be advanced that law of land does not permit any person to accumulate undisclosed income and to hold undisclosed asset. Therefore, if any such asset belonging to any person is found during search operation against an assessee, such books of account, documents or undisclosed assets belonging to other person should also be seized & proceeded with even if initially search action was not undertaken against him. Thus, department comes into possession of evidences relating to undisclosed income belonging to other person, such person should not be spared of the consequences. This concept has also been legislated by way of introduction of section 153C which empowers the department to assess or reassess income of such other person.

In view of the above discussion, there seems to be a tilt in favour of the view that evidences relating to undisclosed income or undisclosed asset found in the course of a search, belonging to other person(s) can also be seized unless it is an admitted fact that such assets exclusively belong to the other persons.

In the case of *S.R. Batliboi & Co.* v. *DIT (Inv.)* [2009] 181 Taxman 9, Delhi High Court directed to return the laptop which was seized from the possession of the auditors who were present in the premises at the time of search for conducting audit of the assessee client. It was held that Department is not entitled to demand unrestricted access or right to acquire the electronic records present in the laptops belonging to the auditor of the assessee pertaining to third parties unconnected to the person against whom the search and seizure operations under section 132 have been conducted.

However, in the above case reported at *DIT (Inv.)* v. *S.R. Batliboi & Co.* [2010] 186 Taxman 350/[2009] 227 CTR 238 (SC), Supreme Court held that two laptops in question which were seized from the possession of the respondent's auditor firm are directed to be desealed and the data is to be examined by the Director General of National Informatics Centre in the presence of the representatives of the Income Tax Department and the assessee and all the data on the laptops is to be made available for inspection by the Income Tax Department to verify whether it pertains to the assessee in question. It is open to the Income Tax Department to copy the data relating to the specified three entities of the assessee group.

(v) In case of search or survey at the premises of the Counsel/Chartered Accountant, whether files/documents of other clients can be seized?

In the case of search operation planned by the department at some business house, generally it has been seen that the counsel/Chartered Accountant of the assessee is also covered by the department, particularly when department is having the credible information that his counsel/Chartered Accountant is deeply involved in assisting the client in managing his financial and tax affairs, which are not recorded in the books of account. Generally, in such cases survey u/s 133A is conducted at the business premises of the Counsel.

In exceptional cases, when there is credible information with the department that the Counsel/Chartered Accountant of the assessee is himself involved in undertaking undisclosed transactions and tax evasion, department undertakes search operation u/s 132 with respect to business and residential premises of the counsel/Chartered Accountant.

At the business premises of the counsel/Chartered Accountant, files of various clients are mentioned and kept. A question obviously arises as to whether in the case of search or survey operation at the business premises of the counsel/Chartered Accountant, files relating to other clients can be inspected and seized by the department?

As per the law contained in this regard, advocates enjoy the confidentiality Privilege with respect to the correspondence, files and information while discharging professional obligations relating to their clients. Therefore, it can be said that in such cases department owes a duty to honour the privilege available to the advocates and the inspection of correspondence files has to be restricted only in respect to the person for whom search or survey action has been undertaken. In the case of counsel being Chartered Accountant or some other professional, such privilege is not available. However, in practice it has been observed that generally department restricts its investigation and inspection with respect to the files of the target person for whom search or survey action has been undertaken. It can however be stated that there is no specific denial or restriction to look into and inspect files of other persons/clients in case there is information or suspicion by the department that incriminating material or data relating to the target person are kept or has relation to target person are kept or has relation with such other person.

In case of data kept in the soft form *i.e.* in hard disk, pen drive etc. which comprises the data relating to target person along with the other persons, it is difficult and almost impossible to segregate the data and seize the data related to target person. In such situation, entire hard disk or pen drive is seized but even at the later stage, inspection should be restricted only to the data related to the target person. However, nothing precludes the department to inspect all the files contained in the storage medium.

For such a situation, the judgment of *S. R. Batliboi & Co.* v. *DIT (Inv.)* [2009] 181 Taxman 9 (Delhi) is significant wherein Delhi High Court directed to return the laptop which was seized from the possession of the auditors who were present in the premises at the time of search for conducting audit of the assessee client. It was held that department is not entitled to demand unrestricted access or right to acquire the electronic records present in the laptop belonging to the auditor of the assessee pertaining to third parties unconnected to the person against whom the search and seizure operations under section 132 have been conducted.

(*vi*) **Seizure of asset acquired prior to 7 assessment years preceding to the year of search - Whether valid?**

Assessee may be found in possession of movable or immovable assets which have been acquired during the period which is beyond the period of limitation for making assessment u/s 153A or 148. Even if assessee is not able to explain the source and produce the evidences of acquiring such asset, the same cannot be treated as undisclosed asset and seizure of such asset is not valid. As per the Act, assessee is not supposed to maintain and keep the evidences relating to asset acquired prior to above mentioned limitation period. Such asset even if undisclosed cannot be assessed u/s 153A or u/s 147 and therefore is not liable to be seized.

However, it is important to mention that in case any such asset is covered within the ambit of Wealth Tax Act and has not been shown for the purpose of wealth tax, it can be seized for the evasion of wealth tax. Further, the burden to establish that the asset in question has been acquired beyond the above mentioned limitation period would lie on the assessee.

6.3 Manner of seizure

(*i*) **Opportunity to assessee before seizure is made**

There is no prescribed procedure or requirement to grant opportunity to the assessee to prove whether the assets are disclosed or not before making seizure of the assets. However, in practice it has been observed that whenever any assets are intended to be seized by the authorized officer, either assessee is asked by the authorised officer or assessee himself pleads his case to prove that the assets are disclosed assets. In the absence of all the evidences available with the assessee to show to the authorized officer at the time of search, even disclosed assets of the assessee are also sometimes seized. The onus certainly lies with the assessee to prove with cogent evidences that the assets are disclosed assets. He is entitled to refer to his records *i.e.* bank passbook, income tax return, books of account or other documents to support his explanation to satisfy the authorized officer. In case the assets are belonging to other family members or to some third person, evidences to this effect are required to be produced.

In *L.R. Gupta* v. *Union of India* [1991] 59 Taxman 305, at page 55, Delhi High Court observed:

".... We, however, feel that while it is for the authorized officer to decide about the manner in which the search is to be conducted and statements recorded before any seizure is effected or a restraint order passed, some sort of an opportunity should be granted to the person from whose custody the seizure is effected. It is not every article which is found as a result of the search which has to be seized. *Prima facie* it is only those valuable articles which are seized or in respect of which a restraint order is passed with regard to which, ultimately, an order u/s 132(5) may be passed. Before any seizure is effected then, if possible, a statement of the person from whom the seizure is being effected should be recorded. He may have an effective explanation with regard to items which are found as a result of the search. For example, there should have been no occasion to remove the files or documents of the clients of petitioner No. 1, in the absence of a valid authorization in respect thereto. If an opportunity had been granted, this would have been pointed out. Over enthusiasm or over-zealousness on the part of the raiding party should not cause unnecessary harassment. In the present case, the statement of petitioner No. 1 was recorded before the search commenced but, surprisingly enough, no statement was recorded after the search was concluded even though the said petitioner was not permitted to attend to the work in the courts on the pretext that his presence may be necessary for recording of his statement. We hasten to add that non-recording of such statement will not invalidate a search but it will be prudent that one or more statements are recorded after the search is completed and the persons in possession of immovable articles or documents are asked questions so that the authorized officer is in a position to decide whether the seizure of all or any of the items is necessary or not."

(ii) Seizure of disclosed assets for want of evidences

Another situation may be one when disclosed assets are seized during the search by authorized officer due to non-availability or non-production of the relevant evidences by the assessee at the time of search. Such seizure cannot be said to be illegal seizure.

A distinction is required to be drawn in the case of seizure of those disclosed assets with respect to which, evidences of disclosure are made available to the authorized officer at the time of search and yet the seizure is made and the case of those disclosed assets where evidence of disclosure are not readily available & could not be shown to the authorized officer and the seizure is made.

In the case of those assets which are disclosed but evidence of which could not be shown to the authorized officer and therefore seized, remedy would lie under the first and second proviso to section 132B(1) where such situation has been contemplated by the legislature and mechanism for the release of such assets has been provided therein. However, it is seen in practice that despite such provision existing on the statute under the first and second proviso to section 132B(1), even disclosed assets once seized are not easily released on one pretext or the other such as necessity of obtaining the requisite approval of higher authorities and subjective considerations in the matter of satisfaction regarding nature and source of the acquisition of the assets. Moreover, power to release such disclosed assets as per the first proviso of section 132B(1) has been given to the assessing officer and not to the authorized officer. This also creates delay in the release of the assets.

There is a strong case to make amendment to section 132B or to provide a clear cut provision and procedure for the release of disclosed assets by the authorized officer after examining the evidences of the disclosure of asset. There does not seem be any intention of Legislature to seize the disclosed assets and in case evidences of disclosure could not be made available during the course of search and the same are made available by the assessee to the authorized officer after the search, there is no reason why such asset should remain lying seized and the same should be released to the assessee immediately. Once authorized officer is convinced that seizure of disclosed asset has been made, the power should be given to take corrective action for releasing the same. Since the seizure is made by authorized officer, the corrective action should also be permitted to be taken by the authorized officer himself.

(iii) **Release of assets illegally seized**

In case disclosed assets are seized even after showing the evidence of disclosure and its explained source, such seizure is illegal. In such a case, action of the authorized officer is illegal and on application made by the assessee as per the proviso to section 132B, such assets should be released to the assessee by the department. However in case of failure in releasing such seized assets, action would lie under Article 226 of the Constitution by way of filing writ to the High Court against such an illegal seizure.

(iv) Location of the asset seized - Significance

At the time when *Panchnama* is prepared mentioning the details of assets seized, it is important to ensure that the location of the asset or the person from whose possession, the particular asset has been found is clearly mentioned. It may be significant not only from the point of view of the assessee but from the point of view of the department as well so as to enquire, establish and assess undisclosed income in the hands of proper person.

There may be a situation where assessee owns any asset which is found from the possession of some other person during the course of search and which is liable to be seized. It should be ensured that since asset belongs to the assessee, it should be seized in the name of the assessee only. This decision may be important so as to prevent the other person to be roped in within the ambit of section 153C. For example, if jewellery is found from the locker of wife but is owned as undisclosed assets by assessee himself, wife may then not be required to be covered and assessed u/s 153C. There may be a case where cash is found from the possession of senior employee or director of a company. Such cash may be liable to be seized as their undisclosed income and in that situation they will be covered within the ambit of section 153C unless such cash is owned by the company.

(v) Illegal Seizure v. Illegal Search

In case seizure of the disclosed asset is made illegally, the action of search cannot said to be illegal for this reason alone. In case of illegal seizure, department may be asked to release the assets seized or in appropriate cases pay interest upto the date of release of assets or pay damages or compensation. In case any *mala fide* is proved on the part of the authorized officer in making such an illegal seizure, the authorized officer may be personally held liable for the consequence. But the overall action of search due to above reason cannot be said to be illegal and the assessee would be required to face the consequences of search.

In case search action u/s 132 is declared to be illegal, all consequential actions following the search would also become illegal. In case a search is declared illegal, all assets seized whether disclosed or undisclosed are liable to be released to the assessee.

(vi) Seizure of asset whose location is known

Location of movable assets can never be static and even at a particular point of time, the location of a movable asset may be in the knowledge of the department, the same can be seized during search operations.

The observations of the Supreme Court in the case of *CIT* v. *Tarsem Kumar* [1986] 27 Taxman 305 (SC) were made with regard to the location of asset in the peculiar circumstances of that case, as there the assets were in the custody of custom authority and therefore no search was considered necessary in the light of the fact that precise knowledge about the location was already available to the department. These observations are not of universal application and after the introduction of section 132A w.e.f. 1st October 1985; they have lost their relevance in the context of the documents or assets being held by another department.

The observation of Delhi High Court in the case of *L.R. Gupta* v. *Union of India* [1991] 59 Taxman 305 (Delhi) that where existence of the money or asset is known to the income tax department, then the provisions of clause (*c*) of section 132(1) would not be attracted, has been made in the case where the department knew about the existence of the property which were acquired from the known sources.

Insofar as the application of these observations to other cases is concerned it would be relevant to refer to the observation of the Supreme Court in the case of *Pooran Mal* v. *Director of Inspection* [1974] 93 ITR 505 (SC). If the director of investigation gets timely information about the undisclosed assets and its location, he can direct a search and seizure. Otherwise it is futile to direct a search and seizure because the whole endeavour will be fruitless.

(vii) Whether search has to precede the seizure

In *Mohd. Kunhi* v. *Mohd. Koya* [1973] 91 ITR 301 (Mad.), the Madras High Court held that to say that the power of seizure is not exercisable unless it is preceded by the search of a building or breaking open the locks is to confuse ends with the means and to caricature the intention of Legislature which in order to facilitate the power of seizure has provided also for ancillary power of invading the privacy of people by entering and searching their buildings and breaking open the receptacles where things to be seized might remain concealed. The section does not say that the officer can enter and search the building of the person who has failed to disclose his income, but says that he can enter and search any building, place, etc. where he has reason to suspect that any incriminating material or concealed assets are kept.

In *I. Devarajan* v. *Tamil Nadu Farmers Service Co-operative Federation* [1981] 131 ITR 506 (Mad.), the High Court observed that the actual physical search need not precede the seizure.

6.4 Deemed seizure

Second proviso to section 132(1) lays down that where it is not possible or practicable to take physical possession of any valuable article or thing and remove it to a safe place due to its volume, weight or other physical characteristics or due to its being of a dangerous nature, the authorized officer may serve an order on the owner or the person who is in immediate possession or control thereof that he shall not remove, part with or otherwise deal with it, except with the previous permission of the authorized officer and such action of the authorized officer shall be deemed to be seizure of such valuable article or thing under clause (*iii*) of section 132(1).

It is further provided with effect from 1st June 2003 that nothing contained in the second proviso shall apply in case of any valuable article or thing being stock-in-trade of the business.

The concept of deemed seizure or constructive seizure was introduced in the Act by the Finance Act, 1988 with effect from 1st April 1989. The objective is to facilitate the authorized officer in making seizure of such valuable article or thing which cannot be seized and kept due to peculiar nature of the asset and non-availability of adequate space with him. Some important features of this proviso may be noted as under:-

(*i*) **Only valuable article or thing covered**

Deemed seizure cannot be made of books of account, documents, loose papers, files or assets consisting of cash, money, bullion or jewellery. It is only valuable article or thing which can be put under deemed seizure. It may include paintings, carpets, valuable household articles, silver utensils etc. It is only those items which cannot be removed or seized to a proper and safe place due to heavy volume, weight or other physical characteristics or dangerous nature of such items. Cash, money, bullion or jewellery have not been covered for the purpose of deemed seizure since the same are capable of being removed and kept in possession of the department. Books of account or other documents are since required to be examined, therefore, the same have to remain in the custody of the authorised officer.

1. In the case of *Rajendra Singh Nayak* v. *Dy. CIT* [2014] 50 taxmann. com 218/227 Taxman 13 (Mag.)(MP)(HC). The Petitioner's premises was subjected to search and his immovable properties, namely,

agricultural lands and plots total 14 in numbers were placed under deemed seizure on the strength of second proviso to section 132(1). The Petitioner, being aggrieved, filed applications requesting for release of the attached immovable property but the revenue authorities did not pay any heed to his prayer.

On writ in High Court, the court allowed the writ petition and held that where it was not revenue's case that there was any valuable article or thing described in clause (*iii*) of section 132(1) such as books of account, other documents, money, bullion, jewellery and other valuable article or thing found as a result of search which was of a nature that it was not possible or practicable to take physical possession of same and remove to a safe place due to its volume, weight or other physical characteristics or due to its being of a dangerous nature necessitating seizure of immovable properties, action of revenue of seizure of petitioner's immovable properties which were in nature of agricultural lands and open plots was wholly without any authority of law and could not be sustained.

(*ii*) "Not Possible or Practicable"

Deemed seizure has been provided in the situation when it is either not possible or not practicable to take physical possession of any valuable article or thing.

Needless to say that deemed seizure can also be made only of those articles or things which can be seized *i.e.* those items which represents wholly or partly undisclosed income of the assessee.

For making deemed seizure, the authorized officer is required to serve an order under second proviso to section 132(1). On service of such notice, it shall be deemed that the seizure has taken place and the assessee shall not remove, part with or otherwise deal with it except with the previous permission of the authorized officer. In fact assessee will be deemed henceforth to possess such valuable article or thing on behalf of income tax department.

(*iii*) No deemed seizure of stock-in-trade

By Finance Act, 2003 w.e.f. 1st June 2003, third proviso to section 132(1) has been inserted providing that the concept of deemed seizure shall not be applicable in the case of stock-in-trade of the business. This is a welcome relief from the point of view of the businessmen. Prior to this amendment, deemed seizure of stock-in-trade was causing lot of hardships to the assessees. Due to deemed seizure of stock inventory, normal business operations used to get hampered. With the passage of time, stock items put under deemed seizure also used to get outdated, obsolete and damaged. Even department was not able to realize substantial taxes out of the same.

(iv) **Deemed seizure not applicable to Bank Lockers, FDRs, Deposits etc.**

The provisions of deemed seizure can be applied only under the circumstances mentioned under the second proviso *i.e.* when seizure is not possible due to volume, weight, etc. of the items. The provision of deemed seizure can thus not be extended to items such as bank lockers, bank deposits, FDRs, cheques, drafts, deposits with third parties, promissory notes etc.

(v) **Deemed seizure v. Restraint u/s 132(3)**

Restraint u/s 132(3) is a different concept and it need not be mixed or treated as alternative to deemed seizure. The objective of putting restraint u/s 132(3) is to provide reasonable time to the authorized officer before taking action of seizure which could not be done during search since it was not practicable to do so. Restraint u/s 132(3) can be put on any books of account, other documents or any kind of assets which are liable to be seized. It is important to note that restraint u/s 132(3) can be put only on those assets which can be seized or in which case order of deemed seizure can be passed. Since there cannot be any deemed seizure of stock-in-trade in the business, no restraint on stock items or for production of goods or dispatch of goods can be put.

Restraint u/s 132(3) can remain in force for a period not exceeding 60 days from the date of such order and before the expiry of the period of 60 days the authorized officer has to lift the restraint order passed u/s 132(3) and take decision whether to seize such items or not.

6.5 Nature and procedure of seizure

(i) **Not to record reason for seizure**

There is no requirement in section 132 or Rule 112 for the authorized officer to record the reasons before seizure of the documents and/or assets. Section 165 of the Criminal Procedure Code cannot be held to require the authorized officer to record reasons. It is not a statutory requirement to record at the time of search and seizure the relevancy of document. [*Balwant Singh* v. *R.D. Shah, Director of Inspection* [1969] 71 ITR 550 (Delhi); *Hindustan Metal Works* v. *CIT* [1968] 68 ITR 798 (All.)].

(ii) **To take actual possession of assets**

The seizure envisaged in section 132(1)(*iii*) is effected only when the authorized officer takes possession of the seized articles to enable the revenue to appropriate the same towards the payment of the amount that may be determined to be due under the Act. A mere order issued for taking possession of the keys to the bank locker will not constitute 'seizure' as contemplated by section 132(1). [*Mrs. Kanwal Shamsher Singh* v. *UOI* [1974] 95 ITR 80 (Delhi)]

(iii) Immediate realization of seized assets illegal

Section 132 does not confer any authority on the Assessing Officer to realize the assets and convert them into cash. That could be possible only when the demand is finally quantified and the assets have to be realized in discharge of the liability. [*Dheer Singh* v. *Asstt. DIT* [1997] 90 Taxman 392 (All.)] [*Smt. Bimla Singh* v. *Chief CIT* 1997 Tax LR 873/[1998] 96 Taxman 114 (Pat.)]

(iv) Arbitrary seizure held illegal

All this supports and substantiates the case of the petitioner that the books of account and documents had been seized in their entirety from the premises and whatever was found lying there was taken into possession irrespective of any consideration of the question, which it was mandatory both under the provisions of section 132 and under the warrant of authorization for the income tax officer, whether it was relevant or useful for the purposes of the proceedings for the assessment year 1962-63 onwards or not. The search and the seizure, in the circumstances, must be held to be illegal as being arbitrary and an abuse of power. [*N.K. Textile Mills* v. *CIT* [1966] 62 ITR 58 (Punj. & Har.) [judgment delivered by *A.N. Grover, J.*]

(v) Volume of papers seized is irrelevant

It was finally contended that, because of the large quantity of papers seized, the seizure was "enormous" and amounted to an abuse of power. The use of the word "enormous" is rather inappropriate with reference to the searches and seizures because in this, as in other things, the quantitative test is likely to be misleading. Whether, in a given case, the authorities effecting the search and seizure have exceeded their powers and acted arbitrarily and excessively depends upon the facts of that case. It may be that in a given case, having regard to the nature of the assessment proceedings and the magnitude of the suspected evasion, a large quantity of material may have to be seized. That by itself does not render the search excessive or *mala fide*. [*Sri Venkateswara Lodge* v. *CIT* [1969] 71 ITR 629 (AP)]

(vi) No power to seal

There is no provision for sealing of a business premises either under section 133A or section 132 or any other section of the Act,.................. Sealing of the business premises of the petitioner was in violation of the fundamental rights guaranteed to a citizen under Article 19(1)(*g*) of the Constitution of India which guarantees right to practice any profession, or to carry on any occupation, trade or business and also under Article 300A of the Constitution of India inasmuch as the same amounted to temporary deprivation of the property without authority of law. *[Shyam Jeweller* v. *Chief Commissioner (Admin.)* [1992] 196 ITR 243 (All.)]

6.6 Seizure of different kind of assets

(*i*) Money

Money is a wide term and it means coins and paper currency used as medium of exchange.

Undisclosed cash is most-sought asset looked for by the search team in any search operation. Cash may be kept at secret places within the premises and search is targeted to find such places.

(*ii*) Cash found at business premises

When cash is found at office or at other business premises and it is as per balance of "cash in hand" reflected in the cash book of the business firm maintained in the ordinary course of business, the same is disclosed cash and cannot be seized. If cash found is in excess of the balance as per cash book, assessee has to explain the source with evidences of such cash found alongwith reason why the same could not be entered in the cash book to the satisfaction of authorized officer. It may be amount of cash sales of preceding day as per cash memos which is pending to be entered in the cash book. If cash is withdrawn from the bank, entry in the bank statement may be shown to explain the source. In the absence of satisfactory explanation, unaccounted cash is likely to be seized.

(*iii*) Cash found at residential premises

When cash is found at residential premises, before making seizure of such cash, certain credit is given for reasonable cash to be out of past savings and towards *stridhan* or kept for meeting out day to day household expenses depending upon the facts of each individual case. But huge amount of cash cannot be claimed to be kept for such purposes or out of past saving, unless otherwise proved, as the assessee is not expected to keep such amount in cash without any valid and plausible reason.

Source of cash found is required to be explained by the assessee with evidences. In case assessee claims the cash found at residence belongs to the business concern, proper authorization or receipted voucher or any other contemporary evidence is expected to be available. Mere statement in this regard may not be sufficient. In case cash has been generated out of sale proceeds of some asset or property, evidence of sale and cash receipt from the buyer may be produced as evidence. In case when there is long gap from the date of sale of asset, it may create doubt and assessee will have to explain why such cash was not kept in cash at residence.

In the case of seizure of cash, the person from whose possession cash has been found should be clearly mentioned in search memo. This would help the assessee in explaining the source of the cash at the time of assessment and for the department also, to determine undisclosed income in the hands of proper person. There may be several sources of cash found at residence. At the time of search while recording his statement u/s 132(4), the source of cash can be explained. The cash found may be related to sale of jewellery, loans or gifts from friends or relatives, repayment of advances earlier given, maturity of FDRs or insurance policy, sale of scrap or other goods, advance received for sale of property etc. In the absence of proper evidences available and shown to the authorized officer, cash may be seized at that point of time. However, at the stage of assessment proceedings assessee may lead relevant evidences.

(iv) Jewellery

Jewellery is the other popular item of undisclosed asset looked for by the search team at residential premises or from the bank lockers of the assessee and his other family members.

As a matter of custom prevailing in the society, jewellery ornaments are acquired, inherited or received as gifts on different occasions from parents or other relatives or friends.

Assessee is required to explain the source of acquisition of jewellery. Mere assertion by the assessee that it represents the jewellery received at the time of marriage, birth of the children or other occasions or the same has been inherited from the parents or parents-in-law may not be sufficient.

Jewellery is an item of taxable asset covered under Wealth Tax Act. The jewellery and ornaments which have been disclosed in the wealth tax return & source of which is explained, cannot be seized. Assessee is required to produce copy of wealth tax return and the valuer's report or any other evidence to explain the source. Assessee might have declared jewellery under the VDIS, relevant evidences of declaration may be produced in that case. In case value of jewellery found is less than the amount for which wealth tax return is required to be filed, assessee may produce copy of bills of purchasing jewellery alongwith evidence for source of payment made. In the absence of proper evidence regarding the source of acquisition of jewellery, it is likely to be seized by the income tax department.

(*a*) **Minimum jewellery not to be seized**

As it is customary in our society to receive jewellery at the time of marriage or other occasion, Board has issued instructions not to seize jewellery as per the following limits or such higher quantum of jewellery at the discretion of authorized officer keeping in view the status of the assessee.

   a. 500 gms of gold jewellery in the case of each married lady.

   b. 250 gms of gold jewellery in the case of each unmarried female member.

   c. 100 gms of gold jewellery in the case of each male member.

Copy of instruction issued by Board in this regard is reproduced below.

Guidelines for seizure of jewellery and ornaments in course of search - Instruction No. 1916 [F. No. 286/63/93-IT (Inv. II)], dated 11-5-1994:

Instances of seizure of jewellery of small quantity in course of operations under section 132 have come to the notice of the Board. The question of a common approach to situations where search parties come across items of jewellery, has been examined by the Board and following guidelines are issued for strict compliance—

   (*i*) In the case of a wealth-tax assessee, gold jewellery and ornaments found in excess of the gross weight declared in the wealth-tax return only need be seized.

   (*ii*) In the case of a person not assessed to wealth-tax, gold jewellery and ornaments to the extent of 500 gms per married lady, 250 gms per unmarried lady and 100 gms per male member of the family, need not be seized.

   (*iii*) The authorised officer may, having regard to the status of the family and the custom and practices of the community to which the family belongs and other circumstances of the case, decide to exclude a larger quantity of jewellery and ornaments from seizure. This should be reported to the Director of Income-tax/Commissioner authorising the search at the time of furnishing the search report.

   (*iv*) In all cases, a detailed inventory of the jewellery and ornaments found must be prepared to be used for assessment purposes.

The choice of selecting the items not to be seized is, in practice, given to the assessee so as to select those items which may be useful to be used by the assessee or his wife or other family members for their personal purpose as per need by them.

Minimum jewellery not required to be seized as per above Instruction and the jewellery regarding which the evidences of source are produced by the assessee cannot be said to be mutually exclusive. It may be difficult for the assessee to claim the benefit of both. In case evidences for source of jewellery produced is in excess of the minimum amount of jewellery not required to be seized as per above instructions, no further credit may be given for not seizing the jewellery in accordance with the above instruction.

(b) Seizure in case of diamond/other precious stones jewellery

The above instruction of the Board regarding non-seizure of the specified quantity of the jewellery refers to jewellery made of gold. Nothing is mentioned in the said Instruction about the diamond/other precious stone jewellery. Now-a-days, jewellery is generally found which contain diamond and other precious stones and are quite valuable. The said instruction of the Board cannot be interpreted that jewellery of the specified quantity of gold which contain diamond/other precious stones cannot be seized. On the other hand, it cannot also be said that diamond/other precious jewellery in all cases will be seized. Reasonable interpretation can be put that in case jewellery items are made of diamond or other precious stone, jewellery of equivalent value as per above limit of gold jewellery are not required to be seized.

In the case of *Tilak Raj Sharma* v. *Dy. CIT* [2014] 41 taxmann.com 432/221 Taxman 123 (Mag.)(All.)(HC), during the search certain documents, loose papers, cash, jewellery, etc. were found. The assessee submitted that the jewellery belonged to his mother and wife and had been acquired over a period of more than 40 years. The AO accepted the explanation given by the assessee but contended that gold sovereigns were not jewellery and since no explanation was given by the assessee in that respect, the AO added it to the income of the assessee. The CIT(A) and the Tribunal confirmed the findings of the AO.

The High Court observed that when the jewellery was being inventoried, the gold sovereigns had been included in it and that the term 'jewellery' was used as a loose term. The High Court accordingly held that since the explanation regarding jewellery had been accepted by the department, the remaining part relating to gold sovereigns which were a part of 'jewellery' did not belong to the assessee and explanation thereof had to be accepted.

(c) Valuation of jewellery

For valuation of jewellery, departmental approved valuer is called during search or at the time of operation of locker at later stage by the search team. Valuation report is prepared by the valuer mentioning the weight and quality of the jewellery. In the absence of proof regarding the date of acquisition of jewellery, current rate of gold or diamond is taken into consideration. Unaccounted jewellery is seized treating the same as undisclosed income of the current year.

In case assessee has any valid objection to the value adopted by the valuer, he may lodge his objection and in such a case another valuer may be called by the authorized officer for making the valuation so as to rule out any bias & maintain independence to the valuation.

(d) Matching of items of jewellery

Whenever any evidence regarding acquisition of jewellery is produced by the assessee such as wealth tax return, valuation report, copy of invoices, VDIS declaration containing details of items of jewellery, the ideal situation is that the item of jewellery found matches with the item of jewellery mentioned in such list. But in practice, it may not happen even in genuine cases since ladies are in the habit of getting the items altered from time to time. In case evidence of alteration is available, there should not be any problem. In the absence of any such evidence, it may take pains for the assessee to convince to the authorized officer that the jewellery found is represented by the above mentioned evidences produced.

In such a situation decision of seizure depends upon satisfaction of the authorized officer. Some may take the view that in case gross weight declared and the gross weight of the jewellery found match, no seizure is required. But in some cases, the authorized officer may take strict view and may seize the jewellery which do not match, on the pre-text that the jewellery found is some other jewellery which is undisclosed and the declared jewellery might have been kept somewhere else or might have been dealt in some other manner by the assessee.

It is for the assessee to handle the situation tactfully in such cases.

(e) Jewellery in person

Jewellery which is being put on body in person forms part of total jewellery and the same is also valued as part of total jewellery found. As a matter of social decorum, the same is usually given back to be used by the person wearing it and in any case the same may form part of the jewellery not required to be seized as per the instruction of the Board as discussed above.

(f) Jewellery of others kept with the assessee in safe custody

There may be cases when jewellery of the married daughter of the assessee or mother of the assessee or some other person who are not presently residing with the assessee, may be kept with the assessee or in his bank locker. In such cases assessee should declare this fact in his statement before the jewellery is searched or locker is opened. In case any evidence to this effect is found along with the jewellery to the satisfaction of the authorized officer, authorized officer cannot seize the same under the law.

In the absence of any evidence to prove the ownership of the other person, jewellery found may be seized as belonging to assessee and legal presumption in terms of the provision of section 132(4A) will be raised against the assessee.

(g) Pledged gold ornaments

Department has right to seize only those articles which absolutely belong to the person in possession. This is evident from use of the words 'possession' and 'represent' in section 132(1). These words denote ownership. In a case where the assessee was found having unaccounted loan transaction where the advances were made on security of gold pledged by the customers, and the gold so pledged was seized by the department, it was held that the assessee with whom the gold ornaments were pledged, had right to retain possession of the pledged goods only till such time that the debt was discharged. The assessee was not the owner of the seized ornaments and the department had no right to seize them. *[Alleppey Financial Enterprises* v. *Asstt. DIT* [1999] 102 **Taxman** 309 (Ker.)]

(h) Jewellery short found

There may be situation when jewellery found during the course of search is less than the jewellery declared by the assessee in his Wealth Tax or Income Tax Returns. Assessee is asked to explain the reason of such difference in the quantum of such jewellery. It is suggested as a practical measure in case of jewellery that jewellery of entire family should be clubbed, compared and explained. This is so because jewellery is generally exchanged or kept with other family members. Secondly, it may be appreciated that there may, in all likelihood, not be any negative inference leading to any addition in the assessment in case jewellery is found short. The reason of short jewellery may be many *e.g.* some jewellery may have been kept with parents/in-laws residing at different locations. No negative inference can be drawn against the assessee in case he is not able to explain the short fall at the time of search itself. Assessee can very well explain the reason of jewellery found short after enquiring the facts properly at later stage or at the time of assessment proceeding.

(v) Seizure of immovable properties

Immovable properties cannot be seized in the proceedings u/s 132. No restraint on opening of shop can be put u/s 132(3). Seizure of immovable property is not within the ambit of section 132.

In the case of *Sardar Paraduman Singh* v. *Union of India* [1987] 31 Taxman 515 (Delhi), the court observed that a plain reading of section 132 shows that its scope is limited to article and things mentioned in section 132(1)(*a*), (*b*) or (*c*) and it does not include within its ambit "immovable property" because of the reason that the location of an immovable property is known and no search has to be made for it and if no search is called for, a question of seizure does not arise. U/s 132 the search and seizure go together. It was further held that the action of Directorate in sealing the shop and in passing the restraint order u/s 132(3) was totally illegal and without jurisdiction. It was also held that the refusal to release the shop to assessee after repeated requests was also illegal and the illegality was further aggravated by requiring to furnish bank guarantee equal to the value of the shop or to prove his ownership in case he wanted to open the shop. The court also held that the action of the Directorate in breaking seals in the absence of the assessee and handing over the possession of the shop to the Rehabilitation authorities was wholly illegal and also smacked of mala fides.

In the case of *Nand Kishore Mangharani* v. *DIT* [1994] 210 ITR 1071 (All.), before Allahabad High Court it was submitted by the counsel for the revenue that under the Income tax Act even immovable property can be attached. Repelling this contention, the High Court observed, no doubt, that the provisions of section 281B of the Act are emphatic in this regard and if the proceedings are for provisional attachment, certainly immovable property can be attached. But in the case before the High Court, since admittedly the proceedings which were started under section 132 of the Act related only to movable property the impugned seizure of immovable property was apparently without jurisdiction. The High Court followed the judgments in *Sardar Paraduman Singh* v. *Union of India* [1987] 31 Taxman 515 (Delhi) and *CIT* v. *M.K. Gabrial Babu* [1991] 57 Taxman 146 (Ker.).

Kerala High Court in *M.K. Gabriel Babu* v. *Asstt. DIT* [1991] 55 Taxman 18 (Ker.) has observed that the words 'other valuable article or thing' used in association with the words 'money, bullion, jewellery' cannot be understood differently. The section therefore cannot be said to include in its ambit immovable property also. Immovable properties cannot be seized u/s 132. In coming to this conclusion, Kerala High Court rejected the plea based on *CIT* v. *N.C. Budharaja & Co.* [1980] 121 ITR 212 (Ori.) and *CIT* v. *Pressure Piling Co. (India) (P.) Ltd.* [1979] 1 Taxman 406 (Bom.), that the word, 'article' occurring in section 84 is capable of meaning anything corporeal and observed that the meaning of the word 'article' is used in a different context in section 132 and, therefore, the aforesaid two decisions have no relevance.

1. In the case of *Rajendra Singh Nayak* v. *Dy. CIT* [2014] 50 taxmann. com 218/227 Taxman 13(Mag.) (MP)(HC). The Petitioner's premises was subjected to search and his immovable properties, namely, agricultural lands and plots total 14 in numbers were placed under deemed seizure on the strength of second proviso to section 132(1). The Petitioner, being aggrieved, filed applications requesting for release of the attached immovable property but the revenue authorities did not pay any heed to his prayer.

On writ in High Court, the court allowed the writ petition and held that where it was not revenue's case that there was any valuable article or thing described in clause (*iii*) of section 132(1) such as books of account, other documents, money, bullion, jewellery and other valuable article or thing found as a result of search which was of a nature that it was not possible or practicable to take physical possession of same and remove to a safe place due to its volume, weight or other physical characteristics or due to its being of a dangerous nature necessitating seizure of immovable properties, action of revenue of seizure of petitioner's immovable properties which were in nature of agricultural lands and open plots was wholly without any authority of law and could not be sustained.

(vi) Seizure of title deeds of immovable property

Seizure of Title deeds of Immovable Property does not tantamount to seizure of immovable property. It is well established that immovable property cannot be seized which implies that immovable property cannot be sealed, locked; possession or keys of the same cannot be taken over by the department. But by this proposition it cannot be interpreted that original Title Deeds of the immovable property can also not be seized.

In the case of *Bhagwandas Narayandas* v. *CIT* [1975] 98 ITR 194 (Guj.), it has been held that title deeds have only evidentiary value. They do not possess any intrinsic market value and are therefore not includible in the category of 'valuable article or thing'. It cannot be negotiable or transferred for valuable considerations.

A Title Deed of immovable property being a valuable document, can be seized u/s 132(1) and retained u/s 132(8), but its retention itself will not confer any special right on the department unless simultaneous action is taken by exercising the powers of provisional attachment of the property in question u/s 281B.

The issue regarding seizure of title deeds of immovable property is a debatable issue. Title Deeds are no doubt valuable document and there is power to seize books of account or other documents and therefore, title deeds being in the nature of document can be seized.

On the other hand one may argue that every registered document is a public document and readily available with the registering authority and there is no chance of there being any manipulation. The same in original are not required to be seized; the authorized officer may well take its copy of extracts. Secondly when immovable properties cannot be seized, original title deeds representing immovable properties can also not be seized and thirdly the reference of 'other document' for the purpose of seizure alongwith books of account is with reference to those documents which are in juxtaposition with books of account and the documents and the nature of original title deeds of immovable property cannot be covered for this purpose.

Apart from original Registered Title Deeds, other documents relating to immovable property *e.g.* agreement to sale, MOU, buyers agreement, collaboration agreement, cash receipts of payment etc. are very well covered within the ambit of document and can be seized.

In practice, it has been seen that department seizes photocopy of title deeds or other documents of immovable property which are recorded in the books of account. Further, it has been observed in practice that in case original title deeds are seized at the time of search, the same are released by the department after retaining the certified photocopy of such documents.

In case there are certain documents, agreement to sell, MOU, Collaboration Agreement etc. which are not recorded in the books of account, the same are seized in original.

(vii) Seizure of Will or other confidential documents

In the case of search, department may discover some Will written by some person/some other confidential documents, photographs etc. There is no restriction on the powers of the department not to seize such documents or material. However, department generally seizes only such documents or material or assets which are of incriminating nature and which has evidentiary value to unearth the unaccounted income.

In case such documents or material does not have any such evidentiary value, it may not be seized by the department. The confidentiality of the documents to the assessee cannot be deterrence for the department not to seize such document if it has evidentiary value to unearth the unaccounted income. However, in appropriate cases, department may seize certified photocopy of such document and return the original thereof.

(viia) Valuable article or thing

All kind of articles are not covered u/s 132. It is only the valuable articles which can be seized. The word 'value' refers to the monetary value in commercial terms. It does not include articles of sentimental or personal value.

'Article' refers to tangible substance and 'thing' covers intangible substance within its fold as observed by Madras High Court in the case of *I. Devarajan* v. *Tamil Nadu Farmers Service Co-operative Federation* [1981] 131 ITR 506 (Mad.).

The addition of the word 'thing' in section 132(1)(c) of the Income-tax Act, 1961, as contrasted with sections 69A and 69B is significant. What is not contemplated by the expression "Valuable article" which would refer to tangible assets is sought to be brought in by using the expression "valuable thing" in order to describe or bring in intangible assets also. A "chose-in-action" would also be a thing and hence money kept in a bank will be a "valuable thing" so as to be covered by the provisions of section 132.

(viii) Seizure of passport

Passport provides the right to travel out of India to the passport-holder. Passport Authority is empowered to impound passport under certain circumstances as provided under Passport Act, 1867 and as per the order of the competent Court. Seizure of passport would mean to deny the constitutional right of the holder of the passport to go abroad. Therefore it will not be within the powers of Income Tax Authority to deny this right to the assessee.

In case there is material to believe that foreign travels have been made out of unaccounted money and passport can be used as an evidence to establish the concealment of income, it would be open to the authorized officer to take photocopy of the passport and in case required at any later stage assessee may be asked to produce original copy of passport for verification.

The power to impound or cancel a passport falls in the jurisdiction of the passport authority under the Passport Act. [*Smt. Maneka Gandhi v. UOI* AIR 1978 SC 597].

There will be similar position with reference to other licenses, Permits, Registration Certificates, PAN Card, Ration Card, Voters Identity Card, Driving License, Drug License, Factory License, SSI Certificate, Sales Tax or Excise Registration Certificate etc. These cannot be seized in original. However certified photocopy can be obtained and seized.

(ix) Immunity from seizure of special bearer bonds

As per departmental instruction, assessee possessing special bearer bonds cannot be enquired about the source of acquisition and no seizure can be made of such bonds. There should be no reference to these bonds even in the *panchnama*.

(x) Gold bonds

Gold bonds acquired by surrender of gold are exempt in the hands of such person from any enquiry about the source of investment under the Income tax Act or under the Wealth tax Act. The subsequent purchaser of such bonds does not enjoy the immunity regarding source of investment and in his hands, gold bonds can be seized.

(xi) Seizure of fixed deposit, NSC, KVP, shares etc.

These certificates or receipts representing deposits of the assessee with the bank, Govt. or other authority can be seized.

When such certificates are seized, an order u/s 132(3) is served on the assessee as well as the concerned branch of the bank to guard against the issue of duplicate receipts. Though validity of order under section 132(3) is for a period of 60 days only from the date of order, it has been noticed in practice that once such order is served on a bank, they do not release the proceeds of fixed deposits to the assessee without the permission of the income tax authority.

In case assessee attempts to get the duplicate copy of such receipts issued from the bank on the pretext of theft or misplacement, he is liable to be criminally prosecuted.

(xii) **Seizure of bank deposits in saving or current accounts**

There remains a question in the mind of the assessee whether during the course of search, operation of regular and declared bank accounts of the assessee or its business entities can be stopped or the deposits in these accounts can be seized. There is no power to stop the operation or seize the deposits lying in the disclosed saving or current accounts of the assessee maintained with the banks. In case there comes to the knowledge of the authorized officer any undisclosed or *Benami* bank account wherein unaccounted deposits are kept, prohibitory orders u/s 132(3) can be passed for such accounts and proceeds in such account can be seized by the authorized officer.

It has been held in the case of *Visa Comtrade Ltd.* v. *Union of India* [2011] 113 taxmann.com 44/201 Taxman 413 (Ori.) that prohibitory order under section 132(3) and the subsequent authorization and panchnama, *vis-à-vis* current account issued without forming any reasonable belief that the money lying in the current account wholly or partly represents undisclosed income of the petitioner were not valid and consequently action of the department in converting the money lying in the current account into demand draft/pay order in favour of CIT and withdrawing the same from the current account was also not valid. Department was directed to return the amount along with accrued interest into the current account of the petition-er-company.

It has been held in the case of *Strategic Credit Capital P. Ltd.* v. *Ratna-kar Bank Ltd.* [2017] 81 taxmann.com 408/395 ITR 391 (Delhi) that "Any money" and "other valuable article or thing does not exclude money in bank account. In a case where restraint order was issued on bank accounts of persons not subjected to search & where reason-able belief exists that these persons are in possession of undisclosed income of person subjected to search, it is then not necessary for separate search warrant in names of such persons & such person in respect of whom search is conducted is beneficial owner of monies in such accounts & thus restraint order and direction for provisional attachment of such accounts are valid.

(xiii) **Seizure of contents of bank locker**

Contents of Bank Locker of the assessee or his family members can be searched and seized.

In case information is already available with the authorized officer regarding the bank locker of the assessee, warrant of authorization may be issued to search such locker. If the information of bank locker is obtained during the course of search, separate authorization may be obtained by the authorized officer. In some cases, authorized officer passes order u/s 132(3) and assessee is asked to operate the locker alongwith authorized officer, bring the contents of the locker to his residence and then the same are seized.

In the case of bank lockers, authorized officer ensures soon after the information is obtained regarding the existence of some locker by issuing prohibitory order u/s 132(3) so that the same is not operated by the assessee. In case of any violation by the assessee, action under Indian Penal Code may be taken by the income tax department.

The order u/s 132(3) should be addressed to the assessee and copy of the same should be served to the bank. However, it is seen in practice, that order u/s 132(3) is addressed to the bank with respect to particular assessee prohibiting the operation of the locker. Technically, this procedure does not seem to be correct. An order u/s 132(3) can be addressed & served to the bank when authorization is obtained in the name of the bank itself.

(xiv) Seizure of antiques, paintings or work of art

Antiques being in the nature of valuable article or thing can be seized.

In case assessee is able to produce evidence regarding acquisition and holding of such items beyond the search years, the same cannot be treated as undisclosed income of the assessee u/s 153A and therefore, the same are not liable to be seized. In the case of antiques, registration certificate from the concerned authority in the name of assessee can be one of the evidences. In the absence of any evidence regarding the year and source of acquisition, the same may be treated as undisclosed income of the assessee for the current year and therefore such items are liable to be seized.

Seizure of such items can be either under clause (iii) by taking physical possession or under second proviso to section 132(1) by passing an order of deemed seizure.

Income tax authority cannot undertake any sale or auction of antiques or work of art in view of the provision of the Antiquities and Art Treasures Act, 1972 and any auction in this respect at any stage has to be taken in accordance with the provision of this Act.

It may be carefully noted that in view of the provisions of the Antiquities and Art Treasurer Act, the income tax authorities cannot undertake any sale/auction of antiquities. When an antiquity or art treasure is compulsorily acquired by the government, the compensation amount will be dealt with in accordance with the provisions of section 132/132B of the Income tax Act. If the Director General, Archaeological Survey of India advises that the Government is not interested in acquiring an antiquity, it will have to be sold, where necessary, through a licensed dealer. [Instruction No. 994-CBDT F. No. 286/37/76-IT (Inv.), dated 31-7-1976].

(xv) **Seizure of stock-in-trade**

After amendment of clause *(iii)* of section 132(1) and insertion of third proviso, by Finance Act, 2003 w.e.f. 1st June 2003, no seizure or deemed seizure of stock-in-trade of the business can be made.

Authorized officer is required to prepare inventory of such stock-in-trade of the business and decision regarding any undisclosed income with respect to the stock-in-trade shall be taken by the assessing officer at the time of assessment proceedings.

In case there are any items found from the possession of the assessee for which assessee is not doing any business activity, the same can be seized in the hands of the assessee as valuable article or thing and cannot be claimed to be in the nature of stock-in-trade.

It has been held in the case of *Puspa Ranjan Sachoo* v. *Asstt. Director of IT (Inv.)* [2012] 26 taxmann.com 83/210 Taxman 217 (Mag.) (Ori.) that in view of the specific provision contained in proviso to section 132(1)(*iii*) and third proviso to section 132(1)(*v*), bullion, jewellery or other valuable article or things being stock in trade of business found as a result of search could not be seized, even if said stock-in-trade represents wholly or partly undisclosed income or property of the assessee.

It has been held in the case of *Khem Chand Mukim* v. *Principal Director of IT (Inv.) & Ors.* 186 DTR (Del) 145 that reasons were, firstly, not recorded before undertaking the search and was therefore, completely unauthorized and a high-handed action on the part of the respondents. Also, Respondents do not state that Jewellery was concealed, or was kept by the assessee surreptitiously. Jewellery found in the assessee's possession was his stock-in-trade and consequently, he was entitled to the protection provided in the proviso appearing after sub-cl. *(iii)* to sub-s. (1) of s. 132 & thus search and seizure and *ex post facto* warrant of authorization dt.11th Sept., 2018 issued by respondent No. 2 under s. 132 was quashed with costs of Rs. 50,000 payable by Revenue.

It has been held in the case of *Harshvardhan Chhajed* v. *Director General of IT (Inv.)* [2021] 133 taxmann.com 478 (Raj.) that as to the search and seizure and authorisation under section 132(1), if the concerned person has shown documents in order to explain the goods which he is carrying and also gives a statement like in the present case that the articles were belonging to a firm and were part of stock-in-trade, there should be no seizure.

(*xvi*) **Seizure of foreign liquor or excess liquor**

No person is supposed to keep liquor or imported liquor in excess of quantity permitted under Excise or Customs laws. Any excess quantity found would be in violation of law. In suitable cases, the authorized officer may bring the matter to the notice of concerned authorities for taking appropriate action by them. The authorized officer may inventorize the quantity of liquor bottles which are found, so as to examine unaccounted investment, if any.

(*xvii*) **Seizure of fire arms or other weapons**

No person is permitted to keep unlicensed pistols, fire arms or other weapons. In case such arms are found in violation of the Arms Act, intimation may be sent to the concerned authority.

So long as any fire arms represent unaccounted income or asset whether such arms are licensed or unlicensed, it will be covered under clause (*c*) of section 132(1) and such unaccounted income is liable to be assessed in the hands of the assessee.

(*xviii*) **Seizure of foreign exchange**

In case foreign currency is found in excess of foreign currency permitted to be kept in accordance with the provision of FEMA, it may be reported to the concerned authority or Reserve Bank of India.

The decision of the seizure of the foreign exchange may be taken by the authorized officer keeping in view whether the same has been acquired out of unaccounted income.

(*xix*) **Seizure of promissory notes, hundies**

Promissory Notes and Hundies can be seized as these are assets falling in the category of valuable articles or things. Before the maturity of such Notes & Hundies, these should be realized and proceeds thereof can be retained, otherwise department may be dragged into litigation by the assessee for the loss.

As per Negotiable Instruments Act, a negotiable instrument means a promissory note, bill of exchange or cheque, payable either to order or to bearer. Therefore, cheques, pay orders, demand drafts, hundies or other instrument of the similar nature will also fall under the same category.

(xx) **Seizure of computers**

There is, now-a-days, more and more use of computers and electronic devices for maintaining records & books of account. Definition of "books of account" has been amended by the Finance Act, 2001, and now it includes printouts of data stored in a floppy, disc, tape or any other form of electromagnetic data storage device. Therefore, the authorized officer can seize computers and other electromagnetic device in which the data is stored.

The definition of "books of account" given u/s 2(*12A*) is debatable as, wordings used in the definition refer to books in the written form or printouts of data stored in hard disc or computers. Thus, one may argue that it is the printout of data stored in a floppy or disc etc. alone which can be said to be covered with in the definition of books of account and not the hard disc or floppy or pen drive etc. But, this interpretation is too mechanical and defies the well established principle that what is important is the substance and not the form. By this logic, floppy, pen drive or hard disc etc. containing the financial data would be treated as books of account and are liable to be seized.

Earlier department used to seize complete computer hardware (CPU) or laptop but they were finding it difficult to store the same in their possession due to lack of space. There hardly remains any material value of the hardware with the passage of time. The objective of seizure was never hardware but the software and data stored in it. Of late, it has been observed that as per internal departmental instruction, now only hard disc containing data is seized.

(xxi) **Seizure of books of account or other documents**

The authorized officer is empowered to seize any books of account or documents which in his opinion will be useful or relevant to any proceedings under the Income-tax Act. Books of account or other documents will include loose papers, diaries, registers, files, agreements, MOUs, affidavits etc.

In a business premises there are large volume of books of account, records, and files available. Authorized officer is not supposed to seize all such records. He is supposed to apply his mind and seize only those books of account or documents which may be useful and relevant for assessment proceedings.

"When in the course of a search, voluminous documents and books of account are to be examined with a view to judge whether they would be relevant, a certain amount of latitude must be permitted to the authorities. It is true that when particular documents are asked to be seized, unnecessary examination of other documents may conceivably make the search excessive. But, when documents, pieces of papers, exercise books, account books, small memos etc. have all to be examined with a view to see how far they are relevant for the proceeding under the Act, error of judgment is not unlikely. At the most this would be an irregularity, not an illegality". [*Pooran Mal* v. *Director of Inspection* [1974] 93 ITR 505 (SC)]

It is scarcely to be expected that at the stage of seizure there must be conclusive proof of the relevancy or usefulness of the material seized. [*Sri Venkateswara Lodge* v. *CIT* [1969] 71 ITR 629 (AP)]

In the case of *ITO* v. *Seth Bros.* [1969] 74 ITR 836, the Supreme Court held that where the warrant is issued in relation to a firm, the authority is not restricted to searching for and taking possession of only those books of account and other documents which directly relate to the business carried on by the partners in the name of the firm. The books of account and other documents in respect of other businesses carried on by the partners would certainly be relevant because they would tend to show the inter-relation between the dealings and supply materials having a bearing on the case of evasion of income tax by the firm. Entire search and seizure does not become illegal merely because the ITO, in a search of the firm, seized books of account and documents in relation to the business carried on by any one or more of the partners in the names of other firms or companies or of themselves.

In the case of *Naraindas* v. *CIT* [1983] 14 Taxman 447 (M.P.), it was held that search and seizure of books of the assessee in respect of business carried on in other commodities like oils, oil-seeds, grains, etc., in different names was justified on the ground that the clandestine business in coal was believed to be carried on by the assessee and that he would not produce the books pertaining to any suppressed business because a tax-evader normally does not produce such books of account, as and when required.

The principle that the seizure of any books of account or documents irrespective of whether they relate to some other person or to some other business will be justified, if they are found in the possession and control of the assessee against whom the search warrant is issued, is based on the premise that the books of account or other documents, though in the name of the other person or other business, will not or would not be produced in response to summons u/s 131 or notice u/s 142(1) and to that extent the conditions laid down in clauses (*a*) and (*b*) of sub-section (1) or section 132 are satisfied.

However, if there is no such inter-connection or likely detection of tax evasion, the seizure of books of account or other documents belonging to other persons would not be justified as in relation thereto it cannot be said that they would not be produced.

In *ITO* v. *Seth Bros.* [1969] 74 ITR 836 (SC), it was held that the mere fact that it may ultimately be found that some document seized is not directly relevant to any proceeding under the Act or that another officer with more information at his disposal may have come to a different conclusion will not be a ground for setting aside the order and the proceeding for search and seizure.

In *Balwant Singh* v. *Shah (R.D.), Director of Inspection* [1969] 71 ITR 550 (Delhi), it was held that while conducting the search, the authorized officer has necessarily to apply his mind and look for only such books of account and documents which will be relevant or useful to any proceedings. In searching or seizing the documents, the officers might have erred slightly here or there and seized documents, which on closer scrutiny, might ultimately turn out to be irrelevant but that does not vitiate the search.

(*xxii*) Seizure of deposits or proceeds from third parties

In the case of bank deposits with the bank, FDRs, claim of debt against promissory notes or bill of exchange, realization of National Saving Certificates or Kisan Vikas Patra or post office certificates or other Govt. securities, how to seize the same and realize the proceeds from third parties *i.e.* Bank, post office or other persons by the authorized officer is a grey area and proper procedure of the same is not laid down.

As discussed above, such instruments are valuable articles or things and can be seized by the department. But by seizing the document of such instruments, department does not get actual money. There is fixed maturity date of such instruments or time barring date of realization. After maturity date, assessee starts losing interest unless the instruments are renewed and in case of time barring instruments, assessee loses its rights to get the proceeds at all.

Any order passed u/s 132(3) is valid only for 60 days and order passed u/s 132(3) is not in the nature of order of seizure. The authorized officer does not have any power to direct or compel the third party to send the proceeds of such instruments to the income tax department. It can be done only by the Assessing Officer by passing order u/s 226(3) after demand is raised and recovery of demand remains outstanding.

The ideal situation for the authorized officer is to persuade the assessee and get the proceeds of such instruments realized through assessee and seize the amount in the account of the assessee. But in all cases this procedure may not be practicable to be adopted. In case demand of the assessee remains outstanding and assessee keeps on losing interest or other benefit on such instruments which remained seized, department may be dragged into litigation and authorized officer or Assessing Officer may be held responsible for carelessness in this regard and may be punished. There is need to provide proper system and procedure for such cases.

(xxiii) **Seizure of gifted items**

In case assessee claims that assets found from his possession are gifted or acquired as inherited, he is required to produce relevant evidences of such claim. Unless the authorized officer is satisfied regarding the genuineness of such claim and evidences, these assets are likely to be seized. After introduction of section 56(2)(*vii*), items of gifts received from other than relatives or on the occasion of wedding etc., are taxable in the hands of the recipients subject to specified limits.

In case assessee claims the gifts or jewellery received on the occasion of wedding, list of the donors along with their names and addresses should be prepared and produced. In the case of expensive gifts, the donors may be examined as to the source of gifts made in their hands.

In case imported items are gifted by friends visiting from abroad, the same may be taxable in the hands of the assessee in view of the latest amendment u/s 56(2) wherein receipt of movable assets without consideration or without adequate consideration have been made taxable in the hands of the recipients in certain circumstances. Assessee is required to keep and produce the evidence of their visit, letter declaring gift, evidence regarding payment of custom duty if applicable. The same may be useful to claim exemption if any allowable under the Act at the relevant time. In case such gifts are not taxable or if taxable, have been declared in the return of income and applicable taxes have been paid, no seizure of such gifted assets can be made.

(xxiv) **Seizure of loose papers or evidences, attempting to be destroyed by assessee**

In search cases, such kind of situation is encountered when assessee or his representative may try to run away with the assets, records or files. Sometimes papers, cash or jewellery may be thrown at the adjoining house with the neighbours, or assessee or some other person may try to run away with the same. The authorized officer can seize such records or assets after recording the complete incident in the presence of the witnesses. Any plea of the assessee at later stage that these evidences or assets have not been found and seized from his premises is of no consequence.

(xxv) Seizure of papers brought from outside

In some cases it has been experienced in practice that papers, diary or files purportedly found are brought from outside, and are made part of seizure and *Panchnama* of the assessee.

In one of the cases, department was having the information that assessee is keeping some diary containing details of undisclosed transactions at a shop in front of his residence. Some official from the search team went there, found the diary, brought it and included it in the evidences found and seized from the assessee. At later stage when this plea was taken by the assessee, the same could not be accepted since there was no mention in *Panchnama* that diary was brought from outside.

As per law there is no power to the authorized officer to bring any material or diary from outside even if it may be relating to assessee and it cannot be seized as part of seizure in his *Panchnama*. In case it is being so done, this fact should be got recorded in seizure memo or in the statement of the assessee recorded during search or immediate intimation of such fact should be given by the assessee to the authorized officer and to the higher authorities.

There is no power to seize any material or asset found and brought from outside or from the possession of some other person not within the premises of the assessee. The evidentiary value of such material is considerably reduced. Presumption of section 292C is not available to the department and onus to prove undisclosed income of the assessee based upon such document or diary is shifted to the department.

In case authorized officer wishes to seize such material, he has to obtain separate search warrant for that separate premises, wherein he suspects incriminating material relating to assessee is kept therein.

6.7 Manner of seizure - Taking physical possession

Seizure by its very meaning implies taking over physical possession. It means to take over actual physical possession and to keep the books of account, documents or assets in physical possession of the department by the authorized officer. For the sake of convenience, the concept of deemed seizure or constructive seizure has also been provided under second proviso to section 132(1) and is regarded as good as physical seizure by the department.

The procedure regarding manner and how assets seized are to be kept in physical possession of the department by the authorized officer are given under sub-rules (8), (9), (10), (11) & (12) and have been discussed in detail while analyzing the rules in **Chapter 5** regarding actual conduct of search:

(*i*) Assets found but not seized

There may be certain assets which are found during search but it is decided by the authorized officer not to seize the same. There may be cheque books, pass books of different bank accounts maintained in the name of different entities. Stock-in-trade of business is another item which cannot be seized but list of physical inventory found is prepared. There may be NSCs, KVPs, share certificates, FDRs, which are not seized by the authorised officer. Cash and jewellery to certain extent is not required to be seized as discussed earlier. However, in all such cases lists are prepared making notes of inventory of such items found but not seized. The objective is to make verification and to inquire regarding the source of such assets during assessment stage.

(*ii*) Placing of mark of identification on books of account and other documents

It is neither practical nor desirable to seize each and every book of account or document whether disclosed or undisclosed found at the premises during the course of search. The authorized officer using his discretion may seize only such books of account and other documents which he considers may be useful or relevant to any proceedings under the Act. Clause (*iv*) of section 132(1) empowers him to place marks of identification on any books of account or other documents. Proper list of books of account or documents identified is prepared mentioning the page No. on which identification has been marked. The manner of identification with a specimen is also recorded in the list. The objective is to call and verify the identified books of account or other documents at any stage later or during assessment proceedings.

(*iii*) Whether taking over keys amounts to seizure

Merely taking over keys of any locker, safe or almirah does not tantamount to seizure. Even order passed u/s 132(3) by putting seal or restraint does not mean seizure. For valid seizure, order under clause (*iii*) of section 132(1) has to be passed, Panchnama is to be prepared and physical possession has to be taken over by the authorized officer.

In *Bhagwandas Narayandas* v. *CIT* [1975] 98 ITR 194 (Guj.), Gujarat High Court held that by taking away of the keys, the seizure had not taken place. Commenting on the Gujarat High Court, Madras High Court observed at page 199 that the officer concerned was obliged to take the keys only with a view to see that the articles in the cupboard were not tampered with. [*Punamchand R. Shah* v. *ITO* [1975] 101 ITR 373 (Mad.)]

In *Mrs. Kanwal Shamsher Singh* v. *Union of India* [1974] 95 ITR 80 (Delhi), it was held that taking possession of the keys to the lockers in a safe deposit of company or restraining that company from operating on the lockers or making out inventories will not amount to 'seizure' of articles within the meaning of section 132(1).

7

RESTRAINT ORDER - SECTION 132(3) AND SECTION 132(8A)

In this Chapter, sub-section (3) and sub-section (8A) of section 132 are being discussed and analyzed.

7.1 Text of Section

Sub-section (3) of section 132 reads as under—

Sub-section (3)

(3) The authorized officer may, where it is not practicable to seize any such books of account, other documents, money, bullion, jewellery or other valuable article or thing {for reasons other than those mentioned in the second proviso to sub-section (1)}, serve an order on the owner or the person who is in immediate possession or control thereof that he shall not remove, part with or otherwise deal with it except with the previous permission of such officer and such officer may take such steps as may be necessary for ensuring compliance with this sub-section.

Explanation—For the removal of doubts, it is hereby declared that serving of an order as aforesaid under this sub-section shall not be deemed to be seizure of such books of account, documents, money, bullion, jewellery or other valuable article or thing under clause (*iii*) of sub-section (1).

Sub-section (8A) of section 132 reads as under—

Sub-section (8A)

(8A) An order under sub-section (3) shall not be in force for a period exceeding 60 days from the date of the order.

7.2 Legislative History

W.e.f. 1st April, 1989, concept of deemed seizure was introduced under section 132 by way of insertion of second proviso to section 132(1) by Finance Act, 1988. It was also provided u/s 132(3) that restraint order under this sub-section can be passed for reasons other than those mentioned in

265

the second proviso to sub-section (1). The nature of restraint order passed under this sub-section is different from the order of deemed seizure passed under the second proviso to sub-section (1) of section 132. Further by way of *Explanation* to sub-section (3) introduced by Direct Tax Laws (Amendment) Act, 1987 with effect from 1-4-1989, it was clarified that order passed under this sub-section shall not be treated as order of seizure of books of account, other documents or assets.

Sub-section (8A) of section 132 was substituted w.e.f. 1st June 2002, providing that order under sub-section (3) shall not be in force for a period exceeding 60 days from the date of the order. Earlier, this sub-section used to provide for extension of this period with the approval of Director or Commissioner up to 30 days after the completion of all the proceedings under the Act. Due to the provision of extension given earlier in this sub-section, it was not serving the purpose for which the sub-section was intended to be legislated and it was felt that the power of restraint was prone to be misused. The assessees were facing a lot of practical hardships and inconvenience in smooth operation of the business.

7.3 Objective

The objective of giving powers to the authorized officer to pass the order of restraint under section 132(3) seems to provide him reasonable time to take decision regarding seizure of books of account, other documents or assets before concluding the search. It may not be possible for the authorized officer to operate all the bank lockers, appraise all the evidences found, take decision regarding seizure after being satisfied whether the same are undisclosed or not and to conclude the search proceedings at a stretch. The authorized officer gets reasonable time for taking such decision before concluding the search due to the presence of this power to pass order of restraint. On the other hand, assessee also gets an opportunity to produce evidences to prove whether the assets are disclosed so that the same may not be seized and further also, he gets opportunity to make declaration of undisclosed income etc. under section 132(4) before conclusion of the search.

7.4 When can restraint order under section 132(3) be passed?

Restraint order u/s 132(3) can be passed when it is not practicable to seize any such books of account, other documents, money, bullion, jewellery or other valuable article or thing.

In case seizure of any valuable article or thing is not possible due to its volume, weight or other physical characteristics or due to being of dangerous nature, the authorized officer has the powers to make deemed seizure of such assets as prescribed under second proviso to section 132(1). Restraint order under this sub-section (3) can be passed for reasons other than those mentioned in the second proviso to sub-section (1). Such other reasons may be, *inter alia*, long search hours causing fatigue to the assessee and search team members, coordination with the banker to be done for operation of the locker, time to be given to the assessee to produce evidences regarding disclosure of assets etc.

(*i*) Not practicable to seize - Meaning

The words used in this sub-section *"not practicable to seize"* are significant. It indicates impliedly that restrain under section 132(3) can be passed only under the circumstances when it is not practicable to seize the books of account, other documents or assets found during search. There may be various reasons for such situation such as-

   a. Long hours of search causing fatigue to the assessee and search team members.

   b. Coordination with the banker to be done for operation of the locker.

   c. Time to be given to the assessee to produce evidences regarding disclosure of assets etc.

   d. Bank deposits or debts recoverable are not practicable to be seized under section 132(1)(*iii*) due to the nature of such assets but restraint under section 132(3) can be passed pending decision for seizure in appropriate manner.

Power under this sub-section to impose restraint order has been given when there is practical difficulty in making effective seizure during search. To take the decision of seizure in an effective, equitable and just manner, this power provides reasonable time on the part of authorized officer to make correct decision of seizure. At the same time, it gives reasonable time to the assessee to explain the source or produce the evidences regarding disclosed nature of the assets so that the same are not seized.

The contingencies contemplated by sub-section (3) of section 132 of the Act, could be other than those provided in the second proviso to sub-section (1) of section 132. Such a contingency could be due to physical causes or mental incapacity of the concerned officer due to over strain. The reasons as contemplated under sub-section (3) of section 132 of the Act pertain to impracticability rather than impossibility. [*State of Maharashtra* v. *Narayan Champalal Bajaj* [1993] 201 ITR 315 (Bom.)]

There may be a number of reasons which can make it impracticable to seize documents and valuable things. The word "impracticable" indicates that, for some good and valid reason, it is not possible to seize the valuable articles or the books of account. Section 132(3) would apply only in those cases where the second proviso to section 132(1) does not apply. Where it is not practicable to seize the account books and valuable articles for the reason stated in the second proviso to section 132(1), a restraint order would not be applicable. But where it is not practicable to do so for any other reason, then a restraint order will be regarded as having been validly passed under section 132(3) and the restraint order will continue till a formal seizure is effected. *B.K. Nowlakha* v. *Union of India* [1991] 192 ITR 436 (Del.)

In the case of *B.K. Nowlakha* v. *Union of India* [1991] 192 ITR 436 (Del.) it was held that not knowing the value of the articles or whether they are antiques or not cannot be regarded as a practical difficulty on the part of the authorized officer in effecting seizure.

In practice it has been observed that restraint order under section 132(3) is passed with respect to some bank locker or almirah, safe with certain documents or loose papers or jewellery kept inside for some oblique purpose such as to keep the search pending. That is a different thing that this practice does not have statutory backing & administratively also, it is not considered desirable. This time may be utilized by the authorized officer for recording statement of the assessee under section 132(4), getting explanation regarding the seized documents and for enabling the assessee to make surrender of undisclosed income. Technically, search is concluded when all restraint orders passed under this sub-section are lifted.

(ii) **Restraint order only for books of account, other documents or assets which can be seized**

Use of the words *"not practicable to seize"* in this sub-section clearly implies that only those books of account, other documents or assets which are liable to be seized can alone be put under restraint by the authorized officer. Disclosed assets cannot be seized. Therefore, restraint order cannot be passed in respect of the disclosed assets. Immovable property cannot be seized under the law. Therefore, no restraint order can be passed in respect of the immovable property either for sealing of whole of the shop or the office premises or otherwise. No restraint order can be passed against the operation of regular bank account of the assessee unless the same is benami or undisclosed account.

After insertion of proviso to clause *(iii)* to section 132(1), stock-in-trade of the business cannot be seized. Therefore, it implies that no restraint order on stock-in-trade can be passed. In practice, it has however been observed that restraint order is passed under section 132(3) on business inventory items or on the movement of goods *i.e.* receipt and dispatch of the goods on the pretext that physical counting of inventory items is pending. The impracticability of physical counting of inventory items during search and to defer this exercise by putting restraint order does not seem to be a situation covered within the scope of section 132(3). The reason of impracticability can be applied only for those assets which can be seized. The test of impracticability cannot be extended for any other circumstances other than for seizure.

Order prohibiting the bank from honouring the cheques for payment to employees, was held not valid. *Windson Electronics Pvt. Ltd.* v. *Union of India* [2004] 141 Taxman 419 (Cal.)

When the authorized officer is not satisfied or he has doubts as to whether particular ornaments found during search are undisclosed property, he cannot have recourse to provisions contained in sub-section (3) of section 132. *Om Parkash Jindal* v. *Union of India* [1976] 104 ITR 389 (P&H).

The articles or things referred to in sub-section (3) of section 132 are those which authorized officer was empowered to search for and seize and no other. *Ramesh Chander* v. *CIT* [1974] 93 ITR 244 (P&H).

Obviously the authorized officers conducting a search cannot be expected to be continuously present in the searched premises till the entire exercise is over. There may be administrative and other practical difficulties in continuing the search for days together. In case of such practical difficulties, where the search is not completed sub-section (3) authorizes the Officer to serve a restraint order.............. such an order can be passed even where a part of the premises could not be covered during the search and where for administrative or several other reasons the Officers conducting the search are obliged to leave the premises............The officers place a restraint on the owner or the person in possession for the temporary period so that search can be revived at a later point of time and continued. Taking all these into consideration, it is not possible to jump-if the expression can be used- to the conclusion that the passing of a prohibitory order under sub-section (3), is in all cases only to extend the period of limitation, without any fact any circumstances or evidence justifying the conclusion. It may happen in extreme cases that prohibitory order was passed without justification. In such cases courts have come down heavily on such attempts and have seen through the game and held that the restraint orders have no useful purpose to serve and therefore the search must be deemed to have been concluded much earlier. But, in a *bona fide* case where there is no such attempt and the prohibitory order is passed in the normal course and for *bona fide* reasons, the search cannot be deemed to have been concluded on the day on which the said order was passed ....section 132(8A) gives a period of sixty days for the tenure of the restraint order. In the present case the restraint order was effective only for a period of 34 days, which is well in the period of 60 days mentioned in section 132(8A). It cannot be therefore said to be operative for an unreasonably long period. What seems to have happened in the present case is that the documents in the drawer at the ground floor of the premises were not examined by the authorized officers and that is the reason why they resorted to section 132(3), so that they can be seized at a later point of time to find out whether they represent any undisclosed income.............. [*Smt. Krishna Verma* v. *Asstt. CIT* [2008] 113 ITD 655 (Delhi-Trib.) (SB)].

If it is practicable to seize the books of account u/s 132(1), then the Authorized Officer should do so. If it is not possible to do so, authorized officer may then pass a restraint order u/s 132(3). Prior to its amendment in 2002, section 132(8A) provided that an order passed u/s 132(3) shall not be in force for a period exceeding sixty days, except where an extension is granted for reasons to be recorded in writing. Assuming for the sake of argument that the books of account of the petitioner could be seized but were not seized (wrongly), the seizure could have been affected on 22.06.1998, (the first day). The last Panchnama was drawn on 5.08.1998 well before the sixty days period was to expire. Therefore, no ulterior motives can be attributed to the respondents in failing to seize the books of account and instead passing a restraint order in this respect. [*VLS Finance Ltd.* v. *CIT* [2007] 159 Taxman 102 (Delhi)]

(*iii*) Restraint order only in respect of an asset representing concealed income

In the case of *Om Prakash Jindal* v. *Union of India* [1976] 104 ITR 389, Punjab and Haryana High Court observed on this aspect as follows:

> "Before making a seizure the authorized officer has to investigate the matter. The provisions contained in section 132(4) empower him to examine the person found in possession and control of assets. The said investigation may not be full enquiry or of the nature as contemplated by sub-section (5) of section 132. It may be summary, oral or otherwise as permissible in the circumstances of a given case. The result of the said investigation or enquiry may be:
>
> a. that there are no grounds to believe reasonably that the same are undisclosed property; or
>
> b. that the authorized officer has reason to believe that the particular ornaments etc., found in the search, are undisclosed property; or
>
> c. that he has doubt respecting the said ornaments and jewellery being undisclosed property.

It is only in the case of his satisfaction in (*b*) above that the authorized officer would seize the ornaments, jewellery, money, etc., under clause (*iii*) of sub-section (1) of section 132. In the cases mentioned in (*a*) or (*c*), the authorized officer would not be competent or empowered to seize the ornaments, jewellery or money and it is also doubtful that he can take action under sub-section (3) of section 132 respecting those ornaments, bullion or money."

Hon'ble Punjab and Haryana High Court has taken a very strict view and has held that the authorized officer before passing order u/s 132(3) should have reason to believe that the asset is undisclosed property. In case he has any doubt, restraint order cannot be passed for such asset.

The amount declared under the Amnesty Scheme, by each of the petitioners was deposited in their own names and the petitioners were actually the account holders. In that view of the matter, the prohibitory order u/s 132(3) in respect of the bank accounts were held liable to be quashed. [*Mst. Anisa Bano* v. *CIT* [1989] 42 Taxman 184 (MP)]

In practice it does not so happen. With respect to any asset found during search, onus lies upon the assessee to prove that it is a disclosed asset. The authorized officer goes with the presumption that any asset found during search is undisclosed unless otherwise proved by the assessee. The authorized officer usually passes order u/s 132(3) for any asset unless assessee proves that it is a disclosed asset.

(*iv*) **Restraint order not to be used as a tool for temporary suspension of search**

The powers of passing restraint order u/s 132(3) cannot be used by the authorized officer to defer the search operation and resume it on a later date. The search operation of the entire premises is expected to be completed at a stretch as far as possible having regard to human limitations. Due to long hours of working and resultant tiredness of the search team, search operations may be temporarily suspended but it should be resumed as early as possible thereafter. Restraint order cannot be passed for a portion of premises or for certain place to gain time and keep the search pending for oblique purposes.

By simply stating in the Panchnama that the search was temporarily suspended, the authorized officer could not keep the search proceedings in operation by passing a restraint order u/s 132(3). *CIT* v. *Sandhya P. Naik* [2002] 124 Taxman 384 (Bom.)

(*v*) **Power under section 132(3) not to be used to keep the search operation pending**

Powers of restraint order u/s 132(3) should not be used by the department to keep the search operation pending. In practice it has however been observed that the department uses this power for deferring the conclusion of search for several reasons which may not have statutory backing. The deferment of the conclusion of search may be useful to the authorized officer-

a. to enable the assessee to give statement u/s 132(4) and explain the nature and contents of documents seized.

b. to enable the assessee to make surrender of undisclosed income by way of statement u/s 132(4).

c. to get extended time for preparation of appraisal report.

d. to obtain extended time for limitation for assessment u/s 153A.

It has also been observed in practice that the powers of restraint u/s 132(3) are used by the authorized officer to build pressure and to persuade the assessee for declaration of undisclosed income. The search team may visit the premises of the assessee again on the ground of lifting restraint order. As a result, assessee always remains under pressure till all the restraints are lifted and search is concluded.

Action under section 132(3) can be resorted to only if there is any practical difficulty in seizing the item which is liable to be seized. When there is no such practical difficulty, the officer is left with no other alternative but to seize the item, if he is of the view that it represented undisclosed income. The position has become much clear after the insertion of the *Explanation* to section 132(3) effective from 1.4.1989 that a restraint order does not amount to seizure. Therefore, by passing a restraint order, the time limit available for framing of the order cannot be extended.

CIT v. *Sandhya P. Naik* [2002] 124 Taxman 384 (Bom.)

Delhi High Court in the case of *CIT* v. *S.K. Katyal* [2009] 177 Taxman 380 (Delhi), after taking into account the decisions of *CIT* v. *Sarb Consulate Marine Products (P.) Ltd.* [2007] 164 Taxman 299 (Delhi), *CIT* v. *Deepak Aggarwal* [2008] 175 Taxman 1 (Delhi), *M.B. Lal* v. *CIT* [2005] 149 Taxman 490 (Del.), *VLS Finance Ltd.* v. *CIT* [2007] 159 Taxman 102 (Del.), *Dr. C. Balakrishna Nair* v. *CIT* [1999] 103 Taxman 242 (Ker.) and *CIT* v. *Sandhya P. Naik* [2002] 124 Taxman 384 (Bom.) held

"....these decisions clearly establish - (*i*) a search is essentially an invasion of the privacy of the person whose property or person is subjected to search (*ii*) normally a search must be continuous (*iii*) if it cannot be continuous for some plausible reason, the hiatus in the search must be explained (*iv*) if no cogent or plausible reason is shown for the hiatus in the search, the second or 'resumed' search would be illegal (*v*) by merely mentioning in panchnama *i.e.* search has been temporarily suspended does not, *ipso facto*, continue the search. It would have to be seen as a fact as to whether the search continued or had concluded (*vi*) merely because a panchnama is drawn up a particular date, it does not mean that a search was conducted and/or concluded on that date (*vii*) the panchnama must be a record of search or seizure for it to qualify as the panchnama mentioned in *Explanation 2(a)* to section 158BE of the said Act".

7.5 Manner of passing order under section 132(3)

(*i*) Broad Framework

The broad framework according to which order under section 132(3) is passed is as under:

     a. Order under section 132(3) is passed by the authorized officer during the course of search.

     b. An order under section 132(3) is passed against the owner or the person who is in immediate possession or control of the things to be put under restraint.

     c. Order under section 132(3) is passed with a specific direction that he shall not remove, part with or otherwise deal with it except with the previous permission of such officer.

     d. Such officer may take such steps as may be necessary for ensuring compliance with this sub-section.

The effect of passing restraint order is to keep the books of account, other documents or assets with respect to which order is passed on *"as is where is basis"*.

Also, the restraint order has to be in writing and oral order is without jurisdiction. [*Raj Kumar* v. *Union of India* [2000] 110 Taxman 483 (P&H)].

Assessee cannot be held responsible for the contravention of restraint order under section 132(3) unless the authorized officer takes effective steps in matter of ensuring compliance with his order under section 132(3). Steps that can be taken to ensure the compliance of order may include putting lock or sealing of box, almirah or door of the room etc. In case of doubt, proper security arrangements can be made. This will also include preparation of proper inventory before leaving the contents in the custody of assessee or his representative.

In the case of *Sriram Jaiswal* v. *Union of India* [1989] 42 Taxman 83 (All.), Hon'ble Allahabad High Court pointed out that according to provisions of section 132(3), the restrained assets cannot be dealt with, except with the prior permission of the officer passing the restraint order, but there is no machinery provided in the section to deal with the situation arising out of refusal by the officer of the permission sought by the assessee in terms of section 132(3) for dealing with the assets. However, now after amendment to sub-section (8A), this problem has been mitigated because in any case, authorized officer has to lift restraint order passed by him within a period of sixty days.

(ii) Whether reasons to be recorded before passing restraint order

The authorized officer is not required to record reasons before passing an order under section 132(3). It is the subjective satisfaction of the authorized officer. He has to satisfy himself on two counts:-

  a. There exist books of account, other documents or assets which are liable to be seized. The assets represent concealed income of the assessee not disclosed to the department.

  b. It is not practicable to seize such assets, books of account, and documents due to some reason.

The satisfaction of the authorized officer that assets to be put under restraint represent concealed income may be based upon the facts coming to his knowledge at the time of search or as per evidences produced before him by the assessee during the course of search. It is not as if he must have "reason to believe" that assets to be put under restraint represent undisclosed income. It can be on the basis of reason to suspect particularly when nature of assets is not clear. In case of bank locker which could not be operated during the search and put under restraint u/s 132(3), the contents inside the locker are not known to the authorized officer and he has reason to suspect that it may contain undisclosed assets.

(iii) Prohibitory order, to be addressed to the assessee

The moneys deposited in an account, current or saving, in a bank by a customer, belong to the bank and the bank has full control and right to use the money as it likes. The bank is only obliged to honour the cheques issued by the customer if it is a proper cheque and drawn up in a proper manner. The proper way in which an order under section 132(3) should be worded in such a situation, is to address the customer who had deposited the money in the bank account or accounts directing him not to remove, part with or otherwise deal with the money except with the permission of the "Officer". If, therefore, instead of addressing the order to the customer, the order is addressed to the bank, the customer cannot be said to have been aggrieved.

ITO v. *M. Shajahan* [1976] 104 ITR 347 (Ker.)

Jain & Jain v. *UOI* [1982] 8 Taxman 48 (Bom.)

Where a firm was operating with their own undisclosed income, a number of bank accounts in benami names, issue of a prohibitive order under section 132(3) cannot to be held to be illegal or unsustainable.

7.6 Period of validity of restraint order

(i) Restraint order to expire after sixty days

After substitution of sub-section (8A) w.e.f. 1st June, 2002, a restraint order passed under section 132(3) shall remain in operation upto sixty days from the date of order. After expiry of sixty days, such order will lapse automatically and no seizure of any asset can be made thereafter which were put under restraint. The authorized officer is required to lift the restraint within sixty days and take decision regarding seizure of the assets. There is no provision u/s 132(8A) for extension of time limit to keep the restraint order pending as it used to be earlier prior to 1-6-2002.

Time limit of 60 days provided under section 132(8A) is mandatory and the authorized officer had no jurisdiction to withhold the seized articles after expiry of the said period. - *Mahesh Kumar Agarwal* v. *Dy. DIT (Inv.)* [2003] 133 Taxman 520 (Cal.)

(ii) Restraint order cannot be renewed from time to time

When section 132(8A) clearly provides that a restraint order in relation to one set of search and seizure action will lose its force upon the expiry of sixty days, the same cannot be brought back to life in any manner whatsoever. A fresh restraint order can be issued in relation to fresh and different action and not in relation to the same action previously taken. The submission that, in the absence of a contrary provision, it is open for the Revenue officials to pass under section 132(3) afresh in relation to the same search and seizure action is unacceptable.

Windson Electronics (P.) Ltd. v. *UOI* [2004] 141 Taxman 419 (Cal.)

The provision of section 132(8A) cannot be bypassed or rendered nugatory by revoking an order under section 132(3) and thereafter passing another order on the same date. [*B.K. Nowlakha* v. *Union of India* [1991] 192 ITR 436 (Del.)]

(iii) To complete proceedings expeditiously

It has been held in the case of *Shri Ganesh Enterprises Pvt. Ltd.* v. *Union of India* [1994] 75 Taxman 239 (Delhi) that enquiry under section 132(3) should be completed expeditiously.

7.7 Restraint order in respect to which kind of assets

(i) Immovable property

Restraint order can be passed with respect to assets which are liable to be seized. Immovable property cannot be seized and therefore, restraint order with respect to immovable property is not valid.

CIT v. *M.K. Gabrial Babu* [1991] 57 Taxman 146 (Ker.)

Sardar Paraduman Singh v. *Union of India* [1987] 31 Taxman 515 (Delhi), SLP dismissed in 168 ITR (St.) 3 (SC)

(ii) Bank lockers

Restraint order can be passed with respect to bank lockers of the assessee when authorized officer believes that the bank locker contains evidences relating to undisclosed income of the assessee. Restraint order can be served on the banker who is in immediate possession or control thereof with a copy to the assessee.

(iii) Intangible assets, debts recoverable

Intangible assets, debts recoverable, equity shares, bonds, promissory notes, hundis, chose-in-action, are covered within the definition of *"valuable article or thing"* and are liable to be seized. Such assets don't have value of physical contents but nevertheless are valuable assets which may be converted into money by realization. Restraint order can be passed under section 132(3) with respect to such assets. In what manner seizure of such assets can be made has been discussed in the chapter of seizure of assets. The object behind using the expression "valuable thing" is to describe and to bring in intangible assets also within the purview of section 132.

Order under section 132(3) may also cover debts, notwithstanding the specific provisions of sections 226(5) and 281B. *I. Devarajan* v. *Tamil Nadu Farmers Service Co-operative Federation* [1981] 131 ITR 506 (Mad.)

(iv) Bank accounts, fixed deposits

Disclosed bank accounts are not liable to be seized. Therefore, no restraint order under section 132(3) can be passed with respect to the disclosed bank accounts. However, undisclosed bank accounts or benami bank accounts representing undisclosed income of the assessee can be put under restraint under section 132(3).

The credit balance in an account is money kept in the bank and does not cease to be money merely because the relationship between the banker and customer is that of creditor and debtor. Even assuming that a bank deposit is not money, it would at any rate be covered by the expression "valuable thing". Thus, an order under section 132(3) can be made in respect of bank balance including fixed deposit. *I. Devarajan* v. *Tamil Nadu Farmers Service Co-operative Federation* [1981] 131 ITR 506 (Mad.).

The Madras High Court in the case of *I. Devarajan (supra)* held that they did not find the Gujarat High Court's decision in *Bhagwandas*

Narayandas v. *CIT* [1975] 98 ITR 194 to assist the contention that no action under section 132 could be taken in respect of a bank deposit. High Court further observed that the decision of Kerala High Court in *ITO* v. *M. Shajahan* [1976] 104 ITR 347 also did not support the contention that prohibition orders could not be issued under section 132(3) in respect of a credit bank balance.

In *M.V. Gnanendra Nath* v. *Union of India* [2004] 134 Taxman 766 (Kar.), it was held that as the amount of the fixed deposit has remained with the bank or other financial institution on account of prohibitory order u/s 132(3) even after the date of maturity, the bank and other financial institution were directed to pay interest on the deposit amount from the date of maturity till actual payment at the contract rate subject to fluctuations in the rates as prescribed by the Reserve Bank of India from time to time.

(*v*) **Indiscriminate restraint on Bank Accounts**

As and when places or persons of diverse activities and unconnected with each other are searched and their bank accounts are frozen by the authority to get or gather materials and information to form a belief that the assessee is avoiding tax, it is wholly outside the scope of the search and seizure under the said Act. *Mahesh Kumar Agarwal* v. *Dy. DIT (Inv.)* [2003] 133 Taxman 520 (Cal.)

It has been held in the case of *Maa Vaishnavi Sponge Ltd.* v. *Director General of Income-tax (Investigation)* [2012] 21 taxmann.com 512 (Orissa) that in view of no evidence that deposits in banks constituted undisclosed income of assessee, prohibitory order u/s 132(3) was not valid.

(*vi*) **Stock-in-trade**

Prior to insertion of proviso to section 132(1)(*iii*) by the Finance Act, 2003, providing that the stock-in-trade in business cannot be seized, there was no dispute regarding restraint order to be passed in respect of godown, warehouse where stock-in-trade is kept. In the case of *Sriram Jaiswal* v. *UOI* [1989] 42 Taxman 83 (All.), issuance of prohibitory order on warehouse was upheld.

But the position has changed w.e.f. 1st June, 2003. Now since stock-in-trade cannot be seized, one can safely interpret that no restraint order under section 132(3) can be passed with respect to stock-in-trade.

There is however a practical difficulty faced by the Department in the conduct of search regarding preparation of the list of physical inventory of stock-in-trade. As per clause (*v*) of section 132(1) authorized officer is required to prepare list of physical inventory of items of stock but at times it is a very lengthy process. Inventory list may not be possible to be prepared within one or two days and the process of conduct of search has to be deferred. Question as to whether restraint order can be passed with respect to stock-in-trade till physical stock inventory is not completed remains a disputed point. One can argue that to achieve the purpose of the search, it may be possible for the authorized officer to issue restraint order for limited purpose of quickly preparing inventory of stock-in-trade. But any such restraint order creates other hindrance to the assessee. The movement of goods cannot take place even for conducting the business. The incoming of material and dispatch of goods cannot take place. Now-a-days, manufacturers work on zero inventory concept and any delay in dispatch of goods may cause stoppage of manufacturing line and financial damages to the assessee. The normal business operations of the assessee get hampered and the very purpose of making amendment under clause (*iii*) gets defeated.

In view of the above, the tilt of the arguments is more in favour of the assessee and restraint order on stock-in-trade does not seem to be possible any more and does not accord with the legislative intent in the context of the provisions presently contained under section 132(1)(*iii*).

(*vii*) Operation of Computers

It has been observed that sometimes restraint order is passed with respect to operation of computers, particularly those devices which contain financial & production/dispatch data. Now-a-days, books of account are maintained on computers or other electronic devices. Books of account are liable to be seized. Therefore, restraint order can be passed with respect to computers containing data in electronic devices. But it should be done only when it is not practicable to seize the electronic data during search.

The restraint order passed, if any, with respect to operation of computers has to be lifted as early as possible. Non-operation of computers may bring the whole business operation to halt and under such circumstances, normal business activities may be hampered.

(*viii*) Whether restraint order can be put on whole premises

Sealing of whole of the premises is not permissible under section 132. Restraint can be put on some box, almirah or room containing undisclosed material which is not practicable to be seized due to some reason during search. But to put restraint on whole premises is not permissible.

However, there may be situation when premises could not be searched since the same was found locked and occupant of the premises was not available. Instead of breaking the lock and entering into the premises, the authorized officer may decide to wait for the occupant to reach and in the meanwhile, the premises may be sealed for intermediary period. Such act undertaken in *bona fide* manner to carry the legal compliance of search warrant is justified.

Question is that the seizure or restraint of the unaccounted wealth is not in violation of the constitutional provision including Article 19(1)(*g*). How can an act of ensuring the compliance of legal order of restraint may be so? But, at the same time, the sealing of a shop or an office or a factory beyond the time minimum required for the purpose of ensuring compliance with the order under section 132(3) may become invalid, but not the basic act of sealing itself so long as it is *bona fide* and not for collateral purposes as was found by High Court in the case before their Lordships. [*Shyam Jewellers* v. *Chief Commissioner (Admn.) UP* [1992] 196 ITR 243 (All.).]

7.8 Nature of restraint order

(*i*) Restraint order doesn't amount to seizure

Explanation to sub-section (3) has been inserted w.e.f. 1-4-1989 by Direct Tax Laws (Amendment) Act, 1987 which provides, *inter alia*, that serving an order under section 132(3) shall not be deemed to be seizure of such books of account, other documents, money, bullion, etc., under clause (*iii*) of sub-section (1).

After insertion of above *Explanation* and further substituting sub-section (8A) of section 132 by which validity of order under section 132(3) has been restricted to sixty days, the legislative intent has been made very clear regarding nature of power of restraint order given under section 132(3). Even prior to above amendment, Delhi High Court in the case of *Mrs. Kanwal Shamsher Singh* v. *UOI* [1974] 95 ITR 80 (Punj. & Har.) and Punjab and Haryana High Court in the case of *Ramesh Chander* v. *CIT* [1974] 93 ITR 244 (Punj. & Har.) have held that an exercise of power under section 132(3) does not amount to seizure. Delhi High Court in the case of *B.K Nowlakha* v. *UOI* [1991] 192 ITR 436 (Delhi) had also held that the powers under section 132(3) cannot be used to circumvent the provisions of section 132(1) or the erstwhile section 132(5).

Where there is a restraint under section 132(3) it cannot be deemed to be a seizure. *CIT* v. *Sarb Consulate Marine Products (P.) Ltd.* [2007] 164 Taxman 299 (Delhi)

After amendment to section 132(3), the above ratio pronounced by the Courts has been legislated and there does not remain any iota of confusion regarding nature of the restraint order. Restraint order is not an order of seizure and in case authorized officer wants to seize the asset put under restraint, he has to pass separate order seizing the assets under section 132(1)(*iii*).

This proposition has been confirmed by Bombay High Court in the case of *CIT* v. *Sandhya P. Naik* [2002] 124 Taxman 384 (Bom.).

(*ii*) Restraint order, not for recovery-

As section 132(3) contemplates a prohibitory order not to deal with, *inter alia*, the monies deposited by the petitioner with the bank, except with the prior permission of the authorized officer, such a prohibitory order cannot direct to convert the amount so deposited by the petitioner by preparing a draft in favour of the Commissioner. *Santosh Verma* v. *UOI* [1991] 189 ITR 549 (Patna)

It may however be clarified that the ratio of these judgments is to be interpreted only to the extent to mean that in exercise of powers under section 132(3), the authorized officer cannot direct the bank to convert an FDR into cash or bank account into demand draft, payable to the Tax Department. But it does not mean that FDRs cannot be restrained under section 132(3). The FDRs being in the nature of debt due by bank fall in the category of the term "valuable thing", which is liable to be seized as well as restraint.

Since the authorized officer has power under section 132(3) to serve a restraint order on the person who is in immediate possession or control thereof, the authorized officer may restrain bank authority not to allow the person searched to operate the bank account, locker etc.

7.9 Consequences of contravention

(*i*) Consequences of invalid restraint order passed

In case restraint order is passed which is held to be invalid, it will not vitiate the whole process of search. Search cannot be treated as illegal for this reason only. This is an irregularity and at the most assessee can claim to set right adverse consequences, if any, fallen back on assessee due to such invalid restraint order having been passed.

In case the officers of the department on the basis of the material before them have decided to pass order of restraint, the same cannot be said to be an act of bad faith, nor could the act be *mala fide*. Actions of the department at times may be erroneous, but all erroneous actions cannot be said to be *mala fide*.

Bansal Exports (P.) Ltd. v. *UOI* [1996] 84 Taxman 373 (Delhi)

(*ii*) **Prosecution for contravention of restraint order passed under section 132(3)**

Contravention of an order under sub-section (3) of section 132 is punishable under section 275A of the Income Tax Act, 1961 with rigorous imprisonment which may extend to two years and shall also be liable to fine.

Accused cutting the almirah under prohibitory orders of ITO under section 132(3) and removing jewellery therefrom was rightly pro-secuted for offences under section 275A of Income Tax Act. *State of Maharashtra* v. *Narayan Champalal Bajaj* [1993] 201 ITR 315 (Bom.)

However, in *State* v. *Rakesh Aggarwal* [1995] 80 Taxman 539 (Del.), there was no material on record to show that the order u/s 132(3) was served on the accused. Neither the missing documents were recovered from the accused nor accused was entrusted with the responsibility of guarding the seal. It was held that merely on suspicion it could not be held that the accused was guilty of offence of breaking the seal.

(*iii*) **Undue delay in lifting restraint order**

Restraint order has to be lifted as early as possible. After amendment to sub-section (8A), now the maximum time available with the authorized officer for continuing the restraint order is sixty days from the date of the order. As per internal departmental instructions, authorized officer is not supposed to wait till the last day for lifting restraint but he is required to do it as early as possible.

Lifting of restraint order at an early date is very important. Search can be technically said to be concluded when all the authorizations are executed. A search authorization can be said to be executed when all the restraint orders passed in pursuance to that authorization are lifted. Any delay in lifting restraint order keeps the search pending. Non-conclusion of search within a reasonable time has got further consequences regarding subsequent time barring actions to be taken in pursuance of search.

........Section 132(3) comes into operation when it is not possible to seize any valuable article or thing for reason, other than those mentioned in the second proviso to sub-section (1) and by an *Explanation* added to section 132(3), it is made clear that the serving of an order u/s 132(3) shall not be deemed to be seizure of such valuable article or thing...........Passing an order under section 132(3) was not at all warranted given the nature of the articles, *i.e.* fishing trawlers. The action for seizing the fishing trawlers ought to have been taken by the revenue u/s 132(1) and not u/s 132(3). By merely resorting to restraining order u/s 132(3),........The revenue could not have extended the time limit for passing an assessment order. *CIT* v. *Sarb Consulate Marine Products (P.) Ltd.* [2007] 164 Taxman 299 (Delhi).

It has been held in the case of *CIT* v. *Ritika Limited* [2017] 80 taxmann. com 255/[2016] 384 ITR 434 (Cal.) that for the purpose of limitation, period is to be reckoned from date of conclusion of search & thus where restraint order was not extended and no action was taken pursuant to search after three months, Search has to be taken to have been concluded on expiry of restraint order & visit of officers to assessee's premises two years later to record conclusion of search is not material & the period of limitation to pass assessment order is not to be reckoned from such date & thus the assessment is barred by limitation.

(iv) **Restraint order cannot be used to dump articles and documents in a particular place and seal it**

Action of search party in dumping the documents, passbook etc. in an almirah and sealing it without ordering seizure; suspending the search for fourteen days and then resuming it for no valid reason; retaining the documents for more than fifteen days without handing them over the ITO and taking away of number of documents from petitioner's premises without their knowledge and consent is clearly an arbitrary exercise of power and, therefore, the whole action taken under section 132 is vitiated.

Dr. C. Balakrishna Nair v. *CIT* [1999] 103 Taxman 242 (Ker.).

However this decision was reversed by the division bench in the case of *CIT* v. *Dr. C. Balakrishnan Nair* [2005] 148 Taxman 172 (Ker.) by noting on facts that there being no infirmity in the action of the department in keeping the documents found at the time of search in an almirah in the premises of the assessee after issuing an order under section 132(3) or on account of delay of 14 days in completing the search, and the petitioners having failed to prove their allegation that the search party had taken away some documents on the first day of search, and has planted some other documents on resuming the search, there was no procedural violation by the search party or violation of fundamental rights guaranteed under Article 21 of the Constitution and, therefore the search and seizure operation was not vitiated.

7.10 Other Judicial Pronouncements

(*i*) Constitutional validity

In the case of *I. Devarajan* v. *Tamil Nadu Farmers Service Co-operative Federation*[1981] 131 ITR 506 (Mad.) it was observed that sub-section (3) of section 132 is not violative of Article 14 of the Constitution.

(*ii*) No abuse of process of Court

The Supreme Court in the case of *Dy. Director of Inspection (Intelligence)* v. *Vinod Kumar Didwania* [1986] 160 ITR 969 (SC) held that the assessee could not be allowed to abuse the process of Court for circumventing the prohibitory orders issued by income-tax authorities under section 132(3). This is a case where the Supreme Court found that the process of law has been abused for the purpose of gaining undeserved advantage.

The Supreme Court observed that they were not concerned whether the prohibitory orders were valid or not. It was enough that the prohibitory orders were there and by using the stratagem, the goods were removed from the three godowns. The Court finally held that the assessee had abused the process of Court for securing removal of goods and he could not be allowed to retain that advantage. The Court permitted an enquiry into the value of goods removed by the assessee and ultimately passed an order directing the assessee to pay to the Department a sum of ₹ 14 lakhs within six weeks by way of restitution for the quantity of the goods removed from the two godowns so that the position as it obtained prior to the removal of the goods from the three godowns were restored.

8

RECORDING OF STATEMENT - SECTION 132(4)

Section 132(4) of the Income Tax Act, 1961 empowers the authorized officer to record statement of any person during the course of search proceeding. Section 132(4) reads as under:-

8.1 Text of Section 132(4)

'(4) The authorized officer may, during the course of search or seizure, examine on oath any person who is found to be in possession or control of any books of account, documents, money, bullion, jewellery or other valuable article or thing and any statement made by such person during such examination may thereafter be used in evidence in any proceeding under the Indian Income-tax Act, 1922 (11 of 1922), or under this Act.

Explanation—For the removal of doubts, it is hereby declared that the examination of any person under this sub-section may be not merely in respect of any books of account, other documents or assets found as a result of the search, but also in respect of all matters relevant for the purposes of any investigation connected with any proceeding under the Indian Income-tax Act, 1922 (11 of 1922), or under this Act.'

8.2 Legislative History - Significant Amendment

The *Explanation* to sub-section (4) was added w.e.f. 1st April 1989, by Direct Tax Laws (Amendment) Act, 1987. Prior to insertion of this *Explanation*, it was interpreted by some of the Courts that scope of recording of a statement under this sub-section was restricted relating to books of account, documents or assets found as a result of search. The *Explanation* clarifies that examination of any person under this sub-section can be made in respect of all matters relevant for the purposes of any investigation connected with any proceeding under the Income Tax Act.

(i) Scope of Explanation to section 132(4)

The above *Explanation* was inserted under sub-section (4) by Direct Tax Laws (Amendment) Act, 1987, w.e.f. 1st April, 1989. Prior to insertion of this *Explanation*, there used to be controversy regarding interpretation of sub-section (4). In the case of *R.R. Gavit v. Smt. Sherbanoo Hasan Daya* [1986] 28 Taxman 349 (Bom.), Bombay High Court had held that the authorized officer under section 132(4) was empowered to examine the accused on oath during the course of search only in the event the accused was found in possession or control of the things mentioned in the section. It is not disputed that the accused's impugned statement was recorded at 6.30 PM *i.e.* before the commencement of search. Therefore, the complainant has exceeded his authority under the provisions of the said section by putting certain questions to the accused before commencing the search. But after the insertion of *Explanation* to section 132(4), the above Bombay High Court ruling at 28 Taxman 349 is no more good law on the point.

The controversy was with respect to the following two issues—

(a) whether the person whose statement is being recorded under section 132(4) can be examined with respect to merely in respect of the books of account, other documents or assets found as a result of search or he may be examined in respect of all matters relevant for the purposes of any investigation connected with any proceeding under the Income Tax Act?

(b) whether statement under section 132(4) in the course of search proceeding can be recorded of any person at any stage or it can be recorded only of the person when he is found to be in possession or control of any books of account, documents, money, bullion, jewellery or any other valuable article or thing?

So far as the first controversy is concerned, the same has been addressed by insertion of the *Explanation* to sub-section (4). The *Explanation* clearly mentions that the examination of any person under this sub-section may be not merely in respect of any books of account, other documents or assets found as a result of the search, but also in respect of all matters relevant for the purposes of any investigation connected with any proceeding under the Income Tax Act. It clearly implies that the examination of the person during search under section 132(4) can be made with respect to any matter relevant for the purpose of Income Tax and it cannot be said to be restricted only relating to the books of account, documents or assets found as a result of search.

But even after the above *Explanation*, the second controversy has not been properly addressed and there can still be two opinions about the same. As per plain reading of the language of sub-section (4), it comes out that statement under section 132(4) can be recorded of any person who is found to be in possession or control of any books of account, documents or assets in the course of search. It implies that the initiating point for recording statement of any person in the course of search is that such person is found to be in possession or control of any books of account, document or assets. Prior to this, no statement of any person could be recorded under section 132(4) in the course of search. It is all together a different matter that once statement under section 132(4) is recorded, the person may be examined with respect to any matter relating to Income Tax as stated in the *Explanation* inserted to sub-section (4).

In case the above interpretation is accepted, it would mean that no preliminary statement of the person searched or any other person present in the premises under search, can be recorded by the authorized officer even after commencement of search unless the person whose statement is sought to be recorded is found to be in possession or control of any books of account, documents or assets. However in practice, it has been observed that preliminary statement of the person searched is generally recorded with the commencement of search. In such a situation, it can be argued that in case such preliminary statement is not regarded as a statement recorded under section 132(4), it may be treated as statement recorded under section 131(1A) and it will have the same evidentiary value as both the statements are recorded on oath. The above discussion will still keep the controversy open regarding recording of preliminary statement in the course of search under section 132(4) of any person other than the person against whom search is authorized, prior to such person having been found in possession or control of any books of account, documents or assets as a result of search.

On the other hand, it can be argued that the *Explanation* inserted under sub-section (4) enlarges the scope of sub-section (4) and after insertion of the *Explanation*, legislative intent is to clarify that it is possible to examine any person in the course of search with respect to any matter relevant for the purposes of any investigation connected with any proceeding under the Income Tax Act at any stage. It can further be argued that as per the object and purpose of search, sufficient powers are required to be given to the authorized officer for examination of any person during search so as to unearth the undisclosed income and in the absence thereof, it would frustrate the very purpose of search.

All persons who are found at place of search are not automatically covered by action under section 132. There has to be warrant of search in respect of each of the persons. *Jt. CIT* v. *Latika V. Waman* [2005] 1 SOT 535 (Mum.-Trib.)

Even after insertion of *Explanation* to section 132(4), Delhi Bench of ITAT in the case of *Rishab Kumar Jain* v. *Asstt. CIT* [1999] 105 Taxman 74 (Delhi) (Mag.) has held that authorized officer has no power to record the preliminary statement of assessee before start of search proceedings and any such statement is not a statement under section 132(4) and cannot be relied upon; only the statement recorded during the course of search operation is a statement under section 132(4) and it cannot be ignored.

In the case of *CIT* v. *Shri Ramdas Motor Transport* [1999] 102 Taxman 300 (A.P.), Andhra Pradesh High Court had stated that since the Department could not find any unaccounted money, article or thing or incriminating document either at the premises of the company or at the residence of managing director or directors, the finding of the Tribunal that the statement of managing director recorded patently under section 132(4) does not have any evidentiary value is correct and did not raise any question of law.

But Supreme Court in the same case reported at *CIT* v. *Sri Ramdas Motor Transport Ltd.* **[2001] 119 Taxman 490** set aside the above case for reconsideration by A.P High Court in view of the fact that the High Court has, in effect, interpreted section 132(4) and its *Explanation*, which it could not have done without calling for a reference of the concerned questions and hearing it.

In the case of *V. Kunhambu & Sons* v. *CIT* [1996] 86 Taxman 477 (Ker.) it has been held by the High Court of Kerala that authorized officer could record statement on oath on all matters pertaining to the suppressed income. Statement could not be confined only to the books of account. *Explanation* to sub-section (4) inserted w.e.f. 1st April, 1989 merely seeks to clarify the necessary import of the main provision.

8.3 Objective

Income Tax search is the investigation proceeding to collect evidences relating to undisclosed income. The primary objective of this sub-section is to give power to the authorized officer to examine the person and seek explanation regarding books of account, documents or assets found during search. The investigation can further be carried by way of making enquiry relating to any other matter from the person searched which may be relevant relating to any proceeding under the Income Tax Act. The statement is recorded on oath so that it may have evidentiary value during any proceeding under the Income Tax Act. The objective of recording statement is to make enquiry, investigation and gather information relating to any matter connected with Income Tax.

8.4 Significance of statement under section 132(4)

Statement recorded under section 132(4) is significant not only from the point of view of the Department but also from the point of view of assessee who may get immunity from penalty or levy of penalty at staggered rates on undisclosed income as prescribed under section 271AAA/271AAB, if *"undisclosed income"* of the *"specified previous year(s)"* is declared by the assessee during statement recorded under section 132(4) in the course of search. In case 'undisclosed income' as defined under section 271AAA/271AAB is not declared by the assessee in the manner as prescribed therein, during the statement recorded under section 132(4) by the authorized officer, assessee is liable to penalty as prescribed, apart from tax and interest.

From the Department's point of view, recording of statement under section 132(4) during search is significant for the following purposes:-

a. To seek explanation regarding nature and contents of the documents, loose papers or other evidences found during search. The authorized officer makes an attempt to decode the figures and contents written on the documents in secret code. It is believed that at the time of search, assessee may be able to explain the true nature of transactions recorded in the documents or loose papers found.

b. Enquiry is made regarding source of acquisition of money, bullion, jewellery, valuable article or thing consisting of assets in tangible or intangible form found during search to find as to whether the same are disclosed or undisclosed. In case the same are not disclosed, decision to seize such assets is taken by the authorized officer.

c. The authorized officer generally has brief relating to undisclosed income and assets and the *modus operandi* adopted by the assessee to earn undisclosed income. Irrespective of the fact whether evidences relating to the same are found or not during search, the authorized officer makes enquiry from the assessee regarding such unaccounted sources of income.

A power to examine a person on oath is specifically conferred on the authorities only u/s 132(4) in the course of any search or seizure. Thus, Income-tax Act, whenever it thought fit and necessary to confer such power to examine a person on oath, has expressly provided for it, whereas section 133A does not empower any ITO to examine any person on oath. Thus, in contradistinction to the power u/s 133A, section 132(4) enables the Authorized Officer to examine a person on oath and any statement made by such person during such examination can also be used in evidence under the IT Act. On the other hand, whatever statement recorded u/s 133A, is not given an evidentiary value. *[CIT* v. *S. Khader Khan Son* [2008] 300 ITR 157 (Mad.)], *[Paul Mathews & Sons* v. *CIT* [2003] 129 Taxman 416 (Ker.)]

8.5 Manner of recording statement

Statement under section 132(4) starts with the administration of oath to the person by the authorized officer. The authorized officer usually records the statement in English but may record, on request, the same in the language which the person understands. If the authorized officer is not in a position to accede to the request of the person and the statement is not recorded in the language which is understood by the person, then the statement is liable to be explained to him in the language which he understands before he is asked to sign the statement. The person may request the authorized officer to make amendments to his answers in the statement in case he finds that some of the answers are not same or do not convey what was sought to be explained or conveyed by him. Assessee is supposed to understand the question properly before giving his answer. In case of any doubt, he may request the authorized officer to clarify the question. The statement may be recorded in the manner where question put and answer given both are recorded or alternatively question put by the authorized officer is not recorded and only the answer given is recorded in running form.

(*i*) Examination on oath

The statement under section 132(4) is taken on oath. The evidentiary value of the statement recorded on oath is higher and can be used as evidence in any proceedings under the Act. The words used in section 132(4) *'examine on oath'* are very significant. It requires that the oath should be administered & the same should be administered by the authorized officer and there should be evidence to show that the oath was administered.

In the case of *Addl. CIT* v. *Hanuman Agarwal* [1984] 17 Taxman 19 (Pat.) it was held that statements of witnesses taken without administration of oath are equally admissible in evidence. However, the statement recorded under section 132(4) without administering oath will not be admissible in evidence in those proceedings where administration of oath is an essential condition, e.g., in criminal prosecution for making a false statement on oath, but may be possible to use it as evidence in assessment or penalty proceedings. Any deposition not on oath cannot be shut out from consideration in the assessment or penalty proceedings but its evidential weight certainly get reduced by omission to administer on oath but it is not invalid and corroborative and circumstantial evidences are required to substantiate it.

A statement given otherwise than on oath, is also admissible as evidence under the Act. Reference may be made to section 13 of the Indian Oaths Act, 1873 which states that the failure to administer on oath shall not invalidate the statement. It can even be used as evidence in any proceedings under the Act. *Chowkchand Balabux* v. *CIT* [1961] 41 ITR 465 (Assam).

(ii) During the course of Search and Seizure

The statement under section 132(4) is required to be recorded during the course of search and seizure. It implies that statement has to be recorded after commencement of search but before the conclusion of search. A search can be said to be commenced when search warrant is shown to the assessee and his signature is obtained on the same. A search is concluded when last of the authorizations is executed and all restraints put under section 132(3) are lifted. Statutorily there is time of sixty days available to the authorized officer to lift restraint order passed under section 132(3). During this period statement recorded by the authorized officer is the statement under section 132(4).

The statement recorded in the course of search and seizure operation can only be treated as statement recorded under section 132(4) and generally while recording such statement it is mentioned that it is a statement recorded under section 132(4). In case letter is submitted by the assessee making statement in the course of search surrendering undisclosed income or otherwise, it should be clearly stated in the surrender letter that it is the statement being made by the assessee under section 132(4) of the Act. A simple letter written by one of the partners of the firm after conclusion of search was not regarded as statement made under section 132(4) by the assessee as held by Karnataka High Court in the case of *Chief CIT* v. *Pampapathi* [2008] 175 Taxman 318 (Kar.). The High Court held as under:-

Letter dated 25th Jan., 1995 cannot be treated as a statement said to have been made under sub-section (4) of section 132 since the said letter is not recorded on oath by the authorized officer during the course of search or seizure. The search was conducted on the premises of the respondent assessee on 12th and 13th December, 1994. The letter dated 25th Jan., 1995 has been addressed by one of the partners of the assessee and the same is sent through post to the Asstt. Director of IT (Inv.), marking a copy to the Asstt. CIT and the Dy. Director of IT (Inv.). Therefore it is clear that it is an ordinary letter dispatched by the one of partners of the assessee and such letters cannot be considered as a statement said to have been recorded during the course of search invoking sub-section (4) of section 132 in order to use the same against the assessee under the proceedings of the IT Act.

The statement recorded prior to commencement of search cannot be said to be statement recorded under section 132(4). The authorized officer cannot examine on oath any person u/s 132(4) before commencement of search and seizure. However, statement prior to commencement of search can be recorded by the authorized officer under section 131(1A) of the Act.

Further, sub-section (4) of section 132 requires that the authorized officer may examine on oath any person who is found to be in possession or control of any books of account, documents or assets. It implies that the statement u/s 132(4) can be recorded only when the person is found to be in possession or control of any books of account, documents or the assets. Any statement recorded in the course of search prior to the person found in possession of any books of account, documents or assets will be a statement recorded u/s 131(1A).

(iii) **Powers to the authorized officer to record statement under section 131(1A) in the course of search**

Earlier there used to be a controversy on the issue whether statement under section 132(4) can be recorded by the authorized officer in the course of search before the commencement of search or before the person is found to be in possession or control of books of account, documents or assets as a result of search. There was no power under section 131(1) to the authorized officer for recording statement. Therefore as per Taxation Laws Amendment Act, 1975, with effect from 1st October, 1975, sub-section (1A) was inserted under section 131, *inter alia,* empowering the authorized officer to record statement before he takes action under clauses (*i*) to (*v*) of section 132 in the course of search. It implies that after the above amendment, authorized officer can record statement of the person searched before the commencement of search or before the person is found to be in possession or control of books of account, documents or assets etc. Such statement may not be treated as statement recorded under section 132(4) but it will be treated as statement recorded under section 131(1A) and both the statements will have the same evidentiary value as both the statements are recorded on oath.

There can still be a question as to whether such statement under section 131(1A) can be recorded only of the person searched against whom search warrant has been issued or statement of any person present in the premises under search can be recorded. Power under section 131(1A) has been given to the authorized officer to record statement before he takes action under clauses (*i*) to (*v*) of section 132(1). It implies that before he takes action under either of the clauses (*i*) to (*v*) against any person present in the premises, authorized officer is empowered to record statement of such person. It may be noticed that power under clauses (*iia*) and (*iib*) to section 132(1) can be exercised by the authorized officer not only with respect to the person against whom search warrant has been issued but also against any other person present in the premises. In view of this, it can be interpreted that power of the authorized officer for recording the statement before the commencement of search is not restricted to the person against whom search warrant has been issued but it can be extended to any person present in the premises.

(*iv*) Who may record the statement?

The statement may be recorded by the authorized officer or officers who are authorized to conduct the search. A person below the rank of Income Tax Officer cannot be empowered to be the authorized officer and therefore, an Inspector of Income Tax cannot record the statement under section 132(4). An Income-tax Officer who may be part of search team but not designated as authorized officer in search warrant is also not empowered to record statement under section 132(4). In case statement is recorded by such officer or Inspector of Income Tax, there will not be evidentiary value of such statement recorded.

(*v*) Reference of wrong section

Non-mention of section under which statement is recorded will not invalidate statement recorded during the search proceedings. *Asstt. CIT* v. *M.V. Nagaraja* [1999] 70 ITD 318 (Bang.-Trib.)

(*vi*) No protection under Article 20(3) of the Constitution

Assessee cannot refuse to give statement on the plea of testamentary compulsion based on Article 20(3) of the Constitution as he is not an accused. *Dwarka Prosad Agarwalla* v. *Director of Inspection* [1981] 7 Taxman 299 (Cal.)

A person whose house is being searched for gathering the materials as contemplated under sub-section (1) of section 132 is not an accused and, therefore no question of testamentary compulsion arises. *Ramesh Chandra Mehta* v. *State of West Bengal* AIR 1970 SC 940.

8.6 Rights of assessee during statement

(*i*) Signing of the statement

Assessee is required to sign each page of his statement. Statement is signed by the authorized officer and witnesses also. Before signing the statement, assessee should read the statement carefully and ensure that the same has been recorded in the manner and in the words as stated by him. In case of any deviation, he may request the authorized officer to record the correct position in the statement before signing the same. Assessee cannot refuse to sign the statement and in case he does, he may be liable for penalty under section 272A. In case he has any objection regarding the manner of recording of his statement, instead of refusing to sign, it is in his interest to sign the same after recording his objection and bringing the same to the notice of higher authorities as early as possible.

(*ii*) Amending or improving of earlier statement

The assessee may amend, alter or improve the earlier statement given during the course of statement itself. Sometimes it may happen that the assessee might have given incomplete or wrong answer or mis-stated some fact. During the course of statement he may recollect the correct facts. He may place on record the correct position stating clearly that the earlier statement made in this regard is being amended or altered to this extent.

(*iii*) Copy of the statement

Copy of the statement is not given to the assessee at the time of search. Copy of Panchnama prepared along with all annexure is given to the assessee at the time of conclusion of search but statement recorded during search is not part of Panchnama and the copy of the same is not given. As per sub-section (9) of section 132, assessee is entitled to obtain the photocopy of books of account or other documents seized from his possession but he is not entitled to get the photocopy of statement recorded during search. Statement is confronted and copy is supplied to the assessee during the assessment proceedings when statement is used by the Department against the assessee. However, assessee may keep on noting questions put to him and answers given in brief, simultaneously along with recording of his statement and there is no bar in this regard.

(*iv*) Presence of Counsel during recording of the statement

Income Tax search is an investigation process by the Department to collect evidences of undisclosed income and to seize undisclosed assets. The presence of counsel of the assessee at the time of search is not permitted. Presence of counsel of the assessee at the time of recording of his statement during search can also not be insisted upon. The statement is recorded in the presence of two witnesses (Panchas) who witness entire search proceedings and they are required to sign the statement recorded during search as witnesses.

Section 288 of the Income Tax Act allows an assessee to be represented through an authorized representative in connection with any proceedings under the Act except when personal appearance of the assessee is required under section 131 of the Act for examination on oath or affirmation. Statement under section 132(4) is also recorded on oath in the similar manner as statement recorded under section 131 and personal testimony of the assessee is required. As per the provisions of Indian Penal Code and various judicial pronouncements, presence of witness is permitted at the time of recording of the statement as a measure of the principles of natural justice and fairness. The permission of the presence of counsel at the time of recording of the statement by the Courts may be in the capacity as witness of the proceedings and not as representing the person. Courts have consistently held that it is advisable to permit presence of counsel during interrogation but he cannot be allowed to interfere or prompt the person in giving the answers and he cannot be allowed to take active participation in interrogation. The counsel can witness the proceedings and in case any dispute arises in future, the testimony of the witness may play significant role.

Sometimes in practice, statement of the assessee under section 132(4) is recorded by the authorized officer in his office before the conclusion of search. At that point of time, in case no independent witnesses are present, the counsel of assessee may remain present with the assessee in the capacity as witness.

According to the Calcutta High Court in *Sarju Prosad Sharma* v. *ITO* [1974] 93 ITR 36, a witness has no right to take his counsel along at the time when his statement is recorded. In fact there is no provision under the law which authorizes a witness to be represented by or appear with counsel when his statement is recorded.

(v) Right of cross examination

Statement recorded under section 132(4) is different from the statement recorded by the Assessing Officer during assessment proceedings under section 131(1). When statement of the witness of the department is recorded, assessee has a right to cross examination of the said witness. Statement recorded in the course of assessment proceedings under the Income Tax Act are in the nature of proceedings before the Civil Court while trying a suit and the same are quasi-judicial in nature. The procedure of recording the statement is same as before a Civil Court with the distinction that Income Tax authority acts in a dual capacity as a judge as well as a prosecutor.

Statement recorded under section 132(4) in the course of search is statement during the investigation process. Assessee does not have the benefit of presence of his counsel during search and cross examination is not possible. However, assessee may record his objection, if any, during statement being recorded or later on after the statement has been recorded by way of writing letter or filing affidavit to the authorized officer or higher authorities, or at the time when statement is used against the assessee and when same is confronted to him. But objections should be placed on record with evidence, as expeditiously as possible and these should not appear to be afterthought.

8.7 Statement of whom

(i) Statement of any person

As per section 132(4), statement of any person, who is found during the course of search, to be in possession or control of any books of account, documents, money, bullion, jewellery or other valuable article or thing, may be recorded. Statement of the person, against whom search warrant has been issued, can always be recorded even when he may not be in possession of any books of account, documents or assets but he can always be treated as having control of the same. Moreover, such person(s) may be enquired for any matter relevant for the purposes of the investigation under the Income Tax Act.

In case books of account, documents or assets are found in possession or control of ladies, minors or any visitor, their statement may also be recorded by the authorized officer u/s 132(4).

(ii) Statement of Minor

As per section 118 of the Indian Evidence Act, a child of tender age may be allowed to testify if the court is satisfied that he has capacity to understand the question put to him and give rational answers to those questions. Further, it is mentioned that where the witness is under 12 years of age and the court is of the opinion that, though he understands the duty of speaking the truth, he does not understand the nature of an oath or affirmation, he may not administer oath to such a witness. Omission to administer oath does not render the evidence of a child inadmissible.

Thus, statement of minor child may be recorded in the course of search under the Income Tax Act, 1961 and in case he has not been administered oath, the evidentiary value of such statement of the minor shall be less. However it can be used as corroborative evidence.

(iii) Statement of illiterate person

In case statement is recorded of a person who cannot read and write and cannot sign, then a statement is read over to him. After understanding and ensuring the contents written in the statement, he is required to put thumb impression on the same.

(iv) Statement of visitor

In case there is any visitor visiting the place or premises where search operation is going on, such person may be searched by the authorized officer when the authorized officer has the reason to suspect that such person has secreted about his person any books of account, other documents or assets, as per power given under clause (*iia*) of section 132(1). When such person is found to be in possession or control of any books of account, document or assets, the authorized officer may examine him on oath as per power given under section 132(4) of the Act. Even otherwise any visitor visiting the place of search may be examined on oath by the authorized officer when he has reason to suspect that any income has been concealed or is likely to be concealed by any such person, as per power given under section 131(1A) of the Income Tax Act.

8.8 Evidentiary value of statement recorded u/s 132(4)

Though Bombay High Court in the case of *R.R. Gavit* v. *Smt. Sherbanoo Hasan Daya* [1986] 28 Taxman 349 have recognized the fact that the statement is recorded in unusual circumstances and in an atmosphere of high drama liable to cause nervousness and therefore cannot be said reliable yet there is higher evidentiary value of statement recorded u/s 132(4) since examination is on oath and statement is given by the assessee without any external aid or without consultation from any outsider or advisors so as to fuel any speculation of it being tutored & that too on the earliest available occasion. The statement is given by the assessee under specific circumstances of search where the assessee makes depositions/averments instantly without consultation from the counsel or legal advisors and it is expected that at that point of time, there cannot be any possibility of tutoring as to the actual facts and the statement given at that point of time cannot be said to be afterthought. The higher authorities while appreciating the facts of the case in appropriate proceeding, place more reliance on the statement given and averments made by the assessee in the course of search under section 132(4).

AO having found that the assessee had unaccounted income of ₹ 35 lakhs and the search and seizure operation conducted in the premises of the persons who are closely related to the assessee in the business revealed transaction reflecting the undisclosed income, Tribunal was justified in affirming the addition made by AO though on the basis of statement of assessee under section 132(4). *Kesri K. Deboo* v. *Asstt. CIT* [2009] 313 ITR 186 (Bom.).

However statement can't be the only basis for making addition if the facts are different and the same are demonstrated by way of evidences at later stages. In the case of *M.S. Aggarwal* v. *Dy. CIT* [2004] 90 ITD 80 (Del.-Trib.), assessee admitted gift to be non-genuine in his statement recorded during search but during the course of assessment proceedings, it was found that there was ample evidence to show that these transactions was disclosed in the books of donor as well as donee. The addition was deleted. Tribunal considered the judgment of Supreme Court recorded in *Pullangode Rubber Produce Co. Ltd.* v. *State of Kerala* [1973] 91 ITR 18 (SC) and similar other decisions nullifying the effects of surrender in view of evidence found.

In case assessee is able to demonstrate that the facts admitted during statement recorded u/s 132(4) are impractical, can't exist as recorded in the books of account or disclosed in the return of income, are contrary, the authorities accept the reasonable and correct view and only admission in statement can't be the basis of making addition.

Courts have given significance to the statement recorded under section 132(4) observing that surrender made in the course of search by way of statement under section 132(4) has got evidentiary value and it cannot be used to side track the attention of the Department from making deeper investigation in the matter.

In the case of *Ravindra D. Trivedi* v. *CIT* [2008] 215 CTR 313 (Raj.) it has been held by the High Court of Rajasthan that a bare look at the order of the Tribunal, does show that at the time of search, the search team found the stock, available at the business premises, to be in excess of the one, mentioned in the books of account and in his statement, made under section 132(4), the assessee clearly admitted as follows: "I agree for the difference of ₹ 3 lacs in stock and I am ready to disclose the same as my undisclosed income for the current year." This statement was further corroborated by the statement of his son, who was working as a manager on salary. Admittedly this surrender, has not been retracted by the assessee, much less by successfully making out sufficient ground for discrepancy. Then, it has also been found by the Tribunal that the assessee had accepted the discrepancy, rather, as a matter of fact, made disclosure by way of a calculated attempt to sidetrack the attention of the search party and, therefore, sidetracked the investigation of the discrepancy and in the return or at the assessment stage, despite the above statement under section 132(4), the assessee has not disclosed the income in the return. On the basis of language of section 132(4), this addition could rightly be made and has rightly been made.

In the case of *Dy. CIT* v. *Pramukh Builders* [2008] 112 ITD 179 (Ahd.-Trib.) (TM) it has been held that there being no spectre of evidence regarding undisclosed income, addition made only on the basis of statement of managing partner of assessee under section 132(4), given in a state of confusion and later retracted, could not be sustained either in part or as a whole.

In the case of *Dy. CIT* v. *Bhogilal Mulchand* [2005] 96 ITD 344/3 SOT 211 (Ahd.-Trib.), it has been held that addition made by AO on the basis of statement recorded at the time of search, which found corroboration with evidence and loose papers, was sustainable; retraction of statements after three months without any evidence of coercion or threat was not valid.

Admission is one important piece of evidence but it cannot be said that it is conclusive. It is rebuttable. It is open to the assessee who made admission to establish that confession was involuntary and the same was extracted under duress and coercion. The burden of proving that the statement was obtained by coercion or intimidation lies upon the assessee. Where the assessee claims that he made the statements under the mistaken belief of fact or law, he should have applied for rectification to the authority who passed the order based upon his statement. The retraction should be made at the earliest opportunity and the same should be established by producing any contemporaneous record or evidence, oral or documentary, to substantiate the allegation that he was forced to make the statement in question involuntarily..............Assessee Hukum Chand Jain has further stated that he is signing his statement after reading and understanding the same without any coercion and the same has been further countersigned by his three sons/respondents assessees. It is also not in dispute that the assessee did not retract their statements immediately after the search and seizure was over..............The allegation of duress and coercion was made for the first time in the year 2004 i.e. after almost two years when the A.O. confronted them their statements u/s 132(4) and they were asked to explain as to how the above undisclosed income does not find place in their return. The department's contention that there were no mitigating circumstances to show the admission/surrender made by the assessee was retracted at the earliest point of time with corroborative evidence has substance...............The assessee has totally failed to discharge the burden of proving that the statement was obtained under coercion or intimidation. He did not make any complaint to higher authorities alleging intimidation or coercion for retracting the statement u/s 132(4). ......The assessee had failed to discharge the onus of proving that confession made by him u/s 132(4) was as a result of intimidation, duress and coercion or that the same was made as a result of mistaken belief of law or facts. The A.O. was justified in assessing the income of the assessee on the basis of surrender of undisclosed income made by the assessee's u/s 132(4). [*Asstt. CIT* v. *Hukum Chand Jain* [2010] 191 Taxman 319 (Chhattisgarh)]

From the reading of section 132(4), it follows that for a statement to be admissible in evidence in terms of section 132(4) must be the one recorded by the authorized officer during the search and such a statement should have been obtained on oath. Unless these two basic requirements are fulfilled, such a statement cannot be used as evidence in subsequent proceedings under the Act [*Asstt. CIT* v. *Yerra Nagabhushanam* [1997] 93 Taxman 550/226 ITR 843 (AP)]

In the case of *Shree Ganesh Trading Co.* v. *CIT* [2013] 30 taxmann.com 170/214 Taxman 262 (Jharkhand), Statement on oath is a piece of evidence and when there is incriminating admission against himself, then it is required to be examined with due care and caution. Therefore, Addition made only the basis of statement was deleted.

In the case of *Bhagirath Aggarwal* v. *CIT* [2013] 31 taxmann.com 274/215 Taxman 229 (Delhi), the statements recorded under section 132(4) were clearly relevant and admissible and they could be used as evidence. In fact, once there was a clear admission, voluntarily made, on the part of the assessee, that would constitute a good piece of evidence for the Revenue. Appeal of assessee was dismissed.

In the case of *Jyotichand Bhaichand Saraf & Sons (P.) Ltd.* v. *Dy. CIT* [2012] 26 taxmann.com 239/139 ITD 10 (Pune-Trib.). The Tribunal has held that the admission under section 132(4) was made under the mistaken belief of law instead of the correct legal position. The revenue cannot make the addition merely on the basis of statement without any evidence found in the course of the search action or post search enquiries to the effect that the assessee has undisclosed income.

In the case of *Naresh Kumar Verma* v. *Asstt. CIT* [2013] 32 taxmann.com 280/57 SOT 99 (URO) (Chd.-Trib.), addition made merely on the basis of statement of assessee recorded u/s 132(4) without establishing factum that assessee was in fact found in possession or control of any books of account, other documents, money, bullion, jewellery or other valuable article or thing etc. could not be sustained.

In the case of *CIT* v. *Harjeev Aggarwal* [2016] 70 taxmann.com 95/241 Taxman 199 (Delhi), it has been held by High Court that Block assessments can be made on the basis of incriminating material found during the search and the statement under section 132(4) must be relatable to the material found in Search. Statement cannot be sole basis for making Block Assessment. On facts of the case it was held that since assessee had paid cash for the purchase of immovable property which was not recorded in books seized at material time and also diary was found showing undisclosed sales and purchases, therefore department had incriminating material which was relatable to statement and upheld the Block Assessment. On merits also it was held that since source of income/cash were not substantiated, addition of undisclosed income on account of cash purchase of immovable property would be justified.

In the case of *Chetnaben J. Shah* v. *ITO* [2017] 79 taxmann.com 328 (Guj.), it was held that mere voluntary disclosure of undisclosed income by assessee cannot form basis of addition if no evidence is detected in search. It has been held that there is no evidence to support the very existence of the income except the so called statement u/s 132(4) of the Act. It defies logic that an assessee will or should admit any income which he had not earned and which the department had not found out. High Court did not find anything against the arguments that disclosure u/s 132(4) was subject to variation and once the assessee had access to seized documents and he realized subsequently that there was no occasion to make this disclosure, he was having an inherent right to clarify the situation so that he could be taxed only on real income and not on an income which was not there at all, since there was no evidence to prove otherwise too. In addition, the very important fact that remains that inspite of the search, no material/ evidence was found to show that the assessee was having any other undisclosed assets which could be linked with this disclosure.

In the case of *Tribhovandas Bhimji Zaveri (Delhi) P. Ltd.* v. *Asstt. CIT* [2016] 45 ITR 636 (Mum.-Trib.), ITAT held that the statement was obtained under duress and the search officials were posing questions for 4 days and the search was concluded immediately after the Director surrendered the additional income. Thus, the disclosure made by the Director was not voluntary. Further, since no incriminating material was seized during the search except for the discrepancies in stock, the additional income confessed by the Director pertained to the difference in stock.

In the case of *CIT* v. *Dr. P. Sasikumar* [2016] 73 taxmann.com 173 (Ker.), it has been held that not only the books, documents etc. that are unearthed during the course of search but a statement made by such person during such examination can also be used in evidence in any proceeding under the IT Act, 1961.

8.9 Examination at different stages

(i) Recording of Preliminary Statement - Common Issues of examination

A preliminary statement of the person being searched may be recorded by the authorized officer u/s 131(1A) to enquire regarding general business affairs and financial transactions carried on by the assessee. Objective is, *inter alia*, to seek direction of investigation based on the answers and to bind the assessee so that if at later stage, assessee wants to change his position, burden rests on him to lead evidence to establish to contrary to what was stated by him in the preliminary statement. Generally enquiry is made relating to the following matters in the preliminary statement which are illustrative only:-

1. The identity, PAN No., sources of income of the assessee and other family members.

2. Capacity in which the premises under search is occupied i.e. whether as owner, employee, tenant or otherwise.

3. Names and addresses of business concerns, factory, godown, and branches, associate business entities of which assessee or his family members are proprietor, partner, director or share-holder.

4. Investment in immovable properties with addresses and year of acquisition and source of acquisition.

5. Investment in movable assets such as shares, F.D.Rs, Bonds, jewellery, cars, expensive items and source thereof.

6. Particulars of Income Tax and Wealth Tax assessment.

7. Details of cash, jewellery or other valuables lying in the house or in the bank locker, to whom the same belongs and the source thereof.

8. Particulars of bank lockers maintained by the assessee and other family members, contents therein and the location of the keys of the locker(s).

9. Details of bank accounts maintained with the banks with account numbers.

10. Details of household expenses incurred, marriage or functions celebrated, educational expenses of the children and the source of withdrawal for the same.

11. Details of books of account, including stock registers, maintained and the place where these are kept, password and software used for obtaining data kept in computer or other electronic device.

12. Details regarding any secret chamber, locker or false sealing in the premises, if any.

13. Details of any kind of movable assets, books of account or documents of others kept with the assessee or relating to the assessee kept with somebody else.

14. Details of loans and advances, gifts or other credits given or taken by the assessee.

15. Details of foreign travel & source of such expense and copy of passport.

16. Details relating to undisclosed financial transactions carried on by the assessee in respect to which authorized officer have information and the *modus operandi* adopted by the assessee to earn income outside the books.

(*ii*) Recording of final statement

After collecting all the evidences in the search, final statement of the assessee is recorded by the authorized officer u/s 132(4) with a view to enquire following matters which are, however, illustrative in nature:-

1. To get explanation regarding incriminating material found such as pocket diaries, loose papers containing financial transactions, duplicate set of books of account, unaccounted agreements & properties etc.

2. Source of acquisition of assets found such as cash, jewellery, electronic gadgets, A.C, refrigerator, music system etc., stock in business in excess of the amount recorded in the books, investment in immovable properties not recorded in the books, investment made in asset in cash, loans or advances, gifts or any other credit given or taken in cash etc.

3. Authorized officer may cause enquiry to decode the figures or financial transactions recorded by the assessee in some kind of coded form in the seized material.

4. Decision of seizure of assets is taken on the basis of explanation given and evidences produced by the assessee regarding source of acquisition of assets. The undisclosed assets regarding the disclosure of source of which authorized officer is not convinced, are liable to be seized.

5. Enquiry is made regarding any deviation found by the authorized officer in the actual facts and evidences found during search and as stated by the assessee during his preliminary statement.

(*iii*) Recording of statement u/s 132(4) - Before the conclusion of search

Statement under section 132(4) can be recorded in the course of search. Once search proceeding is concluded, no statement under section 132(4) can be recorded by the authorized officer. It is for this reason that sometimes restraint put under section 132(3) on some bank locker or almirah at the premises of the assessee is kept pending till search is not concluded so that statement of the assessee may be recorded by the authorized officer u/s 132(4) only.

In practice, it has been observed that when search is temporarily suspended to be finally concluded later on, assessee is called upon by the authorized officer to appear before him in his office and statement of the assessee is recorded. Such statement is treated as statement of the assessee in continuation of earlier statement recorded under section 132(4). Sometimes, assessee feels uncomfortable and wants to avoid giving further statement. Sometimes, assessee feels harassed when he is called repeatedly for recording his statement. Statement under section 132(4) in the office of authorized officer is recorded generally for the sake of convenience. In case assessee avoids to comply with such requirement or remains absent in the office of authorized officer for giving the statement, the authorized officer may visit his premises again for lifting restraint or otherwise and may record the statement of the assessee relating to any of the matters which may be relevant for seeking explanation of documents/assets found from his possession or for any proceedings under the Act.

In the case of *CIT* v. *Balaji Steel Profiles* [2015] 59 taxmann.com 375/232 Taxman 806 (Andhra Pradesh & Telangana), it has been held that Statement of managing partner of assessee recorded one and half months after search could not be brought under purview of section 132(4), hence could not be basis of assessment.

(iv) **Issuing of summon under section 131(1A) before conclusion of search**

Whether summon under section 131(1A) can be issued by the authorized officer to enforce the presence of the assessee in his office and to submit information and record his statement before the conclusion of the search, has been a controversial issue. When search is not concluded & is still in progress, authorized officer has power to record statement under section 132(4) and in such a situation, there is a strong view that he cannot simultaneously exercise powers to issue summons under section 131(1A). Rationale of this view is that the power to record statement u/s 131(1A) has been given to the authorized officer before he takes action under clauses (*i*) to (*v*) of section 132(1). Once search begins and action under clauses (*i*) to (*v*) of section 132(1) have already been taken, then power to record statement has specifically been granted under section 132(4).

The other view in the matter is that power to record statement u/ss 131(1A) & 132(4) are the powers simultaneously available to the authorized officer in the course of search and he may record the statement in either of these sections.

However in our view, invoking of the provision u/s 131(1A) for summoning the person under search during the course of search itself and recording his statement pursuant to that, appears not to have been intended by the Legislature. When there is specific provision for recording statement u/s 132(4) in the course of search, it is open to record statement under that section only. Second, when a person has already been searched and all incriminating evidences available with him have been investigated and seized, there should not be any reason to again summon the person searched u/s 131(1A) to investigate regarding existence of the undisclosed income with such person. It is to be appreciated that the power u/s 131(1A) for recording statement has been granted when there is reason to suspect that any income has been concealed or likely to be concealed by any person then for the purpose of making any enquiry and investigation relating thereto person may be summoned and statement may be recorded under this section.

Hon'ble Allahabad High Court in the case of *Dr. Mrs. Anita Sahai* v. *DIT* [2004] 136 Taxman 247 (All.) have gone to the extent of holding that where in case a notice is issued under section 131(1A) after search and seizure operation under section 132, it would show that there was neither reason to believe nor material before authorizing officer on basis of which he could issue a warrant under section 132. Search and seizure cannot be a fishing expedition and before search is authorized, Director must on relevant material have reason to believe that assessee has not or would not disclose his income.

In the case of *Emaar Alloys (P) Ltd.* v. *DGIT (Inv) & Ors.* [2015] 64 taxmann.com 67/235 Taxman 569 (Jharkhand), it has been held that summons can be issued before or even after the search proceedings are initiated. High Court held that the words *'referred to in sub-section (1) of section 132 before he takes action under clauses (i) to (v) of that sub-section'* in S. 131(1A) qualify the words 'authorized officer' only and not the other specified authorities named in the section.

In the case of *Ramesh G Dy. DIT (Inv)* v. *Prakash* v. *Sanghvi* [2015] 64 taxmann.com 221/[2016] 236 Taxman 176 (Kar.), it has been held that the Assessing Officer has the power to enforce attendance of the assessee by camping at the residence of the assessee. High Court held that as the Assessing Officer has already entered the premises of the residence, in order to comply with the legal requirement, he has served summons on him calling upon him to depose. To show the place where he should depose, the phrase, "camp at your residence" is mentioned.

In our considered opinion, this decision is of far reaching consequences and may lead to undesirable practices.

(v) Issuing of summons and recording of statement after conclusion of search

Once search is concluded, the authorized officer is required to prepare appraisal report to give his findings regarding the seized material and tentative undisclosed income. In this process, notice may be issued to the assessee to submit his explanation regarding documents or loose papers found from his possession or to obtain some other information from the assessee. In case assessee does not comply with the notice and does not provide the information, it is usually seen in practice that the summons under section 131 is issued.

Summon under section 131(1) can be issued by the assessing officer or higher authorities *"while trying a suit"* i.e. when any proceeding under the Act is pending against the person. Search proceedings are the investigation proceedings for collection of evidences and such proceedings cannot be said to be the proceedings in connection with trying a suit against the assessee. Therefore, summons under section 131(1) cannot be issued after conclusion of the search. Moreover, the powers to issue summons under section 131(1) is available to the assessing officer and higher authorities of the assessment and appellate wing of the Department and not to the Assistant Director of Investigation or higher authorities of the Investigation Wing of the Department.

Power for issuing summons have been given to the Assistant Director of Investigation and higher authorities of the Investigation Wing of the Department, who generally conduct search operation in practice, under sub-section (1A) of section 131. Whether, summons under section 131(1A) can be issued after conclusion of search, is also a controversial issue.

Undoubtedly summon under section 131(1A) can be issued even when no proceedings against the person are pending under the Act. Further, summons under section 131(1A) can be issued on the basis of "reason to suspect" that any income has been concealed or is likely to be concealed by any person and also for the purpose of making any enquiry or investigation relating thereto. But when extreme action of search under section 132 has already been taken and all the evidences available with the person have already been seized, statement under section 132(4) in the course of search has already been recorded; there cannot be a further occasion to make further enquiry or investigation by issuing summon under section 131(1A). Otherwise it shall become an unending exercise and will cause undue harassment to the person searched.

Other practical situation arises when summon under section 131(1A) is issued to the connected persons against whom search was not authorized but evidences are found in a search which may have connection with such person. Power to issue summon under section 131(1A) to the other connected person for the purpose of making any enquiry or investigation regarding concealed income cannot be questioned, in our opinion.

Hon'ble Allahabad High Court in the case of *Dr. Mrs. Anita Sahai* v. *DIT* [2004] 136 Taxman 247 (All.) have gone to the extent of holding that where in case a notice is issued under section 131(1A) after search and seizure operation under section 132, it would show that there was neither reason to believe nor material before authorizing officer on basis of which he could issue a warrant under section 132. Search and seizure cannot be a fishing expedition and before search is authorized, Director must on relevant material have reason to believe that assessee has not or would not disclose his income.

However contrary view has been expressed by Gujarat High Court in the case of *Arti Gases* v. *DIT* [2000] 113 Taxman 68 (Guj.) where it has been held that notices under section 131(1A) can also be issued after completion of the search undertaken under the provisions of section 132. It would be absolutely logical to call for information so as to have better particulars or to have complete idea about the material seized during search. If some material is seized at the time of the search and the authorized officer wants to have some details so as to understand the nature of the documents, he may issue notice under section 131(1A). In a given case such a notice cannot only help the Department but can also help the assessee. If the assessee is called upon to give some information or to explain certain documents or writings seized during the process of search, no harm can be caused to the assessee and as stated hereinabove, such particulars can be helpful not only to the Department but to the assessee also. Moreover, under the provisions of section 133 the AO or the Officers referred to in the said section are having power to call for information. So issuance of such a notice during or after the search cannot be said to be bad in law.

Further, it has been held in the case of *Dr. V.S. Chauhan* v. *Director of Income-tax (Investigations)* [2011] 12 taxmann.com 230/200 Taxman 413 (All.) that discovery of investment in construction of huge hospital being there and thus search was valid and the subsequent notice under section 131(1A) which was in fact notice under section 133(6), would not invalidate search.

It has been held in the case of *Neesa Leisure Ltd.* v. *Union of India* [2011] 16 taxmann.com 163/[2012] 204 Taxman 86 (Guj.) that information giving rise to belief that income would not be disclosed and inquiries and material showing documents would not be produced, search is valid and notice under sections 131(1A) and 133(6) subsequent to search would not invalidate search. Allegation that search proceedings were *mala fide,* is to be proved by the one who so alleges. Burden of proof is on assessee to prove allegation.

It has been held in the case of *CIT* v. *Shankarlal Bhagwati Prasad Jalan* [2017] 84 taxmann.com 275/[2018] 407 ITR 152 (Bom.) that declaration made after search has no evidentiary value & additions cannot be made on basis of such declaration.

It has been held in the case of *Ultimate Builders* v. *Asstt. CIT* 183 DTR (Ind) 179 Trib that search in the case of assessee firm having concluded on 31st Jan., 2014, statement recorded on 2nd Feb., 2014 of assessee's partner in the course of search of other concerns of the group by officer authorized for that group could not be taken to be statement recorded under s. 132(4) *vis-a-vis* assessee firm. Further, no reference has been given by the Revenue authorities to any incriminating material found during the course of search at the business premises of the assessee, which could be correlated to the alleged surrendered income carried by the assessee from undisclosed sources, hence addition was not sustainable.

8.10 Retraction of statement given under section 132(4)

Statement of the person searched is recorded by the authorized officer during search operation primarily to seek explanation regarding incriminating material found and to get declaration of undisclosed income. Though it is denied that any pressure is exerted to obtain confessional statement during search, yet in practice it is not uncommon to observe that assessees are persuaded vigorously by the departmental officials to make declaration of undisclosed income. Sometimes declaration of undisclosed income is made by the assessee so as to quicken the process of the search proceeding being wrapped up at the earliest. Later on after realizing the consequences and understanding the whole process of assessment proceedings to be undertaken after search and based on appreciation of entire evidence, assessee may be prone to retract or modify the statement made during search.

Retraction means to deviate from the earlier statement, *inter alia,* by giving justification and reasons of the circumstances under which the earlier statement was given. The statement under section 132(4) is recorded on oath and the same cannot be dismissed lightly. Retraction is possible depending upon the facts and circumstances of the case. But, retraction simpliciter may not be justified in further proceeding. The retraction of statement should therefore be made carefully justifying the reasons and placing corroborating evidences with the facts being stated including by way of affidavits wherever possible:

> "An admission is an extremely important piece of evidence but it cannot be said that it is conclusive. It is open to the assessee who made the admission to show that it is incorrect." *Nagubai Armul* v. *B. Shama Rao* AIR 1956 SC 100

> "An admission is not conclusive as to the truth of the matters stated therein. It is only a piece of evidence, the weight to be attached to which must depend

on the circumstances in which it is made. It can be shown to be erroneous or untrue." *Sarwan Singh Rattan Singh* v. *State of Punjab* AIR 1957 SC 637

"An admission is the best evidence that an opposite can rely upon and though not conclusive could be decisive of the matter, unless successfully withdrawn or proved erroneous." *Avadh Kishore Das* v. *Ram Gopal* AIR 1979 SC 861

Retraction of statement should be based upon sound reasoning and corroborative evidences. Mere denial of statement is not enough. In the case of *Asstt. CIT* v. *Rameshchandra R. Patel* [2004] 89 ITD 203 (Ahd.-Trib.) (TM) it has been held that in view of repeated admissions of assessee in his statement under section 132(4), amount of ₹ 2 lacs was rightly added in undisclosed income towards renovation of house notwithstanding the assessee's retraction which was not based on any evidence and reasons.

In the case of *Asstt. CIT* v. *Jorawar Singh M. Rathod* [2005] 148 Taxman 35 (Ahd.) (Mag.) it has been held by ITAT, Ahmedabad 'B' Bench that addition made by the AO merely on the basis of retracted statement under section 132(4) could not be sustained in the absence of any evidence, material or recovery of any movable or immovable assets at the time of search to corroborate the disclosure made by the assessee.

(i) Instruction of CBDT on confessional statement

"Confession of additional income during the course of search and seizure and survey operation

Instances have come to the notice of the Board where assessees have claimed that they have been forced to confess the undisclosed income during the course of search and seizure and survey operations. Such confession, if not based upon credible evidence, are later retracted by the concerned assessee while filing returns of income. In these circumstances, such confessions during the course of search and seizure and survey operations do not serve any useful purpose. It is, therefore, advised that there should be focus and concentration on collection of evidence of income which leads to information on what has not been disclosed or is not likely to be disclosed before the Income Tax Department. Similarly, while recording statement during the course of search and seizure and survey operations no attempt should be made to obtain confession as to the undisclosed income. Any action on the contrary shall be viewed adversely.

Further, in respect of pending assessment proceedings also, Assessing Officers should rely upon the evidences/materials gathered during the course of search/survey operations or thereafter while framing the relevant assessment orders".

Instruction : F. No. 286/2/2003-IT (Inv. II), dated 10-3-2003.

The CBDT has issued fresh instruction vide **F.No. 286/98/2013-IT (INV.II), Dated 18-12-2014**, the text is reproduced below:

1. Instances/complaints of undue influence/coercion have come to notice of the CBDT that some assessees were coerced to admit undisclosed income during Searches/Surveys conducted by the Department. It is also seen that many such admissions are retracted in the subsequent proceedings since the same are not backed by credible evidence. Such actions defeat the very purpose of Search/Survey operations as they fail to bring the undisclosed income to tax in a sustainable manner leave alone levy of penalty or launching of prosecution. Further, such actions show the Department as a whole and officers concerned in poor light.

2. *I am further directed to invite your attention to the Instructions/ Guidelines issued by CBDT from time to time, as referred above, through which the Board has emphasized upon the need to focus on gathering evidences during Search/Survey and to strictly avoid obtaining admission of undisclosed income under coercion/undue influence.*

3. *In view of the above while reiterating the aforesaid guidelines of the Board, I am directed to convey that any instance of undue influence/coercion in the recording of the statement during Search/survey/Other proceeding under the I.T. Act, 1961 and/ or recording a disclosure of undisclosed income under undue pressure/coercion shall be viewed by the Board adversely.*

4. *These guidelines may be brought to the notice of all concerned in your Region for strict compliance.*

5. *I have been further directed to request you to closely observe/ oversee the actions of the officers functioning under you in this regard.*

6. *This issues with approval of the Chairperson, CBDT*

(ii) Circumstances prompting assessee to make retraction

According to section 94 of the Evidence Act, presumption can be rebutted by proving that the admission or confession was caused by inducement, threat or promise, thereby making the admission irrelevant.

Ideally assessee should refrain from making retraction of undisclosed income already made during search. It is seen in practice that it is viewed adversely by the departmental officials and assessee should in that case be prepared to face deeper investigation and third party enquiries in such a situation.

There may be case when surrender of undisclosed income was made by the assessee at the time of search under compelling circumstances but neither there exists evidences relating to undisclosed income nor there is availability of resources for making payment of tax with the assessee. Generally under the following circumstances, it is seen in practice that the assessee may take decision of retracting the statement but, it may be noted that, these are by no means exhaustive circumstances:

1. At the time of making the statement, assessee was under wrong impression that by making declaration of undisclosed income and paying the taxes, no further proceedings shall be undertaken against him and it is the end of the matter. Assessee may make declaration in the hope to avoid any future hassles so that he may concentrate on his business activities but in the case of search, it does not happen so. Appreciation of all the evidence found and mandatory assessment of earlier six years under section 153A is a mandatory process in all the search cases. When assessee comes to know this fact, he may realize that there was no advantage of declaration of undisclosed income as initially thought by him.

2. After conclusion of the search and after consulting his counsel & other associates, assessee may realize that there are no evidences of incriminating nature or which cannot be satisfactorily explained.

3. Assessee may realize that making declaration of undisclosed income at his end may create lot of hardships to other business associates, employees or other persons, who may have corresponding impact of the same e.g. loans given in cash - the person taking loan in cash may be penalized under section 271D read with section 269SS. Income having been surrendered towards salaries given out of the books, the concerned employee may be liable to be taxed etc.

4. Assessee may realize that declaration of undisclosed income relating to earlier years is counter-productive inasmuch as, instead of getting immunity from penalty due to which declaration was initially made, he may have no recourse left to avoid penalty, since confession itself may pave the way for the levy of penalty for admitted concealment of undisclosed income relating to earlier years.

(*iii*) Retraction in the nature of amendment/modification of earlier statement given u/s 132(4)

Sometimes, assessee may retract the earlier statement so as to amend, modify or improve upon the manner of making declaration of undisclosed income. Instead of retracting the statement completely, assessee may feel the necessity to amend the manner of declaration. Declaration may be made in the hands of different entities, for different items or for different years. This may be done after going through all the evidences collected from his possession so as to plan the surrender of undisclosed income in a proper and better manner. Generally it is seen in practice that if permitted by the authorized officer, such retraction is not viewed adversely by the department. In such a situation, the later statement made by the assessee may supersede the earlier statement but the statement should be made by the assessee in an unambiguous manner, stating all the facts properly so that there does not remain any scope of confusion. Moreover, the same should be done prior to the conclusion of the search.

Challenging valuation or calculation mistake does not tantamount to retraction in the strict sense of the term. When, say for example, stock list has been prepared and valued at sales price & the same is authenticated by the assessee and surrender of undisclosed income having been made on that basis, assessee may always plead for rectifying the valuation and consequently retract the surrender of undisclosed income, if any, made on the basis of the same.

In yet another case, if any surrender was made keeping in view of peculiar fact situation, such surrender may be retracted later on if there is material alteration in that fact situation. For example, creditors may be surrendered due to non-verifiability but later on, assessee may have collected adequate evidences for due verification which may prompt him to retract the surrender earlier made. Such retraction can be made at any stage up to filing of return of income by the assessee and the same may not be viewed adversely by the Department after finding the justification of retraction.

In the case of *Vasant Thakoor* v. *Asstt. CIT* [2013] 40 taxmann.com 153/[2014] 147 ITD 682 (Mum.-Trib.), since retraction was filed after more than two years of admission by assessee in statement u/s 132(4), the same was not accepted by Tribunal in quantum proceedings. Penalty was held to be justified on these grounds.

(iv) **Manner of retraction**

In case assessee decides to retract the statement, it should be done at the earliest because undue delay in retraction may dilute the impact of retraction, *inter alia*, on the ground of it being after-thought. In case retraction is done for the reason that earlier statement was obtained under pressure or coercion, it is all the more important to make retraction promptly & by showing the circumstantial evidence for the allegation of coercion or pressure. Delay of each day is viewed against the assessee and it may be interpreted as an after-thought excuse.

Retraction may be made, *inter alia,* by way of filing affidavit stating all the facts and prevailing circumstances under which the earlier statement was made. In case statement or affidavit of panch (witness) is also filed as supporting evidence of actual pressure having been brought to bear upon, it may strengthen the case of the assessee. The communication of the retraction should be made to the authorized officer who recorded the statement and to the higher authorities.

Where the affidavit retracting the statement made under section 132(4) was filed after three years, it was held that the admission made earlier in respect of payment of on-money as mentioned in loose papers was to be treated as admissible evidence. *Dhunjibhoy Stud & Agricultural Farm* v. *Dy. CIT* [2002] 82 ITD 18 (Pune-Trib.) (TM).

Where one of the partners and Chief Accountant stated on oath at the time of search that seized sheets recorded details of unaccounted stock and offer its value as additional income, such a disclosure could not be resiled from after 6 months particularly where the surrender made at the time of disclosure was accepted by the departmental authorities and they did not proceed with further investigation and also because the retraction was not supported by any independent and reliable evidence to prove as to what was the correct position of stock. *Hiralal Maganlal & Co.* v. *Dy. CIT* [2005] 96 ITD 113 (Mum.-Trib.).

It has been held in the case of Principal CIT v. *Avinash Kumar Setia* [2017] 81 taxmann.com 476/248 Taxman 106 (Delhi) that Voluntary declaration of unaccounted money by assessee two months after survey & retraction of declaration having been made after two years without satisfactory explanation & failure to show income in return filed for relevant assessment year after surrender of undisclosed Income, is invalid & Appellate Tribunal was not justified in deleting addition of undisclosed income.

It has been held in the case of *Principal CIT* v. *Roshan Lal Sancheti* 172 DTR 313 (Raj.), 306 CTR 140 (Raj.) that while computing undisclosed income, Statement recorded under s. 132(4) and later confirmed in statement recorded under s. 131, **cannot** be discarded simply by observing that the assessee has **retracted** the same, when the retraction was after inordinate delay **of 237 days.**

(*v*) **Consequences of retraction**

Retraction, in practice, is liable to be viewed adversely by the authorized officer & departmental officials who may feel that all the efforts of tracking the undisclosed income have not yielded the desired result. When the retraction of undisclosed income is made, the assessee should be prepared to face the following and it is stated that these are based on practical experience of the authors:-

1. Summon to the assessee u/s 131 to cross examine him to ascertain the correct facts in case affidavit is filed by the assessee making retraction of earlier statement.

2. Conducting deeper investigation relating to the affairs of the assessee or his associates & collecting information and evidences from other government authorities *i.e.* GST, VAT, Registrar office, Banks etc.

3. Summoning third parties and other business associates by issuing notices under section 131 to make enquiries regarding transactions with the assessee to find corroborative evidences.

4. Summoning the assessee, his partners or other associates by issuing notices under section 131 and recording their statements.

5. Highlighting the issues in the appraisal report.

6. Passing information to other government departments regarding any irregularity with respect to them such as GST, VAT and Customs etc.

7. Initiating/instituting prosecution relating to any misstatement or falsification with the Civil Court wherever applicable.

In view of the above and for the fact that these powers are in any case exercisable under the authority of law, assessee has to make decision of retraction after analyzing pros and cons of retraction carefully.

A.O. having issued notice u/s 148 solely on the basis of assessee's statements u/s 132(4) offering certain undisclosed income for assessment which already stood retracted by the assessee twice before the impugned notice was issued and there being no other material on record to make out a *prima facie* case of income escaping assessment within the meaning of section 147, the very issuance of notice u/s 148 was illegal and without jurisdiction. [*CIT* v. *Dr. N. Thippa Setty* [2010] 322 ITR 525 (Kar.)]

Purchaser having admitted in his statement recorded u/s 132(4) that he purchased the land and building from assessee for ₹ 71 lacs as against ₹ 30 lacs declared in sale document and having declared the differential amount of ₹ 41 lacs in return of income and paying the taxes thereon and the actual consideration of ₹ 71 lacs being supported by subsequent valuation report, capital gains in the hands of assessee has to be computed on the basis of sale consideration of ₹ 71 lacs in spite of the fact that the purchaser in cross examination retracted from his earlier statement. [*CIT* v. *Medical Trust Hospital* [2008] 173 Taxman 384 (Ker.)]

(vi) Statement recorded during odd hours

If a statement is recorded during odd hours late in the night or after long search operation when assessee is fully tired and exhausted, retraction of such statement may be accepted by the Courts after taking into account the entire gamut of facts and circumstances of the case. In the case of *Kailashben Manharlal Chokshi* v. *CIT* [2008] 174 Taxman 466 (Guj.) Gujarat High Court has held that statement recorded at odd hours cannot be considered to be a voluntary statement, if it is subsequently retracted and necessary evidence is led contrary to such admission and therefore addition on the basis of retracted statement under section 132(4) was not called for in the facts and circumstances of the case.

In *Deepchand & Co.* v. *Asstt. CIT* [1995] 51 TTJ 421 (Bom.-Trib.), it was held that statements recorded during search proceedings which continued for an unduly long period also cannot be considered to be free, fearless and voluntary. Thus in such circumstances, statements can be successfully retracted contending the same were recorded under pressure and force.

In the case of *Tribhovandas Bhimji Zaveri (Delhi) P. Ltd.* v. *Asstt. CIT* [2016] 45 ITR (Trib.) 636/177 TTJ 306 (Mum.-Trib.), ITAT held that the statement was obtained under duress and the search officials were posing questions for 4 days and the search was concluded immediately after the Director surrendered the additional income. Thus, the disclosure made by the Director was not voluntary. Further, since no incriminating material was seized during the search except for the discrepancies in stock, the additional income confessed by the Director pertained to the difference in stock which too was reconciled later on.

(vii) In case of retraction, burden of proof on assessee

An admission is the best evidence against a person but it is not a conclusive proof. The facts admitted may prove to be wrong on the basis of further evidence and circumstances but the burden would lie upon the person who is claiming it to be wrong.

Admissions are not conclusive proof of the facts admitted and may be explained or shown to be wrong; but they do raise an estoppel and shift the burden of proof on to the person making them or his representative in interest. Unless shown or explained to be wrong, they are an efficacious proof of the facts admitted.

Krishan Lal Shiv Chand Rai v. *CIT* [1973] 88 ITR 293 (P&H)

It is an established principle of law that a party is entitled to show and prove that the admission made by him probably is in fact not correct and true.

Karam Chand v. *Asstt. CIT* [2000] 73 ITD 434 (Chd.-Trib.)

Where the partners of the firm made a voluntary disclosure of ₹ 3 crores comprising earnings from two firms and on account of discrepancies in the books of account and made a retraction after a gap of one month of recording statement under section 132(4), it could not be said that the earlier statement was recorded during duress. Besides, the statement under section 132(4) was fully supported with documents seized during the search. *Video Master* v. *Jt. CIT* [2002] 83 ITD 102 (Mum.-Trib.).

A statement validly recorded by the Assessing Officer under section 132(4) can be used in evidence in block assessment proceedings also even if that statement is later on retracted. *Dhanvarsha Builders & Developers P. Ltd.* v. *Dy. CIT* [2006] 102 ITD 375 (Pune-Trib.).

Where the assessee admitted undisclosed income on the basis of loose papers and cash found during search, his subsequent retraction that the cash represented his agricultural income and income from his other business was not found tenable. *Kantilal Prabhudas Patel* v. *Dy. CIT (Inv.)* [2005] 93 ITD 117 (Indore-Trib.) (TM)

The Managing Director of Assessee Company surrendered ₹ 1.07 crore being 50% of cash receipts not recorded in the regular books of account and did not take any step to rectify the declaration before the search authority before whom it was made, the addition of ₹ 1.07 crore was held to be justified. *Carpenters Classics (Exim) (P.) Ltd.* v. *Dy. CIT* [2007] 108 ITD 142 (Bang-Trib.).

It has been held in the case of *Bannalal Jat Constructions (P.) Ltd.* v. *Asst. CIT* [2019] 106 taxmann.com 128/264 Taxman 5 (SC) that where High Court upheld addition made by authorities below relying upon statement made in course of search proceedings by director of assessee-company, since assessee failed to discharge its burden that admission made by director in his statement was wrong and said statement was recorded under duress and coercion, SLP filed against decision of High Court was to be dismissed. In course of search proceedings, statement of director of assessee-company was recorded under section 132(4) admitting certain undisclosed income. In course of assessment, Assessing Officer made addition to assessee's income on basis of statement given by its director. Subsequently, director of assessee-company retracted said statement. Tribunal, however, finding that statement had been recorded in presence of independent witness, confirmed addition made by Assessing Officer.

High Court also opined that mere fact that director of assessee-company retracted statement at later point of time, could not make said statement unacceptable and it was further opined that burden lay on assessee to show that admission made by director in his statement was wrong and such retraction had to be supported by a strong evidence showing that earlier statement was recorded under duress and coercion. High Court finding that assessee failed to discharge said burden, confirmed order passed by Tribunal, on facts, SLP filed against decision of High Court was dismissed.

(viii) **Shifting stand not acceptable**

During the course of search money deposited in banks was surrendered in a statement made under section 132(4). While filing the return the deposits were not shown as income on the belief that they were out of loan but no evidence for loan was produced. Subsequently, the assessee came out with the story that the banks deposits were out of the withdrawals from the same bank account a few months ago. In view of these shifting stands taken by the assessee, it was held that the Department was justified in relying upon the statement recorded under section 132(4) in preference to subsequent statements. *Mahendra Chiman Lal Shah* v. *Asstt. CIT* [1994] 51 ITD 244 (Ahd.-Trib.).

(ix) **Undisclosed income may be assessed having regard to nature of evidence**

Statement under section 132(4) made by the assessee is one of the evidences regarding acceptance of undisclosed income. Circumstances in which statement was made and retracted later on have to be appreciated & evaluated in its entirety. A statement once made cannot be said to be conclusive proof regarding undisclosed income of the assessee. Courts have consistently opined that ultimately it is the nature of the evidences available with the department which will decide the matter whether on the basis of same, any undisclosed income can be assessed in the hands of the assessee or not.

In the case of *ITO* v. *Ashok Kumar Aggarwal* [1990] 38 TTJ 189 (Del.-Trib.), at the time of search, assessee made statement that cash found from his possession was handed over to him by his father. Later he retracted the statement stating that the money was left by his brother but was delivered to him through his father. It was also stated that the money was collected from various parties including some agriculturists. Statement of assessee, his brother, his father, sarpanch through whom the loans from the agriculturists was said to have been obtained were recorded. The plea of the assessee was accepted since the evidences were reconcilable with the stand of the assessee. Tribunal observed as under:

"Suspicion though a ground for scrutiny of evidence, cannot be made the foundation of a decision. Conjecture is not a substitute for legal proof. Suspicion however strong, cannot take the place of proof. The ITO would not be justified in deciding a case upon his own suspicion or upon mere supposition after discarding the evidence produced by the assessee. One must be careful not to carry caution to an extreme length and not to discard oral evidence merely because it is oral and unless the impeaching and discrediting circumstances are clearly found to exist. In dealing with oral evidence one cannot start with any presumption of perjury. Evidence of persons even though not independent but who are not shaken in cross examination, cannot be rejected on merely suspicion when the story itself as told by them is not improbable. Discrepancies often trifling in themselves when compared with the great mass of fact and small discrepancies quite consistent with the truthfulness of the persons produced cannot be made the ground for disbelief. The general rule is that whenever it is intended to impeach the credit of a person whose statement has been recorded; his attention must be drawn to the discrediting facts so that he may have an opportunity to explaining them".

Retraction from surrender of income made under section 132(4) during search proceedings or even under section 131 may be accepted on facts of the case.

Pullangode Rubber Produce Co. Ltd. v. *State of Kerala* [1973] 91 ITR 18 (SC)

Jodhpur Bench of ITAT in the case of *Dy. CIT* v. *M. L. Jain* [2005] 96 TTJ 362 has held that in the absence of recovery of any unexplained cash during the course of search, addition under section 69A could not be made solely on the basis of statement of the assessee recorded under section 132(4).

In the case of *Asstt. CIT* v. *Anoop Kumar* [2005] 147 Taxman 26 (Asr.) (Mag.) it has been held by ITAT, Amritsar 'SMC' Bench that in the absence of any supportive material or evidence, addition could not be made merely on the basis of statement recorded under section 132(4) when the income computed by the AO on the basis of seized documents and material is less than the income disclosed in the said statement which was subsequently retracted by the assessee.

In the case of *S.R.M.T. Ltd.* v. *Dy. CIT* [2006] 152 Taxman 8 (Visakha.) (Mag.), it has been held that in the absence of any incriminating material with the revenue and in the face of positive evidence adduced by the assessee regarding payment of commission, no disallowance could be made on the basis of retracted admission of assessee. In statement under section 132(4), assessee having produced on record assessment order of authorized dealers to whom commission payment was made, their balance sheet, P&L a/c, statements of 11 and affidavits of 9 dealers, the commission payment was allowable in full.

8.11 Facing examination during search

Recording of statement is an art from the point of view of assessee as well as of the authorized officer. It requires patience, skill and tactfulness. The authorized officer tries to get the truth from the assessee relating to his unaccounted transactions and undisclosed income. It is not an easy task to know from a person something which he does not want to tell. The authorized officer, first of all, tries to bind the assessee with in certain limits through the preliminary statement so that assessee does not try to shift his stand. Sometimes pressure is, in practice, exercised so that assessee does not lie or hide the facts. Assessee, in practice, is grilled and counter questioned from different angles and in different manners. Assessee is usually conveyed that in case replies are not given by him truthfully, he is liable to be prosecuted & it should not be considered as a threat.

Assessee should face the examination in a patient and cool manner. He should understand the question properly and reply the same after proper thinking and analyzing the consequences thereof. While it is emphasized that the facts should be stated in the statement yet some of the points which may be kept in mind are under:-

(*i*) **Exercise of threat or coercion**

In case any threat or coercion is exercised while recording the statement, assessee should not be perturbed or feel pressured by the same. He can politely request the authorized officer not to put pressure upon him. In the case of search proceeding under the Act, the authorized officer does not have power to arrest, to detain, or to use third degree. However, prosecution may be launched against assessee for false statement under the Indian Penal Code.

If a statement is not recorded properly or if any coercion, threat, inducement or undue influence is exercised, the person searched or the person whose statement has been recorded should inform the higher authorities without loss of time and without any exaggerations. Such a statement will be held to be ineffective, being obtained contrary to the provisions of the law. [*P. Mansoor Mohd. Ali Jinnah v. Dy. Director* [1989] 42 Taxman 126 (Mad.)]

(*ii*) **Refusal to reply vis-à-vis evasive reply**

Assessee should not refuse to reply any question. Refusal to reply any question may make him liable for penalty and prosecution. Assessee may show his ignorance or inability to answer depending upon the fact of his ignorance and inability. There is difference between refusal to answer a question in contrast to giving an answer showing ignorance or inability for some valid reason at that point of time.

There is nothing wrong depending upon the facts, in answering as under:

- ◆ I cannot say anything about this paper as I am not able to understand the contents mentioned in it.
- ◆ This paper is not in my hand writing and I cannot explain the details mentioned in it.
- ◆ This paper does not belong to me and I am not able to understand how this paper has come in my office. I will have to enquire regarding the same
- ◆ These matters are looked after by my accountant. I can tell the exact details after consulting with him.

(iii) Not a test of memory

In the course of recording of statement, the authorized officer may put lot of questions where facts and figures are required to be stated. The transactions may be quite old and the assessee may not remember the exact details. Instead of giving incorrect details or on the basis of guess work at the spur of the moment, it may be advisable depending upon the facts to show inability to recollect the correct details. There is nothing wrong depending upon the facts by replying in the following manner:

- ◆ It is a very old matter and I am unable to recollect the details of the same.
- ◆ I do not remember the details. I will have to check the records or consult to my accountant.
- ◆ It is a matter of record and details are contained in the books of account maintained.
- ◆ I do not remember. I will have to look into the records to tell the exact details.

(iv) Enquiry relating to bank accounts, firms and companies to which assessee is associated

Questions are usually asked to provide details of bank accounts maintained by the assessee or his family members. Details of the companies in which assessee is director or firms in which he is partner along with the details of other directors and partners may also be asked. In case complete and correct reply is not given mentioning the details of all the bank accounts or associate companies due to lapse of memory etc., assessee may be held liable for giving false statement and prosecution may be launched on this pretext. Such question may be replied depending upon the facts, with the rider "so far as I remember". There is nothing wrong & Assessee may reply in the following manner depending upon the facts and circumstances of the case:

♦ So far as I remember, the details are as under.

♦ I am highly tired and may not remember the complete details. As soon as I recollect, I will tell the other details.

(v) Enquiry regarding Bank Lockers

The keys of the bank lockers maintained by the person searched are one of the most sought items by the search team. Enquiries are made by the authorized officer from the assessee during his statement being recorded regarding bank lockers maintained with different banks etc. Details of the bank lockers should be provided by the assessee truthfully and carefully without hiding any details. It has been experienced in practice that prosecution is launched by the department for not furnishing complete and correct details regarding bank lockers. In case assessee does not remember the complete details of all the bank lockers, the reply should be given in properly guarded manner.

(vi) Continuous questioning

Sometimes authorized officer may put a question repeatedly in a different manner so as to get more facts or true nature of the transaction. In case assessee has nothing to say further depending upon the facts, he may reply in the following manner & there is nothing objectionable in it:

♦ I am exhausted and I am unable to recall anything further.

♦ I have already replied the question as above and I have nothing to state further in this regard.

(vii) Alleged admission by third party

Sometimes assessee may be communicated during search that the corresponding party has already admitted the unaccounted part of the transaction and assessee should also admit the same otherwise he may be in problem. Assessee may hold his nerves against such alleged admission purportedly made by the other party as he cannot be expected to be sure about the purported fact as communicated to him. He should remain focused on the facts within his knowledge and his replies. He may answer in the following manner depending upon the facts and circumstances of the case:

♦ I do not know about other party but facts in my case are as under.

   ◆ It seems other party has not stated the facts correctly, the actual fact is so and so.

(viii) **Attempt to decode**

Sometimes details are mentioned on the seized material relating to the unrecorded transactions in some kind of code words for example; 54.00 may be fifty four lakhs or 380 may be 380 lakhs. R.S. may be Radhey Shyam, business partner of the assessee. The authorized officer generally makes attempt to decode the details kept in coded format. Assessee should be careful in replying such questions, *inter alia*, to avoid any false reply.

(ix) **Dumb document**

There may be several documents or loose papers found during search which do not speak themselves but may contain vital details of unrecorded transactions. The documents themselves do not contain the nature of transactions or date of transactions. The authorized officer may try to seek details and nature of transactions contained in such documents. Assessee should be careful in replying such questions, *inter alia*, to avoid any false reply.

(x) **Explanation on behalf of others**

Assessee may reply to the questions which are relating to him. In case there are any questions put to him regarding transactions of other business partners or family members, he may pass the burden for reply by those persons only instead of replying such questions as he may not be expected to know the facts relating to others, fully and truly. Any wrong answer may put other into unnecessary avoidable hardships.

(xi) **Explain fully**

Sometimes question may be asked to justify certain expenses or nature of transaction recorded in the books of account. Assessee should furnish complete explanation justifying the nature of transaction as this opportunity can be utilized to strengthen his case.

(xii) **To get recorded**

Certain incidents may take place during search which may unfortunately be illegal or irregular. Before signing the statement, assessee may seek to record such incidents, if permitted, or alternatively he can write a separate letter and send it immediately to the authorized officer and higher departmental officials on the next day. Such incidents may be relating to the following matters:

   ◆ In case disclosed assets are being seized

- Diaries or documents being made part of seized material of the assessee, though the same have not been found from the searched premises but have been brought from outside.

- Quantity of stock items mentioned arbitrarily.

- Excessive exercise of power during search in recording the statement or otherwise.

(*xiii*) Disclosed assets being seized

There may be a situation when assessee believes that certain assets are of disclosed nature, but the same are seized by the authorized officer. The onus lies upon the assessee to produce evidences to the satisfaction of the authorized officer regarding disclosure of the assets in his returns of income filed or otherwise explained nature of such assets to the department. In case the authorized officer is not satisfied with the evidences produced by the assessee, assessee should try to convince him and talk to the higher authorities. The evidences produced by him should be put on record by way of submission of his explanation/letter. In case assets of disclosed nature are still seized, there is a procedure provided under section 132B for release of such assets.

(*xiv*) Password/Software for computer operation

The assessee is under legal obligation to provide password and facilitate operation of computers to the authorized officer so that the data therein may be inspected and/or copied. Any non-cooperation in this respect by the person searched may render him liable to be prosecuted. Therefore, the assessee should never refuse to provide such information to the authorized officer.

(*xv*) Year of acquisition of undisclosed assets

Sometimes, certain assets admittedly of undisclosed nature such as jewellery, valuable household goods etc. are found but the year of acquisition of such assets is not determinable. In case of the enquiry being made regarding the year of acquisition of such assets, assessee may state, depending upon the facts, the year of acquisition which may fall during preceding seven years prior to the year of search. Under such circumstances, the year of undisclosed income relating to such undisclosed assets shall be the year in which asset is stated to have been acquired. Assessee would be in that case liable to pay interest and penalty also in addition to income tax applicable thereon. However, in case such assets are established to have been acquired in the current year, the liability with respect to such undisclosed income shall be restricted upto the income tax applicable thereon when declaration of such undisclosed asset is made u/s 132(4) read with section 271AAA and along with concessional penalty u/s 271AAB as the case may be. Depending upon the actual facts and situation, the assessee should state the facts keeping in view above legal position.

8.12 Handling questions relating to certain specific aspects

(*i*) **Regular books of account not found - Explanation depending upon the facts**

In the course of search, it happens sometimes that the regular books of account may not be available and Authorized Officer may ask for the production of the said books of account. Assessee may tackle the situation depending upon the facts in the following manner:-

♦ Books of account are regularly maintained and must be in the office only. Since all records and files have been disturbed, the same are not readily traceable.

♦ Books of account are maintained on computers and there seems to be some problem in the software, therefore the file is not opening. It seems that virus has infected the computers and data stored in it.

In case books of account are kept somewhere else, before stating this fact assessee should be aware as to the legal position that such other place may also be searched and the books of account may be recovered therefrom.

(*ii*) **About jewellery**

During the course of search, there remains issue regarding seizure of jewellery. Generally, jewellery found during search belongs to all members of the family and there are instructions from the Central Board of Direct Taxes not to seize jewellery up to a prescribed quantity belonging to each family member. In view of the above, question regarding the jewellery may be tackled in the following manner depending upon the actual facts.

♦ Jewellery found at residence and kept in bank lockers belong to all the family members including wife, father, mother, son and daughter-in-law who are residing along with.

♦ It contains jewellery approximately five hundred grams relating to my daughter who is married and resides in U.K. or elsewhere, she has kept her jewellery with me for use whenever she comes to India.

It needs to be emphasized that actual answers would depend upon the facts applicable in each situation.

(*iii*) Investment in movable/immovable assets

Assessee should state the details of investment made in movable and immovable assets as recorded in his books of account. In case he does not remember the complete details, it can be stated that all investments are duly recorded in the books of account, and may be verified therefrom, or the complete details shall be provided after taking the information from the books.

(*iv*) Loans Given/Taken

In case of enquiry being made regarding loans/advances/gifts, given or accepted by the assessee to/from other persons, the reply should be given mentioning the correct details as recollected by him. In case complete details are not within his memory, a well protected reply should be given with the request to provide some time to furnish the complete details after consulting the records.

(*v*) Sources of income and particulars of income tax return filed

Generally, enquiry is made regarding sources of income and particulars of income-tax returns filed by the assessee. Assessee is supposed to know the complete details in this respect, which should be stated by him. In case he does not remember the complete details, the copies of the income tax returns filed may be produced and submitted by him.

(*vi*) Household expenses

Generally, enquiry is made regarding nature and quantum of the household expenses incurred by the assessee. The assessee may state the correct facts as known to him in this respect and further about the details of the expenses and withdrawals as recorded in the books of account. In case complete details are not remembered, he may politely request for further time so as to provide the complete details after consulting the records.

(*vii*) Incomplete Books/Cash Book

In case books of account and particularly cash book is found incomplete as on the date of search, assessee may be asked to explain the reason thereof. The assessee should state the correct facts in this regard. The assessee is supposed to maintain the books of account regularly. At least the primary books/records should be complete on daily & regular basis. Primary books include Cash Book/Day Book/Vouchers regarding receipt/payment of cash etc. In case Cash Book is not complete for some reason such as cashier was absent, or due to excessive work load, the original vouchers regarding receipt/payment of cash along with supporting evidences may be produced, and get recorded. In case primary books of account are not found and are incomplete, it may create serious question regarding the reliability of books of account.

Incompleteness of secondary books of account such as Bank Book, Ledger etc. may be explained with proper reasons but the same may not be very serious since it is a matter of processing which can be undertaken and completed at a later stage also.

(viii) Discrepancy in Inventory

Generally, quantitative detail of all inventory items is prepared and compared with the stock records and other financial records. In case of any discrepancy in the quantities or in the value of the inventory, questions are put to the assessee to explain the discrepancy and in case the explanation of the assessee is not satisfactory, he may be persuaded to make surrender of the undisclosed income.

The assessee, before authenticating the inventory list, must ensure that the quantity and quality of the inventory items have been recorded correctly. In case there are some rejected/slow-moving/damaged goods, this fact should be recorded. In case some of the inventory items are kept somewhere else or dispatched to third parties for job work etc., this fact should be got recorded. In case assessee is not able to furnish proper explanation instantly, he may request to grant some time to furnish the explanation at a later stage after consulting the records.

8.13 Obtaining copy of statement recorded

It has been observed, in practice, that the copy of the statement recorded by the authorized officer under section 132(4) is not supplied to the asses-see. Generally, argument is given from the side of the department that the copy of the statement shall be given by the assessing officer only when it is used against the assessee during assessment proceedings. Further, it is stated that sub-section (9) of section 132 entitles the assessee to obtain photocopy of the books of account or other documents seized during search and it does not empower the assessee to obtain photocopy of the statement recorded during search.

The procedure of recording the statement of the assessee during search proceedings or during any other proceedings under the Income Tax Act is similar to the procedure while recording the statement of any witness by any court. In such a situation, the provisions of Indian Evidence Act regarding recording of statement of the witness become applicable to the income tax proceeding as well. The person is entitled to obtain the copy of the statement recorded during any proceeding in the court immediately thereafter on an application being moved by him. In our opinion, the similar right should be available to the assessee whose statement is recorded during any proceedings under the Income Tax Act. The stand of the department not to supply copy of the statement recorded under section 132(4) does not seem to be reasonable and just. In such a situation assessee may even invoke provisions of Right to Information Act, 2005 to obtain the copy of the statement recorded by the authorized officer.

8.14 Power to issue summons for discovery, production of evidences etc.

Power to issue summons for discovery, production of evidences, enforcing the attendance of any person and examining him on oath are contained under sub-section (1) and sub-section (1A) of section 131 of the Income Tax Act, 1961. The provisions of these sections are quite significant while discussing and analyzing the power of the Income Tax authorities to record statement in the case of search operation. At times, power under section 131 of issuing summons is resorted to by the authorized officer in the case of search operation for enforcing attendance and recording statement of the person searched. It remains a controversial issue as to whether and which stage such power can be exercised by the authorized officer?

Since the provisions of section 131 are quite significant, relevant and debatable in the case of search operations, we are analyzing these provisions in this chapter.

(*i*) **Text of section 131:**

(*1*) *The Assessing Officer, Deputy Commissioner (Appeals), Joint Commissioner, Commissioner (Appeals), Chief Commissioner or Commissioner and the Dispute Resolution Panel referred to in clause (a) of sub-section (15) of section 144C shall, for the purposes of this Act, have the same powers as are vested in a court under the Code of Civil Procedure, 1908 (5 of 1908), when trying a suit in respect of the following matters, namely :—*

(*a*) *discovery and inspection;*

(*b*) *enforcing the attendance of any person, including any officer of a banking company and examining him on oath;*

(*c*) *compelling the production of books of account and other documents; and*

(*d*) *issuing commissions.*

(*1A*) *If the Director General or Director or Joint Director or Assistant Director or Deputy Director, or the authorised officer referred to in sub-section (1) of section 132 before he takes action under clauses (i) to (v) of that sub-section, has reason to suspect that any income has been concealed, or is likely to be concealed, by any person or class of persons, within his jurisdiction, then, for the purposes of making any enquiry or investigation relating thereto, it shall be competent for him to exercise the powers conferred under sub-section (1) on the income-tax authorities referred to in that sub-section, notwithstanding that no proceedings with respect to such person or class of persons are pending before him or any other income-tax authority.*

(2) For the purpose of making an inquiry or investigation in respect of any person or class of persons in relation to an agreement referred to in section 90 or section 90A, it shall be competent for any income-tax authority not below the rank of Assistant Commissioner of Income-tax, as may be notified by the Board in this behalf, to exercise the powers conferred under sub-section (1) on the income-tax authorities referred to in that sub-section, notwithstanding that no proceedings with respect to such person or class of persons are pending before it or any other income-tax authority.

(3) Subject to any rules made in this behalf, any authority referred to in sub-section (1) or sub-section (1A) or sub-section (2) may impound and retain in its custody for such period as it thinks fit any books of account or other documents produced before it in any proceeding under this Act :

Provided *that an Assessing Officer or an Assistant Director or Deputy Director shall not—*

    (a) impound any books of account or other documents without recording his reasons for so doing, or

    (b) retain in his custody any such books or documents for a period exceeding fifteen days (exclusive of holidays) without obtaining the approval of the Chief Commissioner or Director General or Commissioner or Director therefor, as the case may be.

(*ii*) Applicability of sub-section (1) of section 131:

The salient features of sub-section (1) of section 131 may be summarized as under:

    1. It empowers to the Income Tax authorities such as Assessing Officer, Joint Commissioner, Commissioner (Appeals), Chief Commissioner and Dispute Resolution Panel.

    2. It gives the same powers to the above Tax authorities as are vested in a court under Code of Civil Procedure, 1908 in respect of the following matters:

        (*a*) discovery and Inspection

    (*b*) enforcing the attendance of any person and examining him on oath

    (*c*) compelling the production of books of account and other documents

    (*d*) issuing commissions

3. The provisions of this section can be resorted to when trying a suit in the court. With reference to the Income Tax Act, it would imply that the provisions of this Section can be resorted to when any proceeding under the Income Tax Act are pending.

(*iii*) No power to the authorized officer in the course of search to issue summons under sub-section (1):

Since the power under sub-section (1) may be resorted to when any proceedings under the Income Tax Act are pending and therefore for the purpose of making any enquiry or investigation, the Authorized Officer does not have the power to issue summons for examination of any person on oath or for production of books of account or other documents. Moreover, such power cannot be invoked in the course of search proceedings since income tax search proceedings cannot be said to be the pending proceedings under the Income Tax Act in the nature of trying a suit in the court.

The income tax authorities of the Investigation Wing of the Income Tax department, prior to 1st October 1975, were finding themselves handicapped in the absence of such powers to make enquiry or investigation from any person within their jurisdiction prior to taking action of search under section 132 or even during the action of search prior to finding the person searched in possession or control of any books of account, documents or assets. By way of Taxation Laws (Amendment) Act, 1975 w.e.f. 1.10.1975, sub-section (1A) was incorporated under section 131 so as to provide such powers to the Income Tax authorities of the Investigation Wing.

(*iv*) Salient features of sub-section (1A) of section 131:

The salient features of sub-section (1A) of section 131 may be summarized as under:

1. It empowers to issue summons for examination on oath to the Income Tax Authorities of the Investigation Wing of the Income Tax Department i.e. the Director General or Director, Joint Director, Deputy Director or Assistant Director or the Authorized Officer referred to in sub-section (1) of section 132.

2. The power under sub-section (1A) is similar as the power under sub-section (1).

3. The power under sub-section (1A) may be invoked even when no proceedings under the Income Tax Act are pending. Such power can be invoked for the purpose of making any enquiry or investigation relating thereto from any person under the Income Tax Act.

4. Such power can be invoked by:

(*i*) the Director General, Director, Joint Director, Deputy Director or Assistant Director if he has reason to suspect that any income has been concealed or is likely to be concealed by any person or class of persons within his jurisdiction.

(*ii*) the Authorized Officer who has been authorized by the competent authority to conduct search under section 132(1) before he takes action under clauses (*i*) to (*v*) of section 132(1) and has reason to suspect that any income has been concealed or is likely to be concealed by any person or class of persons within his jurisdiction.

In the case of *Sumermal Jain* v. *Dy. CIT* [2014] 43 taxmann.com 57/225 Taxman 282 (Cal.) Reason to suspect that income had been concealed or was likely to be concealed by assessees need not be stated in notice under section 131(1A).Writ petition was held to be not valid.

(*v*) **Certain significant issues**:

From the above, certain practical issues do emerge which may be significant to be examined.

(*vi*) **Validity of Summons issued by ADI/Authorized Officer under sub-section (1) of section 131:**

As discussed above, summons by ADI/Authorized Officer can be issued under sub-section (1A) and not under sub-section (1) of section 131. In case summon is issued by ADI/Authorized Officer under sub-section (1) of section 131, it cannot be said to be a validly issued summon. Non-compliance of such summon may not be held to be a cause to impose penalty for non-compliance of summon under section 272A. However, before taking any such stand, provisions of section 292B introduced by the Taxation Laws (Amendment) Act, 1975 w.e.f. 1.10.1975 regarding ignoring technical default in drawing notice/summon etc. should also be kept in mind.

It has also been observed in practice that sometimes summon is issued by ADI/Authorized Officer simply mentioning as summon under section 131 and without quoting the sub-section. In such cases assessee takes the plea that it is also not a valid summon. In our opinion, such stand of the assessee may not be tenable and it cannot be said to be an invalid summon merely for that reason due to operation of section 292B.

(*vii*) **Whether summon under section 131(1A) can be issued to the person searched:**

This is a debatable issue as to whether summon under section 131(1A) can be issued by the Authorized Officer to the person searched for examining him on oath or for the purpose of production of desired books of account and other documents or for the purpose of seeking explanation from him relating to the seized documents. It has been observed in practice that generally such summons are issued by the Authorized Officer to the person searched so as to put pressure on the searched person to make declaration of undisclosed income. In some other cases summon under section 131(1A) is issued to the person searched to seek information/explanation relating to seized material for the purpose of preparing appraisal report by the Authorized Officer.

Under section 131(1A), there is categorical power to the Authorized Officer for examination on oath to any person before taking action under clauses (*i*) to (*v*) of section 132(1) in the case of search. Once action of search under section 132(1) has been taken, the Authorized Officer further gets power for examination on oath to the person searched under section 132(4) of the Act and such power remains vested with the Authorized Officer till the conclusion of search. In our considered opinion, when power under section 132(4) is vested with the Authorized Officer, he has to examine the person searched under section 132(4). When examination under section 132(4) has been undertaken or may further be undertaken, there should not be any reason to resort to the power of examination under section 131(1A) also.

The intent and object of vesting power under section 131(1A) to the Authorities of Investigation Wing/Authorized Officer was to cover up the deficiency/handicap which these authorities used to face in the absence of such power before taking the action of search as discussed in the earlier Paras also. When the action of search has been taken, all the evidences have been collected, the person searched has been examined under section 132(4), even after that to issue summon for further examination under section 131(1A) do cause unwarranted harassment to the person searched and does not seem to be permitted in the eyes of law. The opinion of the courts in this regard is divided and has been discussed earlier in the preceding part of this chapter.

(viii) **Invoking power under section 131(1A) before taking action under clauses (i) to (v) of section 132(1) by the Authorized Officer- Meaning thereof**

The power of examination under section 131(1A) has been granted to the Authorized Officer *inter alia* to record preliminary statement of the person searched before starting actual search operation. By recording the preliminary statement of the person searched, the Authorized Officer tries to bind the person within certain parameters and further tries to obtain information so as to make the search operation effective. As per language of section 132(4), wherein power of examination on oath during search has been given to the authorized officer, there was controversy and diversant opinion of the courts as to whether statement of the person to be searched may be recorded by the authorized officer before such person is found to be in possession or control of any books of account, documents or assets in the course of search operation. In view of the above controversy prevailing earlier and to strengthen the power of the authorized officer to record preliminary statement the provisions of sub-section (1A) was incorporated under section 131.

The power under sub-section (1A) can be resorted to by the Authorized officer before he takes either of the actions as provided under clauses *(i)* to *(v)* of section 132(1). The interpretation of this language in some of the quarters to this effect that such power is available only *before taking any of the actions* under any of clauses *(i)* to *(v)* of section 132, in our opinion is not reasonable and would make the provision almost redundant. If such interpretation is accepted, it would imply that when the authorized officer enters the premises to be searched, he takes action under clause *(i)* and once he has taken action under clause *(i)*, power under sub-section (1A) cannot be resorted to since such power can be resorted to before taking any action under any of clauses *(i)* to *(v)*. In our opinion, this is not the correct interpretation and rather the object of sub-section (1A) is to examine the person searched on oath before taking either of the actions under clause *(i)* or clause *(ii)* and so on so forth.

(ix) **Whether summon under section 131(1A) can be issued to the persons other than the person searched**

Summon under sub-section (1A) of section 131 can be issued by the prescribed Income Tax Authorities of the Investigation Wing when they have a reason to suspect that any income has been concealed or is likely to be concealed by any person within his jurisdiction. In case there is any material found and seized during search which may create reason to suspect in the opinion of the Authorized Officer that any income has been concealed or is likely to be concealed by any person other than the person searched, then for the purpose of making any enquiry or investigation relating thereto he may resort to power granted under sub-section (1A). Therefore the controversy as to whether after the action of search summon can be issued by the authorized officer under section 131(1A) cannot be extended to the other persons who have not been searched, is misplaced. Such power does remain with the authorized officer for the purpose of making any enquiry or investigation from the other persons.

It is incidental to take notice of the decision of Allahabad High Court in the case of *Dr. Mrs. Anita Sahai* v. *DIT* [2004] 136 Taxman 247 (All.) in which High Court have held that in case a notice is issued u/s 131(1A) after search and seizure operation u/s 132, it would show that there was neither reason to believe nor material before authorizing officer on the basis of which he could issue a warrant u/s 132.

However Gujarat High Court in the case of *Neesa Leisure Ltd.* v. *UOI* have held in its [2011] 16 taxmann.com 163/[2012] 204 Taxman 86 (Guj.)

"This Court does not find any merit in the said contention, in as much as if there is sufficient and tangible material available on record, prior to the search, based on which the concerned officer has formed the requisite belief under section 132(1) of the Act, merely because certain other information has been sought for by the authorised officer or any of the officers mentioned in section 131(1A) of the Act, the same would not render the search proceedings invalid. Even if the contention raised on behalf of the petitioners were to be accepted, viz., the authorised officer does not have any power to issue notices under section 131(1A) of the Act post search, the same at best would render the notices invalid. But issuance of notices under section 131(1A) of the Act post-search would not in any manner render the proceedings under section 132 of the Act invalid, if they were otherwise initiated pursuant to a valid authorization issued after recording satisfaction on the basis of the material available on record. It is difficult to fathom as to how the satisfaction recorded by the Director General of Income Tax (Investigation) on the basis of the material on record, would be rendered invalid merely because the Assistant Director of Income Tax has subsequently issued notices under section 131(1A) of the Act."

Gujarat High Court in the case of *Arti Gases* v. *DIT (Inv.)* [2000] 113 Taxman 68 (Guj.) have held that notices u/s 131(1A) can be issued after completion of search undertaken under the provisions of section 132, as it would be absolutely logical to call for information so as to have better particulars or to have complete idea about the material seized during the search.

(x) **Consequences of non-compliance of summon issued under section 131 to the person searched:**

In case of non-compliance of summon issued under section 131 by the authorized officer to the person searched, the following actions may be taken:

    (i) to take action for imposing penalty under section 272A by Additional/Joint Commissioner/Director. It is also pertinent to note here that penalty provision in this respect contained in clause *(c)* of section ∴72A also refers penalty to be imposed for non-compliance of summon issued under sub-section (1) of section 131 and not the summon issued under sub-section (1A) of section 131. This seems to be drafting error.

    (ii) to enforce attendance of the person to whom summon was issued by way of issue of arrest warrant through police.

(xi) **In case of non-compliance of summon, power of the income tax authorities to enforce attendance through arrest warrant**

The Income Tax authorities issuing summon under section 131 are vested with all the powers as are vested in a court under the Code of Civil Procedure, 1908. Under the Civil Procedure Code, in case summon issued by the court is not complied by any person, the court has power to enforce attendance of such person through police authorities by issue of arrest warrant. The income tax authorities may also exercise the same power in this respect. However in practice it has been observed that the authorized officer exercise such power in extreme cases.

8.15 Introduction of new section 133C by Finance (No. 2) Act, 2014 and as modified by the Finance Act, 2016 and the Finance Act, 2017 granting power to call for information by prescribed income tax authority

Finance (No. 2) Act, 2014 has introduced new section 133C which has been modified by the Finance Act, 2016 and 2017, and which read as under:—

"133C. (1) The prescribed Income Tax Authority may, for the purpose of verification of information in its possession relating to any person, issue a notice to such person requiring him, on or before a date to be specified therein, to furnish information or documents verified in the manner specified therein, which may be useful for, or relevant to, any enquiry or proceeding under this Act.

(2) Where any information or document has been received in response to a notice issued under sub-section (1), the prescribed income-tax authority

may process such information or document and make available the outcome of such processing to the Assessing Officer.

(3) *The Board may make a scheme for centralised issuance of notice and for processing of information or documents and making available the outcome of the processing to the Assessing Officer.*

Explanation.—In this section, the term "proceeding" shall have the meaning assigned to it in clause (*b*) of the *Explanation* to section 133A."

Under the present scheme of the Income Tax Act, power to call for information is vested with the Income Tax Authority in a case when certain proceedings against the person are pending before the Authority. Power to issue summon under section 131(1) is also vested with the Tax Authority in connection with certain proceedings pending before him. Power under section 131(1A) was granted only to the Tax Authority of Investigation wing of the department to make enquiry when such authority has reason to suspect that any income has been concealed or is likely to be concealed by any person. Thus, legislature has not granted power to all tax authorities to make enquiries even when any proceeding is not pending so that powers by the officers are not misused and reasonable safeguard is in-built into the system.

CHAPTER 9

PRESUMPTION UNDER SECTIONS 132(4A) & 292C

9.1 Text of section 132(4A)

Section 132(4A) reads as under—

> *(4A) Where any books of account, other documents, money, bullion, jewellery or other valuable article or thing are or is found in the possession or control of any person in the course of a search, it may be presumed—*
>
> > *(i) That such books of account, other documents, money, bullion, jewellery or other valuable article or thing belong or belongs to such person;*
> >
> > *(ii) That the contents of such books of account and other documents are true; and*
> >
> > *(iii) That the signature and every other part of such books of account and other documents which purport to be in the handwriting of any particular person or which may reasonably be assumed to have been signed by, or to be in the handwriting of, any particular person, are in that person's handwriting, and in the case of a document stamped, executed or attested, that it was duly stamped and executed or attested by the person by whom it purports to have been so executed or attested.*

As per the Finance Act, 2007, legislature has inserted a new section 292C with retrospective effect from 1st October, 1975, i.e. the date from which section 132(4A) was introduced on the statute, which as modified by the Finance Act, 2008, reads as under -

Text of section 292C

> *(1) Where any books of account, other documents, money, bullion, jewellery or other valuable article or thing are or is found in the possession*

*or control of any person in the course of a search **under section 132 or survey under section 133A**, it may, **in any proceeding under this Act**, be presumed—*

  (*i*) *that such books of account, other documents, money, bullion, jewellery or other valuable article or thing belong or belongs to such person;*

 (*ii*) *that the contents of such books of account and other documents are true; and*

(*iii*) *that the signature and every other part of such books of account and other documents which purport to be in the handwriting of any particular person or which may reasonably be assumed to have been signed by, or to be in the handwriting of, any particular person, are in that person's handwriting, and in the case of a document stamped, executed or attested, that it was duly stamped and executed or attested by the person by whom it purports to have been so executed or attested.*

(*2*) *Where any books of account, other documents or assets have been delivered to the requisitioning officer in accordance with the provisions of section 132A, then, the provisions of sub-section (1) shall apply as if such books of account, other documents or assets which had been taken into custody from the person referred to in clause (a) or clause (b) or clause (c), as the case may be, of sub-section (1) of section 132A, had been found in the possession or control of that person in the course of a search under section 132.*

9.2 Legislative History

(*i*) Rationale for introduction of new section 292C

In fact, provisions of section 132(4A) of the Act are analogous to those of section 139 of the Customs Act, 1962. The language of section 292C is also almost same as provided earlier under section 132(4A) except addition of the words mentioned in bold letters (*supra*). The rationale for addition of these words and introduction of new section 292C may be summarized as under-

   1. There was controversy on the issue as to whether presumption under section 132(4A) is applicable only with respect to situations covered under section 132 or more particularly with respect to summary assessment provided under erstwhile sub-section (5) of section 132 or it extends to regular assessment also. The legislative intent was to make presumption of sub-section (4A) applicable to the assessment proceedings as well, but since

sub-section (4A) was part of section 132, this controversy used to be raised in many cases.

In certain judicial pronouncements, Courts had taken the view that presumption under section 132(4A) has limited applicability to section 132 only and it cannot be extended and made use of during assessment proceeding of search cases. One of the arguments in favour of such interpretation was based on this logic that wherever legislature was to extend this presumption u/s 132(4A) to any other proceeding under the Act, it has specifically done so such as in section 278D for the purpose of prosecution. In the case of *Pushkar Narain Sarraf* v. *CIT* [1990] 50 Taxman 213/183 ITR 388 Allahabad High Court held that the presumption under section 132(4A) is for the limited purpose of search and seizure proceedings and for retaining the assets under section 132(5) and nothing more. This ratio was later on approved by the Supreme Court in the case of *P.R. Metrani* v. *CIT* [2006] 157 Taxman 325 (SC) holding that presumption under section 132(4A) is not available to authorities while framing the regular assessment. However the material seized can be used as a piece of evidence in any other proceedings under the Act and all contentions in this regard were left open.

This interpretation coming from the apex court created problem in the matter of regular assessment of search cases. To make the legislative intent clear and unambiguous, separate section has been introduced as section 292C with retrospective effect from 1st October, 1975, i.e. from the inception of sub-section (4A) under section 132. Insertion of section 292C with retrospective effect makes it clear that presumptions prescribed u/s 132(4A) were always available even in regular assessment. Further, addition of the words *"in any proceeding under this Act"* in section 292C leaves no scope for any confusion on this issue and the legislative intent was made amply clear.

Insertion of sub-section (2) under section 292C by Finance Act, 2008 has been made with the objective to make the presumption available in case of requisition under section 132A also. This sub-section has also been made effective retrospectively from 1st October, 1975, and has been discussed in detail in the chapter on requisition under section 132A.

2. The words *"or survey under section 133A"* have been added under section 292C so as to make presumption available to the assessing officer in relation to survey proceedings under section 133A also. These words have been added with retro-

spective effect from 1st June, 2002, the date from which power to impound books of account and other documents was given to the Income Tax authorities during survey proceedings.

Except for the above changes, the language of both the sections viz. section 132(4A) and section 292C is almost identical. Even after insertion of section 292C with retrospective effect, sub-section (4A) has also been retained under section 132 which does not seem to serve any other purpose. Since section 292C is of wider connotation, reference to this section would be more relevant while analyzing the provisions & applicability of this section to the assessment proceeding of search cases. However, from the point of view of analyzing various propositions involved on this issue, it hardly makes any difference whether reference is made to section 132(4A) or to section 292C.

9.3 Objective

The objective of making the presumptions available to the Income Tax authorities as to the books of account, other documents or assets found during search belonging to the person from whose possession or control the same have been found, is to make the person to own such books of account, other documents or assets so as to require him to explain the nature and contents of such material found from his possession. The objective is to place the burden on the assessee so that he may not be permitted to take the plea without cogent evidence that such material does not belong to him or he does not know how such material has come into his possession or contents thereof are incorrect.

This concept is in line with the principle given under Indian Evidence Act. As per section 110 of Indian Evidence Act, 1872, burden of proof as to the actual ownership of a thing lies on the person from whose custody it was found. Section 110 of Indian Evidence Act, 1872 reads as under:-

> "When the question is whether any person is owner of any thing of which he is shown to be in possession, the burden of proving that he is not the owner is on the person who affirms that he is not the owner."

9.4 Broad framework

The broad framework of this section may be described as under-

1. There is legal presumption against the person from whose possession or control any books of account, other documents or assets are found to the effect that the same belongs to him. The onus lies upon him to explain the nature and contents or source of such books of account, other documents or assets found from his possession.

2. There is a further legal presumption that the contents of such books of account or other documents are true and the same are signed and in the handwriting of the person by whom these are purported to be signed or written. Further, in case of a document stamped, executed or attested, there is legal presumption that it has been duly stamped, executed or attested by the person by whom it purports to have been so executed or attested.

3. Possession or control may be different from ownership.

4. This presumption is a rebuttable presumption.

5. The presumption is not binding on Assessing Officer.

6. Presumption is to the extent that books of account, other documents or assets found during search belong to the assessee. The onus to establish that any undisclosed income can be attributed to the assessee out of such evidences remains on Assessing Officer.

7. The presumption is against the person from whose possession or control books of account, other documents or assets have been found during search. This presumption cannot be extended to any third party.

9.5 Legal presumption is against the person having possession or control

This concept of legal presumption has been borrowed in section 132(4A)/292C of the Income Tax Act, from Indian Evidence Act, 1872. Section 110 of the Indian Evidence Act provides that burden to prove as to the actual ownership of a thing lies on the person from whose custody it is found. The section states as under "where the question is whether any person is owner of any thing of which he is shown to be in possession, the burden of proving that he is not the owner is on the person who affirms that he is not the owner."

After insertion of the above provision explicitly in section 132(4A)/292C, one can't get away by merely pleading that it is not for him but it is for the department to establish that books of account or other documents or assets of incriminating nature found during search belong to the assessee or to prove his hand writing or signature thereon or that contents of such books of account or documents are true. One can't possibly take a plea without cogent evidence that such books of account or documents have been left by some stranger and he doesn't know anything about the same. Assessee is required to offer a reasonable explanation regarding the nature of such books of account or documents found in his possession or control and if the same is claimed to be belonging to somebody else, then also assessee is required to explain as to whom the same belong and as to how the same has come into his possession and that too by leading evidence.

It has been observed in practice that when unaccounted jewellery is found at the time of search, assessee usually tries to explain the same taking plea that it belongs to some other relative or friend who has kept with the assessee for safe custody. But in view of the above presumption, the person who is found in possession or control of jewellery is liable to be treated as owner of the same unless it is otherwise proved by him by leading cogent and satisfactory evidences. The evidence may be oral, documentary or circumstantial depending upon the facts of the case. Same position will hold good for unaccounted money, bullion, cash, bonds or other valuable articles or thing found during search.

There may be situation when some transactions are made by the person searched ostensibly in the name of some other person as his benami but the real owner/beneficiary of such transactions is the searched person himself & documents relating to such transactions are found from possession of the searched person. In such a case, searched person is required to explain the nature & source of the transactions recorded in such documents and the presumption would lie against the searched person who is the real owner/beneficiary. The person search cannot be heard saying that he is not required to explain the nature & source of the transactions emanating from such documents.

In the case of *P. K. Narayanan* v. *CIT* [2000] 112 Taxman 667 (Ker.), Hon'ble Kerala High Court has held that the jewellery business standing in another's name in fact belonged to assessee, no interference was called for with such findings of fact and the income from that business was rightly charged in assessee's hands.

The recovery of ledger and other documents entered in Panchnama having been duly proved and they being in the hand and signatures of the accused, it had to be presumed that the contents of such books of account and documents were true in terms of section 132(4A). *ITO* v. *Prem Dass* [1992] 64 Taxman 526 (P&H).

Provisions of section 132(4A) spelt out the presumption that the documents belonged to the person from whom they were seized and that their contents were true. *Kerala Liquor Corporation* v. *CIT* [1996] 222 ITR 333 (Ker.).

Unless cogent evidence is adduced by the assessee, it would have to be presumed that the articles belonged to him and they were owned by the assessee himself. Not only this, unless the assessee sets up a clear case and leads cogent evidence to show that the gold articles were acquired in some different assessment year, there would be a further presumption that the articles were acquired in the year in question and they represented the concealed income of the year in question itself. *CIT* v. *K.I. Pavunny* [1998] 99 Taxman 327 (Ker).

When any person is owner of anything of which he is shown to be in possession, the onus of proving that he is not the owner is on the person who affirms that he is not the owner. *Chuharmal* v. *CIT* [1988] 38 Taxman 190 (SC).

It is not in dispute that the father and son were living jointly in the house. It is also not the case of the Department that the seized books in question were found from the room of the respondent. Indisputably, the father had owned up the books in question. Normally, the presumption that the seized books belonged to the person from whose possession they have been seized has been discharged and it was upon the Department to prove by cogent material and evidence that the entries in the said books were that of the respondent. No such material has been brought on record by the Department and, therefore, the CIT(A) was perfectly justified in accepting the plea raised by the respondent that the books in question did not belong to him but to his father, who had owned up the same by filing affidavit. The finding recorded by the CIT(A) is based on appreciation of evidence and material on record and has rightly been upheld by the Tribunal. *CIT* v. *Ashok Kumar* [2006] 151 Taxman 105 (All.).

In the case of *Hemant Kumar Ghosh* v. *Asstt. CIT(A)* [2015] 126 DTR (Pat.) 396 (HC), it has been held that when investment were found in name of assessee and assessee alone, that too in course of search and seizure under section 132, presumption could only be that they formed part of unaccounted income of assessee and mere fact of producing an affidavit by wife or mother of assessee would not be treated by Assessing Officer as sufficient explanation.

(i) Meaning of possession or control

The words used under this provision are "possession or control". The possession may be with one person and the control with another person with respect to the same item. For example, documents relating to unaccounted sales are found from the possession of employee of the company but the control of the same would lie upon the owner or management of the company and it can't be said to be unaccounted income of the employee but it would relate to the company with whom the control lies. On the other hand, if a personal diary is found from the possession of an employee containing details of personal affairs of the employee, the control of the same would lie with the employee and any undisclosed income on the basis of such diary would relate to the employee and not to the company.

(ii) Possession or control may be different from ownership

Possession or control may be different from ownership and it is the person who owns the assets will ultimately be liable to be taxed. It is the responsibility of the person from whose possession or control documents or assets are found, to explain about the ownership of the same. Courier carrying unaccounted cash is in possession or control of the asset but the owner of the asset is the person or company on whose behalf he is carrying the cash. The income is ultimately liable to be assessed in the hands of owner, but the onus would lie upon the courier to prove as to who is the owner of the asset in question. In the absence of proof as to ownership of the asset, the presumption would operate against the courier that unaccounted cash belongs to him.

In the case of *ITO* v. *W.D. Estate (P.) Ltd.* [1993] 45 ITD 473 (Bom.-Trib.) (TM) it was held that on the basis of a file and table diary belonging to a disgruntled employee of the assessee, no addition could be made to the assessee although these things are found during the course of search conducted at the assessee's premises which showed sales and receipt of on-money. Further there was no other evidence on record to show that the assessee had received any on-money payments.

In the case of *CIT* v. *K.K. Abdul Kareem* [1996] 88 Taxman 323 (Ker.) it was held that no presumption could be raised that the assessee was the owner of cash if assessee was only a carrier of the amount belonging to others and the appellate authorities did not find any material to conclude that cash, in question, belonged to the assessee.

In the case of *CIT* v. *Soorajmall Nagarmull* [1989] 45 Taxman 151 (Cal.) it was held that value of jewellery found during search could not be assessed in the hands of the firm if it was found in possession of wife and mother of the partner of the firm and there was no material to show that the jewellery belonged to the firm.

Three persons having admitted the ownership of primary gold and gold ornaments found in the possession of the assessee and confirmed that they had given the ornaments for making new ornament and the CEGAT too having arrived at the finding that the said gold and gold ornaments belong to them, addition under section 69A could not be made in the hands of the assessee by presuming him to be the owner of such valuable articles merely because said parties have failed to prove their ownership. *Mangilal Agarwal* v. *Asstt. CIT* [2007] 163 Taxman 399 (Raj.).

Certain amount was recovered from a room which was a bedroom of the petitioner-assessee and the same was kept and locked by him even though the house belonged to his only daughter. It was held that there was no irregularity in applying the presumption u/s 132(4A) for treating the amount so seized as belonging to the assessee. - *R. Bharathan* v. *ITO* [1990] 51 Taxman 502 (Ker.).

Paper were found in the car of the assessee which was used by his children, staff, guests, customers, suppliers and other parties and as such these cannot be said to have been found in the possession or control of the assessee and he is not bound by the presumption u/s 132(4A) in respect of these papers. [*Bansal Strips (P.) Ltd.* v. *Asstt. CIT* [2006] 99 ITD 177 (Delhi-Trib.)].

In the case of *CIT* v. *Shravan Kumar Gurjar* [2010] 186 Taxman 291 (Delhi), Delhi High Court have held that assessee who only acted as a booking agent could not be presumed to be the owner of valuable detected in search operations by police where it was established that the seized goods belonged to angaria who had booked the goods with the assessee. Thus, a clear distinction was made between possession/control on the one hand and ownership on the other hand.

(iii) **No addition on the basis of derivative evidence**

Presumption given under section 132(4A) regarding truth of contents of books of account etc. is not available with regard to the seizure, of US $ and gold biscuits from the possession of assessee, made by custom authorities and the addition made on the basis of derivative evidence was not justified. *Sitaram Somani* v. *Asstt. CIT* [1991] 39 TTJ 609 (Jp.-Trib.)

Similar view that no addition could be made on the basis of derivative evidence was taken in *Brijlal, Rupchand* v. *ITO* [1991] 40 TTJ 668 (Ind.-Trib.). Tribunal followed the Allahabad High Court's order in *Pushkar Narain Sarraf* v. *CIT* [1990] 50 Taxman 213/183 ITR 388.

9.6 Presumption is a rebuttable presumption

The use of the words *"may be presumed"* under the section implies that it can't be applied mechanically against the person who is in possession or control. Due consideration is required to be given in each case to the facts and circumstances existing e.g. if cash is found in the possession of cashier of the company, he can't be presumed to be the owner. On the other hand, if cash is found at the residence of the cashier, who is not authorized to keep the cash of the company at his residence, the same can't be presumed to be company's cash and the ownership of the same may lie on cashier unless otherwise is proved.

The presumption under this section is a rebuttable presumption. The onus to rebut the presumption would lie upon the person who is found in possession or control by leading evidence which may be oral, documentary or circumstantial.

Where assessee had proved that documents didn't belong to him, the amounts mentioned in the said documents are not assessable in the hands of the assessee. *CIT* v. *Raj Pal Singh Ram Avtar* [2005] 149 Taxman 32 (All.)

The Rajasthan High Court held that what quantum of evidence would rebut a legal presumption in a given set of facts does not admit of any thumb rule. The evidence may be direct or circumstantial or both and the mere statement of the assessee may be enough in some cases. *Asstt. CIT* v. *Thahrayamal Balchand* [1980] 124 ITR 111, 117 (Raj.).

Presumption under section 132(4A) that articles found in possession or control of person belong to him is rebuttable for purposes of provisions of Income-tax Act. *CIT* v. *P.R. Metrani* [2002] 120 Taxman 612 (Kar.).

Presumption raised by section 132(4A) is a statutory presumption but such presumptions are rebuttable and assessee can lead evidence to show that books of account found from his premises either do not belong to him or entries recorded therein do not relate to assessee's business. It cannot be said that once entries are found in duplicate books of account which are not intended to be produced before the assessing officer, contents of books of account found and seized during course of search should be accepted as true. *Biru Mal Pyare Lal* v. *Asstt. CIT* [2001] 79 ITD 169 (Chd.-Trib.).

Making of presumption under section 132(4A) depends upon the particular facts of the case. Such presumption is rebuttable and the person is free to lead evidence to rebut such evidence. The ITO could not be justified in making such presumptions in all cases without judicial application of mind to the facts of the particular case. *Shashikant M. Zaveri* v. *Sixth ITO* [1990] 37 TTJ 120 (Bom.-Trib.).

The provisions of section 132(4A) should be applied and interpreted in a reasonable manner and in consonance with justice. In the case of *Asstt. CIT* v. *Sri Radheshyam Poddar* [1992] 41 ITD 449 (Cal.-Trib.) it was held that on the basis of unsigned typed memorandum of understanding, no addition can be made if assessee led evidences by way of letters which were sufficient to rebut the presumption. Words, *'may be presumed'* used in section 132(4A) make it clear that the drawing of presumption in such cases depends upon particular facts and circumstances of the case.

When cash was seized from the room of assessee's daughter, which was normally used and kept lock by the assessee himself, it cannot be said that these amounts really belonged to the daughter and accordingly it was held by the Kerala High Court that amount belong to the father. *Bharathan (R.)* v. *ITO* [1990] 51 Taxman 502 (Ker.).

Question whether presumption under section 132(4A) is rebutted or not is always a question of fact. *CIT* v. *Kishanchand* [1993] 45 TTJ 20 (Jp.-Trib.).

No inference could be drawn on the basis of seized papers which were found during the course of search showing calculation of interest on a slip of paper. Although there is a presumption in section 132(4A) about contents of documents seized in search is true but, is rebuttable. Hence reassessment proceedings on the basis of the slip of paper were held as invalid. *CIT* v. *S.M.S. Investment Corporation (P.) Ltd.* [1994] 207 ITR 364 (Raj.).

The Tribunal has taken note of the presumption deemed under section 132(4A) and has held that the respondent has rebutted the presumption by giving plausible explanation that neither the partners nor their employees knew English and they do not read or write in English and further, the said paper was found from the debris in the shop premises and might have been left by someone and it did not belong to them. The Tribunal has further found that when the partners and their employees had made a statement that they did not know English; no attempt was made by the AO to cross examine the partners or their employees to extract the truth. *CIT* v. *Raj Pal Singh Ram Avtar* [2005] 149 Taxman 32 (All.).

Under section 132(4A), the Revenue was entitled to draw a presumption against the assessee in respect of the cash found but since the presumption is rebuttable, an opportunity was given to the assessee to rebut the statutory presumption. Seeking to rebut the presumption, the assessee stated that the cash belonged to the political party and did not belong to him. The assessee did not bring any material on record to substantiate his allegation. It was held that the assessee had not been able to rebut the statutory presumption under section 132(4A) and, therefore, the addition was made under section 69A. *Sukh Ram* v. *Asstt. CIT* [2007] 159 Taxman 385 (Del.).

The onus to rebut the presumption lies on the assessee and if he is not able to discharge his onus by leading satisfactory evidences, adverse inference may be drawn against the assessee. In the case of *Surendra M. Khandhar* v. *Asstt. CIT* [2010] 321 ITR 254 (Bom.) it has been held by the Bombay High Court that assessee having failed to rebut the presumption under section 292C, addition under section 69 on the basis of document seized from the possession of assessee was rightly made by AO and sustained by the Tribunal.

The presumption under section 132(4A) is a rebuttable presumption and it can be rebutted as per facts and evidences of each case. On the basis of facts of the case, statements made and evidences produced by the assessee, the authorities may accept the rebuttal of the assessee, if satisfied. In the case of *CIT* v. *Ved Prakash Choudhary* [2008] 169 Taxman 130 (Delhi) on the basis of facts of the case no addition could be sustained based upon the presumption. Delhi High Court held as under—

The facts of the case make it very clear that there were two MoUs entered into by the assessee with R and M in respect of the purchase of agricultural land. The two MoUs did record that "the purchase consideration shall be ₹ 123.30 lacs. The purchaser having paid to the vendor the sum of ₹ 25,00,000 part of the said purchase consideration as a deposit and shall pay the residual of said purchase consideration to the vendor on or before 30th April, 1999 when the purchase will be completed." Notwithstanding this, the assessee as well R and M denied the money transaction. In addition thereto, the case set up was that the agricultural land had, in fact, been sold to DT (P) Ltd. by R and M. This was confirmed by N, one of the directors of DT (P) Ltd. Quite clearly, the MoUs did not fructify. Section 132(4A) uses the expression *"it may be presumed"*. It not obligatory on the assessing authority to make a presumption. Even if a presumption is required to be made, then, the presumption is a rebuttable one and relates to a question of fact. In so far as the present case is concerned, the assessee had stated that in fact there was no transfer of money between him and R and M. On the other hand, R and M had denied receipt of any money from the assessee. In the fact of these denials there ought to have been corroborative evidence to show that there was in fact such a transfer of money. Both the CIT(A) as well as the Tribunal have come to the conclusion that there was no such material on record. The AO relied on certain other transactions entered into by the assessee with R and M for drawing a presumption in respect of the transfer of money, but the Tribunal rightly held that those were independent transactions and had nothing to do with the MoUs, which were the subject matter of discussion. Even if there was something wrong with some other transactions entered into, that would not give rise to an adverse inference insofar as the subject MoUs are concerned. No substantial question of law arises.

In the case of *CIT* v. *D.R. Bansal* [2010] 191 Taxman 424 (Chhattisgarh), Chhattisgarh High Court have held that though presumption u/s 132(4A) is rebuttable but it must be rebutted with cogent evidence and not merely by taking the bald plea that incriminating papers seized during the search were forged and fabricated documents planted by two accountants with in intention to get undue pecuniary benefit from the assessee by blackmailing them.

In the case of *CIT* v. *Blue Lines* [2014] 50 taxmann.com 425/[2015] 231 Taxman 49 (Kar.) (HC) Tribunal found that though materials were seized in search, said materials did not reflect name of assessee. Most of cheques were stale and some other cheques were either blank or were in name of third parties, therefore, Tribunal held that revenue was not justified in drawing presumption under section 132(4A). Dismissing the appeal of revenue the Court held that since finding recorded by Tribunal could not be found fault with, same was to be upheld.

It has been held in the case of *Ajay Gupta* v. *CIT* 185 DTR (All) 217 that the presumption under section 132(4A) is not in absolute terms but is subject to corroborative evidence and in the absence of corroborative evidence, the Tribunal was not justified in reversing the finding of the CIT(A) deleting addition.

9.7 Not binding on Assessing Officer

The legislature has used the words *"may presume"* and not the words *"shall presume" or "conclusive proof"*. The phrase *"Shall presume"* does not give any option to the Income Tax Authority but to assume it to be so whereas the phrase *"May presume"* means such presumption is optional having regard to facts of the case. It may or may not be invoked depending upon the facts. Even if the court makes such presumption, it is rebuttable. The words "shall presume" leaves no room with the court not to make the presumption and the court is bound to take the fact as proved until evidence is given to disprove it. In that sense, even such presumption is also rebuttable. The words "conclusive proof" gives an artificial probative effect by the law to certain facts. No evidence is allowed to be adduced to combat that effect and in that sense this is irrebuttable presumption which the law makes so peremptorily that it will not permit that to be overturned by any contrary proof, howsoever the strong that proof may be.

As the section is worded, it implies that the decision is to be taken by the assessing officer according to the facts and circumstances of each case. The presumption laid down in this section is however not binding on the Income Tax Authority. The assessing officer is not required to apply the presumption in each and every case without considering its nature and context.

Presumption laid down under section 132(4A) is not binding on assessing officer. It is open to him to record the findings that the contents of books of account and documents found during the course of search are not true. *Pradip Chandulal Patel* v. *P.G. Karode, Asstt. CIT* [1992] 65 Taxman 513 (Guj.).

There is a presumption regarding truth of the contents of books of account, etc. in section 132(4A). But it is in the discretion of the court or the authority, depending upon other factors, to decide whether the presumption must be drawn. The words used in section are "may be presumed" as is used in section 114 of the Evidence Act. So it is not mandatory that whenever the books of account etc., are seized, the court or the authority shall necessarily draw the presumption, irrespective of any other factors which may dissuade the court or the authority from doing so. *ITO* v. *Abdul Majeed* [1987] 34 Taxman 357 (Ker.).

However, Visakhapatnam Bench of Tribunal in the case of *S.R.M.T. Ltd.* v. *Dy. CIT* [2006] 152 Taxman 8 (Visakhapatnam) (Mag.) have held that when entries relating to commission paid appeared in the seized books and contrary evidence was not brought on record by revenue that such books of account and entries are not correct, presumption available u/s 132(4A) would be available in favour of the assessee and the commission paid to the authorized dealers as recorded in the regular books of the assessee will be presumed to be correct and true.

Contention that the entry made in the books of account regarding the expenses and found during the course of search is to be treated as true is not sustainable [*Anjuga Chit Funds (P.) Ltd.* v. *Dy. CIT* [2008] 113 ITD 67 (Chennai-Trib.)].

It has been held in the case of *CIT* v. *Damac Holdings Pvt. Ltd.* [2018] 89 taxmann.com 70/253 Taxman 123 (Ker.) that presumption as to seized documents can be raised in favour of assessee where documents showing expenditure incurred on account of value additions to property were found and there was failure by Assessing Officer to conduct enquiry or investigation regarding source of investment or genuineness of expenditure. It was held that the expenditure to the extent supported by documents is allowable and Presumption is effective only to extent of documents seized.

(*i*) Presumption - Whether available under regular assessment proceedings?

This issue was relevant prior to introduction of section 292C with retrospective effect from 1st October, 1975. The controversy in this regard has been set right after introduction of section 292C and now there is no doubt to this issue and the presumption as given under section 132(4A) is available to the assessing officer during regular assessment proceedings.

Prior to introduction of section 292C by Finance Act, 2007, there were contradictory judgments of different Courts in this regard. In the case of *Pushkar Narain Sarraf* v. *CIT* [1990] 50 Taxman 213/183 ITR 388 (All.) Allahabad High Court held that the presumption under section 132(4A) is for the limited purpose of search and seizure proceedings and for retaining the assets under section 132(5) and nothing more. This ratio was recently approved by the Supreme Court in the case of *P.R. Metrani* v. *CIT* [2006] 157 Taxman 325 (SC) holding that presumption under section 132(4A) is not available to authorities while framing the regular assessment.

On the other hand even prior to introduction of section 292C certain Courts had taken the view that presumption under section 132(4A) is available to the assessing officer during regular assessment proceedings. In the case of *Ashwani Kumar* v. *ITO* [1991] 39 ITD 183 (Del.-Trib.) it was held that presumption under section 132(4A) could be raised in proceedings for the regular assessment otherwise very purpose of provision contained in section 132(4A) would be frustrated. In the given case during the course of search, certain books of account, were seized in which certain cash credits were recorded. In the assessment proceedings the assessee pleaded that by virtue of section 132(4A) the correctness of those credits, as recorded in the books of account, should be presumed.

(ii) **Presumption u/s 292C available not only in regular assessment proceeding but also in any other proceeding under the Act**

Where the books of account, etc. are found in possession or control of a person in the course of search under section 132, the presumption as given under section 292C will apply in any proceeding under the Act qua the person from whose possession or control, such books of account, other documents or assets are found. The said proceedings may include a regular assessment, an assessment made under sections 153A, 153C, reassessment proceedings under section 147, penalty and prosecution proceeding under Chapter XXII of the Act. Further, presumption will apply to the documents etc. found in survey under section 133A and books of account, etc. requisitioned under section 132A as provided u/s 292C itself.

(iia) **Whether presumption under section 292C is available while framing assessment under section 148**

A question may arise whether presumption under section 292C as available to the assessing officer with respect to evidences collected in the course of search would be available even when assessment is being framed not by invoking provision of section 153A but by invoking provision of section 148.

The presumption under section 292C is available to the assessing officer with respect to books of account, other document, assets or any other evidences collected in the course of search under section 132 or survey under section 133A for the purpose of any proceeding under the Act. In the case of survey conducted under section 133A, assessment is framed under section 143(3) or under section 148. When presumption under section 292C is available for framing assessment under the normal provision of the Act in the case of survey, by applying the same rationale presumption under section 292C shall be available to the assessing officer in the case of search also for framing assessment under section 148 or for that matter for any proceeding under the Act. In fact, presumption under section 292C is attracted with respect to the evidences collected from the possession or control of the person to be assessed and it has nothing to do with the nature of proceedings under the Act in which the same is being used. This rationale is further fortified by this fact that section 153A though is not applicable for the year under search yet when assessment is made u/s 143(3), presumption u/s 292C relating to such assessment proceeding is available.

(iii) **Presumption under section 132(4A) *v.* section 68**

In connection with the cash credits recorded in the books of account of the assessee seized during search, applicability of presumption under section 132(4A) does not mean that assessee is discharged from the onus to prove the identity, genuineness and creditworthiness of such cash credits as required under section 68 of the Act:'The assessee will have to fulfil the requirement of section 68 to prove the cash credits.

In the case of *Pushkar Narain Sarraf* v. *CIT* [1990] 50 Taxman 213/183 ITR 388 (All.), cash credits found in the books of account of the assessee seized in the course of search conducted u/s 132 were sought to proved with the help of presumption of correctness of the contents of the books of account u/s 132(4A). This was repelled by the High Court on the ground that the presumption u/s 132(4A) does not override or exclude section 68 and it does not dispense with the necessity of establishing by independent evidence the genuineness of the cash credits u/s 68.

In the case of *Daya Chand* v. *CIT* [2001] 117 Taxman 438 (Delhi) Delhi High Court has held that presumption under section 132(4A) cannot have the effect of excluding operation of section 68 which is applicable in the course of regular assessment. Section 132(4A) does not relieve the assessee of his responsibility under section 68. Where any sum is found credited in the books of an assessee maintained for any previous year and the assessee offers no explanation about the nature and source thereof or the explanation offered by him is not, in the opinion of the Assessing Officer, satisfactory, the sum so credited may be charged to income-tax as the income of the assessee of that previous year.

(iv) **Presumption under section 132(4A) v. section 69**

Availability of presumption under section 132(4A) to the assessing officer does not mean that before making addition under section 69, requirement as given in section 69 are not to be looked into.

In the case of *Ushakant N. Patel* v. *CIT* [2006] 154 Taxman 55 (Guj.) it has been held by the High Court of Gujarat that the pre-requisite conditions of section 69 have to be satisfied and cannot be presumed to have been established on the basis of section 132(4A).

Addition was made u/s 69A relating to receipt on-money on sale of shops, consequent to a search of the premises of the partners of the assessee firm. The on-money had been paid by the purchasers to the managing partners to the firm. High Court held that when the assessee had admitted the seizure of the documents in question from the premises of its partners, it is for them to explain that the documents did not pertain to the partnership concern and to show under what circumstances said documents was in possession of the partners. When such an explanation has not been offered by the partners, High Court upheld the action of A.O. in bringing to tax the said amount in the hands of the assessee firm supported by the provision of section 292C. [*Fifth Avenue* v. *CIT* [2009] 224 CTR 442/319 ITR 127 (Kar.)].

On further appeal Supreme Court held that High Court having not decided the question as to whether the amount allegedly paid by the purchasers to the managing partners of the assessee firm could be brought to tax in the hands of the firm, matter was remanded to the A.O. for fresh consideration. The Supreme Court further held that it was for the assessee firm and its partners to explain and produce relevant documents before the A.O. to show as to when and how much the unaccounted money was received by them and in case partners are unable to produced any material evidence, it would be open to the A.O. to assume that the amount was received during the A.Y. 1993-94 only. [*Fifth Avenue* v. *CIT* [2009] 183 Taxman 216 (SC)].

9.8 Onus to establish income of the assessee remains on Assessing Officer

Presumption available under section 132(4A)/292C is only to the extent that any books of account, other documents, money, bullion, jewellery or other valuable article or thing found in the possession or control of any person in the course of search-

(*i*) belong to such person,

(*ii*) the contents of the same are true and

(*iii*) the same are in the handwriting of the person to whom it is so purported to be.

The presumption regarding books of account or other documents or assets belonging to the person from whose possession it is found is to make such person answerable regarding the existence of such material with him. He cannot be permitted to take the plea that he does not know from where the same have come into his possession. The primary onus is upon him and he can shift the burden by leading cogent evidences in case such material belongs to somebody else.

Further the presumption that the contents of such books of account or other documents are true does not mean that whatever is written in the documents may be construed to be the income of that person. This presumption implies that assessee cannot deny the contents written in the books of account or documents in the form or in the manner in which the same are written therein. There may be so many things which may be written in normal course by a person in the documents or papers found from his possession. It may or may not relate to financial transactions. It may be rough working, future projections or estimates. It may be noting relating to casual discussion held with somebody. It may be notings relating to transaction of somebody else during discussion with him. The presumption is only to the extent that whatever written on the documents or papers is true in the manner it is mentioned. The onus would lie upon the assessing officer to prove that the contents mentioned in the documents or papers result into undisclosed income of the assessee. The primary burden to relate the contents of the documents or papers with the income of the assessee will lie upon the assessing officer. Once this primary burden is discharged by the assessing officer, the onus will shift on the assessee to disprove that such contents are not his income.

In the case of *Doon Valley Roller Flour Mills (P.) Ltd.* v. *IAC* [1989] 31 ITD 238 (Delhi-Trib.), it was held that the burden to prove that the assessee was the real owner of the property was on the revenue, as the burden is on the person who alleges it. Where assessing officer did not state any fact in the assessment order and did not produce any material to show that those books were in the possession or control of the shareholder of the assessee company, mere fact that a person was one of the shareholders of the assessee company was not sufficient to link the books with the assessee even if there were some entries which indicated that they related to business similar to that of the assessee because the same can only raise a suspicion and positive evidence may be required to convert that suspicion into acceptable proof.

To attract the provisions of section 132(4A) it is required that the document should be found in the possession or control of the assessee and a nexus should be established between the document and the undisclosed income of the assessee. Document includes any matter written, expressed or described upon any substance by means of letters, figures or marks or by more than one of those means, which is intended to be used or which may be used for the purposes of recording that matter.

In the case of *Asstt. CIT* v. *Sri Radheshyam Poddar* [1992] 41 ITD 449 (Cal.-Trib.) it was held that no addition can be made on the basis of unsigned typed memorandum of understanding between the assessee employee and his employer because the provisions of section 132(4A) should be applied and interpreted in a reasonable manner and in consonance with justice and drawing of presumption given in section 132(4A) depends upon particular facts and circumstances of the case.

When it was not established by the department as to how the cement purchased by the assessee was used. Tribunal held that in view of the provisions contained under section 132(4A) the addition would be made under section 69, regarding unexplained investments, of the Act. *Kollipara Subba Rao* v. *ITO* [1990] 32 ITD 668 (Hyd.-Trib.).

Delhi High Court in the case of *CIT* v. *D.K. Gupta* [2008] 174 Taxman 476 (Delhi) also held that there was no evidence to presume notings mentioned in the diaries materialized into transactions and assessee would be liable to tax only on receipts proved to be income of assessee.

It has been held in the case of *Asstt. CIT* v. *Buldana Urban Co-operative Credit Society Ltd.* [2013] 32 taxmann.com 69/57 SOT 76 (URO) (Nagpur-Trib.) that inspite of the presumption under s. 292C, if Assessee denied that the loose paper in question belongs to assessee, and the notings on the said paper not being in the handwriting of any employee of the assessee, addition made by the AO on the basis of said notings cannot be sustained in the absence of any corroborative evidence on record to disprove the explanation of the assessee.

(i) What in case of dumb document

No addition could be made on the basis of dumb document. Dumb documents are those documents which are found during the course of search or survey and do not indicate whether the figures mentioned therein refer to anything meaningful or corroborative with the affairs of the assessee.

It is a matter of experience that in the course of survey & search, large number of loose papers are found and seized by the Department. The assessee is required to explain as to the nature and contents of each and every paper particularly giving reference to the presumption available against the assessee. Many times such loose papers contain notings, scribbling or rough estimates which may not mean anything. The assessing officer sometimes ventures into decoding, extrapolating and estimating income based upon surmises and conjectures. The courts have held that no addition can be made on the basis of dumb documents. The presumption is that the document belongs to the assessee and its contents are correct. The presumption cannot be extended to mean that whatever figure mentioned in the loose paper found from the possession of assessee, represent his income.

No decoding is permissible on suspicion, surmise, conjecture and imagination. *Amar Natvarlal Shah* v. *Asstt. CIT* [1997] 60 ITD 560 (Ahd.-Trib.).

In the instant case, the only known facts are that certain papers were found in the business premises of the assessee (at a place and under the conditions not known) and they contained certain calculations (origin and connection of which is not known) and no intelligible inference therefrom can be drawn. No sensible inference of any fact can be drawn from such known facts. In this view of the matter, all the additions made appear imaginary as a result of suspicion. *Brijlal Rupchand* v. *ITO* [1991] 40 TTJ 668 (Indore-Trib.).

In *Asstt. CIT* v. *Ashok Kumar Poddar* [2008] 16 DTR (Kol. - Trib.) 55, it has been held that the action of making addition was wrong where

A.O. made addition only on the presumption made u/s 132(4A), that the loose sheets belong to the assessee without verifying the hand writing and without making any enquiry or bringing any material on record to substantiate that the assessee had actually earned the income recorded in those sheets.

(ii) **Applicable to "Any" books of account .... and not to "Such" books of account ....**

The presumption applies under this section to any books of account, documents or assets found from the possession or control of the assessee. The word used in sub-section *"any"* includes both kind of books of account or assets whether disclosed or undisclosed. In this sub-section, the word *"such"* has not been used which refers only to undisclosed books of account, documents or assets in the context of section 132(1). The presumption relating to regular books of account or disclosed assets found from the possession or control of the assessee shall require him to explain the nature and ownership of the same. In case regular books of account of some other person are found from his possession, the burden upon him will lie to explain the ownership of the same. Once this burden is discharged and ownership belonging to some other person is proved by him, no adverse inference against the assessee can be drawn with respect to such books of account or documents. The burden will shift to the person who is the owner of such books of account or documents to further explain the contents of the same.

(iii) **Presumption as to the signature and handwriting not against the assessee**

There are three limbs of the presumption given under section 132(4A) as discussed above. The first two limbs indicate the presumption towards the person from whose possession or control books of account, documents or assets are found. But the third presumption regarding the signature and handwriting on the books of account or documents cannot be drawn towards the assessee but it is to be drawn against the particular person to whom the signature or handwriting is purported to be.

In the case of *Ushakant N. Patel* v. *CIT* [2006] 154 Taxman 55 (Guj.) it has been held by the High Court of Gujarat that clauses *(i)* and *(ii)* of section 132(4A) raise a presumption that the books of account belong to the person searched, or the person from whose possession or control the books are recovered or found, and that the contents of such books are true. However when it comes to clause *(iii)* of section 132(4A), it raises a presumption in relation to the signature and the handwriting to be of the person in whose handwriting the books, etc.

are purported to be, or a reasonable assumption may be raised that the books, etc. are signed by or in the handwriting of any particular person. The distinguishing feature is, the clause does not necessarily raise a presumption qua the person searched or from whose possession the books are found. The language employed in clauses (*i*) and (*ii*) "such person", meaning thereby the person searched or from whose possession or control the books are found. As against that, the language employed by clause (*iii*) talks of raising a presumption in relation to "any particular person", who may be the person searched, or may not necessarily be the person searched. In the given case, the books might bear the name of the owner and yet they may be found in possession of, or control of another person. Then, in such an eventuality the presumption as to the signature and handwriting would arise against the person in whose name the books stand. By way of illustration, judicial note can be taken note of the fact that books of account are handed over to persons who work as part-time accountants, and in such circumstances, the presumption has to be in relation to the person who writes the accounts. In the present case, at best, the authorities and the Tribunal could have raised presumption that the books have been recovered from the possession of the assessee (though disputed by the assessee), and belong to the assessee and the contents thereof are true; but from that, it does not necessarily follow that a presumption would arise as to the books or the documents being in the handwriting of the assessee. The Tribunal has brushed aside the finding recorded by the CIT(A) regarding the books/documents not being in the handwriting of assessee, by a sweeping statement without taking note of the finding recorded by CIT(A). The Tribunal has committed this error only because it proceeded on the footing that clause (*iii*) of section 132(4A) raises a presumption qua the person searched or the person from whose possession or control the books or documents are recovered when the language does not indicate it to be so in all cases.

9.9 No presumption against third party

Presumption available under section 132(4A) can be drawn against the person in whose case search is authorized and from whose possession or control books of account, documents or assets are found in the course of search. Presumption regarding correctness of contents of books of account etc. cannot be raised against the third party.

For example there may be a case when details of undisclosed cash transaction relating to property belonging to the sister of the person searched are found from the laptop of the person searched in the course of search conducted at his premises. In the case of assessment proceeding relating to the sister of person searched, presumption as given under section 132(4A) cannot be available to the assessing officer. In such a case initial burden will lie upon the assessing officer to make out the case by leading corroborative evidences that cash transaction relating to the property in question belong to the sister of the person searched and the contents of the same as found are correct. Had the transaction related to the person searched and details were found from his possession, since presumption under section 132(4A) is available with the assessing officer the initial burden would have shifted to the person searched to prove that no cash transaction has taken place and the details of the transaction found from his possession are not correct and no undisclosed income arise out of the same.

Presumption under section 132(4A) is only against the person in whose possession the search material is found and not against any other person. It is further held that the presumption is rebuttable and not conclusive and it cannot be applied in the absence of corroborative evidence. *Straptex (India) (P.) Ltd.* v. *Dy. CIT* [2003] 84 ITD 320 (Mum.-Trib.).

In the case of *Rama Traders* v. *First ITO* [1988] 25 ITD 599 (Pat.-Trib.) (TM) it was held that no addition could be made, on the basis of presumption raised by section 132(4A), in the hands of the assessee where in the books of another firm, certain figures were found showing the purchases made by the assessee.

In the case of *Kishanchand Sobhrajmal* v. *Asstt. CIT* [1992] 41 ITD 97 (Jp.-Trib.) it was held that it is not open to the department to raise any presumption partly on the basis of a document and partly by ignoring its contents. It has also been observed by the Tribunal that a document marked as Annexure C could not be proved as recovered from the business premises of the assessee.

In *Asstt. CIT* v. *Kishore Lal Balwant Rai* [2007] 17 SOT 380 (Chd.-Trib.), it has been held that though the diary seized enables the revenue to presume that its contents are true, such presumption is available only against the person to whom it belongs and this is a rebuttable presumption.

Presumption u/s 132(4A) is not available, when the seized paper is recovered from third party and not from the assessee. [*Sheth Akshay Pushpavadan* v. *Dy. CIT* [2010] 130 TTJ 42 (Ahd.-Trib.) (UO)].

9.10 Constitutional validity upheld

A rebuttable presumption is nothing but a rule of evidence. It has the effect of shifting the burden of proof. Therefore, it does not stand to reason as to how it is unconstitutional when the person concerned has the opportunity to displace the presumption by leading evidence. *Sodhi Transport Co.* v. *State of U.P.* [1986] 1986 taxmann.com 862 (SC), *State of Madhya Pradesh* v. *Bharat Heavy Electricals* [1997] 106 STC 604 (SC).

CHAPTER 10

SECTIONS 132(8)/132(10)/ 132(9)/132(9A) TO (9D) & 132B

PART 1

MISCELLANEOUS PROVISIONS RELATING TO SEARCH

In this Chapter following provisions are being analyzed

Section 132(8)	*Retention and release of books of account and other documents.*
Section 132(10)	*Objection by assessee to CBDT for granting extension to retain books of account or other documents by CIT under sub-section (8).*
Section 132(9)	*Obtaining copies of books of account and other documents seized.*
Section 132(9A)	*Handing over of books of account or other documents or assets seized by the authorized officer to the Assessing Officer.*
Section 132(9B), (9C) & (9D)	*Power of provisional attachment of property & to make reference to valuation officer by the authorized officer*

PART 2

Section 132B	*Application and release of seized assets.*

10.1 Text of section 132(8) and section 132(10)

Section 132(8)

(8) The books of account or other documents seized under sub-section (1) or sub-section (1A) shall not be retained by the authorised officer for a period exceeding thirty days from the date of the order of assessment or reassessment or recomputation under sub-section (3) of section 143 or section 144 or section 147 or section 153A or clause (c) of section 158BC unless the reasons for retaining the same are recorded by him in writing and the approval of the Principal Chief Commissioner or Chief Commissioner, Principal Commissioner or Commissioner, Principal Director General or Director General or Principal Director or Director for such retention is obtained :

Provided *that the Principal Chief Commissioner or Chief Commissioner, Principal Commissioner or Commissioner, Principal Director General or Director General or Principal Director or Director shall not authorise the retention of the books of account and other documents for a period exceeding thirty days after all the proceedings under the Indian Income-tax Act, 1922 (11 of 1922), or this Act in respect of the years for which the books of account or other documents are relevant are completed.*

Section 132(10)

(10) If a person legally entitled to the books of account or other documents seized under sub-section (1) or sub-section (1A) objects for any reason to the approval given by the Chief Commissioner, Commissioner, Director General or Director under sub-section (8), he may make an application to the Board stating therein the reasons for such objection and requesting for the return of the books of account or other documents and the Board may, after giving the applicant an opportunity of being heard, pass such orders as it thinks fit.

10.2 Legislative history - Significant amendments

As per Finance Act, 2002, w.e.f. 1st June, 2002, the period of retention of books of account or other documents seized during search was extended upto thirty days from the date of the order of the assessment passed under section 158BC or under section 153A. Earlier the above period was one hundred and eighty days from the date of the seizure of the books of account or documents.

Reference in sub-section (8) for retention of books of account, even after the above amendment, is still to the authorized officer but it should be to the assessing officer since such power cannot now be exercised under any circumstances by the authorized officer. However, assessing officer gets the authority to exercise power of sub-section (8) by virtue of specific mention to such effect as provided under sub-section (9A) of section 132.

Finance Act, 2022 has inserted the words 'order of assessment or reassessment or recomputation under sub-section (3) of section 143 or section 144 or section 147' in sub-section (8) of section 132. This amendment is consequential to new scheme of assessment in search cases as per sections

147-151 introduced by the Finance Act, 2021. This amendment has been made effective from 1st April, 2022.

10.3 Objective

The objective of the provision is to give power to the Department to retain books of account or other documents seized during search till assessment proceedings are completed.

The books of account or other documents seized may be required by the Department even after completion of assessment proceedings under section 153A till completion of other proceedings under the Act i.e. appeals, revision, penalty proceedings etc. Therefore power has been given to retain books of account or other documents till completion of all the proceedings under the Act. But this power can be exercised after recording reasons in writing and taking approval of the higher authorities.

   (*i*) **Retention and release of books of account or other documents covered under section 132(8) while retention and release of assets covered under section 132B**

       From the close reading of sub-section (8) of section 132 and section 132B, it is observed that retention and release of books of account and other documents is covered by section 132(8) whereas retention, application & release of assets seized is covered by section 132B. Further in case of any objection by the assessee for approval granted by CIT to extend period of retention of books of account or other documents, assessee may approach to the Central Board of Direct Taxes (CBDT) as provided under section 132(10).

  (*ii*) **Rationale behind amendment of sub-section (8) of section 132**

       While making amendment to sub-section (8) of section 132 by Finance Act, 2002, the notes on clauses of Finance Bill, 2002 states as under:

       "Under the existing provisions contained in sub-section (8), the books of account or other documents seized shall not be retained by the authorized officer for a period exceeding one hundred and eighty days from the date of the seizure unless the reasons for retaining the same are recorded by him in writing and the approval of the Chief Commissioner, Commissioner, Director General or Director for such retention is obtained. It is proposed to amend the said sub-section to provide that the books of account or other documents seized shall not be retained for a period exceeding thirty days from the date of the order of assessment under clause (c) of section 158BC, unless the reasons for retaining the same are recorded in writing and the approval of the specified authorities is obtained."

       Before amendment of sub-section (8) of section 132, books of account or other documents seized during the search were seldom returned to the assessee within one hundred and eighty days since the same were required by the assessing officer for completion of assessment proceedings and passing assessment orders relating to search years. There were frequent lapses on the part of Departmental officers to fulfil the conditions as laid down under the then provisions of section 132(8) as under:

◆ Reasons for retaining the books of account or other documents not recorded by the authorized officer in writing and,

◆ The approval of the Commissioner or Chief Commissioner for such retention not obtained within prescribed time limit.

◆ The approval regarding retention of the books of account and other documents obtained from the higher authorities not communicated to the assessee in time.

In such circumstances, the courts ordered for the return of books even before assessment was completed and the assessing officers used to face lot of difficulty in conducting assessment proceedings and in framing assessment order in the absence of seized material.

Such situation has been taken care of by making amendment to sub-section (8) of section 132. Amendment to sub-section (8) of section 132 has relieved the officers of the responsibility of obtaining the approval for retention of the books of account and other documents before completion of the assessment proceedings. Now, assessing officers can retain the books of account and other documents upto thirty days from the date of passing the order of assessment under section 153A without the requirement of obtaining approval from the Commissioner for such retention.

The relevant extract from the Board's circular issued in this regard are reproduced below:

> *"Under the existing provisions of sub-section (8) of section 132, the books of account or other documents seized during search cannot be retained by the Authorized Officer or the Assessing Officer beyond a period of 180 days from the date of seizure, unless the approval of the Chief Commissioner, Commissioner, Director General or Director is, obtained for such retention, on the basis of reasons to be recorded in writing.*
>
> *It has been noticed that this limit of 180 days is not practical, as the assessment proceedings relating to the seized records generally take upto 2 years to be finalized. It is only then that the Assessing Officer can come to a conclusion as to whether any of the seized books of account or documents are required to be retained further.*
>
> *Therefore as a measure of rationalization, the Finance Act, 2002 has amended sub-section (8) of section 132 to provide that books of account or documents seized under section 132(1)(iii) shall not be retained beyond 30 days after completion of the relevant block assessment under Chapter XIV-B, unless the approval of the Chief Commissioner, Commissioner, Director General or Director is obtained on the basis of reasons to be recorded in writing."*

Circular No.8/2002 dated 27.8.2002 [2002] 258 ITR (St.) 13

10.4 Scope and manner

(i) No approval of Commissioner required for retention of books of account or other documents till completion of assessment

The books of account or other documents seized under clause (*iii*) of section 132(1) can be retained by the authorized officer/Assessing Officer till finalization of assessment order and further upto thirty days thereafter. For retaining the books of account or other documents upto the above time limit, no approval from higher authorities is required to be obtained.

In fact authorized officer who seized the books of account or other documents is not at all required to take any approval for retaining books of account or other documents since the same are handed over by him to the assessing officer for making the assessment. The assessing officer is also not required to take any approval for retaining books of account or other documents till finalization of the assessment. It implies that books of account and other documents are not released till finalization of the assessment since the same are required to be made use of while framing the assessment. As provided under sub-section (9) assessee can obtain photocopies of books of account or documents seized for his own purpose but he has no right to get the books of account or documents released before the completion of assessment proceedings.

The reference in sub-section (8) has been made to the authorized officer for obtaining approval of Commissioner for retaining books of account or documents after completion of assessment but in practice, this power can be exercised only by the assessing officer and not by the authorized officer at any stage. Sub-section (9A) has provided that after getting the seized records from the authorized officer, the powers exercisable by the authorized officer under sub-section (8) or sub-section (9) shall be exercisable by the assessing officer. However it would have been appropriate to make mention of assessing officer in sub-section (8) instead of making mention of authorized officer for taking approval of the Commissioner for retaining books of account or other documents since authorized officer can never exercise this power.

(ii) Retention of books of account or other documents after completion of assessment - Extension of period

After expiry of the period of thirty days from the date of order of assessment passed under section 153A, the period of retention of books of account or other documents as per the amended provision, may be extended on fulfilment of following two conditions :-

- ◆ Reasons for retaining the books of account or other documents are recorded by assessing officer in writing.
- ◆ Approval of the prescribed authorities is obtained.

Further as per proviso to section 132(8) it has been mentioned that such authorities shall not authorize the retention of books of account or other documents for a period exceeding thirty days after all the proceedings under the Act are completed.

The period till all the proceedings are completed remains up to finalization of all the appellate/revision/rectification/penalty proceedings instituted by the assessee or by the Department. In practice, the above period keeps on going for a considerable long time since either the Department or the assessee remains in appeal up to Tribunal or High Court for some or the other disputed issue(s). In such circumstances, it has been practically noted that the period of extension and approval by CIT etc. becomes a mechanical job and department doesn't release the books of account or other documents and when all the proceedings under the Act are completed, the relevance or utility of the same for the assessee doesn't remain due to considerable lapse of time.

In the case of *Joshi P. Mathew* v. *Dy. CIT* [2013] 29 taxmann.com 76/214 Taxman 267 (Ker.) (HC) Books of account, seized under s.132(1), were retained by the officer for a period exceeding 30 days from the date of order of assessment passed u/s. 153A without communicating to the assessee reasons recorded for the same and approval obtained from the CCIT, Director General, or Director, as the case may be, for such retention. Held that the requirements of s. 132(8) were not satisfied and therefore, the retention of documents beyond 30 days after completion of assessment was illegal.

(iii) Approval for extension to be granted before the expiry of period

The period prescribed by section 132(8), is mandatory and not directory. The period of retention of books of account or other documents could not be extended unless two things are done before the expiry of the said period, viz.:

  (i) Reasons are recorded by the authorized officer in writing; and

  (ii) The approval of the Commissioner etc. is obtained.

Both these are pre-conditions. They must be done before the expiry of specified period. *CIT* v. *Jawahar Lal Rastogi* [1970] 78 ITR 486 (SC); *Metal Fittings (P.) Ltd.* v. *Union of India* [1983] 14 Taxman 261 (Del.) and *Hyderabad Vanaspathi Ltd.* v. *ITO* [1984] 19 Taxman 422 (AP)

Order under section 132(8) for retaining seized document beyond prescribed period should be passed within that period only. *Hanuman Pershad Ganeriwala* v. *Director of Inspection of Income Tax* [1974] 93 ITR 419 (Del.).

In the case of *Sampatlal and Sons* v. *CIT* [1984] 16 Taxman 144 (MP), it has been held that an order granting approval under section 132(8) for retaining certain books or documents seized during the course of a search should be continuous and without a day's break. Filling this, the books or other documents, etc. is to be released to the assessee.

(iv) Communication of Commissioner's approval

Commissioner's approval, regarding extension of time period prescribed by section 132(8), will not become effective unless it is communicated to the person concerned.

In the case of *CIT* v. *Oriental Rubber Works* [1983] 15 Taxman 51 (SC), it was held that it is obligatory upon the revenue to communicate the Commissioner's approval and also the recorded reasons, on the basis of which approval has been obtained, to the person concerned because without the knowledge of the factum of the Commissioner's approval as also of the recorded reasons on the basis of which such approval has been obtained, it will not be possible for the person to whom the seized books or documents belong, to make any effective objection, as provided in section 132(10), to the approval before the Board and get back his books or documents.

There is a statutory obligation on the part of revenue to communicate to the person concerned not only the Commissioner's approval but also the recorded reasons on which the same has been obtained and that such communication must be made as soon as possible after the passing of the order of approval by the Commissioner and in default of such expeditious communication, any further retention of the seized books or documents would become invalid and unlawful.

In the case of *Sampatlal & Sons* v. *CIT* [1984] 16 Taxman 144 (M.P.), it was held that Commissioner's approval must be communicated to the person whose books of account are seized so that he may make an application to the Board stating his objection and requesting the return of the books of account and the other documents seized.

Order of Commissioner granting approval for retention must be communicated to assessee. *Dr. George Philip Modayil* v. *Asstt. CIT* [1999] 238 ITR 517 (Ker.).

There is a statutory obligation to communicate the recorded reasons of the Commissioner's approval, obtained regarding retention of books of account after expiry of period as prescribed by section 132(8), to the appellant despite pendency of an earlier writ petition in the court. *Jorawar Singh Baid* v. *Asstt. CIT* [1991] 192 ITR 502 (Cal.).

In the case of *Tin Box Co.* v. *ITAT* [1990] 52 Taxman 391 (Delhi), it has been held that under sub-section (8) of section 132, the appropriate authority, namely the Commissioner of Income Tax, can order the retention of books, etc., for reasons to be recorded in writing. Against such an order which is passed, the assessee has a right to file an application to the Central Board of Direct Taxes under section 132(10). This right would become meaningless if the passing of the order under section 132(8) is not made known to the assessee within a reasonable time and, what is more important is that the reason for continued retention of the books are not communicated to the petitioner.

It has been held in the case of *Joshi P. Mathew* v. *Dy. CIT* [2013] 29 taxmann.com 76/214 Taxman 267 (Ker.) that the retention of seized documents beyond 30 days becomes illegal as Respondent authorities have not communicated to the assessee the request made by the Dy. CIT seeking approval of the CIT under section 132(8) for the continued retention of the seized documents or the approval granted by the latter and thus the requirement of section 132(8) is not satisfied and therefore, the retention of documents beyond 30 days period after completion of assessment is illegal.

It has been held in the case of *Udaya Sounds* v. *Principal Commissioner of Income Tax* (2022) 113 CCH 188 Ker HC, (2022) 213 DTR 13 (Ker.), (2022) 326 CTR 377 (Ker.), (2022) 444 ITR 428 (Ker), (2022) 138 taxmann.com 415/287 Taxman 251 (Kerala) that t*hough sub-section (8) of Section 132 does not in terms provide that the approval or the recorded reasons on which the retention is based should be communicated to the concerned person, since the person concerned is bound to be materially prejudiced in the enforcement of his right to have such books and documents returned to him being kept ignorant about the factum of fulfilment of either of the conditions, it was obligatory upon the revenue to communicate the Commissioner's approval as also the recorded reasons to the person concerned.*

(v) Effect of belated communication of reasons recorded

In the case of *Arti Gases* v. *DIT (Inv.)* [2000] 113 Taxman 68 (Guj.), it has been held that non-furnishing of reasons at an earlier stage for retention of seized materials beyond the prescribed period would not make proceedings void, especially when decisions had later been communicated to petitioners. It has further been observed that the Supreme Court has taken a view in the case of *State Bank of Patiala* v. *S.K. Sharma* AIR 1996 SC 1669 and *Managing Director, ECIL* v. *B. Karunakar* AIR 1994 SC 1074 that if the principles of natural justice are violated, the impugned action taken or the order passed by the authorities does not become void. If, ultimately, the reasons are supplied to the concerned or aggrieved party, the concerned party can very well take appropriate action upon the perusal of the said reasons. By mere non- furnishing of the reasons, the order does not become void. Even otherwise, the normal principle is that every violation of the principles of natural justice would not make the order void but it remains voidable. It depends upon the facts of the case as to whether the violation of the principles of natural justice would make the order void.

(*vi*) **Extension for retention of books of account or documents - Application of mind**

The Board has issued **Circular No. 25-D of 1965** wherein it was stated that at different stages of proceedings under section 132(1) the Director of Inspection or the Commissioner of Income-tax and the authorized officer must apply their minds and form opinion as to the relevance or usefulness of books of account and other documents. The Board has also stressed that there should be no indiscriminate seizure. The authorized officer must apply his mind and restrict the seizure to such books of account and documents which have not been produced, or in his judgment, would not be produced.

In order to ensure that books, etc. not useful for assessment/prosecution proceedings are not unnecessarily retained by the Department, the Assessing Officer should complete the scrutiny of books well before the period of 180 days. Such of the books as are no longer required to be retained, should be released before proposal for further retention of the books is sent to CIT. Further, the proposals for retention of the books should not be approved as a routine matter and the Assessing Officers should review from time to time whether part of the seized books could further be released. Even in cases where the books cannot be released for any reason, the assessee should be permitted to take extracts/photocopies and it should be ensured that no inconvenience is caused to him.

Circular No. 1526 F. No. 286/26/83-IT (Inv. III), dated 7-9-1983 from CBDT

Though above circular has been issued by the Board for seeking extension of the time limit beyond 180 days as per pre amended section 132(8) yet it is still relevant and applicable for extension of time limit for retention of books of account and documents as required in the amended provision.

In the case of *Krishna Kumar Sharma* v. *CIT* [1991] 192 ITR 57 (All.), Allahabad High Court held that when there is no evidence for order passed under section 132(8) then, the books of account seized from the petitioner's premises, had to be returned to him.

Retention of books and documents beyond the period as specified by section 132(8) was not valid, when there was no reason on record for approval by the Commissioner. *Nutan Sahkari Avas Samiti Ltd.* v. *DIT (Inv.)* [1994] 75 Taxman 486 (All.).

Approval for retention of seized documents beyond prescribed period must be given only for special reasons. *Madhupuri Corporation* v. *S.S. Khan* [2000] 113 Taxman 568 (Guj.).

In the case of *Dr. Nalini Mahajan* v. *DIT (Inv.)* [2002] 122 Taxman 897 (Del.), it has been held that unless reasons are recorded, retention of books of account beyond the period of 180 days would be nullity.

(vii) No opportunity of hearing required to be granted to the assessee before granting approval for extension

Order of the Commissioner, giving approval to retention of documents, beyond period prescribed in section 132(8), can be passed without providing opportunity of hearing to the assessee as this order is only an administrative order. However, approval needs to be communicated. *CIT* v. *Mahabir Prasad Poddar* [1974] 93 ITR 215 (Cal.) and *Hanuman Pershad Ganeriwala* v. *Director of Inspection (Income-tax)* [1974] 93 ITR 419 (Delhi).

(viii) Extension can be granted repeatedly as may be required

The Allahabad High Court in *Smt. Vidya Devi* v. *ITO* 1972 Tax LR 572 held that it cannot be said that the power to grant approval for extension of the period of retention of books can be exercised by the Commissioner only once and that power gets exhausted after it is first exercised. The power is administrative in character and can be exercised from time to time according to the exigencies and the need to retain the books of account and documents.

In the case of *Mohan Magotra* v. *DIT* [2002] 123 Taxman 843/177 CTR 352 (J&K), it has been held that successive approvals obtained under section 132(8) for retention of books of account, etc., beyond 180 days as well as the reasons for retention of such records being addressed to the petitioner the presumption would be that they were duly conveyed and contention regarding non-compliance of section 132(8) was not therefore sustainable.

10.5 Illegal seizure of books of account or other documents

(i) Release of books of account or other documents illegally seized

There may be circumstances when books of account or other documents are illegally seized by the Department. In case search is held to be illegal, the seizure of books of account or documents in consequence to an illegal search will also be illegal. Department is duty bound to release books of account or documents illegally seized immediately or on application being made by the assessee.

Books of account cannot be retained where proceedings under section 158BD are dropped. *K.R. Modi & Co.* v. *Dy. DIT (Inv.)* [2005] 272 ITR 587 (Cal.).

There may be circumstances when books of account or documents are seized by the Department in the course of a search which was otherwise not required to be seized. It is very difficult to mention as to what kind of books of account or documents cannot be seized in the course of a search operation. There are divergent views regarding seizure of regular or disclosed books of account or documents, original title deeds of immovable properties, original agreements of the licenses/certificates etc. or books of account or records relating to other persons/sister concerns which have no connection with the assessee. It can be said that books of account or documents which are not incriminating in nature or which have no connection with the assessee cannot be seized and any seizure of such books of account or documents shall be illegal.

There is no mechanism provided under section 132 for release of books of account or documents seized in the above illegal or irregular manner. As a matter of general rule any such books of account or documents seized should be released immediately by the Department on application being made by the assessee. However in practice it has been observed that it is seldom so done. Under such circumstances assessee has no option but to seek direction from the court by way of filing a writ for the release of such books of account or documents.

(*ii*) **Release of books of account or documents illegally seized - Can the Department compel the attestation of the documents by the assessee?**

Department cannot compel the assessee to attest the copy of books of account or documents, when the same were seized by the Department without the authority of law and in violation of section 132 of Act. It has been held in number of cases as discussed in detail in chapter 4 that books of account or documents seized illegally, could be used by the Department under any other provisions of the Act. This preposition cannot be interpreted to compel the assessee to certify the books of account or documents seized illegally. It is for the Department to decide as to how such books of account or documents can be used against the assessee under any other provision of the Act. Department may take cognizance of such books of account or documents and develop the case against the assessee, if possible, within the framework of law.

(*iii*) **Release of books of account or documents relating to other person seized**

Books of account or documents seized can be released to the person from whose possession seizure was made. In the case of *Wakil Kumar* v. *CIT* [2004] 134 Taxman 733 (Pat.), it was held that the petitioner was not the person from whose possession money had been recovered. His writ petition for release of such seized assets was not maintainable. Further the High Court refrained to look into the question as to whether the petitioner was the owner of the money or not since such issue could not be gone into by the High Court in writ jurisdiction.

In the case of *Raj Kumar Sharma* v. *Secretary, Govt. of India* [2002] 122 Taxman 163/175 CTR 49 (P&H), department was directed to release the National Savings Certificate and the documents relating to the title of the property belonging to the petitioner seized during the raid at the premises of petitioner's son.

(iv) Illegal seizure v. Illegal retention

There is distinction between illegal seizure of books of account or documents and illegal retention thereof in violation of provisions of section 132(8). Illegal seizure of books of account or documents is *void ab initio* and onus cannot be put on the assessee to explain such documents nor can the presumption under section 132(4A)/292C be drawn against the assessee with respect to such books of account or documents. While in the case of illegal retention, assessee is bound to explain the documents and presumption under section 132(4A)/292C with respect to such books of account or documents may be drawn against the assessee.

10.6 Illegal retention of books of account or other documents

There can be illegal retention of books of account or documents when the same are retained in violation of provisions of section 132(8). There can be illegal retention under the following circumstances:-

a. When approval of extension to retain books of account or documents is not obtained by the Assessing Officer from the Commissioner etc. after expiry of thirty days from the date of passing of assessment order under section 153A.

b. When extension obtained is expired and no further extension is obtained by the Assessing Officer.

c. When extension is granted by the Commissioner etc. in a mechanical manner even when all proceedings under the Act have been completed.

d. When extension granted by the Commissioner is not communicated to the assessee.

In the case of *Thanthi Trust* v. *CIT* [1987] 33 Taxman 503 (Delhi), it has been held that one of the conditions precedent mentioned in the aforesaid decision is that the reasons in writing recorded by the authorized officer and the Income Tax Officer concerned seeking the Commissioner's approval must be communicated to the assessee from whom the books or documents have been seized. Admittedly the reasons were not communicated and the petitioner had to go in appeal. In view of the aforesaid decisions, the further retention of the seized documents and the books of account thus become illegal and unauthorized.

In the case of *Krishna Kumar Sharma* v. *CIT* [1991] 192 ITR 57 (All.), where no order was passed for retaining the books beyond 180 days, the Court ordered the release of the seized books.

In the case of *Cowasjee Nusserwanji Dinshaw* v. *ITO* [1987] 165 ITR 702 (Guj.), it has been held that admittedly after the expiry of the period of 180 days, the documents have been retained by the Income Tax Authorities without communicating the reasons stated by the authorized officer and approval of the Commissioner. There can be no doubt that the extended retention of the account books/documents is wholly illegal and unlawful.

In the case of *C.K. Wadha* v. *CIT* [1970] 78 ITR 782 (Cal.), the High Court directed to return all the books and documents seized under section 132(1) in the absence of proper communication for the retention of the seized documents.

(*i*) **Release of books of account illegally retained - Can the department compel the attestation of the documents by the assessee?**

Department cannot compel the assessee to sign the copies of books of account where books were retained by the department without the authority of law and in violation of the provisions of section 132(8).

In the case of *Khandani Shafakhana* v. *Union of India* [1989] 175 ITR 408 (Delhi), it was observed by the High Court that there is no such law as to direct the assessee to attest the copies and it depends upon the circumstances of each case that whether such a direction can be issued or not.

In S.L.P. filed by the department before Supreme Court in the case of *Rakesh Kumar Agarwal* v. *DGIT* [1995] 83 Taxman 76 (Delhi), it has been observed by the Supreme Court that the concession made by the assessee to sign the copies of the books, would be only to the effect that the signatures made will be relevant only for the purpose of proving that the copies which were being signed were the copies of books which were being returned. *S.L.P. No. 6695 of 1975, dated 3rd April, 1995.*

In the case of *Survir Enterprises* v. *CIT* [1985] 22 Taxman 516 (Delhi), it has been held by the Delhi High Court that once the bar set out in section 132(8) is operated, the department had to return books of account and other seized documents to the person concerned and court will not direct the assessee to keep the books intact and produce them as and when required by the Income Tax Authorities.

Copies of seized books of account and other documents even though made after expiry of period as specified in section 132(8) need not be returned to the assessee, because evidence obtained illegally may be taken into consideration, but no system of law recognizes or permits an authority, public or private, to obtain evidence illegally. In any case a court cannot be a source or instrument from which a direction can be obtained to permit an authority to obtain evidence in a manner contrary to law.

The *Director of Inspection* v. *K.C.A. & Co.* [1987] 32 Taxman 495 (J&K), it was held that where the Court after issuing notice to the department, directed them to hand over seized account books to the respondents after every page of those account books was initialled and stamped with official seal of concerned authority and the respondents had given an undertaking that they would make available same to authorities as and when required, the impugned order of the Court under section 132 was valid.

(ii) **Illegal Retention - Remedies with the Assessee**

In practice, it has been observed that books of account or other documents are illegally retained for a long period and the same are not released in accordance with the provision of section 132(8) inspite of repeated request by the assessee. Under such circumstances assessee has following remedies:-

1. Application to the Board under section 132(10) - In the application made to the Board, the applicant should state the reasons for his objection and ask for the return of books.

2. Writ under Article 226 of the Constitution with the High Court - The person aggrieved can approach the High Court by way of a writ petition and ask for the return of books.

3. Approaching to the office of Ombudsman - Recently Central Government has established the office of Ombudsman to take care of irregularities committed by the Departmental Officers and to fix their accountability. In case books of account or other documents are illegally retained in violation of provision of section 132(8), assessee can file petition with the office of Ombudsman for release of the same.

In the case of *Metal Fittings (P.) Ltd.* v. *Union of India* [1983] 14 Taxman 261 (Delhi), it has been observed by the Delhi High Court that when there is clear infringement of the statutory provision contained in sub-section (8) assessee can straightaway file a writ under Article 226 of the Constitution and ask for the return of books because the period as prescribed by section 132(8) has admittedly expired.

(*iii*) Retention and release of computer/laptop

Now a day in most of the cases, books of account or other data are maintained on computer, laptop, CD, pen drive or other electronic gadgets. As per section 2(12A) inserted by the Finance Act, 2001, the definition of "books of account" has been enlarged to include data stored in a floppy, disk, tape or any other form of electro-magnetic data storage device. Computer, laptop or other electronic device containing books of account or other data can be seized and retained in accordance with the provisions of section 132(8). However in practice, now a days, due to storage problem only hard disk or other devices containing data are seized and other computer hardware or laptop are generally not seized. Copy of hard disk in soft form is also given to the assessee so that day to day working is not hampered.

10.7 I. Section 132(10) - Approval for extension to retain books of account or other document by Commissioner etc. - Objection by assessee

Sub-section (10) of section 132 provides that if a person objects for any reason to the approval given by the Commissioner etc. under sub-section (8) granting extension to retain the books of account or other documents, he may approach to the Board stating the reasons of his objection and requesting for the release of books of account or other documents. The Board may after giving the applicant an opportunity of being heard, pass such order as it may deem fit.

It is unusual that a special provision has been made for making an application to the Board in case of any objection by the assessee against the order passed by Commissioner granting extension to retain books of account or other documents. It shows the significance of matter and legislature does not permit to retain books of account or other documents unless there are valid reasons for the same.

There may be several other irregularities committed by the Departmental officers in the course of search for example - retention of disclosed assets, not releasing the assets seized during search when all proceedings are completed under the Act and no tax demand remain outstanding, seizure of disclosed books of account or assets relating to other persons. No specific provision on the lines of sub-section (10) is contained under section 132 under such circumstances, for making application to the higher authorities or to the Board. There is a need to make specific provision covering all the situations where irregularities are involved during the search.

When petitioner has an alternative remedy to go before the Board against the Commissioner's order granting extension, then there is no justification to interfere under Article 226 with an order under section 132(8). *Abdul Sattar* v. *CIT* [1987] 34 Taxman 18 (All.).

II. Section 132(9)

10.8 Text of section

The person from whose custody any books of account or other documents are seized under sub-section (1) or sub-section (1A) may make copies thereof, or take extracts therefrom, in the presence of the authorized officer or any other person empowered by him in this behalf, at such place and time as the authorized officer may appoint in this behalf.

10.9 Legislative history - Significant amendments

There is no significant amendment to this sub-section except reference to sub-section (1A) has been inserted by Taxation Laws (Amendment) Act, 1975 with effect from 1.10.1975. This is consequential amendment simultaneous to the introduction of sub-section (1A) to section 132 by the said Act.

10.10 Objective

Objective of this sub-section is to enable the person from whose custody any books of account or other documents are seized, to obtain copies or extracts so that in case of proceeding to be taken up, suitable replies may be filed by him. This is in consonance with the well established principle of natural justice also.

10.11 Right to obtain copies of books of account or other documents seized - Section 132(9)

As a matter of general principle, copies of any evidences collected by the department are given to the assessee when the same is used against the assessee. The same is applicable in the case of statement of the assessee recorded or the statement of third party recorded or evidences collected from the third party under section 133(6) or otherwise.

However specific provision has been made under section 132(9) entitling assessee to make copies or take extracts of any books of account or other documents seized from the premises of the assessee. Assessee is entitled to get the copies of the documents or books of account immediately after the search has taken place. This position is further strengthened from the fact that the copies may be obtained from the authorized officer who has conducted the search while the same are used against the assessee by the

Assessing Officer when the assessment proceedings are conducted and assessment order is framed.

The provision contained in section 132(9) to get the copies of books of account or other documents seized is based on the principle of natural justice. The same are required to be given to the assessee for the purpose of enabling him to submit explanation in compliance to show-cause notices, if any, issued by the authorized officer. Apart from the same, assessee may require copies of books of account or documents for carrying day to day business activities smoothly e.g. to complete and finalize the books of account, get the same audited, settle the accounts with parties.

In the case of *New Kashmir & Oriental Transport Co. (P.) Ltd.* v. *CIT* [1973] 92 ITR 334 (All.), it was held that a person is entitled to inspect the record of proceedings and can obtain copies of the proceedings, against whom action is taken under section 132, unless there is a statutory prohibition. If such a right is denied—

♦ Assessee will not be able to satisfy himself that the action taken against him was justified and

♦ Cannot effectively seek the redressal of his grievance against the illegal action.

Assessment cannot be sustained if it is made after denying the person an opportunity to obtain the copies from the seized books or documents and extracts therefrom. *Ramesh Chander* v. *CIT* [1974] 93 ITR 244 (P&H). The same view was taken in *Dhaniram Gupta* v. *Union of India* [1973] 89 ITR 281 (Cal.).

(*i*) **Time limit for supply of copies of books of account or other documents seized**

Though there is a specific provision to supply copies of books of account or other documents seized during search but no time limit has been prescribed under the Act. In the absence of any time limit prescribed, in practice, it has been observed that copies of the books of account and the documents seized during search are seldom given by the authorized officer to the assessee. The action of taking photo copies is delayed by the authorized officer on one or the other pretext.

In the course of search, there may be seizure of large volume of documents, loose papers, files or books of account. It may contain documents or papers which are incriminating in nature. Seized material may also contain the books of account, documents, or files which are maintained in regular course of business and the same are required to carry out day to day business activities. In practice, it is seen that assessee faces lot of difficulty in getting copies of such regular books of account and documents. In the absence of any clear cut guidelines, assessee has no option but to follow up the matter administratively with the higher authorities or in the contingency or failure on that score, remedy by way of writ is pressed.

Assessee may opt to make declaration of undisclosed income as provided under section 271AAA to get immunity from penalty. Unless copies of the documents and papers seized are supplied to him or thorough inspection of all the documents and papers seized is permitted before the conclusion of search, assessee cannot be in a position to make declaration of the undisclosed income, if any, in his statement recorded under section 132(4) during the course of search. Therefore, there is a need to rationalize the provisions regarding supplying copies of documents and papers seized so as to achieve the desired objective.

(ii) Copies of books of account or documents before replying show cause notice issued by the authorized officer

Show cause notice is usually issued by the authorized officer to explain the nature and contents of the documents or loose papers seized from the possession of the assessee before finalizing the appraisal report. The assessee is well within his right to ask the authorized officer to supply copies of all the books of account or documents seized so as to co-relate and reconcile the documents before giving reply to the show cause notice and explain any specific document or query posed by the authorized officer. It is also suggested that copies of such books of account or seized documents may be obtained before submitting any reply so as to avoid the consequences of inconsistent replies which may stare an assessee in future assessments and/or appellate proceeding.

(iii) Copies of books of account or documents before filing the return

In case assessee does not get copies of books of account or documents seized from the authorized officer, he gets the opportunity to obtain the same from the Assessing Officer who issues notice for filing returns under section 153A. Assessee, in any case, is, as a matter of fact, entitled to get the copies of books of account or documents seized before filing return of income in pursuance of notice under section 153A. Any undisclosed income emerging from the documents seized can be declared by the assessee in the return of income to be filed only when the copies of same are supplied to him.

In case there is delay in filing the returns of income in pursuance to notice under section 153A due to the reason of the copies of books of account or other documents seized having not been supplied to the assessee in time, this can be a valid reason to plead against levy of any interest under section 234A for the late filing of return of income.

Hon'ble Delhi High Court in the case of *CIT* v. *Mesco Airlines Ltd.* [2012] 20 taxmann.com 549/206 Taxman 91 (Mag.) (Delhi) have held that while computing interest u/s 158BFA, time taken by the department in supplying the copies of the seized records shall be excluded.

Hon'ble Gujarat High Court in the case of *Paras Bansilal Patel* v. *B.M. Jindel* [2004] 135 Taxman 125 have held that the petitioners are entitled to waiver of interest u/s 234A in respect of the period commencing from the date of search till the date on which copies of the seized records were made available to the petitioners.

10.12 Whether inspection of books of account or other documents is permissible to an employee?

Inspection can be allowed to an employee if the books or documents are seized from his custody because as per section 132(9), the person from whose custody the books or documents are seized, may make copies or take extracts thereof. But the authorized officer will be justified to decline the permission, if the assessee, to whom the books and documents belong, objects to the grant of permission to any employee or any other person from whose custody the seizure is made. It is the duty of authorized officer to allow the inspection or give extract to a person in whose assessment the seized material is proposed to be utilized.

In the case of *Manik Chand Gupta* v. *CIT* [1988] 173 ITR 662 (All.) it was held that where the account books are seized from a firm, the partners or their authorized representatives were entitled to take copies of such books under section 132(9) but no undertaking was to be given by the partners that all the books which were seized belonged to the firm.

Therefore it can be said that it is the assessee alone who will be entitled to the benefit of section 132(9). This is because the term 'custody' used in section 132(9) implies actual and constructive possession, as per requirements of law and duty enjoined by it. *[Circular No. 1404 F No. 185/44/81-IT (AT), dated 18-7-1981 from CBDT]*

III. Section 132(9A) - Handing over of seized books of account or documents and assets to the Assessing Officer

10.13 Text of section

Finance Act, 2002 has substituted sub-section (9A) of section 132 as follows:-

> *"(9A) Where the authorized officer has no jurisdiction over the person referred to in clause (a) or clause (b) or clause (c) of sub-section (1), the books*

of account, other documents, or any money, bullion, jewellery or other valuable article or thing (hereafter in this section and in sections 132A and 132B referred to as assets) seized under that sub-section shall be handed over by the authorized officer to the Assessing Officer having jurisdiction over such person within a period of sixty days from the date on which the last of the authorizations for search was executed and thereupon the powers exercisable by the authorized officer under sub-section (8) or sub-section (9) shall be exercisable by such Assessing Officer."

10.14 Legislative history - Significant amendments

Sub-section (9A) was first introduced by the Taxation Laws (Amendment) Act, 1975 with effect from 19th October, 1975, read as under-

"(9A) Where the authorized officer has no jurisdiction over the person referred to in clause (*a*) or clause (*b*) or clause (*c*) of sub-section (1), the books of account or other documents or assets seized under that sub-section shall be handed over by the authorized officer to the Income Tax Officer having jurisdiction over such person within a period of fifteen days of such seizure and thereupon the powers exercisable by the authorized officer under sub-section (8) or sub-section (9) shall be exercisable by such Income Tax Officer."

The above provision was proving of no practical use and was not being complied with since the period of fifteen days was not sufficient for the authorized officer conducting search to appreciate all the seized books of account and documents and prepare his appraisal report. Therefore the above provision was substituted by Finance Act, 2002, with a new provision with effect from 1st June, 2002 to extending the period of fifteen days upto sixty days.

10.15 Objective

Proceeding undertaken under section 132 are the investigation proceeding to collect evidences of the undisclosed income and to seize undisclosed assets and the authorized officer undertaking search operation may or may not be the assessing officer to assess the assessee. Ultimately the power to assess the assessee under section 153A lies with the assessing officer having jurisdiction over the assessee. Therefore section 132(9A) makes the provision for handing over all the books of account, documents and assets seized by the authorized officer to the assessing officer having power to assess the assessee and thereafter the **power** exercisable by the authorized officer under sub-section (8) to retain **the books** of account or other documents or sub-section (9) to supply **copies of the** seized material shall be exercised by such assessing officer.

The objective of this provision is to handover the **seized** material to the assessing officer who has power to assess the assessee, at an early date so that he may get sufficient time to appraise the evidences and conduct the assessment proceedings. There is no need for the authorized officer who has collected the evidences in the course of search, to keep the same with him. His job is to collect the evidences and to hand over the same to the assessing officer along with his remarks and analysis relating to the evidences collected which is popularly known as Appraisal Report. For this purpose Legislature has deemed fit to grant the period of sixty days from the date of conclusion of search.

10.16 Time limit for handing over books of account or documents

(*i*) **Handing over within a period of sixty days from the date on which the last of the authorizations for search was executed**

The time limit as prescribed by pre-amended provision was fifteen days from the date of seizure and this provision has been substituted so as to extend the said time limit to sixty days from the date on which the last of the authorizations for search is executed. Earlier the time limit of fifteen days was from the date of seizure which was not practicably implementable since there could be different dates of seizure of different assets or documents from different premises. As per the amended provision, the time limit of sixty days has been made applicable from the date on which the last of the authorizations for search is executed i.e. the date of the conclusion of the search.

(*ii*) **Rationale for Amendment of section 132(9A)**

Before amendment of section 132(9A) as it stood prior to 2002, the provision was acted upon by the officers concerned generally by breach and almost in no case the seized material was handed over to the Assessing Officer within fifteen days. It was not practically possible for the authorized officer to appraise all the evidences collected, make his analysis and comments and prepare the appraisal report within a period of fifteen days.

In the case of *CIT* v. *K.V. Krishnaswamy Naidu & Co.* [2001] 118 Taxman 889 (SC), the Apex Court approving the judgment of Madras High Court in the same case [1986] 26 Taxman 533, propounded the following ratio-

◆ An authorized officer could not legally retain the seized material beyond fifteen days if he is authorized only to conduct the search and did not have the jurisdiction as an Assessing Officer.

◆ If such an authorized officer made a proposal under section 132(8) and an approval was granted by the Commissioner, such approval was also illegal and without jurisdiction. (It may be noted that this decision was rendered in the backdrop of the language of sub-section (8) of section 132 prior to its amendment in 2002).

By making amendment to sub-section (9A), the Legislature has made an attempt to recognize the law as laid by the Supreme Court in the above case and further by extending the time limit from fifteen days to sixty days, the provision is made more practical and workable for the Department.

It is obligatory to hand over the seized material within fifteen days or at least within a reasonable time to comply with the provisions of section 132(9A) [*Dr. Nalini Mahajan* v. *DIT (Investigation)* [2002] 122 Taxman 897 (Delhi)]

The amended provisions will apply to searches conducted on or after 1-6-2002. The period of 60 days is to be calculated from execution of the last warrant of authorization.

Seized assets if handed over to the Commissioner, who is a superior officer to the Assessing Officer, there was sufficient compliance with the requirements of section 132(9A). [*Narayan R. Bandekar* v. *Second ITO* [1989] 46 Taxman 274 (Bom.).]

(iii) Ambiguity in the provision still prevails

Though provision of sub-section (9A) has been amended to make it practicable and requiring the authorized officer to hand over the seized material to the Assessing Officer having jurisdiction over the person with in a period of sixty days from the date of conclusion of search, the provision, in practice, is still not strictly complied with by the Department due to following reasons-

    a. The sub-section starts with the wordings - "where the authorized officer has no jurisdiction over the person referred to in clause (*a*) or clause (*b*) or clause (*c*) of sub-section (1)." In view of the purposive interpretation of sub-section (9A), the above phrase should be interpreted to mean - where the authorized officer has no jurisdiction to assess the person searched. The reference to clause (*a*) or clause (*b*) or clause (*c*) is with respect to the person and not with respect to the authorized officer.

    But sometimes Department interprets the above phrase to mean - where the authorized officer referred to in clause (*a*), clause (*b*) or clause (*c*) of sub-section (1) has no jurisdiction over the person searched. In the case of search operation, there may be several authorized officers deputed to conduct search on different premises of the assessee at different locations. There may be one or two authorized officers having territorial jurisdiction over the assessee and the other authorized officers may not have any kind of territorial or assessment jurisdiction over the assessee. The above meaning is to misinterpret and preclude only those authorized officers who have no territorial or assessment jurisdiction over the assessee to conduct search.

If such kind of interpretation of sub-section (9A) is made, the very purpose of sub-section is defeated and the authorized officer may pretend to keep seized material for indefinite period. Such interpretation does not seem to be objective of the sub-section.

   b. There is no clarity under the statute regarding the consequences in case seized material is not handed over by the authorized officer to the Assessing Officer within a period of sixty days. The above requirement is interpreted to be an administrative direction and not the judicial one, non-compliance of which cannot make the search vitiated.

   In the case of *Madhupuri Corporation* v. *Prabhat Jha, Deputy DIT (Investigation)*[2002] 126 Taxman 309, Gujarat High Court has held that illegality of retention of seized material by the authorized officer beyond fifteen days does not vitiate the evidence collected during the search operation.

   c. Search cases, in practice, are generally centralized at the Central Circle and the Assessing Officer in-charge of Central Circle gets jurisdiction over the person searched to assess him. Order under section 127 transferring the case of the person searched from normal jurisdiction to Central Circle takes substantial time and generally the same is not passed within a period of sixty days from the date of conclusion of search. Under such circumstances, authorized officer remains in dilemma to which Assessing Officer to hand over the seized material. This is a genuine practical reason due to which compliance of requirement of sub-section (9A) is not usually made in time.

(*iv*) The Authorized Officer having no jurisdiction over the person - Meaning thereof

Sub-section (9A) requires the authorized officer having no jurisdiction over the person referred to in clause (*a*) or clause (*b*) or clause (*c*) of sub-section (1), *inter alia*, to hand over the seized books of account or assets to the Assessing Officer having jurisdiction over such person within a period of sixty days. There is however controversy regarding the interpretation of the phrase *"authorized officer having no jurisdiction over the person"* as to whether the authorized officer referred in this phrase means the authorized officer having jurisdiction to make assessment or it refers to the authorized officer having territorial investigative jurisdiction over the searched person.

This sub-section mandates, *inter alia*, for handing over the seized material to the assessing officer having jurisdiction over the searched person in case authorized officer does not have jurisdiction over the searched person. This suggests that here authorized officer having jurisdiction over the searched person means the authorized officer having the jurisdiction to assess. Obviously, seized material will be required by the Assessing Officer during the course of assessment proceeding for determining the tax liability on the searched persons.

It is however interesting to note that in the case of *Dr. N.S.D. Raju* v. *DGIT (Inv.)* [2006] 151 Taxman 247 (Ker.), it has been held as under:

Where, the ADI (Investigation) was acting as authorized officer, he has to do the work relating to post-search enquiries and preparation of appraisal report. Retention of seized books of account, documents, etc. beyond sixty days by the Assistant Director of Income Tax (Inv.) is not illegal. Now, Assessing Officer includes ADI/DDI as per section 2(7A) w.e.f. 1.10.1996, and, therefore, the ADI is an AO as per section 2(7A) and the retention of seized documents by him was valid as the procedure laid down in section 132(9A) has been complied with.

In the case of *Arti Gases* v. *DIT (Inv.)* [2000] 113 Taxman 68 (Guj.), it has been held as under:

As per the provisions of section 132(9A), if the authorized officer is an officer who is not having jurisdiction over the assessee, he has to hand over the relevant material seized during the process of search to the Income Tax Officer having jurisdiction over the assessee within a period of sixty days from the conclusion of such search. All such powers exercisable by the authorized officer under section 132(8) or 132(9) shall then be exercised by such Assessing Officer having jurisdiction over the assessee. However, if the authorized officer was also an officer having jurisdiction over the assessee, it was not necessary for him to part with the material seized as per the provisions of section 132(9A).

However, in our considered opinion, the purpose of sub-section (9A) is to make available the seized material within reasonable time limit to the Assessing Officer to frame assessment in consequence of search. Therefore, the very purpose of sub-section (9A) is to hand over the seized material to the Assessing Officer having jurisdiction over the person to make assessment within a period of sixty days from the date of conclusion of search. If an authorized officer is not having jurisdiction to make assessment and which is generally the case, since the authorized officer generally being assistant or deputy director from the investigation wing of the income tax department have the jurisdiction to conduct search and not to make assessment, such authorized officer will be required to hand over the seized material to the Assessing Officer having jurisdiction over the person to make assessment. It seems to be more plausible interpretation of sub-section (9A) and also in line with the purpose and intent of this sub-section. In the case of *Dr. C. Balakrishna Nair* v. *CIT* [1999] 103 Taxman 242/237 ITR 70 (Ker.), it has been held that the seized documents and records cannot be retained by the authorized officer for more than fifteen days. They should be handed over to the ITO within fifteen days of the seizure. Section 132(9A) is very clear in this aspect. Where the search operation was planned and executed by the ADI and he could not be the ITO having jurisdiction over the petitioner, retention of documents and records seized by the ADI beyond a period of fifteen days from the date of seizure, would be contrary to the provisions of the Act.

10.17 Not handing over the seized material within sixty days - Consequences thereof

As discussed in preceding para, there is no clarity under the statute regarding consequences for not handing over seized material by the authorized officer to the Assessing Officer having jurisdiction over the assessee within a period of sixty days from the date of conclusion of search. There is need to bring clarity on this issue so that the provision of sub-section (9A) is made effective and the desired objective is achieved.

In the case of *Digvijay Chemicals Ltd.* v. *Asstt. CIT* [2001] 118 Taxman 1 (All.), it has been held that even if the material was handed over beyond the period of fifteen days it could not be said that the said material could not be looked into by the Assessing Officer.

In the case of *Sambhu Prasad Agarwal* v. *DIT* [2002] 125 Taxman 79 (Cal.), dismissing the writ of the assessee Calcutta High Court held as under:

The period so fixed under the statute is not mandatory but directory directing the departmental authority to expedite the process. If such period of fifteen days is deemed to be directory the period at best can be construed as a reasonable period to come to a conclusion. Moreover, if the sub-section is read with the newly introduced chapter, it seems that the period of search and seizure can be taken for a period of two years. Therefore, merely handing over the documents even by the authorized officer to the Assessing Officer within or outside the period of fifteen days does not help an assessee in any manner whatsoever in getting any relief. If the assessee applies for a copy in accordance within law he will be entitled for the same for which jurisdiction of the high prerogative writ cannot be misused. Accordingly, the writ petition was dismissed.

It has been held in the case of *Agni Estates and Foundations Pvt. Ltd.* v. *Dy CIT* [2021] 126 taxmann.com 14/434 ITR 79 (Mad.) that the handing over of seized material by Investigation Officer to Assessing Officer and the provision of time-limit for such handing over under section 132(9A) is not mandatory and failure to hand over seized material by Investigation Officer to Assessing Officer within prescribed time-limit does not render notice under section 153A invalid.

10.18 Scope of handing over

(*i*) **Handing over seized material to the Assessing Officer of the person searched**

The seized material may contain books of account or documents which are not belonging to the person searched but the same may belong to some other person. The authorized officer should handover the entire search material to the Assessing Officer having jurisdiction over the person searched. It is for the Assessing Officer to decide whether certain books of account or documents belong to some other person and it is for him to hand over such books of account or documents to the Assessing Officer having jurisdiction over such other person as provided under section 153C of the Act.

In case seized material belonging to some other person is directly handed over by the authorized officer to the Assessing Officer having jurisdiction over such other person, the very action of seizure of such books of account or documents may be called in question. The authorized officer can seize books of account or other documents in the course of search which are belonging to the person searched or which have any connection or relation with the person searched and first of all the seized material has to be examined with respect to the person searched.

(*ii*) **Handing over of books of account or documents to other Government Agencies/Department**

The authorized officer does not have duty under the Income Tax Act to hand over the books of account or other documents seized in the course of Income Tax search to other Central or State Government Departments if the same is requisitioned by them unless there is any specific overriding provision under the respective statutes authorizing such power of requisition from the income tax department. However, under section 138 of the Income Tax Act, the income tax authority may furnish or share the information with the other government departments in accordance with the procedure provided therein.

It may happen that Excise or Sales Tax Department may find the seized material consisting of incriminating set of books of account, documents or loose papers useful so as to take appropriate action against the assessee for evasion of tax or duty under their respective statutes. They may make requisition from the authorized officer to handover such incriminating material to them but the authorized officer who has conducted the search under the Income Tax Act is not duty bound to hand over such material to the other authorities in absence of any specific provision under the Income Tax Act.

However an order of the competent Court may be required to be complied with by the authorized officer in accordance with the direction given in the order of the Court.

10.18A Incorporation of sub-sections (9B), (9C) and (9D) - Power of provisional attachment of property and to make reference to Valuation Officer by the Authorized Officer

Finance Act, 2017 has incorporated sub-sections (9B), (9C) and (9D) to section 132 and also substituted *Explanation 1* with new *Explanation 1*, text of which is as under:

"(9B) Where, during the course of the search or seizure or within a period of sixty days from the date on which the last of the authorisations for search was executed, the authorised officer, for the reasons to be recorded in writing, is satisfied that for the purpose of protecting the interest of revenue, it is necessary so to do, he may with the previous approval of the Principal Director General or Director General or the Principal Director or Director, by order in writing, attach provisionally any property belonging to the assessee, and for the said purpose the provisions of the Second Schedule shall, mutatis mutandis, *apply.*

(9C) Every provisional attachment made under sub-section (9B) shall cease to have effect after the expiry of a period of six months from the date of the order referred to in sub-section (9B).

(9D) The authorised officer may, during the course of the search or seizure or within a period of sixty days from the date on which the last of the authorisations for search was executed, make a reference to a Valuation Officer referred to in section 142A, who shall estimate the fair market value of the property in the manner provided under that section and submit a report of the estimate to the said officer within a period of sixty days from the date of receipt of such reference.";

'Explanation 1.—For the purposes of sub-sections (9A), (9B) and (9D), with respect to "execution of an authorisation for search", the provisions of sub-section (2) of section 153B shall apply'.

Finance Act, 2023 has substituted *Explanation 1* as mentioned above with the following *Explanation 1*:

'Explanation 1.—For the purposes of sub-sections (9A), (9B) and (9D), the last of authorisation for search shall be deemed to have been executed,-

(a) in the case of search, on the conclusion of search as recorded in the last panchnama drawn in relation to any person in whose case the warrant of authorisation has been issued; or

(b) in the case of requisition under section 132A, on actual receipt of the books of account or other documents or assets by the authorised officer.'

(i) Objective

Memorandum explaining the Object of amendment appended to Finance Bill, 2017 states as under:

In order to protect the interest of revenue and safeguard recovery in search cases, it is proposed to insert sub-section (9B) and (9C) in the said section, to provide that during the course of a search or seizure or within a period of sixty days from the date on which the last of the authorisations for search was executed, the authorised officer on being satisfied that for protecting the interest of revenue it is necessary so to do, may attach provisionally any property belonging to the assessee with the prior approval of Principal Director General or Director General or Principal Director or Director. It has been proposed that such provisional attachment shall cease to have effect after the expiry of six months from the date of order of such attachment.

In order to enable correct estimation and quantification of undisclosed income held in the form of investment or property by the assessee by the Investigation wing of the Department, it is further proposed to insert a new sub-section (9D) in the said section to provide that in a case of search, the authorised officer may, for the purpose of estimation of fair market value of a property, make a reference to a Valuation Officer referred to in section 142A, for valuation in the manner provided under that sub-section. It also provides that the Valuation Officer shall furnish the valuation report within sixty days of receipt of such reference.

It is also proposed to amend Explanation 1 to section 132, so as to provide that for the purposes of sub-sections 9A, 9B and 9D, with respect to "execution of an authorisation for search" under the provisions of sub-section (2) of section 153B shall apply.

These amendments will take effect from 1st April, 2017.

(ii) Power of Provisional attachment granted for six months:

The power of provisional attachment has been granted to the Authorised Officer for a period of six months from the date of passing the order of attachment. Such order of provisional attachment can be passed either during the course of search and seizure operation or within a period of 60 days from the date on which the last of the authorizations for search was executed by the Authorized Officer. Reason for provisional attachment is required to be recorded in writing and previous approval of the prescribed higher authorities has to be obtained in writing. Object of provisional attachment is to enable the Authorized Officer to take immediate action for protecting the interest of revenue so that the searched person may not dispose the property. It is however not clear from the amendment whether such power can be exercised only with respect to undisclosed asset/property or even for disclosed asset/property. It is also to be noted that there is no provision in the amended sub-section for extension of any attachment beyond six months.

It is usually seen in practice that the jurisdiction is transferred after search to the Assessing Officer within six months from the date of last authorizations of search and all the seized materials along with appraisal report are handed over by the Authorised Officer to the Assessing Officer. Therefore, there appears to be no provision made in the above sub-section for extension of the period of six months for which provisional attachment can be done by the Authorised Officer. After the expiry of the period of six months of provisional attachment made by the Authorised Officer, such power may vest with the Assessing Officer under section 281B who can exercise such powers as provided under section 281B of the Act in terms of the requirement of that section.

(iii) Reference to the Valuation Officer:

The Authorised Officer has been granted power to make reference to Valuation Officer referred to under section 142A for making estimation of the Fair Market Value of any property. The Valuation Officer is required to submit the report within 60 days from the date of such reference. Authorized Officer would then handover the report to the Assessing Officer along with appraisal report at a later date for using the same as an evidence for making assessment under section 153A of the Act.

It seems that the above power has been given so as to expedite the process of collecting evidence by way of making estimation of Fair Market Value of any property in case Authorised Officer is of the opinion that there may be undisclosed investment in the property. Thus, power of reference to the Valuation Officer as contained in section 142A is sought to be given to the Authorized Officer also. But the terminology used in sub-section (9D) enables the making of reference only for estimation of fair market value of any property whereas it has been experienced in practice that estimation of value of investment in properties can serve better purpose to determine undisclosed investment. It seems that the language employed in sub-section (9D) has not been happily worded and may not serve the intent with which this has been brought.

Finance Act, 2023 has amended sub-section (9D) providing power of reference also to any other person or entity or any valuer by inserting sub-clause (*ii*) as under:

> "*(ii) any other person or entity or any valuer registered by or under any law for the time being in force, as may be approved by the Principal Chief Commissioner or the Chief Commissioner or the Principal Director General or the Director General, in accordance with the procedure, as may be prescribed, in this regard,*"

(*iv*) **Whether bank account, stock-in-trade, disclosed assets can also be attached:**

Section 281B of the Act empowers the Assessing Officer during the pendency of proceeding for assessment or re-assessment to attach provisionally any property belonging to the assessee, for the purpose of protecting the interest of the revenue, in the manner provided in Schedule-II with the previous approval of the higher authorities. Such power of provisional attachment can be exercised by the Assessing Officer for the undisclosed as well as disclosed properties of the assessee.

Power of attachment granted to the Authorised Officer by way of sub-section (9B) to section 132 are similar in nature as the powers available with the Assessing Officer as provided under section 281B. Therefore, it can be inferred that Authorised Officer can also make provisional attachment even for disclosed assets/properties of the assessee.

There is already power with the Authorised Officer to effect seizure of undisclosed assets/properties except immovable properties or stock-in-trade. The power of provisional attachment as given in sub-section (9B) would extend to all kinds of assets/properties whether movable or immovable. The above interpretation shall lead to the conclusion that even disclosed bank account, stock-in-trade or any other disclosed assets can also be provisionally attached by the Authorised Officer to protect the interest of revenue. In our opinion, such powers granted to the Authorised Officer are too harsh and may lead to harassment of the searched person.

It is also interesting to note that it was not long back when power of seizure and deemed seizure of the stock-in-trade of the business was withdrawn by way of an amendment brought by Finance Act, 2003 with effect from 1st June, 2003. This was done to avoid the disruption of the business activities which such seizure etc. used to result. But power of provisional attachment given to the Authorized Officer under sub-section (9B) may lead to exercising similar kind of situation whereby the disclosed stock-in-trade may also be attached thus disrupting the flow of the business. This amendment in our considered opinion seems to be a regressive amendment.

10.19 Text of section

132B. (1) The assets seized under section 132 or requisitioned under section 132A may be dealt with in the following manner, namely:—

(*i*) the amount of any existing liability under this Act, the Wealth-tax Act, 1957 (27 of 1957), the Expenditure-tax Act, 1987 (35 of 1987), the Gift-tax Act, 1958 (18 of 1958) and the Interest-tax Act, 1974 (45 of 1974), and the amount of the liability determined on completion of the assessment or reassessment or recomputation and the assessment of the year relevant to the previous year in which search is initiated or requisition is made, or the amount of liability determined on completion of the assessment under Chapter XIV-B for the block period, as the case may be (including any penalty levied or interest payable in connection with such assessment) and in respect of which such person is in default or is deemed to be in default, or the amount of liability arising on an application made before the Settlement Commission under sub-section (1) of section 245C, may be recovered out of such assets:

Provided that where the person concerned makes an application to the Assessing Officer within thirty days from the end of the month in which the asset was seized, for release of asset and the nature and source of acquisition of any such asset is explained to the satisfaction of the Assessing Officer, the amount of any existing liability referred to in this clause may be recovered out of such asset and the remaining portion, if any, of the asset may be released, with the prior approval of the Principal Chief Commissioner or Chief Commissioner or Principal Commissioner or Commissioner, to the person from whose custody the assets were seized:

Provided further that such asset or any portion thereof as is referred to in the first proviso shall be released within a period of one hundred and twenty days from the date on which the last of the authorisations for search under section 132 or for requisition under section 132A, as the case may be, was executed;

(*ii*) if the assets consist solely of money, or partly of money and partly of other assets, the Assessing Officer may apply such money in the discharge of the liabilities referred to in clause (*i*) and the assessee shall be discharged of such liability to the extent of the money so applied;

(*iii*) the assets other than money may also be applied for the discharge of any such liability referred to in clause (*i*) as remains undischarged and for this purpose such assets shall be deemed to be under distraint as if such distraint was effected by the Assessing Officer or, as the case may be, the Tax Recovery Officer under authorisation from the Principal Chief Commissioner or Chief Commissioner or Principal Commissioner or Commissioner under sub-section (5) of section 226 and the Assessing Officer or, as the case may be, the Tax Recovery Officer may recover the amount of such liabilities by the sale of such assets and such sale shall be effected in the manner laid down in the Third Schedule.

(2) Nothing contained in sub-section (1) shall preclude the recovery of the amount of liabilities aforesaid by any other mode laid down in this Act.

(3) Any assets or proceeds thereof which remain after the liabilities referred to in clause (*i*) of sub-section (1) are discharged shall be forthwith made over or paid to the persons from whose custody the assets were seized.

(4) (*a*) The Central Government shall pay simple interest at the rate of one-half per cent for every month or part of a month on the amount by which the aggregate amount of money seized under section 132 or requisitioned under section 132A, as reduced by the amount of money, if any, released under the first proviso to clause (*i*) of sub-section (1), and of the proceeds, if any, of the assets sold towards the discharge of the existing liability referred to in clause (*i*) of sub-section (1), exceeds the aggregate of the amount required to meet the liabilities referred to in clause (*i*) of sub-section (1) of this section.

(*b*) Such interest shall run from the date immediately following the expiry of the period of one hundred and twenty days from the date on which the last of the authorisations for search under section 132 or requisition under section 132A was executed to the date of completion of the assessment or reassessment or recomputation.

Explanation 1.—In this section,—

(*i*) "block period" shall have the meaning assigned to it in clause (*a*) of section 158B;

(*ii*) "execution of an authorisation for search or requisition" shall have the same meaning as assigned to it in *Explanation 2* to section 158BE.

Explanation 2.—For the removal of doubts, it is hereby declared that the "existing liability" does not include advance tax payable in accordance with the provisions of Part C of Chapter XVII.

10.20 Legislative history - Significant amendments

This section was first introduced by the Income Tax (Amendment) Act, 1965, when entire section 132 was substituted. It provided application of retained assets under summary assessment as per section 132(5). This section was amended several times and with the abolition of the concept of summary assessment under section 132(5), the provision of this section became redundant. Therefore, this section was again substituted by the Finance Act, 2002, with effect from 1st June, 2002, providing procedure for application of seized assets under present circumstances.

Finance Act, 2013 has inserted *Explanation 2* clarifying that the term "existing liability" in section 132B does not include advance tax payable. This clarification will have wide ramifications as it would imply that cash seized during search cannot be claimed and adjusted as advance tax paid in the return of income for the search year to be filed by the assessee.

Finance Act, 2022 has amended this section to refer to the assessment or reassessment or recomputation which is to be made as per new scheme of assessment in search cases as per sections 147 to 151 as introduced by the Finance Act, 2021. This amendment has been made effective from 1st April, 2022.

10.21 Objective

The objective of this section is to provide methodology regarding application of seized or requisitioned assets. The basic objective of this section is thus to provide that assets seized during search, consisting of cash or assets in kind can be used and applied for recovery of existing liabilities due from the assessee or future liabilities which may be determined on completion of the assessments relating to search year. This section, in our opinion, is not appropriately drafted and leaves many controversial issues.

10.22 Broad framework

Section 132B lays down the procedure to be followed in connection with application and release of assets seized during search. It provides for the following matters-

 a. Recovery of existing liability under all Direct Tax Acts.

 b. Application and release of disclosed assets, if seized.

 c. Application of undisclosed assets against tax liabilities to be determined on completion of assessment including liability relating to interest and penalty.

  d. Realization of seized assets.

  e. Release of surplus assets.

  f. Payment of interest on excess money retained.

10.23 Application and release of disclosed assets seized

In case the disclosed assets are seized by the department during search, the same are required to be released to the person searched as per procedure prescribed under section 132B.

In the case of *Bipin Vimalchand Jain* v. *Asstt. DIT (Inv.)* [2008] 169 Taxman 396 (Bom.), it was held that once the *Explanation* about the nature and source was found to be correct, the amount of cash seized could not be retained.

(*i*) Existing liability under all Direct Tax Acts to be adjusted

The seized assets can be applied for recovery of existing liability not only under the Income Tax Act but also under other Direct Tax Acts *i.e.* Wealth Tax Act, 1957, Expenditure Tax Act, 1987, Gift Tax Act, 1958, and Interest Tax Act, 1974. The liability may be relating to tax, interest or penalty for which person searched is in default and the same is outstanding against him. Though Expenditure Tax Act, Interest Tax Act, Wealth Tax Act and Gift Tax Act have been repealed and presently not in operation yet any old liability against the person searched, outstanding under the provision of any of these Acts, can be recovered by applying the seized assets.

It has been held in the case of *Rich Udyog Network Ltd. & Ors.* v. *Director of IT (Inv.) & Ors.* [2018] 408 ITR 68 (All.)/173 DTR 269 (All.) that So long as assessment under s. 153A is not finalised, unaccounted cash seized during search could not be released.

It has been held in the case of *Dr. R.P. Patel* v. *Asstt. Director of IT (Inv.)* 210 DTR 62 (Ker.) that adjustment of seized IVPs against tax demands by authorized officer and not by assessee's AO. that too after the period of fifteen days as per section 132(9A) was invalid and further, it is evident that the IVPs were adjusted against liabilities that were not determined on the date of such adjustments and hence adjustments are therefore invalid.

(*ia*) Explanation to be applicable prospectively

In the case of *Kanishka Prints Pvt. Ltd.* v. *Asstt. CIT* [2013] 34 taxmann. com 307/143 ITD 716 (Ahmedabad-Trib.), the Tribunal held that when the legislature has made explanation operative prospectively by words expressed therein, its operation shall have to be confined to the future date. Further when a statute and particularly when the same has been made applicable w.e.f. a particular date, should be construed prospectively and not retrospectively. Thus, considering the totality of the aforesaid, interpretation of applicability of explanation, and by virtue of amendment of section 132B which shall take effect from 1st June, 2013, existing liability does not include advance tax payable in accordance with the provisions of Part C of Chapter XVII of the Act.

It has been held in the case of *Gordhanbhai Nagardas Patel* v. *Deputy CIT* [2017] 82 taxmann.com 455/249 Taxman 604 (Guj.) that Explanation 2 to section 132B inserted with effect from 1.6.2011 clarifying that "existing Liability" would not include advance tax is an amendment to overcome effect of judicial decisions and thus the amendment is not retrospective. Therefore, Hon'ble Court held that application of the cash seized towards advance tax was justified and no interest was chargeable for default in payment of advance tax on such amount.

CBDT in its circular number 20 of 2017 dated 12.6.2017 has also clarified that the above Explanation 2 to section 132B shall be applicable prospectively. Extracts of the Circular is as under:

Circular No. 20/2017

F. No. 279/Misc./140/2015/ITJ
Government of India
Ministry of Finance
Department of Revenue
Central Board of Direct Taxes

New Delhi, Dated 12th June, 2017

Subject: Applicability of Explanation 2 to Section 132B of the I.T. Act, 1961- reg. -

Section 132B of the Income Tax Act 1961, provides for adjustment of seized assets/requisitioned assets against the amount of any existing liability under the Income Tax Act, 1961, (the Act), the Wealth-tax Act, 1957, the Expenditure-tax Act, 1987, the Gift-tax Act, 1958 and the Interest-tax Act, 1974, and the amount of the liability determined on completion of the assessment under section 153A of the Act and the assessment of the year relevant to the previous year in which search is initiated or requisition is made, or the amount of liability determined on completion of the assessment under Chapter XIV-B for the block period, as the case may be (including any penalty levied or interest payable in connection with such assessment) and in respect of which such person is in default or is deemed to be in default, or the amount of liability arising on an application made before the Settlement Commission under sub-section (1) of section 245C of the Act.

2. Dispute arose between the Department and the assessees with regard to adjustment of such seized/requisitioned cash against advance tax liability etc. Several Courts held that on an application made by the assessee, the seized money is to be adjusted against the advance tax liability of the assessee. Subsequently, Explanation 2 to Section 132B of the Act was inserted by the Finance Act, 2013 w.e.f. 01-06-2013, clarifying that "existing liability" does not include advance tax payable in accordance with the provisions of Part C of Chapter XVII of the Act. However, the dispute continued on the issue as to whether the amendment was clarificatory in nature having retrospective applicability or it has only prospective applicability.

3. Several Courts have held that the insertion of Explanation 2 to section 132B of the Act, is prospective in nature and not applicable to cases prior to 06.2013. The SLPs filed by the Department against the judgment of the Hon'ble Punjab and Haryana High Court in the case of Cosmos Builders and Promoters Ltd.[1] and the Hon'ble Allahabad High Court in the case of Sunil Chandra Gupta[2], have been dismissed. Subsequently, the CBDT has also accepted the judgment of the Hon'ble Punjab & Haryana High Court in the case of Spaze Towers Pvt. Ltd.[3] dated 17.11.2016, wherein it was held that the Explanation 2 to Section 132B of the Act is prospective in nature.

4. Accordingly, it has now been settled that insertion of Explanation 2 to Section 132B of the Act shall have a prospective application and so, appeals may not be filed by the Department on this issue for the cases prior to 01.06.2013 and those already filed may be withdrawn/ not pressed upon.

5. The above may be brought to the notice of all concerned.

6. Hindi version follows.

(Neetika Bansal)

Deputy Secretary to Government of India

(*ii*) **Liability arising on application to Settlement Commission can also be adjusted:**

Finance Act, 2015 has amended section 132B w.e.f. 01.06.2015 providing that the amount of liability arising on an application made before the Settlement Commission under sub-section (1) of section 245C, may be recovered out of seized assets.

The amount of liability of tax which may arise on an application made before the Settlement Commission may arise at the following two stages:-

    (*a*) Tax liability to be paid on application being made before Settlement Commission relating to additional undisclosed income declared in the application.

    (*b*) Final tax liability as determined by the Settlement Commission while passing order of settlement.

In our view, the above amendment covers adjustment of both kinds of liabilities out of the seized assets, though plain reading of the amendment suggests as if it seeks to cover the adjustment of the seized assets at the time of final determination of tax liability. It needs to be appreciated that while submitting application to Settlement Commission, the declarant-assessees were facing problem that cash seized during search was not being adjusted by the department towards the tax liability arising on application. The above hardship seems to have been removed by the above amendment. Assessee can make a request to the Commissioner and the Settlement Commission along with the application filed for such adjustment of cash seized. Practically it has also been seen that benches of Settlement Commission are permitting and directing the concerned Commissioner for making such adjustment of cash seized. However, assets other than cash seized which are not in liquid form may not be possible to be adjusted towards tax liability on application to Settlement Commission.

All kind of assets seized may however be used by the department for recovery of tax liability determined by Settlement Commission as per final settlement order passed.

(*iii*) Application of disclosed assets, if seized

In the course of search, even disclosed assets relating to the person searched may be seized. Though it is not the objective of search and seizure scheme under section 132 to seize the disclosed assets, yet there may be several reasons as a result of which the person searched could not produce the evidences regarding disclosure of the assets at the time of taking decision regarding seizure by the authorized officer and due to which even disclosed assets are liable to be seized. This may be so that the person searched may not be available at the premises under search to explain the source of the disclosed asset or, he may be unwell or, the evidences may not be readily available with him at that point of time or the authorized officer may not be convinced with the evidences and so on.

First proviso to clause (*i*) of section 132B(1) makes it clear in a way that disclosed assets, if seized can also be applied for recovering any existing liability referred to under clause (*i*) *i.e.* existing outstanding liability under any of the Direct Taxes Acts. It indirectly validates seizure of disclosed assets which is however not the objective of search and seizure scheme under section 132.

If we closely read the first and second provisos to section 132B(1)(*i*), it provides the following framework—-

1. The assessee is required to make application to the Assessing Officer for release of asset within thirty days from the end of the month in which the asset was seized.

2. The nature and source of acquisition of the asset is explained to the satisfaction of the Assessing Officer.

3. The amount of any existing liability referred to in clause (*i*) of section 132B(1) may be recovered out of such asset.

4. The remaining portion, if any, of the asset may be released with the prior approval of the Chief Commissioner or the Commissioner.

5. Second proviso further provides that the asset or any part of the asset in excess of the existing liability shall be released within a period of one hundred and twenty days from the date on which the last of the authorizations for search was executed.

The provision of the first proviso is applicable for release of the disclosed assets, the nature and source of acquisition of which is fully explainable to the satisfaction of the Assessing Officer. This proviso does not pertain to the release of unaccounted assets but it is pertaining to the release of accounted asset which was seized during search. As per clause (*i*) already discussed above, unaccounted assets cannot be released until finalization of all the assessment and penalty proceedings and recovery of outstanding demand relating to the same.

Seizure of disclosed assets is not permitted under section 132(1)(*iii*). As per scheme of search and seizure under section 132, it is not the objective to seize disclosed assets. However during search operation disclosed assets may be seized due to the reason that assessee could not produce the evidence regarding nature and source of acquisition of such assets at that point of time and the authorized officer, conducting search, may seize the same for want of proper evidences available with the assessee. For release of such assets which were never intended to be seized in the scheme of the Act, providing such stringent procedure of release that too after adjusting existing tax liability does not seem to be in the spirit of law and within the parameters of overall scheme of search. Such assets should be, in our opinion, released by the authorized officer on application by the assessee explaining nature and source of acquisition of asset without making any adjustment for recovery of any tax liability. This is a case of unauthorized seizure of the asset and mere application with the authorized officer should be sufficient for release of such asset.

The recovery proceeding for the existing liability is an independent act and sufficient powers have been provided under the Act for recovering the liability outstanding against the assessee. To apply a disclosed but seized asset for recovery of the outstanding liability is, in our opinion, not warranted.

The argument in favour of justification regarding such provision may be that assessee is required to pay the existing liability out of his disclosed assets and money available. If assessee is not paying the tax liability, department has the right to recover the same out of his assets which comes to the knowledge of the department including the disclosed assets seized during search in whatsoever manner.

(iiia) Release of surplus asset

In the case of *Mul Chand Malu (HUF)* v. *Asstt. CIT* [2016] 69 taxmann. com 437/241 Taxman 189 (Gau.), it has been held that when an application was made for the release of the assets under the first proviso to section 132B(1)(i) of the Act explaining the nature and source of the seized assets and if no dispute was raised by the Department during the permissible time of 120 days, it had no authority to retain the seized assets in view of the mandate contained in second proviso to section 132B(1)(ii) of the Act. The authorities were directed to release the seized assets of the assessee immediately.

In the case of *Nadim Dilip Bhai Panjvani* v. *ITO* [2016] 66 taxmann.com 124/237 Taxman 480 (Guj.), it has been held by the High Court that if an application is made under first proviso to section 132B(1)(i) then the same should be disposed of within the time limit given in the second proviso which is 120 days from the date on which of the last of the authorizations for the search was executed. Second proviso though speaks of releasing the assets as referred to in first proviso within the time limit prescribed, still the question of not releasing the asset would arise only upon the decision on the application is taken by the AO. If no decision is taken within the time limit, then the releasing of assets becomes imminent. Further, it was held that such time limit cannot be said to be directory in nature.

It has been held in the case of *Ashish Jayantilal Sanghavi* v. *Income Tax Officer* (2022) 114 CCH 149 Guj HC, (2022) 214 DTR 380 (Guj.), (2022) 139 taxmann.com 126/444 ITR 457 (Guj.)

"24. The statutory provision of Section 132B of the Act is very clear. There appears to be a mandate and such mandate is mandatory and not directory. This is evident from the ratio of the decision of this High Court in the case of Nadim Dilipbhai Panjvani (supra) wherein this Court has taken the view that the Courts should attach considerable importance to the time frame provided under Sections 132A and 132B of the Act when it comes to a question of retention of books of account or of seized assets. It is not permissible for the Court to read the time limit provided in the proviso to clause (*i*) of sub-section (1) of Section 132B of the Act as being merely directory. Any attempt on the part of the Court to read it as directory would substantially dilute the rigors of the statutory provisions and would give an unbridled power to the Assessing Officer to retain the seized assets awaiting the finalization of future possible liability for indefinite period without deciding the application of the person concerned who may be legitimately in a position to explain the source of the asset so seized."

(*iv*) Provision regarding the release of disclosed asset - Difficult to be implemented

The procedure for release of such asset provided under first and second proviso is not practicably implementable. The assessee is required to make application to the Assessing Officer within thirty days from the end of month in which the asset is seized. The authorized officer is never in a position nor required under law to send the record of seized assets after finalizing appraisal report to the concerned Assessing Officer within a period of thirty days. The decision regarding Assessing Officer who is required to assess the case after centralization is generally not finalized upto thirty days or even months thereafter. When the Assessing Officer to whom assessee is required to file application is not finalized, then how assessee can be expected to file the application to the Assessing Officer. In case application is filed by the assessee to the existing Assessing Officer with whom his Income Tax Returns are filed, no action on the application of the assessee is taken by him, in practice, since he is not having any information, records and assets seized in his possession. When he is not having assets in his possession, how can the same be released by him. Moreover, he may be the Assessing Officer who may not get the seized assets and may not make the assessment in consequence to the search.

In practice, it has been observed that once an asset is seized, it is hardly released even if it may be duly accounted for asset. The assessee is required to explain nature and source of acquisition of asset to the satisfaction of the Assessing Officer. The satisfaction of the Assessing Officer is, it is seen in practice, exercised subjectively and the Assessing Officer generally is not satisfied and thus asset is not released.

Further, there is requirement to take prior approval of the Chief Commissioner or Commissioner before the release of such asset or part of the asset. This is an administrative act and the objective of taking administrative approval may be to take higher authority in confidence and explain him all the facts so as to eliminate any possibility of arbitrary exercise of such power. For the release of disclosed asset which was not required to be seized in the first instance, to take such approval is thought laudable but it is seen in practice that such approval is also given mechanically and most of the times, assets may not be released thus frustrating the very purpose of the overall scheme of release.

As per the second proviso, Assessing Officer is required to release the asset within a period of one hundred and twenty days from the conclusion of search. After recovering existing liability, the surplus disclosed asset should be released immediately and to grant a period of one hundred and twenty days for the release of such assets is also not warranted.

It has been held in the case of *Mitaben R. Shah* v. *Dy. CIT* [2010] 42 DTR 124/235 CTR 285 (Guj.)/[2011] 331 ITR 424 that the petitioner having made an application within the permissible time-limit for release of seized gold ornaments and jewellery explaining the nature and source of acquisition thereof, respondents have no authority to retain these assets after the prescribed period of 120 days by rejecting the petitioner's application after the expiry of said period and the respondent authorities were directed to release the seized ornaments and jewellery forthwith.

In the case of *DIT* v. *Gauri Shankar* [2017] 80 taxmann.com 144 (Delhi), it has been held that the premises of the petitioners were raided on July 11, 2005 nearly 11 years ago. 6 kilograms of gold bars and currency were seized therefrom. Till date, there was no justification forthcoming for either the conduct of the raid or for seizure of the articles. There was nothing on record to show that any proceedings for assessment or reassessment were initiated till date against the petitioners in respect of the articles seized in 2005. There was no justification for any further retention of the seized gold bars as well as the currency.

(v) Certain unanswered questions

Several questions may arise as to what would happen if the assessee could not apply for the release within thirty days from the end of the month in which asset was seized, since assessee was not aware who is going to be Assessing Officer for assessing the search cases under section 153A and as to whether release of the asset can be denied only for the reason that assessee did not apply within time limit. What remedy is available with the assessee if Assessing Officer does not release the asset within one hundred and twenty days from the conclusion of search? What remedy is available with the assessee if Assessing Officer is not satisfied regarding the source of the acquisition of the asset inspite of all the evidence produced by the assessee? Whether Assessing Officer is required to pass any speaking order before rejecting application of the assessee for release of the asset?

These are some of the questions which remain unanswered. However, it may be said that when decision for not releasing the asset is taken, it should be taken by way of speaking order. The only remedy available with assessees is to approach to the higher authorities by way of administrative measure or file writ with the High Court.

(vi) Release only upon satisfactory explanation

The onus to prove that the seized assets are of disclosed nature will lie upon the person who is claiming so and he is required to lead the evidences to this effect to the satisfaction of the Income Tax Officer. In the case of *Suresh Val Chand Jain* v. *Union of India* [2006] 156 Taxman 138 (Raj.), it was held by the High Court that the assessee having failed to explain the source to the satisfaction of the Assistant Commissioner, there was no occasion for release of the seized gold.

However, in case the nature and source of seized assets is satisfactorily explained by the assessee, the same should be released immediately. In the case of *Rajesh Sharma* v. *Asstt. CIT (Inv.)* [2001] 119 Taxman 996, Gauhati High Court issued writ for release of seized assets which was satisfactorily explained. The High Court held that there was no reason as to why the impugned order could not be challenged under Article 226 of the Constitution invoking the writ jurisdiction of the Court on the ground that the same was not judicial or quasi-judicial. Accordingly, the availability of alternate remedy was no bar.

In the case of *Jinkal Dineshbhai Virvadiya* v. *CIT* [2014] 42 taxmann. com 543/223 Taxman 26 (Guj.) (HC), the Court held that the petitioner had been taking contradictory stands regarding the source of the amount. Before the police authorities, he had stated that the amount was out of his personal savings and income from brokerage of diamonds. Later on, before the Department, he changed his version and stated that the amount was received from his father and other relatives to enable him to set up his business and that his relatives had raised these amounts by selling their jewellery and ornaments. The source of cash had not been explained satisfactorily. Refusal to release the cash was justified.

(*vii*) **Immediate release of deposits seized from disclosed bank accounts**

In case any seizure of deposits is made from the bank accounts which are duly disclosed by the assessee, the same is not permitted to be retained and immediate release was required to be made in such cases. In the case of *D.R. Benefit Fund Ltd.* v. *Asstt. DIT (Inv.)* [2008] 297 ITR 346/[2006] 203 CTR 453 (Mad.), the High Court held that it would be just and proper that the Income Tax Department should be directed to refund the cash seized and the amounts withdrawn from the current account of the petitioner held with the bank.

(*viii*) **Release of asset in case of requisition under section 132A**

In the case of *Hemal Dilipbhai Shah* v. *Asstt. CIT* [2017] 80 taxmann. com 151 (Guj), in proceedings under section 132A, VS from whom the cash had been seized had clearly stated that it belonged to the assessee and the assessee had also in proceedings under section 153C admitted this. The Department had treated the cash as belonging to the assessee. There was no dispute as regards the title to the seized assets (cash). The Department was, therefore, not justified in not releasing the balance amount to the assessee on the ground that the cash had been seized from VS.

10.24 Application and release of undisclosed assets seized

(*i*) **Liability to be determined on completion of assessment**

As per second limb of clause (*i*) of section 132B(1), seized assets can be applied not only for existing liability but for recovering the amount of the liability which will be determined on completion of the assessment in consequence of search under section 153A (including the year of search) or for the block period determined under section 158BC, as the case may be. It also includes any liability relating to penalty or interest payable in connection with such assessments.

The above provision almost makes it impossible to get the seized assets released till completion of all the proceedings under the Income Tax Act relating to search years. Assessment proceedings are presently completed with in a period of twenty four months or thirty six months as the case may be from the end of financial year in which search takes place and penalty proceedings may further take considerable time in its finalization. Even after completion of assessment proceedings under section 153A including the year of search and after recovery of demand raised as per assessment orders, the seized assets are generally not released on the pretext of pendency of penalty proceedings. Penalty proceedings are kept pending till the finalization of appellate proceedings and as a result assets seized are not released for a considerable time.

It is pertinent to note here that the provision contained under section 132B(1) regarding application of seized assets is restricted towards the tax liability to be determined relating to search years i.e. the years to be assessed under section 153A including the year of search. Any outstanding liability relating to assessment years subsequent to search year cannot be recovered by the application of seized assets.

In the case of *Jinkal Dineshbhai Virvadiya* v. *CIT* [2014] 42 taxmann. com 543/223 Taxman 26 (Guj.), it was held that amount that could be adjusted from such seized cash would not only be existing liability, but those liabilities that might be determined on completion of assessment under section 153A.

It has been held in the case of *Union of India* v. *Rajesh Kumar* 201 DTR 6 (Ker.) that since proceedings under section 153A are pending and it is also pointed out that under section 132B, until conclusion of the proceedings, the IT Department can retain the said amounts and in such circumstance a refund at this stage is not warranted.

(ia) **Liability determined on completion of assessment-including penalty levied or interest payable**

As per the provisions of section 132B, the seized assets can be retained and applied for meeting the existing tax liability and the liability to be determined on completion of assessment of search cases u/s 153A. Liability to be determined on completion of assessment includes not only the amount of tax and interest but also any penalty which may be levied in consequence thereof.

The levy of penalty after passing of the assessment order which is subject matter of further appeal, further takes considerable time and therefore, the seized assets are retained by the department and the assessee is not able to get the assets released even after when no tax demand remains outstanding relating to search cases. The quantum of penalty to be levied is also difficult to be estimated and it may vary from 100% to 300% of the tax sought to be evaded. Thus, there remains uncertainty in this regard and therefore, assessee is not able to get the seized assets released.

It has also been held in the case of *Sree Balaji Refinery* v. *Dy. CIT* [2012] 20 taxmann.com 183/208 Taxman 383 (Ker.) that expression "penalty levied" in section 132B(1) should be read as penalty to be levied in a proceeding under section 271(1)(c) and therefore section 132B(1) entitles the Income Tax Department to retain the seized gold with them until penalty is levied and apply the same towards the liability so determined provided the assessee is in default or deemed to be in default.

(ii) Realization of assets in kind and application thereof

Clause (*ii*) and clause (*iii*) of section 132B(1) lays down the manner in which the seized assets are to be realized and applied for recovering tax liabilities. If the assets seized consist of money, there is no difficulty of adjustment of the same against tax liabilities as provided under clause (*ii*). However if the assets seized are in kind or other than money, the procedure for application of the same has been provided under clause (*iii*).

Clause (*iii*) provides that asset other than money may also be applied for the discharge of any tax liability, existing or to be determined after assessment of search cases as referred to in clause (*i*) and which remains outstanding against the assessee. For this purpose, the seized assets shall be deemed to be under distraint as affected under section 226(5) by the Assessing Officer or by the Tax Recovery Officer. The Assessing Officer or Tax Recovery Officer may recover the amount of tax liabilities by the sale of such assets in the manner as laid down under Third Schedule of the Income Tax Act.

(iii) Conversion of assets in kind into money

Whenever assets in kind are seized, the same are not permitted to be converted in terms of money unless the tax liability is due against the assessee and recovery of the tax liability is contemplated to be made by the department against the seized assets.

In the case of *K.C.C. Software Ltd.* v. *DIT (Inv.)* [2008] 167 Taxman 248, the Supreme Court observed that cash in bank is conceptually different from cash in hand. It was clarified about the impossibility to convert assets to cash, and therefore impound the same. The Supreme Court held that bank deposits cannot be converted into cash and directed the department to keep the amount in interest bearing fixed deposit as ultimately in the event, the assessee succeeds, it would be entitled to interest.

In the case of *Raj Kumar* v. *Union of India* [2000] 110 Taxman 483 (P&H), it was held that where FDRs are seized during search, Income Tax Authorities will have no jurisdiction to order encashment of the

FDR's and recover the proceeds thereof under section 132(1) of the Act.

In the case of *Windson Electronics (P.) Ltd.* v. *Union of India* [2004] 141 Taxman 419 (Cal.), it was held that section 132 does not confer any authority on Income Tax Officer to realize assets and convert them into cash unless the tax becomes due. Therefore, a revenue official cannot compel bank to encash fixed deposit and make over proceeds to him.

In the case of *Jagdish Prasad M. Joshi* v. *Dy. CIT* [2005] 273 ITR 296 (Bom.), when the department encashed the FDs from the bank account of the petitioner, the High Court observed that the action of the respondent *vis-à-vis* appropriation was high-handed. It was not supported by any provisions of the Income Tax Act, particularly when the appropriation was not to be made without the assessment order. The department was directed to bring back encashed amounts into the petitioner's respective bank accounts.

In practice, it has been observed that asset in kind is generally not sold for recovery of the outstanding tax liabilities until all the appellate proceedings with respect to such cases have been finalized. There may be embarrassing situation for the Assessing Officer in case assets are sold to recover tax liabilities raised after assessment but later on the additions made during assessment are deleted by the appellate authorities.

As a matter of clarification, sub-section (2) of section 132B provides that nothing contained in sub-section (1) shall preclude the recovery of the amount of liabilities by any other mode laid down under the Income Tax Act.

(iv) Release of surplus asset

Sub-section (3) of section 132B provides that any assets or proceeds thereof which remain surplus after discharging all the tax liabilities as referred under clause (*i*) shall be paid to the assessee. The provision requires surplus assets to be released after meeting all the tax liabilities as referred under clause (*i*). Clause (*i*) refers to existing tax liabilities, tax liabilities to be determined on completion of assessment under section 153A including year of search, any liability relating to interest payable and liability relating to penalty to be determined on completion of penalty proceedings relating to such assessment. Since it takes lot of time till finalization of all the penalty proceedings, therefore in practice, assessee does not get back the assets seized up to a considerable time. To retain the seized assets till the finalization of the penalty proceedings needs to be reviewed in our opinion. At least the assets which remain surplus even after making provision for the maximum liability likely to be imposed by way of penalty should immediately be released and instruction to this effect needs to be issued.

Sub-section (3) does not require approval of Commissioner before release of surplus assets. In practice, it has been observed that assets are not released unless approval from the Commissioner for release of the same is obtained and due to which the process of release of the assets is delayed. However, first proviso to clause (*i*) dealing with release of disclosed assets after adjusting existing tax liabilities requires approval of the Commissioner prior to the release of seized assets.

In the case of *Sundar Mal Kedia* v. *Union of India* [2000] 110 Taxman 166 (Raj.), it has been held that once an assessment order has been passed determining the liability of the petitioner, the authorities are legally and statutorily, bound to release the seized goods in excess of his liability towards payment of tax in terms of the mandatory direction given out under section 132B itself.

It has been held in the case of *Fatema Hussain* v. *Union of India* [2017] 88 taxmann.com 725 (Patna) that adjustment of seized cash is permissible only towards tax dues already determined & not against amounts that might become due in pending assessments & Department is liable to return remaining cash to assessees with statutorily provided interest.

(*v*) **No retention of seized assets during pendency of appeal by the department**

Pendency of Appeal by the Department cannot be the ground for not releasing the assets when case has been decided in favour of the assessee and the demand raised by the lower authorities has been deleted. In the case of *Naresh Kumar Kohli* v. *CIT* [2004] 137 Taxman 438 (P&H), the High Court observed that no provision of law has been brought to the notice under which the department can retain possession of the seized jewellery during the pendency of appeal filed by the revenue before the High Court.

In the case of *Mukundray K. Shah* v. *DGIT* [2004] 141 Taxman 381 (Cal.), the High Court held that there was force in the argument of the assessee that mere filing of the appeal does not operate as a stay of the order appeal against. Therefore, in view of the order of the CIT(A), there was no existing liability at all, and the determination which was made by the Assessing Officer had been set aside. Section 132B is not intended to be made applicable for future course of action but will be applicable *in praesenti.*

However, retained assets may be used for fresh assessment in case assessment is set aside by the appellate authorities. In the case of *Bhagwat Prasad* v. *CIT* [1982] 11 Taxman 219 (All.), it was held that where assessment was set aside by the appellate authority, and remanded to the Income Tax Officer to make the assessment afresh, the assessment made after the remand of the case, will be either a regular assessment u/s 143(3) or an ex-parte assessment u/s 144 and the seized assets retained would be liable to be utilized for the amount of liability determined on completion of such assessments.

In the case of *Asha Devi* v. *CIT* [2007] 164 Taxman 423 (Delhi), the High Court directed to release the jewellery when the assessee had discharged the tax liability in terms of block assessment. The court held that if the petitioners have discharged their liability, there is no reason to retain the jewellery on any of the grounds mentioned by the department. There is admittedly no stay granted by this court in exercise of jurisdiction under section 260A (of husband). Cost of ₹ 10,000 was also imposed on the department.

In the case of *Bhawna Lodha (Smt.)* v. *DGIT* [2013] 31 taxmann.com 116/214 Taxman 273 (Raj.) (HC), since there is no outstanding demand of tax and penalty against the petitioner due to be recovered from the assessee, there is no justification for detention of seized assets. Pendency of appeal before the ITAT on the issue of penalty which is already deposited by the assessee, can only result in further relief to petitioner to the extent, which may be allowed by the ITAT if the appeal is allowed. Hence, detention of assets was not justified. Assessee cannot be asked to give bank guarantee to extent of seized articles. Circular No. F.No. 286/6/2008-IT(Inv.II) dated 21-January, 2009 was referred.

(*va*) Immediate release of seized assets when no demand pending

In the case of *Shreemati Devi* v. *CIT* [WT No. 805 of 2013, dated 14-9-2016] (All.), it has been held by the High Court that the respondents are directed to release all FDRs seized during seizure and also refund the amount in question, if not already released or refunded. In case FDRs and amount in question are not returned or refunded so far, they shall be returned/refunded forthwith without any further delay along with interest @ 18% per annum from the date of seizure till the date of actual returned/refund. Respondents shall be at liberty to recover the said amount of interest from the official(s) concerned who is/are found responsible for such negligence and illegal act, after making enquiry as permissible under law and since the attitude of the Revenue in not returning seized assets despite assessee having succeeded in appeal is clearly arbitrary and shows an attitude of undue harassment to the assessee in the garb of public revenue, therefore the petitioner shall also be entitled to cost which we quantify to ₹ 25,000.

In the case of *Sushila Devi* v. *CIT* [2016] 76 taxmann.com 163 (Delhi), it has been held by the High Court that Department's recalcitrance to release the assessee's seized jewellery, even though it is so small as to constitute "stridhan" and even though no addition was sustained in the assessee's hands, is not "mere inaction" but is one of "deliberate harassment". The respondents shall also pay costs quantified at ₹ 30,000 to the petitioner, within four weeks, directly.

(vi) Release of jewellery seized

Generally in search cases, undisclosed jewellery ornaments are found and seized by the department. Seizure of jewellery becomes a very personalized and sentimental issue for the ladies and they want the jewellery to be released at the earliest. The objective of the department behind seizure of assets or jewellery is to protect the interest of the department for recovery of the tax liability. There are instructions issued by the department to release jewellery against deposit of cash or furnishing of bank guarantee of the equivalent value by the assessee.

Reference is invited to Board's Instruction No. 11/2006 in F.No. 286/138/2006-IT (Inv. II) dated 1.12.2006 wherein certain issues relating to the release of cash deposits in the PD accounts were dealt with. In respect of release of seized assets, other than cash, there is need to modify the existing instructions for redressal of public grievances.

"......2. In this regard Board has issued direction vide F. No. 286/247/98-IT (Inv. II) dated 2.2.1999 and F.No. 286/97/2003-IT (Inv. II) dated 3.3.2004. In supersession of all instructions on the subject of release of seized assets, other than cash, the following instruction is hereby issued. In this instruction hereinafter reference to seized assets may be construed as reference to seized assets, other than cash.

3. (*a*) Where the nature and source of acquisition of seized assets is explained by the assessee to the satisfaction of the Assessing Officer, such seized assets should be released subject to recovery of outstanding arrear demand and fulfilment of other requirements contained in sub-section (1) of section 132B of the Income Tax Act (hereinafter called the 'Act').

(*b*) Where the seized assets are not released under sub-section (1) of section 132B of the Act such seized assets should be released within one month of passing of the last search and seizure assessment orders under section

153A/153C, 143(3), 148 or 158BC/158BD of the Act. The seized assets should be released only with the prior approval of Commissioner of Income Tax or Chief Commissioner of Income Tax. However, no approval should be given for release of :

(*i*) That part of the seized assets, the value of which is sufficient to adjust any existing liability and the amount of liability determined on completion of the search and seizure assessments and also

(*ii*) That part of seized assets which is sufficient to meet the expected liability on account of the penalty imposable in cases where penalty proceeding connected with search assessments have been initiated.

(*c*) Where assessee is in appeal against search assessment orders and the penalty has not been imposed upto the date of the order of the CIT (Appeals), the position regarding the seized assets lying with the department should be reviewed at the time of giving effect to the order of the CIT (Appeals). Only that part of the seized assets should be retained which is sufficient to meet the demand outstanding against the assessee for any assessment year................

(*d*) The seized assets can also be released, at any time with the approval of the Commissioner of Income Tax or Chief Commissioner of Income Tax provided:

(*i*) The assessee unconditionally accepts the ownership and the valuation of the seized assets determined at the time of search and seizure operation; and

(*ii*) Makes a written request to release the seized assets and provides unconditional and irrevocable bank guarantee to the extent of the value of seized assets.

(*e*) The Board is also aware of the fact that some assessees have great attachment to the seized assets and are willing to exchange such seized assets for an equivalent amount of cash. The replacement of seized assets with cash also makes it easier for the department to adjust this cash against tax liability. Hence it has been decided that the seized assets can also be released at any time, with the approval of the CIT or CCIT provided that:

(*i*) The assessee accepts unconditionally the ownership of the seized assets and also the valuation of the seized assets, determined at the time of search and seizure operation;

(*ii*) Makes a request in writing requesting release of seized assets against equivalent amount of cash to be provided by him;

(*iii*) Pays to the CIT, a draft of an amount equal to the value of seized assets; and

(*iv*) Agrees in writing that the amount may be deposited in the PD Account and may be used for adjustment against tax liability in accordance with the provision of section 132B of the Act.

Such amount should be deposited in PD A/c and dealt in the manner laid out in the Board Instruction No. 11/2006.

(*f*) Notwithstanding anything contained in above paragraphs [except in para 3(*a*) above] where the valuation or the ownership of any particular seized assets is disputed or where the specific items of seized assets have evidentiary value in prosecution proceedings, such seized assets will not be released, till the settlement of the dispute or finalization of such assessment or penalty or prosecution proceedings, whichever is later.

4. All DGsIT/CCsIT/CsIT should review the status of the seized assets lying with the department in view of the guidelines mentioned above. It may be noted that any violation in this regard shall be viewed seriously by the Board.

5. This instruction may be brought to the knowledge of all income tax authorities working in your region."

In spite of the above instruction since there is requirement under section 132B to take the approval of Commissioner of Income-tax/Director of Investigation before release of any asset seized, the process of release of jewellery even against deposit of cash or furnishing of bank guarantee is not quick and smooth. In practice it has been observed that it takes lot of time in getting the approval from higher authorities. There is need to make the above process automatic without the requirement of approval from the Commissioner/Director of Income Tax when assessee is willing to deposit cash or furnish bank guarantee for equivalent amount.

The value of jewellery is taken to be the value as on the date of release of jewellery. In case there has been increase in the value of gold/other precious stones as on the date of release in comparison to the value as determined by the valuer as on the date of seizure, the value of jewellery to be released is increased proportionately for the purpose of obtaining equivalent amount of cash or bank guarantee. As per **CBDT Instruction 286/35/2004-IT(Inv. II) dated 6th April 2004** - It has been stated that in case of release of jewellery and seized assets the bank guarantee has to be obtained to the full extent of the seized jewellery to be valued at the rate applicable at the time of release of jewellery.

(*vii*) **Release of assets against deposit of cash, furnishing of bank guarantee**

The purpose of retaining the assets in kind is to secure the Department against any liabilities to be determined on completion of proceedings relating to search years. In case assessee is ready to deposit cash of equivalent amount or to furnish bank guarantee of the amount equal to the value of the asset, the same should be released immediately. Sometimes assessee may have sentimental value with the seized asset. Generally it happens in the case of jewellery ornaments. The procedure for release of assets against deposit of cash or against furnishing bank guarantee should be simple and automatic without obtaining any approval from the higher authorities due to which the process gets delayed.

As per departmental instructions, it has been stated regarding release of seized assets against furnishing of bank guarantee.

"Release of seized assets ....

2. There are also instances where jewellery or perishable stocks are seized. The searched parties sometimes request for release of jewellery on grounds of need for personal use. The perishable stocks again, if not released, could deteriorate in quality leading to an erosion in their value. In such cases, it has been decided that if an unconditional irrevocable bank guarantee to the full extent of the value of the seized assets is given, the assets could be released to that extent. The valuation is to be done by the Income-tax Department and the guarantee should be clear and unequivocal.

3. The bank guarantee should be valid till the relevant assessment proceedings are complete and taxes are collected. The Department should have the option to enforce the guarantee at any point of time. ...."

Instruction : F.No. 286/247/98-IT(Inv. II), dated 2-2-1999

The courts have consistently held that the seized assets should be returned on furnishing bank guarantee subject to the facts of the case. The following cases are relevant in this regard:

Hasmukhlal Bagdiya v. *Asstt. CIT* [1992] 195 ITR 50 (MP)

Rajinder Pal Mahajan v. *Ralson India Ltd.* [1995] 211 ITR 828 (P&H)

Subodhchandra & Co. v. *ITO* [1995] 80 Taxman 621 (Guj.)

Pooran Sugar Works v. *Asstt. CIT* [1996] 219 ITR 221 (All.)

In the case of *Smt. Surinder Kaur* v. *Union of India* [2000] 112 Taxman 370 (Delhi), when cash was seized by Enforcement Directorate and subsequently requisition under section 132A was made by the income tax department for seizure of the cash, on writ petition filed by the assessee, the High Court decided that it would be in the interest of justice that the seized amount was returned to the petitioners subject to their furnishing bank guarantees for refund of the said amount.

It has been held in the case of *Ramnath Kapoor* v. *CIT* [2011] 57 DTR 311 (MP) that respondents are directed to release the seized FDRs belonging to the petitioner on furnishing of bank guarantee by the petitioner equal to the amount of FDRs, and to pass an order of assessment in respect of FDRs within one year.

It has been held in the case of *Kalpesh Laxmi Narayan Thakkar* v. *Deputy CIT* [2017] 81 taxmann.com 136/[2016] 388 ITR 245 (Guj) in respect of release of seized assets in case of search and seizure, based on the effect of CBDT Circular F.No. 286/6/2008 & letter from Income-tax Department that seized gold ornaments would be released on payment of specified amount & amount was accordingly paid, contention that promise was mistake was held not to be acceptable & assessee was held entitled to release of gold ornaments.

(viii) **Release of assets after all dues are paid**

It has been held consistently by the courts that when all dues of taxes, interest etc. of the department are paid by the assessee, the asset should be released immediately.

In the case of *Tandon Jewellers* v. *Chairman, CBDT* [2002] 124 Taxman 733 (All.), the assessee had paid the entire amount due pursuant to an order passed by the Settlement Commission and also filed an application for discharge of assets retained by the revenue.

When the application for the release of seized assets was filed on 21.6.2001, it should have been disposed of forthwith and if any amount was due, that should have been paid and under such circumstances the assets should have been released. The respondents had unnecessarily retained the assets as a result whereof the petitioner suffered. Therefore, unless it could be shown that any amount was due from the petitioner, the assets were to be released forthwith.

In the case of *Anandapadmanabhan* v. *CIT* [1994] 76 Taxman 233 (Ker.), release of pledged assets on deposit of sum equal to loan where ornaments belonging to the petitioner were pledged with the assessee from whom these were seized, these were ordered to be released on deposit of the amount equal to loan and interest with the Commissioner of Income Tax.

In the case of *Pradeep Mishra* v. *CIT* [2005] 142 Taxman 425 (Delhi), Settlement Commission passed an order to the effect that the assets are to be released after the taxes and interests are fully paid, till the auditor's fees as ordered by the Court are paid, it would be open to the Revenue to retain the jewellery. Assets other than jewellery were directed to be released.

It has been held in the case of *Smt. Bhawna Lodha* v. *DGIT* [2013] 31 taxmann.com 116/214 Taxman 273 (Raj.) that when there is no demand of tax, interest and penalty outstanding against the assessee, the continued detention and retention of gold ornaments and jewellery of assessee by the IT Department is without any valid reason and the Respondents were directed to release the jewellery of the assessee.

(ix) **Release of assets of third party seized**

A number of instances come to notice when assets belonging to third parties may be seized in the case of search of some person. It generally happens when search operation is going on at the premises of some person and during that period some other person, his associate or business constituent may visit the person under search along with some cash or assets to be handed over to him. In such a situation, the authorized officer may seize such cash or asset if the source of the same is not satisfactorily explained.

At the first instance it is submitted that in case seizure of such cash or asset is made as the assets belonging to the third person without issuing authorization of search in his name, such seizure shall be invalid. But in case seizure of such cash or asset is made from the possession of the third person but belonging to the person searched, the seizure may be valid. However, later on Assessing Officer of the person searched may come to conclusion that such cash or assets seized do not belong to the person searched but belong to the third person only.

In case such cash or assets seized are in the nature of disclosed assets in the hands of such third person, the same are required to be released by the department and cannot be retained. In the case of *Jiwan Lal Kapoor* v. *Union of India* [2004] 138 Taxman 25 (P&H), jewellery belonging to the person from Amritsar visiting to the person at Bhopal at the premises where search was going on, was seized after recording the finding that it was the unaccounted jewellery of the person visiting the assessee. The Court held that it was necessary that the Assessing Officer of the person at Amritsar should examine the books of account including the stock register and record a finding whether the seized jewellery lying at Bhopal had been accounted for by him in his books of account or not. In case the Assessing Authority came to conclusion that the jewellery had been accounted for, he should pass an order releasing the same forthwith.

(*x*) Treatment of cash seized and kept in Personal Deposit Account (p.d. A/c) of Commissioner

Cash seized during search is kept in the Personal Deposit Account (P.D. A/c) of Commissioner. The Central Board of Direct Taxes has issued instructions regarding retention and release of cash seized and deposited in the P.D. A/c, which is being reproduced as under:-

"Cash deposited in PD Accounts be dealt with as under:-

    a. Where an application is made in accordance with first proviso to section 132B(1)(*i*) for release of seized cash and the nature and acquisition of such cash is explained to the satisfaction of the Assessing Officer, the seized cash should be released within the time-limit provided under that section after adjustment of any existing liability.

    b. Where seized cash or part thereof was not released under first proviso of section 132B(1)(*i*), the amount lying in PD Account should be released within one month of passing the (search and seizure) assessment order after—

   (*i*) adjusting the seized cash against any existing liability and the amount of liability determined on completion of the search and seizure assessment; and

   (*ii*) in cases where penalty proceedings, connected with such assessment, have been initiated, retaining out of the balance an amount to meet the expected liability on account of the penalty imposable.

c. Where assessee is in appeal against the assessment order and the penalty has not been imposed up to the date of the order of the CIT (Appeals), the position regarding the amount lying in the PD Account should be reviewed at the time of giving effect to the order of the CIT (Appeals). Only such amount thereof should be retained which is sufficient to meet the expected amount of penalty imposable on the assessment as revised in appeal effect. The balance should be released within one month from the order under section 250, after recovery of any existing demand at that time.

d. The amount, which was retained after the assessment order or the order of the CIT (Appeals) for the amount of penalty imposable, should be released within one month from passing of the penalty order, after recovery of demand arising out of the penalty order and any other demand existing at that time.

e. Where assessment was made before issue of this Instruction and cash in PD Account has not yet been dealt with or partly dealt with, all the Assessing Officers should examine such cases and amount lying in the PD Account be released within one month from the date of this Instruction, after adjusting against—

   (*i*) any existing demand; and

   (*ii*) expected amount of penalty, if any, imposable on the basis of assessment order [if no appeal has been filed before CIT (Appeals) or the case has not yet been decided by CIT (Appeals)] or assessment order as revised under section 250 or, as the case may be, under section 254.

It may be noted that any violation in this regard shall be viewed seriously by the Board. All CsIT should review the amounts lying in their PD Accounts and they should ensure that no amount in their PD Accounts is retained merely because of the reason that Department is in appeal before the ITAT/HC/SC. Further, the amount to be retained on account of expected penalty demand should not exceed the amount of penalty imposable on the basis of assessment order [if no appeal has been filed before CIT (Appeals) or the case has not yet been decided by the CIT (Appeals)] or assessment order as revised under section 250 or, as the case may be, under section 254."

10.25 Scope for application and release of seized assets

(i) Application of seized assets only when assessee is in default

Tax liabilities can be recovered by way of application of seized assets only when assessee is in default or is deemed to be in default. Assessee is said to be in default when any tax demand has been raised against him which has become due for payment but the same has not been paid by the assessee.

In case any tax liability raised against the assessee has been stayed for recovery, assessee cannot be said to be in default. In case additions have been deleted by appellate authorities and Department is in appeal with the higher authorities, assessee cannot be said to be in default with respect to tax liability relating to such additions and no recovery for the same can be made by application of the seized assets.

Where in view of the order of the Commissioner (Appeals) there is no existing liability at all and the determination which was made by the Assessing Officer has been set aside, and an appeal against the order of the Commissioner (Appeals), is pending, section 132B is not applicable. Hence seized assets were held to be released to the assessee. [*Mukundray K. Shah* v. *DGIT (Inv.)* [2004] 141 Taxman 381 (Cal.)]

The Division Bench of Calcutta High Court affirmed the aforesaid judgment of ld. Single Judge in *CIT* v. *Mukundray Kumar Shah* [2006] 150 Taxman 151 (Cal.).

Where the addition made on account of deemed dividend on RBI Relief Bond is set aside by the CIT(A) and appeal is pending before the Tribunal, retention of RBI Relief Bonds was not valid - *CIT* v. *Mukundray Kumar Shah* [2006] 150 Taxman 151 (Cal.).

The assessee can be said to be in default when time given for making payment of the tax under notice of demand has expired. No appropriation of the seized assets can be made until expiry of time given under notice of demand. In the case of *Dr. R.P. Patel* v. *Asstt. DIT* [2005] 144 Taxman 79 (Ker.), it was held that recovery of tax and interest by way of adjustment from encashed value of IVPs for various years on any date prior to the expiry of the due date for payment under the notices of demand accompanying the assessment orders was in violation of sec. 132B(1).

In the case of *Hemant Kumar Sindhi* v. *CIT* [2014] 45 taxmann.com 103/224 Taxman 70 (Mag.) (All.) (HC), the Assessing Officer rejected the request made by the petitioners for the sale of seized gold bars for adjustment towards the automatic tax liability of the first petitioner, stating that such action could be taken only after the assessment was completed and a demand had been quantified against the petitioners, on a writ petition.

Dismissing the petition, the Court held that in the case of the present assessee, the conditions specified in the first proviso, were clearly not attracted. The Assessing Officer was justified in his conclusion that it was only when the liability was determined on the completion of the assessment that it would stand crystallised and in pursuance of which a demand would be raised and recovery could be initiated.

(ii) **No application of seized assets for liabilities of subsequent years**

Seized assets can be applied to recover existing tax liabilities or liabilities to be determined relating to the years upto the year of the search. Thus, the seized assets can be applied only for recovering tax liabilities relating to the years upto the year of search and not for the assessment years subsequent to the date of search.

In the case of *Vinod Poddar* v. *CIT* [1994] 76 Taxman 519, Patna High Court observed that it was elementary that the income pertaining to the seized assets can be only of the previous year prior to the date of seizure. Therefore the tax and other liabilities relating to the period subsequent to date of seizure cannot be realized out of seized assets. The High Court relied on the Supreme Court's decision in the case of *J. R. Malhotra* v. *Additional Session's Judge* AIR 1976 SC 219.

(iii) **No application of seized assets against tax liabilities of third person**

Department sometimes retains the assets and makes application of the same towards tax liabilities relating to other persons such as wife of the assessee or sister concern relating to the person. Generally it happens in the case of search on a group consisting many companies or individuals within the group. Courts have disapproved any application of seized assets relating to a person against the tax liability of other person even within the same group and even when they are closely associates.

Seized assets belonging to the assessee cannot be retained on account of demand against him as legal representative of his father - *Naresh Kumar Kohli* v. *CIT* [2004] 137 Taxman 438 (P&H).

Allowing the petition, that it was not the case of the Revenue that anything remained due from the petitioner, the action of the Commissioner of Income Tax in not returning the assets to the assessee was wholly unwarranted and the conduct of the authorities showed that instead of proceeding directly to recover the dues pertaining to the husband of the assessee, the Commissioner of Income-tax had adopted an erroneous approach by retaining the assets of a different assessee, i.e., the petitioner. The dues of the assessee had been paid as far back as in 1989. The respondents should have returned the aforesaid assets to the assessee. The order of the Commissioner of Income-tax was liable to be quashed - *Smt. Shobha Sengar* v. *CIT* [1999] 105 Taxman 142 (All.).

(*iv*) Mandatory for Assessing Officer to adjust seized amount against demand under section 140A

It has been held in the case of *Ravinder Singh* v. *Asstt. CIT* [2003] 132 Taxman 211 (Mag.)/[2004] 89 ITD 477 (Asr.-Trib.) that revenue is under legal obligation to carry out the adjustment as requested by assessee of seized assets against tax payable under section 140A, or even under section 158BC and non-execution of the request of the assessee cannot be attributed as a default against the assessee under section 249(4) to dismiss the appeal in limine.

(*v*) No Civil Suit for non-payment of interest under section 132B(4)

In the case of *Prem Kumar & Sons (HUF)* v. *Union of India* [2005] 48 Taxman 103/[2006] 280 ITR 152 (Delhi), the assessee had filed a civil suit for recovery of interest u/s 132B(4) on securities seized under sec.132. Held that:

(*i*) Appellant could have effectively invoked power of revision u/s 264 by Commissioner of Income-tax. The appellant also failed to make a prayer for this in the writ proceedings.

(*ii*) Such relief of recovery of interest was barred under sec. 293 and assessee was barred from filing a civil suit for recovery.

(*iii*) Therefore a civil suit for recovery is not maintainable. The Court agreed with *Union of India* v. *Natwerlal M. Badiani* [2001] 119 Taxman 931 (Guj.) (FB) relying on *CIT* v. *Parmeshwari Devi Sultania* [1998] 97 Taxman 269 (SC).

10.26 Manner of release of seized assets

(*i*) Release of assets in the presence of witnesses

Rule 112C provides that release of assets under section 132B shall be in the presence of two respectable witnesses. Rule 112C states as under -

Any assets or proceeds thereof which remain after the liabilities referred to in clause (*i*) of sub-section (1) of section 132B are discharged, shall be forthwith made over or paid to the person, from whose custody the assets were seized in the presence of two respectable witnesses.

(ii) Who is entitled to release of seized assets under section 132B

Assets should be released to the person from whose custody the same are seized. First proviso to clause (*i*) of section 132B(1) dealing regarding release of disclosed assets as well as sub-section (3) of section 132B dealing regarding release of surplus assets state that the seized assets should be released to the person from whose custody the assets were seized. Rule 112C also states that seized assets should be released to the person from whose custody the assets were seized.

In the case of *Smt. Kusum Lata Singhal* v. *CIT* [1990] 51 Taxman 300 (SC), it has been held that even though a search is not in accordance with law, the valuables cannot be returned to any person other than the person from whom the seizure was made.

Normally the assets are to be released to the person from whose possession and control they are seized - *Assainar* v. *ITO* [1975] 101 ITR 854 (Ker.)

This situation may change when assets seized are handed over by the Assessing Officer of the person searched to the Assessing Officer of the other person as the assets belong to the other person so as to initiate action under section 153C. In such a situation, assets shall be released to the person to whom the same belong and in respect of whom action under section 153C has been taken.

In a case, a necklace, though seized from the locker belonging to a company, *viz.*, Shakti Trading Co. Pvt. Ltd., belonged to the petitioner, Shri B.R. Ruia. This fact was accepted by the Department and the assessment was made accordingly on Mr. Ruia, who paid the taxes. The company did not object to the return of the necklace to Mr. Ruia and the department had not been able to show any material on the basis of which it could have any claim on the necklace. The High Court held that the necklace should be returned to Mr. Ruia. *Balkrishna Ramgopal Ruia* v. *Union of India* [1990] 52 Taxman 90 (Bom). The contention of the department, on the facts of the case, that the department could not return the necklace to the petitioner, was rejected by the Single Judge.

(iii) Release of assets belonging to third parties

There may be a situation when assets belonging to other persons are seized when search action is undertaken for example - in the case of a company, share certificates of the shareholders received by the company for registering transfer of shares may be seized. In the case of NBFC, FDRs belonging to other persons kept with the company as security or otherwise may be seized. In case assets belonging to third parties are seized and the fact that the assets do not belong to the person searched but to some other person is established, and such assets are not undisclosed assets in the hands of such other person, such assets shall be released immediately.

In the case of *Godrej V. Patel* v. *Union of India* [2003] 133 Taxman 395 (Bom.), the High Court instructed to release FDRs of the depositors with the bank which were seized during search operation on being satisfied that the petitioners were the persons holding FDRs and entitled to the said amount.

(iv) **Power of release of assets with whom**

The power for the release of assets seized during search under section 132B has been given to the Assessing Officer. It is for the reason that seized assets can be released after recovering the existing liabilities or liabilities to be determined on completion of assessment. The recovery of the liabilities can be done by the Assessing Officer who is keeping the record of liabilities due from the assessee.

The authorized officer who has conducted the search has not been given the powers to release the seized assets under section 132B. In case when disclosed assets are seized and there is no existing liability outstanding against the assessee, the same are also not released by the authorized officer, which, in our opinion, is not fair and rational from the point of view of the person from whose custody assets have been seized.

Some of the officers of investigation wing do not release the jewellery even against deposit of cash or furnishing bank guarantee inspite of instructions from the Board to this effect. They hold the view that even jewellery against deposit of cash or furnishing of bank guarantee can be released only by the Assessing Officer. In our opinion, this is not the correct view and necessary instructions should be issued to the officers of the Investigation wing to release the seized assets under such circumstances immediately.

10.27 Recovery of liabilities by any other mode

Sub-section (1) of section 132B prescribes the procedure regarding application of seized assets for recovery of tax liability of the assessee. Sub-section (2) of section 132B clarifies that nothing contained in sub-section (1) shall preclude the recovery of the amount of liabilities aforesaid by any other mode laid down in this Act. It implies that department can make the recovery of the tax liability by any other means e.g., by way of attachment of properties, or through Tax recovery officer, and in the manner as is available under the Act. Department cannot be restricted to make the recovery of the tax liability only by application of the seized assets. It has been held as under in the case of *Harinder Singh* v. *ITO* [1987] 32 Taxman 163 (All.):

"However, the seized asset is subject matter of any case and liable to confiscation, the income tax authorities cannot be forced to appropriate the tax demand from the sale of the seized primary gold. The Income Tax authorities are bound to assess the gold control authorities and are also liable to produce the gold before the gold control authorities. The steps taken by the Income Tax Officer to recover the tax from the petitioner by attachment and sale of the house property cannot, therefore, be illegal or unauthorized."

In the case of *P.P. Kanniah* v. *ITO* [1981] 7 Taxman 96 (Mad.), it has been observed that till the sale takes place, the ownership of the property continues to remain in the hand of petitioner, but under distraint by the Income Tax Officer.

10.28 Delay in release of the seized assets

In practice, it has been observed that surplus seized assets are not released immediately after completion of all the proceedings under the Act. Assessee has to make rigorous follow up with the departmental officials but release of assets is delayed on one or the other pretext.

Sometimes delay in release of assets may cause financial loss to the assessee. There may be perishable or fast obsolescing assets which may decline in value with the passage of time such as electronic items. There may be assets where there is lot of fluctuation in the market value, for example - equity shares of listed companies. There may be assets such as fixed deposits, bonds etc. which if they are not renewed, there may be loss of interest or other benefits attached with them. In such circumstances, it is all the more important that assets should be released in time and proper mechanism for the same should be provided.

(i) Delay in release of assets - Remedies with the assessee

In case seized assets are not released even after completion of all the proceedings and after recovery of all the liabilities raised against the assessee relating to search years, there has to be some mechanism, in our opinion, fixing the accountability on the officer concerned and compensating to the assessee for the delay. In some of the case Courts have lashed out quite harsh on the Department in such circumstances and have awarded compensation to the assessee.

In case of delay in release of seized assets, assessee has following remedies—

a. Approach to the higher administrative authorities. But sometimes it has been experienced that even the higher authorities do not take swift action and the file of the assessee keeps on hanging in the process of bureaucratic approvals.

b. Writ to the High Court claiming compensation for delay in release of the assets. But, filing writ with the High Court entails lot of cost and therefore, small assessees are deprived of taking recourse to this mechanism.

c. File petition with the office of Ombudsman which has recently been established by the Government and it is hoped that the hardship of the assessee for release of the seized assets will be taken care of by such mechanism.

10.29 Payment of interest on release of money seized

Sub-section (4) of section 132B provides for the payment of interest on money released. This provision has been drafted in a cumbersome and vague manner and hardly any benefit of the same is received by the person searched. The salient features of this provision are as under:-

i. Interest is required to be paid on money or surplus proceed of the assets, if sold, after recovering tax liabilities.

ii. No interest is paid on assets which remain in kind such as jewellery, bonds, shares etc. Sometimes assessee may lose interest or appreciation on FDs, bonds, shares, saving certificates etc. seized but not released yet no interest is payable to the assessee under this provision.

iii. Interest is to be paid on surplus money after meeting all the tax liabilities as referred under clause (*i*). Clause (*i*) refers existing tax liabilities, tax liabilities raised on completion of assessment under section 153A and liabilities raised on completion of penalty proceedings relating to such assessments. For the period from the date of seizure till above liabilities are raised and adjusted, no interest is required to be paid which makes the provision ineffective from the assessee's point of view.

iv. Presently interest is to be paid at the rate of six per cent per annum. The rate of interest payable from time to time has been as under-

    a. From 12-3-1965 to 30-9-1967   6% per annum

    b. From 1-10-1967 to 31-3-1972   9% per annum

    c. From 1-4-1972 to 30-9-1984   12% per annum

    d. From 1-10-1984 to 30-5-2002   15% per annum

    e. From 1-6-2002 to 7-9-2003   8% per annum

    f. From 8-9-2003 to 31-3-2008   6% per annum

    g. From 1-4-2008   0.5% for every month or part of a month

v. Interest shall be calculated on the surplus money to be released after expiry of the period of one hundred and twenty days from the date of conclusion of search till the date of completion of assessment under section 153A. To provide the calculation of interest till the date of completion of assessment under section 153A gives the impression that the intent is either to adjust the money seized against the tax liability raised on completion of assessment under section 153A or if there is any surplus at this stage the same should be released. From this requirement, it transpires that surplus money cannot be retained till the finalization of penalty proceedings. But the above interpretation is in contradiction to earlier interpretation made for sub-section (4A) which requires surplus money to be calculated after adjusting all the liabilities as referred to in clause (*i*).

The more plausible interpretation may be to adjust the total amount of money seized against the tax liability raised on completion of assessment and in case there remains any surplus, it would attract interest under section 244A upto the date of refund of the same to the assessee. This position has been affirmed by the Gujarat High Court in the case of *Anil Kumar Bhagwandas* v. *P.K. Tiwari* [1999] 238 ITR 788. The High Court has held that section 132B read with section 132(5) covers the period only upto regular assessment and not thereafter and that the period after regular assessment is governed by sections 243 and 244.

In the case of *Anilkumar D. Gajjar* v. *CIT* [1996] 84 Taxman 85 (Guj.), Gujarat High Court went to the extent to direct making payment of interest as per law and further interest @ 15% till from the date of filing of petition till the date of payment by way of compensation.

A contrary view is expressed by M.P. High Court in the case of *Manohar Lal* v. *CIT* [2001] 118 Taxman 104, wherein it is held that the interest is governed by section 132B and section 244 is not applicable. To our opinion this view, with respect, needs reconsideration.

vi. As per clause (*b*) of sub-section (4), it is provided that interest shall run from the date immediately from the expiry of period of one hundred and twenty days from the date of conclusion of search upto the date of completion of assessment. In all fairness, the interest should be payable from the date of seizure as there is no justification for denying the interest for one hundred and twenty days after seizure.

In the case of *Mohammed Usman* v. *Union of India* [1996] 86 Taxman 165 Delhi High Court directed to pay interest from the date of seizure till the date of refund. The High Court held that it was clear that the use of money was denied to the petitioner by the respondent and, therefore, this Hon'ble Court was pleased to direct payment of interest.

When there is undue delay on the part of assessee, to claim return of seized assets, he may not be entitled to get interest for the delayed period. In the case of *Ashok Kumar Aggarwal* v. *Director (Grievances Cell), CBDT* [2005] 144 Taxman 693 (Delhi), it was held that the right to return of article accrued on the date of appeal against the order of the Assessing Officer or latest on the date of order of the Commissioner (Appeals) and the assessee ought to have approached the Court within a reasonable period from that date. As the assessee had approached the court after seven years, it could not be said that it was within a reasonable period. Therefore, on ground of delay and latches, the petition could not be entertained.

(*i*) **Interest under section 132B(3) & (4) read with section 244**

In the case of *Bhagwan Prasad Agrawal* v. *CIT* [2006] 152 Taxman 472 (All.), excess cash seized by revenue during search was determined by assessment order dated 31st December 1977 but not paid till 5th May, 1980. Held that under sec.132B(3) and (4) read with sec. 244, the revenue should pay interest at 12% for the period 31st March, 1978 to 5th May, 1980 at 12%. Further as assessee has been making repeated claims for interest u/s 244, he was entitled to be paid interest in the refund of interest.

In the case of *Ajay Gupta* v. *CIT* [2008] 162 Taxman 296 (Delhi), on a search on 2.7.2002 an amount of ₹ 33 lakhs was seized. On original assessment on 30.7.2002, balance of ₹ 17,33,529 was released on 27.9.2004. CIT(A) in order dated 15.12.2004 deleted further amounts and Assessing Officer framed a nil assessment on 24.12.2004 releasing the residue amount of ₹ 15,66,471. Thus, entire seized amount of ₹ 33 lakhs was released.

Held (*i*) For release of ₹ 17,33,529 on 27.9.2004 interest u/s 132B(4) became payable on 30th July, 2004 being outer limit prescribed u/s 132B(4)(*a*). So, interest for period 1.8.2004 to 27.9.2004 had also to be paid. Revenue was liable to pay damages for the period 1.8.2004 to 27.9.2004 at the rate of 9%.

(*ii*) For sum of ₹ 15,66,471 the order of Assessing Officer merged with order of CIT(A). Therefore, identical treatment was to be given to this amount of ₹ 15,66,471, interest will be payable from 1.8.2004 to 27.9.2004 as per item (*i*).

(*iii*) Interest is payable from 11.11.2002 to 15.12.2004 at the rate of .66 per cent per month and thereafter 0.5% upto 8.9.2003 – Thereafter u/s 132(4)(*b*) period commences 120 days from date of last authorization.

(*iv*) Compensation for period 1.11.2002 to 1.9.2004 was payable at the rate of 9% and they referred to *Sandvik Asia Ltd.* v. *CIT* [2006] 150 Taxman 591 (SC) that interest is payable as compensation for amounts wrongly retained including an interest on interest wrongly retained.

It has been held in the case of *Sitaram* v. *CIT* [2012] 21 taxmann. com 262/208 Taxman 376 (Bom.) while dealing the seizure of cash *vis-à-vis* tax liability and interest thereupon, amount of ₹ 1,60,000 having been seized and tax ultimately payable by assessee having been determined at ₹ 1,654 on 4th July, 1996, assessee was entitled to interest under section 132(B)(4) on ₹ 1,58,346 from 24th June, 1993 till 4th July, 1996.

It has been held in the case of *Mohit Singh* v. *Asstt. CIT* [2012] 20 taxmann.com 745 (Delhi) that neither the block assessment order nor the assessment under section 143(3) for the following assessment year having resulted in any additional tax liability against the assessee, the amount seized during search proceedings under section 132 against him was refundable along with interest under section 132B(4) and, therefore, assessee is entitled to interest @ 7.5 per cent per annum till the date of refund and not merely upto the date of order of block assessment.

It has been held in the case of *Prem Nath Nagpal* v. *Asstt. CIT* [2010] 128 TTJ 53 (Delhi-Trib.) that amount of liability determined on the completion of assessment means the liability finally determined after appeal and not the one determined by Assessing Officer initially on assessment. Assessee's tax liability after appeal having been come to ₹ 30,461 only as against ₹ 1,57,89,832 determined by Assessing Officer, the assessee was entitled to interest under section 132B(4) on the amount of ₹ 25,65,000 seized from him.

It has been held in the case of *Super Cassettes Industries Ltd.* v. *Chief CIT* [2012] 20 taxmann.com 808/207 Taxman 153 (Delhi) that for assessment years 1999-2000 and 2000-01, Instructions dt. 23rd May, 1996 were applicable for considering waiver or reduction of interest under section 234C, and not the Instruction dt. 26th June, 2006. Since assessee had requested for release of the FDRs for payment of the advance tax instalment, it was therefore entitled to waiver of interest under section 234C to the extent of 40 per cent.

It has been held in the case of *Gurvinder Singh* v. *Director of IT (Inv.)* [2012] 84 DTR 41 (All.) that when assessment under section 158BC was quashed and assessee was allowed interest under section 132B(4) on refund of seized amount, interest under section 244A was still allowable since, section 132B and section 244A operate in different fields.

In the case of *S.K. Jain* v. *CIT* [2013] 33 taxmann.com 36/215 Taxman 237 (Delhi) (HC), the assessee was entitled to be paid interest at the rate of 12 per cent in respect of the amount seized for the period from the date on which assessment was completed till date it was actually released to him.

In the case of *Om Prakash Agrawal* v. *UOI* [2013] 31 taxmann.com 123/214 Taxman 5 (Mag.) (MP) (HC), it has been held that, where the assessment of the assessee was concluded resulting in a refund to the assessee which was not given to the assessee for a long time assessee was entitled to interest on refund under section 132B(4) of the Act.

In the case of *Chironjilal Sharma (HUF)* v. *UOI* [2014] 41 taxmann. com 274/222 Taxman 352 (SC), the department's argument that the refund of excess amount is governed by s. 240 and that section 132B(4)(*b*) has no application is not acceptable. Section 132B(4)(*b*) deals with pre-assessment period and there is no conflict between this provision and s. 240 or for that matter s. 244(A). The former deals with pre-assessment period in the matters of search and seizure and the later deals with post assessment period as per the order in appeal. The department's view is not right on the plain reading of s. 132B(4) (*b*) and the assessee is entitled to simple interest at the rate of 15% per annum u/s 132B(4)(*b*) from 1-12-1990 to 4.3.1994. The interest shall be paid within two months from today.

It has been held in the case of *G.L. Jain* v. *CIT* 87 DTR 255 (Del.) that on account of delay in return of seized cash, there was no justi-fication in reducing the amount refundable for payment of interest on the basis of later event i.e. adjustment under s. 132B(1)(*i*), assessee is entitled to interest on the total amount till date of refund.

It has been held in the case of *Sanjeev Kumar* v. *Union of India* 214 DTR 265 (Bom.) that in case of delay in return of seized cash, Section 132B(4) does not indicate any bar from awarding payment of interest or compensation in a situation where Court finds any delay on the part of the Revenue in releasing the amount within time specifically prescribed under the provisions of law for no fault of the assessee.

(*ii*) **Interest payable upto last assessment order**

In the case of *Dr. R.M. Saboo* v. *Asstt. CIT* [2005] 92 ITD 532/92 TTJ 1078 (Hyd.-Trib.), it was held on plain reading of sec. 132B(4)(*b*), it indicates that alternative modes of computation of interest has been prescribed. In the second part of the clause, the legislature has used the expression "assessment" in contradiction to the expression of "regular assessment" used elsewhere which indicates that if more than one order is passed by the Assessing Officer, interest is payable up to the date of the last of such assessment. Appeal of assessee allowed.

In the case of *Kishore Jagjivandas Tanna* v. *K. Rangrajan* [2008] 175 Taxman 294 (Bom.), ₹ 5 lacs was found in cash on search in hotel room in Delhi where assessee had checked in from Bombay and was explained as cash advance for sale of rice. Order u/s 132(5) was passed without furnishing the assessee copies of all statements and documents and thus without following the mandatory rules of natural justice. Direction issued to respondent to issue a fresh notice under rule 112A within 12 weeks and also to furnish copies of all statements and documents. If no notice was issued, then amount seized would be refunded with 6% interest from date of seizure till the date of release.

(*iii*) **Interest at value of silver bars not payable**

In the case of *Puran Mal & Sons* v. *Union of India* [2008] 166 Taxman 452 (Delhi), when the silver bars seized from the assessee, it was held that no interest was payable under section 132B.

(*iiia*) **Interest on value of shares not payable**

It has been held in the case of *Anil Kedia* v. *Settlement Commission of IT and WT* [2013] 33 taxmann.com 624 (Mad.) that in case of seizure of shares, since shares of assessee seized by Department do not constitute 'money' hence are not eligible for interest under s. 132B(4) (*a*).

(*iv*) **Whether seized cash can be treated as advance tax paid by the assessee**

Sub-section (1) of section 132B requires the seized assets to be appropriated against any existing tax liability or the tax liability to be determined on completion of assessment of search cases. If we go as per literal interpretation of section 132B, cash seized cannot be appropriated towards advance tax liability of the assessee. Even when declaration of undisclosed income is made by the assessee during search, including the amount of unaccounted cash which has been seized during search, the department insists for making payment of tax liability of such declared undisclosed income separately and the cash seized is not appropriated towards the above tax liability.

In our opinion, such interpretation and non-adjustment of cash seized towards tax liability does not seem to be reasonable and in accordance with the legislative intent. The cash seized should be permitted to be appropriated as advance tax liability by the assessee.

The courts have taken different views on the above issue which may be discussed as under:-

It has been held in the case of *Rajesh Kumar Vinit Kumar* v. *CIT* [2006] 283 ITR 395 (All.), that cash seized after close of the previous year cannot be treated and adjusted towards advance tax liability of the assessee relating to the relevant previous year.

Cash seized and retained under section 132(5) is not treated as advance tax by virtue of provisions of section 132B(1). This is so because the amount of adjusted liability as specified under section 132(5)(*iii*) and the amount of liability determined on completion of regular assessment including penalty and interest are recoverable out of the assets retained under section 132(5). Therefore, the amount seized and retained under section 132(5), if not treated and adjusted as advance tax in the assessment under section 143(1)(*a*), it did not give rise to any mistake apparent from record rectifiable under section 154. [*Asstt. CIT* v. *Topsel (P) Ltd.* [1996] 56 ITD 187 (Cal. - Trib.)].

In the case of *Ramjilal Jagannath* v. *Asstt. CIT* [2000] 241 ITR 758 (MP), it was held that adjustment of seized amount towards the advance tax liability of the assessee is not permissible unless an order under section 132(5) is passed.

However, after abolition of the provision of section 132(5), recently, courts have taken liberal view on the above issue and it has been decided in number of cases that where an assessee makes a request for adjustment of cash seized against his tax liability, there should be no difficulty in such tax adjustment.

In the case of *Satpaul D. Agarwal (HUF)* v. *Asstt. CIT* [1999] 105 Taxman 71 (Mum. - Trib.) (Mag.), it has been held that on request having been made by the assessee, cash seized has to be treated as payment towards advance tax of the same year, and liability to pay interest under sections 234A, 234B and 234C should be determined accordingly.

Section 132B and rule 112C empower the Revenue to apply the seized assets which are retained against the tax liability of the assessee unilaterally. But when the assessee himself requests for treating the cash seized as tax paid by him there is no necessity for application to utilize the same against tax liability of the assessee whenever it may arise. Therefore, when the assessee himself requests that the amounts seized may be treated as tax paid by him there cannot be and should not be any objection to the revenue in accepting such a request. [*Gopal Chand Khandelwal* v. *Asstt. CIT* [1995] 52 ITD 661 (Delhi - Trib.)]

In the case of *Asstt. CIT* v. *Raghu Nandan Lal* [2002] 82 ITD 436 (Chd. - Trib.), where the assessee had specifically requested to realize bank guarantee as well as cash seized during search, and to adjust the same as payment of advance tax, it is held by Chandigarh Bench of ITAT that the credit was to be given for the same to the assessee and no interest under section 234C was chargeable for non-payment of instalment. It was further held that seizure of asset is certainly a recovery from the assessee. There is no basic difference between "payment" or "recovery" through seizure and other modes of recovery provided in the statute as far as discharge of tax liability is concerned.

In the case of *Iqbal Chand Khurana* v. *Dy. CIT* [2001] 117 Taxman 31 (Delhi - Trib.) (Mag.), it has been held that in the absence of any working to show that seized cash remained with the Department after the liabilities were fully satisfied upto the date of seizure, interest under section 132B cannot be allowed to assessee on the amounts retained and utilized by the Department during the period from the date of seizure to the date of regular assessment.

It has been held in the case of *CIT* v. *Ashok Kumar* [2012] 20 taxmann.com 432/[2011] 334 ITR 355 (Punj. & Har.) that the assessee requesting to adjust advance tax payable out of cash seized and such request made prior to due date for payment of instalment of advance tax, assessee is entitled to adjustment and no interest can be charged.

It has been held in the case of *CIT* v. *Arun Kapoor* [2012] 20 taxmann. com 431 (Punj. & Har.) that search taking place after close of financial year and request for adjustment of advance tax liability against seized cash is made, assessee is liable to pay interest under sections 234B and 234C and is entitled to benefit of payment out of seized cash from date of making application for adjustment of seized cash towards tax liability.

It has been held in the case of *Vishwanath Khanna* v. *Union of India* [2012] 20 taxmann.com 828 (Delhi) that Assessing Officer failing to accede to request of assessee and adjust advance tax against deposits, interest under sections 234B and 234C for default in payment of advance tax cannot be levied.

It has been held in the case of *CIT* v. *Kesr Kimam Karyalaya* [2005] 196 CTR 611/278 ITR 596 (Delhi) that the Tribunal having deleted the levy of interest under sections 234B and 234C holding that assessee's request for adjustment of seized cash against the advance tax liability ought to have been allowed and further that such requests made by the partners were binding on the firm and no interest could be charged in the case of firm also, no substantial question of law arises.

In the case of *Vijay D. Mehta* v. *Asstt. CIT* [2013] 35 taxmann.com 201/60 SOT 100 (URO) (Mum.) (Trib.), it has been held that, where concerned person/assessee makes an application during course of assessment proceedings to adjust remaining amount of cash seized towards his future liability, AO after passing of 120 days from last date of execution of search and seizure operation is liable, either to return remaining amount to assessee/concerned person and/or to adjust same towards his future liability if a specific request has been made by assessee in this respect.

In the case of *DCIT* v. *Spaze Tower Pvt. Ltd.* [ITA No. 2557/Del./2012, dated 17-10-2014] (Delhi) (Trib.) *Explanation 2* attached to section 132B of the Act, is a clarificatory provision which is of retrospective effect, even if, the same was stated to be applicable from a particular date. We also hold that *Explanation 2* to section 132B of the Act, though inserted w.e.f. 1.6.2013, is retrospectively effective from the date of insertion of provision of section 132B of the Act w.e.f. 1.6.2002. On the basis of foregoing discussion, we reach to a legal conclusion that the assets or cash seized u/s 132 of the Act is adjustable against the amount of any "existing liability" under the Act which does not include "advance tax" payable in accordance with the provisions of Part 'C' of Chapter XVII of the Act.

In the case of *Asstt. CIT* v. *Narendra N. Thacker* [2017] 82 taxmann. com 64 (Kol. - Trib.), it has been held that seized cash can be adjusted against self assessment tax and not advance tax. Further, the ITAT also held that the issue being debatable could not be rectified by the AO u/s 154.

It has been held in the case of *Marble Centre International (P) Ltd.* v. *Asstt. CIT* 192 DTR (Kar) 337 that where adjustment of cash seized against advance tax was sought & assessee has offered a sum of Rs. 50 lakhs on 15th March, 2007 towards the advance tax payable for the asst. yr. 2007-08, Tribunal ought to have held the date of payment of tax by the assessee as 15th March, 2007 for the purpose of charge of interest under ss. 234B and 234C.

(iva) **Cash seized in case of income-tax search not to be treated as advance tax paid but can be claimed as self-assessment tax paid**

Finance Act, 2013 has inserted *Explanation 2* to section 132B which states as under:—

"For the removal of doubts it is thereby declared that the "existing liability" does not include advance tax payable in accordance with the provision of Part C of Chapter XVII".

Section 132B of the Income-tax Act prescribes provisions regarding application of assets/cash seized during income tax search conducted u/s 132 of the Act. It prescribes that seized assets/cash can be utilised for the purpose of recovery and adjustment of the amount of any existing tax liability and the amount of the liability determined on completion of the assessment and in pursuance to search assessment u/s 153A.

The controversy as to whether 'existing tax liability' will include advance tax payable by the assessee relating to the year of search or specified previous year was discussed in several judicial decisions above and it was held that cash seized can be adjusted towards the advance tax payable by the assessee on request to this effect having been made by the assessee and in such cases the courts further held that interest u/ss 234B and 234C should not be charged from the assessee from the date such request for adjustment of seized cash towards advance tax liability was made by the assessee.

It seems that Finance Act, 2013 has inserted *Explanation 2* to section 132B to nullify the effect of the above decisions consistently rendered by different high courts and benches of the Tribunal. The impact of the above clarification as inserted by *Explanation 2* shall be quite harsh on the assessees who have been searched u/s 132 of the Act.

The above *Explanation* shall have the effect that the seized cash cannot be claimed as payment of advance tax by the searched person in the return of income to be filed u/s 153A/139. However, there is no bar or denial for the adjustment of seized cash against the self-assessment tax to be paid while filing return of income under section 153A or 139.

In the case of *Asstt. CIT* v. *Concreta Developers* [2015] 61 taxmann. com 255/155 ITD 65 (Nag. - Trib.), it has been held that *Expln. 2* to section 132B inserted by the Finance Act, 2013, w.e.f. 1st June, 2013, is prospective only.

In the case of *CIT* v. *Sri Chand Gupta* [2015] 125 DTR (Delhi) 137 (HC), it has been held that an 'existing liability' as used in section 132(5)(*iii*) would mean such liability that had already been determined and crystallised in respect of prior years where assessment had been made for an any other liability stood crystallized by any determinative process under Act. Therefore, amount retained under section 132(5) does not amount to payment of taxes and cannot be taken into consideration while calculating interest payable under sections 234A, 234B and 234C.

Further, assets retained by the ITO could not have been appropriated towards the payment of tax until the assessee had filed a return indicating the application of seized cash towards its tax liability or till an assessment was framed.

Income Tax Return to be treated as Defective Return under section 139(9)

Finance Act, 2013 has simultaneously made amendment to sub-section (9) of section 139 by way of insertion of clause (*aa*) providing that Income Tax Return filed by the assessee shall be regarded as defective in case the tax together with interest if any payable in accordance with the provision of section 140A, has not been paid on or before the date of furnishing of the return. Further, section 139(9) provides that in case of defective return, if the defect is not cured within the time limit allowed by the Assessing Officer, the return shall be treated as invalid return and provisions of this Act shall apply as if the assessee has failed to furnish the return.

As discussed earlier, there is no bar for the cash seized to be treated as self-assessment tax provided it is so adjusted and claimed in the return of income & in such a case, return of income cannot be treated as defective.

Enhanced Penalty u/s 271AAB

In the case of Income Tax search u/s 132 initiated on or after 1st July, 2012, assessee is covered by the Penalty provision relating to specified Previous year as contained u/s 271AAB. This section provides that in case of declaration of undisclosed income by the searched person during statement recorded u/s 132(4) and further fulfilling other conditions as prescribed therein, Penalty @10% of undisclosed income is leviable. This concessional rate of penalty is applicable only when assessee pays the tax in respect of the undisclosed income and furnishes the Return of Income declaring such undisclosed income therein, on or before due date of filing of return of Income u/s 139(1)/153A.

In case assessee does not pay the tax due in respect undisclosed income before the due date of filing of return of income, he may be liable to penalty @ 30% to 90% of the undisclosed income as provided u/s 271AAB.

It would imply that in case assessee files his return of Income claiming adjustment of cash seized towards the tax liability, penalty u/s 271AAB even in a case when the declaration of undisclosed income was made during search and other conditions mentioned as prescribed therein were complied with, assessee may still be liable to be saddled with penalty @ 30% to 90% of the undisclosed income u/s 271AAB.

Whether Applicability of Explanation 2 is prospective or retrospective

Explanation 2 has been inserted by Finance Act, 2013 with effect from 1.6.2013. But, this *Explanation* starts with the words "For the removal of doubts, it is hereby declared that...". It appears that this amendment is clarificatory in nature and may be interpreted as if the *Explanation* is applicable from the date section 132B was brought on the statute.

Such an interpretation will create further complications for all the assessees in whose case, income tax search was held in the past and cash seized in the return of income was claimed as advance tax paid. In such cases, assessees may be liable to be penalized u/s 271AAA or 271AAB or other provisions of the Act in much harsh manner. In our opinion, there is a need to bring clarification stating that the above *Explanation* shall be applicable prospectively.

It has been held in the case of *CIT* v. *Pramod Kumar Dang* 98 DTR 33 (Del.) that where the assessee has sought adjustment of the amount admittedly lying with the revenue towards the tax payable on the returned income, the assessee cannot be denied a hearing & Tribunal was found correct in holding that the requirements of s. 249(4)(*a*) were duly complied with.

(*v*) **Reduction or waiver of penal interest for late filing of return of income, etc.**

In exercise of the powers under section 119(2)(*a*) of the Act, the Central Board of Direct Taxes authorized the Chief Commissioner and Director General (Investigation) to reduce or waive the interest in certain circumstances as prescribed by the Board. In this connection, reference is invited to a Press Note released on 21-5-1996 as printed at [1994] 73 Taxman 395 (Cal.) (St.) read as follows:-

Reduction or Waiver of Penal Interest for Late Filing of Return of Income, etc: Authorization of Powers to Chief Commissioners and Director General (Investigation).

1. The Chief Commissioners and Directors-General (Investigation) empowered to reduce or waive penal interest for late furnishing of return of income, non-payment or inadequate payment of advance-tax, etc.

2. Prior to 1989 taxpayers who had failed to furnish the return of income within the specified time-limit were charged penal interest for such defaults and also subjected to penalty proceedings. The Direct Tax Laws (Amendment) Act, 1987, inserted new sections 234A, 234B and 234C in the Income-tax Act from assessment year 1989-90 to provide for penal interest at higher rates for the defaults in late furnishing of the return of income,

defaults in payment of advance-tax and for deferment of advance-tax respectively and omitted separate penalty provisions for these defaults. The interest payable under these sections was mandatory and there was no provision for reduction or waiver of the penal interest, as was provided specifically in this behalf prior to 1989. As a result, several taxpayers faced unintended hardships in certain circumstances.

3. The Central Board of Direct Taxes, in exercise of the powers specified in section 119(2)(*a*) has decided to authorize the Chief Commissioners and Directors-General (Investigation) to reduce or waive penal interest charged under the aforesaid sections in the following circumstances, namely:-

   i. Where, in the course of search and seizure operations, books of account have been taken over by the Department and were not available to the taxpayer to prepare his return of income;

   ii. Where, in the course of search and seizure operations, cash had been seized which was not permitted to be adjusted against arrears of tax or payment of advance tax instalments falling due after the date of the search;

   iii. Any income other than "Capital gains" which was received or accrued after the date of the first or subsequent instalment of advance tax, which was neither anticipated nor contemplated by the taxpayer and on which advance tax was paid by the taxpayer after the receipt of such income;

   iv. Where, as a result of any retrospective amendment of law or the decision of the Supreme Court after the end of the relevant previous year, certain receipts which were hitherto treated as exempt, become taxable. Since no advance tax would normally be paid in respect of such receipts during the relevant financial year, penal interest is levied for the default in payment of advance tax;

   v. Where the return of income is filed voluntarily without detection by the Income-tax Department and due to circumstances beyond the control of the taxpayer such return of income was not filed within the stipulated time-limit or advance tax was not paid at the relevant time.

4. The Chief Commissioners and Directors-General are being authorized to reduce or waive penal interest under sections

234A, 234B and 234C with reference to the assessment year 1989-90 and any subsequent assessment year subject to certain specified conditions. This is a major step taken by the Central Board of Direct Taxes to mitigate the hardships in deserving cases.

(vi) Damages in case of delay and irregularities

The courts have come harsh on the department in case of undue delay and irregularities in releasing the assets which cannot legally be retained. There are instances when, apart from interest, courts have awarded damages on the department for such lapses.

In the case of *DGIT* v. *Diamondstar Exports Ltd.* [2006] 156 Taxman 299 (SC), the Supreme Court directed the department to compensate the assessee when search and seizure of gold ornaments was held illegal and inspite of decision of Delhi High Court for paying interest to the assessee on the value of illegally seized articles, department released the articles after a long delay, and without interest on the ground that the assessee had made no prayer in the writ petition for the payment of interest. In the above case, Supreme Court held that :—

"Even if question of payability of interest was not examined, then also department was liable to compensate assessee at least by way of costs as search and seizure was illegal and loss suffered by assessee was further aggravated by the delay caused by the department in complying with the High Court's decision."

In the case of *Kuber Planters Ltd.* v. *Dy. CIT* [2006] 150 Taxman 11 (Delhi), where FDRs of the petitioner illegally seized in search of a finance company, were not released for several years, Delhi High Court held that in view of the suffering and agony which the applicant had undergone for several years for no fault of his, it would be just to award the applicant, compensation along with his deposits.

(vii) Department's responsibility to take care of seized assets

The assets seized are held by the department on behalf of the concerned person. It is the responsibility of the department to take proper care of the articles or valuables seized and kept in its custody. It has been so held in the case of *Swastik Gear Ltd.* v. *ITO* [1988] 39 Taxman 318 (All.).

In the case of *Shanti Sarup Gupta* v. *Asstt. CIT* [2005] 272 ITR 463 (Punj. & Har.), when the bearer bonds seized by the department were lost from its custody, Punjab and Haryana High Court directed the department to compensate the assessee with the amount of the bonds along with interest. It was held as under:-

"Petitioner cannot be made to suffer for the loss. Accordingly, the Department is directed to refund the amount of the bearer bonds, and also to pay simple interest at the rate of 6% per annum from 1st January, 1992 till the date of payment. However, the Department was let free to recover the same from the persons who may be responsible for causing the loss."

10.30 Release of seized assets when search is held illegal

When search is held illegal by the High Court, Department is required to release the assets seized during search immediately. When the search action is held to be illegal ab initio, there is no right with the Department to retain the seized assets, whether disclosed or undisclosed by the assessee. The assets cannot be retained and applied to recover the existing tax liabilities in case of illegal search. This is altogether a different matter that after release of assets seized in pursuance of search conducted which is held to be illegal; the same assets can again be impounded under section 226(5) of the Act so as to recover the existing tax liabilities, if any.

11

REQUISITION UNDER
SECTION 132A

11.1 Text of section 132A

(1) Where the Director General or Director or the Chief Commissioner or Commissioner, in consequence of information in his possession, has reason to believe that—

(a) any person to whom a summons under sub-section (1) of section 37 of the Indian Income Tax Act, 1922 (11 of 1922), or under sub-section (1) of section 131 of this Act, or a notice under sub-section (4) of section 22 of the Indian Income Tax Act, 1922, or under sub-section (1) of section 142 of this Act was issued to produce, or cause to be produced, any books of account or other documents has omitted or failed to produce, or cause to be produced, such books of account or other documents, as required by such summons or notice and the said books of account or other documents have been taken into custody by any officer or authority under any other law for the time being in force, or

(b) any books of account or other documents will be useful for, or relevant to, any proceeding under the Indian Income Tax Act, 1922 (11 of 1922), or under this Act and any person to whom a summons or notice as aforesaid has been or might be issued will not, or would not, produce or cause to be produced, such books of account or other documents on the return of such books of account or other documents by any officer or authority by whom or which such books of account or other documents have been taken into custody under any other law for the time being in force, or

(c) any assets represent either wholly or partly income or property which has not been, or would not have been, disclosed for the purposes of the Indian Income Tax Act, 1922 (11 of 1922), or this Act by any person

431

from whose possession or control such assets have been taken into custody by any officer or authority under any other law for the time being in force,

then, the Director General or Director or the Chief Commissioner or Commissioner may authorize any Additional Director, Additional Commissioner, Joint Director, Joint Commissioner, Assistant Director or Deputy Director, Assistant Commissioner or Deputy Commissioner or Income Tax Officer (hereafter in this section and in sub-section (2) of section 278D referred to as the requisitioning officer) to require the officer or authority referred to in clause (a) or clause (b) or clause (c), as the case may be, to deliver such books of account, other documents or assets to the requisitioning officer.

(2) On a requisition being made under sub-section (1), the officer or authority referred to in clause (a) or clause (b) or clause (c), as the case may be, of that sub-section shall deliver the books of account, other documents or assets to the requisitioning officer either forthwith or when such officer or authority is of the opinion that it is no longer necessary to retain the same in his or its custody.

(3) Where any books of account, other documents or assets have been delivered to the requisitioning officer, the provisions of sub-sections (4A) to (14) (both inclusive) of section 132 and section 132B shall, so far as may be, apply as if such books of account, other documents or assets had been seized under sub-section (1) of section 132 by the requisitioning officer from the custody of the person referred to in clause (a) or clause (b) or clause (c), as the case may be, of sub-section (1) of this section and as if for the words "the authorized officer" occurring in any of the aforesaid sub-sections (4A) to (14), the words "the requisitioning officer" were substituted.

11.2 Legislative history

Section 132A conferring power to requisition books of account, other documents or assets has been inserted under the Income Tax Act by the Taxation Laws (Amendment) Act, 1975 with effect from 1st October, 1975. Prior to 1975, there was no such provision under the Income Tax Act. Rule 112D has been prescribed regarding procedure to be followed in case of requisition under section 132A.

The provisions of this section were explained by the Central Board of Direct Taxes in its **Circular No. 179 Para 13 dated 30th September 1975 reported in 102 ITR St. 9**. The Circular among other things clarified:

"13. The Amendment Act has substituted the existing section 132A by a new section and has renumbered the existing section 132A as section 132B. The new section 132A provides that where any books of account, other documents or assets have been taken into custody by any officer or authority under any other law (e.g., by Collector of Customs, Sales Tax Commissioner, etc.), the

Director of Inspection or the CIT may, in the circumstances covered by section 132, authorize any Deputy Director of Inspection, Inspecting Assistant Commissioner, Additional Director of Inspection or Income Tax Officer to require such officer or authority to deliver to him such books of account, other documents or assets. Where such a requisition is made, the officer or the authority concerned will be required to deliver the books of account, other documents or assets to the requisitioning officer either forthwith or when such officer or authority is of the opinion that it is no longer necessary to retain the same in his or its custody."

11.3 Objective

There may be cases where incriminating material consisting of books of account, other documents or assets are seized by other Government authorities or officers such as Excise or Sales Tax authorities, Police or Custom officers etc. Legislature wants to investigate the person from whose possession incriminating material was found under the Income Tax Act for evasion of income tax. Legislature does not want such person to go scot free from the point of view of income tax in case he has accumulated unaccounted income without paying due income tax. Provision of section 132A has been inserted in the Income Tax Act so as to give power to the Income Tax Authorities to take possession of such incriminating material from other authorities and treat the person as if he has been searched under the Income Tax Act.

(i)* Circumventing Supreme Court decision in the case of *Tarsem Kumar

Prior to insertion of section 132A under the Income Tax Act, Supreme Court delivered a landmark judgment in the case of *CIT* v. *Tarsem Kumar* [1986] 27 Taxman 305 (SC). Due to above judgment, Department was prohibited from taking delivery of incriminating material from the custody of other Government authorities by serving search warrant and from taking action as per section 132 of the Income Tax Act. The principles laid down by the Apex Court in this judgment were followed in various subsequent decisions *i.e.-*

ITO v. *Bafna Textiles* [1987] 164 ITR 281 (SC)

L.R. Gupta v. *Union of India* [1991] 59 Taxman 305 (Delhi)

Nenmal Shankarlal Partner v. *Asstt. CIT* [1992] 62 Taxman 529 (Kar.)

Harmel Singh v. *Union of India* [1993] 69 Taxman 347 (Punj. & Har.)

The brief facts of this case were as follows—

An amount of ₹ 93,500 was seized by the Custom authorities from a person but the same was ordered by the High Court to be returned. Before the amount could be returned, the Income Tax Department served a search warrant under section 132 of the Income Tax Act on such person as well as on Custom Authorities and they took possession of the above sum. On writ petition filed by such person, High Court held that the Income Tax Department could not seize the amount from the Customs authorities under section 132 and the search warrant issued under the Income Tax Act was liable to be quashed. On appeal, Supreme Court upheld the above decision laying down the following principles—

1. There can be no seizure by Income Tax Authorities when goods are in the custody of another Government Department.

2. When goods are in the custody of another Government Department, there can be no possession of the goods with the assessee and therefore no action under section 132 of the Income Tax Act can be taken.

3. There can be no seizure of goods where location was known. When exact location of the property was known and certain, there was nothing to search or look for.

To circumvent the above decision, legislature had inserted section 132A under the Income Tax Act.

(ii) Rationale of provision of section 132A

In case any undisclosed or incriminating material is seized by other government departments such as Customs, Excise, Enforcement Directorate or Police, etc., such departments are required to make investigation and further take appropriate action for evasion of taxes or any other violation under the respective laws. In case such seized material is of undisclosed nature from the point of view of Income Tax Act also and there has been evasion of income tax by the person with respect to acquisition of such assets/material, Legislature rightly wants to make investigation and collect due income tax relating to such assets/material. The objective of search under the Income Tax Act is to unearth the black money, to seize the undisclosed assets and to collect the due income tax. In case efforts have already been put by some other government department and incriminating material representing undisclosed income from the income tax point of view are already in their possession, there is no reason why action under the Income Tax Act should not be taken against the person who has accumulated such assets without paying due income tax and wealth tax etc. There is no rationale in the argument that undisclosed assets can be seized and action under section 132 can be taken by the income tax department only when such assets are in the possession of the concerned person.

11.4 Nature of provision of section 132A

Section 132A empowers the Income Tax Authorities to take delivery of any books of account, other documents or assets of incriminating nature from the custody of other Government Authorities or officers who are having custody of such material under any other law. Once delivery of such incriminating material is taken, it shall be treated as seizure under the Income Tax Act and the person from whose custody such material was seized shall be treated as if he has been searched under the Income Tax Act. The various ingredients of the provisions of section 132A may be summarized as under—

1.Warrant for requisition under section 132A has to be issued by the competent authority.

2. Warrant can be issued when competent authority has reason to believe in consequence of information in his possession that books of account, other documents or assets in the custody of other Government authority are of undisclosed nature for the purpose of Income Tax Act.

3. Competent authority may authorize any authority below his rank to be called as requisitioning officer to take delivery of such incriminating material from other Government authority.

4. Requisitioning officer is required to serve requisition letter along with authorization issued to him by the competent authority, to the other Government Authority to take delivery of such material.

5. On such requisition, the officer or authority of other Department shall deliver the books of account, other documents or assets to the requisitioning officer either forthwith or when such officer or authority is of the opinion that it is no longer necessary to retain such material in his or its custody.

6. On getting delivery of such books of account, other documents or assets it shall be treated as if seizure has been made under section 132(1) of the Income Tax Act from the possession of the person to whom the same belongs and such person shall be treated as if he has been searched under section 132 of the Income Tax Act.

7. All the provisions of sub-sections (4A) to (14) of section 132 and provision of section 132B shall become applicable, so far as may be possible.

8. Assessment proceedings against such person shall be undertaken in accordance with the provisions of sections 153A/153B/153C and 153D of the Income Tax Act.

9. Provision of section 292C regarding presumption with respect to seized material will also be applicable as specifically provided under sub-section (2) of section 292C.

10. Provision of sections 271AAA & 271AAB regarding imposition of penalty and deeming fiction of undisclosed income as provided therein and provision of sub-section (4) of section 132 regarding recording of statement during search are not applicable in case of requisition under section 132A.

(i) Applicability of section 132(4A) to 132(14)

Section 132A(3) has considered the action of requisition as that of seizure under section 132(1) and, as such, the provisions of sub-sections (4A) to (14) of section 132 would apply *mutatis mutandis* to a case requisition also. [*CIT* v. *Aboo Mohmed* [2000] 111 Taxman 120 (Kar.)]

(ii) Comparison and substitution of various situations under section 132A with section 132

Infact, legislature has treated the situation of requisition under section 132A almost at par as if the person has been searched under section 132. Legislature intends that if a person has accumulated undisclosed income and the same comes to the knowledge of Income Tax Department under whatsoever circumstances, such person cannot go scot free and he has to be treated with the severest treatment which is applicable in the case of a person who is searched under section 132. All provisions of sub-sections (4A) to (14) of section 132, section 132B, sections 153A to 153D, section 292C become applicable with equal force. Provision of sub-section (2) regarding taking services of police officer during search, sub-section (3) regarding putting restraint during search, sub-section (4) regarding recording statement during search are not applicable in case of requisition since such kind of need cannot arise when requisition is made under section 132A. Penalty provision of section 271AAA is also not applicable in case of requisition under section 132A since the same is correlated with the requirement of recording statement during search under section 132(4).

For the purpose of applicability of various provisions of the Act in case of requisition under section 132A and for the purpose of deciding the year of search and relevant assessment years for which subsequent action for assessment under section 153A may be required to be taken, various situations under section 132A may be compared with the corresponding situations under section 132 as under—

S.No.	As per section 132	As per section 132A
1.	Date of signing and issue of warrant of authorization for search by the competent authority.	Date of signing and issue of warrant of authorization for requisition by the competent authority.

S.No.	As per section 132	As per section 132A
2.	Date of commencement of search.	Date on which requisition is served by the requisitioning officer to the other Government officer or authority.
3.	Date of conclusion of search when last of the authorization is executed.	Date on which last delivery of incriminating material is received by the requisitioning officer.
4.	Period of conduct of search from the date of commencement of search till the conclusion of search when last of the authorization is executed.	From the date of serving the requisition to the other authority till getting delivery of the incriminating material from such other authority by the requisitioning officer.
5.	Conditions precedent before issuing authorization as given under clauses (a), (b) and (c) of section 132(1).	Similar conditions have been given under clauses (a), (b) and (c) of section 132A(1).

(iii) **Who can issue authorization for requisition under section 132A?**

The competent authority to issue the authorization for requisition under section 132A can be —

    a. Director General or Director

    b. Chief Commissioner or Commissioner

The powers for issuing authorization for requisition under section 132A has not been given to Additional Director or Additional Commissioner, Joint Director or Joint Commissioner who are empowered by the Board for issuing authorization for search and seizure under section 132.

(iv) **Who can be requisitioning officer?**

Requisitioning officer may be any authority below the rank of competent authority who has issued authorization. It will include any of the following—

    a. Additional Director/Additional Commissioner

    b. Joint Director/Joint Commissioner

    c. Deputy Director/Deputy Commissioner

    d. Assistant Director/Assistant Commissioner

    e. Income Tax Officer

A requisitioning officer referred under section 132A is and acts as authorized officer as referred under section 132 in the case of search.

(v) To form "reason to believe" in consequence of information in possession

The competent authority cannot issue authorization under section 132A in a mechanical manner. Similar kind of safeguard mechanism has been provided before issuing authorization under section 132A as has been provided before issuing authorization for search under section 132. All the discussion regarding formation of "reason to believe" and "in consequence to information in his possession" is relevant here also with the equal force.

It is not that competent authority can issue authorization for requisition in every case when any kind of information is received regarding seizure of books of account, documents or assets by any other Government authority or officer. Before issuing authorization for requisition, he has to satisfy that books of account, other documents or assets requisitioned have not been disclosed or would not be disclosed for the purpose of Income Tax Act. The material to be requisitioned has to be in the nature which contains & represents wholly or partly concealed income.

There are various judicial pronouncements where authorization for requisition under section 132A was held illegal and quashed due to non-fulfilment of above requirement.

♦ Mere unexplained possession of amount without anything more would not constitute sufficient information leading to an inference that amount is income which would not have been disclosed by person in possession, so as to justify issuance of authorization for requisitioning such amount - *CIT* v. *Vindhya Metal Corpn.* [1997] 91 Taxman 192 (SC).

♦ Cash seized by police from possession of an employee of assessee along with two letters indicating that the money was meant for payment of customs duty cannot be treated as undisclosed amount particularly when the assessee is a regular taxpayer; warrant of authorization under section 132A (1) issued merely on the basis of information received from police did not satisfy the requirements of said section and is set aside - *B.R. Metal Ltd.* v. *CIT* [1999] 239 ITR 329 (Gau.).

♦ No warrant of authorization under section 132 could be issued where money and documents were taken possession of by a police inspector and the CIT could have no reason to believe within the meaning of section 132 when he did not know anything about the person concerned and made no enquiry from the ITO concerned as regards evasion of tax - *Ramesh Chander* v. *CIT* [1974] 93 ITR 244 (Punj. & Har.).

◆ Assessee being a regular assessee and having submitted documentary proof showing source of cash seized while cash was withdrawn from bank and duly accounted for in the assessee's books, no case for requisition under section 132A was made out - *Biaora Constructions (P.) Ltd.* v. *DIT (Inv.)* [2006] 153 Taxman 252 (MP).

◆ Conditions precedent must be satisfied before issue of an order for requisition and there should be reason to believe that the books of account or documents may not be produced on issue of summons. Where no such reasons were recorded and the order was issued mechanically without application of mind, it was held liable to be quashed - *Shree Janki Solvent Extraction Ltd.* v. *Dy. DIT* [1996] 85 Taxman 462 (All.).

◆ Silver having been seized by the police under section 102 of CrPC from employee of assessee and CIT not being in possession of such information as to arrive at a conclusion that silver represented undisclosed assets of the assessee, it was fallacy on the part of Chief Judicial Magistrate to entertain an application under section 132A and direct handing over of silver to IT department - *DIT (Inv.)* v. *Payal Selection & Co.* [2008] 175 Taxman 36 (MP).

◆ In the case of *Sudarshan & Company* v. *CIT* [1983] 139 ITR 1032 (All.), it was held that section 132A casts a duty on the authorizing authority to apply his mind and take action only where the grounds for the same exist and Court may interfere in case of any failure to carry out this statutory duty but Courts have no jurisdiction where exercise of power under section 132A is in accordance with law. The court held that the existence of the belief can be challenged by the assessee but not the sufficiency of the reasons for the belief.

◆ In the case of *Ibrahim Othayoth* v. *Sub-Inspector of Police* [1998] 232 ITR 320 (Ker.), gold seized in a police raid, on appeal by the income tax department, was directed to be released to the Assistant Director of Income Tax. Rejecting the revision petition it was held that the Appellate Court was justified in looking into the statements recorded in the course of investigation. The Appellate Court has considered all the aspects and came to right conclusion that the articles should be released to the income tax department and this conclusion did not call for any interference.

◆ In *Arun Kumar Chhajar* v. *Collector of Customs (Preventive)* [1993] 1993 taxmann.com 621 (Cal.), High Court held that ITO is required to at least *prima facie* believe that the amount of money in the custody of the customs, represented income which was not disclosed or which would not be disclosed. The mere fact that there was a large amount of money available with the petitioner would not by itself mean that the petitioner would not disclose the amount. There must have been some other factors which should have induced the ITO to at least believe that the petitioner would not in fact disclose the amount. The notice u/s 132A is issued for the purpose of ensuring that the monies which could have been secreted are in fact brought to light. The object of notice u/s 132A(1) being to force disclosure of secreted amounts and the petitioner having in fact disclosed the amount in the return prior to the filing of Writ Petition, there was no question of either the notice u/s 132A being mentioned or the Income-tax Authorities being made parties. Therefore, Calcutta High Court held that there was no warrant for the Income-tax Authorities to hold on for the amount of ₹ 3,10,000 any more.

◆ In the case of *B.R. Metal Ltd.* v. *CIT* [1999] 239 ITR 329 (Gau.), High Court held that the cash seized by the police from the possession of an employee of assessee along with two letters indicating that the money was meant for payment of custom dues cannot be treated as undisclosed sum more particularly in view of the fact that the assessee was a regular Income tax assessee. High Court held that the Warrant of Authorization u/s 132A(1) was issued merely on the basis of information received from police and did not satisfy the requirements of section 132A and was thus liable to be set aside.

◆ Allahabad High Court in the case of *Ganga Prasad Maheshwari* v. *CIT* [1981] 6 Taxman 363 (All.) held that mere possession of jewellery by the petitioner was not sufficient and the information must be such that the CIT may have reason to believe that it represents undisclosed income of the person in whose possession it is. In this case, CIT having issued warrant of authorization without there being any reason to believe that the jewellery which was in possession of the petitioner represented wholly or partly his undisclosed income, his action u/s 132A was found without jurisdiction.

◆ Allahabad High Court in the case of *Manju Tandon* v. *T.N. Kapoor, Dy. Superintendent of Police* [1978] 115 ITR 473 (All.) held that there was absolutely no material before the CIT to have reason to believe that the gold ornaments in the custody of the CBI represented wholly or partly income or property of the petitioner which had not been or would not be disclosed for the purposes of proceeding under the Act and thus condition precedent for issuing authorization to requisition the ornaments from the officers of the CBI did not exist and thus action of the Tax Authority was liable to be quashed.

In the case of *Prakash Jaichand Shah* v. *DIT (Investigations)* [2012] 23 taxmann.com 8/208 Taxman 136 (Mag.) (Guj.), it was held that in view of the factual background, no reasonable person could have come to the conclusion that the amount of ₹ 11 lakhs belonged to the assessee or that he would not disclose the amount to the income-tax authorities under the provisions of the Act. In the circumstances, on the basis of the material before him, the Director of Income-tax could not have formed the requisite opinion as required under section 132A of the Act. The warrant of authorisation issued by him, therefore, was vitiated as having been issued without the condition precedent for exercise of powers under section 132A being satisfied. The warrant of authorisation as well as the order under section 132A was liable to be quashed. The assessee was entitled to the seized amount along with interest.

It has been held in the case of *Smt. Rewati Singh* v. *Asstt. CIT* [2018] 99 taxmann.com 419 (All.) that *in case of requisition u/s 132A where* Cash was seized by police authorities from accused subsequent to murder of assessee & no information was available with Department as to what documents or books of account were to be requisitioned, Order of requisition was untenable & thus notices were quashed.

However, in the following cases, authorization for requisition under section 132A was held valid:—

In the case of *Krishnagopal* v. *DIT (Inv.)* [2009] 182 Taxman 203 (MP), information came to CIT from police that petitioner was in a hotel in possession of raw silver and silver ornaments. CIT issued a warrant u/s 132A requesting the magistrate to hand over assets. On a writ filed against the warrant u/s 132A, it was held that DI (Inv.) was in possession of information from which he had reason to believe that the money and raw silver seized by police represented wholly or partly assets which had not or would not have been disclosed for purposes of Income Tax. It was also held that the belief required under section 132A is subjective and not open to objective test. Warrant was validly issued.

◆ *Explanation* of the petitioner that the cash found in his possession was the amount withdrawn from one bank being wholly unsatisfactory and *prima facie* unreliable in view of diverse slips found on currency notes, initial statement made to the police and the change of version by the petitioner, there was material to form opinion/reason to believe as required for issuance of requisition under section 132A - *Amar Agarwal* v. *DIT (Investigation)* [2005] 144 Taxman 762 (MP).

It has been held in the case of *Smt. Suman Singhai* v. *DIT (Investigation)* [2012] 20 taxmann.com 835 (MP) that in view of the recovery of unexplained silver weighing 54.078 kgs. and cash of ₹ 16,50,000 from an employee of the petitioner and material on record showing absence of business activity and books of account at the shop, respondent No.1 was in possession of information constituting reason to believe that the seized cash and silver represent assets which would not have been disclosed for the purpose of income-tax and, therefore, issuance of warrant of authorization under section 132A was valid and justified.

It has been held in the case of *M. Manoj Kumar & Co.* v. *DIT (Investigation)* [2011] 200 Taxman 12/11 taxmann.com 364 (MP) that the employee in his statement under section 131 did not state that the money in question belonged to petitioner's firm or it was handed over to him on behalf of the said firm and it was nowhere said in his statement that the money in question was to be delivered to the petitioner's firm and no bank account details were provided though it is alleged that money was withdrawn from firm's bank account, there was sufficient information in possession of the authority in order to enable his to form an opinion/reason to believe that the amount in question has not been or would not have been disclosed for the purpose of section 132A of the IT Act.

It has been held in the case of *Atta Husain* v. *DIT (Inv.)* [2012] 22 taxmann.com 50 (MP) that explanation given by the petitioner that the cash of ₹ 6.5 lacs found on his person represented the amounts received by him on sale of agricultural land and a house over a period of more than six years when it is not clear as to how and under what circumstances the amounts were kept by him or were carried by him on the said date is not a convincing explanation and, therefore, it is not a fit case where the proceedings under section 132A initiated against the petitioner can be quashed by exercising extraordinary jurisdiction on a writ petition under Article 226.

It has been held in the case of *Patel Rajesh Kumar Amrutlal & Co.* v. *DIT (Inv.)* [2012] 23 taxmann.com 132/209 Taxman 368 (MP) that in context of section 132A and in view of statement of person from whom money was seized and absence of bank account details, there was sufficient information in possession of the authority in order to enable him to form an opinion/reason to believe that the amount in question has not been or would not have been disclosed for the purpose of Income Tax Act, and therefore warrant of authorization was rightly issued.

(va)   Disclosure of 'reason to believe'

Finance Act, 2017 has inserted an *Explanation* to sub-section (1) of section 132A with effect from 1st day of October, 1975 as under:

"Explanation.—For the removal of doubts, it is hereby declared that the reason to believe, as recorded by the income-tax authority under this sub-section, shall not be disclosed to any person or any authority or the Appellate Tribunal."

The above *Explanation* sets right the controversy prevailing earlier regarding power of Appellate Authority or Tribunal to seek for the 'reason to believe' while deciding the matter pending before them. Similar *Explanation* has been added in section 132 also. However, High Courts and Supreme Court being the constitutional courts can ask for the disclosure of the 'reason to believe' in connection with any proceeding before them.

It has been held in the case of *N. K Jewellers* v. *CIT* [2017] 85 taxmann. com 361/251 Taxman 7/398 ITR 116 (SC) that when employee of Assessee was found in possession of cash by Railway police & requisition was made by Department but explanation was not accepted and cash was treated as concealed income of assessee, Challenge to validity of proceedings was based on search in train by police but contention was not taken before authorities & hence was not permitted & hence no interference was made on merits.

(vi) Before authorization for requisition - Whether opportunity to be granted to the assessee

Before issuing authorization for requisition, the competent authority is required to satisfy regarding existence of any of the conditions mentioned under clause (*a*), (*b*) or (*c*) of section 132A(1). These conditions are almost of the same nature as are the conditions prescribed under clause (*a*), (*b*) or (*c*) of section 132(1) before issuing search warrant. Basically before issuing authorization for requisition, competent authority has to satisfy that books of account, other documents or assets to be requisitioned are of undisclosed nature. Such satisfaction is an administrative act and it is arrived by the competent authority confidentially as per his personal satisfaction in the case of issue of search warrant under section 132. However in case of requisition under section 132A to be issued, no confidentiality is involved and the books of account, documents or assets taken into custody by other Government authority/officer are already in the knowledge of everybody. It would be appropriate if an opportunity is given to the person to explain whether such books of account, documents or assets are of disclosed nature or not. There is no such provision under the Act to provide opportunity to the person to explain the nature and source of books of account, other documents or assets before issuing authorization for requisition by the competent authority.

In such a situation, in our opinion, it could be reasonable if a provision is provided under section 132A to grant opportunity to the assessee to explain the nature and source of the assets intended to be requisitioned so as to avoid requisition and seizure of the disclosed assets. It would further avoid the situation when disclosed assets are requisitioned and seized and as a consequence thereof the action of the department is later invalidated. It would further avoid unnecessary harassment and litigation for the assessee. At the same time, it would serve the objective of the department and only undisclosed assets which are intended to be seized will be requisitioned.

It has been held in the case of *Shiv Tiwari & Ors.* v. *Principal Director of IT (Inv.) & Anr.* 305 CTR 307 (Raj.)/171 DTR 209 (Raj.) that Information in respect of any action which is required to be taken under section 132A and which comes in the exclusive possession of an officer, is not required to be divulged on merely asking of a person & money which has been seized by the police can always be claimed by the petitioner, after the Income Tax Department concludes its proceedings, which have been initiated by issuing notice to the petitioner.

(*vii*) **Opportunity to the person before taking delivery of material from the possession of other Government Authority/Officer**

Sub-rule (2) of rule 112D prescribing the procedure for requisition of books of account, etc. from the possession of other Government Authority/Officer prescribes that a copy of the requisition, along with a copy of authorization in Form No. 45C shall be forwarded to the person referred to in clause (*a*) or clause (*b*) or, as the case may be, clause (*c*) of sub-section (1) of section 132A. In sub-rule (3), it is further provided that such person or any other person on his behalf shall also be permitted to place his seal on the said package or packages (which have been delivered to the requisitioning officer of the income tax department). A copy of the list of the material prepared is also required to be delivered to such person.

However, there is no provision under section 132A to provide an opportunity to the person to explain as to whether such books of account, other documents or assets are of disclosed nature, before handing over delivery of such material to the requisitioning officer. Taking delivery of books of account, other documents or assets from the custody of other Government Authority/Officer is treated as seizure of assets done under sub-section (1) of section 132. Before making seizure of assets in the case of search under section 132, such opportunity is provided to the person searched but it is strange that in case of requisition under section 132A, no such opportunity is provided to the person at this stage also.

(viii) **There may be huge time gap between requisition made and actual delivery of material affected**

There may be huge time gap between the date of requisition served by the requisitioning officer to the other Government Authority/ Officer and the date on which actual delivery of requisitioned assets is made to the requisitioning officer. In practice it has been observed that this gap may sometimes run into several months and years. There is no time limit prescribed for making delivery by other Government Authority/Officer to the requisitioning officer.

Infact, there cannot be any time limit prescribed for this purpose. The books of account, other documents or assets were taken into custody by other Government Authority/Officer for their own purpose for making investigation or taking action as required under respective law under which action was taken and seizure was made by them. Till their purpose is fulfilled, they cannot be expected and are not required to handover delivery of such seized material to the Income Tax Authorities. Sub-section (2) of section 132A states that books of account, other documents or assets shall be delivered by other Government Authority/Officer to the Income Tax Authority *i.e.* requisitioning officer either forthwith or when such officer or authority is of the opinion that it is no longer necessary to retain the same in his custody.

This time gap may create uncertainty and delay under the Income Tax Act for undertaking assessment proceedings under section 153A and also for the release of the seized assets.

(ix) **No requisition, pending decision about confiscation**

"That the issue before the Special Judge was whether the seized amount was liable to be confiscated under section 62 of the NDPS Act. If it was found that the amount was not to be confiscated under section 62 of the NDPS Act then the question of handing over the amount to the applicant revenue arise. The trial court had rightly held that the application was premature and it had not committed any mistake in rejecting it."

DIT (Inv.) v. Gulamnabi [2006] 152 Taxman 55 (MP)

11.5 Procedure of requisition

(*i*) No format for requisitioning letter to be issued by requisitioning officer

Sub-rule (1) of rule 112D prescribes that authorization under sub-section (1) of section 132A to be issued by the competent authority shall be in Form No. 45C under his signature and seal. Form 45C authorizes requisitioning officer to take delivery of the books of account, other documents or assets from the custody of other Government Authority/Officer.

The requisitioning officer is required to issue requisition letter in writing prescribing the details of books of account, other documents or assets, delivery of which is required to be taken. But there is no form prescribed for issuing such requisition letter by the requisitioning officer to the other Government Authority/Officer. However, it is mentioned in rule 112D that the requisition shall be in writing and accompanied by a copy of authorization in Form No. 45C.

(*ii*) Copy of authorization to the person or the assessee

Sub-rule (2) of rule 112D provides that a copy of the requisition letter along with a copy of the authorization in Form No. 45C shall be forwarded to the person/assessee from whose possession or control books of account, other documents or assets were taken into custody by the other Government Authority/Officer. This requirement of serving copy of authorization and requisition is in deviation from the requirement contained under section 132 in the case of search. In the case of search under section 132, search warrant *i.e.* authorization for search is only shown to the assessee but there is no requirement to serve the copy of the same to the assessee. Probably the requirement of serving authorization in case of requisition under section 132A is with the objective to make the assessee aware that action under section 132A has been initiated against him.

(*iii*) Consequences of not serving the authorization to the assessee

In practice it has been observed in number of cases that the copy of authorization and requisition under section 132A is not served to the assessee. Such non-service of requisition to the assessee cannot make the action under section 132A invalid. It may be an irregularity but it cannot form a valid ground to quash action under section 132A.

Having said the same, it is further added that it may be a debatable point and the same is amenable to the judicial test.

(iv) **Procedure regarding taking delivery of the seized material**

Procedure regarding taking delivery of the books of account, other documents or assets from the custody of other Government Authority or Officer is given under sub-rule (3) and sub-rule (4) of rule 112D. Taking delivery of the books of account, other documents or assets is treated in the same manner as if the same had been seized under sub-section (1) of section 132 in case of search from the possession and control of the assessee.

Sub-rule (3) prescribes that at the time of handing over of the delivery of the books of account, other documents or assets, assessee or any other person on his behalf may remain present and he shall also be permitted to place his signature/seal on the packages to be delivered alongwith the signature and seal of requisitioning officer and delivering officer. A copy of the list, prepared containing details of the books of account, other documents or assets delivered, is also required to be given to the assessee. There is no requirement of two independent witnesses to remain present at the time of handing over of delivery of the requisitioned material.

11.6 Requisition can be made from which authority/officer

(i) **To which Authority or Officer, requisition can be made**

Section 132A empowers the Income Tax Authorities to make requisition to any officer or authority under any other law for the time being in force. The scope of the officer or authority to whom requisition can be made is quite large and it covers any officer or authority prescribed under any other law. It may be Central Government or State Government officer or authority empowered under any law for the time being in force in the country. Generally, in practice requisition is placed to Excise Authority, Sales Tax Authority, and Custom Authority, Police Officers, Enforcement Directorate or other Revenue Authority.

The reference to any officer or authority under any other law is to the authorities who as per legal power available with them had taken custody of the books of account, documents or assets. It cannot cover any officer with whom assessee had deposited the books of account or assets willingly and in the capacity as his agent, custodian or trustee.

     ◆ Power envisaged under section 132A(1)(*c*) should be exercised immediately after the property is seized by making requisition to the police officer who seized the property; such power cannot be exercised in proceeding before a Court, that too when an order of release is made - *Janardan Das* v. *Bindeshwari Prasad Sah* [1999] 238 ITR 65 (Pat.).

♦ In exercise of the powers under section 132A, the Director of Inspection or the Commissioner of Income-tax cannot authorize any of the officers mentioned in this section to require a Treasury Officer to deliver the cash property deposited with him for safe custody under order of a competent criminal Court - *Balbir Singh* v. *CIT* [1984] 18 Taxman 67 (Punj. & Har.) *affirmed in CIT* v. *Balbir Singh* [1994] 76 Taxman 177 (Punj. & Har.).

♦ Assets seized by police officer by exercise of power under section 102, CrPC, when taken in possession of by IT authorities, IT authorities alone have jurisdiction in the matter and thus proceedings under section 132 read with section 132A were validly initiated, it could not be said that the ITO acted in collusion with police authorities. - *Chandra Prakash Agrawal* v. *State of Rajasthan* [1994] 76 Taxman 559 (Raj.)

(ii) No requisition from the possession of Court

It has been held in several cases that Courts cannot be said to be an officer or authority and from the custody of Courts, assets cannot be requisitioned.

♦ Section 132A does not empower the Commissioner of Income-tax to require the Court to deliver the assets lying in its custody; provision is referable only to an 'officer' or 'authority' referred to in sub-section (1) of section 132A; gold directed to be returned to the Magistrate who will consider the petitioner's application for release of gold - *Abdul Khader* v. *Sub-Inspector of Police* [1999] 240 ITR 489 (Ker.).

♦ Cash deposited with treasury officer under orders of Court continued to be in the custody of Court and could not have to be requisitioned by ITO under section 132A as officer or authority under section 132A do not include Court. - *CIT* v. *Balbir Singh* [1994] 76 Taxman 177 (Punj. & Har.)

(iii) No requisition from the possession of bank officers

No requisition under section 132A can be made by the Income Tax Department to the bank officers with whom assessee had deposited documents or assets as security against credit facilities availed. Documents or assets with the bank officers are deposited by the assessee willingly as his agent or trustee. These are not taken by bank officers in their custody forcefully under power of any law. Even if such documents or assets may be of undisclosed nature from the point of view of income tax law, the same cannot be requisitioned under section 132A by the Income Tax Authorities.

♦ When a bank draft is presented for clearing by the customer to the bank it cannot be said to have been taken into custody by the bank under any law and, therefore, the IT authorities cannot requisition it by invoking provisions of section 132A. - *Samta Construction* v. *Pawan Kumar Sharma* [1999] 107 Taxman 198 (MP)

(*iv*) Requisition from the custody of Police Officers

There are contradictory views of the Court on the issue as to whether requisition under section 132A can be served and delivery of assets may be taken by the Income Tax Authorities from the custody of Police. In the case of *Srinivasan* v. *Dy. Superintendent of Police* [1973] 91 ITR 308 (Mad.) it has been held that an ITO authorized under section 132 can claim the cash seized by police lying with the Court. The overwhelming view in this regard is that delivery from the police custody can be taken by the Income Tax Authorities under section 132A with the order of competent Court.

It has been held in the case of *Kamleshbhai Rajnikant Shah* v. *Dy. DIT* [2019] 110 taxmann.com 214/267 Taxman 159/[2020] 420 ITR 274 (Guj.) that in case of requisition of assets under section 132A, Cash seized by police requisitioned by Revenue & no satisfactory explanation is available regarding cash, warrant of authorisation was valid.

(*v*) Assets may be requisitioned from the custody of Police Authorities under order of the Court

♦ Assets seized by police cannot be requisitioned unless seizure is reported to the court. It was held, on facts, that the order of requisition under section 132A was not valid - Income Tax Act, 1961, section 132A - *Sadruddin Javeri* v. *Government of Andhra Pradesh* [1999] 104 Taxman 335 (AP).

♦ High Court has power to examine whether warrant of authorization under section 132A was arbitrary or *mala fide.* Cash amounting to twelve lakhs of rupees seized by police from person travelling by bus is held to be valid where no satisfactory *explanation* regarding cash is given. Cash in custody of Magistrate can be requisitioned by issue of warrant of authorization - *Suresh Bhai Bhola Bhai Jani* v. *Union of India* [2001] 249 ITR 363 (Raj.).

◆ Police Officer cannot hand over articles to Director of Income Tax without order of court - *Amandeep Singh* v. *DIT* [2002] 121 Taxman 110 (Punj. & Har.).

◆ In the case of *Parasnath* v. *Union of India* [1996] 87 Taxman 349 (MP), it was held that neither the judicial magistrate nor the SHO of police holding the seized money which is the subject matter of the warrant under section 132A, had any jurisdiction to inquire into the validity of the warrant of authorization for delivery of that money, to the Income-tax Officer concerned nor of the competence of the officer issuing the warrant of authorization.

◆ In the case of *Babu Rao* v. *Inspector of Police* [1991] 190 ITR 616 (Mad.), it was held that the amount in custody of Court should be handed over to them as it represented undisclosed income, the magistrate was justified in handing over the amount to them.

◆ In the case of *Union of India* v. *Judicial Magistrate (Eastern Railway)* [1983] 12 Taxman 76 (All.), it has been held that CIT having issued warrant of authorization under section 132A read with section 112D in the name of SHO who had seized currency notes from a person the magistrate has no jurisdiction to hand over the property in question to another person, and an order should have been passed in favour of the authorized officer so that the inquiry under section 132, may be conducted by the Income Tax Department.

(vi) Court ordering release of cash seized on furnishing bank guarantee

In the case of *Surinder Kaur* v. *Union of India* [2000] 112 Taxman 370 (Delhi) when cash was seized by the Enforcement Directorate and requisition was made for taking delivery of the cash by the Income Tax Authorities under section 132A, Delhi High Court directed to release the cash to the person concerned after furnishing bank guarantee for the equivalent amount so as to protect the interest of the Income Tax Department.

(vii) Requisition from Excise Department in case of auction

In the case of *Babu Lal* v. *DIT* [2005] 147 Taxman 318 (All.), it was held that when banker cheques/CDRs, etc. were deposited with the District Excise Officer in the name of a non-existent firm for participating in an auction for sale of liquor, there was sufficient material before the concerned authority to reasonably believe, on the basis of information in his possession, that action was required to be taken under the provisions of section 132(1) and hence, powers under section 132 were rightly resorted to by the IT authorities for seizure of said banker cheques, CDRs, etc.; provisions of section 132A do not prohibit seizure of documents from a Government office.

(viii) **Overriding powers to Income Tax Authorities over other Authorities**

It is interesting to note that power under section 132A is an overriding power available to the Income Tax Authorities over other Government Authorities or Officers under any other law in force in the country. There may not be such powers under any other law available to any other authorities to take delivery of the seized books of account, documents or assets from the custody of other authorities/officers unless there is specific order by the competent Court for delivery of seized material by the Income Tax Department to the other authorities for taking appropriate action at their end. It shows the significance and importance attached to the provisions of search and seizure under the Income Tax Act by the legislature.

11.7 Recording of statement in case of requisition

(i) **Recording of statement under section 131(1A)**

In the case of requisition under section 132A, there is no applicability of sub-section (4) of section 132. It means that statement under section 132(4) cannot be recorded by the requisitioning officer at the time of taking delivery of the seized material from the custody of other authority. However, statement under section 131(1A) can be recorded by the requisitioning officer.

◆ Statement under sec.132(4) could not be recorded during the course of a seizure made under sec.132A, and in fact there was a specific exclusion in terms of sec.132A(3). However, A.D.I. is competent to record statement under section 131(1A) during proceedings under section 132A - [*Asstt. CIT* v. *M.V. Nagaraja* [1999] 70 ITD 318 (Bang. - Trib.)]

◆ Issuance of notice under section 131(1A) during post search investigation held to be valid - *Madhupuri Corporation* v. *Prabhat Jha, Dy. DIT (Investigation)* [2002] 125 Taxman 309 (Guj.)

(ii) **Benefit of making declaration of undisclosed income under section 132(4) and also Deeming fiction of "undisclosed income" under section 271AAA not applicable in case of requisition u/s 132A**

Sub-section (3) of section 132A states that where any books of account, other documents or assets have been delivered to the requisitioning officer, the provisions of sub-sections (4A) to (14) of section 132 shall, so far as may be, apply. Provision of sub-section (4) of section 132 regarding recording of statement during search and making declaration of undisclosed income by the assessee has not been made applicable. In the case of requisition under section 132A opportunity to the assessee for making declaration of undisclosed income for the specified years (as defined under section 271AAA/271AAB) has not been given and the deeming fiction of undisclosed income as provided under these sections in the case of search under section 132 is also not applicable in the case of requisition under section 132A. It implies that in case there is any undisclosed income upto the year of requisition relating to the year in which requisition is made, the same may be declared by the assessee in his regular return of income to be filed under section 139. When such undisclosed income is declared in the regular return of income filed by the assessee, no penalty provisions under section 271AAA/271AAB or under section 271(1)(c) shall be applicable. However, when such undisclosed income is not declared by the assessee in the regular return of income filed and the same is added by the Assessing Officer during assessment, penalty provisions even for the year of requisition or specified years shall be applicable as per normal provision of section 271(1)(c) and not as per provision of section 271AAA/271AAB.

In other words, it can be stated that in the case of requisition under section 132A assessee is having opportunity for making declaration of undisclosed income upto the date of filing normal return of income and this opportunity is not limited before the date of conclusion of search/delivery of seized material to the requisitioning officer as is the case under section 132.

Penalty provision of section 271AAA has been brought on the statute with effect from 01.04.2007. Prior to this, for imposition of penalty for concealment of income the above situation was covered by *Explanation 5* to section 271(1)(c). In the case of requisition of assets, provision of *Explanation 5* to section 271(1)(c) shall also not be applicable as per the similar rationale as discussed above. Moreover, it may also be noted that *Explanation 5* to section 271(1)(c) only refers to search initiated under section 132 and it does not refer to requisition made under section 132A. In the case of *Gulamrasul M. Pathan* v. *Asstt. CIT* [1996] 57 ITD 129 (Ahd. - Trib.), this aspect was considered and it was held that *Explanation 5* to section 271(1)(c) cannot be made applicable in relation to assets seized under section 132A.

(*iii*) **Penalty in case of revision of return consequent upon requisition under section 132A**

In the case of *CIT* v. *Aboo Mohmed* [2000] 111 Taxman 120 (Kar.), amount seized as a result of requisition under section 132A was subsequently declared by the assessee by revising the return of income. It was held that the Tribunal was not justified in cancelling penalty in as much as the assessee himself has failed to prove the source and the acquisition of that money and ultimately has offered the amount for taxation by revising his return of income.

11.8 Assessment in case of requisition

(*i*) Assessment in accordance with provisions of section 153A

Section 153A has prescribed procedure for making assessment in case of search undertaken under section 132 or requisition made under section 132A. In the case of requisition under section 132A, assessee is treated as if he has been searched under section 132 and assessment is made in accordance with the provisions of section 153A meaning thereby that notices will be issued for preceding six years to file fresh returns of income and the Assessing Officer shall assess or reassess the total income in respect of each assessment year falling within such six assessment years.

It has been held in the undernoted case that notice issued under section 153A should mention about the material requisitioned under section 132A and thus it would require that before issue of notice under section 153A the assessing officer should receive the requisitioned material from the authorized officer.

It has been held in the case *Underwater Services Co. Ltd.* v. *Asstt. CIT* 209 DTR 476 (Bom) that notice under section 153A should have mentioned whether seized material as under section 132 or books of account, other documents or any assets are requisitioned under section 132A and since notice is absolutely silent as could be seen from it and notice says "you are required to prepare true and correct return of income" and "setting forth such other particulars", such notice is vague and hence in the circumstances, the notice is quashed and set aside.

(*ii*) In case of requisition, which six years to be covered

In the case of requisition under section 132A, it is important to ascertain the triggering point to determine the year of requisition and preceding six years for the purpose of section 153A. Clause (*b*) of section 153A(1) states that where a search is initiated under section 132 or books of account, other documents or any assets are requisitioned under section 132A, the Assessing Officer shall assess or reassess the total income of six assessment years immediately preceding the assessment year relevant to the previous year in which such search is conducted or requisition is made. With reference to search under section 132, the determining factor is the year in which "search is conducted". In the context of search under section 132, it has been concluded that six years shall be the years preceding the previous year in which process of conduct of search is initiated or search is commenced. In the case of requisition under section 132A, section 153A has used the phrase "requisition is made" to determine the year which may be said to be the year of requisition/search and the preceding six years shall be determined prior to this year. "Requisition is made" shall mean when requisition under section 132A is served by the requisitioning officer to the other Government Authority/Officer. This date may be equated with the date on which search is commenced under section 132 with the entry of authorized officer into the premises and showing search warrant to the assessee.

The above situation may be explained by way of an example, say requisition is made by the Income Tax Authority to Enforcement Directorate as on 10th of March 2018 and the actual hand over of the gold seized is made on 10th of June 2019. For the purpose of making assessment under section 153A, preceding six years shall be years beginning from the year ending on 31st March 2012 till the year ending on 31st March 2017.

(*iii*) **Delay in receiving requisitioned material - Assessment for the year of requisition**

In the case of requisition under section 132A, there may be situation when there is huge time gap between the date of service of requisition and the date on which actual delivery of requisitioned material is handed over to the requisitioning officer. This gap may sometimes be of several years. In case income tax return for the year in which requisition is made has already been filed by the assessee and time limit for issuing notice under section 143(2) has already expired for making assessment of such year, Assessing Officer under the Income Tax Act will have no recourse but to take action for such year under section 147/148 of the Act by reopening the case subject to the compliance of the statutory requirements. It is for the reason that the year of requisition is not covered within the provisions of section 153A(1)(*b*) and the selection of case for scrutiny for the year of requisition can be made only as per normal provisions of the Act.

In the example given above, in case requisition was made as on 10th of March 2016 and the actual delivery of gold seized was handed over as on 10th June 2019, the preceding six years to be covered under section 153A shall be the years beginning from the financial year ending on 31st March 2010 till the Financial Year ending on 31st March 2015. The year of requisition is the Financial Year 2015-16 relevant to Assessment Year 2016-17. Notice under section 143(2) for making the scrutiny assessment can be issued for Assessment Year 2016-17 upto 30th September 2017. In such a situation when actual delivery of gold is received by the income tax department in the Financial Year 2019-20 and action for making assessment under section 153A is taken by the department after that, the year of requisition *i.e.*, Assessment Year 2016-17 can be scrutinized if required only under section 147/148 after fulfilling the conditions as given therein.

In fact the above kind of situation has not been envisaged by the legislature in the context of requisition under section 132A. Similar was the position in the context of provision of section 153C but by way of insertion of sub-section (2) under section 153C by Finance Act 2005 retrospectively with effect from 1st June 2003, such anomaly was plugged. However, in the context of requisition under section 132A such anomaly still exists.

Due to the above anomaly, one can take the view that the triggering point to determine the preceding six years and the year of requisition under section 153A shall be the year in which actual delivery of the requisitioned assets is handed over to the income tax department and not the year in which requisition is initially made by the income tax department to the other government authority. But in our considered opinion, this view may not be correct and may throw other complications of interpretation.

(iv) **Time limit for completion of assessment under section 153A in case of requisition under section 132A**

Reference of time limit for completion of assessment under section 153A in the case of requisition has been given under section 153B as the financial year in which last of the authorizations for requisition under section 132A was executed. Last of the authorizations under section 132A can be said to be executed when last delivery of the requisitioned material is handed over to the requisitioning officer. This situation is similar to the situation in the case of search under section 132 where reference under section 153B for time limit for completion of assessment under section 153A is prescribed from the end of the financial year in which last of the authorizations for search under section 132 was executed.

In a case when there is considerable delay in receiving the requisitioned material by the income tax department, such situation may create anomaly and controversy regarding the time limit for completion of assessment under section 153A. In the above example, when requisition was made as on 10th of March 2016 and actual delivery of gold was handed over on 10th of June 2019, the date for the execution of requisition for the purpose of section 153B shall be 10th of June 2019 and time limit for completion of assessments under section 153A shall be 31st March 2021 *i.e.*, 12 months from the end of financial year in which requisition under section 132A was executed, as per the amended provisions of section 153B. The years covered under section 153A for making assessments are the assessment years 2010-11 to assessment year 2015-16. The process of making the assessment under section 153A can be initiated by the Assessing Officer by serving notice for filing the returns as required under section 153A(*a*) at any time after the requisition was made *i.e.*, 10th of March 2016. It will result into a situation when the process of assessment initiated at any time after 10th of March 2016 may remain pending and may be completed till 31st March 2021. Moreover in case the process of initiating assessment proceedings under section 153A is initiated late, say, in the year 2019, assessments will still be required to be made under section 153A for the assessment year 2010-11 to assessment year 2015-16. This is also not reasonable and as per legislative intent to make assessments for a period beyond 8 years for which assessee may not be keeping complete records available with him due to operation of time limit prescribed under Rule 6F.

Since the above anomaly is emerging in the interpretation of the proceeding for assessment to be undertaken as per provision of sections 153A and 153B in the case of requisition under section 132A, it is desired that suitable clarification/amendment is made in the legislation so as to avoid unnecessary litigation on this issue.

(*v*) Nature of assessment proceeding in case of requisition under section 132A

For making assessment for preceding six years under section 153A in the case of requisition under section 132A, the same rationale and principles would be applicable as are applicable for making assessment in the case of search under section 153A/153C. Provision of section 153D would also be applicable and assessments framed under section 153A in case of requisition under section 132A shall be passed by the Assessing Officer after getting prior approval of the Joint Commissioner.

(*vi*) Applicability of provision of section 292C regarding presumption

Provision of section 292C regarding presumption with respect to books of account, other documents or assets to be applied during assessment proceedings is available to the Assessing Officer in the case of requisitioned assets under section 132A in the same manner as the seized assets under section 132(1). Sub-section (2) has been specifically inserted under section 292C providing the above provision with respect to this fact from 1.10.1975. All the principles and issues discussed in the chapter of section 132(4A) and section 292C would be relevant and applicable in the case of requisitioned assets in the same manner.

(*vii*) **Application and release of requisitioned assets**

The assets requisitioned under section 132A are treated at par as if seized under section 132(1) in the case of search. The provision of section 132B regarding retention, application and release of the seized assets are equally applicable in case of the assets requisitioned under section 132A.

Once seized goods are handed over to the income tax authorities in consequence to requisition made by them under section 132A, further release of such assets can be made by the concerned income tax authorities to the persons from whose possession goods were seized or to the persons who are the owner of such assets. In the case of *Patel Rajesh Kumar Arvind Kumar* v. *Union of India* [2010] 33 DTR 230 (Delhi), Police having seized unexplained silver/gold jewellery, bricks and gold biscuits from three persons and later handed over the same to the IT Department pursuant to a warrant of authorization under section 132A(1) and the entire record having been sent to the jurisdictional CITs of the alleged owners of the goods, present claimants of the goods are advised to move an application before the jurisdictional authority for the release of goods and the concerned Assessing Officer is directed to deal with the same and pass appropriate orders thereupon.

In the case of *Wakil Kumar* v. *CIT* [2004] 134 Taxman 733 (Pat.), it was held that question as to whether the petitioner was the owner of the money or not, could not be gone into by the High Court in writ jurisdiction

(*viii*) **Provision of section 153C may also be applicable for requisitioned assets**

The requisitioned assets may belong to some other person instead to the person from whose possession or control the same were seized by the other Government Authority/Officer and later on requisitioned by the Income Tax Department. In case during assessment proceedings under section 153A, Assessing Officer finds that the requisitioned assets belong to some other person, he may handover such assets or books of account etc. to the Assessing Officer of such other person and the provision of section 153C shall become applicable with respect to such other person in the same manner as the same are applicable in the case of seized assets during search under section 132.

However, in the case of *Smt. Mithilesh Kumari Jain* v. *CIT* [1993] 70 Taxman 448, Allahabad High Court directed to release seized assets when it was found that the same were belonging to the wife and mother of assessee and the facts of that case were—

During investigation of criminal case under Prevention of Corruption Act, 1988, against N, Jewellery and cash were recovered from N. Same were requisitioned and taken possession of by IT Authorities under section 132A. On enquiry, IT Authorities came to conclusion that assets belong to wife and mother of N. Assets were not subject matter of criminal case against N. In such circumstance, IT Authorities should not hesitate in passing appropriate orders for release of assets. IT Authorities were directed to do so.

(*ix*) Whether provision of section 153A would be applicable when requisition is made but actual delivery of seized material is not handed over to the requisitioning officer

When books of account, documents or other assets are taken into custody by any Government Authority or Officer, they first make use of such seized material to examine and investigate violation from the point of view of the respective law under which books of account, documents or assets were seized by them. They are not supposed to handover delivery of such material to the Income Tax Department immediately as soon as requisition is received by them from the Income Tax Authorities. Under sub-section (2) of section 132A it is clearly mentioned that such other authority or officer shall deliver the books of account, other documents or assets to the requisitioning officer either forthwith or when such officer or authority is of the opinion that it is no longer necessary to retain the same in his or its custody. There may be cases when other Government Authority or Officer confiscates the seized material within the provisions of respective law under which action was taken by him and he does not deliver such seized material to the Income Tax Authorities.

Under such a situation, a question may arise whether Income Tax Department can still take action for making assessment for preceding six years in accordance with the provision of section 153A. As per plain reading of section 153A, triggering point for making assessment under section 153A is when requisition is made and requisition can be said to be made when it is served to the other Government Authority/Officer. In the absence of original seized material and assets, certified copies of the same may be obtained by the requisitioning officer from the other Government Authority/Officer and further action including action under section 153A may be initiated. Non-receipt of seized assets by the Income Tax Authorities may preclude them from getting security against tax liabilities but it cannot preclude them from making assessment and taking action under section 153A of the Act.

However, Courts are having contradictory views on the above issue. In the case of *Asstt. CIT* v. *Sonu Verma* [2008] 115 ITD 37 (Asr. - Trib.) (SB), the Special Bench of ITAT has held that jurisdiction to complete block assessment under section 158BC is conferred on the assessing officer only on the physical handing over of all the books of account/ documents/assets requisitioned under sec. 132A to the income tax authorities concerned. The special bench followed the judgments of *Amandeep Singh* v. *DIT (Investigation)* [2002] 121 Taxman 110 (Punj. & Har.) and *Chandra Prakash Agrawal* v. *State of Rajasthan* [1994] 76 Taxman 559 (Raj.). The Tribunal impliedly disapproved the view in *Jageshwar Rosin & Turpentine Factory* v. *Asstt. CIT* [2006] 100 ITD 399 (Delhi - Trib.) case and distinguished the view taken in *Smt. Mahesh Kumari Batra* v. *Jt. CIT* [2005] 95 ITD 152/146 Taxman 67 (Mag.) (Asr. - Trib.) (SB) as it refers to initiation of search under section 132.

In our considered opinion and with due respect, the above view is liable to further judicial test and reconsideration.

(x) Delay in issuing requisition

When books of account, other documents or assets are seized by other Government Authorities/Officers, intimation may be sent to the Income Tax Authorities for taking action under section 132A of the Income Tax Act. At times, it has been noted that the Income Tax Authorities do not initiate action under section 132A even after lapse of considerable time or years together. It may be due to carelessness or for the reason that satisfaction could not be arrived and recorded in the manner as required under section 132A. One can understand non-action by Income Tax Authorities under section 132A when satisfaction could not be arrived but in practice, reason of delay generally remains red tapism. Later on when reminder is given or more pressure is put by the other Government Authority, authorization for requisition is issued in a mechanical manner. In case there has been considerable delay in issuing authorization for requisition, assessee may have filed its return of income by then disclosing all the facts and assets which were seized by other Government Authority/Officer. Issue of authorization of requisition in such a case without verifying whether the requisitioned assets have already been disclosed by the assessee in his return of income already filed may be quashed on the ground of the fact that it stands already disclosed in the return of income.

In one of the cases, gold bars of 20 kg. were seized by the Enforcement Directorate from a bullion merchant for alleged violation of FEMA in the year 2014 relevant to A.Y. 2015-16. Intimation was sent to the Income Tax Authorities for taking action under section 132A but the same was not taken at that point of time. Assessee filed writ with the High Court against the Enforcement Directorate alleging that the seizure was illegal. Further, assessee filed return of income for A. Y. 2015-16 disclosing all the assets seized by the Enforcement Directorate in his return of income filed in the regular course. In the year 2018, Income Tax Department issued requisition under section 132A and obtained delivery of the seized material. Authorization for requisition was issued without even verifying that assessee had already disclosed the seized assets in his return of income for A. Y. 2015-16 filed. Such authorization for requisition under section 132A cannot be said to be valid and is liable to be quashed.

Under such a situation when assessee had already declared the requisitioned asset in the return of income filed by him & taxes paid thereon, no concealment of income can be attributed to the assessee as deeming fiction of undisclosed income as contemplated under section 271AAA/271AAB is not applicable in the case of requisition u/s 132A.

11.9 Illegal seizure by other Government authority/officer

There may be cases when books of account, other documents or assets are taken into custody by the Police Officers, Enforcement Directorate, Excise or Custom Authorities etc. There may be irregularities in seizure of assets by such authorities. There may be cases when seizure of assets by such authorities is not made in compliance with the provisions of respective statutes under which assets were taken into custody by them or for any other reason, assets were not seized by them in a lawful manner. Under such circumstances Courts may pass an order for release of books of account, other documents or assets seized by such authorities and the seizure may be declared as illegal.

Action of seizure of other Government Authorities/Officers having been declared illegal by the Courts does not preclude the Income Tax Authorities to take action of requisition under section 132A. In case the conditions regarding forming reason to believe in consequence of information in possession with respect to undisclosed income under the Income Tax Act as provided under sub-section (1) of section 132A are fulfilled, Income Tax Authorities can still take action under section 132A for requisition of seized material.

In the case of *Rajiv Agrawal, Dy. DIT* v. *State of Gujarat* [2006] 154 Taxman 172 (Guj.) Gujarat High Court reversed the decision of Trial Court and permitted requisition by the Income Tax Authorities inspite of the fact that the seizure of cash made by police was not in violation of CrPC and police had not made any report that the amount was received through illegal activities.

It has been held in the case of *Indian Traders* v. *State of Bihar* [2019] 417 ITR 95 (Patna) that where cash was seized under guidelines issued by Election Commission but Election Commission finding that seizure was not valid, Income-tax authorities had no jurisdiction to requisition such cash.

(*i*) **Validity of action under section 132A - Whether can be examined by ITAT**

In the case of *Gaya Prasad Pathak* v. *Asstt. CIT* [2007] 162 Taxman 307 (MP), it was held that validity of requisition under section 132A cannot be decided by the Tribunal in an appeal under section 253. Whether the order passed by CIT under section 132A is without jurisdiction or not cannot be the subject-matter of assessment and hence neither the A.O. nor the appellate authority can dwell upon the said fact.

It has been held in the case of *Shiv Tiwari & Ors.* v. *Principal Director of IT (Inv.) & Anr.* 305 CTR 307 (Raj)/171 DTR 209 (Raj) that Information in respect of any action which is required to be taken under section 132A and which comes in the exclusive possession of an officer, is not required to be divulged on merely asking of a person & money which has been seized by the police can always be claimed by the petitioner, after the Income Tax Department concludes its proceedings, which have been initiated by issuing notice to the petitioner.

NEW ASSESSMENT OR RE-ASSESSMENT SCHEME OF SEARCH CASES AS INTRO-DUCED BY THE FINANCE ACT, 2021

12.1 Background

Finance Act, 2021 has made complete change in the scheme of the assessment & reassessment of income tax search cases. The special provision of assessment of search cases provided under sections 153A to 153D have been done away with & such provisions would not be applicable in the cases of income tax search held after 31st March, 2021.

As per the amendments introduced by the Finance Act, 2021, assessment or reassessment of search cases shall be done as per the normal provisions of the Act as contained in sections 143, 144, 147 to 153 of the Act. Some of these sections have also been amended along with the insertion of new section 148A making over all changes in the scheme of the assessment or reassessment of income tax cases in normal circumstances along with the search & survey cases.

Finance Act, 2022 and Finance Act, 2023 have made certain amendments in these provisions which have been discussed at relevant places in this chapter.

Income escaping assessment.

> **147.** *If any income chargeable to tax, in the case of an assessee, has escaped assessment for any assessment year, the Assessing Officer may, subject to the provisions of sections 148 to 153, assess or reassess such income or recompute the loss or the depreciation allowance or any other allowance or*

deduction for such assessment year (hereafter in this section and in sections 148 to 153 referred to as the relevant assessment year).

Explanation.—*For the purposes of assessment or reassessment or recomputation under this section, the Assessing Officer may assess or reassess the income in respect of any issue, which has escaped assessment, and such issue comes to his notice subsequently in the course of the proceedings under this section, irrespective of the fact that the provisions of section 148A have not been complied with.*

Issue of notice where income has escaped assessment.

148. *Before making the assessment, reassessment or recomputation under section 147, and subject to the provisions of section 148A, the Assessing Officer shall serve on the assessee a notice, along with a copy of the order passed, if required, under clause (d) of section 148A, requiring him to furnish within* a period of three months from the end of the month in which such notice is issued, or such further period as may be allowed by the Assessing Officer on the basis of an application made in this regard by the assessee, *a return of his income or the income of any other person in respect of which he is assessable under this Act during the previous year corresponding to the relevant assessment year, in the prescribed form and verified in the prescribed manner and setting forth such other particulars as may be prescribed; and the provisions of this Act shall, so far as may be, apply accordingly as if such return were a return required to be furnished under section 139:*

Provided *that no notice under this section shall be issued unless there is information with the Assessing Officer which suggests that the income chargeable to tax has escaped assessment in the case of the assessee for the relevant assessment year and the Assessing Officer has obtained prior approval of the specified authority to issue such notice:*

Provided further *that no such approval shall be required where the Assessing Officer, with the prior approval of the specified authority, has passed an order under clause (d) of section 148A to the effect that it is a fit case to issue a notice under this section:*

Provided also *that any return of income, required to be furnished by an assessee under this section and furnished beyond the period allowed shall not be deemed to be a return under section 139.*

Explanation 1.—*For the purposes of this section and section 148A, the information with the Assessing Officer which suggests that the income chargeable to tax has escaped assessment means,—*

   (i) *any information in the case of the assessee for the relevant assessment year in accordance with the risk management strategy formulated by the Board from time to time; or*

  (ii) *any audit objection to the effect that the assessment in the case of the assessee for the relevant assessment year has not been made in accordance with the provisions of this Act; or*

 (iii) *any information received under an agreement referred to in section 90 or section 90A of the Act; or*

(iv) *any information made available to the Assessing Officer under the scheme notified under section 135A; or*

(v) *any information which requires action in consequence of the order of a Tribunal or a Court.*

Explanation 2.—For the purposes of this section, where,—

  (i) *a search is initiated under section 132 or books of account, other documents or any assets are requisitioned under section 132A, on or after the 1st day of April, 2021, in the case of the assessee; or*

  (ii) *a survey is conducted under section 133A, other than under sub-section (2A) of that section, on or after the 1st day of April, 2021, in the case of the assessee; or*

  (iii) *the Assessing Officer is satisfied, with the prior approval of the Principal Commissioner or Commissioner, that any money, bullion, jewellery or other valuable article or thing, seized or requisitioned under section 132 or section 132A in case of any other person on or after the 1st day of April, 2021, belongs to the assessee; or*

  (iv) *the Assessing Officer is satisfied, with the prior approval of Principal Commissioner or Commissioner, that any books of account or documents, seized or requisitioned under section 132 or section 132A in case of any other person on or after the 1st day of April, 2021, pertains or pertain to, or any information contained therein, relate to, the assessee,*

the Assessing Officer shall be deemed to have information which suggests that the income chargeable to tax has escaped assessment in the case of the assessee where the search is initiated or books of account, other documents or any assets are requisitioned or survey is conducted in the case of the assessee or money, bullion, jewellery or other valuable article or thing or books of account or documents are seized or requisitioned in case of any other person.

Explanation 3.—For the purposes of this section, specified authority means the specified authority referred to in section 151.

Conducting inquiry, providing opportunity before issue of notice under section 148.

148A. *The Assessing Officer shall, before issuing any notice under section 148,—*

(a) *conduct any enquiry, if required, with the prior approval of specified authority, with respect to the information which suggests that the income chargeable to tax has escaped assessment;*

(b) *provide an opportunity of being heard to the assessee, by serving upon him a notice to show cause within such time, as may be specified in the notice, being not less than seven days and but not exceeding thirty days from the date on which such notice is issued, or such time, as may be extended by him on the basis of an application in this behalf, as to why a notice under section 148 should not be issued on the basis of information which suggests that income chargeable to tax has escaped assessment in his case for the relevant assessment year and results of enquiry conducted, if any, as per clause (a);*

(c) *consider the reply of assessee furnished, if any, in response to the show-cause notice referred to in clause (b);*

(d) *decide, on the basis of material available on record including reply of the assessee, whether or not it is a fit case to issue a notice under section 148, by passing an order, with the prior approval of specified authority, within one month from the end of the month in which the reply referred to in clause (c) is received by him, or where no such reply is furnished, within one month from the end of the month in which time or extended time allowed to furnish a reply as per clause (b) expires:*

Provided *that the provisions of this section shall not apply in a case where,—*

(a) *a search is initiated under section 132 or books of account, other documents or any assets are requisitioned under section 132A in the case of the assessee on or after the 1st day of April, 2021; or*

(b) *the Assessing Officer is satisfied, with the prior approval of the Principal Commissioner or Commissioner that any money, bullion, jewellery or other valuable article or thing, seized in a search under section 132 or requisitioned under section 132A, in the case of any other person on or after the 1st day of April, 2021, belongs to the assessee; or*

(c) *the Assessing Officer is satisfied, with the prior approval of the Principal Commissioner or Commissioner that any books of account or documents, seized in a search under section 132 or requisitioned under section 132A, in case of any other person on or after the 1st day of April, 2021, pertains or pertain to, or any information contained therein, relate to, the assessee; or*

(d) *the Assessing Officer has received any information under the scheme notified under section 135A pertaining to income chargeable to tax escaping assessment for any assessment year in the case of the assessee.*

Explanation.—For the purposes of this section, specified authority means the specified authority referred to in section 151.

Prior approval for assessment, reassessment or recomputation in certain cases.

148B. *No order of assessment or reassessment or recomputation under this Act shall be passed by an Assessing Officer below the rank of Joint Commissioner, in respect of an assessment year to which clause (i) or clause (ii) or clause (iii) or clause (iv) of* Explanation 2 *to section 148 apply except with the prior approval of the Additional Commissioner or Additional Director or Joint Commissioner or Joint Director.*

Time limit for notice.

149. *(1) No notice under section 148 shall be issued for the relevant assessment year,—*

(a) *if three years have elapsed from the end of the relevant assessment year, unless the case falls under clause* (b);

(b) *if three years, but not more than ten years, have elapsed from the end of the relevant assessment year unless the Assessing Officer has in his possession books of account or other documents or evidence which reveal that the income chargeable to tax, represented in the form of—*

   (i) *an asset;*

   (ii) *expenditure in respect of a transaction or in relation to an event or occasion; or*

   (iii) *an entry or entries in the books of account,*

which has escaped assessment amounts to or is likely to amount to fifty lakh rupees or more:

Provided *that no notice under section 148 shall be issued at any time in a case for the relevant assessment year beginning on or before 1st day of April, 2021, if a notice under section 148 or section 153A or section 153C could not have been issued at that time on account of being beyond the time limit specified under the provisions of clause (b) of sub-section (1) of this section or section 153A or section 153C, as the case may be, as they stood immediately before the commencement of the Finance Act, 2021:*

Provided further *that the provisions of this sub-section shall not apply in a case, where a notice under section 153A, or section 153C read with section 153A, is required to be issued in relation to a search initiated under section 132 or books of account, other documents or any assets requisitioned under section 132A, on or before the 31st day of March, 2021:*

Provided also that for cases referred to in clauses *(i), (iii)* and *(iv)* of *Explanation 2* to section 148, where,—

   (*a*) a search is initiated under section 132; or

   (*b*) a search under section 132 for which the last of authorisations is executed; or

   (*c*) requisition is made under section 132A,

after the 15th day of March of any financial year and the period for issue of notice under section 148 expires on the 31st day of March of such financial year, a period of fifteen days shall be excluded for the purpose of computing the period of limitation as per this section and the notice issued under section 148 in such case shall be deemed to have been issued on the 31st day of March of such financial year:

Provided also that where the information as referred to in *Explanation 1* to section 148 emanates from a statement recorded or documents impounded under section 131 or section 133A, as the case may be, on or before the 31st day of March of a financial year, in consequence of,—

   (*a*) a search under section 132 which is initiated; or

(b) a search under section 132 for which the last of authorisations is executed; or

(c) a requisition made under section 132A,

after the 15th day of March of such financial year, a period of fifteen days shall be excluded for the purpose of computing the period of limitation as per this section and the notice issued under clause (b) of section 148A in such case shall be deemed to have been issued on the 31st day of March of such financial year:

Provided also that for the purposes of computing the period of limitation as per this section, the time or extended time allowed to the assessee, as per show-cause notice issued under clause (b) of section 148A or the period during which the proceeding under section 148A is stayed by an order or injunction of any court, shall be excluded:

Provided also that where immediately after the exclusion of the period referred to in the immediately preceding proviso, the period of limitation available to the Assessing Officer for passing an order under clause (d) of section 148A does not exceed seven days, such remaining period shall be extended to seven days and the period of limitation under this sub-section shall be deemed to be extended accordingly.

Explanation.—For the purposes of clause (b) of this sub-section, "asset" shall include immovable property, being land or building or both, shares and securities, loans and advances, deposits in bank account.

(1A) Notwithstanding anything contained in sub-section (1), where the income chargeable to tax represented in the form of an asset or expenditure in relation to an event or occasion of the value referred to in clause (b) of sub-section (1), has escaped the assessment and the investment in such asset or expenditure in relation to such event or occasion has been made or incurred, in more than one previous years relevant to the assessment years within the period referred to in clause (b) of sub-section (1), a notice under section 148 shall be issued for every such assessment year for assessment, reassessment or recomputation, as the case may be.

(2) The provisions of sub-section (1) as to the issue of notice shall be subject to the provisions of section 151.

Provision for cases where assessment is in pursuance of an order on appeal, etc.

150. (1) *Notwithstanding anything contained in section 149, the notice under section 148 may be issued at any time for the purpose of making an assessment or reassessment or recomputation in consequence of or to give effect to any finding or direction contained in an order passed by any authority in any proceeding under this Act by way of appeal, reference or revision or by a Court in any proceeding under any other law.*

(2) The provisions of sub-section (1) shall not apply in any case where any such assessment, reassessment or recomputation as is referred to in that sub-section relates to an assessment year in respect of which an assessment,

reassessment or recomputation could not have been made at the time the order which was the subject-matter of the appeal, reference or revision, as the case may be, was made by reason of any other provision limiting the time within which any action for assessment, reassessment or recomputation may be taken.

Sanction for issue of notice.

151. *Specified authority for the purposes of section 148 and section 148A shall be,—*

(i) *Principal Commissioner or Principal Director or Commissioner or Director, if three years or less than three years have elapsed from the end of the relevant assessment year;*

(ii) *Principal Chief Commissioner or Principal Director General or Chief Commissioner or Director General, if more than three years have elapsed from the end of the relevant assessment year:*

Provided that the period of three years for the purposes of clause (*i*) shall be computed after taking into account the period of limitation as excluded by the third or fourth or fifth provisos or extended by the sixth proviso to sub-section (1) of section 149.

Faceless assessment of income escaping assessment.

151A. *(1) The Central Government may make a scheme, by notification in the Official Gazette, for the purposes of assessment, reassessment or re-computation under section 147 or issuance of notice under section 148 or conducting of enquiries or issuance of show-cause notice or passing of order under section 148A or sanction for issue of such notice under section 151, so as to impart greater efficiency, transparency and accountability by—*

(a) *eliminating the interface between the income-tax authority and the assessee or any other person to the extent technologically feasible;*

(b) *optimising utilisation of the resources through economies of scale and functional specialisation;*

(c) *introducing a team-based assessment, reassessment, re-computation or issuance or sanction of notice with dynamic jurisdiction.*

(2) The Central Government may, for the purpose of giving effect to the scheme made under sub-section (1), by notification in the Official Gazette, direct that any of the provisions of this Act shall not apply or shall apply with such exceptions, modifications and adaptations as may be specified in the notification:

Provided that no direction shall be issued after the 31st day of March, 2022.

(3) Every notification issued under sub-section (1) and sub-section (2) shall, as soon as may be after the notification is issued, be laid before each House of Parliament.

12.1A Legislative history

Finance Act, 2021 re-enacted section 148 regarding issue of notice for assessment or reassessment of the escaped income. The scheme of assessment or reassessment in case of search is also to be governed by newly drafted sections 147 to 151A. *Explanation* 2 to section 148 provided *inte ralia* that it will be deemed in respect of preceding 3 years from the year of search that there was information suggesting escapement of income.

Finance Act, 2022 has amended *Explanation* 2 to section 148 by deleting the reference of 3 years and deeming fiction has thus been made applicable for all the assessment years involved in the search case.

Finance Act, 2023 has further amended sections 148, 149 & 151 which have been discussed elsewhere in this chapter.

12.2 Memorandum explaining the provisions of the Finance Bill, 2021

Memorandum explaining the provisions of the Finance Bill, 2021 is reproduced below which seeks to explain the purport and object of the amendments under consideration as under:

Income escaping assessment and search assessments

Under the Act, the provisions related to income escaping assessment provide that if the Assessing Officer has reason to believe that any income chargeable to tax has escaped assessment for any assessment year, he may assess or reassess or re-compute the total income for such year under section 147 of the Act by issuing a notice under section 148 of the Act. However, such reopening is subject to the time limits prescribed in section 149 of the Act.

In cases where search is initiated u/s 132 of the Act or books of account, other documents or any assets are requisitioned under section 132A of the Act, assessment is made in the case of the assessee, or any other person, in accordance with the special provisions of sections 153A, 153B, 153C and 153D, of the Act that deal specifically with such cases. These provisions were introduced by the Finance Act, 2003 to replace the block assessment under Chapter XIV-B of the Act. This was done due to failure of block assessment in its objective of early resolution of search assessments. Also, the procedural issues related to block assessment were proving to be highly litigation-prone. However, the experience with this procedure has been no different. Like the provisions for block assessment, these provisions have also resulted in a number of litigations.

Due to advancement of technology, the department is now collecting all relevant information related to transactions of taxpayers from third parties under section 285BA of the Act (statement of financial transaction or reportable account). Similarly, information is also received from other law enforcement agencies. This information is also shared with the taxpayer through Annual Information Statement under section 285BB of the Act. Department uses this information to verify the information declared by a taxpayer in the return and to detect non-filers or those who have not disclosed the correct amount of total income. Therefore, assessment or reassessment or re-computation of income escaping assessment, to a large extent, is information-driven.

In view of above, there is a need to completely reform the system of assessment or reassessment or re-computation of income escaping assessment and the assessment of search related cases.

The Bill proposes a completely new procedure of assessment of such cases. It is expected that the new system would result in less litigation and would provide ease of doing business to taxpayers as there is a reduction in time limit by which a notice for assessment or reassessment or re-computation can be issued. The salient features of new procedure are as under:-

   (*i*) The provisions of section 153A and section 153C, of the Act are proposed to be made applicable to only search initiated under section 132 of the Act or books of account, other documents or any assets requisitioned under section 132A of the Act, on or before 31st March 2021.

  (*ii*) Assessments or reassessments or in re-computation in cases where search is initiated under section 132 or requisition is made under 132A, after 31st March 2021, shall be under the new procedure.

 (*iii*) Section 147 proposes to allow the Assessing Officer to assess or reassess or re-compute any income escaping assessment for any assessment year (called relevant assessment year).

 (*iv*) Before such assessment or reassessment or re-computation, a notice is required to be issued under section 148 of the Act, which can be issued only when there is information with the Assessing Officer which suggests that the income chargeable to tax has escaped assessment in the case of the assessee for the relevant assessment year. Prior approval of specified authority is also required to be obtained before issuance of such notice by the Assessing Officer.

  (*v*) It is proposed to provide that any information which has been flagged in the case of the assessee for the relevant assessment year in accordance with the risk management strategy formulated by the Board shall be considered as information which suggests that the income chargeable to tax has escaped assessment. The flagging would largely be done by the computer based system.

(*vi*) Further, a final objection raised by the Comptroller and Auditor General of India to the effect that the assessment in the case of the assessee for the relevant assessment year has not been in accordance with the provisions of the Act shall also be considered as information which suggests that the income chargeable to tax has escaped assessment.

(*vii*) Further, in search, survey or requisition cases initiated or made or conducted, on or after 1st April, 2021, it shall be deemed that the Assessing Officer has information which suggests that the income chargeable to tax has escaped assessment in the case of the assessee for the three assessment years immediately preceding the assessment year relevant to the previous year in which the search is initiated or requisition is made or any material is seized or requisitioned or survey is conducted.

(*viii*) New Section 148A of the Act proposes that before issuance of notice the Assessing Officer shall conduct enquiries, if required, and provide an opportunity of being heard to the assessee. After considering his reply, the Assessing Officer shall decide, by passing an order, whether it is a fit case for issue of notice under section 148 and serve a copy of such order along with such notice on the assessee. The Assessing Officer shall before conducting any such enquiries or providing opportunity to the assessee or passing such order obtain the approval of specified authority. However, this procedure of enquiry, providing opportunity and passing order, before issuing notice under section 148 of the Act, shall not be applicable in search or requisition cases.

(*ix*) The time limitation for issuance of notice under section 148 of the Act is proposed to be provided in section 149 of the Act and is as below:

◆ In normal cases, no notice shall be issued if three years have elapsed from the end of the relevant assessment year. Notice beyond the period of three years from the end of the relevant assessment year can be taken only in a few specific cases.

◆ In specific cases where the Assessing Officer has in his possession evidence which reveal that the income escaping assessment, represented in the form of asset, amounts to or is likely to amount to fifty lakh rupees or more, notice can be issued beyond the period of three year but not beyond the period of ten years from the end of the relevant assessment year;

◆ Another restriction has been provided that the notice under section 148 of the Act cannot be issued at any time in a case for the relevant assessment year beginning on or before 1st day of April, 2021, if such notice could not have been issued at that time on account of being beyond the time limit prescribed under the provisions of clause (*b*), as they stood immediately before the proposed amendment.

◆ Since the assessment or reassessment or re-computation in search or requisition cases (where such search or requisition is initiated or made on or before 31st March 2021) are to be carried out as per the provision of sections 153A, 153B, 153C and 153D of the Act, the aforesaid time limitation shall not apply to such cases.

◆ It is also proposed that for the purposes of computing the period of limitation for issue of section 148 notice, the time or extended time allowed to the assessee in providing opportunity of being heard or period during which such proceedings before issuance of notice under section 148 are stayed by an order or injunction of any court, shall be excluded. If after excluding such period, time available to the Assessing Officer for passing order, about fitness of a case for issue of section 148 notice, is less than seven days, the remaining time shall be extended to seven days.

(*x*) The specified authority for approving enquiries, providing opportunity, passing order under section 148A of the Act and for issuance of notice under section 148 of the Act are proposed to be -

  (*a*) Principal Commissioner or Principal Director or Commissioner or Director, if three years or less than three years have elapsed from the end of the relevant assessment year;

  (*b*) Principal Chief Commissioner or Principal Director General or where there is no Principal Chief Commissioner or Principal Director General, Chief Commissioner or Director General, if more than three years have elapsed from the end of the relevant assessment year.

(*xi*) Once assessment or reassessment or re-computation has started the Assessing Officer is proposed to be empowered (as at present) to assess or reassess the income in respect of any issue which has escaped assessment and which comes to his notice subsequently in the course of the proceeding under this procedure notwithstanding that the procedure prescribed in section 148A was not followed before issuing such notice for such income.

These amendments will take effect from 1st April, 2021.

[Clauses 35 to 40 and 42 to 43]

12.3 Memorandum explaining the provisions of the Finance Bill, 2022

Rationalization of provisions relating to assessment and reassessment

The Finance Act, 2021 amended the procedure for assessment or reassessment of income in the Act with effect from the 1st April, 2021. The said amendment modified, *inter alia*, section 147, section 148, section 149 and also introduced a new section 148A in the Act. In cases where search is initiated under section 132 of the Act or books of account, other documents or any assets are requisitioned under section 132A of the Act, on or after 1st April, 2021, assessment or reassessment is now made under section 143 or 144 or 147 of the Act after the Finance Act, 2021.

2. As part of the government's policy related to simplification of procedures under the Act, it is proposed to—

(*i*) insert a new proviso to the effect that requirement for approval to issue notice under section 148 shall not be required to be taken by the Assessing Officer if he has passed an order under 148A(*d*) with prior approval in that case stating that the income is escaping assessment.

(*ii*) to omit the requirement of approval of specified authority in clause (*b*) of section 148A.

These amendments will take effect from 1st April, 2022.

3. To correct the inadvertent drafting errors and align the provisions with the intent of the section, following amendments are proposed,

(*i*) in section 148 to omit the word flagged from clause (*i*) of *Explanation 1*,

(*ii*) in clause (*ii*) of *Explanation 2* to section 148 to omit the reference of sub-section (5) of section 133A made therein.

These amendments will take effect from 1st April, 2022.

(*iii*) in *Explanation 2* of section 148 to omit the reference to three assessment years preceding the assessment year relevant to the year of search;

(*iv*) in section 153B by inserting sub-section (4) to provide that nothing contained in the said section shall apply to any search initiated under section 132 or requisition made under section 132A on or after the 1st day of April, 2021.

(*v*) in the first proviso of sub-section (1) of section 149 to provide that no notice under section 148 shall be issued at any time in a case for the relevant assessment year beginning on or before 1st day of April, 2021, if a notice under section 148 or section 153A or section 153C could not have been issued at that time on account of being beyond the time limit specified under the provisions of clause (*b*) of sub-section (1) of section 149 or section 153A or section 153C, as the case may be, as they stood immediately before the commencement of the Finance Act, 2021.

These amendments will take effect retrospectively from 1st April, 2021.

4. In order to align the scheme of search assessments with the intent of the Act, it is proposed to—

(*i*) amend sub-section (8) of section 132 to make the provisions of that section also applicable to assessment or reassessment or recomputation under sub-section (3) of 143 or section 144 or section 147, as the case may be,

(*ii*) amend clause (*i*) of sub-section (1) and sub-section (4) of section 132B to provide that these provisions shall also apply to assessment or reassessment or recomputation.

These amendments will take effect from 1 st April, 2022.

(*iii*) insert a new section 148B to provide that no order of assessment or reassessment or recomputation under the Act shall be passed by an Assessing Officer below the rank of Joint Commissioner, except with the prior approval of the Additional Commissioner or Additional Director or Joint Commissioner or Joint Director, in respect of assessments consequent to search, survey and requisition to reduce avoidable inaccuracies.

This amendment will take effect from 1st April, 2022.

(*iv*) amend section 153, by inserting a new clause to provide for exclusion of the period of limitation for the purpose of assessment, reassessment or recomputation, (not exceeding one hundred eighty days) commencing from the date on which a search is initiated under section 132 or a requisition is made under section 132A and ending on the date on which the books of account or other documents, or any money, bullion, jewellery or other valuable article or thing seized under section 132 or requisitioned under section 132A, as the case may be, are handed over to the Assessing Officer having jurisdiction over the assessee, in whose case such search is initiated or such requisition is made or to whom any money, bullion, jewellery or other valuable article or thing seized or requisitioned belongs to or to whom any books of account or documents seized or requisitioned, pertains or pertain to, or any information contained therein, relates to ;

(*v*) amend section 153B, by inserting a new clause to provide for exclusion of the period (not exceeding one hundred eighty days) commencing from the date on which a search is initiated under section 132 or a requisition is made under section 132A and ending on the date on which the books of account or other documents, or any money, bullion, jewellery or other valuable article or thing seized under section 132 or requisitioned under section 132A, as the case may be, are handed over to the Assessing Officer having jurisdiction over the assessee, in whose case such search is initiated under section 132 or such requisition is made under section 132A.

These amendments will take effect retrospectively from lst April, 2021.

(*vi*) amend the definition of "specified date" in clause (*a*) *Explanation* to section 271AAB to make it also applicable to a notice issued under section 148 in case where search is initiated on or after 1st April, 2021.

This amendment will take effect from l st April, 2022.

5. In order to bring clarification in the existing provisions and to align them with the intent of the Act, it is proposed to—

(*i*) clarify what constitutes information under *Explanation 1* to section 148 so as to include any audit objection, or any information received from a foreign jurisdiction under an agreement or directions contained in a court order, or information received under a scheme notified under section 135A etc.

(*ii*) to amend the clause (*b*) of sub-section (1) of the section 149 to provide that a notice under section 148 shall be issued only for the relevant assessment year after three years but prior to ten years from the end of the relevant assessment year where the Assessing Officer has in his possession books of account or other documents or evidence which reveal that the income chargeable to tax, represented,

(*a*) in the form of an asset; or

(*b*) expenditure in respect of a transaction or in relation to an event or occasion; or

(*c*) an entry or entries in the books of account,

which has escaped assessment amounts to or likely to amount to fifty lakh rupees or more.

(*iii*) insert a new sub-section (1A) in section 149 to provide that notwithstanding anything contained in sub-section (1) of the said section, where the income chargeable to tax represented in the form of an asset or expenditure in relation to an event or occasion of the value referred to in clause (*b*) of sub-section (1) of the said section, has escaped assessment and the investment in such asset or expenditure in relation to such event or occasion has been made or incurred, in more than one previous years relevant to the assessment years within the period referred to in clause (*b*) of sub-section (1) of the said section, notice under section 148 shall be issued for every such assessment year for assessment, reassessment or recomputation, as the case may be.

(*iv*) to provide that the provisions of the section 148A shall not apply in cases where the Assessing Officer has received any information regarding the scheme notified under section 135A, pertaining to income chargeable to tax escaping assessment for any assessment year in the case of the assessee.

These amendments will take effect from lst April, 2022.

[Clauses 35, 36, 44, 45, 46, 47, 48, 49 and 73]

12.4 Memorandum explaining the provisions of the Finance Bill, 2023

Provisions relating to reassessment proceedings

The Finance Act, 2021 amended the procedure for assessment or reassessment of income in the Act with effect from the 1st April, 2021. The said amendment modified, *inter alia*, section 147, section 148, section 149 and also introduced a new section 148A in the Act. In cases where search is initiated under section 132 of the Act or books of account, other documents or any assets are requisitioned under section 132A of the Act, assessment or reassessment is now made under section 147 of the Act for all the relevant years prior to the year in which the search was conducted or requisition was made after the Finance Act, 2021. Further, the provisions of re-assessment proceedings were rationalized by amendments made *vide* Finance Act, 2022.

2. Amendments have been proposed in the provisions relating to conduct of reassessment proceedings under the Act to further streamline them and facilitate their conduct and completion in a seamless manner. It has been proposed that the section 148 of the Act may be amended to provide that a return in response to a notice under section 148 of the Act shall be furnished within three months from the end of the month in which such notice is issued, or within such further time as may be allowed by the Assessing Officer on a request made in this behalf by the assessee. However, any return which is furnished beyond the period allowed in the section 148 to furnish such return of income shall not be deemed to be a return under section 139 of the Act. As a result, the consequential requirements *viz.* notice under sub-section (2) of section 143 etc. would not be mandatory for such returns.

3. Further, section 149 of the Act provides the period of limitation for issuance of notice under section 148 of the Act for commencement of

proceedings under section 147 of the Act. It is imperative to note here that in case of a search action under section 132 of the Act, requisition under section 132A of the Act and cases for which information emanates from the above proceedings are deemed to be information under section 149 of the Act and there is no requirement for proceedings under section 148A of the Act to be conducted prior to re-opening the cases in these cases.

4. In cases where survey under section 133A of the Act is conducted, the Assessing Officer is deemed to have information for the purposes of section 148 of the Act but proceedings under section 148A of the Act need to be conducted prior to issuance of notice under section 148 of the Act. It has been seen that in the cases where the aforementioned search, requisition or survey proceedings are conducted after 15th March of a financial year, there is extremely little time to collate this information and issue a notice under section 148 or show cause notice under section 148A(*b*) of the Act. Moreover, the search is conducted by the Investigation Wing and the notice is required to be issued by the Assessing Officers.

5. However, evidence of tax evasion may be reflected in the statements recorded or documents seized or impounded etc. during such action before 31st March, but issuance of notice related to such information or search may go beyond the time limitation provided due to the procedure involved. Therefore, important information related to revenue leakage cannot be proceeded on due to the paucity of time for searched conducted and information obtained as a consequence of these searches in the last few days of any financial year. Accordingly, it has been proposed to insert a proviso in the said section to provide that in cases where a search under section 132 is initiated or a search for which the last of the authorization is executed or requisition is made under section 132A, after the 15th March of any financial year a period of fifteen days shall be excluded for the purpose of computing the period of limitation for issuance of notice under section 148 and the notice so issued shall be deemed to have been issued on the 31st day of March of such financial year.

6. It is also proposed to insert another proviso in the section 149 of the Act to provide that in cases where the information deemed to be with the Assessing Officer emanates from a statement recorded or documents impounded under summons or survey, as the case may be, on or before the 31st day of March of a financial year, in consequence of, a search 44 initiated or last of the authorization executed under section 132 or a requisition made under section 132A, after the 15th day of March of such financial year, a period of fifteen days shall be excluded for the purpose of computing the period of limitation for issuance of notice under section 148 and the show cause notice issued under clause (*b*) of section 148A in such case shall be deemed to have been issued on the 31st day of March of such financial

year. It has also been provided that the impounding or the recording of the statement in consequence of the search or the search itself should be before the 31st March only. Only extension has been provided for the time consumed in the procedure for issuance of notice under section 148 or 148A, as the case may be.

7. Section 151 of the Act contains provisions relating to the specified authority who can grant approval for the purposes of sections 148 and 148A of the Act. The said section provided that the authority would be the Principal Chief Commissioner and where there is no Principal Chief Commissioner, the Chief Commissioner shall give approvals beyond a period of three years.

8. It was seen that the clause (*ii*) of the said section was resulting in mis-interpretation as well as confusion with regards to the specified authority for the cases where re-opening was being done after three years from the relevant assessment year. Therefore, to clarify the position of law in this regard, an amendment has been proposed to provide that the specified authority under clause (*ii*) of section 151 of the Act shall be Principal Chief Commissioner or Principal Director General or Chief Commissioner or Director General.

9. At the same time, to give further clarity with regards to the specified authority a proviso is proposed to be inserted in the section 151 to provide that while computing the period of three years for the purposes of determining the specified authority the period which has been excluded or extended as per the provisos in section 149 of the Act from the time limit for issuance of notice under section 148 of the Act shall be taken into account.

10. These amendments will take effect from the 1st day of April, 2023.

[Clauses 69, 70 & 71]

12.5 Salient Features of the amendments relating to assessment or reassessment of search cases:

1. Special provisions of assessment and reassessment in search cases as provided under section 153A to section 153D of the Act shall remain applicable in the cases of search held on or before 31st March, 2021. In the case of income tax search to be held on or after 1st April, 2021, assessment or reassessment of such search cases shall be governed by the amended provisions as contained under sections 147 to 151A.

2. In the case of search, it has been provided by the Finance Act, 2021 that there would be mandatory reopening of the assessment of pre-ceding three years prior to the year of search. The provisions have been drafted in such a manner so as to give the interpretation that such reopening is mandatorily required even if no evidence regarding

income escaping assessment relating to such three years have been found during search. However, before issuing notice under section 148, prior approval of the 'specified authority' as provided under section 151(*i*) would be required to be obtained in such cases.

Explanation 2 to section 148 has also been amended by the Finance Act, 2022 and it has been provided that in case of search, survey etc. the assessing officer shall be deemed to have information which suggests that the income chargeable to tax has escaped assessment in the case of the assessee. Prior to amendment of this Explanation by the Finance Act, 2022, such deeming fiction was only for three assessment years immediately preceding the assessment year relevant to the previous year in which the search is initiated. By removing the reference to 3 assessment years, this deeming fiction has been extended for reopening of the cases for all the years up to 10 years from the end of the relevant assessment year.

Therefore, in view of the amended *Explanation* 2 to section 148, the nature of information for reopening of the cases as given in *Explanation* 1 is not relevant for the search cases. However, the conditions as given in section 149(1)(*b*) for reopening the cases beyond 3 assessment years up to 10 assessment years are required to be fulfilled.

3. Provisions of reopening of income tax assessments under section 147 have been amended to provide *inter alia* that no notice for reopening shall be issued if three years have elapsed from the end of the relevant assessment year in normal cases. However, in certain specific cases notice for reopening can be issued up to a period of prior 10 years from the end of the relevant assessment year. Such reopening for earlier 10 years' cases is provided where the Assessing Officer has in his possession evidence which reveal that the income escaping assessment, represented in the form of asset, amounts to or is likely to amount to fifty lakh rupees or more.

Reopening of assessment beyond three years can thus be done as provided by newly drafted section 149(1)(*b*) when Assessing Officer is in his possession books of account or other documents or evidence which reveal that the income chargeable to tax, represented in the form of asset, has escaped assessment. The phraseology *"represented in the form of asset"* needs interpretation which has been discussed later in the controversial issues.

Moreover, approval of the 'specified authority' as provided under section 151(*ii*) is required to be obtained before issuing notice under section 148 for such year(s).

Finance Act, 2022 has amended the above position of law. The earlier provision of this section as introduced by the Finance Act, 2021 and as explained above, required that reopening of an assessment beyond 3 assessment years and up to 10 years could have been done when income chargeable to tax was represented in the form of asset. The scope of this provision has been extended by making the amendment that the income chargeable to tax represented in the form of –

(*i*) An asset.

(*ii*) Expenditure in respect of a transaction or in relation to an event or occasion; or

(*iii*) An entry or entries in the books of account.

Which has escaped assessment amounts to or is likely to amount to fifty lakh rupees or more.

Thus, the scope of nature of escaped income has been extended and enlarged by this amendment. Now any escaped income which is represented in the form of an asset or expenditure or any entry in the books of account may be subject matter of assessment or reassessment.

4. Power of assessment or reassessment of 'other person' corresponding to the 'person' & power as enshrined earlier under section 153C has been incorporated under *Explanation 2(iii)* & (*iv*) of section 148. As per newly drafted provision in this regard, there is no longer any statutory requirement of handing over the seized assets or books of account belonging or pertaining to the 'other person' for assuming jurisdiction to make reassessment of such 'other person' as used to be there under section 153C. Further, there shall no longer be any statutory requirement for the Assessing Officer of the searched person to be satisfied to this effect that seized assets or documents etc. belong or pertain to other person.

As per the amended provision, the Assessing Officer of the 'other person' before issuing notice under section 148 is required to be satisfied that seized assets or books of account etc. belong or pertain to his assessee. However, such Assessing Officer is required to obtain prior approval of the Principal Commissioner or Commissioner before assuming jurisdiction over such 'other person'. This approval is required for assuming jurisdiction over the 'other person' under section 148 itself in which issue to be examined would be as to whether seized assets belong to the other person or seized books of account etc. pertain to the other person. Only when this condition is satisfied, the jurisdiction can be assumed by the Assessing Officer of the 'other person' under section 148. This approval, however, is in addition to the approval which is subsequently required under section 151 before issuing notice under section 148.

As explained above, since there is no requirement of statutory handing over the seized assets or books of account etc. by the Assessing Officer of the searched person to the Assessing Officer of the other person under the amended law, such information is liable to be passed by the Assessing Officer of the searched person to the Assessing Officer of the 'other person' as per the administrative guidelines which may be issued or prescribed for this purpose and in the similar manner as any information of the escaped income is required to be passed on to the concerned Assessing Officer as per the policy of the Board.

5. In the case of assessment or reassessment of 'other person', in spite of the above approvals which are required for assuming jurisdiction and issuing notice under section 148, it has also been provided under *Explanation 2* to section 148 that there would be mandatory reopening of the assessment of preceding three years prior to the year of search. The provisions have been drafted in such a manner so as to give the interpretation that such reopening is mandatorily required even if no evidence regarding income escaping assessment relating to such years have been found during search. However, before issuing notice under section 148, prior approval of specified authority as provided under section 151(*i*) would be required to be obtained.

   Further, law relating to reopening of assessment of the 'other person' for the years beyond three years and up to ten years is identical as is applicable in case of searched person which has been so explained.

   Amendment brought by the Finance Act, 2022 in *Explanation* 2 to section 148 deleting the reference of preceding 3 assessment years will have the same effect in the case of 'other person' as well as applicable to searched person as discussed in point 2 above.

6. The requirement of recording 'reason to believe' under section 147 as provided earlier has been substituted by any information which has been flagged in the case of the assessee for the relevant assessment year in accordance with the risk management strategy formulated by the Board from time to time. The flagging would largely be done by the computer based system. Moreover, reopening may be done on the basis of the final objection raised by C&AG of India regarding escapement of income.

   Finance Act, 2022 has amended *Explanation* 1 to section 148 deleting the word "flagged" and providing further situations which suggest that the income chargeable to tax has escaped assessment.

7. It is also provided by inserting a new section 148A that before issuance of notice under section 148, Assessing Officer shall provide an
   opportunity of being heard to the assessee. After considering the
   reply of the assessee, the Assessing Officer shall decide by passing
   an order as to whether it is a fit case for the issue of notice under
   section 148 and serve a copy of such order to the assessee. However
   such order is not appealable.

   But, requirement of section 148A as discussed above is not applicable
   in the case of assessment or reassessment of the searched person or
   'other person'.

8. Prior approval of the higher authorities under section 151 is required
   to be obtained before issue of notice under section 148. The amendments have been made to authorize the newly prescribed higher
   authorities for this purpose.

9. The amended provisions of reassessment as discussed above are
   applicable in respect of notice to be issued under section 148 on or
   after 1.4.2021. It is also provided that those years' reassessments that
   have become barred up to 31.3.2021 as per the earlier provisions of
   section 149 would not be reopened.

   First proviso to section 149(1) prior to the amendment, provides that
   no notice under section 148 shall be issued at any time in a case
   for the relevant assessment year beginning on or before 1st day of
   April 2021, if such notice could not have been issued at that time on
   account of being beyond the time limit specified under the provisions
   of clause (*b*) of sub-section (1) of this section, as they stood immediately before the commencement of the Finance Act, 2021.

   The above proviso implied that time limit for reopening of the earlier
   years' cases was to be 6 years from the end of the relevant assessment year as per the then existing provisions of section 149(1)(*b*). In
   this proviso there was reference of the notice under section 148 only
   which was not applicable for the search cases. But the assessment of
   search cases have to be conducted after the Finance Act, 2021 under
   new scheme as prescribed under sections 147 to 151. Therefore, the
   reference of time limit of reopening of the assessment as prescribed
   under section 153A or section 153C has also been incorporated herein
   this proviso.

   Finance Act, 2023 has inserted a proviso after second proviso to
   section 149(1) to the effect that in a case where search under section
   132 or requisition under section 132A has been initiated after 15th
   March of any financial year and the period of issue of notice under

section 148 expires on the 31st day of March of such financial year, a period of 15 days shall be excluded for the purpose of computing the period of limitation as per section 149 and the notice issued under section 148 in such case shall be deemed to have been issued on the 31st day of March of such financial year.

Above situation would also be applicable in a case where last of authorisation in relation to a search under section 132 is executed on or after 15th day of March of any financial year.

Similar situation would prevail where the information as referred to in *Explanation 1* to section 148 consequent to which assessment can be reopened, emanates from a statement recorded or documents impounded under section 131 or section 133A before 31st day of March of the financial year.

Thus in such kind of situations, an additional time of 15 days has been granted to the Assessing Officer for issue of notice under section 148.

10. Finance Act, 2022 has introduced a new sub-section (1A) to section 149 by which the limit of escapement of income of Rs. 50 lakhs or more for the previous year as given in section 149(1)(*b*) for reopening the cases beyond 3 assessment years has been amended. As per the newly introduced sub section (1A), it has been provided that where the income chargeable to tax represented in the form of an asset or expenditure in relation to an event or occasion of Rs. 50 lakhs or more has escaped the assessment and the investment in such asset or expenditure in relation to such event or occasion has been made or incurred, in more than one previous years relevant to the assessment years, a notice under section 148 shall be issued for every such assessment year. It would mean that the limit of Rs. 50 lakhs in such cases is not to be seen for single previous year but to be seen on aggregate basis which may be spread in several previous years.

11. Finance Act, 2022 has introduced a new section 148B requiring prior approval of higher authorities before passing the assessment or reassessment orders in search cases. The approval is to be taken from Additional Commissioner or Additional Director or Joint Commissioner or Joint Director as the case may be, if the assessment or reassessment order is passed by an officer below the rank of Joint Commissioner. This section has been inserted with effect from 1st April, 2022.

This provision is identical to the provisions of section 153D in earlier scheme of assessment or reassessment of search cases under section 153A/153C.

12.6 Significant Issues emerging out of new assessment or reassessment provisions of search cases:

(*i*) **In the case of search initiated on or before 31st March, 2021, provisions of sections 153A & 153C shall remain applicable**

Sections 153A & 153C have been amended by the Finance Act, 2021 providing that the provisions of these sections shall be applicable only in case of search initiated on or before 31st March, 2021. It would mean that in case search has been initiated on or before 31st March, 2021 but concluded thereafter, then also the assessment or reassessment of the search cases shall be made under the provisions of section 153A or 153C. The provisions relating to limitation for passing the assessment order as given in section 153B and provision relating to approval as given under section 153D would continue to apply to such assessments made.

In case search is initiated on or after 1st April, 2021, assessment or reassessment pursuant to such search shall be governed by the new assessment provisions as contained in sections 147 to 153.

(*ii*) **As per new assessment or reassessment provisions, reopening of the case under section 147 for three or ten preceding years, as the case may be, can be made year wise, & all such years involved are not required to be reopened & reassessed simultaneously, as happened to be the case under section 153A**

Assessment or reassessment in the case of search under section 153A was a special provision for making assessment or reassessment of prior 6 years' or 9 years' cases, as the case may be, wherein assessment or reassessment for all such years were required to be completed simultaneously within the time limit as prescribed under section 153B. Also, the time limit for passing assessment order under section 153A was reduced to nine months from the end of the year in which search was conducted. There used to be heavy burden on the Assessing Officer to appraise all the incriminating material and pass assessment orders for all such years as the time available appeared to be inadequate.

As per the new procedure of assessment or reassessment of search cases, there is no requirement of passing assessment orders of all the years simultaneously with respect to which information suggesting escaped income has been deemed/found. Now, each assessment year is separate assessment year & notice under section 148 can be issued independently & separately for any of the year(s) before the expiry of the time as prescribed & in accordance with the provisions of section 149. It would mean that assessment or reassessment as a consequence of evidences found during search may be taken up to a period of 10 years from the end of the relevant assessment year, as per the time limitation prescribed under section 149. Even reassessment of prior three years which are mandatory to be reopened in case of search etc. may also be reopened & reassessed in different years in terms of section 149 and section 153 and are not required to be assessed simultaneously.

(*iia*) **Impact of TOLA & Supreme Court's decision in Ashish Agarwal for the purpose of extension of time limitation for reopening of AYs 2013-14 & 2014-15**

Finance Act, 2021 introduced an altogether a new regime of reopening provisions enacting new sections 147, 148, 148A, 149, 151 with effect from 1.4.2021. Time limitation of issuing notice under section 148 under the unamended law of section 149 were about to expire on 31.3.2021 in respect of some of the assessment years. Due to pandemic of Covid 19, time limits were extended initially by issuing Ordinance and later on by enacting Taxation & Other Laws (Relaxation & Amendment of Certain Provisions) Act, 2020 (In brief TOLA) and by issuing the notifications under TOLA. In such circumstances, a raging controversy arose as to whether notice under section 148 under the unamended law of section 149 for AYs 2013-14 & 2014-15 issued after the expiry of normal limitation period, on or after 1.4.2021 but issued up to 30.6.2021 *i.e.* the time limit extended due to the provisions of TOLA can be said to be issued within the permissible time limit. Several High Courts barring Chhattisgarh High Court held that such notices issued under section 148 under the unamended law of section 149 between the period 1.4.2021 to 30.6.2021 were bad in law. Such decisions were *Mon Mohan Kohli* v. *ACIT* 441 ITR 207 (Del.), *Ashok Kumar Agarwal* v. *Union of India* 439 ITR 1 (All.), *Tata Communications Transformation Services Ltd.* v. *ACIT* 443 ITR 49 (Bom.) whereas the decision of Chhattisgarh High Court was in the case of *Palak Khatuja* v. *Union of India* WP(T) No. 149 of 2021, 438 ITR 622 (Chhattisgarh).

Matter was agitated in Supreme Court in the case of *Union of India* v. *Ashish Agarwal* 444 ITR 1 (SC) wherein Hon'ble Supreme Court exercised the provisions of Article 142 of the Constitution of India and directed that these notices issued under unamended section 148 between the period 1.4.2021 to 30.6.2021 be treated as notice under section 148A under the amended law and further directed that after giving opportunity of hearing & supplying the material being relied upon, to the respective assessees, the Assessing Officers should pass the order under section 148A(*d*) of the amended law and follow the new procedure of reassessment. Defence of amended section 149 or of any other law was kept alive for both the assessee and the tax department.

Matter did not rest here and challenge has again been made in various High Courts in respect of such notices issued under old section 149 and now treated as notice under section 148A pursuant to the decision of Hon'ble Supreme Court in the case of Ashish Agarwal, supra.

Hon'ble Gujarat High Court in the case of *Keenara Industries P. Ltd.* v. *Union of India* in its judgment dated 7.2.2023 and Allahabad High Court in the case of *Rajeev Bansal* v. *Union of India* in Writ Tax No. 1086 of 2022 dated 22.2.2023 have held that such notice issued under old law of section 148 between 1.4.2021 to 30.6.2021 by taking the extended period provided by TOLA and treated by Supreme Court as notice under section 148A could not be saved due to the new provisions of section 149 coming into force with effect from 1.4.2021. It was held that Supreme Court in the case of Ashish Agarwal supra did not treat such notice as notice under section 148 issued under the amended law of section 148 and merely held such notice to be treated as notice under section 148A. It has further been held that there is nothing either under Finance Act, 2021 and/or TOLA by which old provisions of sections 147 to 151 could be said to have been saved. Attempt by TOLA to save old provisions of sections 147 to 151 through notifications dated 31.3.2021 and 27.4.2021 issued under TOLA was found by High Courts including Delhi High Court in the case of *Mon Mohan Kohli* v. *ACIT* 441 ITR 207 (Del.) as ultra vires of the provisions of TOLA. Thus, Gujarat High Court in *Keenara Industries P. Ltd., supra*, and Allahabad High Court in Rajeev Bansal, supra, have held that notice under section 148 issued under old provision of section 149 between 1.4.2021 to 30.6.2021 for the AYs 2013-14 & 2014-15 though held to be notice under section 148A by Supreme Court under the amended provisions, still were barred by limitation.

Therefore, interpretation of the first proviso to amended section 149(1) given by Gujarat High Court and Allahabad High Court in Keenara Industries P Ltd., supra & Rajeev Bansal, supra, assume importance in respect of reassessment of AYs 2013-14 & 2014-15.

However, in our considered opinion, the view taken by Gujarat High Court and Allahabad High Court in the above two judicial decisions may require re-consideration as in our considered opinion, these may not be in line with the letter and spirit of the decision of Hon'ble Supreme Court in the case of Ashish Agarwal, supra. It can further be stated & explained that Had the notice been issued under section 148A up to 30.6.2021 in respect of AYs 2013-14 & 2014-15, the same would have been valid and reassessment proceeding could have been taken subject to the other provisions of the new law. Similar interpretation should be applied when Supreme Court had directed that notices issued under section 148 from 1.4.2021 to 30.6.2021 may be treated as notice issued under section 148A and reassessment proceeding in pursuance to such notice for AYs 2013-14 & 2014-15 may also be valid subject to that order under section 148A(*d*) is passed within the time limit prescribed by Supreme Court in the case of Ashish Agarwal, supra and further, notice under section 148 for reopening the case is issued within the prescribed time limit of amended section 149. However, we may hasten to add that controversy is not going to die soon.

(*iib*) In the case of search held on or after 1.4.2021, which assessment years can be reopened as per amended law of section 149

Another issue in the context of interpretation of limitation in the first proviso to amended section 149(1) is the reading of time limit in case of search etc. more so after the insertion of reference, made by the Finance Act, 2022, to section 153A or section 153C as they stood immediately before the commencement of the Finance Act, 2021.

Under section 153A, 6 years' assessment preceding the year of search could be assessed or reassessed in normal situation. However, Fourth proviso to section 153A read with *Explanation 1* was added by the Finance Act, 2017 with effect from 1.4.2017 by which the 10 years' assessment including the year of search year were made assessable subject to the evidence of undisclosed income with monetary limit of 50 lacs or more and subject to other stipulations.

In respect of search initiated on or after 1.4.2021, amended section 149(1) provides, *inter alia*, that assessment of ten years from the end of the relevant assessment year can be reopened. But first proviso to section 149(1) further provides that no notice under section 148 shall be issued at any time in a case for the relevant assessment year if a notice under section 153A or section 153C could not have been issued at that time on account of being beyond the time limit specified under the provisions of section 153A or section 153C, as the case may be, as they stood immediately before the commencement of the Finance Act, 2021.

Therefore, in respect of search initiated on or after 1.4.2021, though assessment of ten years from the end of the relevant assessment years can be reopened as per the mandate of main provisions of section

149(1) but further limitation given in the first proviso to section 149(1) would also be required to be seen.

This can be understood by way an example: If search takes place on 20.2.2023 in a case, then ten years' assessment from the end of the relevant assessment years can be reopened under the main section 149(1), but of course, subject to the fulfilment of conditions as given in clause (*b*) of section 149(1). It means that if notice under section 148 is to be issued, say on 31.3.2023, then notice for AYs 2012-13 & 2013-14 can be issued under the main provision of section 149(1). But restriction on time limitation as per the first proviso to section 149(1) is required to be read further and question would be asked as to whether AYs 2012-13 & 2013-14 could be reopened in terms of fourth proviso read with *Explanation 1* of section 153A. Fourth proviso to section 153A read with *Explanation 1* provides that 10 years assessment including the year of search can be reopened. That would mean that in this example, AYs 2012-13 & 2013-14 would fall beyond the time limit prescribed under the Fourth Proviso read with *Explanation 1* of section 153A and AY 2014-15 would be the first year which could be reopened in the fact given in this example.

It would mean that limitation is to be reckoned as on the date on which notice under section 148 is being issued and the time limit & other conditions are to be seen as prescribed under the amended section 149(1) and Fourth proviso to section 153A read with *Explanation 1*.

(*iii*) **There shall not be any abatement of the pending assessments for which notice under section 143(2) has already been issued or assessment is already in progress**

Under section 153A regarding the assessment or reassessment of search cases, there was provision of abatement of the assessment and reassessment proceeding pending as on the date of search. There is no requirement under new scheme & procedure of assessment or reassessment to abate the pending assessments which are being undertaken under section 143(3). Moreover, notice under section 143(2) may be issued for any year for which there is time limit available as per the proviso to section 143(2). Such assessments shall be completed in the normal course and evidences found during search relating to such year(s) may be considered by the Assessing Officer during such assessment proceedings.

However, this may be noted that it is not mandatory. Further, notice under section 148 shall be required to be issued mandatorily for preceding three years in case of search, as provided under section 148. During such assessment or reassessment proceeding under section 148, incriminating material in possession of the revenue found and seized as a consequence of search or otherwise and which has not been earlier considered during assessment proceeding under section 143(2) if any may be considered in reassessment proceeding under section 147.

In such new assessment or reassessment scheme, a situation may arise when certain incriminating material has already been considered by the Assessing Officer during assessment proceeding under section 143(3) but no addition to income was made relating to such issue. But, when reassessment notice under section 148 is issued for prior three years, there may be possibility that such incriminating material is again considered by the Assessing Officer and addition is made during reassessment proceeding. A question may arise as to whether such treatment by the Assessing Officer is tenable in law. A view may be taken in this regard that it would tantamount to change of opinion by the Assessing Officer and is against the well settled principle of law in this regard that Assessing Officer is not permitted to change his opinion on the same set of facts. Though such law was developed when there was requirement of recording 'reason to believe' for reopening the assessment under section 148 but in our considered opinion, the above principle should be applied in the above situation under the new scheme of assessment also as law has attached great sanctity to the finality of assessment.

There may be another view that in case assessment order has been passed by the Assessing Officer under section 143(3) for any of the preceding three years after the date of search, the incriminating material relating to such years should have been considered in the assessment of these years, and reassessment notice under section 148 should not be issued for such years. However, in case any fresh incriminating material comes into the possession of the Assessing Officer, he can issue notice under section 148 for reopening of the assessment or reassessment as per normal provisions of section 148. This may be a contentious issue which may be settled by the courts in due course.

(*iv*) **Provisions of newly inserted section 148A would not be applicable for reopening of the prior three or ten years' cases as a consequence of search. However approval of the 'specified authority' is required under section 151.**

Under the new scheme of assessment or reassessment under section 147, a new section 148A has been introduced providing *inter alia* an opportunity of hearing to the assessee before issue of notice under section 148. As per proviso to section 148A, it has however been provided that provisions of section 148A shall not be applicable in case of search initiated on or after 1st April, 2021 in respect of searched person and in respect of 'other person'. However, it is significant to note that in the case of survey under section 133A, though preceding three years' reassessment proceedings are mandatory but requirement of section 148A in such cases of survey would have to be complied with. In our considered opinion, such provision of section 148A for survey cases is somewhat contradictory in the sense that on the one hand section 148 provides that in case of survey also, the Assessing Officer shall be deemed to have information which suggests that the income chargeable to tax has escaped assessment in the case of the surveyed assessee for the preceding three assessment years and on the other hand, requirement of section 148A to provide opportunity of hearing to the assessee before issue of notice under section 148 would not serve any meaningful purpose.

It may further be noted that though requirement of section 148A is not applicable in case of search assessment or reassessment under section 148 but such notice under section 148 can be issued only after obtaining approval of the 'specified authority' as prescribed under section 151.

(*v*) **Reopening of the cases beyond three years may be possible when income chargeable to tax is** *represented in the form of asset*

As per section 149(1)(*b*) introduced by the Finance Act, 2021, notice under section 148 may be issued beyond preceding three assessment years when Assessing Officer has in his possession books of account or other documents or evidence which reveal that the income chargeable to tax & which is represented in the form of asset, has escaped assessment & which amounts to or is likely to amount to fifty lakh rupees or more for that year. Thus there are the following two requirements to be fulfilled for reopening of the assessment or reassessment beyond three years up to ten years that:

(*i*) the evidence for escapement of income is rupees fifty lakh or more which has to be seen for each year independently

(*ii*) the escaped income chargeable to tax has to be represented in the form of asset.

Here the words **"represented in the form of asset"** are important to be noted. Generally, the evidences of escapement of income may be of the following types:

(*i*) Evidences which reveal undisclosed income

(*ii*) Evidences which reveal undisclosed asset

(*iii*) Wrongly claimed deduction/exemption/relief/rebate

(*iv*) Additions on account of deeming provisions of income

The evidence relating to undisclosed income points out to the generation of income while the evidences which reveal undisclosed asset points out to the application of income in the form of asset. The above clause has covered only undisclosed income which is represented in the form of asset, which implies that the evidence should reveal that there is some undisclosed asset. It is not necessary that undisclosed asset should exist or should have been found during search. The intent of the legislature is to cover undisclosed asset for assuming jurisdiction beyond three years. In case evidence regarding the generation of income are found, such income in our considered opinion would always come in form of some asset though the asset may exist temporarily or may have been exhausted and may not exist on the date of search.

As per *Explanation* to section 149(1), it has been explained that for the purposes of clause (*b*) of sub-section (1) of section 149, "asset" shall include immovable property, being land or building or both, shares and securities, loans and advances, deposits in bank account. The meaning of 'asset' has been given in inclusive manner which means that above mentioned assets are intended to be covered for this purpose. However, there may be several other assets such as sundry debtors, cash in hand, intangible assets, plant & machinery etc. which are though not part of this definition in explicit manner but in our considered opinion, such assets may also be considered for this purpose. Explaining the 'asset' in the above manner is bound to create more confusion than clarity on this issue & litigation appears to be imminent.

In the case of above mentioned third situation, there may be evidence found during search which reveal that some wrong deduction or exemption etc. has been claimed by an assessee such as wrong claim of deduction under section 80-IA etc., section 54 etc. section 10 etc., such wrong claim of deduction or exemption cannot be said to be in the nature of escaped income **represented in the form of asset** and therefore, interestingly such evidences may not lead to the reopening of the assessment beyond three years.

In the case of above mentioned fourth situation, there may be evidence found during search which reveal that some addition to the income may be required to be made as per various deeming provisions under the Act or for technical reason such as deemed dividend under section 2(22)(*e*), disallowance under section 43B or section 40A(3) or section 40(*a*)(*ia*), or section 40A(2) etc. Such additions to the income or disallowance of expenses cannot be said to be in the nature of escaped income *represented in the form of asset* and therefore, such evidences may not lead to the reopening of the assessment beyond three years.

Such expression of escaped income **represented in the form of asset** was earlier used in fourth proviso to section 153A(1) for reopening the assessment in the case of search beyond preceding 6 years by the Finance Act, 2017 with effect from 1st April, 2017. The interpretation of such expression may be a contentious issue and law in this regard may be evolved in due course of time.

Finance Act, 2022 has however amended the above position of law. The earlier provision of this section as introduced by the Finance Act, 2021 and as explained above, required that reopening of an assessment beyond 3 assessment years and up to 10 years could have been done when income chargeable to tax was represented in the form of asset. The scope of this provision has been extended by making the amendment that the income chargeable to tax represented in the form of –

(*i*) An asset.

(*ii*) Expenditure in respect of a transaction or in relation to an event or occasion; or

(*iii*) An entry or entries in the books of account.

Which has escaped assessment amounts to or is likely to amount to fifty lakh rupees or more.

Thus, the scope of nature of escaped income has been extended and enlarged by this amendment. Now any escaped income which is represented in the form of an asset or expenditure or any entry in the books of account may be subject matter of assessment or reassessment.

Finance Act, 2022 has also introduced a new sub-section (1A) to section 149 by which the limit of escapement of income of Rs. 50 lakhs or more for the previous year as given in section 149(1)(*b*) for reopening the cases beyond 3 assessment years has been amended. As per the newly introduced sub-section (1A), it has been provided that where the income chargeable to tax represented in the form of an asset or expenditure in relation to an event or occasion of Rs. 50 lakhs or more has escaped the assessment and the investment in such asset or expenditure in relation to such event or occasion has been made or incurred, in more than one previous years relevant to the assessment years, a notice under section 148 shall be issued for every such assessment year. It would mean that the limit of Rs. 50 lakhs in such cases is not to be seen for single previous year but to be seen on aggregate basis which may be spread in several previous years.

(vi) **Mandatory reopening of prior three years cases in the case of search even if no incriminating material is found during search. Whether it would be in the nature of *de novo* assessment or additions can be made only relating to the incriminating material found during search?**

As per *Explanation 2* to section 148, it has been provided that in case of search, Assessing Officer shall be deemed to have information which suggests that the income chargeable to tax has escaped assessment in the case of the assessee for preceding three assessment years. It would mean that in the case of search, assessment for preceding three years would mandatorily be reopened irrespective of any incriminating evidence regarding escaped income found during the course of search. Such requirement is similar to the requirement as was there in section 153A where preceding six years' assessment were required to be reassessed.

Explanation 2 to section 148 has also been amended by the Finance Act, 2022 and it has been provided that in case of search, survey etc. the assessing officer shall be deemed to have information which suggests that the income chargeable to tax has escaped assessment in the case of the assessee. Prior to amendment of this Explanation by the Finance Act, 2022, such deeming fiction was only for three assessment years immediately preceding the assessment year relevant to the previous year in which the search is initiated. By removing the reference to 3 assessment years, this deeming fiction has been extended for reopening of the cases for all the years up to 10 years from the end of the relevant assessment year.

Therefore, in view of the amended *Explanation* 2 to section 148, the nature of information for reopening of the cases as given in *Explanation* 1 is not relevant for the search cases. However, the conditions as given in section 149(1)(*b*) for reopening the cases beyond 3 assessment years up to 10 assessment years are required to be fulfilled.

A question may arise as to what kind of additions can be made during such assessment proceeding and as to whether such assessment would be in the nature of *de novo* assessment or addition can be made only on the basis of the incriminating material found during search or otherwise coming into the possession of the Assessing Officer.

In our considered opinion the requirement of mandatory reopening of preceding three years' cases is for the purpose of assuming jurisdiction for reopening of the assessment without complying with the requirement of section 148A. Once jurisdiction for reopening of the preceding three years is assumed, the nature of assessment to be made under section 148 would be governed by the general principles of law as developed by Hon'ble Courts in this respect in the case of erstwhile sections 147 and 148. In our considered opinion, the law developed in this regard under section 153A may not be relevant but the law developed with respect to the nature of reassessment proceeding in the context of old sections 147 & 148 would still be relevant.

(vii) **Burden of proof lies on whom in respect of any other escaped income which comes to the notice of AO during the course of reassessment proceeding under section 148**

Explanation to section 147 provides that for the purpose of assessment or reassessment, the Assessing Officer may assess or reassess the income in respect of any issue, which has escaped assessment, and such issue comes to his notice subsequently in the course of the proceeding under section 147 irrespective of the fact that provisions of section 148A have not been complied with. Similar provision was already there in the earlier section 147 also.

This issue has always been a contentious issue as to whether Assessing Officer can enquire and look into any issue, aspect or facet unconnected with the reason recorded. It has been observed in practice that in case of reassessment proceeding, general and omnibus questionnaire is issued and all kind of information is sought from the assessee as if *de novo* assessment is being made. The judicial precedence in this regard is also not clear as to the scope of power of the Assessing Officer to make omnibus enquiries.

In our considered opinion, primarily the Assessing Officer should restrict himself to seek information relating to the issue for which reassessment proceeding has been initiated. In course of such proceeding, in case any other escaped income comes to his notice, it can be assessed in terms of the language of *Explanation* to section 147. In such a situation the burden to prove that this income is also escaped income should rest on the shoulders of the Assessing Officer. This is primarily because the expression used in the *Explanation* to section 147 is that the Assessing Officer may assess or reassess **escaped** income that comes to his notice subsequently in the course of the proceeding which indicates that notice of such escaped income is incidental to the main issues being examined.

(viii) **In case of search, assessment beyond preceding three years may be reopened when there is information with the Assessing Officer which suggests that the income chargeable to tax has escaped assessment-meaning thereof**

As per substituted section 148, jurisdiction to reassess may be assumed by the Assessing Officer when the information available with the Assessing Officer suggests that the income chargeable to tax has escaped assessment. As per substituted provisions of sections 147 & 148, there is no requirement for forming the 'reason to believe' for escapement of income. *Explanation 1* to section 148 has provided two situations when it can be said that there is information suggesting escapement of income chargeable to tax. These situations are (*i*) any information flagged in the case of the assessee for the relevant assessment year in accordance with the risk management strategy formulated by the Board from time to time & (*ii*) any final objection raised by the Comptroller & Auditor General of India to the effect that the assessment in the case of the assessee for the relevant assessment year has not been made in accordance with the provisions of this Act.

Finance Act, 2022 has amended *Explanation* 1 to section 148 in which reference to word "flagged" has been omitted and has amended clause (*ii*) & has inserted new clauses (*iii*), (*iv*), (*v*). The amended clause (*ii*) & newly inserted clauses (*iii*), (*iv*), (*v*) of the *Explanation* 1 to section 148 read as under:

(*ii*) any audit objection to the effect that the assessment in the case of the assessee for the relevant assessment year has not been made in accordance with the provisions of this Act; or

(*iii*) any information received under an agreement referred to in section 90 or section 90A of the Act; or

(*iv*) any information made available to the Assessing Officer under the scheme notified under section 135A; or

(*v*) any information which requires action in consequence of the order of a Tribunal or a Court.

(*ix*) In what manner, jurisdiction over 'other person' may be assumed under section 148, as a consequence of search?

Power of assessment or reassessment of 'other person' corresponding to the person & power as enshrined earlier under section 153C has been incorporated under *Explanation* 2(*iii*) & (*iv*) of section 148. As per newly drafted provision in this regard, there is no statutory requirement of handing over the seized assets belonging to the other person or seized books of account pertaining to the other person for assuming jurisdiction to make assessment or reassessment of such other person. Further, there shall not remain any statutory requirement for the Assessing Officer of the searched person to be satisfied to this effect that seized assets or documents etc. belong or pertain to other person.

As per the amended provision, the Assessing Officer of the other person is required to be satisfied that seized assets or seized books of account etc. belong or pertain to his assessee before issuing notice under section 148. Moreover, such Assessing Officer is required to obtain prior approval of the Principal Commissioner or Commissioner before assuming jurisdiction over the other person. This approval is required for assuming jurisdiction over the other person under section 148 in which issue to be examined would be as to whether seized assets belong to the other person or seized books of account etc. pertain to the other person. Only when this condition is satisfied, the jurisdiction can be assumed by the Assessing Officer of the other person under section 148. This approval is in addition to the approval which is subsequently required under section 151 before issuing notice under section 148.

In section 153C, there is a provision that the Assessing Officer of the other person should be satisfied that the books of account or documents or assets seized have a bearing on the determination of the total income of such other person. Such requirement is not provided in the amended law. However, there is additional requirement of obtaining approval from the higher authorities before assuming jurisdiction and issue of notice under section 148 and at this stage, it may be examined and decided as to whether there is any escapement of income for particular assessment year and it is therefore required to be reassessed. Moreover, for reopening the assessment beyond three years, there is provision under section 149 that the escapement of income should be of Rs. 50 lakhs or more & the income chargeable to tax is represented in the form of assets. Such provision of section 149 has also to be complied with while reopening the assessment of other person beyond three years as a consequence of search.

As explained above, since there is no requirement of statutory handing over the seized assets or books of account etc. by the Assessing Officer of the searched person to the Assessing Officer of the other person under the amended law, such information is liable to be passed by the Assessing Officer of the searched person to the Assessing Officer of the other person as per the administrative guidelines which may be prescribed for this purpose and in the like manner as any information of the escaped income is required to be passed to the concerned Assessing Officer as per the policy of the Board.

(*x*) **Whether penalty provision of section 271AAB shall remain applicable for the 'specified previous year' even after the new assessment scheme of the search cases?**

Penalty provision under section 271AAA or section 271AAB is attracted in the case of search for the 'undisclosed income' of the 'specified previous year'(*s*). For the years preceding to the specified previous year(s), penalty provision as provided under section 271(1)(*c*) or 270A as the case may be are applicable. Even after substitution of new assessment scheme of search cases introduced by the Finance Act, 2021 according to which assessment or reassessment of the search cases shall not be undertaken as per the provisions of section 153A but shall be undertaken under the substituted sections like 147 to 151. However, penalty provision as given under section 271AAB would continue to be applicable in respect of the 'undisclosed income' of the 'specified previous year'(s).

12.7 Relevance of jurisprudence developed with respect to reopening of assessment under the old law contained in sections 147-151 & 153A-153D to the new scheme of assessment or reassessment in search cases

Special provisions of assessment or reassessment as provided in section 153A to section 153D for search cases have been dispensed with in case of income tax search initiated on or after 1st April, 2021. As per new scheme provided, assessment or reassessment in case of search shall be done as per normal provisions provided under the Income Tax Act for assessment or reassessment. The reassessment provisions as provided under section 147 to section 151 for normal cases have also been substituted by new provisions under sections 147, 148, 148A, 149, 151, 151A making substantial deviations from the old law.

We have discussed the salient features of the new scheme of reassessment and significant issues emanating therefrom specifically in the context of search cases, in the earlier part of the chapter. There is substantial amount of jurisprudence which has been developed in the past with respect to various principles of law to be applied in the cases of reopening of the assessment. Such jurisprudence or judgment based law developed in the past may be applicable in the new scheme of assessment or reassessment of search cases also except where there is fundamental change in law made by the new scheme of assessment or reassessment.

We discuss hereunder some of the major principles of law developed in the past which may be still be relevant under the new scheme of reassessment:

(*i*) **What are the consequences if income tax return pursuant to notice under section 148 is not filed?**

Assessee is required to file fresh income tax return in pursuance to notice under section 148 irrespective of the fact as to whether earlier income tax return was filed or not under section 139 or income tax assessment has already been completed under section 143(3). In case income tax return in pursuance to notice under section 148 is not filed, Assessing Officer may complete the assessment/reassessment by passing *ex parte* assessment order as per the provisions of section 144. Second, interest under section 234A for non-filing or delayed filing of such return is liable to be imposed on the amount of the tax demand raised in such assessment/reassessment order.

Sub-section (3) of section 234A speaks of a situation where income has been determined under section 143(1), or the assessment is made under section 143(3) or section 144 or section 147 and thereafter, notice under section 148 is issued. Where the assessee files the return of income after the expiry of the time allowed under such notice or where no return of income is furnished, the assessee shall be liable to pay interest for the delayed period, the starting date being the date immediately following the expiry of the time allowed in the notice under section 148, and ending on (a) the date of furnishing of the return, or (b) in case no return has been furnished, ending on the date of completion of reassessment under section 147. Interest under section 234A(3) shall be paid on the amount by which the tax on the total income determined on such reassessment or re-computation exceeds the tax on the total income determined under section 143(1) or on the basis of earlier assessment under section 143(3) or section 144 or section 147.

Moreover, as per provisions of section 276CC of the Act, assessee is liable to face prosecution for failure to furnish return of income in pursuance to notice issued under section 148.

The above position of law in our considered opinion would apply under the new scheme of assessment or reassessment also.

Finance Act, 2023 has provided that assessee is required to file income tax return in pursuance to notice issued under section 148 within a period of 3 months from the end of the month in which such notice is issued, or such further period as may be allowed by the Assessing Officer on the basis of an application made in this regard by the assessee. It is further provided that any return of income required to be furnished by an assessee under section 148 but is furnished beyond the period allowed, shall not be treated as a return filed under section 139. It means that such return of income shall be treated as non-est and consequences of such failure will follow.

(ii) **Whether fresh notice under section 148 can be issued in case earlier notice is held invalid?**

There may be situations when notice issued under section 148 suffers with legal infirmity and such notice is not a valid notice in the eyes of law. Such infirmity may be observed by the Assessing Officer himself or there may be judicial order passed by the higher authorities holding the infirmity in the notice. In such a case Assessing Officer is entitled to issue fresh notice under section 148 after complying with the correct legal procedure in case time limit permits to issue fresh notice under section 148. The assessment proceeding may be undertaken in pursuance to new notice issued and such proceeding may be treated as valid proceeding. The earlier notice issued shall be treated *non-est* in the eyes of law. Assessee should keep this position of law in mind before raising objections regarding validity of the notice issued under section 148.

Judicial decisions for the above proposition are a plenty and few of them may be discussed hereunder:

Where the first reopening of assessment was set aside by the Tribunal merely because the confessional statement of a creditor which was sought to be relied upon was not available at the time of reopening, second reopening made on the basis of so-called confessional statement after it was recorded in 1968 with the previous sanction of CBDT cannot be said to be invalid as held in the case of *Rawatmall Mohanlal* v. *ITO* (2004) 136 Taxman 140/269 ITR 420/188 CTR (Cal.) 425.

Where the very initiation of the proceeding under section 148 by the first notice has been held to be without jurisdiction, second notice under section 148 can be issued as held in the case of *Sukhlal Ice & Cold Storage Co.* v. *ITO* [1993] 199 ITR 129, 131(All.).

Other decisions are *Kohinoor Enterprises* v. *ITO* [1996] 89 Taxman 587/[1997] 226 ITR 88, 90 (MP), *S.K Gupta & Co.* v. *ITO* [2000] 246 ITR 560 (All.), *Ranjeet Singh* v. *CIT* [2016] 68 taxmann.com 15/238 Taxman 522/382 ITR 409 (P&H).

However, contrary view has been taken in the case of *Smt. Anchi Devi* v. *CIT* 218 CTR 11 (P&H), *Rameshwar Prasad Sharma* v. *CIT* ITA 642 of 2011 dated 4.9.2017 (Raj), *Jaya Publications* [2010] 123 ITD 53 (Chennai), *Babu Lal Lath* v. *Asstt. CIT* [2002] 83 ITD 691 (Mum).

The above position of law would in our considered opinion apply under the new scheme of assessment or reassessment also.

(*iii*) **What is the effect of additional income declared by the assessee in the return filed pursuant to notice under section 148?**

When income tax return is filed by the assessee in pursuance to notice under section 148, additional income may be declared based upon the incriminating material found during search or survey. Assessee has to carefully examine all the incriminating material so found, statements recorded of various persons and take the decision as to whether any additional income not offered to tax earlier is required to be declared now when opportunity has been granted to file fresh return in pursuance to notice under section 148. When additional income is declared by the assessee, he has to pay tax and interest relating to such income along with the filing of return.

Assessee should take a conscious & informed decision of arriving at additional income to be offered in the return of income after carefully examining and analysing all the evidences and incriminating material found during search or survey. Such incriminating material may be of complex nature resulting in the multiple additions and assessee should strategize the whole working carefully after applying the sound accounting and tax principles so as to arrive at the true and correct income earned by him. Once additional income is declared in the return of income, it may not be possible for the assessee to shift his stand easily later on.

There may be situations when declaration of undisclosed income has been made by the assessee during statement recorded at the time of search or survey proceeding. Such undisclosed income may relate to different entities and for different years. In case such undisclosed income declared is relating to the year for which notice for filing of return under section 148 has been received, assessee may offer such undisclosed income in the return of income to be filed unless such declaration of undisclosed income has been retracted by the assessee on some plausible ground.

In case, additional income is declared by the assessee for years prior to the 'specified previous year' as explained under section 271AAB, it may tantamount to admitted concealment or under-reported income and there are judicial decisions that in such case, assessee cannot be absolved from the imposition of penalty, few of which are given as under along with the brief facts:

Revised return showing higher income pursuant to notice under section 148 & Assessee having disclosed higher income after receiving notice under section 148, there was not voluntary surrender of income but a clear cut case of concealment attracting penalty under section 271(1)(c) - *Prempal Gandhi* v. *CIT* 27 DTR 35 (P&H)

Revised return in response to notice under section 148 showing additional income in a return filed pursuant to notice under section 148 clearly attracts penalty under section 271(1)(c). Since assessee itself having admitted that cash credit entry is an income, going back from that saying that it was only to buy peace is not an acceptable explanation to say that it is not an income. - *CIT* v. *Sangmeshwara Associates* 71 DTR 287 (Kar.)

On the other hand, there are certain judicial decisions where penalty has been deleted by the Courts in such circumstances, few of which are given hereunder:

Assessee having surrendered additional income along with an explanation in the revised return filed in pursuance of notice under section 148, and the assessing authority having not taken any objection that the assessee's explanation was not *bona fide*, penalty under section 271(1)(c) is not leviable.-*CIT* v. *Rajiv Garg & Ors.* [2008] 175 Taxman 184/[2009] 313 ITR 256/224 CTR 321 (P&H)

Income declared by the assessee from the long-term capital gain by selling agricultural land & disclosed in his return of income filed under section 148 was accepted by the assessing authority and there being no deliberate concealment, penalty under section 271(1)(c) was rightly cancelled & no substantial question of law arises -*CIT* v. *Pushpendra Surana* 96 DTR 231 (Raj)

Assessee having not disclosed the capital gains in his original return as the taxability thereof was mired in controversy, the said non-disclosure was not wilful, and tax having been paid prior to issuance of notice under section 148 indicating his intention to disclose the same by way of revised return and thereafter disclosed the capital gain voluntarily in the return filed in response to the notice under section 148 before detection of the same by the Revenue authorities, the assessee cannot be held to have concealed particulars of his income relating to capital gains and, therefore, penalty under section 271(1)(c) is not leviable- *Prabhjit Singh Sidhu* v. *ADIT* (*International Taxation*) 159 DTR (Chd.) 244

Withdrawal of inadmissible claim of set off of loss in the return filed pursuant to notice under section 148 & the assessee-company having *suo motu* withdrawn the inadmissible claim of set off of long-term capital gain against the long-term capital loss arising on the sale of shares by the assessee to its hundred per cent holding company as made by it the original return while filing the return in pursuance of notice under section 148 before the same was confronted by the Revenue, the assessee has demonstrated its *bona fides* and, therefore, penalty under section 271(1)(c) is not leviable.-*NSE IT Ltd.* v. *Dy. CIT* 168 DTR (Mumbai 'B') 137

As the legal position as to the levy of penalty under such circumstances is contradictory, assessee has to take the decision keeping in view all the pros and cons.

The above position of law in our considered opinion ought to apply under the new scheme also.

(iv) Time limit for reopening of assessment in the case of income in relation to foreign asset- Applicability after introduction of new scheme of assessment or reassessment

Old section 149 was amended by the Finance Act, 2012 with effect from 1st July, 2012 by inserting clause (*c*) to sub-section (1) providing that in case there is escapement of income chargeable to tax in relation to any asset located outside India, the time limit for reopening of the assessment was extended to 16 years from the end of the relevant assessment year.

A question may arise as to whether such extended time limit would be applicable to the cases for the assessment years, time limit of reopening of which has already expired as on 1.7.2012 *i.e.* the date of amendment to old section 149. In this regard it may be appreciated that an assessee is not expected to maintain and keep the records of the transactions relating to assessment years for which time limit for reopening of the case has already expired as per the earlier provision. There is no other requirement in the Act for maintaining the records relating to the time barred years. Therefore, it can be interpreted that in case time limit for reopening the assessment has already expired as on 1.7.2012 *i.e.* relating to assessment year 2005-06 and earlier years, in such cases the extended time limit as per clause (*c*) of sub-section (1) of old section 149 would not be applicable.

There are various judicial decisions approving the above proposition of law where Courts have held that in case of time barred assessments, assessee obtains the vested right of finality of the assessment and such position of law cannot be amended retrospectively;

Brahm Datt v. *ACIT* [2018] 100 taxmann.com 324/[2019] 260 Taxman 380 (Del), SLP dismissed 105 CCH 155 (SC)

Steel Strips Ltd. v. *Asstt. CIT* [1995] 81 Taxman 369/211 ITR 1021 (P&H)

S.S. Gadgil v. *Lal & Co.* [1964] 53 ITR 231 (SC)

CIT v. *Pushpak Enterprises* [2002] 122 Taxman 478/ 254 ITR 193 (Delhi)

S.C. Prashar v. *Vasantsen Dwarkadas Hungerford Investment Trust Ltd.* [1963] 49 ITR 1 (SC);

J.P. Jani v. *Induprasad Devshankar Bhatt* [1969] 72 ITR 595 (SC);

CIT v. *Onkarmal Meghraj* [1974] 93 ITR 233 (SC)

Another question arises in this regard is with respect to the expressions used in clause (*c*) while bringing this amendment. As per clause (*c*) this amendment is applicable to the income in relation to any asset (including financial interest in any entity) located outside India, chargeable to tax which has escaped assessment. The addition of the words *'in relation to any asset located outside India'* along with the *'income escaped'* gives rise to the interpretation that all kind of incomes escaped assessment are not intended to be covered within the extended time limit. It is only the income chargeable to tax in relation to any asset located outside India which has escaped assessment is to be found for applying the extended time limit.

Now, the question arises what is the meaning of the terminology *in relation to any asset located outside India.* One view may be that escaped income should relate to any asset located outside India and such asset is existing as on the date of issuing the notice under section 148. In case no asset is existing and the income has already been disposed of in some or the other manner, provision of this sub-section may not apply. But in our view, such interpretation may not be correct and there cannot be such intention of the legislature.

Other view may be that this sub-section would cover only those escaped income which results in generation of any asset located outside India at the time when income was accrued or earned. There may be certain income which becomes part of computation of total income as per the Act but such incomes may not result in creating any asset. For example, addition of an income as per section 40(*a*)(*ia*) or section 43B or section 2(22)(*e*) or 40A(2), 40A(3) or 41(1) and so on so forth. Such incomes do not create any asset & therefore such kinds of incomes are not intended to be covered under clause (*c*) of old section 149(1). On the other hand, incomes such as suppressed sale, inflation of expenses, investment in undisclosed property - whether movable or immovable, tangible or intangible, corporeal or non-corporeal, deposit in the foreign bank account are the kind of incomes which create some asset and if such asset was located outside India at the time of generation of income, the intention of legislature is to reopen the assessment with the extended time limit.

However, it may be noted that under the new scheme of assessment or reassessment as given now in sections 147 & 148, & the amended provisions of section 149, there is no provision regarding the reopening of the assessment for earlier sixteen years in respect of any income in relation to foreign asset. This may be for the reason that such income or undisclosed foreign asset may be sought to be covered under the Black Money (Undisclosed Foreign Income & Assets) and Imposition of Tax Act, 2015.

(*v*) **Whether notice under section 143(2) is required to be issued and served before finalizing the reassessment under the new scheme of assessment or reassessment?**

Old section 148 states that income tax return filed in pursuance to notice under section 148 shall so far as may be treated as if such return were a return required to be furnished under section 139. Section 143(2) prescribes the time limit within which notice for scrutiny of the case has to be issued with respect to a return furnished under section 139. If we read both the provisions together, it gives the interpretation that notice under section 143(2) within the prescribed limit is required to be served on the assessee for scrutinizing the assessment with respect to the return filed in response to notice under section 148.

The Finance Act 2006 with retrospective effect from 1st October, 1991 added first and second proviso to section 148(1) to condone the delay in serving the notice under section 143(2) relating to assessment years prior to 30th September, 2005. It was so done as several defaults were noticed in not serving the notice under section 143(2) in time and department wanted such assessment not to be quashed due to such default. However, for future cases to be undertaken for scrutiny, *Explanation* to section 148(1) was enacted.

The above position of law is further clarified by the *Explanation* to sub-section (1) of old section 148 inserted by the Finance Act, 2006 prescribing that the relaxation granted under first proviso or the second proviso shall not be applicable with respect to any return furnished on or after the 1st Day October, 2005 in response to notice served under section 148.

Reliance for the above proposition is placed on the following, amongst others, judicial decisions:

PCIT v. *Silver Line* [2016] 65 taxmann.com 137/383 ITR 455 (Del), *PCIT* v. *Jai Shiv Shankar Traders P Ltd.* [2015] 64 taxmann.com 220/ [2016] 383 ITR 448 (Del), *CIT* v. *Laxman Das Khandelwal* [2019] 108 taxmann.com 183/266 Taxman 171/417 ITR 325 (SC)

In the newly inserted section 148 under the new scheme of assessment or reassessment, there is no explicit corresponding proviso and *Explanation* to the above effect. However, since the return to be filed in response to notice under section 148 under the new scheme would also be treated as return filed under section 139, hence in our considered view, the above principle of law would apply under the new scheme of assessment or reassessment also.

(vi) **Whether under the new scheme, 'reason to believe' is required to be recorded as to the escapement of income as was so required under the old section 148?**

Earlier, old section 147 provided that the assessing officer must have 'reason to believe' that income chargeable to tax has escaped assessment. Old section 148 required the assessing officer to record such 'reason to believe' before issuing notice under section 148.

Now, under the new sections 147 & 148, there is no such explicit requirement. However, a new provision by way of section 148A has been enacted providing *inter alia* that before issuing notice under section 148, the assessing officer shall provide an opportunity of being heard to the assessee as to why notice under section 148 should not be issued on the basis of information which suggests that income chargeable to tax has escaped assessment. Section 148A further provides that after considering the reply of the assessee, the assessing officer may decide as to whether or not this is a fit case for the issue of such notice under section 148 by passing an order with the prior approval of the 'specified authority'.

In view of the above provision of section 148A, it can be taken that the scope of the requirement of recording the 'reason to believe' as to the escapement of income has in a way been enlarged and has become more transparent under the new scheme of assessment or reassessment. The disputes earlier existing relating to non-recording of reason, non-communication of the 'reason' to the assessee & non-disposal of the objection of the assessee etc. appear to have been taken care of by the enactment of section 148A.

However, it is interesting to note that the provision of section 148A has not been made applicable in case of assessment or reassessment of search cases as so given under the proviso to section 148A. It would thus mean that the transparency & safeguard which have been provided while issuing notice under section 148 in cases other than the search cases are made not to exist for assessment or reassessment of search cases. Therefore, the requirement of communication of the information suggesting escapement of income to the assessee may not be required statutorily to be complied with in search cases before the issue of notice under section 148.

It is also to be noted that as per the new provisions of section 148, the assessing officer shall be deemed to have information which suggests that income chargeable to tax has escaped assessment for prior three assessment years in the case of search. It would mean that the assessment of prior three years shall be reopened mandatorily irrespective of any discovery of incriminating material or any evidence relating to escapement of income in possession of the assessing officer.

Further, for reopening of assessments beyond prior three years and up to earlier ten years in cases of search, though provisions of section 148A are not made applicable, but it has been provided that before issue of notice under section 148, prior approval of 'specified authority' as prescribed under section 151 shall be required to be obtained. This would mean in our considered opinion that though there is no explicit requirement of recording as to the information or evidence suggesting escapement of income of the assessee but for taking approval from the higher 'specified authority', such requirement in our opinion should be complied with by the assessing officer. This is for the reason that unless such material or information or evidence is specified and unless it is linked with the escapement of income, there can be no objective consideration before the 'specified authority' before the grant approval. Further, in our considered opinion such approval is subject to judicial review before higher appellate authority or the writ court which would also mean that such information or evidence or material suggesting escapement of income has to be brought on record. Further in our considered opinion, the assessee should be entitled to obtain copy of such approval granted by the higher 'specified authority'.

(*vii*) **Whether additions can be made on issues not covered by the information suggesting escapement of income under the new scheme of assessment or reassessment?**

Earlier section 147 prescribes that if the assessing officer has 'reason to believe' that any income chargeable to tax has escaped assessment for any assessment year, he may issue notice under section 147 for reopening of the case and assess or reassess such income and also any other income chargeable to tax which has escaped assessment and which comes to his notice subsequently in the course of the proceedings under this section. It makes clear that the scope of additions in the assessment to be framed under old section 147 is not restricted to the issues mentioned in the 'reason' recorded but any other income which has escaped assessment and which comes to the notice of the assessing officer in the course of the assessment proceeding, can also be brought to tax.

In fact, P & H High Court in the case of *Vipan Khanna* v. *CIT* [2002] 122 Taxman 1/255 ITR 220 (P&H) had held that the assessing officer cannot make any addition on such issue which does not figure in the reason recorded. This view was followed in yet another case of *CIT* v. *M.P. Iron Traders* (2003) Tax LR 929,931(Punj).

Therefore, the correct position of law was further explained & clarified by inserting an *Explanation 3* to old section 147 prescribing that for the purpose of assessment or reassessment under this section, the assessing officer may assess or reassess the income in respect of any issue, which has escaped assessment, and which comes to his notice subsequently in the course of the proceedings under this section, notwithstanding that such issue had not been included in the 'reason' recorded under sub-section (2) of old section 148.

In the new scheme of assessment or reassessment, *Explanation* to section 147 has been enacted prescribing that for the purpose of assessment or reassessment under section 147, the assessing officer may assess or reassess the income in respect of any issue, which has escaped assessment, and such issue comes to his notice subsequently in the course of the proceedings under section 147 irrespective of the fact that the provisions of section 148A have not been complied with.

Therefore, substantial law on this issue remains more or less similar under the new scheme of assessment or reassessment as prescribed under section 147.

There is also another legal dimension to this issue. In various judicial decisions by Hon'ble Courts, it has been held in the context of old section 147 that addition to income with respect to any other issues can be made only when the addition to income has been made on the issue for which 'reason' was recorded. It was held in those judicial decisions that in case addition is not made on the issue for which 'reason' was recorded for escapement of income, no addition on any other issue can be made.

This is controversial issue and there are divergent views of different Courts:

CIT v. *Jet Airways I Ltd.* [2010] 195 Taxman 117/[2011] 331 ITR 236 (Bom.)

AO may assess or reassess the income in respect of any issue which comes to his notice subsequently in the course of the proceedings though the reasons for such issue were not included in the notice; however, if after issuing a notice under section 148, the AO accepted the contention of the assessee and holds that the income which he has initially formed a reason to believe had escaped assessment, has as a matter of fact not escaped assessment, it is not open to him independently to assess some other income.

CIT v. *Shri Ram Singh* [2008] 306 ITR 343 (Raj)

It is only when, in proceedings under section 147 the AO, assesses or reassesses any income chargeable to tax, which has escaped assessment for any assessment year, with respect to which he had 'reason to believe' to be so, then only, in addition, he can also put to tax, the other income, chargeable to tax, which has escaped assessment, and which has come to his notice subsequently, in the course of proceedings under section 147

Ranbaxy Laboratories Ltd. CIT [2011] 12 taxmann.com 74/336 ITR 136 (Del)

AO had jurisdiction to reassess income other than the income in respect of which proceedings under section 147 were initiated but he was not justified in doing so when the very reasons for initiation of those proceedings ceased to survive; legislature could not be presumed to have intended to give blanket powers to the AO that on assuming jurisdiction under section 147 regarding assessment or reassessment of escaped income, he would keep on making roving inquiry and thereby including different items of income not connected or related with the reasons to believe, on the basis of which he assumed jurisdiction

N Govindaraju v. ITO [2015] 60 taxmann.com 333/233 Taxman 376/ 377 ITR 243 (Kar.)

Once proceedings had been initiated on valid notice, it becomes duty of AO to levy tax on entire income that may have escaped assessment and comes to his notice during course of proceedings initiated u/s 147

However, under the new scheme of assessment or reassessment, the word 'also' is missing under the *Explanation* to section 147 which used to exist in the language of old main section 147 & which expression 'also' led to this interpretation that addition on the issue covered by the 'reason' recorded is *sine qua non* before any other escaped income is brought to tax. Therefore, the above interpretation of law may no longer be applicable in new scheme of assessment or reassessment.

(viii) On whom the burden of proof of escaped income lies?

When there is reopening of the assessment on the basis of formation of belief that income has escaped assessment, obviously the initial burden is on the assessing officer to establish that there is income of the assessee which has gone untaxed or which has escaped assessment. Ideally, the 'reason' recorded for reopening the case should be self-speaking and sufficient enough to discharge such burden. But it is also settled law that it is not necessary that the 'reason' recorded should be based upon any such conclusive evidence. However during the course of assessment proceeding, assessing officer has to lead evidence initially to prove his charge that assessee is having income which is unaccounted and not taxed earlier. Thereafter, the burden should shift on the assessee to disprove the case of the assessing officer.

Assessing officer ought not to require the assessee in the case of assessment under section 148 to justify the taxability of any income without any adverse material being brought on record. For example, there may be certain cash credits or borrowings made by the assessee from third parties appearing in the books of account. Without any adverse material on record, assessing officer cannot shift the burden on the assessee to prove the genuineness of such cash credits on the parameters of section 68.

CIT v. *Pradeep Kumar Gupta* [2008] 303 ITR 95 (Del)

"The facts on which the decision to invoke section 147/148 is predicated may in some cases be sufficient both for decision to carry out a reassessment as well to justify or sustain the fresh assessment. However, there may well be instances where the former said reopening may pass muster in the light of some facts, but those facts by themselves may turn out to be insufficient to preserve the assessment itself. Once sections 147 and 148 are resorted to, the AO must first discharge the burden of showing that income has escaped assessment. It is only thereafter that the assessee has to provide all the answers. We find no reason why the initial burden of proof should not rest on the AO even where the assessment has gone through under section 143(1) of the Act."

The above principle of law developed in the context of old section 147 in our considered opinion should be applicable in the context of new scheme of assessment or reassessment under new section 147 also. This is primarily for the reason that the legislature has used the same phraseology under the new section 147 also *i.e.* income chargeable to tax has escaped assessment. After all, it is the assessing officer who is seeking to disturb the finality of the assessment and that too on this ground that there is income of an assessee and such income has escaped assessment. Therefore, burden to prove that there is income of the assessee and such income has gone untaxed & escaped from assessment should rest on the shoulders of the assessing officer, more so on the principle that one who alleges must prove the allegation.

(ix) **Whether assessing officer may seek omnibus and sweeping details which are unconnected with the information suggesting escapement of income under the new scheme of assessment or reassessment?**

It has been observed in practice when reassessment proceeding are undertaken by the assessing officer under the old provisions of reassessment that assessee is asked to furnish information or details relating to the issues which are not connected with the 'reason' recorded for reopening of the case. Notice is issued to the assessee to furnish information and details in the manner as if such proceeding is *denovo* assessment proceeding as is done during original assessment under section 143(3).

A question arises as to whether the assessing office has to restrict only on the issues on the basis of which assessment has been reopened or he can travel beyond and ask the assessee to submit all other details in sweeping manner. This is a controversial issue and there is no clear judicial opinion expressed by the Courts in this regard. There is no denial to the proposition that assessing officer is empowered also to bring to tax any other escaped income also which comes to his notice during reassessment proceeding. But in such case also, initial burden would be on the assessing officer to establish that there is any other income also which has escaped assessment and which has come to his notice during reassessment proceeding.

But the scope of the assessment proceeding under section 148 cannot be enlarged in our considered opinion to the extent as if it is *denovo* assessment. Assessee may not be required and expected to submit all the details and explanations in sweeping manner. For example, reassessment is reopened on the basis of some specific cash credit received from party A. In case assessee has taken loans from other parties also, details of such loan with justification as per the parameters of section 68 cannot be enforced on the assessee. The principle of finality of assessment has to be respected. P&H High Court in the case of *Amrinder Singh Dhiman* v. *ITO* [2005] 142 Taxman 322/ [2004] 269 ITR 378 held that it was not justified on the part of the assessing officer in calling upon the assessee to furnish information not connected with the reasons on the basis of which reassessment notice had been served on the assessee. However, it was made clear by the High Court that the assessing officer would be competent to frame assessment and to bring to tax any other item of income which might have escaped assessment and which comes to his notice during the proceeding under section 147.

There are contradictory judicial decisions on this issue, one of which may be made reference as under:

V. Jaganmohan Rao v. *CIT* [1970] 75 ITR 373 (SC)

"Once proceedings under section 34 are taken to be validly initiated with regard to two thirds share of the income, the jurisdiction of the ITO cannot be confined only to that portion of the income. Sec. 34 in terms states that once the ITO decides to reopen the assessment he could do so within the period prescribed by serving on the person liable to pay tax a notice containing all or any of the requirements which may be included in a notice under section 22(2) and may proceed to assess or reassess such income, profits or gains. It is, therefore, manifest that once assessment is reopened by issuing a notice under sub-section (2) of section 22 the previous under assessment is set aside and the whole assessment proceedings start afresh. When once valid proceedings are started under section 34(1)(*b*) the ITO had not only the jurisdiction but it was his duty to levy tax on the entire income that had escaped assessment during that year."

In the context of the new scheme of assessment or reassessment also, there remains a grey area on this issue.

(x) Whether reopening is possible based on change of opinion on the same set of facts?

As the law has developed over a period of time, courts have attached lot of sanctity to the finality of the assessment already completed. Therefore the judicial decisions rendered in the matter of reopening of assessment are quite vocal and clear to the effect that reopening is not permissible on the basis of change of opinion on the same set of facts. This is for the reason that there has to be finality of the assessment proceeding. Power of review cannot be permitted into the power of reopening. Reliance for this proposition is placed on *Smt. Jamila Ansari* v. *Income Tax Department* [1997] 92 Taxman 603/225 ITR 490 (All), *Jindal Photo Films Ltd.* v. *Dy. CIT* [1999] 105 Taxman 386/[1998] 234 ITR 170 (Del), *CIT* v. *Malayala Manorama Co. Ltd.* [2018] 95 taxmann.com 136/258 Taxman 238/[2019] 410 ITR 423 (Ker), *CIT* v. *Foramer France* [2003] 129 Taxman 72/264 ITR 566 (SC), *CIT* v. *Kelvinator of India Ltd.* [2010] 187 Taxman 312/320 ITR 561 (SC).

Under the new scheme of assessment or reassessment, there is no reason to deviate from this settled principle of law. Finality of the assessment proceeding is the fundamental to the jurisprudence of reassessment. Therefore, under the new scheme of assessment or reassessment also, change of opinion on the same set of facts would not empower the assessing officer to reopen the assessment.

(xi) Whether another notice under section 148 can be issued if fresh evidences come to the possession of the assessing officer?

Notice under old section 148 could be issued if the assessing officer had 'reason to believe' that the income chargeable to tax has escaped assessment. It is held in the case of *A.S.S.P & Co.* v. *CIT* [1986] 27 Taxman 623/[1988] 172 ITR 274 (Mad.) that even if assessment or reassessment has been done reassessment can be done once again if fresh material leading to the escapement of chargeable income comes into possession of the assessing officer. Reliance is also placed for this proposition on *Kohinoor Enterprises* v. *ITO* [1996] 89 Taxman 587/[1997] 226 ITR 88 (MP).

Under the new law relating to assessment or reassessment also, a notice under section 148 can be issued if there is information suggesting escapement of chargeable income surfaces and comes into possession of the assessing officer. Therefore, under the new scheme of assessment or reassessment, fresh initiation of reassessment proceeding can take place on the receipt of information by the assessing officer which suggests that the income chargeable to tax escaped assessment. There is no reason as to why the principle of fresh initiation of reassessment proceeding should not be applied under the new scheme of assessment or reassessment.

(xii) **Whether reopening is possible on the basis of surmise & suspicion?**

It is settled law under the old provisions of section 147 that there must exist material having live link or nexus with the escapement of income which was chargeable to tax. It was only then the reopening of an assessment could be undertaken. Surmise or conjecture could not be the basis for reopening the concluded assessment. Hon'ble Courts have held that the words " reason to believe" are the words which are stronger than the words 'satisfied' or 'opinion'. (*Ganga Saran & Sons P. Ltd.* v. *ITO* [1981] 6 Taxman 14/130 ITR 1 (SC), *CIT* v. *Gupta Abhushan P Ltd.* [2009] 178 Taxman 473/312 ITR 166 (Del).

Under the new scheme of assessment or reassessment as contained under section 147 read with section 148, reopening of an assessment is possible only when there is information with the assessing officer suggesting escapement of chargeable income. It has been explained under *Explanation 1* to section 148 that final audit objection of C&AG that assessment in the case of the assessee for the relevant assessment year has not been made in accordance with the provisions of the Income Tax Act would be a case of information suggesting escapement of chargeable income. Other situation contemplated under *Explanation 1* to section 148 is when information is flagged in the case of the assessee for the relevant assessment year in accordance with the risk management strategy formulated by CBDT from time to time.

Thus, even under the new law of assessment or reassessment, surmises and conjectures cannot lead to the reopening of the assessment despite the fact that the phrase 'reason to believe' has been substituted by the information suggesting escapement of income chargeable to tax.

But in our considered opinion, the risk management strategy to be formulated by CBDT for flagging any information on the basis of which reopening of the assessment may be undertaken should comply with the above principle in as much as such strategy should not contain element of suspicion, surmise, subjectivity and conjecture. Otherwise such strategy may not pass the test of judicial scrutiny.

(xiii) **Whether reopening of assessment can be made on the basis of heavy cash deposit in Bank account or investment in properties disproportionate to the income?**

Today in the era of digitization, lot of information is available with the income tax department in respect of the financial transactions of an assessee. Moreover, at the time of search & survey information & data contained in the electronic devices and emails etc. are collected by the department which may in turn reveal certain undisclosed or unusual financial transactions. There may be cases where heavy cash has been deposited in the bank accounts or investments have been made in movable or immovable assets which are disproportionate to the income of the assessee.

A question may arise as to whether under such circumstances there may be reopening of the assessment without having evidences that such deposit or investment are out of unaccounted income. Under the old regime of assessment or reassessment, Courts held that merely heavy cash deposit in the bank accounts or investment in asset cannot be the 'reason' to form the belief regarding escapement of income chargeable to tax. In case assessment is reopened only on the basis of such information, such reopening was held liable to be quashed. *Bir Bahadur Singh Sijwali* v. *ITO* [2015] 53 taxmann.com 366/68 SOT 197 (URO) (Del.-Trib.)

Assessing Officer has opined that an income of Rs. 10,24,100 has escaped assessment of income because the assessee has Rs. 10,24,100 in his bank account but then such an opinion proceeds on the fallacious assumption that the bank deposits constitute undisclosed income, and overlooks the fact that the sources of deposit need not necessarily be income of the assessee. Reassessment proceedings cannot be resorted to only to examine the facts of a case, no matter how desirable that be, unless there is a reason to believe, rather than suspect, that an income has escaped assessment.

In fact, before issuing notice for reopening of the case under such circumstances, assessing officer is required to bring material on record to demonstrate that assessee has not been able to explain *prima facie* source of such deposit or investment. Recently, it has been observed that notice under section 133(6) is issued to the assessee requiring the explanation as to the *prima facie* source of such investment and in case assessing officer is not satisfied with the explanation of the assessee, it may lead to the formation of belief that income has escaped assessment and reopening of assessment may be valid.

Under the new scheme of assessment or reassessment, reassessment may be based on the information flagged in the case of the assessee for the relevant assessment year in accordance with the risk management strategy formulated by the CBDT from time to time. This has been so provided under *Explanation 1(i)* of section 148. In all likelihood, heavy deposit of cash or substantial amount of investment disproportionate to the income may be flagged by the Board as information being part of risk management strategy. In that situation, this fact of heavy deposit of cash or investment itself may lead to reopening of the assessment or reassessment under the new scheme.

(xiv) **Whether direction or finding by any appellate authority or court order can be the basis for reopening the assessment under new scheme of assessment or reassessment?**

Section 150 has not undergone any change under the old scheme or new scheme of assessment or reassessment. According to sub-section (1) of section 150, assessment or reassessment or re-computation can be made at any time irrespective of the time limit prescribed under section 149 if such reassessment etc. is in consequence of or to give effect to any finding or direction contained in an order passed by any authority in any proceeding under the Income Tax Act by way of appeal, reference or revision or by a court in any proceeding under any other law. Sub-section (2) of section 150 however puts a time limit on such wide and plenary power contained under sub-section (1).

Thus, the finding or direction referred under sub-section (1) of section 150 used to operate as 'reason to believe' under the old scheme of sections 147-148. Since section 150 has remained unchanged, it can therefore be opined in our considered view that such finding or direction of the nature referred in sub-section (1) of section 150 would operate itself as information suggesting escapement of income under the new scheme leading to assessment or reassessment.

(xv) **Whether reopening of an assessment is possible even in a case when an issue is pending in appeal, revision or reference before any appellate authority or court, under new scheme of assessment or reassessment?**

Under the old section 147, a third proviso was inserted by the Finance Act, 2008 with effect from 1.4.2008 which provided that assessing officer may assess or reassess such income other than the income involving matters which are the subject matters of any appeal, reference or revision which is chargeable to tax and has escaped assessment. Such proviso was inserted in view of the decision of Bombay High Court in the case of *Metro Auto Corporation v. ITO [2006] 286 ITR 618* which held that reopening of an assessment, pending an issue before any appellate authority at the instance of Revenue, is not possible in law. Other decisions on this proposition are:

National Dairy Development Board v. *Dy. CIT* [2013] 353 ITR 538 (Guj.)

Indian Metal & Ferro Alloys Ltd. v. *Asstt. CIT* [2012] 23 taxmann.com 445/209 Taxman 46/[2013] 353 ITR 561 (Ori.)

CIT v. *Mysore Cements Ltd.* [2013] 35 taxmann.com 294/217 Taxman 187/355 ITR 136 (Kar.)

National Dairy Development Board v. *Dy. CIT* [2013] 33 taxmann.com 429/215 Taxman 392/356 ITR 413 (Guj.)

National Dairy Development Board v. *DCIT* [2014] 362 ITR 79 (Guj.)

Radhaswami Salt Works v. *Asstt. CIT* [2017] 83 taxmann.com 195/ [2018] 400 ITR 249 (Guj.)

PCIT v. *ITSC* [2019] 111 taxmann.com 176/[2020] 268 Taxman 234/ 420 ITR 149 (Guj.)

Under the new scheme of assessment or reassessment, there is however no corresponding enabling power or disability on the lines of third proviso of old section 147. It would mean that under the new scheme of assessment or reassessment, there can be reopening of assessment on an issue even if that issue relating to that year is pending in appeal, reference or revision. It is not clear as to whether absence of corresponding provision on the lines of third proviso to old section 147, under the new scheme of assessment or reassessment is an accidental legislative slip or a conscious position. In our considered opinion, there should be corresponding provision in the new scheme also, as the absence of such provision may result in multiplicity of proceeding with different authorities on the same issue which in our considered opinion is not a sound principle in the administration of taxation law.

(xvi) **Whether an assessment can be reopened under the new scheme of reassessment if income has been assessed earlier at too low a rate of tax?**

Under the old section 147, *Explanation 2* was there which provided that for the purpose of section 147, which kind of cases shall also be deemed to be cases where income chargeable to tax escaped assessment. One of the clauses to this effect was where income has been assessed at too low a rate, as given under *Explanation 2(c)(ii)* of old section 147. Therefore, if an income which was to suffer tax at the rate of, say, 30% but actually suffered tax rate of 20%, such case also used to be categorized as a case where income chargeable to tax has escaped assessment under the above mentioned *Explanation*.

Under the new scheme of assessment or reassessment, though word 're-computation' appears along with the words 'assess or reassess' but such re-computation has been used to cover re-computation of loss or the depreciation allowance or any other allowance or deduction. Situation as contemplated under *Explanation 2(c)(ii)* of old section 147 has not been envisaged under the new section 147 thus leading to a situation in our considered opinion that reassessment cannot be undertaken under the new scheme even if some income has been assessed at too low a rate.

(xvii) **Whether reopening notice under section 148 issued under the new scheme of assessment or reassessment can be challenged in Writ before High Court?**

Article 226 of the Constitution provides for the writ remedy against the action or omission of the State or Instrumentality of the State. Writ is an extraordinary jurisdiction vested by the Constitution to the High Courts. In the matter of writ, a general rule is that if there is any other effective and efficacious alternate remedy available, writ would not be issued. But at the same time if there is palpable lack of jurisdiction or breach of the principle of natural justice, writ remedy may be invoked. Reliance is placed on the judicial decisions like *Biswanath Tea Co. Ltd.* v. *Dy. CIT* [2004] 140 Taxman 568/267 ITR 687 (Cal.), *Ajanta Pharma Ltd.* v. *Asstt. CIT* [2004] 135 Taxman 246/267 ITR 200 (Bom.), *Tolin Rubbers P Ltd.* v. *Asstt. CIT* [2003] 130 Taxman 546/264 ITR 439 (Ker), *Amaya Infrastructure P Ltd.* v. *ITO* [2017] 79 taxmann.com 345/[2016] 383 ITR 498 (Bom.), *Jeans Knit (P.) Ltd.* v. *Dy. CIT* [2017] 77 taxmann.com 176/390 ITR 10 (SC).

Under the new scheme of assessment or reassessment also, if it is found that the jurisdiction assumed by the assessing officer is patently bad in law and could not have been so assumed and is thus without the authority of law, challenge can be made by way of writ in the High Court. In other words, the position of law in this regard would continue to be the same as was available hither-to-fore under the old scheme of assessment or reassessment.

(xviii) Whether failure of the assessee to disclose material facts fully & truly in original assessment has become irrelevant under the new scheme of assessment or reassessment while judging the validity of reopening?

Earlier provision of section 147 contained first proviso thereto according to which it was provided therein that if assessment has been made under section 143(3) or under section 147 and reopening is sought to be done in a year which is more than four years after the end of the relevant assessment year, then such reopening of the relevant assessment year concerned could have been done if such reopening was *inter alia* a result of the failure of the assessee to disclose material facts fully and truly. Several judicial decisions as given hereunder went to the extent of holding that the first proviso to section 147 is not only the matter of jurisdiction but also a matter of limitation. Hon'ble Courts held that unless such allegation is mentioned in the 'reason' recorded along with the basis in support of such allegation, limitation to reopen should be read to be within four years and not beyond four years from the end of relevant assessment year:

Reassessment after 4 years from the end of relevant assessment year and original assessment having been made u/s 143(3) and no allegation in the reason recorded about any failure of the petitioner to disclose material facts fully and truly, reassessment held to be bad:

Haryana Acrylic Manufacturing Co. v. *CIT* [2008] 175 Taxman 262/ (2009) 308 ITR 38 (Del).

Wel Intertrade (P) Ltd. v. *ITO* (2009) 178 Taxman 27/308 ITR 22 (Del).

JSRS Udyog Ltd. v. *ITO* (2009) 189 Taxman 477/313 ITR 321 (Del).

Vishwanath Prasad Ashok Kumar Sarraf v. *CIT* (2010) 195 Taxman 19/327 ITR 190 (All).

AO to specify in the reason recorded as to what the nature of failure is there and what material fact has not been disclosed

Himson Textile Engineering Industries Ltd. v. *N.N. Krishnan or His Successors to Office* (2013) 83 DTR 132 (Guj).

Bombay Stock Exchange Ltd. v. *DDIT (Exemption)* (2014) 361 ITR 160 (Bom).

E.I Dupont India (P.) Ltd. v. *Dy. CIT* (2013) 33 taxmann.com 163/215 Taxman 92 (Mag.)/351 ITR 299 (Del).

Under the new scheme of assessment or reassessment, there is no corresponding provision to this effect. Therefore in absence of the provisions on the lines of the first proviso to old section 147 incorporated in new section 147, failure of the assessee to disclose material facts fully and truly is no longer a factor either for jurisdiction or for the purpose of judging the limitation for reopening the assessment. All that is required under the new scheme is that there must be information which suggests that the income chargeable to tax has escaped assessment in terms of the two parameters envisaged under *Explanation 1* to section 148 irrespective as to whether such escapement is as a result of the failure of the assessee or otherwise.

(*xix*) **Whether new scheme of assessment or reassessment applies equally to assessment or reassessment made as a consequence to search as well as survey?**

Under the new scheme of assessment or reassessment prescribed by section 147 etc., all assessments or reassessments including assessments or reassessment as a consequence of search or survey or otherwise are to be assessed or reassessed as per the provisions of sections 147 to 151. There is now no special provision for making assessment or reassessment in search cases as used to be earlier under sections 153A to 153D.

In respect of search initiated on or prior to 31.3.2021, special provisions of assessment or reassessment as contained in sections 153A to 153D were applicable. In case of survey conducted under section 133A, there was no such special assessment provision and assessment in case of survey used to be undertaken under normal provisions of law as contained in sections 143 & 144 or under old section 147 etc. depending upon the income escaping assessment having been discovered as a result of survey.

Under the new scheme of assessment or reassessment under sections 147 & 148, there is mandatory reopening of prior three years' assessment in case of search as well as survey. As per the earlier law, there was mandatory reopening for earlier six years' cases in the case of search as provided under section 153A but there was no mandatory reopening of prior years' cases in the case of survey. Mandatory reopening of prior three years' assessments under the new scheme would mean that assessing officer is not required to bring on record evidence regarding escapement of income and it would be deemed under the *Explanation 2* to section 148 that there is information suggesting escapement of income for these years. It would however remain a controversial issue in our considered opinion as to what would be the nature & scope of additions to be made in the assessment orders of such three years.

(xx) **Whether the law evolved and developed under section 153A is still relevant for assessment or reassessment made under the new scheme for assessment or reassessment as a consequence of search?**

In case of the assessment or reassessment of search cases in respect of search initiated on or prior to 31st March, 2021, provisions of sections 153A to 153D would continue to apply. In case of the return to be filed under section 153A, the law as laid down by Bombay High Court in the case of *PCIT* v. *JSW Steels Ltd.* [2020] 115 taxmann.com 165/270 Taxman 201/422 ITR 71 (Bom.) is to the effect that a fresh and new claim can be made in the return filed in response to notice under section 153A in an abated assessment. We may however hasten to add that this issue is not free from doubt, debate or controversy. But, the law in respect of the return to be filed in response to notice under section 148 has remained that the reassessment proceeding not being a beneficial provision from the standpoint of the assessee, no new or fresh claim can be made in such return of income. Reliance for this proposition is placed on *CIT* v. *Sun Engineering Works P Ltd.* [1992] 64 Taxman 442/198 ITR 297 (SC).

Under the new scheme of assessment or reassessment, since the basic jurisprudence would remain the same in the matter of the nature of assessment or reassessment proceeding, it can therefore be opined that no new or fresh claim can be made under the new scheme, in the return to be filed in response to notice under section 148.

Another issue which was a source of divergent judicial view under section 153A was as to whether any addition which was not based on the incriminating material found as a result of search could be made or not in unabated assessment? View that in unabated assessment, addition could not be made *de hors* the incriminating material found as a result of search, was supported by the following judicial decisions:

CIT v. *Kabul Chawla* [2015] 61 taxmann.com 412/234 Taxman 300/ [2016] 380 ITR 573 (Del), *PCIT* v. *Meeta Gutgutia* [2017] 82 taxmann. com 287/248 Taxman 384/395 ITR 526 (Del), **SLP dismissed** *PCIT* v. *Meeta Gutgutia* [2018] 96 taxmann.com 468/257 Taxman 441 (SC), *PCIT* v. *Ram Avtar Varma* [2017] 88 taxmann.com 666/395 ITR 252 (Del), *PCIT* v. *Dipak Jashvantlal Panchal* [2017] 88 taxmann.com 611/ 397 ITR 153 (Guj.)

Whereas the other view that it could be done, was supported by the following judicial decisions:

CIT v. *Raj Kumar Arora* (2014) 52 taxmann.com 172/367 ITR 517 (All.), *CIT* v. *V. Kesarwani Zarda Bhandar Sahson* ITA 270 of 2014 (All.), *CIT* v. *St. Francis Clay Decor Tiles* (2016) 70 taxmann.com 234/240 Taxman 168/385 ITR 624 (Ker.)

Under the new scheme of assessment or reassessment applicable in case of search or survey, three preceding years' assessments are mandatorily required to be assessed. This is irrespective of the fact as to whether there are any incriminating material found or discovered during the course of search relating to those years. In respect of assessment or reassessment of such cases, what should be the scope of additions to be made is quite interesting & may be debatable.

In our considered opinion, if any or more of these three assessments have been made under section 143(3), it may not be possible for the assessing officer to revisit or review the issues which have already been considered in original assessment. Giving permission to do so in the absence of any incriminating material or information suggesting escapement of income, would amount to review which in our considered opinion is not permissible even under the new scheme of assessment or reassessment.

Of course, the assessing officer may bring to tax any other income which has escaped assessment & which comes to his notice during the reassessment proceeding but as opined by us earlier, the burden to prove so would lie on the shoulders of the assessing officer.

There may be another situation such as when assessment or reassessment is sought to be done in case of search or survey cases for any year beyond three prior years up to preceding ten years which can be done if there is information suggesting escapement of income for an amount of Rs. 50 lacs or more and which is represented in the form of asset.

In such cases, the nature of additions which can be made in such assessment or reassessment may be in respect of such escaped income & also in respect of any such other income which has escaped assessment & which comes to the notice of the assessing officer subsequently during the course of assessment or reassessment proceeding. There can be a view that since the escaped income must be represented in the form of asset, thus additions or disallowances even of escaped income cannot be made when such escaped income is not represented in the form of asset. Thus, if disallowance is to be made in respect of wrongly claimed deduction or exemption or for technical reason such as section 43B, 40(*a*)(*ia*) or 2(*22*)(*e*), as per such interpretation it may not be possible to bring to tax such escaped income as these escaped income is not represented in the form of asset.

The other view may be that escapement of income for an amount of Rs. 50 lacs or more represented in the form of asset is required to be seen for assuming jurisdiction and for issuing notice under section 148. Once jurisdiction is assumed, addition may be made in respect of any income which has escaped assessment even if such escaped income is not represented in the form of asset.

(xxi) Whether initiation of reopening of assessment or reassessment on a non-existing ground can be sustained?

It is settled law in view of the following judicial decisions that initiation of reassessment proceeding on an incorrect or non-existing ground is not possible and permissible in law and if initiation is so done, such initiation cannot be upheld:

Anil Kumar Satish Kumar Nahta v. *IAC* [2000] 242 ITR 238 (MP)

Sagar Enterprises v. *Asstt. CIT* [2002] 124 Taxman 641/257 ITR 335 (Guj)

This principle is so fundamental in nature that it would apply, in our considered opinion, to the new scheme of assessment or reassessment also. This is primarily for this reason that finality of assessment is considered sacrosanct by the legislature and finality cannot therefore be permitted to be disturbed by taking recourse to an incorrect or non-existing ground or basis.

Therefore, if information suggesting escapement of income under the new scheme of assessment or reassessment as per the parameters prescribed under *Explanation 1* to section 148 is based on an incorrect premise or incorrect factual matrix, such reopening cannot be permitted to stand to the test of law.

ASSESSMENT OF SEARCH CASES
UNDER SECTION 153A/153C

The assessment and re-assessment in search cases shall be done as per provisions of sections 153A to 153D, if the search has been initiated on or before 31-03-2021. Please see Chapter 12 if the search has been initiated on or after 01-04-2021. We will analyse sections 153A to 153D with related issues in this Chapter.

A. SECTION 153A - ASSESSMENT IN CASE
OF SEARCH OR REQUISITION

13.1 Text of section 153A

(1) Notwithstanding anything contained in section 139, section 147, section 148, section 149, section 151 and section 153, in the case of a person where a search is initiated under section 132 or books of account, other documents or any assets are requisitioned under section 132A after the 31st day of May, 2003, the Assessing Officer shall —

a. issue notice to such person requiring him to furnish within such period, as may be specified in the notice, the return of income in respect of each assessment year falling within six assessment years and for the relevant assessment year or years referred to in clause (*b*), in the prescribed form and verified in the prescribed manner and setting forth such other particulars as may be prescribed and the provisions of this Act shall, so far as may be, apply accordingly as if such return were a return required to be furnished under section 139;

b. assess or reassess the total income of six assessment years immediately preceding the assessment year relevant to the previous year in which such search is conducted or requisition is made and for the relevant assessment year or years:

Provided that the Assessing Officer shall assess or reassess the total income in respect of each assessment year falling within

510

such six assessment years and for the relevant assessment year or years:

Provided further that assessment or reassessment, if any, relating to any assessment year falling within the period of six assessment years and for the relevant assessment year or years referred to in this sub-section pending on the date of initiation of the search under section 132 or making of requisition under section 132A, as the case may be, shall abate:

Provided also that the Central Government by rules made by it and published in the Official Gazette (except in cases where any assessment or reassessment has abated under the second proviso), specify the class or classes of cases in which the Assessing Officer shall not be required to issue notice for assessing or reassessing the total income for six assessment years immediately preceding the assessment year relevant to the previous year in which search is conducted or requisition is made and for the relevant assessment year or years :

Provided also *that no notice for assessment or reassessment shall be issued by the Assessing Officer for the relevant assessment year or years unless—*

    (*a*) *the Assessing Officer has in his possession books of account or other documents or evidence which reveal that the income, represented in the form of asset, which has escaped assessment amounts to or is likely to amount to fifty lakh rupees or more in the relevant assessment year or in aggregate in the relevant assessment years;*

    (*b*) *the income referred to in clause (a) or part thereof has escaped assessment for such year or years; and*

    (*c*) *the search under section 132 is initiated or requisition under section 132A is made on or after the 1st day of April, 2017.*

Explanation 1.—*For the purposes of this sub-section, the expression "relevant assessment year" shall mean an assessment year preceding the assessment year relevant to the previous year in which search is conducted or requisition is made which falls beyond six assessment years but not later than ten assessment years from the end of the assessment year relevant to the previous year in which search is conducted or requisition is made.*

Explanation 2.—*For the purposes of the fourth proviso, "asset" shall include immovable property being land or building or both, shares and securities, loans and advances, deposits in bank account.*

(2) If any proceeding initiated or any order of assessment or reassessment made under sub-section (1) has been annulled in appeal or any other legal proceeding, then, notwithstanding anything contained in sub-section (1) or section 153, the assessment or reassessment relating to any assessment year which has abated under the second proviso to sub-section (1), shall stand revived with effect from the date of receipt of the order of such annulment by the Principal Commissioner or Commissioner:

Provided that such revival shall cease to have effect, if such order of annulment is set aside.

Explanation—For the removal of doubts, it is hereby declared that—

(*i*) save as otherwise provided in this section, section 153B and section 153C, all other provisions of this Act shall apply to the assessment made under this section;

(*ii*) in an assessment or reassessment made in respect of an assessment year under this section, the tax shall be chargeable at the rate or rates as applicable to such assessment year.

13.2 Legislative history

Before the concept of block assessment in search cases was introduced by way of introduction of Chapter XIVB w.e.f. 01.07.1995, there was no special procedure for assessment of search cases prescribed under the Income Tax Act. The assessment of search cases used to be framed in accordance with the normal provisions of the Act as prescribed for making assessment under section 143 or reassessment under section 147/148. Earlier years' cases were to be reopened on the basis of evidences collected during search depending upon as to whether there was any escapement of income in accordance with the principles and procedure laid down for reopening of the cases under section 147 to section 153.

(*i*) **Concept of block assessment**

As per Finance Act, 1995, concept of block assessment was introduced with effect from 1st July, 1995, by way of introduction of Chapter XIV-B. Up to 31st May, 2001, block period consisted ten assessment years prior to the year of search and the year of search consisting period from 1st April till the date of search. However, as per Finance Act, 2001, ten assessment years were reduced to six assessment years with effect from 1st June, 2001.

The objective of concept of block assessment was to make one assessment for the entire block period so that there was no requirement to reopen earlier years' cases year wise in accordance with the provisions of section 147/148 and there was no need to fulfil the conditions of reopening and limitation as laid down under section 147 to section 153 of the Act.

Under the concept of block assessment, regular income was not covered and there used to be separate assessment for such regular income. It was only the undisclosed income found as a result of search which was covered under the concept of block assessment.

Concept of block assessment was however abolished by the Finance Act, 2003 since it was observed that it is not serving the purpose for which block assessment was introduced. Memorandum of objects of Finance Act, 2003 explaining the reason for abolishing the special procedure of block assessment stated as under—

The existing provisions of the Chapter XIVB provide for a single assessment of undisclosed income of a block period, which means the period comprising previous years relevant to six assessment years preceding the previous year in which the search was conducted and also includes the period upto the date of the commencement of such search, and lay down the manner in which such income is to be computed. The main objectives for the introduction of the Chapter XIVB were avoidance of disputes, early finalization of search assessments and reduction in multiplicity of proceedings. The idea was to have a cost-effective, efficient and meaningful search assessment procedure.

However, the experience on implementation of the special procedure for search assessments (block assessment) contained in Chapter XIVB, has shown that the new scheme has failed in its objective of early resolution of search assessments. The new procedure postulates two parallel streams of assessment *i.e.*, one of regular assessment and the other for block assessment during the same period, *i.e.*, during the block period. Controversies have sprung up questioning the treatment of a particular income as 'undisclosed' and whether it is relatable to the material found during the course of search etc. Even where the facts are clear, litigation on procedural matters continue to persist. The new procedure has thus spawned a fresh stream of litigation.

(ii) **New procedure for assessment as prescribed under section 153A**

As per Finance Act, 2003, concept of block assessment was scrapped and new procedure of assessment in search cases was prescribed with effect from 1st June, 2003. Assessment under section 153A is applicable in case search under section 132 is conducted or requisition under section 132A is made after authorization of search or requisition by the competent authority as provided under section 132 or 132A.

In the case of *CIT* v. *Ramesh D. Patel* [2014] 225 Taxman 411/42 taxmann.com 540 (Guj.), the provisions of section 124 clearly concern the territorial jurisdiction of the Assessing Officer and have no relevance in so far as the inherent jurisdiction for passing an order of assessment under section 153A is concerned, when no search authorisation under section 132 was issued or requisition under section 132A of the Act was made. In the absence of search authorization, the Tribunal was justified in holding that the assessment orders under section 153A could not be passed.

This procedure is being discussed in detail in this chapter.

(iii) **Amendment introduced by Finance Act, 2012**

Finance Act, 2012 has inserted proviso to section 153A w.e.f. 1.7.2012 providing that in certain class of cases as may be notified by the Central Government, Assessing Officer shall not be required to issue notice and frame assessment mandatorily for all the earlier six years. It appears that the objective of the above amendment is to enable the Assessing Officer not to reopen/reassess those cases where no incriminating material relating to any of those earlier years has been found and seized. Rules are to be notified by the Central Government specifying the class of cases where notice u/s 153A shall not be required to be issued mandatorily.

The Central Government has prescribed Rule 112F by the Income-tax (Fourteenth Amendment) Rules, 2012 with retrospective effect from 1.7.2012, specifying such class of cases where income tax search is held u/s 132 or requisition is made u/s 132A, and cash and/or other assets are seized during parliamentary and state assembly election period and where the assets so seized or requisitioned are connected in any manner to the ongoing election. In such cases, Assessing Officer has been empowered not to reopen the cases u/s 153A relating to all the earlier six years mandatorily. It implies that Assessing Officer may decide, keeping in view the facts of each of such case, as to for which of the earlier year(s) assessment may be required to be reopened.

Further, CBDT has issued Circular No. 10/2012, dated 31-12-2012 specifying the procedure regarding the application of this Rule, which is reproduced below:—

"As per provisions contained in sections 153A and 153C of the Income-tax Act, 1961, the Assessing Officer is required to issue notice for assessing or reassessing the total income for six assessment years immediately preceding the assessment year relevant to the previous year in which search is conducted or requisition is made.

2. In consequence of the powers conferred by clauses (*64*) and (*66*) of the Finance Act, 2012 the Central Government amended the Income-tax Rules, 1962, to insert a new Rule 112F after the existing Rule 112E, specifying the class or classes of cases in which the Assessing Officer shall not be required to issue notice for assessing or reassessing the total income for six assessment years immediately preceding the assessment year relevant to the previous year in which search is conducted or requisition is made.

3. The aforesaid amendment was introduced with a view to reduce infructuous and unnecessary proceedings under the Income-tax Act, 1961 in cases where a search is conducted u/s 132 or requisition made u/s 132A and cash or other assets are seized during the election period, generally on a single warrant, and no evidence is available, or investigation required, for any assessment year other than the assessment year relevant to the previous year in which search is conducted or requisition is made.

4. In such cases, the officer investigating the case, with the approval of the Director General of Income Tax, shall certify that—

(*i*) the search is conducted under section 132 or the requisition is made under section 132A of the Act in the territorial area of an assembly or parliamentary constituency in respect of which a notification has been issued under section 30, read with section 56 of the Representation of the People Act, 1951; or

(*ii*) the assets seized or requisitioned are connected in any manner to the ongoing election process in an assembly or parliamentary constituency; and

(*iii*) no evidence is available or investigation is required for any assessment year other than the assessment year relevant to the previous year in which search is conducted or requisition is made.

5. The certificate of the investigating officer shall be communicated to the Commissioner of Income Tax and the Assessing Officer having jurisdiction over the case of such person."

(*iiia*) Amendment introduced by Finance Act, 2017

Finance Act, 2017 has enlarged the scope of assessment years to be covered for making assessment under section 153A from 6 years to 9 years in certain situations.

(iv) **Constitutional validity**

Constitutional validity of the provisions of section 153A has been upheld by Delhi High Court in the case of *Saraya Industries Ltd.* v. *Union of India* [2008] 171 Taxman 194 (Delhi).

13.3 Objective

The objective for prescribing special procedure for assessment for search cases may be summarized as under-

  a. In the case of search, assessments for earlier six years and for the year of search are framed together and there is no reopening of cases year wise at different points of time.

  b. There is no requirement of existence of "reason to believe" for escapement of income before reopening of the earlier years' cases as prescribed under section 147/148 and cases of all the earlier six years are mandatorily reopened.

  c. There is no duality of assessment for the same year as was the case in the concept of block assessment.

  d. Assessments are framed year wise and rate of tax including surcharge is applied as applicable for the relevant assessment year.

13.4 Nature and scope of provision of section 153A

(i) **Mandatory reopening of preceding six years' cases**

The basic requirement of section 153A is to reopen the cases of earlier six years prior to the year of search mandatorily. Section 153A categorically states that in the case of a person where search is initiated, the assessing officer shall issue a notice to such person requiring him to furnish fresh Income Tax returns for earlier six years so as to assess or reassess the total income of the person relating to those years. The six assessment years referred to under section 153A are the assessment years immediately preceding the year of search.

There is an opinion expressed in certain quarters that reopening of cases for earlier six years is not a mandatory requirement and only the cases for the assessment years for which certain evidences regarding undisclosed income are found during search are required to be reopened. In our humble opinion this view is not correct. The language of section 153A is very clear and it requires categorically to assess or reassess earlier six years in all cases where search has taken place. The legislature has further clarified so as to remove any confusion in this regard by way of inserting first proviso to section 153A which clearly states that the Assessing Officer shall assess or reassess the total income in respect of each assessment year falling with in such six assessment years.

It has been held in the case of *CIT* v. *Anil Kumar Bhatia* [2012] 24 taxmann.com 98/211 Taxman 453 (Delhi) that under section 153A, AO has power to assess or reassess the total income of six assessment years in separate assessment orders and the provisions of section 153A can be invoked even where the return filed by the assessee for all the six years preceding the search have already been processed under section 143(1)(*a*).

In the case of *Rupesh Anand* v. *Asstt. CIT* [2015] 67 SOT 227/53 taxmann.com 391 (URO) (Bang. - Trib.), the Assessing Officer gets jurisdiction for passing orders under section 153A, once search action is initiated, whether or not any incriminating material is found during the course of search action.

In the case of *Madugula Venu* v. *DIT* [2013] 215 Taxman 298/29 taxmann.com 200 (Delhi), it has been held that once there is a search, the Assessing Officer has no option but to call upon assessee to file returns of income for earlier six assessment years. Therefore, notice issued under section 153A calling upon assessee to file returns for those years, cannot be challenged merely on ground that it would cause certain degree of hardship to assessee.

In the case of *Scope (P.) Ltd.* v. *Dy. CIT* [2013] 142 ITD 515/33 taxmann.com 167 (Mum. - Trib.), it has been held that once a search/ requisition is made under section 132, Assessing Officer is bound to proceed under section 153A for all six years immediately preceding assessment years relevant to previous year in which search was conducted or requisition was made, even if there is no incriminating material to indicate any undisclosed income during original assessment completed under section 143(3) for any particular year. Once Assessing Officer has issued notice under section 153A inviting return of income, he is duty bound to proceed with reassessment proceedings and apart from income already assessed in original assessment completed under section 143(3), he can assess total income of assessee by making addition on account of undisclosed income or income escaped assessment.

In the case of *Canara Housing Development Co.* v. *Dy. CIT* [2014] 49 taxmann.com 98 (Kar.), it has been held that AO is required to assess the "total income" and is not confined only to income which was unearthed during search.

In the case of *CIT* v. *St. Francis Clay Décor Tiles* [2016] 137 DTR (Ker.) 340, it has been held that neither under section 132 nor under section 153A, the phraseology "incriminating" is used by the Parliament. Therefore, any material which was unearthed during search operations or any statement made during the course of search by the assessee is a valuable piece of evidence in order to invoke section 153A. Tribunal having not considered the issue with specific reference to the facts involved in the case and as provided under section 153A matter is remanded for reconstitution.

As per amendment made by Finance Act, 2012, proviso has been inserted w.e.f. 1.7.2012 prescribing that in certain class of cases as may be notified by the Central Government by way of rules to be made by it, Assessing Officer shall not be required to issue notice for assessment/reassessment the total income of the searched person for preceding six years mandatorily. In such cases those years wherein assessment/reassessment proceedings are not pending as on the date of search and are not required to be abated as per second proviso to section 153A, such years may not be required to be assessed/reassessed again by the Assessing Officer as was required earlier. Earlier in the case of searched person preceding six years were mandatorily required to be assessed or reassessed irrespective of the fact whether any incriminating evidence relating to earlier years were found and seized during search or not. There was judicial controversy on this issue and contrary views were expressed by different benches of the Tribunal. The objective of inserting the above proviso, it appears, is not to frame assessment of those assessment years with respect to which no incriminating evidences have been found and seized during search.

The rules in this regard are yet to be notified by the Central Government specifying the class or classes of cases with respect to which such relaxation is intended to be prescribed by the Central Government.

In exercise of the power as granted above, the Central Government has prescribed Rule 112F and has issued Circular No. 10/2012 dated 31.12.2012 specifying certain class of cases covered under these provisions. Detailed discussion in this regard has been made in para 12.2. The cases prescribed are of limited nature covering only those cases of income tax search or requisition held during parliamentary or state assembly election period and that too when the assets seized are having connection with ongoing election. Thus, the expectation that the cases of search where no incriminating material is found shall not be covered in mandatory six years' assessment requirements, has not been so far materialized.

(ii) Rationale for reopening of preceding six years' cases

There are questions raised on the rationale for reopening of cases of preceding six years in the case of search when no incriminating material or evidences are found during search relating to those years.

It is not as if the requirement of reopening of preceding six years' cases has been prescribed under section 153A for the first time. As per Finance Act, 1995, the concept of block assessment under Chapter XIVB was also introduced with the same intent and during the regime of block assessment also, cases for earlier six years were required to be reopened mandatorily. Under the concept of block assessment, single assessment order consisting the period of all the earlier six years including the period upto the date of search was required to be covered. However, concept of block assessment was restricted to assess or reassess only the undisclosed income found as a result of search.

The rationale for such requirement may be spelt out as under:-

a. 'Reason to believe' for undisclosed income is usually formed by the competent authority before authorization of search. 'Reason to believe' with respect to a person regarding undisclosed income or undisclosed assets, formed by the competent authority is believed to be enough to authorize a drastic action like search. It is at this stage only when "reason to believe" is formed to authorize search and search action is initiated against a person, legislature appears to intend to cover such person for his assessment or reassessment for preceding six years.

b. In case search is conducted and no incriminating material is found from the possession of the person searched, it cannot be held to be a conclusive proof that such person has not accumulated any undisclosed income or undisclosed assets. Search proceeding are the investigation proceeding to collect evidences relating to undisclosed income and to seize the undisclosed assets. By taking search action, Department may or may not succeed in its attempt.

c. In case incriminating material is found in the course of search without evidence regarding the year to which undisclosed income relates, the same is taxed in the current year as per deeming fiction under section 69 and the similar provisions. For example huge cash is found in the possession of the person searched, in the absence of any other evidence regarding year of earning of undisclosed income representing such cash, it is likely to be taxed in the year of search. Though it is legally taxed in the year of search, yet it gives an indication that the person has been earning undisclosed income and the accumulated cash might be relating to the accumulated undisclosed income earned during earlier years. Therefore such person is required to be investigated for all the earlier six years for which legislature provides power to the Department for reopening of the cases.

There may well be contrary arguments against the above points, but there is no utility to harp upon the same. The constitutional validity of such provision under section 153A has been upheld by the Courts.

(iii) Significance of non-obstante clause

Section 153A starts with the non-obstante clause *'notwithstanding anything contained in section 139, section 147, section 148, section 149, section 151 and section 153'.* The object to start section 153A with such non-obstante clause is to clarify the legislative intent to supersede the requirements of the provisions of these sections by the provisions of section 153A which are inconsistent with the provisions contained under those sections.

Section 139 contains provision regarding filing of return, section 147 regarding reopening of assessment where income has escaped assessment, section 148 regarding issue of notice of escapement of income and section 149 regarding time limit for issue of notice where income has escaped assessment, section 151 regarding approval to be taken from higher authorities in certain cases before issue of notice for reopening of the case and section 153 prescribes time limit for completion of assessments and reassessments. Since sections 153A & 153B, in the case of search, contain provisions regarding filing of return, reopening of cases and completion of assessment or reassessment which are inconsistent with the normal provisions of the Act, therefore, sections 153A & 153B start with such non-obstante clause. In the case of search, assessment or reassessment procedure is to be followed as prescribed under section 153A. In the case of search, a person is mandatorily required to be assessed or reassessed for preceding six years only for the reason that search has been authorized and conducted in his case. Nothing more is required to be done for the simple reason that the application of the sections 147, 148, 149, 151 and 153 is stalled. The result is that the safeguard mechanism provided by the legislature for reopening the earlier year cases by way of forming of "reason to believe" is no more required.

A question may arise as to whether the above non-obstante clause stalls the operation and applicability of all the provisions of section 139/147/148/149/151/153 or stalls only those provisions which are inconsistent with the provisions of section 153A. In our opinion, only those provisions which are inconsistent with the provisions of section 153A are superseded in view of the following reasons:—

(a) Clause (a) of section 153A (1) states that the return filed under section 153A shall be treated as return filed under section 139.

In such a case, applicability of all other provisions of section 139 cannot be stalled.

(b) Section 153A does not prescribe procedure and nature of assessment or reassessment proceedings to be undertaken. The same shall be governed by the normal procedure as prescribed under section 143/147.

(c) *Explanation* to section 153A clarifies that save as otherwise provided under section 153A, all the provisions of the Act shall apply to the proceedings under section 153A.

It has been held in the case of *Amar Jewellers Ltd.* v. *Asstt. CIT* 216 DTR (Guj.) 137 that it is difficult to take the view that the non obstante clause in section 153A excludes the very applicability of sections 147 and 148 respectively and that submission of the counsel appearing for the Revenue that the *non obstante* clause in section 153A should be understood as merely dispensing with the procedural aspect of section 147 is sustainable and that Return filed under section 153A(1) is a return furnished under section 139 and therefore, the provisions of the Act which would be otherwise applicable in case of return filed in the regular course under section 139(1) would also continue to apply in case of return filed under section 153A.

(*iv*) **Applicable in case of search initiated after 31st May, 2003**

Provisions of section 153A are applicable in the case of a person where Income Tax search is initiated under section 132 or books of account, other documents or assets are requisitioned under section 132A after 31st May, 2003. It means that the triggering point for applicability of new procedure of assessment as prescribed under section 153A is the initiation of search. If search is initiated on or after 1st June, 2003, the assessment or reassessment relating to search years shall be governed by the provisions of section 153A.

(*v*) **Discrepancy regarding "search is initiated" and "search is conducted"**

Section 153A has used the dual phrases *viz.* "search is initiated" as well as "search is conducted" in different parts of the section, which has created controversy relating to the years to be covered for assessment or reassessment. Opening para of sub-section (1) uses the phrase *'where a search is initiated, section 153A becomes applicable and notices for preceding six years shall be issued'*. Clause (b) of sub-section (1) prescribes the assessment years which are required to be covered for making assessment or reassessment. It makes reference to the preceding six years prior to the previous year in which *'search is conducted'*. It states that Assessing Officer shall assess or reassess the total income of six assessment years immediately preceding the assessment year relevant to the previous year in which search is conducted or requisition is made. Further second proviso which discusses regarding abatement of proceeding relating to any assessment year falling with in the period of six assessment years makes reference to the date of initiation of search. Second proviso prescribes the abatement of proceedings, if pending, relating to any assessment year falling within the period of six assessment years referred to in sub-section (1). The reference of six assessment years in sub-section (1) is under clause (*b*). Use of the phrase "search is conducted" under clause (*b*) of sub-section (1) and use of the words "date of the initiation of the search" under second proviso to sub-section (1) which is referring to the same six years as referred to under clause (*b*), is clearly contradictory in nature. It shows that either the legislature has used these two phrases "search is initiated" and "search is conducted" interchangeably having the same meaning or there is drafting error.

(*vi*) **Meaning of "search is initiated" and "search is conducted"**

The meaning of the phrase "search is initiated" can be interpreted in two ways. If we go as per literal interpretation, the date of the initiation of search is the date on which first step regarding initiation of search is performed. The first step regarding initiation of search can be said to be the date on which search warrant is signed and issued by the competent authority. If this interpretation of initiation of search is accepted, it will lead to unintended situation. There may be a case where search is authorized but it is never conducted. It would mean that when search warrant is issued by the competent authority but search is never conducted, the provision of section 153A may be attracted. It cannot be the legislative intent. In another situation, search warrant may be issued at the fag end of March but actual search is conducted in the month of April. In such a situation, there may create discrepancy regarding which preceding six years to be covered for the purpose of applicability of section 153A.

The other interpretation of the phrase "search is initiated" can be the date on which actual search action is initiated on getting the search warrant signed and the authorized officer entering into the premises authorized for search.

The phrase "search is conducted" would mean the incidence of actual conduct of the search. Actual conduct of the search is not a particular point but it is a process during which search is conducted. The process of conduct of search is commenced with the entry and ingress by the authorized officer in the premises to be searched after getting the search warrant signed from the person to be searched as a proof of showing the search warrant to him. This is the first step in the process of conduct of search and this process of conduct of search keeps on going with the other acts to be undertaken *i.e.* collecting the evidences, recording the statements, seizing the undisclosed assets etc. and the process of conduct of search comes to an end when panchnama is drawn and search is finally concluded. The use of the words "search is conducted" in clause (*b*) of sub-section (1) would mean the date on which the first step regarding conduct of search is undertaken by the authorized officer. In the process of conduct of search, whether incriminating material relating to the person searched is found or not, is not material to decide whether search has been conducted or not. Once search warrant is shown to and got signed from the person to be searched, the process of conduct of search is commenced and that may be said to be the date on which it search is conducted.

It has been held in the case of *Bansilal B. Raisoni & Sons* v. *Asstt. CIT & Anr.* 173 DTR 68 (Bom.) that in the search and seizure assessment under section 153A, contention that there was no search at premises of the firm and in order to issue notice under sub-section (1) of section 153A, there must be initiation of search in case of the notice is sustainable. Mere search authorization would not be sufficient but, writ petition to quash the notice under section 153A is still not maintainable & once the AO passes final order pursuant to the impugned notices, it will always be open to the assessee to pursue the remedy available under the Act.

(*vii*) How to resolve the controversy

If we borrow the above interpretation of the phrase "search is conducted" and the second interpretation of the phrase "search is initiated" as discussed above, the date in both the cases would coincide and there will not be any interpretational controversy with respect to sub-section (1) of section 153A.

In case first interpretation of the phrase "search is initiated" as discussed above is taken to be the correct interpretation, it will lead to unintended complication regarding interpretation of sub-section (1) of section 153A. Therefore, without landing into the controversy regarding interpretation of the phrase "search is initiated", to make the harmonious construction of sub-section (1), it is opined that the phrase "search is initiated" should be interpreted as per second interpretation, so that both the dates i.e. the date of initiation of search and the date of conduct of search is the same. Such interpretation goes in line with the legislative intent and makes the interpretation objective and harmonious without leaving any room for unnecessary controversy. It is cardinal principle of interpretation of statute that in case there exists any contradiction in literal interpretation, one should adopt the principle of purposive interpretation.

It is settled law as held by Hon'ble Supreme Court in the case of *R.K. Upadhyaya* v. *Shanabhai P. Patel* [1987] 33 Taxman 229 (SC) that in the matter of reopening, AO assumes the jurisdiction to reopen an assessment by issuing the notice u/s 148. Therefore, one may be tempted to borrow this argument for the purpose of saying that once search warrant is signed, search can be said to be initiated. In fact, issue of search warrant should not be equated with the issuing of notice under section 148. The issue of search warrant is distinct from the issue of notice under section 148 and both the situations cannot be kept at par and no analogy in this regard can be drawn from the principles laid down regarding issue of notice under section 148. The proceeding under section 148 commences with the issue of notice itself which is part of assessment proceeding and it is regarded as quasi judicial action. On the other hand, issue of search warrant is an administrative act though it has to be performed objectively.

Ahmedabad Bench of ITAT in the case of *Dr. Mansukh Kanjibhai Shah* v. *Asstt. CIT* [2010] 41 DTR 353 has held as under—

The mere issue of warrant of authorization without there being search of the premises mentioned in the warrant of authorization would be meaningless and would not serve the purpose of section 132; therefore, actual search shall have to be carried out necessarily before proceeding under section 153A.

In *CIT* v. *Wipro Finance Ltd.* [2009] 176 Taxman 233 (Kar.), it was held that the search is initiated not on date of signing warrant of authorization but on the date initial search was carried out.

It has been held in the case of *Bansilal B. Raisoni & Sons* v. *Asstt. CIT* [2019] 101 taxmann.com 20/260 Taxman 281 (Bom) that in order to issue notice under sub-section (1) of section 153A, there must be initiation of search in case of noticee and mere search authorisation would not be sufficient.

(*viii*) **Whether drawing of Panchnama is mandatory to decide conduct of search?**

In one of the cases, search warrant was issued in the name of six persons jointly consisting of various group companies, having office at the same place. Search proceedings were conducted and when the Panchnama relating to search was drawn, it was drawn in the name of main company say 'ABC Ltd. and others'. The other five companies' names were not specifically mentioned in the Panchnama. Those companies took the plea that no search can be said to have been conducted in their case as no Panchnama has been drawn in their name. Copy of search warrant was not given and therefore, there is no evidence available with them to show that search was conducted with respect to those companies. Therefore, no proceedings under section 153A can be undertaken.

The precise point to be discussed in this case is as to what is the evidence to show that search has been conducted or not. Whether non-drawing of Panchnama would be a conclusive proof to state that no search has been conducted? In our opinion, this view is not correct. Once search warrant is drawn, search team enters the premises, show the search warrant and gets the same signed from the person to be searched, the first step for conduct of search has taken place. Panchnama contains the details regarding proceedings which have taken place during the conduct of search. Non-drawing of Panchnama cannot be a conclusive plea that no search has been conducted, particularly under the circumstances when Panchnama mentioning name of one company and further adding the words 'and others' for other companies was drawn.

However, in the absence of panchnama drawn in the name of the person searched, heavy burden would lie upon Revenue to prove by circumstantial evidences or by leading any other evidences that in fact, search with respect to such person was actually conducted by them. Merely showing search warrant cannot be treated as if search was conducted.

It has been held in the case of *Unique Star Developers* v. *Dy. CIT* [2017] 83 taxmann.com 83 (Mum.-Trib.) that in case of search and seizure assessment under section 153A & its validity in view of absence Panchanama in the name of the assessee, since the name of the assessee-AOP did not appear in the Panchnama and no incriminating material relating to the assessee was seized during the course of search conducted at the premises of the members of the assessee, and not at the premises of the assessee, there is conclusive proof that no search was at all conducted against the assessee and therefore, proceedings under section 153A taken against the assessee were not valid.

Omission to make out a Panchnama did not vitiate the entire search proceeding where the Magistrate was satisfied that the evidence of police officer was true. [*State* v. *Kuppuswamy Margesh Acharya* AIR 1967 Bom. 199]

(*ix*) **Assessment under section 153A not the assessment only for undisclosed income found as a result of search as was the case in block assessment under Chapter XIVB**

Assessment proceedings under section 153A are the proceedings to frame assessment or reassessment of total income of the assessee relating to the years covered under search. It includes the assessment to be made relating to regular income and undisclosed income found as a result of search. In that sense, assessment proceedings u/s 153A are different from the block assessment proceedings under Chapter XIVB which were applicable in respect of searches held prior to 1.6.2003. Block assessment proceedings were the special assessment proceeding to assess the undisclosed income found as a result of search and the assessment proceeding for regular income used to be undertaken independently and simultaneously.

(*x*) **Concept of undisclosed income under section 271AAA/271AAB entirely from a different perspective**

Concept of undisclosed income as provided under section 271AAA/271AAB is a deeming provision of undisclosed income and has been provided only for the purpose of imposition of penalty in certain cases of search. The concept of undisclosed income provided therein has nothing to do with the nature of assessment proceedings to be undertaken under section 153A.

The provision of section 271AAA/271AAB is regarding levy of penalty with respect to undisclosed income relating to specified previous year. Provisions of section 271AAA/271AAB are applicable in case of search conducted under section 132 and are specific provision with respect to levy of penalty in case of search in certain circumstances. The definition of undisclosed income given under section 271AAA/271AAB is only with respect to the levy of penalty as required under these sections. Concept of undisclosed income given under section 271AAA/271AAB has no correlation and cannot be imported for the purpose of nature of additions to be made during assessment proceedings in search cases under section 153A.

13.5 Assessment years covered under section 153A

(*i*) **Preceding six years covered under section 153A - What about preceding seventh year?**

Section 153A mandates to assess or reassess the total income of six assessment years immediately preceding the assessment year relevant to the previous year in which search is conducted or requisition is made.

As per section 149, a case can be reopened in accordance with provision of section 147 where income has escaped assessment for preceding seven financial years. In case there are any evidence of undisclosed income relating to seventh preceding year, the same cannot be reopened under section 153A. A question arises for making assessment of such income of seventh preceding year as to whether action under section 147/148 can be taken. In our opinion, there is no bar for taking action under section 147/148 in such a situation. However, any undisclosed income relating to the year prior to seven preceding years cannot be brought to tax under any of the provisions of the Act.

This controversy has been discussed by **M.P. High Court** in the case of *Ramballabh Gupta* v. *Asstt. CIT* [2005] 149 Taxman 451 wherein it has been held as under -

Notice under section 148 in relation to an assessment year other than the six assessment years falling within the jurisdiction of section 153A is valid; submission that in cases of search, section 148 has no application and no order for reassessment can be passed beyond six years as provided in section 153A is not correct.

(ii) **What about year of search?**

Section 153A mandates to issue notice and frame assessment relating to six years immediately preceding the year of search. The assessment year relating to the year of search is not covered by section 153A. It is for the reason that time for filing Income Tax return relating to assessment year relevant to the year of search will arise after completion of the financial year in which search is conducted and assessee is required to file return of such year in accordance with the normal provisions of the Act. Return to be filed under section 153A is not a special return or a return of only undisclosed income as was the case regarding block period return under section 158BC. Return to be filed under section 153A is a normal return. It has been specifically clarified under clause *(a)* of sub-section (1) of section 153A by inserting that the provisions of this Act shall, so far as may be, apply accordingly as if such return were a return required to be furnished under section 139.

Therefore, a person is required to file income tax return for the year of search disclosing income relating to such year in normal course as per normal provisions of the Act as contained under section 139. No distinction is to be made and no separate return is required to be filed relating to the income upto the date of search and thereafter upto the closing of the year. For the year of search, single normal return is to be filed under section 139 for the whole year. No distinction is to be made for the period upto the date of search or thereafter. Now there is no concept of block period containing the period upto the date of search for which separate return was required to be filed under section 158BC.

It has been held in the case of *A.N. Rangaswamy* v. *Asstt. CIT* [2011] 45 SOT 106 (Bang.-Trib.) (URO) that there is no requirement in section 153A to record reasons before issuing notice and further that search was conducted on 4th July, 2003 which falls in the accounting year relevant to the assessment year 2004-05 and therefore assessment year 2004-05 is outside the purview of section 153A.

Infact, legislature has not created any distinction regarding the nature of the returns to be filed relating to search years. Income Tax returns to be filed for search years are to be filed in accordance with the normal provisions of the Act. The provisions of section 153A is for dispensing with the requirement regarding recording of satisfaction for income escaping assessment, time limit for reopening of the case, approval of higher authorities etc. As per *Explanation* to section 153A, it has further been clarified that save as otherwise provided in this section, all other provisions of this Act shall apply to the assessment made under this section. Therefore, there is no special provision for filing income tax return for the year of search and it is to be filed in the normal course.

However, it may be mentioned here that with respect to the assessment relating to the assessment year pertaining to the year of search, there are different provision relating to the following two matters specifically provided under the Act—

   a. Time limit for completion of assessment for the assessment year relating to the year of search has been preponed by twelve months as per provision contained under section 153B(1)(*b*).

   b. There is attraction of penalty provision under section 271AAA relating to undisclosed income as defined therein for the period upto the date of search, if such income is not recorded in the books of account maintained in the normal course and further the same is not declared in the course of search.

These issues have been discussed in detail at the respective place while discussing the entire provisions.

(iii) **No duality of assessment as in the case of Block Assessment**

Under section 153A there is no concept of dual assessment as was the case under block assessment provisions. Prior to 1st June, 2003, as per requirement of section 158B, block period return was required to be filed declaring undisclosed income, if any, and normal Income Tax return under section 139 was required to be filed containing disclosed income and there used to be two different assessments framed for the same year. Under section 153A, there is no such concept of separate returns for disclosed and undisclosed income. A person is required to file one return for a year and only one assessment order is required to be framed as per the normal provisions of the Act.

(iv) **Re-opening of assessment for further three assessment years beyond prior six assessment years in certain cases**

As per Finance Act, 2017, Fourth proviso has been inserted under section 153A as under:

Provided also *that no notice for assessment or reassessment shall be issued by the Assessing Officer for the relevant assessment year or years unless—*

(a) the Assessing Officer has in his possession books of account or other documents or evidence which reveal that the income, represented in the form of asset, which has escaped assessment amounts to or is likely to amount to fifty lakh rupees or more in the relevant assessment year or in aggregate in the relevant assessment years;

(b) the income referred to in clause (a) or part thereof has escaped assessment for such year or years; and

(c) the search under section 132 is initiated or requisition under section 132A is made on or after the 1st day of April, 2017.

Explanation 1.—For the purposes of this sub-section, the expression "relevant assessment year" shall mean an assessment year preceding the assessment year relevant to the previous year in which search is conducted or requisition is made which falls beyond six assessment years but not later than ten assessment years from the end of the assessment year relevant to the previous year in which search is conducted or requisition is made.

Explanation 2.—For the purposes of the fourth proviso, "asset" shall include immovable property being land or building or both, shares and securities, loans and advances, deposits in bank account.

The following points are significant to be noted from the above proviso:

(1) The above proviso is applicable relating to the search conducted or requisition is made on or after 1st day of April, 2017.

(2) The Assessing Officer is having the power to make assessment or re-assessment of earlier six assessment years cases prior to the year of search as provided under section 153A(1) of the Act. By way of insertion of the above proviso to section 153A, power of making assessment or re-assessment under section 153A has been extended up to earlier 9 Years prior to the year of search, in certain specific circumstances and cases.

The expression 'relevant assessment year' has been defined in *Explanation 1* to section 153A to mean assessment years which fall beyond six assessment years but not later than ten assessment years from the end of the assessment year relevant to the previous year in which search is conducted or requisition is made. If we read this *Explanation* carefully, ten assessment years referred therein include the year of search also. Therefore, the assessment years to be covered u/s 153A as per this provision shall be the assessment year in which the search is conducted and nine preceding assessment years.

It has been held in the case of *A.R.Safiullah* v. *ACIT* in WP(MD) No. 4327 of 2021 Madras High Court *vide* its order dated 24.3.2021 have held that in terms of *Explanation 1* to sub-section (1) of section 153A, the terminal point is tenth year calculated from the end of the assessment year relevant to previous year in which search is conducted. By this, search assessment year has to be included in the period of 10 years.

(3) The additional preceding three more years can be assessed or re-assessed when the Assessing Officer has in his possession books of account or other documents or evidence which reveal that the income, represented in the form of asset which has escaped assessment amounts to or is likely to amount to ₹ 50 Lac or more in the relevant assessment year or in aggregate in all the three assessment years.

(4) The power of Assessing Officer to make assessment or re-assessment for additional three years is conditional on fulfilment of primarily two conditions *i.e.* the undisclosed income is represented in the form of some asset and quantum of such undisclosed income should not be less than ₹ 50 Lacs.

(5) There is though no mention in the above proviso for recording of 'satisfaction' by the Assessing Officer before assuming jurisdiction for additional three years. However, in our opinion, the Assessing Officer will have to record satisfaction regarding fulfilment of the above conditions so as to assume jurisdiction for additional three years. Since the fact of existence of undisclosed income based on books of account, documents etc. represented in the form of asset and its quantum of not less than ₹ 50 lacs are the pre requisites for assuming jurisdiction for opening and assessing/reassessing additional three more years, action of Assessing Officer would become subject matter of challenge in appropriate cases in this regard. In order to provide objectivity and justiciability, it would be necessary in our considered opinion for an Assessing Officer to record satisfaction about the existence of the pre requisites with reference to which the appellate or revisional authority or writ court may be in position to judge the validity of action taken in this regard.

(6) In the above case, all the prior three years are not mandatorily or cumulatively required to be assessed or re-assessed. The Assessing Officer may issue notice for assessment or re-assessment only for the year(s) for which he is in possession of evidence regarding escapement of income.

(7) Clause (*a*) of the proviso has used the language that the Assessing Officer is in possession of books of account or other

documents or evidence which reveal that the income, **represented in the form of asset,** has escaped assessment. Here the words **"represented in the form of asset"** are important to be noted.

Generally, there may be evidences of two types:

(*i*) The evidences which reveal undisclosed income/credit and

(*ii*) The evidences which reveal undisclosed asset

The evidence relating to undisclosed income points out generation of income while the evidences which reveal undisclosed asset points out application of income. The above clause has covered only undisclosed income which is represented in the form of asset, which implies that the evidence should reveal that there is some undisclosed asset. It is not necessary that undisclosed asset should exist or should have been found during search. The intent of the legislature is to cover undisclosed asset for assuming jurisdiction for additional three years. Such undisclosed asset may be in the nature of income as referred under sections 69, 69A, 69B. The deemed income, it may be argued by the tax payers, which comes within the scope of section 68 relating to unexplained credits in the books of account and section 69C relating to undisclosed expenditure shall not be covered within the ambit of above proviso.

The above interpretation finds rationale in the background due to which the above proviso seems to have been incorporated. Government came out with Income Declaration Scheme (IDS), 2016 applicable from 1st June, 2016 to 30th Sept., 2016 and thereafter Pradhan Mantri Garib Kalyan Yojana (PMGKY) applicable after demonetization during Dec., 2016 to March, 2017, wherein disclosure of undisclosed assets to be made by the assessees was the focus. Under IDS 2016, there was requirement to make declaration of undisclosed assets at its Fair Market Value as on 1st June, 2016 irrespective of the year in which the asset was acquired. Even the assets acquired six years or ten years or even more, prior to A.Y. 2017-18 were required to be declared under the scheme. There was further a provision in the form of section 197C under the scheme (IDS) which stated that there may be re-opening of cases of any earlier year without any limitation, if declaration of undisclosed asset has not been made under the scheme and such asset is discovered later on. However, Government has withdrawn provision of section 197C of the scheme as declared in the Finance Act, 2017 but the requirement of making assessment or re-assessment for additional three years prior to six years as earlier provided under section 153A has been incorporated. It seems from this background that the intent of the legislature is therefore to cover the cases of undisclosed income represented in the form of asset only. Further, *Explanation 2* to proviso clarifies that for this purpose asset shall include immovable property being land or building or both, shares and securities, loans and advances and deposits in bank account. It would mean that the jurisdiction under this proviso for additional three years can be assumed only when there are evidences found relating to undisclosed asset.

The above interpretation may be a contentious issue and there may be divergent views and further clarity may be brought at later stage when the above proviso is judicially interpreted by the Judicial Authorities and Courts.

13.6 Procedure for making assessment under section 153A

(i) Flexibility in issue of notice

Section 153A has been drafted in a very flexible manner without putting any restriction on the Assessing Officer regarding time limit for issue of notice or for filing of return of income in pursuance to such notice. There have been numerous judicial decisions in relation to Chapter XIVB where assessment orders relating to search years were quashed due to technical default by the Assessing Officer such as not granting prescribed time in the notice as required under law for filing the return etc. To take care of the situation that assessment orders relating to search years are not quashed due to technical defaults, such flexible provisions have been incorporated under section 153A.

However, it has been held in the undernoted case that notice issued under section 153A should mention about the material seized under section 132.

It has been held in the case *Underwater Services Co. Ltd. v. Asstt. CIT* 209 DTR 476 (Bom.) that notice under section 153A should have mentioned whether seized material as under section 132 or books of account, other documents or any assets are requisitioned under section 132A and since notice is absolutely silent as could be seen from it and notice says "you are required to prepare true and correct return of income" and "setting forth such other particulars", such notice is vague and hence in the circumstances, the notice is quashed and set aside.

(ii) No time limit for issue of notice

Section 153A requires notice to be issued by the Assessing Officer to the person searched requiring him to furnish fresh Income Tax returns for the preceding six years, but no time limit for issue of such notices has been prescribed. Though under section 132(9A), authorized officer is required to hand over the books of account, other documents or assets seized to the Assessing Officer having jurisdiction over the person searched within a period of sixty days from the date of conclusion of search, yet in practice it has been observed that generally it takes much longer period when search material along with appraisal report is handed over by the authorized officer to the Assessing Officer. Sometimes the decision and approval for centralization of cases take lot of time due to which Assessing Officer who is to frame the assessment is not decided. In view of these uncertainties, section 153A does not put any time limit for issue of notices for filing returns relating to preceding six years. In practice, it has been noted that after getting the seized material, notices under section 153A for filing returns are issued by the Assessing Officer as per his convenience. However it may be noted that time limit for passing the assessment order is fixed as provided under section 153B. In any case, notices under section 153A are to be issued prior to that and after keeping reasonable time for the assessee for filing returns and submitting replies to the queries raised.

(iii) No time limit for filing return

There is no minimum time required to be given in the notice to be issued under section 153A for filing return. There was a minimum time of fifteen days prescribed for filing return of income to be granted in the notice under section 158BC but there is no such requirement under section 153A.

In the case of *Manoj Aggarwal* v. *Dy. CIT* [2008] 113 ITD 377 (Delhi-Trib.) (SB) where time of less than fifteen days was granted in the notice for filing return in terms of section 158BD, notice was held to be invalid and assessment order framed in consequence to such notice was quashed. To take care of such situation so that assessee is not benefited due to technical default of the Assessing Officer, legislature has left it open at the discretion of the Assessing Officer to decide and mention in the notice time period within which return in pursuance to notice under section 153A may be filed by the assessee. However Courts have held that reasonable time should be given to the assessee for filing the return.

(iv) No separate prescribed form for return of income

Clause (*a*) of sub-section (1) of section 153A requires return of income to be furnished in the prescribed form and verified in the prescribed manner and setting forth such other particulars as may be prescribed. However no separate format of return has been prescribed under the Rules for filing return under section 153A. The Income Tax return under section 153A is filed in the normal format in which return under section 139 is filed. Ideally income tax return form should be used which was applicable for the relevant assessment year for which return is now required to be filed in pursuance to notice under section 153A.

In pursuance to notice under section 153A received by the assessee for filing fresh income tax return for preceding six years, sometimes a letter is written by the assessee instead of filing fresh returns, stating that original return filed may be treated as return filed in response to notice under section 153A. This practice has been examined in the context of income tax return required to be filed in response to notice under section 148. In the case of *Tiwari Kanhaiya Lal* v. *CIT* [1984] 19 Taxman 497 (Raj.), it has been held that such letter shall be treated as filing of return and sufficient compliance of the notice.

(*v*) Implication of the phrase 'So far as may be'

Clause (*a*) of section 153A(1) states that the provisions of this Act shall, so far as may be, apply accordingly as if such return were a return required to be furnished under section 139. It means that all the provisions of the Act as contained under Chapter XIV prescribing procedure for assessment or under any other Chapter of the Act with respect to return of income filed under section 139 shall be applicable with respect to returns filed pursuant to notice under section 153A. The words *'so far as may be'* have been used to restrict the applicability of those provisions which are inconsistent with the provision of section 153A.

Hon'ble Supreme Court in the case of *Asstt. CIT* v. *Hotel Blue Moon* [2010] 188 Taxman 113 has repelled the argument of the revenue in the interpretation of section 148 to the effect that the expression "so far as may be applied" indicates that it is not expected to follow the provisions of section 142, sub-sections (2) and (3) of section 143 strictly for the purpose of block assessment. Hon'ble Court did not agree with the submission of the revenue and failed to see any reason to restrict the scope and meaning of the expression, "so far as may be applied".

Hon'ble Gauhati High Court in the case of *Smt. Bandana Gogoi* v. *CIT* [2008] 171 Taxman 1, was clearly of the view that the words, "so far as may be" appearing in section 158BC(*b*) would have to be construed as mandatory or merely directory depending upon what action the Ld. A.O. takes.

Hon'ble Supreme Court in the case of *R. Dalmia* v. *CIT* [1999] 102 Taxman 702, has held that if a notice having been issued u/s 148, the procedure set out in the section subsequent to section 139 has to be followed "so far as may be" and it can be excluded by the reasons of the use of the words "so far as may be".

Thus all provisions and requirement of sections 139, 142, 142(1), 143(2), 143(3), 144, 147, 148, 149, 151, 153 etc. which are not inconsistent with the provisions of section 153A will be applicable.

(vi) All other provisions of the Act to apply

By way of insertion of an *Explanation* below section 153A, it has been clarified that save as otherwise provided under this section, section 153B and section 153C, all other provisions of the Act shall apply to the assessment made under section 153A. It implies that section 153A is having overriding effect with respect to the aspects contained therein to the extent the same are inconsistent with the requirement of the provisions contained in section 139, section 147, section 148, section 149, section 151 and section 153. It further implies that the other requirement of these sections *viz.* sections 139, 147, 148, 149, 151, 153 which are not inconsistent with the requirement of the provisions contained under sections 153A, 153B and 153C shall still be applicable for search cases under section 153A.

The above interpretation further strengthens the view that the assessment proceeding to be undertaken under section 153A is like regular assessment proceeding and assessment/reassessment is to be framed in accordance with the normal provisions of the Act. Assessee will be entitled to all the benefits, exemptions or deductions available as are available under the normal provisions of the Act. At the same time, assessee will be required to comply with all obligations as provided under the normal provisions of the Act. Therefore, it can be said that in the case of assessment under section 153A, for instance assessee will be entitled in terms of law, to —

    a. Get benefit of set off of brought forward losses or unabsorbed depreciation.

    b. Depreciation as per normal provisions of the Act, on the assets, if any, declared during search as undisclosed investment.

    c. Deduction/exemption under sections 10, 10A, 10B, 11, 12 or under Chapter VIA or under any other provisions of the Act.

    d. MAT credit, if available, will also be allowed.

(vii) Rate of tax applicable in the case of assessment under section 153A

It has also been clarified under the *Explanation* that in case of assessment/reassessment under section 153A, rate of tax shall be chargeable as per the normal rate applicable for the respective assessment year. It implies that surcharge or cess shall also be chargeable as applicable for the respective assessment year.

(*viii*) Search warrant/panchnama drawn in joint name

There was a controversy regarding the issue as to where search warrant/panchnama has been drawn in the joint name of more than one person, they are to be assessed under section 153A separately or jointly as Association of Persons or Body of Individuals. In the case of *CIT* v. *Smt. Vandana Verma* [2010] 186 Taxman 88 (All.), High Court has held that it is not possible to assess a person in the individual capacity in respect of the asset found in search carried out on the basis of warrant of authorization issued in the joint names of husband and wife. In such a case, High Court held that assessment can be made only as AOP/BOI.

This controversy has been resolved by the introduction of section 292CC by the Finance Act, 2012 with retrospective effect from 1.4.1976 wherein it has been provided in sub-section (2) that *"notwithstanding that an authorisation under section 132 has been issued or requisition under section 132A has been made mentioning therein the name of more than one person, the assessment or reassessment shall be made separately in the name of each of the persons mentioned in such authorisation or requisition".*

It has been held in the case of *Radan Multimedia Ltd.* v. *Dy. CIT* [2011] 58 DTR 129 (Mum. 'D') (Trib.) that warrant of authorization issued in the name of three companies including assessee, separated only by a comma without the word "and" between the name of the companies is a common warrant in the case of said three companies and not a warrant in the joint name of three companies and, therefore, the block assessment order framed in the individual name of the assessee-company is not invalid.

It has been held in the case of *Rajat Tradecom India (P.) Ltd.* v. *Dy. CIT* [2009] 120 ITD 48 (Indore-Trib.) as to the joint search warrant including the assessee's name that search warrant having been issued in the joint names of a person and the assessee who were carrying on business from the same premises and the premises having been searched and panchnama so prepared, it could not be said that there was no search in the case of assessee. Hence assessment under section 153A in the case of assessee was valid.

In the case of *CIT* v. *Smt. Umlesh Goel* [2016] 141 DTR (Raj.) 25, it has been held that all the family members are separate assessable legal entities under the Act and in a case where search warrant has been issued in the name of OP and family. It cannot be stretched to cover all the family members, namely spouse and children. Search warrant has to be in the name of specific person to initiate proceeding. When names of the two assessee does not find mention in the warrant of authorisation, the A.O. has no jurisdiction to issue notice under section 158BC.

(ix) Notice of assessment in case of Amalgamation

In an unreported case of *CIT* v. *Indu Surveyors & Loss Assessors Pvt. Ltd.* [ITA Nos. 365, 366, 367, 368, 371 & 372 of 2013, dated 15-10-2015] (Delhi), it has been held by the High Court that if the assessee stands amalgamated with another Co., it ceases to exist and all proceedings of search u/s 132, notice and assessment u/s 153C on the assessee are a nullity and *void ab initio.*

(x) Notice of assessment to deceased

It has been held in the case of *Late Bhupendra Bhikhalal Desai (Since Deed.) Through L/H Raju Bhupendra Desai v. ITO* 200 DTR 313 (Guj.) that notice in the name of deceased & Issuance of notice under section 153C in the name of a dead assessee is not a mere technical defect which can be corrected under section 292B and that the issuance of the notice to a dead assessee and the consequent proceedings pursuant thereto would be without jurisdiction and, therefore, *null* and void.

13.7 Abatement of pending assessment or reassessment proceeding(s)

(i) Pending assessment or reassessment to abate

Second proviso to section 153A prescribes that assessment or reassessment, if any, relating to any assessment year falling within the period of six assessment years referred to in this sub-section pending on the date of search shall abate. The word 'abate' means to stop or to put an end. The objective of this proviso is to eliminate the multiplicity of assessment or reassessment proceedings which are pending on the date of search and which are now required to be undertaken afresh in view of section 153A.

In case of a person when search takes place, the status relating to pending assessment proceedings relevant to preceding six years may be in following different stages—

    a. There may be assessment proceedings under section 143(3) pending with the Assessing Officer for some years.

    b. There may be reassessment proceedings under section 147/148 pending with the Assessing Officer for some years.

    c. There may be assessment proceedings pending with the Assessing Officer in pursuance to the direction by Commissioner of Income Tax under section 263 of the Act.

d. There may be assessment proceedings pending with the Assessing Officer to make fresh assessment in pursuance to the direction given by higher appellate authorities setting aside the original assessment.

e. There may be situation when assessment or reassessment proceedings under section 153A are pending in pursuance to earlier search held after 1st June 2003.

f. There may be situation when block assessment proceedings relating to undisclosed income as required under Chapter XIVB may be pending in pursuance to earlier search held prior to 1st June 2003.

In a case where search has taken place, assessee shall be mandatorily required to furnish fresh returns of income for the preceding six years in accordance with provision of section 153A and fresh assessment proceedings shall be held and assessment orders shall be framed by the Assessing Officer for such years irrespective of any incriminating material relating to assessee found during search or not. In case any kind of assessment or reassessment proceedings as discussed above, are already pending with respect to such person with the Assessing Officer, it would lead to a situation towards multiplicity of proceedings relating to the same year. To avoid such situation, legislature had provided that all existing assessment or reassessment proceedings pending as on the date of search shall abate. It would imply that all issues pending thereat shall be merged with the new proceedings to be undertaken in pursuance to notice under section 153A.

There should not be any iota of doubt regarding abatement of pending assessment or reassessment proceedings in the nature as described in point No. (*a*) to (*d*) above. Assessment or reassessment proceedings in the nature as described in point No. (*e*) above shall also abate and will get merged with the new assessment or reassessment proceedings to be undertaken in pursuance to new search having taken place but it can be possible only relating to the years which are covered now under new proceedings to be undertaken under section 153A. In case of any other earlier year covered within the ambit of pending assessment or reassessment proceedings under section 153A in pursuance to earlier search held, the same will not abate and assessment or reassessment with respect to those years shall be finalized by the Assessing Officer independently. In case of block assessment proceedings in the nature as described in point No. (*f*) above, the same shall not abate and independent assessment order relating to undisclosed income for the block period shall be framed and finalized by the Assessing Officer. It is so, in our opinion, because block assessment proceedings under Chapter XIVB are in the nature of special assessment proceedings to assess undisclosed income found as a result of search. Moreover section 153A does not override provision of Chapter XIVB relating to block assessment proceedings.

When pending assessment proceeding with the Assessing Officer relating to search years abates, no assessment or reassessment order with respect to such pending assessment or reassessment can be passed by the Assessing Officer. In case any assessment order is still passed after search in pursuance to the pending proceedings, the same will not have any legal validity and such order is liable to be quashed on this ground alone.

In the case of *Abhay Kumar Shroff* v. *CIT* [2007] 162 Taxman 429 (Jharkhand) High Court of Jharkhand has held as under—

Assessment proceeding pending at the time of search stood abated by virtue of second proviso to section 153A, and the continuation of the assessment proceeding and passing of impugned final order of assessment purportedly under section 143(3), without any notice under section 153A was illegal, arbitrary and wholly without jurisdiction.

It has been held in the case of *Guruprerna Enterprises* v. *Asstt. CIT* [2011] 57 DTR 465 (Mumbai - Trib.) that only the assessments pending before the AO for completion shall abate.

It has been held in the case of *CIT* v. *Smt. Shaila Agarwal* [2011] 16 taxmann.com 232/[2012] 204 Taxman 276 (All.) that only an assessment or reassessment pending on the date of initiation of search u/s 132 or requisition section 132A shall abate under the second proviso to section 153A and that even if an appeal is pending against a completed assessment before the Tribunal on the date of search, such completed proceedings do not abate.

It has been held in the case of *Chintels India Ltd.* v. *Dy. CIT* [2017] 84 taxmann.com 57/249 Taxman 630 (Delhi) that in case of search and seizure assessment under section 153A, if an assessee does not receive a notice under section 143(2) within the period stipulated then such an assessee "can take it that the return filed by him has become final and no scrutiny proceedings are to be started in respect of that return"; Tribunal was held thus not justified in negativing the plea of the assessee that the assessment for asst. yr. 2008-09 had abated, because no notice had been issued to the assessee either under section 143(2) or under section 142(1) within the stipulated time.

(*ii*) Fresh assessments to be framed for all the preceding six years whether assessment proceedings are abated or not

As per requirement of section 153A, fresh assessment or reassessment proceedings are required to be undertaken for all the preceding six years irrespective of the fact whether as on the date of initiation of search, any assessment proceedings are pending or not or whether the same are abated or not. In our opinion, the requirement of abatement is only to do away with the multiplicity of proceedings for the same year. The requirement of abatement of the pending proceeding does not alter the mandate of making fresh assessment or reassessment for all the preceding six years as given in section 153A(1)(*b*) and further reiterated as per first proviso to section 153A.

In some of the ITAT judgments, different interpretation is being made to the interpretation of "abatement" and whether fresh assessment proceedings are to be undertaken relating to the years for which proceedings are not abated.

In the case of *Meghmani Organics Ltd.* v. *Dy. CIT* [2010] 129 TTJ 255 Ahmedabad Bench of ITAT has held as under—

The AO is precluded from re-agitating the assessments that have attained finality in original assessment proceedings, though pending in for the appeals. So far as the AO is concerned, his jurisdiction is ousted and is a *"functus officio"* so far as the original assessments are concerned. Therefore, re-agitating the concluded issues in section 153C proceedings without any documents relating thereto belonging to the assessee cannot be considered in such assessment under section 153C. In assessments under section 153C the issue can be considered only if the pending assessment is abated and not otherwise. If the original assessments are completed which are subject-matter of further litigation and if those very assessments are re-agitated under section 153C proceedings, the same will not only multiply assessment proceedings but will multiply even the appellate proceedings. This can never be the intention of the legislature.

In *LMJ International Ltd.* v. *Dy. CIT* [2008] 22 SOT 315 (Kol. Trib.), it was held that where nothing incriminating is found in the course of search relating to any assessment years, the assessments for such years cannot be disturbed.

Similar views have been expressed in the case of *Anil Kumar Bhatia* v. *Asstt. CIT* [2010] 1 ITR (Trib.) 484 (Delhi) and *Anil P. Khemani* v. *Dy. CIT* [ITA Nos. 2855 to 2860/Mum./2008 dated 23-2-2010].

In our humble opinion, the above view does not seem to be correct and the above decisions require to be reconsidered and adjudicated by the higher authorities.

However, Finance Act, 2012 has with effect from 1.7.2012 inserted proviso to section 153A granting powers to the Central Government to notify rules specifying the class of cases in which earlier six years are not mandatorily required to be assessed/reassessed again under the circumstances when any assessment/reassessment proceedings are not pending as on the date of search. (It implies that, those assessment year(s) for which any assessment or reassessment proceedings were pending on the date of search will not be affected by this newly inserted proviso and assessment/reassessment of those year(s) shall be required to be passed u/s 153A). For other years appropriate rules shall be notified.

It has been held in the case of *CIT* v. *Anil Kumar Bhatia* [2012] 24 taxmann.com 98/211 Taxman 453 (Delhi) that under section 153A, AO has power to assess or reassess the total income of six assessment years in separate assessment orders and the provisions of section 153A can be invoked even where the return filed by the assessee for all the six years preceding the search have already been processed under section 143(1)(*a*).

In the case of *CIT* v. *Raj Kumar Arora* [2014] 120 DTR (All.) 417, it has been held that where the assessment or reassessment proceedings have already been completed and assessment orders have been passed, which were subsisting when the search was made, the Assessing Officer would be competent to reopen the assessment proceeding already made and determine the total income of the Assessee. The Assessing Officer, while exercising the power under section 153A of the Act, would make assessment and compute the total income of the Assessee including the undisclosed income, notwithstanding the Assessee had filed the return before the date of search which stood processed under section 143(1)(*a*) of the Act.

(*iii*) **Abatement of pending assessment proceeding - What remains the status of return filed?**

Abatement of pending assessment proceeding as provided under the second proviso to section 153A will not mean that the income tax return filed by the assessee will no longer remain valid or it will become *non est*. Abatement of assessment proceeding would only mean that no assessment can be framed on the basis of such return filed earlier. After the search, assessee will be required to file fresh returns in pursuance to notice under section 153A and assessment will be framed with respect to fresh returns filed in pursuance to notice under section 153A. Evidences available with Assessing Officer during abated proceedings may be made use of by Assessing Officer during assessment under section 153A now.

Earlier returns filed under section 139 or 142(1) or 148 with respect to which assessment proceeding were pending which were abated after search, will still remain on record as valid returns filed. Interest or penalty may be imposed in case there is any default in filing of such returns as per normal provisions of the Act. Original returns filed shall become relevant in case abatement is revived due to any reason at any later stage.

In the case of *M.M. Sulaiman* v. *Asstt. CIT* [2014] 51 taxmann.com 310/[2015] 67 SOT 32 (URO) (Cochin-Trib.), Tribunal held that where search took place when original assessment of instant year was pending, documents filed along with return of income filed under section 139 also could be considered by Assessing Officer for purpose of making assessment under section 153A.

(iv) Abatement to revive

Sub-section (2) of section 153A provides that if any proceeding initiated or any order of assessment or reassessment made under sub-section (1) has been annulled in appeal or any other legal proceeding then, notwithstanding anything contained in sub-section (1) or section 153, the assessment or reassessment relating to any assessment year which has abated under the second proviso to sub-section (1), shall stand revived with effect from the date of receipt of the order of such annulment by the Commissioner. It is further provided that such revival shall cease to have effect, if such order of annulment is set aside.

The objective of the above provision is to revive the assessment or reassessment proceedings which were pending under the normal provision of the Act but which were abated and merged with the assessment proceedings to be undertaken in pursuance to returns filed under section 153A. There may be situation when proceedings under section 153A are held not to be valid which may happen due to various reasons such as -

    a. Search action under section 132 is held illegal and consequently proceedings under section 153A are also held to be illegal.

    b. Invoking provision of section 153A is held to be illegal due to some other reason by the appellate authorities.

    c. The jurisdiction to assessment or reassessment under section 153A was not validly assumed by the Assessing Officer and therefore assessment or reassessment framed under section 153A is quashed by the appellate authorities.

    d. Assessment or reassessment framed under section 153A was time barred and therefore the same is quashed by the appellate authorities.

    e. Due to some other reason or technical/legal fault on the part of Assessing Officer, order of assessment or reassessment framed under section 153A is quashed in appeal or in any other legal proceedings by the higher authorities.

In sub-section (2) of section 153A, legislature has used the phrase any proceeding initiated or any assessment or reassessment order made is "annulled". The meaning of the word "annulled" is not clear and the same is not defined in the Act. Whether annulment would cover all the situations as mentioned above may be a point of debate. There is no doubt that it would cover situation mentioned at point (*a*) and (*b*) above but it cannot be interpreted to cover the situation mentioned at point (*c*), (*d*) and (*e*) keeping in view the object and intent of the provision.

(v) No other assessment or reassessment proceedings during pendency of proceeding u/s 153A

When cases under section 153A for assessment or reassessment are pending, no other proceeding for reassessment under section 147/148 or in pursuance to direction under section 263 or any other provisions of the Act can be undertaken by the Assessing Officer separately otherwise it would tantamount to duplicate proceedings which is not intended to be undertaken as per the provision of section 153A of the Act.

Situation can be compared to the proceeding u/s 147 where reassessment proceedings initiated under section 147 have not been concluded to the logical end, a fresh reassessment proceeding is initiated which would be invalid and unsustainable as held by Rajasthan High Court in the case of *CIT* v. *Jaideo Jain & Co.* [1997] 227 ITR 302 (Raj.).

However contrary view has been taken by Delhi Bench of Tribunal in the following case:

It has been held in the case of *Trilok Chand Chaudhary* v. *Asstt. CIT* ITA No.5870/Delhi/2017 (Delhi - Trib) that the Act has separate provisions for making assessment in case of material found in the course of search from premises of assessee (section 153A) as well as material found in course of search at premises of third party (section 153C). Even if search happens in case of assessee, the AO cannot initiate proceedings u/s 153A if incriminating material is found during search of other person. Proceedings should be initiated u/s 153C and failure to do so renders the addition in the section 153A assessment *void-ab initio.* (*Vinod Kumar Gupta* 165 DTR 409 (Del.) distinguished).

In our considered opinion, the above view does not seem to be correct. In case assessment proceeding under section 153A is going on with respect of the searched person, & any material of incriminating nature having bearing on the assessment or the searched person is found during the course of search or survey with respect of some other person, such material can be passed on to the Assessing Officer of the searched person who is already undertaking assessment proceeding u/s 153A & can be considered by the Assessing Officer.

The ratio laid down in the decision of Hon'ble Supreme Court in the case of *CIT* v. *S. Ajit Kumar* [2018] 93 taxmann.com 294/255 Taxman 286 though was in the context of Block assessment under section 158BC, is significant in support of the above view.

Thus, during the pendency of proceeding under section 153A, in case there are any issues coming to the knowledge of Assessing Officer based upon new information requiring reopening, or there is any direction by Commissioner under section 263 to re-examine any issue relating to earlier year or any assessment is set aside by higher appellate authorities for making fresh assessment or there is any incriminating material received from the Assessing Officer of some other person searched but belonging to the assessee in accordance with the provision of section 153C, all such information or material shall be merged and considered during the proceedings pending under section 153A only.

(vi) Application for rectification under section 154 not to abate

There may be cases when application for rectification of any earlier order passed by the Assessing Officer has been filed by the assessee under section 154 of the Act which is pending with the Assessing Officer. Such application shall not abate since it is in continuation of the completed assessment proceedings already finalized. Assessing Officer will be required to adjudicate upon the same and pass the necessary order.

(vii) No abatement of pending appellate proceedings

The abatement shall take place only relating to assessment or reassessment proceedings of whatsoever nature pending with the Assessing Officer. Any appeal filed by the assessee or by the Department pending with the higher authorities shall be carried in normal course and it will not abate.

The issues on which a view has been finalized by the Assessing Officer and additions have made in any of the earlier assessment or reassessment proceedings, will not be disturbed and in case the same are agitated by the assessee, appellate authorities will decide the matter on merit.

It has been held in the case of *CIT* v. *Smt. Shaila Agarwal* [2011] 16 taxmann.com 232/[2012] 204 Taxman 276 (All.) that only an assessment or reassessment pending on the date of initiation of search under section 132 or requisition section 132A shall abate under the second proviso to section 153A and even if an appeal is pending against a completed assessment before the Tribunal on the date of search, such completed proceedings do not abate.

It has been held in the case of *Dy. CIT* v. *HML Agencies (P.) Ltd.* [2011] 12 taxmann.com 397/131 ITD 539 (Bang.-Trib.) that the application to rectify the order of the Tribunal under section 254(2) on the ground that in the subsequent proceedings under section 153A the issues which were subject matter of proceedings under section 143(3) were also incorporated, is not maintainable as there is no question of abatement of appeal.

13.8 Issues regarding filing of return under section 153A

(*i*) **Whether exemption/deduction can be claimed first time in the returns filed under section 153A, which could not be made in the original return**

There arises a question whether assessee is entitled to any new claim of exemption/deduction in the income tax return to be filed in pursuance to notice under section 153A which could not be claimed or which was barred while filing original income tax return under section 139 *e.g.* where assessee filed the original return belatedly due to which the deduction u/s 80-IA etc. could not be claimed or where though return was filed in time but a claim of deduction, say, u/s 10B was not made.

This is a debatable issue. Jodhpur Bench of ITAT in the case of *Suncity Alloys (P.) Ltd.* v. *Asstt. CIT* [2009] 124 TTJ 674 (Jodh.-Trib.) has examined this issue and has held that the assessments or reassessments made pursuance to notice under section 153A are not *de novo* assessments and therefore no new claim of deduction or allowance can be made by assessee.

In *Charchit Agarwal* v. *Asstt. CIT* [2009] 34 SOT 348, Delhi Bench of Tribunal held that since the search proceedings under section 153A are for the benefit of the Revenue, assessee is not permitted to value the closing stock for concluded years in a difference manner than the one adopted in earlier years and claim lower income.

In the case of *Jai Steel (India)* v. *Asstt. CIT* [2013] 36 taxmann.com 523/219 Taxman 223/259 CTR 281 (Raj.), it has been held that assessment or reassessment proceedings, which have already been 'completed' and assessment orders have been passed determining the assessee's total income and, such orders are subsisting at the time when the search or the requisition is made, there is no question of any abatement since no proceedings are pending. In such cases, where the assessments already stands completed, the AO can reopen the assessments or reassessments already made without following the provisions of sections 147, 148 and 151 of the Act and determine the total income of the assessee. It is not open for assessee to seek deduction or claim expenditure which has not been claimed in original assessment, which assessment already stands completed, only because assessment u/s 153A in pursuance of search or requisition is required to be made.

On the other hand, there can be another view that section 153A requires to assess or reassess the total income of preceding six years as mentioned under clause (*b*) as well as under first proviso to section 153A(1). When total income is to be assessed, assessee would be entitled to lodge fresh claims which could not be made in the original returns.

It has been held in the case of *CIT* v. *B. G. Shirke Construction Technology (P.) Ltd.* [2017] 79 taxmann.com 306/246 Taxman 300 (Bom.) that in case of assessment in search cases under section I53A, Assessee can claim deduction for first time before appellate authorities. This decision has been rendered after considering the ratio laid down by the apex court in the case of *CIT* v. *Sun Engineering Works (P.) Ltd.* [1992] 64 Taxman 442 (SC).

It has been held in the case of *Principal CIT* v. *Vijay Infrastructure Ltd.* [2018] 402 ITR 363 (All.) that deduction under section 80- IA can be claimed in return filed pursuant to notice under section 153A.

In our opinion, this issue should be decided based upon the principles and ratios applicable in case of reopening of assessment under section 147/148.

In the case of *CIT* v. *Sun Engineering Works (P.) Ltd.* [1992] 64 Taxman 442, Supreme Court has held that by reassessment original assessment is not wiped off. A loss not allowed to be set off due to late filing of return of income, cannot be claimed to be allowed to be carried forward and set off.

It has been held in the case of *Dy. CIT* v. *Eversmile Construction Co. (P.) Ltd.* [2013] 33 taxmann.com 657 (Mum.-Trib.) while dealing the issue of the scope of section 153A *vis-à-vis* new claim for deduction that requirement of section 153A is to compute the total income of each of such assessment years and such determination of the total income has to be done afresh without any reference to what was done in the original assessment and the assessee is entitled to seek relief on any addition which was made in the original assessment.

In our considered opinion, the ratio laid down in the above decision needs reconsideration. There are already judicial decisions taking a contrary view. Any addition made in the original assessment order unless deleted or varied by the higher appellate authorities attains finality and cannot be considered during the assessment proceeding under section 153A.

It has been held in the case of *Principal CIT* v. *JSW Steel Ltd* 187 DTR (Bom) 1 that in view of the second proviso to s. 153A(1), once assessment gets abated, it is open for the assessee to lodge a new claim in a proceeding under s. 153A(1) which was not claimed in his regular return of income, because assessment was never made/finalized in the case of the assessee in such a situation.

(*ii*) Interest provisions applicable as in normal course

Provisions regarding applicability of interest as contained under section 234A, 234B or 234C shall be applicable with respect to income tax returns filed in pursuance to notice under section 153A in the same manner as applicable for income tax return to be filed in pursuance to notice under section 147/148. These sections regarding imposition of interest contain reference to the income tax return filed under section 153A in the same manner as return filed in pursuance to notice under section 148.

There may be a situation when income tax return was originally filed late but return in pursuance to notice under section 153A is filed in time. Therefore, a question arises as to whether interest for delayed filing of the original return would be leviable u/s 234A? Assessee is required under the law to compute interest and pay it while filing the return of income. In case it is not so paid, it has to be levied while processing the return u/s 143(1). In case processing of original return has been done under section 143(1) before the date of conduct of search, interest under section 234A shall be charged thereat. However, in case processing of return under section 143(1) has not been undertaken till the date of conduct of search, then also, interest u/s 234A will be leviable as the return filed originally remains the valid return. Second proviso to section 153A provides for the abatement of the pending assessment or reassessment proceeding. Return filed does not abate and assessee would be liable for interest on account of default in filing such return. Interest under sections 234B and 234C shall be applicable and charged in normal course.

(*iii*) **Applicability of provisions regarding imposition of penalty and prosecution**

Penalty and prosecution provisions will also be applicable for search assessments made in pursuance to notices under section 153A. Specific penalty provisions in the case of search cases are contained under section 271AAA/271AAB and under section 271(1)(*c*) read with *Explanation 5A*. Provisions regarding initiation of prosecution under the Income Tax Act would also be applicable in the search assessment in the same manner as are applicable in case of normal assessments. Detailed discussion in this regard has been made in a separate chapter on Penalty & Prosecution.

(*iv*) **Filing of return after search under normal provisions of the Act -Whether required?**

In a case where search is initiated, there may be cases when original return with respect to any of the preceding six years prior to the date of search as required under section 139 has not been filed. There may be a situation when due date of filing return under section 139 has expired but assessee has not filed the return. There may be another situation when as on the date of search, due date for filing the return had not expired but it falls in between the date of search and the date of getting the notice under section 153A for filing the returns for preceding six years.

There arises a question under above situation as to whether assessee is required to file original return under section 139 or he should wait for notices under section 153A to be received for filing returns of income for preceding six years. Further, in case original return along with tax audit report is not filed in time, whether assessee will be liable to penalty under section 271B or under any other provisions of the Act.

This is a complex issue and there can be two opinions regarding the same. One view can be that in the case of search, requirement of getting notices under section 153A and filing fresh income tax returns for preceding six years is a special provision over and above the normal requirement of filing return under section 139. Assessee should therefore file normal return under section 139 irrespective of search having taken place and in case of failure the consequences thereof will follow. Whenever notices under section 153A are received, assessee shall be required to file fresh returns in pursuance to such notices.

The other view may be that provision of section 153A starts with non obstante clause stating notwithstanding anything contained in section 139 which in turn prescribes time limit for filing Income Tax return, the provision regarding time limit for filing the return under section 139 is superseded by clause (*a*) of section 153A(1). Once search is held, income tax return shall be required to be filed in pursuance to notice under section 153A within such period as may be specified in the notice. Further it is provided under clause (*a*) that provisions of this Act shall, so far as may be, apply accordingly as if such return were a return required to furnished under section 139. Further it is provided that the pending assessment proceeding as on the date of search shall abate. Therefore when no assessment proceeding can be undertaken in pursuance to original return required to be filed under section 139, filing of such return is of no consequence.

In view of the above arguments, one can interpret that assessee may not file pending original return and wait for receiving notice under section 153A and file the return in pursuance to the same. However as a matter of caution, it may be expressed that the above view is liable to judicial test and interpretation.

Further it is submitted that in case proceeding under section 153A is annulled in appeal or any other legal proceedings, income tax returns filed by the assessee in pursuance to notices under section 153A shall become non est or at the best the same may be treated as original returns belatedly filed under section 139 and in that case, all the consequences for non filing or belated filing of income tax return under section 139 will follow.

It has been held in the case of *Shrikant Mohta* v. *CIT* [2018] 257 Taxman 43/95 taxmann.com 224 (Cal.) that when search operations are conducted under section 132, the obligation of the assessee to file any return remains suspended till such time that a notice is issued for such purpose under section 153A(1)(*a*) & if the return is filed by the assessee within the reasonable time permitted by such notice under section 153A(1)(*a*), such return would then be deemed to have been filed within the time permitted under section 139(1) for the benefit of loss under section 139(3) to be availed of by the assessee.

In our considered opinion, the above judicial decision requires re-consideration because such interpretation may lead to undesirable consequence for such assessee in whose case search and search assessment is quashed for some reason.

(*v*) Late filing of return under section 153A - Consequences thereof

There may be cases when returns for the preceding six years are not filed in time as specified in the notice received under section 153A.

Late filing of such return shall attract interest under section 234A. In case late filing of return is for valid reasons, assessee can make out a case for non levy or waiver of interest. Non-receipt of photocopy of the documents, books of account or records seized during search inspite of request by the assessee may be a valid reason for late filing of return.

It has been held in the case of *Mahavir Manakchand Bhansali* v. *CIT* [2017] 88 taxmann.com 609 (Bom.) that when there is delay by Department in supplying seized documents and allowing inspection of records leading to delay in filing return, no interest is chargeable for period of delay before filing of return attributable to Department.

It has been held in the case of *Dy. CIT* v. *Ngenox Technologies (P.) Ltd.* 205 DTR (Del. 'E') 193 that the assessee having filed the return under section 139(1) declaring loss for the relevant year within the due date provided under the Act, it was entitled to carry forward loss and since no assessment was pending as on the date of search, the regular assessment did not abate and therefore, AO was not justified in denying the carry forward of the loss on account of late filing of the return section 153A.

Sometimes, returns in pursuance to notice under section 153A are filed, without any valid reason, at the fag end of time barring limit for completion of assessment as prescribed under section 153B. The Assessing Officer is required to complete the assessment as per time limit prescribed under section 153B and in such a case apart from attraction of interest for late filing of return and any other consequence, it may also be difficult, as is pleaded by the department, for the assessee to take the plea that adequate opportunity was not given to him during assessment proceedings to represent his case. In case no return is filed in pursuance to notice under section 153A, the Assessing Officer will have no option but to frame ex parte assessment.

However, there is no bar under the Act for the AO to proceed with the assessment proceeding without the return having been filed by the assessee. But before making addition, AO is expected to confront the incriminating material to the assessee on the basis of which the additions are proposed to be made in the assessment order. In case no such opportunity is granted by AO, the plea of inadequate opportunity of hearing may still be made by the assessee during appellate proceeding depending upon the facts and circumstances of the case.

(vi) **Whether return filed in pursuance to notice under section 153A can be revised?**

As per clause (*a*) of sub-section (1) of section 153A, income tax return filed in pursuance to notice under section 153A, is treated a return as if such return were a return required to be furnished under section 139. Therefore, such return may be revised in accordance with the provision of sub-section (5) of section 139. This is evident from this fact that wherever legislature has denied the revision of return, it has so provided, for example, as provided in second proviso to section 158BC(*a*). Further, it may be said that such income tax return filed under section 153A may be revised as many times as assessee may opt to revise as the position in the case of income tax return filed under section 139(1).

There may arise another question as to whether income tax return can be filed under section 153A after the due date as provided in the notice issued by Assessing Officer for filing the return under section 153A. This may be a controversial issue. Income tax return filed belatedly under section 139(4) cannot be revised as has been held in various judicial pronouncements. There is no statutory time limit provided under the Act for filing income tax return under section 153A. The due date for filing income tax return under section 153A is prescribed by the Assessing Officer in the notice to be issued for filing the return under section 153A and this time limit may be flexible keeping in view the date of notice and the period for filing the return mentioned therein by the Assessing Officer. In case income tax return required to be filed in pursuance to such notice is filed after the due date as prescribed in the notice, the same may be treated as a belated return and in such a situation it may not be possible to revise such belated return filed under section 153A.

However, it is mentioned here that the above issue should be addressed in accordance with the position prevailing in the case of income tax return filed by the assessee in pursuance to notice under section 148 and the ratio applicable there should be applied in the case of revision of return filed under section 153A.

In the case of *ITO* v. *Banarsilal Satyanarain* [1995] 55 ITD 372 (Patna-Trib.), Tribunal held that a return filed in response to notice under section 148(1) can be validly revised under section 139(5).

In the case of *Asstt. CIT* v. *Cavinkare (P.) Ltd.* [2009] 120 ITD 126 (Chennai-Trib.), Tribunal has held that section 139(5) is a procedural provision although it vests the assessee with a right to revise his return. This right is meant to rectify any omission or any wrong statement made in the return already furnished. Thus the provision in section 139(5) is partly a substantive provision and partly a procedural provision. If that be the case, then it is not difficult to envisage a situation wherein a return filed under section 148 may also contain certain omissions or wrong statement. Therefore, the assessee should have the right vested in him by virtue of section 139(5) to be extended to a return under section 148 also.

It is pertinent to note here that in the case of a revised return u/s 139(5), Assessing Officer gets nine months time to complete assessment but if return filed u/s 153A is revised at the fag end of limitation, Assessing Officer would not get any extension or additional time for passing the assessment order.

(vii) Whether assessee should file income tax returns under section 153A when opting to apply to Settlement Commission?

As per Finance Act, 2010, the option available to the assessee regarding filing of petition with the Settlement Commission so as to have one time settlement in the case of search has been revived which was *hitherto fore*, withdrawn by the Finance Act, 2007. For filing the petition before the Settlement Commission, in the case of a person searched, it is required to make declaration of additional income so as to make payment of minimum tax liability of ₹ 50 lakhs.

In case income tax return is filed by the assessee for the year of search under section 139 or for preceding six years as per provisions of section 153A showing undisclosed income and after that assessee decides for making application to the Settlement Commission, he will be required to declare further additional income so as to pay additional tax liability of minimum rupees fifty lakh. Therefore, it has been observed that a person who is contemplating to file petition with the Settlement Commission does not file regular return for search year under section 139 or for preceding six years as per provision of section 153A.

This kind of approach is not advisable. There may be situation when petition filed by the assessee with the Settlement Commission is not accepted and he is directed to undergo process of regular assessment proceeding. In such a case when income tax returns under section 139 or 153A are filed by the assessee later on, such returns are delayed and assessee may have to face the consequences of late filing of return including interest under section 234A. Therefore, it is advisable that even when assessee is contemplating to file petition with the Settlement Commission, regular returns under section 139 or under section 153A should be filed showing the regular income. The additional income may be declared in the petition to be filed with the Settlement Commission or by revising the earlier returns as the case may be and as situation may require.

However, Finance Act, 2021 has abolished the institution of Settlement Commission and with effect from 1st February, 2021 no new application may be filed for settlement.

(viii) **Cash seized during search - Whether adjustable as advance tax**

There is a controversy regarding this issue. The provision of section 132B regarding retention and application of assets seized during search do not address this question and controversy remains unresolved for the reason that the advance tax payable is not treated as existing tax liability and adjustment contemplated u/s 132B is only against the existing tax liability.

When cash is seized during search, it is kept, as seen in practice, in the Personal Deposit Account (PD A/c) of the Commissioner. It is not transferred to the regular account to be adjusted against his tax liability till final assessment under section 153A are framed and tax demand is created against the assessee. In certain cases, even after completion of assessment, adjustment of the seized cash is delayed by way of transfer from Commissioner's PD account to regular account to be adjusted against tax liability due to procedural delay. Due to late adjustment of cash seized, assessee is charged interest under section 234B/234C on the tax demand raised upto the date of such adjustment and the same becomes a contentious issue.

On the other hand, assessee claims that the amount of cash seized should be treated as advance tax paid as on the date of seizure. The argument of the assessee usually remains that when undisclosed income is declared, the cash representing such undisclosed income which has been seized, is the money out of which advance tax liability is required to be paid. Even when no surrender of undisclosed income is made by the assessee, contention of the assessee still remains that the cash seized should be treated as advance tax paid as on the date of seizure to be adjusted against tax liability to be raised against the assessee. In any case, assessee's contention further remains that sum has been seized by the Department and stands deposited with the Department on behalf of the assessee and therefore it should be treated as advance tax paid.

This controversy further creates complication in the situation when assessee takes credit of such seized cash in the return of income filed which is not admitted by the department and due to this reason, the very maintainability of the first appeal before CIT (A) to be filed by the assessee comes in question because section 249(4)(*a*) provides that tax due on the returned income must be paid.

From the practical point of view, it is suggested that a representation at the earliest stage should be made by the assessee to the Department requesting to treat cash seized as payment of advance tax to be adjusted against tax liability. Such request would be very useful to the assessee to get the matter decided in his favour by higher authorities in future at appellate stage or in case assessee opts to apply to Chief Commissioner for the waiver of the interest.

There are judicial decisions in this regard which hold that the case seized can be adjusted by way of advance tax.

In *Satya Prakash Sharma* v. *Asstt. CIT* [2009] 20 DTR 561(Del.) (Trib.), it was held that adjustment of seized cash towards advance tax liability was possible and AO was directed to adjust the seized cash as requested by the assessee against advance tax from the date on which the assessee made the request and recomputed the levy of interest under section 234B accordingly.

In *Sudhakar M. Shetty* v. *Asstt. CIT* [2008] 10 DTR 173 (Mum.) (Trib.), Tribunal has held that since, assessee has requested the department to adjust the cash seized against his tax liability, the department has to adjust the seized amount towards the advance tax from the date when it was seized.

High Court in the case of *CIT* v. *K.K. Marketing* [2005] 278 ITR 596 (Del.), have held that the offer for adjustment of the seized cash was made by the assessees before advance tax liability became due and therefore, it is not as if the assessees had any intention of shirking their advance tax liabilities. While it is true that tax laws and equity do not always go hand in hand, but in the present cases, since there is nothing to prohibit the assessees from making a request for adjustment of the cash seized against advance tax liabilities, equity demands that the cash amount ought to have been adjusted as paid for the assessees to save it from any liability of interest.

However, in the following judicial decisions, it has been held that cash seized cannot be adjusted straightway as advance tax liability.

In *Gian Chand Gupta* v. *Dy. CIT* [2002] 80 ITD 548 (Del.-Trib.), Tribunal has held that there is no automatic payment of advance tax on the date of seizure and therefore, interest u/ss 234A, 234B and 234C are chargeable up to the date of adjustment on the total amount of tax.

In *Dy. CIT* v. *Gold Tax Furnishing Industries* [2001] 73 TTJ 223 (Del.-Trib.) Tribunal has held, cash seized at the time of search would not be adjusted against the advance tax liabilities and assessee was therefore liable to interest u/ss. 234B and 234C.

Madhya Pradesh High Court in the case of *Ramjilal Jagannath* v. *Asstt. CIT* [2000] 241 ITR 758 (MP) have held that, so long as a final order u/s 132(5) has not been passed, ITO cannot direct that the seized money to be adjusted towards the existing liability for advance tax in accordance with the provisions of the Income-tax Act, 1961. He cannot avoid his liability u/s 234B or 234C irrespective of seizure of cash.

Nagpur Bench of Bombay High Court in the case of *CIT* v. *Pandurang Dayaram Talmale* [2004] 135 Taxman 193 (Bom.), have however held that, only after a final order is made u/s 132(5), the seized amount may be adjusted or appropriated towards the assessee's liability for payment of advance tax.

The above controversy has been set at rest by amendment to section 132B introduced by the Finance Act, 2013 with effect from 1st June, 2013 by inserting *Explanation 2* stating that the 'existing liability' does not include advance tax payable. It would mean that cash seized cannot be adjusted as advance tax paid. However, there is no bar in adjustment of seized cash towards self-assessment tax liability.

13.9 Certain issues relating to assessment under section 153A

(*i*) **No repetition of addition under section 153A for the same issues relating to which addition already made in earlier assessment or reassessment proceedings**

Reassessment proceedings under section 153A are in the same nature as reassessment proceedings under section 148. In pursuance to notice under section 153A, assessee may file Income Tax return in either of the following manners—

1. By making declaration of income relating to those items for which addition was made in the earlier assessment or reassessment proceedings and which have not been agitated by the assessee in the appellate proceedings.

2. Without making declaration of income relating to those items for which addition was made in the earlier assessment or reassessment proceedings and which have not been agitated by the assessee in the appellate proceedings and making declaration of the original income as returned in the earlier returns filed.

In second situation, sometimes, Assessing Officer remains in dilemma whether to repeat or reconsider the additions made in earlier assessment, again in the assessment order to be passed under section 153A.

In fact it is not required to repeat the additions and there should be no dilemma in this regard. The assessment under section 153A is the assessment over and above what has already been done in earlier assessments.

Further, it may be clarified that in case assessee files return under section 153A in the manner as mentioned at second point above, there can be no allegation of concealment of income here with respect to additions made in earlier assessment but not agitated by the assessee as in respect of the additions made in earlier assessment, decision regarding concealment etc. would have already been taken by AO thereat. In case there is any view of the Department regarding concealment of income relating to such additions and penalty proceeding is required to be initiated for the same, it would be appropriate to do in the original assessment proceedings and not in the proceeding u/s 153A. Any assessment or reassessment proceeding under section 153A is the proceeding over and above what has already been done in the earlier concluded proceedings.

(ii) Fresh material found relating to issue with respect to which addition already made in earlier assessment finalized

There may be situation when fresh material/evidences are found and seized relating to certain issue(s) with respect to which addition has already been made during earlier assessment finalized and the assessee is in appeal with respect to such addition *e.g.,* addition for unsecured loan/share capital has earlier been made on the ground of non-confirmation and non-verification. During search, fresh evidences regarding the unsecured loan/share capital being bogus in nature or assessee's own money routed through the same are found and seized. In such a case, no fresh addition for such unsecured loan/share capital under section 68 can be made since addition has already been made but the Assessing Officer is required to forward the fresh evidences available with him to the appellate authority with whom matter may be pending with the request to admit the same as additional evidences in support of earlier addition made.

There may be a situation when the addition made by the Assessing Officer during earlier assessment proceeding was deleted by the appellate authority. In case, department is in appeal against the deletion of the addition, the new evidences found during search may be sent by the department to the appropriate appellate authority for admission of additional evidence. However, in case department is not in appeal and the matter has attained finality, addition can be made again by the Assessing Officer during the assessment u/s 153A having regard to the new evidences found as a result of search.

(iii) Whether to assess or reassess as required under section 153A tantamount to de novo assessment proceeding?

Section 153A requires the assessing Officer to assess or reassess the total income of six assessment years immediately preceding the year of search. There has been lot of debate and judicial controversy regarding the nature of assessment or reassessment proceedings to be undertaken under section 153A.

Legislature requires the Assessing Officer to assess or reassess the total income of preceding six assessment years. The words *'total income'* has been used under clause (*b*) of section 153A(1) as well as under first proviso to section 153A(1).

1. Does it mean that even completed assessments will be required to be reassessed *de novo*?

2. Whether addition can be made with respect to any issue or even for issues which have already been covered in earlier assessment proceedings?

3. Whether additions can be made only relating to undisclosed income detected as a result of search and based upon incriminating material found during search?

These are certain complex issues and contradictory views are being expressed not only in professional circle but by the judicial authorities as well while deciding various case laws. Following discussion is relevant in this regard.

The assessment or reassessment proceedings to be undertaken under section 153A may be classified as under—

a. For the assessment year relating to the year of search—whether normal assessment can be framed examining and making additions relating to all the issues as can be done in normal scrutiny case?

b. In the case when assessment proceedings u/s 143(3) were pending and those proceedings were abated due to search having taken place — whether assessment for such years can be made as normal assessment examining and making additions relating to all the issues as can be done in normal scrutiny case?

c. For the years for which no notice u/s 143(2) was earlier issued and the same having been time barred — whether assessment for such years can be made as normal assessment examining and making additions relating to all the issues as can be done in normal scrutiny case? Such years may further be classified as the years for which processing under section 143(1)(*a*) has been done or

d. In the case of proceedings u/s 153A relating to the years for which assessment order u/s 143(3) has been passed earlier—whether issues already examined in earlier assessment proceedings can be re-examined by the Assessing Officer? Whether there can be change of opinion by the Assessing Officer on the issues already considered without any new evidences coming to his possession?

Before we examine the above issues, there has to be clarity regarding nature of provision of section 153A requiring assessment or reassessment to be made in the case of search cases. Requirement of section 153A is limited to opening or reopening of the cases for the purpose of making assessment or reassessment of the total income of preceding six assessment years prior to the year of search. It does not contain any provision regarding the concept of making assessment of undisclosed income alone as was the case under block assessment regime under Chapter XIVB. It does not contain any provision regarding the nature of additions which can be made under this section. This section has rather provided, for the removal of doubts, by way of insertion of *Explanation* at the end of the section that save as otherwise provided in this section, section 153B and section 153C, all other provisions of this Act shall apply to the assessment made under this section.

It clearly implies that nature of assessment or reassessment to be made under this section 153A shall be governed by the normal provisions of the Act. In case it is an assessment being made for the first time, all principles of assessment which are applicable to assessment under section 143(3) shall become applicable and in case it is a reassessment being made, all principles of reassessment which are applicable in the case of proceedings under section 147/148, shall become applicable.

One may never compare and confuse the nature of provisions contained under section 153A with the nature of provisions contained under Chapter XIVB regarding block assessment proceedings. Concept of block assessment under Chapter XIVB was altogether different. It was a special procedure for assessment of search cases to make assessment relating to only undisclosed income. There was then the concept of dual assessment proceedings. Normal assessment proceedings for other than undisclosed income used to be undertaken independently and simultaneously.

Section 153A does not contain any such special procedure to assess undisclosed income found as a result of search, rather pending normal assessment or reassessment proceedings are abated and in a way merged within the proceedings to be undertaken under section 153A. Assessment proceedings pursuant to notice under section 153A are not intended to be restricted to make assessment of undisclosed income only detected as a result of search.

Following arguments may be advanced in favour of the view that assessment or reassessment proceedings under section 153A are *de novo* assessment proceedings—

1. Section 153A requires total income for preceding six years to be assessed or reassessed in pursuance to notice under section 153A. Total income will include any kind of income and it cannot be restricted to undisclosed income or escaped income.

2. After initiation of search, pending assessment proceedings are abated and the same are merged with the assessment proceedings to be undertaken pursuant to notice under section 153A. Nature of assessment proceedings, so merged, cannot be restricted to make assessment only of undisclosed income.

3. Section 153A requires total income for all the preceding six years to be assessed or reassessed, therefore, nature of assessment proceedings for all the six years will be of the same nature and the nature of completed assessment proceedings to be reassessed pursuant to notice under section 153A cannot be different.

4. There is no concept of assessment of undisclosed income under section 153A as was the case during block assessment regime under Chapter XIVB. Under block assessment, there was concept of dual assessment - one for undisclosed income detected as a result of search and other for normal assessment as per normal provisions of the Act. Since under section 153A, both the assessment proceedings are merged together, the nature of the additions to be made cannot be restricted to assess only undisclosed income detected as a result of search.

5. In case of reopening of assessment under section 147/148, specific reasons of income escaping assessment are recorded and therefore, enquiries are made during assessment proceedings with respect to such issues. However in case of search assessment, there are no specific reasons recorded. In the case of search before issuing search warrant, satisfaction is recorded by the competent authority regarding accumulation of undisclosed income by the person to be searched and legislature requires such person to be mandatorily assessed for preceding six years with respect to his total income. Therefore, enquiries can be made relating to all the issues during section 153A assessment proceedings.

(*iv*) Arguments against the concept of de novo assessment

1. Legislature requires pending assessment proceedings to abate and only such years for which proceedings are abated, may be treated as normal assessment proceedings. For other years, addition can be made only relating to undisclosed income found as a result of search.

2. For making assessment or reassessment under section 153A, no "reason to believe" for income escaping assessment is formed by the assessing officer. "Reason to believe" regarding undisclosed income formed by the competent authority was only for the purpose of authorizing the search. Copy of the same is not made available to the assessing officer. When search has taken place, it is only the seized material and undisclosed income emanating out of the same, which is relevant and useful for the assessing officer, to be considered during assessment proceedings. Therefore, no addition can be made for the matters other than the matters suggesting undisclosed income found as a result of search and emanating out of seized material.

3. The concept of assessment is governed by the time barring provision and assessee acquires a right as to the finality of proceedings. Quietus of the completed assessments can be disturbed only when there is information or evidences regarding undisclosed income or assessing officer had information in his possession showing escapement of income. This principle has been approved by the Apex Court and various High Courts consistently in the context of the provisions of section 147/148.

In view of the above discussion, the nature of additions which can be made during assessment or reassessment proceedings under section 153A which are pending at different stages as described above may be discussed as under—

1. There should not be any meaningful controversy regarding nature of assessment proceedings so far as the situation covered under points (*a*) and (*b*) is concerned. In the above situations covered under points (*a*) and (*b*) above, there can be examination and addition relating to all issues including issues emanating out of incriminating material found as a result of search. These are normal assessment proceedings being undertaken for the first time under normal provisions of the Act. Such assessment proceedings are, undoubtly, fresh assessment proceedings and assessment for such years can be made as normal assessment examining and making additions relating to all the issues as can be done in normal scrutiny case under section 143(3).

It is relevant to note that assessment year relating to the year of search is not covered by the provisions of section 153A and return for the year of search is not filed in pursuance to notice under section 153A but as per normal provisions of section 139. Reliance is placed on the following judicial decisions for this proposition of law:

Seema Mundra v. *DCIT* [ITA] No.431/Jp/2018 dated 21.6.2018 (Jaipur) Trib.

Iqbal Singh v. *DCIT* [ITA] No. 712/Chd/2016 dated 20.9.2017 (Chandigarh) Trib.

Upendra Kumar Sharma v. *DCIT* [ITA] no. 3137/Del/2009 dated 12.4.2010 (Delhi) Trib.

Rajiv Kumar v. *Asstt. CIT* [2017] 88 taxmann.com 793 (Chd.-Trib.)

CIT v. *Sri Ram Dayal Jaiswal* [ITA No. 27 of 2010 dated 28.2.2017] (Allahabad) High Court

However, in *Dy. CIT* v. *Sushil Kumar Jain* [2010] 48 DTR 185 (Ind.), Tribunal has held that the year under search is also covered u/s 153A.

To take a view that assessment proceedings under section 153A for such years will be restricted only to examine and make additions regarding undisclosed income detected as a result of search, is not reasonable and in accordance with the scheme of section 153A. The proceedings under section 153A cannot be viewed and compared with block assessment proceedings under Chapter XIVB, nature of which was entirely different. There is no concept of assessment of only undisclosed income during proceedings under section 153A. It is the total income of the assessee required to be assessed under section 153A. There are no separate assessment proceedings undertaken for normal income as was the case under block assessment, rather pending normal assessment proceedings are abated and merged into assessment proceedings to be undertaken under section 153A.

2. So far as the situation covered under point (*c*) above is concerned i.e. where intimation u/s 143(1)(*a*) has been issued and the time for issuing notice u/s 143(2) has expired, the nature of assessment proceeding to be undertaken u/s 153A in this case would also be the same as in first situation except that in this case, the assessment could not have been taken up by issuing notice under section 143(2). This would be a case of first time

assessment and not the case of reassessment. Section 153A is having overriding effect over section 147 for reopening of the cases. It can be argued that once the assessment proceeding is reopened u/s 153A and assessment is made for the first time, the situation regarding the nature of assessment would be same as situation covered under points (*a*) & (*b*) above.

Processing of return under section 143(1)(*a*) cannot be regarded as assessment made with respect to original return as also held by Hon'ble Supreme Court in the case of *Asstt. CIT* v. *Rajesh Jhaveri Stock Brokers (P.) Ltd.* [2007] 161 Taxman 316. In the case of processing of return under section 143(1)(*a*), no issues are examined by the assessing officer and no opinion is formed by the assessing officer with respect to any of the issues. Since section 153A requires total income to be assessed, therefore all issues may be examined during assessment proceeding.

It may be noticed that under the provisions of the Act, once the power to issue notice for normal assessment has become time barred under the proviso to section 143(2), assessment proceeding in such a case can be reopened in accordance with the provision of section 147/148. In the case of section 153A being made applicable for search case, when assessment proceeding is reopened, it can also be argued alternatively that the nature of assessment proceeding and the nature of additions which can be made in such a case, will also be governed by the same principles as laid down under section 147/148 of the Act.

However, there are contradictory opinions of the Courts on this issue. There are various judicial decisions too holding that in such kind of situation, addition can be made only in respect of the incriminating material found during the course of search which have been discussed in detail in the later part of this chapter.

3. So far as the situation covered under point (*d*) is concerned, we are of the considered opinion that principles of reassessment as contained under section 147/148 and as propounded in accordance with various judicial pronouncements made in this regard shall be applicable for making assessment or reassessment pursuant to notice under section 153A.

The significant provisions regarding nature of assessment proceedings contained under section 147 may be summarized as under—

   i. As per section 147, assessing officer may assess or reassess income chargeable to tax which has escaped assessment and also any other income chargeable to tax which has escaped assessment and which comes to his notice subsequently in the course of the proceedings under this section or recompute the loss or depreciation allowance or any other allowance as the case may be for the assessment year concerned.

ii. Third proviso to section 147 states that the assessing officer may assess or reassess such income other than the income involving matters which are the subject matters of any appeal, reference or revision, which is chargeable to tax and which has escaped assessment.

iii. *Explanation (3)* to section 147 inserted by Finance (No. 2) Act, 2009, with retrospective effect from 1-4-1989 further provides that for the purpose of assessment or reassessment under this section, the Assessing Officer may assess or reassess the income in respect of any issue, which has escaped assessment, and such issue comes to his notice subsequently in the course of the proceedings under this section, notwithstanding that the reasons for such issue have not been included in the reasons recorded under sub-section (2) of section 148.

The position regarding nature of assessment proceedings under section 147/148 has also been clarified after retrospective introduction of *Explanation (3)* to section 147. Earlier there was a view that addition in the case of reassessment under section 147/148 can be made only with respect to those issues for which reasons have been recorded as propounded in the case of *Vipan Khanna* v. *CIT* [2002] 122 Taxman 1 (Punj. & Har.).

This situation was diluted first by substitution of section 147 by Direct Tax Laws (Amendment) Act, 1987 and further by insertion of *Explanation (3)* by the Finance (No. 2) Act, 2009 retrospectively with effect from 1st April, 1989. Now assessing officer may assess or reassess income in respect of any issue which has escaped assessment and which comes to his notice subsequently in the course of proceedings under this section notwithstanding that the reasons for such issues have not been earlier recorded. When addition under section 147/148 can be made on any issue which has escaped assessment, the same situation may be applicable in the case of proceedings under section 153A in our considered opinion.

However there is still controversy regarding assessment proceeding under section 147 as to whether assessing officer is entitled to seek for fresh information/details/explanation/justification regarding any issue or it has to be restricted only relating to the issues for which reasons have been recorded & in that process, if any other income escaping assessment comes to his knowledge, the same may be added.

But in the case of section 153A proceedings, there are no specific reasons recorded. Therefore, it can be interpreted that assessing officer may seek information/explanation/justification with respect to any issues, and additions can be made in that regard.

On the other hand, one can put forth argument that when no specific reasons have been recorded, the enquiry has to be restricted and addition can be made only with respect to the issues which are emanating out of seized material found as a result of search. There are various judicial decisions holding that in such kind of situation, addition can be made only in respect of the incriminating material found during the course of search which have been discussed in detail in the later part of this chapter.

(v) **Change of opinion by the assessing officer during assessment/reassessment proceedings under section 153A relating to issue already considered and examined during earlier assessment proceedings.**

A controversy is also there to this effect as to whether during assessment proceedings under section 153A, assessing officer can be at liberty to re-examine the issues which have already been examined in earlier assessment proceedings or Assessing Officer may not be at liberty to change his opinion on the issues which were already considered during earlier assessment proceedings without any fresh evidences coming to his possession as a result of search?

This is a ticklish issue and the opinion of the experts is divided on the above issue. In our considered opinion, this issue needs to be addressed in the light of various judicial pronouncements rendered with respect to reassessment proceedings under section 147/148. It is settled law that in case of reassessment proceedings under section 147/148, change of opinion on the same set of facts is not permitted as held by Supreme Court in the case of *CIT* v. *Kelvinator of India Ltd.* [2010] 187 Taxman 312. As earlier opined, reassessment proceedings under section 153A are also of the same nature as reassessment proceedings under section 147/148. The above ratio should equally be applied while framing reassessment under section 153A.

It has been held in the case of *Guruprerna Enterprises* v. *Asstt. CIT* [2011] 57 DTR 465 (Mumbai - Trib.) that under section 153A, the issues decided in the assessment cannot be reconsidered and re-adjudicated, unless there is some fresh material found during the course of search in relation to such points.

It has been held in the case of *Asstt. CIT* v. *Mrs. Uttara S. Shorewa-la* [2011] 12 taxmann.com 460/48 SOT 6 (URO) (Mum.-Trib.) that Revenue having accepted the order of CIT (A) deleting the addition under section 69C in reassessment proceedings, AO was not justified in repeating the same addition in the proceedings under section 153A by merely relying on the statement and the affidavit of a third party which was nothing but reiteration of the stand taken by him in the earlier proceedings.

It has been held in the case of *Lord Krishna Dwellers (P) Ltd.* v. *Dy. CIT* [ ]173 DTR 241(Del 'D') that while Computing undisclosed in-come vis-a-vis absence of incriminating material, Copies of sale deeds of land found during the course of search operation which were already considered by the AO while framing the assessment under section 143(3) cannot be considered as incriminating material and, therefore, the assessment framed under section 153A on the basis of the contents of the same sale deeds is bad in law.

(vi) **Judicial controversy regarding de novo assessment**

There are certain complex issues on which there have been con-trary decisions of different Benches of ITAT. Such issues are as to whether assessment in pursuance to notice under section 153A is de novo assessment and whether all issues may be examined or not? Whether additions relating to undisclosed income with respect to incriminating material found as a result of search can only be made during assessment proceedings under section 153A? Whether any other income escaping assessment but not emanating from the incriminating material found during search can be made during assessment proceeding under section 153A?

In the case of *Suncity Alloys Pvt. Ltd.* v. *Asstt. CIT* [2009] 124 TTJ 674 Jodhpur Bench of ITAT has observed as under—

The issuance of notice under section 153A for all the six assessment years also does not entail altogether a fresh exercise of making fresh assessment. Infact, the apparent and logical purpose of calling for return for all the six assessment years immediately preceding the year in which search is initiated is to dispense with the requirement of recording reasons for reopening the assessment and also to avoid any controversy as to the correct year of assessibility of such income falling within such six assessment years. Necessarily the undisclosed income that shall form part of total income would be so taken after defraying for all expenses that are incurred for earning such income by the assessee. Reference to the principle made in judgment ren-dered by Apex Court in *CIT* v. *Piara Singh* [1980] 3 Taxman 67 (SC) is relevant. —This all goes to show that the assessments or reassessment made pursuance to notice under section 153A are not de novo assessments.

Kolkata Bench of ITAT in the case of *LMJ International Ltd.* v. *Dy. CIT* [2008] 22 SOT 315 (Kal.-Trib.), while discussing nature of additions which can be made during assessment proceeding under section 153C (the ratio can be extended to assessment proceeding under section 153A also) has held as under -

Where nothing incriminating is found in the course of search relating to any assessment years, the assessments for such years cannot be disturbed; items of regular assessment cannot be added back in the proceedings under section 153C when no incriminating documents were found in respect of the disallowed amounts in the search proceedings.

Ahmedabad Bench of ITAT in the case of *Meghmani Organics Ltd.* v. *Dy. CIT* [2010] 129 TTJ 255 has made the following observations —

"The power under section 153A of the Act should, therefore, be with reference to assessment or reassessment of pending assessments or qua the materials found during the course of search. Since admittedly nothing was found during the search to suggest that any income has escaped assessment, that AO does not have any jurisdiction for framing assessment under section 153A of the Act."

Ahmedabad Bench in the above case has gone one step further and held that when no incriminating material is found during search, the assessing officer does not have any jurisdiction for framing assessment under section 153A of the Act. In our opinion, it is submitted with great respect that it may not be a correct view. There can be difference of opinion regarding nature of additions which can be made during assessments under section 153A but by no stretch of interpretation, it is correct to hold that when there is no incriminating material found during search, AO does not have any jurisdiction for framing assessment under section 153A of the Act.

Following the above judgment, Delhi Bench of ITAT in the case of *Anil Kumar Bhatia* v. *Asstt. CIT* [2010] 1 ITR (Trib.) 484 has also expressed similar view by holding as under—

"From the aforesaid analysis of judicial precedents, we are of the considered view that since for all the assessment years in consideration, processing of returns under section 143(1)(*a*) stood completed, for returns filed in due course before search, and no material being found in search thereafter, no addition can be made for agricultural income, gifts, unexplained deposit."

Hon'ble Delhi High Court in the case of *CIT* v. *Kabul Chawla* [2015] 61 taxmann.com 412/234 Taxman 300, has summarized the complete provision of section 153A explaining the rationale and nature of assessment/re-assessment to be framed in the case of search as under:

(*i*) Once a search takes place under section 132 of the Act, notice under section 153A(1) will have to be mandatorily issued to the person searched requiring him to file returns for six AYs immediately preceding the previous year relevant to the AY in which the search takes place.

(*ii*) Assessments and reassessments pending on the date of the search shall abate. The total income for such AYs will have to be computed by the AOs as a fresh exercise.

(*iii*) The AO will exercise normal assessment powers in respect of the six years previous to the relevant AY in which the search takes place. The AO has the power to assess and reassess the 'total income' of the aforementioned six years in separate assessment orders for each of the six years. In other words there will be only one assessment order in respect of each of the six AYs "in which both the disclosed and the undisclosed income would be brought to tax".

(*iv*) Although section 153A does not say that additions should be strictly made on the basis of evidence found in the course of the search, or other post-search material or information available with the AO which can be related to the evidence found, it does not mean that the assessment "can be arbitrary or made without any relevance or nexus with the seized material. Obviously an assessment has to be made under this section only on the basis of seized material."

(*v*) In absence of any incriminating material, the completed assessment can be reiterated and the abated assessment or reassessment can be made. The word 'assess' in section 153A is relatable to abated proceedings (i.e. those pending on the date of search) and the word 'reassess' to completed assessment proceedings.

(*vi*) Insofar as pending assessments are concerned, the jurisdiction to make the original assessment and the assessment under Section 153A merges into one. Only one assessment shall be made separately for each AY on the basis of the findings of the search and any other material existing or brought on the record of the AO.

(*vii*) Completed assessments can be interfered with by the AO while making the assessment under Section 153A only on the basis of some incriminating material unearthed during the course of search or requisition of documents or undisclosed income or property discovered in the course of search which were not produced or not already disclosed or made known in the course of original assessment.

It has been held in the case of *CIT* v. *Deepak Kumar Agarwal* [2017] 86 taxmann.com 3/251 Taxman 22 (Bom.) that in case of search and seizure assessment under section 153A, no addition could have been made while completing assessment under section 153A in the case of completed assessment if no incriminating material is recovered and no undisclosed income was determinable from the material found as a result of search.

In the case of *Principal CIT* v. *Mitsui and Co. India (P.) Ltd.* [2017] 81 taxmann.com 85 (Delhi), the Court held that the Tribunal was right in holding that there had to be incriminating material recovered during the search *qua* the assessee in each of the years for the purposes of framing an assessment under section 153A of the Act.

In the case of *Principal CIT* v. *Lata Jain* [2017] 81 taxmann.com 83 (Delhi), it has been noticed by the ITAT in the impugned order that for the AYs in question no incriminating material *qua* the Assessee was found. In that view of the matter, and in light of the decision of this Court in *CIT* v. *Kabul Chawla* [2015] 61 taxmann.com 412/234 Taxman 300 (Delhi), the Court is of the view that the impugned order of the ITAT suffers from no legal infirmity and no substantial question of law arises for determination.

Therefore, assessment cannot be made for the AYs in which incriminating material is not recovered even though incriminating material may be recovered for other years in the block of 6 years.

In the case of *CIT* v. *Lancy Constructions* [2016] 66 taxmann.com 264/237 Taxman 728 (Kar.), it has been held that merely because a search was conducted in the premises of the assessee, would not entitle the revenue to initiate the process of reassessment, for which there was a separate procedure prescribed in the statute. It was only when the conditions prescribed for reassessment were fulfilled that a concluded assessment could be reopened.

The very same accounts which were submitted by the assessee, on the basis of which assessment had been concluded, could not be re-appreciated by the AO merely because a search had been conducted in the premises of the assessee.

In the case of *Principal CIT* v. *Kurele Paper Mills (P.) Ltd.* [2017] 81 taxmann.com 82 (Delhi), Court declined to frame a question of law in a case where, in the absence of any incriminating material being found during the search under section 132 of the Act, the Revenue sought to justify initiation of proceedings under section 153A of the Act and make an addition under Section 68 of the Act on bogus share capital gain. The order of the CIT(A), affirmed by the ITAT, deleting the addition, was not interfered with.

The Supreme Court has dismissed the special leave petition filed by the Department against this judgment [2016] 380 ITR 64 (ST.)

In the case of *Jadau Jewellers & Manufacturers (P.) Ltd.* v. *Asstt. CIT* [2017] 83 taxmann.com 249 (Jodh.-Trib.), it has been held that AO having not issued notice under section 143(2) within the prescribed time limit pursuant to the return filed by the assessee under section 139(1). No proceeding was pending before the AO on the date of initiation of search which had abated, and the Revenue authorities having found no incriminating document during the course of search, the impugned order passed under section 153A r/w s. 143(3) is void ab initio.

In the case of *Sanjay Aggarwal* v. *Dy. CIT* [2015] 117 DTR 40 (Del. 'G') (Trib.), it has been held that the language of section 153A has been structured in such a way so as not to permit the making of addition for the assessment year of which the assessment is not pending as on the date of search, without there being any incriminating material found during the course of search. It is manifest that a duty is cast on the AO to determine the 'total income' of the assessee for such six assessment years. 'Total income' refers to the sum total of income in respect of which a person is assessable and covers not only the income emanating from declared sources or any material placed before the AO but from all sources including the undeclared ones. However, the second proviso to section 153A(1) eclipses the afore discussed determination of 'total income' by mandating that while pending assessments relating to any assessment year falling within the period of six years shall abate and that completed assessments shall remain intact. The effect of the second proviso in the entire setting of section is that the assessment for any assessment year which is not pending as on the date of search cannot include an item of income for which no incriminating material was found.

A contrary view has been taken by Delhi Bench of ITAT in the case of *Shivnath Rai Harnarain (India) Ltd.* v. *Dy. CIT* [2009] 117 ITD 74 it has been held as under —

In view of our above analysis of the provisions of sections, the contentions of the learned counsel for the assessee have no force because there is no requirement for an assessment made under section 153A of the Act being based on any material seized in the course of search. Further, under the second proviso to section 153A pending assessment or reassessment proceedings in relation to any assessment year falling within the period of six assessment years referred to in section 153A(*b*) of the Act shall come to an end (abate), which means that the AO gets jurisdiction for six assessment years referred to in section 153A(*b*) of the Act for making an assessment or reassessment.

It has been held in the case of *CIT* v. *K.P. Ummer* [2019] 413 ITR 251/177 DTR 379 (Ker.) that Tribunal went wrong in holding that assessments carried out under section 153A for the prior years in which the due date for notice under s. 143(2) has expired, can only be with reference to incriminating materials recovered on search.

Further Delhi Bench of ITAT in the case of *Ms. Shyam Lata Kaushik* v. *Asstt. CIT* [2008] 114 ITD 305 has expressed the similar view —

The contention of the assessee was that there was no seized material based on which the assessment was completed by the AO in the case of the assessee and, therefore, the assessment framed should be held to be null and void. It was also submitted that the provisions of section 153A cannot be invoked to make an assessment or reassessment of income just because a search had taken place in the case of an assessee. This contention of the assessee cannot be accepted. There is no requirement for an assessment made under section 153A being based on any material seized in the course of search. Further under the second proviso to section 153A, pending assessment or reassessment proceedings in relation to any assessment years falling within the period of six assessment years referred to in section 153A(*b*) shall abate. Thus the AO gets jurisdiction for six assessment years referred to in section 153A(*b*) for making an assessment or reassessment. It is not the complaint of the assessee that any income, which is already subjected to assessment under section 143(3) or under section 148 completed prior to the search in respect of six assessment years referred to in section 153A(*b*) and in the second proviso to section 153A, has also been included in the assessment framed under section 153A. In such circumstances the plea of the assessee cannot be accepted. There is no requirement for an assessment made under section 153A being based on any material seized in the course of search.

It has been held in the case of *Asstt. CIT* v. *Kamal Kumar S. Agrawal (Indl.)* [2012] 20 taxmann.com 338 (Nag.) that assessee having disclosed all share transactions in the returns of the relevant years in the normal course and the department having accepted the same, these transactions cannot be treated as non-genuine or sham and the sale proceeds of shares cannot be taxed under section 68 in the proceedings under section 153A as no incriminating material was found during the course of search which could cast doubt on the genuineness of such transactions and the majority of the brokers have supported the assessee's claim.

It has been held in the case of *Vishnu Agarwal* v. *Asstt. CIT* [2010] 45 DTR 222 (Hyd. 'A') (Trib.) that while computing the undisclosed income during the assessment under section 153A, it is open to the AO to compute the income under section 153A on the basis of the material available on record and it is not necessary for the AO to confine himself only to the material found during the course of search operation. Revenue authorities having discovered material during the course of search operation indicating suppression of job work receipts only in assessment years 2004-05 and 2005-06 and assessee having admitted that they were following this practice for the past 1-1/2 years, AO was justified in estimating suppressed income duly for assessment years 2004-05 and 2005-06 but not for other years. Revenue authorities found investment for the financial years 1999-2000 to 2004-05 and therefore the AO was directed to estimate profits @ 4 per cent instead of 5 per cent.

In the case of *Nandini Delux* v. *Asstt. CIT* [2015] 54 taxmann.com 162/68 SOT 5 (URO) (Bang.-Trib.). Even in non-pending assessments where no incriminating material is found, AO is not limited to assessing "undisclosed" income. The Assessing Officer can take note of the income disclosed in the earlier return, any undisclosed income found during the course of search and also any other income which is not disclosed in the earlier return of income OR which is not unearthed in the course of search under section 132 of the Act, in order to find out and determine what is the 'total income' of each year and then pass the order of assessment.

It has been held in the case of *All Cargo Global Logistics Ltd.* v. *Dy. CIT* [2012] 23 taxmann.com 103/137 ITD 287 (Mum.-Trib.) (SB) that in assessments that are abated, the AO retains the original jurisdiction as well as jurisdiction conferred on him under section 153A for which assessment shall be made for each of the six assessment years separately. It was further held that in other cases, in addition to the income that has already been assessed, the assessment under section 153A will be made on the basis of incriminating material, which in the context of relevant provisions means -(*i*) books of account, other documents, found in the course of search but not produced in the course of original assessment, and (*ii*) undisclosed income or property discovered in the course of search.

It has been held in the case of *Gurinder Singh Bawa* v. *Dy. CIT* [2012] 28 taxmann.com 328/[2014] 150 ITD 40 (Mum.-Trib.) that where in search assessment under section 153A, all assessments pertaining to six immediately preceding assessment years were complete, Assessing Officer cannot make any addition there under unless there is any incriminating material recovered during search.

It has been held as under in the case of *Asstt. CIT* v. *Pratibha Industries Ltd.* [2012] 28 taxmann.com 246/[2013] 141 ITD 151 (Mum. - Trib.):-

"...................Therefore what emerges is that no doubt under section 153A shall be initiated, and all the six years shall become subject matter of assessment under section 153A. The AO shall get the free hand, through abatement, only on the proceedings that are/is pending. It is, in these abated proceedings, AO can frame the assessment(s) afresh. But in a case or in a circumstances where the proceedings have reached finality, assessment under section 153A read with 143(3) has to be made as was originally made/assessed and in case where certain incriminating documents have been found indicating undisclosed income, then the addition shall only be restricted to those documents/incriminating material, and clubbed only to the assessment framed originally, as the law does not permit the AO to disturb already concluded issues, whether it pertained to any income or expenditure or deduction, as also observed by the Hon'ble Delhi High Court in the case of *Anil Kumar Bhatia* (*supra*),........."

It has been held in the case of *CIT* v. *Lachman Dass Bhatia* [2012] 26 taxmann.com 167/211 Taxman 70 (Mag.) (Delhi) in the context of section 153A that both the CIT(A) and the Tribunal having recorded a concurrent finding that there was no basis for making any addition towards low gross profit since search on the assessee did not yield any incriminating material on the basis of which it can be said that the assessee was indulging in under invoicing or suppression of sales, no interference was called for.

It has been held in the case of *CIT* v. *Anil Kumar Bhatia* [2012] 24 taxmann.com 98/211 Taxman 453 (Delhi) that under section 153A, AO has power to assess or reassess the total income of six assessment years in separate assessment orders and the provisions of section 153A can be invoked even where the return filed by the assessee for all the six years preceding the search have already been processed under section 143(1)(*a*).

In the case of *CIT* v. *Raj Kumar Arora* [2014] 120 DTR (All.) 417 (HC), it has been held that where the assessment or reassessment proceedings have already been completed and assessment orders have been passed, which were subsisting when the search was made, the Assessing Officer would be competent to reopen the assessment proceeding already made and determine the total income of the Assessee. The

Assessing Officer, while exercising the power under section 153A of the Act, would make assessment and compute the total income of the Assessee including the undisclosed income, notwithstanding the Assessee had filed the return before the date of search which stood processed under section 143(1)(*a*) of the Act.

In the case of *Filatex India Ltd.* v. *CIT* [2014] 49 taxmann.com 465/ [2015] 229 Taxman 555 (Delhi), during assessment under section 153A, additions need not be restricted or limited to incriminating material found during course of search and, hence, argument of assessee that addition under section 115JB was not justified in order under section 153A as no incriminating material was found concerning said addition had to be rejected. Appeal of assessee was dismissed.

It has been held in the case of *Principal Commissioner of Income Tax* v. *Shri Mehndipur Balaji* [2023] 147 taxmann.com 201/(2022) 114 CCH 179 All HC. (2022) 447 ITR 0517 (All) that w*hile exercising the power under Section 153A Assessing Officer has the power to reassess the returns of the assessee not only for the undisclosed income, which was found during the search operation but also with regard to the material that was available at the time of the original assessment.*

It is relevant to mention that as on date, Hon'ble Supreme Court has heard the case of *CIT* v. *Abhisaar Buildwell* in which the point in issue involved is one which was involved in the case of Kabul Chawla (Del.) (*supra*) that as to whether any addition can not be made without there being any incriminating material found during the course of search. Decision of Hon'ble Supreme Court is awaited.

So far as our view on the above controversy is concerned, we have opined earlier while discussing the provisions of the section that the principles and ratios laid down with respect to reassessment/ reopening under section 147/148 should be equally applicable during assessment under section 153A as well.

(*via*) No addition in case No Incriminating Material Found during search & Assessment Proceedings not abated

In the case of *Jignesh P. Shah* v. *DCIT* [ITA Nos. 1553 & 3173/ Mum./2010, dated 13-2-2015] (Mum.) (Trib.), it has been held that, since the assessment for the A.Ys. 2002-03 & 2004-05 had attained finality before the date of search and does not get abated in view of second proviso to section 153A, therefore, without there being any incriminating material found at the time of search, no addition over and above the income which already stood assessed can be made. Thus, the addition of deemed dividend made by the assessing officer is beyond the scope of assessment u/s 153A for the impugned assessment years. *Satish L. Babladi* v. *DCIT* passed in ITA Nos. 1732 & 2109 order dated 19.03.2013 distinguished (ITA Nos. 1553 & 3173/Mum/2010, dated 13-02-2015)

In the case of *Gurinder Singh Bawa* v. *Dy. CIT* [2012] 28 taxmann. com 328 [2014] 150 ITD 40 (Mum.-Trib.), when assessments pertaining to six immediately preceding assessment years were complete, AO cannot make any addition there under unless there is any incriminating material recovered during search. Assessment was not abated. Assessment was quashed.

In the case of *CIT* v. *Murli Agro Products Ltd.* [2014] 49 taxmann.com 172 (Bom.), it has been held that no addition can be made in respect of an unabated assessment which has become final if no incriminating material is found during the search.

It has been held in the case of *Asstt. CIT* v. *SRJ Peety Steels (P) Ltd.* [2012] 20 taxmann.com 101 (Pune) that when nothing incriminating was found in the course of search relating to any of the assessment years 2000-01 to 2005-06, the assessments for such years could not be disturbed.

It has been held in the case of *Guruprerna Enterprises* v. *Asstt. CIT* [2011] 57 DTR 465 (Mum. 'G') (Trib.) that only the assessments pending before the AO for completion shall abate and under section 153A the issues decided in the assessment cannot be reconsidered and readjudicated, unless there is some fresh material found during the course of search in relation to such points.

It has been held in the case of *Principal CIT* v. *Smt. Anita Rani* [2017] 88 taxmann.com 591/392 ITR 501 (Delhi) that in case Sale consideration stood duly disclosed by assessee in return, absence of seizure of any new material during search could not have justified fresh examination of the valuation.

It has been held in the case of *CIT* v. *Deepak Kumar Agarwal & ORS.* [2017] 86 taxmann.com 3/251 Taxman 22 (Bom.) that in case of search and seizure assessment under section 153A, no addition could have been made while completing assessment under s. 153A in the case of completed assessment if no incriminating material is recovered and no undisclosed income was determinable from the material found as a result of search.

It has been held in the case of *Principal CIT* v. *Ram Avtar Verma* [2017] 88 taxmann.com 666 (Delhi) that in search and seizure assessment u/s 153A, assessments completed on date of search & no incriminating materials having been found during search, assessment under section 153A was invalid.

It has been held in the case of *Principal CIT* v. *Meeta Gutgutia Prop. M/s. Ferns "N"* Petals [2017] 82 taxmann.com 287/248 Taxman 384 (Delhi) that in assessment of search cases, Assessment having been completed on date of search & no incriminating material pertaining to earlier assessment years having been found during search, invocation of section 153A for assessment years earlier to year of search is invalid.

It has been held in the case of *Principal CIT* v. *Dipak Jashvantlal Panchal* [2017] 88 taxmann.com 611 (Guj.) that in the assessment under section 153A, additions can be made only on basis of material found during search.

It has been held in the case of *CIT* v. *S. Ajit Kumar* [2018] 93 taxmann. com 294/255 Taxman 286 (SC) that material found in any proceedings simultaneously conducted in premises of assessee or persons connected with assessee and having dealings with assessee can be used in the assessment u/s 158BC in a case where search at premises of assessee & simultaneous survey in builder's premises revealing fact of payment of cash by assessee to builder which was not accounted for surfaced and thus adverse material found during survey can be used while making block assessment.

It has been held that in the case of *Principal CIT* v. *Dipak J Panchal* [2017] 98 CCH 0074 (Guj.) that Appellate Tribunal was correct in law in holding that the scope of Section 153A is limited to assessing only search related income, there by denying Revenue the opportunity of taxing other escaped income, that comes to the notice of the Assessing Officer. It was held that AO while framing assessment u/s 153A for block period may make addition considering the incriminating material found for year under consideration only which was collected during search.

It has been held in the case of Smt. Jami Nirmala v. *Principal CIT* 207 DTR 65 (Ori.) *that impugned assessment order under section 153A does not refer to any document unearthed during the course of the search and therefore, the assumption of jurisdiction under section 153A was without legal basis.*

It has been held in the case of Dy. CIT v. *Frost Falcon Distilleries Ltd. 207 DTR 1 (Del 'B') that in the absence of any incriminating material, addition could not be made by treating the share capital received by the assessee as unaccounted money by relying solely on the statement of a dummy director of the investor company recorded during the survey action in the case of that company without confronting the same to the assessee.*

It has been held in the case of Smt. Smrutisudha Nayak v. *Union of India* 208 DTR 1 (Ori.) *that as to scope vis-a-vis absence of incriminating material, there being absolutely no incriminating materials found or seized at the time of search, there was no justification for the initiation of assessment proceedings under section 153A.*

It has been held in the case of *Smt Srnrutisudha Nayak* v. *Union of India* 208 DTR 1 (Ori.) that there being absolutely no incriminating materials found or seized at the time of search, there was no justification for the initiation of assessment proceedings under section 153A.

It has been held in the case of *Principal CIT* v. *Agson Global (P) Ltd.* 210 DTR 225 (Del.) that while making assessment under section 153A, Tribunal noted that the photocopies of documents such as blank share transfer forms, blank receipts and blank power of attorney did not constitute incriminating material and thus view of the Tribunal that assessments concluded in respect of asst. yrs. 2012-13, 2013-14 and 2014-15 under section 143(3) could not be disturbed, as no incriminating material was found was sustainable.

It has been held in the case of *Principal CIT* v. *Bhadani Financiers (P) Ltd.* 218 DTR (Del) 294 that since no incriminating documents or materials had been found and seized at the time of search, consequently, no addition can be made under section 153A as the cases of assessees are of non-abated assessments.

It has been held in the case of *Principal CIT* v. *JPM Tools Ltd.* 219 DTR (Del) 201 that where the assessment of the assessees has attained finality prior to the date of search and no incriminating documents/ materials have been found and seized at the time of search, no additions can be made under section 153A and further that Statements recorded under section 132(4) do not by themselves constitute incriminating material.

It has been held in the case of *PCIT* v. *Suman Agarwal* (Ms) (2022) 289 Taxman 674 (Delhi)(HC) that assessment under section 153A as a result of Search or requisition, addition of Long term capital gains on sale of shares was made but no incriminating material was found and thus merely on the basis of statement of and letter of Managing Director of company, addition cannot be made.

(*vib*) Statement under section 132(4) - Whether to be construed as incriminating material?

It has been held in *Principal CIT* v. *Best Infrastructure (India) (P.) Ltd.* [2017] 84 taxmann.com 287/397 ITR 82/159 DTR 257 (Del) *in the case of* search and seizure assessment under section 153A, while dealing with the scope *vis-a-vis* incriminating material, Statements u/s 132(4) make it plain that the surrender of the sum of ₹ 8 crores was only for the assessment year in question and not for each of the six assessment years preceding the year of search & since statements recorded under section 132(4) do not by themselves constitute incriminating material; assumption of jurisdiction under section 153A was not justified in law.

It has been held in the case of *CIT* v. *S. Ajit Kumar* [2018] 93 taxmann. com 294/255 Taxman 286 (SC) that in case of block assessment u/s 158BC, undisclosed income is computed on the basis of evidence found in course of search "and such other materials or information as are available with the Assessing Officer and relatable to such evidence" but material found in any survey proceedings simultaneously conducted in premises of assessee or persons connected with assessee and having dealings with assessee can be used where there was search at premises of assessee & simultaneous survey in builder's premises revealing fact of payment of cash by assessee to builder which was not accounted for & thus adverse material round during survey can be used while making block assessment.

It has been held in the case of *Principal CIT* v. *Sunrise Finlease (P) Ltd.* [2018] 89 taxmann.com 1/252 Taxman 407 (Guj.) that in search and seizure assessment under section 153A & in computing undisclosed income, if there is absence of any incriminating material found in search, assessment under section 153A and consequent addition under s. 68 on the basis of statement of director of assessee company recorded much after the date of search was invalid.

It has been held in the case of *Dy. CIT* v. *Frost Falcon Distilleries Ltd.* 207 DTR 1 (Del 'B') that in the absence of any incriminating material, addition could not be made by treating the share capital received by the assessee as unaccounted money by relying solely on the statement of a dummy director of the investor company recorded during the survey action in the case of that company without confronting the same to the assessee.

It has been held in the case of *PCIT* v. *Shiv Kumar Agarwal* [2022] 289 Taxman 278 (Delhi)(HC) that when no incriminating material was found during course of search and AO had made additions solely relying on disclosures made by Managing Director of a company on which search was conducted, impugned addition was unjustified.

(vic) What constitutes Incriminating Material?

It has been held in the case of *Dy. CIT* v. *M/s Image Vinimay Limited,* IT(SS) A No. 84/Kol/2017 (Kolkata – Trib.) that the bank statements based on which the cash trail was prepared are part of the disclosed documents and cannot be held as incriminating material. Thus, material gathered by the Assessing Officer cannot be categorized as incriminating material found during the course of search, the addition cannot be upheld.

It has been held in the case of *Principal CIT* v. *Param Dairy Ltd.* 200 DTR 118 (Del.) that since Tribunal has held that since the entries of cash payments were made in the books of account, which had been subjected to audit and which audited financial statements of account were part of the return of income filed and assessment whereof stood concluded, it was not incriminating evidence found during the search.

It has been held in the case of *Asstt. CIT* v. *CMG Steels (P) Ltd.* 205 DTR 6 (Chennai 'A') that the confirmation letters obtained from the loan creditors in connection with unsecured loans taken and disclosed in the books of account which were found and seized during the course of search cannot be treated as incriminating material found as a result of search to make addition towards unsecured loans declared in the regular return.

(vii) **In case of search, whether invoking provision of section 153A is mandatory?**

Section 153A requires the assessing officer to assess or reassess the total income of preceding six years in the case of a person in whose case search is initiated. A question arises as to whether in the case of search, it is mandatory for the assessing officer to invoke the provisions of section 153A or the assessing officer has the option to frame assessment or reassessment by invoking provision of section 148 for any particular year.

This question assumes significance in the circumstances when no incriminating material relating to the person searched is found in the course of search, or the incriminating material relating to the person searched found is only relating to one particular year or when incriminating material found in the course of search is not at all relating to the person searched but relating to some other person.

Section 153A has used the words - *"the assessing officer **shall**- issue notice......."* The use of the word *'shall'* makes it mandatory on the part of assessing officer to issue notice and make assessment/reassessment for the preceding six years in all cases where search has been initiated. Assessment/reassessment under section 153A are not assessment for undisclosed income only. Therefore, the requirement of making assessment/reassessment under section 153A has no relation with the nature of incriminating material found or not found in the course of search. Even if there is no incriminating material relating to the person searched found or the incriminating material found is relating to the some other person and with respect to such other incriminating material, such other person shall be required to be assessed under section 153C, still the person searched shall be required to be assessed/reassessed for preceding six years under section 153A.

There is no material distinction regarding the nature of assessment proceedings to be undertaken when a case is reopened either under section 153A or under section 148. For framing assessment under any of these sections, normal provisions of the Act are applicable in all the cases. Section 153A gives overriding power to the assessing officer to reopen the cases of preceding six years without fulfiling any requirement for recording satisfaction or forming reason to believe regarding income having escaped assessment as required under section 147/148 or to fulfil any other requirement regarding time limit or approval by higher authorities as contained under section 149/151. In a case falling under section 153C, when material found during search belongs or relates to some other person, there is requirement to handover such material to the assessing officer having jurisdiction over such other person and then he shall be assessed in accordance with provisions of section 153A.

There can be an opinion that in case assessing officer does not want to exercise power for reopening of the cases as given under section 153A/153C, there does not, however, appear to be any restriction under the Act for the assessing officer to make assessment in the case of search by invoking provisions of other sections *i.e.* section 148. But, this view does not seem to be correct in the light of settled law that specific provision would prevail over general provision. Moreover, it is in the interest of assessing officer to invoke provision of section 153A/153C since he assumes wider powers under these sections in comparison to powers available under section 147/148.

(*viii*) **Name not appearing in Panchnama- prima facie proof of no search-provision of section u/s 153A can not be invoked**

It has been held in the case of *Unique Star Developers* v. *Deputy CIT* [2017] 83 taxmann.com 83 (Mum.-Trib.) that in case of search and seizure assessment under section 153A & its validity in view of absence Panchnama in the name of the assessee, since the name of the assessee-AOP did not appear in the Panchnama and no incriminating material relating to the assessee was seized during the course of search conducted at the premises of the members of the assessee, and not at the premises of the assessee, there is conclusive proof that no search was at all conducted against the assessee and therefore, proceedings under section 153A taken against the assessee were not valid.

(*ix*) **Invoking provision of section 153C instead of provision of section 153A even in case of searched person**

There may be a situation when invoking of the provision of section 153A in the case of the person searched has become time barred. But, there may be seized material belonging to such person available in the case of search held at some other person relating to his associate, relative or close connection. This situation generally happens in practice. In such a case, assessing officer may resort to invoke provision of section 153C with respect to such other person searched so as to get extended time barring period for framing assessment in accordance with the provision of section 153B/153C as is available to the assessing officer.

This kind of situation may arise particularly under the circumstances when time limit for framing assessment under section 153A as prescribed under the provisions of section 153B had expired but due to oversight or some other reason, such material could not be considered during assessment proceeding under section 153A or action under section 153A could not be taken by the assessing officer. Time limit for framing the assessment available under section 153C may get extended beyond the time limit as available under section 153A as per limitation for framing assessment provided under section 153B. In such a situation when time limit for making assessment under section 153A had expired, assessing officer may resort to such options.

In case assessing officer opts to invoke provisions of section 153C, he has to satisfy himself with respect to material found in the course of search that the material belongs to some other person for whom proceeding under section 153C is purported to be resorted and once section 153C is invoked, all material available with the assessing officer relating to such other person can be examined and assessment can be framed after considering the same.

There may however be another view to the effect that a person who has been searched can be assessed in accordance with the provisions of section 153A only and once limitation for framing assessment u/s 153A has expired, such limitation cannot be circumvented by resorting to the proceeding u/s 153C if available to the Assessing Officer.

(*x*) **Whether provision of section 148 or 263 can be invoked with respect to assessment framed as per provisions of section 153A**

Once assessment or reassessment for preceding six years are framed in accordance with the provisions of section 153A, such orders may be rectified under section 154 or reopened in accordance with the provision of section 147/148 by the assessing officer, revised under section 263 by the Commissioner of Income Tax provided there is fulfilment of the conditions required for taking action under the provisions of these respective sections.

There may be a view that there can be reopening the case under section 147/148 even on the basis of seized material available with the assessing officer which could not be considered at the time of framing assessment or reassessment u/s 153A. But before taking action under section 147/148 or 263, one will have to apply the test and the principles established in accordance with various judicial pronouncements obtaining in this regard, so as to justify the action under these sections.

However, there may be contrary view that unless there is some fresh material coming into the possession of the assessing officer, provision of section 147 can not be invoked on the basis of the material already possessed by the assessing officer before framing assessment under section 153A.

(*xi*) **Seized material from the authorized officer received late - Beyond time limit as prescribed u/s 132(9A) - Validity of assessment proceeding**

As per provision of sub-section (9A) of section 132, authorized officer is required to handover seized material to the assessing officer having jurisdiction over the assessee within a period of sixty days from the date of conclusion of search. There may be cases when seized material is not handed over by the authorized officer to the assessing officer within the above time limit due to which assessment proceeding to be undertaken by the assessing officer as per section 153A may get delayed. Sometimes, delay may be due to the reason that the decision regarding centralization of cases could not be finalized in time and the authorized officer could not decide to which assessing officer to handover the seized material.

Under the above circumstances, a question arises as to whether the assessee can challenge the validity of proceedings to be undertaken under section 153A and assumption of jurisdiction by the assessing officer, since statutory requirement as provided under sub-section (9A) of section 132 has not been fulfilled.

In our opinion, requirement of sub-section (9A) is a procedural requirement which is fortified by the language of section 132(9A) itself according to which, after the receipt of seized material from the authorized officer, the assessing officer shall be entitled to exercise the powers as provided under sub-section (8) or sub-section (9) of section

132. Non-receipt of the seized material within a period of sixty days thus cannot invalidate the assumption of jurisdiction by the assessing officer, as jurisdiction for making assessment is not assumed as a result of handing over the seized material but is assumed as a result of initiation of search itself as provided in section 153A. There is no statutory time limit provided under section 153A for issuing notice to file returns and delayed handover of the seized material does not have any adverse bearing on the issue of the notices u/s 153A.

As per provision of section 153A, jurisdiction to make assessment under section 153A is assumed by the assessing officer as soon as search is initiated against a person. Handing over seized material by the authorized officer is to further assist to the assessing officer and to make him available the incriminating material relating to the assessee collected by the Department during search, so as to make use of the same during assessment proceedings.

(xii) Issue of notice under section 153A prior to receipt of the seized material from the authorized officer

Jurisdiction to frame assessment under section 153A is assumed by the assessing officer in all cases when search is initiated. Once the assessing officer who is required to make assessment is determined and decided and cases are transferred to him, he may issue notices to file return for the preceding six years under section 153A even if seized material has not been received from the authorized officer. In our opinion, receiving of seized material is only an administrative act and seized material is to be considered by the assessing officer during the assessment proceedings and for framing the assessment. Non-receipt of the seized material does not prohibit the assessing officer from issuing notices for filing returns under section 153A.

(xiii) Assumption of jurisdiction - Notice under section 143(2) within time limit - Whether mandatory in case of proceedings u/s 153A?

There is a settled position of law that for making assessment under section 143(3) or for making reassessment under section 147/148, assessing officer is required to issue notice under section 143(2) within the time limit as prescribed therein for the purpose of assuming jurisdiction to assess.

Since income tax return filed under section 153A is treated as if it were a return filed as per section 139 of the Act and all other provisions of the Act are applicable for making assessment or reassessment in pursuance to notice under section 153A, a question arises as to whether to issue notice under section 143(2) within the time limit as prescribed therein is a mandatory requirement. In case notice under section

143(2) is not issued or it is issued beyond the time limit, whether it can be said that there is no valid assumption of jurisdiction and any assessment or reassessment framed under section 153A is liable to be quashed or whether it can be said that in the case of income tax return filed as per provision of section 153A, issuing of notice under section 143(2) is only a procedural requirement which is curable and any discrepancy in this regard cannot make the assessment invalid.

This controversy has been settled by Supreme Court in the case of *Asstt. CIT* v. *Hotel Blue Moon* [2010] 188 Taxman 113 wherein it has been held that if AO for any reason wants to repudiate the return filed, he must necessarily issue notice u/s 143(2) within the time prescribed in the proviso to section 143(2) and non-issue of such notice is not mere procedural irregularity and is not curable. However, this judgment was rendered by Supreme Court in the context of assessment for block period under section 158B.

In *Dy. CIT* v. *Sushil Kumar Jain* [2010] 48 DTR 185 (Ind.), it was held that the time limit of service of notice under section 143(2) shall also apply in respect of assessments framed under section 153A and such time limit would start from the end of the month in which return is filed in response to notice issued under section 153A/142(1) and, in case, no such notice has been issued, then, it shall be construed from the end of month in which return was filed.

It has been held in the case of *Ashok Chaddha* v. *ITO* [2012] 20 taxmann.com 387 (Delhi) that where notice under section 153A and questionnaire calling for details were sent, it is not necessary that further notice under section 143(2) should be sent.

It has been held in the case of *Narendra Singh* v. *ITO* [2011] 9 taxmann. com 227/130 ITD 509 (Agra-Trib.) that while making an assessment under section 153A, service of notice under section 143(2) within the prescribed time is mandatory and in the absence of service of such notice, the AO cannot make the addition to the income of the assessee and the AO is bound to accept the income as returned by the assessee.

It has been held in the case of *B. Kubendran* v. *Dy. CIT* [2021] 126 taxmann.com 107/434 ITR 161 (Mad.) that notice under section 143(2) is not mandatory but principles of natural justice must be followed and since adequate opportunity to be heard was not granted, hence order under section 153A not valid.

It has been held in the case of *E. Shamsudeen* v. *CIT* 209 DTR 440 (Ker.) that notice under section 143(2) is not required to be issued in the case of an assessment under section 153A.

However, it has been held in the undernoted case that notice issued under section 153A should mention about the material seized under section 132 and thus it would require that before issue of notice under section 153A the assessing officer should receive the seized material from the authorized officer.

It has been held in the case *Underwater Services Co. Ltd.* v. *Asstt. CIT* 209 DTR 476 (Bom.) that notice under section 153A should have mentioned whether seized material as under section 132 or books of account, other documents or any assets are requisitioned under section 132A and since notice is absolutely silent as could be seen from it and notice says "you are required to prepare true and correct return of income" and "setting forth such other particulars", such notice is vague and hence in the circumstances, the notice is quashed and set aside.

It has been held in the case of *Principal CIT* v. *Cherian Abraham* 210 DTR 152 (Kar.) even in assessment made under section 153C, absence of service of notice under section 143(2) within limitation period & failure of the AO in issuing the notice within the period of limitation under section 143(2) which is a notice giving jurisdiction to the AO to frame assessment cannot be condoned by referring to section 292BB & there is no ground to interfere with the impugned order of the Tribunal.

(xiv) **Status of assessment order passed under section 153A when search is held illegal**

There may be cases when action of search under section 132 under-taken by the Department is challenged in writ jurisdiction before the High Court and the search is held to be illegal. In such a case provisions of section 153A cannot be invoked and no assessment can be framed in pursuance to notice issued under section 153A. In case search is held illegal before passing the order under section 153A, the assess-ment proceeding shall stand dropped. In case search is held illegal after passing of assessment orders under section 153A, such orders shall be illegal. It is altogether a different matter that Department may use the seized material and take action in whatsoever manner possible under any other provision of the Act in accordance with the fulfilment of the requirement provided therein. In such a situation, so far as the proceeding under section 153A is concerned, there does not remain any validity of the same and assessee cannot be assessed pursuant to notices issued under section 153A.

Income tax return relating to the year of search is however not filed pursuant to notice under section 153A which is filed in the normal course as return under section 139. Moreover, it includes post search period also within the same year and single assessment order is passed consisting of the period upto the date of search and after the date of search. It would be interesting to examine as to whether such assessment order will also be illegal when search is held illegal. In case of illegal search, seized material is required to be returned to the assessee but additions having already been made prior to the search declared illegal on the basis of such seized material may trigger controversy regarding its evidentiary value. It is a settled position of law as held by the Supreme Court in the case of *Pooran Mal* v. *Director of Inspection* [1974] 93 ITR 505 that evidences collected even in illegal search may be used against the assessee in appropriate proceeding under the law. But, the evidentiary value and presumption u/s 292C of such seized material is diluted to a great extent.

In view of the above, we are of the opinion that assessment order passed relating to the year of search, under such circumstances will remain valid and the same cannot be treated as illegal. But assessee would be entitled to plead before the appellate authority regarding the presumption u/s 292C remaining no longer available to Revenue and appellate authority will be obliged to take the diluted impact of such seized material and shift in the rules of burden of proof.

It has been held in the case of *Siksha "O" Anusandhan* v. *CIT* [2012] 20 taxmann.com 798 (Orissa) that the person, in respect of whom search under section 132 is initiated, is the same person against whom notice under section 153A is to be issued for making assessment and if there is any illegality in the search warrant, the same will invalidate the search assessment proceeding initiated under section 153A.

(xv) **"Reason to believe" recorded by the competent authority for authorization of the search not available with the assessing officer**

Copy of "reason to believe" recorded, *inter alia*, regarding undisclosed income by the competent authority for authorization of search as per sub-section (1) of section 132 is neither supplied to the person searched nor to the assessing officer who is going to make assessment in pursuance to the search held. In case the copy of the "reason" recorded regarding undisclosed income is made available to the assessing officer, it may provide guidance to him for framing the assessment. Probably the rationale behind not supplying the copy of "reason" recorded by the competent authority is that the evidences regarding undisclosed income at that stage are gathered by the competent authority in a confidential manner and from the confidential sources even from the informers whose identity is not disclosed. When the above process is confidential, legislature does not want to get the mind of assessing officer influenced by such evidences. Alternatively, appraisal report is prepared by the authorized officer which mentions the basis of search and analysis of evidences collected during search so as to provide input to the assessing officer for framing the assessment.

(xvi) Significance of appraisal report during assessment for search cases

Technically, appraisal report prepared by the authorized officer is only an internal report to be made available to the assessing officer to assist him in framing assessments. Legally, assessing officer is not expected to rely upon solely and be influenced by the finding or analysis in the appraisal report. He is required to apply his independent mind after appraising all the seized material. Assessing officer is expected to go through each and every evidence collected during search and take his independent decision regarding the relevance of the same with respect to the total income of the assessee and frame assessment order accordingly.

However, in practice, it has been observed that appraisal report becomes a very significant document and due to pressure of time barring search cases, assessing officer hardly gets any time to look beyond the issues raised and discussed in the appraisal report.

As per administrative departmental instructions, assessing officer is required to examine all the issues discussed in the appraisal report. In case assessing officer takes a view which is in deviation with the finding given in the appraisal report and which is prejudicial to the interest of revenue, he is expected to consult to the authorized officer who had prepared the appraisal report and try to reach at a consensus view. In case of difference of opinion, matter may be referred to Additional Commissioner or Commissioner who in turn would discuss with the corresponding authority in the investigation wing of the Department in the hierarchy and the issue is required to be decided in consultation with each other. Of course, ultimately final view has to be taken by the assessing officer only in consultation with range in-charge who is the approving authority for the assessment orders to be passed under section 153A as required under section 153D.

Recently departmental internal guidelines have been issued for the authorized officer to prepare a draft of preliminary questionnaire to be issued by and under the authority of the assessing officer to the assessee. In legal terms, any such questionnaire can only be suggestive to the assessing officer and he is not bound to issue the same questionnaire to the assessee. The objective of such requirement is to take benefit of the efforts already put by the authorized officer in appraising the documents and other evidences found during search.

(*xvii*) **For assessment of search cases, integrated investigation approach is adopted**

Generally, search cases with respect to the person searched in whose case action under section 153A is to be taken or related persons in whose case action under section 153C is likely to be taken, are centralized at one place. Departmental instructions have been issued from time to time regarding centralization of all the cases at the Central Circle which has been specially created for making assessment of search cases. The objective is to make integrated investigation and examination of evidences by the same officer relating to all the person/entities falling within a group. Sometimes, there may be evidences which may be common to many persons. In case assessing officers of such persons are different officers, it may create problem in deciding to which assessing officer to handover the evidences and how to make available such evidences to the assessing officer of respective persons. Centralization of cases is from the point of view of administrative convenience and in suitable cases, as the situation may require, this policy may be deviated.

Before transferring the case from one jurisdiction to another in other city, an opportunity is given to the assessee as required under section 127 of the Act to make his objection, if any, and keeping in view the merit of the objection so raised by the assessee, appropriate decision is taken by the competent authorities. In case assessee is not satisfied with the decision of Commissioner or Chief Commissioner in this regard, he may approach to the higher authorities or file writ with the High Court so as to decide the jurisdiction of his cases.

(*xviii*) **Whether ITO can be assessing officer under section 153A?**

For making assessment or reassessment relating to search cases under section 153A, there is no restriction under the Act and even an officer of the rank of Income Tax Officer may be the assessing officer for passing such orders. In the case of block assessment under Chapter XIVB, there was requirement to make assessment by an authority not below the rank of Assistant Commissioner of Income Tax for making assessment of undisclosed income. But there is no such requirement under section 153A.

(*xix*) **Whether authorized officer can be the Assessing Officer?**

There is no restriction under the Act regarding handling of the assessment/reassessment proceedings under section 153A by the authorized officer who conducted the search if he is otherwise vested with the assessment jurisdiction. One view can be that assessment/reassessment proceedings in the capacity as assessing officer may be handled in a better manner by the authorized officer since he has carried the investigation, appraised all the evidences and is having the complete knowledge of the case. On other hand, argument may be given that investigation officer who has carried the investigation should not be deputed as assessing officer as well to make the assessment since he was deeply involved in the investigation process and search operation and he may not be able to apply his independent mind in impartial, fair, objective and just manner. In the interest of equity and justice, an investigation officer should not be an adjudication officer who is a quasi judicial authority.

In practice, it has been observed that generally the job of passing assessment/reassessment order(s) is not assigned to the authorized officer who has carried out the search operation.

Assessment by the Authorized Officer heading search

Officer heading the search - Party cannot make block assessment - hit by judicial bias.

Dy. CIT who was heading the raiding party in the search at the house of petitioner No. 2 and his wife could not be the AO in the case of these petitioners once they are complaining of bias and reasonable apprehension of prejudice to them - *Vipan Kumar Jain* v. *UOI* [2001] 117 Taxman 178 (P&H).

(xx) **Application of presumption under section 292C during assessment of search cases**

Section 292C provides that in the case of books of account, documents or assets found during search, it may be presumed that such books of account, documents or assets belong to the person searched, the contents of such books of account and documents are true and the same are under signature and in the hand writing of the particular person to whom the same are purported to be in.

The provision regarding above presumption was earlier contained under section 132(4A) and there used to be controversy whether the same can be applied by assessing officer during assessment proceedings or it was available only for the purpose of passing order u/s 132(5) as earlier required [*P.R. Metrani* v. *CIT* [2006] 157 Taxman 325 (SC)]. After the retrospective amendment with effect from 1-10-1975 by the Finance Act, 2007, this controversy has been set at rest by introducing the provision regarding presumption as to assets, books of account etc. found during search under section 292C. The presumption is not restricted to books of account, documents or assets found during search under section 132 but it has been extended regarding books of account, documents or assets found during survey under section 133A also.

It implies that in regard to the material discovered during search, provision of presumption contained under section 292C is not restricted to be applied during assessment proceedings under section 153A only but also the same can be applied during any assessment proceedings or any other proceedings undertaken under any of the provisions of the Act. In fact presumption is with respect to books of account, other documents or any assets found during search or survey operation and whenever use of such material found is made by the authorities under any of the provisions of Act, the presumption is applicable and may be used by the authorities.

A detailed discussion regarding applicability of presumption as contained under section 292C has been made under separate chapter and may be referred thereat.

(xxi) **Introduction of section 115BBE & flat rate of tax rate on undisclosed income/investment/expenditure etc.**

This section has been inserted by Finance Act, 2012 applicable from A.Y. 2013-14. It seeks to levy flat rate of tax on any income which are referred in sections 68, 69, 69A, 69B, 69C and 69D.

Section 68 to section 69D contains provisions regarding deeming income in case source of income/expenditure/investment is not explained by the assessee. In the case of search, undisclosed income/expenditure/investment is generally found which are taxed under these sections. Hither-to-fore, such deemed incomes were assessed in the return of income under the head "Income from other sources" and regular rates of tax were applicable on the total income including such deemed incomes.

Finance Act, 2012 has introduced a new section 115BBE providing that such deemed incomes shall be liable to be taxed at the flat rate of 30%. There shall thus not be allowed benefit of basic exemption limit. For example, if an assessee has deemed income under any of these sections, say, of ₹ 2,50,000 and he does not have any other income, the amount of tax applicable would be ₹ 75,000 from A.Y. 2013-14, whereas prior to the insertion of section 115BBE, the amount of tax would have been only ₹ 5,000 after giving benefit of basic exemption limit of ₹ 2,00,000.

Further, after the introduction of this section, the benefit of set off of business losses or unabsorbed depreciation against such deemed incomes shall also not be available to the assessee. In search cases, assessee used to make declaration of undisclosed income and to claim set off of business loss or loss under the other heads brought forward from earlier years or incurred during the year. When such losses were adjustable against the undisclosed income declared during search, the effective tax burden used to get reduced. After section 115BBE, such adjustment or benefit is not permitted.

Under the Income-tax Act, there are several provisions relating to deemed incomes apart from the incomes mentioned in section 68 to section 69D. For example, section 56 deems income relating to amounts/assets received without or inadequate consideration, section 2(22)(e) relating to deemed dividend etc. It may be noticed that the applicability of section 115BBE has been made only to the deemed income covered by section 68 to section 69D. This provision cannot be extended to any other deemed incomes covered under the Act.

There may be cases where assessee claims an income under section 56 or as business income earned from tuitions, dairy, embroidery and stitching etc. but during assessment, if he is not able to prove the character the income as claimed by adducing the evidences to this effect, such income may be re-characterized by the AO as deemed income u/ss 68 to 69D and in such a situation, assessee shall be liable to be taxed u/s 115BBE at the flat rate of 30% of such income. It is to be noted that the applicability of section 115BBE is not dependant upon the observations to be made by the AO in the assessment order. Section 115BBE would still be attracted even if the income is *suo motu* offered by the assessee in his return of income under either of these sections.

Amendment of section 115BBE - Effective Tax @ 75% applicable in the case of deemed income.

Finance Act, 2012 w.e.f. 1st of April, 2013 introduced a new section 115BBE as modified by the Finance Act, 2016 which provided as under:

115BBE. (1) Where the total income of an assessee includes any income referred to in section 68, section 69, section 69A, section 69B, section 69C or section 69D, the income-tax payable shall be the aggregate of—

 (a) the amount of income-tax calculated on income referred to in section 68, section 69, section 69A, section 69B, section 69C or section 69D, at the rate of thirty per cent; and

 (b) the amount of income-tax with which the assessee would have been chargeable had his total income been reduced by the amount of income referred to in clause (a).

(2) Notwithstanding anything contained in this Act, no deduction in respect of any expenditure or allowance or set off of any loss shall be allowed to the assessee under any provision of this Act in computing his income referred to in clause (a) of sub-section (1).

As a result of the above section, any income referred to in section 68, section 69, section 69A, section 69B, section 69C or section 69D became taxable at the flat rate of 30% without giving the benefit of lower slab rate. Further, no deduction in respect of any expenditure or allowance or set off is allowed to the assessee under any provision of the Act against such deemed incomes. It implies that benefit of set off of losses under the business or unabsorbed depreciation or losses under any other head even for the current year are not allowed to be set off against such deemed incomes.

The Taxation Laws (Second Amendment) Act, 2016 w.e.f. A.Y. 2017-18 has substituted sub-section (1) of section 115BBE by introducing the following sub-section:

(*1*)   *"Where the total income of an assessee,—*

   (*a*)   *includes any income referred to in section 68, section 69, section 69A, section 69B, section 69C or section 69D and reflected in the return of income furnished under section 139; or*

   (*b*)   *determined by the Assessing Officer includes any income referred to in section 68, section 69, section 69A, section 69B, section 69C or section 69D, if such income is not covered under clause* (a),

   the income-tax payable shall be the aggregate of—

   (*i*)   *the amount of income-tax calculated on the income referred to in clause* (a) *and clause* (b), *at the rate of sixty per cent; and*

   (*ii*)   *the amount of income-tax with which the assessee would have been chargeable had his total income been reduced by the amount of income referred to in clause* (i).*"*

Further section 2 of Finance Act, 2016 has been amended by introducing a new proviso providing that in respect of any income chargeable to tax under clause (*i*) of sub-section (1) of section 115BBE of the Income-tax Act, 2016, the advance tax computed under the first proviso shall be increased by surcharge, for the purpose of the union, calculated @ 25% of such advance tax.

It would imply that in the case of income referred to in section 68, section 69, section 69A, section 69B, section 69C or section 69D of the Act, the applicable effective rate of tax shall be 75% (tax @ 60% plus surcharge @ 25% of 60% *i.e.* 15%)

Salient Features of section 115BBE :

   1. Background of making amendment under section 115BBE

   2. Rate of tax increased substantially from 30% plus surcharge to 75% plus cess

3. Amended section applicable for A.Y. 2017-18 i.e. F.Y. 2016-17

4. Nature of income covered under section 115BBE

5. Cash deposited in bank or any other income, source of which is not explainable covered within the ambit of section 115BBE

6. Income under section 115BBE can be declared by the assessee himself in the return of income.

7. No set-off of losses or any deduction or allowance allowed against such income.

8. Penalty provision under section 271AAC introduced for deemed income.

Detailed Analysis of Salient Features:

(i) Background of making amendment under section 115BBE

Government introduced Income Declaration Scheme (IDS), 2016 w.e.f. 1st of June, 2016 till 30th of Sept., 2016 enabling declaration of undisclosed income/undisclosed assets by way of payment of tax including interest and penalty at the rate of 45% of such undisclosed income. It is matter within the public domain that quite a good number of assessees did not avail this opportunity, *inter alia*, for the reason that opinion was expressed in certain quarters that rate of tax for deemed incomes related to current year for which source cannot be explained may be 30% plus surcharge as stipulated under section 115BBE. Therefore, it would not make sense to pay higher rate of tax i.e. 45% under Income Declaration scheme (IDS) for declaring cash or current year's income.

Government further came out with demonetization of high denomination old currency w.e.f. 8th of Nov., 2016 mid-night substituting the old currency with the new currency. As per scheme of demonetization, such old currency was required to be deposited in the bank for exchanging with the new currency. Assessees started depositing old currency in the bank and again an opinion was expressed that in case source of such cash deposit is not explainable, it would at best attract tax @ 30% plus surcharge as provided under section 115BBE. However, government made it clear by way of statement issued by Hon'ble Prime Minister as well as Revenue Secretary that such cases would attract heavy penalty apart from tax so that the assessees who did not avail Income Declaration Scheme (IDS) may not be in advantageous position. However, there was no legal back-up for imposing such penalty under the existing provisions of the Income Tax Act. The amendment under section 115BBE has been brought increasing the rate of tax from 30% plus surcharge to 60% plus 15% surcharge i.e. 75%, so that the element of penalty is recovered simultaneously and assessees are discouraged to generate undisclosed income. It is also significant to note that the amendment was not brought under penalty provisions for such cases because retrospective provision in penalty provision, it was feared, could have been struck down by the Courts. Therefore, government thought it fit to increase the rate of tax under section 115BBE.

Such increase in the rate of tax under section 115BBE was brought as per the above background but its effect is not limited in respect of cash deposited during the window provided in demonetization period only. But it is a permanent amendment under section 115BBE which would mean that in future all kind of income covered within the ambit of section 68, section 69, section 69A, section 69B, section 69C or section 69D, which are in the nature of deemed/undisclosed income shall attract higher rate of tax @75%.

(ii) **Rate of tax increased substantially from 30% to 75%**

Section 115BBE was incorporated by Finance Act, 2012 providing flat rate of tax on incomes covered under section 68, section 69, section 69A, section 69B, section 69C or section 69D (hereinafter called deemed incomes) without giving benefit of lower slab tax rate or adjustment for brought forward losses under other heads of income. Legislature provided flat rate of tax @ 30% plus surcharge i.e. Maximum Marginal Rate (MMR) on such incomes. Generally, such incomes are of the nature with respect to which assessee is not able to explain and establish the source of income. Therefore, legislature wanted such cases to be taxed at Maximum Marginal Rate (MMR).

The Taxation Laws (Second Amendment) Act, 2016 has substantially increased the rate of tax on deemed income from 30% plus surcharge to 75% (*i.e.* 60% plus 15% surcharge). The objective of such steep increase in the rate of tax is to discourage generation of such undisclosed or deemed income by the assessee for which source of earning cannot be explained. In a way, element of penalty in such cases has already been embedded in a way in the tax rate itself. It has been observed that undisclosed income or assets detected during search are generally of the nature covered under section 68, section 69, section 69A, section 69B, section 69C or section 69D. In such cases now, assessee shall be liable to pay tax @ 75%.

(iii) **Amended Section applicable for A.Y 2017-18 i.e. F.Y. 2016-17**

Amended sub-section (1) of section 115BBE brought by the Taxation Laws (Second Amendment) Act, 2016 is applicable w.e.f. A.Y. 2017-18 i.e. period commencing from 1st of April, 2016. The above amendment has been brought by the Taxation Laws (Second Amendment) Act, 2016 which was introduced and passed in Parliament in the month of

December, 2016. Therefore, the increase in rate of tax under section 115BBE is having retrospective effect to certain extent.

(*iv*) **Nature of income covered under section 115BBE**

Section 115BBE is applicable relating to any income referred to in under section 68, section 69, section 69A, section 69B, section 69C or section 69D. The income reflected under these sections is of the following nature:

Section 68	Cash Credits
Section 69	Unexplained Investments
Section 69A	Unexplained Money, etc.
Section 69B	Amount of Investment, etc., not fully disclosed in books of account
Section 69C	Unexplained Expenditure, etc.
Section 69D	Amount borrowed or repaid or Hundi

The above referred incomes are of the nature with respect to which assessee is not able to explain the nature and source of earning such income or making investment in assets acquired by the assessee or expenses incurred. The above referred sections cover unexplained or undisclosed incomes or assets, e.g., in the case of search, when cash or jewellery is found, source of which cannot be explained by the assessee, such income is taxed under section 69, section 69A or section 69B of the Act. Similarly, when evidences related to certain unexplained expenditure incurred are found, it is liable to be taxed under section 69C of the Act. Section 68 covers credits found in the books for which no satisfactory explanation regarding nature and source thereof is offered by the assessee. As per amended section 115BBE, all such incomes will attract tax rate @ 75%. In the case of search generally evidences relating to undisclosed income or undisclosed assets are found which would attract tax rate of 75% apart from penalty under section 271AAB which has been discussed separately. Therefore, in the case of search now, declaration of undisclosed income falling within the ambit of above referred sections will have to be made keeping in view that it would attract tax rate at the rate of 75% plus minimum penalty of 30% of undisclosed income even when declaration of undisclosed income is made by the assessee during search while recording statement under section 132(4).

(*v*) **Cash deposited in bank or any other income, source of which is not explainable covered within the ambit of section 115BBE**

It has been observed in practice that in certain cases assessees used to file income tax return by showing cash deposit in bank surrendered for want of evidences regarding source or income from Tuition fees, Tailoring, Knitting, Daily Business etc., proper nature and source of which was difficult to establish. In any case, before amendment of section 115BBE, such incomes were liable to be taxed maximum at the rate of 30% but now after amendment under section 115BBE, the rate of tax has increased to 75%. Assessee will have to be very cautious in declaring any income or cash deposited in bank with respect to which nature and source cannot be establish satisfactorily. In such cases, Assessing Officer may treat such unexplained incomes not as income from business or profession but income under section 68 or section 69 etc. and may impose tax at the rate of 75%.

(*vi*) **Income under section 115BBE can be declared by the assessee himself in the return of income.**

Section 115BBE as amended by the Taxation Laws (Second Amendment) Act, 2016 has been drafted in such a manner that it provides an option to the assessee for making declaration of undisclosed or unexplained income in the return of income by himself. It is pertinent to note that there is no column in the income tax return form prevalent or used so far to show income under section 68, section 69, section 69A, section 69B, section 69C or section 69D by assessee himself. In fact, income referred under these sections are in the nature of deeming income which are triggered when Assessing Officer is not satisfied regarding the nature and source of such income or assets and addition is made by the Assessing Officer under these sections.

The amended provision of sub-section (1) of section 115BBE has two limbs:

Clause (*a*) covers the cases when such incomes is so deemed & offered to tax by the assessee in the return of income under section 139 and;

Clause (*b*) covers the cases when addition is made by the Assessing Officer.

There may be possibility that return of income forms may be revised in future for A.Y. 2017-18 & onwards to provide column for making declaration of such deemed income by assessee himself.

(*vii*) **No set-off of losses or any deduction or allowance allowed against such income.**

Income covered under section 115BBE attracts flat rate of tax and surcharge at the rate of 75%. No set off of losses under any other head of income or unabsorbed losses or unabsorbed depreciation brought forward from earlier year is allowed to be set off against such income. Therefore, in the case of search, any declaration of such income shall be liable to be taxed at the rate 75% without any scope of planning for reducing the income by taking the benefit of set off of losses which used to be done prior to introduction of amendment under section 115BBE.

(viii) Penalty provision under section 271AAC introduced for deemed income.

Penalty provision for under-reporting or mis-reporting of income has been given under section 270A of the Act which ranges from 50% to 200% of the amount of tax payable on under-reported income. In the case of income in the nature covered under section 115BBE since rate of tax has been increased substantially *i.e.* 75% including surcharge, separate penalty provision for such income has been legislated in the Act by way of insertion of new section 271AAC which states as under:

"**271AAC.** *(1) The Assessing Officer may, notwithstanding anything contained in this Act other than the provisions of section 271AAB, direct that, in a case where the income determined includes any income referred to in section 68, section 69, section 69A, section 69B, section 69C or section 69D for any previous year, the assessee shall pay by way of penalty, in addition to tax payable under section 115BBE, a sum computed at the rate of ten per cent of the tax payable under clause (i) of sub-section (1) of section 115BBE:*

Provided *that no penalty shall be levied in respect of income referred to in section 68, section 69, section 69A, section 69B, section 69C or section 69D to the extent such income has been included by the assessee in the return of income furnished under section 139 and the tax in accordance with the provisions of clause (i) of sub-section (1) of section 115BBE has been paid on or before the end of the relevant previous year.*

(2) No penalty under the provisions of section 270A shall be imposed upon the assessee in respect of the income referred to in sub-section (1).

(3) The provisions of sections 274 and 275 shall, as far as may be, apply in relation to the penalty referred to in this section.".

It implies that in case declaration of incomes referred under section 115BBE is made by the assessee himself in the return of income, there is no penalty. However, addition is made by Assessing Officer at later stage in assessment or reassessment, penalty at the rate of 10% of the tax payable under section 115BBE shall be attracted.

B. SECTION 153C - ASSESSMENT OF INCOME OF ANY OTHER PERSON

13.10 Text of section 153C

(1) Notwithstanding anything contained in section 139, section 147, section 148, section 149, section 151 and section 153, where the Assessing Officer is satisfied that,—

(a) *any money, bullion, jewellery or other valuable article or thing, seized or requisitioned, belongs to; or*

(b) *any books of account or documents, seized or requisitioned, pertains or pertain to, or any information contained therein, relates to,*

a person other than the person referred to in section 153A, then, the books of account or documents or assets, seized or requisitioned shall be handed over to the Assessing Officer having jurisdiction over such other person and that Assessing Officer shall proceed against each such other person and issue notice and assess or reassess the income of the other person in accordance with the provisions of section 153A, if, that Assessing Officer is satisfied that the books of account or documents or assets seized or requisitioned have a bearing on the determination of the total income of such other person for six assessment years immediately preceding the assessment year relevant to the previous year in which search is conducted or requisition is made and for the relevant assessment year or years referred to in sub-section (1) of section 153A :

Provided *that in case of such other person, the reference to the date of initiation of the search under section 132 or making of requisition under section 132A in the second proviso to sub-section (1) of section 153A shall be construed as reference to the date of receiving the books of account or documents or assets seized or requisitioned by the Assessing Officer having jurisdiction over such other person:*

Provided further *that the Central Government may by rules made by it and published in the Official Gazette, specify the class or classes of cases in respect of such other person, in which the Assessing Officer shall not be required to issue notice for assessing or reassessing the total income for six assessment years immediately preceding the assessment year relevant to the previous year in which search is conducted or requisition is made and for the relevant assessment year or years as referred to in sub-section (1) of section 153A except in cases where any assessment or reassessment has abated.*

2. Where books of account or documents or assets seized or requisitioned as referred to in sub-section (1) has or have been received by the Assessing Officer having jurisdiction over such other person after the due date for furnishing the return of income for the assessment year relevant to the previous year in which search is conducted under section 132 or requisition is made under section 132A and in respect of such assessment year—

a. *No return of income has been furnished by such other person and no notice under sub-section (1) of section 142 has been issued to him, or*

b. *A return of income has been furnished by such other person but no notice under sub-section (2) of section 143 has been served and limitation of serving the notice under sub-section (2) of section 143 has expired, or*

c. *Assessment or reassessment, if any, has been made.*

Before the date of receiving of books of account or documents or assets seized or requisitioned by the Assessing Officer having jurisdiction over such other person, such Assessing Officer shall issue the notice and assess or reassess total income of such other person of such assessment year in the manner provided in section 153A.

13.11 Legislative history

Prior to the concept of block assessment introduced by Finance Act, 1995, there was no special provision under the Act for making assessment or reassessment of any other person with respect to whom, books of account, documents or assets were found during search of any person. Under such situation, normal provisions of the Act for reopening of the case relating to other persons were applicable.

As per Finance Act, 1995, with the introduction of concept of block assessment, special provision to assess undisclosed income of any other person was legislated under section 158BD.

As per Finance Act, 2003, concept of block assessment was abolished and new procedure for assessment and reassessment in search cases was introduced. Special procedure for assessment or reassessment of preceding six years and the year of search in the case of any other person have been introduced by way of introduction of section 153C. Section 153C has been introduced to make assessment or reassessment of any other person in the same manner as assessment or reassessment of the person searched, if any books of account, documents or assets seized during search belong to the some other person.

Finance Act, 2012 has w.e.f. 1.7.2012 inserted proviso to section 153C providing that in certain class of cases as may be notified by the Central Government, Assessing Officer shall not be required to issue notice(s) and frame assessment(s) mandatorily for all the earlier six years. The objective of the above amendment, it appears, is not to reopen those cases where no incriminating material relating to earlier year(s) has been found and seized.

As per the Finance (No. 2) Act, 2014 with effect from 1.10.2014, section 153C was amended providing that assessing officer of the other person shall proceed against each such other person and issue notice and assess or reassess the income of the other person in accordance with the provisions of section 153A, if that assessing officer is satisfied that the books of account or documents or assets seized or requisitioned have a bearing on the determination of the total income of such other person. Thus, legislature has provided the requirement of the satisfaction of the assessing officer of the other person also before initiating assessment proceeding under section 153C.

Finance Act, 2015 has amended sub-section (1) of section 153C providing that provision of section 153C can be invoked when any money, bullion, jewellery or other valuable article or thing, seized or requisitioned belongs to other person & any books of account or documents, seized or requisitioned pertains or pertain to or any information contained therein, relates to some other person. Thus, the concept of the seized material including books of account or other documents belonging to the other person has been diluted by this amendment & the scope of section 153C has been enlarged.

Finance Act, 2017 has amended provision of section 153C providing the years which can be reopened under section 153C and the controversy in this regard existing due to the earlier judicial decisions has been settled. It has been provided that under section 153C six assessment years immediately preceding the assessment year relevant to the previous year in which search is conducted or requisition is made & the year of search shall be the years which may be covered u/s 153C.

13.12 Objective

In the case of search of a person, if any incriminating material suggesting undisclosed income is found and seized which does not belong to the person searched but to some other person, in such situation, such other person has to be made liable to be assessed with respect to such undisclosed income. The provisions of section 153A/153C are not only to make assessment of undisclosed income but to make assessment or reassessment of the total income including the previously disclosed income as well as the undisclosed income found as a result of search.

13.13 Nature of provision of section 153C

(i) Provision of section 153C - Plain interpretation

For applicability of the provision of section 153C, the following conditions are required to be fulfilled—

1. The assessing officer is satisfied that any money, bullion, jewellery or other valuable article or thing seized or requisitioned belongs to, or books of account or document seized or requisitioned pertains or pertain to, or any information contained therein relates to a person other than the person with respect to whom search has been initiated.

2. The books of account, documents or assets seized or requisitioned shall be handed over to the assessing officer having jurisdiction over such other person.

3. That assessing officer shall proceed against each such other person in the same manner as the person searched, to make assessment or reassessment in accordance with the provisions of section 153A. It implies that such other person shall also be assessed or reassessed for the year of search and for the preceding six years.

(*ii*) Rationale of the provision

A search under section 132(1) may be authorized, *inter alia*, with respect to any person who is in possession or control of any money, bullion, jewellery or other valuable article or thing which represents undisclosed income. The actual owner of such undisclosed assets may be some other person. Undisclosed income is required to be assessed in the hands of the person who is the actual owner of the asset or who has earned the undisclosed income. Therefore, section 153C requires that if any incriminating material or undisclosed asset seized in the course of a search action, belongs or relates to some other person the same shall be handed over to the assessing officer having jurisdiction over such other person for making assessment of such other person.

The incriminating material seized during search may belong to the person searched or may belong to some other person. In case such material belongs to the person searched, it will be considered during his assessment under section 153A. However in case such material belongs or relates to some other person, in that case such other person is roped into for making assessment with respect to such material by way of section 153C.

(*iii*) Provision of section 153C is harsh

Having explained the rationale of section 153C, it can be said that the provision of section 153C is harsh with respect to the person who has not been searched as also echoed by Supreme Court in the context of section 158BD in the case of *Manish Maheshwari* v. *Asstt. CIT* [2007] 159 Taxman 258. The Legislature has however kept both the persons at par- one against whom search warrant has been authorized and search has been conducted and the other person against whom no search warrant has been authorized and no search has been conducted.

A person against whom no search warrant has been authorized should not be equated with the person against whom search is authorized so as to make assessment in his case also in the same manner as in the case of person searched as per provision of section 153A. There are vital points of distinction in both the cases—

    a. Extensive enquiries are conducted and information is collected by high ranking Departmental officials before forming "reason to believe" regarding undisclosed income and issuing search warrant against the person to be searched. No "reason to believe" regarding undisclosed income is formed and recorded by the competent authority with respect to the other person. To make assessment or reassessment of such other person mandatorily for seven years cannot be justified on the ground of plain equity.

    b. No opportunity to explain whether assets are disclosed in the hands of other person is provided to him during search before taking decision of seizure. Third person cannot be put in a worse position than the person searched. Under such situation, even disclosed assets belonging to other person may be seized and in that case invoking provision of section 153C can not be the intention of the Legislature.

In view of the above discussion, it is opined that the provision of section 153C has to be interpreted strictly having regard to the intention of the Legislature. The provision of section 153C needs to be read down in a manner so as to achieve the actual legislative intent. The literal interpretation of the provision of this section needs to be toned down so that there are no unintended severe repercussions on the third person. Interpretation of law in this regard by way of judicial pronouncements is in the developing stage and the literal interpretation of section 153C is liable to judicial test and scrutiny. In our opinion, purposive interpretation of section 153C is required to be adopted so that there is no unintended adverse impact upon the persons against whom no search warrant has been issued and no search has been conducted.

In *Asstt. CIT* v. *Panchuram Deshmukh* [2010] 8 taxmann.com 204/133 TTJ 53 (Bilaspur), Tribunal has however held that as per provisions of section 153C, satisfaction has to be arrived at with regard to the ownership of a document found during the search and not regarding the undisclosed income and in view of sufficient evidence on record to arrive at such satisfaction and appraisal thereof by the AO giving specific particulars of Annexures to the seized material and contents of such material showing application of mind, it cannot be said that the impugned notice was issued without proper satisfaction.

13.14 Analysis of provision of section 153C

Various aspects relating to the provision of section 153C are being analyzed and discussed hereinafter.

(*i*) **"Where the assessing officer is satisfied"**

The reference of the "assessing officer" in the above phrase under section 153C is to the assessing officer who is making assessment of the person searched under section 153A. The satisfaction regarding books of account, documents or assets belonging to some other person is required to be formed by such assessing officer. Satisfaction or recommendation of the authorized officer in his appraisal report for invoking provisions of section 153C with respect to some other person is not sufficient requirement. It is the assessing officer of the searched person while appraising all the seized material of the person searched has to be satisfied that some of the seized material do not belong to the person searched but to some other person.

In the case of block assessment under Chapter XIVB, similar provision was contained more or less under section 158BD which also used the same phrase "where the assessing officer is satisfied that......" Courts have interpreted in the context of the language of section 158BD that the assessing officer referred therein refers to the assessing officer of the searched person.

Supreme Court in case of *Manish Maheshwari* v. *Asstt. CIT* [2007] 159 Taxman 258 (SC) have held that section 158BD provides for taking recourse to a block assessment in terms of section 158BC in respect of any other person, the conditions precedent where for are (*i*) satisfaction must be recorded by the A.O. that any undisclosed income belongs to any person other than the persons with respect to whom search was made under section 132....... As the A.O. has not recorded his satisfaction, which is mandatory nor has he transferred the case to the A.O. having jurisdiction over the matter, the impugned judgment of the High Court cannot be sustained.

Delhi High Court in the case of *CIT* v. *Dawn View Farms (P.) Ltd.* [2009] 178 Taxman 15 (Delhi), have held that plain reading of the provision of section 158BD makes it clear that until and unless the A.O. of the person who is searched is satisfied that there is any undisclosed income belonging to any person, other than the person with respect to whom search was made under section 132, no further step can take place.... It is only the satisfaction of the A.O. of the person in respect of whom the search is conducted that is relevant.

In a recent case of *CIT* v. *Radhey Shyam Bansal* (yet to be reported), Delhi High Court upheld the decision of Tribunal setting aside the assessment framed in pursuance to proceeding u/s 158BD on the ground that no satisfaction was recorded by the Assessing Officer of the person searched to the effect that the undisclosed income belongs to any person other than the searched person.

It has been held in the case of *Asstt. CIT* v. *Jay Dee Securities & Finance Ltd.* [2017] 88 taxmann.com 626 (Delhi-Trib.) that where Satisfaction having been recorded by the AO who has issued notices under s. 153C r/w s. 153A to initiate the proceedings under s. 153C against the assessee and not by the AO of the person who has been searched, initiation of the impugned proceedings under s. 153C is invalid and accordingly, all the assessment orders for the relevant assessment years are quashed.

It has been held in the case of *Vision Promoters & Builders (P.) Ltd.* v. *CIT* [2017] 190 TTJ 398 (Chd.-Trib.) that since no separate satisfaction note was recorded in the case of searched person that the seized documents belonged to the assessee and that the same will have a bearing on the determination of the total income of the assessee, the very assumption of jurisdiction under s. 153C was bad in law and subsequent assessment order passed under s. 153C is null and void and is to be treated as non est in the eyes of law and consequently the subsequent revision order passed by the CIT under s. 263 is also void.

It has been held in the case of *Principal CIT* v. *N.S. Software (Firm)* [2018] 93 taxmann.com 21/255 Taxman 230 (Delhi) that AO's satisfaction note recorded under section 153C nowhere reflects whether any document, seized, on application of his mind, disclosed that it belonged to the assessee, and if so, its *prima facie* nature & also, satisfaction note was not recorded by the AO of searched person from whose premises the documents were seized, assessment was therefore invalid.

Recently CBDT has issued a circular directing to withdraw all pending appeals in case satisfaction has not been recorded by the A.O. of the searched person. Full text of the circular is reproduced below:—

Circular No. 24/2015 dated 31st December, 2015

The issue of recording of satisfaction for the purposes of section 158BD/153C has been subject matter of litigation.

2. The Hon'ble Supreme Court in the case of *CIT* v. *Calcutta Knit-wears* [2014] 43 taxmann.com 446/223 Taxman 115 (SC) (Mag.) (available in NJRS at 2014-LL-0312-51) has laid down that for the purpose of Section 158BD of the Act, recording of a satisfaction note is a prerequisite and the satisfaction note must be prepared by the AO before he transmits the record to the other AO who has jurisdiction over such other person u/s 158BD. The Hon'ble Court held that "the satisfaction note could be prepared at any of the following stages:

(*a*) at the time of or along with the initiation of proceedings against the searched person under section 158BC of the Act; or

(*b*) in the course of the assessment proceedings under section 158BC of the Act; or

(*c*) immediately after the assessment proceedings are completed under section 158BC of the Act of the searched person."

3. Several High Courts have held that the provisions of section 153C of the Act are substantially similar/*pari-materia* to the provisions of section 158BD of the Act and therefore, the above guidelines of the Hon'ble SC, apply to proceedings u/s 153C of the IT Act, for the purposes of assessment of income of other than the searched person. This view has been accepted by CBDT.

4. The guidelines of the Hon'ble Supreme Court as referred to in para 2 above, with regard to recording of satisfaction note, may be brought to the notice of all for strict compliance. It is further clarified that even if the AO of the searched person and the "other person" is one and the same, then also he is required to record his satisfaction as has been held by the Courts.

5. In view of the above, filing of appeals on the issue of recording of satisfaction note should also be decided in the light of the above judgment. Accordingly, the Board hereby directs that pending litigation with regard to recording of satisfaction note under section 158BD/153C should be withdrawn/not pressed if it does not meet the guidelines laid down by the Apex Court.

(*ii*) **Whether satisfaction to be recorded in writing?**

There is no specific requirement under section 153C for the assessing officer to record satisfaction in writing. However, such satisfaction is significant in nature and will have severe consequences on the third person. Therefore, Courts have held that satisfaction should be recorded by the assessing officer in writing. It is thus not only that the assessing officer of the searched person should be satisfied but the satisfaction should be recorded in writing so as to maintain the objectivity and such jurisdictional fact is amenable to be examined by the higher authorities in appropriate proceeding if agitated.

Assessment order passed under section 158BD without recording of satisfaction is not valid. - [*Asstt. CIT* v. *R.P. Singh* [2007] 165 Taxman 147 (Delhi) (Mag.)].

Initiation of proceedings under section 158BD by the AO against the assessee without recording the requisite satisfaction was illegal.—[*CIT* v. *Late Raj Pal Bhatia* [2011] 49 DTR 9/60 taxmann.com 484/233 Taxman 540 (Delhi)]

In the case of *CIT* v. *Mechmen* [2015] 380 ITR (MP) 591(HC), it has been held that the legal position as applicable to section 158BD regarding satisfaction in the first instance of the first Assessing Officer forwarding the items to the Assessing Officer having jurisdiction; and in the second instance of the Assessing Officer having jurisdiction whilst sending notice to such other person (other than the person referred to in section 153A), must apply *proprio vigore*. The fact that incidentally the Assessing Officer is common at both the stages would not extricate him from recording satisfaction at the respective stages. In that, the Assessing Officer is satisfied that the items referred to in section 153C belongs or belong to a person (other than the person referred to in section 153A), being *sine qua non*. He cannot assume jurisdiction to transmit those items to another file which incidentally is pending before him concerning other person (person other than the person referred to in section 153A).

In the present case, the concurrent finding of fact recorded by the Appellate Forums is that, no satisfaction had been recorded by the Assessing Officer before issuing of notice under section 153C. Further, none of the papers seized belonged to assessee in course of search proceedings carried out at premises of its partner (noticee). The Appellate Forums have further found that no addition or even observations have been made by the Assessing Officer in any of the orders for the relevant assessment years in connection with any material found during the course of search. Even for that reason no action under section 153C is justified. These findings of fact need no interference.

In the case of *CIT* v. *Smt. Nirmala Keshwani* [2015] 123 DTR (All.) 177 (HC), it has been held that the section mandates about recording of the satisfaction by the Assessing Officer(s) and it is a pre-condition for invoking jurisdiction and it is not a mere formality because recording of satisfaction postulates application of mind consciously as the documents seized must be belonging to any other person other than the person referred to in section 153A of the Act. In the instant case, the order passed by the Tribunal, a final fact finding authority, clearly states that no "satisfaction note" has been recorded before initiating the proceedings under section 153C of the Income-tax Act. *Therefore*, when no satisfaction was recorded then the requirement of section 153C was not satisfied. Therefore, High Court have no reason to interfere with the impugned order passed by the Tribunal, who has not sustained the proceedings under section 153C of the Act, for the reason that there was no satisfaction at any stage.

In the case of *Dy. CIT* v. *Aakash Arogya Mindir (P.) Ltd.* [2015] 58 taxmann.com 293 (Delhi-Trib.), Assessee submitted that AO of searched person has to record satisfaction that some documents belong to other persons and then hand over same to AO of such persons who again will record his satisfaction. It was submitted that first satisfaction by AO of searched persons has not been done in these cases and therefore assessment proceedings itself were not legal. The Tribunal held, copy of satisfaction note suggested that satisfaction note enclosed with letter was prepared by AO of other entities who had assumed jurisdiction by invoking provisions of section 153C, recording of satisfaction by AO of searched persons is a necessary pre-condition for initiation of proceedings u/s 153C which was not done in present appeals, hence assessment proceedings quashed being illegal.

In the case of *Dy. CIT* v. *Aakash Arogya Mindir (P.) Ltd.* [2015] 58 taxmann.com 293 (Delhi-Trib.) Assessee obtained copies of letters under RTI from various files of assessees whose premises were searched u/s 153A of the Act. It was emerged no satisfaction note was recorded by the A.O of the searched person with respect to other entities. The Tribunal quashed the assessment proceedings u/s 153C as A.O of the searched person had not recorded the requisite satisfaction.

In the case of *Dy. CIT* v. *Qualitron Commodities (P.) Ltd.* [2015] 54 taxmann.com 295 (Delhi-Trib.). It was held that the satisfaction of the Assessing Officer that the said documents 'belong to' the assessee is condition precedent to initiate proceedings under section 153C. In absence of such finding by the Assessing Officer, the notice issued under section 153C in the present case is held invalid. Besides there was no incriminating material found during the course of search and the assessment was not pending or abated to justify the assessment framed under section 132A, read with section 153C as well as section 143(3) against the assessee. The assessment in the question framed in furtherance to the said invalid notice and in absence of incriminating material is thus held as void.

In the case of *Principal CIT* v. *Nikki Drugs & Chemicals (P.) Ltd.* [2015] 64 taxmann.com 309/[2016] 236 Taxman 305 (Delhi), the High Court held that satisfaction by the Assessing Officer of the person searched under section 153A is *sine qua non* for initiation of proceedings under section 153C.

In the case of *CIT* v. *Smt. Nirmala Keshwani* [2017] 79 taxmann.com 399 (All.), *CIT* v. *Smt. Nirmala Keshwani* [2017] 79 taxmann.com 399 (All.) and *CIT* v. *Smt. Nisha Keshwani* [2017] 79 taxmann.com 399/ [2016] 380 ITR 566 (All), it has been held that, the order passed by the Tribunal, the final fact finding authority clearly states that no satisfaction note had been recorded before initiating the proceedings u/s 153C. When no satisfaction was recorded the requirement of section 153C was not satisfied. Therefore, there was no reason to interfere with the order passed by the Tribunal, which had not sustained the proceedings u/s 153C for the reason that there was no satisfaction at any stage.

It was held in the case of *CIT* v. *Calcutta Knitwears* [2014] 43 taxmann. com 446/223 Taxman 115 (Mag.) (SC) that for the purpose of section 158BD, satisfaction note is sine qua non.

However in the following decisions, contrary view was taken.

Whether there is no requirement to record satisfaction in writing for issuing notice under section 158BD; satisfaction of Assessing Officer should, however, be discernible from material on record. - [*Vijay Sehgal (HUF)* v. *Asstt. CIT* [2006] 100 ITD 560 (Asr.-Trib.)]

In the case of *Dy. CIT* v. *Damac Holdings (P.) Ltd.* [2014] 51 taxmann. com 538/[2015] 67 SOT 148 (Cochin-Trib.) (URO), it was held that where same Assessing Officer had completed assessment proceeding of assessee-company and its director, recording of satisfaction may not be necessary because there was no necessity for Assessing Officer to handover document to another Assessing Officer.

Recording of satisfaction of Assessing Officer regarding material is not necessary justifying action under section 158BD. - [*Y. Subbaraju & Co.* v. *Asstt. CIT* [2004] (Bang.-Trib.) (SB)].

(*iii*) **Time limit for recording satisfaction & handing over the seized material**

There is no time limit provided under section 153C for recording satisfaction and further for handing over the seized material belonging or relating to the other person to his assessing officer. Therefore, satisfaction can be recorded either before or after the conclusion of the assessment proceeding of the searched person. In this regard, following two decisions are relevant though these have been rendered in the context of section 158BD but the ratio of these decisions would be applicable to the proceeding under section 153C also.

In the case of *CIT* v. *Calcutta Knitwears* [2014] 43 taxmann.com 446/223 Taxman 115 (Mag.) (SC), it was held that for the purpose of Section 158BD of the Act a satisfaction note is sine qua non and must be prepared by the assessing officer before he transmits the records to the other assessing officer who has jurisdiction over such other person. The satisfaction note could be prepared at either of the following stages: (*a*) at the time of or along with the initiation of proceedings against the searched person under Section 158BC of the Act; (*b*) along with the assessment proceedings under Section 158BC of the Act; and (*c*) immediately after the assessment proceedings are completed under Section 158BC of the Act of the searched person.

In case satisfaction is recorded after completion of the assessment proceeding of the searched person, it should be done within reasonable time without undue delay. Otherwise, it may be held that valid jurisdiction has not been assumed.

In the case of *CIT* v. *Bharat Bhushan Jain* [2015] 61 taxmann.com 89 (Delhi), it was held having regard to the intent of the Supreme Court in Para 44 of the *Calcutta Knitwears, supra,* where it was indicated that the Revenue has to be vigilant in issuing notice to the third party under Section 158BD, immediately after the completion of assessment of the searched person, this Court is of the opinion that a delay ranging between 10 months of 1½ years cannot be considered contemporaneous to assessment proceedings. Thus notices were not issued in conformity with the requirements of Section 158BD, and were unduly delayed, appeals of the Revenue were dismissed.

There may be a view that satisfaction should be recorded by the assessing officer before framing assessment in the case of person searched under section 153A. It is at the stage while appraising all the seized material and before finalizing assessment of the person searched, he has to decide whether the seized material belong or relate to some other person. After framing assessment of the person searched, assessing officer in normal course will not have any opportunity to go through entire seized material and decide whether the same belong or relate to some other person. However, this issue has been settled as of now, as per the ratio laid down by the decision of Hon'ble Supreme Court in the case of *Calcutta Knitwears, supra.*

Once satisfaction is recorded, the process of handing over the seized material belonging or relating to some other person is a procedural act which can be performed after finalization of assessment of the person searched. However handing over of the seized material should also be done at the earliest so that the action of making assessment under section 153C relating to the other person is not delayed.

There are numerous cases coming to the notice when seized material belonging to other person is handed over even after several years from the date of finalization of assessment of the person searched. In our opinion, invoking provision of section 153C under such circumstances is not valid. In the case of proceeding u/s 153C, six preceding years are counted from the date of search held in the case of person searched. In case section 153C is invoked several years after the search, it will cover assessment years prior to beyond seven years at that time. A person cannot be expected to produce books of account and records beyond seven years which are not required to be kept and preserved by him under the Statute.

Therefore under such situation instead of resorting to section 153C, it is desirable on the part of Department to resort to the provision of section 148 relating to the years for which reopening is permissible in accordance to the provisions of sections 147 & 149. However, this view is also not free from controversy and Courts too have differed on this issue.

In *Shoreline Hotel (P.) Ltd.* v. *Dy. CIT* [2010] 37 SOT 7 (Mum.-Trib.) (URO) it has been held that recourse to section 158BD was illegal also on the ground that the impugned satisfaction note is much beyond the period within which the block assessment could be completed in the case of the person searched.

Special larger bench of Tribunal in the case of *Manoj Aggarwal* v. *Dy. CIT* [2008] 113 ITD 377 (Delhi-Trib.) have also held that the requisite satisfaction that undisclosed income belongs to the other person must be arrived at during the proceeding of section 158BC in case of searched person.

It has been held in the case of *Principal CIT* v. *Jitendra H. Modi* [2017] 87 taxmann.com 110/[2018] 403 ITR 110 (Guj.) that recording of satisfaction under section 158BD by the Assessing Officer is to be done even after assessment of person subjected to search but must be done within reasonable time. Recording of satisfaction nine months after assessment of person subjected to search & no reasonable explanation for delay being there, delay was not justified & Assessment under section 158BD was not valid.

(iv) **Nature of Satisfaction**

Satisfaction of the assessing officer regarding seized material belonging or relating to some other person should not be arrived in casual manner or merely on the basis of statement made by the person searched. Satisfaction should be based upon cogent material. This is so because the satisfaction of the assessing officer is going to have severe repercussions on the other person and his seven years' cases may be assessed or reassessed. In view of the severity of consequences u/s 153C, it is absolutely necessary on the part of the Assessing Officer of the searched person to ensure that the seized material in question belong or relate, as the case may be, to other person only. In case of any doubt, it would be appropriate to examine such other person or obtain his confirmation regarding purported seized material belonging to him.

In the case of *Pepsi Foods P. Ltd.* v. *ACIT* [2014] 367 ITR 112 (Delhi) (HC), it has been held that it was evident from the satisfaction note that apart from saying that the documents belonged to the assessee and that the Assessing Officer was satisfied that it was a fit case for issuance of a notice under section 153C, there was nothing which would indicate how the presumptions which were to be normally raised had been rebutted by the Assessing Officer. Mere use or mention of the word "satisfaction" or the words "I am satisfied" in the order or the note would not meet the requirement of the concept of satisfaction as used in section 153C. The satisfaction note itself must display the reasons or basis for the conclusion that the Assessing Officer of the person in respect of whom the search was conducted is satisfied that the seized documents belonged to another person. On going through the contents of the satisfaction note, no "satisfaction" of the kind required under section 153C could be discerned. Thus, the very first step prior to the issuance of a notice under section 153C had not been fulfilled. Inasmuch as this condition precedent had not been met, the notices under section 153C were liable to be quashed.

It has been held in the case of *Ganpati Fincap Services (P.) Ltd.* v. *CIT* [2017] 82 taxmann.com 408 (Delhi) that there is no requirement that satisfaction note should state that documents do not belong to person in respect of whom search conducted.

It has been held in the case of *Tapan Kumar Dutta* v. *CIT* [2018] 92 taxmann.com 367/255 Taxman 200 (SC) that mere disclosure made by assessee before the authority cannot be the basis for reaching a satisfaction for the purpose of section 158BD that any undisclosed income belongs to him unless the seized books of account or other documents or assets are perused, examined or verified by the concerned Assessing Officer.

It has been held in the case of *Shyamraj Singh* v. *Dy. CIT* [2019] 411 ITR 709 (Kar.) that the ingredients of Section 153C should be explicitly expressed in recording the satisfaction report by the Assessing Officer of the searched person. In the said satisfaction note, the seized or requisitioned belongs to a person other than the person referred to the seized person, is not forthcoming. Merely stating that the case is covered under Section 153C of the Act and the case has been notified under Section 153 of the Act would not be suffice and the same cannot be construed as the satisfaction recorded under Section 153C of the Act. On the other hand, the said note would disclose that it is only a note prepared for initiating proceedings under Section 153C of the Act with neither any heading/title to indicate it as a satisfaction recorded nor the contents suggests the satisfaction of the Assessing Officer. Hence, the said note is incomplete in as much as the satisfaction of the Assessing Officer as required under Section 153C of the Act is missing & thus proceedings initiated under Section 153C of the Act are without jurisdiction and are vitiated in law.

It has been held in the case of *Asstt. CIT* v. *Gulshan Kumar Sethi,* I.T.A. No. 5220/DELHI/2015 (Delhi-Trib.) that before issue of a notice under section 153C, the first step was that AO of the searched person must arrive at satisfaction that a document seized from him did not belong to him but to some other person. It was only in the second step that the document was to be handed over to AO of the person to whom the seized document 'belongs'. Therefore, it was for AO of the searched person to rebut that presumption and came to a conclusion or 'satisfaction' that the document in fact belonged to somebody else. Thus, in the case of assessee, AO of the searched person had not rebutted the presumption that the seized documents belonged to M/s. C Ltd. Therefore, the first step itself had not been fulfilled and thus, the issue of notice under section 153C on the assessee was illegal.

It has been held in the case of *Principal CIT* v. *Himanshu Chandulal Patel* [2019] 109 taxmann.com 202/267 Taxman 305 (Delhi) that where proceedings are proposed to be initiated under Section 153C of the Act against the 'other person', it has to be preceded by a satisfaction note by the AO of the searched person. He will record in this satisfaction note that the seized document belongs to the other person. Depending on the nature and contents of the document he may be required to give some reasons for such conclusion. Therefore, it is apparent that if the satisfaction note, does not have any reasons for such conclusion, it is not in accordance with the law for invoking jurisdiction under section 153C of the Income Tax Act.

It has been held in the case of Raju Bhupendra Desai v. ITO 207 DTR 129 (Guj.) that as to validity and recording of satisfaction, submission that the AO had recorded the satisfaction on the borrowed information has no force & that the contention that respondent had initiated the action against the assessee on the basis of a mistaken identity was also not acceptable and that satisfaction under section 153C would be in the realm of subjective satisfaction of the concerned A.O.

(v) Recording of satisfaction when assessing officer is common

Provision of section 153C can be invoked with respect to other person when seized material belongs or relates to other person and assessing officer making assessment of the person searched records his satisfaction to this effect. In case assessing officer is common to both the persons, a question may arise as to whether satisfaction is still required to be recorded in writing.

In our opinion, recording of satisfaction regarding seized material belonging or relating to other person goes to the root of the matter to assume jurisdiction to make assessment of other person under section 153C. For assuming such jurisdiction, recording of satisfaction in writing even when assessing officer is common, is warranted.

In the case of *CIT* v. *Mechmen* [2015] 60 taxmann.com 484/233 Taxman 540/[2016] 380 ITR (MP) 591 (HC), it has been held that recording of satisfaction by Assessing Officer having jurisdiction over person in respect of whom search conducted that money or assets discovered during search belong to third person. Recording of satisfaction is necessary even if Assessing Officer of both the persons is the same.

In the case of *Smt. Rekhaben Thakkar* v. *Asstt. CIT* [2015] 61 taxmann.com 60/155 ITD 54 (Ahd.-Trib.), it has been held that AO of the person searched having not recorded a satisfaction that undisclosed income discovered during search belonged to the assessee, proceedings against assessee under s. 153C were invalid. Recording of satisfaction is must even where the AO of the person searched and that of another person is the same.

In the case of *Dy. CIT* v. *Satkar Roadlines (P.) Ltd.* [2015] 62 taxmann.com 327/155 ITD 501 (Delhi-Trib.), it has been held that Recording of satisfaction by Assessing Officer having jurisdiction over person searched is an essential and prerequisite condition for bestowing jurisdiction to Assessing Officer of 'other person' under section 153C; even where Assessing Officer of searched person and such other person is same, Assessing Officer has to carry out dual exercise, first as Assessing Officer of person searched in which he has to record satisfaction and second as Assessing Officer of 'other person'. Satisfaction note to the effect that documents etc. found during search belonged to person other than the person searched having not been recorded by AO of person searched, assumption of jurisdiction by AO of such other person under section 153C is *void ab initio*, notwithstanding the fact that AO of the person searched and AO of the other person is the same.

In the case of *DSL Properties (P.) Ltd.* v. *Dy. CIT* [2013] 33 taxmann. com 420/60 SOT 88 (Delhi-Trib.) (URO), it has been held that for initiating action under section 153C recording of satisfaction by AO of person searched that any money, bullion, jewellery or other valuable article or thing or books of account or documents seized belong to person other than person searched as well as handing over of books of account, other documents or assets seized to AO of such other person is a *sine qua non*. If AO of person searched and AO of such other person is same, he has to first record satisfaction in file of person searched and then such note along with seized document/ books of account is to be placed in file of such other person and thereafter in capacity of AO such other person, he has to issue notice under section 153C, read with section 153A. On the facts of the case condition were not fulfilled hence notice was barred by limitation. Accordingly assessment completed in pursuance to such notice also quashed.

In the case of *Principal CIT* v. *Nikki Drug & Chemicals (P.) Ltd.* [2015] 64 taxmann.com 309/[2016] 236 Taxman 305 (Delhi), the High Court held that satisfaction by the Assessing Officer of the person searched under section 153A is *sine qua non* for initiation of proceedings under section 153C. The High Court further held that section 153C is not attracted where documents pertaining to the other person is found, it is attracted only in case where documents belonging to the other person is found. It was held that satisfaction must be recorded by the Assessing Officer even if the Assessing Officer of the person searched under section 153A and a person sought to be assessed under section 153C is the same.

Contrary view has been taken by Kerala High Court on this issue in the context of section 158BD.

It has been held in the case of *CIT* v. *Smt. Soudha Gafoor* [2017] 88 taxmann.com 921/[2018] 408 ITR 246 (Ker) that recording of satisfaction that income belonged to third person is not required where Assessing Officer is the same.

Further this issue has been dealt by Hon'ble Supreme Court in the following case:

It has been held in the case of *Super Malls (P) Ltd.* v. *Principal CIT* 187 DTR (SC) 257 that where the AO of the searched person and the other person is the same, it is sufficient for the AO to note in the satisfaction note that the documents seized from the searched person belonged to the other person & since the satisfaction note of the AO clearly states that the documents so seized belonged to the other person i.e., the assessee and not the searched person, the requirement of s. 153C stands fulfilled.

(*vi*) **Material seized - What in case of illegal seizure? - Whether seized material to be of incriminating nature?**

Section 153C can be invoked where the assessing officer is satisfied that any money, bullion, jewellery or other valuable article or thing or books of account or documents seized or requisitioned belong or relate to some other person. The word 'seized' is significant. In the course of search, possibility of seizure of disclosed or regular books of account, documents, records or assets cannot be ruled out. This possibility is further increased regarding books of account, documents or assets belonging or relating to some other person who does not even get opportunity to explain the nature and source of such material at the time of search so as to prevent its seizure.

Several questions may arise as to whether provision of section 153C can be invoked when books of account, documents or assets are seized illegally or in irregular manner and whether provision of section 153C can be invoked on the basis of regular books of account of sister concern seized or whether provision of section 153C can be invoked on the basis of regular passbook of saving account of the father of the assessee seized or whether provision of section 153C can be invoked when gold ornaments in the capacity as mortgagee or files of the client in the capacity as consultant were kept in fiduciary capacity or as custodian and the same are seized by the search team.

The intention of the Legislature cannot be to invoke provision of section 153C under all the above circumstances. Therefore, the word "seized" used under section 153C should be interpreted to mean legally seized or only those books of account, documents or assets which are required to be seized as per provisions of section 132(1). The satisfaction of the assessing officer should not be restricted to the extent that seized material belongs or relates to some other person but such seized material should be of undisclosed or incriminating nature.

As per section 132(1), the material which is intended to be seized and which may belong to some other person can fall under clause (*b*) or clause (*c*) of section 132(1). Situation under clause (*a*) cannot be applicable in the case of other person. Situation under clause (*b*) regarding books of account or other documents and under clause (*c*) regarding assets primarily refer to undisclosed character of books of account, documents or assets. Therefore what is intended to be covered under section 153C is only those books of account, documents or assets seized belonging or relating to other person which are undisclosed in nature.

A detailed discussion has been held regarding books of account, documents or assets belonging to some other person that can be seized in the chapter of seizure of assets and a reference may be made thereat.

However, it is seen in practice, this fine legal aspect is ignored by the Assessing Officer(s) and the moment books of account etc. relating to other person are seized even though such were not to be seized strictly in terms of section 132, action u/s 153C is still initiated against the other person.

As we have opined earlier that the literal interpretation of the provision of section 153C is very harsh and the same is required to be read down so as to make purposive interpretation of this section. There are judicial pronouncements holding that jurisdiction under section 153C can be assumed on the basis of seized material belonging or relating to the other person, to be of incriminating nature.

In a recent judgment *Sinhgad Technical Education Society* v. *Asstt. CIT* [2011] 16 taxmann.com 101/[2012] 50 SOT 89 (Pune-Trib.) (URO), Pune Bench of ITAT has held that to confer jurisdiction u/s 153C with respect to other person, the document must have *prima facie* incriminating information. If the impugned documents merely contain the notings of entries which are already recorded in the books of account or subjected to scrutiny of the A.O. in the past in regular assessment u/s 143(3) of the Act, such document cannot be said to be containing the incriminating information so as to confer jurisdiction u/s 153C.

It has been held in the case of *Dy. CIT* v. *Sandip M. Patel* [2012] 22 taxmann.com 288/137 ITD 104 (Ahd.-Trib.) that if *prima facie*, certain documents are found to be belonging to another person, the AO is duty bound first to investigate and then only be able to decide about the factum of concealed income. AO was therefore justified in issuing notice under s. 153C.

In the case of *CIT* v. *Sinhgad Technical Education Society* [2015] 120 DTR (Bom.) 79, Tribunal found that documents in question were **neither incriminating ones nor recorded unaccounted transactions of assessee. Reasons assigned by Assessing Officer in satisfaction note were found to be silent about assessment year in which specific incriminating information or unaccounted or undisclosed hidden information was discovered or seized by revenue from assessee.** Tribunal, therefore, quashed notice issued under section 153C.

It has been held by Hon'ble Bombay High Court that where loose papers found and seized from residence of President of assessee, an educational institution, indicating some 'on money' receipt during admission process did not establish corelation document-wise with assessment years in question, notice issued under section 153C to assessee was invalid, the general satisfaction as recorded in the note is not enough. No substantial question of law arises out of Tribunal's order quashing notice under s. 153C.

The above view has been approved by the apex court in the case of *CIT* v. *Sinhgad Technical Education Society* [2017] 84 taxmann.com 290/250 Taxman 225 (SC).

It has been held in the case of *Principal CIT* v. *Dreamcity Buildwell (P.) Ltd* [2019] 110 taxmann.com 28/266 Taxman 465 (Delhi) that as per the law applicable for A.Y. 2005-06, the onus is on revenue to show that incriminating material/documents recovered at time of search 'belongs' to a person other than searched person and it is not enough for revenue to show that documents either 'pertain' to assessee or contains information that 'relates to' assessee. During search, various incriminating documents were found and seized which included a letter from Director Town and Country Planning (DTCP) granting licence to assessee for setting up of a residential plot colony and; a letter from DTCP to assessee granting it permission for transfer of aforesaid license number granted to assessee. One DNT who was main controlling person of TP Group of companies, in his sworn statement given under section 132(4), admitted that various group companies including assessee had received bogus accommodation entries from concerns of one SKG who was an accommodation entry operator & on basis of abovesaid documents Assessing Officer issued notice under section 153C against assessee. It was noted that licence issued to assessee by DTCP and letter issued by DTCP permitting it to transfer such licence, had no relevance for purposes of determining escapement of income of assessee & Consequently, even if those two documents could be said to 'belonged' to assessee they were not documents on basis of which jurisdiction could be assumed by Assessing Officer under section 153C. As far as statement of DNT was concerned, though such statement contained information that 'related' to assessee, but it could not said to be a document that 'belonged' to assessee & therefore, assumption of jurisdiction *qua* assessee under section 153C was not valid.

In the case of *CIT* v. *Refam Management Services P. Ltd.* [2017] 80 taxmann.com 251 (Delhi), the Court held that since the only document seized during the search was a cheque book pertaining to the assessee which reflected the issue of cheques during the period and there was no other evidence of undisclosed income, the proceedings under section 153C were not valid.

In the case of *CIT* v. *Promy Kuriakose* [2017] 79 taxmann.com 405 (Ker.), it has been held that in absence of incriminating material, Search material Assessment of third person cannot be made. Recording of satisfaction by AO having jurisdiction over third person in respect of search conducted that such money, asset or valuables belonged to third person is required.

In the case of *CIT* v. *RRJ Securities Ltd.* [2015] 62 taxmann.com 391 (Delhi) (HC), it has been held that where in course of search carried out at premises of Chartered Accountant, a hard disk containing working papers belonging to assessee was seized, since said disk did not contain any incriminating material, rather it supported returns filed by assessee, proceedings under section 153C could not be initiated against assessee on basis of said hard disk.

It has been held in the case of *Asstt. CIT* v. *Dr. Ranjan Pai* [2019] 109 taxmann.com 90/178 ITD 647 (Bang. - Trib.) that for purposes of making any document to be incriminating material, it is necessary that document should be found from lawful custody of a person who is lawfully and naturally responsible for possessing it. Where document was neither written by assessee nor she was aware of content, nor she was aware who had written document, it could be concluded that said document did not belong to assessee and same could not be used as incriminating material on basis of which impugned addition could be made.

It has been held in the case of *Smt. Sunita Bhagchandka* v. *Asstt. CIT* ITA No. 3447/Del/2016 (Delhi-Trib) that if the documents unearthed during the course of search do not indicate existence of any unaccounted income, they are not incriminating in nature. It is important that documents found during the course of search must give some indication about the undisclosed income of the assessee. The impugned certificate did not give any indication about the fact of gift of the shares, which are alleged to be undisclosed income of the assessee.

It has been held in the case of *Sri Sai Cashews* v. *Chief CIT* [2021] 131 taxmann.com 177/[2022] 284 Taxman 593 (Orissa) that in the absence of incriminating materials *vis-à-vis* the assessee being found in the course of the search of the searched persons the impugned assessment order passed under section 153C and the consequent demand order are unsustainable in law and are set aside.

It has been held in the case of *Asstt. CIT* v. *Dr. Ranjan Pai* [2019] 109 taxmann.com 90/178 ITD 647 (Bang.-Trib.) that for purposes of making any document to be incriminating material, it is necessary that document should be found from lawful custody of a person who is lawfully and naturally responsible for possessing it. Where document was neither written by assessee nor she was aware of content, nor she was aware who had written document, it could be concluded that said document did not belong to assessee and same could not be used as incriminating material on basis of which impugned addition could be made.

It has been held in the case of *Nova Iron & Steel Ltd.* v. *DCIT* 190 TTJ 499/160 DTR 142 (Delhi-Trib.) *that where no evidence was found during the course of search that any money (cash credit) belongs to the assessee-company or to prove that assessee had received any accommodation entry or that cash was given by assessee-company to take any loan or credits, condition precedent for issuing notice under s. 153C was not satisfied, hence consequent assessment and addition made under s. 68 were liable to be quashed.*

It has been held in the case of *Principal CIT* v. *N. S. Software (Firm)* [2018] 93 taxmann.com 21/255 Taxman 230 (Delhi) that Satisfaction of Assessing officer that seized material belonged to third person was not recorded by Assessing Officer of party in respect of whom search was conducted & also in view of the failure by Assessing Officer to record specific satisfaction how seized material belonged to assessee, Previous years' assessments cannot be disturbed in absence of incriminating material & Notice u/s 153C was thus invalid.

However, in certain decisions, courts have taken divergent views.

It has been held in the case of *SSP Aviation Ltd.* v. *Dy. CIT* [2012] 20 taxmann.com 214/207 Taxman 260 (Delhi) that Procedure envisaged by s. 153C does not in any way infringe any rights of the petitioner or curtail or curb his right to be heard by the AO or to file appeal and question the assessments made pursuant to the notice under s. 153A. Provision of section 153C authorizes enquiry on satisfaction that valuable article or documents discovered during search belong to third person and that such valuable article or document are to be handed over to Assessing officer having jurisdiction over assessee. It is not necessary that satisfaction should be recorded that valuable article or document showed undisclosed income.

It has been held in the case of *Dr. K.M. Mehaboob* v. *Dy. CIT* [2012] 26 taxmann.com 54/211 Taxman 52 (Ker.) that for transferring any material or evidence collecting in search to the AO of an assessee other than the searched person for the purpose of assessment under s. 153C, what is required to be satisfied is that the money, bullion jewellery or other valuable article or thing or books of account or documents seized in the course of search belong or relate to a person other than the searched person and that no satisfaction is required to be recorded that the books of account or other evidence or material seized in the course of search represent undisclosed income of the other assessee.

It has been held in the case of Principal CIT v. *S.R. Trust* [2021] 123 taxmann.com 311/277 Taxman 133 (Mad.) *that in the absence of any-incriminating documents or evidence discovered during the course of search in the case of searched person against the assessee, the jurisdiction under the provisions of section 153C cannot be assumed.*

It has been held in the case of *Amar Jewellers Ltd.* v. *Asstt. CIT* 216 DTR (Guj.) 137 that it is difficult to take the view that the *non obstante* clause in section 153A excludes the very applicability of sections 147 and 148 respectively and that submission of the counsel appearing for the Revenue that the *non obstante* clause in section 153A should be understood as merely dispensing with the procedural aspect of section 147 is sustainable and that Return filed under section 153A(1) is a return furnished under section 139 and therefore, the provisions of the Act which would be otherwise applicable in case of return filed in the regular course under section 139(1) would also continue to apply in case of return filed under section 153A.

It has been held in the case of *Neesa Technologies (P.) Ltd.* v. *Dy. CIT* 214 DTR 172 (Ahd 'C') that AO having initiated the proceedings under section 153C on the basis of two documents which admittedly did not belong to the assessee and which were not of incriminating nature, the assumption of jurisdiction under section 153C was invalid.

(vii) **"Belongs or belong to other person"**

Assessing officer has to be satisfied that seized material belongs or belong to some other person. The word 'belong' implies that it is the property of some other person. The ownership belongs to him. The objective is to make assessment in the hands of the person to whom the seized material belongs. Either of them can be assessed on the basis of such seized material under section 153A.

The concept of seized material belonging to some other person on the basis of which provisions of section 153C can be triggered is different from the concept of undisclosed income belonging to some other person on the basis of which section 158BD could be invoked in the case of block assessment regime. Under section 153C, the requirement is that the books of account, documents or assets belong to some other person. Provisions of section 153C cannot be invoked on the basis of entries or details of transactions contained in the books of account, documents or loose papers, computer, laptop etc. belonging to the person searched. However in such a situation possibility of invoking provision of section 147/148 with respect to such other person cannot be ruled out.

Infact, there is conceptual difference in the nature of proceeding contained in the erstwhile section 158BD during block assessment regime and provision of section 153C contained in the new assessment procedure. This difference is in tune with the different conceptual framework of these proceedings, one relating to block assessment of only undisclosed income and other for the assessment of the total income including the disclosed income as well as the undisclosed income detected as a result of search or otherwise.

Gujarat High Court in the case of *Vijaybhai N. Chandrani* v. *Asstt. CIT* [2010] 38 DTR (Guj.) 225, elaborating the meaning of the words 'belonging to the assessee' has held as under—

Notice issued under section 153C on the basis of loose papers which bear the name of assessee but actually did not belong to assessee was without jurisdiction, because, under section 153C notice can be issued only where the money, bullion, jewellery or other valuable article or thing or books of account or documents seized or requisitioned actually belong to assessee.

Bangalore Bench of ITAT in the case of *P. Srinivas Naik* v. *Asstt. CIT* [2008] 24 SOT 10 (URO)/[2009] 117 ITD 201 (Bang.-Trib.) has held as under—

Action under section 153C can be taken against a person only if valuable or books of account or documents belonging to that person are seized in the course of a search carried out in the case of some other person; action under section 153A read with section 153C could not be initiated against the assessee on the basis of seizure of books of account and documents from a third party which contained the transactions relating to group concerns of that party and which do not belong to the assessee.

The term "belong" implies something more than a casual connection and it involves the notion of continuity involving intimate connection over a period of time. (*P. Srinivas Naik* v. *Asstt. CIT*) (*supra*).

Ahmedabad Bench of ITAT in the case of *Meghmani Organics Ltd.* v. *Dy. CIT* [2010] 6 ITR(T) 360/129 TTJ (Ahd.) 255, elaborating the meaning of the words 'belonging to the assessee' has held as under—

The AO in the assessment order has categorically held that pp. 87 to 91 of Annex. A-4 seized from LK are his own handwritten estimate for the proposed work of the assessee. Therefore, though these documents may refer to the work proposed on behalf of the assessee, the same cannot be considered as "documents belonging to the assessee". If a person makes some jottings/notes etc. for his own purpose and which has no nexus to hold that it belongs to other person and also does not contain a material which reveals any income therein, cannot be used so as to initiate action under section 153C.

In *Bhajan Das & Brothers* v. *Asstt. CIT* [2009] 119 ITD 76 (Agra-Trib.) (TM) it is held that Assessing Officer assessing the person searched must give a categorical finding that the search material pertains to a third party.

In the case of *CIT* v. *Mohan Meakins Ltd.* [2015] 118 DTR 275 (Delhi) (HC), matter is remitted back to the Tribunal for reconsideration after rendering specific findings as to examine and decide whether any documents or material seized during the course of search proceedings belonged to any of the assessees.

In the case of *Smt. Rekhaben Thakkar* v. *Asstt. CIT* [2015] 61 taxmann. com 60/155 ITD 54 (Ahd.-Trib.), cheque issued by the assessee was in the name of the director of the Group which was searched. The cheque was found from the person upon whom the cheque was drawn. Therefore, the cheque 'belongs to' the person upon whom it was drawn and cannot be said to be continued to 'belonging to' the person who issued the cheque. Therefore, undated cheques recovered in search cannot represent undisclosed income and hence, proceedings under section 153C were liable to be quashed.

In the case of *Kamleshbhai Dharamshibhai Patel* v. *CIT* [2013] 31 taxmann.com 50/214 Taxman 558 (Guj.) (HC), in order to initiate any action under section 153C, it is essential that any money, bullion, jewellery or other valuable article or thing or books of account or documents seized or requisitioned should belong to a person other than person referred to in section 153A. The assessee sold certain land to S group. Subsequently, 'S' group was subjected to search during which sale deeds of land in question and agreements entered into by and between tenants of said property and assessee on various dates regarding eviction of tenants were seized. It has been held that action initiated u/s 153C of the Act cannot be quashed if the documents seized during search belong to the assessee.

It has been held in the case of *Principal CIT* v. *Vinita Charurasia* [2017] 82 taxmann.com 153/248 Taxman 172 (Delhi) that where satisfaction note does record that the document in question does not belong the searched person, AO does not indicate on what basis he proceeds as if the document belonged to the assessee; even according to searched person the document in question did not belong to the assessee; there is no material whatsoever placed on record by the

Revenue to justify the invocation of s. 153C against the assessee on the basis that the above document belonged to her.

It has been held in the case of *CIT* v. *Arpit Land P. Ltd.* 154 DTR 241 (Bom.) that while recording of satisfaction *vis-a-vis* documents belonging to assessee prior to 1st June, 2015, proceedings under s. 153C could be initiated against a party only if the document seized during the search and seizure proceedings of another person belonged to the party concerned; Tribunal having recorded a finding of fact that the seized documents which formed the basis of the proceedings against the assessee do not belong to them, the entire proceedings under s. 153C are null and void; no substantial question of law arises.

It has been held in the case of *Canyon Financial Services Ltd.* v. *ITO* [2017] 84 taxmann.com 71/249 Taxman 493 (Delhi) that while recording of satisfaction *vis-a-vis* documents belonging to the assessee prior to 1.6.2015, application made by the assessee for subscription to the shares of 'DEPL and certificate issued by the assessee confirming the issuance in its favour of the equity shares of 'DEPL' can certainly be said to the 'pertaining' to the assessee but once they were submitted by the assessee to DEPL and found in possession of DEPL, they cannot be said to 'belong' to the assessee. Satisfaction note prepared by the AO of the searched person and satisfaction note of the AO of the assessee, being a carbon copy of the satisfaction note of the AO of the searched person do not fulfil the legal requirement spelled out in s. 153C(1).

It has been held in the case of *Principal CIT* v. *Index Securities P Ltd.* 304 CTR 67/157 DTR 20 (Delhi) that essential jurisdictional requirement for assumption of jurisdiction under s. 153C is that seized documents forming the basis of the satisfaction note must not merely 'pertain' to the other person but must belong to the 'other person'; further, seized documents must be incriminating and must relate to the assessment years whose assessments are sought to be reopened.

It has been held in the case of *CIT* v. *Renu Constructions P. Ltd.* [2018] 99 taxmann.com 426 (Delhi) that prior to the amendment w.e.f. 1st June, 2015, for the purpose of initiating proceedings under s. 153C, the seized documents had to be shown to belong to the other person and not merely pertaining to such other person; change brought about in this regard in s. 153C by way of amendment has been given prospective effect from 1st June, 2015.

It has been held in the case of *CIT* v. *Lavanya Land Pvt. Ltd.* [2017] 83 taxmann.com 161/249 Taxman 275 (Bom.) that money or document found during search should belong to such third person & finding by Tribunal that there was no evidence that documents and money found during search belonged to third person, notice under section 153C is not valid.

It has been held in the case of *Principal CIT* v. *M/s Dreamcity Buildwell Pvt. Ltd.,* [2019] 110 taxmann.com 28/266 Taxman 465 (Delhi) that prior to the amendment to section 153C, onus was on the Revenue to show that the incriminating material/documents recovered at the time of search belongs' to the assessee. In other words, it is not enough for the Revenue to show that the documents either 'pertain' to the Assessee or contains information that 'relates to' the Assessee.

It has been held in the case of *Pr. CIT* v. *Krutika Land (P.) Ltd.* [2019] 103 taxmann.com 9/261 Taxman 454 (SC) that where seized documents were not in name of assessee, no action could be undertaken in case of assessee under section 153C and further entire decision being based on huge amounts revealed from seized documents not being supported by actual cash passing hands, additions under section 69C were not sustainable.

Amendment by Finance Act, 2015-Seized documents 'pertain to' & information contained therein 'relates to' other person

Finance Act, 2015 has amended sub-section (1) of section 153C as under:

153C. (1) *Notwithstanding anything contained in section 139, section 147, section 148, section 149, section 151 and section 153, where the Assessing Officer is satisfied that—*

   (c) *any money, bullion, jewellery or other valuable article or thing, seized or requisitioned, belongs to; or*

   (d) *any books of account or documents, seized or requisitioned, pertains or pertain to, or any information contained therein, relates to,*

a person other than the person referred to in section 153A, then, the books of account or documents or assets, seized or requisitioned shall be handed over to the Assessing Officer having jurisdiction over such other person

Prior to amendment, sub-section (1) of section 153C was as under:

1. Notwithstanding anything contained in section 139, section 147, section 148, section 149, section 151 and section 153, where the Assessing Officer is satisfied that any money, bullion, jewellery or other valuable article or thing or books of account or documents seized or requisitioned belongs or belong to a person other than the person referred to in section 153A, then the books of account or documents or assets seized or requisitioned shall be handed over to the Assessing Officer having jurisdiction over such other person and

that Assessing Officer shall proceed against each such other person and issue notice and assess or reassess the income of the other person in accordance with the provisions of section 153A, if, that Assessing Officer is satisfied that the books of account or documents or assets seized or requisitioned have a bearing on the determination of the total income of such other person for the relevant assessment year or years referred to in sub-section (1) of section 153A :

The above amendment is quite significant and has changed the basic structure of section 153C. It has the following effects:—

(*a*) Earlier prior to amendment, provision of section 153C could be invoked only when seized assets, books of account were belonging to some other person. The basic ingredient of belonging to some other person has been restricted only to seized assets i.e. any money, bullion, jewellery or other valuable articles or things seized or requisitioned in the course of search.

(*b*) For the purpose of books of account or documents seized, the requirement of "belonging to some other person" has been done away with and substituted by the requirement "pertains or pertain to, or any information contained therein, relates to".

Substitution of above terminology has far reaching implications. For invoking provision of section 153C, it is no longer required that the seized books of account or documents should belong to some other person. Even if there is some information contained in books of account or documents seized, which is relating to some other person, provision of section 153C can be invoked.

In our opinion, the above amendment defies the basic rationale of introduction of section 153C under the statute in the case of search. It would mean now after the amendment that if any books of account or documents belonging to the searched person contain certain information relating to some other person, provision of section 153C can be invoked. In such a situation, question would arise as to how such books of account can be handed over to the Assessing Officer of some other person in original as is required u/s 153C, until the proceedings against the searched person are completed. In such a case photocopy of the original document can be handed over but whether on the basis of photocopy, provision of section 153C can be invoked with respect to the other person is a question which would need discussion. Section 153C has the effect to treat the other person in the same manner as if he has also been searched and he is also required to be assessed as per the provisions of section 153A, which in our considered opinion should not be done unless the seized books of account or documents entirely belongs to the other person and is of incriminating nature. In case there is some information relating to the third person, contained in the seized document belonging to the searched person, department can resort to the provision of section 148. Such tool was already available with the department but to amend the provision of section 153C in such harsh manner seems to be unwarranted and in our opinion, constitutional validity of such amendment shall be required to be tested in times to come.

It has been held in the case of *CIT* v. *Renu Constructions P. Ltd.* [2018] 99 taxmann.com 426 (Delhi) that prior to the amendment w.e.f. 1st June, 2015, for the purpose of initiating proceedings under s. 153C, the seized documents had to be shown to belong to the other person and not merely pertaining to such other person; change brought about in this regard in s. 153C by way of amendment has been given prospective effect from 1st June, 2015.

It has been held in the case of *Anil Kumar Gopikishan Agrawal* v. *Asstt. CIT* [2019] 106 taxmann.com 137 (Guj.) that section 153C as amended with effect from 1-6-2015 incorporating the words "pertains to' & 'relates to' instead of 'belongs to' qua books of accounts & documents, would apply to search initiated on or after 1-6-2015 and, thus, it is date of search that has been considered to be relevant date for purpose of applying amended provisions of section 153C(1). Consequently, in relation to searches carried out till 31-5-2015, it is not permissible for Assessing Officer to assume jurisdiction under section 153C on the basis of books of account or documents which did not 'belong' to the other person but may be pertaining to or relating to the other person.

It has been held in the case of Jitendra Mansukhlal Adesara v. *Asstt. CIT 207 DTR 96 (Guj.) that in the satisfaction note, it has been recorded that the version put forth by the searched person that the Jewellery being given to the assessee for job work was found not correct & it is case of the Department that jewellery or other valuable article or things seized 'belong' to the assessee and also "document" 'pertains' to and that any information contained therein relates to the assessee and further that subsequent to 1st June, 2015, the information embedded in the document is sufficient for taking action under section 153C.*

It has been held in the case of *Amar Jewellers Ltd.* v. *Asstt. CIT* 216 DTR (Guj.) 137 that it is difficult to take the view that the *non obstante* clause in section 153A excludes the very applicability of sections 147 and 148 respectively and that submission of the counsel appearing for the Revenue that the *non obstante* clause in section

153A should be understood as merely dispensing with the procedural aspect of section 147 is sustainable and that Return filed under section 153A(1) is a return furnished under section 139 and therefore, the provisions of the Act which would be otherwise applicable in case of return filed in the regular course under section 139(1) would also continue to apply in case of return filed under section 153A.

It has been held in the case of *Neesa Technologies (P.) Ltd.* v. *Dy. CIT* 214 DTR 172 (Ahd 'C') that AO having initiated the proceedings under section 153C on the basis of two documents which admittedly did not belong to the assessee and which were not of incriminating nature, the assumption of jurisdiction under section 153C was invalid.

(*viii*) Belonging to more than one person

There may be situation when an asset or document jointly belongs to several persons. There may be an agreement to buy property entered jointly by person 'A' along with persons 'B' and 'C' while search action is undertaken against "A" only. A question arises as to whether on the basis of such agreement, action under section 153C can be taken against person 'B' or person 'C'?

This is a debatable issue. There can be one view that provision of section 153C can be invoked when the document belongs to a person other than the person referred to in section 153A. In the above example the document belongs to person 'A' also against whom proceeding u/s 153A is to be undertaken as the person searched. For invoking provision of section 153C, the document should belong to the other person exclusively and it should not at all belong to the person covered under section 153A so that the same is not required to be considered in his case under section 153A. Under such situation, instead of invoking provision of section 153C in the case of person 'B' or 'C', Department has powers to invoke provision of section 147/148 by reopening case of person 'B' or 'C'.

The other view may be that since the document belongs to all the three persons namely A, B, C, actions u/s 153A/153C can be undertaken against B & C also.

The above controversy is no more relevant now after amendment to section 153C by the Finance Act, 2015 wherein it has been provided that provision of section 153C can be invoked when any books of account or documents seized pertain to some other person. In view of this amendment, in the above situation action under section 153C can be taken against the person 'B'&'C'.

Another question may arise when assessing officers having jurisdiction over all the persons namely A, B & C are different, as to which assessing officer such material is to be handed over for invoking provision of section 153C. This is a tricky situation. The practical solution to the problem may be to centralize the cases of all such persons with the same assessing officer. The other way may be to hand over photocopies of the seized books of account or documents pertaining to other person.

(ix) To hand over to the Assessing Officer of other person

Books of account, documents or assets seized but belonging to other person are required to be handed over to the assessing officer of such other person. The handing over is a physical act and it implies that seized material belonging to other person should be physically handed over to the assessing officer of such other person. Handing over can be actual physical handing over or constructive handing over. For example: jewellery belonging to other person, kept in safe custody, can be constructively handed over by handing over the keys of the locker, in which jewellery is kept.

It has been held in the case of *CIT* v. *Late J. Chandrasekar (HUF)* [2012] 20 taxmann.com 451 (Mad.) that assessment of third person by issuing notice under section 153C which was not based on seized material is not valid, as the seized material was not handed over to the AO of the assessee by the AO of the searched person.

Generally in practice it has been observed that cases which are required to be covered under section 153C are transferred under section 127 and centralized with the same Assessing Officer who is making assessment of person searched under section 153A. In such a case, when Assessing Officer is common, no physical handing over is required.

(ixa) Satisfaction by the Assessing Officer of the other person

As per the Finance (No. 2) Act, 2014 with effect from 1.10.2014, section 153C was amended providing that assessing officer of the other person shall proceed against each such other person and issue notice and assess or reassess the income of the other person in accordance with the provisions of section 153A, if that Assessing Officer is satisfied that the books of account or documents or assets seized or requisitioned have a bearing on the determination of the total income of such other person. Thus, legislature has provided the requirement of the satisfaction of the Assessing Officer of the other person also before initiating assessment proceeding under section 153C.

The requirement of arriving at the satisfaction by the jurisdictional Assessing Officer has been provided, as such Assessing Officer can only decide as to whether the seized material handed over to him has any bearing on the determination of undisclosed income of such other person. In case jurisdictional Assessing Officer is of the view that seized material does not have any bearing on the determination of the total income of such other person, he may not initiate assessment proceeding under section 153C.

There is no mention in section 153C as to whether satisfaction has to be recorded in writing by the jurisdictional Assessing Officer. However, we are of the view that such satisfaction too should be recorded in writing applying the same principle and decisions as applicable in case of satisfaction by the Assessing Officer of the searched person.

Satisfaction should be recorded before issuing notice under section 153C. In case notice under section 153C is issued and assessment proceeding is initiated without recording such satisfaction, initiation of the proceeding under section 153C would not be valid.

(*x*) **Time limit for issuing notice as per section 153C**

From the above discussion, it can be reasonably inferred that the jurisdiction is assumed by the assessing officer under section 153C to make assessment of other person with the receiving of seized material belonging to such other person. He is required to issue notice to such other person for filing returns for the seven years. There is no time limit prescribed for issuing notice u/s 153C. There is however time limit for completion of assessment prescribed under section 153B. Therefore, assessing officer can issue notice at any time before the final date of completion of assessment as is the case under section 153A. However, there should be sufficient time and reasonable opportunity to be provided to the assessee to file the returns and make submissions in support of his case.

(*xi*) **Law existing on the date of search to apply for cases under section 153C**

The provisions of section 153C have undergone changes from time to time and therefore there remains a controversy as to the law existing on which date would be applicable for the cases under section 153C, particularly when there is substantial gap between the date of search on the person searched, date of handing over the books of accounts etc. of the assessing officer of the other person in whose case action under section 153C is initiated. This controversy has been addressed in the following cases:

It has been held in the case of *Anilkumar Gopikishan Agrawal* v. *Asstt. CIT* [2019] 106 taxmann.com 137/418 ITR 25 (Guj.) that the amendment of section 153C w.e.f. 1-6-2015 expands scope of section 153C and affects substantive rights and thus the amendment is not retrospective since Starting point for action under section 153C is search and thus Section 153C is applicable as it existed on date of search and thus on the Search prior to 1-6- 2015, Section 153C as amended w.e.f. 1-6-2015 is not applicable.

It has also been held in the case of *Principal CIT* v. *Sarwar Agency P Ltd.*[2017] 85 taxmann.com 269/397 ITR 400 (Delhi) that amendment with effect from April 1, 2017 made in section 153C is prospective.

13.15 Assumption of jurisdiction u/s 153C

(*i*) Assumption of jurisdiction u/s 153C at what stage?

This may be a debatable issue as to at what stage jurisdiction is assumed by the assessing officer to make assessment/reassessment under section 153C in the case of other person who has not been searched but some material belonging to him is found and seized in the case of search of some other person. The point regarding the assumption of jurisdiction assumes significance so as to address the following issues:

1. To decide whether jurisdiction has been assumed validly to make assessment/reassessment of the other person for seven years under section 153C.

2. To decide the time barring limit for making assessment/reassessment under section 153C.

There may be different stages in the context of the proceeding under section 153C which can be said to be related with the issue of assumption of jurisdiction and may be described as under:

1. At the time when satisfaction is arrived and recorded by the assessing officer of the person searched that certain books of account, documents or assets seized belong or relate to a person other than the person searched.

2. At the time when such books of account, document or assets seized are handed over to the assessing officer having jurisdiction over such other person.

3. At the time when the assessing officer after receiving such books of account, documents or assets, records his satisfaction to proceed against the other person.

4. At the time when such assessing officer issues notice to the other person for filing returns of income for seven years.

Under section 153C, there is no clarity regarding the stage at which it can be said that jurisdiction is validly assumed by the assessing officer to take action under section 153C. From the language of section, it appears that the stage of handing over of the books of account, documents or assets belonging to other person by the assessing officer of the person searched to the assessing officer of other person is the stage when jurisdiction is assumed by the assessing officer to proceed under section 153C against such other person. Before amendment brought by the Finance Act, 2014, there was no requirement under section 153C for recording of satisfaction by the assessing officer of the other person before assuming jurisdiction for making assessment/reassessment of the other person. However, we had opined earlier that since the provision of section 153C are quite harsh *vis-à-vis* to the other person and in the interest of equity and justice and in accordance with the principle of natural justice, recording of satisfaction by such assessing officer is also warranted before assuming jurisdiction.

For making assessment/reassessment under section 153C in the case of other person, the period of limitation has been provided with reference to the date on which books of account, documents or assets seized are handed over, as provided under first proviso to section 153B(1). It is the settled law in the case of reopening of case under section 147/148 that the limitation of making the reassessment is reckoned with respect to the date on which notice is served by the assessing officer for filing return, as prescribed u/s 153(2). But since there is specific mention in the first proviso to section 153B(1) in this respect, there should not be any scope for controversy in this regard and the date of handing over of the seized material is to be considered as the date applicable for this purpose.

(*ii*) **That assessing officer shall proceed against each such other person - Recording of satisfaction by the assessing officer having jurisdiction over the other person before assuming jurisdiction under section 153C?**

Before amendment by the Finance Act, 2014 and 2015, Section 153C states that once seized material belonging to other person is handed over to the assessing officer having jurisdiction over such other person, that assessing officer shall proceed against each such other person to assess or reassess his income in accordance with the provisions of section 153A. As per above requirement, it appeared that assessing officer of other person assumes jurisdiction under section 153C just by receiving seized material belonging to such other person.

Plain reading of section 153C before the said amendments did not require satisfaction to be recorded regarding undisclosed income of the other person by the assessing officer, before assuming jurisdiction under section 153C against such other person. Assuming jurisdiction under section 153C has severe consequences and on the basis of some paper or document for a particular year, such other person may be liable to be assessed or reassessed for entire seven years. In our opinion, assuming jurisdiction under section 153C against any other person had to be properly guarded and this situation could not be kept at par with the situation of the person against whom search warrant was issued.

Provision of section 153C should be interpreted to contain safeguards that

    a. Assessing officer of such other person should also record his satisfaction that seized materials received by him actually belong to such other person, and

    b. Such seized material *prima facie* represent undisclosed income of such other person.

Assessing officer of the person searched who is not having jurisdiction and records of such other person can not be in a position to decide whether such seized material belong to such other person and represents his undisclosed income. It is the assessing officer of such other person who can look into his records and take a decision whether seized material handed over to him represent undisclosed income of such other person. As discussed earlier, jurisdiction under section 153C cannot be intended to be assumed on the basis of seized material which does not represent undisclosed income though department may take a contrary interpretation.

In the case of person searched, *"reason to believe"* regarding acquisition of undisclosed income is formed by the competent authority before authorizing search. No such "reason to believe" is formed in the case of other person intended to be covered under section 153C. Before assuming jurisdiction under section 153C, assessing officer of such other person should also be satisfied regarding undisclosed income acquired by such person on the basis of seized material belonging to him.

It is further submitted that it would be in the interest of justice if an opportunity is granted of being heard to such other person before assuming jurisdiction under section 153C by the assessing officer. The Apex Court in various pronouncements has held that the principles of natural justice should be observed in the administration and enforcement of fiscal laws. In the case of *Sahara India (Firm)* v. *CIT* [2008] 169 Taxman 328 (SC), the Apex Court approved pre-decisional hearing in section 142A even in the absence of an express provision under the Act to this effect. Applying the same ratio, the assessing officer should afford an opportunity of hearing to such other person before assuming jurisdiction under section 153C against such other person. This will not only be fair and just to such other person but may result in avoidance of unnecessary litigation.

Mere passing of the seized material by the assessing officer of the searched person does not amount to recording of requisite satisfaction and proceeding under section 153C(1) in such a case will be treated as without jurisdiction.

Nauvika Investment and Commercial Enterprises Pvt. Ltd. v. *Dy. CIT* [2008] 5 DTR 479 (Delhi-Trib.).

In the case of *CIT* v. *Classic Enterprises* [2013] 35 taxmann.com 244/219 Taxman 237 (All.) (HC), it has been held that before a notice under section 153C can be issued, the AO ought to be satisfied that undisclosed income belongs to a third person. Such satisfaction should be reasonable but need not be conclusive.

In this context ratio propounded by Apex Court in the case of *Manish Maheshwari* v. *Asstt. CIT* [2007] 159 Taxman 258 (SC) rendered in the context of section 158BD is quite significant.

Enactment of above view by the Legislature

The above view of the authors has been largely enacted by the legislature by way of amendment brought to section 153C(1) by the Finance (No. 2) Act, 2014 which is being discussed in detail as under.

Amendment in Text of section 153C

Finance (No. 2) Act, 2014 has amended sub-section (1) of section 153C which is reproduced as under after showing the deleted portion so as to enable better appreciation of amendment made :—

> *1. Notwithstanding anything contained in section 139, section 147, section 148, section 149, section 151 and section 153, where the Assessing Officer is satisfied that any money, bullion, jewellery or other valuable article or thing or books of account or documents seized or requisitioned belong or belongs to a person other than the person referred to in section 153A, then the books of account or documents or assets seized or requisitioned shall be handed over to the Assessing Officer having jurisdiction over such other person and that Assessing Officer shall proceed against each such other person and issue such other person notice and assess or reassess income of such other person in accordance with the provisions of section 153A:*

*that Assessing Officer shall proceed against each such other person and issue notice and assess or re-assess the income of the other person in accordance with the provisions of section 153A, if, that **Assessing Officer is satisfied that the books of account or documents or assets seized or requisitioned have a bearing on the determination of the total income of such other person** for the relevant assessment year or years referred to in sub-section (1) of section 153A.*

While making the above amendment, the legislature has vindicated the opinion expressed by the authors regarding the issue for recording satisfaction by the Assessing Officer of other person before assuming jurisdiction to assess or reassess such other person as per provisions of section 153C. The above amendment introduced by Finance (No. 2) Act, 2014 shall have the following implications regarding the applicability of the provisions of section 153C:

    a. Assessing Officer of the other person to whom books of account, other documents, or assets seized in the case of searched person have been handed over will also have to record satisfaction before assuming jurisdiction against such other person u/s 153C of the Act.

    b. The satisfaction is to be recorded that the books of account or documents or assets seized or requisitioned have a bearing on the determination of the total income of such other person for the relevant assessment year or years referred to in sub-section (1) of section 153A.

    It would imply that satisfaction is to be recorded for each of the seven assessment years covered for assessment or reassessment u/s 153C. In case, books of account or other documents or asset seized are relating to only one year, there would not now be any requirement to re-open cases of all the seven assessment years mandatorily by the Assessing Officer of such other person u/s 153C.

    c. The legislature has used the language regarding the satisfaction by Assessing Officer of other person to the effect that the *"books of account or documents or assets seized or requisitioned have a bearing on the determination of the total income of such other person"*. This is new terminology which has been used by the legislature while amending sub-section (1) of section 153C by Finance (No. 2) Act, 2014.

Under section 148 of the Act for reopening or making reassessment, legislature has required Assessing Officer to record *reason to believe* that the income has escaped assessment.

Invoking section 153C against other person is in the nature of reopening or reassessing his case(s) of earlier assessment years. The legislature could have used the same language u/s 153C also as used in section 147, for recording satisfaction. Such language *seized material etc. have a bearing on the determination of the total income* seems to give a wider handle to the Assessing Officer to reopen the case in comparison to the situation of income escaping assessment under section 147.

The above terminology that seized material etc. having bearing on determination of total income shall be required to be interpreted by the judiciary and may be prone to litigation. It shall be interesting how such terminology is interpreted by the courts. In our opinion, the interpretation of such terminology should also fall in the same manner as income escaping assessment since the intent of section 153C is of the similar nature but nevertheless by using such ambiguous terminology, new line of litigation may open which could have been avoided.

(*iii*) **The word 'shall' to be interpreted as mandatory or directory? - Whether all search years to be reassessed?**

Once seized material belonging to the other person is received by his assessing officer, section 153C states that such assessing officer shall proceed against such each other person to assess or reassess his income in accordance with the provision of section 153A. It implies that even when the seized material received is relating to a particular year, assessment or reassessment of such other person shall be made for seven years as is the case with respect to person searched to be assessed under section 153A.

A question arises as to whether use of the word 'shall' in this phrase of section 153C(1) is mandatory or it may be interpreted as only an enabling provision conferring the requisite power on the concerned assessing officer.

As per the language of section 153C as it stood prior to the amendment introduced by the Finance (No. 2) Act, 2014, it appears that it is mandatory requirement for assessing officer to issue notice for filing the returns and making assessment/reassessment for seven years, in a case when jurisdiction is assumed by him under section 153C against the other person. The rationale for making assessment of seven years even when the seized material handed over may be relating to some particular year, can be said to be the same as discussed in the context of making assessments for six years under section 153A. But in our opinion, the person who has not been searched cannot be kept at par with the person who has been searched and against whom search was authorized by the competent authority after recording reasons for accumulation of undisclosed income. The provision of section 153C itself is very harsh *vis-à-vis* to the other person and in the interest of the natural justice, it would be reasonable if such other person is assessed/reassessed only with respect to the years to which seized material belonging to him, relates.

In practice, it has however been observed that even in the department, some of the assessing officers take the above view and they issue notice requiring for filing return under section 153C only relating to the years to which seized material relates.

In view of the discussion held above and keeping in view the intention of Legislature, it is further opined that the word 'shall' should be interpreted as only directory. The assessing officer may reopen and assess cases for all the seven years or any of the years as may be required keeping in view the nature of seized material received by him.

The observation of Delhi High Court in the case of *Saraya Industries Ltd.* v. *Union of India* [2008] 171 Taxman 194 (Delhi), while upholding the constitutional validity of sections 153A and 153C, are quite significant. They have observed that seizure or requisition must be of such a character as to persuade the assessing officer to even reopen closed assessments. It implies that reopening of closed assessment under section 153C is not intended to be automatic but it would depend upon the nature of the seized documents.

It has been held in the case of *Sinhgad Technical Education Society* v. *Asstt. CIT* [2011] 16 taxmann.com 101/[2012] 50 SOT 89 (URO) (Pune-Trib.) that where no assessment year specific incriminating material or document is found, assessments of such assessment years cannot be disturbed by invoking the provisions of section 153C and that in the absence of any reference to any assessment year specific incriminating information or document relatable to the assessee for the assessment year in question in the reasons recorded by the AO, impugned assessment under section 153C is bad in law.

The above ration has been approved by the apex court in the case of *CIT* v. *Sinhgad Technical Education Society* [2017] 84 taxmann.com 290/250 Taxman 225 (SC) that in assessment under s. 153C while judging the validity *vis-a-vis* recording of satisfaction. It was noted by the Tribunal that incriminating material which was seized had to pertain to the assessment years in question and it is an undisputed fact that the documents which were seized did not establish any co-relation, document-wise, with four assessment years in question;

order of the High Court affirming this view of the Tribunal is, therefore, without any blemish.

It has been held in the case of *Principal CIT* v. *Index Securities P Ltd.* [2017] 86 taxmann.com 84 (Delhi) that essential jurisdictional requirement for assumption of jurisdiction under s. 153C is that seized documents forming the basis of the satisfaction note must not merely 'pertain' to the other person but must belong to the 'other person'; further, seized documents must be incriminating and must relate to the assessment years whose assessments are sought to be reopened.

After the amendment made by the Finance (No. 2) Act, 2014 in sub-section (1) of section 153C as discussed in point no. (*ii*) above, the Assessing Officer shall not be required to reopen all the seven assessment years of the other persons u/s 153C. He would be required to record the satisfaction with respect to each assessment year and the case(s) shall be reopened only of such assessment years with respect to which assessing officer is satisfied that seized material etc. handed over to him have a bearing on the determination of the total income of such other person.

By making such amendment, controversy in this regard as to whether all seven assessment years are to be reopened u/s 153C or not, has been resolved by the legislature in a way.

(*iv*) **Relaxation regarding requirement of framing assessment or reassessment of earlier six years**

As per Finance Act, 2012 w.e.f 1-7-2012, proviso has been inserted to section 153C prescribing that the Central Government may by rules to be made by it specify the class of cases in which the Assessing Officer shall not be required to issue notice for framing fresh assessment for all the preceding six assessment years except in cases where any assessment/reassessment has abated. It appears that the objective of the above proviso is not to frame fresh assessment for those years with respect to which no incriminating evidences have been found and seized. Income tax Rule 112F has been prescribed by the Central Government specifying the class of persons who may be benefited by this provision.

(*v*) **All provisions of section 153A to apply**

Once jurisdiction under section 153C is assumed by the assessing officer of other person, he is required to issue notice and assess or reassess income of such other person in accordance with the provisions of section 153A. After assuming jurisdiction under section 153C, assessment or reassessment shall be made in accordance with provisions of section 153A and all the requirements mentioned in section 153A will be applicable here also.

It implies that such other person will also be assessed for preceding six years and for the year of search even when seized material handed over may belong to only one particular year. This requirement of section 153C seems to be very harsh. It is opined that such interpretation needs to be read down and the other person should be assessed or reassessed with respect to the seized material belonging to him and with respect to only those years to which seized material belong.

Above view has been upheld by Hon'ble Supreme Court in the case of *CIT* v. *Sinhgad Technical Education Society* [2017] 84 taxmann. com 290/250 Taxman 225 (SC)

Section 153C also starts with the *non obstante* clause ...."Notwithstanding anything contained in section 139, section 147, section 148, section 149, section 151 and section 153.............." it implies that provisions of section 153C which are inconsistent with the provisions of these sections will override in the same manner as is provided under section 153A.

13.16 Issues regarding assessment under section 153C

(*i*) **Assessment or reassessment of seven years - Which seven years?**

Assessment or reassessment of the person covered under section 153C is required to be made for preceding six years as required under section 153A and for the year of search as well. The year of search to be covered for assessment or reassessment has been specifically provided by way of introduction of sub-section (2) to section 153C by Finance Act, 2005, with retrospective effect from 1st June, 2003 i.e. from the date of incorporation of section 153C under the statute.

The year of search and preceding six years shall be the same assessment years with respect to which the person searched is covered. There may be a situation, for example, when seized material belonging to other person is handed over after two years from the date of search but section 153C would cover *qua* the other person, the original years as applicable in the case of person who was searched. Assessment years subsequent to the year of search for which returns might have been filed or assessment might have been completed in the case of such other person are not covered within the ambit of section 153C.

Ahmedabad Bench of ITAT in the case of *Vijay M. Vimawal* v. *Asstt. CIT* [2009] 34 SOT 34 (Ahd.-Trib.) (URO), has held that six assessment years shall be calculated prior to the year in which seized material belonging to the other person is handed over for making assessment under section 153C. It has been held in that case as under—

Documents having been handed over to the AO of the assessee on 3rd November, 2006, relevant assessment year being 2007-08, the AO could reopen the assessments for six preceding years i.e. A.Ys 2001 to 2006-07 and assessment for A.Y. 1999-2000 was barred by limitation. In the above case, the year in which search was conducted was A.Y. 2005-06.

In the case of *CIT* v. *RRJ Securities Ltd.* [2015] 62 taxmann.com 391 (Delhi) (HC), it has been held that six years which can be assessed u/s 153C shall have to be construed from the date on which the books of account or documents are handed over by the AO of the main party subjected to the search to the AO of the other person (the appellant in this case). That accordingly the six years which can be assessed u/s 153C in applicant's case are AYs. 2005-06 to 2010-11. The above view is clear on reading the proviso to sec. 153C(1) r. w. s 153A(1) of the IT Act. Accordingly the initiation of the proceedings for A.Y. 2003-04 (and the other respective AY's as the case may be) which has been made on 8-9-2010 is barred by limitation, and therefore the assessment order passed u/s 153C is held as a nullity.

In the case of *R. L. Allied Industries* v. *ITO* [2015] 54 taxmann.com 222 (Delhi-Trib.), it has been held that the seized material was received on March 12, 2009 from the Assistant Commissioner. Thus, the year in which the seized material was seized was the previous year 2008-09 relevant to the assessment year 2009-10. The preceding six years would be assessment years 2008-09, 2007-08, 2006-07, 2005-06, 2004-05 and 2003-04. Therefore, on the facts of the assessee's case and a combined reading of section 153C and section 153A of the Act, the issue of notice under section 153C of the Act for the assessment years 2001-02 and 2002-03 was barred by limitation and was to be quashed and consequentially, the assessment order passed in pursuance to the notice issued under section 153C of the Act was also to be quashed as was the penalty levied under section 271F of the Act.

In the case of *Jasjit Singh* v. *ACIT* [ITA No. 1436/Delhi/2012, dated 5-11-2014] (Delhi-Trib.) Date of receiving seized documents is the "date of initiation of search" and six years period has to be reckoned from that date. An assessment order passed u/s 143(3) instead of u/s 153C is void.

It has been held in the case of *ARN Infrastructure India Ltd.* v. *Asstt. CIT* [2017] 81 taxmann.com 260 (Delhi) that *six assessment years for which assessments/reassessments could be made under Section 153C of the Act would also have to be construed with reference to the date of handing over of assets/documents to the AO of the Assessee.*

It has been held in the case of *Principal CIT* v. *Sarwar Agency (P.) Ltd.* [2017] 85 taxmann.com 269 (Delhi) that Six assessment years immediately preceding assessment year relevant to previous year in which search was conducted in case of assessment of third person are to be reckoned from date of handing over of assets and documents to Assessing Officer of third person by Assessing Officer of person against whom search was conducted. Amendment with effect from April 1, 2017 that six previous years are to be reckoned from date of search is prospective.

Other judicial decisions on this proposition are as under:

◆ *B N B Investment & Properties Ltd.* v. *DCIT* in ITA No. 506/2015 dated 27.06.2018 (ITAT-Delhi)

◆ *Reliance Estate Agency* v. *ACIT* in ITA No. 1614-1619 dated 30.07.2018 (ITAT-Delhi)

CIT v. *Sh. Jasjit Singh,* ITA 337 of 2015, dated 11.08.2015 (DHC) *Sh. Vishnu Bhagwan* v. *DCIT,* ITA No. 3560 of 2015, dated 04.12.2018 (Delhi)

Sanjay Thakur v. *DCIT,* ITA No. 3559 of 2015, dated 06.11.2018 (Delhi)

M/s Ambawatta Buildwell Pvt. Ltd. v. *DCIT,* ITA Nos. 2592 and 2551 of 2015, dated 18.09.2018 (Delhi)

ACIT v. *M/s Empire Casting Pvt. Ltd.,* ITA No. 4018 of 2011, dated 21.11.2017 (Delhi)

M/s Pavitra Realcon Pvt. Ltd. v. *Asstt. CIT* [2017] 87 taxmann.com 142 (Delhi-Trib.)

Dy. CIT v. *Satkar Roadlines Pvt. Ltd.* [2015] 62 taxmann.com 327/155 ITD 501 (Delhi-Trib.)

In our humble opinion, the above view of various Benches of Tribunal & Hon'ble Delhi High Court is not correct and requires reconsideration. The proviso to section 153C has not been read in right perspective. Infact, the reference made in the proviso regarding assessment years is for the purpose of abatement of pending proceedings and not for assessment years for which assessment proceedings are required to be undertaken after assuming jurisdiction under section 153C.

However, recent decision from Hon'ble Gujarat High Court has laid down that six years' period has to be taken qua the date of search.

It has been held in the case of *Anil Kumar Gopikishan Agrawal* v. *Asstt. CIT* [2019] 106 taxmann.com 137 (Guj.) that. In case any notice under section 153C is issued for assessment years beyond six assessment years, such notices would be beyond jurisdiction as same do not fall within six assessment years as contemplated under section 153A.

In fact this view has later been legislated by bringing amendment to section 153C(1) by the Finance Act, 2017 with effect from 1.4.2017. In our considered view, this amendment should be taken as clarificatory and even in relation to period prior to 1.4.2017.

Finance Act, 2017 has amended provision of section 153C providing the years which can be reopened under section 153C and the controversy in this regard existing due to the earlier judicial decisions has been settled. It has been provided that under section 153C six assessment years immediately preceding the assessment year relevant to the previous year in which search is conducted or requisition is made & the year of search shall be the years which may be covered u/s 153C.

There is another dimension to this issue. In several judgments mentioned above, courts have held that the preceding six years should be considered preceding to the year in which seized material is handed over by the Assessing Officer of the searched person to the Assessing Officer of the assessee. Such view has been rendered emphasizing the issue that in case preceding six years are considered with reference to the year of search and there is substantial gap in the year of search and the year in which seized material is handed over, there may be certain initial years which are time-barred under section 148 and in such cases assessee may not be keeping the books of account and records relevant for the purpose of assessment. In our opinion, under such circumstances preceding six years should be reduced to preceding four years or five years as the case may be, but as per combined reading of sections 153C and 153A, in our opinion the reference to preceding six years has been drawn from the year of search as discussed by us earlier also. The years after the year of search relating to the other person covered under section 153C can be put to scrutiny under normal provisions of the Act as per section 143/148 of the Income Tax Act.

(ii) **Abatement of pending proceedings**

Proviso to section 153C(1) clarifies regarding abatement of pending proceedings in the case of a person against whom provision of section 153C is invoked. It states that the reference to the date of initiation of the search in the second proviso to section 153A(1) shall be construed as reference to the date of receiving the seized material belonging to other person. To have more clarity in this regard, let us read second proviso to section 153A(1) by substituting the above referred date :

"**Provided further** that assessment or reassessment, if any, relating to any assessment year falling within the period of six assessment years referred to in this sub-section pending on the date of *receiving the books of account or documents or assets seized or requisitioned by the assessing officer having jurisdiction over such other person,* as the case may be, shall abate." (Emphasis supplied by us)

There may be situation when between the date of search and the date of handing over of seized material to the assessing officer of the other person, some of his assessment relating to the assessment years referred under section 153A, pending on the date of search might have been finalized. The purpose of this proviso is to clarify that any such finalized assessment between these dates will not be disturbed and the same shall not abate. It is only the pending cases as on the date of receiving seized material of such other person but relating to those years which are covered under section 153A and the year of search, shall abate.

(*iii*) **Assessment of undisclosed income of other person on the basis of entries in books of account or documents of the person searched**

There may be cases where certain details of financial transactions suggesting undisclosed income relating to some other person are detected from the books of account or documents found and belonging to the person searched. In such a case, provision of section 153C could not be invoked against such other person prior to the amendment brought by the Finance Act, 2015 wherein the requirement of books of account or documents belonging to other person has been substituted by the requirement of such books of account or documents 'pertaining to' or information therein relating to the other person. Thus, as per the amended provision, section 153C can be invoked on the basis of entries in the books of account or documents belonging to the searched person having information relating to the other person & which may have bearing on the determination of total income of such other person.

It has been held in the case of *Principal CIT* v. *Anand Kumar Jain (HUF)* [2021] 201 DTR 200 (Del.)/432 ITR 384 (Delhi) that existence of incriminating material found during the course of the search is a *sine qua* non for making additions and further, as per the mandate of section 153C. If statement of PK was to be construed as an incriminating material belonging to or pertaining to a person other than person searched (as referred to in section 153A). then the only legal recourse available to the Department was to proceed in terms of section 153C which was not done and thus Tribunal was justified in deleting addition made by AO.

It has been held in the case of *Principal CIT* v. *Kunvarji Commodities Brokers (P.) Ltd.* [2020] 118 taxmann.com 374/274 Taxman 162/ [2021] 432 ITR 180 (Guj.) that Assessing Officer bifurcating amount disclosed by third person and accordingly making addition in hands of assessee and thus addition made merely on basis of third person's statement and disclosure of income by him is unsustainable.

(*iv*) **Seized material belonging or relating to some other person, whether section 153C is the only recourse?**

Section 153C is a special provision overriding certain requirements provided under section 139/147/148/149/151/153. With respect to the seized material belonging or relating to some other person, assessing officer has the power to make assessment/reassessment of the earlier seven years' cases of such person without fulfilling the conditions for reopening as provided under section 147/148/149/151/153. In case assessing officer opts not to invoke provision of section 153C but opts to invoke provision of section 147/148, there does not seem to be any restriction on the assessing officer for doing so as per the plain reading of the provision.

Sometimes, such option may be resorted to by the assessing officer when there has been considerable delay in invoking provision of section 153C and any such action may encounter the possible hurdle of being held as time barred but the time limit for reopening the case under section 147/148 for a particular year is still available. A question may arise as to whether reopening of case under section 147/148 under such circumstances is valid. An argument may be put on behalf of the assessee that it was mandatory on the part of the assessing officer to take action under section 153C which is special provision for such a situation and in case he has failed to do so, action cannot be taken under any other general provision of the Act. The other view may be that the validity of reopening under section 147/148 cannot be challenged on this ground that action should have been taken by the assessing officer under section 153C only.

It has been held in the case of *ITO* v. *Arun Kumar Kapoor* [2011] 16 taxmann.com 373/[2012] 50 SOT 87 (URO)(ASR.-Trib.) that Reassessment under section 147 on the basis of incriminating material against assessee found in search of third party and forwarded to AO of assessee by the search officer was illegal and *void ab initio* as in such a situation, assessment could be made only under section 153C which specifically ousted the application of sections 147 and 148.

Other judicial decisions for this proposition of law are as under:

Rajat Shubra Chatterji v. *ACIT ITA* No. 2430/Delhi/2015 dated 20.5.2016 (Delhi-Trib.)

Adarsh Agarwal v. *ITO,* ITA No. 777/Delhi/2019, dated 14.01.2020 (Delhi)

Saurashtra Color Tones Pvt. Ltd. v. *ITO,* ITA No. 6276/Delhi/2018, dated 22.01.2020 (Delhi)

Meer Hassan v. *ITO* and *Ali Hassan* v. *ITO,* ITA Nos. 1571 and 1573/Delhi/2015, dated 28.02.2019 (Delhi)

Smt. Sangeeta Chhabra v. *ITO,* ITA No. 1853/Delhi/2017, dated 21.04.2017 (Delhi)

Mohan Thakur v. *ITO,* ITA No. 7413/Mum./2017, dated 09.01.2020 (Mum.)

Girish Chand Sharma v. *ITO,* ITA No. 987/Delhi/2018, dated 30.11.2018 (Del.)

It has been held in the case of *Sanjay Singhal (HUF)* v. *Dy. CIT* 194 DTR (Chd. "A") 209 that the suspicion that some income having escaped assessment cannot by itself be sufficient to sustain the action under s. 147 & further, seizure of documents during search of third person could form the basis for action under s. 153C and not under s. 147.

However, there are contrary judgment from the High Court regarding this issue:

It has been held in the case of *Heval Navinbhai Patel* v. *ITO* [2021] 126 taxmann.com 82/279 Taxman 24 (Guj.) that where the material was seized during search of third person and AO had analyzed the voluminous material collected by the Revenue during the search operations in connection with the VS Group, material at the command of the AO is sufficient to permit the process of reopening and that the contention that proceedings under section 148 are not tenable in law, as the case falls within the ambit of section 153C was not sustainable.

It has been held in the case of Asstt. CIT v. *K.S. Chawla & Sons (HUF)* 203 DTR 180 (Del 'B') *that assessment based upon documents found during the course of search of the premises of a third party can be made only under section 153C and not under section 147.*

It has been held in the case of Karti P. Chidambaram v. *Principal Director of IT (Inv.)* [2021] 128 taxmann.com 116 (Mad.) *that use of the non-obstante clause coupled with the abatement mechanism contained in the provisions of sections 153A and 153C makes it clear that the legislative intent was for AO to proceed only under section 153A or section 153C upon receipt of material seized or requisitioned and that initial materials and information provided to the AO, made him to initiate s. 147 proceedings and on receipt of the seized materials officially in accordance with section 153C, the AO recorded satisfaction and issued notice under section 153C and thus there is no procedural irregularity with reference to the actions initiated under section 147/148 and thereafter, under section153C.*

However, contrary view has been taken in the following judicial decisions:

It has been held in the case of Navkar Electronics v. ITO 208 DTR (Mad.) 320 thatprovisions of sections 153C and 147 are separate, distinct and independent measures that apply to different situations and the impugned assessment is based upon materials found in the course of search under section 132 and thus contention that notice under section 148 was invalid as the action should have been taken under section 153C is no sustainable.

(v) **Once jurisdiction under section 153C is invoked - What kind of additions can be made?**

Once provision of section 153C is invoked with respect to some other person, same principle should apply in respect of the nature of additions to be made during the assessment, which is applicable and discussed in the context of assessment under section 153A. Jurisprudence developed in the context of section 153A would be applicable in the assessment made under section 153C also.

In *LMJ International Ltd.* v. *Dy. CIT* [2008] 22 SOT 315 (Kol.-Trib.), it has been held that items of regular assessment cannot be added back in the proceedings under section 153C when no incriminating documents were found in respect of the disallowed amounts in the search proceedings.

Hon'ble Delhi Bench of Tribunal in the case of *Anil Kumar Bhatia* v. *Asstt. CIT* [2010] 1 ITR (Trib.) 484 (Delhi) have held that no material found in search, no addition can be made for agricultural income, gifts, unexplained deposit.

Similar view has been taken by Mumbai Bench of Tribunal in the case of *Anil P. Khimani* v. *Dy. CIT* [ITA Nos. 2855 to 2860 of 2008, dated 23.2.2010] where Hon'ble Bench has held that addition on account of low household withdrawals cannot be made as it was not based on any material found during the course of search or during the course of assessment proceeding.

Contrary view has however been taken by Delhi Benches in the case of *Ms. Shyam Lata Kaushik* v. *Asstt. CIT* [2008] 114 ITD 305 (Delhi-Trib.) and *Shivnath Rai Harnarain (India) Ltd.* v. *Dy. CIT* [2009] 117 ITD 74 (Delhi-Trib.).

(*vi*) **Presumption under section 292C - Whether available in the case of assessment under section 153C?**

Presumption under section 292C is available to the assessing officer where any books of account, other documents or assets are found in the possession or control of any person in the course of search. Therefore, presumption u/s 292C is available to the assessing officer *qua* the person from whose possession or control such books of account or other documents or assets etc. are found. Section 153C is applicable not to the person searched but to some other person. Books of account, documents or assets are not found from the possession or control of such other person in the course of search. Therefore, it may not be possible to apply presumption of section 292C in the case of such other person who is to be assessed as per provision of section 153C.

(*vii*) **Mention of wrong section/designation of assessee in order does not invalidate the order**

In the case of *DCIT* v. *Damac Holdings (P.) Ltd.* [2014] 51 taxmann.com 538/[2015] 67 SOT 148 (Cochin-Trib.) (URO), originally assessment was made under section 153C, read with section 153A. However, assessment order was framed under section 153C only without mentioning of section 153A. It was held that order passed by Assessing Officer could not be treated as invalid, merely because there was an omission to mention relevant provision of law or wrong mentioning of provisions of law.

In the case of *DCIT* v. *Damac Holdings (P.) Ltd.* [2014] 51 taxmann.com 538/[2015] 67 SOT 148 (Cochin-Trib.) (URO), search was conducted in premises of 'H' who was director of assessee company. But in assessment order his designation was wrongly described as managing director. On said ground assessee challenged validity of assessment order. It was by ITAT that mere wrong description of designation could not be a reason to invalidate order of assessment.

C. SECTION 153D - PRIOR APPROVAL
OF JOINT COMMISSIONER

13.17 Text of section 153D

No order of assessment or reassessment shall be passed by an Assessing Officer below the rank of Joint Commissioner in respect of each assessment year referred to in clause (b) of sub-section (1) of section 153A or the assessment year referred to in clause (b) of sub-section

(1) of section 153B, except with the prior approval of the Joint Commissioner:

Provided *that nothing contained in this section shall apply where the assessment or reassessment order, as the case may be, is required to be passed by the Assessing Officer with the prior approval of the Principal Commissioner or Commissioner under sub-section (12) of section 144BA.*

13.18 Legislative history

Block assessment order under section 158BC was required to be passed with the approval of Joint Commissioner. When block assessment regime was substituted with the new assessment procedure as per sections 153A, 153B, 153C, there was no provision incorporated initially for passing order under section 153A with the approval of the Joint Commissioner. However, as per Finance Act, 2007, section 153D has been legislated with effect from 1st June, 2007, providing prior approval of the Joint Commissioner before passing order under section 153A by the assessing officer.

13.19 Objective

Assessments for search years involve complicated issues. Decision is required to be made regarding undisclosed income of the assessee based upon seized material and on the basis of analysis made by the authorized officer in the appraisal report. Legislature has thought it fit to have application of mind by higher authority i.e. Joint Commissioner also in case assessment order is being passed by an authority below him. The objective is to ensure appraisal of evidences and quality of assessment in a better and objective manner.

13.20 Mandatory requirement

As per Finance Act, 2007, with effect from 1st June, 2007, by way of introduction of section 153D it has been made mandatory that no order of assessment or reassessment shall be passed by an assessing officer below the rank of Joint Commissioner relating to assessment or reassessment made as per provision of section 153A or for the year of search except with the prior approval of the Joint Commissioner/Additional Commissioner. Therefore it is mandatory to pass assessment order in the case of search with the prior approval of range in-charge. There is no requirement to provide opportunity to the assessee to represent his case before granting approval by the Joint Commissioner.

Assessment order passed in the case of other person as per provision of section 153C will also require prior approval of Joint Commissioner as all provisions of section 153A are applicable in such case also.

The provision of section 153D being procedural in nature shall become applicable with respect to all assessment order passed on or after 1st June, 2007, irrespective of the date of search and the assessment year to which the same belongs.

It has been held in the case of *Akil Gulamali Somji* v. *ITO* [2012] 20 tax-mann.com 380/137 ITD 94 (Pune-Trib.) that obtaining prior approval of Jt. CIT for assessment under s. 153A/153C is mandatory and assessment orders framed without obtaining prior approval of the Jt. CIT are invalid, null and void.

It has been held in the case of *Ajay Sharma* v. *Dy. CIT* 187 DTR (Del 'A') 132 that assessment order passed by Dy. CIT under s. 153A without obtaining prior approval of Jt. CIT under s. 153D is *null* and *void* & entire assessment is set aside and quashed.

A. Approval

◆ **No opportunity necessary nor recording of reasons necessary**

Before granting approval to block assessment under the proviso to section 158BG, it is not necessary for the CIT to pass a reasoned order after giving opportunity of hearing to the assessee. *Kailash Moudgil* v. *Dy. CIT* [2000] 72 ITD 97 (Delhi) (SB)

◆ **Approval - Hearing not necessary**

Provisions of section 158BG do not contemplate that CIT should provide opportunity of being heard to the assessee before according approval. *Sree Rama Medical & Surgical Agencies* v. *CIT* [2003] 128 Taxman 288 (AP)

◆ **Opportunity of hearing not required to be given by Commissioner under section 158BG**

Before granting approval to block assessment under the proviso to section 158BG, it is not necessary for the CIT to pass a reasoned order after giving opportunity of hearing to the assessee. The approval of the CIT without recording any reasons in writing for approving the order would not render the order of the AO *void ab initio* and would not invalidate the assessment order. *Kailash Moudgil* v. *Dy. CIT* [2000] 72 ITD 97 (Delhi) (SB).

◆ **Approval - Not obliged to grant opportunity of hearing**

CIT is not obliged to grant opportunity of hearing to the assessee before giving approval under section 158BG; Tribunal can examine the correctness of approval. *Shaw Wallace & Co. Ltd.* v. *Asstt. CIT* [1999] 68 ITD 148 (Cal.).

◆ **No mechanical approval**

In the case of *Smt. Shreelekha Damani* v. *Dy. CIT* [2015] 125 DTR (Mumbai 'F') 263 (Trib.), it has been held that Addl. CIT having expressed his inability to analyze the issues of draft order on merits, clearly staling that no much time is left and granted the approval under section 153D on the very same day, the approval accorded by him was mechanical without considering the materials on record and devoid of any application of mind and, therefore, the impugned assessment made under section 143(3) r/w s. 153A is bad in law and is annulled.

It has been held in the case of *Rajat Minerals (P) Ltd.* v. *Dy. CIT* 190 DTR (Ranchi) 248 where AO having issued questionnaire to assessee on 21st Nov., 2016, for compliance on 28th Nov., 2016 and having made assessment under s. 153A without waiting for assessee's reply which was filed on 29th Nov. 2016 and after obtaining the approval of Jt. CIT on 28th Nov. 2016 itself after preparing draft assessment and furnishing the same to Jt. CIT in 28 cases on 28th Nov. 2016 itself and Jt. CIT granting approval on 28th Nov., 2016 in all cases, this shows colossal abnormality in the conduct of AO and Jt. CIT rendering the approval under s. 153D and consequent assessments invalid.

It has been held in the case of *Dilip Constructions (P) Ltd.* v. *Asstt. CIT* 190 DTR (Ctk) 181 where it is not being discernible from order of approval under s. 153D that the Jt. CIT granted approval after perusing the relevant assessment records and draft assessment orders proposed to be passed by AO, the same was invalid suffering from non-application of mind and assessment made on the basis of said approval was bad in law.

It has been held in the case of *Smt. Indra Bansal* v. *Asstt. CIT* 164 DTR 185/192 TTJ 968 (Jd) that Jt. CIT having granted the approval under s. 153D in all the twenty two cases of the assessee group on the very same day on which the forwarding letter seeking approval was received in his office, and circumstances indicate that this exercise was carried out by the Jt. CIT in a mechanical manner without proper application of mind and even without going through the records as the same were in Jodhpur while the Jt. CIT was at Udaipur and therefore, the approval granted by him cannot be sustained & impugned assessments are annulled.

It has been held in the case of *Geetarani Panda* v. *Asstt. CIT* 169 DTR 18 (ctk) that supervisory authority having himself admitted that he has accorded the approval under s. 153D mechanically without applying his mind to the facts of the case, the alleged approval does not constitute an approval envisaged by the provisions of s. 153D and, therefore, the impugned assessment under s. 153A is void and bad in law.

It has been held in the case of *Principal CIT* v. *Smt. Shreelekha Damani* 174 DTR 86/307 CTR 218 (Bom.) that Addl. CIT for want of time could not examine the issues arising out of the draft order & Tribunal was therefore justified in holding that there was no 'application of mind' on the part of the authority granting approval and therefore approval was invalid.

It has been held in the case of *D.S. India Jewelmart P Ltd.* v. *Asstt. CIT* ITA Nos. 263 to 267/Agr/2017 (Agra-Trib) that the scope and ambit in the present litigation is not that of grant of hearing or representation at the time of approval but whether the approval can be granted by the superior authority without application of mind without looking into seized material, investigation report, the draft assessment order etc. can be sustainable in the eyes of law & such an approval without application of mind is bad in law and cannot be sustained.

It has been held in the case of *Shri Swapan Kumar Paul* v. *Asstt. CIT*, ITA Nos.136-142/Gau/2018 (Gau-Trib.) that Supervisory Authority has himself admitted that because of reasons stated by him, could not apply his mind and has accorded the approval mechanically to meet the requirements of law as the requirement was merely a formality. The said Supervisory Authority had a duty towards both the assessee as well as the Revenue which was failed to be performed in the instant case. Position on the very issue of sec. 153D approval in light of earlier provision of sec. 158BG *vis-a-vis* sec. 153D (*supra*) to conclude that the JCIT is not to accord a mere mechanical approval but he has to apply his mind in order to ensure that the assessing authority conducts appropriate enquiry and investigation.

It has been held in the case of *Dillip Construction Pvt. Ltd.* v. *Asstt. CIT*, IT(ss) A Nos.66 to 71/Ctk/2018 (Ctk-Trib.) that the approval granted by the JCIT in the appeals under consideration has been granted in a mechanical manner without application of mind and that the assessments/reassessment orders passed by the AO on such approval are declared to be void and bad in law.

It has been held in the case of *Rishabh Buildcon P. Ltd., New Delhi* v. *Dy. CIT*, ITA No. 2122/Delhi/2018 (Delhi-Trib) that the statute does not provide for any format in which the approval must be granted or the approval granted must be recorded. Nevertheless, when the Additional CIT while granting the approval recorded that he did not have enough time to analyze the issues arising out of the draft order, clearly this was a case in which the higher Authority had granted the approval without consideration of relevant issues.

It has been held in the case of *M/s. Rajat Minerals Pvt. Ltd. ITAT Ranchi* ITS Nos.41 to 47 /Ran/2019-dt.20.1.2020 that the Process of Approving 'Draft Assessment order' should not be purportedly carried out as the exercise of granting approval in a baffling haste.

The purported act of approval of the JCIT on assessment orders placed before him on that day itself and obtained on the same day (in as many as 28 cases) relating to search is highly improbable and a near impossibility.

It is not humanly possible to look into assessment records as well as draft assessment orders thereon and apply its own mind objectively by a senior designated authority involving such complex matters and grant approval as contemplated under. Section 153D of the Act in a spur. The approval granted by the JCIT, if any, on the same date as noted is thus illusory tantamounting to no approval rendering the entire assessment process void and a nullity.

It has been held in the case of *M/s. Rajat Minerals Pvt. Ltd., ACIT, New Delhi* v .*Sh. Bhupesh Kumar Dhingra,* ITAT-Ranchi-ITA Nos. 41 to 47 of 2019 dt.20.1.2020 Para 14.3 & ITAT - Delhi.. ITA No.5800/Del./2015, dated 31st January, 2020 that AO has prepared the draft assessment order without even waiting for completion of that date of hearing is gross sub-version of the quasi-judicial process.

Aforesaid approval given by the Addl. Commissioner of Income-tax shows that approval to the draft assessment order u/s 153D is granted in case of the assessee, Shri Bhupesh Kumar Dhingra along with 8 other assessees without perusing the draft assessment order.

It has been held in the case of *M/s Rishabh Buildwell P. Ltd ITAT* Delhi- ITA Nos. 2122, 2163, 2123,2162. 2124 & 2491/Del./2018 dt.10.6.2019 para 14 that a conditioned approval subjected 'to modifications by the DCIT after receiving of the approval which makes it an invalid, qualified, uncertain approval.

It has been held in the case of *Principal CIT* v. *Sunrise Finlease (P.) Ltd.* [2018] 89 taxmann.com/252 Taxman 407 (Guj.) that the compliance of Section 153D requirement is absolute, therefore order passed by the Assessing Officer without approval of Joint Commissioner was held to be bad in law.

It has been held in the case of Ch. Krishna Murthy ITA No.766/Hyd/2012 dt. 13.2.2015— that the Assessing Officer should submit the draft assessment order for such approval well in time.

◆ The submission of the draft order must be docketed in the ordersheet.

◆ A copy of the draft order and covering letter filed in the relevant miscellaneous records folder.

◆ Finally once such approval is granted, it must be in writing and filed in the relevant folder indicated above after making a due entry in the ordersheet.

◆ The assessment order can be passed only after the receipt of such approval.

♦ The fact that such approval has been obtained should also be mentioned in the body of the assessment order itself.

It has been held in the case of *Shri Tarachand Khatri* 2020 ITA No. 21/JAB/2019, dated 17-1-2020, No relevant documents were produced before JCIT before granting approval under section 153D of the I.T. Act. Approval have been granted on the same day on 22.12.2017 despite the fact that A.O. was having his office at Jabalpur and JCIT was holding his Office at Bhopal in which there is a significant distance. No record have been produced before JCIT, only draft order have been sent. The A.O. in his letter did not mention if he has forwarded any assessment record before JCIT for his perusal before granting approval under section 153D. No statement of assessee have been recorded under section 132(4). The JCIT did not see any seized material or submission of the assessee brought on record. Therefore, JCIT granted the approval under section 153D without application of mind and in a mechanical manner.

The JCIT also in his approval dated 22.12.2017 (supra) has merely mentioned that A.O. has verified the facts of examining the material Thus, it is clear that JCIT has not gone through the record or the material before granting approval under section 153D of the I.T. Act. The JCIT merely believed the certificate given by the A.O.

It has been held in the case of *M3M India Holdings* v *Dy. CIT* ITA No. 2691/Delhi/2018, dated 15-3-2019 that it is difficult for the Assessing Officer at Faridabad to go through these voluminous papers and prepare a draft order on 30th January 2014, so that the draft order could be transmitted to the Addl. CIT at Chandigarh on same day. In reply to RTI application, the Assessing Officer has reported that no record of mode of dispatch of assessment record to the Addl. CIT is available with the Assessing Officer. Similarly, no record is available as to how the draft order and assessment record have been received by Addl. CIT at Chandigarh. The Addl. CIT, Chandigarh did not mention in his approval dated 31st January 2014 (supra) if he has gone through the assessment record or that assessment record was produced before him. Since no details are available on record about the mode, through which, assessment record was transmitted by the assessing officer at Faridabad to Addl. CIT in Chandigarh and *vice versa* by Addl. CIT, Chandigarh to Assessing Officer at Faridabad on the very next day would lead to suspicion, in explanation of A.O. if any. valid draft order was transmitted to the Addl. within the time or if the Addl. CIT has communicated the approval under section 153D to the Assessing Officer at Faridabad on 31st January 2014. These facts would clearly show that the action of the Addl. CIT. Chandigarh granting approval in this case was, thus, a mere mechanical exercise, accepting the draft order as it is, without any independent application of mind on his part.

It has been held in the case of *Sri Madhusudan Panigrahi* v. *ACIT Corporate* Circle-1(2) ITAT Guwahati -ITA No.136-142/Gau/2018 order dated 31.7.2019 & ITAT Cuttack -, ITA No. IT(S) A No. 44 to 46/CTK/2016 dated 27 September, 2018—The Supervisory Authority has himself admitted that because of reasons stated by him, could not apply his mind and has accorded the approval mechanically to meet the requirements of law as the requirement was merely a formality.

Fresh Assessment pursuant to order u/s 263 - Whether fresh approval u/s 153D required - Debatable

It has been held in the case of *Osho Forge Ltd.* v. *CIT* [2018] 93 taxmann. com 369/255 Taxman 375 (P&H) that AO, while making original assessment under s. 153A, having duly obtained approval under s. 153D, there was no requirement in law for obtaining fresh approval under s. 153D for making fresh assessment in compliance with remand order of CIT passed under s. 263

No Valid order under section 263 without revision of approval order passed under section 153D

It has been held in the case of Smt. Abha Bansal v. Principal CIT 208 DTR 265 (Del 'A') that order passed under section 143(3) r/w section 153B cannot be revised without revising the approval of the Jt. CIT under section 153D and the Principal CIT having not revised the approval of Jt. CIT given under section 153D, he had no jurisdiction to proceed under section 263 in the matter in issue.

It has been held in the case of *Neelachal Carbo Metalicks (P.) Ltd.* v. *Asstt. CIT* 211 DTR 76 (Ctk) that the Competent authority having himself admitted that he could not apply his mind and accorded the approval under section 153D mechanically to meet the requirements of law as the final orders were getting time-barred shortly, the approval was bad-in-law, more so as the approval was not taken after issuance of notice under section 142(1) and thus assessment order is liable to be cancelled.

It has been held in the case of *PCIT* v. *Subodh Agarwal* (2023) 450 ITR 526 (All) that Prior approval of prescribed authority in respect of each assessment year is mandatory & Sanction of prescribed authority for 38 cases granted on single day & the Assessing Officer passing draft assessment order and final assessment order on same day of approval, Approval illegal and non est-order of Tribunal was up held.

It has been held in the case of *PCIT* v. *Siddarth Gupta* [2023] 147 taxmann. com 305/450 ITR 534/ 330 CTR 295 (All)(HC) that Assessing Officer passing draft assessment order and on same day approving authority granting approval for 123 assessees is impossible for a person to apply his mind on all cases for all in a single day and thus Approval is illegal and non est.

D. TIME LIMIT FOR COMPLETION OF ASSESSMENT

(a) Section 153B - Time limit for completion of assessment under section 153A

13.21 Text of section 153B

153B. (1) Notwithstanding anything contained in section 153, the Assessing Officer shall make an order of assessment or reassessment,—

(a) in respect of each assessment year falling within six assessment years and for the relevant assessment year or years referred to in clause (b) of sub-section (1) of section 153A, within a period of twenty-one months from the end of the financial year in which the last of the authorisations for search under section 132 or for requisition under section 132A was executed;

(b) in respect of the assessment year relevant to the previous year in which search is conducted under section 132 or requisition is made under section 132A, within a period of twenty-one months from the end of the financial year in which the last of the authorisations for search under section 132 or for requisition under section 132A was executed:

Provided that in case of other person referred to in section 153C, the period of limitation for making the assessment or reassessment shall be the period as referred to in clause (a) or clause (b) of this sub-section or nine months from the end of the financial year in which books of account or documents or assets seized or requisitioned are handed over under section 153C to the Assessing Officer having jurisdiction over such other person, whichever is later:

Provided further that in the case where the last of the authorisations for search under section 132 or for requisition under section 132A was executed during the financial year commencing on the 1st day of April, 2018,—

(i) the provisions of clause (a) or clause (b) of this sub-section shall have effect, as if for the words "twenty-one months", the words "eighteen months" had been substituted;

(ii) the period of limitation for making the assessment or reassessment in case of other person referred to in section 153C, shall be the period of eighteen months from the end of the financial year in which the last of the authorisations for search under section 132 or for requisition under section 132A was executed or twelve months from the end of the financial year in which books of account or documents or assets seized or requisitioned are handed over under section 153C to the Assessing Officer having jurisdiction over such other person, whichever is later:

Provided also that in the case where the last of the authorisations for search under section 132 or for requisition under section 132A was executed during the financial year commencing on or after the 1st day of April, 2019,—

(*i*) the provisions of clause (*a*) or clause (*b*) of this sub-section shall have effect, as if for the words "twenty-one months", the words "twelve months" had been substituted;

(*ii*) the period of limitation for making the assessment or reassessment in case of other person referred to in section 153C, shall be the period of twelve months from the end of the financial year in which the last of the authorisations for search under section 132 or for requisition under section 132A was executed or twelve months from the end of the financial year in which books of account or documents or assets seized or requisitioned are handed over under section 153C to the Assessing Officer having jurisdiction over such other person, whichever is later:

Provided also that in case where the last of the authorisations for search under section 132 or for requisition under section 132A was executed and during the course of the proceedings for the assessment or reassessment of total income, a reference under sub-section (1) of section 92CA is made, the period available for making an order of assessment or reassessment shall be extended by twelve months:

Provided also that in case where during the course of the proceedings for the assessment or reassessment of total income in case of other person referred to in section 153C, a reference under sub-section (1) of section 92CA is made, the period available for making an order of assessment or reassessment in case of such other person shall be extended by twelve months:

Provided also that in a case where the last of the authorisations for search under section 132 or requisition under section 132A was executed during the financial year commencing on the 1st day of April, 2020 or in case of other person referred to in section 153C, the books of account or document or assets seized or requisitioned were handed over under section 153C to the Assessing Officer having jurisdiction over such other person during the financial year commencing on the 1st day of April, 2020, the assessment in such cases for the assessment year commencing on the 1st day of April, 2021 shall be made on or before the 30th day of September, 2022.

(2) The authorisation referred to in clause (*a*) and clause (*b*) of sub-section (1) shall be deemed to have been executed,—

(*a*) in the case of search, on the conclusion of search as recorded in the last *panchnama* drawn in relation to any person in whose case the warrant of authorisation has been issued; or (*b*) in the case of requisition under section 132A, on the actual receipt of the books of account or other documents or assets by the Authorised Officer.

(3) The provisions of this section, as they stood immediately before the commencement of the Finance Act, 2016, shall apply to and in relation to any order of assessment or reassessment made before the 1st day of June, 2016:

Provided that where a notice under section 153A or section 153C has been issued prior to the 1st day of June, 2016 and the assessment has not been completed by such date due to exclusion of time referred to in the *Explanation*, such assessment shall be completed in accordance with the provisions of this section as it stood immediately before its substitution by the Finance Act, 2016 (28 of 2016).

(4) Nothing contained in this section shall apply to any search initiated under section 132 or requisition made under section 132A on or after the 1st day of April, 2021.

Explanation.—In computing the period of limitation under this section—

(*i*) the period during which the assessment proceeding is stayed by an order or injunction of any court; or

(*ii*) the period commencing from the date on which the Assessing Officer directs the assessee to get his accounts audited under sub-section (2A) of section 142 and—

(*a*) ending with the last date on which the assessee is required to furnish a report of such audit under that sub-section; or

(*b*) where such direction is challenged before a court, ending with the date on which the order setting aside such direction is received by the Principal Commissioner or Commissioner; or

(*iii*) the period commencing from the date on which the Assessing Officer makes a reference to the Valuation Officer under sub-section (1) of section 142A and ending with the date on which the report of the Valuation Officer is received by the Assessing Officer; or

(*iv*) the time taken in re-opening the whole or any part of the proceeding or in giving an opportunity to the assessee of being re-heard under the proviso to section 129; or

(*v*) in a case where an application made before the Income-tax Settlement Commission is rejected by it or is not allowed to be proceeded with by it, the period commencing from the date on which an application is made before the Settlement Commission under section 245C and ending with the date on which the order under sub-section (1) of section 245D is received by the Principal Commissioner or Commissioner under sub-section (2) of that section; or (*vi*) the period commencing from the date on which an application is made before the Authority for Advance Rulings or before the Board for Advance Rulings] under sub-section (1) of section 245Q and ending with the date on which the order rejecting the application is received by the Principal Commissioner or Commissioner under sub-section (3) of section 245R; or

(*vii*) the period commencing from the date on which an application is made before the Authority for Advance Rulings or before the Board for Advance Rulings under sub-section (1) of section 245Q and ending with the date on which the advance ruling pronounced by it is received by the Principal Commissioner or Commissioner under sub-section (7) of section 245R; or

(*viii*) the period commencing from the date of annulment of a proceeding or order of assessment or reassessment referred to in sub-section (2) of section 153A, till the date of the receipt of the order setting aside the order of such annulment, by the Principal Commissioner or Commissioner; or

(*ix*) the period commencing from the date on which a reference or first of the references for exchange of information is made by an authority competent under an agreement referred to in section 90 or section 90A and ending with the date on which the information requested is last received by the Principal Commissioner or Commissioner or a period of one year, whichever is less; or

(*x*) the period commencing from the date on which a reference for declaration of an arrangement to be an impermissible avoidance arrangement is received by the Principal Commissioner or Commissioner under sub-section (1) of section 144BA and ending on the date on which a direction under sub-section (3) or sub-section (6) or an order under sub-section (5) of the said section is received by the Assessing Officer; or

(*xi*) the period (not exceeding one hundred and eighty days) commencing from the date on which a search is initiated under section 132 or a requisition is made under section 132A and ending on the date on which the books of account, or other documents or money or bullion or jewellery or other valuable article or thing seized under section 132 or requisitioned under section 132A, as the case may be, are handed over to the Assessing Officer having jurisdiction over the assessee, in whose case such search is initiated under section 132 or such requisition is made under section 132A, as the case may be,

shall be excluded:

Provided that where immediately after the exclusion of the aforesaid period, the period of limitation referred to in clause (*a*) or clause (*b*) of this sub-section available to the Assessing Officer for making an order of assessment or reassessment, as the case may be, is less than sixty days, such remaining period shall be extended to sixty days and the aforesaid period of limitation shall be deemed to be extended accordingly:

Provided further that where the period available to the Transfer Pricing Officer is extended to sixty days in accordance with the proviso to sub-section (3A) of section 92CA and the period of limitation available to the Assessing Officer for making an order of assessment or reassessment, as the case may be, is less than sixty days, such remaining period shall be extended to sixty days and the aforesaid period of limitation shall be deemed to be extended accordingly:

Provided also that where a proceeding before the Settlement Commission abates under section 245HA, the period of limitation available under this section to the Assessing Officer for making an order of assessment or reassessment, as the case may be, shall, after the exclusion of the period under sub-section (4) of section 245HA, be not less than one year; and where such period of limitation is less than one year, it shall be deemed to have been extended to one year:

Provided also that where the assessee exercises the option to withdraw the application under sub-section (1) of section 245M, the period of limitation available under this section to the Assessing Officer for making an order of assessment or reassessment, as the case may be, shall, after the exclusion of the period under sub-section (5) of the said section, be not less than one year; and where such period of limitation is less than one year, it shall be deemed to have been extended to one year.

13.22 Legislative history

Section 153B has been enacted to prescribe the time limit for completion of assessment under section 153A/153C as per Finance Act, 2003. Further amendments have been made by Finance Act, 2005 to Finance Act, 2012 to bring the provision in conformity with other provisions of the Act.

Provisions of section 153B regarding the time limit for passing the assessment order in search cases shall be applicable in the case of search initiated on or before 31.3.2021. By inserting sub-section (4) to section 153B by the Finance Act, 2022, it has been provided that provisions of section 153B shall not apply to any search initiated on or after 1st April, 2021. In such case, provisions of section 153 shall be applicable.

13.23 Objective

The concept of framing assessment under the Income Tax Act is governed by the principle of time barring limits so that there is finality to the proceedings upto a particular time limit. Provision under section 153B has also been incorporated to meet the above objective in case of assessment or reassessment for search cases.

13.24 Time limit for completing assessment in search cases

Section 153B provides time limit for completion of assessment under section 153A or under section 153C. Normal provisions regarding time limit for completion of assessment and reassessment are contained under section 153 of the Act. Provision of section 153B has overriding effect over the provision of section 153 since section 153B starts with non obstante clause stating —"notwithstanding anything contained in section 153............"

In case of a search, assessment or reassessment is to be made for —

    a. Six assessment years immediately preceding the year in which search is conducted.

    b. Assessment year relevant to the year in which search is conducted.

The phrase *"search is conducted"* has been discussed in detail in the context of provision of section 153A. The year in which search is conducted would be the year in which search operation is commenced.

Time limit for completion of assessment for all the above seven years i.e. preceding six years and the year of search has been prescribed as per sub-section (1) of section 153B read with second proviso which is twenty one months (twenty four months in case search is concluded before 1st April, 2004) from the end of the financial year in which the last of the authorizations for search under section 132 or for requisition under section 132A was executed.

For deciding time limit for completion of assessment, reference under section 153B is to the date on which last of the authorizations for search was executed. Sub-section (2) to section 153B further clarifies that search authorization shall be deemed to have been executed on the conclusion of search as recorded in the last Panchnama drawn in relation to any person in whose case search warrant was issued. In case of any search operation there has to be a search warrant issued and with respect to each search warrant, a panchnama is required to be drawn mentioning the date when search is finally concluded. A search is concluded when all the restraints put under section 132(3), if any, are lifted.

As per amendment brought by Finance Act, 2012, time limit for completion of assessment/reassessment under section 153A or under section 153C has been restored to be 24 months instead of 21 months from the end of the financial year in which the last of the authorizations for search under section 132 or for requisition under section 132A was executed. This amendment shall be applicable with respect to the search concluded on or after 1st April, 2010. For example, in the case of search concluded during financial year 2010-11, as per earlier provision, time limit under section 153B for completion of assessment/reassessment under section 153A relating to assessment year 2011-12 and earlier six years was 31st of Dec., 2012. This time limit has now been extended till 31st of March, 2013.

Thus, under section 153B, the original position of time limit which was existing with respect to Income Tax Search concluded prior to 1st April, 2004 has been restored and the effect of second proviso added to section 153B has been nullified.

Finance Bill, 2016 w.e.f. 01.06.2016 has again proposed to amend section 153B restoring the same position providing time limit for completion of assessment which was existing before the amendment brought by Finance Act, 2012. It would mean that w.e.f. 01.06.2016, time limit for completion of assessment/reassessment u/s 153A or u/s 153C shall be 21 months from the end of the financial year in which the last of the authorizations for search u/s 132 or requisition u/s 132A was executed. Thus, all assessments/ reassessments relating to Income Tax search held during F.Y. 2014-15 shall be time-barred as on 31.12.2016 and shall not be carried up to 31.03.2017.

However, the time-limit in the cases of assessment where reference u/s 92CA has been made i.e. assessments involving transfer pricing issue and cases have been referred to Transfer Pricing Officer, the timelimit for completion of the assessment u/s 153A/153C is thirty-six months (w.e.f. 01.06.2016 thirty-three months).

Finance Act, 2017 has substituted second and third proviso to sub-section (1) of section 153B, which reads as under :

> 'Provided further *that in the case where the last of the authorisations for search under section 132 or for requisition under section 132A was executed during the financial year commencing on the 1st day of April, 2018,—*
>
> (i) *the provisions of clause (a) or clause (b) of this sub-section shall have effect, as if for the words "twenty-one months", the words "eighteen months" had been substituted;*
>
> (ii) *the period of limitation for making the assessment or reassessment in case of other person referred to in section 153C, shall be the period of eighteen months from the end of the financial year in which the last of the authorisations for search under section 132 or for requisition under section 132A was executed or twelve months from the end of the financial year in which books of account or documents or assets seized or requisitioned are handed over under section 153C*

to the Assessing Officer having jurisdiction over such other person, whichever is later:

Provided also *that in the case where the last of the authorisations for search under section 132 or for requisition under section 132A was executed during the financial year commencing on or after the 1st day of April, 2019,—*

(i) *the provisions of clause (a) or clause (b) of this sub-section shall have effect, as if for the words "twenty-one months", the words "twelve months" had been substituted;*

(ii) *the period of limitation for making the assessment or reassessment in case of other person referred to in section 153C, shall be the period of twelve months from the end of the financial year in which the last of the authorisations for search under section 132 or for requisition under section 132A was executed or twelve months from the end of the financial year in which books of account or documents or assets seized or requisitioned are handed over under section 153C to the Assessing Officer having jurisdiction over such other person, whichever is later:*

Provided also *that in case where the last of the authorisations for search under section 132 or for requisition under section 132A was executed and during the course of the proceedings for the assessment or reassessment of total income, a reference under sub-section (1) of section 92CA is made, the period available for making an order of assessment or reassessment shall be extended by twelve months:*

Provided also *that in case where during the course of the proceedings for the assessment or reassessment of total income in case of other person referred to in section 153C, a reference under sub-section (1) of section 92CA is made, the period available for making an order of assessment or reassessment in case of such other person shall be extended by twelve months.'*

Memorandum of object appended to Finance Bill, 2017 states as under:

Since the time limit for completion of assessment under section 153 is proposed to be rationalised, the time limit for completion of assessment under section 153A is also proposed to be consequentially rationalised. It is accordingly proposed to amend sub-section (1) of the said section to provide that for search and seizure cases conducted in the financial year 2018-19, the time limit for making an assessment order under section 153A shall be reduced from existing twenty-one months to eighteen months from the end of the financial year in which the last of the authorisations for search under section 132 or for requisition under section 132A was executed. It is further proposed that for search and seizure cases conducted in the financial year 2019-20 and onwards, the said time limit shall be further reduced to twelve months from the end of the financial year in which the last of the authorizations for search under section 132 or for requisition under section 132A was executed.

It is further proposed to provide that period of limitation for making the assessment or reassessment in case of other person referred to in section

153C, shall be the period available to make assessment or reassessment in case of person on whom search is conducted or twelve months from the end of the financial year in which books of account or documents or assets seized or requisitioned are handed over under section 153C to the Assessing Officer having jurisdiction over such other persons, whichever is later.

These amendments will take effect from 1st April, 2017.

Finance Act, 2017 has also inserted a new proviso to sub-section (3) to section 153 which reads as under:

> "**Provided** *that where a notice under section 153A or section 153C has been issued prior to the 1st day of June, 2016 and the assessment has not been completed by such date due to exclusion of time referred to in the Explanation, such assessment shall be completed in accordance with the provisions of this section as it stood immediately before its substitution by the Finance Act, 2016.";*

Memorandum of object appended to Finance Bill, 2017 states as under:

It is also proposed to amend sub-section (3) of section 153B to provide that where a notice under section 153A or section 153C has been issued prior to 1st day of June, 2016 and the assessment has not been completed by such date due to exclusion of time referred to in the *Explanation*, such assessment shall be completed in accordance with the provisions of this section as it stood immediately before its substitution by the Finance Act, 2016.

This amendment will take effect retrospectively from 1st June, 2016.

Finance Act, 2017 has also inserted a new proviso to explanation to section 153 which reads as under:

In the Explanation, after the second proviso, the following proviso shall be inserted, namely:—

> "**Provided also** *that where a proceeding before the Settlement Commission abates under section 245HA, the period of limitation available under this section to the Assessing Officer for making an order of assessment or reassessment, as the case may be, shall, after the exclusion of the period under sub-section (4) of section 245HA, be not less than one year; and where such period of limitation is less than one year, it shall be deemed to have been extended to one year."*

Memorandum of object appended to Finance Bill, 2017 states as under:

It is also proposed to insert a proviso to the *Explanation* of the said section to provide that where a proceeding before the Settlement Commission abates under section 245HA, the period of limitation available under this section for assessment or reassessment shall after the exclusion of the period under sub-section (4) of section 245HA shall not be less than one year; and where such period of limitation is less than one year, it shall be deemed to have been extended to one year.

These amendments will take effect from 1st April, 2017.

In the case of *CIT* v. *Anil Minda* [2010] 8 taxmann.com 95 (Delhi), Hon'ble High Court held that in the case of block assessment order u/s 158BC, period of limitation of two years starts from the date when last panchnama is drawn in respect of any warrant of authorization, if there are more than one warrant of authorizations. It is interesting to note that the language of *Explanation 2* to section 158BE is identical to the language of sub-section (2) of section 153B.

♦ **Search and seizure - Block assessment - Limitation**

When the search was concluded on 20th Oct., 1996 itself, the subsequent proceedings in which a second restraint order under section 132(3) was passed in respect of sealed cupboard could not be considered as part of execution of search proceedings which had already concluded and, therefore the impugned block assessment made on 31st Dec., 1997 i.e. after 31st Oct., 1997, was barred by limitation and also invalid. *CIT* v. *Sandhya P. Naik* [2002] 124 Taxman 384 (Bom.)

♦ **Search and seizure - Block assessment - Limitation**

Tribunal can examine the search action to determine the period of limitation under section 158BE. It is further held that search is deemed to continue so long all material and valuable are either not seized or released but in respect of which certain prohibitory orders is clamped at the search premises and the time limit will not commence so long as the panchnama declaring conclusion of search is not wrong. It is further held that the search can be said to be continuing during the pendency of prohibitory orders and successive visits of searches which are carried out on the basis of authorization initially issued. *C. Ramaiah Reddy* v. *Asstt. CIT* [2003] 87 ITD 439 (Bang.-Trib.) (SB).

♦ **Search and seizure - Block assessment - Limitation**

Due to the operation of the non obstante clause, this exclusion of time by extending the analogy of section 153, *Expln. 1(iii)* is not possible in cases of block assessment. The wording of *Expln. 1(ii)* of section 158BE and *Expln. 1(iii)* of section 153 are also not in *pari materia*. The conclusion that one can draw on a plain reading of section 153, *Expln. 1(iii)* is that the period as fixed under section 142(2A) alone needs to be excluded and not a period of 180 days referred to in section 142(2C). *Mahakoshan Engineers & Contractors Co. (P) Ltd.* v. *Asstt. CIT* [2003] 85 ITD 267 (Nag.-Trib.).

♦ **Search and seizure - Block assessment - Limitation**

On a plain reading of *Explanation 2(a)* below section 158BE makes it clear that an authorization referred to in sub-section (1) is deemed to have been executed on conclusion of search as record in the last panchnama drawn in relation to a person in whose case warrant was issued. Therefore, the time limit for making an order under section 158BC(c) read with section 158BE(1) will start from the last panchnama. In this case, last panchnama was executed in relation to the almirah and cupboard found in the premises under search which were restraint under section 132(3) and when search was subsequently completed, the last panchnama was drawn. *Babu Lal* v. *DIT* [2005] 147 Taxman 318 (All.).

◆ **Search and seizure - Block assessment - Limitation**

Execution of search warrant is to be inferred from the date of conclusion of search recorded in the last panchnama; since no seizure was made *vide* last panchnama dated 25th April, 1996, and it was drawn after the prohibitory order under section 132(3) ceased to have effect, said panchnama was not valid and therefore, the earlier Panchnama dt. 19th Feb., 1996, whereby certain books of account and documents were seized being the last Panchnama, assessment order passed on 24th April, 1997, was barred by limitation. *DTS Rao* v. *Asstt. CIT* [2007] 106 ITD 570 (Bang.-Trib.).

◆ **Search and seizure - Block assessment - Limitation**

In the facts and circumstances of the case, last authorisation was executed on 19th June, 1998 when scrips were seized and on order under section 132(3) was passed and not on 1st Aug., 1998 when they were released and thus block assessment completed on 28th Aug., 2000 was barred by limitation under section 158BE. *Dy. CIT* v. *Adolf Patric Pinto* [2006] 100 ITD 191 (Mum.-Trib.)

It has been held in the case of *Rakesh Sarin* v. *Dy. CIT* [2011] 12 taxmann.com 319/203 Taxman 58 (Mag.) (Mad.) that panchanamas drawn on 27th and 28th March, 2003 in respect of residential and business premises of the petitioner being the last Panchanamas, the date of the same is the date of conclusion of the search for reckoning the time limit of two years for completion of block assessment and not 17th and 14th June, 2003, on which dated prohibitory orders under s. 132(3) were lifted though time period of 60 days already expired on 27th May, 2003 and, therefore, the impugned assessment order passed on 30th June, 2005, was barred by limitation.

It has been held in the case of *Skyline Builders* v. *CIT* [2019] 105 taxmann.com 207/265 Taxman 38 (Ker.) (Mag.) that question regarding limitation can be raised for first time before High Court.

It has been held in the case of *Srinidhi Karti Chidambaram* v. *Principal CIT* [2018] 92 taxmann.com 392/255 Taxman 495/404 ITR (Mad) 578 that Court cannot extend or reduce time limitation contrary to statutory provisions.

It has been held in the case of *NKG Infrastructure Ltd.* v. *Principal CIT* 171 DTR (Del 'E') 385 that in appeal before the Tribunal against order of revision, assessee can raise the issue of limitation of assessment under s. 153B for the first time.

It has been held in the case of *NKG Infrastructure Ltd.* v. *Principal CIT* 171 DTR (Del 'E') 385 that in the case of search assessment under s. 153A limitation period prescribed under s. 153B and not under s. 153 applies. Search conducted on 23rd Aug. 2012, return filed on 12th Nov., 2014 and order under s. 245D(2C) passed by Settlement Commission on 9th April. 2015, order under s. 153A ought to have been passed by 7th June, 2015 & since same was passed on 31st March, 2016 & the same was thus clearly barred by limitation.

(*i*) **Advancement of time limit for completion of assessment for the year of search by twelve months**

For the year in which search is conducted i.e. the year of search, time limit for completion of assessment has statutorily been preponed by twelve months. As per normal provision of section 153, time limit for completion of assessment is twenty one months from the end of the assessment year while under section 153B, time limit for the year of search is twenty one months from the end of the financial year in which search is concluded. For example: in case a search is conducted and concluded as on 15th March, 2011, the assessment year relating to the year of search in this case is A.Y. 2011-2012. As per normal provision of section 153, time limit for completion of assessment for assessment year 2011-2012 shall be 31st December, 2013. But when search is conducted, time limit for completion of assessment for assessment year 2011-12 shall become 31st December, 2012 as per provision of section 153B.

It appears that the advancement of time limit for completion of assessment of the year of search has been prescribed so that assessment of the year of search may be undertaken and completed along with six preceding years for which assessments are to be undertaken and completed u/s 153A so that assessing officer may be able to undertake coordinated investigation relating to the seized material found in search.

Thus there is heavy burden on assessing officer of time barring limit for completion of assessment of all the seven years simultaneously. In case of search on a group, several persons including companies, firms and individuals are covered and assessments of seven years for all the persons may run into more than hundreds of assessment orders to be passed. Infact, it is seen in practice that due to above time barring provision of section 153B, the assessing officer hardly gets any time to go through the entire seized material, electronic records and to make third party inquiries and investigation in a meaningful and effective manner.

(ii) **Date on which search is conducted and the date on which search is concluded may fall in different financial years**

In case search is commenced as on 15th March, 2011 and the same is concluded as on 30th April, 2011, the year of search in this case in which search is conducted will be A.Y. 2011-12. Assessments with respect to search will be required to be made for A.Y. 2011-12 and preceding six assessment years.

Time limit for completion of assessment in this case shall be reckoned with reference to the date of conclusion of search i.e. twenty one months from the end of financial year in which search is concluded i.e. 31st March, 2012 and in such a situation time limit under section 153B for completion of assessments for A.Y. 2011-12 and for preceding six years will become 31st December, 2013.

Thus, time limit for completion of assessment is extended by twelve months when the date of conclusion of search is crossed over and falls within subsequent financial year.

(iii) **Different time limits for different persons within the group**

Whenever a search action is taken, it is with reference to a group consisting of many persons i.e. companies, firms, individual directors, partners and other associates with in the group. Search is generally commenced at the same time with respect to all the persons but the date of conclusion of search may be different in the case of different persons within the group. Generally in practice, it has been seen that with respect to main business concern and main individual person, search remains pending due to pending restraint order(s) under section 132(3) but in case of all other persons, search is concluded on the same day or on the next day. In case date of conclusion of search in case of some persons with in the group is crossed over to the subsequent financial year, the time limit for completion of assessment may be different for different persons within the group. Time limit for completion of assessment under section 153B is to be decided with respect to each person separately and not for the group as a whole. This situation may create confusion for the assessing officer and may create hindrance in finalizing assessment in a coordinated manner. Therefore, in practice it has been observed, and to be on safer side, assessing officer adopts a cautious approach and the earliest time limit is adhered with respect to all the persons with in the group as a measure of administrative convenience.

(iv) Time limit for completion of assessment in case of the person covered under section 153C

In case of assessment to be made with respect to other person as referred under section 153C, time limit for making assessment or reassessment shall be the date as referred to above in the case of the person covered under section 153A or nine months (one year in the case of search concluded before 1st April, 2004) from the end of the financial year in which seized material belonging to such other person is handed over under section 153C to the assessing officer having jurisdiction over such other person whichever is later.

There may be situation when seized material relating to other person is handed over at the fag end or even after the last date of time limit for completion of assessment of the person searched. Therefore, sufficient time has been granted for finalizing assessment of such other person covered under section 153C.

In case assessing officer is common for both the persons, generally it has been observed in practice that time limit for completion of assessment for the person covered under section 153C is also followed by the assessing officer to be the same time limit which is applicable for person searched and covered under section 153A. Technically as per provision of section 153B, assessing officer may get extended time limit for completion of assessment of other person covered under section 153C depending upon the date on which satisfaction is recorded and constructive handing over of seized material is done from the file of person 'A' who was searched to person 'B' to whom seized material belongs and proceeding u/s 153C has been invoked. But when assessing officer is common, there is no actual physical handing over of seized material to any other assessing officer and to be on safer side, it is seen in practice, cautious approach is adopted by the assessing officer.

(v) "Service of assessment order also should be within the limitation period"

It has been held in the case of *Shanti Lal Godawat* v. *Asstt. CIT* [2009] 30 DTR 413/126 TTJ 135 (Jd.-Trib.) that assessment order having been passed on 28th Dec., 2007 but dispatched and served on 2nd Jan., 2008, beyond the period of limitation of 31st Dec., 2007, was barred by limitation and thus *non est* in law.

It has been held in the case of *A. S. Precision Machines (P) Ltd.* v. *CIT* [2017] 79 taxmann.com 421 (P&H) 161 that Order passed on 20th March 2013 was within the limitation period which expired on 31st March, 2013. There was no requirement to dispatch the order within the period of limitation itself.

It has been held in the case of *Geetarani Panda* v. *Asstt. CIT* 169 DTR (Ctk) 187 that though the impugned order of assessment is dt. 31st March, 2015, it was issued and served manually only on 8th April, 2015 on the authorized representative of the assessee and therefore, the same is barred by limitation.

It has been held in the case of *Rajan Jewellery* v. *CIT* [2019] 109 taxmann.com 104/266 Taxman 357 (Ker.) that Where, pursuant to a search, Assessing Officer passed an assessment order under section 153A on last date of limitation prescribed under section 153B and dispatched it after office hours, said order could not be vitiated on grounds of being passed after limitation period.

It has been held in the case of *Sujata Panda* v. *Asstt. CIT* 220 DTR (Ctk) 185 that as to the limitation under section 153B, in the absence of any documentary evidence on record to show that the impugned assessment order under section 153A purportedly passed on 30th Dec., 2016 which was dispatched by the Department only on 7th Jan., 2017 was in fact passed on 30th Dec., 2016 before the expiry of limitation period, the same is barred by limitation.

(vi) **Last of the Authorisation executed - Meaning thereof**

In the case of *ACIT* v. *Vijay Kumar Raichand* [ITA Nos. 6437-42/ Delhi/2012 and ITA Nos. 101-07/Delhi/2012, dated 13-2-2015] (Delhi-Trib.), A search and seizure action was conducted at the premises of the assessee on 28-2-2007 and a panchnama dated 1-3-2007 was drawn wherein cash amounting to ₹ 18 lakhs and some loose papers were seized. On 1-3-2007, a prohibitory order under section 132(3) of the Act was also passed in respect of some articles. The search was recommenced on 28-4-2007 and concluded on the same day and as per the panchnama for this date, no articles were seized and prohibitory order u/s 132(3) was revoked. Finally, the assessments for the AYs 2001-02 to 2006-07 was completed u/s 153A r.w.s 143(3) on 29-12-2009, which the assessee claimed to have been time barred in view of second proviso to section 153B(1).

Held that if on the date when such prohibitory orders are vacated, it would be relevant to see the action of the department and if no seizure is made on that date and nothing is done except lifting the prohibitory orders then the last punchnama drawn on that date would not be relevant to compute the limitation period for framing the assessment. Hence, period of limitation should have commenced from 1-3-2007 when for all practical purposes the authorization issued by the department for search in the case of the assessee was executed and subsequent panchanama drawn on 28-4-2007 could not be considered as relevant.

Since the period of limitation expired on 31-12-2008, the assessment orders passed on 31-3-2009 were held time barred. ITA Nos. 6437-42/Delhi/2012 & ITA Nos. 101-07/Delhi/2012 dt. 13-2-2015.

It has been held in the case of *K.V. Padmanabhan* v. *Asstt. CIT* [2019] 107 taxmann.com 24/265 Taxman 36 (Mag.) (Ker.) that where during search at premises of assessee, a panchnama was prepared seizing number of documents and, thereafter, a subsequent panchnama was prepared to effect seizure of material or documents which were issued with a restraint order, since subsequent panchnama was last panchnama drawn up of an effective seizure made under section 132, same would be starting point of period of limitation for purpose of section 158BE. In course of block assessment proceedings, one single authorisation can specify more than one officers and, thus, mere fact that search was conducted on separate days by two different officers though duly authorized, would not vitiate search and seizure procedure.

It has been held in the case of *Principal CIT* v. *PPC Business & Products (P.) Ltd.* [2017] 84 taxmann.com 10 (Delhi) that in search and seizure assessment under s. 153A, Search party having neither found anything new nor seized any item belonging to the searched entities during its second visit of the assessee's premises on 15th May, 2007 and only appraised the valuation reports which had been already prepared at the time of the first visit on 21st March, 2007 and released the jewellery items, the search, in fact, stood concluded on 22nd March 2007 itself when the search was closed and not on 15th May 2007 simply because another Panchnama was drawn up on that date and, therefore, the assessments under s. 153A/153C completed on 24th/31st Dec. 2009 were barred by limitation in terms of s. 153B.

It has been held in the case of *Mohd. Yasin* v. *CIT* [2017] 84 taxmann.com 292/398 ITR 33 (Raj.) where Search warrant was issued on 15th May, 1997 and search of factory premises concluded on 16th May, 1997 and restraint order was only for the purpose of seizure and no further search material was found and therefore, limitation started on 26th May, 1997 and not from last Panchnama dt. 14th Aug., 1997 and therefore assessment order passed on 16th Aug., 1999 was barred by limitation.

It has been held in the case of *CIT* v. *Ritika Ltd.* [2016] 384 ITR 434/[2017] 80 taxmann.com 255 (Cal.) that for the purpose of limitation, period is to be reckoned from date of conclusion of search & thus where restraint order was not extended and no action was taken pursuant to search after three months, Search has to be taken to have been concluded on expiry of restraint order & visit of officers to assessee's premises two years later to record conclusion of search is not material & the period of limitation to pass assessment order is not to be reckoned from such date & thus the assessment is barred by limitation.

13.25 Exclusion of time period in certain circumstances

There may be circumstances due to which assessing officer could not complete the assessment within time limit as prescribed under section 153B. Seven such circumstances have been discussed as per *Explanation* given under section 153B and it has been provided to exclude the time period consumed due to such circumstances for calculating the period available to the assessing officer for completion of assessment as provided under sub-section (1) of section 153B.

Such circumstances cover the following situations, as given in the *Explanation* to section 153B, and the corresponding period of limitation which is required to be excluded:

S.No.	Situation	Period to be excluded
1.	Stay of assessment proceedings by an order or injunction of any court	Period during which stay of assessment proceeding is effective
2.	Direction to the assessee to get accounts audited under section 142(2A)	From the date of passing order under section 142(2A) till the date on which assessee is required to furnish report of audit under that sub-section.
3.	Request of assessee for rehearing as provided under proviso to section 129	Time taken in reopening the whole or any part of the proceeding or in giving an opportunity to the assessee of being reheard.
4.	In the case of application made by assessee before the settlement commission under section 245C	The period commencing on the date of making the application to the settlement commission till the date on which the order under section 245D(1) is received by the Commissioner rejecting the application.
5.	In the case of application made by the assessee before the authority for Advance ruling under section 245Q(1)	The period commencing from the date of making the application to the authority for advance ruling till the date on which the order rejecting the application is received by the Commissioner under section 245R(3) or till the date on which the order of the authority for advance ruling pronouncing the ruling is received by the Commissioner under section 245R(7).

S.No.	Situation	Period to be excluded
6.	In the case of annulment of the proceeding or order of assessment or reassessment as referred under section 153A(2)	The period commencing from the date of annulment till the date of receipt of the order setting aside of the order of such annulment by the Commissioner.

The above situation is being explained by way of an example as follows—

In a case when search is concluded on 15th march, 2011, time limit for completion of assessment for A.Y. 2011-12 shall be 31st December, 2012. Assessee files an application with the Settlement Commission under section 245C as on 1st July, 2011 but the same is rejected by the Settlement Commission and the order of rejection is received by the Commissioner as on 25th September, 2011. The time period for completion of assessment shall be extended by two months and twenty five days after 31st December, 2012 and under such a situation now time limit available to the assessing officer for completion of assessment shall be upto 25th March, 2013.

As per proviso to the *Explanation* it is further provided that where after exclusion of the aforesaid period, time limit available to the assessing officer for making assessment is less than sixty days, such remaining period shall be extended to sixty days meaning thereby that assessing officer shall be granted a minimum period of sixty days for completion of assessment.

This kind of situation may, sometimes, arise in certain cases particularly when action for any of the circumstances mentioned in the *Explanation* is initiated during the last two months prior to the final date for completion of assessment. In the above example, if application before Settlement Commission is filed by the assessee as on 15th December, 2011 which is rejected and received by the Commissioner as on 30th April, 2012 the time period to be excluded will be only fifteen days i.e. from 15th December, 2011 to 31st December, 2011. It means when rejection order from the Settlement Commission is received by the Commission on 30th April, 2012, Department will have only fifteen days i.e. upto 15th May, 2012 for finalizing the assessment. For such kind of situation a minimum period of sixty days has been granted and in view of the proviso the time limit available to the Department for finalizing the assessment will be till 29th June, 2012.

In the case of *Tikka Brijendra Singh* v. *CIT* [2015] 127 DTR (HP) 381 (HC), assessment framed by the AO to give effect to the conclusion of the High Court that the properties owned by the assessee were his self-acquired properties and not owned by him in his HUF status was passed under section 153(3) and was not barred by limitation. Further, assessee in fact obtained an advantage from this Court by having the proceedings stayed before the Revenue Department and, therefore, at this stage is now estopped from challenging and questioning the proceedings as being time-barred.

It has been held in the case of *Rohit Kumar Gupta* v. *Principal CIT & Anr.* 181 DTR (Delhi) 185 that Search in the present case took place on 24th May, 2012 and notices to the two assessees under s. 153A were issued on 2nd June, 2014 & proceedings in the ITSC at the instance of the two assessees were pending from 26th Feb., 2015 till 4th Aug., 2016 when order under s. 245D(4) was passed by Settlement Commission rejecting the petitions. In terms of second proviso to Expln. 1 below s. 153, there was time till 16th Aug., 2017 for the AO to complete the assessments & Consequently the notices issued to the assessees on 6th April, 2017 under s. 143(2) r/w s. 153A were not invalid as the limitation period for completing the assessments had not expired by then.

It was held in the case of *Dr. Bharat Mehta* v. *Dy CIT* [2020] 423 ITR 568 (Mad.) that as to the effect of insertion of clause (*iib*) in section 132(1), time taken to obtain information stored in electronic records is to be taken into account and where Search started in January 2001 and Assessee not giving access to records stored in computer till June 2001, block assessment made in June 2003 is not barred by limitation.

(*i*) **Time limit when reference is made to transfer pricing officer under section 92CA**

Third and fourth proviso to section 153B(1) are regarding prescribing extension of time limit when reference is made to transfer pricing officer under sub-section (1) of section 92CA. As per these provisos, a further time limit of twelve months has been granted in addition to the time limit as prescribed under provision of sub-section (1) of section 153B.

Section 153B prescribes the limitation for passing assessment order in the case of search initiated on or before 31.3.2021 for the relevant years. Explanation prescribes that in computing the period of limitation under this section, certain time period as given is required to be excluded.

Clause (*xi*) has been inserted in the Explanation providing for the exclusion of time period (not exceeding 180 days) involved in the case of search commencing from the date on which search is initiated and ending on the date on which books of account and other documents or assets are handed over to the assessing officer having jurisdiction over the assessee.

13.26 Extension of time limit due to Covid-19

Due to pandemic Covid-19, time limit for passing assessment order under sections 153A & 153C has been extended from time to time during March 2020 to February 2021 by way of Ordinance, notifications issued under the Ordinance & Taxation and Other Laws (Relaxation and Amendment of Certain Provisions) Act, 2020. Such Ordinance, Act & notifications are given in the **Appendix 9**.

(b) Section 153- Time Limit for Completion of Assessment of Search Cases initiated on or after 1st April 2021

Text of section 153

Time limit for completion of assessment, reassessment and recomputation.

153. (1) No order of assessment shall be made under section 143 or section 144 at any time after the expiry of twenty-one months from the end of the assessment year in which the income was first assessable:

Provided that in respect of an order of assessment relating to the assessment year commencing on the 1st day of April, 2018, the provisions of this sub-section shall have effect, as if for the words "twenty-one months", the words "eighteen months" had been substituted:

Provided further that in respect of an order of assessment relating to the assessment year commencing on the—

(*i*) 1st day of April, 2019, the provisions of this sub-section shall have effect, as if for the words "twenty-one months", the words "twelve months" had been substituted;

(*ii*) 1st day of April, 2020, the provisions of this sub-section shall have effect, as if for the words "twenty-one months", the words "eighteen months" had been substituted:

Provided also that in respect of an order of assessment relating to the assessment year commencing on or after the 1st day of April, 2021, the provisions of this sub-section shall have effect, as if for the words "twenty-one months", the words "nine months" had been substituted.

(1A) Notwithstanding anything contained in sub-section (1), where a return under sub-section (8A) of section 139 is furnished, an order of assessment under section 143 or section 144 may be made at any time before the expiry of nine months from the end of the financial year in which such return was furnished.

(2) No order of assessment, reassessment or recomputation shall be made under section 147 after the expiry of nine months from the end of the financial year in which the notice under section 148 was served:

Provided that where the notice under section 148 is served on or after the 1st day of April, 2019, the provisions of this sub-section shall have effect, as if for the words "nine months", the words "twelve months" had been substituted.

(3) Notwithstanding anything contained in sub-sections (1) and (2), an order of fresh assessment or fresh order under section 92CA, as the case may

be, in pursuance of an order under section 254 or section 263 or section 264, setting aside or cancelling an assessment, or an order under section 92CA, as the case may be, may be made at any time before the expiry of nine months from the end of the financial year in which the order under section 254 is received by the Principal Chief Commissioner or Chief Commissioner or Principal Commissioner or Commissioner or, as the case may be, the order under section 263 or section 264 is passed by the Principal Commissioner or Commissioner:

Provided that where the order under section 254 is received by the Principal Chief Commissioner or Chief Commissioner or Principal Commissioner or Commissioner or, as the case may be, the order under section 263 or section 264 is passed by the Principal Commissioner or Commissioner on or after the 1st day of April, 2019, the provisions of this sub-section shall have effect, as if for the words "nine months", the words "twelve months" had been substituted.

(4) Notwithstanding anything contained in sub-sections (1), (2) and (3), where a reference under sub-section (1) of section 92CA is made during the course of the proceeding for the assessment or reassessment, the period available for completion of assessment or reassessment, as the case may be, under the said sub-sections (1), (2) and (3) shall be extended by twelve months.

(5) Where effect to an order under section 250 or section 254 or section 260 or section 262 or section 263 or section 264 is to be given by the Assessing Officer or the Transfer Pricing Officer, as the case may be, wholly or partly, otherwise than by making a fresh assessment or reassessment or fresh order under section 92CA, as the case may be, such effect shall be given within a period of three months from the end of the month in which order under section 250 or section 254 or section 260 or section 262 is received by the Principal Chief Commissioner or Chief Commissioner or Principal Commissioner or Commissioner, as the case may be, the order under section 263 or section 264 is passed by the Principal Commissioner or Commissioner:

Provided that where it is not possible for the Assessing Officer or the Transfer Pricing Officer, as the case may be, to give effect to such order within the aforesaid period, for reasons beyond his control, the Principal Commissioner or Commissioner on receipt of such request in writing from the Assessing Officer or the Transfer Pricing Officer, as the case may be, if satisfied, may allow an additional period of six months to give effect to the order:

Provided further that where an order under section 250 or section 254 or section 260 or section 262 or section 263 or section 264 requires verification of any issue by way of submission of any document by the assessee or any other person or where an opportunity of being heard is to be provided to the assessee, the order giving effect to the said order under section 250 or section 254 or section 260 or section 262 or section 263 or section 264 shall be made within the time specified in sub-section (3).

(5A) Where the Transfer Pricing Officer gives effect to an order or direction under section 263 by an order under section 92CA and forwards such order to the Assessing Officer, the Assessing Officer shall proceed to modify the order of assessment or reassessment or recomputation, in conformity with such order of the Transfer Pricing Officer, within two months from the end of the month in which such order of the Transfer Pricing Officer is received by him.

(6) Nothing contained in sub-sections (1) and (2) shall apply to the following classes of assessments, reassessments and recomputation which may, subject to the provisions of sub-sections (3), (5) and (5A), be completed—

   (*i*) where the assessment, reassessment or recomputation is made on the assessee or any person in consequence of or to give effect to any finding or direction contained in an order under section 250, section 254, section 260, section 262, section 263, or section 264 or in an order of any court in a proceeding otherwise than by way of appeal or reference under this Act, on or before the expiry of twelve months from the end of the month in which such order is received or passed by the Principal Commissioner or Commissioner, as the case may be; or

   (*ii*) where, in the case of a firm, an assessment is made on a partner of the firm in consequence of an assessment made on the firm under section 147, on or before the expiry of twelve months from the end of the month in which the assessment order in the case of the firm is passed.

(7) Where effect to any order, finding or direction referred to in sub-section (5) or sub-section (6) is to be given by the Assessing Officer, within the time specified in the said sub-sections, and such order has been received or passed, as the case may be, by the income-tax authority specified therein before the 1st day of June, 2016, the Assessing Officer shall give effect to such order, finding or direction, or assess, reassess or recompute the income of the assessee, on or before the 31st day of March, 2017.

(8) Notwithstanding anything contained in the foregoing provisions of this section, sub-section (2) of section 153A or sub-section (1) of section 153B, the order of assessment or reassessment, relating to any assessment year, which stands revived under sub-section (2) of section 153A, shall be made within a period of one year from the end of the month of such revival or within the period specified in this section or sub-section (1) of section 153B, whichever is later.

(9) The provisions of this section as they stood immediately before the commencement of the Finance Act, 2016, shall apply to and in relation to

any order of assessment, reassessment or recomputation made before the 1st day of June, 2016:

Provided that where a notice under sub-section (1) of section 142 or sub-section (2) of section 143 or section 148 has been issued prior to the 1st day of June, 2016 and the assessment or reassessment has not been completed by such date due to exclusion of time referred to in *Explanation 1*, such assessment or reassessment shall be completed in accordance with the provisions of this section as it stood immediately before its substitution by the Finance Act, 2016 (28 of 2016).

Explanation 1.—For the purposes of this section, in computing the period of limitation—

(*i*) the time taken in reopening the whole or any part of the proceeding or in giving an opportunity to the assessee to be re-heard under the proviso to section 129; or

(*ii*) the period during which the assessment proceeding is stayed by an order or injunction of any court; or

(*iii*) the period commencing from the date on which the Assessing Officer intimates the Central Government or the prescribed authority, the contravention of the provisions of clause (*21*) or clause (*22B*) or clause (*23A*) or clause (*23B*), under clause (i) of the first proviso to sub-section (3) of section 143 and ending with the date on which the copy of the order withdrawing the approval or rescinding the notification, as the case may be, under those clauses is received by the Assessing Officer; or

(*iv*) the period commencing from the date on which the Assessing Officer directs the assessee to get his accounts audited under sub-section (2A) of section 142 and—

  (*a*) ending with the last date on which the assessee is required to furnish a report of such audit under that sub-section; or

  (*b*) where such direction is challenged before a court, ending with the date on which the order setting aside such direction is received by the Principal Commissioner or Commissioner; or

(*v*) the period commencing from the date on which the Assessing Officer makes a reference to the Valuation Officer under sub-section (1) of section 142A and ending with the date on which the report of the Valuation Officer is received by the Assessing Officer; or

(*vi*) the period (not exceeding sixty days) commencing from the date on which the Assessing Officer received the declaration under sub-section (1) of section 158A and ending with the date on which the order under sub-section (3) of that section is made by him; or (*vii*) in a case where an application made before the Income-tax Settlement Commission is rejected by it or is not allowed to be proceeded with by it, the period commencing from the date on which an application is made before the Settlement Commission under section 245C and ending with the date on which the order under sub-section (1) of section 245D is received by the Principal Commissioner or Commissioner under sub-section (2) of that section; or

(*viii*) the period commencing from the date on which an application is made before the Authority for Advance Rulings or before the Board for Advance Rulings under sub-section (1) of section 245Q and ending with the date on which the order rejecting the application is received by the Principal Commissioner or Commissioner under sub-section (3) of section 245R; or

(*ix*) the period commencing from the date on which an application is made before the Authority for Advance Rulings or before the Board for Advance Rulings under sub-section (1) of section 245Q and ending with the date on which the advance ruling pronounced by it is received by the Principal Commissioner or Commissioner under sub-section (7) of section 245R; or

(*x*) the period commencing from the date on which a reference or first of the references for exchange of information is made by an authority competent under an agreement referred to in section 90 or section 90A and ending with the date on which the information requested is last received by the Principal Commissioner or Commissioner or a period of one year, whichever is less; or

(*xi*) the period commencing from the date on which a reference for declaration of an arrangement to be an impermissible avoidance arrangement is received by the Principal Commissioner or Commissioner under sub-section (1) of section 144BA and ending on the date on which a direction under sub-section (3) or sub-section (6) or an order under sub-section (5) of the said section is received by the Assessing Officer; or

(*xii*) the period (not exceeding one hundred and eighty days) commencing from the date on which a search is initiated under section 132 or a requisition is made under section 132A and ending on the date on which the books of account or other documents, or any money, bullion, jewellery or other valuable article or thing seized under section 132 or requisitioned under section 132A, as the case may be, are handed over to the Assessing Officer having jurisdiction over the assessee,—

(*a*) in whose case such search is initiated under section 132 or such requisition is made under section 132A; or (*b*) to whom any money, bullion, jewellery or other valuable article or thing seized or requisitioned belongs to; or

(*c*) to whom any books of account or documents seized or requisitioned pertains or pertain to, or any information contained therein, relates to; or

(*xiii*) the period commencing from the date on which the Assessing Officer makes a reference to the Principal Commissioner or Commissioner under the second proviso to sub-section (3) of section 143 and ending with the date on which the copy of the order under clause (*ii*) or clause (*iii*) of the fifteenth proviso to clause (*23C*) of section 10 or clause (*ii*) or clause (*iii*) of sub-section (4) of section 12AB, as the case may be, is received by the Assessing Officer,

shall be excluded:

Provided that where immediately after the exclusion of the aforesaid period, the period of limitation referred to in sub-sections (1), (2), (3) and sub-section (8) available to the Assessing Officer for making an order of assessment, reassessment or recomputation, as the case may be, is less than sixty days, such remaining period shall be extended to sixty days and the aforesaid period of limitation shall be deemed to be extended accordingly:

Provided further that where the period available to the Transfer Pricing Officer is extended to sixty days in accordance with the proviso to sub-section (3A) of section 92CA and the period of limitation available to the Assessing Officer for making an order of assessment, reassessment or recomputation, as the case may be, is less than sixty days, such remaining period shall be extended to sixty days and the aforesaid period of limitation shall be deemed to be extended accordingly:

Provided also that where a proceeding before the Settlement Commission abates under section 245HA, the period of limitation available under this section to the Assessing Officer for making an order of assessment, reassessment or recomputation, as the case may be, shall, after the exclusion of the period under sub-section (4) of section 245HA, be not less than one year; and where such period of limitation is less than one year, it shall be deemed to have been extended to one year; and for the purposes of determining the period of limitation under sections 149, 154, 155 and 158BE and for the purposes of payment of interest under section 244A, this proviso shall also apply accordingly:

Provided also that where the assessee exercises the option to withdraw the application under sub-section (1) of section 245M, the period of limitation available under this section to the Assessing Officer for making an order of assessment, reassessment or recomputation, as the case may be, shall, after the exclusion of the period under sub-section (5) of the said section, be not less than one year; and where such period of limitation is less than one year, it shall be deemed to have been extended to one year:

Provided also that for the purposes of determining the period of limitation under sections 149, 154 and 155, and for the purposes of payment of interest under section 244A, the provisions of the fourth proviso shall apply accordingly.

Explanation 2.—For the purposes of this section, where, by an order referred to in clause (*i*) of sub-section (6),—

(a) any income is excluded from the total income of the assessee for an assessment year, then, an assessment of such income for another assessment year shall, for the purposes of section 150 and this section, be deemed to be one made in consequence of or to give effect to any finding or direction contained in the said order; or

(b) any income is excluded from the total income of one person and held to be the income of another person, then, an assessment of such income on such other person shall, for the purposes of section 150 and this section, be deemed to be one made in consequence of or to give effect to any finding or direction contained in the said order, if such other person was given an opportunity of being heard before the said order was passed.

Background

In the case of assessment for search cases under section 153A, time limit for completion of assessment was prescribed under section 153B. However, In case of search initiated or after 1st April 2021 the assessment or reassessment of search cases is required to be made under sections 147 to 151A. The time limit for completion of assessment under section 147 etc. has been prescribed under section 153 and hence provisions of section 153B would not be applicable in respect of search initiated on or after 1st April 2021.

Time limit for completion of assessment or reassessment to be undertaken as a consequence of search would also be governed by section 153.

Amendment made by the Finance Act, 2022

Section 153 prescribes the limitation for passing assessment order in the case of search for the relevant years. Explanation prescribes that in computing the period of limitation under this section, certain time period as given is required to be excluded.

Clause (*xii*) has been inserted in the Explanation providing for the exclusion of time period (not exceeding 180 days) involved in the case of search commencing from the date on which search is initiated and ending on the date on which books of account and other documents or assets are handed over to the assessing officer having jurisdiction over the assessee.

Amendment made by the Finance Act, 2023

Finance Act, 2023 has made several amendments in section 153 providing *inter alia,* time barring limit for completion of assessment or reassessment. The amendments as given in the Finance Bill, 2023 are as under:

(Clause 72 of the Finance Bill, 2023 to be reproduced here)

Section 153 as amended by the Finance Act, 2023 stands as under:

(To reproduce section 153 as amended by the Finance Act, 2023)

Significant Amendments by the Finance Act, 2023 in section 153:

(*i*) **Time limit for completion of assessment extended from 9 months to 12 months for assessment year commencing on or after 1st April, 2022 i.e. AY 2022-23 and onwards**

Time limit for completion of assessment was made earlier by the Finance Act, 2022 as 9 months relating to the assessment year commencing on or after 1st April, 2021. Thus, assessment was required to be completed upto 31st December, after the end of the assessment year. It was felt that such time was not sufficient and therefore, amendment has been made by Finance Act, 2023 making the time limit for completion of assessment up to 12 months from the end of the relevant assessment year. After the above amendment, the time limit for completion of assessment shall be 31st March following the relevant assessment year. Such time limit shall be in alignment with the time limit for completion of reassessment under section 147 which is also 12 months from the end of the financial year in which notice under section 148 is served.

(*ii*) **Time limit for completion of pending assessment extended where search has taken place**

There may be cases where assessment or reassessment of a person is pending and limitation period for passing assessment or reassessment is approaching and in the meantime, search takes place in his case. In such cases, time limit for completion of on-going pending assessment or reassessment has been extended by a further period of 12 months so as to enable the Assessing Officer to receive and consider the seized material and evidences etc. which may be relevant to such pending assessment etc.

Such time limit has been similarly extended even in a case where search may not have taken place in case of a person and his assessment is pending and during search of some other person, seized material or asset belonging or pertaining or relating to such person are found.

14

HANDLING OF ASSESSMENT
IN SEARCH CASES

14.1 Certain steps/techniques which may be useful to the assessee during assessment of search cases

(i) Obtaining copies of seized materials

Assessee has legal right to obtain photocopies of all the seized material i.e. books of account, documents, loose papers, files, diaries, etc. In all search cases before replying to the questionnaire of the assessing officer on various aspects, assessee should always obtain photocopies of all the seized materials tagged and numbered in the same manner as with the department. Copies of the seized material should rather be obtained before filing return of income under section 153A. Assessee can plan his affairs and reply to the questions of the assessing officer relating to seized material in proper and effective manner only when copy of the seized material is available with him in organized and systematic manner.

It is the legal right of the person from whose custody any books of account or other documents are seized as provided under section 132(9) to make copies thereof or take extracts therefrom as has been held in number of cases such as *CIT* v. *Oriental Rubber Works* [1983] 15 Taxman 51 (SC), *Jorwar Singh Baid* v. *Asstt. CIT* [1990] 52 Taxman 276 (Cal.). In the case of *Dhaniram Gupta* v. *Union of India* [1973] 89 ITR 281, Calcutta High Court had gone to the extent to hold that any assessment made after denying the person opportunity of inspection or to make copies of documents, etc. seized from him, cannot be sustained.

(ii) Ledgerisation of transactions relating to individuals

Generally, it has been observed that in case of individual case where no business activity is undertaken, assessee does not maintain day

676

to day personal books of account and the flow of funds and its utilization is not readily available.

In the case of search assessment of an individual-assessee, there may be requirement to explain the source of investment made in different assets, household expenses incurred, deposits in the bank account, expenses incurred for functions, foreign travelling and transactions emanating from the seized documents etc. To explain all such issues properly, it is advisable to ledgerize all the bank and cash transactions date wise. It will give clarity regarding flow of funds from different sources and utilization of the same for different purposes. The queries raised by the assessing officer may be explained by the assessee in a proper and effective manner.

(iii) **To avoid duplicate additions - Apply principle of sources of income vs. application in assets**

In the case of search, there are numerous documents/evidences found by the Department. Some of the documents/papers may suggest undisclosed income earned by the assessee which may be taxed under section 28 or under section 68 or some other provision of the Act. At the same time, there may be certain evidences/documents which may suggest investment in unexplained assets or expenses which may be added by the assessing officer in the hands of the assessee under sections 69, 69A, 69C or some other provision of the Act. For example: there may be documents found suggesting sales transaction not recorded in the books resulting in undisclosed income and there may be unaccounted cash found from the possession of the person searched. Assessing officer may be tempted to make addition of both the transactions separately for want of proper explanation co-relating both the kind of evidences from the assessee.

An exercise should be made by the assessee to segregate documents/ evidences suggesting undisclosed income and the documents/evidences suggesting unexplained expenditure or investment in assets. By making a proper fund flow chart, evidences of both the nature *viz.* income and investment/expenditure, may be explained by single source of undisclosed income. In the above example, assessee can explain that cash found from his possession is the cash which has been earned and accumulated out of unrecorded sales transactions. Similarly, investment made in jewellery, stock, immovable properties etc. or expenses incurred on functions, foreign travelling, household expenses etc. may be correlated with the documents found during search suggesting generation of undisclosed income. In this manner, one can make out a case so as to avoid duplicate additions:

◆ **Whether undisclosed income declared in the block return can be used for explaining other proposed addition or undisclosed investment**

Undisclosed income declared by the assessee in the return of block period on the basis of seized material is available to the assessee for the purpose of explaining other additions/investments and the addition on account of undisclosed purchases being less than the said amount, no separate addition is to be made. *Eagle Seeds & Biotech Ltd.* v. *Asstt. CIT* [2006] 100 ITD 301 (Indore - Trib.)

◆ **No separate addition on account of GP after surrender in stock**

Where the assessee surrendered an amount of ₹ 3,70,000 being difference in valuation of stock, no separate addition of ₹ 49,105 was called for on account of low G.P. because the lighter amount merged with the amount surrendered. *Ram Lubhaya* v. *Asstt. CIT* [1995] 52 TTJ (Delhi) 21

◆ **Assessing Officer not justified in adding cash credit as well as the assets acquired out of the money borrowed by the assessee and surrendered as income.**

In this case the Tribunal found that during the course of search some pieces of paper were found containing the names and amounts. Apprehending that the creditors may not come forward to confirm the loans, the amounts were surrendered. The revenue accepted the surrender and also added the cost of assets acquired out of investment of such amounts.

Tribunal made interesting observations and said that the revenue should not act like Sherlock Holmes. It further observed that the concept of 'Head I win and tail you lose' is alien to the principles of justice. *Kantilal & Bros.* v. *Asstt. CIT* [1995] 52 ITD 412 (Pune - Trib.).

It has been held in the case of *Vivek Kumar Kathotia* v. *Dy. CIT* [2013] 32 taxmann.com 331/142 ITD 394 (Kol. - Trib.) in the context of section 153A that since total undisclosed income arising from the seized documents have been already offered for taxation by assessee and cash found in the course of search stood explained from entries recorded in the seized documents, no separate addition can be made in respect of cash found.

(iv) **Principle of peak balance**

There may be evidences found during search suggesting in flow and out flow of funds on different occasions. In such a situation, exercise should be done to workout peak balance by preparing date wise cash flow chart. Assessee can make out his case that it is the same amount which is rolling over and only the addition of the peak balance can be sustained. In some of the following cases, the principle of peak balance has been accepted and approved by the Courts:-

♦ Tribunal deleting addition by way of undisclosed income on the ground that loans advanced by assessee were more than covered by withdrawals in the accounts of the depositors, was justified. No referable question of law arose. *Addl. CIT* v. *Chetan Dass* [1975] 99 ITR 46 (Delhi).

♦ Cash credit found in ten different names in assessee's books. Tribunal found that these cash credits really represented income from undisclosed sources taxed in earlier years and did not represent income earned in relevant accounting year. Addition, therefore, deleted. *Addl. CIT* v. *Dharamdas Agarwal* [1983] 15 Taxman 485 (MP).

♦ It is well settled that where there is an unexplained credit, it is open to the ITO to hold that it is the income of the assessee and no further burden lies on the ITO to show that income is from any particular source. It is for the assessee to prove that, even if the cash credit represents income, it is the income from a source which has already been taxed. *Addl. CIT* v. *Mohan Engineering Co.* [1984] 17 Taxman 6 (Pat.)

♦ Assessee having no other sources of income Tribunal was justified in holding that the additions in respect of extra profit in each of the years under appeal would be nil in the years in which the addition on the basis of the difference in the peak unaccounted money used from year to year exceeds the extra profit and that where the extra profit addition is more than the addition on account of the difference in peak credits, the bigger of the two would remain as the addition. *CIT* v. *Neemar Ram Badlu Ram* [1980] 122 ITR 68 (All.)

In the case of *Sunil Gupta* v. *Dy. CIT* [2015] 174 TTJ 1 (Chd.-Trib.) (UO), it has been held that Revenue authorities having found no evidence or material during the course of search indicating that the assessee has made any undisclosed investment outside his known sources in any forward trading business and the Revenue having not challenged the findings of the CIT(A) that the assessee was not at all indulging in forward trading as claimed by him, the theory of peak credit is not applicable to the facts of the case and, therefore, the impugned additions made by the AO on account of peak undisclosed investment are wholly unjustified.

♦ **Working of Peak Principles regarding**

So far as the working of the peak is concerned, it is again for the assessee to prove that the withdrawals were not utilized for other expenses or investments and were available for making subsequent deposits in the said bank accounts. The benefit of peak can be given only when the recycling of funds is proved, as contended by the Departmental Representative. There is merit in the contention of the counsel for the assessee that the peak of the earlier year should be reduced from the peak of the subsequent year. *Surendra M. Khandhar* v. *Asstt. CIT* [2001] 76 ITD 121 (Mum. - Trib.)

♦ **Adjustment of Peak Cash Deficit**

The assessee's contention that the amount of ₹ 4 Lakhs and odd already considered in earlier assessments should be set-off against the deficit in cash balance as on 31-3-1992 was rejected on the ground that whereas the deficit was worked out as on 1-8-1991, the excess was on 31-3-1992 and that the same could not be available for set-off. *Essem Intra - Port Services (P.) Ltd.* v. *Asstt. CIT* [2000] 72 ITD 228 (Hyd. - Trib.)

(*v*) **Use of affidavits/confirmations**

Assessee should make extensive use of placing affidavits/confirmations of self & from third parties in appropriate situations so as to make assertion regarding his point. In the absence of direct evidence available, such evidence becomes strong evidence in favour of the assessee. Affidavit is a significant evidence to prove or disprove a fact which cannot be proved or disproved by documentary evidence. Courts give lot of weightage to an affidavit filed unless the same is found incorrect by the assessing officer in cross examination. Following decisions in this regard are worth noting—

♦ The Tribunal had not indicated upon what material it held that ₹ 30,000 should be treated as secret profit or profits from undisclosed sources and the order passed by it was bad. The appellants had furnished a reasonable explanation for the possession of the high denomination notes of the face value of ₹ 61,000 and affidavits before AAC to the effect that a sum of ₹ 43,000 were paid in 1000 rupee notes during the relevant period, there was no justification for having accepted it in part and discarded it in relation to a sum of ₹ 30,000. *Mehta Parikh & Co.* v. *CIT* [1956] 30 ITR 181 (SC).

♦ Mere filing of confirmatory letters or particulars does not discharge the onus that lies on the assessee under section 68;

Tribunal was justified in remitting the matter for fresh enquiry as the assessee merely filed an affidavit of the alleged creditor confirming that she had deposited the amount with the assessee and the same was repaid to her and giving other details, but assessee failed to produce her before the assessing authority. *Rajshree Synthetics (P.) Ltd.* v. *CIT* [2003] 131 Taxman 391 (Raj.).

(*vi*) Submit complete and voluminous details

In the case of search, assessments/reassessments of various individuals and entities relating to seven years are undertaken together by the assessing officer. Assessing officer gets very limited time for completing assessment/reassessment of all the cases relating to various individuals and business entities covered within a group. Assessment in search cases under section 153A are undertaken like normal assessment and, *inter alia*, details of all the incomes and expenses, assets and liabilities, incoming and outgoing in the bank accounts, etc. are required to be submitted by the assessee. Assessee is required and should file all such details which may be quite voluminous. Assessee should not refrain from filing all the details for the reason that the details may be voluminous and may run into thousand of pages. It may be in the interest of the assessee since on one hand he would be discharging his onus, and on the other hand in case of additions made in assessment, these very details would prove handy to argue against the additions.

(*vii*) Request for cross examination

In case affidavit or statement of third party is referred as evidence by the assessing officer in making his assertion against the assessee, he should demand and obtain copy of such statement/affidavit. Assessee should controvert the facts mentioned in such statement/affidavit by putting the actual facts to his favour, reading relevant evidences or submitting counter affidavit if required. Further assessee may request for cross examination of the person who has given statement/affidavit against him. The evidentiary value of such statement/affidavit is reduced in case cross examination is not permitted by the assessing officer.

(*viii*) Intangible additions

Intangible additions are the additions made in general without correlating with any corresponding liability or asset in the books of account of the assessee e.g., trading addition made for fall in G.P. rate or *ad hoc* disallowances out of expenses on account of non-verification. Assessee may make out a case to explain cash credits or deposits in the bank as having been made by utilizing such intangible additions.

However, any such explanation should be made keeping in view penalty provisions as given under *Explanation 2* to section 271(1)(*c*). The under noted decisions may be referred in this connection-

The income, described as intangible is as much a part of real income as that disclosed by the account books. It has the same concrete existence. It could be available to the assessee as the book profits could be.

CIT v. *Jawanmal Gemaji Gandhi* [1983] 15 Taxman 487 (Bom.)

Anantharam Veerasinghaiah & Co. v. *CIT* [1980] 123 ITR 457 (SC)

If the tribunal inferred that there was a connection between the profits withheld from the books of account and the unexplained cash credit entries found in the books, and therefore held that the former covered the latter, the court will be reluctant to disturb the finding. *CIT* v. *S. Nelliappan* [1967] 66 ITR 722 (SC).

(*viiia*) Applicability of higher tax rate under section 115BBE

As per the amendment made by the Taxation Laws (Second) Amendment Act, 2016 with effect from 1.4.2017 *viz.* from A.Y. 2017-18, any income from undisclosed source referred to in sections 68, 69, 69A to 69D sufferes higher tax rate under section 115BBE which is as high as 60% of such income plus surcharge @ 25% of such tax rate. While making declaration of undisclosed income, it should be kept in mind that if such declared income is falling within the ambit of any of these sections, such income would attract higher tax rate under section 115BBE. On the other hand, if such income falls under specific head of income, rate of tax in that situation would be normal tax rate. Therefore, declaration of undisclosed income should be made by specifying & substantiating the source of such income falling under specific head of income.

(*ix*) In case of general declaration of undisclosed income, benefit of telescoping

Sometimes declaration of undisclosed income is made by the assessee in the course of search being general in nature without correlating with some specific item. Such declaration is made to cover any kind of undisclosed income which may be found and detected during assessment proceedings out of seized material. Though such manner of declaration is not proper yet in practice declaration is made in the above manner particularly under the circumstances when assessee is compelled to make declaration of undisclosed income without correlating with specific item at the time of search.

During assessment proceedings when additions are made for specific items of undisclosed income emanating from the seized material, assessee can make out a case for telescoping such additions against the general declaration of undisclosed income earlier made so as to avoid duplicate additions.

- ◆ In addition to the bogus cash credit, there is an addition towards the suppression of profit. In such a case as this when there are two additions it is always open to the assessee to explain that the suppressed profits during the year has been brought in as cash credits and, therefore, one has to be telescoped into the other and there can be only one addition. The view taken by the Tribunal that the additions towards the suppressed book profits should be telescoped with the additions towards the cash credit is, therefore, legally tenable. *CIT* v. *K.S.M. Guruswamy Nadar & Sons* [1984] 19 Taxman 533 (Mad.)

(x) Direction by Joint Commissioner under section 144A

Section 144A of the Income Tax Act provides that a Joint Commissioner may on his own motion or on his reference being made to him by the assessing officer or on the application of an assessee, call for and examine the record of any proceeding in which an assessment is pending and if he considers that having regard to the nature of the case or the amount involved or for any other reason, it is necessary or expedient so to do, he may issue such directions as he thinks fit for the guidance of the assessing officer to enable him to complete the assessment and such directions shall be binding on the assessing officer.

Assessee can make use of the above provision under the circumstances when it is felt that assessing officer is acting objectively and thus intervention of the higher authority is desirable. Though, assessment order under section 153A cannot be passed without the approval of Joint Commissioner as provided under section 153D, still provision of section 144A can be invoked and made use of by the assessee in case it is so deemed fit.

(xi) Approaching to Settlement Commission

As per amendment made by the Finance Act, 2010, assessee can approach the Settlement Commission for settlement of search cases at any stage prior to finalization of assessment by the assessing officer. During the pendency of assessment proceedings, assessee has option to avail such opportunity. Keeping in view the tone and tenor of assessment proceedings being undertaken by the assessing officer, assessee can evaluate the situation and take decision as to whether it would be in his interest to make application to the Settlement Commission, in case he is able to fulfil the conditions as required for making application to Settlement Commission. A detailed discussion regarding application to Settlement Commission is given under separate chapter.

However, Finance Act, 2021 has abolished the institution of Settlement Commission and with effect from 1st February, 2021 no new application may be filed for settlement.

14.2 Tools available with Assessing Officer during assessment of search cases

(i) Centralization of search cases

As per Instruction No. 8 dated 14th August 2002 issued by Central Board of Direct Taxes, search cases are normally centralized in Central Circle so as to undertake cases of all the persons or business entities relating to a particular group at one place. It facilitates coordinated investigation relating to all the persons/business entities by the same officer.

◆ **Jurisdiction of Officer u/s 120 to decide search cases of assessment**

A.C. Kottayam was notified as officer having exclusive jurisdiction to make assessment of search cases for certain areas. File of assessee was shifted to officer after search. Held, that this was not a case of transfer of file as visualized under section 127. There was no need to give hearing to assessee. Block assessment was made by A.C. Kottyam held valid. *Alleppey Financial Enterprises* v. *CIT* [2009] 176 Taxman 1 (Ker.)

◆ **Transfer under section 127 of Block Assessment - Valid - Section 158BH**

Supreme Court in *K.P. Mohammed Salim* v. *CIT* [2008] 169 Taxman 465 (SC) has affirmed *K.V. Kader Haji* v. *CIT* [2004] 140 Taxman 527 (Ker.) [Para 12.10.2] and has held:

(a) The power of transfer in effect provides for a machinery provision. It must be given its full effect. It must be construed in a manner so as to make it workable. Even section 127 of the Act is a machinery provision.

(b) Section 158BH categorically states that all other provisions of the Act shall apply to assessment made under this Chapter. Section 127 would therefore *mutatis mutandis* apply to Chapter XIV-B.

(c) The word 'any' must be read in the context of statute and for the said purposive construction for the said propose may be resorted to. Thus in the context of a statute the word 'any' may be read as all in the context of Income-tax Act for which the power of transfer has been conferred upon the authorities specified under section 127.

(d) Power of transfer u/s 127 can also exercised in respect of block assessments.

(ii) Availability of appraisal report

In all the search cases an appraisal report is prepared by the authorized officer heading the search highlighting the areas of concealed income, analyzing and correlating the facts and seized documents, recording the statement of the person searched and other related persons, explaining the nature and contents of all the seized documents and papers, etc. Appraisal report is an internal document which is sent to the assessing officer and it gives suggestion regarding further course of investigation to be carried out by the assessing officer before framing assessment. The assessing officer is largely guided by the finding of the authorized officer containing the appraisal report, though it is not binding on him. As per departmental guidelines issued, any deviation from assessing concealed income contrary to the finding given in the appraisal report has to be discussed with the authorities of the investigation wing before taking a final decision in this regard.

(iii) Summons under section 131

Power under section 131 of the Income Tax Act is similar with that of a civil court while trying a suit under civil procedure code. Such power is extensively used by the assessing officer particularly in search cases for gathering evidences, cross verification of documents and for recording statement of the assessee or third parties. Recording of statement on oath is a tool which is feared most by the assessee and other parties and assessing officers make use of it so as to bring true facts on record.

(iv) Calling for information under section 133(6)

Assessing officer may require any person to furnish information in relation to such points or matters which may be useful or relevant to the assessment proceedings. Such power is extensively used in search cases by the assessing officer for making third party enquiries, for verification of statement of account of the debtors and creditors and for the purpose of confirmation of the financial transaction with other business constituents.

(v) Availability of presumption under section 292C

With respect to seized books of account, documents or assets, assessing officer is having presumption as provided under section

292C that such books of account, documents or assets belong to the person searched and the contents thereof are true. Thus, the initial burden of proving the nature and contents of the books of account and documents rests with the assessee. The earlier controversy as to whether such presumption as contained under section 132(4A) also, is available to the assessing officer during assessment proceedings has been resolved by inserting section 292C by the Finance Act, 2007 with retrospective effect from 1st October 1975.

(*vi*) Reference to valuation officer

As per section 142A, assessing officer has power to make reference to valuation officer for estimating value of any investment in bullion, jewellery or other valuable article including immovable property. In the case of search normally jewellery is found which is got valued by the departmental valuer generally in the course of search before taking the decision of seizure. Immovable properties are also referred by the assessing officer during assessment proceedings for estimating value of investment made by the assessee which may not be fully reflected or disclosed by him.

♦ **Block Assessment - Reference to Departmental Valuer**

Departmental valuer being a civil engineer is an expert in the field of civil construction and, therefore, his opinion is admissible for valuation of properties; if there is significant undervaluation that would be material/evidence of understatement of consideration also in the event of the undervaluation not being satisfactorily explained by the assessee. *Hanemp Properties (P.) Ltd.* v. *Asstt. CIT* [2006] 101 ITD 19 (Delhi - Trib.)

♦ **DVO's report for wealth-tax purposes not relevant**

A report that the DVO prepared for wealth-tax purposes could have hardly been beneficially used for finding out any unexplained investment by the assessee. Addition rightly deleted. *ITO* v. *Hotel Hilltop* [1995] 83 Taxman 355 (Jp. - Trib.)(Mag.)

(*vii*) Protective and Substantive Assessment

In the case of assessment of search cases, assessing officers make use of the method of making protective and substantive assessment. There may be uncertainty regarding the actual owner to whom or as to the relevant year to which undisclosed income based upon the documents or papers found during search can be said to relate. To be on the safe side, assessing officer resorts to the technique of making substantive and protective assessments in the hands of two different persons or for two different years. Ultimately only one addition has to survive. In case substantive addition is confirmed, protective addition is liable to be deleted. On the other hand, if substantive addition is deleted, protective addition takes the character of substantive addition. Such kind of situation may arise in some of the following circumstances—

(*i*) In case relevant year of taxability of income is not clear, addition can be made in two different years on substantive and protective basis.

(*ii*) In case some asset is found held in "benami" name, addition can be made in the hands of benamidar and the real owner who has actually invested in the asset on protective & substantive basis. The burden of proof is however on the Department as to whether a transaction is benami, by leading cogent and reliable evidence.

(*iii*) In the case of share capital, addition can be made in the hands of recipient company as well as in the hands of the investor(s) on protective and substantive basis.

(*iv*) In case of uncertainty as to income/investment/expenditure relating to which person(s), addition can be made in the hands of two different persons on protective and substantive basis.

(*v*) There may be a situation when apparent transaction is something else but real beneficiary is some other person. It may so happen in the case of round trip transactions, raising of bogus share capital or cash credits etc.

It has been held in the case of *Trilok Singh Dhillon* v. *CIT* [2012] 20 taxmann.com 806 (Chhattisgarh) that protective assessment is permissible under section 153C.

(*viii*) Special audit under section 142(2A)

Section 142(2A) empowers the assessing officer to direct the assessee to get his accounts audited by a firm of chartered accountants nominated by the Commissioner/Chief Commissioner. The assessing officer can issue direction for special audit only with the previous approval of the Commissioner/Chief Commissioner when during the assessment proceeding before him the assessing officer forms an opinion to this effect based on the nature and complexity of accounts and the interest of the revenue involved in a matter. The assessing officer can direct for special audit not withstanding that accounts have already been audited under any other law by the firm of chartered accountants.

As per various judicial pronouncements it has been held that before directing special audit, assessing officer is required to grant an opportunity of hearing to the assessee. Further as per amendment brought with effect from 1st June 2007, cost of special audit will not be borne by the assessee but by the Central Government.

Recently in practice it has been observed that the above power of directing special audit is being used frequently by the assessing officers. Sometimes such power is used so as to gain further time for completion of assessment and for circumventing the provision of time barring for finalization of assessment.

◆ **Directing special audit under section 142(2A)**

It is held that since no notice u/s 142(2A) was given to assessee before referring the case, the extended time for completion of assessment is not available to the A.O. and therefore assessment is beyond limitation u/s 153(3)(*iii*). *Maya Spinners Ltd.* v. *Dy. CIT (Assessment)* [2008] 306 ITR (AT) 137 (Indore).

◆ **No recommendation from Assessing Officer - Invoking section 142(2A) invalid**

Assessing officer had forwarded recommendation of ADI and had not made his own recommendation after applying his mind in directing assessee to get accounts audited, recourse to section 142(2A) was not valid. Therefore block assessment completed beyond normal limitation, was invalid under section 158BE. *Rajendra C. Singh* v. *Jt. CIT* [2009] 118 ITD 99 (Mum. - Trib.)

◆ **Opportunity necessary before invoking section 142(2A) - Application of mind by Assessing Officer and CIT**

The Supreme Court in *Sahara India (Firm)* v. *CIT* [2008] 169 Taxman 328 has reversed the order of *Sahara India Financial Corporation Ltd.* v. *CIT* [2006] 157 Taxman 279 (Delhi), the exercise of the power under section 142(2A) leads to serious civil consequences and therefore in the absence of express provision for affording an opportunity to an assessee, the requirement of observance of the principles of natural justice is to be read into the said provision. Accordingly we reiterate, the view expressed in *Rajesh Kumar* v. *Dy. CIT* [2006] 157 Taxman 168 (SC)

As per Finance Act, 2013, with effect from 1st June, 2013, the scope of applicability of special audit provision u/s 142(2A) has been enlarged. Earlier, this section could have been invoked by the AO keeping in view the nature and complexity of the accounts of the assessee and to protect the interest of revenue. But now, as per the amendment introduced, four more parameters have been added which are *"volume of the accounts, doubts about the correctness of the accounts, multiplicity of the transactions in the accounts or specialized nature of business activities of the assessee."* Effect of the above amendment is that in case AO is of the opinion during the assessment proceeding that any of the above parameters exists in a case, he may direct the assessee to get his accounts audited. After such amendment, the power to direct the special audit has been widened to a considerable extent.

(ix) Ex parte assessment

In case of non-co-operation by the assessee and non-submission of required details and information, assessing officer can frame assessment under section 144 as ex parte assessment to the best of his judgment and based upon the material and records available with him.

(x) Provisional attachment under section 281B

As per section 281B of the Income Tax Act where during pendency of any proceeding for the assessment of any income, assessing officer is of the opinion that for the purpose of protecting the interest of revenue it is necessary to do so, he may with the previous approval of the commissioner or chief commissioner, attach provisionally any property belonging to the assessee in the manner provided in the second schedule.

It has been observed in practice that such power is also frequently used by the assessing officer in search cases to protect the interest of revenue and in the cases where huge demand are expected to be fastened on the assessee.

(xi) To undertake proceedings under section 148/153C

In case there are evidences suggesting escapement of income pertaining to seventh year prior to the date of search, assessing officer can issue notice under section 148 and make assessment or reassessment by reopening the case for such year. In case there are evidences of incriminating nature found during search which belong or relate to some other person, assessing officer may proceed against such other person by invoking provisions of section 153C.

(xii) Applicability of deeming provisions of income under sections 68 to 69D

In search cases evidences of incriminating nature are found where year of earning income is not determinable. For such situation legislature has created deeming fiction of income for cash credits under section 68, for unexplained investments under sections 69 and 69B, for unexplained money under section 69A, for unexplained expenditure under section 69C and for amount borrowed or repaid on hundi under section 69D. All these provisions creating deeming fiction of income are extensively used and applied in search cases.

14.3 Constraints with the Assessing Officer

It has been observed, in practice, that quality of assessments for search cases does not remain upto the mark for the reason that there are certain constraints in the working of the department within which assessing officers do perform their functions. No doubt assessees do get advantage of such a situation. Sometimes assessees also resort to dilatory tactics to leave insufficient time to the assessing officers to carry out proper enquiry and investigation before finalizing the assessment. Such constraints may be of the following nature:-

1. **All cases of seven years required to be assessed together**

   As per scheme of sections 153A and 153B all the cases of seven years relating to various individuals and business entities within a group are required to be assessed together by the assessing officer. Normally, on an average in a search case there may be 15 to 20 individuals or business entities. Thus, in a normal search case generally more than 100 scrutiny assessments are required to be framed by an assessing officer. It has been seen that normally an assessing officer in central circle has 3 to 5 group search cases for which assessments are required to be framed by him within a year. Thus, assessing officers at central circle are burdened with huge task and volume of work. Each case requires deep investigation and appraisal of voluminous seized documents. Under such circumstances assessing officers are not generally able to justify the task assigned to them and perform the function of framing assessment in qualitative and efficient manner.

2. **Huge burden of time barring**

   There is time barring limit for framing assessment and under no circumstances assessing officers can cross the time barring limit. They have no option but to pass the assessment orders within the time barring limit. Therefore, it has been observed, in practice, that assessing officers are not able to appraise the whole seized material independently and carry out the investigation and enquiries deeply. Data is collected by the search team in electronic form stored in electronic devices such as hard disk, pen drive, computers, etc. An assessing officer is supposed to go through the whole data and investigate the concealed income if any not disclosed by the assessee in his return of income. In practice it has been observed that due to lack of time and pressure of time barring limit they are able to restrict themselves to the points highlighted in the appraisal report by the authorized officer.

3. Lack of availability of skilled staff

It is also been observed that assessing officer are not equipped with the availability of skilled staff who may assist them in carrying out the proper and deep investigation and enquiry. Sometimes even stenographers for dictating the orders are not available with the assessing officers and they have to discharge this function by themselves or through the inspectors.

4. Indiscriminate seizure of books of account, documents and electronic data

It has been seen, in practice, that indiscriminate seizure of huge records consisting of books of account, loose papers, documents, files, data in electronic devices is made by the search team without looking into the relevance and usefulness of such records during assessment proceedings. Burdened with such voluminous seizure of records and data, the objectivity is lost and concentration is diverted from the relevant and useful evidences. Assessing officer does not remain able to concentrate on the useful and key evidences.

5. Delay in centralization

It has been observed in practice that sometimes process of centralization of cases in central circle takes lot of time particularly under the circumstances when there is shifting of cases from one Commissioner to other Commissioner and objection is filed by the assessee for transferring the cases under section 127. There is no time limit prescribed under the Act for transferring and centralization of cases. Further there is no time limit for issuing of notices for filing return under section 153A by the assessing officer. It has been experienced that sometimes cases are centralized few months prior to the time barring limit for framing the assessment. Under such circumstances, it is difficult to justify and maintain the quality of assessment orders to be framed.

6. Late commencement of assessment proceedings

Legally, assessing officer gets 21 months from the end of the financial year in which search is conducted, for framing assessment or reassessment orders under section 153A. But practically it has been observed that the effective work of assessment proceedings is commenced by the assessing officers five or six months prior to the date of time barring limit. It happens so due to delay in centralization of cases, work pressure of time barring cases of preceding year and other administrative and recovery of demands work pressure with the assessing officers. In such a short span assessing officers find themselves handicapped to produce desired results.

7. Technical defaults.

It has also been observed that sometimes technical defaults are committed by the assessing officers due to which whole assessment may be quashed. Such defaults are committed due to either work pressure or lack of proper exposure regarding the provisions of law. The technical defaults may be in the nature such as delay in issue of notice under section 143(2), defect in issue or service of notice for filing returns, delay in passing of orders, defect in recording satisfaction or non-recording of satisfaction in the case of proceedings under section 147/148/153C, etc. Legislature is aware of this situation and therefore, provision of section 153A/153C have been drafted in such a manner so that there is hardly any scope for making such defaults. Moreover, sections 292B and 292BB have been enacted so that entire assessment order is not quashed due to minor technical defaults but still there are certain grey areas and assessing officers are required to be given proper training and knowledge from this point of view.

14.4 Certain issues relating to assessment in search cases

Handling of assessment proceedings involves application and adherence of various aspects & principles of general nature such as application of principle of natural justice, burden of proof—onus and shifting of burden, circumstances when books of account can be rejected, rules against bias and arbitrariness, doctrine of *res judicata*, benami or bogus transactions, reference to valuation cell, recording of statement, reference to special audit etc.

In this chapter, idea is not to discuss all the gamut of principles and issues of general nature applicable during assessment proceedings but, there may be certain specific issues during assessment proceedings of search cases which are being discussed.

(*i*) General questionnaire requiring explanation of all the documents found during search

It has been observed that during assessment proceeding of search cases, a general and omnibus question is put by the assessing officer to explain nature and contents of all the documents and papers found during search. The documents or papers found during search may run into several hundreds/thousands. Assessing officer may pose the query which may be more or less on the following lines:-

"Kindly explain nature and contents of all the documents and papers found and seized during search along with documentary evidence in proof of your contention. Further explain how the same have been recorded in your books of account regularly maintained.

In case satisfactory explanation with documentary evidence is not provided, the amounts mentioned therein shall be treated as your undisclosed income in view of provision contained under section 292C."

Such kind of query is too general and vague to shift entire burden on the assessee. Presumption under section 292C does not mean to treat each and every amount/figure written in the paper or documents found during search as undisclosed income of the assessee. It is for the assessing officer to prepare a *prima facie* case by corroborating the figures and contents mentioned on the papers or documents found during search that any kind of undisclosed income is emanating out of the same.

Such kind of query may be handled by the assessee by explaining the broad nature of documents or papers found. Assessee may explain loose papers in the following manner which, as a measure of abundant caution it is mentioned, is only indicative or suggestive as actual reply would depend upon the facts and circumstances of each case:-

"These papers appear to contain rough calculation, estimates or jottings during some discussion by somebody. We have gone through all the documents/ papers found during search and no undisclosed income belonging to the assessee is emanating out of the same. In case your good self has observed anything specific in this regard, the same may kindly be communicated so that reply may be given on merit."

Such reply would enable the assessee to understand the mind of AO and inference which is intended to be drawn against the assessee based upon which suitable reply can be furnished.

(*ii*) Conditional Surrender

There may be cases when surrender of undisclosed income was made by the assessee in the course of search but such surrender was under specific circumstances or subject to certain conditions. In case those conditions are now fulfilled in favour of the assessee, assessee can explain his case at the time of filing the return of income or during assessment proceeding. In some cases, such situation may arise under the following circumstances—

(*i*) Surrender of investment in inventory was made on the basis of physical inventory taken during search and valued at that time. In case there was calculation mistake in valuation of inventory e.g. the same was valued at sales price instead of cost price while assessee regularly values inventory at cost price which resulted in difference in the value of inventory due to which surrender was made by the assessee.

(*ii*) There was rejected/damaged or slow moving items of inventory which were valued at full price instead of valuing the same at realizable value as earlier valued by the assessee due to which higher difference was worked out.

(*iii*) Assessee surrendered certain transactions or creditors as unverifiable since requisite evidences for verification were not available at the time of search. Later on, all the evidences could be available.

In case assessee takes a stand not to show such earlier surrendered undisclosed income in his return in view of the explanation and evidences now available, it cannot technically be termed as retraction and the issue has to be decided by the assessing officer in the light of the evidences on its merit.

(*iii*) Explanation of documents/assets not belonging to assessee

There may be cases where certain documents or assets are found which do not belong to the assessee but may belong to his spouse, children or to some close connection. During assessment proceeding, one option with the assessee is to state this fact and not to provide any further explanation with respect to such documents or assets on the ground that these relate to independent assessees. In such a situation, there may be all the possibility of the assessing officer undertaking proceedings by invoking provisions of section 153C or section 148 against such other person. When such other person is spouse or children of the assessee, the rigors of those proceedings may have to be faced by him only in actual practice.

The other option with the assessee in such a situation where the income/investment appears ostensibly standing in the name of third person but actual investment has been made by the assessee, is to own the undisclosed asset or undisclosed income as belonging to him only and pay the taxes in his hands so that other persons may not be required to face proceedings under section 153C/148.

In case the source of the acquisition of asset is explainable in the hand of the other person, all the evidences explaining the source of acquisition of the asset by such other person may be furnished during the assessment proceedings by the assessee himself instead simply saying that the asset does not belong to the assessee but to other person. In case assessing officer is satisfied regarding the source of acquisition of asset and that the asset is not the undisclosed asset in the hands of other person, no further action may be taken by the assessing officer with respect to those persons.

(*iv*) Reliance on statement recorded by authorized officer during search

During the course of search, statements are recorded by the authorized officer u/s 131(1A)/132(4). Question arises as to what extent assessing officer may have reliance and make use of statements recorded by the authorized officer during assessment proceedings. Whether he is required to make independent appraisal of facts recorded in the statements by the authorized officer?

As per specific provision under section 132(4), statement recorded during search under this section may be used in evidence in any proceeding under the Income Tax Act. Though there is no specific mention about the evidentiary value of the statement recorded u/s 131(1A), yet statement recorded by the authorized officer under section 131(1A) are recorded pursuant to powers as are vested in a court under the Code of Civil Procedure, 1908 and will have the same evidentiary value. Assessing Officer is however required to confront the statements during the assessment proceeding before drawing an adverse inference, to the assessee and provide him an opportunity of cross examination if desired by the assessee. In case cross examination is demanded by the assessee, Assessing Officer is obliged under the law to call upon the witness for the cross examination by the assessee. In case cross examination is not allowed by the assessing officer when demanded by the assessee, the evidentiary value of such statement is to be ignored as per the decision of Hon'ble Supreme Court in the case of *Kishinchand Chelaram* v. *CIT* [1980] 4 Taxman 29 (SC).

Delhi Bench of ITAT in the case of *Jindal Stainless Ltd.* v. *Asstt. CIT* [2009] 120 ITD 301 (Delhi - Trib.) has held as under—

Assessee having not been given opportunity to cross examine the person on the basis of whose sole statement addition was made in assessment under section 153A, the addition is liable to be deleted - Addition cannot be made on the basis of documents found from the residential premises of a third person (employee of company) unless positive material is brought on record by the Revenue that the assessee in fact had received any extra money on account of over billing.

In *Kailashben Manharlal Chokshi* v. *CIT* [2008] 14 DTR 257 (Guj.), High Court held that Addition on the basis of retracted statement under section 132(4) recorded at odd hours cannot be considered to be a voluntary statement, if it is subsequently retracted and necessary evidence is led contrary to such admission and therefore addition on the basis of retracted statement under section 132(4) was not called for in the facts and circumstances of the case.

14.5 Decided case laws relating to certain significant issues

(i) Addition for undisclosed jewellery

It has been observed in practice that in most of the cases, evidences regarding acquisition of jewellery are not available with the assessees particularly in the case of those assessees who are not covered within the Wealth Tax limit. In our society, jewellery is usually received as gift on different occasions such as marriage, birth of child etc. and further the same is inherited from the parents/grand parents. In fact, for such kind of acquisition of jewellery, there may not be any direct evidence.

During assessment proceeding, assessee may find it difficult to explain the source of acquisition of jewellery found from his possession. One of the ways can be to submit evidences by way of filing affidavits of the assessee and his spouse and further affidavits can be obtained from parents, parents-in-law, other friends and relatives who may have gifted the jewellery on various occasions. Sometimes it becomes a cumber some exercise and at times it may be difficult for the assessee to procure the affidavits from third persons.

There are instructions from the Board for non-seizure of jewellery to certain extent in the case of search as discussed in the chapter on seizure of assets. There are judicial decisions also wherein it has been held that jewellery to the extent which is not liable to be seized as per instructions of CBDT may be treated as explained and no addition on this account is warranted.

In *Smt. Salochana Devi Jaiswal* v. *Dy. CIT* [2004] 90 TTJ 974 (Jabalpur), Tribunal has held that gold jewellery weighing less than 500 grams found during search cannot be subjected to addition in assessment in view of CBDT Instruction No.1916 dated 1.05.1994.

Total jewellery with the family being 670 gms, undisclosed jewellery can be taken only as 170 gms after allowing credit of 500 gms as per CBDT instructions and addition is to be sustained to the extent of value of 170 gms of jewellery. *Smt. Bommana Swarna Rekha* v. *Asstt. CIT* [2005] 147 Taxman 59 (Visakha.) (Mag.).

Assessee and other members of his family having disclosed the gold jewellery under the VDIS 1997 no part thereof could be treated as unexplained more so, in view of Instruction No.1916, dated 11th May, 1994. Also Silver jewellery weighing 16.895 kgs. is to be regarded as reasonable and could not be treated as unexplained having regard to the large size and status of the assessee's family. *Jai Kumar Jain* v. *Asstt. CIT* [2007] 11 SOT 61 (Jp. - Trib.) (URO).

During course of search certain jewellery was found in assessee's premises. In view of instruction issued by Board, while making addition on account of unexplained investment in jewellery, atleast a credit of 500 gms. per married lady and 250 grams for unmarried girl should be given. *Rajendra C. Shah* v. *Jt. CIT* [2007] 158 Taxman 170 (Mum.) (Mag.)

Tribunal was justified in deleting addition on account of jewellery having regard to CBDT Instruction No. 1916, dated 11th May, 1994. *CIT* v. *M.S. Agrawal (HUF)* [2008] 11 DTR 169 (MP)

Credit of 500 gms. of Jewellery each has to be allowed in respect of jewellery belonging to two deceased ladies of the assessee's family as per CBDT guidelines and, therefore no addition was called for. *Dy. CIT* v. *Gordhandas Lachmandas* [2008] 16 DTR 26 (Mum.)

In the case of *R. Umamaheswar* v. *Dy. CIT* [2015] 60 taxmann.com 400/155 ITD 149 (Hyd. - Trib.), it has been held that the Central Board of Direct Taxes had laid down the guidelines that in the case of a person not assessed to wealth tax, gold jewellery and ornaments to the extent of 500 grams for a married lady need not be seized. Hence, the gold jewellery of 471 grams found during the course of search could reasonably be treated as explained and the addition was to be deleted.

Instruction No. 1916, dated 11-5-1994 which lays down guidelines for seizure of jewellery in the course of search takes into account the quantity of jewellery which would generally be held by the family members of an assessee, and therefore, unless anything contrary is shown, it can be safely presumed that the source to the extent of the jewellery stated in the circular stands explained. *CIT* v. *Ratanlal Vyaparilal Jain* [2010] 45 DTR 290 (Guj.)

◆ **Section 69 provides inclusion of wife's ornaments in the income of a husband**

Whether the Tribunal was justified in law in holding that the value of the jewellery from the room of the wife should be included in the income of husband, gave rise to a question of law. *Lal Chand* v. *CIT* [1993] 69 Taxman 9 (All.)

◆ **Section 69 - Unexplained investment- Seizure of jewellery**

Held, that no addition could also be sustained where the assessee's daughter-in-law and unmarried daughter were in possession of old jewellery below the limits of 500 grams per married lady prescribed by the Board. *Dy. CIT* v. *Dr. Arjun Dass Kalwani* [2006] 101 ITD 337 (Jodh. - Trib.)

♦ **Where addition could not be made under wealth tax Act**

Where during the search cash and gold ornaments were found and seized and a petition was moved before the Settlement Commission. The commission held that these items belong to the assessee and bifurcated the income in different years. The wealth tax officer included the amounts in the net wealth of the assessee on the respective valuation dates. The tribunal held that mere fact that the income tax was levied on estimated basis, was not sufficient to prove that the assessee owned and possessed gold and silver utensil on the respective valuation dates. Additions were deleted. *Manibhai S. Patel* v. *WTO* [1991] 37 ITD 485 (Ahd. - Trib.)

♦ **Valuation report of diamond jewellery**

Section 69 - valuation report of the Departmental Valuer estimating the value of diamond ornaments cannot simply be made the basis for concluding that the assessee spent more money than what was disclosed in bills produced by the assessee.

Legal fiction enacted into section 69B comes into play when all the circumstances enumerated in the section do factually exist. The onus to prove the existence of the circumstances lies on the Department. There is no room or scope for making any presumption about the estimated or hypothetical value of the diamond jewellery, in question. It must be factually established that the real investment made was more than what was stated in the invoices. *Gautam Laljibhai Gajjar* v. *ITO* [1991] 37 ITD 514 (Ahd. - Trib.)

♦ **Jewellery belonging to assessee and family members**

Having regard to the family background and their financial standing, *explanation* tendered by the assessee and his relatives that all the ornaments did not belong in entirety to the assessee, was not improbable. *Asstt. CIT* v. *Smt. Parbati Ganguly* [1992] 44 TTJ (Cal.) 108.

♦ **Excess jewellery to be explained during assessment**

In the case of *V.G.P. Ravidas* v. *Asstt. CIT* [2014] 121 DTR (Mad.) 44 (HC), it has been held by Madras High Court that the Board Instruction dated 11.5.1994 stipulates the circumstances under which excess gold jewellery or ornaments could be seized and where it need not be seized. It does not state that it should not be treated as unexplained investment in jewellery. In this case, the Original Authority had correctly included the excess jewellery other than what had been found in the wealth tax assessment as unexplained investment in jewellery and demanded tax and penalty. No error found in such order passed by the Assessing Officer, which was confirmed by the Commissioner of Income Tax (Appeals) and Tribunal. It was found that there was no justification to interfere with the order of the Tribunal and in our considered opinion, on the facts and circumstances of the case, no substantial question of law arises for consideration in these appeals.

(*ii*) **Assessment when there is retraction of surrender of undisclosed income**

There may be a case when surrender of undisclosed income was made by the assessee in the course of search but later on surrender of undisclosed income was retracted by filing affidavits/letter/evidences before authorized officer who recorded the statement or before the assessing officer. In case surrendered undisclosed-income is not declared in the return of income filed by the assessee, and taxes are not paid with respect to the same, it does tantamount to retraction.

Statement of assessee recorded during search is one of the evidences to be considered by the assessing officer for taking decision regarding addition of such income but statement cannot be treated as the conclusive evidence. The assessing officer has to take into consideration the whole circumstances in totality to decide the matter. He has to consider the circumstances under which statement was recorded, the circumstances under which statement has been retracted, the related evidences available, corroboration of the statement with the evidences available, statement or cross examination of third parties. After taking into consideration all the circumstances and evidences on record, assessing officer has to decide the matter. *Prima facie* the case remains against the assessee and heavy burden lies upon him to prove the case in his favour by leading cogent evidences, filing affidavit himself or through third parties and explaining the circumstances under which surrender was made at the first instance. Delay in retraction, if any, is further required to be explained by the assessee. Delay of each day in retraction may be viewed against the assessee and justification for retraction offered by assessee may be treated as after thought exercise. Ultimately, it is the nature of evidences available on record which will decide the matter as has been held differently in the under noted decisions.

Statement recorded at odd hours cannot be considered to be a voluntary statement, if it is subsequently retracted and necessary evidence is led contrary to such admission and therefore addition on the basis of retracted statement under section 132(4) was not called for in the facts and circumstances of the case. *Kailashben Manharlal Chokshi* v. *CIT* [2008] 14 DTR 257 (Guj.)

Where Assessing Officer made additions merely on basis of confessional statement, made by assessee before DDIT (Inv.), which was not supported by any independent and corroborative evidence and said statement was subsequently retracted by assessee during course of assessment, additions made on basis of said statement were to be deleted. *ITO* v. *Bua Dass* [2006] 155 Taxman 130 (Asr.) (Mag.).

Income from undisclosed sources - Addition on the basis of statement recorded during survey - Where the assessee has been able to explain the discrepancy in stock found during the survey, addition could not have been made by the AO solely on the basis of the statement made by the assessee during the course of survey. *CIT* v. *Dhingra Metal Works* [2010] 48 DTR 230 (Del.)

Addition on the basis of statement recorded during survey - Where the assessee failed to produce books of account which may have been maintained during regular course of business or any other authentic contemporaneous evidence of agricultural income, the retraction of statement of the assessee during the course of survey under section 133A could not be accepted and the statement of the assessee during the survey admitting the investment not recorded in the books of account could certainly be acted upon. - *Bachittar Singh* v. *CIT* [2010] 48 DTR 236 (P&H)

Amount paid towards illegal gratification for securing car agency by assessee which was additional income disclosed in the statement of the assessee recorded following enforcement raid and search under section 132 represented undisclosed income and was rightly taxed ignoring retracted statements made after four months. *CIT* v. *Jagdish Chand Gupta* [2010] 47 DTR 156 (P&H)

In the case of *Urmila & Co. Ltd.* v. *Dy. CIT* [2013] 35 taxmann.com 589 60 SOT 1 (Mum. - Trib.)(URO), in the course of search voluminous records were seized which indicated unaccounted transactions. Director of assessee-company was examined on oath and he conceded that assessee obtained bogus bills. Subsequently, assessee filed affidavit claiming bills to be genuine and contended that disclosure during search was made without reference to records. In appeal retraction of disclosure was accepted by CIT(A). On appeal by revenue since disclosure in statement was found to be correct and complete in all respects and also explained purpose for which bogus bills were raised, retraction of disclosure could not be accepted. Additions made on the basis of disclosure was confirmed.

In the case of *CIT* v. *Muzaffarnagar Kshetriya Gramin Bank Ltd.* [2013] 32 taxmann.com 225/214 Taxman 117 (Mag.) (All.), the Authorized Officer conducted search under section 132 upon assessee and seized certain cash from his possession. At time of search, the assessee surrendered said cash amount as his undisclosed income but after four years, he retracted confessional statement and submitted that aforesaid amount was cash-in-hand as reflected from books of account. The Assessing Officer disbelieved the retraction made by assessee and treated amount in question as undisclosed income of assessee. Held, the retraction made after four years was an after thought and therefore, the action of the Assessing Officer in treating cash amount as undisclosed income was justified.

It has been held in the case of *Bannalal Jat Constructions (P.) Ltd.* v. *Asstt. CIT* [2019] 106 taxmann.com 128/264 Taxman 5 (SC) that where High Court upheld addition made by authorities below relying upon statement made in course of search proceedings by director of assessee-company, since assessee failed to discharge its burden that admission made by director in his statement was wrong and said statement was recorded under duress and coercion, SLP filed against decision of High Court was to be dismissed. In course of search proceedings, statement of director of assessee-company was recorded under section 132(4) admitting certain undisclosed income. In course of assessment, Assessing Officer made addition to assessee's income on basis of statement given by its director. Subsequently, director of assessee-company retracted said statement. Tribunal, however, finding that statement had been recorded in presence of independent witness, confirmed addition made by Assessing Officer. High Court also opined that mere fact that director of assessee-company retracted statement at later point of time, could not make said statement unacceptable and it was further opined that burden lay on assessee to show that admission made by director in his statement was wrong and such retraction had to be supported by a strong evidence showing that earlier statement was recorded under duress and coercion. High Court finding that assessee failed to discharge said burden, confirmed order passed by Tribunal, on facts, SLP filed against decision of High Court was dismissed.

◆ **Block Assessment - Undisclosed income - Admission during search and retraction made subsequently**

Where the assessee admitted undisclosed income before DDIT during search proceedings and retracted the admission after 3 months, it was held that retraction was made after a long interval and also that there was no material to support the retraction, therefore, addition based on addition was justified.

Carpenters Classics (Exim) (P.) Ltd. v. *Dy. CIT* [2008] 299 ITR(AT) 124 (Bang.).

◆ **Retraction not admissible when no ambiguity**

Where the statement is made voluntarily without any coercion and the contents of the statement were clear and unambiguous, the same could be binding on the assessee even if the statement was retracted subsequently. *Hotel Kiran* v. *Asstt. CIT* [2002] 82 ITD 453 (Pune - Trib.)

◆ **Section 132(4) - Retraction of Statement**

Assessing Officer was not justified in drawing adverse inference where the assessee had retracted from statement given on search day. *Asstt. CIT* v. *Mrs. Sushiladevi S. Agarwal* [1994] 50 ITD 524 (Ahd.-Trib.)

◆ **Loose papers - Admission by director - Retracted within 5 days - No material to connect business**

The loose paper did not establish that it pertained to the business transaction of the assessee firm. Addition made was not supported by any material which could point out to unexplained investment outside the books of assessee. *Asstt. CIT* v. *Ravi Agricultural Industries* [2009] 117 ITD 338 (Agra - Trib.) (TM)

It has been held in the case of *Kantilal C. Shah* v. *Asstt. CIT* [2011] 14 taxmann.com 108/133 ITD 57 (Ahd.-Trib.) that while making computation of undisclosed income, confessional statement which was recorded on the date of search under section 132(4) has evidentiary value and retraction after several months, that too without any evidence, is not valid. Further once an investment was witnessed by the search party and the assessee had not furnished any source of investment, then addition was sustainable.

It has been held in the case of *Shree Ganesh Trading Co.* v. *CIT* [2013] 30 taxmann.com 170/214 Taxman 262 (Jharkhand) that addition made on the basis of statement under section 132(4) despite the absence of seizure of any asset or cash and the statement having been retracted, was not sustainable.

It has been held in the case of *Principal CIT* v. *Avinash Kumar Setia* [2017] 81 taxmann.com 476/248 Taxman 106 (Delhi) that Voluntary declaration of unaccounted money by assessee two months after survey and retraction of declaration having been made after two years without satisfactory explanation and failure to show income in return filed for relevant assessment year after surrender of undisclosed Income, such retraction is invalid and Appellate Tribunal was not justified in deleting addition of undisclosed income.

It has been held in the case of *Principal CIT* v. *Roshan Lal Sancheti* 172 DTR 313/306 CTR 140 (Raj.) that while computing undisclosed income, Statement recorded under s. 132(4) and later confirmed in statement recorded under s. 131, cannot be discarded simply by observing that the assessee has retracted the same, when the retraction was after inordinate delay of 237 days.

(*iii*) **Dumb Documents**

During the course of search, large number of loose papers, diaries or note pads may be found and seized by the Department. Such loose papers may contain scribbling, rough notes, estimates, projections or figures recorded during some discussion. Sometimes these papers may contain details of certain financial transactions in coded form or without mentioning details, date and nature of transaction.

Generally in the case of professionals or consultants such as Chartered Accountants, financial advisers, share brokers, real estate dealers, there may be large number of such papers generated in the course of discussion with the clients or customers relating to their financial transactions. Such papers may not have any connection with the affairs of the assessee.

During the course of assessment proceeding, assessee is generally required to explain the nature and contents of such papers. Assessing officer may make attempt to decode the figures, appreciate the nature of transaction and income may be sought to be estimated by applying multiplier of thousand or lakhs depending upon the facts of the case and his interpretation of the evidences.

Under section 292C, there is presumption against the assessee that such loose papers or documents found from his possession belong to him and its contents are correct. However such presumption cannot be extended to mean that any figures mentioned on the loose papers represent the undisclosed income of the assessee. Moreover, such presumption is a rebuttable presumption. It is for the assessing officer to establish that the details mentioned on the loose papers are relating to undisclosed income of the assessee. The nature of transaction should be revealed from the loose paper and any pure guess work in this regard in not acceptable in the eyes of law. Such documents or papers may be in the nature of dumb documents and no adverse inference against the assessee can be drawn based upon suspicion or conjectures alone.

Reference may be made to the following decisions where Courts have held that no addition can be made on the basis of dumb document.

◆ No decoding is permissible on suspicion, surmise, conjecture and imagination. *Amar Natvarlal Shah* v. *Asstt. CIT* [1997] 60 ITD 560 (Ahd.-Trib.)

◆ In absence of any evidence about the nature of figures noted on loose paper seized, date, name of party etc., no addition can be made merely upon suspicion. *Asstt. CIT* v. *Shailesh S. Shah* [1997] 63 ITD 153 (Mum. - Trib.)

◆ *Brijlal Rupchand* v. *ITO* [1991] 40 TTJ (Indore-Trib.) 668

◆ Vague noting on loose paper found in the course of search proceedings of sister concern and there being no material on record to suggest that the assessee has in fact received the amounts written on the loose paper, apart from and in addition to the amount received by the assessee per account payee cheques and entered in its account books, addition was deleted. *Malabar Oil Marketing Co.* v. *Asstt. CIT* [2004] 91 TTJ (Mum.-Trib.) 348

◆ Loose papers containing jottings of certain figures even if seized from the possession of assessee would not come within the compass of the word 'document' and cannot be the basis for treating certain income as undisclosed income of the assessee. *D.D. Malhan* v. *Dy. CIT* [2004] 91 TTJ (Delhi-Trib.) 947

◆ Additions based on jottings on paper found during the course of search could not be sustained in the absence of any corroborative material or evidence on record for rejecting the assessee's contention that jotting was an estimate and not actually expended amount. *Addl. CIT* v. *Prasant Ahluwalia* [2005] 92 TTJ (Ctk.-Trib.) 464.

◆ Addition could not be made on the basis of an unnamed loose paper found at the business premises of the husband of the assessee by treating part of the items noted in the said paper as transactions relating to assessee. *Smt. Bommana Swarna Rekha* v. *Asstt. CIT* [2005] 147 Taxman 59 (Visakha.) (Mag.).

◆ Dumb documents or documents with no certainty have no evidentiary value for purpose of resorting to deeming provisions of sections 68, 69, 69A to 69D. In absence of adequate material as to nature and ownership of transaction, undisclosed income cannot be assessed in hands of assessee merely by arithmetically totalling various figures jotted down on loose documents found during search. *Bansal Strips (P.) Ltd.* v. *Asstt. CIT* [2006] 99 ITD 177 (Delhi-Trib.)

◆ Addition on basis of loose paper which can not be treated as books of account cannot be made under section 68. *Asstt. CIT* v. *Satyapal Wassan* [2007] 295 ITR (AT) 352/[2008] 5 DTR (Jab. - Trib.) 202.

♦ Additions made by the AO, *inter alia,* on the basis of loose papers found during search by making certain presumptions which are found to be inconsistent or contrary to other evidence on record cannot be upheld, especially when no significant asset outside the books or no evidence of ostensible expenditure outside the books is found - *Nirmal Fashions (P.) Ltd.* v. *Dy. CIT* [2009] 23 DTR 386 (Kol. - Trib.).

♦ Assessee's undisclosed income could not be taken as ₹ 48 lakhs on the basis of seizure of a dumb document which showed certain unexplained entries totalling '48' in the absence of any material on record to come to the conclusion that the figure '48' is to be read as ₹ 48 lakhs. Tribunal having rightly deleted the addition of ₹ 48 lakhs, the order of the Tribunal does not give rise to a question of law, much less a substantial question of law. *CIT* v. *Girish Chaudhary* [2007] 163 Taxman 608 (Delhi)

♦ **No evidentiary value of dumb documents**

Dumb documents have no evidentiary value for the purpose of resorting to deeming provisions under sections 68, 69, 69A to 69D and no addition can be made on account of undisclosed income merely by arithmetically totalling various figures jotted down on loose documents found during search in the absence of any adequate material as to the nature and ownership. *Bansal Strips (P.) Ltd.* v. *Asstt. CIT* [2006] 99 ITD 177 (Delhi - Trib.).

♦ **No addition can be made on the basis of dumb documents**

Loose papers found at assessee's premises indicating money-lending transactions without mentioning assessee's name have no evidentiary value and cannot by itself form the basis of addition. *Chander Mohan Mehta* v. *Asstt. CIT* [1999] 71 ITD 245 (Pune - Trib.).

♦ **Notings and jottings in the diaries seized during search**

The search party discovered some notings and jottings in the diaries and documents seized. Additions were made raising presumption under section 132(4A) about the notings. Additions were deleted by CIT(A) and ITAT. Held that, Tribunal had recorded a finding that, there was no corroborative or direct evidence to presume that notings and jottings had materialized into transactions giving rise to income not disclosed in the books. There was no perversity in Tribunal's findings. *CIT* v. *D.K. Gupta* [2008] 174 Taxman 476 (Delhi)

◆ **Block assessment - Addition not justified**

In the absence of corroborative evidence, addition of undis-closed income could not be made simply on the basis of entries on loose papers recovered from the residence of a third party and certain general statements of said party. *T.S. Venkatesan* v. *Asstt. CIT* [2000] 74 ITD 298 (Cal. - Trib.)

(*iv*) **Extrapolation of income**

In the course of search, there may be documents or loose papers found suggesting unrecorded sales for a particular period. Assessee remains under the belief that on the basis of such evidences of un-recorded sales of a particular period or a particular year, it is likely to be extrapolated on the same basis for all the seven years under assessment.

The actual position in this regard will depend on the facts of each case. However, as a matter of general rule, it may be mentioned here that the doctrine of *res judicata* does not apply to tax laws. This is because under the Income-tax Act each year is an independent year and assessment is to be made for each year independently based upon the evidences available for that particular year. Further reference may be made to the following decisions—

◆ Ahmedabad Bench of ITAT in the case of *Dy. CIT* v. *Royal Mar-war Tobacco Product (P.) Ltd.* [2009] 29 SOT 53 (Ahd. - Trib.) (URO), while dealing with the same issue has held as under:

No evidence or material indicating any suppressed sales in assessment years 2000-01 to 2003-04 having been found during search, and no defect in the books having also been found, AO was not justified, on the basis of material seized relating to A.Y. 2004-05 indicating suppressed sales, in assuming suppressed sales for earlier assessment years, estimating the same on the basis of consumption of electricity and making additions.

◆ The decisions given in one assessment year will not be binding on the parties for subsequent years. *ITO* v. *Murlidhar Bhagwan Das* [1964] 52 ITR 335 (SC), *Instalment Supply (P.) Ltd.* v. *Union of India* AIR 1962 SC 53.

◆ Each year is distinct year and any mistakes or errors commit-ted in one assessment year cannot be directed to be repeated in the next year, either on the ground of estoppel or on the ground of *res judicata*. *K. Sadasiva Krishnarao* v. *CIT* [1983] 12 Taxman 231 (AP).

◆ It is true that the past history might be legitimate material, but that by itself may not be sufficient to sustain an assessment order in every case without something more. *CIT* v. *Mahesh Chand* [1992] 63 Taxman 27 (All.)

◆ Sales are to be estimated only for the year for which information or document has been found or seized for a part of the accounting period and not for the period for which no information is available on the basis of seized record. *Asstt. CIT* v. *M.M. Sales Agencies* [2006] 153 Taxman 13 (Jp.) (Mag.).

It has been held in the case of *Fort Projects (P.) Ltd.* v. *Dy. CIT* [2013] 29 taxmann.com 84 (Kol. - Trib.) that AO was not justified in extrapolating few stray notings in seized document to the balance flats in three projects given that no incriminating evidence pertaining thereto was found in course of search.

In the case of *Sunny Jacob Jewellers & Wedding Centre* v. *Dy. CIT* [2014] 48 taxmann.com 347 (Ker.). Though the estimate slip reflected the actual purchase and sale of gold made in the business concerns of the assessees, the sale bill was always for a lesser quantity than the details reflected in the estimate slip. By this process the actual sales were not reflected and this was the information gathered during 2006 by the Commercial Tax Department. The search took place in 2007. There was material at least for these two years. Therefore, there was enough information and material to presume the nature of accounting and also the *modus operandi* in maintaining the records by the assessee. There is also no requirement under section 153A and other provisions requiring the department to collect information and evidence for each and every year for the six years under section 153A. Order of Tribunal was confirmed.

◆ **Block Assessment - Evidence should be found for each year**

It is held that there has to be evidence found as a result of search for each previous year falling within the block period and where there is no material at all found in relation to a particular previous year, even though falling within the block, no undisclosed income can be assessed. Where the undisclosed income is discernible from the seized material itself, there is no need for AO to find out corresponding assets or expenses. *Dr. S. Surendranath Reddy* v. *Asstt. CIT* [2000] 72 ITD 205 (Hyd. - Trib.)

◆ **No presumption to the existence of undisclosed income for the other period**

In the absence of any other evidence, AO is not empowered to estimate the suppression of sales for a larger period on the basis of the diary found in search showing suppression of sales for a particular period. *Samrat Beer Bar* v. *Asstt. CIT* [2000] 75 ITD 19 (Pune - Trib.) (TM)

◆ **Suppression for the whole year could be held though the seized material is found only for five months**

In a case where a regular pattern of suppression is established, it may be presumed that there is suppression for the whole year which may be estimated for the period for which direct evidence is not available. *Dr. S. Surendranath Reddy* v. *Asstt. CIT* [2000] 72 ITD 205 (Hyd. - Trib.)

It has been held in the case of *Ashoka Infrastructure Ltd.* v. *Asstt. CIT* 189 TTJ 749 (Pune)/163 DTR 321 (Pune) that while computing of undisclosed income in the light of the evidence found during the course of search indicating that full toll receipts were not recorded in the books of account for certain period, such evidence can be utilized for extrapolation of income for the relevant financial year(s) and the said material cannot be made the basis for working out the income for other years for which no incriminating documents or entries in any cash book or note books ware found during the course of search.

◆ **No suppression can be presumed for the post search period**

Dr. S. Surendranath Reddy v. *Asstt. CIT* [2000] 72 ITD 205 (Hyd. - Trib.).

◆ **Block assessment - On money**

Documents regarding receipt of "on money" by assessee having been found in respect of sale of flats to one party, addition could not be made in respect of all the parties to whom assessee sold flats merely on the basis of presumption. *D.N. Kamani (HUF)* v. *Dy. CIT* [1999] 70 ITD 77 (Patna - Trib.) (TM)

(v) No addition on estimated/*ad hoc* basis

Addition relating to unexplained household expenditure can be made based on the incriminating evidence whether direct or circumstantial, found in the course of search, suggesting incurring the unrecorded household expenditure. In the absence of any such evidence, it may not be legally permitted to make addition for household expenses on estimated basis during assessments of search cases. This principle is applicable not only in search cases but even in regular assessment cases. But in search case, it needs to be applied more strictly. Courts have consistently opined and rendered various judgments on this aspect in favour of the assessee.

In case any direct or circumstantial evidence is found by the Assessing Officer regarding unrecorded household expense in a particular year and such evidence is of the nature which suggests the possibility of such expenditure in other years as well, extrapolation of household expenditure for other years cannot be ruled out.

This issue assumes more significance in search cases when Assessing Officer are tempted to make addition for low household expenses for all the seven years in search cases which is a controversial issue on which various judicial decisions are available and are being discussed as under:—

Without pointing out any item of suppressed household expenses, AO was not justified in estimating the household expenses by applying inflation index. *Asstt. CIT* v. *Radhey Shyam Poddar (HUF)* [2004] 86 TTJ (Asr.-Trib.) 558.

Unexplained expenses on marriage - In the absence of anything on record to show that the assessee had contributed any amount to the expenses of the marriage of his sister over and above what he had declared, addition could not be made on pure presumption. *Asstt. CIT* v. *Nitin Mukesh Mathur* [2004] 88 TTJ (Mum.-Trib.) 220

Addition - Low household expenses - A.O. having estimated assessee's household expenses on the basis of suspicion and surmises, addition cannot be sustained. *Bajrang Lal Bansal* v. *Dy. CIT* [2006] 150 Taxman 29 (Delhi) (Mag.)

In view of seizure of a loose paper indicating assessee's household expenses without any indication as to the month or year to which it related, the A.O. was entitled to proceed on the basis that it indicated monthly expenses during the entire year in which then search was made. Notwithstanding such document it cannot be assumed that similar expenditure as adjusted for inflation was incurred in the past 10 years also and therefore, addition could not be made in the past assessment years. *CIT* v. *C.L. Khatri* [2005] 147 Taxman 652 (MP).

In the case of *Jagdish Duggal* v. *Asstt. CIT* [2009] 24 DTR (Chd.) (Trib.) 174, Chandigarh Bench of ITAT has held as under in this regard—

The short point revolves around the quantum of household expenses incurred by the assessee. The expenses declared by the assessee have been held to be inadequate by the AO. The reasons advanced by the AO are two-fold. Firstly, the assessee family is enjoying the use of household articles like ACs, TVs, geysers and other electronic gadgets and that during the course of search, one of the lady members admitted that the household expenses were to the extent of ₹ 20,000 per month. In terms of section 153A under which the impugned assessments have been made, the mandate of the AO is to assess or reassess the total income of the assessee in the cases where search has taken place. Admittedly, in the case of the assessee, search operation took place on 15th Oct., 2003. In any case, before the claim of household expenses made by the assessee is to be rejected, the AO must bring out cogent material and evidence. In this case, reasons advanced by the AO are quite general in nature. In fact, the first reason relating to the household articles pointed out, does not turn much on the subject because such articles are a normal occurrence in urban household. There is no allegation by the AO, much less a finding, that the lifestyle or the expenditure on the gadgets was ostentatiously lavish. Secondly, even estimation of household expenses admitted by the lady member of the family, can at best, be a yardstick to consider the acceptability of the expenses incurred by the assessee in the assessment year in question. Considering the amount admitted by the lady member of the family in the year 2003 and also household goods referred to by the AO, in the years under consideration, the amounts returned by the assessee on household expenses cannot be rejected as unbelievable or unreasonable. Considering in the overall light and on the basis of absence of any adverse material on record, there is no justification with the AO to estimate the household expenses over and above those returned by the assessee in the respective assessment years. The order of the CIT (A) is set aside, and the AO is directed to delete the additions.

♦ **No *ad hoc* addition can be made as a result of search**

Additions made by AO in block assessment on estimate basis towards value of furniture, fittings, household expenses, foreign travel, medical expenses and investment and income relating to dairy farm not on the basis of material found during search but on the basis of post-search enquiries were not called for. *Sukh Ram* v. *Asstt. CIT* [2006] 99 ITD 417 (Delhi - Trib.)

♦ **Addition not sustainable merely on the ground of discrepancy in stating exact denomination or on the ground that why the assessee retained so much cash for such a long time.**

Assessee-company having explained that the cash seized by police from its employees belonged to the assessee which was being carried for depositing in the bank and produced its cash book to prove the availability of the cash no addition could be sustained irrespective of some discrepancies in the statements with regard to the timing when the cash was taken by the employees to the bank or with regard to the denomination of the currency notes. *Anand Autoride Ltd.* v. *Jt. CIT* [2006] 99 ITD 227 (Ahd. - Trib.)

♦ **Estimate of income during search period**

In the absence of any evidence, merely on the basis of few loose papers and only two days' transactions hawala business could not be assumed in existence for a period of 18 months. *Kantilal Prabhudas Patel* v. *Dy. CIT* [2005] 93 ITD 117 (Indore) (TM)

♦ **Estimation of income on the basis of blank stamped voucher found during the course of search and seizure operations**

Simply because some blank vouchers were found during search bearing revenue stamps and signature of some unidentified person, no *ad hoc* addition can be made without linking the blank vouchers with inflation of any particular expenditure. *Smt. Rajrani Gupta* v. *Dy. CIT* [2000] 72 ITD 155 (Mum.)?

♦ **Undisclosed income - Estimation of**

Amount due to assessee-doctors but not collected cannot be included in undisclosed income. Amounts collected from patients of assessee-doctor and embezzled by employees partake the characters of receipts in the hands of assessees. *Dr. R.M.L. Mehrotra* v. *Asstt. CIT* [1999] 68 ITD 288 (All. - Trib.).

It has been held in the case of *Mrs. Deepa Bhatia* v. *Asstt. CIT* [2012] 20 taxmann.com 315 (Delhi) that where assessee being a regular income-tax assessee who has been filing her returns, addition made by the AO on estimate basis towards purchase of jewellery by the assessee without bringing any evidence on record exhibiting that the investment was made outside the books is not sustainable.

♦ **Addition on the basis of conjectures**

No addition can be made on the basis of conjectures. There was no justification for making addition for unaccounted cash payments allegedly made by assessee for purchase of shares solely relying on the statements of two witnesses to the sale agreement from which they resiled at the time of assessment when no evidence in the form of receipts or notings of alleged cash payments were discovered during the search at the premises of the either party. *Smt. Purnima Beri* v. *Dy. CIT* [2003] 264 ITR 54 (Asr.-Trib.) (TM)

♦ **Unlawful business**

Where the assessee was unable to explain the source of investment in acquisition of gold found and confiscated by Customs authorities, addition made on estimated value thereof was justified. The Tribunal held that the assessee was not entitled to claim the loss due to confiscation of gold as he was not found to be engaged in the lawful or unlawful business of gold. *ITO* v. *Vijay Kumar Khandelwal* [1994] 50 ITD 405 (Jp. - Trib.).

◆ **Unaccounted sales as per loose sheets found during the search**

Held on facts, following the decision of the Calcutta High Court in the case of *CIT* v. *S.M. Omer* [1992] 62 Taxman 46 that only the net profit rate can be applied on unaccounted sales for the purposes of making addition. *ITO* v. *Gurubachhan Singh J. Juneja* [1995] 55 ITD 75 (Ahd. - Trib.) (TM).

◆ **Withdrawal of money from Bank-Cash seized evidence**

The cash seized from the assessee's employee had been out of cash withdrawn from the Bank. Held the explanation was reasonable—ITAT was not justified in denying the benefit of withdrawal on the ground that the bundles of notes seized were not impressed with seal of Bank but of Bank B. Held it was too technical. *Mansukhlal Ratanlal Jain (Chopra)* v. *Union of India* [2006] 157 Taxman 62 (MP).

◆ **Undisclosed income in block assessment**

Where no evidence of concealment is discovered in search and seizure operation and the addition is made only on estimated value of properties, it is held to be invalid. *CIT* v. *Manoj Jain* [2007] 163 Taxman 223 (Delhi).

◆ **Decoding without corroborative evidence cannot lead to addition**

It has been held in the case of *Asstt. CIT* v. *G.M. Infrastructure* [2011] 135 TTJ (Indore-Trib.) 469 that CIT(A) was justified in deleting the addition made by the AO on the basis of noting in the papers found during search as the AO had treated figures mentioned in the papers as sales rates in codes without bringing any corroborative evidence specifically when the properties were claimed to have been sold at the rate equal to or more than the rates fixed by the registering authorities.

(*vi*) **Unrecorded business expenditure - Whether deduction can be claimed?**

There may be documents or loose papers found in the course of search, suggesting unrecorded business expenditure incurred, the source of which is not explainable. Addition in such a case is made under section 69C as undisclosed income of the assessee. As per proviso to section 69C, such expenditure cannot otherwise be claimed as business expenditure by the assessee under any other provision of the Act.

However, it is to be noted that a proviso is added to section 69C by Finance (No. 2) Act, 1998, w.e.f. 1-4-1994 to the effect that notwithstanding anything contained in any provision of this Act, the unexplained expenditure which is deemed to be income of the assessee shall not be allowed as deductions under any head of income. In view of this amendment the benefit of neutralization cannot be availed by the assessee for the assessment year 1999-2000. *Elite Developers* v. *Dy. CIT* [2000] 73 ITD 379 (Nag. - Trib.)

In case there are documents or loose papers found suggesting generation of undisclosed income and at the same time incurring expenditure not recorded in the books, assessee can make declaration of undisclosed income generated. Regarding unrecorded expenditure, one can make out a case that the same have been incurred out of funds generated from the undisclosed income and no separate addition for such expenditure incurred is warranted. Such situation is not covered within the ambit of the proviso to section 69C as discussed above.

◆ **Allowability of expenditure disclosed in seized documents**

Undisclosed income in the form of 'on money' stood established by seizure of document read with statement recorded under section 132(4); however in computing undisclosed income, expenditure incurred has to be allowed; income discovered has to be taxed in assessment years as per method of accounting followed by assessee. *Dhanvarsha Builders & Developers (P.) Ltd.* v. *Dy. CIT* [2006] 102 ITD 375 (Pune - Trib.)

(vii) **Addition on the basis of Statement**

◆ **Statement has to be accepted as a whole and could not be used in part**

Statement of assessee under section 131 admitting money-lending activities has to be accepted *in toto* and not partly - *Chander Mohan Mehta* v. *Asstt. CIT* [1999] 71 ITD 245 (Pune - Trib.)

In the case of *Shree Ram Balaji Developers and Infrastructure (P.) Ltd.* v. *Asstt. CIT* [2017] 88 taxmann.com 364 (Jp.-Trib.), it has been held that director in his statement under section 132(4) having admitted advancement of undisclosed money but at the same time stated that those amounts were returned and affidavit in support having also been furnished, therefore, addition was not sustainable.

◆ **Revenue to establish income, mere admission not sufficient**

In *CIT* v. *Mrs. Doris S. Luiz* [1974] 96 ITR 646 (Ker.), it was held that even when there was admission, it is incumbent upon Revenue to establish by relevant material that income in question was income in the hands of assessee.

It has been held in the case of *Asstt. CIT* v. *Dr. Raj Dhariwal* [2012] 23 taxmann.com 284 (Jodh. - Trib.) that where addition was made under section 69 on the basis of statements under section 132(4) *vis-à-vis* unexplained investment in purchase of plots and the price of the plots paid by the assessee being consistent with the circle rate at which the stamp duty has been paid and the Department having not found any document or evidence to establish that the assessee has made more payment than that found recorded in his accounts, the statement made by the assessee under section 132(4) surrendering the impugned amount could not have been taken as basis for making addition towards unexplained investment in plots by the assessee.

In the case of *CIT* v. *Jagdish Narain Ratan Kumar* [2015] 61 taxmann.com 173/234 Taxman 39 (Raj.), the Court held that the Commissioner (Appeals) had after taking into account the statement of the assessee, in which it had surrendered the income, and having referred it to the books of account, disagreed with the quantum of the additions made by the assessing authority. The assessment made by the Commissioner (Appeals) was not found to be incorrect by the Tribunal. The decision of the Tribunal was justified. The statements made during search must be correlated with the records which are found, and if there is any ambiguity the explanation given by the assessee should be taken into consideration before making the assessment.

In the case of *Dy. CIT* v. *A. Audinarayana Reddy* [2014] 50 taxmann.com 91 (Hyd. - Trib.), it has been held that the AO cannot presume income of assessee for period covered by section 153A on basis of confession statement and AO is required to bring on record positive material in support of addition.

In the case of *B. Kishore Kumar* v. *Dy. CIT* [2014] 52 taxmann.com 449/[2015] 229 Taxman 614/112 DTR 121/[2015] 273 CTR 468 (Mad.), the Court held that when there is a clear and categoric admission of the undisclosed income by the assessee himself, there is no necessity to scrutinize the documents. The document can be of some relevance, if the undisclosed income is determined higher than what is now determined by the department. Moreover, it is not the case of the assessee that the admission made by him was incorrect or there is mistake. In fact, when there is a clear admission, voluntarily made, by the assessee, that would constitute a good piece of evidence for the Revenue.

In the case of *Mahashian Di Hatti Ltd.* v. *Dy. CIT* [2013] 21 ITR 731 (Delhi - Trib.), the Tribunal held that in the absence of any discrepancy in inventory, no addition could be made. As the figures of discrepancy were not available with the Department and the director of the assessee-company had retracted the surrender made by him on account of stock difference, no addition could be made on the basis of a statement recorded under section 132(4) of the Act. If the Assessing Officer wanted to add the amount of ₹ 11 crores on account of stock inventory, he should have brought material on record.

In the case of *Jyotichand Bhaichand Saraf & Sons (P.) Ltd.* v. *Dy. CIT* [2012] 26 taxmann.com 239/139 ITD 10 (Pune - Trib.). The Tribunal has held that the admission under section 132(4) was made under the mistaken belief of law instead of the correct legal position. The revenue cannot make the addition merely on the basis of statement without any evidence found in the course of the search action or post search enquiries to the effect that the assessee has undisclosed income.

In the case of *Naresh Kumar Verma* v. *Asstt. CIT* [2013] 32 taxmann.com 280/57 SOT 99 (Chd. - Trib.) (URO), addition made merely on the basis of statement of assessee recorded u/s 132(4) without establishing factum that assessee was in fact found in possession or control of any books of account, other documents, money, bullion, jewellery or other valuable article or thing etc. could not be sustained.

In the case of *Shree Ganesh Trading Co.* v. *CIT* [2013] 30 taxmann.com 170/214 Taxman 262 (Jharkhand), statement on oath is a piece of evidence and when there is incriminating admission against himself, then it is required to be examined with due care and caution. Therefore, addition made only the basis of statement was deleted.

In the case of *Bhagirath Aggarwal* v. *CIT* [2013] 31 taxmann. com 274/215 Taxman 229 (Delhi), the statements recorded under section 132(4) were clearly relevant and admissible and they could be used as evidence. In fact, once there was a clear admission, voluntarily made, on the part of the assessee, that would constitute a good piece of evidence for the Revenue. Appeal of assessee was dismissed.

In the case of *P. Kunhiraman Nair* v. *CIT* [2013] 40 taxmann. com 12/219 Taxman 128 (Ker.) (Mag.), a search was conducted in the residential premises of the assessee, which revealed deposits of ₹ 8 lakhs in cash, in three bank accounts. The assessee was examined on oath under section 131 where he offered ₹ 3 lakhs as consultation charges received. Later, he explained that the amount of ₹ 3 lakhs was not his income and belonged to his daughter employed in a bank. The amount was treated as his income and this was confirmed by the CIT(A) and the Tribunal. Held, the assessee, at the time of search, had given a statement and he had no case that he had retracted from the statement on the basis that the statement was procured by unlawful means. Furthermore, circumstances also indicated that the findings of the Tribunal affirming the orders of the authorities were probable in this regard. Hence, the appeal was dismissed.

In the case of *Asstt. CIT* v. *Kunvarji Finance (P.) Ltd.* [2015] 119 DTR (Ahd 'A') 1 (Trib.), it has been held that if there was any discrepancy or defect in the assessee's books of account or the seized documents indicating any undisclosed income, the AO ought to have mentioned the same in the assessment order. However, any defects or discrepancies were not specified. Since neither the AO nor the Departmental Representative having pointed out any defect or discrepancy in any of the seized documents, therefore no addition could be made simply on the basis of the disclosure of unaccounted income made by the director of the assessee-company in his statement during the course of search under the impulsion of the general statement made by the authorized officer that there are defects and discrepancies in the seized documents.

In the case of *CIT* v. *Naresh Kumar Agarwal* [2015] 122 DTR (AP) 339 (HC), it has been held that no incriminating material having been found during search, block assessment made solely on the basis of statement of assessee recorded under section 132(4) was invalid, more so when such statement was recorded after two and a half months of search and was retracted.

It has been held in *Principal CIT* v. *Best Infrastructure (India) (P.) Ltd.* [2018] 94 taxmann.com 115/256 Taxman 63 (SC) in the case of search and seizure assessment under s. 153A, while dealing with the scope *vis-a-vis* incriminating material, Statements u/s 132(4) make it plain that the surrender of the sum of ₹ 8 crores was only for the assessment year in question and not for each of the six assessment years preceding the year of search and since statements recorded under s. 132(4) do not by themselves constitute incriminating material; assumption of jurisdiction under s. 153A was not justified in law.

It has been held in the case of *Principal CIT* v. *Manoj Hora* [2017] 88 taxmann.com 923 (Delhi) that in search and seizure assessment u/s 153A, though statement of third party was recorded under section 132(4) but no incriminating material attributable to assessee was found during search to corroborate statement, additions made by Assessing Officer were unsustainable.

It has been held in the case of *CIT* v. *Dilbagh Rai Arora* [2019] 104 taxmann.com 371/263 Taxman 30 (All.), that if the person can explain with supportive evidence, material or otherwise that the admission by him earlier under s. 132(4) is not correct or contains a wrong statement or that a true state of affairs is different from that represented therein, addition cannot be made solely relying on statement under s. 132(4).

◆ **Statements recorded during the course of search at variance-explanation found reasonable as the deponent was unwell**

Tribunal held that the addition was not justified as there was likelihood of the statement tendered at the time of search being at variance with subsequent statements. The Tribunal observed that for satisfactory reasons, statements made on search day might not be fully relied upon because the assessee was unwell during the search operations. Therefore, variation in the statement was natural. *Asstt. CIT* v. *Mrs. Sushiladevi S. Agarwal* [1994] 50 ITD 524 (Ahd. - Trib.)

◆ **No addition on the basis of statement given under pressure**

In the case of *Basant Bansal* v. *Asstt. CIT* [2015] 122 DTR (Jp.) 118 (Trib.), it has been held that where assessee offered a summary disclosure of an amount due to pressure of proceedings created by the department during search or survey operations which were adversely affecting business, then the same cannot be regarded as voluntary disclosure and no incriminating material was discovered by the department as a result of search or survey operations carried out against the assessee. Therefore, the impugned additions made solely on the basis of said disclosure do not conform to the mandate of section 153A and consequently, the same cannot be sustained.

◆ **No addition can be made on the basis of conflicting statements of the seller of the property**

It is held that the burden is on the revenue to prove that the price of the property purchased is under stated. No addition can be made where no enquiry is made and no such evidence is found during the search except the conflicting statement of the seller. *CIT* v. *P.V. Kalyanasundaram* [2006] 155 Taxman 454 (Mad.) affirmed in *CIT* v. *P.V. Kalyanasundaram* [2007] 164 Taxman 78 (SC).

◆ **Mere statement of the third party that property was sold to the assessee for a higher amount than shown, no protective assessment could be made in the case of the assessees**

The assessee along with others purchased property from Razia Begum for ₹ 4 lacs. Subsequently, a search was conducted at the residence of Razia Begum and her two daughters and cash amounting to ₹ 7,56,600 was recovered. She explained that this was due to sale proceeds of the house sold to the assessee and others for ₹ 11.75 lacs out of which ₹ 4 lacs was received by a demand draft and the balance in cash. The departmental valuation officer first estimated the value of the house at ₹ 4.53 lacs and then at ₹ 11.85 lacs and then at ₹ 4.60 lacs. On these facts, it was held that no protective assessment could be made in the hands of the assessee. *Ramesh Pershad* v. *IAC* [1989] 28 ITD 550 (Hyd. - Trib.)

◆ **Possibility of committing a mistake during surrender/survey**

Where nothing incriminating was found in the survey which was conducted twice and where there was nothing on the record to show that the book results were manipulated and where the original declaration was made by the junior - most partner who was non-matriculate, the possibility of committing a mistake in explaining the affairs of the firm could not be ruled out.

In this case during the course of survey operations an admission of unaccounted income was made to the extent of ₹ 9,25,000. Later on, the assessee retracted the admission on the ground that there was some misunderstanding as what he stated was about sale and not the income. Later on the assessee offered a sum of ₹ 3,00,000. The offer was rejected and an addition of ₹ 9,25,000 was made. The addition in excess of ₹ 3,00,000 was deleted. *Pushpa Vihar* v. *Asstt. CIT* [1994] 48 TTJ (Bom.-Trib.) 389

It has been held in the case of *M. Narayanan & Bros.* v. *Asstt. CIT* [2011] 13 taxmann.com 49/201 Taxman 207 (Mad.) that where addition was made on the basis of statement recorded during search but the assessee has explained on the basis of relevant material that the amount of ₹ 4 lacs surrendered by him as unaccounted income during the search represented loans taken from relations who were already assessed on the said amount, coupled with the fact that the transactions of pawn booking were made by the assessee in the earlier years, the said amount could not be included in the hands of the assessee solely on the basis of the statement made by him at the time of search.

◆ **No further proof necessary to be adduced by the Assessing Officer where a fact is admitted by the assessee**

Where the assessee pleaded that the amount, in question, was his income, this pleading was binding on him. Since the assessee had admitted that the income related to the Assessment Year 1977-78, there was nothing for the ITO to prove or disprove, held the Tribunal in *ITO* v. *Akshay Bhandar* [1990] 33 ITD 13 (Gauhati - Trib.), following *Choudhury Sahu* v. *State of Bihar* AIR 1982 SC 98; *Mahendra Manilal Nanavati* v. *Sushila Mahendra Nanavati* AIR 1965 SC 364 and *Nagindas Ramdas* v. *Dalpat Ram Ichcharam* alias *Brij Ram* AIR 1974 SC 471.

It has been held in the case of *CIT* v. *O. Abdul Razak* [2012] 68 DTR 237 (Ker.) that while making computation of undisclosed income, where additions were made by the AO on the basis of clear admission made by the assessee in the statement recorded under section 132(4) and assessee having not proved any threat or coercion, the Tribunal was not right in deleting the additions.

◆ **Settlement after surrender held as valid**

Madras High Court held in the case of *Madras Bangalore Transport Co.* v. *CIT* [1991] 190 ITR 679 (Bom.) that the settlement arrived at after search was valid if it was based on material on record.

◆ **An admission is an important piece of evidence but not conclusive**

In *S. Arjan Singh* v. *CWT* [1988] 41 Taxman 272, Delhi High Court held that an admission is an important piece of evidence, but it is not conclusive and it is open to the assessee to show that it is incorrect. The Delhi High Court drew support from Supreme Court's decision in *Pullangode Rubber Produce Co. Ltd.* v. *State of Kerala* [1973] 91 ITR 18.

Statement recorded after a search could not be used against assessee in the absence of any incriminating material found during search. *CIT* v. *Ravi Kant Jain* [2001] 117 Taxman 28 (Delhi)

◆ **Block assessment - Undisclosed income under section 158BB**

Where a block assessment is made by estimating the income on the basis of statement recorded during search proceedings and documents seized under section 132, the block assessment is held to be valid. *Hotel Kumar Palace* v. *CIT* [2006] 154 Taxman 10 (P&H)

It has been held that in the case of *Bhagirath Aggarwal* v. *CIT* [2013] 31 taxmann.com 274/215 Taxman 229 (Delhi) that in search and seizure, when undisclosed income was admitted in the statement under section 132(4) and there is no evidence to establish that admission was incorrect in any way, addition made on basis of statement justified.

(*viii*) **Addition on the basis of loose papers, diaries, etc.**

◆ **No addition on the basis of noting on a slip of paper**

Addition in the assessment of assessee on the basis of a document found during search of N was unwarranted as the document was neither recovered from the possession of assessee nor assessee was given an opportunity of cross-examination of N and N having changed his stand and retracted his statement at various levels, his testimony could not be said to be reliable. *Amarjit Singh Bakshi (HUF)* v. *Asstt. CIT* [2003] 263 ITR 75 (Delhi)

It has been held in the case of Kantibhai P. Patel v. Dy. CIT 208 DTR 54 (Ahd 'B') that the addition on account of on money allegedly received by the assessees on sale of land could not be made in the assessment under section 153C simply on the basis of some vague notings on a nondescript loose paper seized from the possession of the searched person (purchaser) and the statement of the said third party without cross-examination, more so when the purchaser has filed an affidavit whereby he has affirmed on oath that the cash payments were not made to the assessees but to some old landowners/Banakhat owners and others who were claiming ownership of the said lands and the contents of the affidavit remain uncontroverted.

◆ **No addition on the basis of undated and unsigned document**

In the case of *CIT* v. *Vivek Aggarwal* [2015] 121 DTR 241 (Delhi) (HC), it has been held that addition made on the basis of undated and unsigned document seized during search is not sustainable.

◆ **No addition unless facts ascertained and verified**

In the case of *CIT* v. *Home Developers (P.) Ltd.* [2015] 117 DTR 248 (Delhi) (HC), it has been held that revenue has not filed any documents or material to show that in fact loan was taken and interest payment was made and the persons to whom allegedly interest was paid, their details and particulars were not ascertained, verified and examined. Therefore, Tribunal was justified in deleting the addition.

In the case of *Bhanuvijaysingh M. Vaghela* v. *ITO* [2013] 33 taxmann.com 555 (Guj.), the loose paper had clearly indicated the amount given by B by way of loan. Based on facts, there was no perversity in the conclusion of the Tribunal. The amount had to be added to the income of the assessee.

◆ **Rough Notes found during search**

Rough notings on seized documents could not be treated as unaccounted expenditure on production of film as it is improbable that actual expenditure on production was not recorded in books; additions deleted. *Pooja Bhatt* v. *Asstt. CIT* [2000] 73 ITD 205 (Mum. - Trib.)

◆ **Diary seized from another city**

Addition could not be made in the hands of assessee-company on the basis of contents of a personal diary of an employee seized from him in another city particularly when he was never summoned and examined by AO. *Associated Stone Industries (Kotah) Ltd.* v. *Dy. CIT* [1999] 68 ITD 312 (Jp. - Trib.)

◆ **Deciphering of figures contained in a loose sheet of paper**

AO was not justified in deciphering the figures on a seized paper at his whims and caprice based on unfounded presumptions and conjectures without bringing any corroborative material evidence in support thereof and same cannot form the basis for assessing undisclosed income by way of sale proceeds of a property. *Atul Kumar Jain* v. *Dy. CIT* [1999] 64 TTJ (Delhi-Trib.) 786.

It has been held in the case of *Principal CIT* v. *Umesh Ishrani* [2019] 108 taxmann.com 437 (Bom.) that where Tribunal noted that such loose papers nowhere showed that any payments were made by such partners and, further, no enquiry or verification was made with seller of shops or developer & Tribunal, therefore, concluded that entries reflected in loose papers were not corroborated with any other evidence on record, Tribunal was justified in deleting impugned additions made by revenue.

◆ **Loose document found during search**

Documents relating to transactions in gold ornaments and household goods found in the premises of assessee goldsmith are presumed to be belonging to him in absence of any contrary evidence; addition on account of amount due from undeclared debtors and unexplained investment sustained partly. *Daulat Ram* v. *Asstt. CIT* [1999] 63 TTJ (Delhi-Trib.) 436.

Document to be read in toto

It has been held in the case of *Dy. CIT* v. *Kanakia Hospitality (P.) Ltd.* [2019] 110 taxmann.com 4/179 ITD 1 (Mum. - Trib.) that Contents of a 'seized document' are to be read in toto, and it is not permissible on part of an Assessing Officer to dissect same and therein summarily accept same in part and reject other part.

◆ **Additions made on the basis of loose sheets of paper and torn paper not justified on facts**

Additions made on the basis of seized loose sheet and torn papers was not justified as the entries found thereon were mere estimates and no corroborating evidence has been brought on record to show that purchases and sales of properties had actually taken place and hence there is no question of any undisclosed income. *S.K. Gupta* v. *Dy. CIT* [1999] 63 TTJ (Delhi-Trib.) 532.

◆ **Opportunity of cross-examination to be given**

In the case of *M.M. Sulaiman* v. *Asstt. CIT* [2014] 51 taxmann. com 310/[2015] 67 SOT 32 (URO) (Cochin-Trib.) CIT (A) quashed assessment order for violation of natural justice as AO did not provide an opportunity to assessee to cross-examine workers who had given statements against assessee. Tribunal held that since power of CIT(A) are co-terminus with that of AO he should have called for a report from AO submitted after providing opportunity of cross examination and also after furnishing relevant documents, accordingly order of CIT(A) was to be set aside.

It has been held in the case of Vetrivel Minerals v. Asstt. CIT 208 DTR 280 (Mad.) that non-furnishing of copies of documents seized and Panchanama to assessees and non-providing of opportunity to cross-examine the persons whose statements were recorded under section 132(4) and used against assessees while framing assessment under section 153A amounted to violation of principles of natural justice and thus assessment orders are set aside and the matter is remanded back to the AO for de nova assessment.

◆ **Cash Credits - Source not proved-stand shifted**

Where certain cash receipts were explained as amounts arranged by one of the Directors of the income and when that stand later on was changed and it was submitted that the said amount represented share application money collected from various persons out of the share application money was not found entered in the accounts, share application form, allotment letter, shareholders register, and share certificates etc. could also not be produced, it was held that the addition was justified. *Essem Intra Port Services (P.) Ltd.* v. *Asstt. CIT* [2000] 72 ITD 228 (Hyd. - Trib.).

◆ **Diary - Entries in the diary of a third person not enough**

A diary was seized from the premises of a third party which indicated the alleged unrecorded sales made to that party by the assessee. Variation in month-wise and other allied enterprises did not indicate that the assessee made any sales to 'H'. Average yield of the assessee was higher than that in comparable cases. The Assessing Officer relied only on the entries of the said diary and did not bring on record any corroborative material to prove that such sales were made outside the books. It was held that mere entries in the accounts of a third party were not sufficient to prove that the assessee indulged in such transactions. *Asstt. CIT* v. *Prabhat Oil Mills* [1995] 52 TTJ (Ahd.-Trib.) 533

◆ **Addition made on the basis of loose documents found during search**

The Tribunal deleted the addition based solely on loose sheets found and seized during the course of search and not supported by any independent evidence is unsustainable, in the eye of the law. The High Court held that The Tribunal neither discussed all the issues nor met the reasoning given by the Assessing Officer and CIT(A) for coming to the conclusion. Tribunal order was set aside and recommended the matter to the Tribunal. *CIT* v. *Multi Tech Auto Ltd.* [2008] 301 ITR 73 (Jharkhand)

◆ **Addition made on the basis of loose documents found during search**

In the case of *Vinit Ranawat* v. *Asstt. CIT* [2015] 126 DTR 73 (Pune 'B') (Trib.), it has been held that addition could not be made in the hands of the assessee simply on the basis of some papers found with a third party when there is no business connection between assessee and that party, particularly when no unaccounted asset, Investment or loose paper evidencing any such unaccounted receipt is found during the course of search earned out at the assessee's premises.

◆ **Addition on the basis of loose documents found during search**

In the case of *CIT* v. *Vivek Aggarwal* [2015] 121 DTR (Delhi) 241, it has been held that addition made only on the basis of some loose papers and a chit could not be sustained without some surveillance of the substantiation.

◆ **Entries in Diary held imaginary**

Tribunal had given a finding of fact while deleting addition made on the basis of diary that all entries made in the diary were imaginary and no reliance could be placed on these entries for making the addition. Held, that no question of law arose on account of the finding fact. *CIT* v. *Khazan Singh & Bros.* [2007] 164 Taxman 30 (Punj. & Har.)

Addition in the year to which incriminating material belongs

It has been held in the case of *Principal CIT* v. *Jayant K. Furnishers* [2019] 109 taxmann.com 52/266 Taxman 91 (SC) that Tribunal finding that no unexplained payment was made in relevant assessment year, deleted addition made by Assessing Officer and High Court by impugned order held that since there was material on record pointing out that unexplained cash payments were made to assessee in earlier assessment year, impugned order passed by Tribunal that no addition could be made in assessment year in question, did not require any interference and Special Leave Petition filed against impugned order was dismissed.

◆ **Addition on the basis of agreement**

In the case of *P. Madhurajan (HUF)* v. *Asstt. CIT* [2015] 61 taxmann.com 274 (Mad.), it has been held that:

> (*i*) this was a question of fact, which the assessee should have pursued before the original authority or before the Commissioner (Appeals). The Tribunal, after examining the issue threadbare, declined to interfere with the order of the Commissioner (Appeals) principally on the ground that no reliability could be placed on the submissions made by the assessee, who had taken different stands

before the authorities below. There was no reason to interfere with the order of the Tribunal.

(*ii*) That the mere statement of Vanaja saying that she did not pay money or receive money was of no avail, when she herself admitted that she signed on the back of the agreement having received the money on the cancellation of the sale agreement. Her statement threw more light on the present case that was not a clear transaction. The entire transaction was shrouded in mystery and the Assessing Officer had correctly made additions.

◆ **Both inflow and outflow cannot be taxed**

In the case of *CIT* v. *Jalaj Batra* [2015] 61 taxmann.com 357/234 Taxman 271 (Bom.), it has been held that the finding of double taxation had been rendered after examining the matter in detail, namely, scrutiny of the bank accounts. Either the inflows had been explained with evidence and then the question of taxing the withdrawals would not arise or because there was no evidence, the taxing of the deposits in the bank was justified. The Tribunal held that both inflow and outflow could not be taxed. No substantial relief had been granted as complained by the Revenue particularly with regard to the items or grounds which had been given up before the Commissioner (Appeals). The findings of fact based thereon, therefore, reflected a possible view of the Tribunal. Such a view did not raise any substantial question of law particularly when it was not perverse as complained.

◆ **No Addition on the basis of journal entries**

It has been held in the case of *Dy. CIT* v. *Aarti Colonizer Company* 183 DTR (Raipur) 345 that in an assessment under s. 153A, computation of undisclosed income & addition made by AO solely on the basis of journal entries obtained from a pen drive, in the absence of any corroborative evidence of actual investment made by assessee could not be sustained.

(*ix*) **Burden of Proof**

◆ **Burden of proof is on the assessee to prove that Benami Bank Account did not belong to him**

Assessee having retracted from the admission made in statement under section 132(4) stating that the bank accounts did not belong to him but they belonged to different concerns which were assessed separately and produced details of such assessments for the first time before the Tribunal, additional evidence filed by the Department to enable the AO examine, verify and judge the correctness of the retraction is admissible. *Surendra M. Khandar* v. *Asstt. CIT* [2001] 76 ITD 121 (Mum. - Trib.)

◆ **Burden of proof**

Burden of proof is held to be on the Department in relation to 2 challans recovered during search and no books of account were found for the relevant period. On the facts of the case, it was held that it was for the Department to prove that the fabrication charges and purchases were not entered in the regular books of account. *Asstt. CIT* v. *Sweety Traders* [2007] 105 ITD 45 (Chd. - Trib.) (TM).

◆ **Section 69 - Difference in stock pledged with the bank - Burden of proof on the revenue**

Where the addition was made due to difference between the value of stock as recorded in the books and as found in the declaration to the Bank for getting overdraft, it was held that the burden of proof lay on the Revenue which could not be discharged merely by referring to the statement of the assessee to a third party. Addition was deleted. *CIT* v. *N. Swamy* [2000] 125 Taxman 233 (Mad.)

◆ **Where creditor did not respond to notice under section 131**

Fact that creditor did not turn up in response to summons under section 131 duly served would not entail adverse inference against the assessee. *G.G. Films* v. *ITO* [1993] 45 TTJ (Coch.-Trib.) 644

◆ **Plea for breach of principles of natural justice**

Where the assessee did not ask for cross examination he could not plead for breach of principles of natural justice. *K. Hari Prasad* v. *IAC* [1995] 52 ITD 563 (Hyd.-Trib.)

◆ **Discharge of burden of proof**

Supreme Court held in the case of *CIT* v. *Mussadilal Ram Bharose* [1987] 30 Taxman 546H/165 ITR 14 that the burden placed upon the assessee is not discharged by any fantastic explanation. Nor is it the law that any and every narration by the assessee must be accepted. It must be an explanation acceptable to the fact finding body.

◆ **Extent to which the Evidence Act is applicable to Income-tax proceedings**

In the case of *Chuharmal* v. *CIT* [1988] 38 Taxman 190, the Supreme Court held that what was meant by saying that the

Evidence Act did not apply to proceedings under Income-tax Act, 1961, was that the rigour of the rules of evidence contained in the Evidence Act was not applicable, but that did not mean that when the taxing authorities were desirous of invoking the principles of Evidence Act in the proceedings before them, they were prevented from doing so. The Supreme Court further held that all that section 110 of the Evidence Act, 1972 did say was to embody a salutary principle of common law jurisprudence, *viz.*, where a person was found in possession of anything, the 'onus of proving that he was not its owner was on that person. This principle could be attracted to a set of circumstances that satisfy the conditions and was applicable to taxation proceedings.

◆ **Onus on the Revenue**

It is held that in case of an addition proposed to be made under section 69, the burden of proof lied on the revenue to show that the payments were made outside the books.

In this case the credits represented credit purchases from blacksmiths. According to the Department, the assessee paid for such purchases in cash but recorded them as if on credit. On these facts it was held that the provisions of section 69 and not section 68 will apply and the onus in relation to section 69 lies on the revenue to show that the payments were made outside the books. No adverse inference could be drawn against the assessee merely because the Assessing Officer could not contact some of the blacksmiths. The credits were in the names of several parties and in odd figures. They did not represent cash credits. Statement of one blacksmith indicated that sometimes the payments were deferred. Even presuming that all the purchases were on cash basis, only the first purchase could be outside the books of account and for the purpose of making the addition the entire amount could not be taken into account. Addition of only small amount of ₹ 10,500 respectively sustained for two years sustained on estimate basis. [*Bafakyh Export House* v. *ITO* [1995] 53 TTJ (Coch.-Trib.) 293]

◆ **Burden of proof with regard to income and expenditure**

The burden is on the Department to prove that any amount received by the assessee is income. The burden is on the assessee to prove the claims that such an amount is exempt under any provisions of the taxing statute. Burden is on the assessee to prove his claim for deduction of any expenditure also. It is well settled in :

G. Venkataswami Naidu & Co. v. *CIT* [1959] 35 ITR 594 (SC);

Janki Ram Bahadur Ram v. *CIT* [1965] 57 ITR 21 (SC);

Saroj Kumar Mazumdar v. *CIT* [1959] 37 ITR 242 (SC);

CIT v. *Premji Gopalbhai* [1978] 113 ITR 785 (Guj.);

ITO v. *Ratnesh Kumari (Rani)* [1980] 123 ITR 343 (All.);

Abubucker Sait (Janab) v. *CIT* [1962] 45 ITR 37 (Mad.);

CIT v. *Raunaq Singh Swaran Singh* [1972] 85 ITR 220 (Delhi);

Dalmia Cement Ltd. v. *CIT* [1976] 105 ITR 633 (SC);

Virani D.S. v. *CIT* [1973] 90 ITR 255 (Guj.);

Deep Chandra & Co. v. *CIT* [1977] 107 ITR 716 (All.);

Lalit Ram Mangilal of Cawnpore v. *CIT* [1950] 18 ITR 286 (All.).

♦ Only because the opinion of registered valuer is not accepted or some other expert gives another opinion, is not by itself sufficient for arriving at a conclusion that the assessee had furnished inaccurate particulars attracting penalty under section 271(1)(*c*). Primary burden of proof of furnishing inaccurate particulars of income is on the Revenue and it is only on discharge of primary burden that secondary burden of proof would shift on the assessee. *Dilip N. Shroff* v. *Jt. CIT* [2007] 161 Taxman 218 (SC)

Burden on proof on Revenue

It has been held in the case of *Asstt. CIT* v. *Buldana Urban Co-operative Credit Society Ltd.* [2013] 32 taxmann.com 69/57 SOT 76 (URO) (Nag. - Trib.) that having regard to the presumption under section 292C, assessee having denied that the loose paper in question belongs to assessee, and the notings on the said paper not being in the handwriting of any employee of the assessee, addition made by the AO on the basis of said notings cannot be sustained in the absence of any corroborative evidence on record to disprove the explanation the assessee.

(*x*) Benefit of Telescoping

In the case of *Uday C. Tamhankar* v. *Dy. CIT* [2015] 127 DTR (Mum. 'F') 41 (Trib.), it has been held that Assessee having offered additional income of about ₹ 20 lakhs over and above the excess cash balance found during the course of search even though the Revenue authorities did not seize any other incriminating material, the additions under section 69C are to be telescoped against the said amount of ₹ 20 lakhs. Impugned additions made under section 69C being a small part of the aforesaid amount, no addition can be sustained.

(xi) **No assessment for non-existent company**

In the case of *CIT* v. *Micron Steels (P.) Ltd.* [2015] 117 DTR 89 (Delhi), during course of search in cases of other person, materials were seized which belonged to assessee-company and, accordingly, Assessing Officer issued notice under section 153 to assessee-company. By that time, assessee was already amalgamated. Assessee contended that on account of amalgamation and by operation of section 170, income-tax authorities were under a duty to initiate complete proceedings against transferee company which had not been done.

It was held that completion of assessment in respect of a non-existent company, due to amalgamation order, would render assessment in name and in respect of original assessee-company, a nullity. Further, if notice, summons or other proceeding taken by an authority suffers from an inherent lacuna affecting his/its jurisdiction, same cannot be cured by having resort to section 292B.

It has been held in the case of *BDR Builders and Developers (P.) Ltd.* v. *Asst. CIT* [2017] 85 taxmann.com 146 (Delhi) that in search and seizure assessment in search cases, where amalgamation of companies has taken place, warrant of authorisation and panchnama issued in the name of transferor company after it ceased to exist is bad and proceedings are void *ab initio.*

(xii) **Notice for filing returns**

◆ **Defect in issue of notice for filing returns**

◆ **Notice u/s 158BC(*a*)**

Notice under section 158BC(*a*) cannot be treated as invalid simply because of defect in specifying the status of assessee when the search was conducted in the case of the assessee in his individual capacity, it was well understood by the assessee and was duly complied with. *Dr. R.M.L Mehrotra* v. *Asstt. CIT* [1999] 68 ITD 288 (All. - Trib.).

◆ **Notice not a mere procedural requirement**

Notice under section 158BC is not merely a procedural requirement but a condition precedent for assuming jurisdiction; notice under s. 158BC addressed to assessee-company and not to its principal officer and not mentioning the status in which return was required to be furnished and not specifying exactly the 'person' who is required to file the return and the block period was wholly deficient; assessment made on the basis of said notice was bad in law and void *ab initio. VVS Alloys Ltd.* v. *Asstt. CIT* [2000] 68 TTJ (All.-Trib.) 516

'Issue of notice u/s 153A - section 292B to be considered'

It has been held in the case of *Dy. CIT* v. *K.M. Nagraj* [2007] 166 ITD 53/82 taxmann.com 170 (Beng. - Trib.) that in the case of Search and seizure assessment under section 153C, when notice under section 153A has been issued & Assessee having responded to the notice issued under section 153A by filing a return and also participated in the proceedings till the matter resulted in framing of the assessment despite the fact that the search operations were conducted in the case of a company and no search warrant was issued in the name of the assessee, the mistake on the part of the AO in mentioning section 153A instead of section 153C in the notice did not invalidate the proceedings initiated pursuant thereto in view of the provisions of section 292B.

(xiii) **Normal disallowances**

◆ **Disallowance of depreciation, interest etc.**

Since the assessee has produced sufficient documentary evidence to prove genuineness of leasing transactions made by it which the AO could not rebut by positive material, he cannot disallow the claim for depreciation on leased assets and interest paid on advance rental and treat it as undisclosed income in block assessment. *Microland Ltd.* v. *Asstt. CIT* [1998] 67 ITD 446 (Bang. - Trib.).

◆ **Block Assessment - Concept of real income**

'Concept of income' is a legal concept and amount of real income has to be arrived at after considering various aspects such as expenditure, year of taxability, etc., and such matters cannot be ignored in making an assessment even if a confessional statement is made. In doing so, the method of accounting followed by the assessee cannot be ignored and if it is found that the assessee confessed some income during search proceedings but none such income is actually found to have been earned on the basis of seized material, no assessment can be made on account of such income, in the year of search. *Dhanvarsha Builders & Developers (P.) Ltd.* v. *Dy. CIT* [2006] 102 ITD 375 (Pune - Trib.)

◆ **Block Assessment - Estimation of income to be made as per Net Profit Rate and not Gross Profit Rate**

Undisclosed income on account of unaccounted purchases is to be worked out by applying net profit rate and not GP rate. *Eagle Seeds & Biotech Ltd.* v. *Asstt. CIT* [2006] 100 ITD 301 (Indore-Trib.)

◆ **Confiscated gold- loss of business**

The amount of gold confiscated by Central Excise cannot be allowed as business loss. *Manharlal C. Soni* v. *CIT* [1996] 86 Taxman 407 (Guj.)

◆ **Valuation under section 16A of the Wealth-tax Act cannot be applied under the Income-tax Act**

Basana Rani Saha v. *ITO* [1990] 33 ITD 574 (Gauhati - Trib.) 188

◆ **Seizure of loose sheets reflecting sales - Only gross profit taxable**

During search some loose sheets were seized reflecting sales of ₹ 10,85,003 not recorded in the books of account. Tribunal held that the assessee could not be taxed on the entire amount but was liable to be taxed on the gross profit earned on the sales on the ground that the purchases had been fully vouched. *CIT* v. *Guru Bachhan Singh J. Juneja* [2008] 171 Taxman 406 (Guj.)

◆ **Addition on account of inadequate household expense**

That addition on account of inadequate household expenses and marriage expenses of children were justified especially considering the assessee maintained high standard of living and he estimated the amount spent on managers, Tribunal was justified in sustaining additions. Further, Tribunal had allowed accrued interest on fixed deposit. Held, it was not contrary to material on record. *CIT* v. *Rameshwar Lal Ahuja* [2009] 312 ITR 217 (Punj. & Har.)

(xiv) **No duplicate additions**

◆ **Cash introduced - Out of addition made in the preceding year after search**

During the assessment year 1987-88 ITO found credits of ₹ 5 lakhs in current account of assessee in the books of 'M'. Wealth-tax statements as on 31-3-1986 showed a cash balance of ₹ 5.17 lakhs. The assessee explained that pursuant to search in 1986, assessment for the assessment year 1986-87 was completed with an addition of ₹ 10 lakhs and cash balance of ₹ 5 lakhs was given out such income which in turn was brought into books as credit in its current account with 'M'. In view of the background of earlier addition, addition of cash credit of ₹ 5 lakhs in the assessment year 1987-88 was to be deleted. *B. Rajasekharan Nair* v. *Asstt. CIT* [1992] 40 ITD 273 (Coch. - Trib.)

♦ **Net Profit applied - No separate addition under section 68**

In the case of a civil contractor, book result was rejected and rate of net profit was estimated. In addition separate addition was made of ₹ 9,25,939 on account of cash introduced in the books and ₹ 9,77,535 on account of payments made for purchases made outside books of account. CIT(A) and ITAT held that when accounts were registered, separate addition for cash credits and purchases were not justified. The court perused the law laid down in *CIT* v. *Banwari Lal Banshidhar* [1998] 229 ITR 229 (All.), where it was observed that:

"When the gross profit rate is applied, there was no need for Assessing Officer to make scrutiny of the amount incurred on the purchases by the assessee and held that CIT(A) and ITAT were justified in holding that once the net profit rate was applied, no further addition was called for in respect of purchases and introduction of cash." - *CIT* v. *Aggarwal Engineering Co.* [2006] 156 Taxman 40 (Punj. & Har.) (Mag.).

♦ **Double assessment not permissible**

A person cannot be taxed twice over the same income. Where the partners admitted on money payment out of the suppressed profits of the firm, the firm was not entitled to set off this amount against its suppressed business profits. *Hotel Kiran* v. *Asstt. CIT* [2002] 82 ITD 453 (Pune - Trib.)

♦ **No addition in the case of director, if added in the name of company**

In the case of *Dr. William Britto* v. *CIT* [2015] 120 DTR (Panji) 289 (Trib.), it has been held that while making assessment order, it is the satisfaction of the Assessing Officer who made the enquiry and it should be a touchstone of the assessment order passed by him, the Commissioner cannot substitute his view in place of finding of the Assessing Officer until and unless the view taken by the Assessing Officer is unsustainable in law. No cogent material or evidence was brought by revenue which may prove that the decision taken by the Assessing Officer that the sum has not to be added in the hands of the company. The order passed by the Commissioner is illegal without jurisdiction. Therefore, on this basis, the order passed by the Assessing Officer is not erroneous and prejudicial to the interest of the revenue and, accordingly, the order passed under section 263 is quashed.

(xv) **No additions possible in block assessment under Chapter XIVB when no incriminating material is found during search**

♦ **Where no incriminating material is found during search, no undisclosed income can be added**

♦ No incriminating material having been found during search that might show that the assessee had made more investment in the properties than their declared value, no addition could be made in block assessment by referring the valuation of properties to the Valuation Officer. *CIT* v. *Ashok Khetrapal* [2008] 166 Taxman 75 (Delhi)

♦ Tribunal having recorded a clear finding of fact that the search at the assessee's premises did not lead to seizure of any incriminating evidence to suggest that any income had not been disclosed or would not have been disclosed, it was correct in holding that the AO was not justified in making additions on account of undisclosed investment in two properties on the basis of the report of the DVO; no substantial question of law arises. *CIT* v. *Manoj Jain* [2007] 163 Taxman 223 (Delhi)

♦ Undisclosed income in question not being determined on the basis of any search material but on the basis of report of special auditors who had given different colour to existing facts and which stood assessed in earlier assessment orders, Tribunal was justified in its view that section 158BA had no application to the facts of the case and therefore, no substantial question of law arises; appeal under section 260A dismissed. *CIT* v. *Ravi Kant Jain* [2001] 117 Taxman 28 (Delhi)

♦ Since the expenditure on fabrication of yarn as shown in the books of account of the relevant period was more than the expenditure found to have been incurred by the assessee on the basis of challans found at the time of search and the purchases of yarn were reflected in the audited accounts of the relevant period, neither the fabrication charges nor the purchases of yarn could be treated as unexplained expenses in the absence of any other material and, therefore, no addition could be made in block assessment. *Asstt. CIT* v. *Sweety Traders* [2007] 105 ITD 45 (Chd. - Trib.) (TM)

(xvi) **Levy of penalty in case of agreed addition during assessment**

♦ **Levy of penalty - Revised return after search**

Omission or wrong statement in the original return not being due to *bona fide* or inadvertent mistake, and revised return having been filed after search, Tribunal was justified in confirming penalty under section 271(1)(*c*). *M.S. Mohammad Marzook* v. *ITO* [2006] 283 ITR 254 (Mad.)

◆ **Section 69A and section 271(1)(*c*) - Levy of penalty on making additions in return**

Addition made under section 69A would not automatically justify levy of penalty under section 271(1)(*c*). *CIT* v. *Dharamchand L. Shah* [1993] 70 Taxman 414 (Bom.)

◆ **Assessing Officer does not have jurisdiction to enter into any contract with the assessee to impose or not to impose any penalty**

The Tribunal has further held that the Assessing Officer does not have any jurisdiction to enter into any contract with the assessee to impose or not to impose any penalty as this would depend on the merits of each case. The applicability of the penal provisions does not depend on the consent or otherwise of the assessee. In support, the Tribunal relied on *Rathnam & Co.* v. *IAC* [1980] 4 Taxman 342 (Mad.). In this case the Tribunal also held that the surrender was not voluntary or *bona fide*. Settlement after surrender held as valid. *ITO* v. *Akshay Bhandar* [1990] 33 ITD 13 (Gauhati-Trib.)

◆ **Section 132(4) read with *Explanation 5* to section 271(1)(*c*) Admission Retraction**

No penalty under section 271(1)(*c*) can be levied where the assessee has given valid, cogent and plausible reasons for the difference between the income declared in the return of income and admitted during the search and seizure proceedings under section 132(4) of the Act. *Pullangode Rubber Produce Co. Ltd.* v. *State of Kerala* [1973] 91 ITR 18 (SC)

(*xvii*) Addition for difference in stock

◆ **Additions to stock when found less - Sections 69B, 133A**

It was not proper to make addition under section 69B when a stock was found less than recorded in the books of account. *ITO* v. *Jewels Emporium* [1994] 48 ITD 164 (Ind.-Trib.)

◆ **Section 69B - Undisclosed income - Stock found short - Addition not justified**

Where the addition was made because stock was found less in the books than the inventory prepared on the date of search by applying gross profit rate, it was held that the addition made on that basis was not justified. *CIT* v. *Hindustan Mills & Electrical Stores* [1997] 95 Taxman 489 (MP)

◆ Unaccounted stock attracts section 69

Where during the course of survey operation under section 133A, a physical inventory was prepared and it was also found that the assessee had not maintained any quantitative stock record item-wise in respect of opening stock plus purchases less sales, so as to give the position of actual stock at any given point of time, it was held by the Tribunal that in the absence of any record, whole quantity of stock attracted the provisions of section 69 and only that part of the funds invested in stock was required to be deleted for which satisfactory *explanation* was offered. *Giggles (P.) Ltd.* v. *ITO* [1992] 43 ITD 388 (Delhi - Trib.)

◆ Difference in Bank statements and Stock Registers

Where a difference was found between the stock hypothecated with the bank and the stock registers and it was explained by the assessee that the stock figures given to the bank were only for the bank purposes and the stock registers were checked from time to time by the Civil Supplies and Sales-tax Department, it is was held that the addition was not justified. *Jai Sharda Rice Mills* v. *ITO* [1991] 36 ITD 254 (Asr. - Trib.)

No addition on the basis of presumptive investment

For an addition under section 69A, the Department must have detected some actual investment which the assessee had failed to explain. The investment must have been established. No addition can be made on the basis of presumptive investment which the assessee had failed to explain. The investment must have been established. No addition can be made on the basis of presumptive investment which would or should have been made. The Tribunal deleted the entire addition of ₹ 24.15 lacs. *ITO* v. *Shyam Sunder Dhoot* [1986] 17 ITD 274 (Jp. - Trib.)

◆ Difference between closing stock declared to bank and that disclosed in Income-tax return

Supreme Court has dismissed SLP by Revenue of Gujarat High Court where appeal by Revenue had been dismissed by Court in a case where Tribunal had deleted the addition under section 69B on account of difference between the closing stock furnished to the bank of availing of credit facility and that disclosed in the books of account furnished before the Income-tax authorities. *CIT* v. *Veerdip Rollers (P.) Ltd.* [2010] 323 ITR 341 (Guj.)

◆ **No addition when process of inventorisation was defective**

It has been held in the case of *CIT* v. *D.D. Gears Ltd.* [2012] 25 taxmann.com 562/211 Taxman 8 (Delhi) (Mag.) that the Tribunal having deleted the additions made by the AO towards the alleged discrepancy in stocks on the ground that the entire process of inventorisation followed by the income tax authorities was inaccurate as it was humanly impossible to complete the entire exercise in a single day and that the AO has not examined the reconciliation of stock filed by the assessee and ignored the value addition made to the semi-finished goods and the discount and profit element in arriving at the value of stocks coupled with the fact that there was no evidence of sale of stocks outside the books, finding of the Tribunal are findings of facts and, therefore, no substantial question of law arises out of the findings of the Tribunal *vis-à-vis* the impugned additions.

◆ **No addition for difference in stock undertaken on guestimate basis**

It has been held in the case of *CIT* v. *Bansal High Carbons (P.) Ltd.* [2007] 165 Taxman 243 (Delhi) that the search party having made a guestimate of enormous quantity of stock held by the assessee by following a short-cut and slipshod procedure rather than actual counting and weighing the bundles, the finding that excess stock was found during the course of search cannot be sustained and, therefore, addition on account of alleged excess stock was rightly deleted.

(xviii) **Addition u/s 68**

◆ **Gifts**

Where affidavits of the donors were filed who were income tax assessees and were also assessed in respect of gifts, it was held that rejection of application without making further enquiry and without issuing summons to donors was not justified. *Satyapal Wassan* v. *ITO* [1991] 39 TTJ (Jab.-Trib.) 72

◆ **Piece of paper seized at the time of search could not be construed to be a book for the purpose for section 68**

A piece of paper seized at the time of search could not be construed to be a 'book of account'. The term "book" is to be construed as is understood in the common parlance. No special meaning is assigned to that term in section 68. *Kantilal & Bros.* v. *Asstt. CIT* [1995] 52 ITD 412 (Pune - Trib.)

◆ **Production of confirmatory letters by assessee in respect of loan advanced by creditor**

Where the assessee produced two informatory letters but the creditors denied to have advanced a loan on a subsequent statement recorded by the Revenue at the back of the assessee they also denied to have signed the confirmatory letters and where the assessee subsequently produced the affidavits from the same creditors giving a completely different version, it, was held that such affidavits could not be relied upon. However, it was held that the matter deserved to be referred to the hand-writing expert for verification of signatures on confirmatory letters and in the event of those being found as genuine, cash credit should be accepted. *K. Hari Prasad* v. *IAC* [1995] 52 ITD 563 (Hyd. - Trib.)

◆ **Burden of proof where sum found is credited in the assessee's books**

In view of section 68 of the Income-tax Act, 1961, where any sum found is credited in the books of the assessee this may be charged to income-tax if the explanation offered about the nature of source thereof is not satisfactory. In such a case there is, *prima facie,* an evidence against the assessee, *viz.,* the receipt of money, and if the fails to rebut the said evidence, it can be used against him by holding that it was a receipt of an income nature. While considering the explanation of the assessee, the Department cannot, however, act unreasonably. *Sumati Dayal* v. *CIT* [1995] 80 Taxman 89/214 ITR 801 (SC)

◆ **Piece of paper would not constitute to be a book**

In *Kantilal & Bros.* v. *Asstt. CIT* [1995] 52 ITD 412 (Pune - Trib.), Pune Bench of the Tribunal held that a piece of paper impounded at the time of search would not constitute to be a book and as to the entries therein it was held that the assessee's case could not be put within the ken of section 68 of the Income-tax Act. The Tribunal observed that the term 'book' is to be construed as it is understood in the common parlance and no said meaning can be assigned to that term.

(xix) Addition u/s 69

◆ **Section 69A - Year in which addition be made**

Provisions of section 69A merely constitute a rule of evidence raising certain presumptions which can be rebutted with expla-nation of the assessee, or other evidence on record. Where the assessee is able to establish that the year of acquisition of an asset was other than the search year, the question of addition should be considered in that year. *Kewal G. Bajaj* v. *Asstt. CIT* [1999] 71 ITD 375 (Mum. - Trib.) (SMC)

◆ **Cash deposited in Bank - No books maintained - Amount assessable u/s 69 or 69B.**

The Special Bench in *Manoj Aggarwal* v. *Dy. CIT* [2008] 113 ITD 377 (Delhi-Trib.) (SB) held that in the case where:

   (*i*) Assessee is not maintaining any books of account, section 68 is not applicable.

  (*ii*) Bank statements cannot be considered as the assessee's books of account yet.

 (*iii*) On the basis of judgment of the Supreme Court in the case of *A. Govindarajulu Mudaliar* v. *CIT* [1958] 34 ITR 807, it is the onus of the assessee to explain the cash received by him.

 (*iv*) If there is no explanation or acceptable evidence to prove the nature and source of the receipt; and

  (*v*) The amount may be added as the assessee's, income on general principles, and it is not necessary for Revenue to point out the source of monies received.

Held further, that even if section 68 is not applicable, the cash deposit in the bank can be asked to be explained by the assessee under section 69 or section 69B.

◆ **Cash deposited in Bank but no books of account maintained - Assessable under section 69 or 69B**

It is held by Special Bench that where no books of account are maintained, and cash of ₹ 15 lac is deposited in assessee's bank and explanation offered is not accepted, "the cash deposited can be asked to be explained u/s 69 or section 69B". *Manoj Aggarwal* v. *Dy. CIT* [2008] 113 ITD 377 (Delhi - Trib.) (SB)

◆ **Not assessable under section 68 - But non-genuine credits assessable under section 69A**

In *Vinod Behari Jain* v. *ITO* [2009] 117 ITD 220 (Delhi - Trib.), it is held that—

Assessee was not maintaining books of account, and hence unexplained cash credit could not be assessed under section 68. Further held that gift amounts were not genuine and represent assessee's own-money introduced as gifts, therefore such amounts were deemed income of assessee. However addition could be made under section 69A and not under section 68.

◆ No addition on the basis of document found from third party

It has been held in the case of *ITO* v. *Dua Auto Components (P.) Ltd.* [2011] 16 taxmann.com 58/[2012] 49 SOT 85 (URO) (Delhi - Trib.) that the addition could not be made in the assessee's hand on the basis of documents found during the search at the premises of a third party which at best only showed the tentative price of a plot and did not indicate that they belong to the assessee or that on-money transaction has taken place in the purchase of said plot by the assessee.

◆ No addition for short cash found

It has been held in the case of *Dy. CIT* v. *Eastern Medikit Ltd.* [2012] 71 DTR 241 (Delhi 'B') that detection of shortage in cash *ipso facto* does not lead to inference of earning unaccounted income and, therefore, in the absence of any evidence of undisclosed income, mere statement of Director-cum-DGM (Finance) of the assessee company surrendering the deficit cash for taxation during the survey proceedings cannot be a ground for sustaining the addition.

◆ No addition on the basis of draft agreement

It has been held in the case of *Dy. CIT* v. *Rajat Agarwal* [2012] 27 taxmann.com 166 (Jp. - Trib.) that alleged amount of ₹ 1.85 crores cannot be said to have been paid by the assessee merely on the basis of the draft agreement and the papers found at the time of survey and when it was established that said deal was finally closed as per revised agreement and there was no evidences to show payment of ₹ 1.85 crores by assessee or his family members.

◆ No addition on the basis future schedule of payment

It has been held in the case of *CIT* v. *Tips Industries (P.) Ltd.* [2010] 190 Taxman 65 (Bom.) that the addition based on the notings on seized paper representing payment schedule of agreement yet to be executed, deletion of addition justified.

Evidence of advance paid unless rebutted may lead to addition

It has been held in the case of *Surendra M. Khandhar* v. *Asstt. CIT* [2010] 321 ITR 254 (Bom.) that the document stating that amount had been advanced by assessee having been discovered during search and the presumption being that contents of document are true which has not been rebutted by assessee, amount shown in document is assessable as unexplained investment in view of the presumption u/s 292C.

Addition on the basis of decoded document is sustainable

It has been held in the case of *Smt. Urmila Gambhir* v. *CIT* [2010] 34 DTR 169 (Delhi) that on the basis of document seized, the AO having concluded that the figures were in hundreds and pertained to land purchased by assessee and assessee having failed to establish that it was only a rough estimate of the cost of setting up a new project, addition was rightly made.

(xx) Assessment based upon instructions of other officers

◆ Block assessment based on instructions of DDI

Assessments made by AO under section 158BC pursuant to directions/instructions given in appraisal report of DDI, which is not produced before Tribunal even on asking for it, are vitiated and not sustainable in law as the act of framing the assessment is a quasi-judicial act which should be discharged independently, by the AO and not on the directions or instructions of superior authorities. *Kirtilal Kalidas & Co.* v. *Dy. CIT* [1998] 67 ITD 573 (Mad. - Trib.)

(xxi) Levy of interest

◆ Delay in supplying copies of seized material, levy of interest not justified

Delay in filing the return of the block period having occurred on account of the failure of the Department to give copies of the seized material and the statements of the assessee recorded in the course of search proceedings and not on account of any element of lack of *bona fides* on the part of assessee, levy of interest under section 158BFA(1) was not justified; interest is not leviable for the period until the xerox copies of all such materials were made available to the assessee. *Bachchubhai S. Antrolia* v. *Asstt. CIT* [2007] 288 ITR (AT) 57 (Rajkot)

(xxii) No addition when income was declared before Settlement Commission

In the case of *CIT* v. *Jever Jewellers* [2015] 64 taxmann.com 277/ [2016] 236 Taxman 282 (Jharkhand), addition was made by the Assessing Officer on account of discrepancy in the physical value and book value of the stock. It was held by High Court that the addition cannot be made in the hands of the assessee as the amount was disclosed by the partner of the assessee-firm before the Settlement Commission and was also accepted by it which was never questioned by the Department. Therefore, addition cannot be made in the hands of the assessee-firm. Further, in respect of method to be adopted for valuation of stock, it was held by the High Court that it is a well-settled principle of accountancy that the stock has to be valued at cost or market price whichever is lower.

(xxiii) Addition relating to Foreign bank account

It has been held by the Tribunal in the case of *Shyam Sunder Jindal* v. *Asstt. CIT* [2017] 81 taxmann.com 123/164 ITD 470/155 DTR 249 (Delhi - Trib.) that when in his statement recorded during search and also in the course of assessment, assessee denied having any bank account abroad in his own name or in the name of any member of his family, addition made by AO relying on copies of the copies which did not have any signature of bank official or name of the bank or the place or the country where the bank was situated was not sustainable. Matter was remanded for decision afresh after giving assessee adequate opportunity of hearing.

(xxiv) Miscellaneous

It has been held in the case of *Vetrivel Minerals* v. *Asstt. CIT* 208 DTR 280 (Mad.) that non-furnishing of copies of documents seized and Panchanama to assessees and non-providing of opportunity to cross-examine the persons whose statements were recorded under section 132(4) and used against assessees while framing assessment under section 153A amounted to violation of principles of natural justice.

15

ATTRACTION OF WEALTH TAX IN SEARCH CASES

The provisions regarding search and seizure under the Wealth-tax Act are almost similar as contained under the Income-tax Act. The provisions regarding search and seizure under the Wealth-tax Act are contained under section 37A, section 37B and section 37C which are almost corresponding to section 132, section 132A and section 132B of the Income-tax Act. Further rules 10 and 10A of the Wealth-tax Rules prescribe detailed procedure to be followed with regard to search and seizure operation. The same are identical to the powers given under the Income-tax Rules.

It may be noted that the Wealth-tax Act, 1957 stands abolished with effect from 1-4-2016 by Finance Act, 2016.

15.1 Text of section

"37A. (1) Where the Director General or Director or the Chief Commissioner or Commissioner or any such Joint Director or Joint Commissioner as may be empowered in this behalf by the Board, in consequence of information in his possession, has reason to believe that—

(a) any person to whom a notice under sub-section (4) of section 16 or a summons under section 37 was issued to produce, or cause to be produced, any books of account or other documents, has omitted or failed to produce, or cause to be produced, such books of account or other documents as required by such notice or summons, or

(b) any person to whom a notice or summons as aforesaid has been or might be issued will not, or would not, produce, or cause to be produced, any books of account or other documents which will be useful for, or relevant to, any proceeding under this Act, or (*c*) any person is in possession of any money, bullion, jewellery or other valuable article or thing disproportionate to his known assets, particulars of which will be useful for, or relevant to, any proceeding under this Act,

then,—

(*A*) the Director-General or Director or the Chief Commissioner or Commissioner, as the case may be, may authorize any Joint Director, Joint Commissioner, Assistant Director or Deputy Director, Assistant Commissioner or Deputy Commissioner or Income-tax Officer; or

(*B*) such Joint Director or Joint Commissioner may authorize any Assistant Director or Deputy Director or Assistant Commissioner or Deputy Commissioner or Income-tax Officer,

(the officer so authorized in all cases being hereafter in this section referred to as the authorized officer) to—

(*i*) enter and search any building, place, vessel, vehicle or aircraft where he has reason to suspect that such books of account or other documents, money, bullion, jewellery or other valuable article or things are kept;

(*ii*) search any person who has got out of, or is about to get into, or is in, the building, place, vessel, vehicle or aircraft, if the authorized officer has reason to suspect that such person has secreted about his person any such books of account or other documents, money, bullion, jewellery or other valuable article or thing;

(*iii*) break open the lock of any door, box, locker, safe, almirah or other receptacle for exercising the powers conferred by clause (*i*) where the keys thereof are not available;

(*iv*) seize any such books of account, other documents, money, bullion, jewellery or other valuable article or thing found as a result of such search;

(*v*) place marks of identification on any such books of account or other documents or make, or cause to be made, extracts or copies therefrom;

(*vi*) make a note or an inventory of any money, bullion, jewellery or other valuable article or thing found which, in his opinion, will be useful for, or relevant to, any proceeding under this Act:

Provided that where any building, place, vessel, vehicle or aircraft referred to in clause (*i*) is within the area of jurisdiction of any Chief Commissioner or Commissioner but such Chief Commissioner or

Commissioner has no jurisdiction over the person referred to in clause (*a*) or clause (*b*) or clause (*c*) of this sub-section, then, notwithstanding anything contained in section 8, it shall be competent for him to exercise the powers under this sub-section in all cases where he has reason to believe that any delay in getting the authorization from the Chief Commissioner or Commissioner having jurisdiction over such person may be prejudicial to the interests of the revenue:

Provided further that where it is not possible or practicable to take physical possession of any valuable article or thing and remove it to a safe place due to its volume, weight or other physical characteristics or due to its being of a dangerous nature, the authorized officer may serve an order on the owner or the person who is in immediate possession or control thereof that he shall not remove, part with or otherwise deal with it except with the previous permission of such authorized officer and such action of the authorized officer shall be deemed to be seizure of such valuable article or thing under clause (*iv*) of this sub-section.

(2) Where any Chief Commissioner or Commissioner, in consequence of information in his possession, has reason to suspect that any books of account or other documents, money, bullion, jewellery or other valuable article or thing in respect of which an officer has been authorized by the Director General or Director or any other Chief Commissioner or Commissioner or any such Joint Director or Joint Commissioner as may be empowered in this behalf by the Board to take action under clauses (*i*) to (*vi*) of sub-section (1) are kept in any building, place, vessel, vehicle or aircraft not mentioned in the authorization under sub-section (1), such Chief Commissioner or Commissioner may, notwithstanding anything contained in section 8, authorize the said officer to take action under any of the clauses aforesaid in respect of such building, place, vessel, vehicle or aircraft.

(3) The authorized officer may requisition the services of any police officer or of any officer of the Central Government, or of both, to assist him for all or any of the purposes specified in sub-section (1) or sub-section (2) and it shall be the duty of every such officer to comply with such requisition.

(3A) The authorized officer may, where it is not practicable to seize any books of account, other documents, money, bullion, jewellery or other valuable article or thing, for reasons other than those mentioned in the second proviso to sub-section (1), serve an order on the owner or the person who is in immediate possession or control thereof that he shall not remove, part with or otherwise deal with it except with the previous permission of such officer and such officer may take such steps as may be necessary for ensuring compliance with this sub-section.

Explanation.—For the removal of doubts, it is hereby declared that serving of an order as aforesaid under this sub-section shall not be deemed to be seizure of such books of account, other documents, money, bullion, jewellery or other valuable article or thing under clause (*iv*) of sub-section (1).

(4) The authorized officer may, during the course of the search or seizure, examine on oath any person who is found to be in possession or control of any books of account or other documents, articles or things including money and any statement made by such person during such examination may thereafter be used in evidence in any proceeding under this Act.

Explanation.—For the removal of doubts, it is hereby declared that the examination of any person under this sub-section may be not merely in respect of any books of account, other documents or assets found as a result of the search, but also in respect of matters relevant for the purposes of any investigation connected with any proceedings under this Act.

(5) Where any books of account or other documents, articles or things including money are found in the possession or control of any person in the course of a search, it may be presumed that—

   (*i*) such books of account or other documents, articles or things including money belong to such person;

   (*ii*) the contents of such books of account or other documents are true; and

   (*iii*) the signature and every other part of such books of account or other documents which purport to be in the handwriting of any particular person or which may reasonably be assumed to have been signed by, or to be in the handwriting of, any particular person, are in that person's handwriting, and in the case of a document stamped, executed or attested, that it was duly stamped and executed or attested by the person by whom it purports to have been so executed or attested.

(5A) Where any money, bullion, jewellery or other valuable article or thing (hereafter in this section and in sections 37B and 37C referred to as the assets) is seized under sub-section (1) or sub-section (2), the Assessing Officer, after affording a reasonable opportunity to the person concerned of being heard and making such inquiry as may be prescribed, shall, within one hundred and twenty days of the seizure, make an order, with the previous approval of the Joint Commissioner,—

(*i*) estimating the undisclosed net wealth in a summary manner to the best of his judgment on the basis of such materials as are available with him;

(*ii*) calculating the amount of tax on the net wealth so estimated in accordance with the provisions of this Act;

(*iii*) determining the amount of interest payable and the amount of any penalty imposable in accordance with the provisions of this Act, as if the order had been the order of regular assessment;

(*iv*) specifying the amount that will be required to satisfy any existing liability under this Act in respect of which such person is in default or is deemed to be in default, and retain in his custody such assets or part thereof as are in his opinion sufficient to satisfy the aggregate of the amounts referred it in clauses (*ii*), (*iii*) and (*iv*) and forthwith release the remaining portion, if any, of the assets to the person from whose custody they were seized:

Provided that where a person has paid or made satisfactory arrangements for payment of all the amounts referred to in clauses (*ii*), (*iii*) and (*iv*) or any part thereof, the Assessing Officer, may with the previous approval of the Chief Commissioner or Commissioner release the assets or such part thereof as he may deem fit in the circumstances of the case.

(5B) The assets retained under sub-section (5A) may be dealt with in accordance with the provisions of section 37C.

(5C) If the Assessing Officer is satisfied that the seized assets or any part thereof were held by such person for or on behalf of any other person, the Assessing Officer may proceed under sub-section (5A) against such other person and all the provisions of this section shall apply accordingly.

(6) The books of account or other documents, seized under sub-section (1) or sub-section (2), shall not be retained by the authorized officer for a period exceeding one hundred and eighty days from the date of the seizure unless the reasons for retaining the same are recorded by him in writing and the approval of the Chief Commissioner or Commissioner for such retention is obtained:

Provided that the Chief Commissioner or Commissioner shall not authorize the retention of the books of account or other documents for a period exceeding thirty days after all the proceedings under this

Act in respect of the years for which the books of account or other documents are relevant are completed.

(6A) An order under sub-section (3A) shall not be in force for a period exceeding sixty days from the date of the order, except where the authorized officer, for reasons to be recorded in writing by him, extends the period of operation of the order beyond sixty days, after obtaining the approval of the Director or, as the case may be, Commissioner for such extension:

Provided that the Director or, as the case may be, Commissioner shall not approve the extension of the period for any period beyond the expiry of thirty days after the completion of the proceedings under this Act in respect of the years for which the books of account, other documents, money, bullion, jewellery or other valuable articles or things are relevant.

(7) The person from whose custody any books of account or other documents are seized under sub-section (1) or sub-section (2) may make copies thereof, or take extracts therefrom, in the presence of the authorized officer or any other person empowered by him in this behalf at such place and time as the authorized officer may appoint in this behalf.

(8) Where the authorized officer has no jurisdiction over the person referred to in clause (*a*) or clause (*b*) or clause (*c*) of sub-section (1), the books of account or other documents seized under that sub-section shall be handed over by the authorized officer to the Assessing Officer having jurisdiction over such person within a period of fifteen days of such seizure and thereupon the powers exercisable by the authorized officer under sub-section (6) or sub-section (7) shall be exercisable by such Assessing Officer.

(9) If a person legally entitled to the books of account or other documents seized under sub-section (1) or sub-section (2) objects for any reason to the approval given by the Chief Commissioner or Commissioner under sub-section (6), he may make an application to the Board stating therein the reasons for such objection and requesting for the return of the books of account or other documents.

(9A) If any person objects for any reason to an order made under sub-section (5A), he may, within thirty days from the date of such order, make an application to the Chief Commissioner or Commissioner stating therein the reasons for such objection and requesting for appropriate relief in the matter.

(10) On receipt of the application under sub-section (9), the Board, or on receipt of the application under sub-section (9A), the Chief

Commissioner or Commissioner, may, after giving the applicant an opportunity of being heard, pass such orders as it or he thinks fit.

(11) The provisions of the Code of Criminal Procedure, 1973 (2 of 1974), relating to searches shall apply, so far as may be, to searches under this section.

(12) The Board may make rules in relation to searches or seizure under this section; and in particular and without prejudice to the generality of the foregoing power, such rules may provide for the procedure to be followed by the authorized officer—

(*i*) for obtaining ingress into any building, place, vessel, vehicle or aircraft to be searched where free ingress thereto is not available;

(*ii*) for ensuring the safe custody of any books of account or other documents seized.

Explanation 1.—In computing the period referred to in sub-section (5A) for the purposes of that sub-section, any period during which any proceeding under this section is stayed by an order or injunction of any court shall be excluded.

Explanation 2.—In this section, the word "proceeding" means any proceeding in respect of any year under this Act which may be pending on the date on which a search is authorized under this section or which may have been completed on or before such date and includes also proceedings under this Act which may be commenced after such date in respect of any year.

37B. (1) Where the Director General or Director or the Chief Commissioner or Commissioner, in consequence of information in his possession, has reason to believe that—

(*a*) any person to whom a notice under sub-section (4) of section 16 or a summons under section 37 was issued to produce, or cause to be produced, any books of account or other documents has omitted or failed to produce, or cause to be produced, such books of account or other documents as required by such notice or summons and the said books of account or other documents have been taken into custody by any officer or authority under any other law for the time being in force, or

(*b*) any books of account or other documents will be useful for, or relevant to, any proceeding under this Act and any person to whom a notice or summons as aforesaid has been or might be issued will not, or would not, produce or cause to be produced such books of account or other documents on the return of such books of account or other documents by any officer or authority by whom or which such books of account or other documents have been taken into custody under any other law for the time being in force, or

(*c*) any assets disproportionate to the known assets of any person, particulars of which will be useful for, or relevant to, any proceeding under this Act, have been taken into custody by any officer or authority under any other law for the time being in force, from the possession of such person,

then, the Director-General or Director or the Chief Commissioner or Commissioner may authorize any Joint Director, Joint Commissioner, Assistant Director or Deputy Director or Assistant Commissioner or Deputy Commissioner or Income-tax Officer (hereafter in this section referred to as the requisitioning officer) to require such officer or authority to deliver such books of account, other documents, or assets to the requisitioning officer.

(2) On a requisition being made under sub-section (1), the officer or authority referred to in clause (*a*) or clause (*b*) or clause (*c*), as the case may be, of that sub-section shall deliver the books of account, other documents, or assets to the requisitioning officer either forthwith or when such officer or authority is of the opinion that it is no longer necessary to retain the same in his or its custody.

(3) Where any books of account, other documents, or assets have been delivered to the requisitioning officer, the provisions of sub-sections (5) to (12) (both inclusive) of section 37A and section 37C shall, so far as may be, apply as if such books of account, other documents, or assets had been seized under sub-section (1) of section 37A by the requisitioning officer from the custody of the person referred to in clause (*a*) or clause (*b*) or clause (*c*) of sub-section (1) of this section and as if for the words "the authorized officer" occurring in sub-sections (5) to (12) aforesaid, the words "the requisitioning officer" were substituted.

37C. (1) The assets retained under sub-section (5A) of section 37A may be dealt with in the following manner, namely :—

(*i*) the amount of the existing liability referred to in clause (*iv*) of the said sub-section and the amount of the liability determined on completion of the regular assessment or reassessment for all the assessment years for which the net wealth referred to in clause (*i*) of that sub-section is assessable to tax (including any penalty levied or interest payable, in connection with such assessment or reassessment) and in respect of which the assessee is in default or is deemed to be in default may be recovered out of such assets;

(*ii*) if the assets consist solely of money, or partly of money and partly of other assets, the Assessing Officer may apply such money in the discharge of the liabilities referred to in clause (*i*) and the assessee shall be discharged of such liabilities to the extent of the money so applied;

(*iii*) the assets other than money may also be applied for the discharge of any such liability referred to in clause (*i*) as remains undischarged and for this purpose such assets shall be deemed to be under distraint as if such distraint was effected by the Assessing Officer under authorization from the Chief Commissioner or Commissioner under sub-section (5) of section 226 of the Income-tax Act as made applicable to this Act by section 32, and the Assessing Officer may recover the amount of such liabilities by the sale of such assets and such sale shall be effected in the manner laid down in the Third Schedule to the Income-tax Act as made applicable to this Act by section 32.

(2) Nothing contained in sub-section (1) shall preclude the recovery of the amount of liabilities aforesaid by any other mode laid down in this Act.

(3) Any assets or proceeds thereof which remain after the liabilities referred to in clause (*i*) of sub-section (1) are discharged shall be forthwith made over or paid to the persons from whose custody the assets were seized.

(4) (*a*) The Central Government shall pay simple interest at the rate of fifteen per cent per annum on the amount by which the aggregate of the money retained under section 37A and of the proceeds, if any, of the assets sold towards the discharge of the existing liability referred to in clause (*iv*) of sub-section (5A) of that section exceeds the aggregate of the amounts required to meet the liabilities referred to in clause (*i*) of sub-section (1) of this section.

(*b*) Such interest shall run from the date immediately following the expiry of the period of six months from the date of the order under sub-section (5A) of section 37A to the date of the regular assessment or reassessment referred to in clause (*i*) of sub-section (1) or, as the case may be, to the date of the last of such assessments or reassessments."

15.2 Legislative history

The provisions regarding search and seizure under the Wealth Tax Act have been enacted and amended from time to time in the same manner and with the same spirit as under the Income-tax Act. Original section 37A was inserted by the Wealth-tax (Amendment) Act, 1964 with effect from 1st April, 1965. Section 37A and section 37B were Substituted for original section 37A by the Taxation Laws (Amendment) Act, 1975 with effect from 1st October, 1975. Further, section 37C has been inserted by the Direct Tax Laws (Amendment) Act, 1987, with effect from 1st April, 1989.

It may be noted that the Wealth-tax Act, 1957 stands abolished with effect from 1-4-2016 by the Finance Act, 2016.

15.3 Objective

Under the Direct Taxes, Wealth-tax is also levied apart from income-tax. Wealth-tax is levied on the value of "net wealth" as on the closing of the financial year, owned by a person. As per Finance Act, 1992, with effect from 1st April, 1993, levy of wealth-tax has been restricted only on individual, HUF and certain class of companies, applicable only on certain class of assets as defined under clause (*ea*) of section 2 of the Wealth-tax Act. The provisions regarding search and seizure under the Wealth-tax Act have been incorporated to collect evidences and seize assets, wherever there is evasion of wealth-tax.

15.4 Similarities between the provisions under both the Acts

The provisions regarding search and seizure under the Income-tax Act and under the Wealth-tax Act are almost on the similar lines and do correspond to each other. The same income-tax authorities discharge the function under the Wealth Tax Act as wealth-tax authorities. Below is a table given describing the corresponding sections under both the Acts—

Wealth Tax Act, 1957	Subject-matter	Income Tax Act, 1961
(Section)		(Section)
37A (1)	Power of search and seizure	132(1)
37A (1), first proviso	Exercising of power by Chief CIT or CIT not having jurisdiction	132(1), first proviso
37A(1), second proviso	Constructive seizure	132(1), second proviso
37A(2)	Exercising the power in respect of building, places, etc., not mentioned in authorization	132(1A)
37A(3)	Requisition of service of police or any Central Government Officer	132(2)
37A(3A)	Restraint order	132(3)

Wealth Tax Act, 1957	Subject-matter	Income Tax Act, 1961
37A(4)	Statement on oath during search	132(4)
37A(5)	Presumption regarding books of account, documents or other valuable articles found during search	132(4A)
37A(5A)	Omitted (Provisional assessment for limited purpose)	132(5)
37A(5B)	Omitted (Dealing with assets retained)	132(6)
37A(5C)	Omitted (Assets related to any other person)	132(7)
37A(6)	Retention of seized books of account, documents, etc.	132(8)
37A(6A)	Expiry of restraint order	132(8A)
37A(7)	Taking copies from seized books of account etc.	132(9)
37A(8)	Seized documents relating to other person	132(9A)
37A(9)	Objection to CBDT (Board)	132(10)
37A(9A)	Omitted (Application to Chief CIT or CIT)	132(11)
37A(10)	Omitted	132(12)
37A(11)	Cr.P.C. to apply.	132(13)
37A(12)	Rule making power of Board	132(14)
37B	Requisition of books of account, documents, money, valuables etc.	132A
37C	Application of retained assets	132B

15.5 Why is there a separate provision under the Wealth-tax Act?

Truly speaking, there is no need of having separate provisions regarding search and seizure under the Wealth-tax Act and there has been hardly any case when powers of search and seizure under the Wealth-tax Act have been exercised independently to collect evidences and seize assets for evasion of wealth tax. Any evasion of wealth tax may very well be protected by action of search and seizure under the Income Tax Act itself. It seems that separate provisions have been made under the Wealth Tax Act just to supplement the action of search and seizure under the Income Tax Act. It has been noticed in practice that authorization for action under the Income Tax Act contains the reference of corresponding section of Wealth Tax Act also.

15.6 Assets on which wealth-tax is leviable

With effect from A.Y. 1993-94, wealth-tax is applicable, in practical sense, with respect to the following assets —

1. Any unproductive building or land appurtenant thereto.
2. Motor cars.
3. Jewellery, bullion, furniture, utensils or any other article made wholly or partly of gold, silver, platinum or any other precious metal other than when used as stock-in-trade in business.
4. Yachts, boats and aircrafts.
5. Urban land.
6. Cash-in-hand in excess of ₹ 50,000 in case of Individual and HUF.

Any other assets of whatsoever nature are not covered for the purpose of levy of wealth-tax.

15.7 Use of the phrase "disproportionate to his known assets"

Under clause (c) to section 37A(1), which is corresponding to clause (c) of section 132(1) of the Income Tax Act, phrase "disproportionate to his known assets" has been used, meaning of which is not very clear. Clause (c) reads as under :

> "Any person is in possession of any money, bullion, jewellery or other valuable article or thing disproportionate to his known assets, particulars of which will be useful for, or relevant to, any proceeding under this Act."

There may be assets which may be disproportionate to the known source of income or declared sources of income but it is difficult to comprehend the meaning of the phrase "assets disproportionate to the known assets". Infact, reference seems to be to the assets not disclosed under the Wealth Tax Act.

Under the Wealth-tax Act, all assets owned by a person are not required to be disclosed. Only those assets which are covered for the purpose of levy of wealth-tax are required to be disclosed in the wealth-tax return and wealth-tax is required to be paid on the same. As discussed above, there are only six categories of assets covered for the purpose of levy of wealth-tax. Therefore, reference can be made only to those undisclosed assets for the purpose of this clause.

15.8 Collection of evidences

The exercise of collection of evidences *i.e.* books of account or other documents will be similar and common under the Income-tax Act as well as under the Wealth-tax Act. It is the same evidences which suggest undisclosed income, would suggest undisclosed wealth for the purpose of Wealth-tax Act.

15.9 Seizure of assets for evasion of wealth-tax

Specific seizure of assets being in the nature of undisclosed assets where evasion of wealth-tax is involved may be in rare cases. Out of six categories of assets on which wealth-tax is leviable, it is only cash and jewellery which may practically be seized. Any cash or jewellery found during search and which is undisclosed in nature, is treated as undisclosed income for the current year as per the deeming fiction under section 69 of the Income-tax Act. There can be no evasion of wealth-tax with respect to such cash or jewellery up to the date of search since wealth-tax can be levied as on the valuation date *i.e.* 31st March following the date of search. In view of the above, such cash or jewellery relating to current financial year cannot be seized for any evasion of wealth-tax under the provisions of Wealth-tax Act.

However, there may be cases where jewellery has been acquired seven years prior to the year of search or cash found in locker is traced to have been kept in the locker since more than seven years prior to the year of search. Such cash or jewellery cannot be seized under the Income-tax Act since no tax liability with respect to assets acquired prior to seven years can be imposed under the Income-tax Act and therefore, such cash or jewellery cannot be treated as undisclosed even if assessee is not able to establish the source of acquisition of such cash or jewellery.

But such cash or jewellery is liable to be covered under the provisions of Wealth-tax Act and it is required to file wealth-tax return and pay wealth-tax every year on the value of such wealth along with other assets, if any, covered in accordance with the provision of Wealth-tax Act. Under such circumstances, such cash or jewellery may be seized for evasion of wealth tax. This is one circumstance where separate provision of search and seizure under Wealth-tax Act become relevant and useful.

There may be another situation when source regarding acquisition of assets is established by the assessee and there is no evasion of income-tax with respect to such assets. However, due to ignorance or some other reason, wealth-tax returns have not been filed by the assessee and wealth-tax has not been paid with respect to such assets though the same are covered within the definition of "assets" on which wealth-tax is leviable. Under such circumstances also, such assets may be seized under the Wealth-tax Act though the same cannot be seized under the Income-tax Act.

PENALTIES AND PROSECUTION
IN SEARCH CASES

16.1 Introduction - Penalty for concealment of income in search cases

Provisions regarding penalty for concealment of particulars of income or furnishing inaccurate particulars of income have been given under section 271(1)(c) read with earlier *Explanation 5* and now *Explanation 5A* of the Income-tax Act, 1961. As per the Finance Act, 2016 with effect from 1st April, 2017 penalty provision has been restructured and now penalty is leviable for under reporting and misreporting of income as provided under section 270A in place of earlier penalty provision contained under section 271(1)(c). Further, provisions for the levy of penalty in respect of "undisclosed income" found during the course of search in respect of the "specified previous year" are contained under section 271AAA/271AAB of the Income Tax Act.

In the case of search initiated before 1st June, 2007, provision of section 271(1)(c) along with *Explanation 5* is applicable. In the case of search initiated on or after 1st June, 2007, provision of section 271(1)(c) along with *Explanation 5A* or with effect from A.Y. 2017-18, provision under section 270A shall be applicable. Penalty for search cases for 'specified previous year' *qua* 'undisclosed income' shall be governed by the provisions of section 271AAA/271AAB.

First of all, we would analyze the provisions regarding penalty as contained under section 271AAA/271AAB and under *Explanation 5A* to section 271(1) (c) which are applicable in the case of search initiated on or after 1st June, 2007. Thereafter, we would analyze the provisions of penalty as contained under *Explanation 5* to section 271(1)(c) which are applicable in the case of search initiated before 1st June, 2007. Provision of section 270A would also be discussed which are applicable from A.Y. 2017-18.

In the case of search initiated on or after 1st June, 2007, penalty provisions are applicable under section 271AAA/271AAB for "specified previous year" with respect to "undisclosed income" as defined under that section whereas penalty provisions for other than "specified previous year" and in respect of concealed income, have been dealt under *Explanation 5A* to section 271(1)(*c*) and now with effect from A.Y. 2017-18, under the provision of section 270A.

16.2 Penalty provision under section 271AAA/271AAB

Penalty provision in the case of search initiated under section 132 on or after 1st June, 2007, with respect to the "undisclosed income" of the "specified previous year" *i.e.* year of search and immediately earlier year if due date of filing of return has not expired and income-tax return for such year has not been filed, are contained and governed by section 271AAA and not by the provisions of section 271(1)(*c*). The quantum of penalty to be levied under section 271AAA is substantially less than the quantum of penalty levied under section 271(1)(*c*) and thus, penalty provisions under section 271AAA are much relaxed in comparison to penalty provisions under section 271(1)(*c*).

However in relation to search initiated on or after 1-7-2012, penalty provision for 'specified previous year' *qua* 'undisclosed income' has been substituted by the provision of section 271AAB according to which higher rate of penalty has been prescribed.

16.3 Text of sections 271AAA and 271AAB

Text of section 271AAA

◆ Section 271AAA

(*1*) *The Assessing Officer may, notwithstanding anything contained in any other provisions of this Act, direct that, in a case where search has been initiated under section 132 on or after the 1st day of June, 2007 but before the 1st day of July, 2012, the assessee shall pay by way of penalty, in addition to tax, if any, payable by him, a sum computed at the rate of ten per cent of the undisclosed income of the specified previous year.*

(*2*) *Nothing contained in sub-section (1) shall apply if the assessee, —*

(i) *in the course of the search, in a statement under sub-section (4) of section 132, admits the undisclosed income and specifies the manner in which such income has been derived;*

(ii) *substantiates the manner in which the undisclosed income was derived; and*

  (iii) *pays the tax, together with interest, if any, in respect of the undisclosed income.*

 (3) *No penalty under the provisions of clause (c) of sub-section (1) of section 271 shall be imposed upon the assessee in respect of the undisclosed income referred to in sub-section (1).*

 (4) *The provisions of sections 274 and 275 shall, so far as may be, apply in relation to the penalty referred to in this section.*

Explanation.—For the purposes of this section,—

 (a) *"undisclosed income" means—*

  (i) *any income of the specified previous year represented, either wholly or partly, by any money, bullion, jewellery or other valuable article or thing or any entry in the books of account or other documents or transactions found in the course of a search under section 132, which has—*

   (A) *not been recorded on or before the date of search in the books of account or other documents maintained in the normal course relating to such previous year; or*

   (B) *otherwise not been disclosed to the Principal Chief Commissioner or Chief Commissioner or Principal Commissioner or Commissioner before the date of search; or*

  (ii) *any income of the specified previous year represented, either wholly or partly, by any entry in respect of an expense recorded in the books of account or other documents maintained in the normal course relating to the specified previous year which is found to be false and would not have been found to be so, had the search not been conducted;*

 (b) *"specified previous year" means the previous year—*

  (i) *which has ended before the date of search, but the date of filing the return of income under sub-section (1) of section 139 for such year has not expired before the date of search and the assessee has not furnished the return of income for the previous year before the said date; or*

  (ii) *in which search was conducted.*

◆ Section 271AAB

Penalty where search has been initiated.

271AAB. (1) The Assessing Officer or the Commissioner (Appeals) may, notwithstanding anything contained in any other provisions of this Act, direct that, in a case where search has been initiated under section 132 on or after the 1st day of July, 2012 but before the date on which the Taxation Laws (Second Amendment) Bill, 2016 receives the assent of the President, the assessee shall pay by way of penalty, in addition to tax, if any, payable by him,—

(*a*) a sum computed at the rate of ten per cent of the undisclosed income of the specified previous year, if such assessee—

    (*i*) in the course of the search, in a statement under sub-section (4) of section 132, admits the undisclosed income and specifies the manner in which such income has been derived;

    (*ii*) substantiates the manner in which the undisclosed income was derived; and

    (*iii*) on or before the specified date—

        (*A*) pays the tax, together with interest, if any, in respect of the undisclosed income; and

        (*B*) furnishes the return of income for the specified previous year declaring such undisclosed income therein;

(*b*) a sum computed at the rate of twenty per cent of the undisclosed income of the specified previous year, if such assessee—

    (*i*) in the course of the search, in a statement under sub-section (4) of section 132, does not admit the undisclosed income; and

    (*ii*) on or before the specified date—

        (*A*) declares such income in the return of income furnished for the specified previous year; and

        (*B*) pays the tax, together with interest, if any, in respect of the undisclosed income;

(*c*) a sum computed at the rate of sixty per cent of the undisclosed income of the specified previous year, if it is not covered by the provisions of clauses (*a*) and (*b*).

(1A) The Assessing Officer or the Commissioner (Appeals) may, notwithstanding anything contained in any other provisions of this Act, direct that, in a case where search has been initiated under section 132 on or after the date on which the Taxation Laws (Second Amendment) Bill, 2016 receives the assent of the President, the assessee shall pay by way of penalty, in addition to tax, if any, payable by him,—

    (*a*) a sum computed at the rate of thirty per cent of the undisclosed income of the specified previous year, if the assessee—

        (*i*) in the course of the search, in a statement under sub-section (4) of section 132, admits the undisclosed income and specifies the manner in which such income has been derived;

        (*ii*) substantiates the manner in which the undisclosed income was derived; and

        (*iii*) on or before the specified date—

            (*A*) pays the tax, together with interest, if any, in respect of the undisclosed income; and

            (*B*) furnishes the return of income for the specified previous year declaring such undisclosed income therein;

    (*b*) a sum computed at the rate of sixty per cent of the undisclosed income of the specified previous year, if it is not covered under the provisions of clause (*a*).

(2) No penalty under the provisions of section 270A or clause (*c*) of sub-section (1) of section 271 shall be imposed upon the assessee in respect of the undisclosed income referred to in sub-section (1) or sub-section (1A).

(3) The provisions of sections 274 and 275 shall, as far as may be, apply in relation to the penalty referred to in this section.

Explanation.—For the purposes of this section,—

    (*a*) "specified date" means the due date of furnishing of return of income under sub-section (1) of section 139 or the date on which the period specified in the notice issued under section 148 or under section 153A, as the case may be, for furnishing of return of income expires, as the case may be;

    (*b*) "specified previous year" means the previous year—

        (*i*) which has ended before the date of search, but the date of furnishing the return of income under sub-section (1) of section 139 for such year has not expired before the date of search and the assessee has not furnished the return of income for the previous year before the date of search; or

        (*ii*) in which search was conducted;

(*c*) "undisclosed income" means—

  (*i*) any income of the specified previous year represented, either wholly or partly, by any money, bullion, jewellery or other valuable article or thing or any entry in the books of account or other documents or transactions found in the course of a search under section 132, which has—

   (*A*) not been recorded on or before the date of search in the books of account or other documents maintained in the normal course relating to such previous year; or

   (*B*) otherwise not been disclosed to the Principal Chief Commissioner or Chief Commissioner or Principal Commissioner or Commissioner before the date of search; or

  (*ii*) any income of the specified previous year represented, either wholly or partly, by any entry in respect of an expense recorded in the books of account or other documents maintained in the normal course relating to the specified previous year which is found to be false and would not have been found to be so had the search not been conducted.

16.4 Legislative history - Significant amendments

Provision of section 271AAA has been inserted by the Finance Act, 2007 and is applicable along with *Explanation 5A* to section 271(1)(*c*) with respect to search initiated under section 132 on or after 1st June, 2007. In case of search initiated on or after 1st June, 2003 but before 1st June, 2007, wherein assessments are framed in accordance with provisions of section 153A, penalty provision with respect to such assessments are contained and governed by section 271(1)(*c*) read with *Explanation 5*.

In the case of block assessment regime applicable to income-tax search initiated on or after 1st July, 1995 till 31st May, 2003, special procedure for assessment of search cases for the block period as per Chapter XIV-B of the Act was applicable and there was no attraction of penalty for concealment of income u/s 271(1)(*c*) with respect to undisclosed income for the block period, as there was specific provision of penalty prescribed u/s 158BFA (2).

Prior to the block assessment regime *i.e.* in case of search conducted before 1st July, 1995, general provision of penalty as contained under section 271(1)(*c*) read with *Explanation 5* thereto was applicable.

Finance Act, 2012 has introduced a new section 271AAB prescribing provision for imposition of penalty in a case where search has taken place on or after 1st July, 2012. The imposition of penalty relating to undisclosed income of the specified previous year in a case where search has taken place on or after 1.7.2012 shall now be governed as per provision of section 271AAB and not as per provisions of section 271AAA. The provisions of section 271AAA shall remain applicable in a case when search has taken place before 1st July, 2012.

The Taxation Laws (Second Amendment) Act, 2016 with respect to search initiated on or after 15th December, 2016 has inserted sub-section (1A) to section 271AAB by which the rate of penalty to be levied under this section was restructured and increased substantially.

Further, as per Finance Act, 2016 with effect from 1st April, 2017 penalty provision for the years prior to 'specified previous year' which were governed by the provision of section 271(1)(c) have been substituted by section 270A.

As per the amendment brought by the Finance Act, 2022 under section 271AAB, the power of levying the penalty under this section has been given to the Commissioner of Income Tax (Appeal) also along with the assessing officer also which was earlier missing.

16.5 Objective

Objective of section 271AAA/271AAB regarding penalty for "undisclosed income" of the "specified previous year" in cases of search initiated on or after 1st June, 2007 may be summarized as under—

1. For the year of search and for immediately earlier year for which income-tax return has not been filed and the due date for filing income-tax return has not expired, the assessee has opportunity to file his return of income and to disclose any income including the "undisclosed income" found during search relating to such years. As a matter of general proposition, there can be no concealment of income till filing of the return as per normal provisions of section 271(1)(c), as the concealment of income can be attributed with reference to the return filed. However, as per provision of section 271AAA/271AAB, deeming fiction of "undisclosed income" has been enacted and it has been provided that any income found as a result of search not recorded in the books of account or other documents maintained in the normal course will be deemed to be "undisclosed income". Therefore, an opportunity has been given to the assessee to come clean and declare such undisclosed income while making statement under section 132(4) in the course of search so that the same would no longer be treated as "undisclosed income" and no or lower penalty for the same is levied.

2. To give an opportunity to the assessee for making declaration u/s 132(4), of undisclosed assets i.e. money, bullion, jewellery or other

valuable article or thing found in the course of search and representing "undisclosed income" of the assessee relating to "specified previous year", without attraction of penalty or attraction of lower rate of penalty for concealment.

3. By obtaining declaration of "undisclosed income" u/s 132(4) relating to "specified previous year", it is intended to settle the issue with the assessee so as to collect tax and interest without levy of any penalty or lower rate of penalty for concealment.

4. The above provision regarding imposition of penalty is available only when assessee comes clean specifying and substantiating the manner in which such undisclosed income has been derived by him and paying the tax together with interest in respect of such undisclosed income.

5. In case declaration of "undisclosed income" is not made by the assessee in the course of search and in the manner as prescribed under section 271AAA/271AAB, penalty on undisclosed income is leviable as per the provision contained therein.

16.6 Rationale of the provisions of section 271AAA/271AAB

The rationale of provision of section 271AAA can be said to have an early settlement with the assessee so that Department is able to obtain the declaration of undisclosed income and collect taxes without prolonged litigation. Further, the quantum of penalty under section 271AAA is substantially less than the quantum of penalty under section 271(1)(c), probably for the reason that there is deeming fiction of "undisclosed income" and legislature intends to levy lesser penalty on such deemed undisclosed income. Provision of section 271AAA is applicable only for "specified previous year" and not for earlier years for which income-tax return has already been filed or due date for filing of return of income has already expired and return has not been filed. Provision of section 271AAA, no doubt, was a beneficial provision to the taxpayers and put the tax evasion at premium and in certain quarters, this provision has been fiercely criticized on this score.

In view of the criticism of the provision of section 271AAA, this section was substituted by section 271AAB in case of search initiated on or after 1st July, 2012. It may be noted that the amended provision of section 271AAB is now very harsh and does not meet the rationale as discussed above in relation to provision of section 271AAA. As per amended provision of section 271AAB, minimum penalty at the rate of 30% of the undisclosed income is leviable even if declaration of undisclosed income is made in the course of search. Therefore, now there is hardly any motivation to the tax payers for making declaration of undisclosed income in the course of search.

16.7 Nature and scope of penalty provision under section 271AAA

(i) Applicable in the case of search initiated on or after 1st June, 2007 but before 1st July, 2012

Provision of section 271AAA is applicable in respect of the "undisclosed income" as a result of income-tax search under section 132 initiated on or after 1st June, 2007 but before 1st July, 2012. In fact, there has been major shift regarding the provision for imposition of penalty in case of search under section 132 initiated on or after 1st June, 2007 by way of introduction of provision of section 271AAA. The rigors of imposition of penalty for concealment of income have been mitigated to a large extent by introduction of section 271AAA in respect of the "undisclosed income" of the "specified previous year". An opportunity has been given to the assessee to come clean by making declaration of undisclosed income u/s 132(4), specifying and substantiating the manner of deriving such income and paying the taxes along with the interest on such income. On the other hand, penalty provision as contained under section 271(1)(*c*) read with *Explanation 5* was comparatively harsh with respect to the quantum of penalty leviable in case of search initiated before 1st June, 2007.

Provision of section 271AAA is applicable with respect to "undisclosed income" of the "specified previous year". Before we proceed further, it is important to understand and analyze the meaning of the words "undisclosed income" and "specified previous year" as defined under section 271AAA.

(ii) "Specified previous year"

Provision of section 271AAA is applicable with respect to "undisclosed income" of the "specified previous year". As per clause (*b*) to *Explanation* given under section 271AAA, "specified previous year" means —

　　a. The year in which search is conducted.

　　b. Immediately preceding year, due date of filing of return of income of which has not expired and return has not been filed.

For example, in a case when search is conducted as on 1st September, 2011 in the case of a company, specified previous year shall be A.Y. 2012-13 and A.Y. 2011-12 (in case return for A.Y. 2011-12 has not been filed and the due date for filing of return being 30th September, 2011 has not yet expired). But, in case company had filed its return for A.Y. 2011-12, say on 16.8.2011 *i.e.* before the date of search, the specified previous year for the purpose of section 271AAA shall only be A.Y. 2012-13.

In another case, when search is conducted as on 5th October, 2011, specified previous year shall be A.Y. 2012-13. In this case A.Y. 2011-12 cannot be treated as specified previous year irrespective of the fact whether return of income for the A.Y. 2011-12 has been filed by the company or not before due date *i.e.* 30th September, 2011.

Thus depending upon the date on which search is conducted, "specified previous year" shall be the year of search only in some cases, whereas in some other cases, one more year may be available to the assessee as "specified previous year" within the provision of section 271AAA as explained above.

In the case of *Mahendra R. Gupta* v. *Dy. CIT* [2013] 38 taxmann.com 391/145 ITD 265 (Ahd.-Trib.), it has been held that when previous year has ended before the date of search and the due date for filing the return of income u/s 139(1) has also expired before the date of search then provisions of section 271AAA(1) will not be applicable.

It has been held in the case of *S&P Foundations (P) Ltd.* v. *Asstt. CIT* 186 DTR (Chennai 'C') 122 that where previous year having ended before the date of search and the date of filing of return of income under s. 139(1) had also been expired, provisions of s. 271AAA were not attracted.

(*iii*) "Undisclosed Income"

Clause (*a*) to *Explanation* to section 271AAA defines "undisclosed income" to mean—

(*i*) Any income of the specified previous year represented, either wholly or partly, by any money, bullion, jewellery or other valuable article or thing which has not been recorded before the date of search in the books of account or other documents maintained in the normal course or otherwise not disclosed to the CCIT or CIT before the date of search, meaning thereby any kind of undisclosed assets.

(*ii*) Any income of the specified previous year represented, either wholly or partly, by any entry in the books of account, other documents, loose papers, diaries etc. or any other transactions found in the course of search which have not been recorded before the date of search in the books of account or other documents maintained in the normal course or otherwise not disclosed to the CCIT or CIT before the date of search.

(*iii*) Any income of the specified previous year represented, either wholly or partly, by any entry in respect of an expense recorded in the books of account or other documents maintained in the normal course which is found to be false and detected as a result of search.

In brief, it can be said that "undisclosed income" means any income of the "specified previous year" represented by—

(*i*) Undisclosed assets

(*ii*) Unrecorded transactions representing undisclosed income

(*iii*) False or bogus expenses claimed.

It is significant to understand the meaning of "undisclosed income" as defined under section 271AAA and the items which are covered within its ambit. This is for the reason that the provision of section 271AAA regarding levy of lesser penalty and further provision regarding getting immunity from penalty by making declaration in the statement recorded under section 132(4) during search is available only with respect to items which may be covered within the definition of "undisclosed income" and not to other income. In case there is an item of undisclosed nature not covered within the definition of "undisclosed income" under section 271AAA, provision of section 271AAA cannot be applied with respect to the same and in that case provision of section 271(1)(*c*) for levy of penalty for concealment may be applicable.

It is important to note here that in such a case, penalty provision u/s 271(1) (*c*) may be attracted when such items of income are not declared by the assessee in the return of income filed for the "specified previous year". In case of such items of undisclosed nature which are not covered within the definition of "undisclosed income" as given under section 271AAA, no penalty either under section 271AAA or under section 271(1)(*c*) can be attracted if such income is shown in the return of income filed. But if the same are not shown in the return of income filed and addition is made by the assessing officer during assessment, penalty for concealment of income may be levied under section 271(1)(*c*) but and under section 271AAA.

"Undisclosed income" relating to the "specified previous year" has been defined under section 271AAA extensively to cover within its ambit all items of undisclosed nature up to the date of search with an opportunity to the assessee to come clean, make declaration u/s 132(4), specify and substantiate the manner of deriving such income and pay the taxes along with interest. Items of undisclosed nature, for example, loans and advances given or taken out of books, unverifiable cash credits not recorded in the books, unaccounted sales, bogus capital gains etc. in respect of which any entry in the books of account or other documents or transactions are found in the course of search shall be covered within the above definition of "undisclosed income".

If we make close scrutiny of the above definition of "undisclosed income", there may well be certain items in the nature of concealed income not found during the course of search and as such may not be covered within the above definition. Some of the examples, which are illustrative and not exhaustive, relating to the disallowance of expense or deduction or exemption or addition to income regarding which addition can be made by the assessing officer during assessment but which are not covered within the definition of "undisclosed income" as per section 271AAA, may be narrated as under:-

1. Wrong claim of deduction/exemption under section 10A/10B/80-IC or similar deduction or exemption made by the assessee in the return of income filed.

2. Excess claim of depreciation made by the assessee in the return of income filed.

3. Loss on sale of assets claimed as allowable business expenditure which is otherwise not allowed as business expenditure.

4. Unverified cash credits/share capital credited in the books of account.

5. Jewellery declared in the wealth-tax return but source of acquisition is not established.

6. Household expenses not shown.

The above list of examples is not exhaustive and there may be other items of income/expense/deduction/exemption which may also be covered for this purpose. The definition of "Undisclosed income" given under *Explanation* to section 271AAA needs to be closely analyzed for this purpose.

There may be different views as to whether or not the above items would be covered within the definition of "Undisclosed Income" under section 271AAA even when nothing is found relating to the above items in the course of search. It would be interesting to examine whether above items are covered within the definition of "undisclosed income" under section 271AAA. In case these are not covered within the definition of "undisclosed income" under section 271AAA and addition/disallowance is made during assessment with respect to such items, penalty provision as contained under section 271(1)(c) may be more appropriate to be applied instead of penalty provision as contained under section 271AAA.

Bombay High Court in the case of *Sheraton Apparels* v. *Asstt. CIT* [2002] 123 Taxman 238/256 ITR 20 have held that the books of account referred to in sub-clause (*1*) of *Explanation 5* to section 271(1) (*c*) means books of account which have been maintained for determining any source of income and whose main object is to provide credible data and information to file tax returns and thus diaries seized during the search could not be regarded as books of account maintained by the assessee as contemplated under *Explanation (5)* to section 271(1)(c) to as to afford immunity from penalty.

It has been held in the case of *Sanjay Dattatray Kakade* v. *Asstt. CIT* 175 DTR 1/198 TTJ 50 (Pune) that only such items of undisclosed income can be considered for imposition of penalty under section 271AAA, which are found in the course of search and if a particular item of income is not found during the course of search but the assessee *suo motu* offers it in his return of income, the same cannot fall within the purview of 'undisclosed income' and escapes the rigour of penalty under section 271AAA.

It has been held in the case of *Savaliya Buildcon* v. *Dy. CIT* [I.T. Appeal Nos. 401 (Ahd.) of 2014 and 3188 (Ahd.) 2015 (Ahd.-Trib.) that one of the significant plea raised on behalf of the assessee is that the income declared in the return of income arises out of regular stream of income from various sources and also *ad hoc* declaration combined made for group concern and included in the return of income towards its share and such disclosure *per se* does not tantamount to 'undisclosed income' as codified in *Explanation (a)* below section 271AAA of the Act.

(iv) ***Non obstante* clause under section 271AAA**

Provision of section 271AAA is with the *non obstante* clause which reads as under - *"Notwithstanding anything contained in any other provisions of this Act—"*. It implies that the provision of section 271AAA regarding imposition of penalty in the case of search with respect to "undisclosed income" of the "specified previous year" is having the overriding effect over the general provision of imposition of penalty for concealment of income as contained under section 271(1)(c).

This legislative intent has further been clarified by way of insertion of sub-section (3) to section 271AAA wherein it has been mentioned that no penalty under the provisions of clause (c) of sub-section (1) of section 271 shall be imposed upon the assessee in respect of the "undisclosed income" of the "specified previous year" as referred to in sub-section (1).

(v) **Whether penalty u/s 271AAA mandatory**

Like other penalty provisions, penalty provision under section 271AAA is also not mandatory. Sub-section (1) of section 271AAA starts as —"the Assessing Officer may, notwithstanding—." The use of the word "may" and not "shall" by the legislature makes it clear that penalty provision under section 271AAA is not mandatory in nature. It would depend upon the judicial satisfaction and judicial discretion of the assessing officer which has to be exercised having regard to justice, equity and good conscience.

This may also be a debatable issue as to whether satisfaction is to be recorded in the assessment order for initiation of penalty under section 271AAA. The language used by the legislature in section 271(1) (c) requires impliedly the recording of satisfaction of the initiation of penalty whereas there is no such language employed in section 271AAA.

It has been held in the case of *Sanjay Dattatray Kakade* v. *Asstt. CIT* 175 DTR (Pune 'A') 1 that as per the language of section 271AAA, the AO is simply to 'direct' that penalty should be paid by the assessee under this provision & Unlike section 271(1)(c), the legislature has not contemplated recording of satisfaction under section 271AAA.

(*vi*) **Penalty at the rate of ten per cent of the "undisclosed income"**

The quantum of penalty with respect to "undisclosed income" relating to "specified previous year" provided under section 271AAA is ten per cent of the "undisclosed income". This rate is concessional rate in comparison to rate of penalty leviable under section 271(1)(*c*). Rate of penalty under section 271(1)(*c*) is hundred per cent to three hundred per cent of "tax sought to be evaded". Under section 271AAA, rate of penalty is ten per cent of undisclosed income which comes to approximately thirty three per cent of the tax sought to be evaded by assuming maximum marginal rate applicable on undisclosed income. Rate of penalty under section 271AAA at the rate of thirty three per cent of tax sought to be evaded in comparison to rate of penalty of hundred per cent to three hundred per cent of tax sought to be evaded under section 271(1)(*c*) is quite less and may be termed concessional. This provision of concessional rate of penalty has been criticized and it is often said that it puts the tax evasion at premium. But since there is deeming fiction of "undisclosed income" on which penalty under section 271AAA is levied, legislature seems to have consciously provided concessional rate of penalty. However, in the case of search initiated on or after 1st July, 2012 penalty provision under section 271AAA has been substituted by section 271AAB in which rate of penalty has been substantially increased.

(*vii*) **Penalty for specified previous year in the case of search initiated on or after 1.6.2007 can be levied u/s 271AAA/271AAB and not u/s 271(1)(c)**

Finance Act, 2007 by inserting provision of section 271AAA and later on substituted by provision of section 271AAB by Finance Act, 2012 has clearly demarcated levy of penalty for specified previous year and for earlier years under two different sections *i.e.* 271AAA/271AAB and section 271(1)(*c*). For specified previous years, penalty can be levied under section 271AAA/271AAB irrespective of the fact that the income was declared or not by the assessee in the return of income filed for earlier years *i.e.* years other than specified previous years, penalty has to be levied under section 271(1)(*c*) read with *Explanation (5A)*. Provision of section 271(1)(*c*) has further been substituted by section 270A with effect from A.Y. 2017-18.

In the case of *Marvel Tea Estate (I) Ltd.* v. *Dy. CIT* [2015] 120 DTR (Delhi 'E') 305 (Trib.), it has been noticed that the AO levied the penalty under section 271(1)(*c*) of the Act. However, for levying the penalty in search cases the Finance Act, 2007 inserted section 271AAA of the Act w.e.f 1st April, 2007 *i.e.* penalty, if any, could be levied under section 271AAA and not under section 271(1)(*c*).

In the case of *Dr. Naman A. Shastri* v. *Asstt. CIT* [2015] 128 DTR (Ahd. "D") 73 (Trib.), it has been held that provisions of sections 271AAA and 271(1)(*c*) are mutually exclusive and, thus, once penalty is initiated under section 271AAA for 'specified previous year', there cannot be any occasion to impose penalty under section 271(1)(*c*).

In the case of *Mahendra R. Gupta* v. *Dy. CIT* [2013] 38 taxmann.com 391/145 ITD 265 (Ahd.) (Trib.), it has been held that on merit of the levy of penalty in both these years, no other argument was advanced by the learned AR of the assessee except arguing this that it is covered in favour of the assessee by these two Tribunal decisions in group cases arising out of the same search. Before the authorities below also, no other argument was advanced by the learned AR of the assessee to contend that there is no concealment except this that penalty is not leviable in terms of sub-sections (2) and (3) of section 271AAA. Under these facts, this court feels that both these matters should go back to the file of the A.O. for a fresh decision about penalty to enable the assessee to make his submissions on applicability of the provisions of section 271(1)(*c*) of the I. T. Act because it seems that under this impression that the provisions of section 271AAA(2) & (3) are applicable, no other argument was advanced by the learned AR of the assessee before this court or before the authorities below about otherwise applicability of section 271(1)(*c*) of the I. T. Act, 1961. Since, these are penalty proceedings, this court feels it proper to provide one more opportunity to the assessee. Hence, this court sets aside the order of the learned CIT(A) in both years and restore the matter back to the A.O. for a fresh decision about applicability of the provisions of section 271(1)(*c*) of the I. T. Act after providing adequate opportunity of being heard to the assessee.

In the case of *Asstt. CIT* v. *A. N. Annamalaisamy (HUF)* [2013] 38 tax-mann.com 440 (Chennai) (Trib.), when the assessee has admitted the income in the course of search and has disclosed income by way of revised return and has explained the nature of sources of undisclosed income and had paid the tax together with interest, penalty cannot be levied u/s 271AAA.

16.8 Provision of section 271AAA in nutshell

(1) There is deeming fiction of "undisclosed income" relating to "specified previous year" as defined under section 271AAA.

(2) With respect to "undisclosed income" relating to "specified previous year", penalty is leviable at the rate of ten per cent of "undisclosed income".

(3) There is provision for immunity from penalty in case declaration of "undisclosed income" is made in the statement recorded under section 132(4) during the course of search provided other conditions mentioned in section 271AAA *e.g.* specifying and substantiating the manner of deriving such income and paying of taxes and interest thereon are fulfilled.

(4) With respect to "undisclosed income" of the "specified previous year", penalty shall be levied as per provision of section 271AAA and the provision of section 271(1)(*c*) will not be applicable.

16.9 Immunity from penalty under section 271AAA - Manner of declaration

Section 271AAA was applicable in connection with the search initiated on or after 1st day of June, 2007 but before 1st day of July, 2012.

Sub-section (2) of section 271AAA provides that no penalty under section 271AAA shall be levied with respect to the "undisclosed income" of the "specified previous year", in case assessee makes declaration of the undisclosed income in the following manner—

(*i*) In the statement recorded under section 132(4) during the course of search, assessee admits the undisclosed income and specifies the manner in which such income has been derived.

(*ii*) Substantiates the manner in which the undisclosed income was derived.

(*iii*) Pays the tax, together with interest, if any, in respect of the undisclosed income.

For getting immunity from penalty under section 271AAA, the above three conditions are required to be fulfilled cumulatively.

(i) Declaration to be made in the course of search

Declaration of undisclosed income is required to be made during the statement under section 132(4) in the course of search. Statement of the assessee in the course of search is recorded under section 132(4) and it can be recorded up to conclusion of the search. Search is concluded when all the authorizations issued are executed, all the restraints put under section 132(3) are lifted, lockers are operated and search is finally concluded after drawing all the Panchnamas. This process of conclusion of search generally may take up to sixty days from the date of initiation of search as is practically observed. Thus assessee gets ample opportunity for making declaration of undisclosed income relating to specified previous year after appreciating all the evidences collected by the search team and after having consultation with his counsel.

In case declaration of undisclosed income is made by the assessee before conclusion of search by way of filing a letter/affidavit to this effect to the authorized officer, it should be clearly mentioned as a measure of caution, in such letter/affidavit that the same may be treated as statement of the assessee made under section 132(4).

Within the group under search, there may be different entities, companies or individuals. Search may be concluded within one or two days with respect to certain entities/individuals and search may remain pending with respect to some of the entities/individuals. Any declaration of undisclosed income made by the person on behalf and for the other persons/entities in whose case search has already been concluded should be made carefully and ensuring that the same is made with respect to those persons/entities before the conclusion of search with respect to them separately.

In *Hissaria Brothers* v. *Dy. CIT* [2009] 31 DTR 223 (Jd.), it was held that the authorized officer having not recorded assessee's statement under section 132(4) during the course of search, the disclosure of additional income made by the assessee through a letter addressed to the *Asstt. Director of IT (Inv.)* immediately after the conclusion of the search which is also included in its return and has been accepted without any variation, has to be construed as a *bona fide* voluntary disclosure and, therefore, penalty under section 271(1)(c) is not leviable in view of *Explanation 5* thereto.

(ii) Specifies and substantiates the manner

The condition regarding specifying and substantiating the manner in which undisclosed income has been derived by the assessee may be difficult to be complied with in strict sense. In case assessee has earned income not recorded in the books of account, it may be difficult for the assessee to specify and more so, to substantiate the manner in which undisclosed income has been derived. The manner of earning the income may be specified in certain cases but its substantiation may still be more difficult and impractical.

The manner of earning undisclosed income may be specified, depending upon the facts, in broad term such as — income earned out of property business not recorded in the books, income earned from gambling/betting/speculation etc. out of books, income earned out of sales not recorded in the books etc. But, to substantiate the manner in which undisclosed income has been derived implies to describe the methodology along with documentary or circumstantial proof by which the undisclosed income was earned. It may not be practically possible for the declarant to comply this requirement. No person usually keeps the evidences of undisclosed income not recorded in the books of account. Practically, it has been observed that Department too does not insist compliance of this requirement in its strict sense. Admission of undisclosed income and describing the broad nature of the same is generally treated as compliance of the above requirement.

In the case of *Mahendra Chimanlal Shah* v. *Asstt. CIT* [1994] 51 ITD 244 (Ahd. - Trib.), it has been held that assessee is not required to specify and substantiate the manner of earning undisclosed income unless the same is specifically asked by the authorized officer during statement recorded under section 132(4).

Allahabad High Court in the case of *CIT* v. *Radha Kishan Goel* [2006] 152 Taxman 290/[2005] 278 ITR 454 has observed that non disclosure of manner of earning the undisclosed income is not relevant for the purpose of availing benefit under *Explanation 5* below section 271(1)(*c*).

In *CIT* v. *Mahendra C. Shah* [2008] 172 Taxman 58/299 ITR 305 (Guj.), it was held that the assessee having declared the value of diamonds in his statement under section 132(4) and paid taxes thereon before assessment, was entitled to immunity from penalty under section 271(1)(*c*) under *Explanation 5* thereof even though the statement did not specify the manner in which the income representing value of diamonds was derived.

The above judicial decisions have been rendered while explaining *Explanation 5* to section 271(1)(*c*) which also had the requirement of specifying the manner of undisclosed income. Recently, following decisions have been rendered by Tribunal with respect to such requirement in relation to section 271AAA.

It has been held in the case of *Pramod Kumar Jain* v. *Dy. CIT* [2013] 33 taxmann.com 651 (Ctk. - Trib.) in the context of penalty under section 271AAA that the disclosure of income under section 132(4) during the search having been made and the assessee having surrendered certain income for the relevant assessment years in the statements during the course of search and filed returns declaring the same pursuant to notice under section 153A and which returns have been accepted by the AO, levy of penalty under section 271AAA was not justified on the ground that the assessee has though made disclosure but failed to specify the manner in which such income had been derived. Hon'ble Tribunal further held that no definition could be given to the "specified manner" and there is no prescribed method given in the statute to indicate the manner in which income was generated.

It has been held in the case of *Ashok Kumar Sharma* v. *Dy. CIT* [2013] 33 taxmann.com 652 (Ctk. - Trib.) that when assessee disclosed concealed income while giving statement under section 132(4) during the course of search and paid tax thereon and showed the said undisclosed income in the return under the head "Income from business" and which undisclosed income has been accepted by the Department, penalty under section 271AAA is not leviable.

It has been held in the case of *Smt. Raj Rani Gupta* v. *Dy. CIT* [IT Appeal No. 3371 (Delhi) 2011, dated 30-3-2012], Delhi Bench of Income Tax Appellate Tribunal held that since nothing was asked from the assessee during the course of search in the statement u/s 132(4) as to the manner of deriving the undisclosed income or its substantiation, no fault can be found with the assessee and penalty levied u/s 271AAA due to non-specification of manner and its substantiation was unjustified.

In the case of *Sunil Kumar Bansal* v. *Dy. CIT* [2015] 62 taxmann.com 78/70 SOT 137 (Chd.) (Trib.), pursuant to search operations the assessee surrendered an amount to tax. The income was assessed on returned income after considering surrendered income and the Assessing Officer imposed penalty under section 271AAA of the Act on the ground that the assessee had not substantiated the manner in which the income was earned or furnished details of commission or of the transaction or property in respect of which income was earned. The CIT(A) confirmed this. On appeal by the assessee contending that no questions were asked regarding the manner of earning income :

Held, allowing the appeal, that if no question was asked during the statement recorded under section 132(4) of the Act, the assessee could not be expected to further substantiate the manner of earning of income. Since taxes were already paid, penalty could not be levied.

In the case of *Neerat Singal* v. *Asstt. CIT* [2014] 146 ITD 152/[2013] 37 taxmann.com 189 (Delhi) (Trib.), the Tribunal held that when authorized officer had not raised any query during course of recording of statement under section 132(4) about manner in which undisclosed income had been derived and about its substantiation. A.O. was not justified in imposing penalty under section 271AAA, specifically when offered undisclosed income had been accepted and taxes due thereon had been paid by assessee.

It has been held in the case of *Gillco Developers & Builders (P.) Ltd.* v. *Dy. CIT* [2017] 85 taxmann.com 339 (Chd. - Trib.) that assessee having surrendered undisclosed income as its 'business income' in the statement under section 132(4), the source and manner of earning the undisclosed income as explained by the assessee stand substantiated and, therefore, the conditions laid down in clauses (*i*) and (*ii*) of section 271AAA(2) have been complied with; further, assessee having deposited part of the tax due along with interest and tendered post-dated cheques for the remaining tax which have been encashed by the AO, the third condition of payment of taxes as per provisions of section 271AAA(2)(*iii*) also stood complied with; levy of penalty under section 271AAA is therefore not sustainable.

It has been held in the case of *Principal CIT* v. *Emirates Technologies Pvt. Ltd.* [2018] 99 taxmann.com 355/[2017] 399 ITR 189 (Delhi) that no query was raised by Assessing Officer regarding manner of derivation of income and its substantiation and thus deletion of penalty u/s 271AAA was justified.

It has been held in the case of *Principal CIT* v. *Swapna Enterprise* [2018] 91 taxmann.com 12/253 Taxman 531 (Guj.) that finding that statement specified manner in which such income was earned and no evidence is there to show that such income was earned from any other source. Payment of tax with interest was made before assessment made and thus satisfaction of conditions laid down in provisions of section 271 AAA(2) was achieved and thus deletion of penalty was justified.

It has been held in the case of *Roshan Lal Jindal* v. *Dy. CIT* 56 CCH 13 (Chd. - Trib) that where assessee was one of persons covered under such search action who had surrendered an additional income and was disclosed in return of income which was accepted by Revenue also and where penalty u/s 271AAA was initiated and thereafter levied on ground that assessee failed to substantiate manner in which undisclosed income was earned by him, disclosure of income u/s

132(4) during search having been made and assessee having surren- . dered same and included same in returns filed which was accepted by Revenue, no penalty u/s 271AAA was leviable for not specifying manner of earning surrendered income.

It has been held in the case of *Asstt. CIT* v. *Shreenarayan Sitaram Mundra* [2017] 83 taxmann.com 231/166 ITD 47 (Ahd. - Trib.) that where assessee filed its return of income declaring unaccounted income of ₹ 2 crores and Income was assessed on returned income and penalty under section 271AAA was imposed on ground that assessee had not specified manner in which income was earned though it was mentioned by assessee in his statement under section 132(4) that income was earned from taxable business and where no further question was asked by revenue during statement recorded under section 132(4), revenue later could not plead deficiency on part of assessee to specify manner of earning income, thus, penalty levied upon assessee was unjustified.

It has been held in the case of *Principal CIT* v. *Smt. Ritu Singhal* [2018] 92 taxmann.com 224 (Delhi) that assessee merely stated that the sums advanced were undisclosed income, however, she did not specify how she derived that income and what head it fell in (rent, capital gain, professional or business income out of money lending, source of the money, etc.) and thus assessee did not, in her statement, substantiate the manner in which the undisclosed income was derived and thus it was held that the Tribunal was not therefore justified in deleting the penalty under section 271AAA.

It has been held in the case of *Asstt. CIT* v. *Shailesh Gopal Mhaske* [2017] 86 taxmann.com 263/167 ITD 344 (Pune - Trib.) *that assessee though specifically questioned but having failed to* explain in his statement under section 132(4) the manner in which undisclosed income was derived and having also failed to pay tax on undisclosed income along with return, was not entitled to benefit of sub-section (2) of section 271AAA, hence penalty was rightly imposed by AO.

It has been held in the case of *Principal CIT* v. *Bhavi Chand Jindal* 170 DTR 401/305 CTR 180 (Delhi) that proceedings u/s 271AAA had been initiated on the ground that the assessee had not substantiated the manner in which the undisclosed income of ₹ 30 crores had been derived whereas Revenue's contention is that statement made under section 132(4) did not indicate and state the manner thereof, Tribunal was therefore justified in deleting penalty.

It has been held in the case of *Narsi Iron & Steel (P) Ltd.* v. *Dy. CIT* 177 DTR (Del 'E') 420 that the Assessee having failed to specify the manner in which the undisclosed income of Rs. 90 lacs surrendered by way of letter to Director of IT (Inv.) was earned, AO was justified in levying penalty of Rs. 9 lacs under s. 271AAA.

It has been held in the case of *Principal CIT* v. *Patdi Commercial & Investment Ltd.* 187 DTR (Guj) 35 that where no question having been put to assessee in his statement under s. 132(4) as regards fulfilment of condition of cl. (*iii*) of sub-s. (2) of s. 271AAA, regarding manner of deriving undisclosed income, Tribunal was justified in affirming order of CIT(A) deleting penalty under s. 271AAA, having found that conditions (*i*) and (*ii*) stood fulfilled.

It has been held in the case of *Principal CIT* v. *Sun Corporation* [2019] 419 ITR 414 (Guj) that the statement under section 132(4) by partner of assessee specifying manner in which disclosed income earned satisfies requirement to claim immunity from penalty under section 271AAA.

(*iia*) Requirement of substantiating the manner of deriving the undisclosed income to be complied with at which stage

It may be seen from the plain reading of sections 271AAA and 271AAB that its language is somewhat different from *Explanation 5* of section 271(1)(*c*) in as much as sections 271AAA and 271AAB require the assessee to substantiate the manner of deriving of undisclosed income also, whereas *Explanation 5* to section 271(1)(*c*) required assessee to specify the manner of deriving undisclosed income only. There was no requirement under that *Explanation* to substantiate the manner of deriving the undisclosed income. To this extent, the present sections 271AAB and 271AAA are more onerous.

Another important feature of section 271AAA and section 271AAB is that requirement of substantiation of the manner of deriving of undisclosed income is *de hors* the statement u/s 132(4) whereas the specification of the manner of deriving the undisclosed income has to be made during the course of search in statement recorded u/s 132(4). There is however no time limit prescribed for "substantiation" of the "manner". Therefore, in our considered opinion, assessee may substantiate the manner during the course of assessment proceeding or penalty proceeding and in our considered opinion, that would be sufficient compliance of the requirement of these sections. This interpretation is clear from the plain reading of these sections and the way various sub-clauses of sub-section (2) of section 271AAA and clause (*a*) of sub-section (1) of section 271AAB are bracketed and placed. This interpretation is further clear from the fact that there was no requirement of any time limit within which the tax etc. was to be paid in respect of the undisclosed income u/s 271AAA. But Hon'ble Supreme Court in the case of *Asstt. CIT* v. *Gebilal Kanhaialal (HUF)*

[2012] 25 taxmann.com 214/210 Taxman 244/348 ITR 561 has held that in absence of any time limit prescribed in this regard, it would be sufficient compliance if the taxes etc. are paid on or before the assessment is made. Thus, Hon'ble Supreme Court also read the requirement of payment of taxes etc. *de hors* the statement u/s 132(4). This interpretation is further clear from the present language of sub-clause (*iii*) of section 271AAB(1) where the time limit is prescribed for payment of taxes and no time limit is prescribed for "substantiation of the manner". Therefore, there may well be circumstances where assessee may not have substantiated the "manner" during the statement u/s 132(4) but should do so at least before the conclusion of assessment proceeding and/or during penalty proceeding u/s 271AAA/271AAB.

Another significant problem which is often encountered is in regard to "substantiation of the manner". "Substantiation" means "to establish" or "to prove". Specifying the "manner" of deriving the undisclosed income may not pose much problem but "substantiation of the manner" may pose problem depending upon the facts and circumstances of the case. It may in fact proliferate litigation and at times may make the immunity provision as paper immunity only, as despite such provision remaining on the statute, one may not be able to obtain the benefit conferred by such provision. There may well be situations where it may be difficult to "substantiate the manner" of deriving the undisclosed income. In the situation of such statutory requirement remaining uncomplied with, Revenue may deny the benefit of concession in penalty/immunity from the levy of penalty u/ss 271AAA and 271AAB. It will be the insistence of the Revenue to strictly comply with the conditions of these sections to avail the benefit envisaged under these sections.

It has been held in the case of *Principal CIT* v. S *wapna Enterprise* [2018] 91 taxmann.com 12/253 Taxman 531 (Guj.) that Partner of assessee having disclosed in statement recorded during search that undisclosed income constituted on-money received in building project, no question about substantiating the manner of earning that income was asked by Revenue and tax on undisclosed income having been paid much before making of assessment, all conditions of s. 271AAA stood satisfied and Tribunal rightly deleted penalty under s. 271AAA.

It has been held in the case of *Principal CIT* v. *Mukeshbhai Ramanlal Prajapati* [2018] 99 taxmann.com 447/[2017] 398 ITR 170 (Guj.) that Additional condition u/s 271AAA(2) of having to substantiate manner in which undisclosed income was earned is applicable only if Revenue raises question regarding manner in which undisclosed income was earned while recording assessee's statement under section 132(4).

It has been held in the case of *Principal CIT* v. *Phoenix Mills Ltd.* 175 DTR 433/307 CTR 700 (Bom.) that unless the authorized officer recording the statement under s. 132(4) puts the specific question with regard to the manner in which income has been derived, it cannot be expected from a person to make a statement in this regard and in case in the statement the manner in which income has been derived has not been stated, but has been stated subsequently, it amounts to compliance with s. 271AAA(2)(*i*) and penalty thus levied was deleted.

(*iii*) Pays the tax and interest in respect of the undisclosed income

The third condition for getting immunity from penalty under section 271AAA is that the assessee makes payment of tax and interest in respect of the undisclosed income declared by him in the course of search. Of course the objective of getting declaration from the assessee is to collect taxes and assessee is supposed to pay the same along with interest under sections 234B and 234C, if applicable.

The amount of tax is not required to be paid by the assessee immediately at the time of making declaration of undisclosed income u/s 132(4) but the same may be paid as and when due and finally before filing return of income for the relevant year. In case, for example, search is held as on 30th April, 2011 and declaration of undisclosed income is made relating to current year *i.e.* for A.Y. 2012-13 the instalment for payment of advance tax for A.Y. 2012-13 shall fall due subsequently in the months of June/September/December or March, as the case may be, and assessee can make the payment of the taxes relating to such undisclosed income declared as and when the same becomes due subsequently. In case of late payment, tax can be paid along with interest under sections 234B and 234C up to the filing of the return.

Punjab & Haryana High Court in the case of *Ashok Kumar Gupta* v. *CIT* [2006] 157 Taxman 339 have held that immunity from penalty is to be availed of by the assessee by invoking the provisions of *Explanation 5* to section 271(1)(*c*) of the Act, and the tax on the surrendered income along with the interest is required to be paid immediately and in any case before the due date of return. High Court held that the plea of non availability of funds for payments of tax due on the surrendered income is not tenable and payment of tax along with interest before the date of assessment or payment of interest for delayed payment of tax cannot be the circumstances which could be pleaded by the assessee to claim immunity from levy of penalty in terms of *Explanation 5.*

Allahabad High Court, however, in the case of *CIT* v. *Nem Kumar Jain* [2006] 151 Taxman 187 have held that clause (2) of *Explanation 5* to section 271(1)(c) does not say that the tax along with interest should be deposited before filing the return and merely because tax has not be deposited before filing of the return would not make *Explanation 5(2)* inapplicable.

Rajasthan High Court also in the case of *Gebilal Kanhaialal (HUF)* v. *Asstt. CIT* [2005] 143 Taxman 42 have held that if assessee has disclosed and surrendered concealed income during the search and has paid the tax along with interest on the said income before assessment, penalty u/s 271(1)(c) was not leviable in view of clause (2) of *Explanation 5* to section 271(1)(c).

In the case of *Asstt. CIT* v. *Munish Kumar Goyal* [2014] 45 taxmann. com 563/[2015] 152 ITD 453 (Chd.-Trib.), if the assessee during the course of search admits certain undisclosed income and pays taxes on the same then penalty cannot be levied in terms of sub-section (1) of this section. In the instant case, the amount of ₹ 4 crores which was surrendered during search has been declared by the assessee in the return and taxes have been paid accordingly. Therefore the assessee is normally entitled for the immunity provided in section 271AAA itself. The assessee has disclosed the manner in which income has been earned. Thus, impugned penalty order deserve to be set aside.

In the case of *Uday C. Tamhankar* v. *Dy. CIT* 127 DTR (Mumbai 'F') 41 (Trib.), it has been held that assessee having disclosed undisclosed income as his professional income in the statement under section 132(4) and paid tax together with interest in respect of said undis-closed income, he has complied with all the three conditions specified in section 271AAA(2) and, therefore, penalty under section 271AAA is not leviable.

In the case of *SPS Steel & Power Ltd.* v. *Asstt. CIT* [2015] 122 DTR (Kol. 'B') 248 (Trib.), it has been held that penalty under section 271AAA could not be levied merely on admission of assessee during search proceedings and there must be some conclusive evidence before Assessing Officer that entry made in seized documents represented undisclosed income of assessee.

In the context of penalty under section 271AAA, recently it has been held in the case of *Dy. CIT* v. *Pioneer Marbles & Interiors (P.) Ltd.* [2012] 19 taxmann.com 301/50 SOT 571 (Kol.-Trib.) while dealing with a case of penalty under section 271AAA and the conditions precedent thereto, that no time limit is set out for payment of taxes along with interest by the assessee for availing of the immunity under section 271AAA(2) and, therefore, once the entire tax and interest has been duly paid well within the time-limit as per the notice of demand under section 156 and well before the conclusion of the impugned penalty proceedings, the assessee cannot be denied immunity under section 271AAA(2) and the penalty under section 271AAA rightly cancelled.

It has been in the case of *Duraipandi & S. Thalavaipandian AOP* v. *Asstt. CIT* [2019] 106 taxmann.com 20 (Mad.) that where assessee made disclosure of undisclosed income in statements recorded under section 132 (4) during course of search and had also specified manner in which such income was derived but paid tax in respect of such income belatedly, since there is no time frame prescribed for payment of tax in *Explanation 5(2)* to section 271(1)(*c*), assessee was entitled to immunity from penalty under section 271(1)(*c*).

Hon'ble Supreme Court in the case of *Asstt. CIT* v. *Gebilal Kanhaialal (HUF)* [2012] 25 taxmann.com 214/210 Taxman 244 have held that in absence of any time limit prescribed in this regard, it would be sufficient compliance if the taxes etc. are paid on or before the assessment is made.

It would be noticed that though above cases were decided by Hon'ble High Courts in the context of *Explanation 5* to section 271(1)(*c*) of the Act yet the language of the statute used being almost identical, ratio of these decisions would be applicable in case of penalty u/s 271AAA also. However, it may be noted that Hon'ble Punjab and Haryana High Court in the above case have taken a narrow view whereas Allahabad and Rajasthan High Court have taken a broad view in the matter of timing of payment of tax and interest. Rajasthan High Court view was upheld by the Supreme Court also as mentioned above.

It is also to be noticed that the requirement of payment is with respect to tax, as may be applicable, for the relevant A.Y. in accordance with the provisions of the Act after availing the benefits/adjustment for any kind of deduction/exemption/set off of losses available to the assessee. For example—declaration of undisclosed income is made by the assessee for the previous year relevant to A.Y. 2012-13 in the course of search. At the same time there are business losses available to the assessee for the A.Y. 2012-13 which can be set off against the undisclosed income declared and due to such set off, tax liability is substantially reduced or becomes nil. In such a case, assessee may not be required to pay any taxes with respect to undisclosed income declared during search and the declaration would still be valid.

It has also been held in the case of *Principal CIT* v. *Surinder Kumar Khindri* [2017] 88 taxmann.com 673 (Punj. & Har.) that Cash seized from assessee could be adjusted against advance-tax liability and penalty imposed by AO under s. 271AAA by refusing to make such adjustment was rightly deleted by Tribunal.

16.9A Nature and Scope of Provision under section 271AAB

(*i*) **Applicable in the case of search initiated on or after 1st day of July 2012:**

In the case of search initiated on or after 1st day of July 2012, provision regarding imposition of penalty for undisclosed income shall be governed by section 271AAB and not by section 271AAA. Finance Act, 2012 has inserted section 271AAB which shall be applicable for imposition of penalty in the case of search initiated under section 132 on or after 1st day of July, 2012. However, in the case of search initiated on or after 15th December, 2016, sub-section (1A) was inserted to section 271AAB according to which rate of penalty under this section was substantially increased.

The concept of "undisclosed income" and "specified previous year" as are there in section 271AAA would continue to remain the same under section 271AAB as well.

(*ii*) **Rationale of introducing section 271AAB:**

Under section 271AAA, penalty with respect to "undisclosed income" relating to the "specified previous year" was applicable at the rate of 10% of the "undisclosed income". There was however immunity from imposition of the said penalty under section 271AAA in case declaration of undisclosed income was made during the statement recorded under section 132(4) in the course of search and other conditions regarding specifying and substantiating the manner of declaration of undisclosed income and payment of taxes relating to such undisclosed income were being fulfilled.

The provision of section 271AAA was drafted in such a manner that even when no declaration of income was made by the assessee during search or even while filing the return of income relating to specified previous year but addition is made by the Assessing Officer during assessment proceedings, penalty could be levied only to the extent of 10% of undisclosed income. While in the normal case, when a person has not been searched but addition is made during normal assessment proceeding, penalty is applicable under section 271(1)(*c*) which can be levied equal to 100% to 300% of the tax sought to be evaded. Thus, in a case when additions are made by the Assessing Officer during assessment proceedings, the quantum of penalty applicable in the case of searched person was much lower in comparison to a normal case. There was no rationale putting the searched person at premium in comparison to the normal case. Therefore, there was a need to suitably modify provision of section 271AAA. However, the amendment made by way of section 271AAB has been drafted in a much stricter manner.

(*iii*) Staggering of quantum of penalty under section 271AAB

In respect of search initiated on or after 1st day of July, 2012 but before 15th December, 2016, section 271AAB has prescribed three different rates of penalty for undisclosed income relating to specified previous year in the following manner:

    (*i*) Penalty at the rate of 10% of undisclosed income is leviable even when declaration of undisclosed income is made in the statement under section 132(4) recorded during the course of search.

    (*ii*) Penalty at the rate of 20% of undisclosed income is leviable when undisclosed income is not declared during the course of search but is declared in the return of income furnished for the specified previous year.

    (*iii*) Penalty at the rate of 30% to 90% of the undisclosed income is leviable when undisclosed income is not declared even while filing the return of income for the specified previous year but addition is made by the Assessing Officer during the assessment proceedings.

Finance Act, 2016 has however amended above penalty rate of 30% to 90% and has prescribed rate of 60% of undisclosed income of the specified previous year with effect from 1-4-2017 *viz.* A.Y. 2017-18. Its effect would be that in case of search initiated on or after 1st April, 2016 but before 15th December, 2016, new rate of penalty of 60% as aforesaid would be applicable for (*iii*) above. It is pertinent to note that in case of search initiated on or after 15th December, 2016, penalty provision under section 271AAB has been prescribed by newly inserted sub-section (1A) by the Taxation Laws (Second Amendment) Act, 2016.

(*iv*) Levy of penalty at the rate of 10% of undisclosed income when declaration of undisclosed income is made during search initiated on or after 1-7-2012 but before 15-12-2016

Clause (*a*) of sub-section (1) of section 271AAB has prescribed the levy of penalty at the rate of 10% of undisclosed income even when declaration of undisclosed income is made by the searched person in the statement under section 132(4) recorded during the course of search. Following conditions are required to be satisfied so that penalty under section 271AAB is attracted only at the rate of 10% of undisclosed income:

    (*a*) income in the nature of "undisclosed income" relating to "specified previous year" is found with respect to the searched person.

    (*b*) declaration of undisclosed income is made by the searched person in a statement under section 132(4) during the course of search and he specifies and substantiates the manner in which such undisclosed income has been derived

(c) payment of the tax along with interest in respect of such un-disclosed income is made before the "specified date".

(d) return of income for the "specified previous year" is furnished declaring such "undisclosed income" therein.

The salient features of sub-section (1) to section 271AAB for impo-sition of penalty under section 271AAB as discussed above may be noted as under :

(i) penalty @ 10% of undisclosed income seems to be mandatory in nature

(ii) penalty @ 10% of undisclosed income is to be levied even when declaration of undisclosed income is made during search.

(iii) concept and definition of "undisclosed income" and "specified previous year" are the same as have been given under section 271AAA

(iv) penalty @ 10% of undisclosed income is the minimum penalty which shall be applicable only when all the four conditions as mentioned above are complied with by the searched person. In case any of the conditions as mentioned above is not complied with, assessee would fall in a category where higher penalty is applicable

(v) a new condition regarding the payment of tax with interest in respect of the undisclosed income *before the "specified date"* has been prescribed under this section. Under section 271AAA, though there was also requirement regarding payment of tax in respect of undisclosed income but there was no requirement for payment of such tax before the specified date.

"Specified date" has been defined to mean the due date of furnishing of return of income under sub-section (1) of section 139 or the date on which the period specified in the notice issued under section 153A for furnishing of return of income expires, as the case may be.

It has been held in the case of *Asstt. CIT* v. *Vishal Agarwal* [2018] 100 taxmann.com 283/[2019] 174 ITD 125 (Kol.-Trib.) that assessee hav-ing made disclosure of undisclosed income in the course of search, having substantiated the manner in which it was earned and having paid tax along with interest thereon and filed return, penalty is at-tracted at 10 per cent under section 271AAB(1)(*a*) and not at 30 per cent under section 271AAB(1)(*c*).

(v) Levy of penalty at the rate of 20% of undisclosed income when decla-ration of undisclosed income is made not during the course of search but in the return of income filed for the specified previous year in case of search initiated on or after 1-7-2012 but before 15-12-2016

Clause (*b*) of sub-section (1) of section 271AAB prescribes levy of penalty at the rate of 20% of undisclosed income when declaration of undisclosed income is not made by the searched person in the course of search but is made in the return of income for the specified previous year furnished by him.

This clause requires that the return of income for the specified previous year declaring the undisclosed income has to be furnished on or before the "specified date" along with the payment of tax and interest accrued thereon. In the earlier situation where penalty is leviable at the rate of 10% of the undisclosed income, there is a condition of making the payment of tax before the specified date but there is no condition for filing the return of income before the specified date. However under this clause, there is a condition for filing the return of income as well as payment of tax relating to undisclosed income before the specified date. It implies that in case a person furnishes return of income for the specified previous year making declaration of undisclosed income after the specified date, he may be liable to be penalized under this section interestingly at a higher rate and not at the rate of 20% of the undisclosed income.

(*vi*) **Levy of penalty at the rate of 30% to 90% (60% for A.Y. 2017-18) of undisclosed income when declaration of undisclosed income is not made by the searched person but additions are made by the Assessing Officer during assessment proceedings, in respect of search initiated on or after 1-7-2012 but before 15-12-2016**

Clause (*c*) of sub-section (1) of section 271AAB prescribes levy of penalty at the rate of 30% to 90% of undisclosed income when declaration of undisclosed income is neither made by the searched person in the course of search nor in the return of income furnished for the specified previous year before the specified date. When no declaration of undisclosed income is made by the assessee himself and addition is made by the Assessing Officer during assessment proceedings, it tantamounts in a way to concealment of income as prescribed under section 271(1)(*c*) of the Act. In such a situation, penalty under this section has been prescribed at the rate of 30% to 90% of the undisclosed income which is equivalent to 100% to 300% of the tax sought to be evaded assuming applicable rate of tax at maximum marginal rate of 30%.

As per the Finance Act, 2016 penalty provision under section 271(1)(*c*) was replaced by section 270A which prescribes the maximum penalty at the rate of 200% of the amount of tax payable on under-reported income. In line with the insertion of section 270A, the penalty rate in section 271AAB(1)(*c*) was also rationalized to 60% of the undisclosed income applicable for and from A.Y. 2017-18. However, this provision was further amended and substituted by sub-section (1A) to section 271AAB with respect to search initiated on or after 15-12-2016.

It has been held in the case of *Harshvardhan* v. *Dy. CIT* 195 DTR (Bang 'B') 145 that assessment resulting in a loss and the same having been accepted by AO, penalty under s. 271AAB could not be imposed.

(vii) Provisions of section 274 and section 275 to apply

Sub-section (3) of section 271AAB prescribes that the provisions of sections 274 and 275 shall, as far as may be, apply in relation to the penalty referred to in this section. This provision is similar to the provision as has been given in the case of section 271AAA as well.

(viii) Analysis of Significant issues

(i) Interpretation of the definition of "Undisclosed Income"

As a general rule, undisclosed income can be said to exist *qua* a person when return of income for a particular year is filed by him and such income is not declared by him in the return of income so filed. Thus, by necessary implication, it cannot be said in normal circumstances, before filing the return of income that a person has not disclosed his income or a person is having any undisclosed income.

However, section 271AAA created a deeming provision as to the undisclosed income prescribing that any income of the specified previous year represented by any assets or any entry in the books of account or other documents found in the course of search would be in the nature of undisclosed income, in case it has not been recorded before the date of search in the regular books of account or other documents maintained in the normal course relating to such previous year or otherwise it has not been disclosed to the Income-tax Department. Penalty u/s 271AAA has been prescribed on such undisclosed income at the rate of 10% thereof. At the same time, remedy was provided in section 271AAA prescribing immunity from such penalty in case declaration of such undisclosed income is made by the searched person during search. Therefore, practically levy of penalty u/s 271AAA gets attracted only when undisclosed income is found during search but declaration of the same is not made by the searched person during the course of search. The language of the definition of undisclosed income given in section 271AAA though was ambiguous but since it was not having much implication due to the reason mentioned above, one would have tended not to be so vigilant as to its interpretation.

But now, sub-section (1) of section 271AAB has however prescribed the penalty at the rate of 10% of undisclosed income even when declaration of undisclosed income is made by the searched person in the course of search. Under sub-section (1A) of section 271AAB, rate of penalty has been enhanced from 10% to 30% of undisclosed income even when declaration of undisclosed income is made by the searched person in the course of search. Under such circumstances, interpretation of the definition of "undisclosed income" assumes enough significance. If we closely scrutinize the definition of "undisclosed income" given u/s 271AAB which is in any way identical to one given u/s 271AAA, it may give rise to several debatable issues relating to the point as to whether an income of the "specified previous year" shall be in the nature of "undisclosed income" or not. Some issues which may create litigation in this respect may be as under:

(*a*) What is the meaning of the books of account or other documents maintained in the normal course?

(*b*) What would happen in the case of an individual who is not having business income and is thus not required to maintain regular books of account?

(*c*) What is the meaning of "other documents" maintained in normal course?

(*d*) What is the meaning of the phrase - *"otherwise not been disclosed to the Chief Commissioner or Commissioner before the date of search?"* There does not seem to be any procedure or system of making disclosure of income by any person to the Chief Commissioner or Commissioner. The concept of undisclosed income created in this section is related to the income for the period for which return of income has not yet been filed. In such a situation, therefore, question is as to what is the meaning of this phrase?

(*e*) In case of false expenses claimed by the searched person in his books of account, undisclosed income relating to such expenses can be attributed when such expenses are found to be false and would not have been found to be so, had the search not been conducted. Does it imply that certain evidences indicating the falsity of such expenditure should be found in search so as to classify such expense in the nature of undisclosed income?

(*f*) Whether excess or false claim of deduction/exemption/allowance under any other provision of the Act claimed by the assessee having not been expressly provided in the definition of undisclosed income, can be termed as undisclosed income for the purpose of this section?

It has been held in the case of *SEL Textiles Ltd.* v. *Dy. CIT* 181 DTR (Chd 'B') 217 that additions made by AO on debatable issues like s. 14A, s. 36(1)(*iii*) and s. 36(1)(*v*) did not attract penalty under s. 271AAB but however, as regards addition towards profits on stock found short, penalty @ 10 per cent of the surrendered amount was leviable under s. 271AAB(1)(*a*).

It has been held in the case of *Ajanta Pharma Ltd.* v. *Dy. CIT* 187 DTR (Mumbai 'A') 159 that simply because assessee has admitted the amount of certain expenses as its income in its statement recorded under s. 132(4) to avoid litigation and to buy peace of mind, penalty under s. 271AAB is not leviable in the absence of any allegation of the Revenue that the said expenses have been found to be false or the same are inadmissible as deduction.

(*ia*) **'Penalty' u/s 271AAB imposable if income declared falls within the definition of 'Undisclosed Income'**

It has been held in the case of *Asstt. CIT* v. *Marvel Associates* [2018] 92 taxmann.com 109/170 ITD 353/194 TTJ 338/166 DTR 409 (Visakha-Trib.) that imposition of penalty under s. 271AAB is directory and not mandatory and assessee having admitted additional income during the course of search and the Revenue authorities having found no incriminating material except a loose sheet of paper which shows certain projections and not real figures, or any other material indicating any undisclosed income/assets, no case is made out for imposing penalty under s. 271AAB.

It has been held in the case of *Dy. CIT* v. *Manish Agarwala* [2018] 92 taxmann.com 81 (Kol.-Trib.) that once the AO has accepted the assessee's statement of total income and the return wherein the assessee has shown the income out of speculative business from sale of commodities under the head 'Income from other sources', he cannot treat the same as 'income from business' in the penalty proceedings and also since the income in question was in fact entered in the "other documents" maintained in the normal course which was retrieved during the search, the amount of ₹ 3 crores offered by the assessee does not fall in the ken of "undisclosed income" defined in s. 271AAB and, therefore, penalty under s. 271AAB cannot be levied.

It has been held in the case of *Rambhajo's* v. *Asstt. CIT* 175 DTR 161 (Jp.) that in the absence of detection of any discrepancy by the AO either during the assessment or penalty proceedings, the amount surrendered by the assessee on account of unspecified discrepancies may form the basis for assessment but cannot form the basis for levy of penalty under s. 271AAB.

It has been held in the case of *Padam Chand Pungliya* v. *Asst. CIT* [2020] 113 taxmann.com 446/181 ITD 261 (Jp.-Trib), that the penalty under section 271AAB is not mandatory but the AO has the discretion to take a decision and the same should be based on judicious decision of the AO. AO has a discretion after considering all the relevant aspects of the case and then to satisfy himself that the case of the assessee falls in the definition of undisclosed income as provided in the *Explanation* to section 271AAB of the Act. Further, both the show-cause notices issued by the AO for initiation of penalty proceedings under section 271AAB are very vague and silent about the default of the assessee and further the amount of undisclosed income on which the penalty was proposed to be levied. Further, the statement recorded under section 132(4) itself would not either constitute an incriminating material or undisclosed income in the absence of any corresponding asset or entry in the seized document representing the undisclosed income. Accordingly, the penalty levied by the AO under section 271AAB of the Act is deleted.

It has been held in the case of Laxman Nainani v. Dy. CIT 204 DTR 97 (Jp 'B') that as to the penalty under section 271AAB, in the absence of any enquiry by the AO that the entries/notings on the loose papers found during the course of search represent real transactions or any finding in the penalty order that the income surrendered by the assessee during the course of search is "undisclosed income" as defined in section 271AAB, penalty levied under section 271AAB cannot be sustained, more so as the entries in the loose papers are related to the business of the company in which the assessee is a director and not to the assessee in his individual capacity.

It has been held in the case of *Shiv Bhagwan Gupta* v. *Asstt. CIT* 200 DTR 65 (Pat 'SMC') that AO has been given discretion in the matter of levy of penalty under section 271AAB & if the surrendered income does not fall in the definition of "undisclosed income" as defined under section 271AAB, penalty is not warranted and since assessee having not surrendered any undisclosed income during the search action, penalty under section 271AAB levied by AO solely on the basis of disclosure of certain income from undisclosed sources by the assessee in the return is not sustainable.

It has been held in the case of *Garg Brothers (P.) Ltd.* v. *Dy. CIT* 212 DTR 256 (Kol 'A') that additional income conditionally offered by the assessee in its disclosure petition out of abundant caution to cover any undisclosed income, other than the income disclosed in the statement under section 132(4), which is not attributable to any money, bullion, jewellery, article or transaction or entry or documents which has not been recorded in the books cannot fall in the ken of definition of 'undisclosed income' for the purpose of penalty under section 271AAA and, therefore, penalty is not leviable in respect of the said income.

(*ib*) **Declaration of Undisclosed Income in the statement recorded u/s 132(4) would not *ipso facto* be regarded as Undisclosed Income.**

It has been held in the case of *Smt. Aparna Agarwal* v. *Dy. CIT* [2019] 105 taxmann.com 233/176 ITD 753 (Jp.-Trib.) that disclosure of income in statement recorded under section 132(4) would not *ipso facto* be regarded as undisclosed income unless and until it is tested as per definition provided in *Explanation* to section 271AAB. In course of search proceedings, statement of assessee was recorded under section 132(4) wherein she surrendered long-term capital gain arising from sale of shares. Assessing Officer while completing assessment added said amount to assessee's taxable income and also passed a penalty order under section 271AAB. Since, all transactions of purchase and sale and LTCG arising from sale of equity shares of listed companies were duly recorded in books of account, primary condition for treating such income as undisclosed income in terms of section 271AAB was not satisfied and therefore, penalty order was to be set aside.

(*ii*) **Ambiguity in the definition of "Specified Date"**

For the levy of penalty u/s 271AAB at different rates, it has been provided that tax relating to "undisclosed income" declared in the income-tax return for the "specified previous year" has to be paid before the specified date and also the income-tax return has to be furnished before the specified date.

As per *Explanation* given for the purpose of section 271AAB, "specified date" has been defined to mean the due date of furnishing of return of income under sub-section (1) of section 139 or the date on which the period specified in the notice issued u/s 153A for furnishing of return of income expires, as the case may be.

If we closely scrutinize the above definition of "specified date", it is likely to create ambiguity in certain situations. There may emerge three different kinds of situations regarding filing of return:

(*a*) Income-tax return for the year of search being "specified previous year" shall be required to be filed u/s 139(1).

(b) Income-tax return for the earlier five years or six years (in certain situations years have been increased to total nine), as the case may be, not being specified previous years may be required to be filed u/s 153A.

(c) Income-tax return for the immediate previous year prior to the year of search, being in the nature of specified previous year, Income-tax return may be required to be filed u/s 153A.

Whereas there may not be any controversy in determining the "specified date" in the first two situations, however in the third situation, it may so happen that date for filing the return of income would fall due u/s 139(1) after the date of search as well as at a later stage when notice u/s 153A will also be received for filing the return for such year. In such a situation, question would be as to which of the date out of the above two dates shall be treated to be "specified date" for this section.

(iii) **Cash seized - Whether to be treated as payment of tax before the "specified date"?**

As per the amendment brought under section 132B by the Finance Act, 2013, it has been provided with effect from 1-6-2013 that cash seized cannot be adjusted towards advance tax liability payable for the year of search. However, there is no restriction in adjusting the cash seized towards the self assessment tax liability. Therefore, if cash seized is adjusted towards self assessment tax, in the return of income to be filed by the assessee for the year of search and return is filed on or before the due date prescribed under section 139(1), it would be treated as payment of tax made before the 'specified date'.

Prior to the above amendment, it was decided in the case of *Principal CIT* v. *Surinder Kumar Khindri* [2017] 154 DTR 157 (P&H) that Cash seized from assessee could be adjusted against advance-tax liability; and thus penalty imposed by AO under section 271AAA by refusing to make such adjustment was rightly deleted by Tribunal.

(iv) **Decision regarding declaration of "undisclosed income" during search to be made more cautiously**

After introduction of penalty provision u/s 271AAB, decision regarding declaration of undisclosed income during search will have to be taken by the searched person more cautiously and after weighing all the *pros* and *cons*. During applicability of the provision of penalty u/s 271AAA, there was a legal advantage to the assessee in the form of immunity from penalty by making declaration of "undisclosed income" during search. But after introduction of provision of penalty u/s 271AAB, there is no immunity from penalty even by making declaration of undisclosed income during search. Rather by making declaration of undisclosed income during search, assessee may be liable to pay penalty at the rate of 10% or 30% of the undisclosed income (later on 30% or 60%) as the case may be depending upon the date of search initiated.

As it is observed in all search cases in practice, the ultimate thrust of the department remains to get declaration of "undisclosed income". The parameter for success of search operation is decided by the tax authorities by the quantum of declaration of "undisclosed income" obtained by them during search. After applicability of penalty provision u/s 271AAB, there may be higher amount of resistance by the searched person from making any declaration of undisclosed income during search. The searched person may no more be inclined towards declaration as he will not get any immunity from penalty. Rather he would put himself in a situation when penalty on undisclosed income declared is also levied upon him.

There may well be situations where it may be in the interest of the assessee not to make declaration of "undisclosed income" relating to "specified previous year" during the course of search but to make declaration of such income in the return of income to be filed for the "specified previous year" and then try to make out a case that such income does not fall within the ambit of definition of "undisclosed income" as given u/s 271AAB. This is possible in view of the ambiguity in drafting of the definition of "undisclosed income" under this section and controversy may emerge regarding interpretation of this definition as discussed in the earlier paras. The other option with the assessee may now be to opt for filing application for settlement of cases with the Settlement Commission along with application for immunity from penalty under this section.

(v) Application with Settlement Commission may be opted by searched person

After introduction of penalty provision under section 271AAB where penalty has been prescribed to be levied even with respect to the "undisclosed income" declared during the course of search relating to "specified previous year", the searched person may find it more useful to exercise the option of filing application with the Settlement Commission and get his search cases settled by the Settlement Commission. As per section 245H of the Income-tax Act, 1961, Settlement Commission has been granted power to grant immunity from imposition of penalty in appropriate cases. Such power to grant immunity from imposition of penalty will cover penalty leviable u/s 271AAB as well.

Finance Act, 2021 has abolished the institution of Settlement Commission and with effect from 1st February, 2021 no new application may be filed for settlement. Therefore such option is no longer available to the searched person.

(vi) Whether penalty u/s 271AAB is mandatory in nature?

A question may arise as to whether penalty provision prescribed u/s 271AAB is mandatory in nature and as to whether penalty u/s 271AAB shall be levied in all cases of search covered within its ambit when conditions of that section are fulfilled.

The provision of section 271AAB has been drafted in such a manner which indicates as if penalty is leviable in all cases when declaration of undisclosed income is made by the assessee in the course of search or at the time of filing of the Income Tax Return for the specified previous year, as the case may be. Similarly, when undisclosed income of the nature as defined u/s 271AAB is assessed in assessment and is not covered by clause (a) or clause (b) of sub-section (1) of section 271AAB, identical question would arise as to whether penalty on undisclosed income is mandatorily leviable.

Proponents of the mandatory character of this penalty draw attention to the definition of 'undisclosed income' given in section 271AAB. According to such view, when undisclosed income of the nature as envisaged in section 271AAB is found in search and is so assessed, there should not be any good ground or justification for not imposing penalty on such undisclosed income.

On the other hand, one may argue that imposition of penalty u/s 271(1)(c) depends upon the judicial satisfaction and judicial discretion of the Assessing Officer. Like any other penalty provisions, penalty provision u/s 271AAB can not be said to be mandatory.

Though no clear cut answer can be given but one thing which may be said in this regard is that the phrase "concealment of particulars of income" has not been defined u/s 271(1)(c) but the term "undisclosed income" has been exhaustively defined in the *Explanation* to section 271AAB. If income assessed is held as a matter of fact as concealed income or undisclosed income, there is no escape from the rigor of section 271(1)(*c*) or 271AAB.

It has been held in the case of *Padam Chand Pungliya* v. *Asstt. CIT* [2020] 113 taxmann.com 446/181 ITD 261 (Jp.-Trib.), that the penalty under section 271AAB is not mandatory but the AO has the discretion to take a decision and the same should be based on judicious decision of the AO. AO has a discretion after considering all the relevant aspects of the case and then to satisfy himself that the case of the assessee falls in the definition of undisclosed income as provided in the *Explanation* to section 271AAB of the Act. Further, both the show cause notices issued by the AO for initiation of penalty proceedings under section 271AAB are very vague and silent about the default of the assessee and further the amount of undisclosed income on which the penalty was proposed to be levied. Further, the statement recorded under section 132(4) itself would not either constitute an incriminating material or undisclosed income in the absence of any corresponding asset or entry in the seized document representing the undisclosed income. Accordingly, the penalty levied by the AO under section 271AAB of the Act is deleted.

It has been held in the case of Laxman Nainani v. *Dy. CIT 204 DTR 97 (Jp 'B') that levy of penalty under section 271AAB is not mandatory and it depends upon specific facts and circumstances of each case and the AO has to issue a show-cause granting an opportunity to the assessee.*

(via) **Penalty provision under section 271AAB amended in case of search initiated on or after 15th of December, 2016**

As per the Taxation Laws (Second Amendment) Act, 2016, penalty provision in the case of search under section 271AAB has been amended. The existing provision of section 271AAB shall remain applicable in the case of search initiated up to 14th of December, 2016. In the case of search held on or after 15th of December, 2016 *i.e.* the date on which the Taxation Laws (Second Amendment) Act, 2016 received the assent of the President and the bill became an Act, a new Penalty provision has been introduced under section 271AAB by way of insertion of sub-section (1A) to section 271AAB which is reproduced as under:

"(1A) The Assessing Officer may, notwithstanding anything contained in any other provisions of this Act, direct that, in a case where search has been initiated under section 132 on or after the date on which the Taxation Laws (Second Amendment) Bill, 2016 receives the assent of the President, the assessee shall pay by way of penalty, in addition to tax, if any, payable by him,—

(a) *a sum computed at the rate of thirty per cent of the undisclosed income of the specified previous year, if the assessee—*

  (i) *in the course of the search, in a statement under sub-section (4) of section 132, admits the undisclosed income and specifies the manner in which such income has been derived;*

  (ii) *substantiates the manner in which the undisclosed income was derived; and*

  (iii) *on or before the specified date—*

     (A) *pays the tax, together with interest, if any, in respect of the undisclosed income; and*

     (B) *furnishes the return of income for the specified previous year declaring such undisclosed income therein;*

(b) *a sum computed at the rate of sixty per cent of the undisclosed income of the specified previous year, if it is not covered under the provisions of clause (a)."*

Penalty at the rate of 10% of undisclosed income increased to 30%, in case of declaration of undisclosed income in case of search:

The penalty provision in the case of search has become very harsh. As per sub-section (1A), there is penalty of 30% of the undisclosed income of the specified previous year in case any declaration of undisclosed income is made by the assessee in the course of search during statement recorded under section 132(4) of the Act. This penalty of 30% is leviable when assessee fulfils other conditions as stipulated in this sub-section *i.e.* assessee specifies and substantiates the manner in which undisclosed income was derived, makes payment of applicable tax and interest and furnishes the return of income on or before the specified time.

In case searched person does not make declaration of undisclosed income during search and does not fulfil other conditions as specified under section 271AAB, penalty may be imposed at the rate of 60% of undisclosed income.

The above penalty provision shall have the effect that in the case of search, total tax liability for undisclosed and unexplained income assessed under sections 68 to 69D detected in search would be as provided under section 115BBE at the rate of 75% (60% tax *plus* 15% as surcharge) *plus* minimum penalty as provided under section 271AAB at the rate of 30% *i.e.* total 105%, cess liability over and above the prescribed tax rate.

As we know that in practice lot of pressure is exercised by the tax authorities on the searched person for making declaration of undisclosed income at the time of search even when evidences relating to undisclosed income of substantive nature are not found. Searched person due to pressure makes declaration of undisclosed income so as to buy peace and get the search operation concluded but now searched person should make declaration of undisclosed income very cautiously and after taking into consideration the fact that on any undisclosed income declared during search and assessable under sections 68 to 69D and chargeable to tax under section 115BBE, he would be liable to pay total tax liability *i.e.* tax, surcharge and penalty of approximately 105%.

(*vii*) Enhancement of penalty by the first appellate authority

It has been held in the case of *Sanjay Dattatray Kakade* v. *Asstt. CIT* 175 DTR (Pune 'A') 1 that CIT(A) can make enhancement of penalty under section 271AAA imposed by the AO, if it was wrongly levied at a rate less than 10 per cent or the AO considered a particular amount of income in the penalty order but was satisfied with the explanation tendered by the assessee and chose not to impose penalty thereon and If, however, a particular item of income was not at all considered by the AO in his penalty order, the same cannot come within the purview of power of enhancement by the CIT(A).

16.10 Penalty under section 271AAA/271AAB v. Penalty under section 271(1)(c)

(*i*) Penalty provision u/s 271AAA applicable even when no declaration of "undisclosed income" relating to "specified previous year" is made during search and such "undisclosed income" is declared in the return of income filed or such "undisclosed income" is added by AO in the assessment order in respect of search initiated after 1-6-2007 but before 1-7-2012

It would be interesting to note that penalty provision under section 271AAA alone is applicable with respect to "undisclosed income" relating to "specified previous year". There may be a situation where the declaration of "undisclosed income" of the "specified previous year" is made by the assessee in the return of income filed or addition of such undisclosed income is made by the assessing officer in the assessment order, still the penalty in respect of such undisclosed income shall be governed by the provisions of section 271AAA only and not by section 271(1)(*c*). Infact, there is compartmentalization of the provisions regarding imposition of penalty for concealment of income between section 271AAA and section 271(1)(*c*)—

(*1*) It is the penalty provision of section 271AAA which is applicable with respect to "undisclosed income" of the "specified previous year" as defined under this section, in all situations *viz.* whether such income is declared in the return or addition is made by AO in the assessment order.

(*2*) Provisions of section 271(1)(*c*) read with *Explanation 5A* will be applicable —

    (*i*) with respect to any other income/additions which are not covered within the definition of "undisclosed income" as given under section 271AAA relating to "specified previous year".

    (*ii*) With respect to any undisclosed income or concealment of income relating to the years prior to the "specified previous year".

It may further be noted that by making declaration of undisclosed income during search in the manner as provided therein, assessee gets immunity from penalty under section 271AAA and such penalty is not leviable. It therefore follows, that it is the penalty under section 271AAA with respect to "undisclosed income" of the "specified previous year" which alone is liable to be imposed when declaration of such undisclosed income is not made by the assessee in the course of search or in the manner as provided therein.

There may be situation such as—

(*1*) When "undisclosed income" is though declared by the assessee during search u/s 132(4) but other conditions spelt out in sub-section (2) of section 271AAA are not fulfilled.

(*2*) When "undisclosed income" is declared by the assessee after conclusion of the search so that it cannot be treated as declared in statement u/s 132(4).

(*3*) When "undisclosed income" is not declared in statement u/s 132(4) but is declared and shown by the assessee in the return of income filed for the "specified previous year" under section 153A/139.

(*4*) When addition of undeclared "undisclosed income" is made by the assessing officer during assessment for "specified previous year".

In all the above cases, penalty provision in respect to the "undisclosed income" as contained under section 271AAA will be applicable and not the penalty provisions for concealment of income as contained under section 271(1)(c). This legislative intent has further been clarified specifically by way of insertion of sub-section (3) to section 271AAA which states that no penalty under the provision of section 271(1)(c) shall be imposed upon the assessee in respect of the "undisclosed income" of the "specified previous year".

It may be observed that in case where assessee is not in a position to specify and substantiate the manner of earning the "undisclosed income", he would not get the immunity from penalty u/s 271AAA and in that case, whether declaration of undisclosed income is made during search or at later stage while filing the return or it is not at all made, penalty will be leviable in all the cases under section 271AAA only *i.e.* at the rate of ten per cent of the undisclosed income.

In view of the above discussion, it is clear that the provision of section 271AAA was putting searched person at premium in comparison to any other person with respect to levy of penalty for the undisclosed income relating to the 'specified previous year' even if declaration of undisclosed income was not being made by the searched person. Therefore, provision of section 271AAA appears to have been substituted by new penalty provision of section 271AAB by the Finance Act, 2012 in respect of search initiated on or after 1-7-2012.

(ia) **Penalty under section 271AAB v. Penalty under section 271(1)(c)**

Penalty provision under section 271AAB has the same concept of specified previous year and undisclosed income as was there in section 271AAA. Therefore, attraction of penalty for different situations and different years would be applicable under section 271AAB or section 271(1)(c) in the same manner as discussed earlier with respect to section 271AAA. However, rate of penalty has been increased substantially.

Moreover, penalty under section 271AAB is leviable even if declaration of undisclosed income is made in the statement under section 132(4) and there is no immunity as was there in case of section 271AAA.

(ii) **Situation when penalty for "specified previous year" may be applicable/leviable under section 271(1)(c)**

From the above discussion, it should not be construed that penalty for concealment of income relating to "specified previous year" can be imposed only under section 271AAA/271AAB in all the circumstances. There may be situations when even for "specified previous year", penalty for concealment of income can be imposed under section 271(1)(c) in the following cases—

(*i*) With respect to concealed income/additions relating to the period after the date of search till the closing of the year of search.

(*ii*) With respect to any concealed income/additions other than those covered within the definition of "undisclosed income" as defined under section 271AAA/271AAB and relating to the period upto the date of search.

Thus, penalty provision for concealment of income for the same year may be attracted under section 271AAA/271AAB as well as under section 271(1)(c) depending upon the nature of disallowance/addition/concealment.

(*iia*) **Judicial decisions to the effect that penalty under section 271(1)(c) not applicable at all for specified previous year in the case of search.**

There are however following judicial decisions to the effect that penalty under section 271(1)(c) is not applicable at all for specified previous year in case of search for any kind of income or disallowance made in the assessment order and in such cases penalty provision of section 271AAA can only be applied. This view is contrary to the view as expressed by us in the preceding para and with due respect, we are of the considered view that these judicial decisions are prone to be reviewed by higher judicial forum.

Ashwani Kumar Arora v. *Asstt. CIT* [2017] 81 taxmann.com 440 (Delhi-Trib.)

Raj Katha Products (P.) Ltd. v. *ACIT* IT Appeal No. 401 (Delhi) 2017, dated 12-7-2017]

Asstt. CIT v. *Saviour Builders Pvt. Ltd.,* [2019] 105 taxmann.com 119 (Delhi-Trib.)

Shri Sureshkumar Jethalal Shah v. *ACIT* [IT Appeal No. 2228 (Ahd.)/2014, dated 28-11-2019]

(*iii*) **No penalty u/s 271(1)(c) for concealment of income if income not covered within the definition of "undisclosed income" under section 271AAA/271AAB, is declared in the return of income relating to 'specified previous year'**

There may be cases where certain items of income are not found as a result of search and are thus not covered within the definition of "undisclosed income" as given under section 271AAA/271AAB. Examples (which are not exhaustive) of such income may be—

(*a*) Creditors no longer payable

(b) Bogus share capital

(c) Unverified cash credits

(d) Low household expenses.

As a matter of broad general proposition, it can be said that there can be no concealment of income if the same is declared in the return of income filed by the assessee if the due date of filing of return was not over prior to search. Penalty under section 271AAA/271AAB is however attracted relating to "undisclosed income" of the "specified previous year" due to the specific deeming fiction of "undisclosed income" given under that section, even if such "undisclosed income" is declared in the return of income to be filed by the assessee falling due after the date of search and for which no declaration was made in the course of search and in the manner as provided under section 271AAA/271AAB.

In case any item of income is not covered within the definition of "undisclosed income" as given under section 271AAA/271AAB and when such item of income is included by the assessee in the return of income filed after the date of search, no penalty for concealment of income with respect to such items can be imposed either under section 271AAA/271AAB or under section 271(1)(c). It goes without saying that concealment of income may not be attached to the assessee for the items which have been declared by him in the return of income filed first time under section 139 as per normal provisions of the Act.

It may also be noted that *Explanation 5A* to section 271(1)(c) is applicable for the years prior to specified previous year(s) as per plain reading of the said *Explanation* and therefore, in the above situations, penalty provision under section 271(1)(c) read with *Explanation 5A* can also not be made applicable.

16.11 Penalty for undisclosed income relating to earlier years

(i) **Provision of section 271AAA/271AAB applicable only for "specified previous year" and not for earlier years - Declaration of undisclosed income for earlier years may be treated as admitted concealment for those years**

It is very significant to note that any declaration of undisclosed income during search relating to the years prior to specified previous year may tantamount to admitted concealment and penalty provision shall be applicable as provided under section 271(1)(c).

Declaration of undisclosed income should be made by the assessee in the course of search after due consideration and consultation regarding the legal position. At the time of search, it is often seen that assessee remains under stress and he may not be in a position to take a fair and rational decision. Legally speaking, assessee gets immunity from penalty under section 271AAA or concessional penalty under section 271AAB with respect to declaration of "undisclosed income" pertaining to "specified previous year". In case of declaration of undisclosed income made during search relating to earlier years, there is no immunity from penalty available to assessee and rather admission of undisclosed income by the assessee may be treated as admitted concealment and it may be difficult for the assessee to defend penalty under section 271(1)(c) under such circumstances. However, this is seen in practice that sometimes undisclosed income for earlier years is admitted by the assessee during search for other practical reasons such as to prompt the winding up of the search proceedings at an early stage or to mitigate the depth of investigation and rigors of search by the Income Tax Department.

It is also not necessary that in all cases where undisclosed income for earlier years is admitted by the assessee during search, penalty for concealment under section 271(1)(c) may be levied. It is the nature of evidences available which will decide whether there is any concealment of income in the nature so as to attract penalty under section 271(1)(c). Mere admission by the assessee in his statement during search may not be sufficient evidence to attract penalty for concealment.

In *CIT* v. *Punjab Tyres* [1986] 162 ITR 517 (M.P.); it was held that, agreed addition to income to purchase peace or for other similar reasons cannot amount to an admission constituting evidence of concealment in penalty proceedings. Mere surrender of income by itself will not justify the imposition of penalty.

Hon'ble Supreme Court in the case of *CIT* v. *Suresh Chandra Mittal* [2001] 119 Taxman 433 (SC); have held that though, the assessee surrendered additional income in the revised return after persistent queries by A.O., yet once the revised returns have been regularized by revenue, the explanation of the assessee that additional income was declared to buy peace and to come out of the vexed litigation, could be treated as *bona fide* and penalty was rightly cancelled. Hon'ble Supreme Court affirmed the decision of Madhya Pradesh High Court in the case of *CIT* v. *Suresh Chandra Mittal* [2002] 123 Taxman 1052.

In *CIT* v. *Rajiv Garg* [2008] 175 Taxman 184 (Punj. & Har.); it was held that the assessee having surrendered additional income alongwith an explanation in the revised return filed in response to notice u/s 148 and there being no objection from the A.O. that the explanation of the assessee was not *bona fide*, penalty u/s 271(1)(c) was found rightly cancelled.

(ia) **Judicial decisions to the effect that in case undisclosed income is shown in the return filed under section 153A for years prior to specified previous year, no penalty under section 271(1)(c) can be levied**

There are judicial decisions to the effect that penalty under section 271(1)(c) is not leviable for the years prior to specified previous year in case of search, for any undisclosed income declared in the return of income filed under section 153A even if such income was not shown in the original return filed under section 139. This view is contrary to the view as expressed by us in the preceding para & with due respect, we are of the considered view that these judicial decisions are prone to be reviewed by higher judicial forum.

Prem Arora v. *Dy. CIT* 78 DTR 91 (Delhi)

Sanjay Tapriya v. *DCIT* 35 CCH 563 (Delhi-Trib.)

DCIT v. *Pratap Properties(P.) Ltd.* 46 CCH 106 (Kol.-Trib.)

Principal CIT v. *Neeraj Jindal* [2017] 79 taxmann.com 96 (Delhi)

(ii) **Clinching evidences of undisclosed income for earlier years**

There may be cases where clinching evidences suggesting undisclosed income for earlier years are found and seized during search. In practice, it has been seen that the assessee often remains under stress for making admission of such undisclosed income pertaining to earlier years. Under such circumstances, assessee at times, has no option but to admit the undisclosed income for earlier years. In such cases, assessee may explore the possibility of making petition with the Settlement Commission for settlement of cases subject to applicable conditions as prescribed for filing petition with the Settlement Commission which has got power to grant immunity from penalty and prosecution under the Income-tax Act.

(iii) **Declaration made for earlier years subject to no penalty**

Sometimes, declaration of undisclosed income for earlier years is made by the assessee stating that the same is subject to no penalty for concealment under section 271(1)(c). There is judicial controversy on this issue whether under such circumstances penalty can be imposed or not. As per analysis of various judicial decisions on this aspect and as per latest trend of judicial judgments, the overwhelming view is that there can be no estoppel against law by making surrender of undisclosed income in such a manner. Decision for imposition of penalty for concealment is to be taken by the assessing officer based upon the nature of evidences and material available with him. Few of the decisions which may be relevant to the issue at hand are given hereunder:-

In *CIT* v. *D.K.B & Co.* [2003] 128 Taxman 552 (Ker.); it was held that there is no principle of universal application that whenever an assessment has been completed by accepting the offer of assessee, the penalty cannot be imposed. There cannot be estoppel against a statute. Department can levy penalty u/s 271(1)(c) in respect of additional income offered by assessee if the explanation offered for not including such amount in the return is not found acceptable.

In *CIT* v. *Rakesh Suri* [2011] 9 taxmann.com 5 (All.); it was held that, where the assessee was found to have tried his best to escape from communicating the relevant information called for by the A.O. regarding the genuineness of the sale of shares, surrender of income cannot be said to be voluntary after being cornered by revenue and levy of penalty u/s 271(1)(c) for concealment of income was justified.

In *Bhagat & Co.* v. *Asstt. CIT* [2006] 10 SOT 37 (Mum.-Trib.) (URO); it was held that conditional surrender to income with request not to impose penalty having been accepted by revenue, no penalty for concealment could be levied when there was no other evidence to prove concealment.

In *Addl. CIT* v. *Prem Chand Garg* [2009] 31 SOT 97 (Delhi-Trib.) (TM); it was held that assessee having surrendered the amount of N.R.I. gift on a general query raised by A.O. on the condition of not initiating penalty proceedings before assessment was taken up, A.O. could not have imposed penalty u/s 271(1)(c).

In *Asstt. CIT* v. *Indica Exports* [2010] 129 TTJ 269 (Delhi-Trib.); it was held that penalty u/s 271(1)(c) was not called for when addition was made pursuant to the offer of the assessee surrendering ₹ 10 lakhs u/s 68 in view of the inability to produce books of account and the creditors, subject to the condition of non-levy of penalty.

In *Trivium Power Engineers (P.) Ltd.* v. *ITO* [2011] 44 SOT 1 (Delhi-Trib.) (URO); it was however held that the condition imposed by the assessee that no penalty u/s 271(1)(c) should be levied on surrender has no force in the eyes of law when surrender was made by the assessee on account of alleged loans deposits only after receiving a show cause notice from the A.O. intimating it about the outcome of his inquiry and thus, surrender was not voluntary and *bona fide* but was under compulsion.

Hon'ble Supreme Court in *Sir Shadi Lal Sugar & General Mills Ltd.* v. *CIT* [1987] 33 Taxman 460A (SC); held that from agreeing to the addition, it does not follow that the amount agreed to be added was concealed as there may be hundred and one reasons to such admission.

Hon'ble Supreme Court, however, in the case of *K.P. Madhusudhanan* v. *CIT* [2001] 118 Taxman 324; have held that the decision in the case of *Sir Shadi Lal Sugar & General Mills Ltd.* v. *CIT* [1987] 33 Taxman 460A (SC) was no longer a good law in view of the *Explanation* appended to section 271(1)(*c*). Hon'ble Supreme Court held that, express invocation of the *Explanation* to section 271 in the notice u/s 271 is not necessary before the provisions of the *Explanation* therein, are applied.

(*iv*) **Penalty for concealment of income for earlier years applicable under section 271(1)(c) read with *Explanation 5A***

In the case of search under section 132 initiated on or after 1st June, 2007 *Explanation 5A* was inserted under section 271(1)(*c*) by the Finance Act, 2007 with effect from 1st June, 2007 but the same was substituted by the Finance (No. 2) Act, 2009, in the present form with retrospective effect from 1st June, 2007 with minor amendments.

Explanation 5A has been inserted under section 271(1)(*c*) along with the incorporation of section 271AAA/271AAB under the Act. Penalty provisions under section 271AAA/271AAB are applicable with respect to "specified previous year" while penalty provisions contained under the *Explanation (5A)* to section 271(1)(*c*) are applicable with respect to the years prior to the "specified previous year". There is compartmentalization between section 271AAA/271AAB and *Explanation 5A* to section 271(1)(*c*) so far as the issue regarding the years to which the same are applicable, is concerned.

(*v*) **No Penalty merely on surrender of Income**

In the case of *Marvel Tea Estate (I) Ltd.* v. *Dy. CIT* [2015] 120 DTR (Delhi 'E') 305 (Trib.), it has been held that assessee having admittedly disclosed all the information relating to the increase in share capital and the AO having accepted the explanation of the assessee during the course of regular assessment proceedings under section 143(3), it cannot be said that the assessee concealed the particulars or information relating to the increase in share capital and therefore, AO was not justified in levying penalty under section 271(1)(*c*) merely because the assessee surrendered the amount of its paid-up share capital during the course of assessment under section 153A.

16.12 Text of *Explanation 5A* to section 271(1)(c)

Where, in the course of a search initiated under section 132 on or after the 1st day of June, 2007, the assessee is found to be the owner of—

(*i*) any money, bullion, jewellery or other valuable article or thing (hereafter in this *Explanation* referred to as assets) and the assessee claims that such assets have been acquired by him by utilizing (wholly or in part) his income for any previous year; or

(*ii*) any income based on any entry in any books of account or other documents or transactions and he claims that such entry in the books of account or other documents or transactions represents his income (wholly or in part) for any previous year,

which has ended before the date of search and—

(*a*) where the return of income for such previous year has been furnished before the said date but such income has not been declared therein; or

(*b*) the due date for filing the return of income for such previous year has expired but the assessee has not filed the return,

then, notwithstanding that such income is declared by him in any return of income furnished on or after the date of search, he shall, for the purposes of imposition of a penalty under clause (*c*) of sub-section (1) of this section, be deemed to have concealed the particulars of his income or furnished inaccurate particulars of such income.

16.13 Rationale for insertion of *Explanation 5A* to section 271(1)(c)

(*i*) To cover a situation where due date of filing of return is expired but concealed income is included in the return filed after search

In fact, penalty for concealment of income which is otherwise not covered by the provisions of section 271AAA/271AAB, is covered and attracted as per normal provisions of section 271(1)(c). Provisions of section 271AAA/271AAB are applicable with respect to the "undisclosed income" of the "specified previous year". Any concealment of income other than the one covered within the definition of "undisclosed income" as given under section 271AAA/271AAB for the "specified previous year" and any concealment of any income for the years prior to the "specified previous year" may attract penalty in accordance with the normal provisions of section 271(1)(c).

However there could have been a situation where penalty provision under section 271(1)(c) for the years prior to the "specified previous year", could not have been attracted but for the existence of the *Explanation 5A* to section 271(1)(c). Such situation could have been like where after search having taken place, the return of income for earlier years are pending to be filed by the assessee up to the date of search even though the due date for filing the return had expired and the same is filed by the assessee after the date of search within the time limit prescribed u/s 139(4) showing such undisclosed income found as a result of search pertaining to such year. In order to cover such a situation, *Explanation 5A* to section 271(1)(c) has been enacted.

Undisclosed assets or undisclosed income are generally detected during the search and when such income comes to the knowledge of the assessee who having sufficient time from the date of search till the receiving of the notices under section 153A for filing fresh returns of income, may file pending belated return u/s 139(4), showing such undisclosed income/assets detected as a result of search and thereby may avoid the penalty u/s 271(1)(c). In this manner, he may have avoided the levy of penalty for concealment of income under the normal provisions of section 271(1)(c). To take care of such situation, *Explanation 5A* has been inserted to section 271(1)(c) due to which such assessee would no longer be able to avoid the penalty on that score. *Explanation 5A* to section 271(1)(c) is with the same intent, as *Explanation 3* to section 271(1)(c) is there on the statute for roping in a situation where notice under section 142(1) or under section 148 has been issued.

(ii) **After search having taken place, return of income already filed is revised showing undisclosed income found as a result of search pertaining to such year.**

There may be another situation when search having taken place, return of income already filed is revised showing undisclosed income found as a result of search pertaining to such year before receiving the notices for filing returns of income u/s 153A. Revision of income-tax return showing undisclosed income detected as a result of search cannot absolve the assessee from the penal consequences and such situation is also covered under *Explanation 5A* to section 271(1)(c). Concealment of income may be attributed to the assessee depending upon nature of revision even in non search cases when there is revision of return.

However, courts have taken divergent views on the above issue and even in the case of search when income-tax return is revised after search having taken place, concealment of income has been attributed depending upon the facts of the case, nature of evidences found and the *Explanation* furnished by the assessee. There are instances when even under such circumstances, penalty for concealment has been deleted by the courts. Some of the case laws on this issue having both kind of interpretation are given below:

In *CIT* v. *Shyamlal M. Soni* [2005] 144 Taxman 666 (MP), High Court held that no penalty under section 271(1)(c) could be levied in a case, where income returned in revised returns was accepted and assessed in hands of assessee even though revised returns were filed after search and subsequent to inquiries made by department during course of assessment proceedings.

In *Dy. CIT* v. *S. Kumar* [2008] 15 DTR 34 (Bang.), it was held that the assessee having admitted undisclosed income representing bogus gifts recorded in the books in his statement under section 132(4) during search and declared the same in return under section 153A and paid taxes thereon, was eligible for immunity from penalty under section 271(1)(*c*) under *Explanation 5* thereof.

In *CIT* v. *Suresh Chand Bansal* [2009] 22 DTR 1 (Cal.), High Court held that disclosure of additional income after search in revised return under section 153A and such additional income offered by assessee after the search having been accepted in its entirety without detailed discussion of the seized documents and without making any attempt to obtain the *Explanation* of the assessee, penalty under section 271(1)(*c*) is not leviable.

In *Dy. CIT* v. *K. Natarajan* [2010] 34 DTR 414 (Bang.), it was held that penalty under section 271(1)(*c*) is leviable in respect of unaccounted sales detected on the basis of documents found during the search and unaccounted debtors which were not declared in the statement under section 132(4). AO having estimated the income from sale of scrap at 7 per cent as against 5 per cent shown by the assessee, penalty is leviable only to the extent of net profit estimated at 5 per cent by the assessee. In view of *Explanation 5,* no penalty is leviable is respect of the amount of debtors declared in the statement under section 132(4) for which the tax stands paid.

In *Asstt. CIT* v. *Rupesh Bholidas Patel* [2008] 16 DTR 369 (Ahd.), it was however been held that assessment of assessee having already been completed before the date of search on a return filed under section 139, said assessment did not abate and return filed in response to notice under section 153A could not be treated as one filed under section 139 so as to extend benefit of *Explanation 5* to section 271(1)(*c*) to the assessee.

In *Dy. CIT* v. *Omkareshwar R. Kalantri* [2010] 42 DTR 489 (Pune), it was held that the assessee having disclosed additional income during the search and in the return filed in response to notice under section 153A which was neither recorded in the books of account nor disclosed to the CIT/chief CIT before the search nor the source of the same was explained, immunity under *Explanation 5* to section 271(1)(*c*) is not available to the assessee and, therefore penalty under section 271(1)(*c*) is leviable on the difference between income returned in the original return under section 139(1) and in the return under section 153A.

In *CIT* v. *A. Sreenivasa Pai* [2000] 109 Taxman 267 (Ker.); it was held that penalty u/s 271(1)(c) was leviable in respect of additional income offered by assessee in the revised return as the same was filed only after the revenue had impounded assessee's books and started inquiries. Return filed so as to include concealed income cannot be treated as revised return.

However, ratio of the above decisions may not apply to the cases covered under *Explanation 5A* to section 271(1)(c) as there is considerable change in the language of *Explanations 5* and *5A*. Therefore, caution is desired to be exercised while dealing with the new *Explanation 5A*.

However, Delhi Bench of Tribunal has held in the case of *Prem Arora* v. *Dy. CIT* [2012] 24 taxmann.com 260/[2013] 56 SOT 14 (URO) (Delhi-Trib.) that when scheme of search assessment as designed by the Legislature does not prescribe to take into account the earlier assessment proceedings whether abated or not, it will not be proper or justified to refer to returned income u/s 139 for the purpose imposition of penalty u/s 271(1)(c) of the Act. For the purpose of imposition of penalty u/s 271(1)(c) resulting as a result of search assessments made u/s 153A, the original return of income filed u/s 139 cannot be considered. When there is no concealment, question levy of penalty u/s 271(1)(c) of the Act will not arise. Where returned income filed u/s 153A is accepted by the Assessing Officer, there will be no concealment of income and consequently penalty u/s 271(1)(c) cannot be imposed.

In *CIT* v. *Shankerlal Nebhumal Uttamchandani* [2009] 311 ITR 327 (Guj.), High Court held that during Search proceedings, Queries though were raised but no detection of undisclosed income was made and the assessee filed the revised return surrendering amount standing in names of family members who were assessed on such income, no concealment of income can be said to have taken place and penalty could not be imposed under section 271(1)(c).

(iii) **Whether *Explanation 5A* to section 271(1)(c) shall be attracted regarding normal profits as per balance sheet finalized but income-tax return pending on the date of search**

In the case of search, a situation may arise, for example, as follows—

   (i) A search takes place as on 15th October, 2010 when date of filing of income-tax return for A.Y. 2010-11 had expired on 30-9-2010 but the return of income could not be filed by the assessee.

(*ii*) Balance sheet for the F.Y. 2009-10 was finalized showing net profit of ₹ 2 crores but income-tax return could not be filed for the reason that self assessment tax could not be paid or return could not be signed by the M.D. as he was out of the country at relevant time.

(*iii*) Similarly in the case of individuals, there may be cases when there is regular income of salary/rent/interest etc. but return could not be filed in time due to carelessness. T.D.S. has been deducted by the payer but self assessment tax may be pending on the part of assessee.

(*iv*) Assessee files return for A.Y. 2010-11 after the date of search under section 139(4)/153A.

A question may arise as to whether such a situation is hit by *Explanation 5A* to section 271(1)(*c*) and whether with respect to the regular income of the assessee, penalty for concealment can be attracted under section 271(1)(*c*) for the reason that the return could not be filed by the assessee in time and before he could file the return, search has taken place?

Explanation 5A is attracted when in the course of search initiated under section 132, assessee is found to be the owner of —

(*i*) Any money, bullion, jewellery or other valuable article or thing (hereafter in his *Explanation* referred to as assets) and the assessee claims that such assets have been acquired by him by utilizing (wholly or in part) his income for any previous year, or

(*ii*) Any income based on any entry in any books of account or other documents or transactions and he claims that such entry in the books of account or other documents or transactions represent his income (wholly or in part) for any previous year.

As per the plain reading of clause (*ii*) above, it transpires that above situation shall be covered within the ambit of *Explanation 5A* to section 271(1)(*c*) and penalty may be exigible.

However, a close reading of the above provision indicates that the legislative intent is to cover within the ambit of *Explanation 5A* to section 271(1)(*c*) such undisclosed assets or undisclosed income found in the course of search which assessee had not disclosed or would not have disclosed to the Department. It does not seem to cover those incomes which assessee would have disclosed in regular course but could not disclose to the Department since the income-tax return could not be filed in time.

However, as a matter of caution it may be added that the above view is not free from debate and the same is liable to the judicial test and interpretation. Arguments on behalf of the taxpayers are more amenable to acceptance when advance tax relating to such income already stood paid by the assessee but return of income could not be filed in time due to some other plausible reason. However in the situation when advance tax relating to such income was also unpaid, it may take lot of pains to the assessee to avoid the levy of penalty.

16.14 Provision of section 271AAA/271AAB and *Explanation 5A* to section 271(1)(c) not applicable to requisition made under section 132A

Provision of section 271AAA/271AAB is applicable only in a case where search has been initiated under section 132 and is thus not applicable when requisition is made under section 132A. It means that in the case of requisition made under section 132A, deeming provision of "undisclosed income" relating to "specified previous year" is not applicable. One can understand the rationale since there is no opportunity available to the assessee for making declaration of undisclosed income under section 132(4) in the case of requisition made under section 132A. Therefore, section 271AAA/271AAB does not cover within its scope requisition under section 132A. It, therefore, implies that assessee can make declaration of undisclosed income/assets relating to "specified previous year" found and requisitioned under section 132A at the time of filing of return of income for such year and there cannot be any concealment of income which may be attached to the assessee with respect to the requisitioned assets and no penalty relating to the same can be imposed.

It may further be observed that even under *Explanation 5A* to section 271(1)(c), requisition made under section 132A has not been covered as the said *Explanation* refers only to search initiated under section 132. It, therefore, implies that relating to the earlier years for which income-tax returns are filed late u/s 139(4) after the date of requisition, showing further income covering the assets/evidences found and requisitioned under section 132A, no penalty for concealment may be attracted under section 271(1)(c) as no concealment can be attributed to the assessee relating to income declared in the return filed.

It is further interesting to observe that the situation may remain the same even when notices under section 153A for filing fresh returns have been issued. It is for the reason that *Explanation 3* to section 271(1)(c) does not cover notice under section 153A though it covers notice issued under section 142(1) or section 148. Though in our opinion, this is an anomaly in the provision and it cannot be the legislative intent.

In *Vinod Goyal* v. *Asstt. CIT* [2009] 28 SOT 9 (Nag.-Trib.) (URO), it was held that no search under section 132 having been conducted in the case of assessee, penalty under section 271(1)(c) could not be imposed by invoking *Explanation 5* thereof in a case where cash seized by police from assessee's employee was requisitioned by the Department under section 132A and which was surrendered by assessee as his income during survey under section 133A and which was returned by assessee in his regular return and accepted by A.O. in assessment under section 153A.

Karnataka High Court, however, in the case of *CIT* v. *Aboo Mohmed* [2000] 111 Taxman 120 have held that requisition u/s 132A is deemed as seizure u/s 132(1) and since it is deemed search, *Explanation 5* to section 271(1) (c) would also apply to a proceeding u/s 132A.

16.15 New Penalty provision under section 270A made applicable with effect from A.Y. 2017-18 in place of section 271(1)(c)

As per the Finance Act, 2016 with effect from 1st April, 2017, *i.e.* from A.Y. 2017-18, new penalty provision for concealment of income under section 270A has been enacted. It means that up to A.Y. 2016-17 penalty provision for concealment of income would be governed by section 271(1)(c) and thereafter by provision of section 270A. There is conceptual change between the two provisions. As per section 270A, penalty is leviable for under-reporting and misreporting of income while under section 271(1) (c), penalty was leviable for concealment of particulars of income and/or furnishing of inaccurate particulars of income. Moreover, rate of penalty has also been rationalized.

Text of section 270A

Penalty for under-reporting and misreporting of income.

270A. (1) The Assessing Officer or the Commissioner (Appeals) or the Principal Commissioner or Commissioner may, during the course of any proceedings under this Act, direct that any person who has under-reported his income shall be liable to pay a penalty in addition to tax, if any, on the under-reported income.

(2) A person shall be considered to have under-reported his income, if—

  (a) the income assessed is greater than the income determined in the return processed under clause (a) of sub-section (1) of section 143;

  (b) the income assessed is greater than the maximum amount not chargeable to tax, where no return of income has been furnished or where return has been furnished for the first time under section 148;

  (c) the income reassessed is greater than the income assessed or reassessed immediately before such reassessment;

(d) the amount of deemed total income assessed or reassessed as per the provisions of section 115JB or section 115JC, as the case may be, is greater than the deemed total income determined in the return processed under clause (a) of sub-section (1) of section 143;

(e) the amount of deemed total income assessed as per the provisions of section 115JB or section 115JC is greater than the maximum amount not chargeable to tax, where no return of income has been furnished or where return has been furnished for the first time under section 148;

(f) the amount of deemed total income reassessed as per the provisions of section 115JB or section 115JC, as the case may be, is greater than the deemed total income assessed or reassessed immediately before such reassessment;

(g) the income assessed or reassessed has the effect of reducing the loss or converting such loss into income.

(3) The amount of under-reported income shall be,—

(i) in a case where income has been assessed for the first time,—

(a) if return has been furnished, the difference between the amount of income assessed and the amount of income determined under clause (a) of sub-section (1) of section 143;

(b) in a case where no return of income has been furnished or where return has been furnished for the first time under section 148,—

(A) the amount of income assessed, in the case of a company, firm or local authority; and

(B) the difference between the amount of income assessed and the maximum amount not chargeable to tax, in a case not covered in item (A);

(ii) in any other case, the difference between the amount of income reassessed or recomputed and the amount of income assessed, reassessed or recomputed in a preceding order:

Provided that where under-reported income arises out of determination of deemed total income in accordance with the provisions of section 115JB or section 115JC, the amount of total under-reported income shall be determined in accordance with the following formula—

$$(A - B) + (C - D)$$

where,

A = the total income assessed as per the provisions other than the provisions contained in section 115JB or section 115JC (herein called general provisions);

B = the total income that would have been chargeable had the total income assessed as per the general provisions been reduced by the amount of under-reported income;

C = the total income assessed as per the provisions contained in section 115JB or section 115JC;

D = the total income that would have been chargeable had the total income assessed as per the provisions contained in section 115JB or section 115JC been reduced by the amount of under-reported income:

Provided further that where the amount of under-reported income on any issue is considered both under the provisions contained in section 115JB or section 115JC and under general provisions, such amount shall not be reduced from total income assessed while determining the amount under item *D*.

Explanation.—For the purposes of this section,—

    (*a*) "preceding order" means an order immediately preceding the order during the course of which the penalty under sub-section (1) has been initiated;

    (*b*) in a case where an assessment or reassessment has the effect of reducing the loss declared in the return or converting that loss into income, the amount of under-reported income shall be the difference between the loss claimed and the income or loss, as the case may be, assessed or reassessed.

(4) Subject to the provisions of sub-section (6), where the source of any receipt, deposit or investment in any assessment year is claimed to be an amount added to income or deducted while computing loss, as the case may be, in the assessment of such person in any year prior to the assessment year in which such receipt, deposit or investment appears (hereinafter referred to as "preceding year") and no penalty was levied for such preceding year, then, the under-reported income shall include such amount as is sufficient to cover such receipt, deposit or investment.

(5) The amount referred to in sub-section (4) shall be deemed to be amount of income under-reported for the preceding year in the following order—

    (*a*) the preceding year immediately before the year in which the receipt, deposit or investment appears, being the first preceding year; and

    (*b*) where the amount added or deducted in the first preceding year is not sufficient to cover the receipt, deposit or investment, the year immediately preceding the first preceding year and so on.

(6) The under-reported income, for the purposes of this section, shall not include the following, namely:—

(*a*) the amount of income in respect of which the assessee offers an explanation and the Assessing Officer or the Commissioner (Appeals) or the Commissioner or the Principal Commissioner, as the case may be, is satisfied that the explanation is *bona fide* and the assessee has disclosed all the material facts to substantiate the explanation offered;

(*b*) the amount of under-reported income determined on the basis of an estimate, if the accounts are correct and complete to the satisfaction of the Assessing Officer or the Commissioner (Appeals) or the Commissioner or the Principal Commissioner, as the case may be, but the method employed is such that the income cannot properly be deduced therefrom;

(*c*) the amount of under-reported income determined on the basis of an estimate, if the assessee has, on his own, estimated a lower amount of addition or disallowance on the same issue, has included such amount in the computation of his income and has disclosed all the facts material to the addition or disallowance;

(*d*) the amount of under-reported income represented by any addition made in conformity with the arm's length price determined by the Transfer Pricing Officer, where the assessee had maintained information and documents as prescribed under section 92D, declared the international transaction under Chapter X, and, disclosed all the material facts relating to the transaction; and

(*e*) the amount of undisclosed income referred to in section 271AAB.

(7) The penalty referred to in sub-section (1) shall be a sum equal to fifty per cent of the amount of tax payable on under-reported income.

(8) Notwithstanding anything contained in sub-section (6) or sub-section (7), where under-reported income is in consequence of any mis-reporting thereof by any person, the penalty referred to in sub-section (1) shall be equal to two hundred per cent of the amount of tax payable on under-reported income.

(9) The cases of misreporting of income referred to in sub-section (8) shall be the following, namely:—

(*a*) misrepresentation or suppression of facts;

(*b*) failure to record investments in the books of account;

(*c*) claim of expenditure not substantiated by any evidence;

(*d*) recording of any false entry in the books of account;

(*e*) failure to record any receipt in books of account having a bearing on total income; and (*f*) failure to report any international transaction or any transaction deemed to be an international transaction or any specified domestic transaction, to which the provisions of Chapter X apply.

(10) The tax payable in respect of the under-reported income shall be—

(*a*) where no return of income has been furnished or where return has been furnished for the first time under section 148 and the income has been assessed for the first time, the amount of tax calculated on the under-reported income as increased by the maximum amount not chargeable to tax as if it were the total income;

(*b*) where the total income determined under clause (*a*) of sub-section (1) of section 143 or assessed, reassessed or recomputed in a preceding order is a loss, the amount of tax calculated on the under-reported income as if it were the total income;

(*c*) in any other case, determined in accordance with the formula—

$$(X–Y)$$

where,

X = the amount of tax calculated on the under-reported income as increased by the total income determined under clause (*a*) of sub-section (1) of section 143 or total income assessed, reassessed or recomputed in a preceding order as if it were the total income; and

Y = the amount of tax calculated on the total income determined under clause (*a*) of sub-section (1) of section 143 or total income assessed, reassessed or recomputed in a preceding order.

(11) No addition or disallowance of an amount shall form the basis for imposition of penalty, if such addition or disallowance has formed the basis of imposition of penalty in the case of the person for the same or any other assessment year.

(12) The penalty referred to in sub-section (1) shall be imposed, by an order in writing, by the Assessing Officer, the Commissioner (Appeals), the Commissioner or the Principal Commissioner, as the case may be.

(*i*) Applicability of provision of section 270A in case of search

In the case of search, penalty provision under section 271AAB is applicable for 'specified previous year' in respect of 'undisclosed income'. 'Specified previous year' is the year of search and in certain cases would include the preceding year also as defined therein. In the case of search, assessment under section 153A is made for preceding six years (nine years in certain cases). For the years prior to 'specified previous year', penalty is leviable under section 271(1)(*c*) for and up to assessment year 2016-17, and from A.Y. 2017-18, penalty would be leviable under section 270A. There may be situations when in the case of same search, penalty for years prior to specified previous year is leviable under section 271(1)(c) as well as under section 270A depending upon the year for which assessment is being framed under section 153A.

For example, in case search is initiated as on 15-2-2020, penalty provision for different assessment years may be as under:

For A.Y. 2020-21 being 'specified previous year' - penalty under section 271AAB

For A.Y. 2014-15 to 2016-17- penalty under section 271(1)(c)

For A.Y. 2017-18 to 2019-20- penalty under section 270A

(ii) **No provision under section 270A corresponding to *Explanation 5A* to section 271(1)(c)**

There is no provision under section 270A which can be said to be corresponding to *Explanation 5A* to section 271(1)(c). Therefore, implication of applicability of *Explanation 5A* to section 271(1)(c) is not attracted under section 270A.

16.16 Miscellaneous

(i) **Instructions of the CBDT regarding not pressurizing for declaration of undisclosed income during search**

The CBDT has issued Instruction F. No. 286/2/2003-IT (Inv), dated 10-3-2003 to the Income Tax Officials not to insist for declaration of undisclosed income from the assessee during search and survey. The objective of search was stated to be an exercise to collect evidences of undisclosed income use of which can be made during assessment proceedings. Such Instruction is reproduced as under:

F. No. 286/2/2003-IT (Inv)
GOVERNMENT OF INDIA
MINISTRY OF FINANCE &COMPANY AFFAIRS
DEPARTMENT OF REVENUE
CENTRAL BOARD OF DIRECT TAXES
Room No. 254/North Block, New Delhi, the 10th March, 2003

To

All Chief Commissioners of Income Tax, (Cadre Contra) & All Directors General of Income Tax Inv.

Sir

Subject : Confession of additional income during the course of search and seizure and survey operation -regarding

Instances have come to the notice of the Board where assessees have claimed that they have been forced to confess the undisclosed income during the course of the search and seizure and survey operations. Such confessions, if not based upon credible evidence, are later retracted by the concerned assessees while filing returns of income. In these circumstances, on confessions during the course of search and seizure and survey operations do not serve any useful purpose. It is, therefore, advised that there should be focus and concentration on collection of evidence of income which leads to information on what has not been disclosed or is not likely to be disclosed before the Income Tax Departments. Similarly, while recording statement during the course of search it seizures and survey operations no attempt should be made to obtain confession as to the undisclosed income. Any action on the contrary shall be viewed adversely.

Further, in respect of pending assessment proceedings also, Assessing Officers should rely upon the evidences/materials gathered during the course of search/survey operations or thereafter while framing the relevant assessment orders

Yours faithfully,

Sd/-

(S. R. Mahapatra)

Under Secretary (Inv. II)

F.No. 286/98/2013-IT (Inv.II)
Government of India
Ministry of Finance
Department of Revenue
Central Board of Direct Taxes

Dated- 18th December, 2014

To

1. All Principal Chief Commissioners of Income Tax

2. All Chief Commissioners of Income Tax

3. All Directors General of Income Tax (Inv.)

4. Director General of Income Tax (I & CI), New Delhi

Subject: Admissions of Undisclosed Income under coercion/pressure during Search/Survey - reg.

Ref: (1) CBDT letter F.No. 286/57/2002-IT(Inv.II) dated, 03-07-2002

(2) CBDT letter F.No. 286/2/2003-IT(Inv.11) dated, 10-03-2003

(3) CBDT letter F.No. 286/98/2013-IT(Inv.11) dated, 09-01-2014

Sir/Madam

Instances/complaints of undue influence/coercion have come to notice of the CBDT that some assessees were coerced to admit undisclosed income during Searches/Surveys conducted by the Department. It is also seen that many such admissions are retracted in the subsequent proceedings since the same are not backed by credible evidence. Such actions defeat the very purpose of Search/Survey operations as they fail to bring the undisclosed income to tax in a sustainable manner leave alone levy of penalty or launching of prosecution. Further, such actions show the Department as a whole and officers concerned in poor light.

2. I am further directed to invite your attention to the Instructions/Guidelines issued by CBDT from time to time, as referred above, through which the Board has emphasized upon the need to focus on gathering evidences during Search/Survey and to strictly avoid obtaining admission of undisclosed income under coercion/undue influence.

3. In view of the above, while reiterating the aforesaid guidelines of the Board, I am directed to convey that any instance of undue influence/coercion in the recording of the statement during Search/Survey/Other proceeding under the I.T. Act, 1961 and/or recording a disclosure of undisclosed income under undue pressure/coercion shall be viewed by the Board adversely.

4. These guidelines may be brought to the notice of all concerned in your Region for strict compliance.

5. I have been further directed to request you to closely observe/oversee the actions of the officers functioning under you in this regard.

6. This issues with approval of the Chairperson, CBDT

(K. Ravi Ramchandran)

Director (Inv.)-II, CBDT

The spirit of the above instructions issued by the Government to the Tax Officials is not to pressurize the assessees for making declaration of undisclosed income in the course of search. In case an assessee wants to make declaration of undisclosed income *suo motu* to take advantage of the provision of section 271AAA/271AAB so as to get immunity from penalty, it can be done by the assessee and such declaration of the undisclosed income may be accepted by the Tax Officials. However, in practice, it has generally been observed that the above instructions issued by the Government are not followed by the Tax Officials and the person searched is put under enormous pressure for making declaration of undisclosed income in the course of search.

(ii) **Provisions of sections 274 and 275 to apply**

Sub-section (4) to section 271AAA and sub section (3) to section 271AAB provide that provisions of sections 274 and 275, so far as may be, shall apply in relation to penalty to be levied under section 271AAA/271AAB. Section 274 requires reasonable opportunity of hearing to be given to the assessee before imposition of any penalty. It further provides approval of the Joint Commissioner to be taken before imposition of penalty in certain cases. Section 275 contains provision regarding limitation for imposing penalty. All the requirement of provisions of these sections shall be applicable with equal force with respect to penalty to be levied under section 271AAA/271AAB.

Further, it may be mentioned that basic general principles for imposition of penalty as are applicable in other cases for imposition of any other penalty will be applicable with respect to penalty to be imposed under section 271AAA/271AAB. These principles may include principle regarding initiation of penalty during assessment proceedings, satisfaction of assessing officer during the course of assessment etc.

It has been held in the case of *Ramgopal Ochhavlal Maheshwari* v. *Deputy CIT* [2019] 109 taxmann.com 184/417 ITR 710 (Guj) that where notice was issued under section 271AAA & subsequent corrigendum was issued stating notice was under section 271AAB, there is no substantial difference between sections 271AAA and 271AAB & thus notice and consequential order of penalty is valid.

It has been held in the case of *Sandeep Chandak* v. *Asstt. CIT* 150 DTR (Lucknow 'B') 247 that the provisions of ss. 271(1)(c) and 271AAB being entirely different, notice issued under s. 271(1)(c) was not valid for initiation of proceedings under s. 271AAB. Also, AO should record satisfaction before initialing the proceedings under s. 271AAB. Also, levy of penalty under s. 271AAB cannot be sustained also for the reason that the assessee was given only two working days to reply the said notice.

It has been held in the case of *Principal CIT* v. *Sandeep Chandak* 169 DTR (All) 449 that assessees having admitted undisclosed income and specified the manner in which such income has been derived in their statements recorded under s. 132(4) during the course of search, provisions of s. 271AAB are attracted & further, Assessing authority having clearly indicated in the penalty notice issued under s. 274 r/w 271 that the proceedings are being initiated under s. 271AAB, and initiated no proceedings under s. 271(1)(c), the penalty proceedings under s. 271AAB were not invalid.

16.17 Attraction of penalty for concealment in cases covered u/s 153C

It may be interesting to examine the applicability of penalty provision as contained under section 271AAA/271AAB and under *Explanation 5A* to section 271(1)(c) in respect of the cases covered u/s 153C.

For this purpose, it may be observed that situation u/s 153C is similar to the situation of requisition made under section 132A to the extent and in as much as there is no opportunity available in both the cases, to the person covered under sections 153C and 132A to make declaration of undisclosed income in the course of search. There can thus, not be any deeming fiction of "undisclosed income" created under section 271AAA/271AAB applicable in such circumstances and, therefore, application of the provision of penalty as contained under section 271AAA/271AAB with respect to the person covered under section 153C is also neither practical nor possible under the express provision of law.

It has been held in the case of *Dy. CIT* v. *Velji Rupshi Faria* [2018] 97 taxmann.com 460/172 ITD 445 (Mumbai - Trib.) that only in case of a person in whose case search and seizure operation under section 132(1) is carried out, penalty proceedings under section 271AAA can be initiated and not in a case where action u/s 153C was taken.

It has been held in the case of *Principal CIT v. Silemankhan & Mahaboob Khan* [2021] 130 taxmann.com 62/282 Taxman 403 (AP) When return of income is filed in response to notice under section 153C by a person other than the person who has been searched in execution of warrant under section 132, penalty under section 271AAB cannot be imposed.

Insofar as the applicability of the provision of *Explanation 5A* to section 271(1)(*c*) in respect of the person covered u/s 153C is concerned, it may be a debatable issue. In such a case, on the one hand it can be argued that:—

(*a*) Since situation covered u/s 153C is similar to the situation covered u/s 132A in as much as opportunity to declare u/s 132(4) is not available in both the cases and jurisdiction to assess is assumed u/s 153C not on the initiation of search but at a later stage, and requisition under section 132A is not covered by *Explanation 5A* to section 271(1)(*c*), the person covered by the provision of section 153C, should therefore, not be hit by the penalty provision of *Explanation 5A* to section 271(1)(*c*).

(*b*) *Explanation 5A* to section 271(1)(*c*) is applicable when the assessee is found to be the owner of undisclosed income/assets in the course of search initiated under section 132. This situation may be applicable in case of the person against whom the search warrant has been issued and not to any other person who is covered later on u/s 153C and in whose case search was not initiated. Thus, *Explanation 5A* to section 271(1)(*c*) should not be applicable in such a case.

(*c*) Jurisdiction to make assessment u/s 153C in case of other person is assumed by the assessing officer when seized material belonging to such other person is handed over by the assessing officer of the person searched to the assessing officer of such other person. Prior to this stage, there cannot even be any argument that search has been initiated with respect to such other person and he can be said to be the owner of any undisclosed income/asset so as to press the applicability of *Explanation 5A* to section 271(1)(*c*).

On the other hand, opposing the above view, it can be argued that *Explanation 5A* to section 271(1)(*c*) is triggered when in the course of search initiated u/s 132, the assessee is found to be the owner of undisclosed income/undisclosed asset. It does not refer to search of any particular person. Action u/s 153C is undertaken against other person when any seized asset/material belonging to such other person is found in the course of search initiated u/s 132. Therefore, though the jurisdiction to make assessment of such other person may be assumed at a later stage but the seized material found belonging to such other person is as a result of search initiated u/s 132. Therefore, *Explanation 5A* should be applicable in his case also.

In our considered opinion, the above view does not seem to be reasonable since *Explanation 5A* cannot be said to be applicable to a person who has not been searched till the time the books of account, other documents or assets belonging to the other person are handed over to the assessing officer of such person and jurisdiction under section 153C is assumed by the assessing officer with respect to such person. At the most, penalty for concealment u/s 271(1)(*c*) read with *Explanation 5A* can be applicable when any return of income is filed by such other person with the assessing officer after assumption of jurisdiction under section 153C showing further income detected as a result of search.

It has been held by the Apex Court in the case of *Principal CIT* v. *Rajkumar Gulab Badgujar* [2019] 111 taxmann.com 257/267 Taxman 488 (SC) **by approving the Bombay High Court's decision titled identically and reported at 111 taxmann.com 256 (Bom.)** that *Explanation 5A* to section 271(1)(*c*) would apply to searched person and not to other person covered under section 153C.

16.17A Penalty provision relating to search initiated before 1st June, 2007 - *Explanation 5* to section 271(1)(*c*)

In connection with income-tax search initiated under section 132 before 1st June, 2007, penalty for concealment of income is governed by provision of section 271(1)(*c*) read with *Explanation 5.*

Explanation 5 was inserted under the Income-tax Act by Taxation Laws (Amendment) Act, 1984 with effect from 1st October, 1984. Prior to this, penalty for concealment in case of search was governed by normal provisions of section 271(1)(*c*). It may further be noted that penalty provisions for concealment of income under section 271(1)(*c*) were not at all applicable during block assessment regime commencing from 1st July, 1995 till 31st May, 2003 since there was specific penalty provision u/s 158BFA(2).

In connection with search initiated after 1st June, 2007 penalty provision for concealment of income has been segregated for undisclosed income relating to specified previous year and for the years prior to the specified previous year by the provisions of section 271AAA and *Explanation 5A* to section 271(1)(*c*) respectively. There was no such segregation regarding penalty provision in connection with search initiated before 1st June, 2007 and penalty provision under section 271(1)(c) read with *Explanation 5* was applicable relating to concealed income for specified previous year as well as for earlier years.

(i) Text of *Explanation 5* to section 271(1)(c)

Where in the course of a search initiated under section 132 before the 1st day of June, 2007, the assessee is found to be the owner of any money, bullion, jewellery or other valuable article or thing (hereafter in this *Explanation* referred to as assets) and the assessee claims that such assets have been acquired by him by utilizing (wholly or in part) his income,—

(a) for any previous year which has ended before the date of search, but the return of income for such year has not been furnished before the said date or, where such return has been furnished before the said date, such income has not been declared therein; or

(b) for any previous year which is to end on or after the date of the search,

then, notwithstanding that such income is declared by him in any return of income furnished on or after the date of the search, he shall, for the purposes of imposition of a penalty under clause (c) of sub-section (1) of this section, be deemed to have concealed the particulars of his income or furnished inaccurate particulars of such income, unless,—

(1) such income is, or the transactions resulting in such income are recorded,—

(i) in a case falling under clause (a), before the date of the search; and

(ii) in a case falling under clause (b) on or before such date,

in the books of account, if any, maintained by him for any source of income or such income is otherwise disclosed to the Chief Commissioner or Commissioner before the said date; or

(2) he, in the course of the search, makes a statement under sub-section (4) of section 132 that any money, bullion, jewellery or other valuable article or thing found in his possession or under his control, has been acquired out of his income which has not been disclosed so far in his return of income to be furnished before the expiry of time specified in sub-section (1) of section 139, and also specifies in the statement the manner in which such income has been derived and pays the tax, together with interest, if any, in respect of such income.

(ii) Salient features of *Explanation 5* to section 271(1)(c)

(1) *Explanation 5* is applicable in connection with assessments made relating to search initiated under section 132 before 1st June, 2007 except for the block assessment regime.

(2) It is applicable when in the course of search assessee is found to be the owner of any assets and income representing such assets —

  (a) has not been declared in the return of income already filed by the assessee;

  (b) income representing such assets has not been recorded in the books of account maintained by him or such income is otherwise not disclosed to the Income Tax Department on or before the date of search.

(3) Assessee may get immunity from penalty in connection with the above deemed concealed income in case declaration of undisclosed income is made in the statement under section 132(4) in the course of search, specifying the manner in which such income has been derived and payment of tax along with interest is made.

(4) *Explanation 5* covers only undisclosed assets while *Explanation 5A* covers apart from undisclosed assets, any undisclosed income based on any entry in any books of account or documents or any other transactions. However, there is no distinction between tangible and intangible undisclosed asset. Rajasthan High Court in the case of *CIT* v. *Mishrimal Soni* [2007] 162 Taxman 53, have held that *Explanation 5* to section 271(1)(c) applies to the disclosure of both tangible as well as intangible undisclosed assets and penalty u/s 271(1)(c) cannot be levied in respect of unexplained investment in money lending business and loan advanced by the assessee evidenced by promissory notes found during search.

(5) *Explanation 5* may be applicable when due date for filing of return has expired but return has not been filed by the assessee while *Explanation 5A* is applicable when due date for filing return of income has not expired and assessee has not filed the return of income.

(6) For seeking immunity from penalty under *Explanation 5* to section 271(1)(c), disclosure in the statement during search has been contemplated only with respect to the undisclosed assets relating to current year for which deeming fiction has been created. There is no requirement of making declaration

with respect to other nature of undisclosed income relating to the current year which is not covered within the purview of deeming fiction of undisclosed income as created under *Explanation 5*. Such income can be declared at any time till the filing of the return of income without attracting any penalty for concealment under normal provision of section 271(1)(*c*).

In *CIT* v. *S.D.V. Chandru* [2004] 136 Taxman 537 (Mad.), Madras High Court have gone to the extent of holding that para (2) in *Explanation 5* does not make any distinction between the previous year which has ended before the date of search and the previous year which is to end on or after the date of search and therefore when the assessee filed his returns for earlier years admitting a larger income and also paid tax together with interest after his statement was recorded under section 132(4), he was entitled to immunity under *Explanation 5* to section 271(1)(*c*) and penalty was not leviable.

However it is submitted with great respect that the above view requires reconsideration because if the above view is accepted, then there will hardly be any case for imposition of penalty for concealment for earlier years even when undisclosed income is detected by the department in the course of search and assessee declares such income in his return of income filed subsequent to the search.

In *Ajit B. Zota* v. *Asstt. CIT* [2010] 40 SOT 543 (Mum.-Trib.); it was held that since the assessee disclosed additional income consequent to the search and seizure proceedings, penalty u/s 271(1)(*c*) was rightly levied and no immunity was available to the assessee under *Explanation 5* to section 271(1)(*c*), when additional income was disclosed in the income-tax return filed u/s 153A.

Following decisions rendered by Courts in this respect merit consideration:-

It has been held in the case of *Dy. CIT* v. *Purti Sakhar Karkhana* [2013] 84 DTR 65 (Nagpur) that penalty under section 271(1)(*c*) is not leviable where Assessee's assessments are framed by the AO at the same income or loss at which the assessee has filed the return including the surrendered income in pursuance of the notice issued under section 153A despite surrender of certain amount by the assessee by reduction of capital work in progress.

It has been held in the case of *Shourya Tower (P.) Ltd.* v. *Dy. CIT* [2013] 30 taxmann.com 10/213 Taxman 20 (Mag.) (Delhi) in the context of penalty under section 271(1)(*c*) and applicability of *Explanation 5* that assessee having not filed return in pursuance of notice under section 153A, clause (2) of *Explanation 5* to section 271(1)(*c*) was not attracted and further, clause (2) extends to those cases falling in clause (*b*) of the excepted part *i.e.* where the return is yet to be filed, in respect of a previous year, during which search took place.

It has been held in the case of *CIT* v. *Smt. Meera Devi* [2012] 26 tax-mann.com 132/[2013] 212 Taxman 68 (Mag.) (Delhi) that there being neither any search of assessee's premises nor any disclosure or state-ment or surrender of income in the course of search, *Explanation 5* of section 271(1)(*c*) was not applicable and further that the assessee having filed return in response to notice under section 153C, which disclosed concealed income, not shown earlier, penalty under section 271(1)(*c*) was sustainable.

It has been held in the case of *Shreeji Traders* v. *Dy. CIT* [2012] 21 tax-mann.com 541/136 ITD 249 (Mum.-Trib.) that the additional income declared after search constituted concealment attracting penalty under section 271(1)(*c*) and that the provisions of *Explanation 5(2)* to section 271(1)(*c*) clearly shows that if income has not been declared before the expiry of time under sub-section (1) of section 139 then immunity is not available.

It has been held in the case of *Shabbir Allauddin Latiwala* v. *Dy. CIT* [2011] 16 taxmann.com 177/[2012] 49 SOT 137 (URO) (Rajkot-Trib.) that when disclosure of additional income is made in the return fur-nished in response to notice under section 153A and the Revenue having failed to identify the very foundation on the basis of which the assessees have offered additional income in the returns filed in response to notice under section 153A and to link such foundation to the documents or other records that were found during the course of the search, the charge of concealment of income is not established and therefore, penalties under section 271(1)(*c*) levied by the AO on a common charge of concealment of income and furnishing of inaccurate particulars of income cannot be sustained even though the assessees are not eligible for claiming any immunity from levy of penalty under *Explanation 5* to section 271(1)(*c*).

It has been held in the case of *Asstt. CIT* v. *Gebilal Kanhaialal (HUF)* [2012] 25 taxmann.com 214/210 Taxman 244 (SC) that no time limit has been prescribed for payment of tax under clause (*2*) of *Explana-tion 5* and the assessee having paid tax with interest up to the date of payment in respect of the undisclosed income surrendered by it in the course of search, all the three conditions laid down in clause (*2*) of *Explanation 5* to section 271(1)(*c*) stood fulfilled and, therefore, assessee is entitled to immunity under clause (*2*) of *Explanation 5* to section 271(1)(*c*).

In *Smt. Kiran Devi* v. *Asstt. CIT* [2009] 125 TTJ 631 (Delhi-Trib.); it was held that income disclosed in the return filed in response to notice u/s 153C which was not shown in the original return filed u/s 139, there was clear concealment of income attracting penalty u/s 271(1)(c) and it was unnecessary to invoke *Explanation 5* to section 271(1)(c).

It has been held in the case of *Principal CIT* v. *Gopal Das Kothari* (HUF) [2017] 88 taxmann.com 723 (Cal.) that in view of the finding that assessee declared additional income in return filed under section 153A in response to notice under section 153C and assessee fulfilling conditions for being entitled to immunity from penalty under *Explanation 5(2)* to section 271(1)(c), disclosure in return filed under section 153A amounts to extension of disclosure made under section 132(4) and penalty cannot be levied.

16.18 Penalty for other defaults

Assessment/reassessment to be made in pursuance to provision of section 153A after search having taken place, are in the nature of normal assessment/reassessment proceedings. Various other defaults committed by the assessee may come to the knowledge of the assessing officer in the course of such proceedings and penalty provisions as provided for various defaults under Chapter XXI of the Income-tax Act shall be attracted with respect to such defaults as are there in the normal course. All the penalty provisions are therefore not being discussed here. However, attention is invited to some of the defaults which are generally found to have been committed in relation to search cases:—

(*i*) **Failure to answer questions, sign statements recorded u/s 132(4) or u/s 131(1A)**

In the course of search, statements are recorded by the authorized officer u/s 132(4) or under section 131(1A). Assessee is required to give answer to the questions addressed to him and sign the statement made by him. Failure to answer questions and/or sign statements may attract penalty under section 272A which may amount to ₹ 10,000 for each default or failure. In case statement of the assessee is not recorded in legal manner by the authorized officer, assessee may record his objection to this effect instead of refusing to answer the question and/or sign the statement.

(*ii*) **Failure to comply with the summons issued under section 131**

In the case of summon issued u/s 131 either to attend to give evidence or produce books of account or other documents at a certain place and time and the assessee omits to attend or produce books of account or documents at the specified place or time, penalty u/s 272A may be levied which may amount to ₹ 10,000 for each default or failure.

In the case of search, summon u/s 131 are issued by the authorized officer during post search investigation and proceeding. There is legal controversy on the issue whether summon u/s 131 can be issued by the authorized officer during the post search proceeding. There are divergent views of the courts on this issue. Generally it has been observed that assesses avoid to comply with such summons and penalty proceedings are initiated u/s 272A for such default on the part of the assessees.

It may be interesting to note in this regard that clause (c) of section 272A(1) covers the default of non-compliance of summon issued under sub-section (1) of section 131 and it does not refer to summon issued under sub-section (1A) of section 131. The authorized officer does not have the power to issue summon under sub-section (1) but he can issue summon under sub-section (1A). For this reason also, assessee may defend the levy of the penalty for such default. Reliance can be placed on the decision of Delhi Bench of Tribunal in the case of *Rajiv Kumar* v. *Additional DIT (Inv)* [ITA 3634 (Delhi) of 2012, dated 30.8.2013].

However, Delhi Bench of Income Tax Appellate Tribunal in the case of *Young Indian* v. *Additional DIT (Inv)* [IT Appeal No. 5303 (Delhi) of 2016, dated 30-8-2018] have held that penalty u/s 272A(1)(c) can be levied for the non-compliance of summon issued under section 131(1A).

(iii) **Penalty for unaccounted business transactions**

In the course of search, details or evidences may be found relating to unaccounted business transactions, unrecorded sales or parallel business carried on but not shown in the regular books of account and return of income filed by the assessee. In such a case, there may be an issue regarding levy of penalty for various defaults which may have been committed by the assessee in the course of carrying on such unaccounted business transactions. Such defaults may be of the nature where penalty may be attracted, inter alia, under various provisions of the Act such as:

   (a) Penalty under section 271A for failure to maintain books of account;

   (b) Penalty under section 271B for failure to get books of account audited;

   (c) Penalty under section 271C for failure relating to deduction of tax at source;

   (d) Penalty under section 271(1)(c) for concealment of particulars of income or for furnishing inaccurate particulars of income.

It may be mentioned that "undisclosed income" relating to such unaccounted business transactions may relate to the "specified previous year" as defined under section 271AAA/271AAB or may relate to the earlier years prior to the "specified previous year" and we will examine the above issue as to the levy of penalty for above stated defaults, in both the situations.

In the case of "specified previous year"

In case "undisclosed income" relating to unaccounted business transactions relate to the "specified previous year", penalty provision is governed under section 271AAA/271AAB in the case of search. Sub-section (1) of section 271AAA provides that the assessing officer may, notwithstanding anything contained in any other provisions of this Act, direct that, in a case where search has been initiated under section 132 on or after the first day of June, 2007, the assessee shall pay by way of penalty, in addition to tax, if any, payable by him, a sum computed at the rate of ten per cent of the "undisclosed income" of the "specified previous year".

It is significant to note here that penalty provided under section 271AAA/271AAB is not termed as penalty for concealment of income and the amount of penalty to be levied under this section is not linked with the "tax sought to be evaded" but it is linked with the "undisclosed income" of the "specified previous year". Moreover, section 271AAA/271AAB starts with the *non obstante* clause stating *"notwithstanding anything contained in any other provisions of this Act..."* One may argue that the manner section 271AAA/271AA has been worded implies that section 271AAA/271AAB has overriding effect over the other provisions of the Act and which would include other penalty provisions of the Act as well. Therefore, a view may be taken keeping in mind the language of section 271AAA/271AAB that once a person falls within the ambit of section 271AAA/271AAB, no other penalty provision for any other default under the Income-tax Act may be attracted. It may further be articulated that when a person avails immunity from penalty as provided under sub-section (2) of section 271AAA or concessional levy of penalty under sub-section (1) or (1A) to section 271AAB making the declaration of undisclosed income in the course of search during statement recorded under section 132(4) and after fulfilling other conditions as provided therein, he should not be liable to any other penalty under this Act. Such immunity or concessional rate of penalty, as the case may be, proponents of this argument may canvass, is not restricted to the default of concealment of income but for any other defaults also as mentioned above, penalty for which may be attracted under any other provisions of the Act.

Arguments may further be taken forward by such persons that in case conditions for availing immunity as provided under sub-section (2) of section 271AAA are not fulfilled and penalty is levied under sub-section (1), it would cover any kind of penalty applicable for any other default under this Act. As per the nature and language of provision of section 271AAA, the situation will remain the same when such undisclosed income is not declared by the assessee during search or in his return of income filed under section 139/153A and addition is made by the assessing officer at the assessment stage.

Such interpretation is highly tilted in favour of the person searched and may not be tenable in the light of the language of provision of sub-section (3) of section 271AAA which specifically provides that once the penalty u/s 271AAA is levied, penalty u/s 271(1)(c) cannot be imposed in respect of the undisclosed income of the specified previous year. Thus, opponent of the above view may argue that wherever legislature wanted to exclude specific penalty, it has so provided and in absence of exclusion of any other penalty, it can not be said that once penalty u/s 271AAA is imposed, no other penalty can be imposed.

In the case of earlier years

In case undisclosed income pertaining to unaccounted business transactions relate to the earlier years prior to the "specified previous year", normal penalty provisions shall be applicable as provided under various provisions of the Act for various defaults committed by the assessee. Declaration of such undisclosed income by the assessee in the course of search cannot absolve him from penalty for concealment of income or for other defaults under the Income-tax Act. Issue relating to attraction of penalty for concealment of income under such circumstances has already been discussed earlier.

There may be attraction of penalty for other defaults under such circumstances in accordance with various provisions of the Act and applicability thereof under the given circumstances. Assessee can, however, make out a case of "reasonable cause" as provided under section 273B for non-imposition of penalty and decision may be taken by the assessing officer and/or Joint Commissioner based upon facts and circumstances of the case.

(iv) **Penalty for loans or deposits or 'specified sum' taken or repaid in cash**

No person is permitted to take or repay loans or deposits in cash in violation of the provisions of section 269SS/269T of the Income-tax Act and in such cases, penalty provisions are attracted under section 271D/271E of the Act. In the case of search, generally it has been observed that details of transactions of loans and deposits taken or repaid in cash are found. A question may arise as to whether in such cases, penalty under section 271D/271E may be attracted or not.

In case when such loans or deposits are admitted by the assessee or treated by the assessing officer as undisclosed income of the assessee, the character of such transactions does not remain that of loan or deposit and in such a case, penalty under section 271D/271E cannot be legally imposed as has been held in *Diwan Enterprises* v. *CIT* [2000] 246 ITR 571 (Delhi), *CIT* v. *Standard Brands Ltd.* [2006] 155 Taxman 383 (Delhi).

However in case, such transactions are accepted in the nature of loan or deposits taken or repaid in cash, penalty provision under section 271D/271E gets attracted under such circumstances and penalty may be imposed depending upon the facts and pleadings made by the assessee. The above situation will hold good for the "specified previous year" as well as for the earlier years. In practice, such situation may generally arise when such transactions in cash are found recorded during search at the premises of both the parties *i.e.* the borrower and the lender.

Finance Act, 2015 with effect from 1st June, 2015 has added 'specified sum' and 'specified advance' within the scope of sections 269SS and 269T. 'Specified sum' has been defined to mean any sum of money receivable, whether as advance or otherwise, in relation to transfer of an immovable property, whether or not the transfer takes place. Similarly, 'specified advance' under section 269T means any sum of money in the nature of advance, by whatever name called, in relation to transfer of an immovable property, whether or not the transfer takes place. Therefore, now penalty under sections 271D and 271E is leviable even for accepting or repaying the amount of advance accepted or repaid in cash above the prescribed threshold in relation to immovable property.

(v) Whether penalty is attracted for non-filing or late filing of Income-tax Returns under section 153A

As per penalty provisions contained under the Income-tax Act, there is no penalty provided in case of non-filing or late filing of income tax returns under section 153A. Section 271F provides penalty when a person fails to furnish his return of income as required under section 139(1) before the end of the relevant assessment year. But such penalty cannot be attracted for default in filing returns under section 153A.

In the case of default for filing returns under section 153A, assessee shall be liable for interest under section 234A and may be liable for prosecution as provided under section 276CC.

(*vi*) **Power to reduce or waive penalty etc. in certain cases as provided under section 273A**

Sub-section (1) of section 273A of the Income-tax Act gives powers to the Commissioner to reduce or waive penalty imposed or imposable under section 271(1)(*c*) of the Act, *suo motu* or on an application made by the assessee, on his being satisfied that:

(*a*) The assessee has fully cooperated in any enquiry relating to the assessment of his income.

(*b*) The assessee has either paid, or made satisfactory arrangements for payment of tax and interest, if any in respect of the relevant assessment year(s) and

(*c*) The assessee has prior to detection by the Assessing Officer, of the concealment of particulars of income or of the inaccuracy of particulars furnished in respect of such income, voluntarily and in good faith, made full and true disclosure of such particulars.

Under sub-section (1) of section 273A, where the amount involved exceeds ₹ 5 lakhs, the Commissioner needs to take prior permission from the Chief Commissioner or Director General, as the case may be. It is further provided in sub-section (3) of section 273A that such an order of reduction or waiver of penalty u/s 271(1)(*c*) can be made in the favour of the assessee once in his lifetime.

Sub-section (4) of section 273A empowers the Commissioner to reduce or waive or stay the recovery of any kind of penalty payable by the assessee, after recording the reasons thereof in writing, if he is satisfied that:

(*a*) To do otherwise would cause genuine hardship to the assessee, having regard to the circumstances of the case, and

(*b*) The assessee has cooperated in any inquiry relating to the assessment or any proceeding for the recovery of any amount due from him.

In case of sub-section (4) of section 273A, if the amount involved exceeds ₹ 1 lakh, the Commissioner needs to take prior permission from the Chief Commissioner or Director General, as the case may be.

The order under section 273A is final and no appeal is provided against it.

(vii) **Power of Commissioner to grant immunity from penalty under section 273AA**

A person may make an application to the Commissioner for granting immunity from penalty, if—

(a) He has made an application for settlement under section 245C and the proceedings for settlement have abated under section 245HA, and

(b) The penalty proceedings have been initiated under this Act.

Such application ought to have been made after abatement, but before the imposition of penalty.

Section 273AA empowers the Commissioner to grant to a person, immunity from penalty under this Act, if he is satisfied that the person has, after abatement, co-operated with the income-tax authority in the proceedings before him and has made full and true disclosure of his income and the manner of its derivation.

Such immunity may stand withdrawn if—

(a) Such person fails to comply with any condition subject to which immunity was granted.

(b) Such person had, in the course of the proceedings after abatement, concealed any particular material or had given false evidence in the assessment

On withdrawal of such immunity, all provisions of the Act shall apply as if such immunity had never been granted.

16.19 Offences and Prosecution

Apart from imposition of penalty applicable for various defaults as discussed under Chapter XXI of the Act, assessee may also be prosecuted for various offences committed under this Act. Provisions relating to attraction of prosecution in the case of certain offences, which have generally been seen applicable in practice are being discussed as under :

(i) **Contravention of prohibitory order passed under section 132(3) - Section 275A**

In the case of contravention of any prohibitory order passed by the authorized officer under section 132(3) or order of deemed seizure passed under second proviso to section 132(1), the person concerned shall be punishable with rigorous imprisonment which may extend to two years and shall also be liable to fine as prescribed in section 275A. The contravention of prohibitory order passed under section 132(3) may, *inter alia*, be in the nature when seal put by the authorized officer is damaged or broken or the items put under restraint are removed or replaced. The contravention of order of deemed seizure passed may, *inter alia*, be in the nature when such items are removed or replaced.

(ii) **Non-compliance of provision of section 132(1)(*ii*)(*b*) - Section 275B**

If a person who, in the course of search, is required to afford the authorized officer the necessary facility to inspect the books of account or other documents, as required under section 132(1)(*iib*) fails to afford such facility to the authorized officer, he shall be punishable with rigorous imprisonment for a term which may extend to two years and shall also be liable to fine as prescribed in section 275B. Such contravention may, *inter alia*, be in the nature when software or password for opening a file in the computer is not made available to the authorized officer.

(iii) **Wilful attempt to evade tax - Section 276C**

As provided under section 276C, if a person wilfully attempts in any manner whatsoever, to evade any tax, penalty or interest chargeable or imposable under this Act or wilfully evades payment thereof, he shall in addition to any penalty, that may be imposable on him, be punishable with prosecution also which may extend up to seven years with fine depending upon the quantum of amount sought to be evaded. Prosecution under this section is, *inter alia*, applicable for concealment of income or furnishing inaccurate particulars of income, in addition to penalty which may be imposed for such default.

(iv) **Failure to furnish return of income in search cases - Section 276CC**

If a person wilfully fails to furnish in a due time, the return of income, as required under section 139(1) or under section 153A, he shall be punishable with imprisonment for a term which may extend up to seven years and with fine depending upon the quantum of amount of tax which would have been evaded if the failure had not been discovered.

(v) **False statement and verification - Section 277**

Section 277 of Income-tax Act provides that in case a person makes a false or untrue statement at the time of recording of his statement by the authorized officer under section 132(4) or under section 131 or any other provisions of the Act, he shall be punishable with imprisonment which may extend up to seven years and with fine. Provision under this section may be attracted when a person delivers an account or submit details, information or evidences which are false or forged.

(vi) **Falsification of books of account or documents, etc. - Section 277A**

Section 277A inserted w.e.f. 1-10-2004 seeks to provide punishment with rigorous imprisonment for a term not less than 3 months but which may extend to 3 years and with fine for falsification of books of account or documents for inducing or abetting any other person to evade any tax, penalty or interest chargeable or impossible under the Act. This section was inserted to provide for a situation which was not covered under section 278 *i.e.* abatement of false return.

As far section 278, punishment to a person could be sustained only if tax evasion by the other person was established. However, there was no deterrent provision against making false books or document with an intent to enable other person to evade tax, penalty or interest when there was no tax evasion by the other person established. That in why and in order to provide for such a situation, section 277A came into existence. Its explanation clarifies that for the purpose of establishing the charge u/s 277A, it shall not be necessary to prove that the second person has actually evaded any tax, penalty or interest chargeable or imposable under the Act.

(vii) **Abatement of false return - Section 278**

Section 278 is based on the principle of criminal jurisprudence that any person who abets, aids, counsels or procures the commission of an offence is liable to be tried, proceeded against, and punished as a principal offender. It provides for that if a person abets or induces in any manner to another person to make or deliver to the income tax authorities an account, statement or declaration relating to any income chargeable to tax and which that a better knows to be false or does not believe to be true, he may be punishable with imprisonment up to 7 years and with fine depending upon the quantum of tax etc. which would have been evaded, if the declaration etc. made be accepted as true.

(viii) **Presumption as to assets, books of account in case of search for the purpose of prosecution - Section 278D**

Section 278D provides the rule of evidence as contained in section 132(4A) also in respect of assets, books of account or other documents found in the course of search or obtained on requisition from other authorities u/s 132A, according to which presumption u/s 132(4A) will apply for the purpose of evidence in prosecution proceedings under section 278. However such presumption can be rebutted. It is in the discretion of the criminal court whether presumption must be drawn or not depending upon the cumulative effect of all the factors.

(*ix*) **Whether there can be prosecution for non-compliance of summons issued under section 131**

In the case of non-compliance of summons issued under section 131 by the authorized officer, there is provision for imposition of penalty as discussed earlier. Further, the attendance of such person may be enforced by way of arrest through police authorities as prescribed under rule 10(3) of Order XVI of Civil Procedure Code. There is no provision for prosecution in such cases under the Income-tax Act, 1961.

(*x*) **Refusal to answer questions or to give incorrect reply to questions put during recording of statement under section 132(4)/131**

There is no provision under the Income-tax Act, for initiating prosecution for the refusal to answer question. There is penalty prescribed for such a situation in section 272A(1)(*a*). However, a person may be prosecuted for perjury for giving incorrect reply to the questions under the Indian Penal Code.

(*xi*) **Offences by companies**

Section 278B of the Act provides that where an offence under this Act has been committed by a company, every person who at the time the offence was committed, was in charge of, and was responsible to, the company for the conduct of the business of the company, as well as the company shall be deemed to be guilty of the offence.

In case of offence by the company, the proceeding of prosecution shall be liable to be proceeded against the above person. It is further provided that nothing contained in this sub-section shall render any such person liable to any punishment if he proves that the offence was committed without his knowledge or that he had exercised all due diligence to prevent the commission of such offence.

(*xii*) **Principles emerging from decided cases about prosecution proceedings**

The various principles which emerge from various decisions considered in *Madan Lal* v. *ITO* [1998] 98 Taxman 395/144 CTR 57 (Raj.), are as follows: (1) if the finding of the false statement in respect of income has been set aside by the Tribunal, the criminal proceedings cannot be allowed to be continued, (2) if the proceedings for levy of penalty have been dropped, the question of any criminal prosecution to continue does not arise, (3) if the penalty has been set aside on the ground not deciding the factual position of the matter, the trial court can continue with the criminal prosecution, (4) the criminal proceedings are independent proceedings and mere expectations of success in appeal or reference would not come in the way of the Department for institution of criminal proceedings, (5) the question whether any offence has been committed requires investigation of the fact by the trial court and the High Court in jurisdiction under Article 226 of the Constitution or section 482 of the Criminal Procedure Code cannot adjudicate the same. It is for the Magistrate who can record a finding as to whether an offence has been committed or not, (6) the finding recorded by the Tribunal on facts is final and the High Court cannot go behind such finding, (7) the order of the Tribunal is a good piece of evidence and unless something contrary is shown or exceptional circumstances are pointed out, the trial court would not deviate from such finding of fact recorded, (8) the power under section 482 of the Criminal Procedure Code can be exercised for quashing the criminal proceedings very sparingly and with circumspection in rarest of rare cases, (9) *mens rea* is an essential ingredient and the burden to establish the offence is on the prosecution, (10) it would not be proper to continue with the criminal proceedings during the pendency of appeal before the first appellate authority or Tribunal.

(*xiii*) Power of Commissioner to grant immunity from prosecution

Section 278AB gives power to Commissioner to grant immunity from prosecution but such power is restricted to cases of abatement of settlement proceedings. In respect of other offences, Commissioner does not enjoy power to grant immunity from prosecution.

APPLICATION TO SETTLEMENT COMMISSION IN SEARCH CASES

Amendment by the Finance Act, 2021

Institution of Settlement Commission has been abolished by the Finance Act, 2021 and no new application shall be permitted to be filed on or after 1st February, 2021. As per the provisions of the new scheme, even the pending cases with the Settlement Commission shall not be adjudicated/ settled by Settlement Commission and it has been provided that an interim Board shall be constituted by the CBDT for this purpose.

Memorandum explaining the provisions contained in the Finance Bill, 2021 relating to Income Tax Settlement Commission, is as under:

Discontinuance of Income-tax Settlement Commission

It is proposed to discontinue Income-tax Settlement Commission (ITSC) and to constitute Interim Board of settlement for pending cases. The various amendments proposed are as under:

- ◆ *ITSC shall cease to operate on or after 1st February, 2021*
- ◆ *No application under section 245C of the Act for settlement of cases shall be made on or after 1st February, 2021;*
- ◆ *All applications that were filed under section 245C of the Act and not declared invalid under sub-section (2C) of section 245D of the Act and in respect of which no order under section 245D(4) of the Act was issued on or before the 31st January, 2021 shall be treated as pending applications.*
- ◆ *Where in respect of an application, an order, which was required to be passed by the ITSC under section 245(2C) of the Act on or before the 31st day of January, 2021 to declare an application invalid but such order has not been passed on or before 31st January, 2021,*

such application shall be deemed to be valid and treated as pending application.

♦ *The Central Government shall constitute one or more Interim Board for Settlement (hereinafter referred to as the Interim Board), as may be necessary, for settlement of pending applications. Every Interim Board shall consist of three members, each being an officer of the rank of Chief Commissioner, as may be nominated by the Board. If the Members of the Interim Board differ in opinion on any point, the point shall be decided according to the opinion of majority.*

♦ *On and from 1st February, 2021, the provisions related to exercise of powers or performance of functions by the ITSC viz. provisional attachment, exclusive jurisdiction over the case, inspection of reports and power to grant immunity shall apply* mutatis mutandis *to the Interim Board for the purposes of disposal of pending applications and in respect of functions like rectification of orders for all orders passed under sub-section (4) of section 245D of the Act. However, where the time-limit for amending any order or filing of rectification application under section 245(6B) of the Act expires on or after 1st February, 2021, in computing the period of limitation, the period commencing from 1st February, 2021 and ending on the end of the month in which the Interim Board is constituted shall be excluded and the remaining period shall be extended to sixty days, if less than sixty days.*

♦ *With respect to a pending application, the assessee who had filed such application may, at his option, withdraw such application within a period of three months from the date of commencement of the Finance Act, 2021 and intimate the Assessing Officer, in the prescribed manner, about such withdrawal.*

♦ *Where the option for withdrawal of application is not exercised by the assessee within the time allowed, the pending application shall be deemed to have been received by the Interim Board on the date on which such application is allotted or transferred to the Interim Board.*

♦ *The Board may, by an order, allot any pending application to any Interim Board and may also transfer, by an order, any pending application from one Interim Board to another Interim Board.*

♦ *Where the pending application is allotted to an Interim Board or transferred to another Interim Board subsequently, all the records, documents or evidences, with whatever name called, with the ITSC shall be transferred to such Interim Board and shall be deemed to be the records before it for all purposes.*

◆ *Where the assessee exercises the option to withdraw his application, the proceedings with respect to the application shall abate on the date on which such application is withdrawn and the Assessing Officer, or, as the case may be, any other income-tax authority before whom the proceeding at the time of making the application was pending, shall dispose of the case in accordance with the provisions of this Act as if no application under section 245C of the Act had been made. However, for the purposes of the time-limit under sections 149, 153, 153B, 154 and 155 and for the purposes of payment of interest under section 243 or 244 or, as the case may be, section 244A, for making the assessment or reassessment, the period commencing on and from the date of the application to the ITSC under section 245C of the Act and ending with the date on which application is withdrawn shall be excluded. Further, the income-tax authority shall not be entitled to use the material and other information produced by the assessee before the ITSC or the results of the inquiry held or evidence recorded by the ITSC in the course of proceeding before it. However, this restriction shall not apply in relation to the material and other information collected, or results of the inquiry held or evidence recorded by the Assessing Officer, or, as the case may be, other income-tax authority during the course of any other proceeding under this Act irrespective of whether such material or other information or results of the inquiry or evidence was also produced by the assessee or the Assessing Officer before the ITSC.*

◆ *The Central Government may make a scheme, by notification in the Official Gazette, for the purposes of settlement in respect of pending applications by the Interim Board, so as to impart greater efficiency, transparency and accountability by eliminating the interface between the Interim Board and the assessee in the course of proceedings to the extent technologically feasible; optimising utilisation of the resources through economies of scale and functional specialisation; and introducing a mechanism with dynamic jurisdiction. The Central Government may, for the purposes of giving effect to the said scheme, by notification in the Official Gazette, direct that any of the provisions of this Act shall not apply or shall apply with such exceptions, modifications and adaptations as may be specified in the notification. However, no such direction shall be issued after the 31st March, 2023. Every such notification issued shall, as soon as may be after the notification is issued, be laid before each House of Parliament.*

These amendments will take effect from 1st February, 2021.

[Clauses 54 to 65]

17.1 Introduction

The powers and functions of Income Tax Settlement Commission are contained in Chapter XIX-A of the Income-tax Act, 1961 and are covered by sections 245A to 245V. The concept of Settlement Commission was first introduced by the Taxation Laws (Amendment) Act, 1975, w.e.f. 1st April 1976 and since then provisions contained in this regard have been amended several times.

The institution of Settlement Commission was introduced under the Income-tax Act with the intention to reduce the litigation and speedy settlement of the complicated cases. In the case of search, cases of seven years are undertaken for assessment/reassessment. These cases are, *inter alia*, based upon incriminating material seized during search which may involve lot of complications. Assessee may find it useful, depending upon the facts of the case, to approach to the Settlement Commission for settlement of search cases.

However, it is apt to take note of the observations of the Supreme Court in the case of *CIT* v. *Express Newspaper Ltd.* [1994] 72 Taxman 438 in which Hon'ble Apex Court have held that the disclosure u/s 245C must be of an income not disclosed before the Assessing Officer. If the Assessing Officer has already discovered it and has either gathered the material to establish the particulars of such income or fraudfully or is at a stage of investigation/enquires, where the material gathered by him is likely to establish the particulars of such income or fraud. The assessee cannot be allowed to defeat or forestall, as the case may be, the entire exercise, of the income-tax authority just by approaching the Commission. In such a case, it cannot be said that he is acting voluntarily or in good faith. He should not be allowed to take advantage of the comparatively easy course of settlement. The Chapter is meant for those assessees who want to disclose income not disclosed till then together with the manner in which the said income is derived. It is not meant for those who come after the event *i.e.* after the discovery of the particulars of income and its source - or discovery of particulars of fraud perpetrated by the assessee, as the case may be - nor even to those who come to the Commission to forestall the investigation/enquires which have reached a stage where the department is in possession of material which though not sufficient to establish such concealment or fraud, is such that it is likely to establish it - may be some more material is required to establish it fully.

17.2 Legislative history

The law regarding application to be filed with the Settlement Commission during different periods may be divided into five parts:

i. **Search held before 1st July, 1995**

ii. **Search held between 1.7.1995 till 31.5.2003 when concept of block assessment for undisclosed income was applicable**

iii. **Search held between 1st June 2003 till 31st May 2007**

iv. **Search held between 1st June 2007 till 31st May 2010 - Revised Settlement Scheme - No Application to Settlement Commission permitted**

v. **Search held on or after 1st June, 2010**

(*i*) **Search held before 1st July, 1995:**

In the case of search held before 1st July 1995, the normal procedure of assessment and consequently the normal procedure of filing application with the Settlement Commission were applicable. Prior to amendment brought under section 245A, w.e.f. 1.6.2007, application to Settlement Commission could have been filed during the pendency of any proceeding of assessment/reassessment/appeal or revision before an income-tax authority. But now, application to Settlement Commission can be filed only during the pendency of assessment proceedings before the Assessing Officer.

Earlier there was a requirement to give an opportunity to the Commissioner of Income-tax to make appearance before the Commission and argue his case as to why application made by the assessee may not be admitted by the Settlement Commission. At this stage, the copy of the application made by the assessee was also available with the Commissioner and he could make out his case as to whether true and full disclosure of undisclosed income has been made by the assessee or not. Later on, the above requirement has been dispensed with. In the earlier situation, an application could be made to the Settlement Commission in the case of search only after the filing of income-tax returns. The assessee was under obligation to establish his case for admission of his application by the Settlement Commission that the additional income declared by him in the application has not been discovered either during search or has not been disclosed by him in the income-tax returns filed after search. Such requirement used to create a lot of practical problems and the assessees used to face uphill task in getting the application admitted by Settlement Commission.

(*ii*) **Search held between 1.7.1995 till 31.5.2003 when concept of block assessment for undisclosed income was applicable**

There was initially a controversy as to whether a person covered by block assessment procedure for assessment of undisclosed income relating to income-tax search conducted between 1-7-1995 to 31-5-2003 would be entitled to make application to the Settlement Commission. The Settlement Commission was having the view in favour of the above position but the Income Tax Department had questioned the jurisdiction of the Settlement Commission under such circumstances and had filed SLP before the Supreme Court against the decision of the Settlement Commission. This controversy was set right by CBDT withdrawing all pending SLPs before the Supreme Court and it was clarified that application to Settlement Commission could be moved by the assessee during Block Assessment regime.

(*iii*) **Search held between 1st June 2003 till 31st May 2007**

With effect from 1st June 2003, the procedure of Block Assessment of undisclosed income in search cases was abolished and new procedure under sections 153A to 153D was prescribed. There was no legal bar on making an application to Settlement Commission in the cases of search held on or after 1st June 2003 provided the prerequisite conditions for moving application to Settlement Commission were fulfilled.

(*iv*) **Search held between 1st June 2007 till 31st May 2010 - Revised Settlement Scheme - No Application to Settlement Commission permitted**

The scheme and procedure regarding moving application to Settlement Commission was revised w.e.f. 1st June, 2007 as per Finance Act, 2007. As per the revised scheme, assessee is entitled to make application to Settlement Commission with respect to assessment proceedings pending before Assessing officer. The assessee has been prohibited to make application to the Settlement Commission when proceedings are pending during reassessment stage, or in appeal or in revision. Further, it was also provided that application to Settlement Commission could not be moved with respect to assessment/re-assessment proceedings undertaken in search cases as provided under sections 153A, 153B and 153C of the Act. Thus, the assessee, in whose case income-tax assessment or reassessment proceedings were pending before the Assessing Officer as per provisions of sections 153A, 153B and 153C, was debarred from making application to the Settlement Commission. In this manner, the jurisdiction of the Settlement Commission was restricted to a large extent.

(*v*) **Search held on or after 1st June 2010**

As per Finance Act, 2010, the jurisdiction of Settlement Commission in the case of assessment or reassessment proceedings with respect to search cases pending with the Assessing Officer on or after 1st June 2010 has been revived. Now, an assessee in whose case assessment or reassessment proceedings under section 153A or 153C are pending with the Assessing Officer on or after 1st June 2010, can make application to the Settlement Commission for the purpose of settlement of assessment/reassessment of search cases which are required to be assessed/reassessed as per provisions of sections 153A to 153D. Such application can be made before finalization of assessment/ reassessment order as per provisions of sections 153A to 153D.

Detailed analysis of the provisions for making application to the Settlement Commission, which are applicable presently in the case of search held on or after 1st June 2010 is being made further in this Chapter.

The salient features of the present scheme for making application to the Settlement Commission in search cases may be summarized as under:

1. Application to Settlement Commission can be made by any person in respect of any assessment proceedings, which may be pending before an Assessing Officer on the date on which an application under sub-section (1) of section 245C is made.

2. The pending assessment proceedings before the Assessing Officer would include assessment or reassessment proceedings, which may be pending before him in search cases in pursuance to notices issued for filing income-tax returns under section 153A. Such proceedings shall be deemed to have commenced on the date of issue of notice initiating such proceedings and concluded on the date on which the assessment is made.

   Thus, it implies that application to Settlement Commission in search cases can be made after issuance of notice by the Assessing Officer for filing income-tax returns for earlier six years prior to the year of search. However, the year of search shall be governed by the normal provision and application to Settlement Commission for such year may be filed on or after 1st day of April following the financial year in which search was conducted. Further, it may be noted that the application to the Settlement Commission can be made before finalization of the assessment order for the relevant assessment year.

3. The application to the Settlement Commission is required to be made in Form No. 34B containing a full and true disclosure of the income which has not been disclosed before the Assessing Officer, and stating the manner in which such income has been derived.

4. The additional amount of income-tax payable on the income disclosed in the application exceeds ₹ 50 lakhs. This additional amount of income tax payable is to be seen with respect to each

person relating to all the seven years *i.e.* the year of search and earlier six years.

As per Finance Act, 2011, this requirement of additional income-tax payable of ₹ 50 lakhs with respect to each person covered under search has been diluted and now it is provided in the Finance Act, 2011, that w.e.f. 1st June 2011, in the case of a defined related person/entity covered under search, the additional amount of tax payable may be ₹ 10 lakhs provided application has been made to the Settlement Commission by the specified person searched offering additional tax liability of ₹ 50 lakhs.

5. The additional amount of income-tax and interest u/ss 234A, 234B and 234C thereon is paid on or before the date of making the application to the Settlement Commission and the proof of such payment is attached with the application.

6. Once an application is filed with the Settlement Commission, it shall not be allowed to be withdrawn by the applicant.

7. The intimation of making the application to the Settlement Commission shall be given by the assessee to the Assessing Officer, in Form No.34BA as provided under rule 44C.

8. On receipt of an application under section 245C, the Settlement Commission shall, within 7 days, from the date of receipt of the application, issue a notice to the applicant requiring him to explain as to why the application made by him be allowed to be proceeded with, and on hearing the applicant, the Settlement Commission shall, within a period of 14 days from the date of the application, by an order in writing, reject the application or allow the application to be proceeded with. It is further provided that where no order has been passed within the aforesaid period by the Settlement Commission, the application shall be deemed to have been allowed to be proceeded with.

9. The Settlement Commission is further required to call for a report from the Commissioner and based upon the application filed by the assessee and report received from the Commissioner, the Commission may declare the application in question as invalid after giving an opportunity of hearing to the applicant-assessee.

10. As per the revised scheme, an assessee has one time opportunity to make an application to the Settlement Commission for settlement of his cases.

11. Order shall be passed by the Settlement Commission as provided under sub-section (4) of section 245D after giving opportunity of hearing to the assessee, calling the report from the Commissioner and examining the evidences produced by the assessee within a period of eighteen months from the end of the month in which application was made.

12. The order of settlement passed by the Settlement Commission shall be conclusive and the assessee or Revenue shall not have any right to file an appeal against such order.

(*vi*) **Taxpayers can approach Settlement Commission even for pending reassessment cases:**

As per section 245C of the Act, an assessee may apply to Settlement Commission for settlement of cases at any stage of a case relating to him. The term 'case' as per section 245A(*b*) shall mean any proceeding for assessment which may be pending before an Assessing Officer on the date on which application is made before Settlement Commission.

Before June 1, 2007 an assessee was allowed to apply for settlement of cases even when the proceedings for reassessment were pending before the Assessing Officer. Subsequently, Finance Act, 2007 restricted the scope of the provisions by providing that an assessee shall not be allowed to make the application before the Commission during the pendency of reassessment proceedings or during pendency of proceedings of making fresh assessment where original assessment was set aside.

Finance Act, 2007 inserted a proviso for the purpose of section 245A(*b*) to provide that proceedings for reassessment or fresh assessment where original assessment was set aside shall not be deemed to a proceeding pending before the Assessing Officer. Consequently, a taxpayer was not able to file an application for settlement of cases in cases where reassessment was pending before the Assessing Officer. Effectively, the scope of the term 'case' for which an application could be made was curtailed by the Finance Act, 2007.

Finance Act, 2010 enlarged the scope of settlement commission providing that in case of income-tax search taking place and assessment or reassessment proceedings are undertaken u/s 153A of the Act during pendency of assessment or reassessment proceedings u/s 153A or u/s 153C assessee can file application with the settlement commission for the purpose of settlement of assessment or reassessment of search cases.

The Finance Minister during his budget speech while presenting budget proposals 2014 has proposed to enlarge the scope of the Income-tax Settlement Commission so that taxpayers could approach the Commission for settlement of disputes. Accordingly, the Finance (No. 2) Bill, 2014 as passed by Lok Sabha has deleted the proviso which restricted the scope of the term 'case' to the pending assessment cases only. Such amendment would reinstate the position and now an assessee would be eligible to apply for settlement of even those cases which are pending for reassessment proceedings. The changes in the provisions shall take effect from October 1, 2014.

The above amendment will enlarge the scope of making application to the settlement commission to the effect that any kind of assessment or re-assessment proceedings pending before the Assessing Officer may be subject matter of application to be filed before settlement commission for settlement of cases. Such proceedings pending before Assessing Officer may *inter alia* include following:—

  (*i*) Reassessment proceedings pending before Assessing Officer re-opened under section 148 of the Act;

  (*ii*) Assessment or reassessment set aside by Income Tax Appellate Tribunal under section 254 or by Commissioner of Income Tax under section 263 or under section 264 for fresh examination by the Assessing Officer;

Finance Act, 2015 w.e.f. 1.6.2015 has substituted clause (*i*) to *Explanation* to section 245A. Earlier, it provided that the proceeding for assessment or reassessment under section 147 of the Act is deemed to commence from the date of issue of notice under section 148 of the Act. It has been observed that issue relating to escapement of income is often involved in more than one assessment year. In such case, the assessee becomes eligible to approach Settlement Commission only for the assessment year for which notice under section 148 has been issued. Therefore, to take the proceeding for all other assessment years where there is escapement, the assessee becomes eligible only after notice under section 148 has been issued for all such assessment years.

In order to obviate the need for issue of notice in all such assessment years for commencement of pendency of the proceeding, it has been amended under clause (*i*) of the said *Explanation* to provide that where a notice under section 148 is issued for any assessment year, the assessee can approach Settlement Commission for other assessment years as well even if notice under section 148 for such other assessment years has not been issued. However, a return of income for such other assessment years should have been furnished under section 139 of the Act or in response to notice under section 142 of the Act.

17.3 Whether to approach the Settlement Commission in search cases

(*i*) **Decision by the assessee for approaching the Settlement Commission - Merits and Demerits**

It remains a dilemma in the mind of the assessee whether to approach the Settlement Commission or not for settling his case of search. Decision for making application to the Settlement Commission has to be taken by the assessee keeping in view merits and de-merits of the proceedings of the Settlement Commission, which may be discussed as under:

Merits

(*a*) Assessee may approach the Settlement Commission in complicated cases since Settlement Commission takes broad, objective and practical view.

(*b*) Assessee may approach the Settlement Commission when evidences found during search are relating to undisclosed income earned during earlier years since in normal assessment, it may be difficult to avoid the penalty and prosecution.

(*c*) Assessee may approach the Settlement Commission when it is felt that it is difficult to defend penalty for concealment of income under section 271(1)(*c*) and prosecution under the Income-tax Act, 1961 since Commission has power to grant immunity from penalty and prosecution.

(*d*) The settlement by the Settlement Commission makes early disposal of the search cases and neither of the parties have right to take the proceeding to the higher authorities in appeal.

Demerits

(*a*) For making application to the Settlement Commission, the assessee should come clean declaring all the undisclosed income himself in the application.

(*b*) The amount of admitted tax liability is required to be paid by the assessee before making an application to the Settlement Commission.

(*c*) In search cases, minimum amount of additional tax payable should exceed ₹ 50 lakhs, otherwise application to Settlement Commission is not maintainable.

(*d*) The order of the Settlement Commission is final and binding on the assessee and he does not have the opportunity to file an appeal against such order.

(*e*) As per amended scheme by Finance Act, 2007, assessee has only one time opportunity for making application to the Settlement Commission for settling his cases.

(*ii*) Nature of proceedings before Settlement Commission vs. Assessing Officer

Proceedings before the Settlement Commission are almost similar in nature as the proceedings before the Assessing Officer for making assessment/reassessment of the year of search and earlier six years based upon the material seized during search, income-tax returns filed and undisclosed income declared by the assessee. The Settlement Commission makes an attempt to determine the true and correct taxable income of the assessee relating to the seven years covered under search. However, there remains distinction in the approach of both the authorities. The proceedings before the Settlement Commission can be said to be distinct from the proceedings before the Assessing Officer in following respects:

(*a*) The proceedings of the Settlement Commission are conducted by high ranked officials who have held the office of Chief Commissioners or above having specialised knowledge of and experience in problems relating to direct taxes and business accounts.

(*b*) The approach of the Settlement Commission remains broad, objective and practical. Instead of making high-pitched assessment, Commission tries to settle the cases and determine the income of the assessee with a fair and just approach to both the parties. The Commission remains conscious of the fact that the Settlement Commission is the first and last forum with the assessee and assessee cannot file appeal with the higher authorities against the order of the Settlement Commission.

(*c*) The Settlement Commission generally determines income of the assessee based upon the material seized during search. Commission does not concentrate too much on the small issues relating to income already declared by the assessee in his returns of income filed unless there are any apparent or glaring mistakes.

(*d*) The Settlement Commission generally appreciates the books of account, documents and other evidences found and seized during search from the practical and objective approach.

(*e*) The Settlement Commission discharges the function of quasi-judicial nature so as to determine true and correct taxable income of the assessee. The nature of proceedings before the Settlement Commission are judicial in nature and it provides equal opportunity to the assessee as well as to the department to represent their respective case and point of view.

(*iii*) **Circumstances under which application to Settlement Commission may be advisable to the assessee**

In case of the following circumstances, it may be in the interest of the assessee to approach the Settlement Commission for settling his cases in the case of search:

(*a*) When the seized material indicates undisclosed income relating to earlier years and assessee feels that during normal assessment proceedings, it may not be possible to defend penalty for concealment of income under section 271(1)(*c*) read with *Explanation 5A* and prosecution under the Income-tax Act.

(*b*) When incriminating material has been seized consisting of numerous documents, loose papers, diaries etc. containing details of unrecorded transactions and there are cross-references, duplicate notings, multiple incoming and outgoing of funds, undisclosed income generated and applied/spent out of the books. In such a situation, there may be duplicate/multiple additions of undisclosed income by the Assessing Officer, while the Settlement Commission generally takes practical and reasonable view.

(*c*) When the issues are such that the assessee expects to be embroiled in long drawn litigation with the Revenue. Settlement order is passed by the Settlement Commission expeditiously and neither of the parties have any right to file appeal against such order. Thus, assessee may settle the litigation with the department at an early stage through the institution of the Settlement Commission.

17.4 Filing and admission of application with Settlement Commission - Certain conditions to be fulfilled

(*i*) **Stage for filing application to Settlement Commission in search cases**

A person is required to be assessed/reassessed for earlier six years prior to the year of search in accordance with the provisions of section 153A/153C. Application to Settlement Commission can be filed by the assessee after receiving the notices from the Assessing Officer for filing fresh returns for earlier six years as provided under clause (*a*) of section 153A(1). The year of search is not covered under section 153A but is covered under the normal provisions of the Act. The application to the Settlement Commission with respect to the year of search can be filed on or after 1st day of April following the year in which search was held. Since the application for all the years is filed by the assessee in a consolidated manner, practically application can be filed after commencement of both the above dates.

Further, it may be mentioned that the application to Settlement Commission may be filed at any stage after the above dates and before finalization of the assessment order by the Assessing Officer. This shall be the period during which assessment proceedings may be said to be pending.

(*ii*) Application to Settlement Commission may be filed when assessment proceedings are pending with the Assessing Officer

As per amendment made by the Finance Act, 2010, application to Settlement Commission in search cases has been revived and such application may be filed by assessee when assessment or reassessment proceedings in pursuance to notices under section 153A or 153C are pending with the Assessing Officer on or after 1st day of June 2010. Assessment or reassessment proceedings may be pending with the Assessing Officer on or after 1st June 2010 for search held between the period on or after 1st April 2008 till 31st May 2010. It would imply that even for such cases with respect to which assessment or reassessment proceedings under section 153A/153C are lying pending with the Assessing Officer, application to Settlement Commission can be made by the assessee.

It may further be pointed out as per new scheme for filing application to the Settlement Commission introduced by the Finance Act, 2007, application to Settlement Commission can be filed only when assessment proceedings are pending with the Assessing Officer and the assessment order has not been finalized. Now assessee has no opportunity to apply to the Settlement Commission when the case is pending before the Commissioner (Appeals) at appellate stage. Further, there is no opportunity now, to the assessee to apply to the Settlement Commission when the case is reopened for reassessment under section 148 or any proceedings pending with the Assessing Officer for making fresh assessment in pursuance of an order under section 254 by Tribunal or under section 263/264 by the CIT, setting aside or cancelling an assessment.

(iii) **For admission of application by Settlement Commission, there has to be additional income-tax payable by the assessee**

An application to Settlement Commission can be admitted only when application has been made fulfilling, *inter alia,* the following conditions:

1. The application shall contain a full and true disclosure of the income of the assessee, which has not been disclosed before the Assessing Officer.

2. The assessee shall state the manner in which such income has been derived.

3. The additional amount of income-tax payable on such undisclosed income shall exceed ₹ 50 lakhs in a case of search where assessment/reassessment proceedings are pending under section 153A. In normal case, when assessment proceedings are pending otherwise than in search case, the additional amount of income-tax payable for admission of application by Settlement Commission is ₹ 10 lakhs.

   As per Finance Act, 2011, there is an amendment under section 245C providing for admission of application by the Settlement Commission in the case of defined associated persons and entities covered under search other than the specified person when additional income-tax payable is exceeding ₹ 10 lakhs. It means that if a person referred in this section as a specified person and covered under search makes application to the Settlement Commission offering additional tax payable exceeding ₹ 50 lakhs, the other associated person covered under search may be eligible to file the application to the Settlement Commission when additional tax payable in his case exceeds ₹ 10 lakhs.

4. The additional amount of income-tax payable shall be calculated with respect to the assessee relating to all the years cumulatively.

(iv) **Additional Tax Payable - Meaning thereof**

With respect to the meaning of additional tax payable for admission of application by Settlement Commission, the following points may be noted:

1. The additional income-tax payable referred under section 245C will not include interest. In case undisclosed income offered by the assessee before the Settlement Commission is relating to earlier years, assessee shall be liable to pay interest u/ss 234A, 234B and 234C in addition to income-tax applicable on such

undisclosed income and the amount of such interest shall not be considered for the purpose of calculating additional income-tax payable for admission of application by the Settlement Commission.

2. Any amount of income-tax paid by the assessee on the income declared in the income-tax returns filed under section 153A/139 will not be treated as additional income-tax payable.

3. The amount of income tax deposited by the assessee after the date of search on the undisclosed income declared or to be declared before receiving notices under section 153A shall be considered for the purpose of calculating additional tax payable under section 245C.

It may be a point of debate as to whether the following amounts paid by the assessee may be treated as additional tax payable. In practice, it has been observed that the Settlement Commission is accepting such amounts in the nature of additional income tax payable for the purpose of admission of the application of the assessee.

     a. Advance tax paid or tax of the assessee deducted at source prior to the date of search and credit of which has not been taken by the assessee in the income-tax return, if any filed by him subsequently.

     b. Any amount of cash or money seized during search.

(v) Whether regular income-tax return for which has not been filed, may be part of additional income to be disclosed before Settlement Commission

There may be a situation when income-tax return relating to regular income has not been filed by the assessee but amount of tax applicable on such income has been deposited as advance tax or tax has already been deducted at source. A question may arise as to whether such income may be considered as part of additional income to be disclosed before the Settlement Commission and the amount of tax relating to the same already deposited may be considered for calculating additional tax liability of ₹ 50 lakhs or ₹ 10 lakhs, as the case may be.

On the one side, there can be a view that section 245C(1) requires disclosure of income before the Settlement Commission which has not been disclosed before the Assessing Officer. Since the assessee has not filed his return of income disclosing such income to the Assessing Officer and when such income is disclosed first time in the application before the Settlement Commission, it fulfils the requirement of section 245C(1) and should be considered as part of additional income offered by the assessee for the purpose of admission of his application. As per the revised scheme of settlement as per Finance Act, 2007, there is no requirement of filing regular return of income before making application to the Settlement Commission.

On the other hand, there can be a view that regular income of the assessee for which tax has already been deposited cannot be treated in the nature of additional income to be disclosed before the Settlement Commission. Even if income-tax return has not been filed by the assessee declaring such income to the Assessing Officer, such income cannot be treated in the nature of additional income as such income was always intended to be disclosed by the assessee to the Assessing Officer and the amount of income-tax already deposited/deducted at source cannot be treated as part of additional tax payable for making application to the Settlement Commission. The legislative intent for declaring additional income and paying additional amount of tax to the Settlement Commission is over and above the regular income and the tax already deposited by the assessee with respect to such income.

However in practice, it has been observed that the Settlement Commission is accepting the first view and application submitted to the Settlement Commission making such declaration are being accepted.

(vi) **Whether seized cash, money, FDRs etc. may be adjusted towards additional tax payable?**

In the course of search, certain assets such as cash, money, FDRs, bank deposits etc. may be seized. A question may arise as to whether such liquid assets seized by the Income-tax Department may be adjusted towards additional tax payable relating to additional income disclosed by the assessee in his application to the Settlement Commission. Such additional income offered to the Settlement Commission may or may not include the above mentioned assets as part of additional undisclosed income depending upon whether the same are of disclosed or undisclosed nature.

Logically speaking, such assets seized by the department are the assets belonging to the assessee out of which assessee is entitled to make payment of his tax liability and when such assets are already in the possession of the department, the same should be allowed to be adjusted towards liability of the assessee for additional tax payable. In practice, it is sometimes also permitted by the department. But in some cases, such adjustment is not permitted and technical objection is created on the ground that until such assets seized are transferred from Personal Deposit Account (PD A/c) of the Commissioner in which seized assets are first kept, to the account of the assessee with the Assessing Officer, it is not possible. In our view, this is an internal administrative matter on the part of the department and due to non action on this account, assessee may not be asked to deposit separate tax, pending such transfer entry on the part of the income-tax Department.

Finance Act, 2015 w.e.f. 1-6-2015 has amended section 132B of the Income-tax Act, providing that the amount of liability arising on an application made before the Settlement Commission under sub-section (1) of section 245C may be recovered out of the seized assets.

The above amendment is in line with the views expressed by us and it has removed the hardship being faced by the assessees to get adjustment of cash or liquid assets seized during search towards the tax liability arising on an application to Settlement Commission.

(vii) **Application to Settlement Commission separately by each person, but for all the years together**

Application to the Settlement Commission is required to be filed separately by each person and the requirement of additional income tax payable for admission of application by Settlement Commission is required to be fulfilled by each person separately. However, the application may be the consolidated application for all the seven years covered under search and the amount of additional income tax payable for admission of the application by the Settlement Commission has to be considered as total amount of additional income tax payable relating to all the years covered under search.

In the case of *Airtech Pvt. Ltd.* v. *ITSC* [1994] 209 ITR 21 (ITSC) (SB), the Special Bench of the Settlement Commission held that the minimum additional tax prescribed in proviso to section 245C(1) applies to the application as a whole and not to each and every year covered in the application separately.

The application should be prepared by each person declaring his disclosed income and additional income and covering all the issues involved as per material seized during search. Even when additional income to be declared is relating to some of the years covered under search, the person should cover all the years involved in the search in the application to be filed with the Settlement Commission so that there is no duplication of proceedings with the Settlement Commission as well as with the Assessing Officer with respect to such person.

(*viii*) Assessee is required to make full and true disclosure of his undisclosed income in the application

As per sub-section (1) of section 245C, assessee in his application submitted to the Settlement Commission, is required to make full and true disclosure of his income which has not been disclosed before the Assessing Officer and state the manner in which such income has been derived by him. The Commission ensures before admitting the application of the assessee that assessee has made before it, the full and true disclosure of his undisclosed income.

Supreme Court in the case of *Ajmera Housing Corporation* v. *CIT* [2010] 193 Taxman 193 have held that a full and true disclosure of income, which has not been earlier disclosed by the assessee is a precondition for a valid application u/s 245C(1) and scheme of the Settlement Commission does not contemplate revision of income so disclosed in the application of settlement. Hon'ble Supreme Court further held that the disclosure of additional undisclosed income in the revised annexure was enough to establish that the application made by the assessee u/s 245C(1) did not contain a full and true disclosure of its undisclosed income and the manner in which such income was derived and, thus, settlement application could not be entertained.

Under the present scheme, the Commissioner of Income-tax, in his report submitted to the Commission, cannot file the objection as to whether full and true disclosure of undisclosed income has been made or not by the assessee. It is for the reason that before passing order for rejection of application under section 245D, copy of the application submitted by the assessee is not made available to the Commissioner and it is kept confidential. When the copy of the application is not available with the Commissioner, and the contents thereof are not within his knowledge, any objection on the point that assessee has not made full and true disclosure of his undisclosed income may not be tenable. The satisfaction regarding the issue as to whether full and true disclosure of his undisclosed income has been made by the assessee, has to be arrived by the Commission itself on the basis of the contents of the application and on hearing the applicant if required by the Commission.

(*ix*) All taxes to be paid otherwise application may be rejected

In the case of *CIT* v. *Keti Construction Ltd.* [2016] 65 taxmann. com 263 (MP.), it has been held that the assessee had not paid the self-assessment tax in the return of income under sections 153A and 143(2) for the assessment years 2007-08 to 2012-13, the application for settlement was not valid and quashed the order dated 26-5-2014 passed by the Settlement Commission.

(x) Whether undisclosed income declared by the assessee during search in the statement under section 132(4), may be considered as additional income to be declared before Settlement Commission

This is a controversial issue. On the one side, there is a view that once an undisclosed income has been admitted and declared by the assessee in his statement recorded under section 132(4) in the course of search, such income cannot be treated as income not disclosed before the Assessing Officer and therefore, cannot be declared before the Settlement Commission for admission of application filed by the assessee. On the other hand, the view on behalf of the assessee is usually that the income which has not been disclosed in the return of income filed before the Assessing Officer but declared in the statement u/s 132(4) is in the nature of income not disclosed before the Assessing Officer and therefore such additional income has to be considered for the purpose of admission of application of the assessee. In such a case, it can further be argued that there are sufficient grounds to prove the complexity of investigation in respect of what is not disclosed to the Assessing Officer, but is being disclosed for the first time to the Settlement Commission.

However, in practice it has been observed that the Settlement Commission is accepting the application filed before it treating such declaration as income not disclosed before the Assessing Officer where the same has not been included in the return of income, if any earlier filed.

(xi) Copy of application to be given to the Assessing Officer simultaneously

Sub-section (4) of section 245C provides that the assessee shall, on the date on which he makes an application to the Settlement Commission, also intimate the Assessing Officer of having made such application to the Settlement Commission. The application is required to be made in Form No. 34BA as provided under rule 44C. The requirement of simultaneous intimation to the Assessing Officer is with the object to ensure that as soon as the application to the Settlement Commission is made by the assessee, the proceedings with the Assessing Officer are stayed and jurisdiction for making assessment is shifted from Assessing Officer to the Settlement Commission. At the time of making decision regarding admission of the application, the Settlement Commission ensures and obtains report from the Commissioner that such intimation has been given by the assessee to the Assessing Officer in time.

(xii) Application to be submitted carefully, in case of any default application is liable to be rejected

The application to the Settlement Commission should be filed by the assessee very carefully fulfilling all the requirements as provided under section 245C. The calculation of additional tax payable and the interest under section 234A/234B/234C applicable thereon should be made properly and evidence of payment of tax and interest should be enclosed with the application. In case of any default in fulfilling the prescribed requirements or in case of less deposit of tax or interest, the application is liable to be rejected by the Commission. In such cases, Settlement Commission does not generally grant opportunity to the assessee to make further payment of the shortfall in the amount of additional tax or interest. Once the application is rejected, assessee may be exposed regarding declaration of undisclosed income made to the Commission before the Assessing Officer with whom, in such circumstances, he will have to undergo the normal assessment proceedings.

(xiii) Consequences when application is not proceeded with/rejected by the Settlement Commission

There are two stages when an application filed by the assessee before the Settlement Commission may be rejected by the Commission as provided under sub-section (1) and sub-section (2C) of section 245D:

(a) On receipt of an application made by the assessee, the Settlement Commission shall within seven days from the date of receipt of application, issue a notice to the applicant requiring him to explain as to why the application made by him be allowed to be proceeded with. On hearing the assessee, the Settlement Commission shall within a period of fourteen days from the date of the application reject the application or allow the application to be proceeded with, by passing the order in writing. The copy of the order shall be communicated to the assessee and to the Commissioner. In case no such notice is issued by the Settlement Commission within a period of seven days or no such order rejecting the application is passed by the Settlement Commission within the aforesaid period, the application shall be deemed to have been allowed to be proceeded with. In practice, it has been observed that the above required notice is not in all cases issued by the Settlement Commission particularly when the Commission is *prima facie* satisfied regarding fulfilment of all the requirements for admission of the application.

At this stage, application may be rejected by the Settlement Commission, in case the applicant prima facie does not fulfil the basic requirement provided under the Act for admission of the application. For example, case of the assessee not falling within the jurisdiction of the Settlement Commission, additional tax payable less than the prescribed limit or the payment of tax not made by the assessee before making application, disclosure of additional income not found *prima facie* to be full and true etc.

(b) In respect of an application, which is allowed to be proceeded with, the Settlement Commission shall within thirty days from the date on which the application was made, call for a report from the Commissioner and the Commissioner is required to furnish the report within a period of thirty days of the receipt of communication from the Settlement Commission. In this report, the Commissioner is required to specify as to whether the applicant has filed Form No. 34BA to the AO in time and the calculation of tax and interest payable on the additional income is correct or not. After considering such report, the Settlement Commission may declare the application in question as invalid by passing an order in writing after giving an opportunity of hearing to the assessee.

At this stage, application may be declared invalid by the Settlement Commission when the defects in the application are brought to the notice of the Settlement Commission by the Commissioner of Income-tax in his report submitted. The defects pointed out by the Commissioner may be of the nature which would make the application inadmissible.

When an application is rejected by the Settlement Commission under the above situations, the proceedings before the Assessing Officer shall be revived and the Assessing Officer shall proceed to frame assessment/reassessment in accordance with the provisions of section 153A/153C. It is provided under section 153B(1) that the time-barring limit for making the assessment under section 153A shall be extended by the period commencing from the date on which application is made by the assessee and ending with the date on which order under sub-section (1) of section 245D rejecting the application is received by the Commissioner.

It may be pointed out here that clause (*iv*) of the *Explanation* to section 153B(1) prescribing the extension for period of limitation refers only to the first situation of rejection of application as discussed above and not the second situation. The above situation is however covered under sub-section (4) of section 245HA wherein it has been *inter alia* provided for exclusion of the time commencing from the date of making the application to the Settlement Commission till the date of declaring the application invalid by the Commission for the purpose of calculating the time limit for framing assessment u/s 153B. Sub-section (4) of section 245HA is a provision of general nature and extends time limit covered under limitation sections 149, 153, 153B, 154, 155, 158BE and 231 and covers both the situations discussed above for this purpose.

(xiv) **Filing application with the Settlement Commission, jurisdiction of the Assessing Officer to be excluded**

When an application is filed by the assessee before the Settlement Commission under section 245C, Settlement Commission alone would have the exclusive jurisdiction as provided under the proviso to section 245F(1), the effect of which is that the pending assessment proceedings before the Assessing Officer would in a way get stayed and the Assessing Officer is not required to proceed with the matter. In case application made by the assessee is not allowed to be proceeded with or is rejected by the Settlement Commission, the proceedings before the Assessing Officer are revived and the Assessing Officer shall proceed further to frame the assessment as per the normal procedure. In such a case, it is provided under *Explanation* to section 153B(1) that in a case where an application made before the Settlement Commission under section 245C is rejected by it or is not allowed to be proceeded with by it, and it is also provided under sub-section (4) of section 245HA that in a case where application made before the Settlement Commission is declared invalid, the period commencing from the date on which such application is made and ending with the date on which the order under sub-section (1) of section 245D is received by the Commissioner, shall be excluded for the purpose of calculating time limit for completion of assessment under section 153A/153C.

The proceedings before the Assessing Officer are stayed with respect to the person relating to the years for which application has been filed with the Settlement Commission. With respect to the other persons, the Assessing Officer shall proceed in the normal course for framing assessment as per provisions of section 153A/153C.

(xv) **Before filing application to Settlement Commission, whether Income-tax Returns under section 153A to be filed? - Consequences of non filing of returns?**

As per provisions of section 245A as revised by the Finance Act, 2007, it is not statutorily required for the assessee to file income-tax returns in pursuance to notice under section 153A or under section 139 before filing application to Settlement Commission. Application to Settlement Commission can be filed immediately after receiving notices from the Assessing Officer for filing returns under section 153A/153C.

However, it is in the interest of the assessee first to file income-tax returns under section 153A/139 before making application to the Settlement Commission. This is for the reason that in case application filed by the assessee is rejected by the Settlement Commission, the assessee may not be held liable for non-filing of income-tax returns in time and further consequences thereof regarding levy of interest and penalty for late filing/non-filing of income-tax returns. However, Hon'ble Supreme Court in the case of *Brij Lal* v. *CIT* [2010] 194 Taxman 566 have observed that the settlement application filed is akin to return of income.

It is important to note here that in case income-tax returns are filed by the assessee before making application to the Settlement Commission, adequate margin for additional income-tax payable should be kept so that application to the Settlement Commission may be maintainable.

17.5 Proceedings before Settlement Commission - Nature and scope

(*i*) **Procedure of proceedings before Settlement Commission**

The proceedings before the Settlement Commission are almost of the same nature as assessment proceedings before the Assessing Officer and the objective of the Settlement Commission remains to determine the true and correct income of the assessee relating to the years covered under the application. However, the proceedings before the Settlement Commission are of judicial nature within the meaning of Indian Penal Code, 1860. The Settlement Commission provides equal opportunity to the assessee as well as to the Commissioner to make submissions and produce records. The Settlement Commission may direct the Commissioner to make enquiry or investigations, if deemed fit, and submit report of his findings.

The proceedings before the Settlement Commission are held before the bench consisting of minimum two members and the bench may take assistance of its secretariat/junior officers in conducting the enquiry or in appreciating the evidences. The approach of the Settlement Commission remains practical and objective.

After hearing both the parties and after examining all the evidences produced, the Settlement Commission may pass such order as it thinks fit on the matters covered by the application and any other matter relating to the case not covered by the application, but referred to in the report of the Commissioner. The order passed by the Settlement Commission shall provide for the terms of settlement including any demand by way of tax, interest or penalty and the manner in which any sum due under the settlement shall be paid and all other matters to make the settlement effective.

(ii) Limitation for passing order by Settlement Commission

Sub-section (4A) of section 245D provides limitation for passing order by Settlement Commission. In respect of an application made on or after 1st June 2010, Settlement Commission shall pass order within 18 months from the end of the month in which the application was made. For the applications filed on or after 1st June 2007 but before 1st June 2010, the above period was 12 months from the end of the month in which the application was made.

(iii) Application once filed with the Settlement Commission under section 245C cannot be withdrawn

Application must be filed by the assessee before the Settlement Commission after due consideration and weighing all the *pros* and *cons*. Once an application by the assessee is filed before Settlement Commission, sub-section (3) of section 245C provides that it shall not be allowed to be withdrawn by the applicant. Such provision may apparently look to be harsh but keeping in view the special nature of proceedings before the Settlement Commission, it appears to be justified that a person cannot be permitted to go back on his own admission of undisclosed income.

17.6 Power of Settlement Commission to grant immunity from levy of interest, penalty or prosecution

(i) Whether Settlement Commission has the power to grant waiver from levy of interest?

The levy of interest under sections 234A, 234B and 234C is mandatory in nature and Settlement Commission does not have the power to reduce or waive such interest. Any controversy in this regard which used to prevail earlier, has come to an end by decision of Supreme Court in the case of *CIT* v. *Anjum M.H. Ghaswala* [2001] 119 Taxman 352, holding that

    (a) Settlement Commission cannot either equate itself with the CBDT or claim the right to exercise the power vested in the Board under section 119 which is an administrative power.

    (b) While exercising its quasi judicial power of arrival at a settlement under section 245D, the Settlement Commission cannot have the administrative powers of issuing directions to other income-tax authorities. The Commissioner cannot exercise the power of relaxation found in section 119(2)(*a*) in the manner provided therein; it cannot invoke that power under section 119(2)(*a*) to exercise the same in its judicial proceedings by following a procedure contrary to that provided under section 119(2).

(*c*) That expression 'shall' used in sections 234A, 234B and 234C cannot be construed as 'may'. The intention of the legislature was to make the collection of statutory interest mandatory. That expression is used deliberately.

(*d*) The Commission in exercise of its power under section 245D(4) and (6) does not have the power to reduce or waive interest statutorily payable under sections 234A, 234B and 234C except to the extent of granting relief under the circulars issued by the Board under section 119 of the Act.

Recently, Supreme Court in the case of *Brij Lal* v. *CIT* [2010] 194 Taxman 566 have held that interest u/ss 234A, 234B and 234C are applicable to the proceedings of the Settlement Commission under Chapter XIX-A, and the terminal point for the levy of interest u/s 234B would be up to the date of the order u/s 245D(1) and not up to the date of the order of settlement u/s 245D(4).

(*ii*) Power of Settlement Commission to grant immunity from Penalty and Prosecution

As per section 245H of the Income-tax Act, 1961, Settlement Commission has been empowered to grant immunity from penalty and prosecution. The Settlement Commission may, if it is satisfied that any person who made the application for settlement under section 245C has co-operated with the Settlement Commission in the proceedings before it and has made a full and true disclosure of his income and the manner in which such income has been derived, grant to such person immunity from prosecution for any offence under the Income-tax Act, 1961. The Settlement Commission may impose such conditions as it may think fit while granting immunity. The power of the Settlement Commission regarding granting of immunity from prosecution for any offence under the Indian Penal Code or under any Central Act, which was available hitherto before, has been withdrawn in the cases when application under section 245C is made to the Settlement Commission on or after 1st June 2007. Further, it has been provided that no such immunity shall be granted by the Settlement Commission in cases where the proceedings for the prosecution for any offence under the Income-tax Act has been instituted before the date of receipt of the application by the Settlement Commission under section 245C.

Immunity from imposition of penalty for any default under the Income-tax Act may also be granted by the Settlement Commission, either wholly or in part, with respect to the case covered by the settlement.

The power to grant immunity from penalty and prosecution is at the judicial discretion of the Settlement Commission and it would *inter alia* depend upon the conduct of the assessee also. Immunity from penalty and prosecution is not automatic or it cannot be said to be a legal right of the assessee in all cases of settlement.

It is further provided under sub-section (1A) of section 245H that immunity granted to a person shall stand withdrawn if such person fails to pay any sum specified in the order of settlement within the time permitted or fails to comply with any other condition subject to which the immunity was granted.

It is further provided under sub-section (2) of section 245H that immunity granted to a person may be withdrawn by the Settlement Commission if it is satisfied that such person had in the course of the settlement proceedings concealed any particulars, material to the settlement, or had given false evidences.

17.7 Certain post settlement issues

(*i*) Payment of Demand raised as per order of Settlement Commission

Assessee is required to make payment of demand raised in the order of Settlement Commission within thirty five days of the receipt of the copy of order by him. In case payment is not made within the above period by him, and whether or not the Settlement Commission has extended the time for payment of tax or has allowed payment by instalments, the assessee shall be liable to pay simple interest at the rate of 15% per annum, as provided under sub-section (6A) of section 245D. This provision seems to have been incorporated corresponding to the provision of charging interest under section 220(2) in the normal case and further to curtail the power of Settlement Commission to reduce or waive levy of such interest.

It is significant to note that the demand raised in the order of settlement should be paid by the assessee in time as per manner provided in the order. In case there is default made by the assessee in making payment of such demand in time, the order of settlement may become void and in such a situation, the matters covered by the settlement shall be deemed to have been revived from the stage at which the application was allowed to be proceeded with by the Settlement Commission and the concerned income-tax authority may complete such proceedings at any time before the expiry of two years from the end of the financial year in which the settlement became void. To avoid such situation and in the case when assessee is not able to make the payment of demand raised in the order of the Commission within the time permitted, the only recourse available with the assessee is to approach the Settlement Commission itself for extension of time for making the payment or for granting instalments for making such outstanding payment.

(ii) **Settlement to become void if it is found that it was obtained by fraud or misrepresentation of facts**

Sub-section (6) of section 245D further provides that the settlement shall be void if it is subsequently found by the Settlement Commission that it has been obtained by fraud or misrepresentation of facts.

Supreme Court in the case of *CIT* v. *Om Prakash Mittal* [2005] 273 ITR 326/143 Taxman 373 have held that if the revenue has material to show that the Settlement Order passed u/s 245D(4) was obtained by fraud or misrepresentation of facts, it can move the Commission for decision on that issue and it is open to the Commission to decide the same.

Sub-section (7) further provides that when the settlement becomes void, the proceedings with respect to the matters covered by the settlement shall be deemed to have been revived from the stage at which the application was allowed to be proceeded with by the Settlement Commission and the concerned income-tax authority may complete such proceedings at any time before the expiry of two years from the end of the financial year in which the settlement became void.

In the case of assessee making application to the Settlement Commission for settlement of the cases, this is a high risk which shall always be carried by the assessee even after settlement had been arrived and all taxes had been paid by the assessee. There is no time limit prescribed under this sub-section and the provision of this sub-section may be triggered at any stage in future during the life-time of the assessee, whenever the fact of any kind of fraud or misrepresentation is brought to the notice of the Settlement Commission.

Such harsh provision has been provided since the underlying principle for making application to the Settlement Commission is that the assessee should come clean and make declaration of all of his undisclosed income relating to the period covered under the application.

Practically, instances are not uncommon where an assessee gets his case of search settled with the Settlement Commission. Subsequently, search may be conducted second time and certain evidences regarding undisclosed income relating to the earlier period for which settlement had earlier been arrived by the Settlement Commission, may be found by the Income Tax Department. In such a case, Department may file application with the Settlement Commission contending and representing that the assessee had obtained the order of settlement earlier by misrepresentation of facts and full and true disclosure of undisclosed income was not made by the assessee at that stage. In such a situation, assessee may have to face lot of hardships as settlement order may be declared void. Therefore, it is advised that assessee should ensure that full and true disclosure of all the undisclosed income is made by the assessee in the application to the Settlement Commission because once the order of settlement is passed by the Commission, any evidence of incriminating nature relating to the period covered under the settlement retained by the assessee and found subsequently may pave the way of declaration of the earlier settlement as void.

(iii) Order of Settlement Commission not appealable

The order passed by the Settlement Commission is final and binding on the assessee as well as on the department and no appeal against such order may be filed.

This is another risk which is carried by the assessee while opting to make application with the Settlement Commission. In the case of normal assessment proceedings before the Assessing Officer, assessee gets different stages for filing appeal with the higher authorities but the order of the Settlement Commission is final and conclusive and no appeal against such order may be filed by the assessee. However, the right of the assessee to file writ/SLP with the High Court/Supreme Court as provided under the Constitution of India is available with in the scheme of the constitutional provisions.

Supreme Court in the case of *R.B. Shreeram Durga Prasad & Fatehchand Nursing Das* v. *Settlement Commission* [1989] 176 ITR 169/43 Taxman 34 have held that in exercise of power of judicial review of the decision of the Settlement Commission, the Supreme Court is concerned with the legality of the procedure followed and not with validity of the order.

Karnataka High Court in the case of *N. Krishnan* v. *Settlement Commission* [1989] 47 Taxman 294 have held that though the order of Settlement Commission is made final and conclusive by section 245-I, the assessee is entitled to seek judicial review under Articles 226 and 227 of the Constitution of India. However, the scope for interference against a decision of the Settlement Commission is restricted and when there is neither violation of any mandatory procedure nor any violation of any of the rules of natural justice and the reasons for rejecting the settlement petition had nexus to the decision taken by the Settlement Commission, no interference can be made by the Court.

(*iv*) **Power of review/revision/rectification by Settlement Commission**

As per the scheme of settlement, as given under Chapter XIX-A of the Income-tax Act, 1961, there is no power with the Settlement Commission for review/revision of its order. There was no specific power to carry out rectification of the apparent errors. Moreover, the order of the Settlement Commission is not appealable. It was quite surprising to note that in case if there occurred any mistake apparent from record in passing the settlement order by the Settlement Commission, power of rectification was not there in the Act specifically. Though section 245F(1) provides that the Settlement Commission shall have all the powers which are vested in an income tax authority under the Act, which implies that the power to rectify the order when there was apparent mistake, which is vested in an income-tax authority u/s 154 should also be attached to the Settlement Commission yet Hon'ble Supreme Court's Constitution Bench in a recent case of *Brij Lal* v. *CIT* [2010] 194 Taxman 566 have held that power to rectify an apparent error can not be conceded to the Settlement Commission, first, in the absence of such specific power conferred on the Settlement Commission under the Act and second, it would militate against the finality of the order of the settlement.

Recently Finance Act, 2011 has made necessary amendment by inserting sub-section (6B) to section 245D so as to specifically provide that the Settlement Commission may, at any time within a period of six months from the date of its order, with a view to rectifying any mistake apparent from the record, amend any order passed by it under section 245D(4). It has also been provided further that a rectification which has the effect of modifying the liability of the applicant shall not be made unless the Settlement Commission has given notice to the applicant and the Commissioner of its intention to do so and has allowed the applicant and the Commissioner an opportunity of being heard. It may be noted that power to carry out rectification has to be exercised within 6 months from the date of its order whereas income-tax authorities have been given this power to be exercised within a period of 4 years from the end of the year in which the order sought to be rectified was passed.

(v) Abatement of proceeding before Settlement Commission

Section 245HA was introduced by Finance Act, 2007 w.e.f. 1-6-2007 providing the abatement of proceeding before the Settlement Commission in certain circumstances. According to the plain provisions of law contained in this regard u/s 245HA, proceeding in the following cases before the Settlement Commission shall abate on the specified dates:—

a. If an application is made u/s 245C on or after 1-6-2007 which has been rejected under section 245D(1) then, the proceeding before the Settlement Commission in such a case shall abate on the day when such application was rejected.

b. If application made u/s 245C was made before 1-6-2007 and no order u/s 245D(1) was passed before 1-6-2007, such application shall be deemed to be allowed to be proceeded with, if additional tax on the income disclosed in such application and interest thereon was paid on or before 31-7-2007. In case such tax and interest has not been paid before such date, such application shall be deemed to be rejected on 31-7-2007 and in such a case proceeding before Settlement Commission shall abate on 31-7-2007. In case on such application, order u/s 245D(1) was passed before 1.6.2007 and order u/s 245D(4) was not passed before 1-6-2007, such application shall be deemed to be rejected unless tax along with interest disclosed in such application was not paid on or before 31-7-2007. In respect of such applications, proceedings before the Settlement Application shall also abate on 31-7-2007.

c. If an application made u/s 245C is declared invalid under section 245D(2C) by the Settlement Commission, proceeding before the Settlement Commission shall abate on the last day of the month in which application was declared invalid.

d. If an application has been made u/s 245C and order u/s 245D(4) was not passed before 31-3-2008 in case application u/s 245C was made before 1-6-2007, and within twelve months from the end of the month in which application was made if such an application was made on or after 1-6-2007 but before 1-6-2010, and within eighteen months from the end of month in which application was made where application was made on or after 1-6-2010, proceeding before Settlement Commission shall abate on the date on which time for passing the order u/s 245D(4) expires.

It is further provided that where the proceeding before the Settlement Commission abates, the AO or any other Income-tax authority before whom the proceeding at the time of making the application was pending shall dispose the case in accordance with the provision of the Act, by taking as if no application was made u/s 245C and such authority shall be entitled to use all other material and information produced by the assessee before the Settlement Commission. Such authority shall further be entitled to use the results of the enquiry held or evidence recorded by Settlement Commission in the course of the proceedings before it as if such material, information, enquiry and evidence had been produced before the Assessing Officer or other income-tax authority in the course of the proceedings before him.

The period commencing from the date of application to the Settlement Commission and ending with the specified date shall be excluded while computing the limitation period and tax and interest paid before the date of making the application or during the pendency of the case before the Settlement Commission shall be allowed as credit.

Hon'ble Bombay High Court in the case of *Star Television News Ltd.* v. *Union of India* [2009] 184 Taxman 400 have held that the provision fixing the cut of date as 31-3-2008 for disposal of all Settlement Applications filed prior to 1-6-2007 is unjust, arbitrary, discriminatory and operation of consequences of section 245HA(3), wherein application so reverts to income-tax authority upon abatement are arbitrary and unreasonable. Therefore Bombay High Court held that the time limit for disposal of application u/s 245D(4A)(*i*) has to be read as not applicable where there is no fault of the applicant. Bombay High Court further held that the words "any other application made u/s 245C" in section 245HA(1)(*iv*) have to be read as "any other application made under section 245C, where due to reasons attributable to the assessee" so as to avoid rendering any part of section 245C(4A) (*i*) or section 245HA(1)(*iv*) otherwise, meaningless or redundant and unconstitutional.

18

PRECAUTIONS BEFORE FACING SEARCH ACTION

18.1 Menace of black money

The primary objective of undertaking search action by the Income tax Department, *inter alia*, is to unearth black money and uncover the evasion of income tax. Black money is generated by entering into the financial transactions which are not recorded in the books of account and the taxes applicable relating to such transactions are not paid to the government. Taxes may be in the nature of direct taxes or indirect taxes payable to Central Government, State Government or local authorities. Direct taxes generally include income tax and wealth tax. Indirect taxes generally include excise duty, custom duty, sales tax or VAT, service tax etc. Other taxes prominently may include stamp duty on registration of immovable property, octroi etc.

Legally and ethically, nobody is supposed to generate black money. All the taxes applicable on any kind of financial transactions are expected to be paid by all citizens to the respective authorities truthfully and honestly. But in real life situation, everybody does not carry such moral and ethical values and there remains temptation not to pay due taxes to the government. Deterioration of the values in the society is largely responsible to this phenomenon. No section of the society can be permitted to resort to any such undesirable practices. Unfortunately such undesirable practices travel from the top and most influential section of the society to the bottom and the masses.

The practice of evasion of Income Tax is resorted to so as to avoid income tax liability on the income earned which is otherwise liable to be taxed. Sometimes, primary motivating factor for entering into unrecorded transactions may not be the evasion of income tax but the evasion of excise duty, VAT or stamp duty. But irrespective of the motive for entering into unrecorded transactions, income tax search operation covers all kind of unrecorded financial and business transactions and the unrecorded assets generated.

(*i*) It is in the interest of the assessee not to generate black money

There may be temptation on the part of the taxpayers to enter into unrecorded financial transactions so as to avoid various kind of direct and indirect taxes and in this process, unaccounted funds and assets are generated. Such funds are not kept in the banking channel and are generally kept in cash form. A person carries a lot of risk in keeping the funds in cash and its transportation. Moreover, safety and management of such funds and assets are likely to disturb the mental peace.

The capitalist model of the economy has taught that there can be growth in the business and assets can be created manifold by utilizing and circulating the funds in a better, efficient and speedy manner. The utilization and circulation of funds kept in cash is liable to be reduced considerably in comparison to the utilization and circulation of funds through banking channels and thus in long term, the business growth is hampered to a large extent. For steady and speedy growth of the business in long term, mobilization of funds through regular banking channels is warranted.

High growth in business can be achieved by making high investment from all kind of sources. One cannot remain restricted to one's own funds only for investing in the business for achieving high growth. One has to generate funds for investment in business from different sources such as financial institutions, from the public through IPO or other capital market instruments, from overseas as FDI or in any other manner. The funds from such sources can be tapped by achieving and showing good business results including heavy top line and bottom line in the financial statement of the business. This can be possible only when all business transactions are fully and completely reflected in the books of account in a truthful manner. Therefore, it is in the interest of the taxpayer not to enter into unrecorded business and other transactions so as to open the floodgates for better and huge business opportunities.

The security of funds which are kept in the form of unrecorded cash and assets is always in danger. The fear of danger looms large not only from thieves and unscrupulous persons but even from the near and dears, family members, friends and business associates also. Another risk is the disturbance of the peace of mind and at the end of the day, one may be compelled to think why to indulge in such activities at the cost of peace of his mind.

(ii) Though unacceptable, sometimes circumstances may compel for evasion of income tax

In spite of the issue of ethical and moral values, and the factual & legal risks involved, one has to concede that there is unfortunate practice of generation of black money in our society. By no means such practice can be legitimized and recognized but still this is hard reality prevailing in the society. Sometimes it has been felt that a person may be willing to record the transactions from the income tax point of view and pay the income tax thereon so as to bring the funds and assets in the regular channels, but he is not able to do the same due to other compelling reasons such as inconsistency and inequity prevailing and perceived in other laws, corrupt practices prevailing in the society and in the systematic set up and political system. Attention may be invited to some of the following points in this regard:

1. There are rampant corrupt practices in our political, bureaucratic and business set up. On-money transactions and other unethical practices are the hard business and social realities. Cash funds are generated at both the ends for this purpose *i.e.* at the end of the recipient as well as at the end of the payer.

2. With the deterioration of the value system in the society and lack of confidence of the citizens in the government regarding proper utilization of funds collected by way of taxes paid by them, there is tendency to resort to such practices which generate unaccounted income, cash and other assets.

3. Due to various scams and numerous instances of misutilization of public funds, tax payer - citizens have gradually lost confidence in the government, and therefore such section of the society remains apprehensive, scary, slow and reluctant towards payment of taxes to the government. In public perception in general, there is gradual erosion of faith in the motive and ability of the government to utilize the public funds in a proper and judicious manner.

4. For buying immovable property in most of the cases, payment of unrecorded cash is a hard reality. A person is compelled to generate unrecorded cash whenever he is required to make investment in immovable property. The stamp duty rate structure and other policies framed by the government in this regard are irrational and leave scope for such practices.

5. A vicious circle is created when a person is compelled to enter into unrecorded business transactions without payment of

PERIODICAL REVIEW AND COUNSELLING **Para 18.2**

excise, VAT and other indirect taxes so as to meet the competition in the market created by such other persons.

18.2 Periodical review and counselling

(i) Periodical review of unwarranted papers, documents

In the course of business, a lot of unwarranted or waste papers, documents, rough details are generated which are of no use. Such papers may relate to future projections, informal discussions, and impractical ambitious plans and may have details containing huge financial figures which have no meaning. Such papers may relate to the assessee himself or somebody else, generated during discussion with other persons. In the case of consultants, papers may be found in their possession relating to affairs of their clients. Such papers may typically be termed as dumb documents.

In some of the cases, it has been observed that backside of papers is used for further working and such papers are preserved in some drawer for such purpose, though the details contained on the back side are cancelled and are of no use. For example, such papers may contain provisional or projected statement of affairs generated at some point of time containing imaginary or ambigous figures or targets to be achieved. Such papers being of no relevance may be marked as cancelled but preserved for using back side for further working.

In case of any income tax search action, when such papers or documents are found in the control or possession of the assessee, he is under legal obligation to explain the contents of such papers and documents as presumption under section 292C is applicable with respect to the same. At times, assessee may have to face a lot of problems in explaining such documents and papers and convincing the authorized officer that such papers have no relevance with his financial affairs or unrecorded income.

Therefore, the assessees should periodically review all such unwanted loose papers, documents, rough pads and waste papers for elimination. Availability of such useless papers or details may unnecessarily invite problems for the assessee. Drawers and working place of the assessee and his employees at business and residential premises may be checked and reviewed on regular basis.

(*ii*) **Incriminating Documents/Details Found in Search may Fasten Huge Tax Liability**

It has been observed in practice that certain persons tend to keep details/papers relating to certain transactions which may not be of any use to them in future, such as :—

(*a*) Details of household expenses incurred, invoices/cash memos of regular shopping items.

(*b*) Cash Receipts, duplicate sale agreement, details of cash account etc., in the case of purchase or sale transactions of immovable properties.

(*c*) Details or papers relating to unaccounted cash transactions including that of past several earlier years.

(*d*) Duplicate or parallel books of account/cash book/day book containing details of unrecorded cash transactions.

(*e*) Details regarding temporary loans or advances taken or given in cash along with details and calculation of periodic interest relating to the same.

(*f*) Details or papers regarding suppressed sales, bogus bills of expenses, unrecorded sale of scrap, etc.

(*g*) Details or evidences relating to benami share capital introduced in the books of account.

Such kind of transactions should not be entered as it erodes the valuable tax base of our country and is illegal at the same time. But it is unfortunate that such transactions are not only found entered by the unscrupulous taxpayers but such details or documents do exist for various reasons including the one so as to settle account amongst the partners or family members. So much so, even after the settlement of the account, such details or papers are found during search in the custody of the person. Needless to say that when such documents, papers or details are found during search, these may pave the way of fastening huge tax liability on the taxpayers including the penal consequences.

(*iii*) **Vigilant Family Members - Counselling required**

It has been observed that in the Indian joint family structure, the financial affairs relating to wife, mother, children and other members are generally planned and maintained by male members/spouse. Family members including the ladies of the house do work as working directors in the companies or working partners in the firms and remuneration paid to them is claimed as deduction against the taxable profits in the business entities. Income Tax Returns of such family members are filed showing various kind of incomes which are earned by them. At the time of search, when enquiry is made from them, they may not be able to withstand pressure of search and show ignorance about their working for which they even received remuneration and facts are not correctly stated by them about their working and consequent remuneration earned by them and this creates inconsistency in their statements and the income tax returns filed by them. Therefore, it is advisable that the ladies or other family members should be given regular counselling regarding the financial transactions entered by them so that in the event of search and enquiry, there may not be any mismatch between the return of income and their statement.

(*iv*) **Mock search exercise**

In case assessee apprehends the action of income tax search, it may be a useful exercise to get the mock search conducted at his business or residential premises from the team of his income tax consultants who are having fair and reasonable experience regarding the manner in which income tax search action is undertaken. Such exercise may give first hand experience to the assessee regarding the manner in which search is conducted and the ways how to handle the situation. Such exercise may further provide an opportunity to the assessee, his family members and employees to put the house in order. In the course of such exercise, all the related persons/employees may be educated regarding their rights and duties and the powers of the tax authorities.

18.3 Approach to maintain records

(*i*) **Details of unrecorded transactions in coded form are also liable to be decoded**

At the cost of repetition, it is stated and advised that no person should indulge in unaccounted cash transactions as it is, *inter alia,* not in his interest. However it is seen in practice that people tend to keep such details in coded form so that these may not be decipherable by any one including by the tax sleuths. But it is also experienced in practical life that despite all such care of keeping the details in coded form, some trace is left so as to make such coded details amenable to decoding. For example, details of cash transactions are mixed along with details of bank (accounted) transactions and once that is done, such transactions are liable to be decoded with the help of full and true particulars of the bank transactions. Further may be an example where the details kept in coded manner may seem to be absolutely unrealistic keeping in view the nature of transaction.

(ii) Details beyond earlier seven years

As per the present provisions of the Income-tax Act, 1961, the cases of the assessee may be reopened under section 153A or 148 relating to earlier seven years prior to the year of search. Details of the transactions and evidences of the assets relating to the period prior to the above period may be found with the assessee, but he cannot legally be asked to prove the source and genuineness of the transactions relating to the above period. Even if such details are found during search, assessment cannot be reopened and no undisclosed income relating to the above period can be attributed to the assessee.

However, use of the diary of the current year for keeping details of the transaction relating to earlier year would cast serious doubt regarding the genuineness of the period to which such details or transactions actually relate.

18.4 Availability of evidences so as to avoid seizure

(i) Separate file of jewellery containing evidences of acquisition

It has been observed that even in the cases when jewellery is acquired with the disclosed and explained sources, evidences of acquisition explaining the source are not readily available at the time of search action and in the absence of such evidence, even such otherwise explained jewellery may be liable to be seized. Therefore, it is advised that in connection with the jewellery, a separate file should be maintained containing the following details:—

(a) Copy of wealth tax return along with the Registered Valuer's certificate, if any available.

(b) Even when filing of wealth tax return is not applicable, Registered valuer's certificate valuing the jewellery may be obtained.

(c) Copy of invoices and details of payments made regarding jewellery acquired.

(d) In case jewellery of some other person/family member of the assessee is kept with the assessee or in his bank locker, an authorization to this effect containing the item wise details of such jewellery should be kept.

(e) It has been observed that jewellery are prone to periodic alteration, remaking and exchange of items at the instance of the owner. Some evidence in this regard should be kept so that in case items of jewellery do not match with the wealth tax return/valuer's certificate/VDIS declaration earlier made etc., the fact may be explained and authorized officer may be convinced.

(*f*) In case jewellery has been inherited or acquired by way of gift, copy of will or copy of gift deed may be kept.

(*g*) Photographs of marriage or other occasions taken place in the past including the period earlier to more than seven years, wearing the items of jewellery may also be kept as evidence to justify that such items of jewellery have been acquired in the past including during the period which falls beyond past seven years and therefore, may not be liable to be taxed as deemed income under section 69. This may, however, not be a very sound evidence and department may attempt to trash it on the ground that jewellery shown in the photograph may be imitating jewellery.

(*h*) Copy of the statement of affairs, if any filed with the Income tax Department containing the details of jewellery owned by the assessee.

In case a file containing above evidences is separately kept, it may be very handy to convince the authorized officer regarding source of acquisition of the jewellery and unwarranted seizure in the absence of evidences may be avoided.

(*ii*) Cash belonging to business firm, kept at residence

In case cash belonging to the business entity is kept at the residence of owner, director, partner or senior employee of such entity, it should be kept along with proper evidence authorizing the same. Evidence or copy of such authorization should be available at the premises of the business entity also. It would be ideal if requisite accounting entry to this effect is also passed in the books of account of the business entity. Availability of such evidences at both the premises would be quite useful in explaining the source of cash found and seizure of cash may be avoided.

(*iii*) Evidence regarding assets of other persons kept

There may be cases when cash, jewellery, property documents or other assets belonging to other family members or friends of the assessee may be kept by him at his residence or his bank locker. Assessee may keep such assets as trustee for others. Sometimes, such assets or documents may be in the possession of assessee in the capacity as mortgagee against the money lent by him. In such cases, assessee should keep with him proper evidences or authorization along with such assets. In the case of any search action at his premises, such assets may be protected from seizure and consequent action under section 153C against such other persons may also be avoided.

(iv) Tangible assets to be duly recorded

It is advisable that all tangible assets whether movable or immovable should be duly recorded in the books of account and be acquired out of the explained sources of investment. This issue is significant particularly in the case of those assets, date and year of acquisition of which may be inquired and established easily. Such assets may include immovable properties, vehicles *i.e.* cars, scooters etc., shares and bonds, NSCs and KVPs which are not bearer in nature. In case unrecorded assets of such nature are found during search, unaccounted income of the assessee shall relate to the year in which such assets were acquired and if the year of acquisition is the year prior to current year for which return of income had already been filed, it may be difficult to defend penalty for concealment of income.

Similarly, certain expenses incurred should also be duly recorded and sources explained properly. Such expenses may include foreign travel undertaken, details of which are easily available from the passport, expenses incurred through credit cards, electricity expenses, tuition fees of children, telephone expenses etc. The year of incurring these expenses can easily be enquired and established and addition for unexplained expenditure under section 69A of the Act may be attributed to the earlier years and assessee may be liable not only for the tax and interest, but for penalty also.

(v) In case of joint premises, clear cut demarcation desirable

There may be cases when several business entities do exist at one & the common premises. Search warrant is issued qua-premises as well as qua-assessee. In case of search action, whole premises may be covered under the investigation and all the books of account, documents or assets belonging to the targeted assessee along with belonging to other persons or entities may be seized. In case such joint premises are having clear cut demarcation, earmarking, separate place, almirah or room for each entity, assessee can plead and protect the other entities from the investigation and seizure of books of account, documents or assets of other entities may be avoided.

18.5 Vigilance with respect to others

(i) In case of financial disputes, handle the situation tactfully

It has been experienced that financial information and evidences regarding unrecorded transactions are generally supplied to the income tax authorities by disgruntled employees, rival business associates, ex-business partners, jealous family members and friends or family-in-laws members having matrimonial disputes etc. Such kind of situation may arise particularly when there are financial or other disputes of the assessee with such persons. Assessee should be vigilant and handle the situation tactfully and with maturity. Exit of any employee who was handling the affairs of the assessee should be made amicably and respectfully without creating the feeling of hostility or vengeance. It goes without saying that the incriminating evidences in possession of hostile person may give sleepless nights to the assessee.

(*ii*) **Damaging details/evidences available with the corresponding person may be a source of expensive long drawn litigation**

Any kind of financial transaction may be entered into between or managed by two or more parties and the details or evidences relating to such transactions may remain in the possession of all the parties. It has been experienced at times that such evidences or details may not be retained by the assessee but may be retained by any other party and in such circumstances assessee may feel the heat of the complexities of the investigation by the tax authorities. In case any action is undertaken by the Department at the premises of such other party which is retaining the evidence or details, it is not only the person against whom action has been taken but all other related persons may also have to face the consequences thereof.

There may be cases when an employee is entrusted with the job of managing the affairs of the assessee-employer. The assessee may not be maintaining any unwanted details or evidences but the employee may be retaining such details on the ground that he may be questioned and be required to show the account of the financial affairs at any point of time by his employer. In another situation, in the case of transfer of immovable property transaction, buyer may not be keeping any unwarranted records but the seller or middleman may be preserving such details or evidences.

In practice, such situation is encountered quite frequently. It is therefore very important for a person to keep his house in order, and at the same time, ensure the same for others also. This situation is similar to the situation that while driving a car on road, accident of vehicle may take place even for a very efficient and alert driver due to mistake of other driver of another vehicle. Therefore, a driver can be said to be an efficient driver only when he remains alert and takes precaution from the anticipated faults of the other drivers on road.

(*iii*) **Senior employees or consultants to remain vigilant**

Whenever search action is planned by the income tax authorities, senior employees or consultants of the assessee who are deeply involved in managing the financial affairs of the assessee are also roped in search action may be undertaken at their residential premises also. In case search action is undertaken at their residential premises, investigation is not restricted relating to the affairs of the person/ entity only with respect to whom search was primarily planned but their personal affairs and that of their family members shall also be covered under investigation.

Such persons should always remain vigilant and manage the affairs in such a manner that unnecessary problems are not invited relating to personal affairs of themselves or their other family members.

18.6 Powers of department

(i) To be aware regarding powers of tax authorities

An assessee should be well aware of the duties and powers of tax authorities in case of any kind of search action. At the same time, he should remain aware of his own rights and duties. In this connection, following points are noteworthy-

(a) Under the Income Tax Act, in case of search action there is no power to the tax authorities to put a person under arrest or confinement. Tax authorities do not have any power to slap, use derogatory language or resort to third degree treatment. Such power of arrest may be available to custom and excise authorities, Enforcement Directorate, CBI etc. It remains grievance of income tax authorities that in the absence of such powers, they find themselves handicapped to get honest and truthful admission of unrecorded transactions from the assessee. To some extent, there may be justification in their stand but the legislature in its wisdom has thought it fit not to equip income tax authorities with such power for detecting economic offence of evasion of direct taxes.

(b) Sometimes, threat is exercised by the authorized officer particularly on the employees of the employer-assessee to give the statement in the manner as desired by him, otherwise search action may be taken against him also at his residential premises. One should be aware of the fact that legislature has provided number of safeguards before taking extreme action of search against a person. It takes lot of efforts in preparing a case fit for search and in obtaining approval and search warrant against a person from the higher competent authorities. A person should not come under such pressure unless the facts and the situation indicate otherwise.

(c) No documents or papers can be seized and made part of panchnama of the person under search which are not found in control or possession of person searched but is brought from outside, even when such papers or documents may relate to the financial affairs of the person searched.

It is important to keep the above points in mind so that assessee does not remain under any kind of fear and may handle the situation properly. It is also important to educate senior employees of the employer-assessee who may be required to handle the search operation at some of the premises in the absence of the assessee.

(ii) Lot of information relating to assessee within the domain of income tax department

It is felt that the most effective way to curb the menace of black money is the development and establishment of technology based systems with all the revenue departments of the government and having inter-departmental access and cross reconciliation and verification amongst themselves. Any kind of detection at the end of any of the departments may trigger signal bells to the other departments also and a person may be held responsible and be penalized from different quarters. Such kind of system in place and investigation undertaken by the government may act as catalyst so as to create deterrence effect in the society and discourage the persons from entering into unrecorded transactions.

Government is trying to achieve the above objective by establishing technology driven systems in all the revenue departments. Information regarding high value financial transactions is collected by the Income Tax Department from various sources such as:-

(a) banks relating to high value cash transactions in the bank accounts

(b) stock exchanges relating to settlement in cash

(c) banks relating to unidentified or doubtful bank accounts

(d) registration authorities relating to purchase and sale of immovable properties exceeding ₹ 30 Lakhs

(e) details of investment in mutual funds exceeding ₹ 5 Lakhs

(f) credit card transactions during the year exceeding ₹ 2 Lakhs in a single account during the year

(g) high value cars sold by the dealers

Further, it is significant to note that quoting of Permanent Account Number (PAN) has almost been made compulsory substantially for all kinds of financial transactions and the Income Tax Department may track such transactions with the help of PAN.

Thus, with the spread of technology, income tax department is gradually having access to lot of information regarding the financial transactions of the assessees. Further, there may be information available with the tax department, regarding any person with the help of internet or search engines like google, yahoo etc. Information is also required to be submitted by every assessee in his return of income regarding major financial transactions and information furnished therein may be reconciled with the information collected by the department from various sources and in case of any discrepancy, suitable action may be taken.

Assessees should remain aware and vigilant regarding the above system and working of the department and should try to manage their affairs cautiously and in a transparent manner.

APPENDICES

APPENDICES

TAXPAYERS' CHARTER

Every taxpayer is entitled to expect the income-tax department:

To be fair

- in deciding tax matters, by providing a right to be heard and by being objective and impartial
- in collecting the taxes that are legitimately due.

To provide quality service

- be settling tax affairs promptly
- by keeping personal and private information furnished to the Department confidential
- by being courteous to the taxpayers

To assist him

- in understanding the rights and duties under the tax laws
- in availing of the benefits and concessions due to him
- in getting information and assistance at the enquiry counters

And in return, the Income-tax Department expects the taxpayer

- to extend co-operation to tax officials in the matter of assessment and collection
- to voluntarily disclose his correct income and pay the taxes due
- to discharge his statutory obligations in time
- to provide true and complete information

Charter of rights and duties of persons searched:

Rights of the person searched

- to see the warrant of authorization duly signed and sealed by the issuing authority
- to verify the identity of search of each member of the search party
- to make personal search of all members of the search party before the start of the search and on conclusion of the search.
- To insist on personal search of ladies being taken only by a lady, with strict regard to decency.
- To have at least two respectable and independent residents of the locality as witnesses.

- A lady occupying an apartment being searched has a right to withdraw before the search party enters, if, according to custom, she does not appear in public.
- To call a medical practitioner in case of emergency.
- To allow the children to go to school, after checking their bags.
- To have the facility of having meals, etc., at the normal time.
- To inspect the seals placed on various receptacles, sealed in course of search and subsequently at the time of reopening of the seals.
- Every person who is examined under section 132(4) has a right to ensure that the facts so stated by him have been recorded correctly.
- To have a copy of the panchnama together with all the annexures.
- To have a copy of any statement that is used against him by the Department.
- To have inspection of the seized books of account, etc., or to take extracts therefrom in the presence of any of the authorised officers or any other person empowered by him.
- To make an application objecting to the approval given by the Commissioner of Income-tax for retention of books and documents beyond 180 days from the date of the seizure.
- To make an application under section 132(11) to the Commissioner of Income-tax against an order under section 132(5).
- To get back the assets found to be in excess of the liability determined in the order under section 132(5).

Duties of the person searched

- To allow free and unhindered ingress into the premises.
- To see the warrant of authorisation and put signature on the same.
- To identify all receptacles in which assets or books of account and documents are kept and to hand over keys to such receptacles to the authorised officer.
- To identify and explain the ownership of the assets, books of account and documents found in the premises.
- To identify every individual in the premises and to explain their relationship to the person being searched. He should not mislead by personation. If he cheats by pretending to be some other person or knowingly substitutes one person for another, it is an offence punishable under section 416 of the Indian Penal Code.
- Not to allow or encourage the entry of any unauthorized person into the premises.
- Not to remove any article from its place without notice or knowledge of the authorised officer. If he secretes or destroys any document with the intention of preventing the same from being produced or used as evidence before the court or public servant, he shall be punishable with imprisonment or fine or both, in accordance with section 204 of the Indian Penal Code.

- To answer all queries truthfully and to the best of his knowledge. He should not allow any third party to either interfere or prompt while his statement is being recorded by the authorised officer. In doing so, he should keep in mind that—

  (*i*) If he refuses to answer a question on a subject relevant to the search operation, he shall be punishable with imprisonment or fine or both, under section 179 of the Indian Penal Code.

  (*ii*) Being legally bound by an oath or affirmation to state the truth, if he makes a false statement, he shall be punishable with imprisonment or fine or both under section 181 of the Indian Penal Code.

  (*iii*) Similarly, if he provides evidence which is false and which he knows or believes to be false, he is liable to be punished under section 191 of the Indian Penal Code.

- To affix his signature on the recorded statement, inventories and the panchnama.

- To ensure that peace is maintained throughout the duration of the search, and to co-operate with the search party in all respects so that the search action is concluded at the earliest and in a peaceful manner.

- Similar co-operation should be extended even after the search action is over, so as to enable the authorised officer to complete necessary follow-up investigations at the earliest.

GROUND RULES FOR SEARCH AND SEIZURE

RULE 1
COMPETENT AUTHORITY

1. Authorization for a search can only be ordered by a competent officer after considering the information he has in his possession provided he has reasons to believe that a search is justified. Before the issue of a search warrant, a formal order is required to be passed by the competent authority.

Information may come from external sources like informers, other Government departments or newspaper, magazines and publications. In the case of an informer, it is generally made clear to him that he is liable to be prosecuted under section 182 of the IPC if his allegations are proved false. Internal sources comprise cases developed *suo motu* on the basis of records and investigation and intelligence gathered by the intelligent wing of the department.

RULE 2
OBJECTIVES OF THE SEARCH

2. A search is necessary to secure evidence which is not likely to be made available by issue of summons or by visiting, in ordinary course, the premises concerned. Tax authorities have powers to summon persons and documents. Tax authorities have to resort to search and seizure when there is evidence of undisclosed documents or assets which have been and would not be disclosed in ordinary course.

RULE 3
SEARCH PARTY

3. Search party has to be led by an officer of a certain rank in case of major searches. The party must be led by an officer of at least the rank of Assistant Collector or equivalent. The team must include two respectable witnesses of the locality and technical persons like valuers, etc.

RULE 4
RIGHTS OF THE PERSON TO BE SEARCHED

4. (*A*) To see the warrant of authorisation duly signed and sealed by the issuing authority.

(*B*) Verify the identity of each member of the search party.

(*C*) To have at least two respectable and independent residents of the locality as witnesses.

(*D*) To have personal search of all members of the party before the start of the search and after conclusion of the search.

(*E*) To insist on a personal search of females by another female only with strict regard to decency.

(*F*) To have a copy of the panchnama together with all the Annexures.

(*G*) To put his own seals on the packages containing the seized assets.

(*H*) Woman having the occupancy of an apartment, etc., to be search has right to withdraw before the search party enters, if, according to custom, she does not appear in public.

(*I*) To call medical practitioner if he is not well.

(*J*) To have his children permitted to go to school, after the examination of their bags.

(*K*) To inspect the seals placed on various receptacles sealed in course of searches and subsequently reopened by continuation of searches.

(*L*) To have the facilities of having meals, etc., at the normal time.

(*M*) To have a copy of any statement before it is used against him in an assessment or prosecution proceedings.

(*N*) To have inspection of the books of account, etc., seized or to take extracts therefrom in the presence of any of the authorised officer or any other person empowered by him.

RULE 5
EXAMINATION

5. Tax authorities thereafter examine the person searched. In the case of income-tax, the person has to take an oath. In the case of other Acts, it is made clear to him that proceedings are judicial and he is bound to tell the truth. It is also explained to him that the statement is liable to be used against him. The examination is deemed as a judicial proceeding and this statement is admissible as evidence. The purpose of this examination is statement is admissible as evidence. The purpose of this examination is to secure the explanation of the person regarding the documents and properties before he has an opportunity to concoct an explanation and fabricate evidence. He is not allowed the services of a lawyer at this stage.

RULE 6
REPORT TO THE SENIOR AUTHORITY

6. After the search, the party has to submit a report to the senior authority like Collector, Commissioner, etc. The outcome of search is given to enable the senior officer to judge the *bona fide* of the search and to exercise control over searches carried out.

RULE 7

SAFEGUARDS

7. Section 136(2) of the Customs Act provides for deterrent punishment in-cluding imprisonment of the Customs Officer held responsible for vexatious searches. In the cases of Excise and FERA, vexatious searches are punishable by a fine.

RULE 8

ARRESTS

8. The power of arrest vests with the Customs, Central Excise and Enforcement Officers. Income-tax Officers have no powers of arrests. Arrests are generally resorted to in cases where the detected offence is of a serious nature and the case appears to be fit for criminal prosecution. Persons are generally not arrested when the intention is only to have departmental proceedings. Persons are arrested when there is a gravity of offence, evidence of personal culpability, a strong *prima facie* case and a likelihood of person tampering with the evidence by remaining at large or absconding.

RULE 9

DEPARTMENTAL PROCEEDINGS

9. Under the Income-tax Act, the Income-tax Officer concerned must make a summary assessment within 120 days of the seizure estimating the undisclosed income and calculating the amount of tax on income so estimated along with the interest and penalty payable. Thereafter, he retains in his custody only such assets as are in his opinion, sufficient to satisfy the aggregate amount of tax, penalty and interest due.

Books of account and documents seized cannot be restrained for more than 180 days except for specially recorded reasons and with the approval of the Commissioner. Law specifically provides that the person concerned may make copies of the documents concerned.

In the case of the Customs Act, the period for retaining the contraband cannot be extended beyond one year. The adjudicating officer can impose penalties up to five times the foreign exchange involved. Penalty in the case of income-tax can be up to 200% of tax evaded. The contraband goods can be absolutely confiscated or allowed to be redeemed on payment of fine. No imprisonment can be awarded by an adjudicating officer.

Instructions are being issued that the time-limit of completing search cases will be strictly adhered to future and no undue extension will be given.

RULE 10

PROSECUTION

10. Apart from departmental proceedings, the law provides for criminal pros-ecution in certain cases. The complaint made by the tax department is treated as a personal criminal complaint as these offences under the Acts are treated as non-cognisable. The chief offences on which prosecutions are

launched are customs and excise duties or income-tax evasion, and in the case of FERA, contravention of the provisions of the Act.

In the case of offences by companies, every person who was in-charge at the time when the offence was committed and was responsible for the conductor business of the company as well as the company itself, are liable to be prosecuted provided that the offence was committed with the knowledge of such person or that he did not exercise all due diligence to prevent the commission of such offence.

Publicity - The raiding party will not make any statement to the press. Statement to the press, if any, will be made by the head of the department and will be factual in nature. It may be necessary in some cases to give out a press note especially where distorted versions have been released to the press by other parties.

WARRANT OF AUTHORISATION

FORM NO. 45

[*See* rule 112]

Warrant of authorisation under section 132 of the Income-tax Act, 1961, and rule 112(1) of the Income-tax Rules, 1962

To

The Deputy Director,

The Deputy Commissioner,

The Assistant Director,

The Assistant Commissioner,

The Income-tax Officer,

....

Whereas information has been laid before me and on the consideration thereof I have reason to believe that—

a summons under sub-section (1) of section 37 of the Indian Income-tax Act, 1922, or under sub-section (1) of section 131 of the Income-tax Act, 1961, or a notice under sub-section (4) of section 22 of the Indian Income-tax Act, 1922, or under sub-section (1) of section 142 of the Income-tax Act, 1961, was issued by the Deputy Commissioner/the Assistant Commissioner/the Income-tax Officer, ... to .... [name of the person] on .... [date] to produce, or cause to be produced, books of account or other documents specified in the relevant summons or notice and he has omitted or failed to produce, or cause to be produced, such books of account or other documents as required by such summons or notice;

a summons under sub-section (1) of section 37 of the Indian Income-tax Act, 1922, or under sub-section (1) of section 131 of the Income-tax Act, 1961, or a notice under sub-section (4) of section 22 of the Indian Income-tax Act, 1922, or under sub-section (1) of section 142 of the Income-tax Act, 1961, has been issued by the Deputy Commissioner/the Assistant Commissioner/the Income-tax Officer, ... to .... [name of the person] on .... [date] to produce, or cause to be produced, books of account or other documents specified in the relevant summons or notice and he will not produce or cause to be produced, such books of account or other documents as required by such summons or notice;

if a summons under sub-section (1) of section 37 of the Indian Income-tax Act, 1922, or under sub-section (1) of section 131 of the Income-tax Act, 1961, or a notice under sub-section (4) of section 22 of the Indian Income-tax Act, 1922, or under sub-section (1) of section 142 of the Income-tax Act, 1961, is issued to .... [name of the person] to produce, or cause to be produced, books of account or other documents which will be useful for, or relevant to, proceedings under the Indian Income-tax Act, 1922, or under the Income-tax Act, 1961, he would not produce, or cause to be produced, such books of account or other documents as required by such summons or notice;

Sarvashri/Shri/Shrimati .... are/is in possession of any money, bullion, jewellery or other valuable article or thing and such money, bullion, jewellery or other valuable article or thing represents either wholly or partly income or property which has not been, or would not be, disclosed for the purposes of the Indian Income-tax Act, 1922, or the Income-tax Act, 1961;

And whereas I have reason to suspect that such books of account, other documents, money, bullion, jewellery or other valuable article or thing have been kept and are to be found in ... . (specify particulars of the building/place/vessel/vehicle/aircraft); This is to authorise and require you ....
....

name of the Deputy Director or of the Deputy Commissioner or of the Assistant Director or of the Assistant Commissioner or the Income-tax Officer—

 (*a*) to enter and search the said building/place/vessel/vehicle/aircraft;

 (*b*) to search any person who has got out of, or is about to get into, or is in the building/place/vessel/vehicle/aircraft if you have reason to suspect that such person has secreted about his person any such books of account, other documents, money, bullion, jewellery or other valuable article or thing;

 (*c*) to place identification marks on such books of account and documents as may be found in the course of the search and as you may consider relevant to or useful for the proceedings aforesaid and to make a list thereof together with particulars of the identification marks;

 (*d*) to examine such books of account and documents and make, or cause to be made, copies or extracts from such books of account and documents;

 (*e*) to seize any such books of account, documents, money, bullion, jewellery or other valuable article or thing found as a result of such search and take possession thereof;

 (*f*) to make a note or an inventory of any such money, bullion, jewellery, or other valuable article or thing;

 (*g*) to convey such books of account, documents, money, bullion, jewellery or other valuable article or thing to the office of the Deputy Commissioner of Income-tax or any other authority not below the rank of the Income-tax Officer employed in the execution of the Income-tax Act, 1961; and

 (*h*) to exercise all other powers and perform all other functions under section 132 of the Income-tax Act, 1961, and the rules relating thereto.

You may requisition the services of any police officer or any officer of the Central Government, or of both, to assist you for all or any of the purposes specified in sub-section (1) of section 132 of the Income-tax Act, 1961.

Director-General or Director
(SEAL)   *Chief Commissioner or Commissioner of Income-tax*
                                                                                        Deputy Director
                                                                    Deputy Commissioner of Income-tax

FORM NO. 45A

[*See* rule 112(2)(*b*)]

**Warrant of authorisation under the proviso to sub-section (1) of section 132
of the Income-tax Act, 1961**

To

The Deputy Director,

The Deputy Commissioner,

The Assistant Director,

The Assistant Commissioner,

The Income-tax Officer,

....

Whereas information has been laid before me and on the consideration thereof I have reason to believe that—

a summons under sub-section (1) of section 37 of the Indian Income-tax Act, 1922, or under sub-section (1) of section 131 of the Income-tax Act, 1961, or a notice under sub-section (4) of section 22 of the Indian Income-tax Act, 1922, or under sub-section (1) of section 142 of the Income-tax Act, 1961, was issued by the Deputy Commissioner/the Assistant Commissioner/ the Income-tax Officer,..............to........[name of the person] on........[date] to produce, or cause to be produced, books of account or other documents specified in the relevant summons or notice and he has omitted or failed to produce, or cause to be produced, such books of account or other documents as required by such summons or notice ;

a summons under sub-section (1) of section 37 of the Indian Income-tax Act, 1922, or under sub-section (1) of section 131 of the Income-tax Act, 1961, or a notice under sub-section (4) of section 22 of the Indian Income-tax Act, 1922, or under sub-section (1) of section 142 of the Income-tax Act, 1961, has been issued by the Deputy Commissioner/the Assistant Commissioner/the Income-tax Officer,........to........[name of the person] on........[date] to produce, or cause to be produced, books of account or other documents specified in the relevant summons or notice and he will not produce or cause to be produced, such books of account or other documents as required by such summons or notice ;

if a summons under sub-section (1) of section 37 of the Indian Income-tax Act, 1922, or under sub-section (1) of section 131 of the Income-tax Act, 1961, or a notice under sub-section (4) of section 22 of the Indian Income-tax Act, 1922, or under sub-section (1) of section 142 of the Income-tax Act, 1961, is issued to.....[name of the person] to produce, or cause to be produced, books of account or other documents which will be useful for, or relevant to, proceedings under the Indian Income-tax Act, 1922, or under the Income-tax Act, 1961, he would not produce, or cause to be produced, such books of account or other documents as required by such summons or notice ;

Sarvashri/Shri/Shrimati.............are/is in possession of any money, bullion, jewellery or other valuable article or thing and such money, bullion, jewellery or other valuable article or thing represents either wholly or partly income or property which has not been, or would not be, disclosed for the purposes of the Indian Income-tax Act, 1922, or the Income-tax Act, 1961 ;

And whereas I have reason to suspect that such books of account, other documents, money, bullion, jewellery or other valuable article or thing have been kept and are to be found in.............(specify particulars of the building/place/vessel/vehicle/aircraft) which is within the area of my jurisdiction ;

And whereas I have reason to believe that any delay in getting an authorisation under sub-section (1) of section 132 from the Chief Commissioner or Commissioner having jurisdiction over Sarvashri/Shri/Shrimati.................may be prejudicial to the interests of the revenue ;

This is to authorise and require you ....

....

name of the Deputy Director or of the Deputy Commissioner or of the Assistant Director or of the Assistant Commissioner or the Income-tax Officer—

    (a) to enter and search the said building/place/vessel/vehicle/aircraft ;

    (b) to search any person who has got out of, or is about to get into, or is in, the building/place/vessel/vehicle/aircraft if you have reason to suspect that such person has secreted about his person any such books of account, other documents, money, bullion, jewellery or other valuable article or thing ;

    (c) to place identification marks on such books of account and documents as may be found in the course of the search and as you may consider relevant to or useful for the proceedings aforesaid and to make a list thereof together with particulars of the identification marks ;

    (d) to examine such books of account and documents and make, or cause to be made, copies or extracts from such books of account and documents ;

    (e) to seize any such books of account, documents, money, bullion, jewellery or other valuable article or thing found as a result of such search and take possession thereof ;

    (f) to make a note or an inventory of any such money, bullion, jewellery, or other valuable article or thing ;

    (g) to convey such books of account, documents, money, bullion, jewellery, or other valuable article or thing to the office of the Deputy Commissioner of Income-tax or any other authority not below the rank of the Income-tax Officer employed in the execution of the Income-tax Act, 1961 ; and

    (h) to exercise all other powers and perform all other functions under section 132 of the Income-tax Act, 1961 and the rules relating thereto.

You may requisition the services of any police officer or any officer of the Central Government, or of both, to assist you for all or any of the purposes specified in sub-section (1) of section 132 of the Income-tax Act, 1961.

(SEAL)   *Chief Commissioner or Commissioner of Income-tax*

FORM NO. 45B

[*See* rule 112(2)(*c*)]

Warrant of authorisation under sub-section (1A) of section 132 of the Income-tax Act, 1961

To

The Deputy Director,

The Deputy Commissioner,

The Assistant Director,

The Assistant Commissioner,

The Income-tax Officer,

....

Whereas information has been laid before me and on the consideration thereof I have reason to suspect that the books of account, other documents, money, bullion, jewellery or other valuable article or thing in respect of which..
[name and designation of authorised officer]

has been authorised by the Director-General or Director/Chief Commissioner or Commissioner of Income-tax/Deputy Director/Deputy Commissioner of Income-tax................ to take action under clauses (*i*) to (*v*) of sub-section (1) of section 132 are or is kept in ....
....;
[specify particulars of the building/place/vessel/vehicle/aircraft]

And whereas the building/place/vessel/vehicle/aircraft specified above has/have not been mentioned in the authorisation under sub-section (1) of section 132 by the Director General or Director/Chief Commissioner or Commissioner of Income-tax/Deputy Director/Deputy Commissioner of Income-tax;

This is to authorise and require you..

name of the Deputy Director or of the Deputy Commissioner or of the Assistant Director or of the Assistant Commissioner or the Income-tax Officer—

- (*a*) to enter and search the said building/place/vessel/vehicle/aircraft;
- (*b*) to search any person who has got out of, or is about to get into, or is in, the building/place/vessel/vehicle/aircraft, if you have reason to suspect that such person has secreted about his person any such books of account, other documents, money, bullion, jewellery or other valuable article or thing ;
- (*c*) to place identification marks on such books of account and documents as may be found in the course of search and as you may consider relevant to, or useful for, proceedings under the Indian Income-tax Act, 1922, or under the Income-tax Act, 1961, and to make a list thereof together with particulars of the identification marks ;
- (*d*) to examine such books of account and documents and make, or cause to be made, copies or extracts from such books of account and documents ;
- (*e*) to seize any such books of account, documents, money, bullion, jewellery or other valuable article or thing found as a result of such search and take possession thereof ;
- (*f*) to make a note or an inventory of any such money, bullion, jewellery or other valuable article or thing ;

(g) to convey such books of account, documents, money, bullion, jewellery or other valuable article or thing to the office of the Deputy Commissioner of Income-tax or any other authority not below the rank of the Income-tax Officer employed in the execution of the Income-tax Act, 1961 ; and

(h) to exercise all other powers and perform all other functions under section 132 of the Income-tax Act, 1961, and the rules relating thereto.

You may requisition the services of any police officer or any officer of the Central Government or of both, to assist you for all or any of the purposes specified in sub-section (1) of section 132 of the Income-tax Act, 1961.

(SEAL)   *Chief Commissioner or Commissioner of Income-tax*

FORM NO. 45C

[*See* rule 112D(1)]

Warrant of authorisation under sub-section (1) of section 132A of the Income-tax Act, 1961

To

The Deputy Director,

The Deputy Commissioner,

The Assistant Director,

The Assistant Commissioner,

The Income-tax Officer,

....

Whereas information has been laid before me and on the consideration thereof I have reason to believe that—

a summons under sub-section (1) of section 37 of the Indian Income-tax Act, 1922, or under sub-section (1) of section 131 of the Income-tax Act, 1961, or a notice under sub-section (4) of section 22 of the Indian Income-tax Act, 1922, or under sub-section (1) of section 142 of the Income-tax Act, 1961, was issued by the Deputy Commissioner/the Assistant Commissioner/the Income-tax Officer,...

[name of the person]

to produce, or cause to be produced, books of account or other documents specified in the relevant summons or notice and he has omitted or failed to produce or cause to be produced, such books of account or other documents as required by such summons or notice, and the said books of account or other documents have been taken into custody by................................

....

[name and designation of the officer or authority]

certain books of account or other documents which will be useful for, or relevant to, proceedings under the Indian Income-tax Act, 1922 or under the Income-tax Act, 1961, have been taken into custody by...

[name and designation of officer or authority]

And Sarvashri/Shri/Shrimati..

[name of the person]

to whom a summons under sub-section (1) of section 37 of the Indian Income-tax Act, 1922, or under sub-section (1) of section 131 of the Income-tax Act, 1961, or a notice under sub-section (4) of section 22 of the Indian Income-tax Act, 1922, or under sub-section (1) of section 142 of the Income-tax Act, 1961, has been or might be issued by the Deputy Commissioner/ the Assistant Commissioner/the Income-tax Officer,...............will not, or would not, produce or cause to be produced, such books of account or other documents on their return by the said officer/authority ;

the assets taken into custody by...

[name and designation of the officer or authority]

represent either wholly or partly income or property which has not been or would not have been disclosed for the purposes of the Indian Income-tax Act, 1922, or the Income-tax Act, 1961, by ....

[name of the person]

from whose possession or control such assets have been taken into custody by the officer/ authority aforesaid ;

This is to authorise you...

name of the Deputy Director or of the Deputy Commissioner or of the Assistant Director or of the Assistant Commissioner or the Income-tax Officer—

to require the said officer or authority to deliver to you the books of account, other documents or assets as aforesaid.

Director-General or Director

Chief Commissioner or Commissioner of Income-tax

(SEAL)

PROFORMA OF PANCHNAMA

(To be prepared in quadruplicate)

A. Warrant in the case of :

B. Warrant to search

(Details & Ownership of Place of search)

Telephone Numbers

C. (A) and (B) stated to be assessed by   (A)   (B)

D. Search Party consisting of

Authorised Officer

Full Designation

Name

    1.

    2.

    3.

    4.

    5.

    6.

    7.

    8.

Other officials who assisted the authorized officers

    1.

    2.

    3.

    4.

    5.

    6.

E. Name and complete address of panchas:

    1.

    2.

On being called by Shri .... on .... at .... a.m./p.m.; we, the above named Panchas presented ourselves at the above place of search. The Authorised Officer, Shri ....showed the warrant of authorization dated .... issued under section 132 of the Income-tax Act, 1961/37A of the Wealth-tax Act, 1957 in the case of (A) above, to search the place mentioned at (B) above and duly signed and sealed by the Director of Inspection (Investigation), New Delhi/Commissioner of Income-tax, New Delhi/Deputy Director of Inspection (Investigation) New Delhi/Inspecting Assistant Commissioner of Income-tax Range ....New Delhi to Shri/Smt. ....who was present in the said place at the time and who after reading the said authorization/after the authorization was explained in local language, *viz.,*...................by Shri/Smt. .... signed in, in our presence and along with us, in token of having perused the same.

2. As today's search was in continuance of the proceedings on ....we, along with the aforesaid authorized officers, before the commencement of proceedings today, inspected the seals which had been placed on that date and found them to be intact/tampered with as narrated in enclosures.

3. The above-mentioned search party offered themselves for personal search before commencing the search, which was taken/declined.

4. A search of the above-mentioned place was carried out by the said party in our presence in an orderly manner without hurting the sentiments of any of the occupants of the premises. Nothings untoward/the events narrated in the enclosure, happened in the course of search.

5. In the course of the search:—

    (*a*) The following were found and seized:

        (*i*) Books of account and documents as per Annexure .... (sheets)

        (*ii*) Bullion, *i.e.*, gold, silver, etc., as per Annexure................. (sheets)

        (*iii*) Cash as per Annexure .... (sheets)

        (*iv*) Jewellery, ornaments, etc., which have been inventoried separately for each place .... from where recovered, as per Annexure ....(sheets)

        (*v*) Silver articles and silverware as per Annexure ....(sheets)

        (*vi*) Other values, locker keys, F.Ds., etc., as per Annexure...................(sheets)

    (*b*) The following were found but not seized:—

        (*i*) Books of account and documents as per Annexure .... Marks of identification were placed on these and the specimen of the marks and the pages where these have been placed are shown in the inventory prepared, *viz.*, Annexure ....

        (*ii*) The other valuable articles or things (including money) as per Annexures ....

(Separate inventories of jewellery, ornaments, silverware, etc. were prepared for items found in different places or claimed to be belonging to different persons.)

6. In the course of the search the authorized officer Shri .... recorded the statement(s) of Shri .... on solemn affirmation/oath, in our presence. No coercion, threat, inducement, promise or other undue influence was brought to bear on the above deponent. The statement was read over/explained in the local

language, *viz.* .... to the deponent who signed the statement in token of having understood its contents and of agreeing that it had been correctly recorded.

7. The following other important persons were present in the place of search and either took an active part in or helped the search proceedings;

Name

Relationship

8. The search commenced on..............at.....................a.m./p.m. The proceedings were closed on...............at...................a.m./p.m. as finally concluded/as temporarily concluded for the day to be commenced subsequently for which purpose seals were placed on the entire place/on.................in our presence.

9. An order under section 132(3) of the Income-tax Act, 1961 in respect of the sealed premises/was served on Shri/Smt.......................by the said authorized officer Shri......................

10. Before leaving the above-mentioned place of search, the entire search party again offered themselves for personal search which was taken/declined. The above panchnama has been read by us explained to us in local language................. by Shri/Smt.........................and it is certified that it has been correctly recorded.

Signature of the Panchas with Dates

   1.

   2.

Signature of the Authorised	Signature of the person receiving
Officer...............................	the copy of the panchnama............
Name	Name
Designation	Position in/relationship to 'A'
Date:	Date
Seal	

MODEL FORMS USED DURING SEARCH

Inventory of Cash Found/Seized

Annexure...................... Page......................

Date of Search/Survey...............................

Particulars of cash found/seized in the case of M/s./Shri/Smt......................
at........................... during the course of search/survey

Sl. No.	Bundle No.	Denomination	No. of Pieces	Amount
		Total		

Signature of Panchas

(in case of search only)

1.
2.

Signature of officers authorized to

Search/survey (with name and designation)

1.
2.

Signature of Party

(with name and position)

LIST/INVENTORY OF JEWELLERY, ETC., FOUND/SEIZED

Annexure.............. Page................

Date of Search........................

List of Bullion (Primary gold, silver, etc.)/gold ornaments and jewellery/silver articles found/seized in the case of

M/s./Shri/Smt.. at ....

Specific place where found ....

Item claimed to be belonging to ....

Sl. No.	Description of the articles	No.	Metal	Gross wt.	Estimated Net Wt.	Value ₹
	Total					

Signature of Panchas

    1.

    2.

Signature of Authorised Officers

    1.

    2.

Signature of party

Notes.—*1.* Separate list to be prepared for items found at different places or claimed to be belonging to different persons.

2. Ornaments on body of person should be indicated separately person-wise.

LIST/INVENTORY OF JEWELLERY, ETC., FOUND/SEIZED

Annexure...................... Page................

Date of Search ....

List of books of account, documents, etc., found/seized in the case of M/s. Shri/Smt. ....

....

....

....

....

....

Sl. No.	Description	Total Pages	Written pages	Period written for		Pages on which identification marks placed
				From	To	

Total No. of items of books of Specimen marks of

Account, documents, etc., on this

identification placed

Page ....

in various pages

Total up to this page...............

listed out.

Signature of Panchas (in case of Search only)

    1.

    2.

Signature of officers authorized to search/survey

(with name and designation)

1.

2.

Signature of party

(with name and position)

ORDER UNDER SECTION 132(3) OF THE INCOME-TAX ACT, 1961

By virtue of the powers vested in me under the warrant of authorization dated.............
issued by the Commissioner of Income-tax, New Delhi/Director of Inspection (Investigation), New Delhi/Deputy Director of Inspection (Investigation), New Delhi under section 132(1) of the Income-tax Act, 1961 and in exercise of the authority conferred on me by section 132(3) of the Income-tax Act, 1961, I hereby order you not to remove, part with or otherwise deal with the articles mentioned below without my previous permission.

Detail of Articles

1.

2.

3.

4.

5.

6.

Seal

To   Signature of the Authorised   Officer

Name:

Full:

Designation

Copy to   1. Tel. No.:

Date: Time:

2. Dy. Director of Inspection (Inv.)

C.R. Building, New Delhi

Tel. Nos.:

Note—The authorized officers are advised to prepare five copies of this order and serve once copy on the concerns/persons in charge of place sealed with a copy to the assessee/owner concerned. Two office copies may be kept. If a locked premises is sealed, a copy of this order may be prominently pasted at the entrance with a notice requesting the owner/occupant to contract the authorized officers immediately on arrival. In the case of a bank lockers, the order may be addressed to the owner of the locker with copy to the Manager of the bank.

**SUMMONS TO ASSESSEE/WITNESSES UNDER
SECTION 131OF THE INCOME-TAX ACT, 1961**

Ref: ADI (Inv.)/CR/DLH　　　　　　　　　　　Dated.......................

To

....

....

....

Whereas your attendance is required in connection with the proceedings under the Income-tax Act in your case/the case of...............you are hereby required personally to attend my office at.................on the.................day of .... 20............ at.....................
o'clock a.m./p.m. thereto give evidence and/or to produce either personally or thorough an authorized representative the books of account or other documents specified below and not to depart until you receive my permission to do so. Without prejudice to the provisions of any other law for the time being in force, if you intentionally omit to so attend and give evidence or produce the books of account or documents, a fine up to ₹ 500 may be imposed upon you under section 131(2) of the Income-tax Act, 1961.

　　　　　　　　　　　　　　　　　　　Asstt. Director of Inspection (Inv.)

　　　　　　　　　　　　　　　　　　　　C.R. Building, New Delhi

Books of account or documents to be produced:-

FORM 'B'

**Authorisation under section 133A(1)
of the Income-tax Act, 1961 (43 of 1961)**

1. In exercise of the powers conferred by clause (*b*) of the Income-tax Act, 1961 (43 of 1961), in hereby authorize Shri ....

....

....

....

in respect of whom I exercise jurisdiction at which a business or profession is carried on, whether such place be the principal place or not of such business or profession and require any proprietor, employee or any other person who may at the time and place be attending in any manner to, or helping in, the carrying on of such business or profession to afford him the necessary facility to inspect such books of account or other documents as he may require and which may be available at such place, and on the inspection of such account or documents he may, if he so deems necessary, place marks of identification of the books of account or other documents inspected by him and make or cause to be made extracts or copies therefrom.

2. The inspector of Income-tax enter any place of business referred to in paragraph 1 only during such hours at which such place is open for the conduct of the business or profession.

3. The Inspector of Income-tax shall not remove or cause to be removed from the place, which he has entered, and books of account or other documents.

Delhi:

Date:

Official Seal

ORDER UNDER RULE 112(6) OF INCOME-TAX RULES, 1962 READ WITH SECTION 132 OF THE INCOME-TAX ACT, 1961

To

Whereas the undersigned has been authorized to make a search under section 132 of Income-tax Act, 1961 and your services are forthwith required as a witness for the said search, you are hereby directed to attend and witness the search and not to depart till such time as the search is complete.

This order is issued under rule 112(6) of Income-tax Rules, 1962, read with section 132 of the Income-tax Act, 1961.

Signature:

Designation:

Date:

Seal

Note.—The following provisions of law are reproduced below for the information of the witness:

Rule 112(6) of Income-tax Rules, 1962: Before making a search the authorized officer about to make is shall call upon two or more respectable inhabitants of the locality in which the building or place to be searched is situated to attend and witness the search and may issue an order is writing to them or any of them to do.

Rule 112(7) of Income-tax Rules, 1962: The search shall be made in the presence of the witnesses aforesaid and a list of all things seized in the course of such search and of the places in which they were respectively found shall be prepared by the authorized officer and signed by such witness; but no person witnessing a search shall be required to attend as a witness of the search in any proceedings under the Indian Income-tax Act, 1922 (11 of 1922) of the Act unless specifically summoned.

Section 103(5) of Cr PC: Any person who, without reasonable cause, refused or neglects to attend any witness a search under this section, when called upon to do so by an order in writing delivered or tendered to him, shall be deemed to have committed an offence under section 117 of the Indian Penal Code (45 of 1860).

RELEVANT PROVISIONS OF CODE
OF CRIMINAL PROCEDURE, 1973

Search of place entered by person sought to be arrested.

47. (1) If any person acting under a warrant of arrest, or any police officer having authority to arrest, has reason to believe that the person to be arrested has entered into, or is within, any place, any person residing in, or being in charge of, such place shall, on demand of such person acting as aforesaid or such police officer, allow him free ingress thereto, and afford all reasonable facilities for a search therein.

(2) If ingress to such place cannot be obtained under sub-section (1), it shall be lawful in any case for a person acting under a warrant and in any case in which a warrant may issue, but cannot be obtained without affording the person to be arrested an opportunity of escape, for a police officer to enter such place and search therein, and in order to effect an entrance into such place, to break open any outer or inner door or window of any house or place, whether that of the person to be arrested or of any other person, if after notification of his authority and purpose, and demand of admittance duly made, he cannot otherwise obtain admittance:

Provided that, if any such place is an apartment in the actual occupancy of a female (not being the person to be arrested) who, according to custom, does not appear in public, such person or police officer shall, before entering such apartment, give notice to such female that she is at liberty to withdraw and shall afford her every reasonable facility for withdrawing, and may then break open the apartment and enter it.

(3) Any police officer or other person authorised to make an arrest may break open any outer or inner door or window of any house or place in order to liberate himself or any other person who, having lawfully entered for the purpose of making an arrest, is detained therein.

** ** **

Search of arrested person.

51. (1) Whenever a person is arrested by a police officer under a warrant which does not provide for the taking of bail, or under a warrant which provides for the taking of bail but the person arrested cannot furnish bail, and whenever a person is arrested without warrant, or by a private person under a warrant, and cannot legally be admitted to bail, or is unable to furnish bail, the officer making the arrest or, when the arrest is made by a private person, the police officer to whom he makes over the person arrested, may search such person, and place in safe Custody all articles, other than necessary wearing-apparel, found upon him and where any article is seized from the arrested person, a receipt showing the articles taken in possession by the police officer shall be given to such person.

(2) Whenever it is necessary to cause a female to be searched, the search shall be made by another female with strict regard to decency.

Power to seize offensive weapons.

52. The officer or other person making any arrest under this Code may taken from the person arrested any offensive weapons which he has about his person, and shall deliver all weapons so taken to the court or officer before which or whom the officer or person making the arrest is required by this Code to produce the person arrested.

Examination of accused by medical practitioner at the request of police officer.

53. (1) When a person is arrested on a charge of committing an offence of such a nature and alleged to have been committed under such circumstances that there are reasonable grounds for believing that an examination of his person will afford evidence as to the commission of an offence, it shall be lawful for a registered medical practitioner, acting at the request of a police officer not below the rank of sub-inspector, and for any person acting in good faith in his aid and under his direction, to make such an examination of the person arrested as is reasonably necessary in order to ascertain the facts which may afford such evidence, and to use such force as is reasonably necessary for that purpose.

(2) Whenever the person of a female is to be examined under this section, the examination shall be made only by, or under the supervision of, a female registered medical practitioner.

Explanation.—In this section and in sections 53A and 54,—

  (a) "examination" shall include the examination of blood, blood stains, semen, swabs in case of sexual offences, sputum and sweat, hair samples and finger nail clippings by the use of modern and scientific techniques including DNA profiling and such other tests which the registered medical practitioner thinks necessary in a particular case;

  (b) "registered medical practitioner" means a medical practitioner who possess any medical qualification as defined in clause (h) of section 2 of the Indian Medical Council Act, 1956 (102 of 1956) and whose name has been entered in a State Medical Register.

**   **   **

Examination of arrested person by medical officer.

54. (1) When any person is arrested, he shall be examined by a medical officer in the service of Central or State Government, and in case the medical officer is not available, by a registered medical practitioner soon after the arrest is made:

Provided that where the arrested person is a female, the examination of the body shall be made only by or under the supervision of a female medical officer, and in case the female medical officer is not available, by a female registered medical practitioner.

(2) The medical officer or a registered medical practitioner so examining the arrested person shall prepare the record of such examination, mentioning therein any injuries or marks of violence upon the person arrested, and the approximate time when such injuries or marks may have been inflicted.

(3) Where an examination is made under sub-section (1), a copy of the report of such examination shall be furnished by the medical officer or registered medical practitioner, as the case may be, to the arrested person or the person nominated by such arrested person.

** ** **

Form of warrant of arrest and duration.

70. (1) Every warrant of arrest issued by a court under this Code shall be in writing, signed by the presiding officer of such court and shall bear the seal of the court.

(2) Every such warrant shall remain in force until it is cancelled by the Court which issued it, or until it is executed.

** ** **

Warrants to whom directed.

72. (1) A warrant of arrest shall ordinarily be directed to one or more police officers; but the court issuing such a warrant may, if its immediate execution is necessary and no police officer is immediately available, direct it to any other person or persons, and such person or persons shall execute the same.

(2) When a warrant is directed to more officers or persons than one, it may be executed by all, or by any one or more of them.

Warrant may be directed to any person.

73. (1) The Chief Judicial Magistrate or a Magistrate of the first class may direct a warrant to any person within his local jurisdiction for the arrest of any escaped convict, proclaimed offender or of any person who is accused of a non-bailable offence and is evading arrest.

(2) Such person shall acknowledge in writing the receipt of the warrant, and shall execute it if the person for whose arrest it was issued, is in, or enters on, any land or other property under his charge.

(3) When the person against whom such warrant is issued is arrested, he shall be made over with the warrant to the nearest police officer, who shall cause him to be taken before a Magistrate having jurisdiction in the case, unless security is taken under section 71.

Warrant directed to police officer.

74. A warrant directed to any police officer may also be executed by any other police officer whose name is endorsed upon the warrant by the officer to whom it is directed or endorsed.

** ** **

Warrant forwarded for execution outside jurisdiction.

78. (1) When a warrant is to be executed outside the local jurisdiction of the Court issuing it, such court may, instead of directing the warrant to a police officer within its jurisdiction, forward it by post or otherwise to any Executive Magistrate or District Superintendent of Police or Commissioner of Police within the local limits of whose jurisdiction it is to be executed; and the Executive Magistrate or District

Superintendent or Commissioner shall endorse his name thereon, and if practicable, cause it to be executed in the manner herein before provided.

(2) The Court issuing a warrant under sub-section (1) shall forward, along with the warrant, the substance of the information against the person to be arrested together with such documents, if any, as may be sufficient to enable the Court acting under section 81 to decide whether bail should or should not be granted to the person.

Warrant directed to police officer for execution outside jurisdiction.

79. (1) When a warrant directed to a police officer is to be executed beyond the local jurisdiction of the court issuing the same, he shall ordinarily take it for endorsement either to an Executive Magistrate or to a police officer not below the rank of an officer in charge of a police station, within the local limits of whose jurisdiction the warrant is to be executed.

(2) Such Magistrate or police officer shall endorse his name thereon and such endorsement shall be sufficient authority to the police officer to whom the warrant is directed to execute the same, and the local police shall, if so required, assist such officer in executing such warrant.

(3) Whenever there is reason to believe that the delay occasioned by obtaining the endorsement of the Magistrate or police officer within whose local jurisdiction the warrant is to be executed will prevent such execution, the police officer to whom it is directed may execute the same without such endorsement in any place beyond the local jurisdiction of the court which issued it.

**   **   **

Power to take bond for appearance.

88. When any person for whose appearance or arrest the officer presiding in any court is empowered to issue a summons or warrant, is present in such court, such officer may require such person to execute a bond, with or without sureties, for his appearance in such court, or any other court to which the case may be transferred for trial.

**   **   **

Summons to produce document or other thing.

91. (1) Whenever any court or any officer in charge of a police station considers that the production of any document or other thing is necessary or desirable for the purposes of any investigation, inquiry, trial or other proceeding under this code by or before such Court or officer, such Court may issue a summons, or such officer a written order, to the person in whose possession or power such document or thing is believed to be, requiring him to attend and produce it, or to produce it, at the time and place stated in the summons or order.

(2) Any person required under this section merely to produce a document or other thing shall be deemed to have complied with the requisition if he causes such document or thing to be produced instead of attending personally to produce the same.

(3) Nothing in this section shall be deemed—

   (*a*) to affect sections 123 and 124 of the Indian Evidence Act, 1872 (1 of 1872), or the Bankers' Books Evidence Act, 1891(13 of 1891), or (*b*) to apply to a letter, postcard, telegram or other document or any parcel or thing in the custody of the postal or telegraph authority.

Procedure as to letters and telegrams.

92. (1) If any document, parcel or thing in the custody of a postal or telegraph authority is, in the opinion of the District Magistrate, Chief Judicial Magistrate, Court of Session or High Court wanted for the purpose of any investigation, inquiry, trial or other proceeding under this Code, such Magistrate or court may require the Postal or Telegraph authority, as the case may be, to deliver the document, parcel or thing to such person as the Magistrate or Court directs.

(2) If any such document, parcel or thing is, in the opinion of any other Magistrate, whether Executive or Judicial, or of any Commissioner of Police or District Superintendent of Police, wanted for any such purpose, he may require the postal or telegraph authority, as the case may be, to cause search to be made for and to detain such document, parcel or thing pending the order of a District Magistrate, Chief Judicial Magistrate or Court under sub-section (1).

When search warrant may be issued.

93. (1) (*a*) where any court has reason to believe that a person to whom a summons or order under section 91 or a requisition under sub-section (1) of section 92 has been, or might be, addressed, will not or would not produce the document or thing as required by such summons or requisition, or

(*b*) where such document or thing is not known to the Court to be in the possession of any person, or

(*c*) where the court considers that the purposes of any inquiry, trial or other proceeding under this Code will be served by a General search or inspection,

it may issue a search-warrant; and the person to whom such warrant is directed, may search or inspect in accordance therewith and the provisions hereinafter contained.

(2) The court may, if it thinks fit, specify in the warrant the particular place or part thereof to which only the search or inspection shall extend; and the person charged with the execution of such warrant shall then search or inspect only the place or part so specified.

(3) Nothing contained in this section shall authorize any Magistrate other than a District Magistrate or Chief Judicial Magistrate to grant a warrant to search for a document, parcel or other thing in the custody of the postal or telegraph authority.

Search of place suspected to contain stolen property, forged documents, etc.

94. (1) If a District Magistrate, Sub-divisional Magistrate or Magistrate of the first class, upon information and after such inquiry as he thinks necessary, has reason to believe that any place is used for the deposit or sale of stolen property, or for the deposit, sale or production of any objectionable article to which this section applies, or that any such objectionable article is deposited in any place, he may by warrant authorize any police officer above the rank of a constable—

(*a*) to enter, with such assistance as may be required, such place,

(*b*) to search the same in the manner specified in the warrant,

(c) to take possession of any property or article therein found which he reasonably suspects to be stolen property or objectionable article to which this section applies,

(d) to convey such property or article before a Magistrate, or to guard the same on the spot until the offender is taken before a Magistrate, or otherwise to dispose of it in some place of safety,

(e) to take into custody and carry before a Magistrate every person found in such place who appears to have been privy to the deposit, sale or production of any such property or article knowing or having reasonable cause to suspect it to be stolen property or, as the case may be, objectionable article to which this section applies.

(2) The objectionable articles to which this section applies are—

(a) counterfeit coin;

(b) pieces of metal made in contravention of the Metal Tokens Act, 1889 (1 of 1889), or brought into India in contravention of any notification for the time being in force under section 11 of the Customs Act, 1962 (52 of 1962);

(c) counterfeit currency note; counterfeit stamps;

(d) forged documents;

(e) false seals;

(f) obscene objects referred to in section 292 of the Indian Penal Code (45 of 1860);

(g) instruments or materials used for the production of any of the articles mentioned in clauses (a) to (f).

Power to declare certain publications forfeited and to issue search warrants for the same.

95. (1) Where—

(a) any newspaper, or book, or

(b) any document,

wherever printed, appears to the State Government to contain any matter the publication of which is punishable under section 124A or section 153A or section 153B or section 292 or section 293 or section 295A of the Indian Penal Code (45 of 1860), the State Government may, by notification, stating the grounds of its opinion, declare every copy of the issue of the newspaper containing such matter, and every copy of such book or other document to be forfeited to Government, and thereupon any police officer may seize the same wherever found in India and any Magistrate may by warrant authorize any police officer not below the rank of sub-inspector to enter upon and search for the same in any premises where any copy of such issue or any such book or other document may be or may be reasonably suspected to be.

(2) In this section and in section 96,—

(a) "newspaper" and "book" have the same meaning as in the Press and Registration of Books Act, 1867 (25 of 1867);

(*b*) "document" includes any painting, drawing or photograph, or other visible representation.

(3) No order passed or action taken under this section shall be called in question in any court otherwise than in accordance with the provisions of section 96.

Application to High Court to set aside declaration of forfeiture.

96. (1) Any person having any interest in any newspaper, book or other document, in respect of which a declaration of forfeiture has been made under section 95, may, within two months from the date of publication in the Official Gazette of such declaration, apply to the High Court to set aside such declaration on the ground that the issue of the newspaper, or the book or other document, in respect of which the declaration was made, did not contain any such matter as is referred to in sub-section (1) of section 95.

(2) Every such application shall, where the High Court consists of three or more Judges, be heard and determined by a Special Bench of the High Court composed of three Judges and where the High Court consists of less than three Judges, such Special Bench shall be composed of all the Judges of that High Court.

(3) On the hearing of any such application with reference to any newspaper, any copy of such newspaper may be given in evidence in aid of the proof of the nature or tendency of the words, signs or visible representations contained in such newspaper, in respect of which the declaration of forfeiture was made.

(4) The High Court shall, if it is not satisfied that the issue of the newspaper, or the book or other document, in respect of which the application has been made, contained any such matter as is referred to in sub-section (1) of section 95, set aside the declaration of forfeiture.

(5) Where there is a difference of opinion among the Judges forming the Special Bench, the decision shall be in accordance with the opinion of the majority of those Judges.

Search for persons wrongfully confined.

97. If any District Magistrate, Sub-divisional Magistrate or Magistrate of the first class has reason to believe that any person is confined under such circumstances that the confinement amounts to an offence, he may issue a search-warrant, and the person to whom such warrant is directed may search for the person so confined; and such search shall be made in accordance therewith, and the person, if found, shall be immediately taken before a Magistrate, who shall make such order as in the circumstances of the case seems proper.

Power to compel restoration of abducted females.

98. Upon complaint made on oath of the abduction or unlawful detention of a woman, or a female child under the age of eighteen years, for any unlawful purpose, a District Magistrate, Sub-divisional Magistrate or Magistrate of the first class may make an order for the immediate restoration of such woman to her liberty, or of such female child to her husband, parent, guardian or other person having the lawful charge of such child, and may compel compliance with such order, using such force as may be necessary.

Direction, etc., of search warrants.

99. The provisions of sections 38, 70, 72, 74, 77, 78 and 79 shall, so far as may be, apply to all search-warrants issued under section 93, section 94, section 95 or section 97.

Persons in charge of closed place to allow search.

100. (1) Whenever any place liable to search or inspection under this Chapter is closed, any person residing in, or being in charge of, such place, shall, on demand of the officer or other person executing the warrant, and on production of the warrant, allow him free ingress thereto, and afford all reasonable facilities for a search therein.

(2) If ingress into such place cannot be so obtained, the officer or other person executing the warrant may proceed in the manner provided by sub-section (2) of section 47.

(3) Where any person in or about such place is reasonably suspected of concealing about his person any article for which search should be made, such person may be searched and if such person is a woman, the search shall be made by another woman with strict regard to decency.

(4) Before making a search under this Chapter, the officer or other person about to make it shall call upon two or more independent and respectable inhabitants of the locality in which the place to be searched is situate or of any other locality if no such inhabitant of the said locality is available or is willing to be a witness to the search, to attend and witness the search and may issue an order in writing to them or any of them so to do.

(5) The search shall be made in their presence, and a list of all things seized in the course of such search and of the places in which they are respectively found shall be prepared by such officer or other person and signed by such witnesses; but no person witnessing a search under this section shall be required to attend the court as a witness of the search unless specially summoned by it.

(6) The occupant of the place searched, or some person in his behalf, shall, in every instance, be permitted to attend during the search, and a copy of the list prepared under this section, signed by the said witnesses, shall be delivered to such occupant or person.

(7) When any person is searched under sub-section (3), a list of all things taken possession of shall be prepared, and a copy thereof shall be delivered to such person.

(8) Any person who, without reasonable cause, refuses or neglects to attend and witness a search under this section, when called upon to do so by an order in writing delivered or tendered to him, shall be deemed to have committed an offence under section 187 of the Indian Penal Code (45 of 1860).

Disposal of things found in search beyond jurisdiction.

101. When, in the execution of a search-warrant at any place beyond the local jurisdiction of the court which issued the same, any of the things for which search is made, are found, such things, together with the list of the same prepared under the provisions hereinafter contained, shall be immediately taken before the court issuing the warrant, unless such place is nearer to the Magistrate having jurisdiction therein than to such court, in which case the list and things shall be immediately taken before such Magistrate; and, unless there be good cause to the contrary, such Magistrate shall make an order authorising them to be taken to such court.

Power of police officer to seize certain property.

102. (1) Any police officer may seize any property which may be alleged or suspected to have been stolen, or which may be found under circumstances which create suspicion of the Commission of any offence.

(2) Such police officer, if subordinate to the officer in charge of a police station, shall forthwith report the seizure to that officer.

(3) Every police officer acting under sub-section (1) shall forthwith report the seizure to the Magistrate having jurisdiction and where the property seized is such that it cannot be conveniently transported to the court or where there is difficulty in securing proper accommodation for the custody of such property, or where the continued retention of the property in police custody may not be considered necessary for the purpose of investigation, he may give custody thereof to any person on his executing a bond undertaking to produce the property before the Court as and when required and to give effect to the further orders of the Court as to the disposal of the same:

Provided that where the property seized under sub-section (1) is subject to speedy and natural decay and if the person entitled to the possession of such property is unknown or absent and the value of such property is less than five hundred rupees, it may forthwith be sold by auction under the orders of the Superintendent of Police and the provisions of sections 457 and 458 shall, as nearly as may be practicable, apply to the net proceeds of such sale.

Magistrate may direct search in his presence.

103. Any Magistrate may direct a search to be made in his presence of any place for the search of which he is competent to issue a search warrant.

Power to impound document, etc., produced.

104. Any court may, if it thinks fit, impound any document or thing produced before it under this Code.

Reciprocal arrangements regarding processes.

105. (1) Where a court in the territories to which this Code extends (hereafter in this section referred to as the said territories) desires that—

(*a*) a summons to an accused person, or

(*b*) a warrant for the arrest of an accused person, or

(*c*) a summons to any person requiring him to attend and produce a document or other thing, or to produce it, or

(*d*) a search warrant,

issued by it shall be served or executed at any place,—

(*i*) within the local jurisdiction of a court in any State or area in India outside the said territories, it may send such summons or warrant in duplicate by post or otherwise, to the presiding officer of that court to be served or executed; and where any summons referred to in clause (*a*) or clause (*c*) has been so served, the provisions of section 68 shall apply in relation to such summons as if the presiding officer of the court to whom it is sent were a Magistrate in the said territories;

(*ii*) in any country or place outside India in respect of which arrangements have been made by the Central Government with the Government of such country or place for service or execution of summons or warrant in relation to criminal matters (hereafter in this section referred to as the contracting State), it may send such summons or warrant in duplicate in such form, directed to such court, Judge or Magistrate, and sent to such authority for transmission, as the Central Government may, by notification, specify in this behalf.

(2) Where a court in the said territories has received for service or execution—

(*a*) a summons to an accused person, or

(*b*) a warrant for the arrest of an accused person, or

(*c*) a summons to any person requiring him to attend and produce a document or other thing, or to produce it, or

(*d*) a search warrant,

issued by—

(*i*) a court in any State or area in India outside the said territories;

(*ii*) a court, Judge or Magistrate in a contracting State,

it shall cause the same to be served or executed as if it were a summons or warrant received by it from another court in the said territories for service or execution within its local Jurisdiction; and where—

(*i*) a warrant of arrest has been executed, the person arrested shall, so far as possible, be dealt with in accordance with the procedure prescribed by sections 80 and 81,

(*ii*) a search warrant has been executed, the things found in the search shall, so far as possible, be dealt with in accordance with the procedure prescribed by section 101:

Provided that in a case where a summons or search warrant received from a contracting State has been executed, the documents or things produced or things found in the search shall be forwarded to the court issuing the summons or search warrant through such Authority as the Central Government may, by notification, specify in this behalf.

**   **   **

Search by police officer.

165. (1) Whenever an officer in charge of a police station or a police officer making an investigation has reasonable grounds for believing that anything necessary for the purposes of an investigation into any offence which he is authorised to investigate may be found in any place within the limits of the police station of which he is in charge, or to which he is attached, and that such thing cannot in his opinion be otherwise obtained without undue delay, such officer may, after recording in writing the grounds of his belief and specifying in such writing, so far as possible, the thing for which search is to be made, search, or cause search to be made, for such thing in any place within the limits of such station.

(2) A police officer proceeding under sub-section (1), shall, if practicable, conduct the search in person.

(3) If he is unable to conduct the search in person, and there is no other person competent to make the search present at the time, he may, after recording in writing his reasons for so doing, require any officer subordinate to him to make the search, and he shall deliver to such subordinate officer an order in writing, specifying the place to be searched, and so far as possible, the thing for which search is to be made; and such subordinate officer may thereupon search for such thing in such place.

(4) The provisions of this Code as to search-warrants and the general provisions as to searches contained in section 100 shall, so far as may be, apply to a search made under this section.

(5) Copies of any record made under sub-section (1) or sub-section (3) shall forthwith be sent to the nearest Magistrate empowered to take cognizance of the offence, and the owner or occupier of the place searched shall, on application, be furnished, free of cost, with a copy of the same by the Magistrate.

**   **   **

Prosecution for contempt of lawful authority of public servants, for offences against public justice and for offences relating to documents given in evidence.

195. (1) No court shall take cognizance—

(*a*)(*i*) of any offence punishable under sections 172 to 188 (both inclusive) of the Indian Penal Code (45 of 1860), or

  (*ii*) of any abetment of, or attempt to commit, such offence, or

  (*iii*) of any criminal conspiracy to commit, such offence,

   except on the complaint in writing of the public servant concerned or of some other public servant to whom he is administratively subordinate;

(*b*)(*i*) of any offence punishable under any of the following sections of the Indian Penal Code (45 of 1860), namely, sections 193 to 196 (both inclusive), 199, 200, 205 to 211 (both inclusive) and 228, when such offence is alleged to have been committed in, or in relation to, any proceeding in any court, or

  (*ii*) of any offence described in section 463, or punishable under section 471, section 475 or section 476, of the said Code, when such offence is alleged to have been committed in respect of a document produced or given in evidence, in a proceeding in any court, or

  (*iii*) of any criminal conspiracy to commit, or attempt to commit, or the abetment of, any offence specified in sub-clause (*i*) or sub-clause (*ii*),

   except on the complaint in writing of that court, or by such officer of the Court as that Court may authorise in writing in this behalf, or of some other Court to which that Court is subordinate.

(2) Where a complaint has been made by a public servant under clause (*a*) of sub-section (1) any authority to which he is administratively subordinate may order the withdrawal of the complaint and send a copy of such order to the court; and upon its receipt by the court, no further proceedings shall be taken on the complaint:

Provided that no such withdrawal shall be ordered if the trial in the court of first instance has been concluded.

(3) In clause (*b*) of sub-section (1), the term "court" means a Civil, Revenue or Criminal Court, and includes a tribunal constituted by or under a Central, provincial or State Act if declared by that Act to be a court for the purposes of this section.

(4) For the purposes of clause (*b*) of sub-section (1), a court shall be deemed to be subordinate to the court to which appeals ordinarily lie from the appealable decrees or sentences of such former court, or in the case of a civil court from whose decrees no appeal ordinarily lies, to the principal court having ordinary original civil jurisdiction within whose local jurisdiction such civil court is situate:

Provided that—

(*a*) where appeals lie to more than one court, the Appellate Court of inferior jurisdiction shall be the court to which such court shall be deemed to be subordinate;

(*b*) where appeals lie to a Civil and also to a Revenue Court, such court shall be deemed to be subordinate to the Civil or Revenue Court according to the nature of the case or proceeding in connection with which the offence is alleged to have been committed.

**   **   **

What persons may be charged jointly.

223. The following persons may be charged and tried together, namely:—

(*a*) persons accused of the same offence committed in the course of the same transaction;

(*b*) persons accused of an offence and persons accused of abetment of, or attempt to commit, such offence;

(*c*) persons accused of more than one offence of the same kind, within the meaning of section 219 committed by them jointly within the period of twelve months;

(*d*) persons accused of different offences committed in the course of the same transaction;

(*e*) persons accused of an offence which includes theft, extortion, cheating, or criminal misappropriation, and persons accused of receiving or retaining, or assisting in the disposal or concealment of, property possession of which is alleged to have been transferred by any such offence committed by the first-named persons, or of abetment of or attempting to commit any such last- named offence;

(*f*) persons accused of offences under sections 411 and 414 of the Indian Penal Code (45 of 1860) or either of those sections in respect of stolen property the possession of which has been transferred by one offence;

(g) persons accused of any offence under Chapter XII of the Indian Penal Code (45 of 1860) relating to counterfeit coin and persons accused of any other offence under the said Chapter relating to the same coin, or of abetment of or attempting to commit any such offence; and the provisions contained in the former part of this Chapter shall, so far as may be, apply to all such charges:

Provided that where a number of persons are charged with separate offences and such persons do not fall within any of the categories specified in this section, the Magistrate or Court of Session may, if such persons by an application in writing, so desire, and if he or it is satisfied that such persons would not be prejudicially affected thereby, and it is expedient so to do, try all such persons together.

RELEVANT PROVISIONS OF INDIAN PENAL CODE, 1860

**   **   **

Refusing to answer public servant authorized to question.

179. Whoever, being legally bound to state the truth on any subject to any public servant, refuses to answer any question demanded of him touching that subject by such public servant in the exercise of the legal powers of such public servant, shall be punished with simple imprisonment for a term which may extend to six months, or with fine which may extend to one thousand rupees, or with both.

Refusing to sign statement.

180. Whoever refuses to sign any statement made by him, when required to sign that statement by a public servant legally competent to require that he shall sign that statement, shall be punished with simple imprisonment for a term which may extend to three months, or with fine which may extend to five hundred rupees, or with both.

False statement on oath or affirmation to public servant or person authorized to administer an oath or affirmation.

181. Whoever, being legally bound by an oath or affirmation to state the truth on any subject to any public servant or other person authorized by law to administer such oath or affirmation, makes, to such public servant or other person as aforesaid, touching that subject, any statement which is false, and which he either knows or believes to be false or does not believe to be true, shall be punished with imprisonment of either description for a term which may extend to three years, and shall also be liable to fine.

False information, with intent to cause public servant to use his lawful power to the injury of another person.

182. Whoever gives to any public servant any information which he knows or believes to be false, intending thereby to cause, or knowing it to be likely that he will thereby cause, such public servant—

    (*a*) to do or omit anything which such public servant ought not to do or omit if the true state of facts respecting which such information is given were known by him, or

    (*b*) to use the lawful power of such public servant to the injury or annoyance of any person,

shall be punished with imprisonment of either description for a term which may extend to six months, or with fine which may extend to one thousand rupees, or with both.

Illustrations

(*a*) A informs a Magistrate that Z, a police-officer, subordinate to such Magistrate, has been guilty of neglect of duty or misconduct, knowing such information to be false, and knowing it to be likely that the information will cause the Magistrate to dismiss Z. A has committed the offence defined in this section.

(*b*) A falsely informs a public servant that Z has contraband salt in a secret place, knowing such information to be false, and knowing that it is likely that the consequence of the information will be a search of Z's premises, attended with annoyance to Z. A has committed the offence defined in this section.

(*c*) A falsely informs a policeman that he has been assaulted and robbed in the neighbourhood of a particular village. He does not mention the name of any person as one of his assailants, but knows it to be likely that in consequence of this information the police will make enquiries and institute searches in the village to the annoyance of the villagers or some of them. A has committed an offence under this section.

Resistance to the taking of property by the lawful authority of a public servant.

183. Whoever offers any resistance to the taking of any property by the lawful authority of any public servant, knowing or having reason to believe that he is such public servant, shall be punished with imprisonment of either description for a term which may extend to six months, or with fine which may extend to one thousand rupees, or with both.

Obstructing sale of property offered for sale by authority of public servant.

184. Whoever intentionally obstructs any sale of property offered for sale by the lawful authority of any public servant, as such, shall be punished with imprisonment of either description for a term which may extend to one month, or with fine which may extend to five hundred rupees, or with both.

Illegal purchase or bid for property offered for sale by authority of public servant.

185. Whoever, at any sale of property held by the lawful authority of a public servant, as such, purchases or bids for any property on account of any person, whether himself or any other, whom he knows to be under a legal incapacity to purchase that property at that sale, or bids for such property not intending to perform the obligations under which he lays himself by such bidding, shall be punished with imprisonment of either description for a term which may extend to one month, or with fine which may extend to two hundred rupees, or with both.

Obstructing public servant in discharge of public functions.

186. Whoever voluntarily obstructs any public servant in the discharge of his public functions, shall be punished with imprisonment of either description for a term which may extend to three months, or with fine which may extend to five hundred rupees, or with both.

Omission to assist public servant when bound by law to give assistance.

187. Whoever, being bound by law to render or furnish assistance to any public servant in the execution of his public duty, intentionally omits to give such assistance, shall be punished with simple imprisonment for a term which may extend to one month, or with fine which may extend to two hundred rupees, or with both;

and if such assistance be demanded of him by a public servant legally competent to make such demand for the purposes of executing any process lawfully issued by a Court of Justice, or of preventing the commission of an offence, or of suppressing a riot, or affray, or of apprehending a person charged with or guilty of an offence, or of having escaped from lawful custody, shall be punished with simple imprisonment for a term which may extend to six months, or with fine which may extend to five hundred rupees, or with both.

Disobedience to order duly promulgated by public servant.

188. Whoever, knowing that, by an order promulgated by a public servant lawfully empowered to promulgate such order, he is directed to abstain from a certain act, or to take certain order with certain property in his possession or under his management, disobeys such direction,

shall, if such disobedience causes or tends to cause obstruction, annoyance or injury, or risk of obstruction, annoyance or injury, to any persons lawfully employed, be punished with simple imprisonment for a term which may extend to one month or with fine which may extend to two hundred rupees, or with both;

and if such disobedience causes or tends to cause danger to human life, health or safety, or causes or tends to cause a riot or affray, shall be punished with imprisonment of either description for a term which may extend to six months, or with fine which may extend to one thousand rupees, or with both.

Explanation.—It is not necessary that the offender should intend to produce harm, or contemplate his disobedience as likely to produce harm. It is sufficient that he knows of the order which he disobeys, and that his disobedience produces, or is likely to produce, harm.

Illustration

An order is promulgated by a public servant lawfully empowered to promulgate such order, directing that a religious procession shall not pass down a certain street. A knowingly disobeys the order, and thereby causes danger of riot. A has committed the offence defined in this section.

Threat of injury to public servant.

189. Whoever holds out any threat of injury to any public servant, or to any person in whom he believes that public servant to be interested, for the purpose of inducing that public servant to do any act, or to forbear or delay to do any act, connected with the exercise of the public functions of such public servant, shall be punished with imprisonment of either description for a term which may extend to two years, or with fine, or with both.

Threat of injury to induce person to refrain from applying for protection to public servant.

190. Whoever holds out any threat of injury to any person for the purpose of inducing that person to refrain or desist from making a legal application for protection against any injury to any public servant legally empowered as such to give such protection, or to cause such protection to be given, shall be punished with imprisonment of either description for a term which may extend to one year, or with fine, or with both.

CHAPTER XI
OF FALSE EVIDENCE AND OFFENCES
AGAINST PUBLIC JUSTICE

Giving false evidence.

191. Whoever, being legally bound by an oath or by an express provision of law to state the truth, or being bound by law to make a declaration upon any subject, makes any statement which is false, and which he either knows or believes to be false or does not believe to be true, is said to give false evidence.

Explanation 1.—A statement is within the meaning of this section, whether it is made verbally or otherwise.

Explanation 2.—A false statement as to the belief of the person attesting is within the meaning of this section, and a person may be guilty of giving false evidence by stating that he believes a thing which he does not believe, as well as by stating that he knows a thing which he does not know.

Illustrations

(a) A, in support of a just claim which B has against Z for one thousand rupees, falsely swears on a trial that he heard Z admit the justice of B's claim. A has given false evidence.

(b) A, being bound by an oath to state the truth, states that he believes a certain signature to be the handwriting of Z, when he does not believe it to be the handwriting of Z. Here A states that which he knows to be false, and therefore gives false evidence.

(c) A, knowing the general character of Z's handwriting, states that he believes a certain signature to be the handwriting of Z; A in good faith believing it to be so. Here A's statement is merely as to his belief, and is true as to his belief, and therefore, although the signature may not be the handwriting of Z, A has not given false evidence.

(d) A, being bound by an oath to state the truth, states that he knows that Z was at a particular place on a particular day, not knowing anything upon the subject. A gives false evidence whether Z was at that place on the day named or not.

(e) A, an interpreter or translator, gives or certifies as a true interpretation or translation of a statement or document, which he is bound by oath to interpret or translate truly, that which is not and which he does not believe to be a true interpretation or translation. A has given false evidence.

RELEVANT PROVISIONS OF CODE OF CIVIL PROCEDURE, 1908

Summons to defendants.

27. Where a suit has been duly instituted, a summons may be issued to the defendant to appear and answer the claim and may be served in manner prescribed on such day not beyond thirty days from date of the institution of the suit.

Service of summons where defendant resides in another State.

28. (1) A summons may be sent for service in another State to such Court and in such manner as may be prescribed by rules in force in that State.

(2) The Court to which such summons is sent shall, upon receipt thereof, proceed as if it had been issued by such Court and shall then return the summons to the Court of issue together with the record (if any) of its proceedings with regard thereto.

(3) Where the language of the summons sent for service in another State is different from the language of the record referred to in sub-section (2), a translation of the record,—

(a) in Hindi, where the language of the Court issuing the summons in Hindi, or

(b) in Hindi or English where the language of such record is other than Hindi or English,

shall also be sent together with the record sent under that sub-section.

Service of foreign summonses.

29. Summonses and other processes issued by—

(a) any Civil or Revenue Court established in any part of India to which the provisions of this Code do not extent, or

(b) any Civil or Revenue Court established or continued by the authority of the Central Government outside India, or

(c) any other Civil or Revenue Court outside India to which the Central Government has, by notification in the Official Gazette, declared the provisions of this section to apply,

may be sent to the Courts in the territories to which this Code extends, and served as if they were summonses issued by such Courts.

Power to order discovery and the like.

30. Subject to such conditions and limitations as may be prescribed, the Court may, at any time, either of its own motion or on the application of any party,—

(a) make such orders as may be necessary or reasonable in all matters relating to the delivery and answering of interrogatories, the admission of documents and facts, and the discovery, inspection, production, impounding and return of documents or other material objects producible as evidence;

(*b*) issue summonses to persons whose attendance is required either to give evidence or to produce documents or such other objects as aforesaid;

(*c*) order any fact to be proved by affidavit.

Summons to witness.

31. The provisions in sections 27, 28 and 29 shall apply to summonses to give evidence or to produce documents or other material objects.

Penalty for default

32. The Court may compel the attendance of any person to whom a summons has been issued under section 30 and for that purpose may—

(*a*) issue a warrant for his arrest;

(*b*) attach and sell his property;

(*c*) impose a fine upon him not exceeding five thousand rupees;

(*d*) order him to furnish security for his appearance and in default commit him to the civil prison.

**   **   **

Power of court to issue commissions.

75. Subject to such conditions and limitations as may be prescribed, the court may issue a commission—

(*a*) to examine any person;

(*b*) to make a local investigation;

(*c*) to examine or adjust accounts; or

(*d*) to make a partition;

(*e*) to hold a scientific, technical, or expert investigation;

(*f*) to conduct sale of property which is subject to speedy and natural decay and which is in the custody of the Court pending the determination of the suit;

(*g*) to perform any ministerial act.

Commission to another Court.

76. (1) A commission for the examination of any person may be issued to any Court (not being a High Court) situate in a State other than the State in which the Court of issue is situate and having jurisdiction in the place in which the person to be examined resides.

(2) Every Court receiving a commission for the examination of any person under sub-section (1) shall examine him or cause him to be examined pursuant thereto, and the commission, when it has been duly executed, shall be returned together with the evidence taken under it to the Court from which it was issued, unless the order for issuing the commission has otherwise directed, in which case the commission shall be returned in terms of such order.

**   **   **

Commissions issued by foreign Courts.

78. Subject to such conditions and limitations as may be prescribed, the provisions as to the execution and return of commissions for the examination of witnesses shall apply to commissions issued by or as the instance of—

    (*a*) Courts situate in any part of India to which the provisions of this Code do not extend; or

    (*b*) Courts established or continued by the authority of the Central Government outside India; or

    (*c*) Courts of any State or country outside India.

Suits by or against Government

79. In a suit by or against the Government, the authority to be named as plaintiff or defendant, as the case may be, shall be—

    (*a*) in the case of a suit by or against the Central Government, the Union of India, and

    (*b*) in the case of a suit by or against a State Government, the State.

** ** **

Exemption from arrest and personal appearance.

81. In a suit instituted against a public officer in respect of any act purporting to be done by him in his official capacity—

    (*a*) the defendant shall not be liable to arrest nor his property to attachment otherwise than in execution of a decree, and

    (*b*) where the Court is satisfied that the defendant cannot absent himself from his duty without detriment to the public service, it shall exempt him from appearing in person.

EXTENSION OF TIME LIMITS DUE TO COVID-19

TAXATION AND OTHER LAWS (RELAXATION OF CERTAIN PROVISIONS) ORDINANCE, 2020

Promulgated by the President in the Seventy-first Year of the Republic of India.

An Ordinance to provide relaxation in the provisions of certain Acts and for matters connected therewith or incidental thereto.

WHEREAS, in view of the spread of pandemic COVID-19 across many countries of the world including India, causing immense loss to the lives of people, it has become imperative to relax certain provisions, including extension of time limit, in the taxation and other laws;

AND WHEREAS, Parliament is not in session and the President is satisfied that circumstances exist which render it necessary for him to take immediate action;

NOW, THEREFORE, in exercise of the powers conferred by clause (*1*) of article 123 of the Constitution, the President is pleased to promulgate the following Ordinance:—

CHAPTER I

PRELIMINARY

Short title and commencement.

1. (1) This Ordinance may be called the Taxation and Other Laws (Relaxation of Certain Provisions) Ordinance, 2020.

(2) Save as otherwise provided, it shall come into force at once.

Definitions.

2. (1) In this Ordinance, unless the context otherwise requires,—

    (*a*) "specified Act" means—

        (*i*) the Wealth-tax Act, 1957 (27 of 1957);

        (*ii*) the Income-tax Act, 1961 (43 of 1961);

        (*iii*) the Prohibition of *Benami* Property Transactions Act, 1988 (45 of 1988);

        (*iv*) Chapter VII of the Finance (No. 2) Act, 2004 (22 of 2004);

    (*v*) Chapter VII of the Finance Act, 2013 (17 of 2013);

    (*vi*) the Black Money (Undisclosed Foreign Income and Assets) and Imposition of Tax Act, 2015 (22 of 2015);

    (*vii*) Chapter VIII of the Finance Act, 2016 (28 of 2016); or

    (*viii*) the Direct Tax *Vivad se Vishwas* Act, 2020 (3 of 2020);

  (*b*) "notification" means the notification published in the Official Gazette.

(2) The words and expressions used herein and not defined, but defined in the specified Act, the Central Excise Act, 1944 (1 of 1944), the Customs Act, 1962 (52 of 1962), the Customs Tariff Act, 1975 (51 of 1975) or the Finance Act, 1994 (32 of 1994), as the case may be, shall have the meaning respectively assigned to them in that Act.

CHAPTER II

RELAXATION OF CERTAIN PROVISIONS OF SPECIFIED ACT

Relaxation of certain provisions of specified Act.

3. (1) Where, any time limit has been specified in, or prescribed or notified under, the specified Act which falls during the period from the 20th day of March, 2020 to the 29th day of June, 2020 or such other date after the 29th day of June, 2020 as the Central Government may, by notification, specify in this behalf, for the completion or compliance of such action as—

  (*a*) completion of any proceeding or passing of any order or issuance of any notice, intimation, notification, sanction or approval or such other action, by whatever name called, by any authority, commission or tribunal, by whatever name called, under the provisions of the specified Act; or

  (*b*) filing of any appeal, reply or application or furnishing of any report, document, return, statement or such other record, by whatever name called, under the provisions of the specified Act; or

  (*c*) in case where the specified Act is the Income-tax Act, 1961 (43 of 1961),—

    (*i*) making of investment, deposit, payment, acquisition, purchase, construction or such other action, by whatever name called, for the purposes of claiming any deduction, exemption or allowance under the provisions contained in—

      (*I*) sections 54 to 54GB or under any provisions of Chapter VI-A under the heading *"B.—Deductions in respect of certain payments"* thereof; or

      (*II*) such other provisions of that Act, subject to fulfilment of such conditions, as the Central Government may, by notification, specify; or (*ii*) beginning of manufacture or production of articles or things or providing any services referred to in section 10AA of that Act, in a case where the letter of approval, required to be issued in accordance with the provisions of the Special Economic Zones Act, 2005 (28 of 2005), has been issued on or before the 31st day of March, 2020,

and where completion or compliance of such action has not been made within such time, then, the time limit for completion or compliance of such action shall, notwithstanding anything contained in the specified Act, stand extended to the 30th day of June, 2020, or such other date after the 30th day of June, 2020, as the Central Government may, by notification, specify in this behalf:

Provided that the Central Government may specify different dates for completion or compliance of different actions :

Provided further that such action shall not include payment of any amount as is referred to in sub-section (2).

(2) Where any due date has been specified in, or prescribed or notified under, the specified Act for payment of any amount towards tax or levy, by whatever name called, which falls during the period from the 20th day of March, 2020 to the 29th day of June, 2020 or such other date after the 29th day of June, 2020 as the Central Government may, by notification, specify in this behalf, and such amount has not been paid within such date, but has been paid on or before the 30th day of June, 2020, or such other date after the 30th day of June, 2020 as the Central Government may, by notification, specify in this behalf, then, notwithstanding anything contained in the specified Act,—

(*a*) the rate of interest payable, if any, in respect of such amount for the period of delay shall not exceed three-fourth per cent for every month or part thereof;

(*b*) no penalty shall be levied and no prosecution shall be sanctioned in respect of such amount for the period of delay.

Explanation.—For the purposes of this sub-section, "the period of delay" means the period between the due date and the date on which the amount has been paid.

CHAPTER III

AMENDMENT TO THE INCOME-TAX ACT, 1961

Amendment of sections 10 and 80G of Act 43 of 1961.

4. In the Income-tax Act, 1961 (43 of 1961), with effect from the 1st day of April, 2020,—

(*i*) in section 10, in *clause* (*23C*), in sub-clause (*i*), after the word "Fund", the words and brackets "or the Prime Minister's Citizen Assistance and Relief in Emergency Situations Fund (PM CARES FUND)" shall be inserted;

(*ii*) in section 80G, in sub-section (2), in clause (*a*), in sub-clause (*iiia*), after the word "Fund", the words and brackets "or the Prime

Minister's Citizen Assistance and Relief in Emergency Situations Fund (PM CARES FUND)" shall be inserted.

CHAPTER IV
AMENDMENTS TO THE DIRECT TAX
VIVAD SE VISHWAS ACT

Amendment of section 3 of Act 3 of 2020.

5. In section 3 of the Direct Tax *Vivad se Vishwas* Act, 2020,—

(*a*) in third column, in the heading, for the figures, letters and words "31st day of March, 2020", the figures, letters and words "30th day of June, 2020" shall be substituted;

(*b*) in fourth column, in the heading, for the figures, letters and words "1st day of April, 2020", the figures, letters and words "1st day of July, 2020" shall be substituted.

CHAPTER V
RELAXATION OF TIME LIMIT UNDER
CERTAIN INDIRECT TAX LAWS

Relaxation of time limit under Central Excise Act, 1944, Customs Act, 1962, Customs Tariff Act, 1975 and Finance Act, 1994.

6. Notwithstanding anything contained in the Central Excise Act, 1944 (1 of 1944), the Customs Act, 1962 (52 of 1962) (except sections 30, 30A, 41, 41A, 46 and 47), the Customs Tariff Act, 1975 (51 of 1975) or Chapter V of the Finance Act, 1994 (32 of 1994), as it stood prior to its omission *vide* section 173 of the Central Goods and Services Tax Act, 2017 with effect from the 1st day of July, 2017, the time limit specified in, or prescribed or notified under, the said Acts which falls during the period from the 20th day of March, 2020 to the 29th day of June, 2020 or such other date after the 29th day of June, 2020 as the Central Government may, by notification, specify, for the completion or compliance of such action as—

(*a*) completion of any proceeding or issuance of any order, notice, intimation, notification or sanction or approval, by whatever name called, by any authority, commission, tribunal, by whatever name called; or

(*b*) filing of any appeal, reply or application or furnishing of any report, document, return or statement, by whatever name called,

shall, notwithstanding that completion or compliance of such action has not been made within such time, stand extended to the 30th day of June, 2020 or such other date after the 30th day of June, 2020 as the Central Government may, by notification, specify in this behalf:

Provided that the Central Government may specify different dates for completion or compliance of different actions under clause (*a*) or clause (*b*).

CHAPTER VI
AMENDMENT TO THE FINANCE (NO. 2) ACT, 2019

Amendment of section 127 of Act 23 of 2019.

7. In section 127 of the Finance (No. 2) Act, 2019,—

(*i*) in sub-section (1), for the words "within a period of sixty days from the date of receipt of the said declaration", the words, figures and letters "on or before the 31st day of May, 2020" shall be substituted;

(*ii*) in sub-section (2), for the words "within thirty days of the date of receipt of the declaration", the words, figures and letters "on or before the 1st day of May, 2020" shall be substituted;

(*iii*) in sub-section (4), for the words "within a period of sixty days from the date of receipt of the declaration", the words, figures and letters "on or before the 31st day of May, 2020" shall be substituted;

(*iv*) in sub-section (5), for the words "within a period of thirty days from the date of issue of such statement", the words, figures and letters "on or before the 30th day of June, 2020" shall be substituted.

CHAPTER VII
AMENDMENT TO THE CENTRAL GOODS AND SERVICES TAX ACT, 2017

Insertion of new section 168A in Act 12 of 2017.

8. After section 168 of the Central Goods and Services Tax Act, 2017, the following section shall be inserted, namely:—

'**168A.** *Power of Government to extend time limit in special circumstances.*—(1) Notwithstanding anything contained in this Act, the Government may, on the recommendations of the Council, by notification, extend the time limit specified in, or prescribed or notified under, this Act in respect of actions which cannot be completed or complied with due to *force majeure*.

(2) The power to issue notification under sub-section (1) shall include the power to give retrospective effect to such notification from a date not earlier than the date of commencement of this Act.

Explanation.—For the purposes of this section, the expression "*force majeure*" means a case of war, epidemic, flood, drought, fire, cyclone, earthquake or any other calamity caused by nature or otherwise affecting the implementation of any of the provisions of this Act.'.

2

TAXATION AND OTHER LAWS (RELAXATION AND AMENDMENT OF CERTAIN PROVISIONS) ACT, 2020

An Act to provide for relaxation and amendment of provisions of certain Acts and for matters connected therewith or incidental thereto

BE it enacted by Parliament in the Seventy-first Year of the Republic of India as follows:—

CHAPTER I

PRELIMINARY

Short title and commencement.

1. (1) This Act may be called the Taxation and Other Laws (Relaxation and Amendment of Certain Provisions) Act, 2020.

(2) Save as otherwise provided, it shall be deemed to have come into force on the 31st day of March, 2020.

Definitions.

2. (1) In this Act, unless the context otherwise requires,—

(*a*) "notification" means the notification published in the Official Gazette;

(*b*) "specified Act" means—

(*i*) the Wealth-tax Act, 1957 (27 of 1957);

(*ii*) the Income-tax Act, 1961 (43 of 1961);

(*iii*) the Prohibition of Benami Property Transactions Act, 1988 (45 of 1988);

(*iv*) Chapter VII of the Finance (No. 2) Act, 2004 (22 of 2004);

(*v*) Chapter VII of the Finance Act, 2013 (17 of 2013);

(*vi*) the Black Money (Undisclosed Foreign Income and Assets) and Imposition of Tax Act, 2015 (22 of 2015);

(*vii*) Chapter VIII of the Finance Act, 2016 (28 of 2016); or

(*viii*) the Direct Tax *Vivad* se *Vishwas* Act, 2020 (3 of 2020).

(2) The words and expressions used herein and not defined, but defined in the specified Act, the Central Excise Act, 1944 (1 of 1944), the Customs Act, 1962 (52 of 1962), the Customs Tariff Act, 1975 (51 of 1975) or the Finance Act, 1994 (32 of 1994), as the case may be, shall have the same meaning respectively assigned to them in that Act.

CHAPTER II

RELAXATION OF CERTAIN PROVISIONS OF SPECIFIED ACT

Relaxation of certain provisions of specified Act.

3. (1) Where, any time limit has been specified in, or prescribed or notified under, the specified Act which falls during the period from the 20th day of March, 2020 to the 31st day of December, 2020, or such other date after the 31st day of December, 2020, as the Central Government may, by notification, specify in this behalf, for the completion or compliance of such action as—

(*a*) completion of any proceeding or passing of any order or issuance of any notice, intimation, notification, sanction or approval, or such other action, by whatever name called, by any authority, commission or tribunal, by whatever name called, under the provisions of the specified Act; or

(*b*) filing of any appeal, reply or application or furnishing of any report, document, return or statement or such other record, by whatever name called, under the provisions of the specified Act; or

(*c*) in case where the specified Act is the Income-tax Act, 1961 (43 of 1961),—

(*i*) making of investment, deposit, payment, acquisition, purchase, construction or such other action, by whatever name called, for the purposes of claiming any deduction, exemption or allowance under the provisions contained in—

(*I*) sections 54 to 54GB, or under any provisions of Chapter VI-A under the heading *"B.—Deductions in respect of certain payments"* thereof; or

(*II*) such other provisions of that Act, subject to fulfilment of such conditions, as the Central Government may, by notification, specify; or

(*ii*) beginning of manufacture or production of articles or things or providing any services referred to in section 10AA of that Act, in a case where the letter of approval, required to be issued in accordance with the provisions of the Special Economic Zones Act, 2005 (28 of 2005), has been issued on or before the 31st day of March, 2020,

and where completion or compliance of such action has not been made within such time, then, the time limit for completion or compliance of such action shall, notwithstanding anything contained in the specified Act, stand extended to the 31st day of March, 2021, or such other date after the 31st day of March, 2021, as the Central Government may, by notification, specify in this behalf:

Provided that the Central Government may specify different dates for completion or compliance of different actions:

Provided further that such action shall not include payment of any amount as is referred to in sub-section (2):

Provided also that where the specified Act is the Income-tax Act, 1961 (43 of 1961) and the compliance relates to—

(i) furnishing of return under section 139 thereof, for the assessment year commencing on the—

(a) 1st day of April, 2019, the provision of this sub-section shall have the effect as if for the figures, letters and words "31st day of March, 2021", the figures, letters and words "30th day of September, 2020" had been substituted;

(b) 1st day of April, 2020, the provision of this sub-section shall have the effect as if for the figures, letters and words "31st day of March, 2021", the figures, letters and words "30th day of November, 2020" had been substituted;

(ii) delivering of statement of deduction of tax at source under sub-section (2A) of section 200 of that Act or statement of collection of tax at source under sub-section (3A) of section 206C thereof for the month of February or March, 2020, or for the quarter ending on the 31st day of March, 2020, as the case may be, the provision of this sub-section shall have the effect as if for the figures, letters and words "31st day of March, 2021", the figures, letters and words "15th day of July, 2020" had been substituted;

(iii) delivering of statement of deduction of tax at source under sub-section (3) of section 200 of that Act or statement of collection of tax at source under proviso to sub-section (3) of section 206C thereof for the month of February or March, 2020, or for the quarter ending on the 31st day of March, 2020, as the case may be, the provision of this sub-section shall have the effect as if for the figures, letters and words "31st day of March, 2021", the figures, letters and words "31st day of July, 2020" had been substituted;

(iv) furnishing of certificate under section 203 of that Act in respect of deduction or payment of tax under section 192 thereof for the financial year commencing on the 1st day of April, 2019, the provision of this sub-section shall have the effect as if for the figures, letters and words "31st day of March, 2021", the figures, letters and words "15th day of August, 2020" had been substituted;

(v) sections 54 to 54GB of that Act, referred to in item (I) of sub-clause (i) of clause (c), or sub-clause (ii) of the said clause, the provision of this sub-section shall have the effect as if—

(a) for the figures, letters and words "31st day of December, 2020", the figures, letters and words "29th day of September, 2020" had been substituted for the time limit for the completion or compliance; and (*b*) for the figures, letters and words "31st day of March, 2021", the figures, letters and words "30th day of September, 2020" had been substituted for making such completion or compliance;

(*vi*) any provisions of Chapter VI-A under the heading *"B.—Deductions in respect of certain payments"* of that Act, referred to in item (*I*) of sub-clause (*i*) of clause (*c*), the provision of this sub-section shall have the effect as if—

(*a*) for the figures, letters and words "31st day of December, 2020", the figures, letters and words "30th day of July, 2020" had been substituted for the time limit for the completion or compliance; and

(*b*) for the figures, letters and words "31st day of March, 2021", the figures, letters and words "31st day of July, 2020" had been substituted for making such completion or compliance;

(*vii*) furnishing of report of audit under any provision thereof for the assessment year commencing on the 1st day of April, 2020, the provision of this sub-section shall have the effect as if for the figures, letters and words "31st day of March, 2021", the figures, letters and words "31st day of October, 2020" had been substituted:

Provided also that the extension of the date as referred to in sub-clause (*b*) of clause (*i*) of the third proviso shall not apply to *Explanation 1* to section 234A of the Income-tax Act, 1961 (43 of 1961) in cases where the amount of tax on the total income as reduced by the amount as specified in clauses (*i*) to (*vi*) of sub-section (1) of the said section exceeds one lakh rupees:

Provided also that for the purposes of the fourth proviso, in case of an individual resident in India referred to in sub-section (2) of section 207 of the Income-tax Act, 1961 (43 of 1961), the tax paid by him under section 140A of that Act within the due date (before extension) provided in that Act, shall be deemed to be the advance tax:

Provided also that where the specified Act is the Direct Tax *Vivad Se Vishwas* Act, 2020 (3 of 2020), the provision of this sub-section shall have the effect as if—

(*a*) for the figures, letters and words "31st day of December, 2020", the figures, letters and words "30th day of December, 2020" had been substituted for the time limit for the completion or compliance of the action; and

(*b*) for the figures, letters and words "31st day of March, 2021", the figures, letters and words "31st day of December, 2020" had been substituted for making such completion or compliance.

(2) Where any due date has been specified in, or prescribed or notified under the specified Act for payment of any amount towards tax or levy, by whatever name called, which falls during the period from the 20th day of March, 2020 to the 29th day of June, 2020 or such other date after the 29th day of June, 2020 as the

Central Government may, by notification, specify in this behalf, and if such amount has not been paid within such date, but has been paid on or before the 30th day of June, 2020, or such other date after the 30th day of June, 2020 as the Central Government may, by notification, specify in this behalf, then, notwithstanding anything contained in the specified Act,—

      (*a*) the rate of interest payable, if any, in respect of such amount for the period of delay shall not exceed three-fourth per cent for every month or part thereof;

      (*b*) no penalty shall be levied and no prosecution shall be sanctioned in respect of such amount for the period of delay.

Explanation.—For the purposes of this sub-section, "the period of delay" means the period between the due date and the date on which the amount has been paid.

CHAPTER III

AMENDMENTS TO THE INCOME-TAX ACT, 1961

Amendment of Act 43 of 1961.

4. In the Income-tax Act, 1961,—

    (*I*) in section 6, with effect from the 1st day of April, 2021,—

      (*a*) in clause (*1*), in *Explanation 1*, in clause (*b*), for the words "the citizen or person of Indian origin", the words "such person" shall be substituted;

      (*b*) in clause (*1A*), the following *Explanation* shall be inserted, namely:—

        "*Explanation.*—For the removal of doubts, it is hereby declared that this clause shall not apply in case of an individual who is said to be resident in India in the previous year under clause (*1*).";

      (*c*) in clause (*6*), in the *Explanation*, the words "and which is not deemed to accrue or arise in India." shall be added at the end;

    (*II*) in section 10,

      (*a*) in clause (*4D*), with effect from the 1st day of April, 2021,—

        (*i*) for the words "convertible foreign exchange, to the extent such income accrued or arisen to, or is received in respect of units held by a non-resident", the words and brackets 'convertible foreign exchange or as a result of transfer of securities (other than shares in a company resident in India) or any income from securities issued by a non-resident (not being a permanent establishment of a non-resident in India) and where such income otherwise does not accrue or arise in India or any income from a securitisation trust which is chargeable under the head "profits and gains of business or profession", to the extent such income accrued or arisen to, or is received, is attributable to units held by non-resident (not being the permanent establishment of a non-resident in India) computed in the prescribed manner' shall be substituted;

(*ii*) in the *Explanation*, after clause (*b*), the following clauses shall be inserted, namely:—

'(*ba*) "permanent establishment" shall have the same meaning assigned to it in clause (*iiia*) of section 92F;

(*bb*) "securities" shall have the same meaning as assigned to it in clause (*h*) of section 2 of the Securities Contracts (Regulation) Act, 1956 (42 of 1956) and shall also include such other securities or instruments as may be notified by the Central Government in the Official Gazette in this behalf;

(*bc*) "securitisation trust" shall have the same meaning assigned to it in clause (*d*) of the *Explanation* to section 115TCA;';

(*b*) in clause (*23C*),—

(*i*) in sub-clause (*i*), after the word "Fund", the words and brackets "or the Prime Minister's Citizen Assistance and Relief in Emergency Situations Fund (PM CARES FUND)" shall be inserted and shall be deemed to have been inserted with effect from the 1st day of April, 2020;

(*ii*) for the first and second provisos,—

(*A*) with effect from the 1st day of June, 2020, the following provisos shall be substituted and shall be deemed to have been substituted, namely:—

"Provided that the fund or trust or institution or any university or other educational institution or any hospital or other medical institution referred to in sub-clause (*iv*) or sub-clause (*v*) or sub-clause (*vi*) or sub-clause (*via*) shall make an application in the prescribed form and manner to the prescribed authority for the purpose of grant of the exemption, or continuance thereof, under sub-clause (*iv*) or sub-clause (*v*) or sub-clause (*vi*) or sub-clause (*via*) :

Provided further that the prescribed authority, before approving any fund or trust or institution or any university or other educational institution or any hospital or other medical institution, under sub-clause (*iv*) or sub-clause (*v*) or sub-clause (*vi*) or sub-clause (*via*), may call for such documents (including audited annual accounts) or information from the fund or trust or institution or any university or other educational institution or any hospital or other medical institution, as the case may be, as it thinks necessary in order to satisfy itself about the genuineness of the activities of such fund or trust or institution or any university or other educational institution or any hospital or other medical institution, as the case may be, and the compliance of such requirements under any other law for the time being in force by such fund or trust or institution or any university or other educational institution or any hospital or other medical institution, as the case may be, as are material for the purpose of achieving its objects and the prescribed authority may also make such inquiries as it deems necessary in this behalf:";

(B) with effect from the 1st day of April, 2021, the following provisos shall be substituted, namely:—

"**Provided** that the exemption to the fund or trust or institution or university or other educational institution or hospital or other medical institution referred to in sub-clause (*iv*) or sub-clause (*v*) or sub-clause (*vi*) or sub-clause (*via*), under the respective sub-clauses, shall not be available to it unless such fund or trust or institution or university or other educational institution or hospital or other medical institution makes an application in the prescribed form and manner to the Principal Commissioner or Commissioner, for grant of approval,—

(*i*) where such fund or trust or institution or university or other educational institution or hospital or other medical institution is approved under the second proviso [as it stood immediately before its amendment by the Taxation and Other Laws (Relaxation and Amendment of Certain Provisions) Act, 2020], within three months from the 1st day of April, 2021;

(*ii*) where such fund or trust or institution or university or other educational institution or hospital or other medical institution is approved and the period of such approval is due to expire, at least six months prior to expiry of the said period;

(*iii*) where such fund or trust or institution or university or other educational institution or hospital or other medical institution has been provisionally approved, at least six months prior to expiry of the period of the provisional approval or within six months of commencement of its activities, whichever is earlier;

(*iv*) in any other case, at least one month prior to the commencement of the previous year relevant to the assessment year from which the said approval is sought,

and the said fund or trust or institution or university or other educational institution or hospital or other medical institution is approved under the second proviso:

Provided further that the Principal Commissioner or Commissioner, on receipt of an application made under the first proviso, shall,—

(*i*) where the application is made under clause (*i*) of the said proviso, pass an order in writing granting approval to it for a period of five years;

(*ii*) where the application is made under clause (*ii*) or clause (*iii*) of the said proviso,—

(*a*) call for such documents or information from it or make such inquiries as he thinks necessary in order to satisfy himself about—

(*A*) the genuineness of activities of such fund or trust or institution or university or other educational institution or hospital or other medical institution; and

(*B*) the compliance of such requirements of any other law for the time being in force by it as are material for the purpose of achieving its objects; and

(*b*) after satisfying himself about the objects and the genuineness of its activities under item (*A*), and compliance of the requirements under item (*B*), of sub-clause (*a*),—

(*A*) pass an order in writing granting approval to it for a period of five years;

(*B*) if he is not so satisfied, pass an order in writing rejecting such application and also cancelling its approval after affording it a reasonable opportunity of being heard;

(*iii*) where the application is made under clause (*iv*) of the said proviso, pass an order in writing granting approval to it provisionally for a period of three years from the assessment year from which the registration is sought, and send a copy of such order to the fund or trust or institution or university or other educational institution or hospital or other medical institution:";

  (*iv*) for the eighth and ninth provisos,—

    (*A*) with effect from the 1st day of June, 2020, the following provisos shall be substituted and shall be deemed to have been substituted, namely:—

    "**Provided also** that any notification issued by the Central Government under sub-clause (*iv*) or sub-clause (*v*), before the date on which the Taxation Laws (Amendment) Bill, 2006 receives the assent of the President, shall, at any one time, have effect for such assessment year or years, not exceeding three assessment years (including an assessment year or years commencing before the date on which such notification is issued) as may be specified in the notification:

    Provided also that where an application under the first proviso is made on or after the date on which the Taxation Laws (Amendment) Bill, 2006 receives the assent of the President, every notification under sub-clause (*iv*) or sub-clause (*v*) shall be issued or approval under sub-clause (*iv*) or sub-clause (*v*) or sub-clause (*vi*) or sub-clause (*via*) shall be granted or an order rejecting the application shall be passed within the period of twelve months from the end of the month in which such application was received:";

    (*B*) with effect from the 1st day of April, 2021, the following provisos shall be substituted, namely:—

    "**Provided also** that any approval granted under the second proviso shall apply in relation to the income of the fund or trust or institution or university or other educational institution or hospital or other medical institution,—

      (*i*) where the application is made under clause (*i*) of the first proviso, from the assessment year from which approval was earlier granted to it;

      (*ii*) where the application is made under clause (*iii*) of the first proviso, from the first of the assessment years for which it was provisionally approved;

      (*iii*) in any other case, from the assessment year immediately following the financial year in which such application is made:

    Provided also that the order under clause (*i*), sub-clause (*b*) of clause (*ii*) and clause (*iii*) of the second proviso shall be passed, in such form and manner as may be prescribed, before expiry of the period of three months, six months and one month, respectively, calculated from the end of the month in which the application was received:";

(*iv*) in the twelfth proviso, for the word, figures and letters "section 12AA", the words, figures and letters "section 12AA or section 12AB" shall be substituted with effect from the 1st day of April, 2021;

(*v*) after fifteenth proviso, with effect from the 1st day of June, 2020, the following proviso shall be inserted and shall be deemed to have been inserted, namely:—

"**Provided also** that in case the fund or trust or institution or any university or other educational institution or any hospital or other medical institution referred to in the first proviso makes an application on or after the 1st day of June, 2006 for the purposes of grant of exemption or continuance thereof, such application shall be made on or before the 30th day of September of the relevant assessment year from which the exemption is sought:";

(*vi*) with effect from the 1st day of April, 2021, the sixteenth proviso as so inserted, shall be omitted;

(*vii*) for the eighteenth proviso,—

(*A*) with effect from the 1st day of June, 2020, the following proviso shall be substituted and shall be deemed to have been substituted, namely:—

"**Provided also** that all pending applications, on which no notification has been issued under sub-clause (*iv*) or sub-clause (*v*) before the 1st day of June, 2007, shall stand transferred on that day to the prescribed authority and the prescribed authority may proceed with such applications under those sub-clauses from the stage at which they were on that day:";

(*B*) with effect from the 1st day of April, 2021, the following proviso shall be substituted, namely:—

"**Provided also** that all applications made under the first proviso [as it stood before its amendment by the Taxation and Other Laws (Relaxation and Amendment of Certain Provisions) Act, 2020] pending before the Principal Commissioner or Commissioner, on which no order has been passed before the 1st day of April, 2021, shall be deemed to be applications made under clause (*iv*) of the first proviso on that date:";

(*c*) after clause (*23FBB*), the following clause shall be inserted, with effect from the 1st day of April, 2021, namely:—

"(*23FBC*) any income accruing or arising to, or received by, a unit holder from a specified fund or on transfer of units in a specified fund.

Explanation.—For the purposes of this clause, the expressions—

(*a*) "specified fund" shall have the same meaning as assigned to it in clause (*c*) of the *Explanation* to clause (*4D*);

(*b*) "unit" means beneficial interest of an investor in the fund and shall include shares or partnership interests.";

(*d*) in clause (*23FE*), in the *Explanation*, with effect from the 1st day of April, 2021,—

(*i*) in clause (*a*), in sub-clause (*ii*), for the words "United Arab Emirates", the words "Abu Dhabi" shall be substituted;

(*ii*) in clause (*b*), in sub-clause (*vi*), after the words "for this purpose", the words "and fulfils conditions specified in such notification" shall be inserted;

(*iii*) in clause (*c*), in sub-clause (*iv*), for the words "for this pur-pose", the words "for this purpose and fulfils conditions specified in such notification" shall be substituted;

(*III*) in section 11,—

(*a*) in sub-section (1), in *Explanation 2*, after the word, figures and letters "section 12AA", the words, figures and letters "or section 12AB, as the case may be" shall be inserted with effect from the 1st day of April, 2021;

(*b*) in sub-section (7),—

(*i*) for the words, figures and letters "under section 12AA or section 12AB", the words, brackets, letters and figures "under clause (*b*) of sub-section (1) of section 12AA" shall be substi-tuted and shall be deemed to have been substituted with effect from the 1st day of June, 2020;

(*ii*) for the words, brackets, letters and figures "under clause (*b*) of sub-section (1) of section 12AA", the words, figures and letters "under section 12AA or section 12AB" shall be substi-tuted with effect from the 1st day of April, 2021;

(*iii*) in the second proviso,—

(*A*) with effect from the 1st day of June, 2020, for the words, figures and letters "under section 12AB", the words, figures and letters "under section 12AA," shall be substi-tuted and shall be deemed to have been substituted;

(*B*) with effect from the 1st day of April, 2021, after the words, figures and letters "under section 12AA", the words, figures and letters "or section 12AB" shall be inserted;

(*IV*) in section 12A,—

 (*a*) in sub-section (1),—

  (*i*) with effect from the 1st day of June, 2020, clause (*ac*) shall be omitted and shall be deemed to have been omitted;

  (*ii*) with effect from the 1st day of April, 2021, after clause (*ab*), the following clause shall be inserted, namely:—

   "(*ac*) notwithstanding anything contained in clauses (*a*) to (*ab*), the person in receipt of the income has made an application in the prescribed form and manner to the Principal Commissioner or Commissioner, for registration of the trust or institution,—

    (*i*) where the trust or institution is registered under section 12A [as it stood immediately before its amendment by the Finance (No. 2) Act, 1996 (33 of 1996)] or under section 12AA [as it stood immediately before its amendment by the Taxation and Other Laws (Relaxation and Amendment of Certain Provisions) Act, 2020 (38 of 2020)], within three months from the 1st day of April, 2021;

    (*ii*) where the trust or institution is registered under section 12AB and the period of the said registration is due to expire, at least six months prior to expiry of the said period;

    (*iii*) where the trust or institution has been provisionally registered under section 12AB, at least six months prior to expiry of period of the provisional registration or within six months of commencement of its activities, whichever is earlier;

    (*iv*) where registration of the trust or institution has become inoperative due to the first proviso to sub-section (7) of section 11, at least six months prior to the commencement of the assessment year from which the said registration is sought to be made operative;

    (*v*) where the trust or institution has adopted or undertaken modifications of the objects which do not conform to the conditions of registration, within a period of thirty days from the date of the said adoption or modification;

    (*vi*) in any other case, at least one month prior to the commencement of the previous year relevant to the assessment year from which the said registration is sought,

and such trust or institution is registered under section 12AB;";

(*b*) in sub-section (2),—

  (*A*) with effect from the 1st day of June, 2020,—

    (*i*) the first proviso shall be omitted and shall be deemed to have been omitted;

    (*ii*) in the second proviso, for the words, figures and letters **"Provided further** that where registration has been granted to the trust or institution under section 12AA or section 12AB", the words, figures and letters **"Provided** that where registration has been granted to the trust or institution under section 12AA" shall be substituted and shall be deemed to have been substituted;

    (*iii*) in the third proviso, for the words **"Provided also"**, the words **"Provided further"**, shall be substituted and shall be deemed to have been substituted;

    (*iv*) in the fourth proviso, for the words, figures and letters "section 12AA or section 12AB", the word, figures and letters "section 12AA" shall be substituted and shall be deemed to have been substituted;

  (*B*) with effect from the 1st day of April, 2021,—

    (*i*) in the first proviso, for the words figures and letters **"Provided** that where registration has been granted to the trust or institution under section 12AA", the following shall be substituted, namely:—

    "Provided that the provisions of sections 11 and 12 shall apply to a trust or institution, where the application is made under—

      (*a*) sub-clause (*i*) of clause (*ac*) of sub-section (1), from the assessment year from which such trust or institution was earlier granted registration;

      (*b*) sub-clause (*iii*) of clause (*ac*) of sub-section (1), from the first of the assessment year for which it was provisionally registered:

    Provided further that where registration has been granted to the trust or institution under section 12AA or section 12AB";

    (*ii*) in the second proviso, for the words **"Provided further"**, the words **"Provided also"** shall be substituted;

    (*iii*) in the fourth proviso, for the word, figures and letters "section 12AA", the words, figures and letters "section 12AA or section 12AB" shall be substituted;

(*V*) in section 12AA,—

(*a*) sub-section (5) shall be omitted and shall be deemed to have been omitted with effect from the 1st day of June, 2020;

(*b*) after sub-section (4), the following sub-section shall be inserted with effect from the 1st day of April, 2021, namely:—

"(5) Nothing contained in this section shall apply on or after the 1st day of April, 2021.";

(*VI*) section 12AB shall be omitted and shall be deemed to have been omitted with effect from the 1st day of June, 2020;

(*VII*) after section 12AA, the following section shall be inserted with effect from the 1st day of April, 2021, namely:—

"**12AB.** *Procedure for fresh registration.*—(1) The Principal Commissioner or Commissioner, on receipt of an application made under clause (*ac*) of sub-section (1) of section 12A, shall,—

(*a*) where the application is made under sub-clause (*i*) of the said clause, pass an order in writing registering the trust or institution for a period of five years;

(*b*) where the application is made under sub-clause (*ii*) or sub-clause (*iii*) or sub-clause (*iv*) or sub-clause (*v*) of the said clause,—

(*i*) call for such documents or information from the trust or institution or make such inquiries as he thinks necessary in order to satisfy himself about—

(*A*) the genuineness of activities of the trust or institution; and

(*B*) the compliance of such requirements of any other law for the time being in force by the trust or institution as are material for the purpose of achieving its objects;

(*ii*) after satisfying himself about the objects of the trust or institution and the genuineness of its activities under item (*A*) and compliance of the requirements under item (*B*), of sub-clause (*i*),—

(*A*) pass an order in writing registering the trust or institution for a period of five years; or

(*B*) if he is not so satisfied, pass an order in writing rejecting such application and also cancelling its registration after affording a reasonable opportunity of being heard;

(*c*) where the application is made under sub-clause (*vi*) of the said clause, pass an order in writing provisionally registering the trust or institution for a period of three years from the assessment year from which the registration is sought,

and send a copy of such order to the trust or institution.

(2) All applications, pending before the Principal Commissioner or Commissioner on which no order has been passed under clause (*b*) of sub-section (1) of section 12AA before the date on which this section has come into force, shall be deemed to be applications made under sub-clause (*vi*) of clause (*ac*) of sub-section (1) of section 12A on that date.

(3) The order under clause (*a*), sub-clause (*ii*) of clause (*b*) and clause (*c*), of sub-section (1) shall be passed, in such form and manner as may be prescribed, before expiry of the period of three months, six months and one month, respectively, calculated from the end of the month in which the application was received.

(4) Where registration of a trust or an institution has been granted under clause (*a*) or clause (*b*) of sub-section (1) and subsequently, the Principal Commissioner or Commissioner is satisfied that the activities of such trust or institution are not genuine or are not being carried out in accordance with the objects of the trust or institution, as the case may be, he shall pass an order in writing cancelling the registration of such trust or institution after affording a reasonable opportunity of being heard.

(5) Without prejudice to the provisions of sub-section (4), where registration of a trust or an institution has been granted under clause (*a*) or clause (*b*) of sub-section (1) and subsequently, it is noticed that—

(*a*) the activities of the trust or the institution are being carried out in a manner that the provisions of sections 11 and 12 do not apply to exclude either whole or any part of the income of such trust or institution due to operation of sub-section (1) of section 13; or

(*b*) the trust or institution has not complied with the requirement of any other law, as referred to in item (*B*) of sub-clause (*i*) of clause (*b*) of sub-section (1), and the order, direction or decree, by whatever name called, holding that such non-compliance has occurred, has either not been disputed or has attained finality,

then, the Principal Commissioner or the Commissioner may, by an order in writing, after affording a reasonable opportunity of being heard, cancel the registration of such trust or institution.";

(*VIII*) in section 13, in *Explanation 1*, after the figures and letter "12A", the figures and letters ", 12AA, 12AB" shall be inserted with effect from the 1st day of April, 2021;

(*IX*) in section 35,—

(*a*) in sub-section (1),—

(*i*) with effect from the 1st day of June, 2020, in clause (*iii*), in the *Explanation*,—

(*A*) for the words, brackets, figures and letter "to which clause (*ii*) or clause (*iii*) or to a company to which clause (*iia*)", the words, brackets and figures "to which clause (*ii*) or clause (*iii*)" shall be substituted and shall be deemed to have been substituted;

(*B*) for the words, brackets, figures and letter "clause (*ii*) or clause (*iii*) or to a company referred to in clause (*iia*)", the words, brackets and figures "clause (*ii*) or clause (*iii*)" shall be substituted and shall be deemed to have been substituted;

(*ii*) with effect from the 1st day of April, 2021, in sub-clause (*iii*), in the *Explanation*,—

(*A*) for the words, brackets and figures "to which clause (*ii*) or clause (*iii*)", the words, brackets, figures and letter "to which clause (*ii*) or clause (*iii*) or to a company to which clause (*iia*)" shall be substituted;

(*B*) for the words, brackets and figures "clause (*ii*) or clause (*iii*)", the words, brackets, figures and letter "clause (*ii*) or clause (*iii*) or to a company referred to in clause (*iia*)" shall be substituted;

(*iii*) the fifth and sixth provisos occurring after clause (*iv*) shall be omitted and shall be deemed to have been omitted with effect from the 1st day of June, 2020;

(*iv*) after the fourth proviso occurring after clause (*iv*), the following provisos shall be inserted with effect from the 1st day of April, 2021, namely:—

"**Provided also** that every notification under clause (*ii*) or clause (*iii*) in respect of the research association, university, college or other institution or under clause (*iia*) in respect of the company issued on or before the date on which this proviso has come into force, shall be deemed to have been withdrawn unless such research association, university, college or other institution referred to in clause (*ii*) or clause (*iii*) or the company referred to in clause (*iia*) makes an intimation in such form and manner, as may be prescribed, to the prescribed income-tax authority within three months from the date on which this proviso has come into force, and subject to such intimation the notification shall be valid for a period of five consecutive assessment years beginning with the assessment year commencing on or after the 1st day of April, 2022:

Provided also that any notification issued by the Central Government under clause (*ii*) or clause (*iia*) or clause (*iii*), after the date on which the Taxation and Other Laws (Relaxation and Amendment of Certain Provisions) Bill, 2020 receives the assent of the President, shall, at any one time, have effect for such assessment year or years, not exceeding five assessment years as may be specified in the notification.";

(*b*) sub-section (1A) shall be omitted and shall be deemed to have been omitted with effect from the 1st day of June, 2020;

(*c*) after sub-section (1), the following sub-section shall be inserted with effect from the 1st day of April, 2021, namely:—

"(1A) Notwithstanding anything contained in sub-section (1), the research association, university, college or other institution referred to in clause (*ii*) or clause (*iii*) or the company referred to in clause (*iia*) of sub-section (1) shall not be entitled to deduction under the respective clauses of the said sub-section, unless such research association, university, college or other institution or company—

(*i*) prepares such statement for such period as may be prescribed and deliver or cause to be delivered to the said prescribed income-tax authority or the person authorised by such authority such statement in such form, verified in such manner, setting forth such particulars and within such time, as may be prescribed:

Provided that such research association, university, college or other institution or the company may also deliver to the prescribed authority a correction statement for rectification of any mistake or to add, delete or update the information furnished in the statement delivered under this sub-section in such form and verified in such manner as may be prescribed;

(*ii*) furnishes to the donor, a certificate specifying the amount of donation in such manner, containing such particulars and within such time from the date of receipt of sum, as may be prescribed.";

(*X*) in section 35AC, with effect from the 1st day of November, 2020,—

(*i*) in sub-section (4)—

(*a*) in clause (*i*), for the word "Committee", the words and brackets "the Principal Chief Commissioner of Income-tax (Exemption) or the Chief Commissioner of Income-tax (Exemption)" shall be substituted;

(*b*) in clause (*ii*), for the words "National Committee", the words and brackets "the Principal Chief Commissioner of Income-tax (Exemption) or the Chief Commissioner of Income-tax (Exemption)" shall be substituted;

(*c*) in the long line, for the words "National Committee", the words and brackets "the Principal Chief Commissioner of Income-tax (Exemption) or the Chief Commissioner of Income-tax (Exemption)" shall be substituted;

(*d*) in the proviso, for the words "National Committee", the words and brackets "the Principal Chief Commissioner of Income-tax (Exemption) or the Chief Commissioner of Income-tax (Exemption)" shall be substituted;

(*ii*) in sub-section (5),—

    (*a*) in clause (*i*), for the words "National Committee", the words and brackets "the Principal Chief Commissioner of Income-tax (Exemption) or the Chief Commissioner of Income-tax (Exemption)" shall be substituted;

    (*b*) in the first proviso, for the words "National Committee", the words and brackets "the Principal Chief Commissioner of Income-tax (Exemption) or the Chief Commissioner of Income-tax (Exemption)" shall be substituted;

(*iii*) in sub-section (6), in clause (*ii*), after the words "National Committee", the words and brackets "or the Principal Chief Commissioner of Income-tax (Exemption) or the Chief Commissioner of Income-tax (Exemption), as the case may be," shall be inserted;

(*XI*) in section 56, in sub-section (2),—

    (*a*) with effect from the 1st day of June, 2020,—

       (*i*) in clause (*v*), in the proviso, in clause (*g*), for the words, figures and letters "section 12AA or section 12AB", the word, figures and letters "section 12AA" shall be substituted and shall be deemed to have been substituted;

      (*ii*) in clause (*vi*), in the proviso, in clause (*g*), for the words, figures and letters "section 12AA or section 12AB", the word, figures and letters "section 12AA" shall be substituted and shall be deemed to have been substituted;

    (*iii*) in clause (*vii*), in the second proviso, in clause (*g*), for the words, figures and letters "section 12AA or section 12AB", the word, figures and letters "section 12AA" shall be substituted and shall be deemed to have been substituted;

    (*b*) with effect from the 1st day of April, 2021,—

       (*i*) in clause (*v*), in the proviso, in clause (*g*), for the word, figures and letters "section 12AA", the words, figures and letters "section 12AA or section 12AB" shall be substituted;

      (*ii*) in clause (*vi*), in the proviso, in clause (*g*), for the word, figures and letters "section 12AA", the words, figures and letters "section 12AA or section 12AB" shall be substituted;

    (*iii*) in clause (*vii*), in the second proviso, in clause (*g*), for the word, figures and letters "section 12AA", the words, figures and letters "section 12AA or section 12AB" shall be substituted;

    (*c*) in clause (*x*), in the proviso, in clause (*VII*),—

       (*i*) for the words, figures and letters "section 12A or section 12AA or section 12AB", the words, figures and letters "section 12A or section 12AA" shall be substituted and shall be deemed to have been substituted with effect from the 1st day of June, 2020;

    (*ii*) for the words, figures and letters "section 12A or section 12AA", the words, figures and letters "section 12A or section 12AA or section 12AB" shall be substituted with effect from the 1st day of April, 2021;

 (*XII*) in section 80G,—

   (*a*) in sub-section (2), in clause (*a*), in sub-clause (*iiia*), after the word "Fund", the words and brackets "or the Prime Minister's Citizen Assistance and Relief in Emergency Situations Fund (PM CARES FUND)" shall be inserted and shall be deemed to have been inserted with effect from the 1st day of April, 2020;

   (*b*) in sub-section (5),—

    (*i*) with effect from the 1st day of June, 2020,—

     (*A*) in clause (*vi*), for the words "approved by the Principal Commissioner or Commissioner;" the words "approved by the Commissioner in accordance with the rules made in this behalf; and" shall be substituted and shall be deemed to have been substituted;

     (*B*) clauses (*viii*) and (*ix*) shall be omitted and shall be deemed to have been omitted;

    (*ii*) with effect from the 1st day of April, 2021,—

     (*A*) in clause (*vi*), for the words "approved by the Commissioner in accordance with the rules made in this behalf; and", the words "approved by the Principal Commissioner or Commissioner;" shall be substituted;

     (*B*) after clause (*vii*), the following clauses shall be inserted, namely:—

      "(*viii*) the institution or fund prepares such statement for such period as may be prescribed and deliver or cause to be delivered to the prescribed income-tax authority or the person authorised by such authority such statement in such form and verified in such manner and setting forth such particulars and within such time as may be prescribed:

       Provided that the institution or fund may also deliver to the said prescribed authority, a correction statement for rectification of any mistake or to add, delete or update the information furnished in the statement delivered under this sub-section in such form and verified in such manner as may be prescribed; and

      (*ix*) the institution or fund furnishes to the donor, a certificate specifying the amount of donation in such manner, containing such particulars and within such time from the date of receipt of donation, as may be prescribed:

Provided that the institution or fund referred to in clause (*vi*) shall make an application in the prescribed form and manner to the Principal Commissioner or Commissioner, for grant of approval,—

(*i*) where the institution or fund is approved under clause (*vi*) [as it stood immediately before its amendment by the Taxation and Other Laws (Relaxation and Amendment of Certain Provisions) Act, 2020], within three months from the 1st day of April, 2021;

(*ii*) where the institution or fund is approved and the period of such approval is due to expire, at least six months prior to expiry of the said period;

(*iii*) where the institution or fund has been provisionally approved, at least six months prior to expiry of the period of the provisional approval or within six months of commencement of its activities, whichever is earlier;

(*iv*) in any other case, at least one month prior to commencement of the previous year relevant to the assessment year from which the said approval is sought:

Provided further that the Principal Commissioner or Commissioner, on receipt of an application made under the first proviso, shall,—

(*i*) where the application is made under clause (*i*) of the said proviso, pass an order in writing granting it approval for a period of five years;

(*ii*) where the application is made under clause (*ii*) or clause (*iii*) of the said proviso,—

    (*a*) call for such documents or information from it or make such inquiries as he thinks necessary in order to satisfy himself about—

        (*A*) the genuineness of activities of such institution or fund; and

        (*B*) the fulfilment of all the conditions laid down in clauses (*i*) to (*v*);

    (*b*) after satisfying himself about the genuineness of activities under item (*A*), and the fulfilment of all the conditions under item (*B*), of sub-clause (*a*),—

          (*A*) pass an order in writing granting it approval for a period of five years; or

          (*B*) if he is not so satisfied, pass an order in writing rejecting such application and also cancelling its approval after affording it a reasonable opportunity of being heard;

      (*iii*) where the application is made under clause (*iv*) of the said proviso, pass an order in writing granting it approval provisionally for a period of three years from the assessment year from which the registration is sought,

and send a copy of such order to the institution or fund:

Provided also that the order under clause (*i*), sub-clause (*b*) of clause (*ii*) and clause (*iii*) of the first proviso shall be passed in such form and manner as may be prescribed, before expiry of the period of three months, six months and one month, respectively, calculated from the end of the month in which the application was received:

Provided also that the approval granted under the second proviso shall apply to an institution or fund, where the application is made under—

      (*a*) clause (*i*) of the first proviso, from the assessment year from which approval was earlier granted to such institution or fund;

      (*b*) clause (*iii*) of the first proviso, from the first of the assessment years for which such institution or fund was provisionally approved;

      (*c*) in any other case, from the assessment year immediately following the financial year in which such application is made.";

  (*c*) sub-section (5E), shall be omitted and shall be deemed to have been omitted with effect from the 1st day of June, 2020;

  (*d*) after sub-section (5D), the following sub-section shall be inserted with effect from the 1st day of April, 2021, namely:—

"(5E) All applications, pending before the Commissioner on which no order has been passed under clause (*vi*) of sub-section (5) before the date on which this sub-section has come into force, shall be deemed to be applications made under clause (*iv*) of the first proviso to sub-section (5) on that date.";

(*e*) *Explanation 2A* shall be omitted and shall be deemed to have been omitted with effect from the 1st day of June, 2020;

(*f*) after *Explanation 2*, the following *Explanation* shall be inserted with effect from the 1st day of April, 2021, namely:—

"*Explanation 2A.*—For the removal of doubts, it is hereby declared that claim of the assessee for a deduction in respect of any donation made to an institution or fund to which the provisions of sub-section (5) apply, in the return of income for any assessment year filed by him, shall be allowed on the basis of information relating to said donation furnished by the institution or fund to the prescribed income-tax authority or the person authorised by such authority, subject to verification in accordance with the risk management strategy formulated by the Board from time to time.";

(*XIII*) in section 92CA, after sub-section (7), the following sub-sections shall be inserted with effect from the 1st day of November, 2020, namely:—

"(8) The Central Government may make a scheme, by notification in the Official Gazette, for the purposes of determination of the arm's length price under sub-section (3), so as to impart greater efficiency, transparency and accountability by—

(*a*) eliminating the interface between the Transfer Pricing Officer and the assessee or any other person to the extent technologically feasible;

(*b*) optimising utilisation of the resources through economies of scale and functional specialisation;

(*c*) introducing a team-based determination of arm's length price with dynamic jurisdiction.

(9) The Central Government may, for the purpose of giving effect to the scheme made under sub-section (8), by notification in the Official Gazette, direct that any of the provisions of this Act shall not apply or shall apply with such exceptions, modifications and adaptations as may be specified in the notification:

Provided that no direction shall be issued after the 31st day of March, 2022.

(10) Every notification issued under sub-section (8) and sub-section (9) shall, as soon as may be after the notification is issued, be laid before each House of Parliament.";

(*XIV*) in section 115AD, with effect from the 1st day of April, 2021,—

(*a*) in sub-section (1),—

(*i*) in the opening portion, for the words "Foreign Institutional Investor", the words "Specified Fund or Foreign Institutional Investor" shall be substituted;

¹[*(ii)* *for clause (i), after the long line, the following clause shall be substituted, namely:—*

"*(i)* *the amount of income-tax calculated on the income in respect of securities referred to in clause (a), if any, included in the total income,—*

(A) *at the rate of twenty per cent in case of Foreign Institutional Investor;*

(B) *at the rate of ten per cent in case of specified fund:*

Provided that the amount of income-tax calculated on the income by way of interest referred to in section 194LD shall be at the rate of five per cent;]

(*iii*) in clause (*iv*), for the words "Foreign Institutional Investor", the words "specified fund or Foreign Institutional Investor" shall be substituted;

(*b*) after sub-section (1), the following sub-section shall be inserted, namely:—

"(1A) Notwithstanding anything contained in sub-section (1), in case of specified fund, the provision of this section shall apply only to the extent of income that is attributable to units held by non-resident (not being a permanent establishment of a non-resident in India) calculated in the prescribed manner.";

(*c*) in sub-section (2), for the words "Foreign Institutional Investor", at both the places where they occur, the words "specified Fund or Foreign Institutional Investor" shall be substituted;

(*d*) in the *Explanation*, for clause (*b*), the following clauses shall be substituted, namely:—

'(*b*) the expression "permanent establishment" shall have the meaning assigned to it in clause (*iiia*) of section 92F;

(*c*) the expression "securities" shall have the meaning assigned to it in clause (*h*) of section 2 of the Securities Contracts (Regulation) Act, 1956 (42 of 1956);

(*d*) the expression "specified fund" shall have the same meaning assigned to it in clause (*c*) of the *Explanation* to clause (*4D*) of section 10.';

(*XV*) in section 115BBDA, in the *Explanation*, in clause (*b*), in sub-clause (*iii*),—

(*i*) for the words, figures and letters, "under section 12A or section 12AA or section 12AB", the words, figures and letters "under section 12A or section 12AA" shall be substituted and shall be deemed to have been substituted with effect from the 1st day of June, 2020;

1. Substituted by the Finance Act, 2021, w.e.f. **1-4-2021**.

(*ii*) for the words, figures and letters, "under section 12A or section 12AA" the words, figures and letters "under section 12A or section 12AA or section 12AB" shall be substituted with effect from the 1st day of April, 2021;

(*XVI*) in section 115JEE, after sub-section (2), the following sub-section shall be inserted with effect from the 1st day of April, 2021, namely:—

"(2A) The provisions of this Chapter shall not apply to specified fund referred to in clause (*c*) of the *Explanation* to clause (*4D*) of section 10.";

(*XVII*) in section 115TD,—

(*i*) for the words, figures and letters "under section 12AA or section 12AB" wherever they occur, the words, figures and letters "under section 12AA" shall be substituted and shall be deemed to have been substituted with effect from the 1st day of June, 2020;

(*ii*) for the words, figures and letters "under section 12AA" wherever they occur, the words, figures and letters "under section 12AA or section 12AB" shall be substituted with effect from the 1st day of April, 2021;

(*XVIII*) after section 129, the following section shall be inserted with effect from the 1st day of November, 2020, namely:—

"130. *Faceless jurisdiction of income-tax authorities.*—(1) The Central Government may make a scheme, by notification in the Official Gazette, for the purposes of—

(*a*) exercise of all or any of the powers and performance of all or any of the functions conferred on, or, as the case may be, assigned to income-tax authorities by or under this Act as referred to in section 120; or

(*b*) vesting the jurisdiction with the Assessing Officer as referred to in section 124; or

(*c*) exercise of power to transfer cases under section 127; or

(*d*) exercise of jurisdiction in case of change of incumbency as referred to in section 129,

so as to impart greater efficiency, transparency and accountability by—

(*i*) eliminating the interface between the income-tax authority and the assessee or any other person, to the extent technologically feasible;

(*ii*) optimising utilisation of the resources through economies of scale and functional specialisation;

(*iii*) introducing a team-based exercise of powers and performance of functions by two or more income-tax authorities, concurrently, in respect of any area or persons or classes of persons or incomes or classes of income or cases or classes of cases, with dynamic jurisdiction.

(2) The Central Government may, for the purpose of giving effect to the scheme made under sub-section (1), by notification in the Official Gazette, direct that any of the provisions of this Act shall not apply or shall apply with such exceptions, modifications and adaptations as may be specified in the notification:

Provided that no direction shall be issued after the 31st day of March, 2022.

(3) Every notification issued under sub-section (1) and sub-section (2) shall, as soon as may be after the notification is issued, be laid before each House of Parliament.";

(*XIX*) in section 133A, with effect from the 1st day of November, 2020,—

    (*i*) in sub-section (6), for the proviso, the following proviso shall be substituted, namely:—

"**Provided** that no action under this section shall be taken by an income-tax authority without the approval of the Principal Director General or the Director General or the Principal Chief Commissioner or the Chief Commissioner.";

    (*ii*) in the *Explanation*, for clause (*a*), the following clause shall be substituted, namely:—

'(*a*) "income-tax authority" means—

        (*i*) a Principal Commissioner or Commissioner, a Principal Director or Director, a Joint Commissioner or Joint Director, an Assistant Director or a Deputy Director or an Assessing Officer, or a Tax Recovery Officer; and

        (*ii*) includes an Inspector of Income-tax, for the purposes of clause (*i*) of sub-section (1), clause (*i*) of sub-section (3) and sub-section (5),

who is subordinate to the Principal Director General of Income-tax (Investigation) or the Director General of Income-tax (Investigation) or the Principal Chief Commissioner of Income-tax (TDS) or the Chief Commissioner of Income-tax (TDS), as the case may be;';

(*XX*) in section 133C, with effect from the 1st day of November, 2020,—

    (*a*) in sub-section (2), for the words "such information or document and make available the outcome of such processing to the Assessing Officer", the words, brackets, figures and letter "and utilise such information and document in accordance with the scheme notified under sub-section (3) or the provisions of section 135A" shall be substituted;

    (*b*) after sub-section (3), the following sub-section shall be inserted, namely:—

"(4) The scheme made under sub-section (3) shall cease to have effect from the date on which the scheme notified under section 135A in respect of this section comes into effect.";

(*XXI*) after section 135, the following section shall be inserted with effect from the 1st day of November, 2020, namely:—

"135A. *Faceless collection of information.*—(1) The Central Government may make a scheme, by notification in the Official Gazette, for the purposes of calling for information under section 133, collecting certain information under section 133B, or calling for information by prescribed income-tax authority under section 133C, or exercise of power to inspect register of companies under section 134, or exercise of power of Assessing Officer under section 135 so as to impart greater efficiency, transparency and accountability by—

(*a*) eliminating the interface between the income-tax authority and the assessee or any other person to the extent technologically feasible;

(*b*) optimising utilisation of the resources through economies of scale and functional specialisation;

(*c*) introducing a team-based exercise of powers, including to call for, or collect, or process, or utilise, the information, with dynamic jurisdiction.

(2) The Central Government may, for the purpose of giving effect to the scheme made under sub-section (1), by notification in the Official Gazette, direct that any of the provisions of this Act shall not apply or shall apply with such exceptions, modifications and adaptations as may be specified in the notification:

Provided that no direction shall be issued after the 31st day of March, 2022.

(3) Every notification issued under sub-section (1) and sub-section (2) shall, as soon as may be after the notification is issued, be laid before each House of Parliament.";

(*XXII*) after section 142A, the following section shall be inserted with effect from the 1st day of November, 2020, namely:—

"142B. *Faceless inquiry or Valuation.*—(1) The Central Government may make a scheme, by notification in the Official Gazette, for the purposes of issuing notice under sub-section (1) or making inquiry before assessment under sub-section (2), or directing the assessee to get his accounts audited under sub-section (2A) of section 142, or estimating the value of any asset, property or investment by a Valuation Officer under section 142A, so as to impart greater efficiency, transparency and accountability by—

(*a*) eliminating the interface between the income-tax authority or Valuation Officer and the assessee or any person to the extent technologically feasible;

(*b*) optimising utilisation of the resources through economies of scale and functional specialisation;

(*c*) introducing a team-based issuance of notice or making of enquiries or issuance of directions or valuation with dynamic jurisdiction;

(2) The Central Government may, for the purpose of giving effect to the scheme made under sub-section (1), by notification in the Official Gazette, direct that any of the provisions of this Act shall not apply or shall apply with such exceptions, modifications and adaptations as may be specified in the notification:

Provided that no direction shall be issued after the 31st day of March, 2022.

(3) Every notification issued under sub-section (1) and sub-section (2) shall, as soon as may be after the notification is issued, be laid before each House of Parliament.";

(*XXIII*) in section 143, with effect from the 1st day of April, 2021,—

(*i*) in sub-section (3B), in the proviso, for the figures "2022", the figures "2021" shall be substituted;

(*ii*) after sub-section (3C), the following sub-section shall be inserted, namely:—

"(3D) Nothing contained in sub-section (3A) and sub-section (3B) shall apply to the assessment made under sub-section (3) or under section 144, as the case may be, on or after the 1st day of April, 2021.";

(*XXIV*) after section 144A, the following section shall be inserted with effect from the 1st day of April, 2021, namely:—

'144B. *Faceless Assessment.*—(1) Notwithstanding anything to the contrary contained in any other provisions of this Act, the assessment under sub-section (3) of section 143 or under section 144, in the cases referred to in sub-section (2), shall be made in a faceless manner as per the following procedure, namely:—

(*i*) the National Faceless Assessment Centre shall serve a notice on the assessee under sub-section (2) of section 143;

(*ii*) the assessee may, within fifteen days from the date of receipt of notice referred to in clause (*i*), file his response to the National Faceless Assessment Centre;

(*iii*) where the assessee—

(*a*) has furnished his return of income under section 139 or in response to a notice issued under sub-section (1) of section 142 or under sub-section (1) of section 148, and a notice under sub-section (2) of section 143 has been issued by the Assessing Officer or the prescribed income-tax authority, as the case may be; or (*b*) has not furnished his return of income in response to a notice issued under sub-section (1) of section 142 by the Assessing Officer; or

(*c*) has not furnished his return of income under sub-section (1) of section 148 and a notice under sub-section (1) of section 142 has been issued by the Assessing Officer,

the National Faceless Assessment Centre shall intimate the assessee that assessment in his case shall be completed in accordance with the procedure laid down under this section;

(*iv*) the National Faceless Assessment Centre shall assign the case selected for the purposes of faceless assessment under this section to a specific assessment unit in any one Regional Faceless Assessment Centre through an automated allocation system;

(*v*) where a case is assigned to the assessment unit, it may make a request to the National Faceless Assessment Centre for—

(*a*) obtaining such further information, documents or evidence from the assessee or any other person, as it may specify;

(*b*) conducting of certain enquiry or verification by verification unit; and

(*c*) seeking technical assistance from the technical unit;

(*vi*) where a request for obtaining further information, documents or evidence from the assessee or any other person has been made by the assessment unit, the National Faceless Assessment Centre shall issue appropriate notice or requisition to the assessee or any other person for obtaining the information, documents or evidence requisitioned by the assessment unit;

(*vii*) the assessee or any other person, as the case may be, shall file his response to the notice referred to in clause (*vi*), within the time specified therein or such time as may be extended on the basis of an application in this regard, to the National Faceless Assessment Centre;

(*viii*) where a request for conducting of certain enquiry or verification by the verification unit has been made by the assessment unit, the request shall be assigned by the National Faceless Assessment Centre to a verification unit in any one Regional Faceless Assessment Centres through an automated allocation system;

(*ix*) where a request for seeking technical assistance from the technical unit has been made by the assessment unit, the request shall be assigned by the National Faceless Assessment Centre to a technical unit in any one Regional Faceless Assessment Centres through an automated allocation system;

(*x*) the National Faceless Assessment Centre shall send the report received from the verification unit or the technical unit, based on the request referred to in clause (*viii*) or clause (*ix*) to the concerned assessment unit;

(*xi*) where the assessee fails to comply with the notice referred to in clause (*vi*) or notice issued under sub-section (1) of section 142 or with a direction issued under sub-section (2A) of section 142, the National Faceless Assessment Centre shall serve upon such assessee a notice under section 144 giving him an opportunity to show-cause, on a date and time to be specified in the notice, why the assessment in his case should not be completed to the best of its judgment;

(*xii*) the assessee shall, within the time specified in the notice referred to in clause (*xi*) or such time as may be extended on the basis of an application in this regard, file his response to the National Faceless Assessment Centre;

(*xiii*) where the assessee fails to file response to the notice referred to in clause (*xi*) within the time specified therein or within the extended time, if any, the National Faceless Assessment Centre shall intimate such failure to the assessment unit;

(*xiv*) the assessment unit shall, after taking into account all the relevant material available on the record make in writing, a draft assessment order or, in a case where intimation referred to in clause (*xiii*) is received from the National Faceless Assessment Centre, make in writing, a draft assessment order to the best of its judgment, either accepting the income or sum payable by, or sum refundable to, the assessee as per his return or making variation to the said income or sum, and send a copy of such order to the National Faceless Assessment Centre;

(*xv*) the assessment unit shall, while making draft assessment order, provide details of the penalty proceedings to be initiated therein, if any;

(*xvi*) the National Faceless Assessment Centre shall examine the draft assessment order in accordance with the risk management strategy specified by the Board, including by way of an automated examination tool, whereupon it may decide to—

(*a*) finalise the assessment, in case no variation prejudicial to the interest of assessee is proposed, as per the draft assessment order and serve a copy of such order and notice for initiating penalty proceedings, if any, to the assessee, alongwith the demand notice, specifying the sum payable by, or refund of any amount due to, the assessee on the basis of such assessment; or

(*b*) provide an opportunity to the assessee, in case any variation prejudicial to the interest of assessee is proposed, by serving a notice calling upon him to show-cause as to why the proposed variation should not be made; or (*c*) assign the draft assessment order to a review unit in any one Regional Faceless Assessment Centre, through an automated allocation system, for conducting review of such order;

 (*xvii*) the review unit shall conduct review of the draft assessment order referred to it by the National Faceless Assessment Centre whereupon it may decide to—

     (*a*) concur with the draft assessment order and intimate the National Faceless Assessment Centre about such concurrence; or

     (*b*) suggest such variation, as it may deem fit, in the draft assessment order and send its suggestions to the National Faceless Assessment Centre;

 (*xviii*) the National Faceless Assessment Centre shall, upon receiving concurrence of the review unit, follow the procedure laid down in—

     (*a*) sub-clause (*a*) of clause (*xvi*); or

     (*b*) sub-clause (*b*) of clause (*xvi*);

 (*xix*) the National Faceless Assessment Centre shall, upon receiving suggestions for variation from the review unit, assign the case to an assessment unit, other than the assessment unit which has made the draft assessment order, through an automated allocation system;

 (*xx*) the assessment unit shall, after considering the variations suggested by the review unit, send the final draft assessment order to the National Faceless Assessment Centre;

 (*xxi*) the National Faceless Assessment Centre shall, upon receiving final draft assessment order follow the procedure laid down in—

     (*a*) sub-clause (*a*) of clause (*xvi*); or

     (*b*) sub-clause (*b*) of clause (*xvi*);

 (*xxii*) the assessee may, in a case where show-cause notice has been served upon him as per the procedure laid down in sub-clause (*b*) of clause (*xvi*), furnish his response to the National Faceless Assessment Centre on or before the date and time specified in the notice or within the extended time, if any;

 (*xxiii*) the National Faceless Assessment Centre shall,—

     (*a*) where no response to the show-cause notice is received as per clause (*xxii*),—

         (*A*) in a case where the draft assessment order or the final draft assessment order is in respect of an eligible assessee and proposes to make any variation which is prejudicial to the interest of said assessee, forward the draft assessment order or final draft assessment order to such assessee; or

(B) in any other case, finalise the assessment as per the draft assessment order or the final draft assessment order and serve a copy of such order and notice for initiating penalty proceedings, if any, to the assessee, alongwith the demand notice, specifying the sum payable by, or refund of any amount due to, the assessee on the basis of such assessment;

(b) in any other case, send the response received from the assessee to the assessment unit;

(xxiv) the assessment unit shall, after taking into account the response furnished by the assessee, make a revised draft assessment order and send it to the National Faceless Assessment Centre;

(xxv) the National Faceless Assessment Centre shall, upon receiving the revised draft assessment order,—

(a) in case the variations proposed in the revised draft assessment order are not prejudicial to the interest of the assessee in comparison to the draft assessment order or the final draft assessment order, and—

(A) in case the revised draft assessment order is in respect of an eligible assessee and there is any variation prejudicial to the interest of the assessee proposed in draft assessment order or the final draft assessment order, forward the said revised draft assessment order to such assessee;

(B) in any other case, finalise the assessment as per the revised draft assessment order and serve a copy of such order and notice for initiating penalty proceedings, if any, to the assessee, alongwith the demand notice, specifying the sum payable by, or refund of any amount due to, the assessee on the basis of such assessment;

(b) in case the variations proposed in the revised draft assessment order are prejudicial to the interest of the assessee in comparison to the draft assessment order or the final draft assessment order, provide an opportunity to the assessee, by serving a notice calling upon him to show-cause as to why the proposed variation should not be made;

(xxvi) the procedure laid down in clauses (xxiii), (xxiv) and (xxv) shall apply *mutatis mutandis* to the notice referred to in sub-clause (b) of clause (xxv);

(xxvii) where the draft assessment order or final draft assessment order or revised draft assessment order is forwarded to the eligible assessee as per item (A) of sub-clause (a) of clause (xxiii) or item (A) of sub-clause (a) of clause (xxv), such assessee shall, within the period specified in sub-section (2) of section 144C, file his acceptance of the variations to the National Faceless Assessment Centre;

(*xxviii*) the National Faceless Assessment Centre shall,—

(*a*) upon receipt of acceptance as per clause (*xxvii*); or

(*b*) if no objections are received from the eligible assessee within the period specified in sub-section (2) of section 144C,

finalise the assessment within the time allowed under sub-section (4) of section 144C and serve a copy of such order and notice for initiating penalty proceedings, if any, to the assessee, alongwith the demand notice, specifying the sum payable by, or refund of any amount due to, the assessee on the basis of such assessment;

(*xxix*) where the eligible assessee files his objections with the Dispute Resolution Panel, the National Faceless Assessment Centre shall upon receipt of the directions issued by the Dispute Resolution Panel under sub-section (5) of section 144C, forward such directions to the concerned assessment unit;

(*xxx*) the assessment unit shall in conformity of the directions issued by the Dispute Resolution panel under sub-section (5) of section 144C, prepare a draft assessment order in accordance with sub-section (13) of section 144C and send a copy of such order to the National Faceless Assessment Centre;

(*xxxi*) the National Faceless Assessment Centre shall, upon receipt of draft assessment order referred to in clause (*xxx*), finalise the assessment within the time allowed under sub-section (13) of section 144C and serve a copy of such order and notice for initiating penalty proceedings, if any, to the assessee, alongwith the demand notice, specifying the sum payable by, or refund of any amount due to, the assessee on the basis of such assessment;

(*xxxii*) the National Faceless Assessment Centre shall, after completion of assessment, transfer all the electronic records of the case to the Assessing Officer having jurisdiction over the said case for such action as may be required under the Act.

(2) The faceless assessment under sub-section (1) shall be made in respect of such territorial area, or persons or class of persons, or incomes or class of incomes, or cases or class of cases, as may be specified by the Board.

(3) The Board may, for the purposes of faceless assessment, set up the following Centres and units and specify their respective jurisdiction, namely:—

(*i*) a National Faceless Assessment Centre to facilitate the conduct of faceless assessment proceedings in a centralised manner, which shall be vested with the jurisdiction to make faceless assessment;

(*ii*) Regional Faceless Assessment Centres, as it may deem necessary, to facilitate the conduct of faceless assessment proceedings in the cadre controlling region of a Principal Chief Commissioner, which shall be vested with the jurisdiction to make faceless assessment;

(*iii*) assessment units, as it may deem necessary to facilitate the conduct of faceless assessment, to perform the function of making assessment, which includes identification of points or issues material for the determination of any liability (including refund) under the Act, seeking information or clarification on points or issues so identified, analysis of the material furnished by the assessee or any other person, and such other functions as may be required for the purposes of making faceless assessment;

(*iv*) verification units, as it may deem necessary to facilitate the conduct of faceless assessment, to perform the function of verification, which includes enquiry, cross verification, examination of books of account, examination of witnesses and recording of statements, and such other functions as may be required for the purposes of verification;

(*v*) technical units, as it may deem necessary to facilitate the conduct of faceless assessment, to perform the function of providing technical assistance which includes any assistance or advice on legal, accounting, forensic, information technology, valuation, transfer pricing, data analytics, management or any other technical matter which may be required in a particular case or a class of cases, under this section; and

(*vi*) review units, as it may deem necessary to facilitate the conduct of faceless assessment, to perform the function of review of the draft assessment order, which includes checking whether the relevant and material evidence has been brought on record, whether the relevant points of fact and law have been duly incorporated in the draft order, whether the issues on which addition or disallowance should be made have been discussed in the draft order, whether the applicable judicial decisions have been considered and dealt with in the draft order, checking for arithmetical correctness of variations proposed, if any, and such other functions as may be required for the purposes of review.

(4) The assessment unit, verification unit, technical unit and the review unit shall have the following authorities, namely:—

(*a*) Additional Commissioner or Additional Director or Joint Commissioner or Joint Director, as the case may be;

(*b*) Deputy Commissioner or Deputy Director or Assistant Commissioner or Assistant Director, or Income-tax Officer, as the case may be;

(*c*) such other income-tax authority, ministerial staff, executive or consultant, as considered necessary by the Board.

(5) All communication among the assessment unit, review unit, verification unit or technical unit or with the assessee or any other person with respect to the information or documents or evidence or any other details, as may be necessary for the purposes of making a faceless assessment shall be through the National Faceless Assessment Centre;

(6) All communications between the National Faceless Assessment Centre and the assessee, or his authorised representative, or any other person shall be exchanged exclusively by electronic mode; and all internal communications between the National Faceless Assessment Centre, Regional Faceless Assessment Centres and various units shall be exchanged exclusively by electronic mode:

Provided that the provisions of this sub-section shall not apply to the enquiry or verification conducted by the verification unit in the circumstances referred to in sub-clause (*g*) of clause (*xii*) of sub-section (7);

(7) For the purposes of faceless assessment—

(*i*) an electronic record shall be authenticated by—

(*a*) the National Faceless Assessment Centre by affixing its digital signature;

(*b*) assessee or any other person, by affixing his digital signature if he is required to furnish his return of income under digital signature, and in any other case, by affixing his digital signature or under electronic verification code in the prescribed manner;

(*ii*) every notice or order or any other electronic communication shall be delivered to the addressee, being the assessee, by way of—

(*a*) placing an authenticated copy thereof in the assessee's registered account; or

(*b*) sending an authenticated copy thereof to the registered email address of the assessee or his authorised representative; or

(*c*) uploading an authenticated copy on the assessee's Mobile App,

and followed by a real time alert;

(*iii*) every notice or order or any other electronic communication shall be delivered to the addressee, being any other person, by sending an authenticated copy thereof to the registered email address of such person, followed by a real time alert;

(*iv*) the assessee shall file his response to any notice or order or any other electronic communication, through his registered account, and once an acknowledgement is sent by the National Faceless Assessment Centre containing the hash result generated upon successful submission of response, the response shall be deemed to be authenticated;

(v) the time and place of dispatch and receipt of electronic record shall be determined in accordance with the provisions of section 13 of the Information Technology Act, 2000 (21 of 2000);

(vi) a person shall not be required to appear either personally or through authorised representative in connection with any proceedings before the income-tax authority at the National Faceless Assessment Centre or Regional Faceless Assessment Centre or any unit set up under this sub-section;

(vii) in a case where a variation is proposed in the draft assessment order or final draft assessment order or revised draft assessment order, and an opportunity is provided to the assessee by serving a notice calling upon him to show-cause as to why the assessment should not be completed as per the such draft or final draft or revised draft assessment order, the assessee or his authorised representative, as the case may be, may request for personal hearing so as to make his oral submissions or present his case before the income-tax authority in any unit;

(viii) the Chief Commissioner or the Director General, in charge of the Regional Faceless Assessment Centre, under which the concerned unit is set up, may approve the request for personal hearing referred to in clause (vii) if he is of the opinion that the request is covered by the circumstances referred to in sub-clause (h) of clause (xii);

(ix) where the request for personal hearing has been approved by the Chief Commissioner or the Director General, in charge of the Regional Faceless Assessment Centre, such hearing shall be conducted exclusively through video conferencing or video telephony, including use of any telecommunication application software which supports video conferencing or video telephony, in accordance with the procedure laid down by the Board;

(x) subject to the proviso to sub-section (6), any examination or recording of the statement of the assessee or any other person (other than statement recorded in the course of survey under section 133A of the Act) shall be conducted by an income-tax authority in any unit, exclusively through video conferencing or video telephony, including use of any telecommunication application software which supports video conferencing or video telephony in accordance with the procedure laid down by the Board;

(xi) the Board shall establish suitable facilities for video conferencing or video telephony including telecommunication application software which supports video conferencing or video telephony at such locations as may be necessary, so as to ensure that the assessee, or his authorised representative, or any other person is not denied the benefit of faceless assessment merely on the consideration that such assessee or his authorised representative, or any other person does not have access to video conferencing or video telephony at his end;

(*xii*) the Principal Chief Commissioner or the Principal Director General, in charge of the National Faceless Assessment Centre shall, with the prior approval of the Board, lay down the standards, procedures and processes for effective functioning of the National Faceless Assessment Centre, Regional Faceless Assessment Centres and the unit set up, in an automated and mechanised environment, including format, mode, procedure and processes in respect of the following, namely:—

(*a*) service of the notice, order or any other communication;

(*b*) receipt of any information or documents from the person in response to the notice, order or any other communication;

(*c*) issue of acknowledgement of the response furnished by the person;

(*d*) provision of "e-proceeding" facility including login account facility, tracking status of assessment, display of relevant details, and facility of download;

(*e*) accessing, verification and authentication of information and response including documents submitted during the assessment proceedings;

(*f*) receipt, storage and retrieval of information or documents in a centralised manner;

(*g*) circumstances in which proviso to sub-section (6) shall apply;

(*h*) circumstances in which personal hearing referred to clause (*viii*) shall be approved;

(*i*) general administration and grievance redressal mechanism in the respective Centres and units.

(8) Notwithstanding anything contained in sub-section (1) or sub-section (2), the Principal Chief Commissioner or the Principal Director General in charge of National Faceless Assessment Centre may at any stage of the assessment, if considered necessary, transfer the case to the Assessing Officer having jurisdiction over such case, with the prior approval of the Board.

(9) Notwithstanding anything contained in any other provision of this Act, assessment made under sub-section (3) of section 143 or under section 144 in the cases referred to in sub-section (2) (other than the cases transferred under sub-section (8), on or after the 1st day of April, 2021), shall be *non-est* if such assessment is not made in accordance with the procedure laid down under this section.

[1][*(10)* *Notwithstanding anything contained in this section the function of verification unit under this section may also be performed by a verification unit located in any other faceless center set up under the provisions of this Act or under any scheme notified under the provisions of this Act; and the request for verification may also be assigned by the National Faceless Assessment Centre to such verification unit.*]

Explanation.—In this section, unless the context otherwise requires—

(*a*) "addressee" shall have the same meaning as assigned to it in clause (*b*) of sub-section (1) of section 2 of the Information Technology Act, 2000 (21 of 2000);

(*b*) "authorised representative" shall have the same meaning as assigned to it in sub-section (2) of section 288;

(*c*) "automated allocation system" means an algorithm for randomised allocation of cases, by using suitable technological tools, including artificial intelligence and machine learning, with a view to optimise the use of resources;

(*d*) "automated examination tool" means an algorithm for standardised examination of draft orders, by using suitable technological tools, including artificial intelligence and machine learning, with a view to reduce the scope of discretion;

(*e*) "computer resource" shall have the same meaning as assigned to it in clause (*k*) of sub-section (1) of section 2 of the Information Technology Act, 2000 (21 of 2000);

(*f*) "computer system" shall have the same meaning as assigned to it in clause (*l*) of sub-section (1) of section 2 of the Information Technology Act, 2000 (21 of 2000);

(*g*) "computer resource of assessee" shall include assessee's registered account in designated portal of the Income-tax Department, the Mobile App linked to the registered mobile number of the assessee, or the registered email address of the assessee with his email service provider;

(*h*) "digital signature" shall have the same meaning as assigned to it in clause (*p*) of sub-section (1) of section 2 of the Information Technology Act, 2000 (21 of 2000);

(*i*) "designated portal" means the web portal designated as such by the Principal Chief Commissioner or Principal Director General, in charge of the National Faceless Assessment Centre;

(*j*) "Dispute Resolution Panel" shall have the same meaning as assigned to it in clause (*a*) of sub-section (15) of section 144C;

(*k*) "faceless assessment" means the assessment proceedings conducted electronically in 'e-Proceeding' facility through assessee's registered account in designated portal;

---

1. Inserted by the Finance Act, 2021, w.e.f. **1-4-2021**.

(*l*) "electronic record" shall have the same meaning as assigned to it in clause (*t*) of sub-section (1) of section 2 of the Information Technology Act, 2000 (21 of 2000);

(*m*) "eligible assessee" shall have the same meaning as assigned to in clause (*b*) of sub-section (15) of section 144C;

(*n*) "email" or "electronic mail" and "electronic mail message" means a message or information created or transmitted or received on a computer, computer system, computer resource or communication device including attachments in text, image, audio, video and any other electronic record, which may be transmitted with the message;

(*o*) "hash function" and "hash result" shall have the same meaning as assigned to them in the *Explanation* to sub-section (2) of section 3 of the Information Technology Act, 2000 (21 of 2000);

(*p*) "Mobile App" shall mean the application software of the Income-tax Department developed for mobile devices which is downloaded and installed on the registered mobile number of the assessee;

(*q*) "originator" shall have the same meaning as assigned to it in clause (*za*) of sub-section (1) of section 2 of the Information Technology Act, 2000 (21 of 2000);

(*r*) "real time alert" means any communication sent to the assessee, by way of Short Messaging Service on his registered mobile number, or by way of update on his Mobile App, or by way of an email at his registered email address, so as to alert him regarding delivery of an electronic communication;

(*s*) "registered account" of the assessee means the electronic filing account registered by the assessee in designated portal;

(*t*) "registered e-mail address" means the e-mail address at which an electronic communication may be delivered or transmitted to the addressee, including—

   (*i*) the e-mail address available in the electronic filing account of the addressee registered in designated portal; or

   (*ii*) the e-mail address available in the last income-tax return furnished by the addressee; or

   (*iii*) the e-mail address available in the Permanent Account Number database relating to the addressee; or

   (*iv*) in the case of addressee being an individual who possesses the Aadhaar number, the e-mail address of addressee available in the database of Unique Identification Authority of India; or

   (*v*) in the case of addressee being a company, the e-mail address of the company as available on the official website of Ministry of Corporate Affairs; or (*vi*) any e-mail address made available by the addressee to the income-tax authority or any person authorised by such authority.

(*u*) "registered mobile number" of the assessee means the mobile number of the assessee, or his authorised representative, appearing in the user profile of the electronic filing account registered by the assessee in designated portal;

(*v*) "video conferencing or video telephony" means the technological solutions for the reception and transmission of audio-video signals by users at different locations, for communication between people in real-time.';

(*XXV*) in section 144C, after sub-section (14A), the following sub-sections shall be inserted with effect from the 1st day of November, 2020, namely:—

"(14B) The Central Government may make a scheme, by notification in the Official Gazette, for the purposes of issuance of directions by the dispute resolution panel, so as to impart greater efficiency, transparency and accountability by—

(*a*) eliminating the interface between the dispute resolution panel and the eligible assessee or any other person to the extent technologically feasible;

(*b*) optimising utilisation of the resources through economies of scale and functional specialisation;

(*c*) introducing a mechanism with dynamic jurisdiction for issuance of directions by dispute resolution panel.

(14C) The Central Government may, for the purpose of giving effect to the scheme made under sub-section (14B), by notification in the Official Gazette, direct that any of the provisions of this Act shall not apply or shall apply with such exceptions, modifications and adaptations as may be specified in the notification:

Provided that no direction shall be issued after the 31st day of March, 2022.

(14D) Every notification issued under sub-section (14B) and sub-section (14C) shall, as soon as may be after the notification is issued, be laid before each House of Parliament.";

(*XXVI*) after section 151, the following section shall be inserted with effect from the 1st day of November, 2020, namely:—

"**151A**. *Faceless assessment of income escaping assessment.*—(1) The Central Government may make a scheme, by notification in the Official Gazette, for the purposes of assessment, reassessment or re-computation under section 147 or issuance of notice under section 148 or sanction for issue of such notice under section 151, so as to impart greater efficiency, transparency and accountability by—

(*a*) eliminating the interface between the income-tax authority and the assessee or any other person to the extent technologically feasible;

(*b*) optimising utilisation of the resources through economies of scale and functional specialisation;

(*c*) introducing a team-based assessment, reassessment, re-computation or issuance or sanction of notice with dynamic jurisdiction.

(2) The Central Government may, for the purpose of giving effect to the scheme made under sub-section (1), by notification in the Official Gazette, direct that any of the provisions of this Act shall not apply or shall apply with such exceptions, modifications and adaptations as may be specified in the notification:

Provided that no direction shall be issued after the 31st day of March, 2022.

(3) Every notification issued under sub-section (1) and sub-section (2) shall, as soon as may be after the notification is issued, be laid before each House of Parliament.";

(*XXVII*) after section 157, the following section shall be inserted with effect from the 1st day of November, 2020, namely:—

"**157A.** *Faceless rectification, amendments and issuance of notice or intimation.*—(1) The Central Government may make a scheme, by notification in the Official Gazette, for the purposes of rectification of any mistake apparent from record under section 154 or other amendments under section 155 or issue of notice of demand under section 156, or intimation of loss under section 157, so as to impart greater efficiency, transparency and accountability by—

(*a*) eliminating the interface between the income-tax authority and the assessee or any other person to the extent technologically feasible;

(*b*) optimising utilisation of the resources through economies of scale and functional specialisation;

(*c*) introducing a team-based rectification of mistakes, amendment of orders, issuance of notice of demand or intimation of loss, with dynamic jurisdiction.

(2) The Central Government may, for the purpose of giving effect to the scheme made under sub-section (1), by notification in the Official Gazette, direct that any of the provisions of this Act shall not apply or shall apply with such exceptions, modifications and adaptations as may be specified in the notification:

Provided that no direction shall be issued after the 31st day of March, 2022.

(3) Every notification issued under sub-section (1) and sub-section (2) shall, as soon as may be after the notification is issued, be laid before each House of Parliament.";

(*XXVIII*) in section 196D, after sub-section (1), the following sub-section shall be inserted with effect from the 1st day of November, 2020, namely:—

"(1A) Where any income in respect of securities referred to in clause (*a*) of sub-section (1) of section 115AD, not being income by way of interest referred to in section 194LD, is payable to a specified fund [referred to in clause (*c*) of the *Explanation* to clause (*4D*) of section 10], the person responsible for making the payment shall, at the time of credit of such income to the account of the payee, or at the time of payment thereof by any mode, whichever is earlier, deduct the income-tax thereon at the rate of ten per cent:

Provided that no deduction shall be made in respect of an income exempt under clause (*4D*) of section 10.";

(*XXIX*) after section 197A, the following section shall be inserted and shall be deemed to have been inserted with effect from the 14th day of May, 2020, namely:—

"197B. *Lower deduction in certain cases for a limited period.*—In case the provisions of sections 193, 194, 194A, 194C, 194D, 194DA, 194EE, 194F, 194G, 194H, 194-I, 194-IA, 194-IB, 194-IC, 194J, 194K, 194LA, sub-section (1) of section 194LBA, clause (*i*) of section 194LBB, sub-section (1) of section 194LBC, sections 194M and 194-O require deduction of tax at source during the period commencing from the 14th day of May, 2020 to the 31st day of March, 2021, then notwithstanding anything contained in these sections the deduction of tax shall be made at the rate being the three-fourth of the rate specified in these sections.";

(*XXX*) in section 206C, after sub-section (10), the following sub-section shall be inserted and shall be deemed to have been inserted with effect from the 14th day of May, 2020, namely:—

"(10A) In case the provisions of sub-section (1) [except the goods referred at serial number (*i*) in the TABLE], (1C), (1F) or (1H) require collection of tax at source during the period commencing from the 14th day of May, 2020 to the 31st day of March, 2021, then, notwithstanding anything contained in these sub-sections the collection of tax shall be made at the rate being the three-fourth of the rate specified in these sub-sections.";

(*XXXI*) after section 230, the following section shall be inserted with effect from the 1st day of November, 2020, namely:—

"231. *Faceless collection and recovery of tax.*—(1) The Central Government may make a scheme, by notification in the Official Gazette, for the purposes of issuance of certificate for deduction of income-tax at any lower rates or no deduction of income-tax under section 197, or deeming a person to be an assessee in default under sub-section (1) of section 201 or sub-section (6A) of section 206C, issuance of certificate for lower collection of tax under sub-section (9) of section 206C or passing of order or amended order under sub-section (3) or sub-section (4) of section 210, or reduction or waiver of the amount of interest paid or payable by an assessee under sub-section (2A), or extending the time for payment or allowing payment by instalment under sub-section (3), or treating the assessee as not being in default under sub-section (6) or sub-section (7) of section 220, or levy of penalty under section 221, or drawing of certificate by the Tax Recovery Officer under section 222, or jurisdiction of Tax Recovery Officer under section 223, or stay of proceedings in pursuance of certificate and amendment or cancellation thereof by the Tax Recovery Officer under section 225, or other modes of recovery under section 226 or issuance of tax clearance certificate under section 230 so as to impart greater efficiency, transparency and accountability by—

(*a*) eliminating the interface between the income-tax authority and the assessee or any other person to the extent technologically feasible;

(*b*) optimising utilisation of the resources through economies of scale and functional specialisation;

(*c*) introducing a team-based issuance of certificate for deduction or collection of income-tax at lower rate, or for no deduction, or for deeming a person to be an assessee in default, or for passing of an order or amended order, or extending the time for payment, or allowing payment by instalment, or reduction or waiver of interest, or for treating the assessee as not being in default, or for levy of penalty or for drawing of certificate or stay of proceedings in pursuance of certificate and amendment or cancellation thereof, by, or jurisdiction of, Tax Recovery Officer or other modes of recovery or issuance of tax clearance certificate, with dynamic jurisdiction.

(2) The Central Government may, for the purpose of giving effect to the scheme made under sub-section (1), by notification in the Official Gazette, direct that any of the provisions of this Act shall not apply or shall apply with such exceptions, modifications and adaptations as may be specified in the notification:

Provided that no direction shall be issued after the 31st day of March, 2022.

(3) Every notification issued under sub-section (1) and sub-section (2) shall, as soon as may be after the notification is issued, be laid before each House of Parliament.";

(*XXXII*) in section 253,—

(*a*) in sub-section (1), in clause (*c*),—

(*i*) for the words, figures and letters "under section 12AA or section 12AB", the words, figures and letters "under section 12AA" shall be substituted and shall be deemed to have been substituted with effect from the 1st day of June, 2020;

      (*ii*) for the words, figures and letters "under section 12AA" the words, figures and letters "under section 12AA or section 12AB" shall be substituted with effect from the 1st day of April, 2021;

    (*b*) after sub-section (7), the following sub-sections shall be inserted with effect from the 1st day of November, 2020, namely:—

"(8) The Central Government may make a scheme, by notification in the Official Gazette, for the purposes of appeal to the Appellate Tribunal under sub-section (2), so as to impart greater efficiency, transparency and accountability by—

    (*a*) optimising utilisation of the resources through economies of scale and functional specialisation;

    (*b*) introducing a team-based mechanism for appeal to the Appellate Tribunal, with dynamic jurisdiction.

(9) The Central Government may, for the purpose of giving effect to the scheme made under sub-section (8), by notification in the Official Gazette, direct that any of the provisions of this Act shall not apply or shall apply with such exceptions, modifications and adaptations as may be specified in the notification:

Provided that no direction shall be issued after the 31st day of March, 2022.

(10) Every notification issued under sub-section (8) and sub-section (9) shall, as soon as may be after the notification is issued, be laid before each House of Parliament.";

(*XXXIII*) in section 263, in sub-section (1), in *Explanation 1*, in clause (*b*), and in *Explanation 2*, after the words "the Principal", the words "Chief Commissioner or Chief Commissioner or Principal" shall be inserted with effect from the 1st day of November, 2020;

(*XXXIV*) in section 264, in sub-section (1), in sub-section (2), in proviso to sub-section (3), in sub-section (4), in *Explanation 1* and in *Explanation 2*, after the words "the Principal", the words "Chief Commissioner or Chief Commissioner or Principal" shall be inserted with effect from the 1st day of November, 2020;

(*XXXV*) after section 264, the following section shall be inserted with effect from the 1st day of November, 2020, namely:—

"264A. *Faceless revision of orders.*—(1) The Central Government may make a scheme, by notification in the Official Gazette, for the purposes of revision of orders under section 263 or section 264, so as to impart greater efficiency, transparency and accountability by—

    (*a*) eliminating the interface between the income-tax authority and the assessee or any other person to the extent technologically feasible;

    (*b*) optimising utilisation of the resources through economies of scale and functional specialisation;

(*c*) introducing a team-based revision of orders, with dynamic juris-diction.

(2) The Central Government may, for the purpose of giving effect to the scheme made under sub-section (1), by notification in the Official Gazette, direct that any of the provisions of this Act shall not apply or shall apply with such exceptions, modifications and adaptations as may be specified in the notification:

Provided that no direction shall be issued after the 31st day of March, 2022.

(3) Every notification issued under sub-section (1) and sub-section (2) shall, as soon as may be after the notification is issued, be laid before each House of Parliament.

264B. *Faceless effect of orders.*—(1) The Central Government may make a scheme, by notification in the Official Gazette, for the pur-poses of giving effect to an order under section 250, 254, 260, 262, 263 or 264, so as to impart greater efficiency, transparency and account-ability by—

(*a*) eliminating the interface between the income-tax authority and the assessee or any other person to the extent technologically feasible;

(*b*) optimising utilisation of the resources through economies of scale and functional specialisation;

(*c*) introducing a team-based giving of effect to orders, with dynamic jurisdiction.

(2) The Central Government may, for the purpose of giving effect to the scheme made under sub-section (1), by notification in the Official Gazette, direct that any of the provisions of this Act shall not apply or shall apply with such exceptions, modifications and adaptations as may be specified in the notification:

Provided that no direction shall be issued after the 31st day of March, 2022.

(3) Every notification issued under sub-section (1) and sub-section (2) shall, as soon as may be after the notification is issued, be laid before each House of Parliament.";

(*XXXVI*) section 271K shall be omitted and shall be deemed to have been omitted with effect from the 1st day of June, 2020;

(*XXXVII*) after section 271J, the following section shall be inserted with effect from the 1st day of April, 2021, namely:—

"271K. *Penalty for failure to furnish statements, etc.*—Without preju-dice to the provisions of this Act, the Assessing Officer may direct that a sum not less than ten thousand rupees but which may extend to one lakh rupees shall be paid by way of penalty by—

(*i*) the research association, university, college or other institution referred to in clause (*ii*) or clause (*iii*) or the company referred to in clause (*iia*), of sub-section (1) of section 35, if it fails to deliver or cause to be delivered a statement within the time prescribed under clause (*i*), or furnish a certificate prescribed under clause (*ii*) of sub-section (1A) of that section; or

(*ii*) the institution or fund, if it fails to deliver or cause to be delivered a statement within the time prescribed under clause (*viii*) of sub-section (5) of section 80G, or furnish a certificate prescribed under clause (*ix*) of the said sub-section.";

(*XXXVIII*) in section 274, in sub-section (2A), in clause (*a*), for the words "Assessing Officer and the assessee in the course of proceedings", the words "income-tax authority and the assessee or any other person" shall be substituted and shall be deemed to have been substituted with effect from the 1st day of April, 2020;

(*XXXIX*) in section 279, after sub-section (3), the following sub-sections shall be inserted with effect from the 1st day of November, 2020, namely:—

"(4) The Central Government may make a scheme, by notification in the Official Gazette, for the purposes of granting sanction under sub-section (1) or compounding under sub-section (2), so as to impart greater efficiency, transparency and accountability by—

(*a*) eliminating the interface between the income-tax authority and the assessee or any other person to the extent technologically feasible;

(*b*) optimising utilisation of the resources through economies of scale and functional specialisation;

(*c*) introducing a team-based sanction to proceed against, or for compounding of, an offence, with dynamic jurisdiction.

(5) The Central Government may, for the purpose of giving effect to the scheme made under sub-section (4), by notification in the Official Gazette, direct that any of the provisions of this Act shall not apply or shall apply with such exceptions, modifications and adaptations as may be specified in the notification:

Provided that no direction shall be issued after the 31st day of March, 2022.

(6) Every notification issued under sub-section (4) and sub-section (5) shall, as soon as may be after the notification is issued, be laid before each House of Parliament.";

(*XL*) after section 293C of the Income-tax Act, the following section shall be inserted with effect from the 1st day of November, 2020, namely:—

"293D. *Faceless approval or registration.*—(1) The Central Government may make a scheme, by notification in the Official Gazette, for the purposes of granting approval or registration, as the case may be, by income-tax authority under any provision of the Act, so as to impart greater efficiency, transparency and accountability by—

(*a*) eliminating the interface between the income-tax authorities and the assessee or any other person to the extent technologically feasible;

(*b*) optimising utilisation of the resources through economies of scale and functional specialisation;

(*c*) introducing a team-based grant of approval or registration, with dynamic jurisdiction.

(2) The Central Government may, for the purpose of giving effect to the scheme made under sub-section (1), by notification in the Official Gazette, direct that any of the provisions of this Act shall not apply or shall apply with such exceptions, modifications and adaptations as may be specified in the notification:

Provided that no direction shall be issued after the 31st day of March, 2022.

(3) Every notification issued under sub-section (1) and sub-section (2) shall, as soon as may be after the notification is issued, be laid before each House of Parliament.".

CHAPTER IV

AMENDMENTS TO THE DIRECT TAX VIVAD SE VISHWAS ACT

Amendment of section 3 of Act 3 of 2020.

5. In section 3 of the Direct Tax *Vivad Se Vishwas* Act, 2020,—

(*a*) in the opening portion, for the words, "under the provisions of this Act on or before the last date" the words "under the provisions of this Act on or before such date as may be notified" shall be substituted and shall be deemed to have been substituted;

(*b*) in the Table,—

(*i*) in third column, in the heading, for the figures, letters and words "31st day of March, 2020", the figures, letters and words "31st day of December, 2020 or such later date as may be notified" shall be substituted and shall be deemed to have been substituted;

(*ii*) in fourth column, in the heading, for the figures, letters and words "1st day of April, 2020", the figures, letters and words "1st day of January, 2021 or such later date as may be notified" shall be substituted and shall be deemed to have been substituted;

CHAPTER V

RELAXATION OF TIME LIMIT UNDER
CERTAIN INDIRECT TAX LAWS

Relaxation of time limit under Central Excise Act, 1944, Customs Act, 1962, Customs Tariff Act, 1975 and Finance Act, 1994.

6. Notwithstanding anything contained in the Central Excise Act, 1944 (1 of 1944), the Customs Act, 1962 (52 of 1962) (except sections 30, 30A, 41, 41A, 46 and 47), the Customs Tariff Act, 1975 (51 of 1975) or Chapter V of the Finance Act, 1994 (32 of 1994), as it stood prior to its omission *vide* section 173 of the Central Goods and Services Tax Act, 2017 (12 of 2017) with effect from the 1st day of July, 2017, the time limit specified in, or prescribed or notified under, the said Acts which falls during the period from the 20th day of March, 2020 to the 29th day of September, 2020 or such other date after the 29th day of September, 2020 as the Central Government may, by notification, specify, for the completion or compliance of such action as—

(*a*) completion of any proceeding or issuance of any order, notice, intimation, notification or sanction or approval, by whatever name called, by any authority, commission, tribunal, by whatever name called; or

(*b*) filing of any appeal, reply or application or furnishing of any report, document, return or statement, by whatever name called,

shall, notwithstanding that completion or compliance of such action has not been made within such time, stand extended to the 30th day of September, 2020 or such other date after 30th day of September, 2020 as the Central Government may, by notification, specify in this behalf:

Provided that the Central Government may specify different dates for completion or compliance of different actions under clause (*a*) or clause (*b*).

CHAPTER VI

AMENDMENT TO THE CENTRAL GOODS
AND SERVICES TAX ACT, 2017

Insertion of new section 168A in Act 12 of 2017.

7. After section 168 of the Central Goods and Services Tax Act, 2017, the following section shall be inserted, namely:—

'**168A.** *Power of Government to extend time limit in special circumstances.*—(1) Notwithstanding anything contained in this Act, the Government may, on the recommendations of the Council, by notification, extend the time limit specified in, or prescribed or notified under, this Act in respect of actions which cannot be completed of complied with due to *force majeure.*

(2) The power to issue notification under sub-section (1) shall include the power to give retrospective effect to such notification from a date not earlier than the date of commencement of this Act.

Explanation.—For the purposes of this section, the expression "*force majeure*" means a case of war, epidemic, flood, drought, fire, cyclone, earthquake or any other calamity caused by nature or otherwise affecting the implementation of any of the provisions of this Act.'.

CHAPTER VII

AMENDMENT TO THE FINANCE (NO. 2) ACT, 2019

Amendment of section 127 of Act 23 of 2019.

8. In section 127 of the Finance (No. 2) Act, 2019,—

(*i*) in sub-section (1), for the words "within a period of sixty days from the date of receipt of the said declaration", the words, figures and letters "on or before the 31st day of May, 2020" shall be substituted;

(*ii*) in sub-section (2), for the words "within thirty days of the date of receipt of the declaration", the words, figures and letters "on or before the 1st day of May, 2020" shall be substituted;

(*iii*) in sub-section (4), for the words "within a period of sixty days from the date of receipt of the declaration", the words, figures and letters "on or before the 31st day of May, 2020" shall be substituted;

(*iv*) in sub-section (5), for the words "within a period of thirty days from the date of issue of such statement", the words, figures and letters "on or before the 30th day of June, 2020" shall be substituted.

CHAPTER VIII

AMENDMENT TO THE FINANCE ACT, 2020

Amendment of Act 12 of 2020.

9. In the Finance Act, 2020, in section 2, with effect from the 1st day of April, 2020,—

(*i*) in sub-section (6),—

(*A*) in clause (*a*), for the words "being a non-resident", the words, figures and letter "being a non-resident, except in case of deduction on income by way of dividend under section 196D of the Income-tax Act" shall be substituted and shall be deemed to have been substituted;

(*B*) after clause (*a*), the following clause shall be inserted and shall be deemed to have been inserted, namely:—

"(*aa*) in the case of every individual or Hindu undivided family or association of persons or body of individuals, whether incorporated or not, or every artificial juridical person referred to in sub-clause (*vii*) of clause (*31*) of section 2 of the Income-tax Act, being a non-resident, in case of deduction on income by way of dividend under section 196D of that Act, calculated,—

(*i*) at the rate of ten per cent of such tax, where the income or the aggregate of such incomes paid or likely to be paid and subject to the deduction exceeds fifty lakh rupees but does not exceed one crore rupees;

(*ii*) at the rate of fifteen per cent of such tax, where the income or the aggregate of such incomes paid or likely to be paid and subject to the deduction exceeds one crore rupees;";

(*ii*) in sub-section (9), in the third proviso, in clause (*aa*),—

(*A*) in sub-clause (*iii*), for the words "excluding the income", the words "excluding the income by way of dividend or income" shall be substituted and shall be deemed to have been substituted;

(*B*) in sub-clause (*iv*), for the words "excluding the income", the words "excluding the income by way of dividend or income" shall be substituted and shall be deemed to have been substituted;

(*C*) in sub-clause (*v*), for the words "including the income", the words "including the income by way of dividend or income" shall be substituted and shall be deemed to have been substituted;

(*D*) in the proviso, for the words "any income", the words "any income by way of dividend or income" shall be substituted and shall be deemed to have been substituted.

Power to remove difficulties.

10. (1) If any difficulty arises in giving effect to the provisions of this Act, the Central Government may, by order, not inconsistent with the provisions of this Act, remove the difficulty:

Provided that no such order shall be made after the expiry of a period of two years from the end of the month in which this Act has received the assent of the President.

(2) Every order made under this section shall be laid before each House of Parliament.

Repeal and savings.

11. (1) The Taxation and Other Laws (Relaxation of Certain Provisions) Ordinance, 2020 (Ord. 2 of 2020) is hereby repealed.

(2) Notwithstanding such repeal, anything done, any notification issued or any action taken under the said Ordinance, shall be deemed to have been done, issued or taken under the corresponding provisions of this Act.

$$\boxed{3}$$

PRESS RELEASE, DATED 30-12-2020

In view of the challenges faced by taxpayers in meeting the statutory and regulatory compliances due to the outbreak of COVID-19, the Government brought the Taxation and Other Laws (Relaxation of Certain Provisions) Ordinance, 2020 ('the Ordinance') on 31st March, 2020 which, *inter alia*, extended various time limits. The Ordinance has since been replaced by the Taxation and Other Laws (Relaxation and Amendment of Certain Provisions) Act.

2. The Government issued a Notification on 24th June, 2020 under the Ordinance which, *inter alia*, extended the due date for all Income-tax Returns for the FY 2019-20 (AY 2020-21) to 30th November, 2020. Hence, the returns of income which were required to be filed by 31st July, 2020 and 31st October, 2020 were required to be filed by 30th November, 2020. Consequently, the date for furnishing various audit reports including tax audit report under the Income-tax Act, 1961 (the Act) was also extended to 31st October, 2020.

3. In order to provide more time to taxpayers for furnishing of Income-tax Returns, the due date was further extended *vide* Notification No. 88/2020/F. No. 370142/35/2020-TPL dated 29th October, 2020:

(A) The due date for furnishing of Income-tax Returns for the taxpayers (including their partners) who are required to get their accounts audited [for whom the due date (*i.e.* before the said extension) as per the Act was 31st October, 2020] was extended to 31st January, 2021.

(B) The due date for furnishing of Income-tax Returns for the taxpayers who are required to furnish report in respect of international/specified domestic transactions [for whom the due date (*i.e.* before the said extension) as per the Act was 30th November, 2020] was extended to 31st January, 2021.

(C) The due date for furnishing of Income-tax Returns for the other taxpayers [for whom the due date (*i.e.* before the said extension) as per the Act was 31st July, 2020] was extended to 31st December, 2020.

(D) Consequently, the date for furnishing of various audit reports under the Act including tax audit report and report in respect of international/specified domestic transaction was also extended to 31st December, 2020.

4. Considering the problems being faced by the taxpayers, it has been decided to provide further time to the taxpayers for furnishing of Income-tax Returns, tax audit reports and declaration under Vivad Se Vishwas Scheme. Further, in order to provide more time to taxpayers to comply under various ongoing proceedings, the dates of completion of proceedings under various Direct Taxes & *Benami* Acts have also been extended. These extensions are as under:

a. The due date for furnishing of Income-tax Returns for the Assessment Year 2020-21 for the taxpayers (including their partners) who are required to get their accounts audited and companies [for whom the due date, as per the provisions of section 139(1) of the Income-tax Act,1961, was 31st October, 2020 and which was extended to 30th November, 2020 and then to 31st January, 2021] has been further extended to 15th February, 2021.

b. The due date for furnishing of Income-tax Returns for the Assessment Year 2020-21 for the taxpayers who are required to furnish report in respect of international/specified domestic transactions [for whom the due date, as per the provisions of section 139(1) of the Income-tax Act,1961, was 30th November, 2020 and which was extended to 31st January, 2021] has been further extended to 15th February, 2021.

c. The due date for furnishing of Income-tax Returns for the Assessment Year 2020-21 for the other taxpayers [for whom the due date, as per the provisions of section 139(1) of the Income-tax Act, 1961, was 31st July, 2020 and which was extended to 30th November, 2020 and then to 31st December, 2020] has been further extended to 10th January, 2021.

d. The date for furnishing of various audit reports under the Act including tax audit report and report in respect of international/specified domestic transaction for the Assessment Year 2020-21 has been further extended to 15th January, 2021.

e. The last date for making a declaration under Vivad Se Vishwas Scheme has been extended to 31st January, 2021 from 31st December, 2020.

f. The date for passing of orders under Vivad Se Vishwas Scheme, which are required to be passed by 30th January, 2021 has been extended to 31st January, 2021.

g. The date for passing of order or issuance of notice by the authorities under the Direct Taxes & *Benami* Acts which are required to be passed/issued/made by 30th March, 2021 has also been extended to 31st March, 2021.

5. Further, in order to provide relief for the third time to small and middle class taxpayers in the matter of payment of self-assessment tax, the due date for payment of self-assessment tax date is hereby again being extended. Accordingly, the due date for payment of self-assessment tax for taxpayers whose self-assessment tax liability is up to Rs. 1 lakh has been extended to 15th February, 2021 for the taxpayers mentioned in para 4(*a*) and para 4(*b*) and to 10th January, 2021 for the taxpayers mentioned in para 4(*c*).

6. The Government has also extended the due date of furnishing of annual return under section 44 of the Central Goods and Services Tax Act, 2017 for the financial year 2019-20 from 31st December, 2020 to 28th February, 2021.

7. The necessary notifications in this regard shall be issued in due course.

SECTION 3 OF THE TAXATION AND OTHER LAWS (RELAXATION OF CERTAIN PROVISIONS) ORDINANCE, 2020 - RELAXATION OF CERTAIN PROVISIONS OF SPECIFIED ACTS - NOTIFIED DATES FOR EXTENSION OF DUE DATES OF VARIOUS COMPLETIONS OR COMPLIANCES UNDER SPECIFIED ACTS

NOTIFICATION NO. S.O. 2033(E) DATED 24-6-2020
AS AMENDED BY NOTIFICATION S.O. 2512(E), DATED 29-7-2020 AS
CORRECTED BY CORRIGENDUM S.O. 2126(E), DATED 29-6-2020

In exercise of the powers conferred by sub-section (1) of section 3 of the Taxation and Other Laws (Relaxation of Certain Provisions) Ordinance, 2020 (2 of 2020) (hereinafter referred to as the Ordinance), the Central Government hereby specifies, for the purposes of the said sub-section (1),—

(*i*) the 31st day of December, 2020 shall be the end date of the period during which the time limit specified in, or prescribed or notified under, the specified Act falls for the completion or compliance of such action as specified under the said sub-section; and

(*ii*) the 31st day of March, 2021 shall be the end date to which the time limit for completion or compliance of such action shall stand extended:

Provided that where the specified Act is the Income-tax Act, 1961 and the compliance relates to—

(*i*) furnishing of return under section 139 thereof, for the assessment year commencing on the—

(*a*) 1st day of April, 2019, the end date shall be extended to [1][the 30th day of September, 2020];

(*b*) 1st day of April, 2020, the end date shall be extended to the 30th day of November, 2020;

(*ii*) delivering of statement of deduction of tax at source under sub-section (2A) of section 200 or statement of collection of tax at source under sub-section (3A) of section 206C thereof for the month of February or March, 2020, or for the quarter ending on the 31st day of March, 2020, as the case may be, the end date shall be extended to the 15th day of July, 2020;

(*iii*) delivering of statement of deduction of tax at source under sub-section (3) of section 200 or statement of collection of tax at source under proviso to sub-section (3) of section 206C thereof for the month of February or March, 2020, or for the quarter ending on the 31st day of March, 2020, as the case may be, the end date shall be extended to the 31st day of July, 2020;

---

1. Substituted for "the 31st day of July, 2020" by Notification No. S.O. 2512(E), dated 29-7-2020 w.e.f. 29-7-2020.

(*iv*) furnishing of certificate under section 203 thereof in respect of deduction or payment of tax under section 192 of that Act for the financial year 2019-20, the end date shall be extended to the 15th day of August, 2020;

(*v*) [1][sections 54 to 54GB] referred to in item (I) of sub-clause (*i*) of clause (*c*) of sub-section (1) of section 3 of the Ordinance or sub-clause (*ii*) of the said clause, the end date in respect of the time limit for the completion or compliance and the end date for making the said completion or compliance, shall be the 29th day of September, 2020 and the 30th day of September, 2020 respectively;

(*vi*) any provisions of Chapter VI-A under the heading "B.—Deductions in respect of certain payments" thereof, referred to in item (I) of [1][sub-clause (*i*) of clause (*c*)] of sub-section (1) of section 3 of the Ordinance, the end date in respect of the time limit for the completion or compliance and the end date for making the said completion or compliance, shall be the 30th day of July, 2020 and the 31st day of July, 2020 respectively; and

(*vii*) furnishing of report of audit under any provision thereof for the assessment year commencing on the 1st day of April, 2020, the end date shall be extended to the 31st day of October, 2020:

Provided further that the extension of the date as referred to in sub-clause (*b*) of clause (*i*) of the first proviso shall not apply to *Explanation 1* to section 234A of the Income-tax Act, 1961 in cases where the amount of tax on the total income as reduced by the clauses (*i*) to (*vi*) of sub-section (1) of the said section exceeds one lakh rupees :

[2][**Provided also** that for the purposes of the second proviso, in case of an individual resident in India referred to in sub-section (2) of section 207 of the Income-tax Act, 1961 (43 of 1961), the tax paid by him under section 140A of that Act within the due date (before extension) provided in that Act, shall be deemed to be the advance tax:]

Provided also that where the specified Act is the Direct Tax Vivad se Vishwas Act, 2020, the 30th day of December, 2020 shall be the end date of the period during which the time limit specified in, or prescribed or notified thereunder falls for the completion or compliance of the action and the 31st day of December, 2020 shall be the end date to which the time limit for completion or compliance of such action shall stand extended.

2. This notification shall come into force from the 30th day of June, 2020.

---

1. Corrected by Corrigendum S.O. 2126(E), dated 29-6-2020.
2. Inserted by Notification No. S.O. 2512(E), dated 29-7-2020 w.e.f. 29-7-2020.

5

SECTION 3 OF THE TAXATION AND OTHER LAWS (RELAXATION AND AMENDMENT OF CERTAIN PROVISIONS) ACT, 2020, READ WITH SECTIONS 139 AND 44AB OF THE INCOME-TAX ACT, 1961 - RELAXATION OF CERTAIN PROVISIONS OF SPECIFIED ACT - EXTENSION OF DUE DATE FOR FURNISHING OF RETURN AND AUDIT REPORT FOR ASSESSMENT YEAR 2020-21 - SUPERSESSION OF NOTIFICATION NO. S.O. 3906(E), DATED 29-10-2020

NOTIFICATION NO. S.O. 4805(E), DATED 31-12-2020

In exercise of the powers conferred by sub-section (1) of section 3 of the Taxation and Other Laws (Relaxation and Amendment of Certain Provisions) Act, 2020 (38 of 2020) (hereinafter referred to the Act) and in supersession of the notification of the Government of India in the Ministry of Finance, (Department of Revenue) No. 88/2020 dated the 29th October, 2020, published in the Gazette of India, Extraordinary, Part-II, Section 3, Sub-section (*ii*), *vide* number S.O. 3906(E), dated the 29th October, 2020, except as respects things done or omitted to be done before such supersession, the Central Government hereby specifies, for the completion or compliance of action referred to in—

(A) clause (*a*) of sub-section (1) of section 3 of the Act, —

   (*i*) the 30th day of March, 2021 shall be the end date of the period during which the time limit specified in, or prescribed or notified under, the specified Act falls for the completion or compliance of such action as specified under the said sub-section; and

   (*ii*) the 31st day of March, 2021 shall be the end date to which the time limit for completion or compliance of such action shall stand extended:

Provided that where the specified Act is the Direct Tax Vivad Se Vishwas Act, 2020 (3 of 2020), the provision of this clause shall have the effect as if—

   (*a*) for the figures, letters and words "30th day of March, 2021", the figures, letters and words "30th day of January, 2021" had been substituted; and

   (*b*) for the figures, letters and words "31st day of March, 2021", the figures, letters and words "31st day of January, 2021" had been substituted:

Provided further that where the specified Act is the Income-tax Act, 1961 (43 of 1961) and completion or compliance of action referred to in clause (*a*) of sub-section (1) of section 3 of the Act is an order under sub-section (3) of section 92CA of the Income-tax Act, 1961, the provision of this clause shall have the effect as if—

   (*a*) for the figures, letters and words "30th day of March, 2021", the figures, letters and words "30th day of January, 2021" had been substituted; and

   (*b*) for the figures, letters and words "31st day of March, 2021", the figures, letters and words "31st day of January, 2021" had been substituted;

(B) clause (*b*) of sub-section (1) of section 3 of the Act, where the specified Act is the Income-tax Act, 1961 (43 of 1961) and the compliance for the assessment year commencing on the 1st day of April, 2020 relates to —

(*i*) furnishing of return under section 139 thereof, the time limit for furnishing of such return, shall —

(*a*) in respect of the assessees referred to in clauses (*a*) and (*aa*) of *Explanation 2* to sub-section (1) of the said section 139, stand extended to the 15th day of February 2021; and

(*b*) in respect of other assessees, stand extended to the 10th day of January, 2021:

Provided that the provisions of the fourth proviso to sub-section (1) of section 3 of the Act shall, *mutatis mutandis* apply to these extensions of due date, as they apply to the date referred to in sub-clause (*b*) of clause (*i*) of the third proviso thereof;

(*ii*) furnishing of report of audit under any provision of that Act, the time limit for furnishing of such report of audit shall stand extended to the 15th day of January, 2021.

2. This notification shall come into force from the date of its publication in the Official Gazette.

6

SECTION 3 OF THE TAXATION AND OTHER LAWS (RELAXATION AND AMENDMENT OF CERTAIN PROVISIONS) ACT, 2020, READ WITH SECTIONS 153 AND 153B OF THE INCOME-TAX ACT, 1961 AND SECTION 26 OF THE PROHIBITION OF BENAMI PROPERTY TRANSACTIONS ACT, 1988 - RELAXATION OF CERTAIN PROVISIONS OF SPECIFIED ACT - EXTENSION OF DUE DATE FOR COMPLETION AND COMPLIANCE OF ANY ACTION IN RELATION TO IMPOSITION OF PENALTY, ASSESSMENT OR REASSESSMENT AND ADJUDICATION OF BENAMI PROPERTY

NOTIFICATION NO. S.O. 966(E), DATED 27-2-2021

In exercise of the powers conferred by sub-section (1) of section 3 of the Taxation and Other Laws (Relaxation and Amendment of Certain Provisions) Act, 2020 (38 of 2020) (hereinafter referred to as the said Act), and in partial modification of the notification of the Government of India in the Ministry of Finance, (Department of Revenue) No. 93/2020 dated the 31st December, 2020, published in the Gazette of India, Extraordinary, Part II, Section 3, Sub-section (*ii*), *vide* number S.O. 4805(E), dated the 31st December, 2020 (hereinafter referred to as the said notification), the Central Government hereby specifies, for the purpose of sub-section (1) of section 3 of the said Act, that,—

(A) where the specified Act is the Income-tax Act, 1961 (43 of 1961) (hereinafter referred to as the Income-tax Act) and the completion of any action, as referred to in clause (*a*) of sub-section (1) of section 3 of the said Act, relates to passing of any order—

  (*a*) for imposition of penalty under Chapter XXI of the Income-tax Act, —

      (*i*) the 29th day of June, 2021 shall be the end date of the period during which the time limit specified in or prescribed or notified under the Income-tax Act falls, for the completion of such action; and

      (*ii*) the 30th day of June, 2021 shall be the end date to which the time limit for completion of such action shall stand extended;

  (*b*) for assessment or reassessment under the Income-tax Act, and the time limit for completion of such action under section 153 or section 153B thereof, —

      (*i*) expires on the 31st day of March, 2021 due to its extension by the said notification, such time limit shall stand extended to the 30th day of April, 2021;

      (*ii*) is not covered under (*i*) and expires on 31st day of March, 2021, such time limit shall stand extended to the 30th day of September, 2021;

(B) where the specified Act is the Prohibition of *Benami* Property Transaction Act, 1988 (45 of 1988) (hereinafter referred to as the *Benami* Act) and the completion of any action, as referred to in clause (*a*) of sub-section (1) of section 3 of the said Act, relates to issue of notice under sub-section (1) or passing of any order under sub-section (3) of section 26 of the *Benami* Act,—

  (*i*) the 30th day of June, 2021 shall be the end date of the period during which the time limit specified in or prescribed or notified under the *Benami* Act falls, for the completion of such action; and

  (*ii*) the 30th day of September, 2021 shall be the end date to which the time limit for completion of such action shall stand extended.